TRUST THE LEADER IN BUSINESS EDUCATION

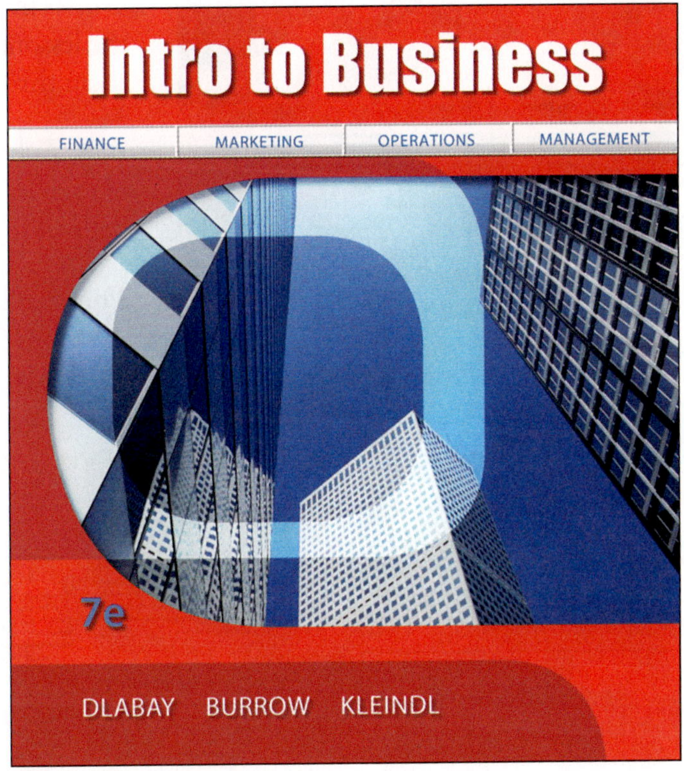

Intro to Business 7E introduces students to the concepts and skills required for success in today's workplace. This market-leading text provides an abundance of practical applications that connect students to the business world. Extensive coverage of finance, marketing, production, and management allows students to explore the foundations of business operations, while topics such as ethics, economics, career planning, and technology take them beyond the basics. The text also helps students prepare for competitive events, internships, and other job opportunities.

ORGANIZED FOR SUCCESS

Each chapter and lesson opener in the text clearly identifies the learning expectations for the student.

Every chapter is organized into *short, succinct lessons* for ease of instruction. Detailed lesson plans are included in the margin.

Teaching Resources, including Web activities, for the chapter are identified in the teaching notes.

Goals list the key concepts at the start of the lesson, while *Main Ideas* identify them throughout.

Key Terms are listed at the beginning of each lesson then are highlighted and defined for easy reference.

Focus on Real Life introduces real-world situations that get students thinking about a topic to be covered in the lesson

FYI offers interesting information related to the lesson topic.

BUSINESS-FOCUSED FEATURES

Business Outside the Box spotlights companies that have used innovative techniques to meet customer demands.

Business Improving Society shows how organizations can use business knowledge to improve the world.

Doing Business In … takes an in-depth look at how businesses operate in other countries.

NEW! Corporate Social Responsibility focuses on business interaction with the community and its positive role on environmental and social issues.

End-of-Unit ***Global Business Project*** offers an opportunity for students to plan, organize, and implement global business activities.

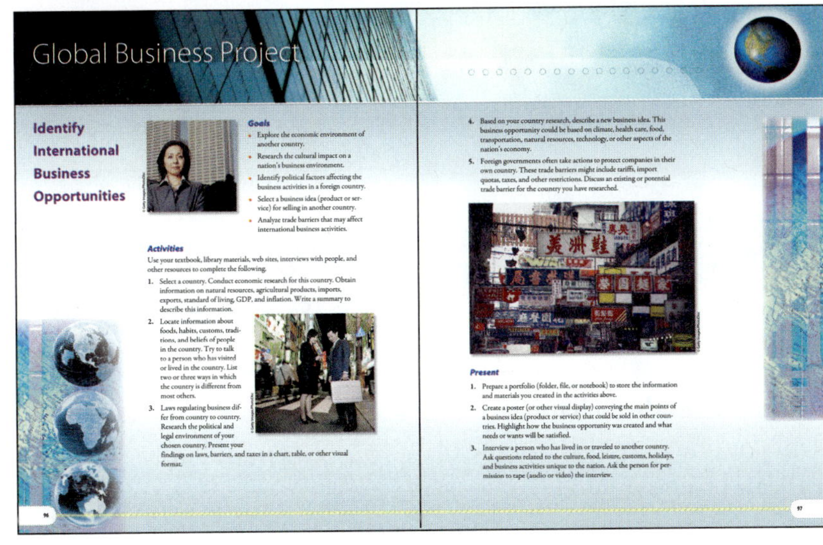

A STEP BEYOND THE REST

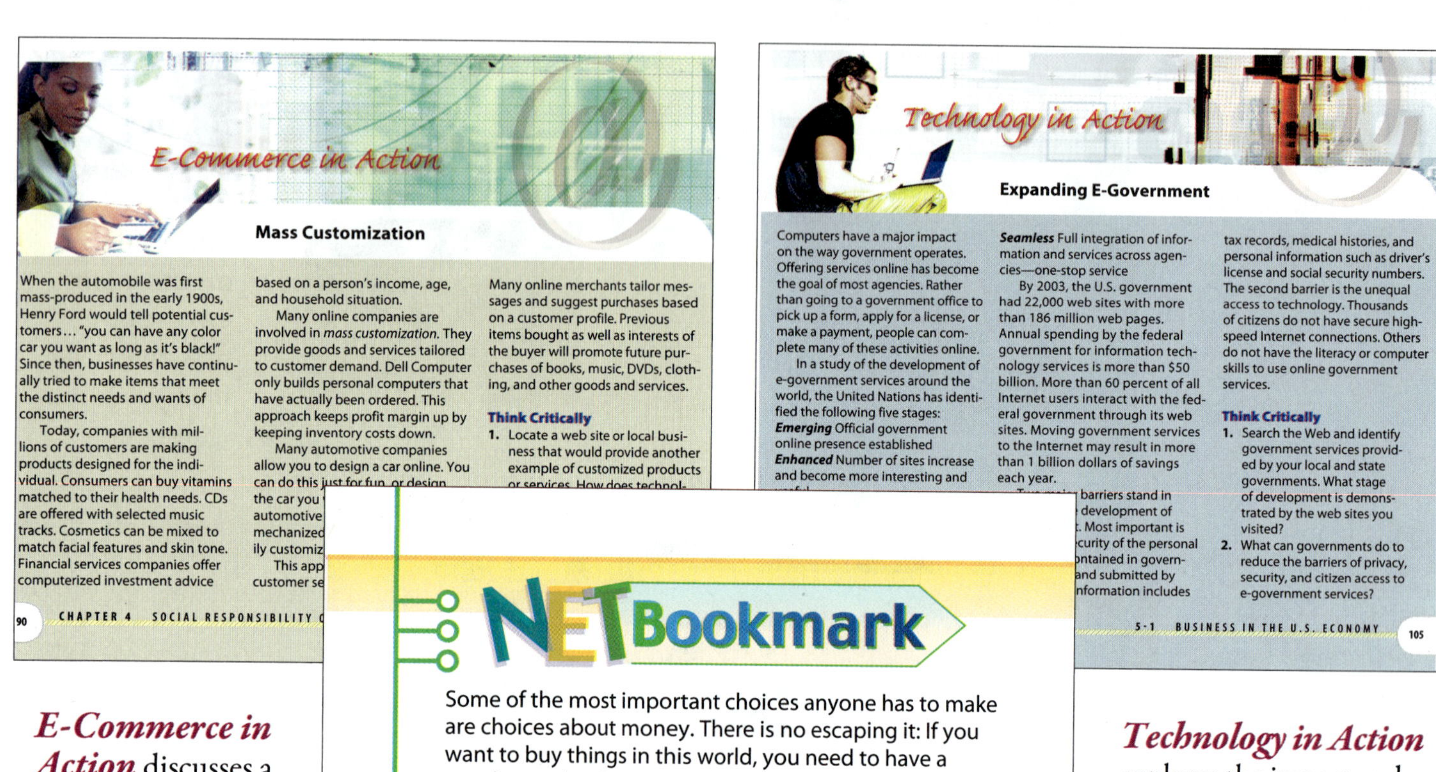

E-Commerce in Action discusses a variety of ways organizations use e-commerce to conduct business.

Technology in Action explores the impact and use of technology in today's businesses.

Net Bookmark encourages students to use the wealth of resources available free at the Xtra! Web site to do research and gather data for analysis.

Xtra! Study Tools and ***Quiz Prep*** offer free online review and study materials at the click of a button.

NEW! Web Workout is an end-of-chapter activity that gets students online to research some of the latest business topics and trends.

">

DEVELOPMENT FOR THE FUTURE

Life-Span Plan offers various activities for students to complete and incorporate into a comprehensive portfolio for use beyond the classroom.

A Question of Ethics asks students to consider ethical challenges in the workplace and research alternative solutions.

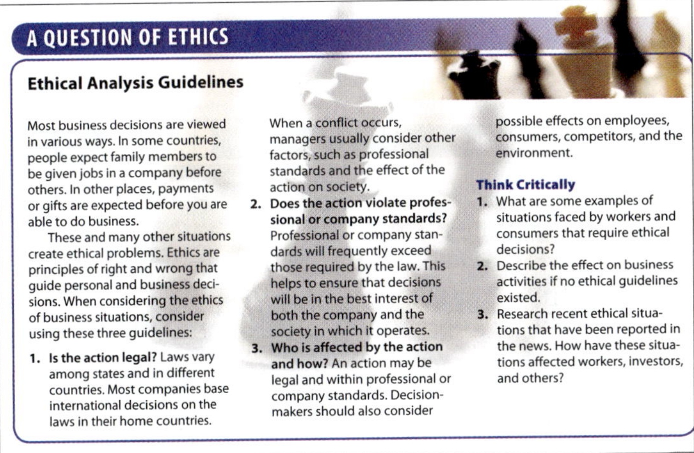

A QUESTION OF ETHICS

Ethical Analysis Guidelines

Most business decisions are viewed in various ways. In some countries, people expect family members to be given jobs in a company before others. In other places, payments or gifts are expected before you are able to do business.

These and many other situations create ethical problems. Ethics are principles of right and wrong that guide personal and business decisions. When considering the ethics of business situations, consider using these three guidelines:

1. **Is the action legal?** Laws vary among states and in different countries. Most companies base international decisions on the laws in their home countries.

When a conflict occurs, managers usually consider other factors, such as professional standards and the effect of the action on society.

2. **Does the action violate professional or company standards?** Professional or company standards will frequently exceed those required by the law. This helps to ensure that decisions will be in the best interest of both the company and the society in which it operates.

3. **Who is affected by the action and how?** An action may be legal and within professional or company standards. Decision-makers should also consider possible effects on employees, consumers, competitors, and the environment.

Think Critically

1. What are some examples of situations faced by workers and consumers that require ethical decisions?

2. Describe the effect on business activities if no ethical guidelines existed.

3. Research recent ethical situations that have been reported in the news. How have these situations affected workers, investors, and others?

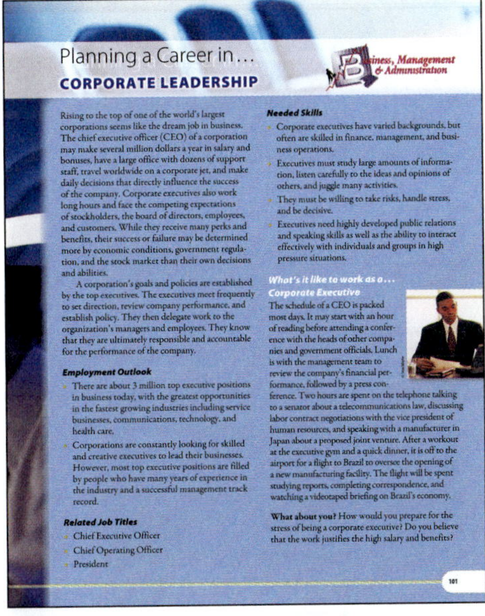

Planning a Career In . . .

features relate to Career Clusters and present the skills, education, and work experience needed for a variety of career paths.

Sharpen Your Life Skills

exposes students to important everyday skills—such as making presentations, resolving conflict, and understanding stock tables.

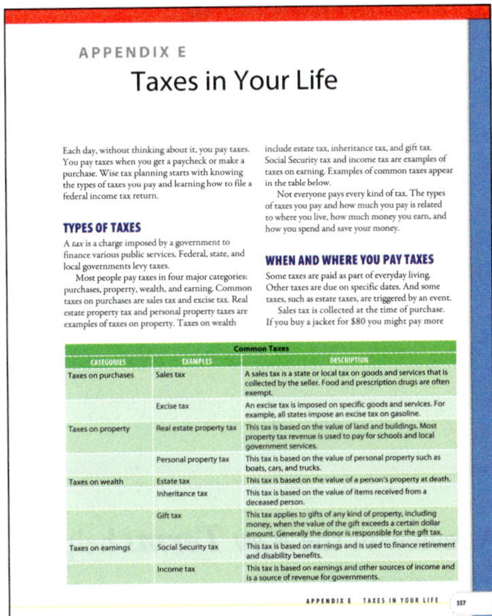

NEW! Taxes in Your Life

appendix covers types of taxes, federal income tax basics, completing a Form 1040, and tax planning strategies.

BELIEVE IN THE BEST

From the latest technology to exceptional instructor support, *Intro to Business 7E* has all the tools necessary for teaching business success.

Student Text (hardcover, 4-color, 624 pages)	0-538-44561-0
Text/eBook bundle	0-324-60366-5
Text/iMPACT Interactive Text CD bundle	0-324-69092-4
Instructor's Resource Box (see contents below)	0-538-44565-3
Instructor's Resource CD (Lesson Plans, PowerPoint, Video Guide)	0-538-44563-7
Instructor's Wraparound Edition	0-538-44562-9
Chapter and Unit Tests	0-538-44573-4
Video	0-538-44082-1
ExamView	0-538-44564-5
Activities and Projects	0-538-44571-8
Xtra! Web site	school.cengage.com/business/introtobiz

Instructor's Resource Box Includes:

- Instructor's Edition Activities and Projects Chapters 1–20
- Instructor's Edition Chapter and Unit Tests
- Spanish Resources
- BPA/FBLA Competitive Event Prep
- Communications Activity Masters
- Ethics Activity Masters
- School-to-Work/SCANS Activity Masters and Resources
- Business Math Activity Masters
- International Business Activity Masters
- Internet Activity Masters and Solutions
- Distance Learning
- Using Technology and the Internet
- Diverse Populations and Learning Styles
- Involving Families and the Community
- Strategies for Block Scheduling
- Alternative Assessment
- Test Prep and Study Skills

ABOVE AND BEYOND

The new *iMPACT Interactive Text* is a fully functioning text on CD that highlights key learning elements and hyperlinks to text subsections, key term definitions, and forms for completing end-of-chapter assessment activities.

INSTRUCTOR'S WRAPAROUND EDITION

Intro to Business

SEVENTH EDITION

LES R. DLABAY

JAMES L. BURROW

BRAD KLEINDL

SOUTH-WESTERN
CENGAGE Learning

Australia • Brazil • Japan • Korea • Mexico • Singapore • Spain • United Kingdom • United States

Intro to Business, Instructors Wraparound Edition, Seventh Edition
Les Dlabay, Brad Kleindl, James Burrow

VP/Editorial Director: Jack W. Calhoun

VP/Editor-in-Chief: Karen Schmohe

VP/Marketing: Bill Hendee

Acquisitions Editor: Eve Lewis

Developmental Editor: Karen Hein

Marketing Manager: Valerie Lauer

Marketing Coordinator: Kelley Gilreath

Content Project Manager: Darrell E. Frye

Manager of Technology, Editorial: Liz Wilkes

Technology Project Editor: Sally Nieman

Website Project Manager: Ed Stubenrauch

Manufacturing Coordinator: Kevin Kluck

Production Service: Integra Software Services

Art Director: Tippy McIntosh

Internal and Cover Designer: Liz Harasymczuk

Cover Image: Donovan Reese, Getty Images

For product information and technology assistance, contact us at
Cengage Learning Academic Resource Center, 1-800-423-0563

For permission to use material from this text or product,
submit all requests online at **www.cengage.com/permissions**
Further permissions questions can be emailed to
permissionrequest@cengage.com

ISBN 13: 978-0-538-44562-7

ISBN 10: 0-538-44562-9

South-Western Cengage Learning
5191 Natorp Boulevard
Mason, OH 45040
USA

Cengage Learning products are represented in Canada by Nelson Education, Ltd.

For your course and learning solutions, visit **school.cengage.com**

Printed in the United States of America
1 2 3 4 5 6 7   11 10 09 08 07

About the Authors

Les R. Dlabay, Ed.D., is a Professor of Business in the Department of Economics and Business at Lake Forest College in Illinois. He has taught more than 30 different business courses in high school, community college, university, teacher preparation, and adult education programs. Dr. Dlabay has presented over 250 teacher workshops and seminars emphasizing team projects and field research activities. His "hobbies" include a cereal package collection (from over 100 countries) and banknotes from 200 countries; these are used to teach economic, cultural, and political aspects of global business. In an effort to distribute the great wealth of our society with the less fortunate, Professor Dlabay makes extensive use of community service class assignments related to world hunger, poverty, and economic development.

James L. Burrow, Ph.D., has a background in marketing and human resource development. He works regularly with the business community and other organizations as a consultant on marketing and performance improvement strategies including the use of the Internet as an education and training resource. He recently retired from the faculty of North Carolina State University where he served as the coordinator of the graduate Training and Development Program for over 15 years. Dr. Burrow received degrees from the University of Northern Iowa and the University of Nebraska in Marketing and Marketing Education.

Brad Kleindl, Ph.D., is Dean of The Robert W. Plaster College of Business Administration at Missouri Southern State University. He has taught courses in marketing, international business, entrepreneurship, and Internet marketing and has presented at conferences and industry meetings across the U.S., Europe, Africa, and Asia. In the Spring of 2003 Dr. Kleindl was a Senior Fulbright Scholar in South Africa lecturing on Internet marketing, e-business, and e-commerce.

Contents

© Getty Images/PhotoDisc

© Digital Vision

© Getty Images/PhotoDisc

© Digital Vision

Chapter 18
Consumer Credit   448

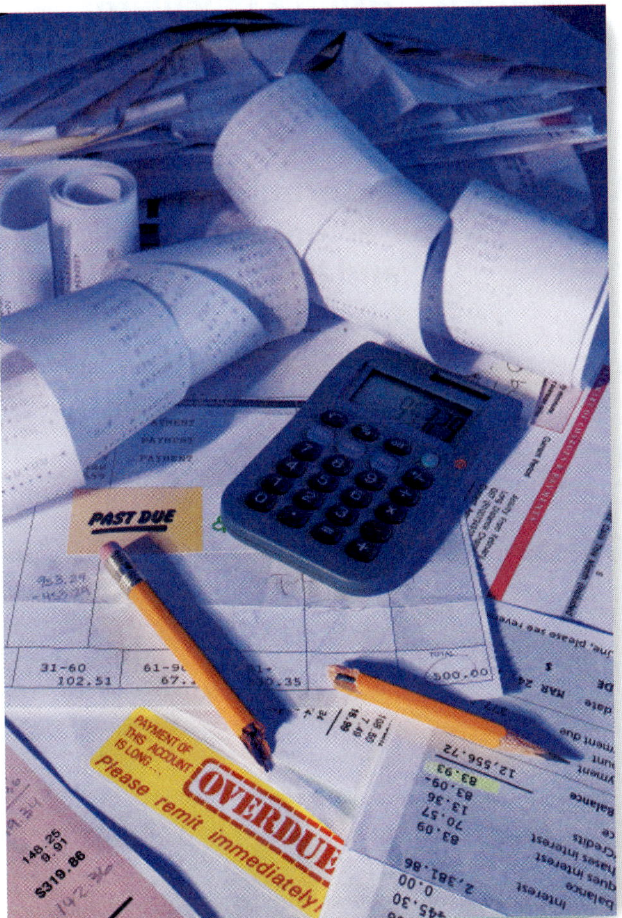

© Getty Images/PhotoDisc

Chapter 19
Savings and Investment
Strategies   478

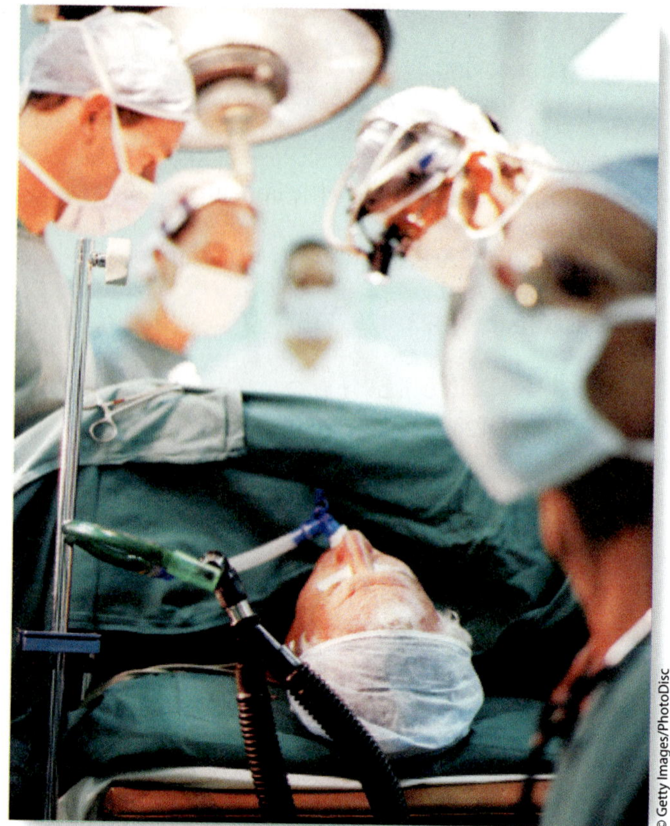

© Getty Images/PhotoDisc

© Comstock Images

Reviewers

Gina Allen
Teacher, Business Department
Union Public School
Tulsa, Oklahoma

Ian A. Barnes
Teacher, Finance Academy
Shades Valley High School
Birmingham, Alabama

Sharon Bokamper
Business Teacher
North Pulaski High School
Jacksonville, Arkansas

Scott Christy
Business and Information
Technology Instructor
Green Bay Public Schools
Green Bay, Wisconsin

Madge Gregg
Finance Academy Director
Hoover High School
Hoover, Alabama

Susan E. Hall
Business and Marketing Educator
University at Buffalo
State University of New York
Buffalo, New York

Steve Jostworth
Department Chair, Business Technology
Sycamore High School
Cincinnati, Ohio

Dennis R. Krejci
Teacher, Business Department
Tri County High School
DeWitt, Nebraska

Kathleen Lehman
Business and Computer
Technology Teacher
Sulphur High School
Sulphur, Oklahoma

Roger C. Lyder
Teacher
Pelham High School
Pelham, New Hampshire

Azzie L. Olds
Business Department Chair
North Caddo Magnet High School
Vivian, Louisiana

Joseph W. Quesnelle
Program Manager, Academy of Finance
Golightly Career and Technical Center
Detroit, Michigan

Shelli Ray
Teacher
Blue Springs South High School
Blue Springs, Missouri

Julia Ruffin
Teacher, Business Department
North Caddo Magnet High School
Vivian, Louisiana

Donald William Shumaker
Teacher and DECA Advisor
Spring Valley High School
Las Vegas, Nevada

Lola Walter
Business Teacher
Parkland High School
Allentown, Pennsylvania

Mary Williamson
Business Teacher
Peabody Magnet High School
Alexandria, Louisiana

Welcome to Intro to Business

"Using credit to buy that home theater system resulted in a much higher cost."

"The interviewer asked me some questions I didn't expect."

"Higher taxes in our community may be necessary to maintain quality police and fire protection.

These comments represent your economic roles as a consumer, worker, and citizen. Each day, you encounter many situations that require knowledge and experience to plan and make decisions. That's what we offer you.

Intro to Business will introduce you to the exciting and challenging world of business. Through the information and activities in the book you will increase your preparation to be a knowledgeable consumer, well-prepared employee, and effective citizen in our economy. This course will serve as a background for other business courses you will take in high school and in college, prepare you for future employment or business ownership, and make you a better informed citizen for an expanding international economy.

This book, along with the supplementary instructional resources, will make it possible for you to learn about many topics you will encounter throughout your life as a consumer, worker, and citizen.

GETTING STARTED

The text is carefully designed and written to present an interesting discussion of business and to help you learn important business principles. It is organized into 20 chapters with each chapter divided into several lessons. Lessons are organized around short *Goals* that identify the important ideas you will learn. You are also given a list of *Key Terms* at the beginning of every lesson that introduces the vocabulary of business. You will find a variety of figures, illustrations, and photographs that offer additional insights and interesting ideas.

Business Outside the Box

These actual stories start each unit and will help you think about business in a different way. The company situations represent some unusual and innovative business enterprises. These articles are just the start of many real-world examples you will encounter throughout the book.

Planning a Career In . . .

What would you like to do in the future? Each chapter starts with information about a career field. These features will help you think about the many career opportunities from which you might choose.

Focus on Real Life

Daily situations provide the basis for learning. These situations at the start of each lesson can get you thinking about the topic to be covered. Put yourself in the situation and decide what you might do.

HELPING YOU LEARN

Many features are included especially to assist you in your learning by providing enhancements to your textbook.

FYI

Did you know that …? These short items provide solid information that can make a difference in your life. Provided are information about effective business management, wise consumer decisions, and career planning suggestions.

Net BookMark

No greater research source is available to enhance your learning than the Internet. These features refer you to school.cengage.com/business/introtobiz to gain additional information on various business topics.

Work as a Team

As a matter of work and life, you will work on a team at some point in time. These exercises will allow you to experience dynamics that enhance the learning process. You will also learn about the benefits and concerns of shared decision making.

Think Critically Through Visuals

"A picture is worth a thousand words." A picture is also the basis for expanded knowledge. Throughout the chapter, you will view various photos. Then, a question will challenge you to apply your learning to these visual situations.

ALSO OF INTEREST TO YOU

Many special features have been developed and placed within the chapters and lessons to encourage you to think about business in new ways and to study innovative examples of business practices.

Business Improving Society

While businesses must earn a profit to survive, most companies also have other goals. These essays provide examples of organizations that are attempting to enhance economic development and improve the quality of life in the United States and around the world.

Corporate Social Responsibility

In addition to economic development, businesses can also play a positive role environmentally. This feature highlights businesses that interact with the community in ways that result in beneficial effects on society and the environment.

Doing Business in . . .

Every organization is affected by international business activities. A basic knowledge of doing business in other countries is vital for living and working in the global economy.

E-commerce in Action

Today, doing business around the world can be as easy as doing business around the block. E-commerce makes use of the Internet and other technology to buy, sell, promote, and communicate information about goods and services.

A Question of Ethics

Each day, decisions are made that may not seem fair for some in our society. You will consider many ethical issues in your life. This feature can help you better prepare for those situations.

Technology in Action

What types of companies do not use computers in some way? There are very few. Your computer skills and technology knowledge are necessary for every work situation as well as for many consumer activities.

Sharpen Your Life Skills

Certain skills are vital in every school and work setting. For example, researching, working in teams, and making effective presentations are abilities that will serve you today and in the future.

MEASURING YOUR PROGRESS

Intro to Business provides you with various kinds of assessment. After each main topic, a *Checkpoint* is provided that asks you a questions about the material. At the end of each lesson there is a *Lesson Assessment* that provides exercises to help you master the concepts in the lesson. At the end of each chapter is an extensive *Chapter Assessment* that provides a number of ways for you to test and apply what you have learned.

Checkpoint

After every section of reading, you will encounter a review question. These will help you determine if you have learned the main idea for this material.

Lesson Assessment

At the end of each lesson, you will have a few *Key Concept* questions to help you test your knowledge of the material. In addition, *Make Academic Connections* are exercises that will enhance your learning by showing you the relationship of business to other courses in your school.

Chapter Assessment

At the end of every chapter, a variety of exercises and activities will give you the opportunity to check your progress. Study questions, vocabulary exercises, decision-making cases, and research projects are offered to measure and expand your learning.

The chapter assessment begins with **Business Notes** that summarize each lesson. The next section is **Communicate Business Concepts** that ask you to think about ideas from the chapter as you solve a problem or gather information. In **Develop Your Business Language** you match the key terms from the chapter with the correct definitions. A short case problem is presented in **Decision-Making Strategies** with challenging questions to demonstrate your problem-solving and critical thinking skills. **Make Academic Connections** are activities that show the relationship of business to other courses in your school's curriculum. **Linking School and Community** offers an opportunity to see how what you are learning in Intro to Business can be applied in your neighborhood and your community. The **Portfolio Activity**, located on the Xtra! web site, asks you to select an activity completed in the chapter to put into a portfolio.

THERE'S STILL MORE

WINNING EDGE

Your ability to work under pressure is a vital skill for business. At the end of each chapter, these activities are based on competitive events for the FBLA (www.fbla-pbl.org) and the BPA (www.bpanet.org).

GLOBAL BUSINESS PROJECT

How might you do business in Asia or Africa? This end-of-unit project provides an opportunity to plan, organize, and implement global business activities.

LIFE-SPAN PLAN PROJECT

Several decision areas must be considered throughout your life. The Life-Span activities will guide you when making choices related to your education, career, family, personal finances, and community involvement.

Now it's time get started on your educational journey using *Intro to Business*. We wish you a life of great success and personal satisfaction.

Les Dlabay
Jim Burrow
Brad Kleindl

The fact that you are reading a copy of *Intro to Business* shows a number of things about you. It probably means you have chosen to sign up for a course that will teach you about businesses and how they operate in the United States. Studying the role businesses play in the nation's society, politics, or economy may interest you. Questions such as, "What causes some businesses to prosper while others fail?" or "What types of people become successful business leaders?" are ones that you may have asked yourself. You may have wondered whether a career in business is right for you. Becoming a success in business, either as an employee or owner, may already be a basic goal you have set for yourself. Whether or not this is true of you, this book will provide you with knowledge and skills you may use to make better decisions throughout your life.

YOUR PERSONAL GOALS

Goals are the things that people want most to achieve in their lives. They are the things that hold the greatest value to them. Most people have set a wide range of goals for themselves. Some are *short-term goals* that they hope to achieve within a year. Others are *long-term goals* that will require many years to attain. Individuals' goals are likely to involve family, living conditions, education, careers, community, and many other aspects of their lives. The goals you set for yourself are based on your personal values, your hopes, and your dreams. Although many people share common goals, most people also have unique goals that set them apart from others.

There is no way to judge most goals as right or wrong, or better or worse. Your most important goal may be to study law and become a judge while your best friend might want to own a farm and grow tomatoes. Your brother may want to start a family at a young age while you prefer to put off marriage and family responsibilities until well into the future. As long as a person's goals are based on what she or he really wants from life, there is no reason for them to be the same as other people's goals.

Almost every important goal you could set for yourself involves topics you will learn about while studying this textbook. Suppose, for example, your most important personal goal is to have a happy and secure family life. You might think that this goal has little to do with what you will learn about businesses this year. But, if what you learn about businesses helps you make a better career choice, then you may be able to earn a greater income and be more satisfied with your life. This will also allow you to provide a better standard of living for a family. The same is true for almost any other personal goal you might set.

A LIFE-SPAN PLAN

As you grow older you should expect the things you want most in your life to change. Today you might believe that owning a nice car is your most important goal. In ten years you may be more concerned with having a rewarding career, buying a home, or saving for your children's education. Even later you will want to have a satisfying retirement. Important events in you life, such as preparing for a career, raising a family or enjoying retirement are parts of your *life cycle*.

Your *life span* is the time from your birth to your death. It includes the events that make up your life cycle. When you are young, you will set long-term goals that you want to achieve over a period of years during your life span. You may think of your life span as a straight line that contains the events of your life cycle.

The *life-span timeline* above can help you understand the relationship between a life span and events in a person's life cycle. It shows a life span as a straight line along the top of the figure. Examples of events in the life cycle appear beneath the time in a person's life when they might happen. If you construct a figure like this for yourself, it is likely to have different events taking place at different times because your life will not be exactly the same as anyone else's.

Life-span goals are long-term goals that you want most to reach during your life. They shape many of the most important decisions you will make. Examples of life-span goals include earning a college degree, owning a business, raising a family, or achieving financial security. For most people, life-span goals don't just happen. Successful people create long-term plans for how they can achieve their life-span goals. These plans are called *life-span plans.* You will be asked to choose life-span goals that you will use to create a life-span plan of your own. This text is specially designed to help you complete this assignment. You will see Life-Span Plan icons, like the one in the margin, placed near parts of the text that can be helpful in setting your life-span goals and preparing a life-span plan for yourself. For each icon, an assignment or activity is listed at the end of this introduction by page number. Completing these assignments and saving them to use later will help you construct your life-span plan.

A LIFE-SPAN PLAN FOR KELLY

To help you prepare your own life-span plan, consider the example of Kelly. Kelly is fifteen years old and a high school sophomore. Roy, a senior at her school, is her steady boyfriend. They have talked about their future and getting married someday, but not for several years. They have agreed to wait until they both finish their educations, get jobs, and save some money.

Kelly's favorite subject in school is art. She has signed up for every art class that she could fit into her schedule. Kelly wants a career in the art world, but not as an artist. She likes the idea of working in an art museum or gallery, but she also thinks of herself as an entrepreneur. Kelly dreams of owning a gallery where she will showcase and sell the works of local artists.

In addition to continuing to develop her skills as an artist, Kelly knows that she will need to learn how to run a business. This is one of the reasons she chose to take a class titled *Intro to Business.* While taking this class, Kelly completed a variety of assignments that helped her learn many things about herself. She saved all

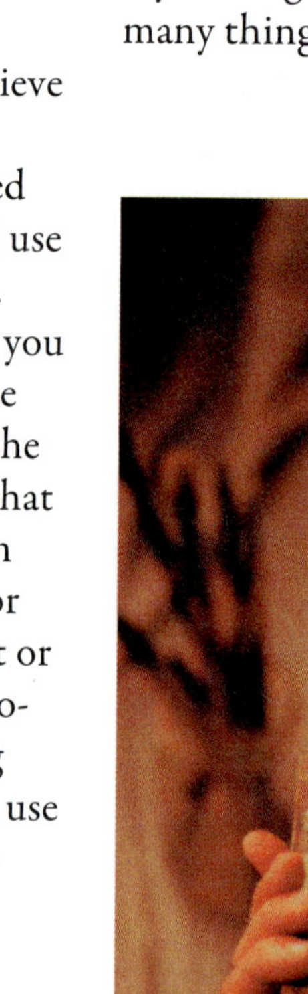

of these assignments and used them to help her complete her life-span plan by taking these steps.

FIRST THINGS FIRST

To begin her life-span plan, Kelly identified six central life-span goals that she most wants to achieve over the next 50 years. These goals fit in well with her values, interests, and personality. They are to:

1. Gain training and education needed to work in a retail art gallery.

2. Own and operate a successful retail art gallery.

3. Get married, have several children, and own a house in a nice neighborhood.

4. Become financially secure.

5. Be active in community, church, and local government.

6. Be able to retire and take up other interests by the age of 65.

Kelly realizes that achieving these life-span goals will involve careful planning and many trade-offs. Almost all life-span goals people set require money. To pay for her education, a business of her own, a home, and a secure retirement she will need to save and invest part of the income she receives during her working life. At times, she may need to borrow funds from others. She will need to construct and follow a budget that allows her to do this. At the present, Kelly may decide to limit the amount she spends on eating out, clothing, and entertainment so she can save more to pay for college tuition later. Kelly will also need to identify related short-term goals that can help her achieve her more-important life-span goals in the future.

RELATED GOALS

Kelly's central life-span goals are related to each other. Saving and investing to achieve financial security, for example, will help her pay for training and later to start a business. If her business is successful, she will be able to afford the house she wants to own. Financial security will also allow Kelly to enjoy a few luxuries. For example, Kelly would like to visit Ireland and see where her ancestors lived. If her business is a success, she will be able to take this trip.

Kelly wants to achieve many short- and long-term goals that are not central goals in her life. These include buying cars, furniture, and owning a sailboat. Although these goals are important, they aren't among the things Kelly cares most about in life, and so they are not listed in her life-span plan. In preparing her life-span plan, Kelly listed and evaluated her goals to decide which ones were the most important. The most important goals are part of her life-span plan.

USING A TABLE FOR ORGANIZATION

Kelly organized her life-span goals in a table as shown below. Across the top she placed six categories to represent her six central life-span goals. On the left side she placed periods of time. These started with the next two years at the top and went fifty years into the future at the bottom. She then placed her goals according to when she would like to achieve them and how they contribute to her central life-span goals. In this way, she created a life-span plan that she believes will help her accomplish what she wants most in life.

Kelly feels a sense of satisfaction with her work. She knows that she will almost surely revise her plan in the future, but she has a foundation on which to build. She can use her plan to help make decisions now. When she makes her class schedule for next year she will sign up for accounting, business management, and more art classes. She knows what type of work to look for and how to spend and save her income. Because she has definite goals, she is better able to make good spending decisions. Having goals makes it easier not to spend money for things she doesn't really need.

KELLY'S LIFE-SPAN PLAN

TIME	EDUCATION	CAREER	FAMILY	FINANCIAL	COMMUNITY	RETIREMENT
Next 2 years	Complete high school. Apply to college.	Find a part-time job in an art gallery or museum.	Help parents with younger children.	Save $2,500 each year to help pay tuition.	Be an active member of my church.	No action is required at this time.
5 years from now	Graduate from college.	Work full-time in an art gallery or museum.	Find a nice apartment in a good location.	Save and invest income to buy a home.	Teach art classes to children at my church.	Open a retirement account.
10 years from now	Take classes in small business management.	Accept a managerial position at an art gallery.	Get married and buy a small home. Have one child.	Save and invest to buy an art gallery.	Teach art classes at a local community college.	Buy life insurance.
20 years from now	Travel to Ireland to see local artist's work.	Buy or start an art gallery.	Buy a larger house. Have another child.	Start a fund for children's education.	Continue teaching art classes.	Continue saving in retirement account.
35 years from now	Teach art store management classes at a community college.	Build a successful business and look for a person to help run it.	See children graduate from college. Buy a vacation home at the beach.	Increase saving and investments now that children have moved out.	Run for town council or participate in government in some other way.	Investigate volunteer work I might enjoy.
50 years from now	Take classes in Irish cooking and history.	Sell business. Take part-time job in art store.	Buy a retirement home in a place where it's warm.	Manage investments carefully.	Volunteer to advise people who have small businesses.	Take at least one long trip each year and visit grandchildren.

Kelly's life-span plan is right for her. It fits her values, personality and family situation. Her plan, however, would not be right for most students, including you. You aren't Kelly. You have other values, abilities, and interests. Her personality is not your personality. Her family is not your family. You need to make your own life-span plan.

YOUR OWN LIFE-SPAN PLAN

Near the end of this class you will be asked to prepare a life-span plan for yourself. To do this, you should reflect on what you've leaned throughout this course. You will study numerous topics and finish many activities that you can use to help you complete this assignment. You will also want to consider things about yourself that were not directly covered in this course. The type and size of family you want to have is important, but will not be discussed in this course. The same is true of where you want to live and the role you wish to play in your community. Preparing your life-span plan will require you to consider all of your values and goals, not just those that are related to businesses and your career choice.

After you accumulate as many useful resources as you can, use these materials as references as you write a list of your goals. Base your goals on what you want from life for yourself, your family, and your community. Sort them according to whether they are short- or long-term goals, and then classify them into overall life-span goals. Place your goals on a grid similar to Kelly's to construct your life-span plan.

When you have finished your life-span plan, it would be helpful to ask an experienced person to review your plan with you. A teacher, guidance counselor, or other adult you respect would be a good choice. Discuss your choices and the feasibility of your plan. This person can offer advice and encouragement for achieving your goals.

Making a life-span plan is an important first step. But, it is only a first step. Putting your life-span plan into action can make the difference between just thinking about your future and actually achieving the life-span goals that are most important to you. If you fail to act on your life-span plan, it will only be a piece of paper.

A table showing the locations of Life-Span Plan icons and activities you may complete to help you create your own life-span plan appears on the next two pages.

© Getty Images/PhotoDisc

LIFE-SPAN PLAN ACTIVITIES

PAGE	ACTIVITY
14	Write an essay that describes how you could use the decision-making process to choose classes for next year that will help you achieve your life-span goals. In what other ways will the decision-making process benefit you in the future?
44	Calculate your savings rate (percent of your current income that you save). Do you believe you save enough of your income? Explain how saving is related to people achieving their life-span goals. Set a short-term saving goal that you could achieve now to help you eventually reach future life-span goals.
55	Identify your special aptitudes or abilities that you believe could help you achieve your life-span goals. Explain how these aptitudes or abilities are similar to nations that have an absolute or comparative advantage in production and trade.
76	Explain how environmental issues might affect the life-span goals you set for yourself.
79	Do you have a personal code of ethics? Explain how your ethics might affect the life-span goals you set for yourself.
90	Explain how government taxing and spending could affect the life-span goals you set for yourself as well as your ability to achieve these goals.
108	Is owning a business a life-span goal you have set for yourself? Describe steps you would need to take to achieve this life-span goal.
128	What personal characteristics do you have that could help you become a successful entrepreneur? Describe how these characteristics may affect the life-span goals you set for your future.
138	What hobbies, interest, and experiences do you have that could help you achieve your life-span goals? Describe steps you could take now that would expand your experiences and opportunities for achieving your life-span goals.
157	List and evaluate your own leadership abilities. Explain how your leadership skills may affect the life-span goals you set for yourself.
176	Why might it not make sense to set a life-span goal of becoming a telephone switchboard operator? Explain why it is necessary to understand changes that are taking place in the workplace when you set your life-span goals.
189	How important do you believe family leave policies, flextime, or job sharing would be to you in choosing a career? Explain why work-life relationships are important when people set their life-span goals.
203	Describe a career planning process you might complete that would help you achieve your life-span goals.
209	Complete a personal assessment of yourself. It should include listings of your interests, values, talents and abilities. Explain how these lists may help you create your own life-span plan.
217	Complete a resume for yourself similar to the one in Figure 9-4 in your text. Identify steps you could take over the next year that would improve your resume and increase your chances of being hired. Explain how these short-term steps might help you achieve your life-span goals.
240	How easily are you able to communicate with other people? Explain how an ability to communicate with other people can affect the life-span goals you set and your ability to achieve them.

  LIFE-SPAN PLAN PROJECT

PAGE	ACTIVITY
266	Do you believe that you are *computer literate* (able to understand and use computers efficiently)? Are you comfortable using computers? Describe how the computerization of our society and economy may affect your ability to achieve your life-span goals.
278	Explain how you believe the growth of e-commerce will affect the life-span goals you set or your ability to achieve them.
302	Describe ways in which the financial planning functions of a business are similar to the financial planning that must be done by people to achieve their life-span goals. Evaluate the status of your own financial planning. How will you know if you have the financial resources to achieve your life-span goals?
310	Explain why making good financial decisions is no less important to individuals than it is to businesses. How do you make your financial decisions? Will this process help you achieve your life-span goals?
324	Identify and describe similarities between production planning and life-span planning. Describe steps you could take to produce success in achieving your life-span goals.
351	Describe several examples of losses you might suffer that would prevent you from achieving your life-span goals. Explain why buying adequate insurance is an important part of every person's life-span plan.
377	Explain why an ability to make wise buying decisions is important for achieving your life-span goals. Do you believe buying skills contribute to your ability to reach your life-span goals? What could you do to improve your buying skills?
404	Explain why it is important for people to create and use a budget process when they are young even if they have only small amounts of income and make few expenditures. Do you have a budget process that you use? How can a budget process help you achieve your life-span goals?
410	Describe the role of financial planning in the creation of a person's life-span plan. Do you have a financial plan? Explain why people who fail to create and follow a financial plan often fail to achieve their life-span goals.
424	Do you believe that people need a safe and reliable banking system to achieve their life-span goals? Describe how you expect to use banks and other financial institutions to reach the goals you set in your life-span plan.
450	What life-span goals might you set that would require you to use credit? Describe steps you can take in the next few years to create a credit history that will help you borrow funds in the future.
460	Describe why the excessive use of credit can prevent people from achieving their life-span goals. How would you decide when, or when not, to borrow funds?
481	Explain why people who have created life-span plans are often more successful in saving than those who have not. How might your life-span plan help you save?
489	Describe how a life-span plan can influence the types of investment choices a person makes. How much risk are you willing to take? How may your willingness to accept risk affect the life-span goals you set for yourself?
498	Will home ownership be one of your life-span goals? Explain how buying a home is different from other types of investments you may make.
517	Why is the purchase of property and liability insurance important to all life-span plans? What amounts and types of insurance should you plan to buy in the next few years?
524	Most life-span plans are created to serve a family. Explain why these plans should include life insurance for all adult members. When do you expect to purchase life insurance? How much and what type will you buy?

UNIT 1 BUSINESS IN THE GLOBAL ECONOMIC ENVIRONMENT	OVERVIEW	SPECIAL FEATURES	LESSON ASSESSMENT	
Chapter 1 Economic Decisions and Systems, pp. 4–31	Chapter 1 introduces the important economic concepts that determine the products and services available for consumers and how economic systems are structured.	Business Improving Society: Heifer International, p. 27; Focus on Real Life, pp. 6, 12, 17, 23; FYI, pp. 9, 18; Life-Span Plan, p. 14; Net Bookmark, p. 13; Planning a Career in Corporate Economics, p. 5; Sharpen Your Life Skills: Research Skills, p. 16; Technology in Action: Online Micropayments, p. 10; Winning Edge BPA: Entrepreneurship Event, p. 31; Work as a Team, pp. 7, 15, 20, 25	Checkpoints, pp. 7, 8, 11, 13, 15, 18, 21, 22, 25, 26 Key Concepts, Make Academic Connections, pp. 11, 15, 22, 26	
Chapter 2 Economic Activity, pp. 32–51	Chapter 2 provides students with an understanding of measurements commonly used to gauge economic activity and business conditions in our society.	Corporate Social Responsibility: Cleantech: Energy Alternatives and Environmentally Friendly Products, p. 45; Doing Business in Ecuador, p. 43; Focus on Real Life, pp. 34, 38, 44; FYI, pp. 37, 40; Life-Span Plan, p. 44; Net Bookmark, p. 39; Planning a Career in Economic Development, p. 33; A Question of Ethics: Ethical Analysis Guidelines, p. 39; Winning Edge FBLA: Emerging Business Issues Event, p. 51; Work as a Team, pp. 35, 42, 46	Checkpoints, pp. 35, 37, 40, 41, 42, 45, 46, 47 Key Concepts, Make Academic Connections, pp. 37, 42, 47	
Chapter 3 Business in the Global Economy, pp. 52–73	Chapter 3 provides students with a foundation for understanding business in the global economy. It focuses on exporting, international trade, and global business activities.	Business Improving Society: The Hunger Site, p. 69; Focus on Real Life, pp. 54, 60, 65; FYI, pp. 59, 67; Life-Span Plan, p. 55; Net Bookmark, p. 68; Planning a Career in International Business, p. 53; A Question of Ethics: Bribery and Gift Giving, p. 57; Technology in Action: Language Translation, p. 63; Winning Edge FBLA: Desktop Publishing Event, p. 73; Work as a Team, pp. 57, 61, 66	Checkpoints pp. 56, 57, 59, 61, 63, 64, 66, 67, 68 Key Concepts, Make Academic Connections, pp. 59, 64, 68	
Chapter 4 Social Responsibility of Business and Government, pp. 74–95	Chapter 4 offers a basic understanding of social responsibility along with discussion of the various roles of government in relation to business.	Doing Business in Vietnam, p. 86; E-Commerce in Action: Mass Customization, p. 90; Focus on Real Life, pp. 76, 82, 87; FYI, pp. 77, 83; Life-Span Plan, pp. 76, 79, 91; Net Bookmark, p. 88; Planning a Career in Government, p. 75; Sharpen Your Life Skills: Working in Teams, p. 81; Winning Edge FBLA: Community Service Project Event, p. 95; Work as a Team, pp. 79, 84, 88	Checkpoints, pp. 78, 80, 83, 84, 85, 88, 89, 91 Key Concepts, Make Academic Connections, pp. 80, 85, 91	

CHAPTER ASSESSMENT	TEACHING RESOURCES	TEACHING STRATEGIES
Business Notes, Communicate Business Concepts, Develop Your Business Language, Decision-Making Strategies, Make Academic Connections, Linking School and Community, Web Workout, pp. 28–31	*Activities and Study Guide,* Ch. 1 *Chapter and Unit Tests,* Ch. 1 *Spanish Resources,* Ch. 1 **Exam***View*® CD, Ch. 1 *Instructor's Resource CD* *Xtra! Web Site*	**Applied Skills** Building Study Skills, p. 21; Communication, pp. 8, 27; Mathematics, p. 13; Technology, p. 18; Writing Across the Curriculum, p. 16 **Different Learning Abilities** At-Risk, p. 14; Hearing Impaired, pp. 10, 19; Limited English Proficiency, pp. 8, 25; Visually Impaired, p. 17 **Different Learning Styles** Auditory Learner, p. 7; Kinesthetic Learner, p. 23; Print Learner, p. 20; Visual Learner, pp. 6, 12, 24 **Teaching Strategies** Expand Beyond the Classroom, pp. 7, 9
Business Notes, Communicate Business Concepts, Develop Your Business Language, Decision-Making Strategies, Make Academic Connections, Linking School and Community, Web Workout, pp. 48–51	*Activities and Study Guide,* Ch. 2 *Chapter and Unit Tests,* Ch. 2 *Spanish Resources,* Ch. 2 **Exam***View*® CD, Ch. 2 *Instructor's Resource CD* *Xtra! Web Site*	**Applied Skills** Communication, p. 46; Language Arts, p. 43; Mathematics, p. 35; Technology, p. 45 **Different Learning Abilities** At-Risk, p. 40; Gifted, p. 41; Hearing Impaired, p. 44 **Different Learning Styles** Auditory Learner, p. 38; Tactile Learner, p. 39; Visual Learner, p. 34 **Teaching Strategies** Expand Beyond the Classroom, p. 36
Business Notes, Communicate Business Concepts, Develop Your Business Language, Decision-Making Strategies, Make Academic Connections, Linking School and Community, Web Workout, pp. 70–73	*Activities and Study Guide,* Ch. 3 *Chapter and Unit Tests,* Ch. 3 *Spanish Resources,* Ch. 3 **Exam***View*® CD, Ch. 3 *Instructor's Resource CD* *Xtra! Web Site*	**Applied Skills** Building Study Skills, p. 55; Communication, p. 56; Mathematics, p. 62; Writing Across the Curriculum, p. 66 **Different Learning Abilities** Attention Deficit Disorder, p. 65; Dyslexia, p. 61; Specific Learning Disability, p. 54; Visually Impaired, p. 60 **Different Learning Styles** Auditory Learner, p. 67; Kinesthetic Learner, p. 69; Print Learner, p. 58
Business Notes, Communicate Business Concepts, Develop Your Business Language, Decision-Making Strategies, Make Academic Connections, Linking School and Community, Web Workout, pp. 92–95	*Activities and Study Guide,* Ch. 4 *Chapter and Unit Tests,* Ch. 4 *Spanish Resources,* Ch. 4 **Exam***View*® CD, Ch. 4 *Instructor's Resource CD* *Xtra! Web Site*	**Applied Skills** Communication, p. 88; Geography, p. 86; Language Arts, p. 79; Science, p. 76; Word Processing/Office Technology, p. 83 **Different Learning Abilities** Gifted, p. 84; Limited English Proficiency, p. 90; Specific Learning Disability, p. 82; Visually Impaired, p. 77 **Different Learning Styles** Tactile Learner, p. 78; Visual Learner, p. 87 **Teaching Strategies** Expand Beyond the Classroom, pp. 81, 89

UNIT 1

Business in the Global Economic Environment

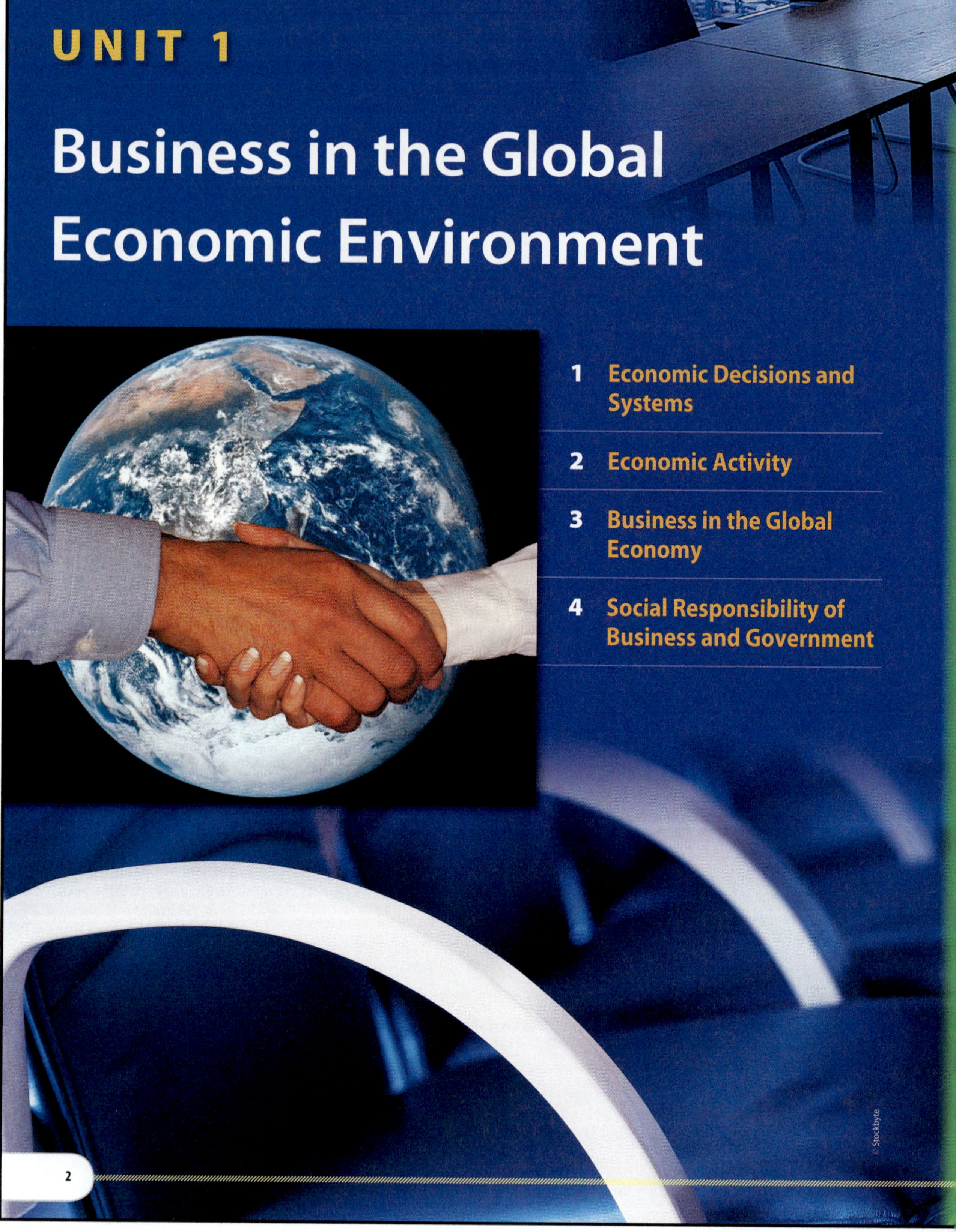

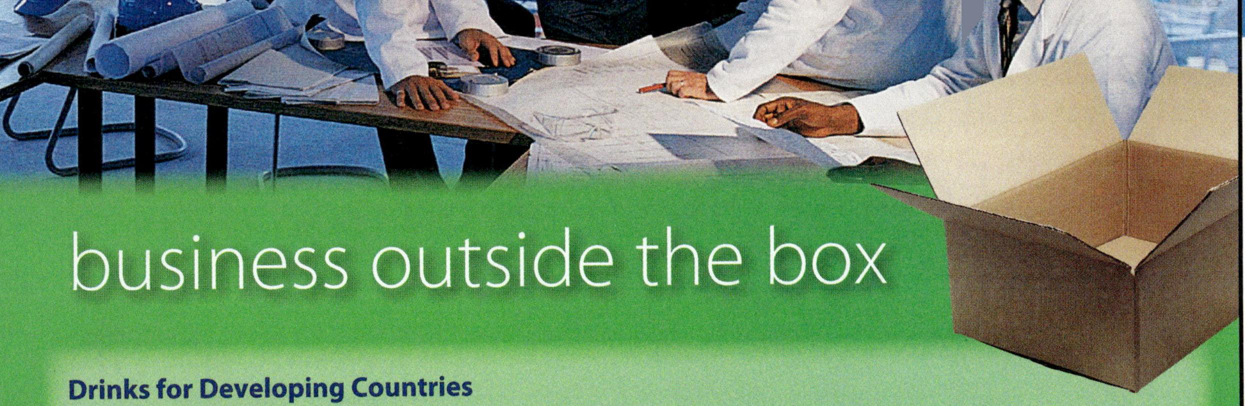

business outside the box

Drinks for Developing Countries

Vitingo, an orange-flavored drink, not only provides refreshment but also could save lives. The Coca-Cola Company offers the product in Botswana and other countries. This juice drink contains 12 vitamins and minerals to help reduce anemia, blindness, and other health problems among children in developing economies.

The drink originally sold for about 20 cents for an 8-ounce liquid serving. Even at that price, few could afford it in these very poor nations. A revised formula of the drink reduced costs—and the price—making Vitingo more affordable to those who need it most. This effort is a part of Coca-Cola's strategy to increase sales of its major products. In addition, the company is contributing to the health and well-being of people living in very difficult situations.

Think Critically

What are some products and services that companies could offer to improve quality of life around the world?

Is It Really Organic?

Increasing health consciousness and concerns about food safety have led to a strong growth in demand for organic foods. Organic crops are raised without using pesticides and without fertilizers derived from petroleum or sewage sludge. Organically raised animals eat organic feed and have access to the outdoors. They are not given antibiotics or growth hormones.

Organic food sales in the United States have grown an average of 20 percent each year since 1997. Organic foods are more expensive to produce but they return a greater profit.

Most organic foods are sold to customers who purchase from small local farmers.

Large companies have been working to develop ways to capture a part of the growing market but have struggled to gain consumer confidence. Some consumers don't trust that a large corporation can actually produce organic food. They are more likely to believe that a local organic farmer follows the practices required to insure organic quality standards.

Dole Foods places a sticker on each of its organic bananas, but it is no ordinary sticker. The sticker includes a three-digit farm code and an invitation to visit their web site. When the farm code is entered, the visitor is linked to a profile of the farm where the fruit was grown. In addition to the name and location of the farm, information about organic certification is included.

Think Critically

Why are people willing to pay higher prices for organic foods? If large companies are able to sell organic products successfully, what kinds of problems will small organic farmers face?

After reading Business Outside the Box, ask students what they think about the topics. Have they heard or read about these products and businesses before? At the conclusion of the discussion, direct students to answer the Think Critically questions that follow the features.

Drinks for Developing Countries

Point out that many companies offer different products in different countries. These products may be quite different from U.S. products and meet consumers' needs that are not apparent to U.S. consumers.

Think Critically *Answer*

Answers will vary, but could include low-spoilage food products, cell phone service, water purifying systems, improved crops and livestock, and cheap and sturdy housing materials.

Is It Really Organic?

Explain that usually small businesses are trying to find ways to compete with larger businesses. Ask students to explain why the organic foods market might be different.

Think Critically *Answer*

Answers will vary. People who buy organic foods are willing to pay higher prices because they believe organic foods are safer and healthier. If large companies can produce and distribute the products more cheaply, small organic farmers may have to reduce their prices.

Portfolio Activity

Portfolio work samples validate skill level and a student's ability to accomplish tasks frequently performed on the job. The most important reason for including samples in a portfolio is to demonstrate a student's abilities and skills. In selecting work samples for each unit, students should always have a choice of which activities to include. Students might be encouraged to include samples from the end-of-chapter activities, particularly Communicate Business Concepts, Decision-Making Strategies, Make Academic Connections, and Linking School and Community.

CHAPTER OVERVIEW

This chapter introduces the important economic concepts that determine the products and services available for consumers and how economic systems are structured.

1-1 Satisfying Needs and Wants

In this lesson, students learn to distinguish between wants and needs and between goods and services.

1-2 Economic Choices

This lesson presents the basic economic problem facing consumers and businesses and the steps in making effective decisions.

1-3 Economic Systems

In this lesson, students learn how the main types of economic systems answer three economic questions.

1-4 Supply and Demand

This lesson discusses supply and demand and how they affect the prices of goods and services offered for sale.

CHAPTER 1

Economic Decisions and Systems

© Getty Images/PhotoDisc

4

Teaching Resources

Activities and Study Guide, Ch. 1
Chapter and Unit Tests, Ch. 1
Spanish Resources, Ch. 1

ExamView® *CD,* Ch. 1
Instructor's Resource CD
- PowerPoint Slides, Ch. 1
- Lesson Plans, Ch. 1

Xtra! Web Site

school.cengage.com/business/introtobiz
- Study Tools, 1-1, 1-2, 1-3, 1-4
- Quiz Prep, Ch. 1
- Net Bookmark, Ch. 1
- Crossword Puzzle, Ch. 1
- Portfolio Activity, Ch. 1

Planning a Career in…
CORPORATE ECONOMICS

Economists play an important role in the business world. They are often asked to be fortunetellers. They try to predict what economic changes are coming. This is a very important task, as businesses and government officials use these predictions to make decisions that affect the economic future. Most economists work in government positions, for businesses and business associations, or as teachers and professors in colleges and universities.

Economists working for corporations forecast the size of markets, changes in consumer demand, and changes in sales and costs. They analyze competitors' growth and market share and advise their company on how to plan. Today, economists pay attention to the international economy and the economic conditions in countries where the company currently operates or plans to expand.

Employment Outlook

- More than half of all economists work for corporations or industry associations that provide research and information to businesses.
- Opportunities for corporate economists should be good in the future. The need for economists results from increased competition and the importance of the global economy. Businesses increasingly rely on statistical analysis to support decisions.
- Economists need at least a master's degree and many obtain a doctorate as they move into senior-level positions.
- Specialized opportunities are available in banking, finance, insurance, and the securities industry.

Related Job Titles

- Senior Economist
- Quantitative Analyst
- Forecaster
- Research Assistant

Needed Skills

- Mathematics, statistics, econometrics, research design, and computer science
- Attention to detail to ensure accuracy of data analysis
- Work independently and for long hours gathering and analyzing information
- Present findings, both orally and in writing, in a clear, concise manner

What's it like to work in… Corporate Economics

Pierre Latrobe is on his way to the office at 4 a.m. each morning. As an associate analyst, he helps prepare a morning briefing. He is responsible for tracking changes in the European economy.

Each morning the senior economist participates in a video-conference connecting eight international offices. She uses the information prepared by her team to review daily changes in financial markets, preview trends in interest rates and costs of commodities, and identify any important government actions. A summary report is e-mailed to the executives and team members are available after the conference to further interpret the information.

On the commuter train, Pierre uses his PDA to get the latest information from the major stock markets. Then he checks the international news services for important stories that might affect the European economy. He updates forecast charts and enters notes.

What about you? What do you like and dislike about Pierre Latrobe's schedule and activities? What do you think happens in the team meetings as Pierre and his colleagues prepare the morning briefing?

Planning a Career in…
CORPORATE ECONOMICS

Many people are not aware that there are job opportunities in the area of economics. Yet, economists help to make some of the most important decisions that affect the lives of consumers. Ask students: In what ways might the health of the U.S. economy affect you, your family, and your community?

What About You? Answers

Student answers will require thinking beyond what is presented and formulation of their own reactions. The following are possible answers:

1. Students will have varying responses to the early start time of Pierre Latrobe's day.

2. The morning team meeting likely includes a great deal of information covered quickly, with the senior economist requiring team members to present their parts of the daily report.

Additional Career Information

Additional information on careers can be found in the *Occupational Outlook Handbook,* an online publication (www.bls.gov/oco) of the federal government. Tell your class about this resource and how to use it. This description of job duties can be used to demonstrate the relevancy of skills learned in this course.

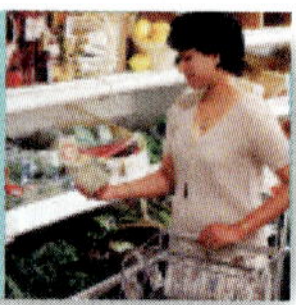

THINK CRITICALLY THROUGH VISUALS

The ease of meeting basic needs will vary in different communities, but is generally easier in the United States than in many other countries of the world.

1-1   Satisfying Needs and Wants

Goals

Explain the difference between needs and wants.

Distinguish between goods and services.

Describe the types of economic resources.

Key Terms

needs

wants

goods

services

economic resources

Focus on Real Life

Gina and Jermaine walked into an electronics store to look at the new portable digital video and music player that had just been released. It could store more than 2,000 songs in memory, and the small ear bud headphones were supposed to have an amazing sound reproduction capability.

As they stood in line, Jermaine said, "I don't know if the player is worth the $400 price. I hear you can get the older model for only $150."

Gina responded, "I know. The size is smaller, it is much more durable, and holds large digital files of music or video. If the sound quality is as good as they say it is, I think many people will want to buy one. If we wait a few months, the price might drop. Are you sure you need it right now?"

Jermaine's decision is one you often face. You often hear about exciting new products, but you do not need and cannot afford all of them. How do you decide what to buy and how much to pay?

---

main idea

Explain the difference between needs and wants.

NEEDS AND WANTS

Hardly a day goes by that you don't see a product or service that you would like to have. You see them in the shopping mall, the grocery store, or while surfing the Web. Advertisements on television, radio, or the Internet attempt to convince you that you need whatever is new. How do you decide what to buy or even if you need to buy at all?

Needs Are Essential

You want many things, but do you really need them? Determining what is a need and what is a want is an important part of making good decisions.

Things that are required in order to live are known as **needs**. Everyone needs food, water, clean air, clothing, and shelter. Other needs in today's economy are a good education, employment, and safety. Most people need transportation to get to and from school and work. People who have health problems need medical care and medicines.

How easy is it for you to meet your basic needs?

Different Learning Styles

Visual Learner Provide students with copies of catalogs from retail businesses. Have them page through the catalog identifying products they believe satisfy needs and those that appeal to wants.

Wants Add to the Quality of Life

Things that add comfort and pleasure to your life are **wants**. You may believe you can't live without the latest fashion, CD, or movie, but you can and many people do. A small apartment meets the need for shelter, but many people want a large house or a vacation home at the beach. It is possible to use public transportation to get around in the city, but driving a new car with luxury options adds convenience and an image of success.

It is not always easy to determine products and services that are needs and those that are wants. The country in which you live, the economic status and lifestyle of your family, and the work you do help determine whether something is really necessary or not. Most products and services you purchase do more than meet your needs. They make your life easier and more comfortable.

Needs and Wants Are Unlimited

Your needs and wants never end. You are limited only by your imagination and by what businesses make available for sale. A new style convinces you your current jacket is no longer adequate. One purchase leads to another. You purchase the latest model video game player and now you need a new set of games. A new pair of shoes may require matching accessories.

Your wants can go on and on. They change from day to day. Something you thought you couldn't live without two days ago now doesn't seem as important and is replaced by a new want. Everyone has unlimited wants. Those wants are not the same for each person.

> *checkpoint* »
> What is the difference between a need and a want?

Work as a Team

Do you believe your needs are very similar to or quite different from those that your parents had when they were your age? As a team, prepare a list of five needs that you agree would be similar to those of your parents when they were young and a list of five needs that you agree would likely be different. Justify why those listed are needs and not wants.

GOODS AND SERVICES

You satisfy your needs and wants by purchasing and consuming goods and services. **Goods** are things that you can see and touch. They are the products you can purchase to meet your wants and needs. **Services** are activities that are consumed at the same time they are produced. Services are intangible, meaning they have no physical characteristics. You use services as well as goods to satisfy your wants and needs, but they must be provided to you at the time you want to consume them.

main idea

Distinguish between goods and services.

Does the service industry satisfy more needs or more wants?

Work as a Team

After students have identified similar and different needs, ask them to determine what products their parents might have used to satisfy their needs. Encourage them to ask their parents about those products or use the Internet to determine products that were sold when their parents were younger.

ONGOING ASSESSMENT

checkpoint » **ANSWER**

Needs are those things required to live, such as food, clothing, and shelter. Wants are things that add comfort and pleasure to our lives such as television, music CDs, and movies.

TEACH

Tell students that the word "product" and the word "goods" mean the same thing. Thousands of products and services are produced and provided by businesses to meet the needs and wants of consumers. Ask students why more and more services are being developed by businesses today.

THINK CRITICALLY THROUGH VISUALS

The service industry generally addresses more wants than needs, but there are important service businesses that satisfy needs. Examples include hospitals, schools, and government agencies such as police and fire department.

Different Learning Styles

Auditory Learners Encourage auditory learners to repeat the definitions of goods and services aloud until they are certain of the meanings and differences.

Teaching Strategies

Expand Beyond the Classroom Have students locate and bring to class a picture or description of a product that can be used by both consumers and businesses and a service that can be used by both.

Goods and Services for Businesses and Consumers

Goods and services are purchased by businesses as well as by consumers. Some goods and services are unique for business or consumer use. Others are similar but meet different needs.

A business needs steel, plastic, gasoline, and computers in order to operate. It must have a constant supply of electricity, security for buildings and equipment, and accountants who maintain records and file tax returns.

Consumers buy watches, televisions, cell phones, and books. They eat at restaurants, go on vacations, and take their car to the auto dealer for service and repairs. Businesses supply the goods and services that meet business and consumer needs and wants.

main idea

Describe the types of economic resources.

The U.S. Economy

The United States is the largest producer of goods and services in the world. Americans consume more than any other country. In fact, America has twice as many shopping malls as it does high schools! America's lead in consuming goods and services increased throughout the 20th century and continues today. The move to an industrialized economy resulted in higher incomes which could be spent on consumer products. The consumer economy provides many advantages, but also results in problems. For example, Americans produce more garbage per person per year than the residents of any other country.

Americans often incur debt through obtaining loans and using credit cards. Not all consumption is excessive and not all Americans purchase beyond their means to pay. In fact, many demonstrate financial responsibility through saving and investing their money rather than spending. This enables them to accumulate enough money to finance a car, pay for additional education, or save for retirement.

Some believe the high level of U.S. consumer demand stems from the sheer quantity of goods and services available and the amount of money businesses spend to advertise their offerings. Spending opportunities occur daily and require careful decisions to make sure important needs and wants are satisfied in the future as well as today.

checkpoint >>
How do people satisfy their wants and needs?

ECONOMIC RESOURCES

How do you get the goods and services you need and want? Few are free. Individuals no longer create most of the products and services they consume as they did many years ago. Economic resources are needed. **Economic resources** are the means through which goods and services are produced. Economic resources are called *factors of production*. The three kinds of economic resources are natural resources, human resources, and capital resources. Businesses and individuals use resources to produce goods and services.

© Getty Images/PhotoDisc

What natural resources are found near your home?

Natural Resources

Raw materials supplied by nature are *natural resources.* The earth contains oil, minerals, and the nutrients needed to grow crops and timber and to feed animals. Rivers, lakes, and oceans are the sources of both food and water. The air you breathe comes from the atmosphere that surrounds you. All products you consume begin with one or more natural resources.

Consider something as simple as a can of chicken noodle soup. What natural resources were used in its production? The chickens, vegetables, and spices are the result of crops and animals raised on rich farmland. The water is extracted from wells or reservoirs that were filled by rain. Aluminum was extracted from the ground and used to produce the container.

The earth contains a variety of minerals, plants, fish, and animals. However, the supply of many natural resources is limited. Increased consumption as well as damage to the environment threatens the natural resources of many regions of the world. Conservation practices as well as the production of more efficient products help to preserve resources.

Human Resources

The people who produce goods and services are known as *human resources.* In the example of the chicken noodle soup, many people are needed to complete the work required to produce that product. Farmers raise the livestock and crops. Factory workers and managers use equipment designed by engineers and manufactured by the employees of other businesses to process the food. Truck drivers, salespeople, advertisers, and supermarket employees are also involved in producing the product and making it available to consumers for purchase.

One type of human resource is an entrepreneur. An *entrepreneur* is the

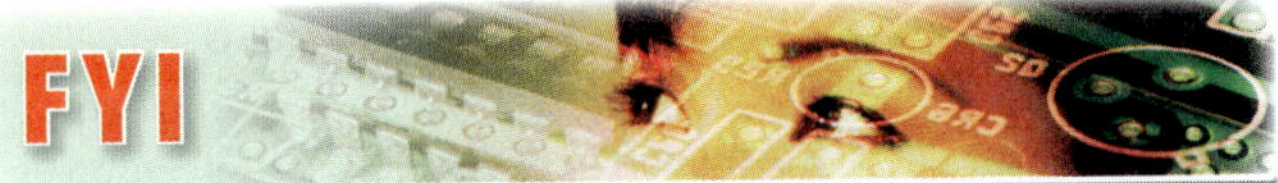

FYI

Even water, one of the most common substances on the planet, is a scarce natural resource, especially in the western United States. Disputes among southwestern states over water rights and access to the major riverways result in frequent political debate and court actions. Water will likely become a more important natural resource in the future.

risk taker who uses resources in an entirely new way to create a new product or service. Without the creative ideas of entrepreneurs and their belief that they can develop a successful business, there would be fewer choices of goods and services and fewer employment opportunities.

In what ways does water contribute to the U.S. economy?

© Getty Images/PhotoDisc

9

TEACH

As each type of economic resource is introduced, ask students to provide examples of the resources that are used by businesses in your community—natural resources such as water, lumber, and minerals; human resources such as the owners, managers, and employees of a business; and capital resources including money from investors, buildings, and equipment.

Ask students to name several ways the demand for human resources has changed in business in the past decade. Examples might be the need for more education and higher skills, requirement for more service workers, and having jobs performed by workers in other countries.

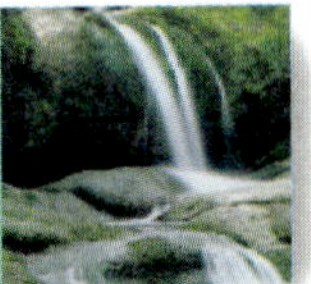

THINK CRITICALLY THROUGH VISUALS

Water contributes to the U.S. economy in the following ways: as an energy source, in growing crops and raising livestock, in many manufacturing processes, as a method of transportation, and as a commodity sold to consumers for their personal consumption and uses inside and outside their homes.

Teaching Strategies

Expand Beyond the Classroom Relating to the FYI and photo on this page, assign students to research a current environmental problem such as rain forest destruction, ozone layer depletion, pollution, or endangered species. Have them prepare a written and/or oral report that includes causes, long-term consequences, controversies surrounding the issue, and possible solutions.

TEACH

If they were entrepreneurs starting a new business, ask students what type of capital they would need and what might be some sources of the needed capital.

THINK CRITICALLY THROUGH VISUALS

Economic resources that go into the construction of a house could include natural resources, such as wood and water; human resources such as the architect, builder, and construction workers; and capital resources, such as the tools and machinery used by the builder and the money loaned by the bank for the home construction.

Technology in Action

New digital and video content is being developed every day. The individuals and businesses developing the content and the consumers who want to purchase it must have an easy and safe way to complete low-cost transactions known as micropayments.

Think Critically
Answers

1. If consumers have to pay for the same type of products and services they purchase from a local retailer, they will be comfortable paying for online access if the cost is comparable and the payment process is safe and easy.

2. Ask students to give oral presentations on the information they find on new micropayment systems.

Capital Resources

People must have access to tools and equipment in order to convert natural resources into products. The products and money used in the production of goods and services are *capital resources.* Capital resources include buildings, equipment, and supplies. They also include the money needed to build a factory, buy or lease vehicles, pay employees, or purchase goods and services required to manufacture and distribute other goods and services.

Some people invest money in businesses so the business will have the capital needed to operate. Those people expect they will make money from the profits earned by the business. Other people receive

What economic resources can you think of that go into the construction of a house?

© Getty Images/PhotoDisc

Technology in Action

Online Micropayments

In the early years of the Internet, users expected information to be available free to anyone. Over time, Internet consumers started to accept that many web sites restricted access to content through the use of registrations, passwords, or, in some cases, annual or monthly membership fees. Today, due to the quality and variety of online content, consumers are more willing to pay for the types of products and services they otherwise would have to purchase elsewhere—music CDs, video games, movie tickets, magazines, and newspapers. The digital content business is growing rapidly and is expected to generate $50 billion by 2009.

In 2005, more than 350 million songs were purchased for download. While that number sounds impressive, there is a major gap between online digital content sales of very low-cost products and services and that of higher priced ones. People are willing to pay a small amount to use an online game, download a song, view a new music video, or watch a sporting event online but they want a quick and easy payment method. Businesses will make such products available if they can collect the small fees in an efficient and profitable way.

Micropayments are online payments too small to be affordably processed by credit card or other electronic payment methods. Most micropayments are under $5 and may be as low as a few cents per transaction. Because of the limitations in payment options, micropayments currently make up less than 3 percent of all online digital content purchases.

New companies as well as industry giants are looking at ways to solve the micropayments problem. Peppercoin allows online merchants to combine many small individual purchases into one larger transaction for processing so the cost and time required to process separate payments are reduced. Microsoft is testing its Microsoft Points system. With this system, consumers buy points in advance (1,600 points sell for $20) and redeem them at the Xbox Live Marketplace. It is certain that new technologies will soon solve the micropayment problem due to the almost unlimited potential for digital content sales.

Think Critically

1. Why have consumers changed their views about the value of online content so they are now willing to pay small fees?
2. Research micropayments and identify new methods being used by companies to accept and process these small payments.

Different Learning Abilities

Hearing Impaired Speak clearly, and be certain that you face the student so lip reading will be possible. Also make use of printed materials and visuals.

income by selling their knowledge and skills to businesses in the form of labor. Those with special skills or knowledge of important business processes often command higher incomes than those with knowledge and skills that are more common.

Resources Are Limited

All economic resources have a limited supply. Most resources can be used to produce several different products and services. If resources are used to produce one type of product, they will not be available for the production of something else.

Individuals, businesses, and even countries compete for access to and ownership of economic resources. Those resources that are in very high demand or that have a limited supply will command high prices. Because there is a limited amount of natural resources, there will also be a limit to the amount of goods and services that can be produced.

checkpoint >>
What are the three types of economic resources? Give an example of each type of resource.

How can a country plan for future limits on its natural resources?

© Getty Images/PhotoDisc

1-1 Assessment

Xtra! Study Tools
school.cengage.com/business/introtobiz

Key Concepts

Determine the best answer.

1. True or False. It is not always easy to determine the products and services that are needs and those that are wants.

2. Which of the following would an economist most likely classify as a need?
   a. gasoline
   b. a college degree
   c. a television
   d. a part-time job to earn extra money

3. An example of a natural resource is
   a. sunlight
   b. a computer programmer
   c. a fishing net
   d. money

Make Academic Connections

4. *Economics* List the three types of economic resources. Choose a product and describe how each economic resource is needed and used in its production. (Hint: refer to the chicken noodle soup example in the lesson.)

5. *Communication* Locate an article from a business publication or newspaper that illustrates the concepts of unlimited wants and needs and limited resources. Write a two-paragraph summary of the article that incorporates several of the key terms from the lesson.

11

Answers will vary, but will likely include a discussion of the importance of needs and wants and the resources and choices available to satisfy them.

1-2 Economic Choices

Goals

Understand the basic economic problem.

Explain the steps in the decision-making process.

Key Terms

scarcity

economic decision-making

trade-off

opportunity cost

Focus on Real Life

Tom is faced with a difficult decision. His friend Jacque just called and told him he had won two tickets to a concert, and he invited Tom to attend. Tom already promised his family that he would go with them to a restaurant to celebrate his father's birthday. Both activities are scheduled for the same evening, so it would be almost impossible to do both. He really wants to go with Jacque to the concert, but missing his father's birthday celebration might cause hard feelings. What advice would you give Tom about how he can resolve the dilemma?

main idea

Understand the basic economic problem.

THE BASIC ECONOMIC PROBLEM

Individuals and businesses have unlimited wants and needs. The economic resources they have are limited. The mismatch of unlimited wants and needs and limited economic resources is called *the basic economic problem.* You may want to purchase several products but have a limited amount of money. Your school may have to cut back on certain classes or extracurricular activities because operating costs are increasing faster than the annual budget. A business may want to expand but does not have access to adequate land for a new larger building. A country may not be able to provide adequate health care for all of its citizens because it does not have enough doctors or hospitals.

The basic economic problem results from scarcity.

Scarcity means not having enough resources to satisfy every need. Scarcity affects everyone, but some people are more affected than others. People with limited incomes have to carefully choose the best way to spend their money to meet their needs and wants. Countries with few natural resources or people with limited education and low skills may not be able to produce enough products and services for their citizens. Areas with poor

How do you make personal choices between your wants and your needs?

Different Learning Styles

Visual Learner Ask students to close their eyes and mentally picture situations that illustrate scarcity. This will help them remember the basic economic problem.

transportation or distribution systems or where few businesses are located may not have access to the variety of products and services found in other areas.

Choices

Everyone makes decisions based on scarcity. Individuals and families must decide how to spread their income among all of the things they want and need. City, state, and national governments must cope with the problem of providing the many services citizens demand using the tax dollars they collect. In each case, someone has to make the difficult choices.

Scarcity forces you to make *choices* or decisions among the alternatives. How do you decide which option is best? You usually choose the things you want the most or can afford. Suppose you earn $75 a week from a part-time job. If you spend the money you earned this week on a new pair of shoes, you will not have enough left over to spend on a movie and pizza with your friends on Saturday night. Due to the limited resource or amount of money you have, you cannot afford everything. You must make a choice. You must decide which of your wants—the shoes or pizza and movie—you want the most. How do you determine which of these two options will satisfy you the most?

Following a logical process can help you make better decisions. It is a proven way to make many decisions, but is especially useful for making important economic decisions. **Economic decision-making** is the process of choosing which wants, among several options, will be satisfied. Once you learn the process, your decision-making will be easier and the process may lead to better choices.

Trade-offs and Opportunity Costs

Most of the choices you make result from considering a number of alternatives. When you decide on one alternative, you give up on the other alternatives you might have chosen. When you give up something to have something else, you are making a **trade-off**. You aren't able to buy a pair of shoes because you decided to spend your money on a movie and pizza with your friends.

The decision-making process helps you select the best and most satisfying alternative from among a set of choices. Economists evaluate an alternative by considering the opportunity cost of a decision. The **opportunity cost** is the value of the next-best alternative that you did not choose. In making a personal decision, part of your choice will be what you are giving up by the choice you make. The benefit you get from your choice should be greater than the benefit from the next-best choice.

Businesses carefully calculate the opportunity costs of decisions before they make a decision about how they will invest their money. If they use money to purchase land for a new building, what choices must they give up? Would there be a greater value if they spent the money to purchase new equipment that is faster and more reliable? Part of the cost of the land is the missed opportunity to have better equipment.

NETBookmark

Some of the most important choices anyone has to make are choices about money. There is no escaping it: If you want to buy things in this world, you need to have a steady supply of money on hand. A great way of ensuring that you won't overspend is to make a budget. Access the web site shown below and click on the link for Chapter 1. Click on the Activities link to learn the important factors that make up a personal budget. How might following this process help you make good choices about your spending?

school.cengage.com/business/introtobiz

NETBookmark

Students should learn about creating a personal budget. Discussion should show that students have understood how budgets help make better personal choices.

TEACH

Have students think of an important need or want and three possible products or services that would satisfy that need or want. Then have them describe how they would go about making a choice among the alternatives. Use their examples to discuss the concepts of "trade-off" and "opportunity cost."

ONGOING ASSESSMENT

checkpoint >> **ANSWER**

Opportunity cost is the value of the next best alternative that you don't choose. It is what you are willing to give up in order to have your first choice.

Mathematics Have students determine the opportunity cost of purchasing a new car versus a three-year-old used car of the same model. Ask them to use the Internet to determine the price of each choice, calculate the opportunity cost, and decide what they would have to give up to choose the new car.

TEACH

Use Figure 1-1, The Decision-Making Process, to review with students the steps in the process. Have students explain each one and give an example from their own lives or experiences with which they are familiar. Select a local community or school problem, such as urban renewal planning, and have the class go through the steps in the decision-making process considering the many factors and decisions that must be taken into account. Point out that the process leads to better choices because it forces you to think about the steps as you make them and to learn from each decision you make. Review and use the steps in the decision-making process throughout the course.

FIGURE 1-1 *ANSWER*

The decision-making process causes you to carefully consider each step rather than rushing to a decision without adequate information.

PROJECT

Provide the following instructions to students. (These instructions also appear on page xxiv of the student text.) Write an essay that describes how you could use the decision-making process to choose classes for next year that will help you achieve your life-span goals. In what other ways will the decision-making process benefit you in the future?

Explain the steps in the decision-making process.

THE DECISION-MAKING PROCESS

There are six steps in the decision-making process. You will use the model shown in Figure 1-1 many times as you proceed through the chapters in this book. You will also use it in day-to-day decisions you make. Businesses and individuals use the process as they choose the best uses for their limited resources.

1. Define the problem.

For every decision, the problem must be clearly defined in order to make a decision that will lead to a satisfying solution. If you only have two hours available to study for three tests, your problem is how to best use the limited amount of time to prepare for the tests.

2. Identify the choices.

It is common for you to face choices with many alternatives. Earlier we identified a problem deciding on the best use of $75. Along with spending money on shoes or the movies and pizza, some other choices you might face are the cost of your lunch and the need to save money for college. In fact, there are many ways you might choose to spend (or save) your $75. It is important to identify and then consider all of the alternatives when making a decision.

3. Evaluate the advantages and disadvantages of each choice.

You might find it helpful to write down your choices and then list the advantages and disadvantages of each choice. If you buy the new shoes, you will be able to wear them many times. It means you will miss the fun of pizza and a movie with friends on the weekend. If you choose to save some of the money, you may be able to make a

The Decision-Making Process
1. Define the problem.
2. Identify the choices.
3. Evaluate the advantages and disadvantages of each choice.
4. Choose one.
5. Act on your choice.
6. Review your decision.

FIGURE 1-1

How does the decision-making process lead to better choices?

larger purchase later. You and your friends may determine a less expensive way to spend your time on the weekend.

4. Choose one.

Select the choice that you believe will be the best for you at this particular time. Even if you have done a good job with the first three steps, this is often a difficult step. Realize that choices have consequences that can lie in the future. If you choose option A, how might it affect you later, as well as right now?

5. Act on your choice.

Once you have made what you believe is the best decision, do whatever you have chosen. If you have decided to spend your money on a movie and pizza with your friends, go and enjoy yourself. Try not to worry about the choices you have decided against. Agonizing over a choice or regretting your decision after it is made can take away from the activity you decided upon. Life is full of choices. No matter what you do, there will be times when you will regret a decision even if you carefully considered the alternatives. The next step will help you with those situations.

Life-Span Plan Answer

Answers will vary. Essays should demonstrate an understanding of how the decision-making process could be used to choose classes or make other important future decisions.

Different Learning Abilities

At-Risk Have students identify a personal decision they are facing. Ask them to list each step of the decision-making process and describe how they would use that step to help them make their decision.

6. Review your decision.

After you have had a chance to experience the results of your choice, it is important to review your choice. On a scale of one to ten, how would you rank your decision in terms of the level of satisfaction it provided? What was good and not so good about it? If you had to do it over again, would you make the same choice? Given what you know now, do you think there was a better alternative? Were there consequences you hadn't identified?

Based on your review of the decision, how well did you follow the steps of the decision-making process? This step gives you an opportunity to think about your decision and learn from it. Next time you face a similar decision, you may be more comfortable with your choices.

You and some friends are meeting with city council members to ask them to build a skateboarding park that would cost $30,000. They ask you to identify the opportunity costs of other recreation alternatives for teenagers. As a team identify two other alternatives for the city and discuss how you would determine the opportunity cost of each.

Some decisions have to be made quickly and some with very little information available. For most decisions, the decision-making process will help you make wiser choices.

> *checkpoint* >>
> What are the six steps in the decision-making process?

Work as a Team

Have students use a brainstorming strategy to identify possible alternatives. Then ask them to discuss each one to come up with the two that the team will evaluate for the city council.

ONGOING ASSESSMENT

checkpoint >> **ANSWER**

The six steps of the decision-making process are

1. Define the problem.

2. Identify the choices.

3. Evaluate the advantages and disadvantages of each alternative.

4. Choose one.

5. Act on your choice.

6. Review your decision.

ASSESS

Key Concepts Answers

1. False. The basic economic problem is satisfying unlimited wants and needs with limited resources.

2. b. you have adequate time to identify and analyze several choices

3. b. the score he will earn on the math exam

Make Academic Connections

4. Essays will vary. Ask volunteers to share their thoughts with the class.

5. Offer suggestions for how students should report their findings—oral presentation, role playing, one-page report, etc. Consider allowing students to work in pairs.

1-2 Assessment

Xtra! Study Tools
school.cengage.com/business/introtobiz

Key Concepts

Determine the best answer.

1. True or False. The basic economic problem is that consumers have too many products and services to choose from.

2. The decision-making process is best to use when
   a. you already know the choice you will make
   b. you have adequate time to identify and analyze several choices
   c. groups rather than individuals are making a choice
   d. you don't have enough money to pay for any of the choices

3. John has two hours before having to go to his part-time job. He is deciding between studying for a math exam and taking a nap. If John chooses to take a nap, the opportunity cost of his decision is
   a. the rest he is getting
   b. the score he will earn on the math exam
   c. the wages from his part-time job
   d. all of the above

Make Academic Connections

4. **Communication** Write a one-page essay about a decision you made recently. Describe how you did or did not use the steps of the decision-making process. Discuss the outcome of your decision.

5. **Economics** Locate and read a news report describing a decision made by a business. Describe what you believe could be the opportunity cost of their choice. Justify your answer.

RETEACH

Have students locate the vocabulary terms from the lesson and write the definition of each in their own words. Then compare the written definitions with those in the lesson.

ENRICH

Have students use the decision-making process to choose between participating in an after-school activity and holding a part-time job.

CLOSE

Have students state the basic economic problem and provide one example of how it has affected them.

Sharpen Your Life Skills

Decision-making will not be effective if students do not have access to and use information. Research skills will help them gather the information they need to make decisions. Effective research skills will help them in their current classes and in their future education and careers, as well as in their personal life.

Think Critically Answers

1. Opinions vary and are not objective. They are formed by a variety of factors and may or may not be reliable. True data, or fact, is generally objective.

2. Some questions may be answered this way, but in order to formulate the best possible decision, it is usually wise to include your own specific observations and data. Other information sources may not be entirely accurate, complete, or relative to your question.

Research Skills

Your abilities are more than just the sum of your experiences. Whether the goal is to improve a business or your own performance, you need to make sound decisions based on the best information available. Research skills are needed to improve decision-making.

Research is a systematic, objective study to establish facts and principles. The research process begins with a question or problem and results in a possible answer that can become the basis for further research.

Here are the steps to follow when conducting research.

Formulate a question. What is the problem you are facing or what is the issue you are trying to resolve? The question should be as specific as possible and relate to an important personal or business issue.

Gather and review information related to the question. Determine if others have studied the same problem and if they have reported on the results of their study. This step usually involves a careful search of library information, including books, magazines, and documents.

Separate fact from opinion. Effective research relies on objective data. The opinions of others may provide interesting ideas to consider but should not be relied on for answers to your question. Consider if the sources of information are credible and if the information provided is factual.

Propose a hypothesis. A hypothesis is a prediction about the answer to your research question. The hypothesis can be based on the information gathered, your experience, or your beliefs. You will conduct a study to gather information that will either support the hypothesis or determine that it is wrong.

Collect data to test the hypothesis. Researchers carefully design studies to gather information related to the question and hypothesis. The common methods of collecting data are the use of surveys, making observations, or conducting an experiment.

Analyze the data. After data has been collected, it is organized and then analyzed using statistical procedures. Careful review of the results of the data analysis will provide evidence to support or disprove the hypothesis.

© Digital Vision

Report the results. It is important that researchers document and report the results of their research. The report will help others understand the research and repeat it or improve upon it. It will also provide evidence that you were objective in the way you completed your research.

Put the research results into practice. You began the research process to answer a question or solve a problem. You need to apply what you learned and determine if what you learned makes a difference. No matter the results, you will want to continue to conduct research and study the research of others. It will help you make sound decisions and have confidence in your knowledge and abilities.

Think Critically
1. Why should you be careful of basing your actions on opinions rather than facts?
2. Do you believe some questions can be answered by just gathering and reviewing information rather than collecting data? Why or why not?

Applied Skills

Writing across the Curriculum Have students prepare a paragraph that shows how they can use the research process they just studied in another of their classes.

Goals

Identify the three economic questions.

Differentiate among the main types of economic systems.

Describe the economic system of the United States.

Key Terms

economic system

command economy

market economy

traditional economy

mixed economy

capitalism

Focus on **Real Life**

Jiang Liang is a resident of modern-day China. His family lived for decades in a small farming community outside of Beijing. There, they faced strict government regulations on what they could and could not grow. Jiang was able to attend Beijing University, where he learned a great deal about computers. With this valuable skill, Jiang moved to Hong Kong, where he worked for a large multinational computer corporation. Jiang was surprised to learn that this company operated without any direct government oversight. The company produced as many computers as it desired and set prices at whatever level it thought best. Jiang has experienced two very different economic systems. Which seems the most like the economic system in the United States?

THE THREE ECONOMIC QUESTIONS

All economies (or nations) of the world face the basic economic problem of scarcity of resources. They also have citizens with many basic needs as well as unlimited wants. Each country must decide how the available resources will be used to meet the needs and wants. All economies must answer three economic questions.

1. What goods and services will be produced?

2. How will the goods and services be produced?

3. What needs and wants will be satisfied with the goods and services produced?

How the questions are answered indicates the type of economic system that exists in each country.

What to Produce?

Nations differ in the type and amount of resources just as individuals differ in their skills and abilities. Some nations have rich soil and regular rains that yield large food supplies. Other nations have desert climates or long, cold winters that make farming difficult. Some countries have abundant supplies of oil, coal, and other energy sources, while many countries have only a limited supply. A nation will use its natural resources to

main idea

Identify the three economic questions.

What resources are necessary for large farm yields?

© Getty Images/PhotoDisc

Focus on **Real Life**

Ask any students who have lived in or visited another country for a length of time if they noticed any differences in the economic system of the country compared with the U.S. system. Suggest that international business makes those differences more apparent to people.

TEACH

Ask students how they would answer the three economic questions. Ask if they think the answers would change if they lived in a different country.

THINK CRITICALLY THROUGH VISUALS

Resources necessary for large farm yields include farm workers, investment money, seeds and fertilizers, water, and machinery and equipment.

Technology and mechanization have changed the way work is done. Today's jobs require less than one percent of the total muscle power used before the Industrial Revolution.

TEACH

Ask students why fewer businesses produce agricultural products in the United States today than two centuries ago. Does that change have a greater effect on the question of what to produce or on how to produce it?

ONGOING ASSESSMENT

checkpoint >> **ANSWER**

The three economic questions are

1. What goods and services will be produced?

2. How will the goods and services be produced?

3. What needs and wants will be satisfied with the goods and services?

determine what can be produced. It can also decide to trade some of its resources with other countries to obtain those it needs.

Just as nations differ in the type and amount of resources, they also differ in their needs. One country may invest heavily in manufacturing, another in agriculture, and a third in security. Some nations have colleges and universities that produce a large number of skilled engineers and technology experts. Other countries have low literacy rates and many unskilled workers. Highways, roads, airports, and shipping ports may be highly developed and functional or transportation may be very difficult.

Deciding how to use resources and what to produce is a very difficult decision. If a country spends too much in one area, there may not be enough resources to meet other needs. If most resources are used to produce the products consumers want, not enough attention may be paid to meeting business needs.

How to Produce?

Nations must decide what combination of resources will best suit their circumstances. As a country develops, tasks that were traditionally performed using human skills, such as farming, are now performed with faster, more efficient tools and equipment. Two centuries ago, more than 80 percent of U.S. citizens were involved in agriculture. Today, less than 3 percent of the U.S. population produces the food the country consumes. The labor needs of the U.S.

economy have changed. The complex 21st-century economy requires highly specialized health care professionals, financial managers, computer specialists, and others who can design and produce the goods and services that you need and want.

Each country decides how to use its resources to produce the goods and services it needs. It may rely on unskilled or skilled labor, on advanced or simple technology, on its own resources or on those it obtains from other countries. Economic resources can be combined in different ways to produce similar goods and services.

What Needs and Wants to Satisfy?

Because wants and needs are unlimited, many will remain unmet when a country decides what goods and services to produce. A country must determine which needs and wants are the most critical when deciding what goods and services to produce. Some countries may decide to invest in capital goods, while others produce more consumer goods. Some countries devote more resources to producing the goods and services required by the government. Other economies respond to those citizens who have the most money or the most political power.

In the United States, goods and services are plentiful. What wants and needs you satisfy largely depends on how much money you have and how you choose to spend or save it. The amount of money you have available to spend depends a great deal on your education and ability and how you decide to use them to earn income.

> *checkpoint* >>
> What are the three economic questions?

Applied Skills

Technology Have students use the Internet to compare the number of businesses involved in farming and manufacturing today compared with 50 years ago. Have them create a chart or graph to display the results.

TYPES OF ECONOMIC SYSTEMS

A nation's plan for answering the three economic questions is called its **economic system**. The type of system is based on how much the government is involved in the marketplace. There are several kinds of economic systems operating in the world today. Each is based on one of the three main types.

Command Economy

In a **command economy**, the resources are owned and controlled by the government. Government officials decide what and how goods are produced and how they will be distributed and shared. They decide how much of the resources will be used to produce goods and services for consumers, such as food products, vehicles, or houses. They also decide how much of the resources will be used to produce capital goods, including machinery, equipment, and factories.

In a command economy, the government may decide to build a superior military or a world-class education system. They may decide to spend money to research new technologies or to build housing for the poor. Some command economies are so strict that government officials assign people to specific schools and even careers. Personal economic freedom is limited in a command economic system.

Market Economy

In a **market economy**, the resources are owned and controlled by the people of the country. The three economic questions are answered by individuals through buying and selling of goods and services in the marketplace. The *marketplace* is anywhere that goods and services exchange hands. This includes a supermarket, the Internet, a business office, or even a flea market.

When a business buys a new truck or orders several tons of steel, it is making an economic decision. An individual consumer who orders a movie on a pay-per-view channel, takes a vacation, or enrolls in college is also making an economic decision. No one directs consumers to make a particular purchase or tells businesses what they must produce. The government has limited involvement in a market economy.

Consumers and businesses make decisions based on their own self-interest. Every time consumers buy products in the marketplace, they "vote" with their dollars. They send a message to businesses regarding their buying preferences, helping to direct the use of resources. Businesses make decisions on what goods and services will be produced based on how they decide to use their resources. When they offer the products and services consumers want, they are rewarded with profits. By those independent decisions, individual

What are some disadvantages of living in a market economy?

Differentiate among the main types of economic systems.

TEACH

Divide the class into three teams. Assign each team one of the main types of economic systems. After each system has been discussed, have that team report on how their economy would answer the three economic questions.

THINK CRITICALLY THROUGH VISUALS

Many answers are possible. Some disadvantages of living in a market economy are too many choices, too much emphasis on consumerism, overuse of environmental resources, and too much waste.

Different Learning Abilities

Hearing Impaired As you speak to students and as teams make their reports, make sure everyone speaks clearly and that they face toward the students who are listening.

producers and consumers answer the three economic questions.

Traditional Economy

Before complex economic systems developed, simple economies operated according to tradition or custom. In a **traditional economy**, goods and services are produced the way it has always been done. The traditional economy is used in countries that are less developed and are not yet participating in the global economy.

How would business ownership be affected by different types of economic systems?

In those countries, the answers to the three economic questions are still established by their traditions. Goods are produced the way they have always been produced, generation after generation. Children are taught to use the same methods to make the same goods their ancestors produced. They often use the natural resources readily available to them and the hand tools they make. They will consume most of what they produce and sell or trade the rest with people who live close to them.

The traditional economy is usually centered on meeting the basic needs of people, such as food, clothing, and shelter. While the global economy has brought change and growth to the farthest corners of the world, there are still pockets of people living in traditional economic systems. Because these economies lack the many formal structures found in more advanced systems, they usually have limited amounts of material wealth and limited investment in improving their conditions.

Mixed Economies

Most nations of the world can be classified as a mixed economy. A **mixed economy** combines elements of the command and market economies. While the past half-century has seen a shift away from command economies and toward market economies, various degrees of government involvement in the marketplace exist.

The former Soviet Union disbanded and became 15 independent nations in the early 1990s. For more than 70 years, the Soviet Union operated under a command economic system called *communism*. Under communism, the Soviet Union underwent a series of government-led plans to direct resources toward economic growth. This led to a limited choice and supply of consumer goods. Often, consumers found it difficult to find such products as bread or a hammer.

During the past decade, several of the Eastern European nations that had used a command economy have made major progress in changing over to a mixed economy. Some of these countries made such economic progress that they were granted membership into the European Union.

More than 1.3 billion Chinese citizens have a communist government that controls most of the resources and decisions. The economy of China is adopting elements of a market system for a growing number of economic decisions. Entire regions of the country, particularly the eastern cities bordering the ocean, are enjoying a booming consumer economy based on greater individual freedom of choice. China is fast becoming a world leader in goods and services produced. A competitive education system produces many skilled workers who are earning money to pay for the goods and services they want.

As many countries with traditional economies develop, they often adopt mixed economies. The government makes many of the decisions about how the country's resources will be used to develop schools, hospitals, roads, and utilities. As people become educated and develop new skills, they are able to obtain jobs and earn money. They then have the resources to purchase more goods and services. Often businesses from other countries will begin to sell products and services in the developing country or even open a business there, offering jobs and locally produced products to the citizens.

THE U.S. ECONOMIC SYSTEM

Can you identify the economic system of the United States? Because individual businesses and consumers make most of the decisions about what will be produced and consumed, the U.S. system best fits the definition of the market economy.

Another name for the economic system in the United States is capitalism. **Capitalism** refers to the private ownership of resources by individuals, rather than by the government. Individual owners are free to decide what to produce. Individual consumers are also free to decide what they want to buy. This freedom of production and consumption decisions lends itself to another name often associated with the U.S. economy— *free enterprise* or *private enterprise.* Individual freedom is vital to the success of the U.S. economy.

The U.S. economic system is based on four important principles. They are private property, freedom of choice, profit, and competition.

Private Property

The right of *private property* means you can own, use, or dispose of things of value. In the United States, you can own anything you want and decide what you want to do with it, as long as it does not violate the law. If you invent something of value, you are protected from others taking your idea.

Freedom of Choice

The private enterprise economy is based on freedom of choice. *Freedom of choice* means that you can make decisions independently and must accept the consequences of those decisions. Business owners can decide where to open a business, what to sell, and how to operate the company. Consumers can decide where to shop, what to buy, and what they want to spend. Only when individual decisions

Profit

Businesses invest resources and take risks for one primary purpose—to earn a profit. *Profit* is the money left from sales after all of the costs of operating a business have been paid. Because businesses are not guaranteed a profit, they may lose the money they have invested. They are challenged to work hard, invest wisely, and produce goods and services that are needed in order to make a profit.

Profit is at the heart of the private enterprise system. Earning a profit is not the only reason for investing money and operating a business. People enjoy the challenge and freedom of business ownership, as well as the satisfaction of providing goods and services that other people want.

Competition

The rivalry among businesses to sell their goods and services is known as *competition*. Consumers have many choices of products and services and will select the one they believe will provide the greatest satisfaction for the money. Businesses must work to improve their products and reduce their costs. If customers are not satisfied with one company's offerings, they will look for another choice. Competition forces businesses to improve products, keep costs low, provide effective customer service, and search for new ideas.

> *checkpoint* >>
> Name the four principles of the U.S. economic system.

TEACH

Write on the board, "Profit is the heart of the private enterprise system." Ask students why profit is necessary for the economy to work effectively and whether they can see any benefits to consumers when a business makes a profit.

ONGOING ASSESSMENT

checkpoint >> **ANSWER**

The four principles of the U.S. economic system are private property, freedom of choice, profit, and competition.

ASSESS

Key Concepts Answers

1. b. requiring individuals to work in a particular career

2. d. command

3. a. make a profit

Make Academic Connections

4. Provide guidance regarding the acceptable length of reports and the preferred style for reference citations.

5. Prices will vary. Graphs should accurately illustrate the data students collect.

CLOSE

Have students list the three common types of economic systems and identify their main differences.

1-3	Assessment	

Key Concepts

Determine the best answer.

1. Which of the following addresses the economic question of how to produce?
   a. growing corn instead of potatoes
   b. requiring individuals to work in a particular career
   c. producing more capital goods and fewer consumer products
   d. selling natural resources to other countries

2. In which of the following economic systems is the government's role greatest?
   a. mixed
   b. traditional
   c. market
   d. command

3. The primary reason business owners make investments and take risks is to
   a. make a profit
   b. satisfy customer needs
   c. develop new products
   d. make their own decisions

Make Academic Connections

4. **Research** Choose one of the following five countries. Research that country and write a report describing its current economic system.
   Chile
   Latvia
   Costa Rica
   Zimbabwe
   Singapore

5. **Math** Use an Internet search engine to gather pricing information on each of the products listed. Identify the highest and lowest price at which each of the products is sold. Calculate the difference in the prices for each product. Create a bar chart that illustrates each of the prices and the amount of difference between the high and low prices.
   a. Ford Focus
   b. Apple iPod
   c. one year of college tuition

RETEACH

Ask students to individually list the three economic questions. As a group, check the answers and discuss why these answers are important to consumers and businesses.

ENRICH

Have students prepare a three-paragraph response to the question, "How would you improve the U.S. private enterprise economy?"

Goals

Describe supply and demand orally and with graphs.

Discuss how supply and demand affect prices of products and services.

Key Terms

consumer

producers

demand

supply

market price

Focus on **Real Life**

Jody and Dennis are both in the mood for some Italian food. Their town has two Italian restaurants, Restaurant Italia and Mamma's Pizzeria. Both Jody and Dennis are on a limited budget, so they are always careful about how they spend their money. Mamma's Pizzeria is famous for its delicious pizza and has excellent service. Restaurant Italia has a broader menu offering both pizza and pasta dishes. Jody and Dennis both feel the food is good but doesn't have that authentic Italian flavor. Often, the restaurant is crowded with slow service. Because Momma's is known for the best pizza in town, the prices are quite a bit higher than at Restaurant Italia. If you were going to eat with Jody and Dennis, how would you decide which restaurant to choose?

PARTICIPATING IN A MARKET ECONOMY

In a market economy, buyers and sellers use the marketplace to make economic decisions. Buying decisions are made by consumers—including individuals, businesses, and government. A **consumer** is a person who buys and uses goods and services. The individual buying decisions of consumers have a tremendous influence on the market economy. Consumers decide what to buy, where to buy, from whom to buy, and what price they are willing to pay.

Producers pay close attention to the needs and activities of consumers. **Producers** are individuals and organizations that determine what products and services will be available for sale. Producers invest resources and take risks in order to make a profit. They determine what products and services will be available in the economy, what needs and wants they will try to satisfy, and the prices they want to receive.

It may seem that the economy is a big, unorganized system in which everyone pursues his or her own self-interest. You may wonder how the system can work when each business makes its own decisions about what to produce, while each consumer makes a decision about what and where to buy. The system does work

main idea

Describe supply and demand orally and with graphs.

What are the advantages of being a consumer in a free enterprise economy?

Focus on **Real Life**

Ask students to suggest ways that each of the restaurants can attract new customers and make sure the customers are happy with their experience.

TEACH

Explain to students that, in order for a market economy to work well, consumers must be able to satisfy their needs and businesses must be able to make a profit. Ask them what they predict will happen to an economy when one of those results is not achieved.

THINK CRITICALLY THROUGH VISUALS

A consumer in a market economy has the freedom to choose what to buy, where to buy, from whom to buy, and what price to pay. These choices exert a great deal of influence on the market.

Different Learning Styles

Kinesthetic Learner Ask students to create a diagram or picture of how consumers and producers interact in a market economy. Have students explain the information included in their diagram.

and works well based on the principles of supply and demand.

Consumers Set Demand

When consumers make decisions about what they will purchase, they determine the demand for goods and services. **Demand** is the quantity of a good or service that consumers are willing and able to buy. A business can prosper or fail based on the demand for their products and services. For example, if a new restaurant opens in your town, but the service is slow, the quality of the food is poor, and the noise level is high, will consumers continue to eat there? It is not likely. Suppose a new restaurant opens with terrific food as well as fast and friendly service. That restaurant will probably be packed with people waiting in line for dinner.

Producers Establish Supply

Understanding demand tells a business what type and what quantity of products and services to supply. **Supply** refers to the quantity of a good or service that businesses are willing and able to provide. If consumers are seeking a popular product and are willing to pay a high price for it, businesses will provide the product to meet customer needs. On the other hand, if there is heavy competition for a product keeping the prices low or if customers are tiring of an

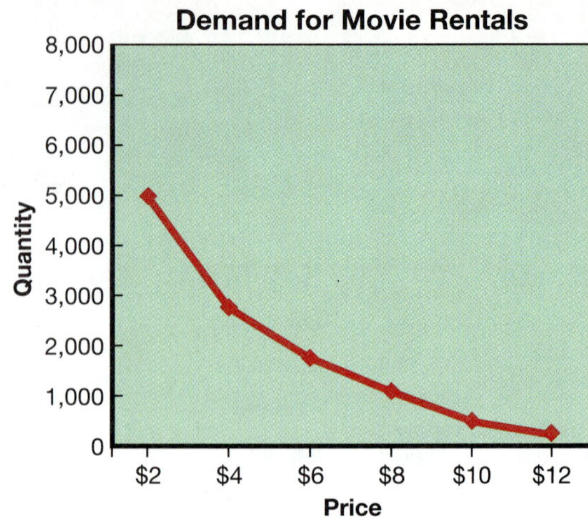

FIGURE 1-2

The quantity of a product customers are willing to purchase at various prices can be illustrated with a graph known as a demand curve.

older product, businesses are less likely to want to offer the product for sale.

A Graphic View

Demand and supply for a product or service can be illustrated using graphs know as demand curves and supply curves. The *demand curve* for a product illustrates the relationship between the price of a

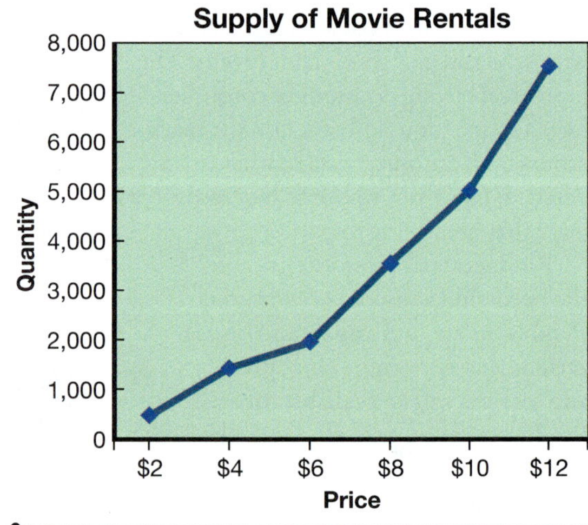

FIGURE 1-3

The quantity of a product businesses are willing to supply at various prices can be illustrated with a graph known as a supply curve.

product and the quantity demanded by consumers. As the price decreases, the number of consumers willing and able to purchase the product will increase. Figure 1-2 illustrates the possible demand for movie rentals at various prices.

In the same way, the *supply curve* for a product illustrates the relationship between the price of the product and the quantity businesses will supply. As the price increases, businesses will be willing to supply larger quantities of the product. Figure 1-3 illustrates the possible supply of movie rentals at various prices.

> *checkpoint* >>
> How does the price of a product affect demand and supply?

DETERMINING PRICE

Why is the price of a hotel room in Phoenix, Arizona, higher in winter than summer? Why do the prices of many of the products sold by farmers remain quite low? Prices are affected by the relationship between supply and demand, plus other factors.

Factors Influencing Demand

If many consumers want (or demand) a particular good or service, its price will tend to go up. More people vacation in Phoenix in the winter than in the summer so demand and prices for hotel rooms rise. When fewer people visit that area during the hot summer, the supply of hotel rooms is greater than the demand. Therefore, prices will decline.

When customers see a number of products that they believe will satisfy a particular want or need, demand for any one of those products will not be as high. Customers will be willing to switch from one product to another if the price of one is much higher than the others. When customers cannot find a good substitute

for a product they want, demand for that product will be high. Even if the price increases, they will be willing to pay the higher price because they are unwilling or unable to switch to another choice.

Factors Influencing Supply

The supply of a product can also affect the price. Because the supply of many of the crops and livestock raised on farms is large, prices remain low. If a drought cuts the quantity of corn grown by Midwest farmers one year, the price of corn will increase.

Competitors are businesses offering very similar products to the same customers. As the number of competitors increases, so does supply. A business will not be able to easily raise its prices. It will have to be much more sensitive to the prices charged by its competitors.

When competition is limited, consumers cannot find good alternatives. If you live in a part of town where there is only one supermarket, the prices at that store will often be higher due to a lack of competition. The prices of products featuring new technology will often be high because the company offering the new product seldom has direct competition.

Sometimes a natural disaster or other unforeseen circumstance affects supply. If the supply of oil, gasoline, or water is disrupted, their prices will increase. The supply of other products that use those resources in production may also be affected and their prices can increase as

Discuss how supply and demand affect prices of products and services.

Work as a Team

The prices of some products change a great deal in a short time, while the prices for other products remain quite stable. Work as a team to identify several products that experience regular price changes and several that do not. Discuss how supply and demand appear to affect the prices of the products in each of the teams.

well. Sometimes businesses will try to restrict supply of products in order to obtain a higher price. That will only work if customer demand is high and if there are no good substitutes for the product.

Determining Market Price

Supply, demand, and competition determine the market price for a product or service. The **market price** is the point where supply and demand are equal. Figure 1-4 shows the market price for movie rentals. Consumers are willing to rent nearly 2,000 movies and businesses are willing to supply that same number of movies if the rental price is just below $6.00 per movie.

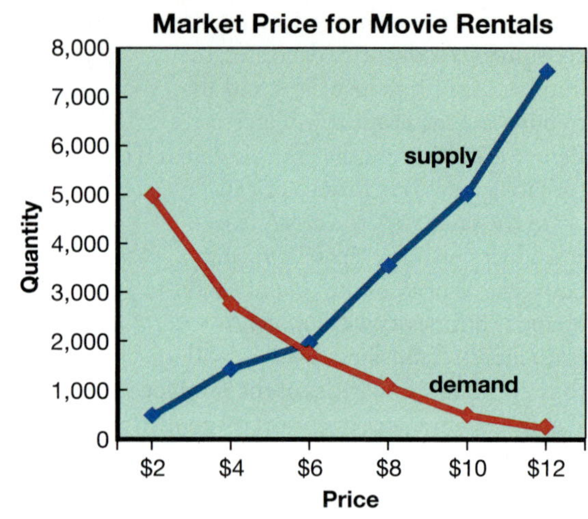

FIGURE 1-4

The market price for a product is the point where supply and demand are equal.

checkpoint >>

How is the market price for a product determined?

1-4 Assessment

Key Concepts

Determine the best answer.

1. True or False. Both individuals and organizations can be producers.

2. True or False. Supply is the quantity of a good or service that a consumer is willing and able to buy at a particular price.

3. As competition increases, prices
  a. usually increase as well
  b. are not affected so will usually not change
  c. usually will decrease
  d. There is no way to predict what will happen to prices due to competition.

Make Academic Connections

4. *Math* Calculate the total value of sales at each possible price for a product with the consumer demand shown in the table.

Price	Quantity demanded
$20.00	8,500
$22.50	7,800
$25.00	6,200
$27.50	5,900
$30.00	4,300

5. *Communication* Write a memo to an entrepreneur who is opening a new restaurant in your community. Explain the importance of supply and demand in determining the prices to charge at the restaurant. Give the new business owner advice on how to avoid lower prices due to competition.

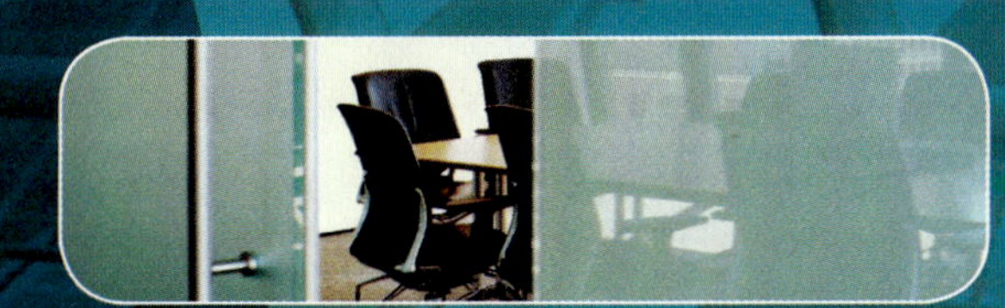

Heifer International

Ending hunger and poverty around the world! It sounds like such a big dream that no one would undertake it. Nevertheless, since 1944, Heifer International has had that dream as its goal. Through a unique program of giving communities a source of food rather than just distributing food, the organization has reached millions of families in more than 115 countries.

Dan West was a Midwestern farmer serving as a relief worker during the Spanish Civil War. With a limited supply of milk and food, he had to decide who would receive the rations and who would not.

As a farmer, Mr. West realized that if people had livestock, farming tools, and some assistance in learning effective farming practices, they would have the capability to raise food for themselves and their families for a lifetime.

He returned to the United States and formed Heifers for Relief. He asked other farmers to donate a heifer. Dan delivered the first shipment of 17 heifers to Puerto Rico, giving them to families with malnourished children who had never tasted milk before. Why heifers? The young cows would give birth to a new calf. Each family that received a heifer and training in how to raise and maintain dairy animals was asked to "pass on the gift" by donating a calf to another family.

For more than 60 years, Heifer International has been developing new projects around the world. Their mission is to work with communities to end hunger and poverty and to care for the earth. They envision a world of communities living together in peace and sharing the resources of a healthy planet. Today, hundreds of thousands of people continue to donate heifers, rabbits, goats, and chickens. Others make cash contributions to purchase livestock and supplies. Many people volunteer their time to travel to the rural communities with the animals to provide training and assistance so that the livestock will remain healthy, grow, and multiply for further distribution.

Recent projects of Heifer International include:

- Sending five rural veterinarians to Mongolia to work with animal herders to teach them improved animal management. These herders will then work with 500 additional herding families.
- Distributing 140 dairy cattle to 100 farm families in Kosovo who were victims of the war in their country in 1999.
- Placing 500 hives of bees in five Adaklu communities in Ghana, Africa. The communities will be taught hive management and honey harvesting techniques that do not harm the environment. Honey is a major source of nutrition in an otherwise malnourished area that suffers from illiteracy and high child mortality.

Think Critically

1. How does this approach to solving world hunger differ from other relief efforts that distribute food, milk, clothing, and health supplies?
2. Use the Internet to locate examples of other organizations that are working to reduce hunger around the world. How are they similar to or different from Heifer International?

© Getty Images/PhotoDisc

Heifer International has a long history of helping improve the economic well-being of families. The organization's projects also strengthen the traditional economies of the countries and regions in which they work.

Think Critically Answers

1. Answers will vary, but should reflect an understanding that providing a one-time supply of food will not meet long-term needs. Creating self-sufficiency through programs such as Heifer International enables communities to address the unlimited need for food.

2. Answers will vary. Encourage interested students to give short presentations about one of the organizations they discover.

Applied Skills

Communication Have students compose an essay on the ways that the work of Heifer International improves relationships between people from the United States and those from other countries around the world.

27

1. Examples will vary, but should demonstrate an understanding that needs and wants often overlap and that wants for some people may be needs for others. A professional football player may be required to wear a team jersey in order to receive payment for doing his job, making it a need, but the same jersey becomes a want for the student who simply wants to make a fashion or fan statement.

2. Answers will vary, but should demonstrate an understanding of the role of natural, human, and capital resources in the chosen business.

3. Answers will vary.

4. Answers will vary.

5. An opportunity cost for

a. trying out for an athletic team might be time lost from some other activities.

b. accepting a part-time job might be time away from friends, family, or other activities.

c. studying for an important exam might be time lost from other activities, such as sleep.

d. saving money for a car might be the amount of money you would otherwise spend on snacks, clothing, music CDs, or doing things with friends.

e. obtaining a loan might be the cost of the money you would save on interest if you purchase the item without a loan.

6. [Student answers are to be in table format.]

What goods and services will be produced?

Command: The government decides what goods and services will be produced or offered.

CHAPTER 1 Assessment

Business Notes

1-1 SATISFYING NEEDS AND WANTS

1. Things that are necessary in order to live are needs. Things that add comfort and pleasure to life are wants.

2. Goods are things that you can see and touch. Services are intangible, meaning they have no physical characteristics.

3. Economic resources are the means through which goods and services are produced. Economic resources are also known as factors of production. The three kinds of economic resources are natural resources, human resources, and capital resources.

1-2 ECONOMIC CHOICES

4. Most choices result from considering a number of alternatives. When you give up some thing to have something else, you are making a trade-off. The opportunity cost is the value of the next best choice.

5. The six steps in the decision-making process are: define the problem, identify the choices, evaluate each choice, make a choice, act on the choice, and review your decision.

1-3 ECONOMIC SYSTEMS

6. All economies must answer three economic questions: What goods and services will be produced? How will the goods and services be produced?

What needs and wants will be satisfied with the goods and services produced?

7. A nation's plan for answering the three economic questions is its economic system. In a command economy, the resources are owned and controlled by the government. In a market economy, the resources are owned and controlled by the people of the country. In a traditional economy, goods and services are produced the way it has always been done. A mixed economy combines elements of command and market economies.

8. Capitalism refers to the private ownership of resources by individuals rather than by the government. The U.S. economic system is based on the principles of private property, freedom of choice, profit, and competition.

1-4 SUPPLY AND DEMAND

9. In a market economy, buyers and sellers use the marketplace to make economic decisions. Demand is the quantity of a good or service that consumers are willing and able to buy. Supply is the quantity of a good or service that businesses are willing and able to provide.

10. If many consumers demand a particular good or service, its price will go up. If competition increases and therefore customers have choices, businesses will not be able to easily raise their prices. The market price is the point where supply and demand are equal.

Communicate Business Concepts

1. Identify five products or services that could be either a need or a want. Provide an example for each that illustrates when it would be considered a need and when it would be considered a want.

2. Select a business with which you are familiar. Describe factors of production used by the business that fit within each of the three kinds of economic resources.

3. Find a newspaper or magazine article that deals with scarcity of a product, service, or natural

resource. Write a summary of the article in which you identify who is affected by the scarcity and the effect it is having on business or consumer markets.

4. Identify a problem you will face in the near future, such as selecting a college or career or making a major purchase. Describe how you would complete each step in the decision-making process for the problem.

Market: The choices of consumers and producers determine which products and services are offered. Competition drives producers to provide new and better products and services based on buying trends.

Traditional: The same products and services that have always been produced continue to be produced.

How will the products and services be produced?

Command: The government decides whether new ways of producing will be adopted and which ways will be best for its country.

Market: Competition drives businesses to find new ways of doing things more quickly, less expensively, and on a larger scale.

5. Identify a possible opportunity cost for each of the following:

    a. Trying out for an athletic team
    b. Accepting a part-time job
    c. Studying for an important exam
    d. Saving money to buy a used car
    e. Obtaining a loan to start a business

6. Develop a table that compares the answers to the three economic questions in a command economy, a market economy, and a traditional economy.

7. Explain how freedom of choice can affect the availability of products and services for consumers. Now explain how it can also affect the profit a business might make on the products and services it sells.

8. Do you agree that the term "private enterprise" is a good description of the U.S. economy? Why or why not?

9. Select a product that is a regular purchase of many consumers. Use a graphing program to develop an illustration of a supply and demand curve for the product. Prepare a brief oral description of the illustration.

10. Review recent news reports of products and services where the price has been affected by supply and demand factors. Write a report using those examples that discusses the effect of supply and demand on prices.

Develop Your Business Language

Match the terms listed with the definitions.

11. Process of choosing which wants, among several options, will be satisfied.

12. Individuals and organizations that determine what products and services will be available for sale.

13. A nation's plan for answering the three economic questions.

14. Means through which goods and services are produced.

15. Things that are required in order to live.

16. Not having enough resources to satisfy every need.

17. Quantity of a good or service that businesses are willing and able to provide.

18. Person who buys and uses goods and services.

19. System in which resources are owned and controlled by the government.

20. Things that you can see and touch.

21. Private ownership of resources by individuals rather than by the government.

22. System in which goods and services are produced the way they have always been done.

23. System that combines elements of the command and market economies.

24. Quantity of a good or service that consumers are willing and able to buy.

25. Point where supply and demand are equal.

26. Things that add comfort and pleasure to your life.

27. Activities that are consumed at the same time they are produced.

28. Giving up on something to have something else.

29. Value of the alternative you did not choose.

30. System in which the resources are owned and controlled by the people of the country.

KEY TERMS

a. capitalism
b. command economy
c. consumer
d. demand
e. economic decision-making
f. economic resources
g. economic system
h. goods
i. market economy
j. market price
k. mixed economy
i. needs
m. opportunity cost
n. producers
o. scarcity
p. services
q. supply
r. trade-off
s. traditional economy
t. wants

Develop Your Business Language Answers

11. e. economic decision-making

12. n. producers

13. g. economic system

14. f. economic resources

15. l. needs

16. o. scarcity

17. q. supply

18. c. consumer

19. b. command economy

20. h. goods

21. a. capitalism

22. s. traditional economy

23. k. mixed economy

24. d. demand

Traditional: Things are done the same way they have always been done, often regardless of their effectiveness.

What needs and wants will be satisfied?

Command: The government decides which needs and wants will take priority. Some are strict and limit available goods and services to those that meet the most basic needs.

Market: Consumers and businesses make decisions based on their own self-interest. Consumers make purchases based on needs, wants, current trends, prices, and supply—decisions which businesses respond to in such a way as to make a profit.

Traditional: The focus of traditional economies is usually placed on the most basic needs.

7. Freedom of choice produces a greater variety for consumers, along with greater competition among products and services. This greater competition creates a drive for improvements and better pricing by businesses. Businesses can use this to their advantage by consistently introducing new or better products, for which they can increase their prices and thus their profits.

8. Private enterprise does describe the U.S. economy in that we each have at least some personal freedom of choice among products and services and some measure of opportunity to market our own product or service. It does not apply in the sense that we are interdependent upon one another and therefore affect the development of goods and services with each of our buying decisions.

9. Answers will vary.

10. Answers will vary.

Make Academic Connections

25. j. market price

26. t. wants

27. p. services

28. r. trade-off

29. m. opportunity cost

30. i. market economy

Make Academic Connections

31. Answers will vary.

32. As advantages for choosing to continue her dance lessons, Sheila might list the fact that she enjoys dance, that she will improve her skills by continuing, and that there are advantages to remaining physically active. The disadvantages she might list are that she will miss the pleasure of attending the later performances for the season and the social aspect of attending with friends or family. The advantages of choosing the theater tickets would be that she would be able to see all of the performances and enjoy the company of friends or family as she attends. The disadvantage would be the loss of time in developing her talent, the loss of physical exercise, and the possible loss of future opportunities as a professional dancer.

33. Answers will vary.

34. a. $56.0 - 17.0 = 39.0$; $56.0 - 29.0 = 27.0$

b. Country 1: $65.0 \div 8 = 8.125$; Country 2: $132.0 \div 8 = 16.5$; Country 3: $701.0 \div 8 = 87.625$

c. Country 1: $17.0 + 65.0 + 16.0 + 7.0 + 8.0 + 18.6 = 131.6$;

Country 2: $29.0 + 132.0 + 13.0 + 11.0 + 7.0 + 24.7 = 216.7$;

Country 3: $56.0 + 701.0 + 27.0 + 3.0 + 25.0 + 53.5 = 865.5$

Make Academic Connections

31. **RESEARCH** Identify a product for which you believe there is a great deal of competition and one that you believe has very little competition. Use the Internet, newspapers, or personal shopping to identify the prices charged by three companies offering the product. Prepare a table to show the information you collected. Based on that information, do you believe you were correct in your original decision about the amount of competition for each product? How does the information support your belief?

32. **DECISION-MAKING** Sheila's father told her that with the family's limited resources, she would have to choose between continuing her dance lessons or a season ticket to the monthly performances of the local theater. This means that Sheila is on step 3 of the decision-making process. Complete step 4 for Sheila, listing the advantages and disadvantages of the two choices.

33. **COMMUNICATION** Your community has received a gift of 100 acres of land from a long-time citizen. A community group is encouraging the city council to use the land to develop a park. Another group would prefer that it be developed as an area for new small businesses. Prepare a one-page report for the city council comparing the two choices based on opportunity costs.

34. **MATH** The table below shows the average number of working hours it takes a worker in three cities in different countries to earn enough money to purchase several products and services. Use the information to answer the following questions:

a. How much longer than the worker in Country 1 must a worker in Country 3 work to earn enough to buy food for a family of four for a total of four weeks? Than a worker in Country 2?

b. How many eight-hour days would a worker in each country have to work to buy a large-screen TV?

c. What is the total amount of time a worker in each country would have to work to purchase each of the products and services listed?

	COUNTRY 1	COUNTRY 2	COUNTRY 3
1 lb. of ground beef	17.0 min.	29.0 min.	56.0 min.
Large-sceen TV	65.0 hr.	132.0 hr.	701.0 hr.
1 tube of toothpaste	16.0 min.	13.0 min.	27.0 min.
City bus fare	7.0 min.	11.0 min.	3.0 min.
1 pair of men's shoes	8.0 hr.	7.0 hr.	25.0 hr.
1 week of food for a family of 4	18.6 hr.	24.7 hr.	53.5 hr.

Linking School and Community

Interview the manager of a local grocery store or specialty retail store to learn more about how supply and demand work to establish the market price for products and services. Find one example where there appears to be evidence of high consumer demand, another with evidence of a great deal of competition among businesses, and a third where other factors seem to be influencing the market price of a product or service. Prepare an oral report to describe what you learned about supply, demand, and price to other students in your class.

Web Workout

The U.S. government collects and reports information about the U.S. economy that is useful to businesses and individuals. The U.S. Census Bureau features economic data on its web site, including economic indicators that provide important information about changes in the U.S. economy. Use your web browser to access the Census Bureau's web site and locate the link to "Economic Indicators." Select one of the indicators and investigate how it has changed over the past 10 years.

Think Critically

1. Prepare a table to present the economic information you found. Use the data in your table to prepare a chart or graph.
2. Write a one-paragraph description of your findings. Include a statement explaining how the economic indicator helps people understand the U.S. economy. Also include information about how the indicator you selected might be used by businesses or individual citizens.

Linking School and Community

Ask students to present their findings to the class.

Web Workout

Encourage students to use a computer spreadsheet to organize their data and prepare a chart or graph.

Students should understand that businesses make plans to expand or reduce operations based on changes in the economy. Individuals need to understand how the economy is changing to make choices about how to use their resources. A growing economy increases business and consumer confidence, while a shrinking economy usually causes concerns.

Decision-Making Strategies

35. Countries that make efficient use of capital goods can produce more with fewer people in a shorter time than countries in which many workers perform the work by manual labor. Study the figures below for farm workers and their yearly output in two different kinds of economic systems, then answer the questions that follow.

a. How many more people were working in agricultural jobs in the traditional economy than in the market economy?

b. In which system was each farm worker more productive?

c. In terms of people supplied from the output of each farm worker, how much more productive was the worker in (b)?

	TRADITIONAL ECONOMY	MARKET ECONOMY
Size of the agriculture labor force	34,350,000	4,380,000
Number of people supplied with food from the labor of each agriculture worker	7	49

Entrepreneurship Event

Entrepreneurs are leaders who take the risk of starting new business ventures. Individuals who are willing to start a business face more than a 50 percent chance of failure within the first five years of operation. Successful entrepreneurs must conduct research, secure financing, and convince consumers to purchase the goods/services they offer.

You must develop a business plan for a new business in your community. The business plan must not exceed 10 single-spaced pages.

Your business plan must include the products or services to be provided, market analysis, customer profile, competition, short-range operational goals, financial analysis (income statement, balance sheet, cash flow statement, and other analyses), and supporting research documents.

You will orally present your business plan to the class/judges for 10 minutes. Class members or judges have up to five minutes to ask you questions about your business plan.

PERFORMANCE INDICATORS EVALUATED

- Develop a written business plan for a start-up business.
- Identify the customer base, including consumer and organizational markets and highlighting demographics.
- Analyze financial data.
- Demonstrate successful price selection methods.
- Identify and use internal and external resources.

You will be evaluated for your

- Knowledge and understanding of entrepreneurship
- Communication of research in a clear and concise manner both orally and in writing
- Demonstration of effective persuasive and informative communication and presentation skills

For more detailed information about performance indicators, go to the BPA web site.

Think Critically

1. Why does your community need the business you have selected?
2. What are your strengths, weaknesses, opportunities, and threats with this business proposal?
3. What is the most effective means to advertise your business?
4. Who are the sources to finance your business idea?
5. When do you plan on first making a profit with this business venture?

http://www.bpanet.org/

Portfolio Activity

school.cengage.com/business/introtobiz

Access the web site shown here to find portfolio activities for this chapter. Use the activities to provide tangible evidence of your learning.

Decision-Making Strategies Answers

35. a. 29,970,000

b. market economy

c. seven times more productive

Winning Edge
Entrepreneurship Event

Think Critically
Answers

1. Answers will vary depending on the type of business selected.

2. Answers will vary.

3. Advertisements may include local newspaper, local radio, cable television, bulk mailing, billboards, and so forth.

4. Financial sources include, but are not limited to, banks, venture capitalists, family investment, and corporate ownership.

5. Answers will vary. Most businesses take up to three years to make a profit.

Economic Activity

CHAPTER OVERVIEW

This chapter provides students with an understanding of measurements commonly used to gauge economic activity and business conditions in our society.

2-1 Measuring Economic Activity

This lesson provides information about foundation economic data used in our society.

2-2 Economic Conditions Change

In this lesson, students will learn about business cycles, consumer prices, and interest rates.

2-3 Other Measures of Business Activity

Investing, borrowing, and various economic challenges are addressed in this lesson.

Teaching Resources

Activities and Study Guide, Ch. 2
Chapter and Unit Tests, Ch. 2
Spanish Resources, Ch. 2

Exam_View_® *CD*, Ch. 2
Instructor's Resource CD
- PowerPoint Slides, Ch. 2
- Lesson Plans, Ch. 2

Xtra! Web Site

school.cengage.com/business/introtobiz
- Study Tools, 2-1, 2-2, 2-3
- Quiz Prep, Ch. 2
- Net Bookmark, Ch. 2
- Crossword Puzzle, Ch. 2
- Portfolio Activity, Ch. 2

Planning a Career in...
ECONOMIC DEVELOPMENT

A career in the economic development field could involve a variety of employment opportunities. If you have the interest and obtain the required training, you could be a corporate executive, a government research director, or a field training consultant. Each of these jobs provides contributions to economic growth.

As you study various topics in this book, your awareness of economic development work will expand. Many positions in the economics profession are related to employment in government, technology, research, engineering, health care, nutrition, marketing, and financial planning. Every country in the world is in need of efforts to enhance its economic development and improve the quality of life for its citizens. Your decision for a career in economic development will have you participating in how a society allocates its scarce resources among its unlimited wants and needs.

Employment Outlook

- Job growth in the economic development field will continue over the next decade.
- Specialized technical skills (engineering, health care, computer technology, food processing) will be in demand, especially in the developing economies of the world.

Related Job Titles

- Economist
- Transportation Engineer
- Urban and Regional Planner
- Survey Researcher
- Statistician
- Statistical Assistant
- Budget Analyst
- Financial Analyst
- Operations Research Analyst

Needed Skills

- Requires a bachelor's degree. More advanced positions need a master's degree or even a doctorate.
- Sociology and cultural knowledge are needed for work in urban settings and in developing nations.
- Special training in statistics, research, health care, technology, nutrition, and other fields will be helpful.

What's it like to work in...
Economic Development

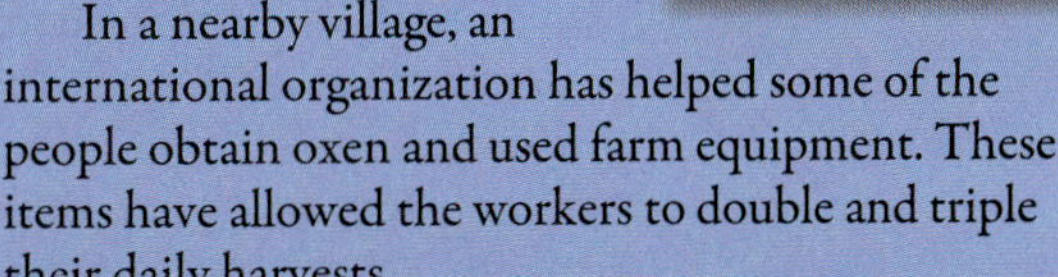

As the sun rises over the mountains, hundreds of workers are already on the job. The people in this village know that they have to harvest enough crops to sell for their family income. The task is difficult, as working by hand has limits.

In a nearby village, an international organization has helped some of the people obtain oxen and used farm equipment. These items have allowed the workers to double and triple their daily harvests.

Many government and private agencies work to help people improve their labor productivity. The use of new growing methods, machinery, and other agricultural advances can provide families with more money for food, housing, clothing, and health care. Funding for these improvements is often uncertain. Money may come from private investors or government grants and loans.

What about you? What aspects of working in economic development interest you?

ECONOMIC DEVELOPMENT

Creation of jobs and improved educational systems provide the foundation of economic development. Students should be made aware of the importance of these efforts in relation to improved quality of life for countries around the world. Ask students: In what ways are you affected by people around the world who live in difficult economic conditions? Students might point out that raw materials and products used in the United States come from many different countries. Also, disease and hunger can cause health concerns and political unrest that affect people in the United States.

What About You?
Answer

Student answers will require thinking beyond what is presented and formulating their own reactions. Students might be interested in knowing that it is possible to have a career in improving living conditions and quality of life around the world. They may have thought that such opportunities only existed for volunteer work.

Additional Career Information

Additional information on careers can be found in the *Occupational Outlook Handbook,* an online publication (www.bls.gov/oco) of the federal government. Tell your class about this resource and how to use it. This description of job duties can be used to demonstrate the relevancy of skills learned in this course.

2-1 Measuring Economic Activity

Goals

Define gross domestic product.

Describe economic measures of labor.

Identify economic indicators for consumer spending.

Key Terms

gross domestic product (GDP)

GDP per capita

unemployment rate

productivity

personal income

retail sales

Focus on **Real Life**

Measuring performance is common in many aspects of life. In a recent basketball game, Rosa Rivera of Middletown High School scored 19 points, pulled down 8 rebounds, and had 7 assists.

Later that day, the school's marching band was in competition and received a score of 88.3. By most standards, this was a good performance.

How about you? How much have you grown in the past 10 years? You can say, "I am 10 years older." Or, "I am 50 pounds heavier." Or, "I now wear shoe size 10C."

Several ways can be used to measure personal growth. In a similar manner, business and economic activity are measured to determine progress.

main idea

Define gross domestic product.

GROSS DOMESTIC PRODUCT (GDP)

Economic growth refers to a steady increase in the production of goods and services in an economic system. Just as you use different ways to measure your own growth, different methods can be used to measure the growth of an economy.

One way to find out how well an economy is doing is to compare output from year to year. Governments collect information from producers and estimate national output. The most widely used measure is gross domestic product. **Gross domestic product** or **GDP** is the total dollar value of all final goods and services produced in a country during one year. Figure 2-1 reports the GDP of various countries in a recent year.

Components of GDP

Gross domestic product includes four major categories of economic activity:

1. Consumer spending for food, clothing, housing, and other aspects

FIGURE 2-1

Which country has the highest GDP per capita? The lowest?

COMPARISON OF GDP IN SELECTED COUNTRIES					
COUNTRY	TOTAL GDP (U.S. $)	GDP PER CAPITA ($)	COUNTRY	TOTAL GDP (U.S. $)	GDP PER CAPITA ($)
United States	13.0 trillion	43,500	Mexico	1.1 trillion	10,600
China	10.0 trillion	7,600	South Africa	576.4 billion	13,000
Japan	4.2 trillion	33,100	Poland	542.6 billion	14,100
India	4.0 trillion	3,700	Saudi Arabia	374.0 billion	13,800
Germany	2.6 trillion	31,400	Vietnam	258.6 billion	3,100
Brazil	1.6 trillion	8,600	Nigeria	188.5 billion	1,400
Canada	1.2 trillion	35,200	Bolivia	27.2 billion	3,000

Source: CIA World Factbook

2. Business spending for buildings, equipment, and inventory items

3. Government spending to pay employees and to buy supplies and other goods and services

4. The exports of a country less the imports into the country

Some goods and services are not included. For example, GDP does not include the value of the work you do for yourself, such as cutting your own lawn or building a picnic table for your yard. If you buy the lawn service or the picnic table from a business, they would be included.

Only final goods, such as cars, are counted when you measure GDP. Intermediate goods used in manufacturing, such as steel and fabrics, are not included. If intermediate goods were counted as well, the value of these intermediate goods would be counted twice.

If the GDP increases from year to year, this usually signals that an economy is growing and is healthy.

Comparing GDP

The United States had an annual GDP of about $12.4 trillion in recent years. The more the goods and services produced, the healthier an economy is considered to be.

The GDP of a country presents information about the economic output of a country. Work as a team to prepare a list of drawbacks resulting from only looking at GDP when evaluating the economic progress of a nation. What aspects of economic growth may not be reflected in the GDP of a country?

Just referring to the dollar value of GDP as a measure of economic growth does not tell the whole story.

Another way to measure economic growth is **GDP per capita** or output per person. GDP per capita is calculated by dividing GDP by the total population (see Figures 2-1 and 2-2). For example, suppose that there is no change in GDP this year compared to last year. Suppose, also, that the population increases. The same output would have to be divided among more people.

An increase in GDP per capita means that an economy is growing. A decrease may mean that an economy is facing difficulties.

> *checkpoint* >>
> What types of economic activities are not included in GDP?

FIGURE 2-2

How does this figure help you see how per capita output is measured?

This activity will allow students to interact on the basic aspects of the GDP. Encourage students to create a list that considers other economic indicators of a society. Ask them to point out valuable activities in our society that are not measured by GDP.

TEACH

Emphasize that many actions that benefit a society are not included in the GDP.

Explain the need to compare GDP and other economic activities among various countries. Point out that these comparisons can assist when business and government are making decisions regarding investing and spending.

FIGURE 2-2 *ANSWER*

Use this figure to point out the process for calculating the GDP per capita. Refer students to Figure 2–1 to view the GDP per capita for various countries.

ONGOING ASSESSMENT

checkpoint >> **ANSWER**

GDP only applies to reported *final* goods and services. Money earned for goods or services that are not reported would not be included. Goods and services used in the manufacture of other products are only counted once—in the final product.

Applied Skills

Mathematics Have students use library resources and Internet sources to obtain the GDP and population statistics for three countries. Have students use the data to calculate the GDP per capita. Ask them to explain differences among the countries.

TEACH

Explain that the unemployment rate does not include all people out of work, but only those who are "looking for work and willing to work."

Have students give reasons why unemployment rates are different in different parts of the country. Reasons may include differences in wages, changing economic conditions, and the skills of available workers.

Describe ways in which productivity is measured, such as manufacturing output, the number of customers served, and reduced production costs per unit.

Ask students to name actions that might be taken to increase productivity in a society.

Discuss problems that can occur from actions to increase productivity. Problems may include technology causing unemployment or increased job accidents as workers attempt to do their jobs faster.

THINK CRITICALLY THROUGH VISUALS

Answers will vary. Students might suggest that money or personal satisfaction motivates them to work harder and faster.

Describe economic measures of labor.

LABOR ACTIVITIES

The workers of a country contribute to the economy in several ways. First, their labor activities create needed goods and services. In addition, the wages they receive are spent to create demand for various items.

Employment

Today, more than 145 million people work in the United States. These members of the labor force are employed in thousands of different jobs. They produce thousands of different products and services. The labor force consists of all people above age 16 who are actively working or seeking work. Students, retired people, and others who cannot or do not wish to work are not part of the labor force.

One economic statistic of concern is the **unemployment rate**. The unemployment rate is the portion of people in the labor force who are not working. People are considered to be "unemployed" if they are looking for work and willing to work but unable to find a job.

Unemployment rates vary from year to year and in different areas of the country. The main cause of unemployment is reduced demand for the goods and services being provided by various workers. If fewer people travel by bus, for example, bus companies will need fewer workers.

Productivity

A vital source of economic growth is an increase in output per worker. **Productivity** is the production output in relation to a unit of input, such as a worker. Improvements in capital resources (equipment and technology), worker training, and management techniques can result in more output per worker.

Over time, the rate of growth in labor productivity has ups and downs. While increases in productivity occur in many years, the amount of the increase often becomes smaller. Sometimes, productivity may actually decrease.

If wages increase faster than gains in productivity, the cost of producing goods increases and prices rise. Even though workers earn more money, they are not able to improve their standard of living because of rising prices. For that reason, strong attention has been focused on ways of motivating workers to increase productivity. By doing so, workers will be contributing to a higher standard of living in the nation while also improving their own life situation.

An ability to produce more goods and services makes it possible to reduce the number of hours in a workweek. In the 1890s, the average worker in the United States put in about 60 hours a week. Today, the average workweek for many factory and union-contracted jobs has decreased to less than 40 hours. At the same time, some people have decided to take positions that require working more than 40 hours a week.

In many industries, even though U.S. employees work fewer hours, more is produced and earned than ever before. More can be produced in less time

What motivates you to work harder and faster?

Teaching Strategies

Expand Beyond the Classroom Have students talk to people who have been in the labor force for more than a few years about ways in which technology and other actions might be used to improve the productivity of workers. What are the benefits and drawbacks of efforts to increase productivity?

because of technology and efficient work methods. The training and skill of workers also contribute to improved productivity.

How can productivity be increased?

CONSUMER SPENDING

The money you earn and spend is one of the most important factors for economic growth.

Personal Income

Each day, people receive money from their participation in production. **Personal income** refers to salaries and wages as well as investment income and government payments to individuals.

These funds provide the foundation for buying needed goods and services.

Retail Sales

On a monthly basis, the U.S. Department of Commerce measures

The labor force in many countries around the world may not be well defined. Poor economic conditions may require family members of all ages to work on farms or in home factories to provide an income to cover basic living expenses.

retail sales, or the sales of durable and nondurable goods bought by consumers. These retail sales are an indicator of general consumer spending patterns in the economy. Increasing retail sales usually points toward economic growth.

The main items whose sales are measured for estimating retail sales include automobiles, building materials, furniture, gasoline, and clothing, as well as purchases from restaurants, department stores, food stores, and drug stores.

main idea

Identify economic indicators for consumer spending.

checkpoint >>
What are the main sources of personal income?

2-1 Assessment

Xtra! Study Tools
school.cengage.com/business/introtobiz

Key Concepts

Determine the best answer.

1. Which of the following would *not* be included in GDP?
   a. exports to other countries
   b. purchases of computers by government
   c. automobiles purchased
   d. dinner preparation for your family

2. Productivity would likely increase as a result of
   a. higher taxes
   b. expanded production technology
   c. decreased training programs
   d. lower government spending

3. Retail sales include
   a. taxes collected
   b. companies buying new equipment
   c. borrowing by business
   d. school supplies bought by students

Make Academic Connections

4. *Technology* Using the data in Figure 2-1, create a graph with a spreadsheet program to compare the total GDP and GDP per capita for five countries you select.

5. *Visual Art* Create a collage or photo essay to illustrate one or more of the ideas presented in the lesson.

ONGOING ASSESSMENT

checkpoint >> **ANSWER**

Productivity may be increased by improvements in capital resources (equipment and technology), worker training, and management techniques.

TEACH

Ask students to explain how personal income and retail sales affect economic activity in a country.

Use the FYI feature to point out that measurement of labor force and other business activities in other countries may be affected by economic, cultural, and political influences.

ONGOING ASSESSMENT

checkpoint >> **ANSWER**

Sources of personal income include wages, salaries, investment income, and government payments.

ASSESS

Key Concepts Answers

1. d. dinner preparation for your family

2. b. expanded production technology

3. d. school supplies bought by students

Make Academic Connections

4. Graphs should accurately illustrate the data students select from Figure 2-1. A column graph showing a pair of columns for each country is appropriate for this kind of data. Line graphs and pie charts should not be used.

5. Collages and photo essays will vary, but should clearly depict one or more ideas related to this lesson.

RETEACH

Prepare a one-sentence summary of each of the economic indicators in this lesson.

ENRICH

Have students research current data for one or more of the economic data items in this lesson.

CLOSE

Ask students to choose one of the economic indicators mentioned in this lesson and explain why it is important that people understand it.

TEACH

Provide an overview of the four phases of the business cycle.

Explain the prosperity phase of the business cycle.

Ask students to suggest reasons why an economy does not stay in the prosperity phase. Students should understand that when people have an adequate amount of a product, demand will decline and the economy will slow down.

THINK CRITICALLY THROUGH VISUALS

Answers will vary, but will likely include a discussion of how a small business owner might have difficulty during a period of low consumer spending, especially if the business fulfills wants rather than needs.

2-2 Economic Conditions Change

Goals

Describe the four phases of the business cycle.

Explain causes of inflation and deflation.

Identify the importance of interest rates.

Key Terms

business cycle

prosperity

recession

depression

recovery

inflation

price index

deflation

Focus on Real Life

As you mature, your abilities increase. You depend less on your family and begin to plan for your future and look toward a career. You might be concerned about earning and saving money. You might also be concerned about how your grades will affect plans for continuing your education. Various elements of your life change—both up and down. Your grades are likely to vary based on study skills and class efforts. The size of your savings account changes based on earning, saving, and spending.

Change is also true for the economy. Ups and downs occur for business activities. As economic conditions improve, quality of life in a country is enhanced. In contrast, downward economic trends result in greater hardships for workers and consumers.

---

main idea

Describe the four phases of the business cycle.

THE BUSINESS CYCLE

Economists have observed that economic activity tends to move in cycles. All nations experience economic good times and bad times. Fortunately, over time, bad conditions disappear and good conditions return.

Looking at the economic changes during the history of the United States shows a pattern of good times to bad times and back to good times. This movement of the economy from one condition to another and back again is called a **business cycle**.

Business cycles are the recurring ups and downs of GDP. Business cycles have four phases: prosperity, recession, depression, and recovery.

Prosperity

At the peak of the business cycle is prosperity.

Prosperity is a period in which most people who want to work are working, businesses produce goods and services in record numbers, wages are good, and the rate of GDP growth increases.

The demand for goods and services is high. This period is usually the high point of the business cycle. Prosperity, though, does not go on forever. The economy eventually cools off and activity slows down.

Think of ways in which spending habits change during a dramatic economic shift. How might this affect the small business owner?

© Getty Images/PhotoDisc

Different Learning Styles

Auditory Learner Ask students to say and repeat each of the phases of the business cycle. Then, describe a phase of the cycle and have students say the name for that phase.

Recession

When the economy slows down, a phase of the business cycle known as recession occurs. **Recession** is a period in which demand begins to decrease, businesses lower production, unemployment begins to rise, and GDP growth slows for two or more quarters of the calendar year.

This phase may not be too serious or last very long, but it often signals trouble for workers in related businesses. For example, if people buy fewer cars, a number of workers who make batteries, tires, and other parts may lose their jobs. This drop in related businesses is called the ripple effect.

Eventually, production weakens throughout the economy, and total output declines in the next quarter. Some recessions last for long periods as fewer factors of production are used and total demand falls.

Depression

If a recession deepens and spreads throughout the entire economy, the nation may move into the third phase, depression. **Depression** is a phase marked by a prolonged period of high unemployment, weak consumer sales, and business failures.

GDP falls rapidly during a depression. Fortunately, our economy has not had a depression for more than 65 years. The period 1930–1940 in U.S. history is referred to as the Great Depression. Approximately 25 percent of the U.S.

A QUESTION OF ETHICS

Ethical Analysis Guidelines

Most business decisions are viewed in various ways. In some countries, people expect family members to be given jobs in a company before others. In other places, payments or gifts are expected before you are able to do business.

These and many other situations create ethical problems. Ethics are principles of right and wrong that guide personal and business decisions. When considering the ethics of business situations, consider using these three guidelines:

1. **Is the action legal?** Laws vary among states and in different countries. Most companies base international decisions on the laws in their home countries.

When a conflict occurs, managers usually consider other factors, such as professional standards and the effect of the action on society.

2. **Does the action violate professional or company standards?** Professional or company standards will frequently exceed those required by the law. This helps to ensure that decisions will be in the best interest of both the company and the society in which it operates.

3. **Who is affected by the action and how?** An action may be legal and within professional or company standards. Decision-makers should also consider possible effects on employees, consumers, competitors, and the environment.

Think Critically

1. What are some examples of situations faced by workers and consumers that require ethical decisions?
2. Describe the effect on business activities if no ethical guidelines existed.
3. Research recent ethical situations that have been reported in the news. How have these situations affected workers, investors, and others?

TEACH

Point out the characteristics of a recession.

Explain that the difference between a recession and depression is the severity of economic difficulties.

A QUESTION OF ETHICS

The three guidelines provided in this feature can be used throughout the course as a framework for the analysis and discussion of various ethical situations.

Think Critically Answers

1. Answers will vary, but might include situations involving race and gender bias, sexual harassment, theft, falsifying information, and breaking confidentiality.

2. Answers will vary, but should reflect an understanding of the effect on a company's reputation, employee morale, productivity, and profit.

3. Offer suggestions for how students should report their findings—oral presentation, role-playing, one-page report, etc. Consider allowing students to work in pairs.

Different Learning Styles

Tactile Learner Use samples of various items to represent a range of economic indicators. A brick could represent business spending or a price tag from a package might represent retail sales. Have students suggest items for each economic indicator. Create a display or use the items as a review tool.

FYI

labor force was unemployed. Many people could not afford to satisfy even their basic needs.

main idea

Explain causes of inflation and deflation.

Recovery

Economic downturns do not go on forever. A welcome phase of the business cycle, known as recovery, begins to appear. **Recovery** is the phase in which unemployment begins to decrease, demand for goods and services increases, and GDP begins to rise again.

People gain employment. Consumers regain confidence about their futures and begin buying again. Recovery may be slow or fast. As it continues, the nation moves back into prosperity.

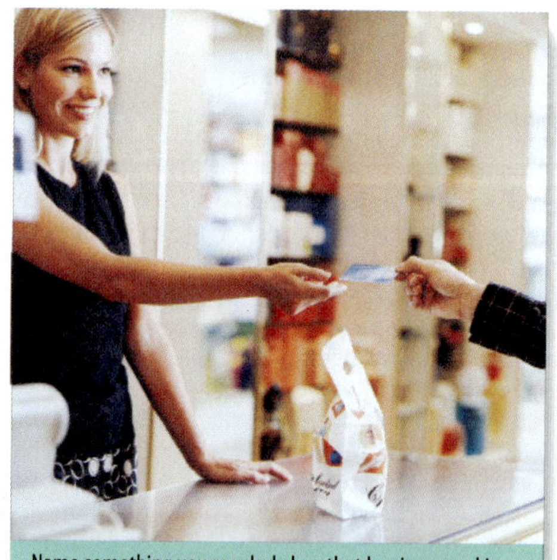

Name something you regularly buy that has increased in price while decreasing in size. How does this affect your decision to purchase the item?

CONSUMER PRICES

Have you ever noticed that packages of some items get smaller while the price stays the same? Have you bought new technology products that are less expensive than earlier ones? These are examples of changes in the buying power of your money.

Inflation

A problem with which most nations have to cope is inflation. **Inflation** is an increase in the general level of prices. In times of inflation, the buying power of the dollar decreases. For example, if prices increased 5 percent during the last year, items that cost $100 then would now cost $105. This means it now takes more money to buy the same amount of goods and services.

Inflation is most harmful to people living on fixed incomes. Due to inflation, retired people and others whose incomes do not change are able to afford fewer goods and services.

Causes of Inflation

One type of inflation occurs when the demand for goods and services is greater than the supply. When a large supply of money, earned or borrowed, is spent for goods that are in short supply, prices increase.

Even though wages (the price paid for labor) tend to increase during inflation, prices of goods and services usually rise so fast that the wage earner never seems to catch up.

Most people think inflation is harmful. Consumers have to pay higher prices for the things they buy. Therefore, as workers, they have to earn more money to maintain the same standard of living. Producers may receive higher prices for the goods and services they sell. If wages go up faster than prices, businesses tend to hire fewer workers and so unemployment worsens.

Measuring Inflation

Inflation rates vary. During the late 1950s and early 1960s, the annual inflation rate in the United States was in the 1 to 3 percent range. During the late 1970s and early 1980s, the cost of living increased 10 to 12 percent annually.

Mild inflation (perhaps 2 or 3 percent a year) can actually stimulate economic growth. During a mildly inflationary period, wages often rise more slowly than the prices of products. The prices of the products sold are high in relation to the cost of labor. The producer makes higher profits and tends to expand production and hire more people. The newly employed workers increase spending, and the total demand in an economy increases.

In the United States, one of the most watched measures of inflation is called the Consumer Price Index (CPI). A **price index** is a number that compares prices in one year with prices in some earlier base year. There are different types of price indexes.

Inflation rates can be deceptive because the Consumer Price Index is based on a group of selected items. Many people face hidden inflation given that they may not buy the exact items used to calculate the index. The cost of necessities (food, gas, health care) may increase faster than that of nonessential items, which could be dropping. This results in a reported inflation rate much lower than the actual cost-of-living increase being experienced by consumers.

Deflation

The opposite of inflation is called deflation. **Deflation** means a decrease in the general level of prices. It usually occurs in periods of recession and depression. Prices of products are lower, but people have less money to buy them.

Significant deflation occurred in the United States during the Great Depression of the 1930s. For example, between 1929 and 1933, prices declined about 25 percent. Deflation may occur for specific products. In recent years, the cost of computers and many other electronic products have declined mainly due to improved technology.

> *checkpoint* >>
> What are the main causes of inflation?

INTEREST RATES

In simple terms, interest rates represent the cost of money. Like everything else, money has a price. Interest rates have a strong influence on business activities. Companies and governments that borrow money are affected by interest rates. Higher interest rates mean higher business costs.

As a consumer, you are affected by interest rates. The earnings you receive as a saver or an investor reflect current

main idea

Identify the importance of interest rates.

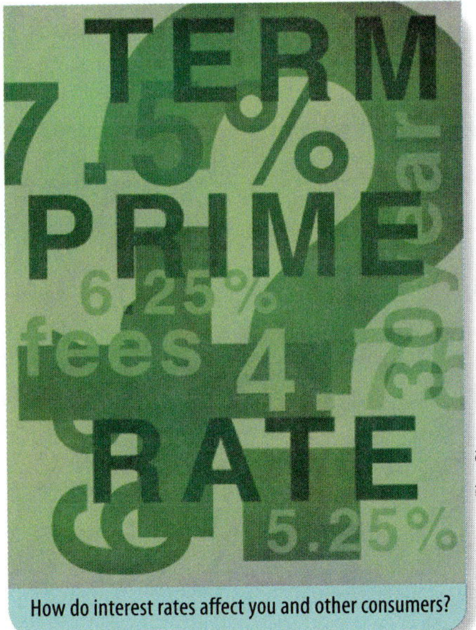

How do interest rates affect you and other consumers?

© Getty Images/PhotoDisc

TEACH

Provide an overview of the seven types of interest rates. Explain that many types of interest rates exist for various borrowing and saving situations of consumers, businesses, and government.

Describe how the supply and demand for money are the main forces affecting interest rates.

ONGOING ASSESSMENT

checkpoint >> **ANSWER**

Interest rates can encourage or discourage borrowing and spending. Lower interest rates allow consumers greater spending power, which increases demand, productivity, and employment. Businesses will likely pass on the cost of higher interest rates to consumers.

ASSESS

Key Concepts Answers

1. False. Deflation is the general decrease of prices.

2. False. Interest rates go up as borrowing increases.

3. d. depression

Make Academic Connections

4. Offer suggestions for how you would like students to report their findings.

5. Suggest that students use the FYI feature on page 40 as a starting point for their research.

Work as a Team

Interest rates influence many aspects of our economy. Working as a team look over the seven "Types of Interest Rates" discussed. Then, prepare a description of who in our economy would be most likely to be affected by each of these types of interest rates.

interest rates. Consumers also borrow. People with poor credit ratings pay a higher interest rate than people with good credit ratings.

Types of Interest Rates

Many types of interest rates exist in every economy. These rates represent the cost of money for different groups in different settings. Some of the types of interest rates include the following:

- The *prime rate* is the rate banks make available to their best business customers, such as large corporations.

- The *discount rate* is the rate financial institutions are charged to borrow funds from Federal Reserve banks.

- The *T-bill rate* is the yield on short-term (13-week) U.S. government debt obligations.

- The *treasury bond rate* is the yield on long-term (20-year) U.S. government debt obligations.

- The *mortgage rate* is the amount individuals pay to borrow for the purchase of a new home.

- The *corporate bond rate* is the cost of borrowing for large U.S. corporations.

- The *certificate of deposit rate* is the rate for time deposits at savings institutions.

Changing Interest Rates

Each day, the cost of money (interest) changes because of various factors. The supply and demand for money is the major influence on the level of interest rates. As amounts saved increase, interest rates tend to decline. This occurs because more funds are available. When borrowing by consumers, businesses, and government increases, interest rates are likely to rise.

checkpoint >>
How do interest rates affect business activities in our economy?

| 2-2 | **Assessment** |  |

Key Concepts

Determine the best answer.

1. True or False. Deflation results in lower buying power of money.

2. True or False. When consumers increase their borrowing, interest rates tend to decline.

3. The phase of the business cycle in which unemployment is highest is
   a. recession
   b. recovery
   c. prosperity
   d. depression

Make Academic Connections

4. *Geography* Obtain information about business cycles in other countries. Do these other economies face similar changes in economic activities?

5. *History* Conduct research about *hyperinflation*. What caused high inflation in various countries? What actions were taken to solve this problem?

RETEACH

Divide the class into four groups. Ask each group to prepare a short drama to help classmates better understand one phase of the business cycle.

ENRICH

Ask students to describe how inflation and interest rates are connected.

CLOSE

Ask students to name an action that might reduce inflation or encourage lower interest rates.

Doing Business in…Ecuador

Official name
Republic of Ecuador (Republica del Ecuador)

Capital
Quito

Population
13.8 million

Currency
U.S. dollar

Major exports
petroleum, bananas, cut flowers, shrimp

Major export partners
United States, Peru, Germany, Colombia

Major imports
vehicles, medicinal products, telecommunications equipment, electricity

Major import partners
United States, Colombia, Venezuela, Brazil, China

Source: CIA World Factbook

© Daniel Acker/Bloomberg News/Landov

Vendors and shopkeepers in Ecuador are happy to take your U.S. dollars for purchases, but your change might not include the familiar quarters, dimes, nickels, and pennies you see in the United States. Although Ecuador adopted the U.S. dollar in 2000, they minted their own coins. Both U.S. and Ecuadorian coins are in circulation.

In the late 1990s, Ecuador faced many economic difficulties, including high inflation, increased poverty, and a declining value of the sucre (its previous currency). Actions to address these concerns included adoption of the U.S. dollar. Dollarization generally helps control inflation and makes the country more attractive to investors.

When doing business in Ecuador, you will be expected to wear conservative clothing for business settings. You are likely to greet others with a handshake. As you get to know your business contacts, an embrace is likely; women may give "air" kisses on both cheeks.

Business meetings will likely start with an exchange of pleasantries. The importance of family in Ecuador is often reflected in these conversations. Avoid discussion of politics and the country's relations with Peru.

You will be expected to be on time for a business meeting, but don't expect it to start on time. For social gatherings, plan to arrive approximately 30 minutes after the appointed time. Lunch is usually taken between 1 p.m. and 2 p.m. For dinner invitations, prepare to eat as late as 11 p.m.

A local agent for selling goods and services is vital. This representative is necessary to do business with the Ecuadorian government. The use of a local attorney will ease the difficulty of maneuvering the country's complex legal system.

Think Critically

1. What are the benefits and possible disadvantages of a country using the U.S. dollar as its official currency?
2. How do business customs in Ecuador differ from others with which you are familiar?
3. Conduct library or Internet research to obtain additional information about business activities and economic conditions in Ecuador.

Doing Business in…

This feature will provide students with a better understanding of business activities in other countries and different cultures.

Have students who lived in or visited other countries describe their observations and experiences.

Ask students: What are the educational and economic benefits of understanding other cultures?

Think Critically Answers

1. Another country could benefit from using the U.S. dollar because its global acceptance helps to create stronger trade relations. Disadvantages could be that a country using the dollar is also subject to fluctuations in its value. Also, the country may loose some of its national identity without its own currency.

2. Differences in business practices in Ecuador include embracing when meeting; referring to family in business meetings, which is not as common in formal U.S. meetings; starting meetings late; eating later; and the use of agents, which is more common in Ecuador than in the United States.

3. Consider offering students suggestion for how they should report their findings.

Applied Skills

Language Arts Have students who speak different languages explain how some words may change meaning when translated. Point out the importance of language skills when doing business in the United States and other countries.

Focus on Real Life

Ask students to suggest actions that individuals, businesses, and governments might take when considering the purchase of expensive items.

TEACH

Ask students to name examples of capital projects in your community and around the world.

Explain how savings makes it possible for economic growth to occur.

Possible long-term goals might include an education, car, apartment, or travel.

PROJECT

Provide the following instructions to students. (These instructions also appear on page xxiv of the student text.) Calculate your savings rate (percent of your current income that you save). Do you believe you save enough of your income? Explain how saving is related to people achieving their life-span goals. Set a short-term saving goal that you could achieve now to help you eventually reach future life-span goals.

2-3 Other Measures of Business Activity

Goals

Discuss investment activities that promote economic growth.

Explain borrowing activities by government, business, and consumers.

Describe future concerns of economic growth.

Key Terms

capital project

stock

bond

budget surplus

budget deficit

national debt

Focus on Real Life

You can't expect to have enough money for a large purchase in the future if you always spend everything you receive. Today's savings makes tomorrow's economic growth possible. The concept is simple, but implementing it can prove difficult.

Governments, businesses, and consumers each must learn to save and invest for their futures. Government must have funds available for needed services desired by citizens. Companies must obtain equipment and other productive resources for a profitable future. Individuals must make choices that balance current spending with future financial security.

---

main idea

Discuss investment activities that promote economic growth.

INVESTMENT ACTIVITIES

Investing for the future can happen in several ways. Your time in school is an investment for your future. When companies buy buildings and equipment, they are also investing in their future.

Capital spending refers to money spent by a business for an item that will be used over a long period. **Capital projects** involve spending by businesses for items such as land, buildings, equipment, and new products. The money for capital projects comes from three main sources: personal savings, stock investments, and bonds.

Personal Savings

A major source of investment funds is personal savings. Companies use money you deposit in a bank or other financial institution. These funds provide the money necessary for buying expensive equipment or creating new products. In return,

savers are paid interest on the money they deposit.

The savings rate of a country is an important factor for economic growth. In recent years, the personal savings rate of the United States has been quite low,

Name some long-term goals you might set for your savings account.

Life-Span Plan Answer

Answers will vary. Check to see that students correctly calculated their saving rates. Their explanations should demonstrate an understanding of how short-term saving goals that they set now can contribute to their ability to achieve their life-span goals in the future.

Different Learning Abilities

Hearing Impaired Speak clearly, and be certain that you face the student so lip reading will be possible. Also make use of printed materials and visuals.

often below one percent. This situation can cause economic concerns in the future.

The Stock Market

Corporations are a major type of business organization. Many people invest by becoming part owners of a corporation. **Stock** represents ownership in a corporation. Stock ownership is commonly called *equity*. This term means "ownership."

The value of shares of stock is affected by many factors. Once again, supply and demand are the major influences. If a company has higher earnings, more people will want to buy its stock. This causes the value to increase.

The Bond Market

Another investment activity involves the sale of bonds. A **bond** represents *debt* for an organization.

If you purchase a corporate or government bond, you are a *creditor*. This means you have lent money to the organization. In return, bondholders are paid interest for the use of their money.

> *checkpoint* »
> Name some examples of capital projects.

BORROWING

"Buy now, pay later" commonly occurs in most economies of the world. Borrowing by governments, businesses, and consumers can have an important economic influence.

Government Debt

People expect services from federal, state, and local governments. Those services cost money. Often, government uses borrowing to finance various projects. New schools, public buildings, highways, and parks are often financed by borrowing.

main idea

Explain borrowing activities by governments, businesses, and consumers.

CORPORATE SOCIAL RESPONSIBILITY

Cleantech: Energy Alternatives and Environmentally Friendly Products

The phrase *cleantech* refers to various goods and services that are environmentally friendly. It is also part of the name of an organization that promotes clean technology among investors, entrepreneurs, and service providers.

The Cleantech Venture Network provides a network of information, online services, and educational events to promote innovations that do not harm the environment. The emphasis of the group's efforts is to balance profit-making and environment-friendly business activities. Cleantech is not just interested in being socially responsible. It also recognizes the need for financial success.

Cleantech attempts to encourage and publicize investment and development for various *clean*, or environment-friendly, technologies. The companies in the Cleantech network are involved in a wide range of products, services, and processes designed to provide superior performance at lower costs. At the same time, these business activities must reduce or eliminate environmental concerns in an effort to improve the quality of life.

A concern for both companies and investors is that the "cleantech" label is often used for products and services that do meet the standards of the Cleantech Venture Network.

Many organizations attempt to attract investors by calling their enterprise "cleantech" even though their business activities are not improving the environment.

Think Critically

1. How do consumers, businesses, and the economy benefit by cleantech activities?
2. What concerns might be associated with cleantech companies?
3. Conduct library or Internet research to obtain examples of various environment-friendly products and services.

Applied Skills

Technology Technology can be part of the problem or part of the solution where the environment is concerned. Technology is used in many ways in various business settings such as banking, health care, manufacturing, financial services, and education. Ask students to identify some business activities where the use of technology benefits the environment and other activities where technology hurts the environment.

Many economic and social concerns are present in the world. Encourage students to recommend specific actions to address the issue they discuss.

TEACH

Point out the difference between a budget surplus and a budget deficit.

Explain what factors cause the national debt to increase.

Ask students why debt can be important for businesses and consumers.

ONGOING ASSESSMENT

checkpoint >> **ANSWER**

A budget deficit occurs when a government or organization spends more than it takes in.

TEACH

Ask students to name causes for various economic problems.

THINK CRITICALLY THROUGH VISUALS

A small business may use more credit than it can afford. For example, payments on the debt might exceed the revenue being generated. Even if revenue exceeds the amount needed to repay a loan, there might not be enough money to pay employees, buy merchandise, or make improvements to keep up with competition. The company may eventually be forced out of business.

Getting involved in economic and social issues is a vital role for citizens. Working as a team, select a current topic that needs attention. Prepare a list of actions that governments, businesses, and consumers might take to address this concern.

main idea

Describe future concerns of economic growth.

A government may spend less than it takes in. When this occurs, a **budget surplus** is the result. If a surplus exists, government may reduce taxes or increase spending on various programs.

In contrast, a government may spend more than it takes in. This situation is called a **budget deficit**. Over time, deficits build up. The total amount owed by the federal government is called the **national debt**.

Business Debt

Loans, bonds, and mortgages are common borrowing methods used by businesses. Most companies, large and small, use debt at some time.

Efficient use of borrowing can be helpful to companies. Using the funds of others can help expand sales and profits. Sometimes, when poor decisions are

---

made, debt creates problems. Poor debt management can result in a company going out of business.

Consumer Debt

People commonly use credit cards, auto loans, and home mortgages to finance their purchases. The use of credit can be convenient. Often, overuse of credit results in financial difficulties for individuals and families.

Careful use of credit can be important for economic growth. In contrast, unwise borrowing can result in legal action and other trouble.

checkpoint >>
What is the cause of a budget deficit?

FUTURE ECONOMIC CHALLENGES

The ability of an economy to produce output determines its growth. The private enterprise system in the United States has worked quite well. Government leaders and citizens know that it can be made to

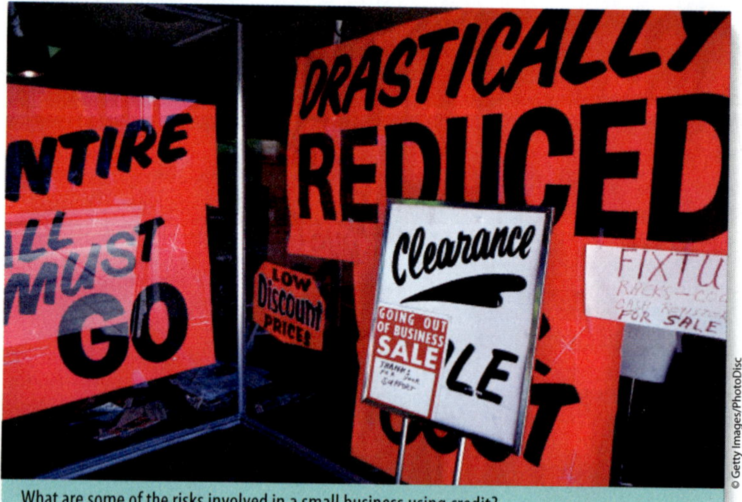

What are some of the risks involved in a small business using credit?

Communication Have students create a visual presentation to communicate various uses of debt by families, businesses, and governments.

Ask students to explain potential benefits and drawbacks in these various situations.

work even better as they strive to develop new technologies and find solutions for economic problems.

Various economic problems exist that need to be solved. Many people do not have access to adequate health care. Some people do not have proper housing, especially in large cities. Traffic and crime are also matters of concern for many. Too many workers are unemployed or do not have appropriate employment.

No one knows for sure what the future economic situation will be. In order to maintain or increase a country's standard of living and to prevent unemployment from rising, economic growth is needed. Economic growth is important because it provides jobs and allows people an opportunity to better meet their needs and wants.

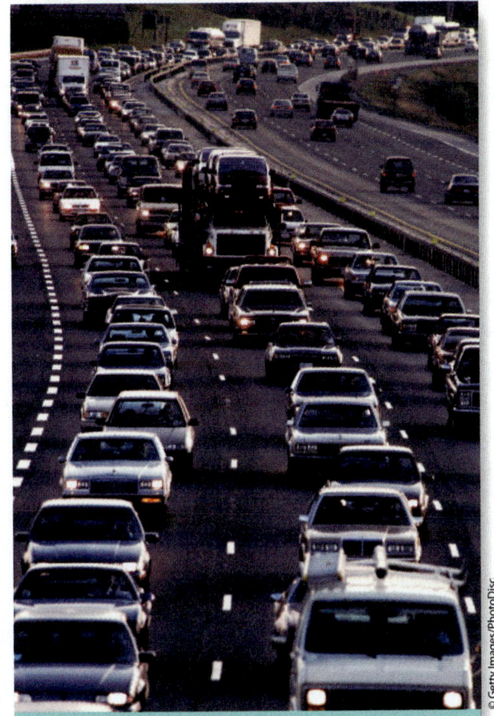

© Getty Images/PhotoDisc

Which economic problem concerns you the most? Why?

2-3 Assessment

Xtra!
Study Tools
school.cengage.com/business/introtobiz

Key Concepts

Determine the best answer.

1. Equity refers to
   a. reduced spending by government
   b. ownership in a company or other asset
   c. borrowing to finance a capital project
   d. increased government taxes

2. Which of the following would most likely cause a budget surplus for government?
   a. higher spending
   b. lower spending
   c. higher borrowing
   d. lower taxes

Make Academic Connections

3. *Economics* Taxes are a necessity. They provide necessary money for government services. What types of taxes do you believe would be best for a society?

4. *Social Issues* How might the future economic concerns of other countries differ from those of the United States?

TEACH

Ask students to suggest actions that might be taken to solve various economic problems around the world.

ONGOING ASSESSMENT

checkpoint >> **ANSWER**

Future economic concerns for any country include the ability to increase its output and provide a means for its citizens to meet the basic needs of food and shelter, adequate health care, education, transportation, employment, and safety.

THINK CRITICALLY THROUGH VISUALS

Answers will vary, but could include housing, health care, crime, traffic, or unemployment.

ASSESS

Key Concepts Answers

1. b. ownership in a company or other asset
2. b. lower spending

Make Academic Connections

3. Answers will vary, but might include taxes (income taxes, sales taxes, property taxes) relevant to the services they finance (e.g., transportation, education).

4. Answers will vary, but should reflect an understanding of various levels of economic development. Some countries are similar to the United States in their need to continue increasing production, while others will be focused on building infrastructure, literacy, and political stability.

RETEACH

Explain possible causes for various economic problems in our society and around the world.

ENRICH

Have students research a comparison of investing in stocks and bonds.

CLOSE

Have students develop a list of economic benefits of higher savings by consumers.

Communicate Business Concepts Answers

1. GDP may not be entirely accurate in reflecting the economic standing of a country. GDP per capita is a more accurate measure of the production of a country, and "real" GDP will allow for variations in prices. Other economic activities might indicate a healthy economy for developing countries such as new businesses, technology, and rising literacy rates.

2. No, not unless Country B had the same population as Country A, which would be unlikely. GDP per capita is determined by dividing GDP by the total population. In the example, if Country B had twice the population of Country A, the per capita output would be about the same in both countries. In order for Country B to have twice the per capita output of Country A, the population would have to be the same in both countries.

3. Improvements in capital resources (equipment and technology), worker training, and management techniques can each result in more output per worker (productivity).

4. Increased productivity means that workers are able to work fewer hours to produce the same amount or more products, leaving leisure time. Increased productivity usually indicates an increased demand for skilled workers, including those hired for production, as well as marketing and management personnel.

5. The country might be headed into a recession. If so, the auto and steel workers who have lost their jobs will reduce their demand for other goods and ser-

Business Notes

2-1 MEASURING ECONOMIC ACTIVITY

1. Gross domestic product (GDP) is the total dollar value of all final goods and services produced in a country during one year. GDP per capita is calculated by dividing GDP by the total population.

2. There are several economic measures of labor. The labor force of an economy consists of all people above age 16 who are actively working or seeking work. The unemployment rate is the portion of people in the labor force who are not working. People are considered to be unemployed if they are looking for work and willing to work but unable to find a job. Productivity is the production output in relation to a unit of input, such as a worker.

3. There are several economic indicators for consumer spending. Personal income refers to salaries and wages, as well as investment income and government payments to individuals. Retail sales measure the sales of durable and nondurable goods bought by consumers.

2-2 ECONOMIC CONDITIONS CHANGE

4. The movement of the economy from good times to bad and back again is called a business cycle. A business cycle has four phases: prosperity, recession, depression, and recovery.

5. Inflation is a general rise in the level of prices. Inflation can occur when the demand for goods and services is greater than the supply. Deflation is a decrease in the general price level. Deflation can occur when prices of products are lower, but people have less money to buy them.

6. Interest rates represent the cost of money. The level of interest rates in an economy is affected by the supply and demand for money. Interest rates affect both consumer and business activities.

2-3 OTHER MEASURES OF BUSINESS ACTIVITY

7. Investment activities that promote economic growth involve personal savings, buying stock as ownership in a corporation, and purchasing bonds from businesses and government.

8. Governments, businesses, and consumers commonly use borrowing to finance various purchases. Careful borrowing can be important for economic growth. In contrast, unwise borrowing can result in legal action and other problems.

9. Economic growth in the future will require consideration of various issues related to unemployment, housing, traffic, and crime. Economic growth is important because it provides jobs and allows people an opportunity to better meet their needs and wants.

Communicate Business Concepts

1. "GDP is the best measurement of a country's economy." Explain why you agree or disagree with this statement.

2. The GDP of Country A is $400,000. The GDP of Country B is $800,000. Does this mean that the per capita output of Country B is about twice that of Country A? Explain.

3. Name three factors that can contribute to increased output of goods and services in a country. Explain how these factors can improve productivity.

4. What is the effect of increased productivity on a country's leisure time? How might increased productivity affect career opportunities?

5. Suppose that many auto and steel plants close in a country. Thousands of workers lose their jobs in a short period. If the country has been enjoying prosperous times, it may now be headed into what phase of the business cycle? Describe other conditions that might begin to occur.

vices, causing other businesses to lose business and perhaps lay off more workers. This lowered demand, lowered production, and increasing unemployment might spread throughout the economy.

6. Retail sales is a measure of durable and nondurable goods bought by consumers. What are some examples of durable and nondurable goods?

7. What actions might be taken by businesses and government in each phase of the business cycle?

8. Why is a high rate of inflation generally considered harmful to an economy?

9. Other than the economic indicators discussed in this chapter, what are some other data items that might be used to measure business and economic activities?

10. What are some economic concerns that may need to be addressed in the future?

Develop your Business Language

Match the terms listed with the definitions.

11. A decrease in the general price level.

12. The movement of an economy from one condition to another and back again.

13. Spending by businesses for items such as land, buildings, and equipment.

14. The total value of all final goods and services produced in a country in one year.

15. Government spends less than it takes in.

16. A phase marked by a long period of high unemployment, weak consumer sales, and business failures.

17. Represents debt for an organization.

18. Salaries and wages as well as investment income and government payments to individuals.

19. The GDP divided by the total population of a country.

20. Production output in relation to a unit of input, such as a worker.

21. The phase in which unemployment decreases, demand for goods and services increases, and GDP begins to rise.

22. An increase in the general price level.

23. Represents ownership in a corporation.

24. Government spends more than it takes in.

25. The portion of people in the labor force who are not working.

26. The sales of durable and nondurable goods bought by consumers.

27. A period in which unemployment is low, businesses produce many goods and services, and wages are good.

28. A number that compares prices in one year with prices in some earlier base year.

29. A period in which demand, production, and GDP growth decrease and unemployment begins to rise.

30. The total amount owed by the federal government.

KEY TERMS

a. bond
b. budget deficit
c. budget surplus
d. business cycle
e. capital project
f. deflation
g. depression
h. gross domestic product (GDP)
i. GDP per capita
j. inflation
k. national debt
l. personal income
m. price index
n. productivity
o. prosperity
p. recession
q. recovery
r. retail sales
s. stock
t. unemployment rate

Develop Your Business Language Answers

11. f. deflation

12. d. business cycle

13. e. capital project

14. h. gross domestic product (GDP)

15. c. budget surplus

16. g. depression

17. a. bond

18. l. personal income

19. i. GDP per capita

20. n. productivity

21. q. recovery

22. j. inflation

23. s. stock

24. b. budget deficit

6. Durable products are those that will not have to be repeatedly replaced within a short amount of time. Examples include furniture, appliances, vehicles, and office equipment. Non-durable products include food, electricity, and gasoline.

7. In prosperity, businesses hope to continue their profits; government will try to control any inflation. During a recession, businesses hope to stimulate demand; government may cut interest rates to stimulate demand. During a depression, businesses hope to avoid going out of business; government may increase spending to stimulate job creation. During recovery, businesses will likely expand hiring; government may encourage business expansion with tax incentives.

8. Inflation makes it difficult for businesses and consumers to plan for the future. It also slows economic growth.

9. New businesses, new types of business, new technology, home buying, and interest rates are all indicators of business and economic activity. Improved health care, housing, transportation, and an increase in literacy and skilled labor could also indicate increased economic activity.

10. Some people in our country—not to mention the millions throughout the world—still do not have enough food, proper housing, and medical care. We need to develop ways and means to satisfy the basic human needs of all of our citizens. Other possible answers are up to the imagination of students.

25. t. unemployment rate

26. r. retail sales

27. o. prosperity

28. m. price index

29. p. recession

30. k. national debt

Make Academic Connections

31. Technology would likely have a positive effect on a country's GDP by increasing productivity and broadening job opportunities. Other answers will vary.

32. Students are to research the Index of Leading Economic Indicators and prepare a summary of their findings.

33. Students create a map showing economic statistics for five countries. They then explain possible reasons for the differences among the countries.

34. Students are to create a poster or other visual showing how the use of computers or other technology can improve productivity.

35. Answers will vary, but should include a discussion of how some cultures value and encourage hard work and high productivity, while the political climate in other cultures might discourage initiative and productivity.

36. 2002: 30 (25 + (0.2 × 25))
2007: 36 (30 + (0.2 × 30))
2012: 43.2 (36 + (0.2 × 36))

37. 2002: $9.00 (30 × 0.30)
2007: $12.60 (36 × 0.35)
2012: $17.28 (43.2 × 0.40)

38. Students research phases of the business cycle during the past 200 years and create a graph showing changes in the economy.

39. Answers will vary. Students are to prepare a visual presentation on the reasons govern-

---

Make Academic Connections

31. TECHNOLOGY Describe ways in which computers and other technology might affect a country's GDP.

32. RESEARCH Conduct research on the "Index of Leading Economic Indicators." Prepare a short written or oral summary to explain what this index involves.

33. GEOGRAPHY Select five countries. Create a map showing various economic statistics for each country. Explain reasons for differences among the countries.

34. SCIENCE Technology is often the basis for increased productivity. Prepare a poster or other visual presentation to demonstrate how the use of computers or other technology might make workers more productive.

35. CULTURE How might culture affect opportunities to increase productivity in different countries? Describe cultural and political factors that may enhance or limit actions to increase productivity.

36. MATH Productivity for a small country was 25 units per worker hour in 1997. Productivity increased 20 percent between 1997 and 2002. What was the productivity figure for 2002? If the rate of increase is maintained, what will the figure be in 2007? In 2012?

37. MATH Workers are paid a rate of $0.30 per unit. Using productivity figures from the previous question, determine how much workers earned per hour in 2002. If their rate increases to $0.35 in 2007 and to $0.40 in 2012, how much would they earn per hour in those years?

38. HISTORY Research various phases of the business cycle in the United States during the past 200 years. Create a graph showing the ups and downs of the economy. What conclusions could be drawn from this research?

39. COMMUNICATION Prepare a visual presentation to report (a) reasons government, businesses, and consumers borrow, and (b) potential problems that could occur for each group if credit is not used properly.

40. LAW What are some of the legal concerns that can result from unwise use of credit by businesses and consumers?

41. ECONOMICS Compare the use of stocks and bonds by companies to raise funds. Describe situations in which each would be most effective.

42. COMMUNICATION Select two interest rates from the list in the chapter. Create a chart showing these rates for the past four or five years. Explain possible reasons for changes in these rates.

Linking School and Community

Locate two or three people in your community who work in various jobs. Ask them about changes that have occurred in their work situation over the years. Did any of these changes occur in an attempt to increase productivity? Are there other changes that might be made to increase productivity? Prepare a short report to summarize your findings.

Web Workout

Web logs, called *blogs*, provide comments, news, and observations. These online journals communicate experiences along with other thoughts and information. Blogs are available on every business topic. The sources of blog postings can range from an economist at the Tax Foundation to a dissatisfied consumer. You should be cautious before believing or acting on information from a blog. Always confirm the information with other sources.

Think Critically

1. Locate a blog that relates to current economic conditions. Describe some recent postings.
2. What actions might you take to make sure the information on this blog is accurate?
3. Without actually posting it, write a comment that you would like to post on this blog.

---

ment, businesses, and consumers borrow and the problems that could occur if credit is used unwisely.

40. If companies or consumers use credit unwisely, they could be sued for recovery of payments or might have to declare bankruptcy.

41. Both stocks and bonds are used by companies to raise funds. Stocks represent ownership in the company and are more effective if a company has high earnings. Bonds, representing debt, are sold to bondholders who must be paid interest for the use of their money.

42. Students are to select two interest rates, create a chart showing how the rates changed over the past four or five years, and explain possible reasons for the changes in rates.

Decision-Making Strategies

In determining GDP, only final goods and services are included. This avoids having some items counted more than once. For example, a mining company sells iron ore to a steel-producing firm. That firm sells the steel to an auto manufacturer who uses it to produce a car. The iron ore, converted to steel, is counted once—in the price paid for the car, the final product. Read carefully the following list of goods and services produced in our economy and then answer the questions.

a. Electric toaster oven bought as a gift
b. Telephone service installed in a government office
c. Fiberglass sold to a company for use in making boats
d. Grooming services for your pet
e. Paper sold to a newspaper publishing company
f. Computer paid for by a city government
g. Computer bought for your family's use
h. Broccoli bought by a food-processing firm

43. Which of these items should be listed as a good and counted in GDP? Give reasons for your answer.

44. Which of these items should be listed as a service and counted in GDP? Give reasons for your answer.

Emerging Business Issues Event

This team event (two or three members) challenges FBLA members to develop and demonstrate research and presentation skills for an emerging business issue. Your team must research one of the following emerging business issues. Your research should find affirmative and negative arguments for each topic.

- Changing the federal income tax to a federal sales tax
- Strengthening the economy with tax refunds
- Alternative plans for Social Security
- Changing careers in a highly productive economy
- Providing more people with health insurance

Fifteen minutes before your presentation, you will draw to determine whether you will present an affirmative or negative argument for your emerging business issue. Any presentation that lasts more than five minutes will receive a five-point deduction. Following each oral presentation, the judges have five minutes to ask questions.

PERFORMANCE INDICATORS EVALUATED

- Understand the given emerging business issue.
- Present a relevant affirmative or negative argument for the topic.
- Conduct research to support your argument with relevant quality evidence.
- Demonstrate persuasive speaking and oral presentation skills.
- Involve all team members in the research and presentation.

For more detailed information about performance indicators, go to the FBLA web site.

Think Critically

1. Why must entrepreneurs pay attention to emerging business issues?
2. List two advantages and two disadvantages of changing federal income tax to federal sales tax.
3. Why is health care such a hot topic during an election year?
4. How has a productive economy influenced the types of jobs available to Americans?
5. How can young people successfully prepare for future careers when considering outsourcing of manufacturing and production jobs?

http://www.fbla-pbl.org/

Portfolio Activity

school.cengage.com/business/introtobiz

Access the web site shown here to find portfolio activities for this chapter. Use the activities to provide tangible evidence of your learning.

This chapter provides students with a foundation for understanding business in the global economy. It focuses on exporting, international trade, and global business activities.

3-1 International Business Basics

Importing, exporting, trade relations, and global currencies are covered in this lesson.

3-2 The Global Marketplace

Geographic, economic, cultural, and political aspects of international business, along with trade relations, are the focus of this lesson.

3-3 International Business Organizations

Methods of organizing international business activities, such as joint ventures and multinational corporations, are the basis for this lesson.

CHAPTER 3

Business in the Global Economy

3-1 International Business Basics

3-2 The Global Marketplace

3-3 International Business Organizations

52

Teaching Resources

Activities and Study Guide, Ch. 3
Chapter and Unit Tests, Ch. 3
Spanish Resources, Ch. 3

ExamView® *CD,* Ch. 3
Instructor's Resource CD
- PowerPoint Slides, Ch. 3
- Lesson Plans, Ch. 3

Xtra! Web Site

school.cengage.com/business/introtobiz
- Study Tools, 3-1, 3-2, 3-3
- Quiz Prep, Ch. 3
- Net Bookmark, Ch. 3
- Crossword Puzzle, Ch. 3
- Portfolio Activity, Ch. 3

Planning a Career in…
INTERNATIONAL BUSINESS

Global business activities create many employment opportunities. Jobs could include directing foreign sales, negotiating with foreign distribution centers, arranging shipping, and planning conversion of products from American to foreign specifications. While the skills necessary to perform these tasks are increasingly important, job titles often will not reflect them directly because the people will also have duties unrelated to importing and exporting. Transportation managers, for example, oversee both foreign and domestic shipping, including settlements between shippers. U.S. Customs Service agents investigate persons, common carriers, and merchandise arriving in or departing from the United States to prevent prohibited importing or exporting.

Employment Outlook

- Strong growth is expected for interpreters and translators.

- Employment of inspectors and compliance officers is not usually affected by economic fluctuations. Recently, increased security concerns have expanded demand for federal, state, and local government examiners.

- Continued growth of many international business positions is expected as companies expand global operations.

Related Job Titles

- Customs Inspector
- Interpreter/Translator
- Global Purchasing Manager
- Transportation/Freight Inspector
- Cross-Cultural Trainer
- International Sales Representative
- International Marketing Manager
- Import/Export Coordinator
- Freight Forwarding Specialist

Needed Skills

- Language skills, cultural awareness, and knowledge of geography provide the foundation for most international business work.

- Many international business positions require knowledge in a field such as accounting, marketing, finance, or information technology.

What's it like to work in… International Business

"I'm sorry, your shipment is being held at the Port of Hong Kong until the proper documentation is prepared."

These are words no exporter wants to hear. To avoid this type of situation, exporters turn to companies such as M.E. Day, which exist to help them ship their products around the world.

M.E. Day and other freight forwarders specialize in shipping goods to customers in other countries. These global intermediaries also help companies selling around the world with other services. Areas of expertise include export regulations, costs for various shipping methods, and the customs process.

M.E. Day also serves as a customs broker, helping international companies pass inspections when goods enter another country. Customs brokers prepare needed documents and make sure the required tariffs are paid.

What about you? What are some aspects of international business that you might find of interest in the future?

Planning a Career in…
INTERNATIONAL BUSINESS

International career opportunities exist in many settings. Use the career feature to point out how most careers are directly or indirectly related to global business activities. Ask students to name some skills and competencies that might be important when working in an international career. You could also use the "What About You?" question that follows this feature as the basis for a class discussion.

What About You? Answer

Student answers will require thinking beyond what is presented and formulating their own reactions. You may want to develop a class list of the interesting aspects of international business such as opportunity for travel and proficiency in multiple languages, job security and varied career opportunities, and intimate knowledge of other cultures and ways of life.

Additional Career Information

Additional information on careers can be found in the *Occupational Outlook Handbook,* an online publication (www.bls.gov/oco) of the federal government. Tell your class about this resource and how to use it. This description of job duties can be used to demonstrate the relevancy of skills learned in this course.

3-1 International Business Basics

Goals

Describe importing and exporting activities.

Compare balance of trade and balance of payments.

List factors that affect the value of global currencies.

Key Terms

imports

exports

balance of trade

balance of payments

exchange rate

Focus on Real Life

What did you and your family have for breakfast this morning? Coffee, cereal, and sliced bananas, perhaps? If it were not for trading with Brazil for coffee and with Honduras for the bananas, you might have had only cereal. The sugar on your table may have come from the Philippines. Even the morning newspaper was printed on paper that may have come from Canada.

As you look around your home, you will find many products made in other countries. For example, you may find a TV made in Japan or Korea, an MP3 player made in Taiwan or China, clothing made in the Philippines or Honduras, kitchen appliances made in Hong Kong or Malaysia, and cocoa from Brazil or Colombia. Look around your classroom. Can you identify products made in other countries?

main idea

Describe importing and exporting activities.

TRADING AMONG NATIONS

Most business activities occur within a country's own borders. *Domestic business* is the making, buying, and selling of goods and services within a country. *International business* refers to business activities needed for creating, shipping, and selling goods and services across national borders. International business is frequently referred to as *foreign* or *world trade.* Evidence of foreign trade is everywhere.

Although the United States has many natural resources, a skilled labor force, and modern production facilities, American companies and consumers go beyond the U.S. borders to obtain many things. The United States conducts trade with more than 180 countries.

In the past, economies were viewed in terms of national borders. With international trade expanding every day, these boundaries are no longer fully valid in defining economies. Countries are interdependent and so are their economies. Consumers have come to expect goods and services from around the world.

© Getty Images/PhotoDisc

What are some of the advantages and disadvantages of international trade?

Absolute Advantage

Two economic principles define buying and selling among companies in different countries. *Absolute advantage* exists when a country can produce a good or service at a lower cost than other countries. This may result from an abundance of natural resources or raw materials in a country. For example, some South American countries have an absolute advantage in coffee production, and Saudi Arabia has an absolute advantage in oil production.

Comparative Advantage

A country may have an absolute advantage in more than one area. If so, it must decide how to maximize its economic wealth. A country may be able to produce both computers and clothing better than other countries. The world market for computers might be stronger than the market for clothing. This means it would be better for the country to produce computers but to buy clothing from other countries. *Comparative advantage* is a situation in which a country specializes in the production of a good or service at which it is relatively more efficient.

Importing

Imports are items bought from other countries. Did you know that imports account for the total supply of bananas, coffee, cocoa, spices, tea, silk, and crude rubber in the United States? The United States buys about half of its crude oil and fish from other countries. Imports also account for 20 to 50 percent of the supply of carpets, sugar, leather gloves, dishes, and sewing machines. U.S. companies must import tin, chrome, manganese, nickel, copper, zinc, and several other metals to manufacture certain goods. Figure 3-1 shows how dependent the United States is on imported raw materials.

Without foreign trade, many things you buy would cost more or not be available. Other countries can produce some goods at a lower cost because they have the needed raw materials or have lower labor costs. Some consumers purchase foreign goods, even at higher prices, if they perceive the quality to be better than domestic goods. They may simply enjoy owning products made in other countries. French perfumes, Norwegian sweaters, and Swiss watches are examples.

Exporting

Goods and services sold to other countries are called **exports**. Just as imports benefit you, exports benefit consumers in other countries. Workers throughout the world use factory and farm machinery

U.S. Import Reliance for Selected Raw Materials

Material	Import	U.S. Production
Mica 30%		70%
Nickel 60%		40%
Silver 65%		35%
Chromium 75%		25%
Tin 79%		21%
Cobalt 81%		19%
Industrial Diamonds 82%		18%
Bauxite and Alumina 100%		0%
Manganese 100%		0%

Import U.S. Production

Source: United States Geological Survey Minerals Information.

FIGURE 3-1

How would U.S. manufacturing be affected if these imports were not available?

TEACH

Explain the difference between an absolute advantage and a comparative advantage.

Ask students to name benefits and concerns associated with importing.

Name various problems that can result from extensive importing.

PROJECT

Provide the following instructions to students. (These instructions also appear on page xxiv of the textbook.) Identify your special aptitudes or abilities that you believe could help you achieve your life-span goals. Explain how these aptitudes or abilities are similar to nations that have an absolute or comparative advantage in production and trade.

Life-Span Plan Answer

Answers will vary. Students should identify aptitudes or abilities they possess and logically explain how these may contribute to them achieving their life-span goals.

FIGURE 3-1 *ANSWER*

The graph in Figure 3-1 indicates that without imports, there would be shortages of these raw materials used in U.S. manufacturing.

Applied Skills

Building Study Skills Have students develop a summary of various international business concepts such as absolute advantage, comparative advantage, importing, and exporting. Encourage students to include visuals such as photos and sketches.

made in the United States. They eat food made from U.S. agricultural products and use chemicals, fertilizers, medicines, and plastics from the United States. People in other countries like to view U.S. movies. They also watch CNN and ESPN. They read books, magazines, and newspapers published by U.S. companies. The goods and services exported by the United States create many jobs. One of every six jobs in the United States depends on international business. Figure 3-2 shows U.S. balance of trade with various nations.

	U.S. Trade Balances		
GOODS EXPORTED (IN BILLIONS)	COUNTRY	GOODS IMPORTED (IN BILLIONS)	U.S. TRADE BALANCE
1,437.8	All Countries	2,201.0	−763.2
230.6	Canada	303.4	−72.8
134.2	Mexico	198.3	−64.1
59.6	Japan	148.0	−88.4
31.1	Netherlands	17.3	+13.8
17.8	Australia	8.2	+9.6
19.2	Brazil	26.4	−7.2
23.0	Taiwan	38.2	−15.2
55.2	China	287.8	−232.6
214.0	European Union	330.6	−116.6

Source: U.S. Census Bureau

FIGURE 3-2

Which country has the largest trade imbalance with the United States?

---

checkpoint >>

How does importing differ from exporting?

---

main idea

Compare balance of trade and balance of payments.

MEASURING TRADE RELATIONS

A major reason people work is to earn money to buy things. First, they sell their labor for wages. They then spend the major part of those wages for goods and services. People usually try to keep their income and spending in balance. They know that if they spend more than they earn, they can experience financial problems. Nations are also concerned about balancing income with expenditures. When people buy more than their income allows, they go into debt. In the same way, when a country has an unfavorable balance of trade it owes money to others. *Foreign debt* is the amount a country owes to other countries.

Balance of Trade

The difference between a country's total exports and total imports is called the **balance of trade**. If a country exports (sells) more than it imports (buys), it has a *trade surplus*. Its trade position is said to be favorable. If it imports more than it exports, it has a *trade deficit* and its trade position is unfavorable.

A country can have a trade surplus with one country and a trade deficit with another. Overall, a country tries to keep its international trade in balance. Figure 3-3 shows the two possible trade

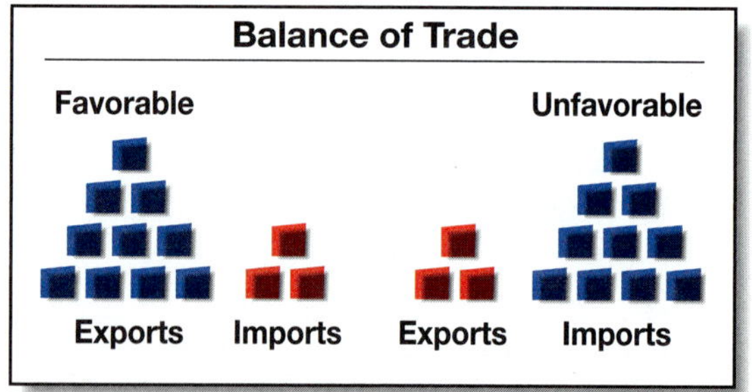

FIGURE 3-3

Why is it better to export more than you import?

---

positions. After a long history of a favorable balance of trade, the United States has had a trade deficit in recent years.

Balance of Payments

In addition to exporting and importing goods and services, other forms of exchange take place among nations. Money goes from one country to another through investments and tourism. A citizen of one country might invest in a corporation in another country. A business may invest in a factory in another country. One government might give financial or military aid to another nation. Banks may deposit funds in foreign banks.

When tourists travel, they add to the flow of money from their country to the country they are visiting. Some countries limit the amount of money their citizens can take out of the country when they travel.

The **balance of payments** is the difference between the amount of money that comes into a country and the amount that goes out of it. A *positive* or *favorable* balance of payments occurs when a nation receives more money in a year than it pays out. A *negative* balance of payments is *unfavorable*. It is the result of a country sending more money out than it brings in.

checkpoint >>

How does balance of trade differ from balance of payments?

A QUESTION OF ETHICS

Bribery and Gift Giving

In the United States, it is considered unethical for a businessperson to pay bribes to government officials or to other businesspersons in exchange for favorable treatment, such as the awarding of well-paid contracts. In fact, it is against the law, whether the recipient is an American or someone in another country. The Foreign Corrupt Business Practices Act of 1977 outlawed the payment of bribes by Americans to foreign officials, companies, or individuals. At times, not doing so may put U.S. businesses at a competitive disadvantage. In some countries, paying and accepting bribes of various sorts is common, even expected. As more countries recognize how harmful bribes are to economic progress, the practice is ending.

While it is relatively easy to outlaw bribes, it is much harder to define and identify what is a bribe and what is a gift given as a token of appreciation. Gift giving among businesspeople is relatively limited and infrequent in the United States and Canada. In other cultures, it is very common and regarded as entirely appropriate. Many organizations have policies that limit the monetary value and type of gifts that are acceptable. Policing intent is much more difficult because it is highly subjective. A social dinner invitation is usually meant to influence the recipient's behavior, even if in a subtle way.

Think Critically

1. How can U.S. businesspeople handle situations in foreign countries where officials expect bribes to be paid as a condition for doing business there?
2. Suppose you work for a manufacturing company. A plastics supplier who is trying to get more business sends you a case of golf balls made with one of its high-tech composite materials. What would you do?

---

services as compensation for not participating in the gift-giving custom.

2. The employee at the manufacturing company who received the case of golf balls could send the balls to the company's technical department for evaluation and send the plastics supplier a letter of thanks for allowing the company to test the product. To further emphasize that this was not accepted as a personal gift, the letter could mention that the leftover balls will be donated to a local school golf team.

TEACH

Ask students to describe factors that could affect the value of a country's currency.

Have students conduct an online search to find photos of currencies from various countries.

THINK CRITICALLY THROUGH VISUALS

Also point out that images on currencies reflect the history, culture, geography, and economic activities of a country.

FIGURE 3-4 *ANSWER*

Figure 3-4 shows that Britain's pound is worth the most in terms of U.S. dollars. Point out that these values change on a daily basis. Encourage students to find a web site that gives the current value of these currencies.

List factors that affect the value of global currencies.

INTERNATIONAL CURRENCY

One challenge faced by businesses involved in international trade is the various currencies used around the world. Nations have their own banking system and money. For instance, Russia uses the *ruble*; the European Union, the *euro*; Brazil, the *real*; India, the *rupee*; and Saudi Arabia, the *riyal*.

Foreign Exchange Rates

The process of exchanging one currency for another occurs in the *foreign exchange market,* which consists of banks that buy and sell different currencies. Most large banks provide currency services for businesses and consumers. The **exchange rate** is the value of a currency in one country compared with the value in another. Supply and demand affect the value of currency. The approximate values of various currencies on a recent date in relation to the U.S. dollar (USD) are given in Figure 3-4.

Travelers and businesspeople must deal with currency exchanges as they go from one country to another. Travelers in another country can go to a currency exchange window and buy any amount of local currency they want. The amount of local currency they receive depends on the value of the two currencies at that time. Current rates are posted at exchange windows. Although locations vary throughout the world, exchange windows generally are found at airports, train stations, hotels, and local banks. Operators of exchange windows charge a fee for their services.

Factors Affecting Currency Values

Three main factors affect currency exchange rates among countries: the country's balance of payments, economic conditions, and political stability.

Balance of Payments When a country has a favorable balance of payments, the value of its currency is usually

Why do many countries use a variety of colors in their currency?

© Digital Vision

Recent Values of Currencies			
COUNTRY	**CURRENCY**	**UNITS PER USD***	**VALUE IN USD***
Britain	pound	0.50 pounds	1.99
Brazil	real	2.03 reals	0.49
Canada	dollar	1.13 dollars	0.88
European Union	euro	0.74 euro	1.35
Japan	yen	119.78 yen	0.0083
Saudi Arabia	riyal	3.75 riyal	0.27
South Africa	rand	7.09 rand	0.141
South Korea	won	931.35 won	0.00107
Venezuela	bolivar	2,144.00 bolivars	0.00047

*United States Dollar

Different Learning Styles

Print Learner Use text and visuals on pages 58–59 to present and reinforce various factors that affect the value of a country's currency.

Tactile Learner Set up a foreign exchange window in your classroom using "play" money from several of the countries listed in Figure 3-4.

constant or rising. An increased demand for both the nation's products and its currency causes this situation. When a nation has an unfavorable balance of payments, its currency usually declines in value.

Economic Conditions When prices increase and the buying power of the country's money declines, its currency is not as appealing. Inflation reduces the buying power of a currency. High inflation in Brazil, for example, would reduce the demand for the real.

Interest rates are the cost of using someone else's money. These rates can affect the value of a country's currency. Higher interest rates usually create lower consumer demand. This often results in a reduced demand for a nation's currency, causing a decline in its value.

Political Stability Companies and individuals want to avoid risk when they do business in other nations. If a government changes suddenly, this may create an unfriendly setting for

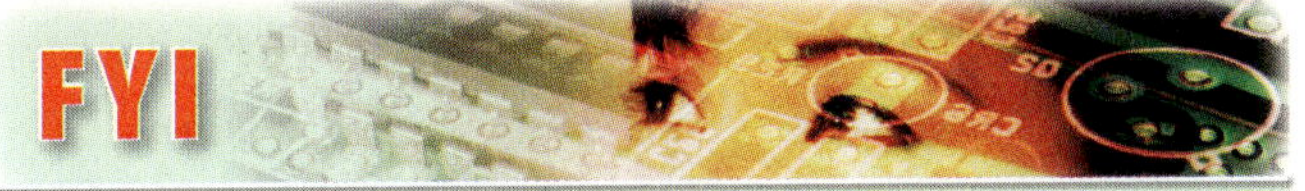

FYI

The U.S. dollar is the official currency of Ecuador, El Salvador, and Panama. A country may adopt a "dollarization" policy in an attempt to reduce economic troubles and enhance trade with other nations. The dollar is also the unofficial monetary unit for tourist transactions in countries such as the Bahamas and Haiti.

foreign business. A company could lose its tbuilding, equipment, or money on deposit in banks.

Political instability may also occur when new laws are put in place. These laws may not allow foreign businesses to operate as freely as they did under the old laws. Uncertainty in a country reduces the confidence that businesspeople have in its currency.

checkpoint >>
What factors affect the value of a country's currency?

3-1 Assessment

Key Concepts

Determine the best answer.

1. Which of the following would be an example of international business?
   a. A farmer in Iowa using U.S. produced equipment
   b. A sales staff in South Carolina representing a foreign producer
   c. A restaurant in Chicago offering Asian menu items
   d. A retail store in Oregon selling craft items from local artists

2. When a country's imports exceed its exports, there is a trade
   a. surplus
   b. deficit
   c. exchange
   d. balance

3. The value of a country's currency is likely to decline as a result of
   a. higher inflation
   b. lower interest rates
   c. a trade surplus
   d. a favorable balance of payments

Make Academic Connections

4. *Culture* While business knowledge is important, often cultural awareness in foreign markets is even more important. Interview someone who has lived in or visited another country about cultural factors that affect business activities in that country.

5. *Technology* Explain how the Internet and other technology help to expand international trade and global business activities.

TEACH

Explain the three main factors that affect the value of a country's currency.

Use the FYI feature to describe how countries can become interrelated through their currencies.

ONGOING ASSESSMENT

checkpoint >> **ANSWER**

The three main factors affecting the value of a country's currency are the country's balance of payments, economic conditions, and political stability.

ASSESS

Key Concepts Answers

1. b. A sales staff in South Carolina representing a foreign producer
2. b. deficit
3. a. higher inflation

Make Academic Connections

4. Consider allowing students to choose how they would like to report their findings. For example, students might prepare an oral report that includes a short video clip from their actual interview. This assignment is appropriate for pairs or small groups.

5. Students should identify ways businesses can use the Internet and other technology in international trade. For example, the Internet and computers can help businesses calculate exchange rates. Businesses can appeal to customers anywhere in the world over the Internet. Satellites can carry television and radio broadcasts, including advertisements, around the planet, thus increasing demand for products in many countries.

RETEACH

List the main ideas on the board. Ask students to describe each concept.

CLOSE

Ask students to list the main reasons why international business activities continue to expand.

ENRICH

Have students research what their state, or a neighboring state, is doing to encourage international trade. Most states have an exporting program in their state department of commerce.

3-2 The Global Marketplace

Goals

Describe the components of the international business environment.

Identify examples of formal trade barriers.

Explain actions to encourage international trade.

Key Terms

Infrastructure

trade barrier

quota

tariff

embargo

Focus on Real Life

Clear and complete exchange of ideas among international business partners is vital. A U.S. retail company contracted with a foreign shirt maker to make men's shirts. The contract stated that the shirts must be made of 60 percent cotton and 40 percent polyester. While the manufacturer supplied shirt labels to that effect, the actual shirts were 35 percent cotton and 65 percent polyester.

Without verifying the material content, the U.S. company accepted the shirts. It sold them with the incorrect information on the label. The Federal Trade Commission fined the company for deceptive labeling.

---

main idea

Describe the components of the international business environment.

INTERNATIONAL BUSINESS ENVIRONMENT

Doing business in other countries requires knowledge of the differences that exist among people and places. As shown in Figure 3-5, businesses must consider four main factors—geography, cultural influences, economic development, and political and legal concerns.

Geography

The location, climate, terrain, seaports, and natural resources of a country influence business activity. Very hot weather will limit the types of crops that can be grown. A nation with many rivers or ocean seaports can easily ship products for foreign trade. Countries with few natural resources must depend on imports.

Cultural Influences

In some societies, hugging is an appropriate business greeting. In other societies, a handshake is the custom. These differences represent different cultures.

Culture is the accepted behaviors, customs, and values of a society. A society's culture has a strong influence on business activities. In Mexico, many businesses close in the afternoon by tradition while people enjoy lunch and a siesta (relaxing rest period).

The main cultural and social factors that affect international business are language, religion, values, customs, and social relationships. These relationships include interactions among families, labor unions, and other organizations.

Economic Development

Every country and every individual faces the problem of limited resources to satisfy needs and wants. You continually make decisions about the use of your time, money, and energy. In a similar way, every country plans the use of its land, natural resources, workers, and wealth to best serve the needs of its people.

In some countries, people travel on a high-speed bullet train to manage a

  CHAPTER 3   BUSINESS IN THE GLOBAL ECONOMY

Visually Impaired Use five pieces of colored paper to create a large display of the information presented in Figure 5-3 to assist students who might need this type of visual assistance.

Use the display to help all students understand the components of the international business environment.

computer network in a high-rise building. In other countries, people go by oxcart to a grass hut to operate a hand loom to make cloth for people in their village. These differences in living and work environments reflect the level of economic development. The key factors that affect a country's level of economic development are:

- **Literacy Level** Countries with better education systems usually provide more and better goods and services for their citizens.
- **Technology** Automated production, distribution, and communications systems allow companies to create and deliver goods, services, and ideas quickly.
- **Agricultural Dependency** An economy that is largely involved in agriculture does not have the manufacturing base to provide citizens with great quantity and high quality of a product.

Another factor that supports international trade in industrialized countries is **infrastructure**. Infrastructure refers to a nation's transportation, communication, and utility systems. A country such as Germany—with its efficient rail system, high-speed highways, and computers—is better prepared for international business activities than other nations with a weaker infrastructure.

Political and Legal Concerns

Each day you come upon examples of government influence on business. Governments regulate fair advertising and enforce contracts. They require safety inspections of foods and medications. People in the United States have a great deal of freedom in their business activities. This is not true in all countries. In many places, the activities of consumers and business operators are restricted. The most common political and legal factors that affect international business activities

Knowledge of the international business environment is important for all global activities. As a team, create a list of items for each of the following categories: geography, cultural influences, economic development, and political-legal concerns. Explain how these items could affect a company when doing business in another country.

include the type of government, the stability of the government, and government policies toward business.

checkpoint »
List the four main elements of the international business environment.

GEOGRAPHY	ECONOMICS
• location	• technology
• climate	• education
• terrain	• inflation
• waterways	• exchange rate
• natural resources	• infrastructure

INTERNATIONAL BUSINESS ENVIRONMENT

CULTURE	POLITICAL–LEGAL FACTORS
• language	• government system
• family	• political stability
• religion	• trade barriers
• customs	• business regulations
• traditions	
• food	

FIGURE 3-5

Explain the difference between formal and informal trade barriers.

Describe examples of quotas that might be used by a country.

Explain the purpose of a tariff in international trade relations.

THINK CRITICALLY THROUGH VISUALS

Tariffs on imported goods do not help consumers because they lead to higher prices, lower quantities of products, and less competition among manufacturers.

---

main idea

Identify examples of formal trade barriers.

INTERNATIONAL TRADE BARRIERS

Government actions can create **trade barriers**, which are restrictions to free trade. These political actions are *formal* trade barriers. Three common formal trade barriers are quotas, tariffs, and embargoes.

The culture, traditions, and religion of a country can create *informal* trade barriers. These situations are not based on formal government actions but they do restrict trade.

Quotas

To regulate international trade, governments set a limit on the quantity of a product that may be imported or exported within a given period. This limit is called a **quota**.

Do tariffs on imported goods help consumers or hurt them?

Quotas may be set for many reasons. Countries that export oil may put quotas on crude oil so that the supply will remain low and prices will stay at a certain level. Quotas may be set on imports from another country to express displeasure at the policies of that country.

Quotas can also be set by a country to protect one of its industries from too much competition from abroad. This often is done by a nation to shield its "infant industries," which need protection to get started. In the past, the U.S. government has imposed quotas on sugar, cattle, dairy products, and textiles.

Tariffs

Another device that governments use to control international trade is the tariff.

A **tariff** is a tax that a government places on certain imported products. Suppose you want to buy an imported bicycle. The producer charges $140, but the government collects a 20 percent tariff ($28) on the bicycle when it is imported. Therefore, you will have to pay $168 plus shipping charges for the bike. The increased price may cause you to decide to buy a U.S. manufactured bike at a lower price.

Some tariffs are a set amount per pound, gallon, or other unit, while others are figured on the value of the good, as in the example of the bicycle. A tariff increases the price for an imported product. A high tariff tends to lower the demand for the product and reduce the quantity of that import. Many people believe that tariffs should be used to protect U.S. jobs from foreign competition.

Applied Skills

Mathematics Have students calculate different tariff amounts. Ask them to explain the benefits and drawbacks of tariffs for countries, companies, and consumers.

Embargoes

If a government wishes to do so, it can stop the export or import of a product completely. This action is called an **embargo**. Governments may impose an embargo for many reasons. They may wish to protect their own industries from international competition more than either the quota or the tariff will achieve. The government may wish to prevent sensitive products, especially those vital to the nation's defense, from falling into the hands of unfriendly groups or nations. A government sometimes imposes an embargo to express its disapproval of the actions or policies of another country.

checkpoint »
What are three formal trade barriers?

ENCOURAGING INTERNATIONAL TRADE

Specific actions by governments can promote international business activities. Governments view exporting as an effective way to create jobs and foster economic prosperity. Common efforts to encourage international trade include free-trade zones, free-trade agreements, and common markets.

Free-Trade Zones

To promote international business, governments often create free-trade zones in their countries. A *free-trade zone* is a selected area where products can be imported duty-free and then stored, assembled, and/or used in manufacturing. A free-trade zone is usually located around a seaport or airport. The importer pays duty only when the product leaves the zone.

TEACH

Describe how a country might use an embargo.

ONGOING ASSESSMENT

checkpoint » **ANSWER**

Three formal trade barriers are quotas, tariffs, and embargoes.

TEACH

Provide an overview of actions that might be used to encourage international business trade activities.

Explain the purpose of a free-trade zone.

Technology in Action

Many technological developments are allowing an easier flow of information, goods, and services among countries with different languages and cultures. This feature provides one example of this use of technology in a global business setting.

Ask students to suggest other uses of technology for improved international business activities.

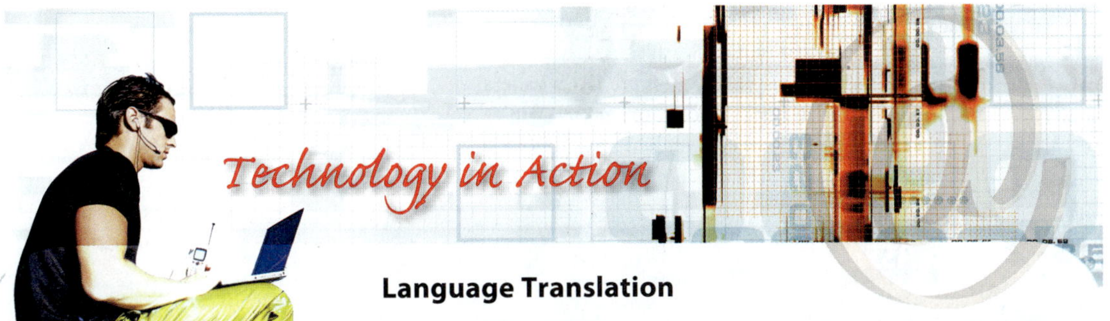

Technology in Action

Language Translation

While on the job at an exporting company, you receive a phone call from a customer in Kenya. Unable to understand the caller's language, you switch on the language translation service. This software allows you to understand, in your language, the product questions of your customer.

Computerized translators recognize speech in one language and convert the spoken words into another language. In a language translation system, three components work together—speech recognition, machine translation, and speech synthesis. The computer recognizes words spoken in the first language and converts them into a computer-readable file. Then, the words are translated into the second language. Finally, a voice synthesizer "speaks" the translated version.

Today, translation technology exists for all commonly used international business languages, such as Arabic, Chinese, English, French, German, Italian, Japanese, Korean, Portuguese, Russian, Spanish, and Vietnamese. In addition, hand-held, low-cost electronic language translators are available for use by businesspeople, travelers, and students.

These technologies allow you to say, "I would like to register for the conference" to a person who only speaks German. Then, using language translation technology, the German businessperson will hear, "Ich möchte für die Konferenz registrieren."

Think Critically

1. What are the possible benefits and drawbacks of computerized language translators?
2. Conduct a Web search to obtain information about the latest technologies for language translation systems.

Think Critically
Answers

1. Benefits of computerized language translators include being able to communicate with customers and suppliers in their native languages, needing to hire fewer translators, and speeding up business transactions. Drawbacks include problems in translating idioms and humor, frustration with the mechanized process, and dependence on computer equipment and software for communication.

2. Students should report their findings to the class using the method you specify—oral report, written report, or e-mail message to you.

Free-Trade Agreements

Many countries set up free-trade agreements with other nations. Under a *free-trade agreement,* member countries agree to remove duties, also called import taxes, and trade barriers on products traded among them. This results in increased trade between the members. For example, the United States, Canada, and Mexico began implementing the North American Free Trade Agreement (NAFTA) in 1994. This pact does away with tarrifs on goods traded among the three countries and eases the movement of goods. NAFTA is designed to enlarge the markets and economic bases of the countries involved.

Common Markets

In a *common market,* members do away with duties and other trade barriers. They allow companies to invest freely in each member's country. They allow workers to move freely across borders. A common market is also called an *economic*

Why do you think U.S. businesses would be interested in exporting?

community. Common market members have a common external duty on products being imported from nonmember countries. Examples of common markets include the European Union (EU) and the Latin American Integration Association (LAIA). The goals are to expand trade among member nations and promote regional economic integration.

checkpoint >>
What actions could be taken to encourage international trade?

3-2 Assessment

Key Concepts

Determine the best answer.

1. True or False. Infrastructure is a significant factor that affects the economic development of a country.

2. True or False. An informal trade barrier is created by government actions.

3. Religion is an element of the _?_ component of the international business environment.
   a. geographic
   b. economic
   c. cultural
   d. political

4. A country that wishes to enhance international trade activities would most likely use
   a. a tariff
   b. a common market
   c. an embargo
   d. a quota

Make Academic Connections

5. *Law* Use the Internet to locate information about laws in foreign countries that are different from those in the United States.

6. *Geography* Using library resources or the Internet, obtain copies of maps for various geographic regions. On your map, indicate how the terrain, climate, and waterways might influence international trade activities. Present a 1–2 minute summary of your findings.

7. *History* Conduct research on the history of a common market such as the EU or the LAIA. Describe some of the benefits the community provides to its member nations.

RETEACH

Provide examples for each component of the international business environment and the various actions to encourage or discourage trade activities.

ENRICH

Have students debate various types of actions that countries might take to encourage or discourage international trade.

3-3 International Business Organizations

Goals

Discuss activities of multinational organizations.

Explain common international business entry modes.

Describe activities of international trade organizations and agencies.

Key Terms

multinational company (MNC)

joint venture

Focus on Real Life

Before taking a new course of action, Ghana, located on the west coast of Africa, had many economic problems. Inflation was 120 percent. Exports had declined by 50 percent. The nation had a crumbling infrastructure. An overvalued currency did not promote widespread exporting of cocoa, Ghana's main export.

Ghana obtained suggestions from the International Monetary Fund. The actions that were implemented, along with lower tax rates, helped to improve the country's balance of payments and stimulate economic growth. Today, Ghana is one of the best-performing economies in Africa with consistent growth. Improved government policies and expanded investment in infrastructure and basic services have also helped reduce the country's poverty level.

MULTINATIONAL COMPANIES

A **multinational company (MNC)** is an organization that does business in several countries. MNCs usually consist of a parent company in a *home country* and divisions or separate companies in one or more host countries. The country in which the MNC places business activities is called the *host country*.

MNC Strategies

Multinational corporations can use either a global or multinational strategy. A *global strategy* uses the same product and marketing strategy worldwide. The same product is sold in essentially the same manner throughout the world. One example with which you are probably familiar is Coca-Cola.

A *multinational strategy* treats each country market differently. Firms develop products and marketing strategies that adapt to the customs, tastes, and buying habits of a distinct national market. Many restaurant chains employ a multinational strategy when they modify their menus to local tastes.

> **main idea**
>
> Discuss activities of multinational organizations.

What are some of the advantages of being a multinational corporation?

Focus on Real Life

Discuss the actions taken in this situation. Ask students to comment on whether these policies would be useful in other countries.

TEACH

Ask students to name reasons for the expansion of multinational companies.

Explain the difference between a "global" (standardized) strategy and a "multinational" (adapted) strategy.

THINK CRITICALLY THROUGH VISUALS

Advantages of being a multinational corporation include having larger markets, benefiting from economies of scale, being able to provide consumers with more goods at lower prices, and being able to offer employees more career opportunities.

Different Learning Abilities

Attention Deficit Disorder Clearly explain global and multinational strategies so students can write a definition and examples. Slowly present these items to allow a focus by students.

Good prices and extensive consumer choice are two advantages of international business.

© Getty Images/PhotoDisc

main idea

Explain common international business entry modes.

MNC Benefits

Many benefits are associated with international business. Consumers have a large amount of goods available. Often, these goods are at lower prices than goods made domestically. Career opportunities also expand as a company does business in a variety of countries.

Global business activities may also foster understanding, communication, and respect among people of different nations. Nations that are business partners usually try to maintain friendly relations for economic reasons.

Work as a Team

International business success often increases when a company works with a local business partner in another country. Choose a company or product that could be sold in other countries. Identify the types of companies that you might consider as a partner in the other countries. Then identify information sources that you might contact to make sure these potential partners would be suitable companies with which to do business.

Drawbacks of Multinational Companies

An MNC can become a major economic power in a host country. The workers of the host country may depend on the MNC for jobs. Consumers become dependent upon it for goods and services. The MNC may actually influence or control the political power of the country.

checkpoint >>
What are two strategies commonly used by multinational companies?

GLOBAL MARKET ENTRY MODES

As companies expand into other countries, several methods are available for their use.

Licensing

Some companies want to produce items in other countries without being actively involved. They may allow a foreign company to use a procedure they own. *Licensing* is selling the right to use some intangible property (production process, trademark, or brand name) for a fee or royalty.

The Gerber Company started selling its baby food products in Japan by means of licensing. The use of television characters or sports team emblems on hats, shirts, jackets, notebooks, luggage, and other items also involves a licensing agreement. Licensing has a low financial investment, so the potential financial return is often low. The risk for the company is also low.

Franchising

Another method often used to expand into other countries is the *franchise*. A franchise is the right to use a company name or business process in a specific way. Organizations enter into contracts with people in other countries to set up a business that looks and runs like the parent company. The company obtaining the franchise will usually adapt a range of business elements. Marketing elements such as food products, packaging, and advertising messages must meet both cultural sensitivities and legal requirements.

Both franchising and licensing involve a royalty payment for the right to use a process or company name. Licensing usually involves a manufacturing process. Franchising commonly involves selling a product or service. Franchise agreements are popular with fast-food companies. McDonald's, Burger King, Wendy's, KFC, and Pizza Hut all have used franchising to increase their presence in foreign markets.

Joint Venture

Business partnerships can provide benefits to all parties involved. One type of global partnership is the joint venture. A **joint venture** is an agreement between two or more companies to share a business project.

The main benefit of a joint venture is the sharing of raw materials, shipping facilities, management activities, or production facilities. Concerns about this type of partnership include sharing of profits and not as much control because several companies are involved.

This arrangement is very popular for manufacturing. Joint ventures between Japanese and U.S. automobile manufacturers have been common. For example, the Ford Motor Company entered a joint venture with Mazda Motor Corporation. Ford used Mazda-produced parts for several of its cars. Mazda set up assembly plants for Ford Motor vehicles.

checkpoint >>

How does licensing differ from a franchise?

FYI

Cereal Partners Worldwide (CPW) is a joint venture between General Mills and Nestle to sell cereal in Latin America, Europe, the Middle East, and other areas of the world. General Mills brought popular products, such as Cheerios, Lucky Charms, and Trix, into the partnership. Nestle, well known all over the world, has a broad distribution system and is a well-known brand in most foreign countries.

INTERNATIONAL TRADE ORGANIZATIONS

International business activities can be very complex. As a result, several organizations have been created to help companies with global trade activities.

World Trade Organization

The World Trade Organization (WTO) was created in 1995 to promote trade around the world. With more than 150 member countries, WTO settles trade disputes and enforces free-trade agreements between its members. Other goals of WTO include the following.

- Lowering tariffs that discourage free trade

- Eliminating import quotas

- Reducing barriers for banks, insurance companies, and other financial services

- Assisting poor countries with economic growth

International Monetary Fund

The International Monetary Fund (IMF), with more than 150 member nations, helps to promote economic cooperation. It maintains an orderly system of world trade and exchange rates. The IMF was established in 1946 when the economic interdependence among nations was growing at a greater pace than ever before in history.

> **main idea**
>
> Describe activities of international trade organizations and agencies.

TEACH

Explain the use of joint ventures by companies.

Use the FYI feature to provide an example of a joint venture.

ONGOING ASSESSMENT

checkpoint >> **ANSWER**

Licensing does not require as much financial investment or risk as franchising. Both licensing and franchising involve royalty payments, but licensing usually involves a manufacturing process, while franchising commonly involves selling a product or service.

TEACH

Explain the activities of the World Trade Organization (WTO).

Describe methods used in the International Monetary Fund (IMF) to assist countries.

Different Learning Styles

Auditory Learner Encourage auditory learners to repeat the names of the organizations discussed on pages 67–68. Ask them to describe one activity of each organization.

TEACH

Describe services provided by the World Bank.

ONGOING ASSESSMENT

checkpoint >> **ANSWER**

The International Monetary Fund assists countries by promoting economic cooperation and maintaining an orderly system of world trade and exchange rates. This cooperation makes harmful trade wars among IMF nations less likely.

ASSESS

Key Concepts Answers

1. d. licensing agreement

2. a. WTO

Make Academic Connections

3. Students are to list information that indicates a licensing agreement found in stores or online sites that sell toys, sporting goods, or other merchandise printed with logos or images belonging to other companies.

4. Invite students to share their presentations with the class.

CLOSE

Ask students to name the three international organizations that promote international trade.

NETBookmark

The U.S. Department of Commerce and other federal government agencies provide extensive help to companies involved in exporting. Access the web site shown below and click on the link for Chapter 3. Review the various information sources available to exporters. Select one of the categories of services offered. Describe how companies that are starting or expanding their exporting activities could use the services.

school.cengage.com/business/introtobiz

Before the International Monetary Fund was instituted, a country could often change the value of its legal tender to attract more foreign customers. As other countries lose business, they may impose trade restrictions or lower the value of their currency. As one nation tries to outdo another, a trade war may result. Today, cooperation among IMF nations makes trade wars less likely.

World Bank

The International Bank for Reconstruction and Development is commonly called the *World Bank*. It was created in 1944 to provide loans for rebuilding after World War II. Today, the bank's key function is to give economic aid to less developed countries. These funds build communications systems, transportation networks, and energy plants.

The World Bank, with more than 180 member countries, has two main divisions: the International Development Association and the International Finance Corporation. The International Development Association (IDA) makes loans to help developing countries. The International Finance Corporation (IFC) provides capital and technical help to private businesses in nations with limited resources. The IFC promotes joint ventures between foreign companies and local companies to further capital investment in developing nations.

checkpoint >>
How does the International Monetary Fund assist countries?

3-3 Assessment

Key Concepts

Determine the best answer.

1. A company is planning to sell the rights to its brand name for use in other countries. This is an example of a
   a. joint venture
   b. trade agreement
   c. franchise
   d. licensing agreement

2. The international organization that settles trade disagreements and enforces free-trade agreements is the
   a. WTO
   b. United Nations
   c. IMF
   d. World Bank

Make Academic Connections

3. *Economics* Visit a store or online site that sells toys, sporting goods, or other merchandise printed with logos or images belonging to other companies. List the information given that indicates a licensing agreement.

4. *Communication* Create a visual presentation (using software, photos, or a poster) that communicates the purpose of the International Monetary Fund or the World Bank.

RETEACH

Using the Business Notes on page 70, have students create an example or expanded explanation for one of the points in this chapter summary.

ENRICH

In small groups, have students prepare a brief drama to communicate one of the points in the Business Notes (chapter summary) on page 70.

The Hunger Site

Each day, more than 1,000 tons of edible food is thrown away in the United States. Elsewhere, several million people go hungry. Around the world, more than 20,000 people die every day from hunger-related causes. But what can one person do to solve this problem?

Tim Kunin and Greg Hesterberg decided to take action with The Hunger Site. On average, 220,000 people from around the world visit the web site each day to click the "Help Feed the Hungry" button.

Kunin and Hesterberg launched The Hunger Site in June 1999. The Hunger Site focuses the power of the Internet on a specific charitable cause: the elimination of world hunger. Since it started, more than 200 million visitors have given more than 300 million cups of staple food to the hungry all over the world. Site sponsors pay for the staple food, distributed to those in need by Mercy Corps and America's Second Harvest.

When visitors to The Hunger Site homepage click on the "Help Feed the Hungry" button, they view sponsor banner ads on the "Thank You" page. Money from banner advertising fees goes to the charity partners. Funds are divided among the organizations to help hungry people in more than 74 countries. Included are those in Africa, Asia, Eastern Europe, the Middle East, Latin America, and North America. Tim and Greg,

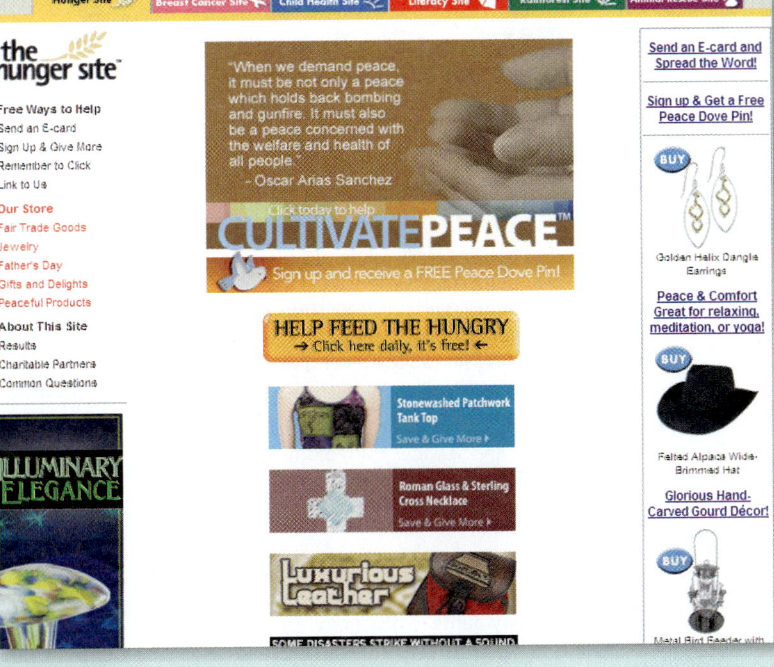

Reproduced courtesy of The Hunger Site.

long-time friends and social activists, are committed to using this online effort to end world hunger.

Sponsors on The Hunger Site benefit in several ways. First, they are able to reach well-educated, upper-income consumers who are a desired target audience for many goods and services. Also, advertising on The Hunger Site creates good-will. Consumers usually appreciate a company's support of a cause they care about. Sponsorship builds customer loyalty. Research shows that at least three-fourths of adults are more likely to buy a product linked with a cause they care about. More than half would be willing to pay a higher price for the product if it benefits a social cause in which they believe.

Think Critically

1. Locate another web site that promotes awareness of and attempts to solve a social issue or concern facing society today. Write a brief description of the web site, the issue, and the goals. Include your opinion about the likelihood of success.

2. Identify a social issue that is of interest to you and plan a web site that might be used to help raise awareness of the concern and lead to a solution.

BUSINESS IMPROVING SOCIETY

Use this feature to point out how the actions of businesses and other organizations can help to solve various problems.

Think Critically Answers

1. Student answers will vary depending on the sites they locate. Be sure students give reasons why they think the sites will succeed or fail.

2. You may want students to share their web site plans with the class. Invite class members to evaluate the proposed web sites and predict whether the sites will be successful.

Different Learning Styles

Kinesthetic Learner Have students create a visual that might be used on a web site to encourage people to donate or volunteer their time for a community service group or a world relief organization. Encourage students to communicate using various visuals and messages that motivate people to take action.

Communicate Business Concepts Answers

1. Examples will vary, but should incorporate the idea that having an absolute advantage in a product means that the country will experience strong demand for the good. It can sell its good abroad at a profit, allowing the country to import items in which it does not have an advantage.

2. Most communities and nations will not have all the raw materials and resources necessary to supply all the wants and needs of their people.

3. International business allows countries to export the items that they can produce most efficiently and cheaply while importing items they cannot produce as efficiently as other countries. Free trade allows these items to flow to consumers around the world, giving them the lowest prices possible. When markets are open across international borders, consumers have many products from which to choose. International trade also brings jobs, giving workers more purchasing power and thus a higher standard of living.

4. The perception that the foreign-based company is taking jobs away from U.S. workers could make it difficult for the company to gain loyal customers. The foreign-based company's products may be perceived as inferior. Foreign-based companies may not understand the cultural preferences of U.S. consumers or common U.S. business practices or U.S. laws regulating businesses.

Business Notes

3-1 INTERNATIONAL BUSINESS BASICS

1. Domestic business is the making, buying, and selling of goods and services within a country. International business refers to the business activities needed for creating, shipping, and selling goods and services across national borders.

2. A country is said to have an absolute advantage when it can produce a good or service at a lower cost than other countries. If a country specializes in the production of a good or service at which it is more efficient, it is said to have a comparative advantage.

3. Imports are items bought from other countries. Exports are goods and services sold to other countries. Nations do business with each other to increase the variety of goods and services available to their consumers.

4. Balance of trade is the difference between a country's exports and imports. The difference between a country's total payments to other countries and its total receipts from other countries is the balance of payments.

5. The exchange rate is the value of a currency in one country compared with the value of a currency in another country.

6. The value of global currencies is affected by three main factors: balance of payments, economic conditions, and political stability.

3-2 THE GLOBAL MARKETPLACE

7. The international business environment involves four main components: geography, cultural influences, economic development, and political and legal concerns.

8. Three formal barriers to international trade are quotas, tariffs, and embargoes. A quota is a limit set on the quantity of a product that may be imported or exported within a given period. A tariff is a tax placed on certain imported products. An embargo stops the import or export of a product completely.

9. Actions to encourage international trade include free-trade zones, free-trade agreements, and common markets.

3-3 INTERNATIONAL BUSINESS ORGANIZATIONS

10. Multinational companies conduct business activities in several countries and have management capable of doing business worldwide.

11. Common methods used for global business include licensing, franchising, and joint ventures.

12. The World Trade Organization was created to promote trade around the world. The International Monetary Fund helps to promote economic cooperation by maintaining a system of world trade and exchange rates. The World Bank provides economic assistance to less developed countries.

Communicate Business Concepts

1. Describe how an absolute advantage might affect a country's imports and exports.

2. Explain why it is difficult for a community or a nation to be completely independent.

3. How does international business contribute to a better standard of living for many people in various countries?

4. What are some attitudes and behaviors that might make it difficult for a foreign-based company to do business in the United States?

5. For the following situations, decide whether this is an example of an *informal* or *formal* trade barrier.

  a. Law requiring that stores be closed on Sunday
  b. Beliefs about not eating certain foods
  c. Special tax on the sale of books
  d. Required nutritional information on food packaging
  e. Hiring family members when jobs are available in an organization

6. Describe situations in which a joint venture would benefit a company involved in international business.

7. A country sometimes uses high tariffs to protect its new and developing industries. What are two examples of new and developing industries either in the United States or in other countries? Do you think that such industries should be protected by high tariffs? If so, how long should they be protected?

8. Some people believe that the United States should place stiff controls on imports of goods that compete with U.S. businesses to prevent the "exporting of American jobs" to other countries. Give arguments for and against such a position.

Develop Your Business Language

Match the terms listed with the definitions.

9. Goods and services sold to another country.

10. A limit on the quantity of a product that may be imported and exported within a given period.

11. Government restrictions to reduce free trade.

12. An organization that conducts business in several countries.

13. The value of money of one country expressed in terms of the money of another country.

14. Goods and services bought from another country.

15. Stopping the importing or exporting of a certain product or service.

16. An agreement between two or more companies from different countries to share a business project.

17. The difference between a country's total exports and total imports of goods.

18. A tax that a government places on certain imported products.

19. The difference between a country's total payments to other countries and its total receipts from other countries.

20. A nation's transportation, communication, and utility systems.

KEY TERMS

a. balance of payments
b. balance of trade
c. embargo
d. exchange rate
e. exports
f. imports
g. infrastructure
h. joint venture
i. multinational company (MNC)
j. quota
k. tariff
l. trade barrier

5. a. formal trade barrier

b. informal trade barrier

c. formal trade barrier

d. formal trade barrier

e. informal trade barrier

6. Answers may vary, but a joint venture will be especially helpful when a company is introducing a product or service that is new to a particular country. The joint venture partner brings insight into the country's culture and business climate and appropriate ways to manufacture and market the product.

7. Answers will vary. Make sure students have reasons to support their opinions as to whether a particular developing industry should be protected by tariffs and how long that protection should last. Remind them to consider the tariff's potential effect on consumers.

8. The argument for stiff controls on imports of goods that compete with U.S. products is to protect jobs held by U.S. workers. The argument against such controls is fear of retaliation against U.S. exports and higher prices and less selection for U.S. consumers.

Develop Your Business Language Answers

9. e. exports

10. j. quota

11. l. trade barrier

12. i. multinational company (MNC)

13. d. exchange rate

14. f. imports

15. c. embargo

16. h. joint venture

17. b. balance of trade

18. k. tariff

19. a. balance of payments

20. g. infrastructure

Make Academic Connections

21. **GEOGRAPHY** Locate examples of multinational companies in different countries. Create a map showing where the companies are based and the other nations in which the companies operate.

22. **ECONOMICS** Go to the web site of an economic community (common market) or a regional trade organization. Make a list of the countries involved and describe some of the organization's activities.

23. **HISTORY** Conduct research on the history of money systems that have been used in other countries. Find examples of the use of a country's currency in another country.

24. **MUSIC** Very often, the music of a country reflects its history, culture, and religion. Find examples of music from other nations that reflect the past and current culture. What aspects of the music are distinctive to that country?

25. **METRIC CONVERSION** To make their exports suitable for use in other countries, U.S. manufacturers must produce goods that are measured in the metric system. For example, if a manufacturer wanted to export paint, which is sold in gallons in this country, it would probably export the paint in 4-liter cans (about 11.4 gallons). To what sizes would the items listed be converted for export to countries using the metric system? (See Appendix D.)

a. A quart bottle of liquid detergent
b. A 50-yard bolt of fabric
c. An automobile engine measured in cubic inches
d. A 12-inch ruler
e. A bathroom scale that measures in pounds

26. **TECHNOLOGY** Using a spreadsheet program, create a table and graph to report the changing value of the U.S. dollar compared with currencies of three other countries.

27. **MATH** Using the information in Figure 3-4 on page 58, determine how many U.S. dollars someone could buy for these amounts of currencies from other countries.

a. In Japan, 1,200 yen
b. In Canada, 5 Canadian dollars
c. In Saudi Arabia, 150 riyals

28. **CAREER PLANNING** Investigate what types of legal agreements a person would encounter when applying for a job to work for a multinational company in another country.

Linking School and Community

Visit a retail store in your community and select 10 clothing items you would like to own. Being careful not to damage the clothing, create a list of the items and indicate the countries in which these items were manufactured. Prepare a summary with the following information:

- Which countries are most often on your list?
- Are there several countries from the same geographic region?
- What are some possible similarities among these countries?
- What are possible economic advantages of these countries involved in clothing manufacturing?

Web Workout

Sold in more than 200 countries, Coca-Cola is one of the most recognized brand names in the world. A visit to the company's web site provides some insight into how the company has tailored its products and image to address cultural differences around the globe.

Think Critically

1. Locate a web site with information about the culture of a specific country. Write a paragraph describing an element of the culture that Coca-Cola might need to consider when doing business in that country.
2. Visit the web site of a company that produces another popular American product and locate information about its international operations. Write a paragraph summarizing content that demonstrates the company's sensitivity to the cultural differences of customers around the world. Illustrate your work with several images from the web site.

Decision-Making Strategies

Assume you have started a business that manufactures electric toasters that you want to sell to the people of China.

29. What are some potential difficulties that you might encounter when doing business in the Chinese market?

30. What actions could your company take to help improve your opportunities for success?

Desktop Publishing Event

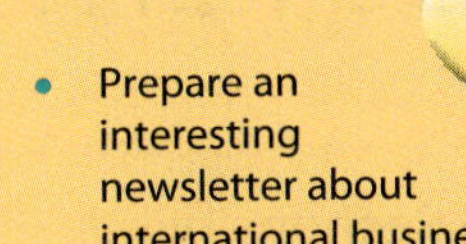

You and a partner have been hired to create, design, and produce a business publication using desktop publishing software. You have two hours of class time to prepare a newsletter that focuses attention on *International Business Basics, The Global Marketplace,* and *Organization for International Business.* Your team is allowed to use two computers, a scanner, and/or clip art. No other equipment may be used. The finished product may be submitted in black and white or in color on plain paper. Word division manuals and dictionaries may be used as reference materials. The second part of this competition includes a one-hour written objective test to determine your knowledge of desktop publishing; the score received on this portion of the event will equal 15 percent of the final event score.

PERFORMANCE INDICATORS EVALUATED

- Understand graphics, text creation, layout, creativity, and selection of appropriate fonts and type sizes for desktop publishing.

- Prepare an interesting newsletter about international business.
- Incorporate graphics and layout that is pleasing to the reader.
- Incorporate correct punctuation, grammar, and sentence structure.
- Illustrate creativity throughout the publication.

For more detailed information about performance indicators, go to the FBLA web site.

Think Critically

1. What is the difference between an average publication and a great publication?
2. What strategies can be used to make a publication more reader-friendly?
3. Who should be considered when producing a publication?
4. Give two examples of items that are distracting on publications

http://www.fbla-pbl.org/

Access the web site shown here to find portfolio activities for this chapter. Use the activities to provide tangible evidence of your learning.

school.cengage.com/business/introtobiz

Web Workout

1. Paragraphs will vary. Students might mention flavor and color preferences. Depending on the country, students could identify the language or languages that need to be used in labeling. Advertising themes might reflect the culture or traditions of a specific country.

2. Paragraphs and images will vary. Summaries should focus on the Web content that relates to cultural differences.

Decision-Making Strategies Answers

29. The Chinese people may not eat bread or other items that fit into toasters. Domestically produced toasters might be cheaper or more durable. The supply of electricity in rural areas of China might not be reliable enough for consumers to desire electrical products. Your company might not understand Chinese businesses or laws.

30. Start by conducting research about the market situation. Next, you could enter into a joint venture with a manufacturing company already established in China. Alternatively, your company could hire Chinese nationals who are knowledgeable about the Chinese business scene.

Winning Edge
Desktop Publishing Event

Think Critically Answers

1. A great publication has a balance between the amount of text and graphics. A great publication uses proper grammar, has good sentence structure, and clearly presents the major ideas.

2. Larger print, fewer words to make a point, and bulleted items make a publication more reader-friendly.

3. Consider the audience or customer who will be reading the publication when planning the content and designing the layout.

4. Too many graphics, not enough white space, and too much written text are examples of distracting items in publications.

This chapter offers a basic understanding of social responsibility along with discussion of the various roles of government in relation to business.

4-1 Social Responsibility

Various actions that businesses take to improve society are covered in this lesson.

4-2 Government Protection Activities

This lesson addresses actions by government to protect workers, consumers, and business activities.

4-3 Government Regulation and Assistance

Regulation of utilities, unfair business practices, and government spending and borrowing are the main focus of this lesson.

CHAPTER 4

Social Responsibility of Business and Government

4-1 Social Responsibility

4-2 Government Protection Activities

4-3 Government Regulation and Assistance

Teaching Resources

Activities and Study Guide, Ch. 4
Chapter and Unit Tests, Ch. 4
Spanish Resources, Ch. 4

ExamView® *CD,* Ch. 4
Instructor's Resource CD
- PowerPoint Slides, Ch. 4
- Lesson Plans, Ch. 4

Xtra! Web Site

school.cengage.com/business/introtobiz
- Study Tools, 4-1, 4-2, 4-3
- Quiz Prep, Ch. 4
- Net Bookmark, Ch. 4
- Crossword Puzzle, Ch.4
- Portfolio Activity, Ch. 4

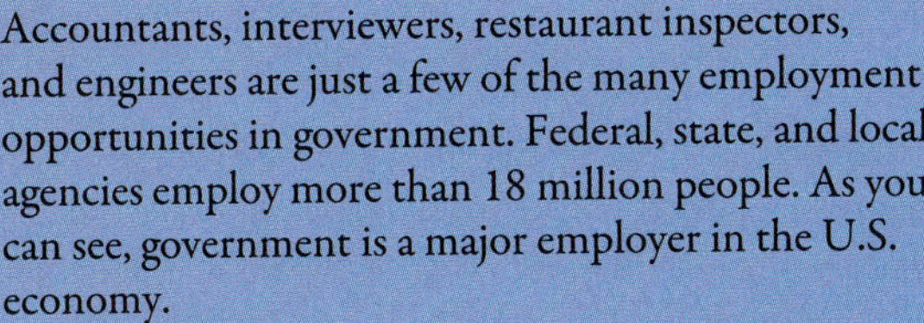

Planning a Career in…

GOVERNMENT

Accountants, interviewers, restaurant inspectors, and engineers are just a few of the many employment opportunities in government. Federal, state, and local agencies employ more than 18 million people. As you can see, government is a major employer in the U.S. economy.

About 60 percent of federal workers hold managerial, business, financial, and professional positions. While some government jobs require training similar to that of business workers, other positions demand training that is more specialized. Food production regulators and homeland security officials need academic and practical experiences related to their fields.

Employment Outlook

- Increased job opportunity in some federal agencies is being offset by slow growth and declines in other federal sectors.
- Despite increased demand for services from state and local governments, employment levels will be affected by economic conditions and the availability of tax revenues.
- Staffing of government positions is directly affected by budget levels approved by legislative bodies and local governing boards.

Related Job Titles

- Purchasing Agent
- Conservation Scientist
- Correctional Officer
- Firefighter
- Highway Maintenance Engineer
- Municipal Clerk
- Registered Nurse
- Revenue Agent
- Social Worker
- Urban Planner
- Job Placement Counselor

Needed Skills

- Education level and experience required vary by occupation.
- Specialized training and field experience will vary depending on the occupational field in which you desire to work.
- Elected government positions will require skills in communication, organization, and leadership.

What's it like to work in… Government

Kathleen works for her local school district, but her job lasts all year. She is the assistant accountant for the district. Her accounting job is just like an accounting job at a nonpublic business. Kathleen is responsible for collecting expense and payment records. She must make sure that incoming bills are correct and that payments are made in a timely manner. Kathleen also works with the school district's head accountant to develop expense reports and budgets. Throughout the year, Kathleen helps the head accountant present reports to the school board. Kathleen uses computer software for accounting records, report writing, and presentations. She could use her accounting skills in the private sector and perhaps earn more money. Although a higher salary would be nice, Kathleen enjoys working for the school district and is happy with her career choice.

What about you? What are some government jobs that might interest you?

GOVERNMENT

A wide variety of government employment positions are available. Point out to students that most types of business jobs are also available with government agencies. After reading this career feature, ask students what they think about the position described. Do they know anyone who holds a similar job? At the conclusion of the discussion, direct students to answer the "What About You?" question that follows this feature.

What About You? Answer

Answers will vary, but could include discussion of the variety of government jobs; virtually all sectors of employment are found within federal, state, or local governments.

Additional Career Information

Additional information on careers can be found in the *Occupational Outlook Handbook,* an online publication (www.bls.gov/oco) of the federal government. Tell your class about this resource and how to use it. This description of job duties can be used to demonstrate the relevancy of skills learned in this course.

4-1 Social Responsibility

Goals

Describe social responsibility issues.

Identify benefits and costs of social responsibility.

Explain the purpose of a code of ethics.

Key Terms

social responsibility

non-renewable resource

ethics

business ethics

code of ethics

Focus on Real Life

Jo Ann Homer, owner of JA Kitchen Crafts, considers herself a socially responsible person and employer. She serves on the board of the local United Way and chairs the job training committee of the local economic development board. She is also involved in literacy and mentoring programs.

JA Kitchen Crafts participates in United Way fundraising and donates to charities that assist the homeless and hungry. The company also participates in a school-to-work program.

The company encourages employees to be active in community affairs and to volunteer with a variety of organizations. In some cases, the company provides paid time off for volunteer commitments during work hours.

In a recent interview, Jo Ann said, "Workers are likely to be more satisfied on the job if they believe their company actively contributes to community life."

main idea

Define social responsibility issues.

SOCIAL RESPONSIBILITY ISSUES

Social responsibility refers to the duty of a business to contribute to the well-being of a community. In considering its responsibility to society, a business must weigh the interests and concerns of many groups. A broadened view of social responsibility of business calls for more attention to social concern. This includes protection of the environment, inclusion of minorities and women in the workplace, employment of physically challenged and older workers, and a healthy and safe work environment.

Environmental Protection

Conservation is saving scarce natural resources. It is a goal of many companies. For example, lumber companies that consume trees have reforestation programs. Some natural resources cannot be replaced. A **non-renewable resource** is a natural resource that cannot be replaced when used up. Examples are gas, oil, and minerals, such as copper and iron ore.

Pollution occurs when the environment is tainted with the by-products of human actions. Some production methods cause pollution of lakes, rivers,

How does preserving the environment benefit business?

© Getty Images/PhotoDisc

Applied Skills

Science Have students identify various health concerns associated with environmental issues in the United States and around the world. Point out that many industries in developing economies use older manufacturing methods and more polluting energy sources that can result in environmental damage.

and air. A socially responsible business takes action to improve or change operations that cause pollution. For example, engineers design new equipment for reducing pollution.

The federal government has set measurable standards for water and air quality. The Environmental Protection Agency (EPA) monitors and enforces those standards. Businesses and the EPA work together to reduce pollution. They try to make the environment healthier.

Workplace Diversity

Businesses are more and more sensitive to the role of women, ethnic groups, and physically challenged and older workers. The workforce of a business should reflect the groups in a community. Members of these groups must have equal access to education, training, jobs, and career advancement. A major challenge facing businesses today involves learning how to manage a workforce made up of workers who represent the diverse cultures in society.

Another issue involves the removal of employment barriers for women. For example, employers are not allowed to exclude women applicants from a physically demanding job unless the business can prove the job requires physical skills that women do not have.

Employers also have taken steps to accommodate individuals who are physically challenged. Passage and enforcement of the Americans with Disabilities Act (ADA), along with other federal and state legislation, has resulted in major improvements in accommodating workers who are physically challenged. Buildings must have access for wheelchairs. People with sight or hearing limitations must be accommodated on the job.

Other laws have been passed to eliminate bias against older workers. The passage of the Age Discrimination in Employment Act bars employers from using age as a basis for employment

Company safety programs often reward employees with cash bonuses, prizes, or additional vacation days for ideas that improve the safety of the workplace.

decisions, including hiring, promotions, or termination from a job. The law protects persons aged 40 and older.

Job Safety

Having a safe place in which to work is important to all employees. They should be able to work in an office or factory free from risks that could cause accidents. The work environment should provide full protection from fire and other hazards. In addition to protection from physical harm, workers need to know how to manage the unexpected. Safety also involves employee training in how to work safely and what to do in case of an emergency.

To ensure the right to safety, most employers have put a variety of programs into practice to protect workers. Federal and state governments have also passed laws to make the workplace safer. Safety standards are regulated and enforced by agencies such as OSHA, the Occupational Safety and Health Administration.

How has the Americans with Disabilities Act increased employment opportunities for people who are physically challenged?

TEACH

Use the FYI feature to highlight some of the programs used by businesses to encourage safety.

Explain the economic and social value of workplace diversity.

Have students describe situations that could be avoided by creating a safer workplace.

THINK CRITICALLY THROUGH VISUALS

The Americans with Disabilities Act has made it necessary for workplaces to provide accommodation for physically challenged workers. Examples of accommodation include designated parking spaces, entrance ramps, automatic doors, elevators, wider doorways, and accessible restroom facilities.

---

main idea

Identify benefits and costs of social responsibility.

Employee Wellness

A healthy workforce is a productive workforce. Workers who have good physical health are valuable assets. Businesses today do a number of things to improve the health of their workforce. Among programs offered are stop-smoking seminars, counseling for employees with drug problems, and weight-loss sessions.

Your general well-being as an employee needs to be protected, too. Clauses that relate to employee well-being are often included in labor contracts and company policy manuals. These clauses are *conditions of work* that pertain to the health and safety of employees while on the job.

Many companies offer programs to promote good health. Seminars on eating a balanced diet, getting proper exercise, and maintaining a healthy lifestyle are a few examples. Some businesses sponsor sports teams and encourage employees to take part.

checkpoint »

What are four areas of social responsibility that may require the attention of business?

How do employees who are healthy benefit their employers?

SOCIAL RESPONSIBILITY EVALUATION

Socially responsible actions can cause controversy. While a number of benefits exist, these actions also have various costs.

Benefits

Common benefits of socially responsible activities include the following:

- Expanded justice for groups of a society
- Enhanced company image
- Reduced need for government actions
- Improved quality of life in a community and around the world
- Increased awareness of social issues among workers, consumers, and others

Costs

There are costs involved when a business takes socially responsible actions. Money must be spent for new non-polluting or safer equipment, for building repairs to remove risks, for wellness and rehabilitation programs, and for social projects sponsored by a company.

A business must make a profit to stay open. If a business does not earn a profit, the business will close and employees will lose their jobs. Spending on social programs must be at a suitable level so a business can still earn a reasonable profit.

checkpoint »

What are the main benefits of social responsibility?

BUSINESS ETHICS

A socially responsible business engages in ethical business practices. **Ethics** are principles of morality or rules of conduct. **Business ethics** are rules about how businesses and their employees ought to behave. Ethical behavior involves conforming to these rules. Unethical behavior violates them. In dealing with business ethics, a code of ethics can help a business identify proper employee behavior.

Code of Ethics

A **code of ethics** is a set of rules for guiding the actions of employees or members of an organization. Codes of ethics address topics such as confidentiality of business information. Figure 4-1 lists other topics to consider when developing a code of ethics. Once established, the code should be a guide of values for all employees within that company.

A code must be worded in terms of acceptable behavior rather than forbidden action. Even with a code of ethics, the choice of proper behavior can cause dilemmas for decision-makers within a business. Here are some examples of ethical dilemmas.

- Should a company expand into a profitable market in another country where doing business requires giving expensive gifts to key government officials?

- Should a company continue to produce a popular product after it discovers a minor defect in it?

Ethical Conduct Guidelines

The ethical conduct of a business is greatly determined by its top management. Executives who show strong moral character and make ethical business decisions set the ethical standards for a business.

Using the three ethical guidelines on this page, select a situation in a work setting that might be considered unethical. As a team use these three questions to assess the ethical aspects of the situation.

Companies concerned about ethical behavior in their employees have set up educational programs on ethical conduct. These programs are designed to promote employee honesty and integrity. Program topics range from making personal phone calls during work hours to taking supplies for personal use. Employees are also trained on how to make ethical decisions on the job.

When considering the ethics of business situations, you could follow these guidelines.

1. Is the action legal?

2. Does the action violate professional or company standards?

3. Who is affected by the action and how?

main idea

Explain the purpose of a code of ethics.

Guidelines for Writing a Code of Ethics
1. Determine the purpose of the code.
2. Tailor the code to the needs and values of the organization.
3. Consider involving employees from all levels of the company in writing the code.
4. Determine the rules or principles that all members of the organization will be expected to adhere to.
5. Include information about how the code will be enforced.
6. Determine how the code will be implemented and where it will be published or posted.
7. Determine how and when the code will be reviewed and revised.

FIGURE 4-1

Do you think a code of ethics can increase a business' profits? How?

The situations used for this activity might include engaging in personal activities on company time, taking of company items for personal use, or revising reports for personal gain.

TEACH

Ask students to describe a society in which laws and rules were not implemented consistently.

Describe various issues related to business ethics.

Explain the purpose of a code of ethics.

FIGURE 4-1 *ANSWER*

A code of ethics can increase business profits. Employees are encouraged to be honest on the job, and the company is committed to providing excellent customer service, which will translate into increased profits.

 **PROJECT**

Provide the following instructions to students. (These instructions also appear on page xxiv of the textbook.) Do you have a personal code of ethics? Explain how your ethics might affect the life-span goals you set for yourself.

Life-Span Plan Answers

Answers will vary. Students should identify their ethics and explain how ethics might affect the life-span goals they set for themselves.

Language Arts Have students adapt the code of ethics presented in Figure 4-1 to a business in your community. As an alternative, this assignment could be based on another company with which students are familiar.

TEACH

Highlight the three guidelines that could be used to assess various ethical issues.

Have students describe situations in which ethical concerns might arise.

ONGOING ASSESSMENT

checkpoint >> **ANSWER**

The purpose of a code of ethics is to guide actions and decisions of employees or members of an organization.

THINK CRITICALLY THROUGH VISUALS

Some costs to society of unethical business behavior include higher prices on products and services, substandard or defective products, and unfair benefits due to conflicts of interest.

ASSESS

Key Concepts Answers

1. gold

2. find ways to help workers who are physically challenged

3. provide guidelines for proper behavior

Make Academic Connections

4. Examples will vary, but should include natural resources such as water, minerals, and land. Businesses might employ various methods such as recycling or replacement programs, following EPA standards, and changing methods and designs in order to reduce pollution.

5. Provide instructions for how you would like students to report their findings.

A common concern in ethical decision-making involves a *conflict of interest.* This can occur when an action by a company or individual results in an unfair benefit. For example, it would be a conflict of interest if a person serving on a company's board pressured the company to buy items only from businesses that the board member owns or controls.

In addition to workplace codes of ethics, many employees, including accountants and engineers, adhere to codes of professional conduct established by their professional associations. They also participate in continuing education related to ethical issues specific to their professions.

checkpoint >>
What is the purpose of a code of ethics?

What are some costs to society of unethical behavior?

© Getty Images/PhotoDisc

4-1 Assessment

Xtra! Study Tools
school.cengage.com/business/introtobiz

Key Concepts

Determine the best answer.

1. An example of a non-renewable resource would be
   a. solar energy
   b. gold
   c. agricultural products
   d. a library book

2. The Americans with Disabilities Act (ADA) requires that a company
   a. provide training to people with disabilities
   b. find ways to help workers who are physically challenged
   c. hire a certain number of people with special needs
   d. adapt products manufactured for special-needs customers

3. A code of ethics is designed to
   a. meet government regulations
   b. reduce operating costs of a company
   c. provide guidelines for proper behavior
   d. improve employee productivity

Make Academic Connections

4. *Science* List a variety of natural resources and agricultural products used in the production of goods and services. What actions might be taken by companies to improve the efficient use of these resources?

5. *Technology* Search the Internet to locate an example of a code of ethics. Describe the benefits of this code of ethics for the organization.

RETEACH

Have students create an example for each of the categories of social responsibility discussed in this chapter.

ENRICH

Have students talk to relatives or friends about ethical situations they have encountered or observed in business activities.

CLOSE

Ask students to list the various actions a company might take related to social responsibility.

Working in Teams

Each day, thousands of workers make decisions and apply business actions in team settings. The ability to work in a team is rated by most employers as one of the most important career skills. The combined skills of the people in a team are greater than that of individuals working alone. When working in a team in class or on the job, consider the following:

- Be prepared for minor conflicts in the first phase of a team project. Differences in opinions will surface. Be ready to adapt to the personalities, behaviors, and actions of others.
- Agree upon guidelines for project goals, meeting times, location, agenda, missed meetings, conflict resolution, and other procedures.
- Define leadership and other roles. Some team members will keep notes and bring needed materials. Others will conduct research or create visuals for a presentation.
- Determine methods for decision-making. Usually this will be done based on agreement among team members after discussion of various issues and opposing points of view.

- Keep focused on your goals. Avoid being distracted by minor issues and personality conflicts. Maintain a team-oriented environment by saying "we, us, ours." Avoid using "I, me, my, mine."
- Be courteous to others. Respect differences in opinions, personalities, and decision-making styles.

Working in teams is something you are likely to do throughout your life. These experiences can be enjoyable and productive. Members of an effective team take responsibility for its work and take pride in its accomplishments. Some team projects will be frustrating. It is important to maintain a positive attitude. Some of the best learning and most valuable experiences result from encounters with others with different backgrounds and diverse points of view.

Think Critically

1. What do you like about working in teams? Are there any aspects about working in teams that you dislike? Describe them.
2. Describe a problem that might occur when working in teams. Explain how this situation might be resolved.

© Getty Images/PhotoDisc

Sharpen Your Life Skills

Emphasize the importance of being able to successfully work in teams. Point out some of the situations in school, community organizations, and other settings in which students might obtain experience working in teams.

Ask students to point out some concerns associated with working in teams. What actions might be taken to reduce those problem areas?

Think Critically Answers

1. Answers will vary.

2. Answers will vary, but most conflicts can be avoided or resolved by following the guidelines listed.

Teaching Strategies

Expand Beyond the Classroom Cross-cultural teams are becoming more common in both domestic and international work settings. Remind students that cross-cultural teams can provide (1) improved cultural understanding, (2) increased creativity from diverse points of view, and (3) expanded global business effectiveness.

4-2 Government Protection Activities

Goals

Identify the roles and levels of government.

Explain government protection activities.

Describe types of intellectual property.

Key Terms

contract

patent

copyright

trademark

Focus on Real Life

Brenda Hiam was driving to school when, all of a sudden, a crack in the road caused her car to swerve and hit a bump. While there was no obvious damage to the vehicle, this was a disturbing event.

At this point, Brenda wanted to contact a government agency to notify them of this potentially dangerous driving hazard. She asked her friend, Kevin, if she should contact the city, county, state, or federal highway department.

"That depends if the road is a city, county, state, or federal highway," he answered.

"Well, this might not be as easy as I thought," said Brenda in a confused tone.

main idea

Identify the roles and levels of government.

GOVERNMENT IN SOCIETY

Government plays a role in all economic systems. Your role as a citizen and voter has an effect on the decisions and actions taken by government. In a private enterprise system, government's role is much less extensive than in other economic systems. It is still a vital one. The role of government in the economy often changes as newly elected officials take office.

Roles of Government

As issues facing society change, so must government change. There are some basic roles of government.

Government is mainly concerned with these areas:

- Providing services for members of society
- Protecting citizens, consumers, businesses, and workers
- Regulating utilities and promoting competition
- Providing information and support to businesses

- Buying goods and services
- Hiring public employees
- Raising revenue

Each of these roles has either a direct or indirect impact on business expansion, consumer affairs, and economic growth in the economy.

Levels of Government

The main goal of the federal government is to oversee the activities that involve two or more states or other countries. In general, the Constitution gives the federal

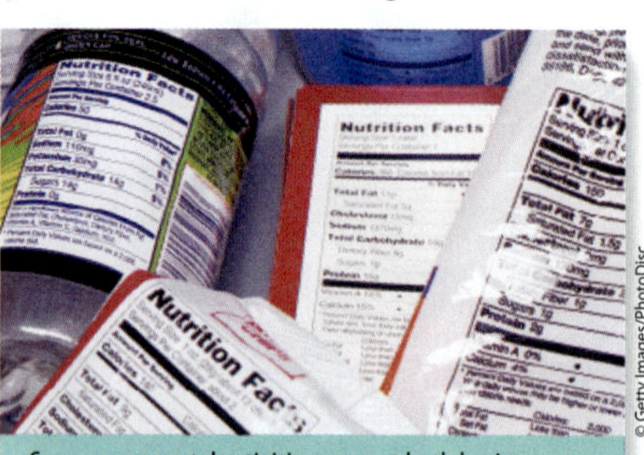
Can governmental activities support both businesses and consumers?

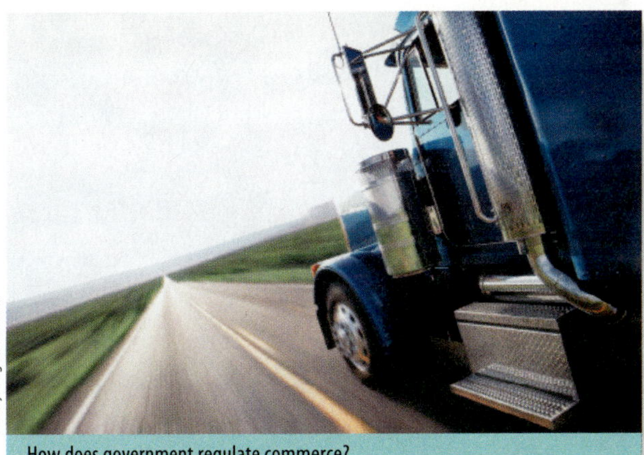

How does government regulate commerce?

government the power to regulate foreign and interstate commerce.

Interstate commerce is business dealings involving companies in more than one state. The federal government would regulate a trucking company that ships products to several states.

State governments regulate business actions within their own borders. *Intrastate commerce* refers to business dealings involving companies that do business in only one state. A trucking company that hauls products only within a state's boundaries would be regulated by that state and not the federal government.

All states have assigned some of their legislative power to local governments. Local governments include county boards and city or town councils. Local governments provide services needed for an orderly society, such as police and fire protection.

> *checkpoint* >>
> What are the three levels of government?

GOVERNMENT PROTECTION ACTIVITIES

Government protects your rights in a number of ways. Citizens are protected through police and fire-fighting services. The armed forces provide for national defense. National security is a chief concern of the federal government.

Worker Protection

Laws have been established to help provide a safe work environment. As a worker, you have a basic right to safe working conditions. Safety standards for buildings, machines, and chemicals are set by government agencies. Government inspection and regulation of work areas help reduce the number of job-related accidents.

More government regulations result from the need to protect the basic human rights of workers. For example, you cannot be denied work because of your race, religion, sex, or age. Selection of someone for a job must be based on job requirements, training, and experience. Prejudices and personal biases must not affect a hiring decision.

Contract Enforcement

Contracts are another example of government protection. A **contract** is an agreement to exchange goods or services for something of value, usually money. It is a basic part of doing business. A contract may be written or unwritten. Certain elements must be included for the contract to be enforceable. Figure 4-2 highlights

main idea

Explain government protection activities.

FYI

It is important to read and understand a contract before signing it. The court system does not protect you from your own lack of common sense.

Explain the main activities of the three levels of government—federal, state, and local.

Ask students to name services commonly provided by each level of government.

THINK CRITICALLY THROUGH VISUALS

Government regulates commerce by overseeing and regulating business activities.

ONGOING ASSESSMENT

checkpoint >> **ANSWER**

The three levels of government are local, state, and federal.

TEACH

Describe some of the services provided by government that protect workers.

Ask students to name some examples of contracts in our society.

Use the FYI feature to explain a common action that can help avoid legal problems.

Word Processing/Office Technology Use database software to categorize various types of government services and activities. Have students sort the items into three groups: local, state, and federal government.

Contract Basics	
Valid, enforceable contracts must contain:	
Agreement	An offer must be made, and an acceptance must occur.
Competent Parties	Those entering into the contract must be of legal age and must be mentally competent.
Consideration	Something of measurable value must be exchanged by the parties involved.
Legality	The contract must be for a product or service that may be legally sold; also, no fraud or deception exists in the agreement.

FIGURE 4-2

Provide examples of contracts you might encounter in the future.

the main provisions of every enforceable contract.

These four elements—agreement, competent parties, consideration, and legality—are the basis for many legal disputes. An item seen as having different values (*consideration*) by different people can result in a legal dispute. Examples of contracts include a lease to rent an apartment, a credit card agreement, and documents that state the terms of a purchase.

Both consumers and businesses benefit from government enforcement of contracts. If you agree to have repairs made on your car for $65, the business firm must do the work as agreed upon. You must pay for the work when it is finished. If work is not done correctly or if you fail to pay, legal action can be taken to force the work to be corrected or force you to pay. Without enforcement, dishonest consumers or business owners could refuse to honor their agreements. Daily business activities would be very difficult.

> **main idea**
>
> Describe types of intellectual property.

checkpoint >>

What are the main elements of a contract?

PROTECTION OF INTELLECTUAL PROPERTY

Intellectual property is purely intangible, with no physical characteristics—a person cannot touch it. Intellectual property includes patents, copyrights, and trademarks.

Patents

When individuals or companies create new products, they may obtain a patent. A **patent** gives the inventor the sole right to make, use, or sell the item for 20 years. A company that creates a new means to record programs from television could get a patent for this process. It would prevent other companies from making or selling recorders using this process.

Work as a Team

Intellectual properties are also called intangible assets. As a team, prepare a list of various patents, copyrights, and trademarks owned by companies and nonprofit organizations. Explain how these assets contribute to the success of the organization. Why is protection of intellectual property important?

Copyrights

A **copyright** protects the creative work of authors, composers, and artists. Copyright protection lasts for the life of the person receiving the copyright. It also extends for 70 years after the person's death. Examples of copyright statements can be found on the front pages of most books. Copyrights are identified with the symbol ©.

Trademarks

A **trademark** is a word, letter, or symbol linked with a specific company or product. Businesses register company names, team emblems, and label designs with the government. A trademark can be very valuable. Many are famous all over the world and are often identified with a symbol, called a *logo*. Can you think of some logos that you see frequently?

Can you think of any kinds of publications that would not be copyrighted?

> *checkpoint* >>
> What are three types of intellectual property?

4-2 Assessment

Xtra! Study Tools
school.cengage.com/business/introtobiz

Key Concepts

Determine the best answer.

1. True or False. International trade with other countries is the responsibility of state and local governments.

2. True or False. An oral contract can be legally binding.

3. Fire and police protection is the main responsibility of
   a. local government
   b. state government
   c. federal government
   d. all levels of government

4. A _?_ would protect the composer's musical score.
   a. patent
   b. trademark
   c. copyright
   d. contract

Make Academic Connections

5. *Math* A city government spends $186,000 a month on public services. Of that amount, 46 percent is used for fire and police protection.
   a. How much is spent each month for fire and police protection?
   b. How much is spent each month for other services?
   c. How much is spent by the city in a year for fire and police protection?

6. *Math* In a city in which there are 90,000 employed workers, 18,000 are public employees. Of this number, the federal government employs 6,000; the state, 8,000; and the city, 4,000.
   a. What percentage of all workers are public employees?
   b. What percentage of the public employees does the federal government employ?
   c. What percentage of all employees are employees of the state government?

7. *Law* Prepare a list of possible problems that could occur in a contract situation.

TEACH

Point out the importance of copyrights. Ask students to explain how technology has affected copyrights. Explain how businesses use trademarks.

THINK CRITICALLY THROUGH VISUALS

Answers will vary. Examples of works protected by copyright include paintings, music, lyrics, plays, wallpaper designs, and greeting cards.

ONGOING ASSESSMENT

checkpoint >> **ANSWER**

Patents, copyrights, and trademarks are types of intellectual property.

ASSESS

Key Concepts Answers

1. False. International trade is the responsibility of the federal government.

2. True.

3. **a.** local government

4. **c.** copyright

Make Academic Connections

5. **a.** $186,000 \times 46\% = \$85,560$

b. $186,000 - \$85,560 = \$100,440$

c. $85,560 \times 12 = \$1,026,720$

6. **a.** $18,000 \div 90,000 = 0.20$ or 20%

b. $6,000 \div 18,000 = 0.30$ or 30%

c. $8,000 \div 90,000 = 0.088$ or 9%

7. Answers will vary. Many contract problems are related to complying with contract agreements, such as completing work or making payments.

RETEACH

Name various government activities. Ask whether each is a local, state, or federal government responsibility.

ENRICH

Have students use the Internet to find examples of patents, copyrights, and trademarks.

CLOSE

Name various items and ask if they would be protected by a patent, copyright, or a trademark.

Many countries in Asia are becoming new markets and new competitors in the world economy. Encourage students to develop an awareness of the economic, cultural, and political differences that exist in various countries in Asia and other regions of the world.

Ask students who have lived in or visited other countries to explain some of the cultural differences they have observed.

Think Critically
Answers

1. Answers will vary and might include age preferences, the value of family, and various rules of etiquette, including those pertaining to greeting one another, meals, and meeting procedures.

2. In order to conduct business in Vietnam, one must have approvals from various levels of government. Vietnam is also relatively new to capitalism. Proceedings move slowly, in contrast to the American tendency to get things done quickly.

3. Let students know how you would like them to report their findings. Consider allowing students to work in pairs.

Doing Business in…Vietnam

Official name
Socialist Republic of Vietnam

Capital
Hanoi

Population
85.3 million

Currency
dong

Major exports
crude oil, marine products, rice, coffee, rubber, tea, garments, shoes

Major export partners
United States, Japan, China, Australia

Major imports
machinery and equipment, petroleum products, fertilizer, steel products, raw cotton

Major import partners
China, Singapore, Taiwan, Japan, South Korea

Source: CIA World Factbook

One minute you see peaceful villages with carts pulled by animals. A moment later, you see busy city streets in which seven of ten Vietnamese families use a motorcycle as their main method of transportation.

Vietnam is a country of contrasts, combining traditional production methods with modern business activities. The nation is moving from decades of strong central planning to emerging areas of capitalism.

Even as Vietnam transitions to a modern market economy, the Vietnamese people continue to place a high value on traditions and family relationships. Several generations may live together in the same home. Children show great respect for the elders of the family, even their older brothers and sisters.

When doing business in Vietnam, you will need to get approvals from several levels of government agencies. In recent years, the government has tried to attract foreign investment for factories, technology, and infrastructure. Making connections with government officials and joint venture partners is especially important for business success.

At the start of a meeting, the exchange of business cards occurs. Cards should be presented and received with both hands. If your card is printed in both English and Vietnamese, it is polite to have the Vietnamese side facing up. You may be asked how old you are. This classifies you as either older or younger than the Vietnamese person in order to determine the correct form of address.

The business meal is likely to include tea and perhaps some exotic foods. You may be served bat meat, stir-fried baby birds, dog, or snake, as well as many types of seafood. It is polite to taste and drink small amounts of all items you are offered.

The conversation will slowly lead to business negotiations. Take care to not move too quickly through the agenda because this is considered rude. Use a low-pitched voice and low-key gestures. Do not allow your hosts to see the soles of your shoes.

Think Critically
1. What cultural factors affect business activities in Vietnam?
2. How do business activities in Vietnam differ from those in other countries?
3. Conduct library or Internet research to obtain additional information about business and economic activities in Vietnam.

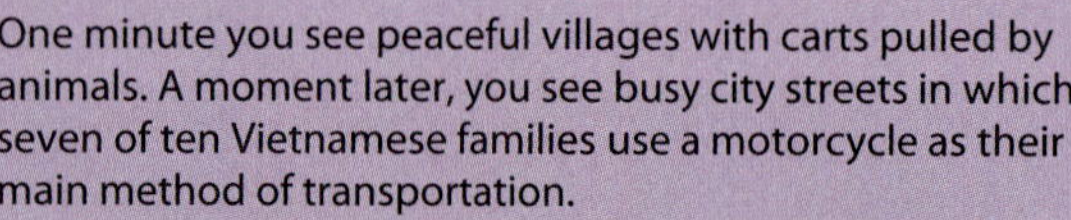

Geography Create a list of 15 to 20 countries. Consider asking students to help develop the list based on recent newspaper and magazine articles. Using a blank sheet or an outline of a world map, have students identify the general location of each country.

Government Regulation and Assistance

Goals

Explain actions by government to regulate business.

Discuss efforts of government to assist businesses.

Identify methods used by government to raise money.

Key Terms

public utility

monopoly

antitrust laws

Focus on Real Life

The skateboard park in the city is one of the most popular areas. Kent Walling recently noticed that due to extensive use, the ramps, jumps, and tracks are wearing out. Using the skate park is not as much fun.

Money is needed by the city government to maintain the skate park. Currently, the city faces many financial needs.

Kent believes that the city should increase taxes to pay for the skate park improvements. His friend, Galib, thinks the city could sell bonds to raise funds for the upgrade. Another friend, Marcus, has heard a fee might be charged to use the skateboard facilities.

REGULATORY ACTIVITIES

Business activity in the United States is structured as a private enterprise or free market system. Private organizations own the factors of production. They choose efficient methods of production in order to earn a profit. Price and output decisions are made not by the government, but by businesses and consumers acting under varying economic conditions.

Government does get involved in some areas of business activities. These include regulating utilities and preventing unfair business practices.

Regulation of Utilities

Most goods and services you use come from private businesses. These businesses are for the most part free of government regulation. A **public utility** is an organization that supplies a service or product vital to all people. These include companies that provide

main idea

Explain actions by government to regulate business.

Is it better for consumers if utilities are offered by competing businesses?

Focus on Real Life

This feature can be used to introduce students to the financial needs and funding methods used by governments.

TEACH

Provide an overview of the various regulatory activities of government.

Explain the importance of public utilities for business operations and economic activities.

THINK CRITICALLY THROUGH VISUALS

It could be better for consumers if utilities compete for business because that keeps prices low; however, utilities are regulated so that their products are reliable and efficient.

Different Learning Styles

Visual Learner Encourage visual learners to create a drawing or sketch that depicts one or more public utilities in your community. Have students explain the services provided by these companies.

TEACH

Explain various types of monopolies that might exist in an economy.

Describe the purpose of antitrust laws.

NET Bookmark

Students should access the product web site and select a topic area of interest to them. Students should be able to describe information that could be of value to consumers or business.

ONGOING ASSESSMENT

checkpoint >> **ANSWER**

Reasons for government regulation of utilities might include the assurance of fair prices, the conservation of resources, and to avoid overcrowding of utility poles and other facilities, such as power plants.

TEACH

Point out ways in which government interacts with businesses.

Work as a Team

Companies can take actions that reduce competition and give consumers fewer choices. Describe some advertising, pricing, or branding actions that could result in unfair competition.

local telephone service, water, and electricity. A public utility is chosen to serve a community. If your city had six different electric companies, each might have its own utility poles, lines, and expensive equipment. The service you would get would be more expensive and less efficient. The extra poles and wires would create an unattractive environment.

While many utility companies are privately owned, usually government closely regulates them. The rates they can charge for things such as electricity, water, or natural gas have to be approved by government agencies. In recent years, there has been a trend toward deregulation of prices where competition can be introduced.

main idea

Discuss efforts of government to assist businesses.

Prevent Unfair Business Practices

Most businesspeople are fair and honest. A few may try to take advantage of their customers or competitors. Government attempts to promote fair competition. If a company charges different prices to different people for the same product, it is treating its customers unfairly. If

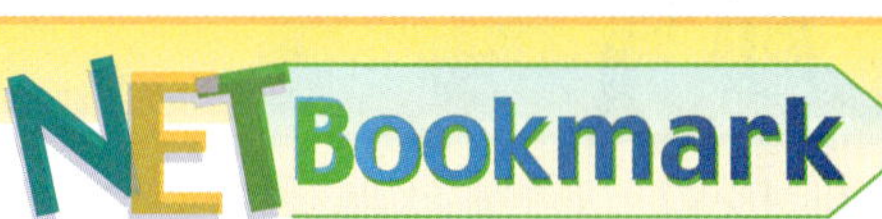

With hundreds of agencies, the U.S. federal government has created a web site to assist citizens. Access the web site shown below and click on the link for Chapter 4. This web site offers information about everything from Amtrak to zoos. Select a topic area of interest to you. Obtain information on the topic and prepare a written summary of how this information might be used by consumers or business.

school.cengage.com/business/introtobiz

one business receives lower rates for the same quality and quantity of supplies than other businesses receive, it has an advantage. Such action may result in unfair competition.

A **monopoly** exists when a business has control of the market for a product or service. A public utility monopoly may benefit consumers by making sure they receive a needed service at a fair price. Other monopolies may not be good for the economy. If the same company owned all food stores in your city, consumers might not be treated fairly. This business could charge high prices and sell poor-quality products. When competition is present, consumers get the best values at the fairest prices.

One government action meant to promote competition and fairness and to avoid monopolies was the passage of **antitrust laws**. Antitrust laws prevent other unfair business practices such as false advertising, deceptive pricing, and misleading labeling. Each of these unfair practices hurts competition and reduces consumer choice.

> *checkpoint* >>
> Why does government regulate utilities?

GOVERNMENT ASSISTS BUSINESS

Government helps businesses by collecting and reporting valuable information. Data gathered by the government can help with planning. Information about incomes, prices, worker availability, and business failures can help a businessperson make wiser choices. For example, census information can help a business decide where a majority of potential customers live. The Bureau of Labor Statistics, the Department of Agriculture, and the

---

Communication Ask students to locate an advertisement with wording that may not be completely clear. Have students explain how this creates an unfair business practice that could be deceptive to consumers.

Department of Commerce are a few of the government agencies that provide information.

The federal government, through the Small Business Administration (SBA), helps new businesses get started by guaranteeing private bank loans. The new businesses must develop an acceptable business plan. Farmers and others may receive financial help in times of great hardship, such as during a drought, flooding, or other natural disasters. Destruction of home and property by a tornado may make a person eligible for a low-interest government loan. These programs are designed to promote the financial well-being of society.

Government Buys Goods and Services

Government spends a great deal of money each day to buy an array of products and services. Total federal, state, and local government spending make up about 20 percent of all the goods and services produced in the United States.

Governments buy everything from file cabinets to buildings to military jet aircraft. In this role, government is a key economic force. Many businesses depend on government contracts for their survival. For instance, government pays businesses to construct highways and build schools.

Government Employs Workers

Government is the single largest employer in the U.S. economy. About 16 percent of workers are public employees. Most people think only of police officers, firefighters, and sanitation workers as government workers. Government also employs the same types of workers as private businesses. Administrative assistants, lawyers, teachers, meat inspectors, and data analysts are all employed by

© Digital Vision

Why do you think a company would want to perform work for the government?

government. Although the number of employees has grown slowly in recent years, good employment opportunities in government continue—in spite of efforts to eliminate or reduce the size of some agencies.

checkpoint »
How does government assist business?

GOVERNMENT RAISES MONEY

Government must have a way to raise money to fund operations and pay wages to workers. Government income is called *revenue*. Governments can obtain

main idea

Describe how the government raises money.

Companies might want to work for the government because governmental purchases and contracts are often for large and ongoing projects.

TEACH

Highlight methods in which government assists businesses.

Ask students to name various goods and services commonly bought by governments.

ONGOING ASSESSMENT

checkpoint » ANSWER

The government assists businesses in a variety of ways, including providing demographic data, buying goods and services, and employing workers who then have the means to buy goods and services.

PROJECT

Provide the following instructions to students. (These instructions also appear on page xxiv of the textbook.) Explain how government taxing and spending could affect the life-span goals you set for yourself as well as your ability to achieve these goals.

Life-Span Plan Answers

Answers will vary. Students should explain how taxes could impact their ability to accumulate funds they need to achieve their life-span goals.

Technology allows companies to serve individual needs and wants in a cost-efficient manner. Ask students to suggest benefits and potential drawbacks of mass customization efforts.

Think Critically
Answers

1. Answers will vary. Students should provide specific examples of customized products or services and explain how technology makes the customization possible.

2. Answers will very. Students should describe specific ideas for offering a customized product or service in their community or online.

revenue through taxes and borrowing. In addition, governments can raise revenue in other ways. Fines for traffic violations and other violations of the law provide revenue for government. Fees and licenses are a source of income. Certain types of ventures require a business license. For example, insurance and real estate agents pay a fee for the privilege of running a business. Governments also charge fees for such things as driver's licenses and fishing privileges.

Taxes

A government creates tax policies to pay for the services it provides. Taxes are levied on earnings, the value of property, and on the sale price of goods and services.

Your earnings as an individual are subject to an income tax. *Income taxes* are levied on the income of individuals. The individual income tax is the largest source of revenue for the federal government. Corporate income taxes also provide government revenue. The corporate income tax is based on business profits.

A major source of revenue for local governments is the real estate *property tax.* This tax is based on the value of land and buildings. Most property tax revenue is used to pay for schools and other local government services, such as police protection and community parks. Businesses also pay a property tax.

The cost of buying things is increased by a sales tax. A *sales tax* is a state or local tax on goods and services that is collected

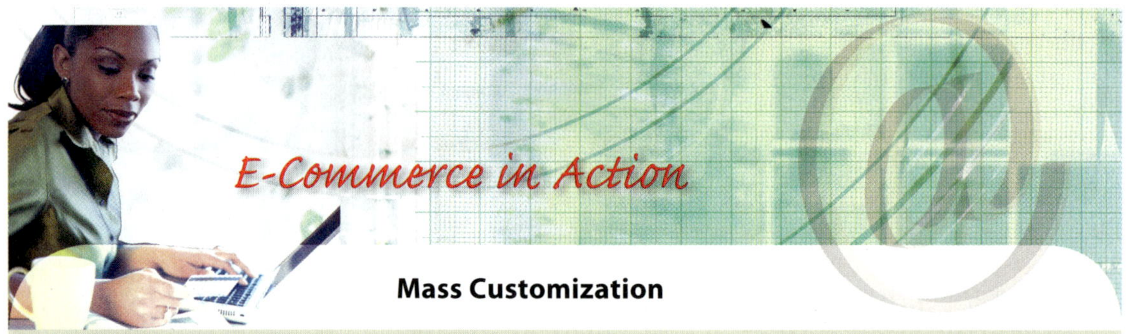

E-Commerce in Action

Mass Customization

When the automobile was first mass-produced in the early 1900s, Henry Ford would tell potential customers… "you can have any color car you want as long as it's black!" Since then, businesses have continually tried to make items that meet the distinct needs and wants of consumers.

Today, companies with millions of customers are making products designed for the individual. Consumers can buy vitamins matched to their health needs. CDs are offered with selected music tracks. Cosmetics can be mixed to match facial features and skin tone. Financial services companies offer computerized investment advice based on a person's income, age, and household situation.

Many online companies are involved in *mass customization.* They provide goods and services tailored to customer demand. Dell Computer only builds personal computers that have actually been ordered. This approach keeps profit margin up by keeping inventory costs down.

Many automotive companies allow you to design a car online. You can do this just for fun, or design the car you want to buy. Because automotive manufacturing is highly mechanized, assembly lines can easily customize the design.

This approach can improve customer service and add to sales.

Many online merchants tailor messages and suggest purchases based on a customer profile. Previous items bought as well as interests of the buyer will promote future purchases of books, music, DVDs, clothing, and other goods and services.

Think Critically

1. Locate a web site or local business that would provide another example of customized products or services. How does technology make this situation possible?

2. Describe an idea to offer a customized product or service online or in your community..

Different Learning Abilities

Limited English Proficiency (LEP) Obtain translations of various government activities and services to reinforce these concepts in both English and other dominant languages used by students.

by the seller. If you buy a can of paint for $15.00 and the state sales tax is 6 percent, the seller collects $15.90 from you. The seller then will pay 90 cents to the state. You were the one who provided the money for the tax.

Paying taxes is a duty of citizens and businesses. You should pay your taxes, but not more than your share. Tax laws and policies are set to help make the paying of taxes fair. Whether a particular tax or tax policy is fair is always subject to debate. Businesses, in spite of public misconceptions, pay a lot of taxes to all levels of government.

Borrowing

Government income from taxes and other sources may not always be enough to cover the costs of providing services. Borrowing is another activity of government. When a government wants to construct a building, such as a new courthouse or convention center, the funds needed are often raised through borrowing.

Government borrows money by selling bonds. When you buy a government bond, you are helping to fund the services provided by government. Banks, insurance companies, and other financial institutions help finance governments by purchasing bonds in large numbers.

By borrowing money, the government becomes a debtor and must pay interest on its debt. Bonds issued by the U.S. government are backed by the "full faith and credit" of the federal government. Bonds issued by the federal government are considered the least risky of all debt.

> *checkpoint* >>
> What is the difference between tax revenue and borrowing by government?

4-3 Assessment

Key Concepts

Determine the best answer.

1. Antitrust laws are designed to
   a. reduce utility rates
   b. lower taxes
   c. create more jobs
   d. maintain competition

2. A(n) _?_ tax is a common source of revenue for state and local governments.
   a. sales
   b. import
   c. gift
   d. unemployment

3. True or False. A monopoly is never a benefit to consumers.

Make Academic Connections

4. **History** Conduct research about various antitrust laws. What situations caused the creation of these laws?

5. **Communication** Conduct a survey of people to obtain their opinions about which types of taxes are most appropriate to raise government revenue. Prepare a summary data table with your findings.

6. **Economics** Describe government actions to raise money that might have a positive or negative influence on business activities.

Communicate Business Concepts Answers

1. Examples of natural resources used everyday can include water, natural gas, gasoline, tin, and other minerals. All of these resources need to be protected. Strategies to avoid depleting natural resources include avoiding the waste of water, recycling cans and bottles, driving only when necessary, and minimizing the use of electricity.

2. Examples will vary, but might include following all manufacturing procedures accurately, keeping electrical cords secured and walkways clear of objects, maintaining adequate lighting, keeping first aid and emergency exits posted, and providing security in areas where needed.

3. Answers will vary. The term "discrimination" could mean an individual is denied a chance for employment or a promotion because of gender, race, or age. The term could also mean not giving some people the same opportunities available to others. Examples of discrimination will vary.

4. Healthy employees are generally more productive employees. The cost of health care insurance is also a concern to employers. One estimate attributes 15–25 percent of corporate health care costs to the unhealthy lifestyles of some employees.

5. The list may include water, sanitation, electric, gas, and cable television.

a. These utilities provide things that make life healthier and more convenient. We have water purification sites, waste removal, and electricity for our homes, schools, hospitals, and businesses.

Business Notes

4-1 SOCIAL RESPONSIBILITY

1. Socially responsible businesses care about their communities. They help make them better places in which to live. Social responsibility concerns relate to environmental protection, workplace diversity, safety on the job, and employee wellness.

2. Benefits of social responsibility include expanded justice for societal groups, enhanced company image, reduced need for government action, improved quality of life, and increased awareness of social issues. Costs of social responsibility are that money must be spent for new or safer equipment, for building renovations to remove hazards, for wellness and rehabilitation programs, and for social projects sponsored by a company. These costs must be balanced with profits to make sure the business stays viable.

3. A code of business ethics is a guide for behavior within an organization.

4-2 GOVERNMENT PROTECTION ACTIVITIES

4. The primary roles of government are to provide services to society; protect citizens, consumers, businesses, and workers; regulate utilities and promote competition; provide information and help to businesses; buy goods and services; hire public employees; and raise revenue. The levels of government are federal, state, and local.

5. Government protects citizens through police and fire services, protects consumers and business owners by enforcing contracts and intellectual property rights, and protects workers through laws that require safe working conditions.

6. The three types of intellectual property are patents, copyrights, and trademarks.

4-3 GOVERNMENT REGULATION AND ASSISTANCE

7. Government regulates utilities and prevents unfair business practices.

8. Government buys a wide range of goods and services and employs workers. Governments also collect and report valuable information and provide loans to help businesses get started or overcome natural disasters.

9. Governments raise needed funds through taxes and borrowing.

Communicate Business Concepts

1. What are some natural resources that you use every day? Which of those natural resources need to be protected? What can you as an individual do to avoid using up non-renewable resources?

2. Safety is often a matter of individuals being careful about where they place things and how they conduct their own business. Name some ways in which you and others can help make a workplace safe.

3. What does the term "discrimination" mean to you? What examples of discrimination in the workplace are you aware of?

4. Why do you think employers are willing to spend money to help employees improve their general health? Be specific about how a company might benefit.

5. Make a list of public utilities that serve your community.

   a. What services do they provide?
   b. Do you think it would be better for these services to be offered by several competing businesses? Explain your answer.

6. Here is a list of some of the public services provided by government. For each item, tell whether the federal, state, or local government would most likely have the responsibility for the service. (Some services may be provided by more than one level of government.)

   a. Fire protection
   b. Education
   c. Parks and recreation
   d. Water supply

b. Some resources, and the resources used to process them, would have a greater demand put upon them if they were privatized and could become scarce. As private companies would compete for the same source and would have to pay for its own equipment, these types of utilities would become more expensive for the provider as well as the consumer. Competition might improve the quality of some services and could reduce costs.

e. Highways between cities
f. Assistance to low-income families
g. Sewage and trash disposal
h. Public buses
i. Police protection
j. Public libraries
k. Street maintenance
l. National defense

7. Each day people enter into many contracts, both written and unwritten.

a. Give examples of contracts between a consumer and a business, between two businesses, and between a worker and a business.

b. What services does government provide to enforce contracts?

Develop Your Business Language

Match the terms listed with the definitions.

10. Principles of morality or rules of conduct.

11. The obligation of a business to contribute to the well-being of a community.

12. Rules about how businesses and their employees ought to behave.

13. A natural resource, such as gas, coal, copper, or iron ore, that cannot be replaced once it is used up.

14. A statement of values and rules that guides the behavior of employees or members of an organization.

15. A business that supplies a service or product vital to all people; the price charged for the service (or product) is determined by government regulation rather than by competition.

16. Laws designed to promote competition and fairness and to prevent monopolies.

17. Protection of the work of authors, composers, and artists.

8. Two students are discussing the topic "Government Is Our Biggest Business." Dan believes that some government activities are in direct competition with private businesses. He thinks that this is unfair. He believes that government should limit its activities to those that private businesses cannot or will not take on. Brian thinks that government should undertake any business activities that it can perform better or at a lower cost than private business. What do you think? Give some examples of business activities undertaken by both private businesses and by government.

9. Why do you suppose government raises revenue through bonds that create debt and require interest payments when government could raise the revenue through an increase in taxes?

18. An agreement to exchange goods or services for something of value.

19. The exclusive right given to a person to make, use, or sell an invention for a period of 20 years.

20. A word, letter, or symbol associated with a specific product or company.

21. A business that has complete control of the market for a product or service.

KEY TERMS

a. antitrust laws
b. business ethics
c. code of ethics
d. contract
e. copyright
f. ethics
g. monopoly
h. non-renewable resource
i. patent
j. public utility
k. social responsibility
l. trademark

Develop Your Business Language Answers

10. f. ethics

11. k. social responsibility

12. b. business ethics

13. h. non-renewable resource

14. c. code of ethics

15. j. public utility

16. a. antitrust laws

17. e. copyright

18. d. contract

19. i. patent

20. l. trademark

21. g. monopoly

6. a. Fire protection, local

b. Education, local and state

c. Parks and recreation, local, state, federal

d. Water supply, local

e. Highways between cities, state and federal

f. Assistance to low-income families, state and federal

g. Sewage and trash disposal, local

h. Public buses, local

i. Police protection, local and state

j. Public libraries, local

k. Street maintenance, local

l. National defense, federal

7. a. A contract between a homeowner and an electrician, a contract between an advertising agency and a soap manufacturer, and a work-for-hire agreement are examples of these types of contracts.

b. The government has established laws regarding the definition of contracts and their enforcement. Court systems exist to settle disputes. Other forms of government protection, such as the protection of workers and intellectual property, often contribute to the regulation of many contracts.

8. Answers will vary. Education, transportation, and health care are all examples of services that can be both public and private.

9. Taxes reduce the consumer's ability to buy goods and services, which weakens the economy as a whole. By providing bonds, governments can increase the consumer's ability to contribute to the flow of the economy, while covering its cost for public services.

22. Reports will vary. Several definitions and examples should be included.

23. a. pollution control: $37,500 ÷ $750,000 = 5%; community projects: $22,500 ÷ $750,000 = 3%; employee fitness: $7,500 ÷ $750,000 = 1%; Total spent: $37,500 + $22,500 + $7,500 = $67,500

b. pollution control: $37,500 × 1.15 = $43,125; community projects: $22,500 × 1.15 = $25,875; employee fitness: $7,500 × 1.15 = $8,625; Total spent: $43,125 + $25,875 + $8,625 = $77,625

24. Technology makes it more difficult to protect intellectual property rights. The electronic transmission and duplication of data is easy and fast, and it is more difficult to regulate the use and sale of products.

25. Students find examples of U.S. and foreign logos and trademarks and design a brand name or trademark that would be effective in countries around the world.

26. Students are to research different systems of government and explain how history and culture affect business regulations in various countries.

27. Reports will vary depending on the product selected. Reports should identify the product, the inventor, the year of the patent, and the product function. They then prepare a summary report.

28. Students are to investigate various legal restrictions they might encounter when applying for a job.

Make Academic Connections

22. **COMMUNICATION** Interview various people to ask them for a definition and an example of "conflict of interest." Prepare a summary report of two to three paragraphs.

23. **MATH** The Johnson Manufacturing Co. has an annual operating budget of $750,000. Each year it budgets for the following expenses: pollution control equipment, $37,500; contributions to community projects, $22,500; employee fitness/sports programs, $7,500.

  a. What percentage of the annual budget is allocated to each socially responsible action (pollution control, community projects, fitness/sports)? What is the total spent?

  b. What will be the amount budgeted for each expense category next year if there is a 15 percent increase? What will be the total spent?

24. **TECHNOLOGY** Explain how new technology is making it more difficult to protect intellectual property rights.

25. **VISUAL ART** Look for examples of trademarks and logos of products from companies based inside and outside of the United States. Design a brand name or trademark that might be effective in several countries around the world.

26. **CULTURE** Research different systems of government. Explain how history and culture can affect business regulations in various countries.

27. **SCIENCE** Research a patent on a product. Identify the inventor, the year the patent was granted, and the product's function. Prepare a summary report of your findings.

28. **CAREER PLANNING** Investigate various legal restrictions that might be encountered when applying for a job position.

Linking School and Community

Interview someone in your community who owns a business or works for a large company or organization. Obtain information about actions that need to be considered when hiring people, designing products, and making other business decisions. Ask them how ethics might affect their daily lives and the lives of others.

Based on their answers, create a short code of ethics that might be used to guide the decisions made by managers and employees in a company.

Web Workout

Global warming is a hot topic. There is strong consensus that the world is getting warmer. Eleven of the last 12 years have been the warmest on record.

Although the warming trend is well documented, there is considerable debate about the cause. Could it be part of a natural cycle? Or, is it due to human activity? Scientists, environmentalists, and policymakers who believe that human activity is the cause of global warming point to the reduction of carbon emissions as part of the solution.

Think Critically
1. Use the Internet to learn more about global warming and get some different perspectives on the issue. Visit at least one web site for each of the following categories: government agency, environmental advocacy organization, large manufacturer, and energy company. In a short report, summarize what you find and offer an opinion about what should be done to combat global warming.

2. Use the Internet to identify actions and strategies that businesses, governments, and individuals could adopt to limit greenhouse gases. Report your findings in a table.

3. Choose three actions or strategies that could help reduce greenhouse gases and write a short explanation of how they might impact business practices.

Linking School and Community

Answers will vary. Students are to talk to people about ethics in business and in daily life, then create a code of ethics for a company.

Web Workout

1. Reports will vary. Students should summarize their findings and offer their opinion about what should be done to combat global warming.

Decision-Making Strategies

Centerville wants to build a new sports complex near the center of town. The complex will cost $250,000. There are two financing proposals:

Proposal A Issue $250,000 worth of bonds at an interest rate of 4 percent. The town will pay $10,000 per year in interest for 15 years. The total interest would be $150,000. The amount borrowed ($250,000) would have to be paid off in 15 years. Fees charged to users of the complex would pay the interest each year and the amount due bondholders ($250,000). Construction could begin right away.

Proposal B Establish a 1/4 percent city sales tax on all purchases. The revenue needed could be raised in about five years. There would be no user fee charged to residents of Centerville. Construction would be delayed a few years.

29. What are the advantages and disadvantages of the two proposals?

30. Which proposal do you favor, and why?

Access the web site shown here to find portfolio activities for this chapter. Use the activities to provide tangible evidence of your learning.

Decision-Making Strategies Answers

29. With Proposal A, construction could begin right away. Fees charged to users of the complex will pay for it. With Proposal B, construction would be delayed a few years, and all consumers in the city would pay for it via the ¼ percent city sales tax, but there would be no fees to residents for use of the complex.

30. Answers will vary.

Winning Edge
Community Service Project Event

Think Critically Answers

1. Answers will vary, depending on the project chosen.

2. Answers will vary, depending on the project chosen.

3. Answers will vary, but should include: recognize members for their involvement and provide publicity for participants in the local and school newspapers.

4. Businesses participate in community service to show their commitment to the community and to present positive public relations.

---

2. Tables will vary. For example students might suggest that businesses could use energy-saving equipment, governments could offer tax incentives to businesses to encourage green business practices, and consumers could plant a tree.

3. Explanations will vary depending on the actions or strategies selected.

This project will allow students the opportunity to work as a team and develop better group decision-making skills.

Explain to students that this team project can provide (1) improved understanding of others, (2) increased creativity from diverse points of view, and (3) expanded awareness of global business activities.

Remind students that effective teams

- clearly define roles and behavior guidelines,
- adapt to differences to allow a focus on tasks of the project,
- value diverse points of view, and
- plan for unexpected situations.

For the outcome, select one or more items in the "Present" section of the project.

Global Business Project

Identify International Business Opportunities

Goals

- Explore the economic environment of another country.
- Research the cultural impact on a nation's business environment.
- Identify political factors affecting the business activities in a foreign country.
- Select a business idea (product or service) for selling in another country.
- Analyze trade barriers that may affect international business activities.

Activities

Use your textbook, library materials, web sites, interviews with people, and other resources to complete the following.

1. Select a country. Conduct economic research for this country. Obtain information on natural resources, agricultural products, imports, exports, standard of living, GDP, and inflation. Write a summary to describe this information.

2. Locate information about foods, habits, customs, traditions, and beliefs of people in the country. Try to talk to a person who has visited or lived in the country. List two or three ways in which the country is different from most others.

3. Laws regulating business differ from country to country. Research the political and legal environment of your chosen country. Present your findings on laws, barriers, and taxes in a chart, table, or other visual format.

4. Based on your country research, describe a new business idea. This business opportunity could be based on climate, health care, food, transportation, natural resources, technology, or other aspects of the nation's economy.

5. Foreign governments often take actions to protect companies in their own country. These trade barriers might include tariffs, import quotas, taxes, and other restrictions. Discuss an existing or potential trade barrier for the country you have researched.

© Getty Images/PhotoDisc

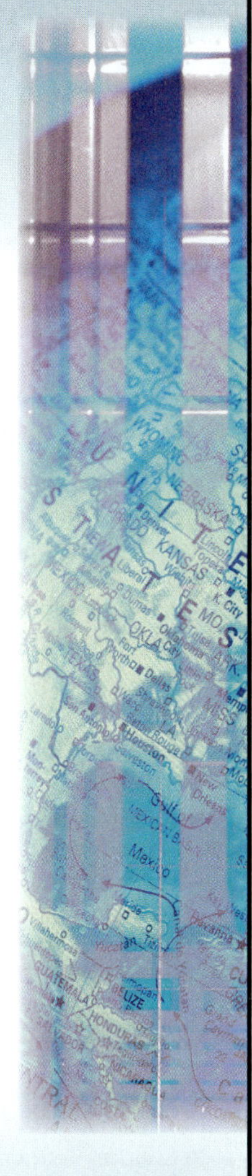

Present

1. Prepare a portfolio (folder, file, or notebook) to store the information and materials you created in the activities above.

2. Create a poster (or other visual display) conveying the main points of a business idea (product or service) that could be sold in other countries. Highlight how the business opportunity was created and what needs or wants will be satisfied.

3. Interview a person who has lived in or traveled to another country. Ask questions related to the culture, food, leisure, customs, holidays, and business activities unique to the nation. Ask the person for permission to tape (audio or video) the interview.

UNIT 2 BUSINESS ORGANIZATION AND MANAGEMENT	OVERVIEW	SPECIAL FEATURES	LESSON ASSESSMENT	
Chapter 5 Business Organization, pp. 100–123	Chapter 5 examines the forms of business ownership and the role of each in the U.S. economy.	Business Improving Society: Electricity Where There Was None, p. 119; Focus on Real Life, pp. 102, 108, 115; FYI, pp. 111, 116; Life-Span Plan, p. 108; Net Bookmark, p. 103; Planning a Career in Corporate Leadership, p. 101; Sharpen Your Life Skills: Understanding Stock Tables, p. 114; Technology in Action: Expanding E-Government, p. 105; Winning Edge BPA: Prepared Speech Event, p. 123; Work as a Team, pp. 105, 110, 118	Checkpoints, pp. 103, 106, 107, 109, 112, 113, 117, 118 Key Concepts, Make Academic Connections, pp. 107, 113, 118	
Chapter 6 Entrepreneurship and Small Business Management, pp. 124–147	Chapter 6 describes the role that small business plays in the U.S. economy and how to start and manage a small business.	Corporate Social Responsibility: Global Social Responsibility, p. 142; Focus on Real Life, pp. 126, 132, 138; FYI, pp. 133, 143; Life-Span Plan, p. 128, 138; Net Bookmark, p. 127; Planning a Career in Consulting, p. 125; Sharpen Your Life Skills: Writing with Technology, p. 137; Winning Edge FBLA: American Enterprise Project, p. 147; Work as a Team, pp. 130, 135, 139	Checkpoints, pp. 129, 131, 134, 135, 136, 140, 141, 143 Key Concepts, Make Academic Connections, pp. 131, 136, 143	
Chapter 7 Management and Leadership, pp. 148–171	In Chapter 7, students learn about the role of management in organizational success, the activities managers complete, and how leadership differs from management.	Doing Business in South Africa, p. 155; Focus on Real Life, pp. 150, 156, 163; FYI, pp. 152, 157; Life-Span Plan, p. 157; Net Bookmark, p. 164; Planning a Career in Management, p. 149; A Question of Ethics: Where Are the Jobs?, p. 166; Technology in Action: Assistive Technology for Disabilities, p. 159; Winning Edge FBLA: Partnership with Business Project, p. 171; Work as a Team, pp. 151, 159, 166	Checkpoints, pp. 151, 152, 154, 158, 160, 162, 165, 167 Key Concepts, Make Academic Connections, pp. 154, 162, 167	
Chapter 8 Human Resources, Culture, and Diversity, pp. 172–199	In Chapter 8, students learn about the role and importance of human resources and how to manage a diverse workforce and an effective organizational culture.	Business Improving Society: Coffee and a Conscience, p. 195; Corporate Social Responsibility: What About Corporate Profits?, p. 182; Focus on Real Life, pp. 174, 180, 187; FYI, pp. 184, 188; Life-Span Plan, p. 176, 189; Net Bookmark, p. 190; Planning a Career in Human Resources, p. 173; Winning Edge FBLA: Emerging Business Issues Event, p. 199; Work as a Team, pp. 176, 189, 192	Checkpoints, pp. 177, 179, 183, 184, 186, 191, 194 Key Concepts, Make Academic Connections, pp. 179, 186, 194	
Chapter 9 Career Planning and Development, pp. 200–229	In Chapter 9, students study the variety of career opportunities in business and learn how to prepare a career plan and apply for a job.	Doing Business in Ukraine, p. 207; Focus on Real Life, pp. 202, 208, 215, 221; FYI, pp. 212, 222; Life-Span Plan, pp. 203, 209, 217; Net Bookmark, p. 204; Planning a Career in Employment Assistance, p. 201; A Question of Ethics: Discriminatory Hiring Practices, p. 210; Sharpen Your Life Skills: Effective Presentations, p. 214; Winning Edge FBLA: Job Interview Event, p. 229; Work as a Team, pp. 205, 209, 219, 223	Checkpoints, pp. 203, 205, 206, 210, 211, 213, 218, 219, 220, 223, 225 Key Concepts, Make Academic Connections, pp. 206, 213, 220, 225	

CHAPTER ASSESSMENT	TEACHING RESOURCES	TEACHING STRATEGIES
Business Notes, Communicate Business Concepts, Develop Your Business Language, Decision-Making Strategies, Make Academic Connections, Linking School and Community, Web Workout, pp. 120–123	*Activities and Study Guide,* Ch. 5 *Chapter and Unit Tests,* Ch. 5 *Spanish Resources,* Ch. 5 **Exam***View*® CD, Ch. 5 *Instructor's Resource CD* *Xtra! Web Site*	**Applied Skills** Building Study Skills, p. 112; Language Arts, p. 115; Technology, pp. 114, 117; Writing Across the Curriculum, p. 108 **Different Learning Abilities** At-Risk, p. 106; Attention Deficit Disorder, p. 116; Gifted, p. 110; Specific Learning Disability, p. 111; Visually Impaired, p. 105 **Different Learning Styles** Kinesthetic Learner, p. 103; Visual Learner, pp. 102, 109 **Teaching Strategies** Collaborative Learning, p. 104; Expand Beyond the Classroom, p. 119
Business Notes, Communicate Business Concepts, Develop Your Business Language, Decision-Making Strategies, Make Academic Connections, Linking School and Community, Web Workout, pp. 144–147	*Activities and Study Guide,* Ch. 6 *Chapter and Unit Tests,* Ch. 6 *Spanish Resources,* Ch. 6 **Exam***View*® CD, Ch. 6 *Instructor's Resource CD* *Xtra! Web Site*	**Applied Skills** Communication, pp. 128, 137; Language Arts, p. 139; Mathematics, p. 133; Word Processing/Office Technology, p. 134; Writing Across the Curriculum, p. 141 **Different Learning Abilities** Attention Deficit Disorder, p. 132; Dyslexia, p. 130; Gifted, p. 129; Limited English Proficiency, p. 126; Specific Learning Disability, p. 142; Visually Impaired, p. 140 **Different Learning Styles** Kinesthetic Learner, pp. 135, 138; Visual Learner, p. 127
Business Notes, Communicate Business Concepts, Develop Your Business Language, Decision-Making Strategies, Make Academic Connections, Linking School and Community, Web Workout, pp. 168–171	*Activities and Study Guide,* Ch. 7 *Chapter and Unit Tests*, Ch. 7 *Spanish Resources,* Ch. 7 **Exam***View*® CD, Ch. 7 *Instructor's Resource CD* *Xtra! Web Site*	**Applied Skill**s Building Study Skills, p. 152; Language Arts, p. 156; Mathematics, p. 166; Word Processing/Office Technology, p. 165; Writing Across the Curriculum, p. 160 **Different Learning Abilities** At-Risk, p. 158; Attention Deficit Disorder, p. 151; Gifted, p. 159; Limited English Proficiency, pp. 150, 163 **Different Learning Styles** Tactile Learner, p. 155; Visual Learner, p. 157 **Teaching Strategies** Collaborative Learning, p. 161; Expand Beyond the Classroom, pp. 153, 164
Business Notes, Communicate Business Concepts, Develop Your Business Language, Decision-Making Strategies, Make Academic Connections, Linking School and Community, Web Workout, pp. 196–199	*Activities and Study Guide,* Ch. 8 *Chapter and Unit Tests,* Ch. 8 *Spanish Resources,* Ch. 8 **Exam***View*® CD, Ch. 8 *Instructor's Resource CD* *Xtra! Web Site*	**Applied Skills** Building Study Skills, p. 184; Communication, pp. 178, 192; Language Arts, p. 182; Mathematics, p. 180; Technology, p. 191 **Different Learning Abilities** At-Risk, p. 177; Gifted, p. 190; Limited English Proficiency, p. 183; Specific Learning Disability, p. 176; Visually Impaired, pp. 175, 189 **Different Learning Styles** Kinesthetic Learner, p. 185; Tactile Learner, p. 188; Visual Learner, p. 187 **Teaching Strategies** Collaborative Learning, p. 181; Expand Beyond the Classroom, pp. 174, 193
Business Notes, Communicate Business Concepts, Develop Your Business Language, Decision-Making Strategies, Make Academic Connections, Linking School and Community, Web Workout, pp. 226–229	*Activities and Study Guide,* Ch. 9 *Chapter and Unit Tests,* Ch. 9 *Spanish Resources*, Ch. 9 **Exam***View*® CD, Ch. 9 *Instructor's Resource CD* *Xtra! Web Site*	**Applied Skills** Building Study Skills, p. 223; Communication, pp. 212, 222; Geography, p. 207; Mathematics, p. 209; Technology, p. 211; Word Processing/Office Technology, p. 217; Writing Across the Curriculum, p. 219 **Different Learning Abilities** At-Risk, pp. 208, 218; Attention Deficit Disorder, p. 202; Dyslexia, p. 216; Hearing Impaired, p. 221; Limited English Proficiency, p. 210 **Different Learning Style**s Auditory Learner, p. 205; Kinesthetic Learner, p. 215; Print Learner, p. 203 **Teaching Strategies** Expand Beyond the Classroom, pp. 204, 214, 224

Business Organization and Management

The chapters in this unit describe various forms of business ownership and organization, the role and work of management, and how to undertake career planning.

Chapter 5 Business Organization This chapter focuses on the major forms of business ownership in the United States and the role each plays in the economy.

Chapter 6

Entrepreneurship and Small Business Management The chapter helps students develop an understanding of the steps in starting a new business and the characteristics of entrepreneurs.

Chapter 7 Management and Leadership The chapter presents information on the major activities common to all managers and how to be an effective leader.

Chapter 8 Human Resources, Culture, and Diversity This chapter describes the important role of human resources in businesses and ways to build a positive and diverse work environment.

Chapter 9 Career Planning and Development In this chapter students study the variety of career opportunities in business and learn how to prepare a career plan and apply for and secure a job.

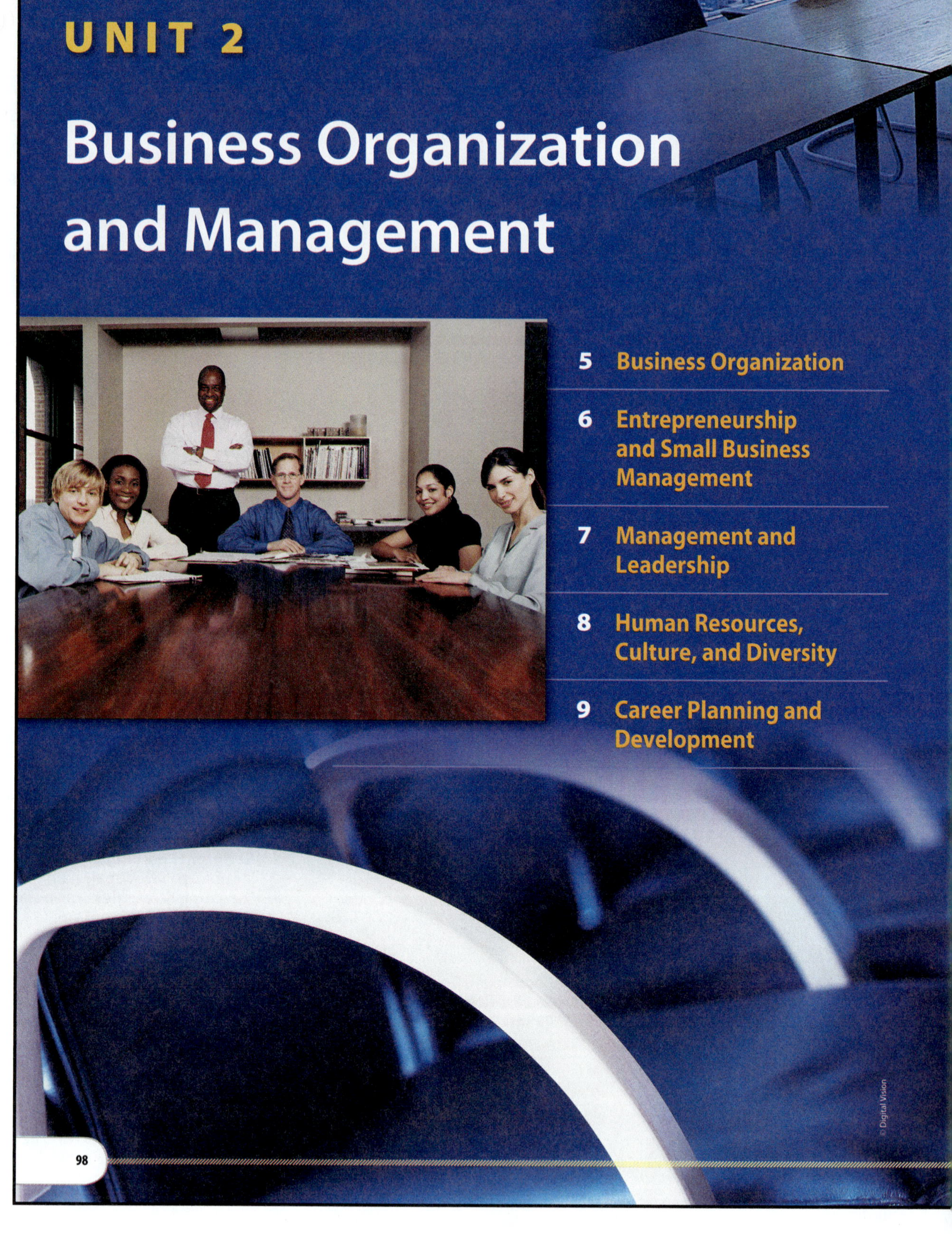

UNIT 2

Business Organization and Management

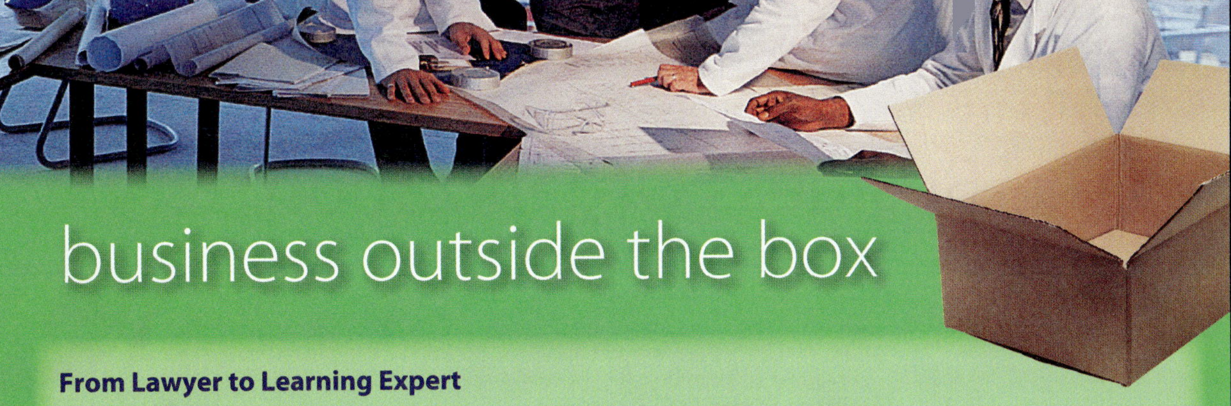

business outside the box

From Lawyer to Learning Expert

Trained as a lawyer, Gene Wade realized the importance of education. Today, his emphasis is in the classroom instead of the courtroom. Wade is the head of Platform Learning, a tutoring service that assists more than 50,000 underprivileged students each year. The company, based in New York City, makes use of "Learn-to-Succeed" tutoring. The program brings together parents, schools, community organizations, and local educators. These groups combine to provide appropriate motivation and teaching materials for individual student needs.

Wade has had a strong influence on the lives of many young people who come from difficult situations. Wade was raised in a Boston housing project laced with gang activity. He was an average student who was helped by a community youth leadership program. After achieving success as a lawyer, Wade was drawn to helping students. Wade's Platform Learning organization tutors students in 18 states to "Believe… Achieve… Succeed." The young people gain confidence, improve academic skills, and gain a foundation for lifelong learning.

Think Critically

What are needs in your community that could result in a business for improving people's lives?

Comfortable and Profitable

A product you create for yourself can result in a company with more than $100 million in sales. That's exactly what happened for Karen Neuburger. She was a stay-at-home mom who wanted to avoid being part of a major corporation. A former fashion industry executive, Karen created comfortable, oversized pajamas for herself to wear around the house. She then realized others might also want this product. Now, Karen is CEO of Karen Neuburger, a company that specializes in pajamas, pillows, socks, and other comfort products. Her products are sold in more than 10,000 outlets around the world.

Karen started her career in the fashion and clothing business as a buyer at Maurice's, a small women's clothing store in Minnesota. Then, she became a merchandise manager as the company grew into a 700-store chain. After moving to the San Francisco area, she began her pajama business. She designed a pair for herself based on her husband's pajamas. Karen sewed a pair of ultra soft, comfortable, fun pj's to wear around the house. Soon her friends at Macy's and Nordstrom were asking for the product. Karen maintains strong enthusiasm for her products. This helps convince others to carry them in their stores.

Think Critically

What are your ideas for a product or service that could be the basis for a start-up company?

---

business outside the box

After reading Business Outside the Box, ask students what they think about the topics. Have they heard or read about these topics before? At the conclusion of the discussion, direct students to answer the Think Critically questions that follow the features.

From Lawyer to Learning Expert

Ask students what values Mr. Wade demonstrated when he made the decision to give up his successful law career to help underprivileged students succeed through learning.

Think Critically *Answer*
Answers will vary. For example, students might identify the need for convenient banking, shopping, transportation, recreation, and social services.

Comfortable and Profitable

Have students discuss how Ms. Neuburger's experience may have helped her start a successful business. She was a fashion buyer, manager of a large chain store, and a stay-at-home mom.

Think Critically *Answer*
Answers will vary. For example, students might be interested in developing a hobby or interest into a business.

Portfolio Activity

Portfolio work samples validate skill level and a student's ability to accomplish tasks frequently performed on the job. The most important reason for including samples in a portfolio is to demonstrate a student's abilities and skills. In selecting work samples for each unit, students should always have a choice of which activities to include. Students might be encouraged to include samples from the end-of-chapter activities, particularly Communicate Business Concepts, Decision-Making Strategies, Make Academic Connections, and Linking School and Community.

Business Organization

CHAPTER OVERVIEW

The chapter examines the forms of business ownership and the role of each in the U.S. economy.

5-1   Business in the U.S. Economy

This lesson describes changes that have occurred in U.S. employment and changes in the types and numbers of businesses.

5-2   Forms of Business Ownership

This lesson introduces the major forms of business ownership and outlines the strengths and limitations of each.

5-3   Organizational Structure for Businesses

The lesson provides information on how to organize effective businesses and alternative structures for businesses.

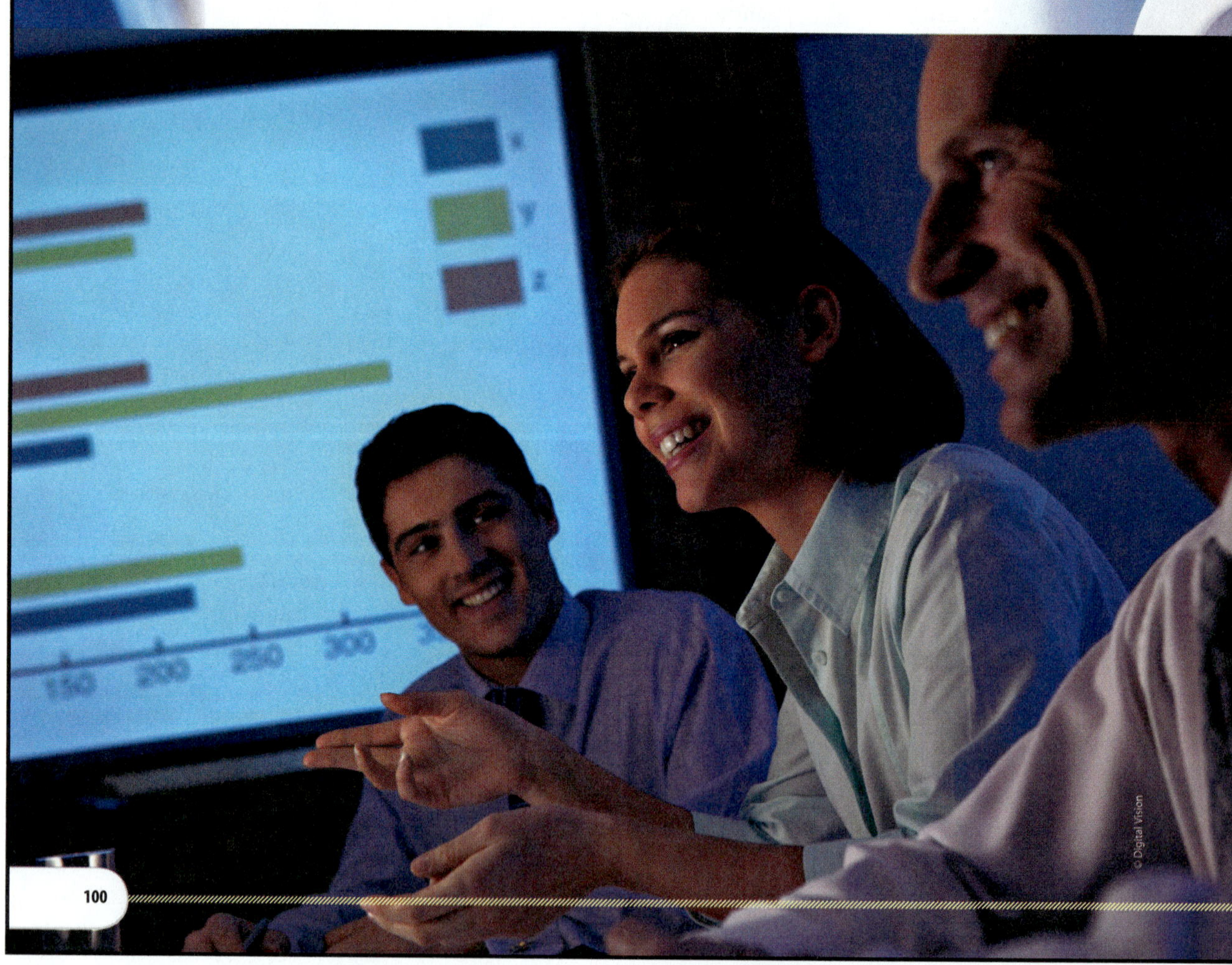

Teaching Resources

Activities and Study Guide, Ch. 5
Chapter and Unit Tests, Ch. 5
Spanish Resources, Ch. 5

ExamView® *CD,* Ch. 5
Instructor's Resource CD
- PowerPoint Slides, Ch. 5
- Lesson Plans, Ch. 5

Xtra! Web Site

school.cengage.com/business/introtobiz
- Study Tools, 5-1, 5-2, 5-3
- Quiz Prep, Ch. 5
- Net Bookmark, Ch. 5
- Crossword Puzzle, Ch. 5
- Portfolio Activity, Ch.5

CORPORATE LEADERSHIP

Rising to the top of one of the world's largest corporations seems like the dream job in business. The chief executive officer (CEO) of a corporation may make several million dollars a year in salary and bonuses, have a large office with dozens of support staff, travel worldwide on a corporate jet, and make daily decisions that directly influence the success of the company. Corporate executives also work long hours and face the competing expectations of stockholders, the board of directors, employees, and customers. While they receive many perks and benefits, their success or failure may be determined more by economic conditions, government regulation, and the stock market than their own decisions and abilities.

A corporation's goals and policies are established by the top executives. The executives meet frequently to set direction, review company performance, and establish policy. They then delegate work to the organization's managers and employees. They know that they are ultimately responsible and accountable for the performance of the company.

Employment Outlook

- There are about 3 million top executive positions in business today, with the greatest opportunities in the fastest growing industries including service businesses, communications, technology, and health care.

- Corporations are constantly looking for skilled and creative executives to lead their businesses. However, most top executive positions are filled by people who have many years of experience in the industry and a successful management track record.

Related Job Titles

- Chief Executive Officer
- Chief Operating Officer
- President

Needed Skills

- Corporate executives have varied backgrounds, but often are skilled in finance, management, and business operations.

- Executives must study large amounts of information, listen carefully to the ideas and opinions of others, and juggle many activities.

- They must be willing to take risks, handle stress, and be decisive.

- Executives need highly developed public relations and speaking skills as well as the ability to interact effectively with individuals and groups in high pressure situations.

What's it like to work as a… Corporate Executive

The schedule of a CEO is packed most days. It may start with an hour of reading before attending a conference with the heads of other companies and government officials. Lunch is with the management team to review the company's financial performance, followed by a press conference. Two hours are spent on the telephone talking to a senator about a telecommunications law, discussing labor contract negotiations with the vice president of human resources, and speaking with a manufacturer in Japan about a proposed joint venture. After a workout at the executive gym and a quick dinner, it is off to the airport for a flight to Brazil to oversee the opening of a new manufacturing facility. The flight will be spent studying reports, completing correspondence, and watching a videotaped briefing on Brazil's economy.

What about you? How would you prepare for the stress of being a corporate executive? Do you believe that the work justifies the high salary and benefits?

The life of a corporate executive can seem glamorous and exciting. Along with the glamour goes immense responsibilities and challenges, as well as long hours and varied duties. It takes both education and years of experience to become the top leader of a business.

What About You? Answers

Answers will vary, but could include discussion of the need for a broad range of experience and years spent at lower levels in an organization.

Additional Career Information

Additional information on careers can be found in the *Occupational Outlook Handbook,* an online publication (www.bls.gov/oco) of the federal government. Tell your class about this resource and how to use it. This description of job duties can be used to demonstrate the relevancy of skills learned in this course.

TEACH

Ask students whether they believe the jobs that interest them today will be available in 10 years. As young people begin career planning, they need to pay attention to the types of jobs that are increasing and declining.

Have students identify any information in the section on employment data that surprises them. Ask them to discuss how employment changes have affected employers.

THINK CRITICALLY THROUGH VISUALS

Over the next decade, the average age of U.S. workers will increase, and there will be a mini-boom of younger workers aged 20–30. Also, the percentage of white workers will decrease, and the percentage of women in the workforce will increase.

5-1 Business in the U.S. Economy

Goals

Describe the changing status of U.S. employment.

Discuss the role of business in the U.S. economy.

Describe three major types of businesses.

Key Terms

contingent worker

intermediary

service business

Focus on Real Life

Sami Rehm loves digital photography. Last year she bought a professional-quality camera with several lenses. She has become very good at using photo editing software. While Sami's photography is currently a hobby, she has framed and sold several of her photographs at local art shows.

Sami has started to wonder if she might be able to use her interest and skills in photography for a career. She knows newspapers, magazines, advertising agencies, and other businesses use photographers. She also knows that people have their own photography studios.

Sami expressed her feelings to her mother. "I know I love photography now. Would I like it as much if I did it every day as a job? I wonder what training and skill a business expects when they hire a photographer?"

---

main idea

Describe the changing status of U.S. employment.

THE CHANGING U.S. JOB MARKET

As the 21st century begins, there are striking changes in employment and careers in the United States. The beginning of the 21st century saw many new career prospects in the dot-com world. It also saw the decline of some traditionally important jobs in manufacturing and agriculture.

Employment Data

From 1996 to 2006 total employment grew by nearly 14 percent. In 2007, 144 million people held jobs. That number is projected to reach 165 million by 2014, an increase of almost 13 percent.

The term "baby boomers" refers to the large number of people born between 1946 and 1964. They have dominated the labor market since they began working in the 1960s. They will continue to do so until they begin retiring in the 2010s. The average age of U.S. workers in 2020 will be over 50. A mini-boom of younger workers will cause the 20- to 30-year-old age group to grow faster than the overall labor force for the first time in 25 years. Other groups that will go through higher employment growth rates are Asian-, Hispanic-, and African-American workers. Currently, white non-Hispanic workers make

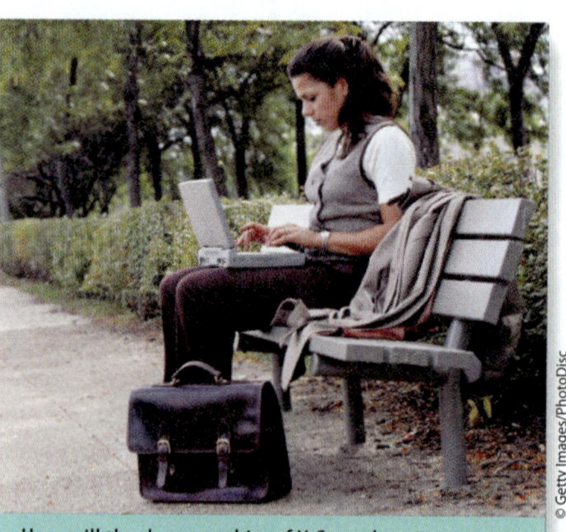

How will the demographics of U.S. workers change over the next decade?

Different Learning Styles

Visual Learner Have students search through magazines and newspapers to locate photographs that illustrate the changes in the workforce described in the chapter. If possible, they should clip or copy the picture and create a photo essay, poster, or collage that visually illustrates the changes.

up 70 percent of the labor force. That number will drop to 66 percent by 2014. Over the last 50 years, one of the most striking trends in employment has been the participation of women. In the early 1960s, 35 percent of women were working outside the home. The number of working women doubled by 2000. By 2014 nearly one half of all jobs (47 percent) in the United States will be held by women.

Pressures on Employees

At one time, it was thought that technology would allow people to work fewer hours. This has not occurred. Economic stress has led to downsizing of the number of people employed by many companies. Companies streamlined production and implemented other cost-cutting procedures. Businesses required employees to take on new tasks and work extra hours. Some full-time jobs were reduced to part-time. Wage rates decreased. Many people were forced to find second jobs to meet their economic needs.

A recent survey reported that 7 of 10 parents felt they were not able to spend enough time with their children. At the same time, children see their parents changing jobs, taking on more responsibility, completing additional education to improve career opportunities, and making important decisions to balance work and family life. Those experiences will likely shape the career and family decisions of the next generation.

Economic pressures also resulted in the increased use of contingent workers. A **contingent worker** is one who has no explicit or implicit contract for long-term employment. About 5 percent of the U.S. workforce (nearly 6 million people) is made up of contingent workers. Some estimates project that number will double in 10 years. Some people take contingent work because they cannot find permanent employment. Others choose contingent work because they like the flexibility it offers.

checkpoint >>
List several groups that will increase as a percentage of the total U.S. workforce in the next decade.

BUSINESS AND THE ECONOMY

Businesses make the goods and services you use each day. That includes the products and services used by other businesses as well as those needed by individual consumers. In 2002, all businesses worldwide produced more than $40 trillion of goods and services. U.S. businesses were responsible for almost 29 percent of that production. Nearly 24 million full- and part-time businesses produce those goods and services.

Size of Businesses

Most U.S. businesses are quite small. The largest number, nearly 19.5 million businesses, have no employees other than the owner. About 4.5 million companies employ less than 20 people. Just over 26,000 employ 20–100 people. About 107,000 large U.S. businesses employ 100 or more workers. Of those large companies, 890 employ more than 10,000 people. Figure 5-1 shows the distribution of U.S. businesses by employment size.

main idea

Discuss the role of business in the U.S. economy.

TEACH

Ask students whether they believe today's workers have more or fewer pressures on them than workers in the past. Have them identify the work, family, and personal pressures that can affect employees.

ONGOING ASSESSMENT

checkpoint >> **ANSWER**

Younger workers (16–24 years of age); Asian-, Hispanic-, African-American groups; and women will compose larger percentages of the workforce in the next decade.

TEACH

Before students read the information, ask them whether they believe that most U.S. businesses are large or small. Have them guess the average number of employees that work for most businesses. Then have them read the paragraph and ask for their reactions.

Different Learning Styles

Kinesthetic Learner Have students write $40 trillion numerically on the board or a piece of paper. Then have them determine what 29 percent of that amount is and write that number, describing the total of U.S. business production.

The numbers are: $40,000,000,000,000
$11,600,000,000,000

Roles of Business

Businesses play several key roles in the U.S. economy. They provide employment for millions of people. Employee wages are used to purchase goods and services. Profits earned by businesses are used to compensate owners and investors. Most businesses pay taxes to federal, state, and local governments. Governments spend these taxes to provide services such as clean water, well-maintained streets, police and fire protection, hospitals, and schools.

The most important role of businesses is to make and distribute products and services needed by consumers, government, and other businesses. Businesses make the clothing, movies, music, food, and other items you use every day.

Impact on a Community

A business can have an important impact on the community in which it operates. When a new business opens, it pays wages to its workers. It also buys goods and services from other businesses in the area. This money has not been in the community before. Employees and businesses in turn spend much of the money to purchase things they need.

The money spent may result in the need for more employees in the community. They will need housing, automobiles, food, and entertainment. They will pay taxes to the community to support needed community services.

When a large business opens in an area, other businesses will often locate there to support the larger business. Small businesses may be started to meet the needs of the residents and other businesses. Successful businesses contribute to more jobs, more income, and a thriving economy in the communities where they operate.

Business Activities

Businesses may be large or small, simple or complex. A business might operate in only one community. It may have many

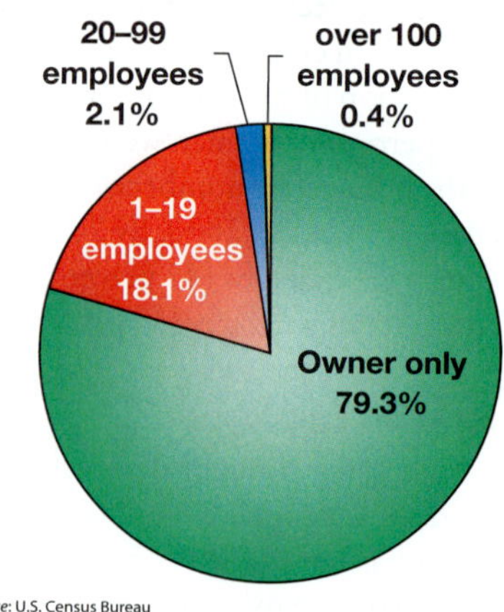

Source: U.S. Census Bureau

FIGURE 5-1

Would you prefer to work in a large or small business? Explain your answer.

locations across the nation or around the world. Although there are many types and sizes of businesses, all firms perform six basic activities.

Generating Ideas A business begins with a new idea. Someone must have an idea for a new product or service or a new way to carry out a business process. A business must continue to improve and develop new ideas in order to remain successful. Businesses must remain competitive with other firms that sell similar goods and services. Many companies have a research and development department that works full-time to discover new product, service, and operating ideas.

Raising Capital Businesses need financial resources to operate. They use these financial resources to buy buildings and equipment, hire and train workers, and complete day-to-day business operations. A large amount of capital is needed to start most businesses. Some capital comes from owners. Most is obtained through loans from financial institutions or from investors.

A business needs more capital as it develops and grows. Some of that capital

Teaching Strategies

Collaborative Learning Divide the class into several three- to four-person teams. Ask each team to identify an industry that they would like to study. The team should use the Internet to identify the five largest U.S. and international businesses in their industry based on the number of employees and develop a chart to present their findings.

will come from reinvested profits. A business will need to continue to work with banks and attract additional investors to have enough money for ongoing operations.

Employing and Training Personnel

Businesses need human resources. Even businesses that begin with no employees other than the owner will add part- and full-time employees as they grow. Businesses have procedures for recruiting, hiring, and training employees. They pay wages, benefits, and employment taxes. New employees receive training in order to perform their jobs correctly. Further training will be necessary when procedures change, new tasks are added, or technology is introduced.

Buying Goods and Services All businesses buy goods and services. Businesses use many of the purchases for their own operations. Other purchases are resold. Manufacturers of automobiles must buy steel, aluminum, and plastics to be used to form the frame and body of new cars. They will also purchase tires, batteries, airbags, and air conditioning units that will be installed on the production line.

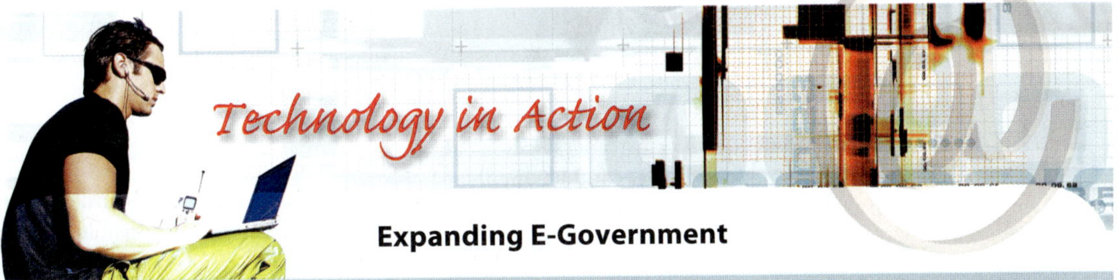

Technology in Action

Expanding E-Government

Computers have a major impact on the way government operates. Offering services online has become the goal of most agencies. Rather than going to a government office to pick up a form, apply for a license, or make a payment, people can complete many of these activities online.

In a study of the development of e-government services around the world, the United Nations has identified the following five stages:

Emerging Official government online presence established

Enhanced Number of sites increase and become more interesting and useful

Interactive Users can download forms, e-mail officials, and interact through the Web

Transactional Users can complete transactions and pay for services online

Seamless Full integration of information and services across agencies—one-stop service

By 2003, the U.S. government had 22,000 web sites with more than 186 million web pages. Annual spending by the federal government for information technology services is more than $50 billion. More than 60 percent of all Internet users interact with the federal government through its web sites. Moving government services to the Internet may result in more than 1 billion dollars of savings each year.

Two major barriers stand in the way of the development of e-government. Most important is privacy and security of the personal information contained in government records and submitted by citizens. That information includes tax records, medical histories, and personal information such as driver's license and social security numbers. The second barrier is the unequal access to technology. Thousands of citizens do not have secure high-speed Internet connections. Others do not have the literacy or computer skills to use online government services.

Think Critically

1. Search the Web and identify government services provided by your local and state governments. What stage of development is demonstrated by the web sites you visited?
2. What can governments do to reduce the barriers of privacy, security, and citizen access to e-government services?

Different Learning Abilities

Visually Impaired Help students to locate government web sites and services that have been developed to effectively accommodate citizens with visual impairments. Have them report on the accommodations that have been made and any ways they believe further accommodation could be provided.

After students have discussed the question and developed their lists, ask them whether their decision might be different based on the type of business or whether the business was new or well established.

TEACH

List the six basic business activities on the board. As you introduce each one, ask students to think about two questions: How does the activity contribute to business success? If the activity is not done well, what problems might result? Discuss students' answers to the questions.

Technology in Action

Explain to students that government agencies and offices often cite two reasons for their increased use of the Internet—savings in the cost of offering the services and time savings for citizens. Yet these services are often very complex, and not all citizens want to use or have easy access to the Internet.

Think Critically Answers

1. Answers will vary depending on the web sites visited. Consider asking volunteers to showcase examples of web sites that fit into the various stages.

2. To overcome privacy and security barriers, governments can utilize strong encryption on their sites. Access and help with computer skills can be provided in government agency locations and in libraries.

A retailer buys an assortment of products to sell to customers. It must also buy the display equipment, computers, and cleaning supplies used to operate the business. Businesses purchase an array of services from other companies. These include advertising, legal and accounting services, lawn care and building maintenance, and security.

Marketing Goods and Services Marketing refers to the activities directed at providing the goods and services wanted by a business's customers. Without marketing, even the best products and services may remain unsold. Businesses need to understand and perform many marketing activities. They must satisfy customers who usually can choose to buy from competitors offering similar products and services.

Maintaining Business Records All businesses must have some type of record-keeping system. Owners and managers need records to track performance and make decisions. Customers need information about orders and payments. Businesses are required by government to keep records and submit information.

main idea

Describe three major types of businesses.

How does marketing affect a consumer's decision to purchase a product?

Today, technology is available to make record keeping easy and accurate. With computer technology, business owners and employees can quickly access information needed to understand business performance and solve problems.

checkpoint >>

What are the six basic activities completed by all businesses?

TYPES OF BUSINESSES

You, your family, and your friends use a variety of businesses to buy the things you want and need. You recognize other businesses but never use them. And, you don't even know about many others. There are three major categories—producers, intermediaries, and service businesses.

Producers

Producers create the products and services used by individuals and other businesses. They are responsible for using resources to make something that is needed by others. A business that takes resources from nature for direct consumption or for use in developing other products is an *extractor*. Extractors pump oil, mine coal, or cut timber. *Farmers* cultivate land and use other natural resources to grow crops and raise livestock for consumption. *Manufacturers* get supplies from other producers and convert them into products. They sell their products to consumers and other businesses.

Business activities start with producers. A builder obtains lumber, cement, shingles, carpet, and paint to construct a house, factory, or office building. A cereal manufacturer buys wheat and oats,

---

sugar, and dried fruit as well as cardboard, glue, and ink to process and package your favorite breakfast food.

Intermediaries

Intermediaries are businesses involved in selling the goods and services of producers to consumers and other businesses. The most common types of intermediaries are retailers and wholesalers. Many other businesses focus on one or a few activities that assist in distributing and selling products and services. Specialized intermediaries include transportation companies, advertising agencies, storage centers, sales offices, and data processing centers.

Service Businesses

Many businesses do not make products. They offer something that is intangible, meaning it has no physical qualities. A **service business** carries out activities that are consumed by its customers. It does not offer products for sale. Service businesses include dentists, physicians, and lawyers as well as pet sitters, painters, and furniture movers. New types of service businesses are Internet service providers, web designers, and online travel agents. Businesses as well as final consumers use services. A business might contact an international trade specialist to help it set up a sale to a new customer in Africa. A communications firm could design and install a new phone system for large telemarketing businesses.

Service businesses are the fastest growing part of the economy. More than 60 percent of all U.S. employment is now in service-producing businesses. While you often hear about low-pay and low-skill service jobs, there are many new businesses offering professional and technical services requiring highly educated employees.

checkpoint >>

How does a manufacturer differ from an extractor?

5-1 Assessment

Key Concepts

Determine the best answer.

1. The largest number of U.S. businesses employ
   a. more than 100 people
   b. between 50 and 100 people
   c. between 10 and 20 people
   d. no employees other than the owner

2. Which of the following is *not* one of the common activities of all businesses?
   a. producing goods and services
   b. employing and training personnel
   c. marketing goods and services
   d. maintaining business records

3. A retailer is an example of a(n)
   a. extractor
   b. producer
   c. intermediary
   d. service business

Make Academic Connections

4. *Math* If 71 percent of all people working in the United States are employed in service occupations, how many people held service jobs in 2007? How many will hold service jobs in 2014 if the percentage increases to 64%? Use employment information from the lesson to make the calculations.

5. *Visual Arts* Select a product that involves all of the types of businesses in its production and marketing. Draw an illustration that shows each business and its role in the successful production and sale of the product. Title your illustration and label the component parts.

TEACH

Have students identify service businesses with which they are familiar. Encourage them to think about businesses that offer professional and technical services and employ a number of highly educated employees.

ONGOING ASSESSMENT

checkpoint >> **ANSWER**

An extractor takes natural resources, such as oil or timber, for direct consumption or for use in developing other products. A manufacturer takes resources supplied by others and converts them into useable products.

ASSESS

Key Concepts Answers

1. d. no employees other than the owner

2. a. producing goods and services

3. c. intermediary

Make Academic Connections

4. In 2007: 146 million × 71% = 103,660,000

   In 2014: 165 million × 79% = 130,350,000

5. Answers will vary depending on the product selected. Illustrations should depict the business and its role in the production and sale of the product.

CLOSE

Remind students that the business world and employment opportunities have changed a great deal in the lifetimes of their parents and grandparents. Ask them what changes they predict will occur in their lifetimes.

RETEACH

Ask students to write two ideas they learned from the lesson that help to describe the role of businesses in the U.S. economy. Have each student read his or her ideas. Discuss and clarify the ideas to ensure understanding.

ENRICH

Have students contact and interview the human resources director for a major company in your community. The interview should focus on the changes and challenges in employment facing the company. Have students record the interview if possible so others can listen to it.

5-2 Forms of Business Ownership

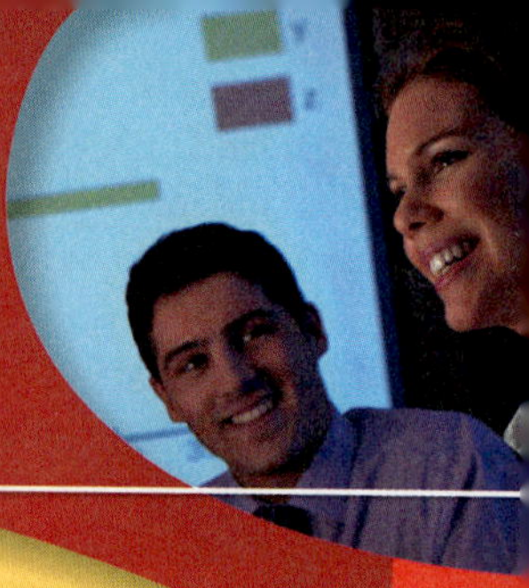

Goals

Understand the three major forms of business ownership.

Determine when each form of business ownership is most appropriate.

Recognize other specialized business ownership forms.

Key Terms

proprietorship

partnership

corporation

partnership agreement

articles of incorporation

franchise

Focus on Real Life

Jaden looked through the daily stock market update in the evening newspaper. He was searching for the listing of the stock he owned—GMS. His grandparents had given him five shares of stock in General Motors Corporation when he was born. He didn't get interested in it until recently when he learned more about the stock market. Now he knew he was an owner of the auto company. The success of the company determined the value of his ownership. While the stock price had gone up and down, it was now at its highest point since he began following the stock price.

While Jaden couldn't make day-to-day decisions as a stockholder, he liked to think what it would be like to be the top executive of GM. He knew that if he was responsible for major decisions about the company's products and operations, thousands of stockholders would be watching to see how those decisions affected the value of their stock.

main idea

Understand the three major forms of business ownership.

BUSINESS OWNERSHIP

Many people think they would like to own a business. The chance to be in control, make decisions, and invest money to make a profit is challenging and exciting. Thousands of people are business owners. The amount of control they have, how decisions are made, the sources of money for the business, and control over profits is not the same for every business owner. The form of ownership affects each of those aspects of the business.

There are three major forms of business ownership—proprietorship, partnership, and corporation. There are also several other specialized forms of ownership.

Proprietorship

A **proprietorship** is a business owned and run by just one person. It is the easiest form of business to start and end. There are very few legal requirements regarding the business ownership or capital needs that must be met.

What are the advantages and disadvantages of owning your own business?

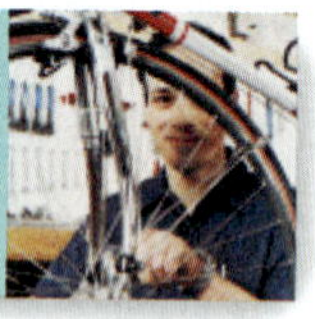

Applied Skills

Writing Across the Curriculum Have students prepare a paragraph that shows the connection between successful business ownership and what they are learning in another class they are currently taking.

Forms of Ownership Among U.S. Businesses				
FORM OF OWNERSHIP	**NUMBER OF BUSINESSES (2000)**	**TOTAL REVENUE (THOUSANDS)**	**PERCENT OF ALL BUSINESSES**	**PERCENT OF TOTAL REVENUE**
Proprietorship	18,925,517	$1,029,691,760	72%	5%
Corporation	5,266,607	19,749,426,052	20%	85%
Partnership	2,242,169	2,582,060,669	8%	11%

Source: Internal Revenue Service

FIGURE 5-2

Why are there so many proprietorships?

Many individuals like the proprietorship form of ownership. It gives them sole control over all business decisions. The owner receives all profits made by the business. He or she can determine how those profits are used. The owner is also responsible for all debts of the business. If the business fails, the owner has almost no shelter from creditors. Any money and other assets owned by the proprietor, whether used in the business or not, can be claimed by creditors to pay the business debts.

Partnership

A **partnership** is a business owned and controlled by two or more people who have entered into an agreement. A partnership is very similar to the proprietorship in several ways. It is quite easy to start. The owners are both responsible for key business decisions and functions. The partners share both investments and profits based on the terms of the partnership agreement. Each partner is liable for all of the debts of the business should it fail.

Corporation

A **corporation** is a separate legal entity formed by documents filed with a state. It is owned by one or more shareholders and managed by a board of directors. Most corporations have several owners who invest in the business by purchasing shares of stock. Corporations are more difficult to form than either proprietorships or partnerships. They must also meet more legal requirements. Not all owners have direct involvement in decision-making about business functions. They will not have access to profits unless the board of directors approves it. Corporations protect the liability of stockholders to only the amount of money they have invested.

Most U.S. businesses are organized as proprietorships. However, as shown in Figure 5-2, proprietorships have a very small percentage of business revenues.

> *checkpoint* >>
> What are the differences between the three main forms of business ownership?

CHOOSING A FORM OF BUSINESS OWNERSHIP

When a new business is started, the owner should carefully consider the form of ownership. While it is possible to change the form of ownership for an existing business, it is best to decide which form to use both for the long-term future of the business as well as for its first few years.

Choosing a Proprietorship

Most businesses begin as a proprietorship. They remain in that form for the life of the owner. Often people choose to start a

main idea

Determine when each form of business ownership is most appropriate.

TEACH

Tell students that, because starting a proprietorship is so easy, it often leads to busi-ness failure. Without careful thought and planning, the proprietor may not be well prepared for the challenges he or she will likely face.

THINK CRITICALLY THROUGH VISUALS

A partnership might be more advantageous than a propri-etorship because two owners can share the responsibilities and costs of the business, as well as combining their expertise.

business because they prefer the freedom of working for themselves rather than for another person. They want to be in total control of the business. Many new busi-ness owners have limited knowledge of the forms of ownership and want to begin the business as easily as possible. Some people form a business from a hobby or operate a business on a part-time basis. They may expand the business over a few years and spend little time thinking about other ways the business could be organized.

Starting a proprietorship is easy. You just have to begin buying and selling as a business. You don't even need a business name. You do need to obtain any required government licenses and permits. You will need to account for income and expenses and pay taxes on the profits of the business. If operating the business for several years will be your primary job, it is best to choose a name for the business. You will need to register the name with local, state, and federal governments.

A proprietorship provides a tax advan-tage for the owner. All income is taxed as a part of your personal income. Many business expenses can be used to reduce the income. That benefit also carries the most significant disadvantage of a propri-etorship. In the eyes of the law, the owner is the same as the business. Any debts of the business are the responsibility of the owner. Personal assets not connected to the business will need to be used to pay business debts if the business assets are not adequate to cover those debts. In that way, a failed business may result in the owner losing almost everything.

For people who want total independence, do not want to be exposed to significant government regulation, want to be in control of all business deci-sions, and are willing to take on the entire risk of a business, the proprietorship offers an effective form of ownership. For a person who wants to expand the business, is willing to share control and decision-making in return for additional resources and reduced risk, and wants some protection for money invested, other forms of ownership are better.

Choosing a Partnership

A partnership is a bit more complex and formal than a proprietorship. In many states, a partnership can be formed by the verbal agreement of two or more people. It is usually better to have a written partnership agreement. The **partnership agreement** is a written agreement among all owners. It details the rules and procedures that guide ownership and operations. It typically

How might a partnership be more advantageous than a proprietorship?

identifies the business name, the investments, and other contributions of each partner. The agreement shows how profits and losses will be divided among the partners. It defines the authority and responsibilities granted to each person and how the partnership can be dissolved. Most states require that partnerships register a business name as well as the name of each person in the partnership.

The advantage of a partnership is that two or more people can contribute to the investment needed to start the business as well as the expertise required to run a business. At the same time, each partner is responsible for decisions made by all other partners. There is no protection for the personal assets of any partner. If the business fails, each person can lose much more than the amount of the original investment. If a partner chooses to leave the partnership or dies, the partnership normally must be dissolved.

A partnership is a good ownership form for people who share an idea for a business. They want to cooperate in managing and investing in the business. It is the easiest form for people who work well together and want to share the risks and rewards of the business. It has the same liability of a proprietorship and presents problems if other people want to join the partnership or if it needs to be dissolved.

Choosing a Corporation

Most people think of corporations as very large businesses. It is the most popular form of ownership for large businesses. It is becoming increasingly popular for new and small businesses as well. Corporations are subject to many more laws and are more difficult to form than either proprietorships or partnerships. They offer a number of advantages to the owners as well.

FYI

Proprietors must pay self-employment taxes in addition to their income tax. Self-employment taxes are contributions to Medicare and Social Security. People employed by another business have those payments deducted from their paychecks, and employers contribute half of the required payments.

Corporations are treated as an "individual" by governments. They must follow the laws of the state in which they are organized. To form a corporation, you must file articles of incorporation with the appropriate state government office. The **articles of incorporation** is a written legal document that defines ownership and operating procedures and conditions for the business. Each state has specific information that must be included. States usually provide a form that can be filled out. The business must create *corporate bylaws* that are the operating procedures for the corporation. It must name a *board of directors,* the people who will make the major policy and financial decisions for the business. The corporation also issues shares of stock to the investors and details how more investments can be made.

Even though a corporation is more difficult to form and is subject to more government rules, it offers several advantages to owners. The liability of any owner is limited to the amount of money invested. The amount of debt of the business does not matter. People can invest in the business and receive some of the profit without having to take part in the day-to-day management and operations. The business can be easily expanded and ownership can be changed by the sale of stock.

Disadvantages of corporate ownership are that decision-making is shared among managers, the board of directors, and shareholders. Many more records

Most states have a relatively simple form that a small business can use to prepare the articles of incorporation for their business. Locate a copy from your state or an adjoining state and let students examine it to observe that it does not have to be a complex document.

Different Learning Abilities

Specific Learning Disability (SLD) Give students a business or telephone directory. Have them locate the name of a business that is clearly a partnership and another that is clearly a corporation. Have them write the name of each business and explain why each fits the correct category.

112

ONGOING ASSESSMENT

checkpoint >> **ANSWER**

The corporation is more complex to begin than other business forms. Forming a corporation requires much more bureaucracy, is more subject to government regulations, requires the organization of a board, and must have clearly defined bylaws.

TEACH

For each of the specialized forms of business ownership, ask students to identify why they believe it is necessary rather than using one of the traditional forms of ownership.

THINK CRITICALLY THROUGH VISUALS

Answers will vary. Encourage students to think about the businesses they frequent, organizations they have heard about, and services they use. Encourage volunteers to share their answers and create a master list on the board.

---

are required and more laws regulate operations than for other forms of ownership. Because corporations are treated as individuals by governments, they must pay corporate taxes on profits earned. Then the investors also pay taxes on their individual earnings from the business.

> *checkpoint* >>
> Which form of business ownership is the most complex and difficult to form?

main idea

Recognize other specialized business ownership forms.

OTHER FORMS OF OWNERSHIP

Most businesses are organized as one of the three common forms just discussed. There are other choices of ownership. Some are specialized forms of partnerships and corporations. Others are totally unique forms.

Specialized Partnerships and Corporations

In a general partnership, all partners take part in ownership and operation of the business. A *limited liability partnership* identifies some investors who cannot lose more than the amount of their investment, but they are not allowed to participate in the day-to-day management of the business. This type of partnership is difficult and costly to set up. A *joint venture* is a unique business organized by two or more other businesses to operate for a limited time and for a specific project. It is a type of partnership.

A corporate form that is favored by many small businesses is the

S-corporation. An *S-corporation* offers the limited liability of a corporation. All income is passed through to the owners based on their investment and is taxed on their individual tax returns. A newer ownership form is the limited liability company (LLC). It combines the best features of a partnership and a corporation. A *limited liability company* provides liability protection for owners. It has a simpler set of organizing and operating requirements than a corporation. No articles of incorporation or bylaws are needed. A simple document much like a partnership agreement must be developed.

A *nonprofit corporation* is a group of people who join to do some activity that benefits the public. They work in areas such as education, health care, charity, or the arts. Nonprofit corporations are free from corporate income taxes. They can raise funds by receiving grants and donations from individuals and businesses. As with other corporations, they must organize as a corporation. The government must approve their purpose and operations.

Cooperatives and Franchises

Sometimes a group of people forms a cooperative to provide goods and services

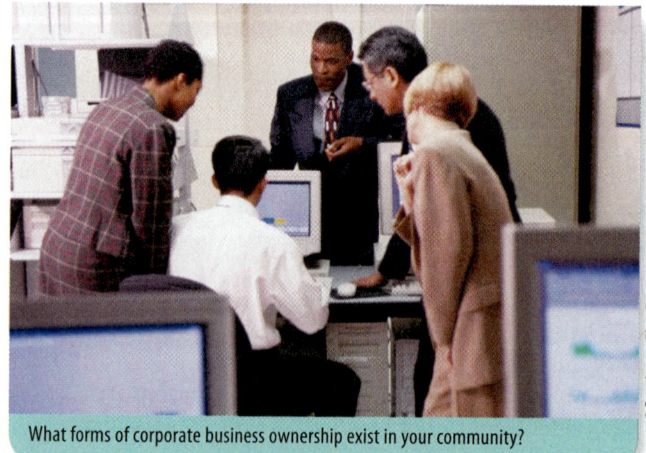

What forms of corporate business ownership exist in your community?

© Getty Images/PhotoDisc

Applied Skills

Building Study Skills Have students prepare an outline with each of the common and specialized forms of business ownership as a major heading. Ask them to prepare a study guide by listing the major features of each form under the appropriate heading. Consider allowing students to work in pairs.

that they all need. A *cooperative* is owned by members, serves their needs, and is managed in their interest. Members form a consumer cooperative so that they can purchase goods and services cheaper as a group than they could individually. A business cooperative forms to market the products produced by members or to purchase products needed by the members. Large numbers of small businesses will have greater bargaining power than the individual businesses.

A **franchise** is a written contract granting permission to operate a business to sell products and services in a set way. The company that owns the product or service and grants the rights to another business is known as the *franchiser*. The company purchasing the rights to run the business is the *franchisee*. A franchise is a way to expand a business using the investments of others while maintaining control over the name, product quality, and operating procedures.

The franchisee maintains day-to-day operations and receives the profits of the business. It pays a fee and percentage of the profits to the franchiser in return for operating assistance. Some popular and successful franchises include Jiffy Lube, Century 21 real estate offices, Mail Boxes Etc., Wild Birds Unlimited, Merry Maids, CD Warehouse, MAACO Collision Repair and Auto Painting, and New York NY Fresh Deli.

> *checkpoint* >>
> What are the other specialized forms of business ownership?

5-2 Assessment

Key Concepts

Determine the best answer.

1. The form of ownership that gives one person sole control over all business decisions is the
   a. proprietorship
   b. partnership
   c. corporation
   d. franchise

2. True or False. All investors in a general partnership have full liability for the debts of the business.

3. The people who make the major policy and financial decisions in a corporation are the
   a. investors
   b. board of directors
   c. managers
   d. owners

4. A special form of business organization that combines advantages of a corporation and a partnership is a
   a. franchise
   b. nonprofit corporation
   c. cooperative
   d. limited liability company

Make Academic Connections

5. **Communication** Two friends who want to open a store to sell the work of local artists ask you to explain the advantages and disadvantages of the three common forms of business ownership. Write a memo outlining the advantages and disadvantages. Include a list of questions that might help your friends make a decision.

6. **Research** Use the Internet to find information on a franchise opportunity related to a current career interest. Prepare a table that describes the franchise, the products or services, the investment requirements, and the benefits of becoming a franchisee.

TEACH

Ask students to use the telephone directory to identify any business and consumer cooperatives that operate in your community.

ONGOING ASSESSMENT

checkpoint >> **ANSWER**

Specialized forms of business ownership include limited liability partnership, joint venture, S-corporation, limited liability companies (LLC), and nonprofit corporations. Cooperatives and franchises could also be discussed here.

ASSESS

Key Concepts Answers

1. a. proprietorship
2. True
3. b. board of directors
4. d. limited liability company

Make Academic Connections

5. Memos will vary but should include the advantages and disadvantages mentioned in this lesson. The questions should reflect an understanding of how the forms of ownership differ.

6. Tables will vary depending on the franchise selected. Charts should include all the information listed in the instructions.

CLOSE

Ask students to write a brief description of the three common forms of business ownership without referring to the lesson or their notes. Have students read their answers aloud and compare them with those of other students.

RETEACH

Divide students into teams of three. Ask each team member to assume one of the roles of a business owner—a proprietor, a partner, and a corporate stockholder. The teams should prepare a short script and role-play a conversation about important advantages and disadvantages of each form of ownership.

ENRICH

Have students use the Internet to determine the percentage of businesses in your state by the number of employees. Have them prepare a chart of the results and present the information to other students. Data for this activity can be found at the U.S. Census Bureau web site. Choose the link for Economic Census and use the Reports by State feature.

113

Many people of all ages own shares of stock in companies. For those who do not, it is often because they do not understand how to evaluate and compare stocks. If you are comfortable with reading stock tables, you are more likely to want to be a stock owner.

Think Critically Answers

1. Answers will vary. A stock owner would likely find the Dividend Yield and the Closing Price to be most important and the 52 Week Hi-Lo to be least important.

2. Stock tables provide the Yield of the Dividend Paid information, which makes it easier to compare stocks with different prices.

Sharpen Your Life Skills

Understanding Stock Tables

Monday, October 23, 20xx			STOCK TABLE EXAMPLE					
52 WK HI-LO	SYM	DIV	VOL	YLD	PE	HI-LO	CLOSE	NET CHG
28–13	LZD	1.1	228	4.58	10.53	25–23.5	24	0.5

People who own stock in a publicly traded company must be able to read a stock table. It provides information on the performance of the stock each day and over an extended period of time. By understanding stock tables, investors can determine how well the company is performing. They can decide whether to maintain their investment, buy additional stock, or sell and move their money to another investment.

Stock tables are available in most daily newspapers. They can also be accessed online. They report on the performance of publicly traded stocks on all of the major stock exchanges. Tables may be organized a bit differently, but will contain the same information shown in this example. On weekends, many newspapers report stock performance for the entire week.

52 WK HI-LO is the highest and lowest prices at which the stock was sold in the past year (52 weeks). In the example, the highest price was $28 and the lowest was $13.

SYM is the company symbol or abbreviation that identifies the firm issuing the stock. This symbol is sometimes referred to as the company's "ticker symbol." The fictitious symbol in the example is LZD.

DIV represents dividends, which are the amount of money approved by the board of directors of the company to be paid to stockholders. The column shows the most recent dividend paid per share—$1.10. Dividends are a measure of the health of the business. They are one way that stockholders earn a return on their investment in addition to gains in the value of the stock.

VOL shows the volume of shares (in 100s) traded on the date of the table. In the example, 22,800 shares were traded by LZD. Volume gives information on the change in demand for the company's shares.

YLD approximates the yield of the dividend paid. The dividend yield is the current rate of return on all capital invested in the company. This allows easier comparison of the performance of companies with different stock prices. The yield is calculated by dividing the current dividend by the closing stock price.

$$\frac{\text{Dividend}}{\text{Price}} = \frac{\$1.10}{\$24.00} = 4.58\% \text{ yield}$$

PE is the comparison of the price per share to the earnings per share. It is called the price/earnings ratio. It shows how much an investor is willing to pay for $1 of current earnings by one share of stock. The ratio is calculated by dividing the price by the earnings per share (EPS). In the example, LZD stock is selling for more than 10 times the current earnings.

$$\frac{\text{Price}}{\text{Eps}} = \frac{\$24.00}{\$2.28} = 10.53 \text{ PE}$$

HI-LO represents the highest and lowest prices of all trades made during the date of the table. In the example, the high was at $25.00 and the low was $23.50.

CLOSE is the last price at which a trade was made during the trading day. In the example, $24.00 is the close.

NET CHG is the difference between the closing price for the previous day and the current day. Because the net change listed is 0.5, the price of the stock on the previous day was $23.50.

Think Critically
1. What information from the stock table do you think is most important for a stock owner to watch on a regular basis? What is the least important?
2. How do stock tables help in comparing the performance of two stocks with very different prices?

Applied Skills

Technology Have students select and track a stock for one week. Use a spreadsheet program to prepare a stock table example, as shown in the Sharpen Your Life Skills example. The table should show information for each of the five days in the business week.

5-3 Organizational Structure for Businesses

Goals

Understand important principles in designing an effective organization.

Compare alternative organizational structures for businesses.

Key Terms

mission statement

goal

policies

procedures

organization chart

Focus on Real Life

Mary Jo's company has just approved a policy that allowed some employees to telecommute. This means employees can work from home and complete their work using a computer and other technology. Mary Jo is interested in the idea but isn't sure if she should apply.

She is afraid she might not be as motivated to complete her work every day if she doesn't have to go to the office and keep a regular schedule. She also is concerned that it may be much more difficult to communicate with coworkers and get feedback from her manager using the technology. Mary Jo also wonders if she will be viewed as a productive and valued employee if people don't see her at work every day.

DESIGNING AN EFFECTIVE BUSINESS ORGANIZATION

It is not easy to create a successful business. Many new businesses fail in the first few years. Few businesses maintain their success for the lifetime of the owner. Successful businesses need more than a good product or service. Skilled managers, well-prepared and motivated employees, adequate resources, and effective procedures add to business success. A business needs to be well organized to help people do their work properly. An effective business begins with a clear purpose and the application of key principles for organizing work.

Setting Direction

The direction for a business comes from its **mission statement**. A mission statement is a short, specific written statement of the reason a business exists and what it wants to achieve. The mission statement for Starbucks is to "Establish Starbucks as the premier purveyor of the finest coffee in the world while maintaining our uncompromising principles while we grow." Starbucks uses six guiding principles to measure their progress: their work environment, diversity, high standard, satisfied customers, clean environment, and profits.

> **main idea**
>
> Understand important principles in designing an effective organization.

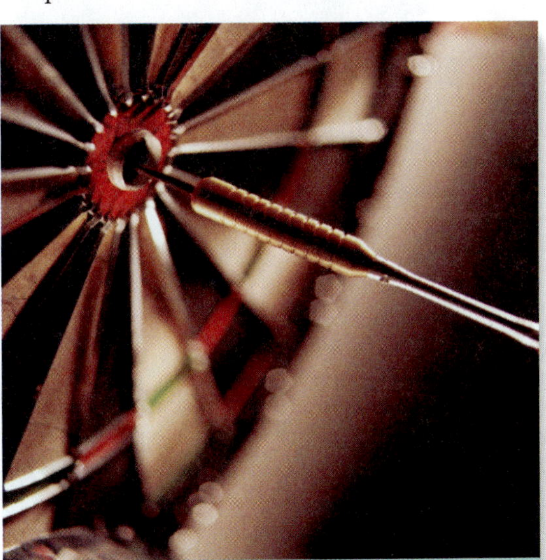

How does effective organization help a business "hit the mark"?

Focus on Real Life

Ask students to define telecommuting. Ask them whether they believe it will become more popular in the future or whether employees will prefer to work face to face with their colleagues.

TEACH

Have students brainstorm a list of factors that would suggest an organization is effective and then do the same for factors that would suggest an organization is ineffective. Have them review the lists and discuss why some organizations are effective while others are not.

THINK CRITICALLY THROUGH VISUALS

Effective organization provides a business with a clear purpose and key principles to follow that help employees and managers do their work well.

Applied Skills

Language Arts Suggest to students that they are the owner of a fitness center. Have them write a two-sentence mission statement for their business that describes the reason the business exists and what they want the business to achieve. Consider allowing students to work in pairs.

THINK CRITICALLY THROUGH VISUALS

Some organizational roles include managers, workers, supervisors, creative people, record keepers, and sales personnel. Encourage students to think of a specific organization as they describe roles.

FYI

In a recent Junior Achievement survey, 41 percent of teens believe starting and operating their own business will offer greater job security than being an employee in another company. Nearly 75 percent of the teens indicated they would like to start their own business someday.

After a mission statement is developed, the business sets goals. A **goal** is a precise statement of results the business expects to achieve. Goals are used to define what needs to be accomplished and to determine if the business is successful. An example of a goal for an automobile manufacturer is "to produce the top-rated brand for quality and customer satisfaction."

Finally, the business sets policies and procedures for the organization. **Policies** are guidelines used in making consistent decisions. **Procedures** are descriptions of the way work is to be done. Effective policies and procedures provide guidance and direction to people working in the organization.

Principles of Effective Organization

When several people work together, their work needs to be organized so they work together well and achieve their tasks. Several principles guide the effective organization of work.

Responsibility, Authority, and Accountability *Responsibility* is the obligation to complete specific work. *Authority* is the right to make decisions about how responsibilities should be accomplished. *Accountability* is taking responsibility for the results achieved. In an effective organization, all managers and employees have a set of responsibilities as a part of their jobs. With every job assignment, they know they have the authority to make the decisions and obtain the resources needed to complete the assignment. They know they will be recognized and rewarded if they are successful. They

In an organization, every member has a specific role to fill. Describe some roles.

Different Learning Abilities

Attention Deficit Disorder Tell the student to think of a specific task they complete regularly, such as brushing their teeth or using an ATM machine. Have them carefully review how they complete the task and list at least four procedures they use in the correct order they need to be completed.

will be held accountable if the work is not completed well.

Unity of Command A key organizing principle is to provide unity of command. *Unity of command* means there is a clear reporting relationship for all staff of a business. If there is confusion in assignments and unclear relationships among people who are working together, it will be hard for people to know what to do or where to go for help. For each work assignment, people need to know who is the leader and how decisions will be made.

Span of Control The last organizing principle is span of control. *Span of control* is the number of employees who are assigned to a particular work task and manager. A large number of people working with little support from their manager cannot be effective. In the same way, a manager with only a very small number of people may provide too much control. Organizations need to make sure that workers have a balance of supervision and freedom to do their work. The span of control for well trained, experienced, and motivated employees can be much greater than for new and inexperienced employees who are not enthused about their work.

TYPES OF ORGANIZATIONAL STRUCTURES

main idea

Compare alternative organizational structures for businesses.

When only one person works in a business, there is little need for an organizational structure. The sole employee is responsible for all of the work. When more people are hired, there will need to be an agreement on what work each person will do and if one person has authority over the work of others. An **organization chart** is a diagram that shows the structure of an organization, classifications of work and jobs, and the relationships among those classifications. You can see a simple organization chart for a business in Figure 5-3.

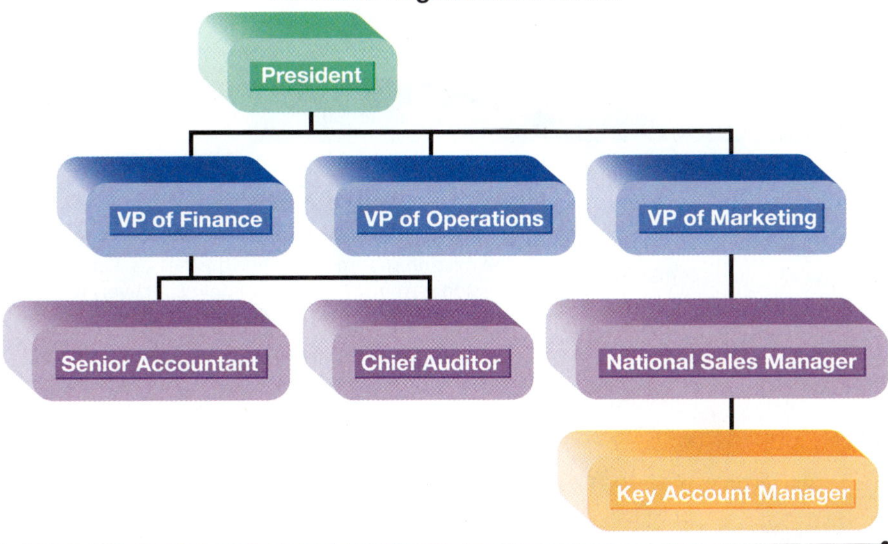

FIGURE 5-3

Why is it important for employees to understand the structure of the company where they work?

Work as a Team

Your class is responsible for selling advertising for the school's yearbook. Work as a team to identify the tasks that will need to be completed to sell 50 ads in the next three weeks. Describe how a project team can be organized to achieve that goal.

Functional Organization Structure

Most businesses use a *functional organizational structure.* In this type of organization, work is arranged within main business functions such as production, operations, marketing, and human resources. All of the people with jobs related to one of the functions will work together. They report to managers who are responsible for that function. The advantage of a functional organization is that people work with others who have the same skills. A drawback is that people become more focused on their specific function than on the success of the whole business. Often, people working in one function have little interaction with people in other parts of the business.

Matrix Organizational Structure

A newer organizational structure designed to overcome the drawbacks of the functional structure is the matrix organization. In a *matrix organizational structure,* work is structured around specific projects, products, or customer groups. People with varied backgrounds are assigned together because their expertise is required for the project or to serve the customer. The assignment may be temporary or long-term.

A matrix organization can be interesting and motivating to employees. They work with many different people. They are focused on a specific project or task. However, it can be confusing and inefficient without effective leadership and communication.

checkpoint >>
What problems can result from the use of a functional organizational structure?

5-3 Assessment

Key Concepts

Determine the best answer.

1. True or False. The direction for a business comes from its policies and procedures.

2. The obligation to complete specific work is
   a. responsibility
   b. authority
   c. accountability
   d. recognition

3. Which of the following is *not* shown on an organizational chart?
   a. the structure of an organization
   b. work relationships
   c. job descriptions
   d. classifications of jobs

Make Academic Connections

4. *Technology* Use the Internet to collect examples of the mission statements of five businesses. Rate each mission statement in terms of how effectively it communicates the purpose and direction of the company.

5. *Critical Thinking* Many schools are organized using a functional organizational structure. Teachers are organized into departments such as English, Mathematics, Science, and Business. How could a school be organized using a matrix structure? Design an organizational chart that illustrates a matrix structure for your school. Describe the advantages and disadvantages of the matrix structure.

Electricity Where There Was None

More than 30 percent of the world's population does not have electricity. Not only does that mean a very difficult day-to-day existence, but also no real chance to improve the standard of living with factories, modern stores, and technology. Fabio Rosa believes that for the same amount of money people spend on kerosene, candles, and batteries, he can rent them low-cost solar kits. Using the "free" energy of the sun, electricity can be delivered to rural areas, mountaintops, and villages in his home country of Brazil in South America. It can also be delivered to the many other places in the world with no access to power lines and generators.

When Mr. Rosa was 22, he was named Secretary of Agriculture in a city in rural southern Brazil. He saw hundreds of people leaving their farms and moving to the city. The lack of electricity made it hard to earn a living in agriculture. That put stress on city services and created the likelihood that there would be few farms in the future. Fabio thought that if low-cost solar energy could be supplied, it would result in higher levels of food production. At the same time, improved health and education services could be provided, pollution levels would be reduced, and people could come back to their farms. He envisioned small business communities springing up to serve the local farmers powering their stores with solar energy.

Based on his work, Mr. Rosa knew that farm families spent at least $11 per month on kerosene, candles, and batteries. This was about the same amount that would be needed to rent a simple solar system that would provide enough electricity for one farm.

© Getty Images/PhotoDisc

With that knowledge, he set out to electrify the rural areas of his country with solar energy kits.

Currently, the solar systems come in three standard sizes: Kit Number 1 rents for $10 per month. It comes complete with a 60-watt solar panel, high-performance battery, all the wiring, plus a number of 12-volt fluorescent lights and electrical outlets for appliances. The system provides, on average per day, six to seven hours of light and several hours for running appliances, equipment, and a water pump. Kits 2 and 3 rent for, respectively, $16 and $24 per month and come with more lights, outlets, and wattage. The installation cost for a kit—about $150—can be paid off over the first 12 months. When Rosa distributes the solar systems to farmers, he includes materials to develop an irrigation system and build electric fences to protect farm animals as well as information on modern farming practices. New tools and equipment are being developed that can be powered with the solar system including saws, drills, refrigerators, and even a  solar water heater to provide warm showers.

Fabio Rosa is currently installing about 1,500 new solar systems each year. He wants to increase the rate at which poor families can obtain electricity, so he is traveling worldwide to seek investors who will provide money to expand his work. "At this moment," he states, "we have millions of people without energy, just like we did 10 years ago, just like we did 20 years ago. Brazil has this problem. India has this problem. China has this problem. Bangladesh has this problem. Two billion people have this problem. First, we will demonstrate results on a small scale, then on a regional scale, then all over Brazil, and then the world."

Think Critically

1. Use the Internet to locate additional information on Fabio Rosa's work.
2. Suggest ways the standard of living of poor families and communities will improve when they have access to electricity.

When people lose their jobs in rural areas and small towns, they usually stream to large cities. That results in problems for both the cities and the rural areas. Fabio Rosa has devoted most of his life to that problem by developing low-cost solutions to help people stay on their farms and in small towns.

Think Critically Answers

1. Offer suggestions for how students are to report their findings.

2. Answers will vary. Some possible answers include indoor and outdoor lighting and ability to use appliances, hot water heaters, power tools, water pumps, and electric fences for easier farming.

Teaching Strategies

Expand Beyond the Classroom Have students review local newspapers, business magazines, and other information sources to identify local businesses or nonprofit organizations that are offering services and support to help low-income individuals and families improve their standard of living.

Communicate Business Concepts Answers

1. Rapidly growing employment opportunities include those in service industries, communications, technology, and health care.

2. Sole proprietorships make up the majority of businesses. Some proprietors may make their entire income from these businesses, as many leave little time for other employment. Others may depend on other sources of income when first starting a business until it becomes profitable.

3. Answers will vary.

4. Answers will vary.

5. Julie may want to consider a partnership, a limited liability partnership, or limited liability company. Each would allow her control over decisions, as well as the benefit of having other investors.

Business Notes

5-1 BUSINESS IN THE U.S. ECONOMY

1. The employment status of the United States is changing. New jobs develop as older jobs disappear. The labor pool is currently getting older, but that will begin to change as baby boomers retire. Minority groups make up a larger percentage of the workforce.

2. Businesses play several key roles in the U.S. economy. They provide employment for millions of people. They compensate owners and investors. They pay taxes to federal, state, and local governments. They make and distribute products and services needed by consumers, government, and businesses.

3. The three major categories of businesses are producers, intermediaries, and service businesses. Producers create the products and services used by individuals and other businesses. Intermediaries sell goods and services. A service business carries out activities that are consumed by its customers.

5-2 FORMS OF BUSINESS OWNERSHIP

4. Most businesses are organized as proprietorships, partnerships, and corporations. A proprietorship is a business owned and run by one person. A partnership is a business owned and controlled by two or more people. A corporation is a separate legal entity owned by one or more shareholders and managed by a board of directors.

5. For people who want to work and make decisions independently, do not want to be exposed to significant regulation, and are willing to take on the risk of a business, the proprietorship is an effective form of ownership. A partnership is good for people who share an idea for a business, want to cooperate in managing and investing, and want to share the risks and rewards of the business. A corporation is more difficult to form and is subject to more regulations. Investors' liability is limited to the amount invested, and they can invest without taking part in the day-to-day management.

6. Other forms of ownership include limited liability partnership, joint venture, S-corporation, limited liability company, nonprofit corporation, cooperative, and franchise.

5-3 ORGANIZATIONAL STRUCTURE FOR BUSINESSES

7. Successful businesses have an effective organizational structure. A mission statement, goals, policies, and procedures guide them.

8. The specific structure of a business can be illustrated with an organizational chart. Traditionally, businesses have used a functional structure but now many are using a matrix organizational structure.

Communicate Business Concepts

1. What are some rapidly growing employment opportunities? What types of jobs are declining in numbers? How can you predict what job categories may grow or decline in the future?

2. Why do most businesses have no employees other than the owner? Do you believe most of those business owners earn their entire income from that business? Why or why not?

3. Identify several businesses from your community that fit within each of the three categories of businesses listed in Lesson 5-1. Do you believe your community has more producers, intermediaries, or service businesses? Justify your answer.

4. Would you like to start and own your own business? Why or why not? What do you believe are the risks and benefits you would face if you decided to start a business?

5. Julie states that she wants to be her own boss. If she starts a business, it will be a proprietorship rather than a partnership or corporation. Explain to Julie why she might want to consider another ownership form. Is it possible for her to be her own boss and yet not use the proprietorship form of ownership?

6. Use a business directory to identify several non-profit corporations in your area. What public service is each providing? Why do you think each is a public rather than a private corporation?

7. "An effective organizational structure is as important to a business as the quality of its products and services." Do you agree or disagree with that statement? Discuss your beliefs with another student who has the opposing view.

8. You are starting a shopping service for elderly people in your community who cannot leave their homes. Write a mission statement that clearly communicates the purpose of your business.

9. How will the appearance of an organizational chart for a business using a functional organizational structure be different from one using a matrix organizational structure? What should you be able to learn about a business by studying its organizational chart?

Develop Your Business Language

Match the terms listed with the definitions.

10. A business owned and controlled by two or more people who have entered into a written agreement.

11. A short, specific written statement of the reason a business exists and what it wants to accomplish.

12. One who has no explicit or implicit contract for long-term employment.

13. Descriptions of the way work is to be done.

14. A specific statement of results the business expects to achieve.

15. A written legal document that identifies ownership and operating procedures and conditions for the business.

16. Businesses involved in selling the goods and services of producers to consumers and other businesses.

17. A separate legal entity, formed by documents filed with the state, which is owned by one or more shareholders and managed by a board of directors.

18. A written contract granting permission to operate a business to sell products and services in a prescribed way.

19. Businesses that complete activities that are consumed by customers rather than offering products for sale.

20. A business owned and controlled by just one person.

21. A written agreement among all owners that specifies the rules and procedures that guide ownership and operations.

22. Guidelines used in making consistent decisions.

23. A diagram that shows the structure of an organization, classifications of jobs, and the relationships among those classifications.

KEY TERMS
a. articles of incorporation
b. contingent worker
c. corporation
d. franchise
e. goal
f. intermediaries
g. mission statement
h. organization chart
i. partnership
j. partnership agreement
k. proprietorship
l. policies
m. procedures
n. service business

6. Answers will vary.

7. Answers will vary.

8. Answers will vary.

9. A functional chart would consist of a list of groups of people, arranged under various functions of the business. A matrix organizational chart will arrange teams under their respective projects, with functions appearing across each project. By studying an organizational chart, one can learn how a company organizes its work load, how it views the significance of each of its employees and their respective roles, and what type of goal setting it uses to motivate them.

Develop Your Business Language Answers

10. i. partnership

11. g. mission statement

12. b. contingent worker

13. m. procedures

14. e. goal

15. a. articles of incorporation

16. f. intermediaries

17. c. corporation

18. d. franchise

19. n. service businesses

20. k. proprietorship

21. j. partnership agreement

22. l. policies

23. h. organization chart

Make Academic Connections

24. **MATH** To provide additional employment and add to its tax base from businesses, Yorketowne's city council opened a business park on the edge of the city. After five years, they had attracted two new manufacturers and four supporting service businesses to the park. The total value of the property of all six businesses was $15,825,500. The companies paid $0.78 per $1,000 of property value each year as property tax. In addition, the businesses employed 328 people at an average salary of $36,000. Each person paid a 1 percent city income tax each year.

   a. What is the total amount of taxes the city collected as a result of opening the business park?
   b. In addition to the tax dollars, what other benefits might the city receive from opening the business park?

25. **TECHNOLOGY** Use a spreadsheet and graphics program to make a chart or graph showing one of the following sets of data: (a) the five largest employers in the world and the number of employees for each, (b) the composition of the U.S. workforce by the age of employees, (c) the average size of U.S. business by annual sales revenues.

26. **COMMUNICATION** The DECA chapter in your school is planning to open a school store to sell school supplies, school-related apparel, and spirit items before and after school. Prepare a mission statement for the store. Write one goal that identifies a specific result the store should achieve. Write a policy statement for accepting returns of merchandise purchased by customers.

27. **SCIENCE** Identify five types of natural resources that are extracted in the United States for use in manufacturing. For each, identify the leading states where the natural resources are extracted and important products for which the natural resource is needed.

28. **PUBLIC SERVICE** Most communities have non-profit corporations that support education. Find out if one or more organizations is working to support your school. If so, contact a leader of the organization. Determine how the organization is structured, if it is has articles of incorporation and bylaws, and its purpose. Find out how students in your school can support the organization through volunteer activities.

Linking School and Community

Interview a stockbroker or financial advisor in your community about the process of selecting and purchasing stock. Ask the professional to share information about how people decide which stock to purchase and how a stockholder can track the stock's performance. Ask the broker or advisor if he or she has any general advice for young investors.

Web Workout

The U.S. government provides support to small businesses through the Small Business Administration (SBA). Visit the SBA web site to learn more about this resource. Browse or search for information about forms of ownership that small businesses might consider. Be sure to read the advantages and disadvantages of each form or ownership.

Think Critically

1. Use information from your textbook and the SBA web site to identify and make a list of factors that influence the form of ownership choice.

2. Provide an example of business that might benefit from choosing the proprietorship form of ownership. Provide an example for each of these other types of ownership: partnership and corporation.

3. Based on one of your examples from above, write a short scenario describing the advantages and disadvantages of the chosen form of ownership. Describe how the business plans to use the form of ownership to its advantage and how it plans to deal with the disadvantages.

Decision-Making Strategies

Sonja Bartholomew started a lawn mowing service. She could not charge as much as she needed to make the profit she desired. Her competitors only charged $15 per lawn while she charged $20, but she did a superior job cutting lawns. Still, potential customers did not want to pay the extra $5.

A friend, Eduardo Guadalupe, suggested that they work together. He was good at trimming shrubs and had ideas for improving landscapes with flowers and lawn ornaments. They would offer a unique service when they combined their businesses. They could charge an amount that would result in a good profit for both of them. They would seek out homes in neighborhoods with above-average income levels.

29. What will be special about the services that Sonja and Eduardo can offer together? What other services might they include?

30. Why would they target above-average income levels?

31. Should Sonja continue to run her business as a proprietorship and hire Eduardo as an employee? If not, what other form of business ownership would you recommend? Justify your choice.

Prepared Speech Event

Small businesses hire the greatest number of employees in the United States. Entrepreneurship and small business ownership have made the United States great.

You have decided to run for Congress. One of the hottest topics in your congressional district is support for small business ownership. Your constituents want to know your plan to stimulate and support small business ownership. You must come up with a specific plan to encourage more minority and female business ownership. You are also challenged to develop a strategy to bring business back to the inner city. Entrepreneurs want to know the incentives for taking the risk of starting businesses in your congressional district.

You will have three to five minutes to present your plan to strengthen and encourage small business ownership. Audiovisual equipment and visual aids may be used in this presentation.

PERFORMANCE INDICATORS EVALUATED

- Define demographics of your congressional district.
- Explain the importance of small business ownership.
- Describe strategies to encourage/support increased small business ownership.
- Outline the greatest obstacles for small businesses to overcome.
- Explain how government assistance to small businesses will be monitored and improved.

You will be evaluated for your

- Knowledge of the topic
- Organized presentation of the topic
- Confidence, quality of voice, and eye contact
- Relationship of the topic to business strategy

For more detailed information about performance indicators, go to the BPA web site.

Think Critically

1. Why is small business ownership important in the United States?
2. What types of government programs or assistance will encourage more small business ownership?
3. Why is it important to meet with community and congressional district leaders to develop a strategy that enhances small business ownership?

http://www.bpanet.org/

Portfolio Activity

school.cengage.com/business/introtobiz

Access the web site shown here to find portfolio activities for this chapter. Use the activities to provide tangible evidence of your learning.

Decision-Making Strategies Answers

29. By combining their businesses, they are offering a complete landscape service with customized plans to meet client needs. They might also consider seeding, fertilizing, and tree care.

30. Above-average income homeowners are more likely to pay someone to care for their lawns and can afford to pay higher rates for special services.

31. Answers will vary. A partnership would allow each to participate in the decision-making and bring their existing assets to the combined business. This would also allow Sonja to share liability with Eduardo. They might also consider an LLC.

Winning Edge
Prepared Speech Event

Students will prepare a political speech to demonstrate support for small business ownership.

Think Critically
Answers

1. Small businesses hire the largest number of people in the United States. Small businesses make up the fabric of the free enterprise system.

2. Tax breaks for small businesses, tax incentives to encourage location of small businesses in certain regions, and assistance to help small businesses offer health care and other benefits to employees will encourage more small business ownership.

3. Decisions made by local, state, and national legislators can have a large effect on small business success. Support of others will be needed to implement plans.

Web Workout

1. Answers will vary. Students should consider costs, liability, sources of financing, and tax issues.

2. Examples will vary. Many small businesses are proprietorships. Professionals such as doctors and accountants often form partnerships. Most large businesses are corporations.

3. Answers will vary. Students should match the business type to the issues outlined in the answer to the first question.

CHAPTER 6

Entrepreneurship and Small Business Management

124

Planning a Career in…
CONSULTING

When businesses face unique problems or undertake major changes, they often turn to consultants for advice and help. Consultants are not long-term employees of a company, but are hired to complete a specific task or to focus on an important challenge facing the business. Consultants may be self-employed and work independently, or they may be part of a large consulting business that employs many specialists. Large companies often form teams of specialists to work with a client.

Consultants bring expertise to a business that may not exist among its employees and that would be difficult to develop quickly enough to solve a current problem. Consultants also may be more objective about the business than people who are working there. The primary work of consultants is to conduct research and complete other types of analysis that help businesses address important challenges they are facing. Consultants often prepare written reports and plans, provide advice to decision-makers, and may even offer help in reorganizing the company and redirecting its efforts.

Employment Outlook

- The employment outlook for business consultants varies by industry, but is generally growing at a better than average rate.
- Employment demand is based on the expertise and reputation of the individual consultant and the consulting business.
- Most consultants have expertise in organizational change, finance, technology, and management.

Related Job Titles

- Business Analyst
- Management Consultant
- Performance Consultant
- Quality Control Consultant
- Security Consultant
- Training Consultant

Needed Skills

- Ability to problem-solve with innovative solutions
- Research and analytical skills
- Specialization in specific aspects of business operations and management
- Effective written and oral communication skills

What's it like to work in … Consulting

Erin Gerrard works as a small business consultant for Security Savings Bank. The bank is committed to strengthening its services to small businesses. Security employs a 10-person team to support its small business customers.

Erin has a degree in accounting, worked five years for a major accounting business, and then operated her own accounting service for five years. The bank asked her to work for them as a small business consultant because of her accounting expertise and reputation in the community. She decided the consulting opportunity would be an interesting challenge.

This morning, Erin is meeting with Dawn Perrot, who is planning to open a florist shop. Dawn has submitted a business plan, but the financial plan is incomplete. Erin is looking forward to helping Dawn gather information and develop a complete picture of the financial needs of her business. Later today, Erin and the bank's information management specialist are visiting The Sherron Company to help them plan a new computerized payroll system.

What about you? How do you believe Erin's work as a consultant is similar to and different from the work she did as the owner of a small accounting business?

Additional Career Information

Additional information on careers can be found in the *Occupational Outlook Handbook,* an online publication (www.bls.gov/oco) of the federal government. Tell your class about this resource and how to use it. This description of job duties can be used to demonstrate the relevancy of skills learned in this course.

Planning a Career in…
CONSULTING

Consultants work for a number of businesses on a variety of activities. When businesses need help on a new project or expertise that the owners do not have, they will often work with a business consultant.

What About You? Answer

Student answers will require thinking beyond what is presented and formulating their own reactions. As a consultant, Erin probably does less hands-on accounting and more research and advising. She uses both her accounting expertise and her experience as a small business owner to provide advice and support to her clients.

6-1 Becoming an Entrepreneur

Goals

Identify characteristics of successful entrepreneurs.

Recognize the importance of entrepreneurship in the economy.

Describe opportunities and risks of entrepreneurship.

Key Terms

entrepreneur

entrepreneurship

venture capital

innovation

improvement

Focus on Real Life

Jerelyn Frank has been working as an aerobics instructor for the Phase 4 Fitness Center for the past six years. Jerelyn enjoys her work because she has always been active and athletic. Since high school, she has taken wellness, first aid, and nutrition classes at the local adult education center. She has completed a number of certification courses in aerobics instruction and yoga. In her spare time, she has developed fitness programs for some of her friends and members of the fitness center where she works.

Jerelyn is seriously thinking about starting a personal fitness service. She wants to go to people's homes and offices to help them plan and maintain a fitness schedule and offer half-hour to one-hour workouts. She already has a number of contacts to help her get underway. Jerelyn is single with no family responsibilities, and she has no debts. She has been able to save more than $15,000 in her bank account.

Jerelyn decides to go forward with the plan just as thousands of other entrepreneurs do each year. Those that become new business owners are willing to contribute a great deal of time and energy and risk personal economic resources for their venture. They hold the hope of a successful business and a reasonable profit.

main idea

Identify characteristics of successful entrepreneurs.

CHARACTERISTICS OF ENTREPRENEURS

An **entrepreneur** is someone who takes a risk in starting a business to earn a profit. Some key factors in starting your own business are having a real desire to be your own boss and developing a good initial plan. Having special skills and abilities and coming up with innovative ideas are also important.

Can you think of some service or product that is not being offered at this time but that could be in demand? Is there some service or product that you could offer more efficiently than others are doing now? Is there some special talent you have that could become the starting point for a business of your own? If so, you have the basis for a new business enterprise. There are good opportunities for entrepreneurship through small business ownership. **Entrepreneurship** is the process of starting, organizing, managing, and assuming the responsibility for a business. Here are some real-life examples of young entrepreneurs.

Entrepreneurs in Action

Joshua Moore was a high school student and brother to four-year-old Sophie when he developed an idea for a baby stroller braking system. To fund work on his invention, Josh started Personal

Affections, selling key chains, picture frames, mirrors, and personalized stickers at his Walhalla, South Carolina, high school. He received an Entrepreneur of the Year award for an operational business from the National Foundation for Teaching Entrepreneurship. At age 15, he was on his way to his dream of becoming an inventor and business owner.

Pankaj Arora was not a typical high school student in Rochester, Minnesota. In addition to a busy schedule of schoolwork and after-school activities, he also ran two business ventures. Using his advanced computer skills, Pankaj created and distributed software through his company, Pankaj Arora Software. His second company, paWare, specialized in custom-built computer systems and web design. Along with his college degree, Pankaj's technical and entrepreneurial skills helped him get a job at General Electric.

Rich Stachowski of Moraga, California, is an avid scuba diver. While enjoying his hobby, he recognized that he was unable to talk to others who were snorkeling with him. He put his imagination to work and invented Water Talkies™. These walkie-talkies can be used under water. Rich worked with a family friend who developed the manufacturing process. He then opened a business to make and sell his product before he was even a teenager. His Short Stack line of water toys is now sold by 100 chain retailers in the United States and several other countries.

Sometimes ideas for new products come from problems in daily life. Abbey Fleck was watching her father use a microwave oven to cook bacon one morning in their White Bear Lake, Minnesota, home. The bacon came out soaked in grease. Abbey had an idea to develop a pan that would cook the bacon while letting the grease drain out below. She and her father tested several designs that resulted in the Makin Bacon® microwave bacon tray.

Do you have ideas or skills that you could use to start a small business?

They were able to convince the producers of Armour brand bacon to sell the tray with an advertisement and order form printed on each package of bacon. The product was an instant hit. Abbey's company, A de F, Inc., has sold more than $3 million worth of Makin Bacon® trays.

NETBookmark

The U.S. government is taking steps to support the more than 6 million women who own their own businesses. One of the resources is a web site dedicated to providing information and networking opportunities to women entrepreneurs. Access the web site shown below and click on the link for Chapter 6. Read the latest news on women's entrepreneurship. Review the types of resources that can be accessed through the web site. Locate other government web sites that provide information and help for people wanting to starting their own businesses.

school.cengage.com/business/introtobiz

127

TEACH

Ask students why they believe that people their age and even younger have been successful in starting their own businesses. Discuss what they think it would take for a young person to actually go ahead with an idea and turn it into a business.

THINK CRITICALLY THROUGH VISUALS

Answers will vary, but could include discussion of hobbies and interests as well as skills.

NETBookmark

The U.S. government, as well as state and local governments, offer support to entrepreneurs. They particularly encourage people who have not had opportunities in business, such as women and racial minorities. Most government agencies and other organizations have developed web sites to make it easier for entrepreneurs to access information.

Different Learning Styles

Visual Learner Have students sketch an illustration of a new product or the front of the building for a new business idea they have. Ask students to show their sketches to other students and describe why the idea interests them. Consider allowing students to work in pairs.

TEACH

Ask students why they believe that young entrepreneurs today are more evenly divided between men and women even though most business owners are male. Some entrepreneurs have not completed any formal education beyond high school. Ask students how these entrepreneurs are able to compensate for having less education than college-educated managers of competing businesses.

THINK CRITICALLY THROUGH VISUALS

Some advantages of turning a hobby into a business are that the knowledge and expertise for the activity are already there. Disadvantages are that the hobby might not be a good basis for a business and that it might not be as enjoyable if it becomes a business.

FIGURE 6-1 *ANSWER*

Answers will vary. Ask volunteers to share their answers with the class.

PROJECT

Provide the following instructions to students. (These instructions also appear on page xxiv of the textbook.) What personal characteristics do you have that could help you become a successful entrepreneur? Describe how these characteristics may affect the life-span goals you set for your future.

The experiences of these entrepreneurs are examples of the thousands of young people who have creative ideas and turn them into businesses each year. Not all ideas lead to successful businesses, but each provides evidence of the opportunities that exist for people who believe they can turn their idea into a profitable business.

What Does It Take?

Not all people who own or manage a business are entrepreneurs. It takes unique skills and personal characteristics to develop a new idea for a product or service. A person must also have both the confidence and capability to turn an idea into a business.

Entrepreneurs come from all age categories and racial and ethnic groups. They represent both genders as well as varied amounts and types of education. Many entrepreneurs own their first business while in their teens. Others do not take the step until retirement. More business owners are male, but young entrepreneurs are more equally divided between male and female.

It is important to have an understanding of business operations and management. This understanding does not always come from getting a business degree in college. People learn how to run a business in many ways. They may work in a business or ask for help and advice from an experienced business owner. They may read and study on their own as well as in school.

There are personal traits that are common to successful entrepreneurs, as shown in Figure 6-1. While some people already have many of these qualities, others do not. If you have a desire to become an entrepreneur, you can work to develop these characteristics.

What are some advantages and disadvantages of turning a hobby into a business?

FIGURE 6-1

Which characteristics of successful entrepreneurs do you possess? Which ones would you like to develop?

Personal Characteristics of Successful Entrepreneurs	
ENTREPRENEURS ARE MORE	**THEY HAVE**
• persistent	• problem-solving skills
• inquisitive	• tolerance for ambiguity
• energetic	• strong integrity
• goal oriented	• personal initiative
• independent	• ability to secure resources
• self-confident	• capability to learn from failure
• creative	• willingness to work hard
• reliable	
• competitive	

Life-Span Plan Answer

Answers will vary. Students should identify personal characteristics and explain how these might affect their ability to achieve their life-span goals.

Applied Skills

Communication Have students create an advertisement or brochure that showcases the personal characteristics of an effective entrepreneur. Encourage students to use a computer to complete this assignment.

ENTREPRENEURSHIP AND THE ECONOMY

Entrepreneurship is a key part of the U.S. economy. Nearly one in ten of all Americans 18–64 years old is involved in some type of entrepreneurship activity. More than 670,000 new businesses are created annually. Entrepreneurship is also risky. Nearly as many small businesses close as begin each year.

Employment

Small businesses are responsible for most new employment. Figure 6-2 shows employment growth by firm size between 1993 and 2003. Over 60 percent of new jobs were created by businesses with fewer than 500 employees.

Financing

Most of the money needed to start a new business comes from the entrepreneur and his or her family and friends. One in five Americans has invested in a business of someone they know well. More than 50 percent lend financial support for the business of a family member or relative. Twenty nine percent give money to neighbors and friends. Eight percent invest in businesses started by work colleagues. Family and friends invest more than $100 billion in new businesses each year.

Another source of money for some new businesses is venture capital. **Venture capital** is money provided by large investors to finance new products and new businesses that have a good chance to be very profitable. In the late 1990s, many venture capital companies were formed. They supplied more than

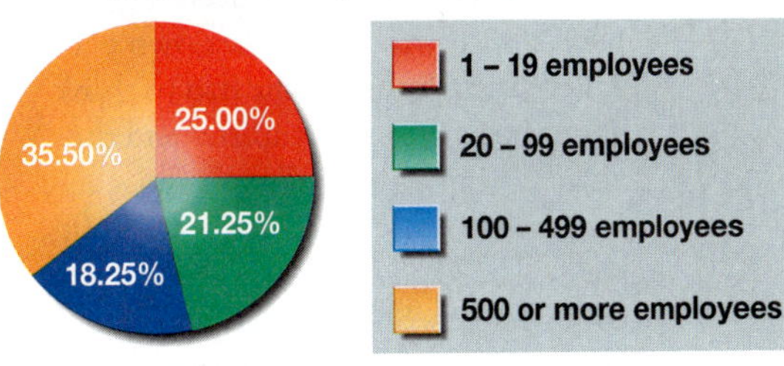

FIGURE 6-2

What percentage of job growth came from businesses with fewer than 100 employees?

$100 billion each year to new businesses. Many of the businesses receiving those funds were e-commerce and high-tech start-ups. When many of those businesses failed, the amount of venture capital declined to less than $22 billion in 2005. More than 2,900 companies receive venture capital each year. That shows that many people think new businesses provide a good investment opportunity. The other sources of financing for new businesses are loans from banks and financial institutions and credit given by businesses that sell products and services to the new business.

Productivity

New and small businesses produce a large volume of goods and services for the economy. Businesses with just a single owner and no staff account for more than $600 billion in sales annually. Small businesses are responsible for more than half of the U.S. gross domestic product each year. They account for 55 percent of all innovative products and services developed.

ONGOING ASSESSMENT

checkpoint >> **ANSWER**

Any characteristics listed in Figure 6-1 are acceptable, such as persistence, inquisitiveness, self-confidence, creativity, and so forth.

FIGURE 6-2 *ANSWER*

Businesses with fewer than 100 employees created 46.25 percent of new jobs. The answer is the result of adding 25 percent and 21.25 percent.

TEACH

Ask students to consider ways that people can be involved in an entrepreneurship activity without actually being the entrepreneur. Possible answers are by lending money, working with the entrepreneur to plan the business, and being an employee.

Explain to students that most new entrepreneurs have difficulty obtaining enough financing to start the business, so they often turn to family and friends. Businesses will usually fail if there is inadequate financing.

ONGOING ASSESSMENT

checkpoint >> **ANSWER**

Sources of financing for entrepreneurs include personal savings, friends and family, venture capital, and bank loans.

Different Learning Abilities

Gifted Have students use the Internet and library resources to research and prepare a report on the dot-com bust of the late 1990s. Ask them to present a summary to other students that highlights the major reasons for the large number of start-up business failures.

TEACH

Ask students to identify the difference between an opportunity and a risk. Do they believe all opportunities have risks? Can an opportunity that is not very risky result in a profitable business?

Explain to students that most new businesses offer improvements to existing products or current business operations rather than offering innovations. Ask them whether they believe the process to develop an innovation is different from the process to design a major improvement to an existing product.

THINK CRITICALLY THROUGH VISUALS

Entrepreneurship opportunities emerge from innovation, invention, and improvement.

Work as a Team

When students have completed their lists, have them rank the questions in order from most important to least important to help determine whether to invest in the business or not.

Describe opportunities and risks of entrepreneurship.

OPPORTUNITIES AND RISKS

When Jerelyn Frank was deciding whether she would open her own personal fitness business, she had to think about both the opportunities and the risks. Giving up a regular job and stable income is a difficult choice. As benefits, she will have personal control over her own business. She can take personal satisfaction if her idea develops into a successful, profitable company.

New Business Opportunities

The American private enterprise economy promotes innovation and new business development. Individuals are able to take the risk to start a new business. They can compete with other businesses to sell their products and services and make a profit. Consumers are always looking for new and better choices to meet their wants and needs.

Many opportunities are open to prospective entrepreneurs. The opportunities begin with the creation of new or improved products and services. An **innovation** is an invention or creation that is brand new. An **improvement** is a designed change that increases the usefulness of a product, service, or process.

Inventors often develop innovations. Those inventions may become the basis for a new business. The inventor may sell them to another company for development and sale. Examples of well-known innovations include the Apple personal computer developed by Steven Jobs and Stephen Wozniak and Post-it Notes created by Arthur Fry and Spencer Silver. Recent innovations that

What do innovation, invention, and improvement have to do with entrepreneurship opportunities?

may become successful products include a miniaturized artificial heart, a virtual computer keyboard, and an optical camouflage system that allows people wearing a special reflective material to seem to disappear.

In addition to inventions, innovators create new services that become the basis for a business. Frederick Smith envisioned an economical worldwide system for quickly and efficiently shipping packages. The creation of FedEx was the result. After graduating from college, Paul Orfalea developed neighborhood walk-in photocopying centers known as Kinko's. When the Internal Revenue Service no longer prepared individual tax returns for free, two brothers, Henry and Richard Bloch, created the H & R Block Company. They trained people to provide efficient, low-cost tax preparation services to individual taxpayers.

Not all entrepreneurship opportunities emerge from those types of inventions and innovations. Many come from an improved design, more effective procedures, or greater attention to quality. Entrepreneurs are creative problem-solvers. Those traits lead to ideas for improved products and services.

Work as a Team

New businesses usually need investments from other people. As a team, develop a list of questions you would ask an entrepreneur to determine if the new business would be one in which you would want to invest some of your money.

Different Learning Abilities

Dyslexia Have the student read each paragraph carefully. After reading each paragraph, have the student write a few words or a short sentence that summarizes the information.

Recognizing Risks

Many successful entrepreneurs and their businesses are well known. Their success encourages others to think about starting a new business. Developing a successful new business is not easy. Many more new businesses fail than succeed. The time and energy required of new business owners is much higher than most people expect.

The National Federation of Independent Business reports that of all new businesses, about one-third are profitable, one-third do not make a profit but continue to operate, and the remaining third lose money. Over a 10-year period, more than 50 percent of all new businesses are discontinued. The primary reasons that businesses started by entrepreneurs close are

- Lack of adequate capital
- Low sales
- Higher than expected expenses
- Competitive pressure
- An owner unprepared to manage a growing business
- Operations requiring more time than the owner is willing to commit

Entrepreneurs need to be aware of the many risks they may face and prepare for them. Most entrepreneurs are willing to take risks. They will work hard to make their businesses succeed. However, many entrepreneurs have seen one or more of their business ideas fail before they are able to grow a successful company.

checkpoint >>
Where do entrepreneurship opportunities begin?

6-1 Assessment

Key Concepts

Determine the best answer.

1. True or False. Everyone who owns or manages a business is an entrepreneur.

2. Which of the following is *not* a characteristic of entrepreneurship in the United States?
   a. About 3 percent of people aged 18–64 are involved in entrepreneurship activity.
   b. About 670,000 new businesses are created each year.
   c. Forty percent of new businesses have no employees.
   d. One in every five Americans has invested in a business of someone who they know well.

3. Money provided by large investors to finance new products and new businesses that have a good chance to be very profitable is known as
   a. a loan
   b. credit
   c. venture capital
   d. start-up funding

4. True or False. The primary reason that businesses started by entrepreneurs close is disagreements with business partners.

Make Academic Connections

5. **Math** Ronaldo Jacarda is opening a manufacturing business. It will produce a new type of USB flash storage card for cell phones and digital cameras. He has several sources for the money needed to start his business. Those sources and amounts are personal savings, $56,500; loans from family and friends, $38,000; venture capital investment, $128,000; bank loan, $22,500. Determine the total amount of capital he has accumulated and the percentage of that total from each of the sources. Prepare a pie chart that illustrates the answers.

6. **History** Use the Internet to identify important inventions and innovations developed in the past 50 years. Select the five you believe have had the greatest business success. Now select the five you believe have been most important in improving society. Prepare a short report in which you identify and briefly describe each of the inventions and innovations you selected and justifications for your choices.

RETEACH

Ask students to review the lesson goals and write a sentence about each goal.

CLOSE

Ask students to discuss their feelings about becoming an entrepreneur.

ENRICH

Have students identify their favorite interest, hobby, or activity. Then have them use a telephone directory or the Internet and identify small businesses that offer related products or services.

ONGOING ASSESSMENT

checkpoint >> **ANSWER**

Opportunities begin with innovations (ideas about new products and services) or improvements (ideas for changes to existing products, services, or processes).

TEACH

List each of the reasons that entrepreneur's businesses fail on the board. Ask students why each reason has a negative effect on the business.

ASSESS

Key Concepts Answers

1. False. Not everyone who owns or manages a business is an entrepreneur.

2. a. About three percent of people aged 18–64 are involved in entrepreneurship activity.

3. c. venture capital

4. False. Primary reasons involve being inexperienced in management and unprepared for the financial and time commitments involved.

Make Academic Connections

5. Total: 56,500+38,000 +128,000+22,500= 245,000

Personal savings: 56,500÷245,000=23%

Family and friends: 38,000+245,000=15%

Capital investment: 128,000÷245,000=52%

Bank loan: 22,500÷245,000=9%

6. Reports will vary. Offer suggestions regarding an acceptable format for reports.

Focus on Real Life

Ask students whether any of them have family members who used to own a small business, but no longer do so. Discuss reasons why people might enjoy owning a business but decide to sell it.

TEACH

Students are usually surprised to learn that the federal government defines small businesses as those with fewer than 500 employees. Before disclosing that information, ask students how many employees they believe a business must have before it is no longer considered small.

Write the following phrase on the board: 18.6 million businesses. Ask students what they believe makes that many U.S. businesses alike. After they have guessed, have them read the statement in the text that identifies that those businesses have no employees; the owner is the only person who works in the business. Ask them to think of businesses in their community that might fit that condition.

6-2 Small Business Basics

Goals

Identify important characteristics of small businesses.

Recognize the competitive advantages of small businesses.

Identify problems faced by many small businesses.

Key Terms

small business

Small Business Admintistration (SBA)

Focus on Real Life

During dinner, Jasmine excitedly told her family what happened in her Intro to Business class. The class had spent the time thinking about opportunities for owning a small business. Jasmine knew that is what she wanted to do.

Jasmine's grandfather said, "Did you know I ran a small business for almost 10 years when I was young? I was as excited as you are about starting a business when I graduated from high school. I went to work for the owner of a small hardware store. I hoped that I could save enough money to open my own store. Luckily, after eight years, he decided to retire. We worked out an arrangement where I could buy the store from him over a number of years."

"What happened to the business?" Jasmine asked.

"Being a small business owner is exciting, but it is a difficult life," explained her grandfather. "As the bigger stores moved in, I found it more and more difficult to attract customers. I decided to sell the business. I'm excited for you, but I want you to know that achieving your goals will be challenging.

---

main idea

Identify important characteristics of small businesses.

SMALL BUSINESS OWNERSHIP

Business is often viewed as very large corporations. These companies employ thousands of people with locations all over the country and the world. That is not the true picture of most businesses. By far the greatest percentage of businesses in the United States is small businesses. Small businesses employ half of all private sector employees.

You may be surprised by the definition of small business used by the federal government. According to the Small Business Administration (SBA), a **small business** is an independent business with fewer than 500 employees. Using that standard, 99.9 percent of the roughly 26 million U.S. businesses are small businesses.

A more specific description of a small business includes the following points.

- The owner is usually the manager.
- It operates in one or very few locations.
- It typically serves a small market.
- It is not dominant in its field.

Most people would probably not consider businesses with 500 employees to be small. Even if you use a standard of fewer than 100 employees, 25 million businesses fit that description. Nearly 18.6 million businesses have no staff other than the owner. Many of those businesses are run on a part-time basis from the owner's home. Twenty million businesses are set up as proprietorships. No matter how you identify small businesses, they are by

---

Different Learning Abilities

Attention Deficit Disorder Ask the student to be the recorder at the board. As other students read the information on page 132 aloud, the recorder should write the numbers on the board that describe small business ownership in the United States.

far the greatest number of businesses operating today.

Small Business Employment

On average, small businesses are responsible for creating 60–80 percent of all new jobs. Figure 6-3 shows some of the common types of small business. It is not surprising that there are a large number of service businesses. Many small business services are professional and technical. Many construction companies operate as small businesses.

Ownership Diversity

Women own more than one-fourth of all small businesses. More than 18 percent of small businesses have African-American, Asian-American, or Hispanic-American ownership. The

Small business owners report that the Internet is having a positive impact on their companies. In a recent survey, 51 percent said the Internet helped increase their profits and 49 percent said its use resulted in reduced operating costs.

majority of small business owners are over 35 years old, but nearly 25 percent are under 35. Today, almost all people starting small businesses have at least a high school diploma. Nearly 60 percent have finished some college work.

Half of all small businesses are home-based businesses. Because many businesses are part-time ventures or service businesses, the owners report that

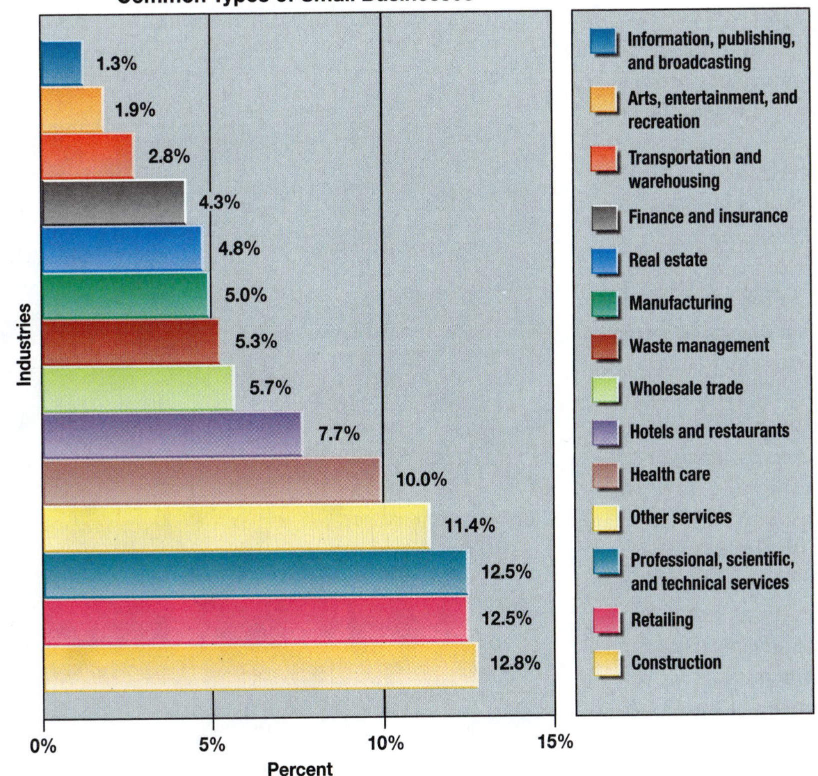

FIGURE 6-3

Why are so many small businesses in services and retailing?

TEACH

Ask students how many of them have family members who work in small businesses. Remind students that small businesses employ fewer than 500 people. Have those students stand and have the class calculate the percentage of students who have family members employed in small businesses.

FYI

Ask students to suggest reasons why the use of the Internet can save money and increase profits for small businesses.

TEACH

Have students use the Internet to determine what percentage of the U.S. population is female and what percentage is African-American, Asian-American, and Hispanic-American. Compare those percentages to the percentage of small business ownership listed for each group. Discuss the findings.

FIGURE 6-3 *ANSWER*

Services and retailing are two categories in which small businesses can get a start and provide customer service and value that large businesses may not be able to match.

Mathematics Have students determine the total number of small businesses in the United States as listed in the lesson. Using the information in Figure 6-3, then have students calculate the number of businesses for each of the categories listed in the figure. Show the results in a table.

ONGOING ASSESSMENT

checkpoint >> **ANSWER**

Nearly 50 percent of the American workforce is employed by small businesses. Small businesses are also responsible for 60–80 percent of all new jobs.

TEACH

Ask students why small service businesses may be able to respond to customer needs better than small businesses that sell products. After students present their ideas, have them read the information on pages 134 and 135 to see whether their ideas are similar or different.

THINK CRITICALLY THROUGH VISUALS

Small businesses can provide more personalized service and satisfy customers' unique needs. They are able to work more directly with fewer customers than larger businesses.

on average they needed $5,000 or less to start that type of business. Full-time businesses with buildings, equipment, and employees may require more than $100,000 of initial capital.

checkpoint >>

What percentage of employees in the United States work for small businesses?

main idea

Recognize the competitive advantages of small businesses.

SMALL BUSINESS ADVANTAGES

You need someone to mow your lawn, make a gourmet meal in your home for a few close friends, build a custom display case for a model train, or repair hardware on your home computer. Where would you turn for help? It's not likely that you will find a large business for any of those services.

Meeting Customer Needs

Small businesses play a vital role in the economy. They often serve customers where the number of products and services needed is small or the requirements are too specialized for large businesses to make a profit. It is easier for a small business to meet the precise needs of customers than a large business. Even though a large business has more resources, to operate efficiently it must focus on products and services that meet the needs of a large group of customers. That makes it harder to satisfy the unique needs of single customers.

Small businesses often are not able to match the lower operating costs

of larger businesses. They can compete by paying attention to their customers. Small businesses serve fewer customers and usually have more frequent contact with those customers than large businesses. They are more likely to be located close to the customer. They depend less on other businesses to distribute or service their products.

Large businesses often rely on consumer research to gather information. Small businesses usually get direct information from their customers about what they like and dislike.

Providing Unique Services

Small businesses are especially suited to provide unique services for customers. They may plan a wedding or design a customized sound system for your home. Providing those types of services means that business representatives must take a special interest in the customer. They spend time determining needs and

How do small businesses provide unique services that large businesses cannot?

Applied Skills

Word Processing/Office Technology Organize students into small groups. Have each group prepare a visual slide presentation using computer software that describes the competitive advantages and disadvantages of small businesses.

discussing alternatives. They have the expertise to plan and deliver the services that satisfy the customer. Large businesses may not find it profitable to spend that much time with each customer. Each employee that works with customers may not have the expertise to design the needed service.

Big business has a clear advantage when a large number of customers are willing to buy standard products and prefer low cost and efficient delivery. Small businesses gain an advantage when customers have unique needs, want more individual attention, and are willing to pay a bit more for the product or service to obtain what they really want. When asked, "What businesses do you believe are most concerned about you as a customer?" the majority of consumers identify small businesses.

- Lack of management experience
- Lack of experience with the type of business
- Not controlling operating expenses
- Poor location for the business
- Failure to manage credit offered to customers

main idea

Identify problems faced by many small businesses.

checkpoint »
How can small businesses compete successfully with larger businesses?

COMMON SMALL BUSINESS PROBLEMS

Not all small businesses succeed. In fact, their failure rate is much higher than larger businesses. Many failures result from the inability to pay expenses. The business is then forced to close. Some companies quietly go out of business when the owner believes that he or she is not doing well enough to continue. The owner may also get tired of the long hours and hard work.

Reasons for Failure

The following are the most common reasons for small business failure:

- Not keeping adequate records
- Not having enough start-up money

What do you think would be the hardest part of managing a small business?

Ask students whether the team members were in agreement on the success factors for the businesses they identified. Did their opinions change if they were customers of the business or not?

ONGOING ASSESSMENT

checkpoint » **ANSWER**

Smaller businesses are able to provide more personalized products and services to their customers. They are able to provide products and services where smaller orders and projects are required and tend to fill unique customer needs, which larger companies do not provide.

TEACH

List the reasons for small business failure on the board. Ask students to describe things that people who are considering starting a small business could do to avoid most of the problems.

THINK CRITICALLY THROUGH VISUALS

Answers will vary. The hardest part of managing a small business for many people is maintaining accurate records and adequate financial resources.

Different Learning Styles

Kinesthetic Learner Have students write each of the reasons for small business failure on a strip of paper. Then have them select a strip, hold it, and read the reason aloud.

Small Business Assistance

With the right kind of assistance, small businesses can overcome each of the causes of failure listed above. Small business owners can get help from a number of sources. Universities and colleges often have faculty members who can give advice and support to people who are starting or have started their own businesses.

Where can small businesses find assistance?

Local groups of businesspeople, such as Chambers of Commerce, have members who can help others with business problems.

The **Small Business Administration (SBA)** is a government agency that helps small business owners develop business plans and obtain financing and other support for their companies. Information about the SBA and its services can be obtained by visiting www.sba.gov.

The SBA offers information, publications, counseling, and many other forms of support. The SBA sponsors the Service Corps of Retired Executives (SCORE). Members of SCORE are retired local businesspeople who volunteer their services to counsel and mentor new business owners.

checkpoint >>
List common reasons for small business failure.

6-2 Assessment

Key Concepts

Determine the best answer.

1. The Small Business Administration considers a business small if it employs fewer than _?_ employees.
   a. 5
   b. 20
   c. 100
   d. 500

2. A competitive advantage that small businesses have over larger businesses is
   a. lower costs
   b. more consumer research
   c. lower prices
   d. attention to unique customer needs

3. Which of the following is *not* one of the reasons small business fail?
   a. poor customer credit practices
   b. the owner does not have adequate experience
   c. a poor business location
   d. not enough employees to do the work

Make Academic Connections

4. *Technology* eBay has become the home of many small businesses. Thousands of small business owners earn an excellent income by selling their products using the online auction services provided by eBay. Visit the eBay web site and identify three ways a small business can use the web site to support its operations.

5. *Communication* Interview a small business owner who has operated his or her business for at least three years. Determine the factors that have contributed to success as well as the major challenges that have been faced. Prepare an audio or video presentation based on your interview.

6. *Research* Interview 10 people who have recently purchased products or services from a small business. Ask them to list the top three reasons they made the purchase from a small business rather than a large business. Summarize the results from your interviews and present your findings in a table or chart.

Writing with Technology

Today's technology allows written communication to be exchanged at a much faster pace. Traditional forms of written communication, including letters, reports, and brochures, have not changed. However, when composed and completed, they can be sent to recipients in minutes using the Internet.

Many uses of traditional written communication have been replaced by instantaneous informal communications including text messaging, instant messaging, and e-mail. The immediate nature of the technology as well as the informal approach to composing those messages often result in poor communication or even miscommunication. When you use technology for written communication, especially in business, a few basic rules will demonstrate to your recipients that they are important and you want to communicate effectively.

The two primary types of communication used in business are memos and e-mail messages. Memos are formal and are used to convey more complex information. Send a memo when there is a need for a more permanent record of your correspondence or there is a need for formal language, or if the information included would make an e-mail too long. E-mail is more informal and used for direct and brief communication. Here are some important guidelines.

When Composing a Memo

1. *Know your audience*. Direct your memo to one person or a small group of people. Who needs the information? What do they need to know?
2. *Focus on one specific subject*. Make sure the subject is important to the audience. Specifically identify the subject of the memo. Do not stray into other topics.
3. *Select your words carefully*. Use language appropriate for the organization and understandable to your audience. Be clear, direct, and objective.
4. *Start strong*. Have an attention-getting first sentence. Focus the attention of the reader and get to the point.
5. *Provide only needed information*. Keep the memo brief, usually no more than one page, so it can be read in a few minutes. Before you end, be sure the information is complete.
6. *End effectively*. Identify any action needed and emphasize the importance of the information.

When Composing an E-mail Message

1. *Send only to the people who need the information*. Do not "reply to all" or use a mass e-mail list. Use e-mail for more individualized and specific messages.
2. *Use a specific subject line*. People get many e-mails. They can read and respond more efficiently if they can identify a clear subject.
3. *Provide a context*. If you are responding to an e-mail, briefly identify the information to which you are responding. Provide any information needed by the reader to understand your message.
4. *Don't get caught up in the technology*. Avoid "flaming" with all caps or inserting emoticons, flashing text, or other gimmicks that detract from the information.
5. *Keep the message short*. An e-mail should be read in about a minute. If the message is longer, send it in a different format or add an attachment or link.
6. *Don't write in haste*. You may regret an emotional message sent in haste. Consider the effect your message may have on the recipient.
7. *Even when informal, use effective writing skills*. Write in complete, active sentences, organize using paragraphs, and check your spelling.
8. *Use e-mail to create a record*. E-mail servers hold records of your files, even after you think they are deleted. If you need a record of a memo, use e-mail.

Think Critically

1. When should you send a memo rather than an e-mail?
2. What are the communication problems that are most likely to occur when using instant communication methods?

Explain to students that technology may make communications faster and easier, but may also result in less effective communications. It is important to use technology correctly when preparing business communications.

Think Critically
Answer

1. Send a memo when there is a need for a more permanent record of your correspondence, a need for formal language, or if the information included would make an e-mail too long.

2. Misinterpretation is a common problem because e-mail writers tend to write in a brief, casual style. Instant messaging is also more immediate and therefore invites emotional responses that might otherwise be tempered in a more formal letter or printed memo. E-mails can also be disregarded as "spam" if the sender does not use an appropriate subject line or may not be read in entirety if the writer has made the e-mail too long.

Applied Skills

Communication Have each student prepare an e-mail message and a two-paragraph memo using the guidelines provided. The communications should relate to a topic from the current lesson and should be directed to other students in the class.

Focus on Real Life

Explain to students that budgets are very important for businesses because they can alert the business owner to problems before they become too big to solve. Budgets may have to be adjusted if changes occur in the economy or in business operations.

TEACH

List the lesson subheadings on the board. Explain to students that there are several important factors that contribute to the success of a new business. As you disclose each of the factors, ask students to give reasons why each factor can affect the success or failure of the business.

PROJECT

Provide the following instructions to students. (These instructions also appear on page xxiv of the textbook.)

What hobbies, interest, and experiences do you have that could help you achieve your life-span goals? Describe steps you could take now that would expand your experiences and opportunities for achieving you life-span goals.

Goals

Recognize important factors to be considered when starting a business.

Describe the elements of a business plan.

Identify types and sources of financing for a small business.

Key Terms

business plan

start-up financing

short-term financing

long-term financing

Focus on Real Life

Jermaine Anderson turned his baseball card hobby into a business. He had a small store in a mall where he bought and sold collectors' baseball cards and other baseball memorabilia. Jermaine began his business with a small loan from the bank and money saved from working while in college.

The business grew steadily each year. Jermaine prepared a specific budget at the beginning of each year. He was able to spend his money wisely on new inventory, advertising, and improvements to his store.

This year he used the same budgeting process that he had for the past four years. Based on last year's results, he estimated that sales would increase 8 percent. He planned to increase expenses accordingly. Even with the increased expenses, the budget projected another nice profit.

The first two months of the year went well. Then the economy slipped into a recession. Customers cut back on their spending at his store. Jermaine's sales were declining while his expenses continued to increase. Jermaine studied his budget to determine why he had problems in the fifth year when his planning had been so successful in the past.

---

main idea

Recognize important factors to be considered when starting a business.

THE BUSINESS DECISION

Many people think about starting a business. Few actually do. The procedures followed to start a business often determine whether it will be successful. The process begins with an idea and concludes with a careful study of information to establish whether the idea can be successful.

An Idea Plus Experience

Every business begins with an idea. Business ideas come from many sources. Hobbies, interests, and business experiences often give people ideas for new businesses. Books and magazines suggest new business opportunities, including available franchises. Few people should think about starting a business without working for some time in a small business. Several years of training in a range of business operations will prepare you for the role of owner. Having responsibility for decisions and opportunities to manage people is a key part of that experience.

Right Place and Time

Putting your business idea into action means finding the right place to open the business. Most retail businesses need good customer traffic. If the business is not easy to find or requires a great deal of travel time, many potential customers will stay away. A wholesaler needs easy access to manufacturers where products are obtained for resale

---

Different Learning Styles

Kinesthetic Learner As students study the factors to consider when starting a business, encourage them to draw a picture or graphic that illustrates each factor. They can use the illustrations as reminders of the important factors.

to other businesses. Manufacturers must be located in an area with access to the raw materials used in manufacturing. Transportation systems must also be easy to reach for distributing finished products. Timing is another key factor in starting a business. Most successful businesses start during a period when customer demand for certain products or services is high.

Team Approach

Many small business owners are quite independent. They started their businesses because they do not want to take direction from other people. A business is not easy to run without the help of others. Even the smallest businesses need a few full- or part-time employees to grow or cover extended hours. The employees must be chosen carefully for their ability to work as a team. Choosing the "team" members becomes one of the most important initial business decisions.

In addition to employees, small business owners will need assistance from people with specialized business knowledge. These include bankers, lawyers, and accountants. If possible, the new owner should identify business professionals who focus on working with small businesses.

Preparation and Research

The most important step in starting a business is preparation. Preparation includes having enough information to make good decisions about the business. Time spent gathering and studying information before the

You are planning to open a small business that will rent bicycles, rollerblades, push scooters, and electric scooters by the hour for people to use for relaxation and exercise. As a team, identify three possible business locations in your community and discuss which location would be best for the business. Prepare a presentation that compares and contrasts the locations. Use visuals such as maps, photos, and drawings to help illustrate your presentation.

business is started will save time and avoid later problems.

Information is needed about customers, competitors, important operations, government regulations, and many other topics. This information is available through libraries, colleges or universities, and small business assistance centers. At times, the new business owner will have to do further

Is there a small business assistance center in your neighborhood? What resources can you use to locate the closest center?

TEACH

Remind students that many entrepreneurs are independent and not always good team players. Have them discuss how this can result in problems for the business and why working with a team can benefit the new small business owner.

Students should identify locations that will attract a large number of people who are interested in the products and also determine where there is a safe and pleasant area to use them nearby.

ONGOING ASSESSMENT
checkpoint » ANSWER

A team approach allows employees to feel valued and motivated to take personal responsibility for the benefit of the business. Owners cannot expect to be able to do everything alone. Building a team will allow the business to increase productivity and, ultimately, profits.

Answers will vary. Students can determine the answer by searching the local telephone directory.

Language Arts Ask students to write a memo to a friend who is considering starting a new business. In the memo, the student should offer advice on things the friend should consider carefully before making a final decision.

TEACH

If available, bring a copy of a completed business plan for a small business to class. Let students see the plan so they have a visual image of the length, format, and content of the business plan. Tell them that all business plans are not alike, but most include information on a common set of elements.

FIGURE 6-4 *ANSWER*

The elements in Figure 6-4 are important when planning a new business because they force the owners to think about and plan all major business activities and how they will be carried out.

research to gather more current data. Information will help to make sure that decisions are made objectively.

> *checkpoint* »
> Why is it important to use a team approach when starting a new business?

main idea

Describe the elements of a business plan.

DEVELOPING A BUSINESS PLAN

When successful businesses are compared with those that failed, one factor stands out as the most important difference. The owners of successful businesses develop and follow a business plan. The owners of businesses that fail often do not have a business plan.

Elements of a Business Plan
Description of the Business • the business idea • major products and services • ownership structure • strengths/weaknesses • long- and short-term goals
Customer Analysis • description of customers • location, number, and resources of customers • sales forecasts
Operations Plan • organization of the company • description of major operations • analysis of resources needed • human resource plans
Marketing Plan • description of major marketing activities • description of resources needed • schedule of marketing activities
Financial Plans • start-up costs • short- and long-term financial needs • sources of financing • budgets and financial statements

FIGURE 6-4

Why are each of these elements important when planning a new business?

What Is a Business Plan?

A **business plan** is a written description of the business idea and how it will be carried out, including all major business activities. Key features of a business plan are a general description of the company, the credentials of the owner(s), a description of the product or service, an analysis of the market (demand, customers, and competition), and a financial plan. Most business plans are developed for one year and then updated for the next year. If the business owner needs help from others, especially for financing the new business, a business plan will usually be required. Figure 6-4 is an outline of the sections of a business plan.

Even if help is not needed, a business plan should be developed. By developing a plan, the owner is forced to think about important activities, the amount of time they will take, and their cost. This process may identify potential problems. The plan also serves as a guide to keep the business on track.

Steps in Developing the Business Plan

The business owner is in charge of developing the business plan. The most popular use of business plans is to persuade lenders and investors to finance the venture. A well-developed plan will lay out an idea and will require an owner to analyze his or her concept and make decisions about key business activities such as production, marketing, staffing, and financing.

Different Learning Abilities

Visually Impaired Reproduce Figure 6-4 and increase the font size so each section of the business plan is on a separate sheet of paper. This visual aid can be used to highlight the kind of information that should be included in each element of a business plan.

Where can the entrepreneur find help in creating a business plan?

Some owners hire someone to write the plan. Others get help from a bank or a local office of the Small Business Administration. Even if others are involved in developing the plan, the owner must be familiar with all of the information and make the major decisions for the plan.

The first step in developing the business plan is to gather and review information. If possible, the owner should review other business plans and study information on the activities and financial performance of similar businesses, especially potential competitors.

Next, the owner should develop strategic alternatives. Alternative plans for production, marketing, staffing, and financing should be studied and identified. The owner can select the best choices from the alternatives.

Finally, each section of the business plan should be written. A plan devotes several sections to a general description of the business. These sections include the basic legal form of the organization and major products or services. Other sections detail the competition, potential customers, operations, marketing, and finances. Before the plan is completed, the owner should have business experts review the plan and offer their advice about its strengths and weaknesses.

> *checkpoint* >>
> What are "strategic alternatives" in a business plan?

TEACH

Have students debate the question: Should a new business owner write the business plan or hire someone else to write it? Record the major points made for each side of the issue on the board.

ONGOING ASSESSMENT

checkpoint >> ANSWER

Strategic alternatives are alternative plans for production, staffing, financing, and so on. Even the best business plan cannot predict every possible circumstance. An alternate plan allows a business to be prepared for the unforeseeable.

THINK CRITICALLY THROUGH VISUALS

An entrepreneur can find help creating a business plan by consulting business experts and using the support provided by the Small Business Administration and other business support groups.

Writing Across the Curriculum Have students prepare a paragraph that compares planning and writing a business plan to writing assignments they have had in other classes, such as a research report in a science class.

Have students prepare an outline that lists the three major types of financing as headings. Then, as each type is discussed, have students list examples of each type of financing under the appropriate heading.

CORPORATE SOCIAL RESPONSIBILITY

Think Critically
Answers

1. Answers will vary. Students should indicate that earning a profit is the main motivation. They might also mention the need to compete against local and regional businesses.

2. Presentations will vary. Students might report on Coca-Cola's efforts to replace every drop of 290 billion liters of water it uses annually to achieve balance in communities and in nature. Another example is Boeing's commitment to produce aircraft that weigh less. This means more fuel efficiency and less pollution.

3. Summaries will vary. Students should be able to locate the report at the McDonald's Corporation web site. Some of the programs mentioned in the report involve protecting the rainforest, reducing packaging, protecting wildlife, and responsible purchasing.

FYI

Tell students that, in addition to reading the business plan, most bankers and lenders will interview the business owner to make sure he or she understands the details of the written plan.

142

FINANCING THE SMALL BUSINESS

A new business with a good product or service may run out of money before it can become profitable. Several years of operation are required before most new businesses earn a profit. Finding adequate financing is a key step in starting and running a new business.

Types of Financing

Three types of financing must be considered. **Start-up financing** is the amount of money needed to open the business. It includes the cost of buildings, equipment, *inventory* (products or raw materials on hand), supplies, licenses, and the like. **Short-term financing** is the money needed to pay for the current operating activities of a business. Short-term financing is obtained for a period of less than a year and often for one or two months. **Long-term financing** is money needed for the main resources of a business (such as land, buildings, and equipment) that will last for many years. These resources usually require large amounts of money and will be paid over many years.

Sources of Financing

Finding the needed money may be the most difficult part of starting a business. The money required to start and operate a new business usually comes from a mixture of owner-supplied and borrowed funds.

Global Social Responsibility

Many Europeans are concerned about their personal health and the health of their environment. In part, this concern is based on Europe's high population density. There are 3.6 times as many people per square mile in Europe as there are in the United States. Europe's high population density has led to concerns about waste disposal, air quality, and the availability of natural resources such as fresh water.

Some businesses based in the United States and doing business in Europe are working hard to address the concerns of European customers and governments, including that of the European Union. McDonald's wants to be seen as a socially responsible company and is developing policies and practices to address concerns about the nutritional value of their products and the impact of their operations on the environment.

Throughout Europe, McDonald's prints nutrition information directly on food containers and wrappers. This means consumers can see information about calories, fat, and sodium as they pluck fries out of the cardboard pouch.

McDonald's has launched an environmental initiative in southern England to convert used cooking oil into biodiesel. The fuel is used to power the company's delivery vehicles. This program removes cooking oil from the waste stream and reduces the consumption of gasoline.

Think Critically
1. What motivates U.S. companies to tailor their policies and practices to address the social concerns of global customers?
2. Research another company's efforts to be socially responsible and address social concerns around the world. Develop a short presentation about your findings.
3. Use the Internet to locate McDonald's Worldwide Corporate Responsibility Report. Write a summary of one of the programs mentioned in the report.

Different Learning Abilities

Specific Learning Disability (SLD) Have students use a local business directory or business listings in a telephone directory to locate the name of three banks that offer financing and other services to small businesses. Have them record the name of the bank, the address, main telephone number, and the URL for the bank's web site if available.

The source of owner-supplied money depends on the ownership structure. In a proprietorship, one person will supply the money. In most partnerships each partner will be expected to contribute. A corporation is owned and financed by the shareholders.

Borrowed funds are obtained through loans from banks and other financial institutions or through funding provided by other people, such as family and friends. Often companies that sell equipment, materials, or inventory to a business will offer credit if the business does not have financial problems. A new business owner should be careful about accepting credit. The owner must take

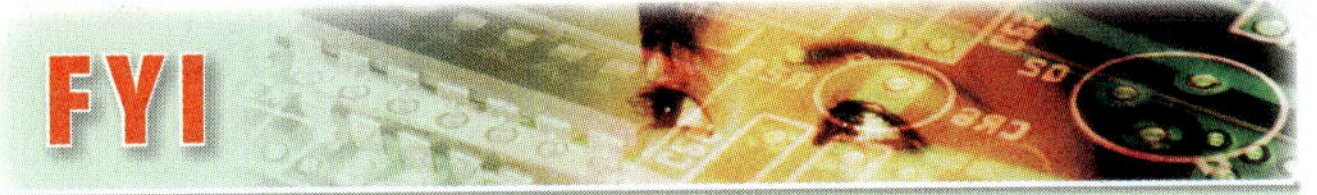

FYI

Bankers and other lenders use a written business plan to determine if the owner really understands the business and is committed to its success.

into account the cost of the credit and when payments are due.

checkpoint >>

In addition to owner-supplied capital, what are several other sources of financing for a small business?

6-3 Assessment

Key Concepts

Determine the best answer.

1. Every business begins with a(n)
   a. customer
   b. profit
   c. idea
   d. invention

2. True or False. Most small business owners enjoy being part of a team.

3. True or False. A business plan does not have to be written because the business owner is well aware of the information in the plan.

4. Money needed for the important resources of a business (such as land, buildings, and equipment) that will last for many years is called
   a. start-up financing
   b. short-term financing
   c. long-term financing
   d. credit

Make Academic Connections

5. *Technology* Locate an outline for a business plan on the Internet. Compare the sections of the plan you found with those in Figure 6-4. Develop a final outline using both resources. Write a two sentence statement for each section of the outline describing why that section is important to a successful small business.

6. *Math* Gwen Osterhaus and Portia Juarez have formed a partnership to open a garden coffee cafe in Central Park. Gwen invests $23,000 and Portia invests $31,000. They get a micro loan from the Small Business Administration for $18,500. They have $9,000 of credit from the Bean Machine Company that sold them some of their equipment. Calculate the total amount of start-up financing available to the partnership. Make a pie chart that shows the percentage of total financing that is provided from each source. How much of the financing is owner supplied and how much is borrowed?

ONGOING ASSESSMENT

checkpoint >> **ANSWER**

Borrowed money may come from banks, finance companies, or other individuals, such as friends and family. Some suppliers may also be willing to extend credit.

ASSESS

Key Concepts Answers

1. c. idea

2. False. Most small business owners are very independent and prefer to work alone. However, most find team work beneficial to their small business.

3. False. A business plan should be written.

4. c. long-term financing

Make Academic Connections

5. Answers will vary. The outlines should show evidence of two sources and should be presented in a logical order. Statements should indicate a clear understanding of the ideas presented in this lesson.

6. Total: $23,000 + 31,000 + 18,500 + 9,000 = 81,500$
   $23,000 \div 81,500 = 28\%$
   $31,000 \div 81,500 = 38\%$
   $18,500 \div 81,500 = 23\%$
   $9,000 \div 81,500 = 11\%$
   Owner supplied: 54,000
   Borrowed: 27,500.

CLOSE

Have each student describe one activity or type of information that is important to a small business owner when planning a new business.

RETEACH

Display Figure 6-4. Have students describe the importance of the business plan and explain the reason for having strategic alternatives for each section of the business plan.

ENRICH

Ask a successful small business owner to speak to the class and discuss the advantages and disadvantages of being a small business owner. Have students prepare questions in advance to ask the entrepreneur based on the information from the lesson.

Communicate Business Concepts Answers

1. Answers will vary depending on students' interests, hobbies, and skills.

2. Small businesses contribute more new jobs because new businesses start frequently. Larger, established businesses have often reached growth limits and have fewer opportunities to offer.

3. Personality plays a key role in the success of many small business owners, a fact well demonstrated. The young entrepreneurs each had marketable skills and good ideas, but their skills and ideas could not sell themselves. Through their persistence, initiative, and ability to secure the help of others, they were able to turn ideas and skills into businesses.

4. By using the Internet, small businesses eliminate some overhead costs, increase the size of available markets, and increase the speed of communication. In doing so, many are able to compete with larger businesses.

5. Freddie can increase his chances for success by considering what type of business he is qualified to manage; how he will finance the start-up, short-term, and long-term goals of the business; how much time he can devote; how he will manage recordkeeping and competition; where he will locate; and who he will enlist for help. Preparing a written business plan will force him to consider each of these questions.

CHAPTER 6 Assessment

Business Notes

6-1 BECOMING AN ENTREPRENEUR

1. Successful entrepreneurs have a real desire to be their own boss. They use special skills and abilities to come up with innovative ideas and then develop a good initial plan for a business. Entrepreneurs come from all age categories, racial and ethnic groups, and both genders, as well as varied educational levels.

2. Entrepreneurship is a key part of the U.S. economy. Money needed to start a new business may come from the owner, family, friends, or venture capital. Other sources of financing are loans from banks and financial institutions and credit given by other businesses. Small businesses are responsible for nearly half of the U.S. gross domestic product each year and 55 percent of all innovative products and services developed.

3. Opportunities open to entrepreneurs include the creation of new or improved products and services, an improved design, more effective procedures, or greater attention to quality. Risks include lack of adequate capital, low sales, higher than expected expenses, competitive pressure, an owner unprepared to manage a growing business, and operations that require more time than the owner is willing to commit.

6-2 SMALL BUSINESS BASICS

4. In a small business, the owner is usually the manager, it operates in one or very few locations, it typically serves a small market, and it is not dominant in its field of operation.

5. Small businesses play an important role in the economy. They often serve customers where the number of products and services needed is small or the requirements are too specialized for large businesses to be profitable.

6. The most common reasons for small business failure are not keeping adequate records, not having enough start-up money, lack of management experience, lack of experience with the type of business, not controlling operating expenses, poor location for the business, and failure to manage customer credit.

6-3 STARTING A SMALL BUSINESS

7. Factors that lead to a successful new business are an idea plus experience, the right time and place, a team approach, and preparation and research.

8. By developing a written business plan, the owner will think about important activities, the amount of time they will take, and their cost. The plan also serves as a guide to keep the business on track.

9. Obtaining adequate financing is an important step in starting and operating a new business. Three types of financing to be considered are start-up, short-term, and long-term financing. The money required to start and operate a new business usually comes from a mixture of owner-supplied and borrowed funds.

Communicate Business Concepts

1. What is a new product or service that could become the basis for a new business that fits your interests, hobbies, or special skills and abilities? What are some reasons you would be interested or not interested in becoming an entrepreneur?

2. Why do you believe that small businesses contribute more of the new jobs to the economy than large established businesses?

3. What are factors that you believe contributed to the success of the young entrepreneurs described in Lesson 6-1? Do you believe the idea for their product or service was more or less important than their personal characteristics?

4. How is the Internet changing the characteristics of small businesses? Do you believe the Internet can make small businesses more competitive with large businesses? Why?

5. Freddie is thinking about starting a small business and has come to you for advice. Using the reasons that most small businesses fail listed in Lesson 6-2, what would you tell Freddie that will help him increase his chances for being successful?

6. In most communities, there are several locations where retail businesses locate but soon fail. They are followed by other businesses that also fail. People say the pattern of failure is because of a poor location. Do you agree that the location is the most likely reason that the businesses fail? Why would a new business consider a location where a previous business has already failed?

7. Identify the three types of people you believe would be the most important to assist a new small business owner. Justify each of your choices.

8. If you were a banker reviewing a business plan to determine if you will provide financing, what information would be most important in determining if you would support the small business or not?

9. What are the advantages and disadvantages of hiring another experienced person to develop and write the business plan for the owner of a new business?

Develop Your Business Language

Match the terms listed with the definitions.

10. A government agency that helps small business owners develop business plans and obtain financing and other support for their companies.

11. Money provided by large investors to finance new products and new businesses that have a good chance to be very profitable.

12. The money needed to pay for the current operating activities of a business.

13. The amount of money needed to open the business.

14. An invention or creation that is brand new.

15. Someone who takes a risk in starting a business to earn a profit.

16. A written description of the business idea and how it will be carried out, including all major business activities.

17. Money needed for the important resources of a business (such as land, buildings, and equipment) that will last for many years.

18. An independent business with fewer than 500 employees.

19. A designed change that increases the usefulness of a product, service, or process.

20. The process of starting, organizing, managing, and assuming the responsibility for a business.

KEY TERMS
a. business plan
b. entrepreneur
c. entrepreneurship
d. improvement
e. innovation
f. long-term financing
g. short-term financing
h. small business
i. Small Business Administration (SBA)
j. start-up financing
k. venture capital

6. This particular location is probably not well suited to retail business. It may not have enough traffic or the traffic may move by too quickly. It may not be visible, have adequate lighting, signage, or walk-by traffic to support a retail business. This does not mean, however, that this same location would not work for a service business for which these elements may not be as critical.

7. A lawyer, accountant, or consultant can assist with a business plan and the necessary legal forms for beginning a business. A loan officer or other finance specialist can assist with securing funds, as can friends and family. Mentors can provide encouragement and insight from their own experience.

8. A banker will want to know that a business owner has considered all aspects important to success. A thorough business plan will provide him or her with answers to critical questions about how well informed and prepared the applicant is. This information will be the most important to consider.

9. The advantages of hiring someone to write a plan would be the insight he or she could offer. A consultant or experienced business owner would recognize any flaws in the plan and could assist the new owner in making needed improvements. The disadvantages might be that another person may not share the same enthusiasm or vision for the business that the prospective owner has.

Develop Your Business Language Answers

10. i. Small Business Administration (SBA)

11. k. venture capital

12. g. short-term financing

13. j. start-up financing

14. e. innovation

15. b. entrepreneur

16. a. business plan

17. f. long-term financing

18. h. small business

19. d. improvement

20. c. entrepreneurship

Make Academic Connections

21. TECHNOLOGY Use the Internet to identify the number of small business owners by race or by age. Then enter the information in a spreadsheet program and calculate the percentage of all small business owners represented by each race or age classification. Then use the graphing function to create a chart or graph illustrating the results.

22. COMMUNICATION Many small business owners obtain some of their start-up financing from family members and friends. Assume you are starting a small Internet business that will develop and maintain low-cost web sites for local organizations, clubs, and nonprofit groups. You have $2,500 of your own money to invest and need to raise an additional $5,000. Develop a letter or one-page brochure that you can use to interest family and friends in investing $500 or more in your new business. Make sure it is persuasive and tells them what benefits they will receive from their investment.

23. PERSONAL DEVELOPMENT The characteristics common to most entrepreneurs are listed in Figure 6-1. Create a table with three columns. In the first column, list each of the characteristics. In the middle column, describe things you have done (hobbies, work, projects, activities) that provide evidence of each characteristic. In the final column, list additional things you can do in the next five years to further develop the characteristic.

24. GOVERNMENT The federal government and most state governments provide many resources as well as financial support for small businesses. Use the Internet to locate two agencies of the federal government that provide services developed specifically for small businesses. Then search the web site for your state's government and locate one state agency that provides small business services. Prepare a three-paragraph report on each of the agencies you identified in which you describe the agency, the services provided, and how a new business can qualify for the services.

25. ECONOMICS The U.S. Census Bureau maintains information on the number of businesses and amount of business activity in every county of each state. Use the Internet to visit the U.S. Census Bureau web site (www.census.gov). Use the search engine on their web site to locate "County Business Patterns." View the county data by clicking on the hypertext table link. When you have accessed that web page, enter the name of your state and then the county in which you live. Find data on the number of businesses with one to four employees in your county. List the total number of businesses of that size, the five industries with the most businesses employing fewer than five employees, and the total number of establishments in each of those industries.

Linking School and Community

Survey at least 10 people in your community about their experiences as consumers with small businesses and large businesses. Ask them to describe the reasons they prefer to buy from small businesses and the reasons they prefer to buy from large businesses. Then ask them to describe the disadvantages of each. Summarize the results of your discussions in a chart or short written report.

Web Workout

The Internet is the ultimate niche small business platform. The Internet can bring together sellers and individual buyers at a very low cost. Many small businesses, including home-based businesses, use portals such as Amazon.com and eBay to sell their products. This way, the small business owner does not need to set up their own web site or e-commerce system.

Think Critically

1. Use the Internet to find a niche seller (a product with a very narrow appeal). Determine if the seller uses a sales portal (like Amazon.com or eBay) or if they have their own web site.

2. Identify a niche product that you would like to sell. Develop a short business plan to determine if it would be better to sell through a sales portal or by developing your own web site.

Decision-Making Strategies

David Obolski completed a community college program in Small Business Management. He now wanted to own his own floral business. He had worked for Flower-a-Bunda during high school and college. In addition, he was able to save almost $20,000 toward starting his own business. However, he knew that he would need more than $20,000 to buy a florist shop. He would need almost double that amount to qualify for the necessary loans to start up the business. David studied three ways he might start his business.

   a. He could find a partner to provide the additional cash.

   b. He could work for the owner of Flower-a-Bunda until she retired in seven years and buy the business with his accumulated savings.

   c. He could purchase a franchise for an investment of $20,000. However, David would have to pay a franchise fee of 6 percent of total sales each year to the franchisor.

26. What are the advantages and disadvantages of each route to small business ownership for David?

27. If you were David, which choice would you make? Why?

American Enterprise Project

The United States takes great pride in the American enterprise system, which encourages individuals to take the risk of starting a business.

Consumers play an important role in the American enterprise system. Their demand for goods and services influences which businesses will be successful. Business success depends upon paying attention to consumer demand.

Your team of three individuals has been challenged to design a presentation that teaches elementary students about the American enterprise system. Your presentation should teach students about supply and demand and the American dream of owning a business. The presentation should include active participation of the elementary students.

You will create a business report with substantiated statements in a clear and concise format. Creativity through design and use of meaningful graphics is encouraged. The report should be a clear presentation about the American enterprise system and your strategy for teaching elementary students key concepts. The report should include the following parts: Purpose of project, Research into school and/or community needs, Description of project, Uniqueness of project, and Evaluation and results. The format of your report will be evaluated for clear and concise presentation with logical arrangements of information; creativity in presentation; and correct grammar, punctuation, spelling, and acceptable business style.

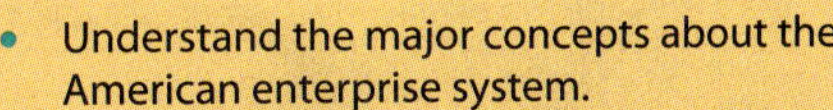
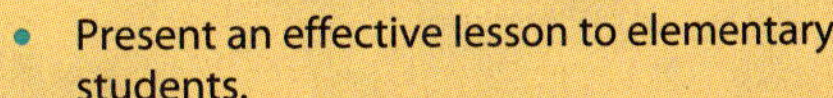

PERFORMANCE INDICATORS EVALUATED

- Understand the major concepts about the American enterprise system.
- Present an effective lesson to elementary students.
- Highlight measurable results from the American Enterprise Project.
- Reach goals for the American Enterprise Project.

For more detailed information about performance indicators, go to the FBLA web site.

Think Critically

1. Why is it important for young Americans to understand the American enterprise system?

2. List two strategies to use during the presentation that will hold the attention of elementary students.

3. List five major concepts that elementary students must understand about the American enterprise system.

4. What would be a good joint project between FBLA/BPA members and elementary students to strengthen understanding about the American Enterprise System?

http://www.fbla-pbl.org/

Access the web site shown here to find portfolio activities for this chapter. Use the activities to provide tangible evidence of your learning.

Decision-Making Strategies Answers

26. a. A partner would provide the additional cash right away, but then David would not be the sole owner of his business.

b. David would be able to buy the business himself, but he would have to wait seven years.

c. He would be able to start his business right away, but he would owe a franchise fee each year that would reduce his profits.

27. Answers will vary.

Winning Edge
American Enterprise Project

Think Critically *Answers*

1. America's economy is based on the principles of private enterprise. Much of the strength of the economy is directly related to the market economy and the incentives it provides to citizens and business owners.

2. Elementary students have short attention spans. Music, props, and audience participation will keep their attention. Give out prizes for students who answer questions correctly.

3. Ownership, supply, demand, consumerism, and profit are five key concepts that should be covered among other possible choices.

4. Answers will vary. Some possible ideas are to design a billboard that emphasizes free enterprise, shadow local businesses, and design a newspaper advertisement that thanks community entrepreneurs and recognizes their spirit of free enterprise.

Management and Leadership

CHAPTER OVERVIEW

In this chapter, students learn about the role of management in organizational success, the activities managers complete, and how leadership differs from management.

7-1   Management

This lesson introduces the five functions of management that are common to all levels of managers and the styles managers use to work with employees.

7-2   Leadership

While studying this lesson, students will compare leadership and management and learn about the characteristics of effective leaders. They will also review human relations skills and types of influence needed by leaders.

7-3   Ethical Management

This lesson focuses on the importance of ethical management and how leaders can increase ethical behavior in their organizations.

© Getty Images-PhotoDisc

Teaching Resources

Activities and Study Guide, Ch. 7
Chapter and Unit Tests, Ch. 7
Spanish Resources, Ch. 7

ExamView® CD, Ch. 7
Instructor's Resource CD
- PowerPoint Slides, Ch. 7
- Lesson Plans, Ch. 7

Xtra! Web Site

school.cengage.com/business/introtobiz
- Study Tools, 7-1, 7-2, 7-3
- Quiz Prep, Ch. 7
- Net Bookmark, Ch. 7
- Crossword Puzzle, Ch. 7
- Portfolio Activity, Ch. 7

Planning a Career in...
MANAGEMENT

A position in management is the goal of many people who enter business careers. The chance to move up in a business and contribute to major decisions is viewed as a challenging goal for many people. Managers are key to the success of a company. Management opportunities exist in all companies and in every part of a business. Whether your interests are in finance, marketing, information management, engineering, or human resources, you can become a manager. You can begin a management career as a team leader, supervisor, or assistant manager after only a few years of experience. You can move up in the company to become a mid or top-level manager with additional experience and education. Your career advancement will be based on your performance as a manager and your contribution to the business' success.

Employment Outlook

- The employment outlook for management jobs is varied, with some high-growth areas and other areas facing increasing competition.
- Mid-level management jobs are more competitive as companies reduce the levels of management and move more decision making and responsibility to employees.
- Entry-level management positions as supervisors or assistant managers are plentiful but often low paying. They usually combine limited management responsibilities with regular job duties.

Related Job Titles

- Assistant Manager
- Coordinator
- Leader
- Supervisor
- Department Head

Needed Skills

- Financial and data analysis skills
- Oral and written communication, listening, and human relations skills
- Leadership and decision-making skills
- Understanding and use of technology with expertise in standard business software

What's it like to work in... Management

Frank faced a number of challenges as he sat at his workstation Monday morning. He is the supervisor of a production line at the Emprex Corporation. Frank had to interview nine people to fill three full-time jobs and one part-time job. He had to meet with his team to let them know they would have to work at least 10 hours of overtime each week for the next two months to meet their quota. He knew the workers would be happy with the extra money but they would be giving up a lot of free time.

Frank was also challenged by some budget problems. While he didn't have full authority over the budget, his manager had warned him that costs were going up, which meant every supervisor had to find ways to reduce expenses. Frank knew that some employees wasted supplies and materials and would have to be watched more carefully. Finally, Frank had to complete one of his least favorite duties. An employee had not met expectations and had to be fired. Frank had a meeting scheduled at 3 p.m. with the employee to break the news.

What about you? What would you find the most and least enjoyable about Frank's work?

Tell students there are many opportunities in management for young people with limited experiences, as well as older, very experienced business people. Management combines knowledge of specific business activities with understanding of the entire business. At the conclusion of the discussion, direct students to answer the "What About You?" question that follows the feature.

What About You? Answer

Answers will vary. Some students will find the manager's work exciting and varied, while others will think it seems too hectic and difficult. You may want to have the class list specific pros and cons of management careers and have them compare different types of management jobs. Ask students how their expectations of management work compare to the description of Frank's activities.

Additional Career information

Additional information on careers can be found in the *Occupational Outlook Handbook,* an online publication (www.bls.gov/oco) of the federal government. Tell your class about this resource and how to use it. This description of job duties can be used to demonstrate the relevancy of skills learned in this course.

7-1 Management

Goals

Define the five functions of management.

Describe the levels of management in businesses.

Discuss when to use the two management styles.

Key Terms

management

planning

organizing

staffing

implementing

controlling

management style

Focus on Real Life

Have you considered a career in management? Do you realize that you might already have experience with activities that are similar in some aspects to those of a managers' work? You manage your time and your money. You might be a leader of a team or organization. Maybe you have taken a leadership role in a group activity. As a leader you probably took responsibility, gave directions, and solved problems.

While not the same as leading a business, these activities give you a taste of the work of managers. Consider what it would be like to be responsible for a million-dollar budget, directing the work of hundreds of people, or making sure an important project involving several parts of a business is completed on schedule.

Do you think you have what it takes to be a manager? Would you find working as a manager exciting as well as challenging? If so, what can you do now to begin to prepare for a management career?

---

main idea

Define the five functions of management.

ROLE AND WORK OF MANAGERS

Managers are responsible for the success or failure of a business. Managers receive recognition and other rewards when a business meets its goals. They also are held accountable when goals are not met. People who want to experience the risks and rewards of business often become managers.

Who Is a Manager?

Management is the process of accomplishing the goals of an organization through the effective use of people and other resources. Managers make things happen in business. The entrepreneur who develops the idea for a new business is a manager. The chief executive of an established firm who decides how to compete in a changing international market is a manager. Supervisors with responsibility for the work of a small number of employees are managers, as are vice presidents with more than 100 employees reporting to them.

What Do Managers Do?

Every manager has specific job duties. Managers must complete similar activities no matter what the size or type of business. Managers' work can be organized within five functions: planning, organizing, staffing, implementing, and controlling.

- **Planning** involves analyzing information, setting goals, and making decisions about what needs to be done.

- **Organizing** means identifying and arranging the work and resources needed to achieve the goals that have been set.

- **Staffing** includes all of the activities involved in obtaining, preparing, and

---

compensating the employees of a business.

- **Implementing** is the effort to direct and lead people to accomplish the planned work of the organization.
- **Controlling** determines to what extent the business is accomplishing the goals it set out to reach in the planning stage.

Large corporations have many managers. Duties for specific management functions are assigned to each manager. Often, due to the size of a business, several managers may have individual responsibilities within just one of the functions. In a partnership, the management functions are usually divided among the partners. Each partner works with functions he or she enjoys and performs well. In a new small business, the owner usually is responsible for all of the management functions. As the business grows, other employees will be moved into management positions.

© Getty Images/PhotoDisc

Think of a business in your neighborhood. What levels of management do you think exist there?

Work as a Team

Your class is responsible for picking up litter on a highway on the edge of your town. Your team has responsibility for managing that project. For each of the five management functions, identify two or three management activities that your team must complete in order for the project to be successful.

They will be assigned one or more of the management functions to complete.

Managing a business or even a part of a business is a very complex process. Managers must make decisions, solve problems, respond to competition, and develop new strategies. Decisions made to complete one management function affect all other functions. The efforts of each manager impact the work of others and the results achieved by the business. Effective managers motivate employees to do their best work. They also use the money and other resources of the business wisely. Successful businesses have managers who are able to complete each of the management functions well.

> *checkpoint* >>
> What are the five management functions?

MANAGEMENT LEVELS

Unless a business is very small, there will be several managers with responsibilities for leading the business. Every manager completes all of the management functions and has authority over other people and their work. Not every manager gives the same amount of attention and time to each of the functions. Most organizations have three levels of managers—executives, mid-managers, and supervisors.

Top Management

Executives are top-level managers with responsibilities for the direction and

main idea

Describe the levels of management in businesses.

Work as a Team

Ask students whether the task could be completed without one or more of the functions being performed. Have them decide whether one of the functions is most important to the success of the task.

TEACH

Provide students with a handout that has a 3×5 table. List the five management functions in the left column. Then have students complete the middle column by listing activities they complete in their personal lives that fit the definition of each function. As a group, complete the final column by listing activities that managers complete in their businesses that fit the function's definition.

ONGOING ASSESSMENT

checkpoint >> **ANSWER**

The five management functions are (1) planning, (2) organizing, (3) staffing, (4) implementing, and (5) controlling.

THINK CRITICALLY THROUGH VISUALS

Answers will vary. Students should identify businesses that have all three levels of managers—executives, mid-managers, and supervisors—as well as some smaller businesses that may have just one or two levels.

Different Learning Abilities

Attention Deficit Disorder Have students prepare flash cards with each management function on one side of a card and the definition of the function on the other side. Have students work with the flash cards in teams of two to learn the terms and definitions.

151

The glass ceiling for women in management still exists when it comes to leading large corporations. There has been some progress, but men still hold a disproportionate number of leadership positions in large corporations. As of 2000, only four women headed Fortune 500 companies. By 2006, that number had grown to 11. Although the number of women leading these companies is growing, more than 97 percent of the top corporations have men in the top job.

success of the entire business. They set long-term direction and plans. They are held accountable for the profitability and success of the business. Job titles of executives include chief executive officer, president, chief operating officer, and vice president.

Executives spend most of their time on planning and controlling activities. They study the economy and competition. They approve all major business communications. Executives are responsible for the work of all other managers and employees.

Mid-Management

Mid-managers are specialists with responsibilities for specific parts of a company's operations. Examples of mid-management jobs are marketing manager, information technology manager, customer service manager, operations manager, and human resources manager. Mid-managers take the company's business plan developed by executives and prepare specific plans for their part of the business. They must coordinate their work with other managers. Much of their time is devoted to the organizing, staffing, and implementing functions.

Supervisors

Supervisors are the first level of management in a business. They are responsible for the work of a group of employees. They plan the day-to-day work of the employees they supervise. They make sure that needed resources are available and used

wisely. Supervisors often evaluate the work of their employees and solve problems that occur in their area. Supervisors spend most of their time implementing the plans of executives and mid-managers. However, they often have non-management duties in addition to their management work.

Management by Others

Employees who are not managers complete work that seems to be a part of one of the management functions. Employees plan and organize their work. They might take part in hiring and training new employees. They may evaluate the quality of the work they complete. Managers are responsible for the work of others and have authority over those employees. Without that authority and responsibility, the work of an employee is not considered part of management.

Some experienced employees are asked to serve as leaders for their work group. They may be asked to lead a project or supervise the work of a new employee.

Many companies are now organizing work teams. They are giving the teams both authority and responsibility for much of their work. The team meets to make plans, determine how work will be completed, and divide the work among the team members. The team is responsible for meeting objectives and may even have some budget control. The team will still report to a manager and can ask for that person's assistance when needed.

Both work group leaders and employee teams are completing a limited number of management activities. Both of those situations are an effective way for employees to have experience with several management activities. They can develop the skills needed by managers and decide whether they are interested in a management career.

> *checkpoint* >>
> What are the differences among the three levels of management?

Applied Skills

Building Study Skills Have students prepare a study guide to understand the three levels of management. In the study guide, have students identify the management functions that are most and least important to each management level.

MANAGEMENT STYLES

Managing a group of people is a very difficult job. It is not easy to get people with different backgrounds, personalities, and experience to work well together. Have you been a part of an athletic team or musical group? If so, you can remember how hard it was at first to coordinate the talents of each group member so the team or group performed well.

Managers approach the task of directing a group in different ways based on their management style. **Management style** is the way a manager treats and involves employees. Two very different styles often used by managers are tactical management and strategic management.

Sometimes a management style is chosen based on the characteristics of the employees being managed. At other times, the choice is based on the work assignment. Figure 7-1 describes situations where each style will be more effective. Experienced and effective managers can change their management style. It should be based on the urgency of the work to be done and the confidence the manager has in the employees.

Tactical Management Sometimes managers are faced with a crisis. They feel they don't have time to let the group decide how to complete the task. In other situations, a manager may be working with a group of new employees or may have work for which the members have no previous experience. In those situations, the manager should use tactical management. *Tactical management* is a style in which the manager is more directive and controlling. The manager will make the major decisions and stay in close contact with employees while they work to make sure the work is done well.

Strategic Management When a group of employees is experienced and work well together, a manager does not have to be as directive and controlling. If there is enough time to bring a team together to help plan a work assignment, team members will

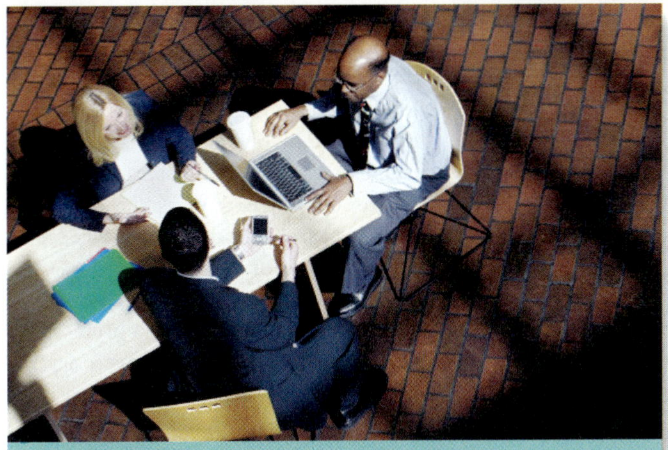

Under which management style would you prefer to work?

main idea

Discuss when to use the two management styles.

Choosing a Management Style	
A MANAGER SHOULD USE TACTICAL MANAGEMENT WHEN	**A MANAGER SHOULD USE STRATEGIC MANAGEMENT WHEN**
• Working with part-time or temporary employees	• Employees are skilled and experienced
• Working with employees who are not motivated	• The work is routine with few new challenges
• Working under tight time pressures	• Employees are doing work they enjoy
• Assigning a new task for which employees are not experienced	• The manager wants to improve group relationships
• Employees prefer not to be involved in decision-making	• Employees are willing to take responsibility for the results of their work

FIGURE 7-1

Why is tactical management appropriate when assigning a new task?

TEACH

Ask students to think of a coach, teacher, or other leader with whom they particularly liked to work. Have them identify the approach the person used in working with people and describe why that approach seemed to be effective.

TEACH

Work with students to prepare a list of several situations in an organization that would require management action such as preparing a budget, handling a conflict among co-workers, or solving a production problem. Have students decide which management style would be most appropriate for each situation and justify their decisions.

THINK CRITICALLY THROUGH VISUALS

Student answers will vary. Encourage students to give specific reasons why they find a particular management style most appealing.

FIGURE 7-1 *ANSWER*

Tactical management allows the manager to be more directive and controlling. The manager will make the major decisions and stay in close contact with employees while they work to make sure the work is done well.

Expand Beyond the Classroom Ask students to talk with several people who have full-time jobs about the management styles of their bosses and what the employees like and don't like about those styles.

154

ONGOING ASSESSMENT

checkpoint >> **ANSWER**

The tactical management style is more directive and controlling than the strategic management style. Using tactical management, the manager makes the major decisions and supervises employees closely to make sure the work is done well. In strategic management, managers are less directive and involve employees in decision-making.

ASSESS

Key Concepts Answers

1. False. An entrepreneur who starts a new business must perform the five management functions.

2. c. producing

3. a. top management

4. False. Effective managers will use the management style best suited to the situation.

Make Academic Connections

5. Reports will vary. Students will prepare a report on one top executive or entrepreneur.

6. Tables will vary. Students will create a table that lists the main duties (classified within the five management functions) of the management job listings they choose.

7. Answers will vary. Students should propose valid situations and should be able to defend their decisions.

CLOSE

Ask students to discuss why the number of managers in organizations might have decreased in the past several years, while the management functions have not changed.

---

usually prefer being involved in the decision-making process. These are examples of strategic management. *Strategic management* is a style in which managers are less directive and involve employees in decision making. A manager using a strategic style will trust employees to work without direct supervision and will seek their advice on important decisions.

Mixed Management Which of the two management styles would you prefer if you were an employee? If you were a manager, which of the styles would you use? Do you believe everyone would answer those two questions the same way? In the past, many managers used the tactical style of management. They believed

they were responsible for getting work done and thus needed to be directive and controlling. That often led to employee frustration because they felt their manager did not trust them. Some employees prefer that the manager make day-to-day decisions. Other employees are not experienced enough to work without close supervision. As a result, effective managers are prepared to use both styles. The combined use of tactical and strategic management is known as *mixed management*.

> *checkpoint* >>
>
> How is tactical management different from strategic management?

7-1 | Assessment

Key Concepts

Determine the best answer.

1. True or False. An entrepreneur who starts a new business is not considered to be a manager.

2. Which of the following is *not* one of the five functions of management?
   a. planning
   b. implementing
   c. producing
   d. controlling

3. Which level of management spends most of its time completing planning and controlling activities?
   a. top management
   b. mid-management
   c. supervisors
   d. team management

4. True or False. Effective managers should use strategic management rather than tactical management.

Make Academic Connections

5. *Research* Use the Internet or library to identify and gather information on the top executive of a large corporation or an entrepreneur. Prepare a report on the manager, describing the person's career path to his or her current position. Identify the important responsibilities of the executive in leading the company.

6. *Careers* Study the classified advertising section of a newspaper or an employment web site. Identify three management job listings. One of the listings should describe a top management position, another a mid-management position, and the third a supervisor position. Develop a table that lists the main duties the person in each position needs to perform. Classify those duties within the five management functions.

7. *Critical Thinking* Imagine you are managing a team of students that is running the snack bar at a basketball game to raise money for your DECA chapter. List two situations that could occur for which a tactical management style would be most appropriate and two other situations when a strategic style would be most appropriate. Discuss the situations with other students and see whether they agree with your decisions.

RETEACH

List each of the vocabulary terms on the board. Have students write their own definition of each term without referring to the lesson. Then have students compare their own definitions with those in the lesson and make any corrections necessary.

ENRICH

Have students locate a magazine article on a successful young manager. Ask them to provide a summary of the article that describes the person's beliefs about management and the preferred management style.

Doing Business in…South Africa

Official name
Republic of South Africa

Capital
Pretoria

Population
44 million

Currency
rand

Major exports
gold, diamonds, platinum, other metals
and minerals, machinery and equipment

Major export partners
Japan, United Kingdom, United States,
Germany, the Netherlands

Major imports
machinery, chemicals, petroleum products,
scientific instruments, food

Major import partners
Germany, China, United States, Japan, Canada, United Kingdom, France, Iran

Source: CIA World Factbook

In 1994, South Africa celebrated the arrival of democracy. After decades of *apartheid*, the government policy that separated blacks and other non-whites from the dominant whites, voting rights were extended to all citizens. Today, the country is often seen as a model for developing economies and emerging markets.

South Africa supplies two-thirds of the electricity used on the African continent. The country has modern seaports, roads, and airports, and is one of the fastest growing countries for mobile communications. This infrastructure makes South Africa one of the best locations for business activity.

The African Growth and Opportunity Act (AGOA) has provided South Africa and other African countries with expanded trade with the United States. AGOA reduces many import taxes and offers incentives for U.S. companies to invest in Africa.

In a business meeting, expect a slow process as you gain the confidence of local businesspeople. While South Africa has 11 official languages, English is most widely used in business activities. The different languages reflect many cultures. Some decision makers may consult with family members before finalizing an agreement. When negotiating, don't be too pushy. Hard-nosed bargaining is not a part of most South African cultures.

Meals at home and away are often a sociable and shared occasion. The foods of South Africa are influenced by the many local, European, and Asian cultures that are part of the country's heritage. A traditional dish is a vegetable and beef stew with a tomato base that may also include pumpkin or cabbage. European foods include a prego roll, a steak sandwich in crispy Portuguese-style bread. Indian and Chinese foods can be found in immigrant communities of people from those countries.

Think Critically

1. What elements of the South African economy make it an attractive location for trade and foreign investment?
2. How does culture affect business activities in South Africa?
3. Conduct library or Internet research to obtain additional information about the history and economic activities of South Africa.

Doing Business in…

South Africa has gone through many political, economic, and social changes. It has made adjustments to those changes much better than many other countries and has become an attractive country for international trade by many companies.

Think Critically Answers

1. The South African economy is an attractive location for trade and foreign investment because it has abundant electricity and modern seaports, roads, and airports, as well as a fast-growing mobile communications infrastructure. The AGOA reduces many import taxes and offers incentives for U.S. companies to invest in Africa.

2. The hard-nosed bargaining often admired in Western culture is not a part of most South African cultures, so those wishing to do business there should not behave too aggressively. Although English is most widely used in business activities, South Africa has 11 official languages reflecting many cultures. Some decision-makers may consult with family members before finalizing an agreement. Meals are often highly social occasions in South African culture.

3. Research results will vary depending on what sources are used. Encourage students to share their findings through displays, written reports, multimedia presentations, and original artwork.

Different Learning Styles

Tactile Learner Have students use a world map or globe to locate South Africa. Have them review the features of the country displayed on the map or globe and identify major cities, rivers, and other geographic features.

Goals

Describe the need for leadership skills and the characteristics of an effective leader.

Identify the human relations skills needed by managers and leaders.

Recognize four types of leadership influence.

Key Terms

leadership

human relations

influence

informal influence

formal influence

Focus on Real Life

The Downtown Business Council's Leadership Award selection committee was meeting. The first item on the agenda was identifying possible nominees for the award.

Janice: I believe we should find out which businesses have been the most profitable during the past year. Each company's top manager should be nominated.

Franklin: I think there is more to leadership than having a profitable company. I don't think we should nominate people just because they managed the most profitable companies.

Jacque: I'm not sure it should be the top manager. Often the managers who work with employees every day are as responsible for a company's success as the top manager.

Felicia: Does the award have to go to a manager? Many employees provide leadership in their organizations.

Janice: I know that management and leadership are not the same thing, but both are important to a successful organization.

main idea

Describe the need for leadership skills and the characteristics of an effective leader.

WHAT IS A LEADER?

A business uses many resources to accomplish its work and make a profit. Those resources include buildings, equipment, money, materials, supplies, and people. One of the most important responsibilities is managing people. Managers have often been very good at managing things but not as good at managing people. Because people are often the most important resource of a business, managers who can effectively manage people are in high demand.

Need for Leadership

The management of people has changed in recent years. In the past, it was thought that if the manager wanted something done, he or she just had to tell the employees and they would do as they were told. Although workers might have done what they were asked, they might not have been doing their best. When employees feel that they are not involved in decisions and are not valued by the business, they will not be as committed to the work.

It is often said that people are the most important resource of a business. The cost

Name an organization or group in which you have been involved. Do you feel there was effective leadership? Why or why not?

Applied Skills

Language Arts Have students write a paragraph on what makes a good leader. Then ask students to work with a partner to create a poem, poster, collage, or skit that incorporates the qualities and characteristics of a good leader.

of hiring, training, and paying employees is usually one of a business' highest expenses. If employees are not satisfied, they might not perform the work correctly, may not treat customers well, or may quit. These problems cost the company money and may require hiring and training new employees. Today, managers are expected to do more than just give orders. They must involve employees and find ways to meet employee needs as well as business needs. Managers must be effective leaders.

Leadership is the ability to motivate individuals and groups to accomplish important goals. When a manager can get individual employees and groups to work well together to accomplish objectives, she or he is an effective leader.

Leadership Characteristics

Leadership is much more than just being friendly with employees. It takes skill to get people with different backgrounds and personalities to work well together and do the work needed by the business. The characteristics of effective leaders are listed in Figure 7-2.

According to the Conference Board, a leading research organization, the four things that most often result in leadership failure are unwillingness to take risks, being arrogant and insensitive, using a controlling style, and avoiding difficult people issues.

You may have heard, "Leaders are born and not made." Most leaders will say that they did not always have the characteristics needed for success. Rather, they worked hard over many years to develop them.

It is harder for some people to develop leadership skills. You may be shy and find it hard to assume leadership roles. You may prefer to let others make decisions while you work to make those decisions successful. You may believe other students seem to be natural leaders or already have mastered many of the leadership characteristics. They are the ones who seem to be willing to take control, take a risk, or make a hard decision. Others look to them for direction and ideas.

Characteristics of Effective Leaders	
CHARACTERISTIC	**DESCRIPTION**
Understanding	Respecting the feelings and needs of the people they work with.
Initiative	Having the ambition and motivation to get work done without being asked.
Dependability	Following through on commitments.
Judgment	Making decisions carefully.
Objectivity	Looking at all sides of an issue before making a decision.
Confidence	Being willing to make decisions and take responsibility for the results.
Stability	Not being too emotional or unpredictable.
Cooperation	Working well with others, recognizing others' strengths, and helping to develop effective group relationships.
Honesty	Being honest and sincere in decision-making and treatment of others.
Courage	Willing to take reasonable risks and make unpopular decisions.
Communication	Able to listen, speak, and write effectively.
Intelligence	Having the knowledge and understanding needed to perform well.

FIGURE 7-2

Identify people who have most of these leadership characteristics. How do they demonstrate their leadership?

Preparing to Be a Leader

You do not have to be a manager to be a leader. You shouldn't wait until you become a manager to begin developing leadership skills. There are several ways you can develop them right now, including:

- *Study leadership.* Many books on the subject of leadership and leadership skills can help you understand what it takes to be a leader. You can also take courses to develop specific leadership skills.

- *Participate in organizations and activities.* Clubs, teams, and organizations need leaders and offer a variety of opportunities to develop leadership skills.

- *Practice leadership at work.* If you have a part-time job, you can develop leadership skills as you help customers, complete work assignments, take initiative to solve problems, and demonstrate dependability and honesty.

- *Observe leaders.* Every day you can observe people in leadership positions in your school and community. You also can see and read media reports about people in leadership positions in business and government. Some are effective, while others are not.

main **idea**

Identify the human relations skills needed by managers and leaders.

Which leadership qualities do you possess? Which qualities do you most need to develop? Are there others that you think you could develop?

- *Work with a mentor.* An older brother or sister, a trusted adult, a teacher or coach, or your supervisor at work may be willing to help you learn about leadership skills and offer direction and feedback on your progress.

- *Do a self-analysis and ask for feedback.* Find opportunities to show leadership characteristics. Review the results to identify what you did well and what you can improve. Ask others for constructive feedback.

checkpoint >>
What are several ways to develop leadership skills?

IMPORTANCE OF HUMAN RELATIONS

Managers and leaders must be able to work well with other people. Most managers spend a majority of their time interacting with people. They work with employees, customers, people from other businesses, and other managers in their own organizations. Human relations largely determines whether a manager is successful or not. **Human relations** is the way people get along with each other.

Human Relations Skills

Effective managers and leaders must be able to get along well with all of the people with whom they work. In addition, they must help their employees develop effective human relations skills. The important human relations skills needed by leaders and managers are (1) self-understanding, (2) understanding others, (3) communication, (4) team building, and (5) developing job satisfaction.

Self-Understanding To be able to meet the expectations of others, leaders must first understand their own strengths and weaknesses. A manager cannot always do exactly what employees would prefer or make decisions with which every employee agrees. In addition, a manager cannot be viewed as either unpredictable or unfair. To improve your human relations skills, study how you get along with others. Try to recognize the ways you communicate and work with others individually and in groups. It is important to understand how you make decisions. You must learn which decisions were effective and which were not so you can improve your decision-making ability over time.

Understanding Others Leaders recognize that people in a business often are more alike than different. Recognizing those similarities will help develop a stronger team. Differences can also improve a business. If everyone thought and acted the same, there would seldom

be new ideas or anyone to question a decision in order to improve it. An effective leader gets to know each person's skills and abilities as well as strengths and weaknesses. The leader will not treat everyone alike, but will attempt to involve each person in the way that is most beneficial to the business and that employee.

List the five human relations skills and rank them 1–5 in the order you believe is most important to effective leadership. Now compare your rankings with those of your team members. As a team agree on a final ranking of the skills. When you are finished, discuss whether the process used to agree on rankings demonstrated effective human relations skills among the team members or not.

Technology in Action

Assistive Technology for Disabilities

People with physical disabilities face special challenges when completing many personal and job functions. Today, assistive technologies are making many tasks possible that previously were difficult or impossible to complete. *Assistive technology* is any unique equipment, modification, or special design used to increase, maintain, or improve the capabilities of persons with disabilities. Companies benefit when providing assistive technology for disabled employees. The technology allows the employee to be productive, often at a level equal to non disabled employees.

The computer industry has developed unique applications so that individuals with disabilities can use computers. For blind persons, software is available that gives audio signals for on-screen images such as windows, menus, icons, and cursor location. A computer can also become a translator for the blind by converting printed pages to speech or Braille. Touch-sensitive Braille displays mechanically lift small rounded plastic or metal pins as needed to form Braille characters. The user reads a line of Braille letters with his or her fingers and then refreshes the display to read the next line. In the same way, a device can monitor computer sounds and alert a deaf computer user with light signals.

Special applications have been designed for people with other physical disabilities. Low-pressure, touch-sensitive keyboards can make typing easier, and special seven-key keyboards are designed primarily for one-handed typists. Special keyboard designs can customize each key's size, position, and function. Touch-screen keyboards and menus allow typing with almost any part of the body. In addition, joysticks, writing pads, and remote-controlled mice can replace the standard mouse when the physical disability requires it.

Think Critically

1. In what ways does a company benefit when it provides assistive technologies for employees with disabilities?
2. What other uses can you see for the technologies described in addition to benefiting physically disabled employees?

Have several teams compare their final team rankings. Note the items that have very similar and very different rankings. Discuss those items and the reasons for the rankings.

Technology in Action

Advances in technology have provided many ways to help people with physical disabilities with their personal and work lives. However, some companies have been slow in adopting the technologies, while others have been leaders in providing assistive technologies for employees with those special needs.

Think Critically Answers

1. A company benefits when it provides assistive technologies for employees with disabilities because it gains a larger pool of potential employees from which to select new hires. Such technologies allow disabled employees to be productive, often at the same level as nondisabled employees.

2. Answers will vary, but should reflect ways assistive technology can help nondisabled individuals. For example, low-pressure, touch-sensitive keyboards can help nondisabled employees avoid carpal tunnel syndrome. On-screen keyboards can be useful in work environments where there may not be room for a keyboard or where its use may be difficult.

Different Learning Abilities

Gifted Have students use the Internet to locate examples of the newest innovations in assistive technologies. Ask students to print pictures of each technology and prepare a display showing the technology and the assistance it offers to users.

Many problems would befall most businesses that lose telephone, fax, and Internet services for a day, and students should have no trouble naming problems that might arise. Customers would not be able to place orders and might become so frustrated they would lose confidence in the company and would move their business to competitors. Managers would not be able to communicate with the home office or other branches or with employees in the field.

TEACH

List each of the classifications of the types of communication on the board. As you discuss each, have students develop a picture or diagram that illustrates the differences in each classification.

TEACH

Ask students to describe why each of the human relations skills listed contributes to a more effective business and better relationships between managers and employees.

ONGOING ASSESSMENT

checkpoint >> **ANSWER**

Managers and leaders need effective human relations skills because their success depends on their ability to get along well with all of the people with whom they work.

Name some problems that might occur if a business lost telephone, fax, and Internet services for a day.

Communication Communication is very important in business. Managers must have effective communication skills. Communication can be classified in several different ways.

- *Formal or informal* Formal communications methods have been established and approved by the organization. Informal communications are common but unofficial ways that information moves in an organization.

- *Internal or external* Internal communications occur between managers, employees, and work groups. External communications occur between those inside the organization and outsiders such as customers, suppliers, and other businesses.

- *Vertical or horizontal* Vertical communications move up or down in an organization between management and employees. Horizontal communications move across the organization at the same level—employee to employee or manager to manager.

- *Oral or written* Oral communications are spoken. Written communications include notes, letters, reports, and e-mail messages.

Managers need to recognize the many ways that communication occurs in the business. They must be able to use all types of communication effectively. Communication must use words that are understandable and meaningful to the people receiving the communications. They must be specific. An effective communicator must be a good listener as well as skilled at providing information. Listening helps managers understand employees and demonstrate respect for their ideas.

Team Building Businesses are organized into groups and teams. The combined skills of the people in an effective team are greater than that of individuals working alone. On the other hand, if there are problems in the team and members cannot get along, the team will not be effective. Managers need team-building skills to help people understand each other and their responsibilities. Managers should be able to identify any problems developing within the group and help resolve issues quickly.

Developing Job Satisfaction Most people are more satisfied than dissatisfied with their work because they have jobs that use their skills and interests. The jobs also provide needed income and benefits. Managers can influence how employees feel about their jobs on a daily basis. Sources of dissatisfaction include assignments employees do not like, poor working conditions, ineffective communication, and lack of recognition. Daily difficulties can lead to long-term dissatisfaction. On the other hand, when a manager pays attention to the needs and concerns of individual employees, they appreciate that effort.

checkpoint >>
Why do managers and leaders need effective human relations skills?

Applied Skills

Writing Across the Curriculum Ask students to prepare a paragraph that shows how another class they are taking contributes to developing or improving one or more of the human relations skills.

INFLUENCING PEOPLE

Have you been a part of a group that seldom agrees on what should be done and spends a long time making decisions? It is interesting to see what the leader of a group does when the group is not working well. Some leaders will complain and criticize group members. Others will give up on the group and attempt to do the work themselves. Neither of those responses improves the group's effectiveness. Effective leaders must be able to influence team members and others. **Influence** enables a person to affect the actions of others.

Kinds of Influence

There are several kinds of influence a leader can use.

Position influence is the ability to get others to accomplish tasks because of the position the leader holds. If the leader has authority over an employee and assigns work tasks it is likely that the employee will choose to respond to the leader's requests.

Reward influence results from the leader's ability to give or withhold rewards. Rewards may be in the form of money or job benefits. Rewards can be non-monetary, such as recognition and praise. Leaders can use rewards in a negative way by requiring people to work overtime or by criticizing rather than praising employees.

Expert influence arises when group members recognize that the leader has special expertise in the area. Suppose a group of inexperienced salespeople have a manager with years of successful selling experience. They will likely look to the manager for guidance.

Identity influence stems from the personal trust and respect members have for the leader. If the leader is well liked and is thought to have the best interests of the group in mind, members are likely to support the leader.

The influence of leaders is not always positive. It may not be effective for a long period. If a manager is not viewed as an expert and is not well liked, he or she will have to rely on position and reward influence. It is not easy to continue to get people to do things for you just because you are their manager. They will probably do just enough to get by, get a reward, or avoid punishment. Most leaders try to develop expert and identity influence.

Formal and Informal Influence

How does a person influence a group to accomplish important goals? It may depend on the person's role within the organization. Managers have formal influence. Others in the organization can have informal influence.

What happens when your teacher assigns a group project and the team members get together for the first time?

Think of a manager, coach, or teacher you've enjoyed working with. What characteristics made it easy to follow his or her lead?

---

main idea

Recognize four types of leadership influence.

TEACH

List the following words on the board: home, school, work. As you discuss each of the four kinds of influence, have students describe an example of that type of influence being used in each of the three situations listed on the board.

THINK CRITICALLY THROUGH VISUALS

Answers will vary. Students should list specific characteristics of the good leader they have identified.

Collaborative Learning Divide students into small learning teams. Assign each of the teams one of the kinds of influence. The teams should prepare a role-play script in which a manager uses that kind of influence ineffectively and then effectively. The teams should present their role-plays to the other students.

ONGOING ASSESSMENT

checkpoint >> **ANSWER**

Managers have formal influence because their leadership position is part of the organization's structure. Managers and non-managers alike can have informal influence when they fill a leadership role that is not part of a formal structure.

ASSESS

Key Concepts Answers

1. d. people

2. False. Most leaders report that they worked hard over many years to develop those qualities.

3. a. human relations

4. d. informal influence.

Make Academic Connections

5. Students are to write a report that describes a project completed by a virtual team and discuss ways technology was used to support successful communication among team members.

6. Students will role-play a discussion between a supervisor and an employee who is reluctant to ask questions of more experienced employees. Students should be sure to keep the discussion positive.

7. Students use the data provided to prepare a chart showing types of influence used most often by managers.

CLOSE

Remind students that all managers need to be good leaders and that employees with effective leadership skills often have opportunities to move into management positions.

Usually one or two people emerge as leaders to help get the group focused and organized. That is known as **informal influence** because the leadership role is not part of a formal structure. Consider another situation where members of the student council meet for the first time. There are bylaws that call for the election of officers. The person elected president has **formal influence** because the leadership position is part of the organization's structure.

Often in organizations, both formal and informal influence will operate at the same time. One person will be the manager and have formal influence.

There may be a well-liked and respected employee in the group who will have informal influence. If there is a conflict between the formal and informal influence, the group will probably not work effectively. Group members will have difficulty deciding whose influence to follow. Effective managers recognize informal influence and work closely with the informal leaders to gain their support and avoid conflicts.

checkpoint >>
What is the difference between formal and informal influence?

7-2 Assessment

Key Concepts

Determine the best answer.

1. It is often said that the most important resource of a business is
   a. cash
   b. technology
   c. customers
   d. people

2. True or False. Research has proven that effective leaders are born and not made.

3. The way people get along with each other is known as
   a. human relations
   b. influence
   c. management style
   d. communications

4. A person who is not a manager but is still able to get a group focused and organized is using
   a. tactical management
   b. strategic management
   c. formal influence
   d. informal influence

Make Academic Connections

5. *Technology* Virtual teams are groups that complete a project by communicating using technology rather than meeting face to face. Complete Internet research on virtual teams. Prepare a report that describes a business project completed by a virtual team. Discuss how technology was used to support communication among team members and successful completion of the project.

6. *Communication* You are the supervisor of a new employee having difficulty completing some tasks. You believe the new employee may be reluctant to ask questions of experienced employees. You encourage your employees to help each other when asked. You want to meet with the new employee to discuss the situation and want the discussion to be positive and result in improved performance. Role-play the discussion with another student using effective oral communication.

7. *Math* A survey of one company's employees asked them to identify which type of influence their managers used most often. Seven hundred employees responded with the following results: Position influence, 305 responses; reward influence, 80 responses; expert influence, 120 responses; identity influence, 195 responses. Prepare a chart that illustrates the percentage of managers using each of the types of influence most frequently.

RETEACH

Divide the class into three groups. Assign each group one of the lesson goals. The team should review the lesson information for that goal and prepare a handout that summarizes the important points.

ENRICH

Invite a successful manager to speak to your class about the importance of human relations in business. Ask the speaker to describe some specific situations he or she has encountered that require effective human relations.

Ethical Management

Goals

Justify the need for ethical management.

Identify the role of leaders in increasing ethical behavior.

Key Terms

ethical business practices

core values

Focus on **Real Life**

The news has been full of information about corporate executives who acted unethically, resulting in the failure of their businesses, loss of employees' retirement savings, and millions of dollars in losses for shareholders. These events suggest that the leaders of businesses operate illegally and unethically with no regard for anything except their personal financial success.

Most executives have a strong personal and professional code of ethics. They insist that their companies, managers, and employees reflect those same values.

The corporate responsibility magazine *CRO,* formerly *Business Ethics,* identifies the 100 best corporate citizens each year. Recognition is given to companies that demonstrate a strong commitment to all of their stakeholders—the community, minorities and women, employees, the environment, non-U.S. stakeholders, and customers. There are 11 companies that have been on the list every year since 2000. You are probably familiar with some of them—Intel, Timberland, Starbucks, and Southwest Airlines. Green Mountain Coffee Roasters made its debut on the list in 2006 at number one. It was number one again in 2007.

IMPORTANCE OF ETHICAL BEHAVIOR

Would you copy a paper from the Internet and submit it to your teacher as your own work? Would you cheat on a test to ensure a higher grade? Is it okay for an employee to call in sick to justify a day off from work or to take office supplies from the company for use at home? Do you believe a manager should ever lie to an employee or ignore unsafe working conditions in order to save money or speed production?

Each of those situations describes an ethical decision you and others may face in your personal life and in business. Not everyone will have the same belief about what is ethical and what is not ethical. It is important for businesses and those

main idea

Justify the need for ethical management.

© Getty Images/PhotoDisc

Name an unethical behavior you would want your employer to discourage.

Focus on **Real Life**

Ask students whether they believe most business executives are ethical or unethical. Tell them that most are ethical, but unethical behavior often gets more attention than ethical behavior. Point out that acting ethically will result in a better reputation among employees, customers, and other businesses.

TEACH

Ask students to list a business activity that they believe almost everyone would recognize as unethical. Then have them list another activity that they believe some people would believe is ethical, while others would believe it is unethical. Discuss why there may be disagreement on what is unethical.

THINK CRITICALLY THROUGH VISUALS

Answers will vary. Students will name a specific behavior they would want their employer to discourage.

TEACH

Ask students: "If an action of a manager or employee has a negative effect on others, is it always unethical?" Remind them that unethical behavior involves both the behavior and the results of that behavior.

Remind students that one of the consequences of unethical behavior is how family and friends feel about you when they learn of your actions. Ask them to consider how they believe the families and friends of executives who have recently been in the news for illegal and unethical behavior felt when those actions were reported in the media.

THINK CRITICALLY THROUGH VISUALS

No, not all unethical activities are illegal, although many are. It is not possible for lawmakers to write legislation to cover every unethical activity that could be performed. On the other hand, all ethical behavior is lawful by definition.

NETBookmark

Since 1996, the Center for the Study of Ethics in the Professions has developed a collection of Codes of Ethics representing nearly 1,000 organizations, professions, and businesses. Access the web site shown below and click on the link for Chapter 7. Select and review several of the ethics codes. Identify principles and values that are common to most of the codes. Develop a sample code of ethics for a business containing 8–10 statements.

school.cengage.com/business/introtobiz

who work in business to develop agreement on behaviors that are acceptable and unacceptable.

Individuals and organizations develop reputations based on their actions and the decisions they make. You can identify people who are not trustworthy and companies that do not compete fairly. When an individual or a company develops that reputation, others will be reluctant to trust them or work with them. Once that reputation is lost, it will be difficult to recover it and build a reputation of honesty and integrity. It is important for an organization to develop a clear view of what is acceptable business behavior and what is not.

What Is Ethical Behavior?

Ethics are the principles of conduct governing an individual or a group. **Ethical business practices** ensure that the highest standards of conduct are observed in a company's relationships with everyone who is a part of the business or is affected by the business' activities. Ethical behavior is not just the decisions and actions of a company's executives and managers. It involves the actions of every employee.

Ethical behavior is made up of two parts: the actions of individuals and groups and the results of those actions. When considering whether behavior is

ethical or not, both the actions taken and the results of those actions should be considered. Ethical behavior meets several standards:

- It is lawful.
- It is consistent with company values and policies.
- It does not harm some while benefiting others.
- If the actions and results become public, it will not embarrass the company.

Ethical Management

Managers are responsible for the success or failure of a business. Success or failure is not just determined by results, such as sales and profits or losses. It is also determined by the actions and activities of the business. Are the actions legal, honest, and ethical? Are people and other companies treated fairly? Does the work of the company improve the communities and countries in which it operates? Does the

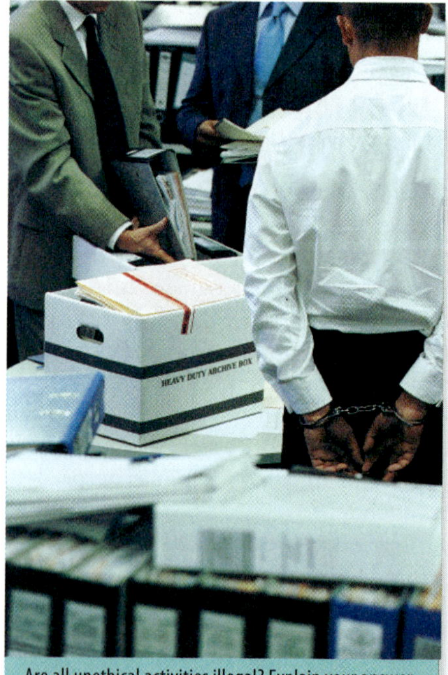
Are all unethical activities illegal? Explain your answer.

© Digital Vision

Teaching Strategies

Expand Beyond the Classroom Tell students that unethical behavior often receives more attention than ethical behavior. Have students find news reports in the media of businesspeople who have demonstrated ethical behavior and share those reports with class members.

company work to protect the environment and conserve natural resources? Besides leadership, managers also provide oversight on employees to make sure their actions are honest, responsible, and ethical.

INCREASING ETHICAL BEHAVIOR THROUGH LEADERSHIP

Most people want to do what is right. When they are under time pressures or facing a major problem, some people act unethically. That unethical behavior ends up harming the business and its relationships with customers and the community. Leaders must take actions to prevent unethical behavior.

Preparing the Organization

It is easier for employees to make the wrong decisions when they do not view ethics as important. It is a manager's duty to create an atmosphere in which all employees know they are expected to act ethically. The employees must know they will be supported when they make the right decision. Leaders also should make it clear that unethical behavior is unacceptable and will be punished if it occurs. Managers can take several steps to develop an ethical environment.

Most organizations have a mission statement. A *mission statement* describes the reason a business exists and what it wants to accomplish. To make ethical behavior a part of a company's mission, many businesses develop a statement of core values. **Core values** are the important principles that will guide

decisions and actions in the company. Figure 7-3 shows the core values statement of the Rite Aid Corporation. As a part of the planning process, managers should work with employees to develop core values that emphasize ethical behavior.

The staffing function offers another chance for managers to emphasize the importance of ethical behavior. The company's commitment to ethical behavior should be made clear when each new employee is hired. In employment interviews, prospective employees should be questioned about ethics and asked to describe how they would handle problems involving ethical behavior. New employee training should include information

Rite Aid Corporation's Core Values
• Rite Aid is a place where customers are treated with respect and they feel appreciated and welcome.
• We are committed to a team work environment where every associate is a valued member, treated with respect, encouraged to contribute, and recognized and rewarded for his/her efforts.
• We value our suppliers as partners.
• We are committed to the highest level of integrity in every aspect of our business.
• We are fiscally responsible and committed to consistently deliver value for our investors.
• We communicate openly, honestly and accurately with our stakeholders: associates, shareholders, and suppliers.
• We are focused on and committed to the healthcare needs of our customers.
• We are caring neighbors, involved in community activities in meaningful ways and committed to reflecting the diversity of each community we serve.

Reprinted by permission of Rite Aid Corporation.

FIGURE 7-3

Can you think of other core values?

TEACH

Have students read the Core Values of the Rite Aid Corporation in Figure 7-3. Ask them to describe activities that employees and managers could complete that would demonstrate each of the core values of the company. Ask students: How can managers make sure that everyone in the company supports the core values?

FIGURE 7-3 ANSWER

Answers will vary. Most often the core values show that the company is concerned about its employees, its customers, and the communities in which it operates. If the core values are specific and related to issues important to students, they will likely have positive feelings about the company.

Word Processing/Office Technology Have students use the Internet to locate core values statements from a company. Have them copy and paste the core values statements into a word processing document. Instruct students to include the name of the company and provide a source. Direct students to adjust the format, if necessary, and print a copy for other students to read.

Work as a Team

Work with your team members to develop four or five statements of core values for your school. The statements should be important principles that guide the actions of students, teachers, administrators, and other school employees. If your school already has a statement of values, compare them with the values statements developed by your team.

about the company's commitment to ethics and values.

In the day-to-day operations of the business, managers and supervisors should often stress the importance of ethics. They should look for situations that might encourage employees to act unethically. Individual employees and work teams should be encouraged to develop ethical solutions to problems.

Ethical behavior should be a part of employee evaluations and promotions. Managers and supervisors should recognize and reward employees who display high ethical standards. They also need to be quick to identify and correct ethical problems if they occur.

Modeling Ethical Behavior

The most important action leaders can take to emphasize the importance of

A QUESTION OF ETHICS

Where Are the Jobs?

Many important business decisions have both positive and negative results. The move toward international outsourcing by many companies has been viewed as both good and bad for the U.S. economy. International outsourcing is a business decision to transfer jobs from the United States to other countries. In an era of international business and the implementation of free trade agreements among many countries, the concept of outsourcing seems to make sense. U.S. companies want to expand their international business and at the same time reduce costs wherever possible. By shifting jobs from the United States to countries where wage rates are much lower, companies can greatly reduce their costs, providing a higher profit for executives and shareholders.

A negative result of outsourcing decisions is that U.S. workers are displaced from their jobs. Forrester Research, Inc., estimates that nearly 1 million jobs have already been lost to outsourcing and that, by 2015, up to 3.4 million U.S. workers will be affected by outsourcing. Lost jobs are found in almost all job categories, from manufacturing and service jobs to high-tech computer and data management jobs. Some suggest that other problems result from outsourcing. Companies are not held to the same strict regulations as when they operate in the United States. That can mean lower environmental standards and poorer working conditions for employees. One of the major issues being raised is the privacy and security of personal consumer data that is transferred from a U.S. company to be handled by unknown employees in other countries.

Those who are in favor of outsourcing argue that in the long run, the movement of jobs to other countries will increase the standard of living for those countries, making them better markets for U.S. products. Opponents say that unless all countries have the same rules and regulations for business operations, U.S. employees do not have a fair playing field and cannot be competitive. The loss of higher paying jobs by many U.S. employees in the past few years combined with increasing profits for many companies has only made the debate more intense.

Think Critically

1. How should companies balance the issue of increasing profits available from outsourcing and the resulting loss of jobs for U.S. employees?
2. Should the U.S. government take action to protect U.S. jobs even if it means that businesses will have lower profits?

Applied Skills

Mathematics Have students use the Internet to find information on how U.S. jobs have been affected by outsourcing. Students should use the information to prepare a graph or chart to illustrate what they have learned.

ethical behavior in an organization is to always act ethically. When it comes to encouraging ethical behavior, actions speak louder than words. If employees read the core values of a company but do not see managers living up to those values, it will be clear that ethics are not that important. On the other hand, if employees see their manager taking actions that demonstrate the company's values, they will be encouraged to act ethically as well.

When managers treat each employee in a respectful way, it demonstrates that everyone is valued in the organization. When a manager rejects a decision that is illegal or would damage the reputation of the company even though it would be profitable, employees learn that ethical behavior is a basic value of the organization. Being an ethical role model inspires others to do the same.

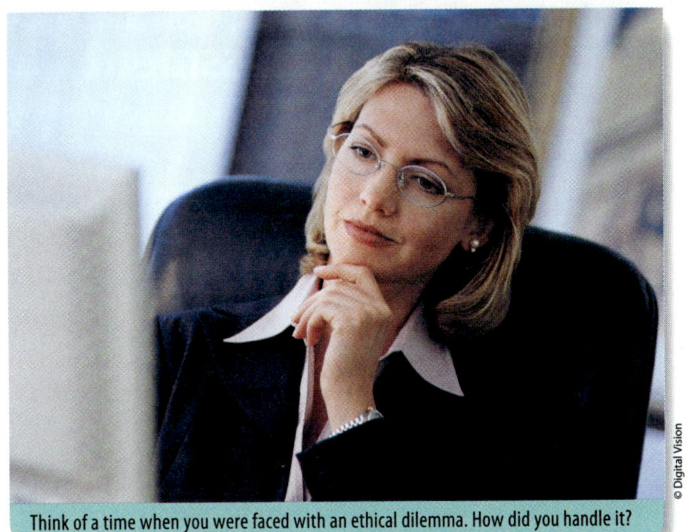
Think of a time when you were faced with an ethical dilemma. How did you handle it?

checkpoint >>
What are the core values of an organization?

Answers will vary. Point out that ethical dilemmas can occur in settings other than employment situations, such as at home or in volunteer organizations.

ONGOING ASSESSMENT

checkpoint >> **ANSWER**

An organization's core values are the principles that guide decisions and actions in the company.

ASSESS

Key Concepts Answers

1. c. It should not give the company a competitive advantage.

2. True

3. d. core values

Make Academic Connections

4. Students prepare a written report on unethical actions taken by a business and the impact of those actions on individuals, as well as the effect of the unethical behavior on the company's image.

5. Students form two teams to debate the statement: "Managers must be responsible for the ethical behavior of every employee." Follow formal debate guidelines for a memorable class activity.

CLOSE

Ask students whether they believe ethical business practices are increasing, decreasing, or remaining about the same in businesses today. Have students representing each viewpoint present reasons for their beliefs.

7-3 Assessment

Key Concepts

Determine the best answer.

1. Which of the following is *not* a standard of ethical behavior?
   a. It should be lawful.
   b. It should not benefit some while harming others.
   c. It should not give the company a competitive advantage.
   d. It should not result in embarrassment for the company.

2. True or False. Managers are responsible for the ethical actions of a business.

3. Important principles that guide decisions and actions in a company are known as
   a. a mission statement
   b. a business plan
   c. ethical behavior
   d. core values

Make Academic Connections

4. *Research* Use the Internet to locate a news report on a business charged with unethical or illegal activities. Gather information to identify the unethical actions taken, the impact of those actions on individuals inside and outside of the company, and the effect of the actions on the image of the company. Prepare a written report on what you learned.

5. *Debate* Form two debate teams. Assign each team the pro or con position on the following statement: "Managers must be responsible for the ethical behavior of every employee." Each team will have five minutes to present their arguments and then two minutes of rebuttal time. At the end of the debate, have class members vote on which team made the most convincing argument.

RETEACH

Ask students to review the lesson and prepare an outline of the important information about the need for ethical business practices and the role of leaders in increasing ethical behavior.

ENRICH

Discuss ways that businesses could identify and reward ethical business practices by their employees.

Communicate Business Concepts Answers

1. Answers will vary, but students should be able to identify similarities and differences between the work of an entrepreneur and that of a top executive. Both are involved in long-range planning and bear the responsibility for the direction and success of the business. Top-level managers, however, are held accountable by the company's board of directors and investors, while an entrepreneur often risks only his or her own resources. Human relations skills will most likely top students' lists of the most important management skills for both types of managers.

2. Student answers will vary, but should describe an activity that involves all five management functions: planning, organizing, staffing, implementing, and controlling.

3. Answers will vary. Some advantages of having fewer levels of management are that employees are empowered, first-level managers can advance to top management more quickly, and the company saves the cost of employing mid-level managers. Disadvantages are fewer experienced managers to guide the company and fewer management positions available. With fewer mid-level managers, employees must assume more responsibility for their work and must make more decisions.

4. Answers will vary, but most students will probably prefer their supervisors to use a strategic management style rather than a tactical one because it allows more independence and less direct supervision. To be successful when working for a manager who uses the tactical management style, an employee

Xtra! Quiz Prep

school.cengage.com/business/introtobiz

Business Notes

7-1 MANAGEMENT

1. Managers' work can be organized within five functions: planning, organizing, staffing, implementing, and controlling. Not every manager devotes the same amount of attention and time to each of the functions.

2. Most organizations have three levels of managers. Executives are top-level managers with responsibilities for the direction and success of the entire business. Mid-managers are specialists with responsibilities for specific parts of a company's operations. Supervisors are the first level of management in a business and are responsible for the work of a group of employees.

3. A manager should use tactical management when working with part-time or temporary employees, working with employees who are not motivated, working under tight time pressures, assigning a new task for which employees are not experienced, or when employees prefer not to be involved in decision-making. A manager should use strategic management when employees are skilled and experienced, the work is routine with few new challenges, employees are doing work they enjoy, the manager wants to improve group relationships, or when employees are willing to take responsibility for the results of their work.

7-2 LEADERSHIP

4. Leadership takes skill to get people with different backgrounds and personalities to work well together and do the work needed by the business. The characteristics of an effective leader are understanding, initiative, dependability, judgment, objectivity, confidence, stability, cooperation, honesty, courage, communication, and intelligence.

5. The important human relations skills needed by leaders and managers are (1) self-understanding, (2) understanding others, (3) communication, (4) team building, and (5) developing job satisfaction.

6. Position influence is the ability to get others to accomplish tasks because of the position the leader holds. Reward influence results from the leader's ability to give or withhold rewards. Expert influence arises when group members recognize that the leader has special expertise. Identity influence stems from the personal trust and respect members have for the leader.

7-3 ETHICAL MANAGEMENT

7. When an individual or a company develops an unethical reputation, others will be reluctant to trust them or work with them. It is important for an organization to develop a clear view of what is acceptable business behavior and what is not.

8. It is the responsibility of managers to establish an atmosphere in which all employees know they are expected to act ethically and believe they will be supported when they make the right decision.

Communicate Business Concepts

1. How are the work of an entrepreneur and the top executive of a large corporation similar? How are they different? What do you believe are the most important management skills both types of managers need for their companies to be successful?

2. Describe a specific activity a manager might complete that illustrates each of the five management functions.

3. The number of mid-managers has been declining in many businesses as companies cut personnel and give employees more responsibilities. In your opinion, what are the advantages and disadvantages of that change for businesses? How will the skills needed by employees change when there are fewer mid-managers?

4. Which type of management style would you personally prefer a manager you work for to have? Why? What would you have to do to successfully work for a manager who used the other style?

would need to be obedient and able to follow directions closely. Employees working for managers who use the strategic management style need to be self-motivated, responsible, and able to work independently.

5. Answers will vary, but one of the first steps an effective team leader should take is to recognize informal leaders within the team and work closely with them to gain their support and lessen conflict within the group. An effective leader also gets to know each person's skills and abilities, as well as strengths and weaknesses, and will attempt to involve each person in the way that is most beneficial to the business and that employee.

5. You have been assigned to be the team leader of a work group that must complete a very important project. What are the first things you would do to inspire and motivate the individuals to work well as a team to complete the assignment?

6. Review the list of leadership characteristics in Figure 7-2. Which three characteristics do you believe are the most important to managers? Which three do you believe are least important? Justify your choices. Compare your decisions with those of other students.

7. To demonstrate your self-understanding, what do you believe are your human relations strengths? What are your current weaknesses? Describe some examples of situations where you get along well with others.

8. In your school or another organization, identify a person that illustrates each of the four kinds of influence. Prepare an example of how each person uses their influence to accomplish the work of the organization.

9. Do you believe the ethical behavior that a person demonstrates in his or her personal life will be the same as the person's ethical behavior in business? Why or why not?

10. As an employee, what would you do if you saw the following individuals behaving unethically: a coworker, a customer, a competitor, the top executive of your company?

Develop Your Business Language

Match the terms listed with the definitions.

11. The leadership role is part of the organization's structure.

12. The important principles that will guide decisions and actions in the company.

13. The effort to direct and lead people to accomplish the planned work of the organization.

14. All of the activities involved in obtaining, preparing, and compensating the employees of a business.

15. Enables a person to affect the actions of others.

16. Ensure that the highest standards of conduct are observed in a company's relationships with everyone who is a part of the business or affected by the business' activities.

17. The process of accomplishing the goals of an organization through the effective use of people and other resources.

18. The way people get along with each other.

19. The effort to inspire and motivate individuals and groups to accomplish important goals.

20. Determines to what extent the business is accomplishing the goals it set out to reach in the planning stage.

21. Analyzing information, setting goals, and making decisions about what needs to be done.

22. The way a manager treats and involves employees.

23. Identifying and arranging the work and resources needed to achieve the goals that have been set.

24. The leadership role is not part of a formal structure.

KEY TERMS

a. controlling
b. core values
c. ethical business practices
d. formal influence
e. human relations
f. implementing
g. influence
h. informal influence
i. leadership
j. management
k. management style
l. organizing
m. planning
n. staffing

6. Students will list what they consider to be the three most and three least important leadership characteristics from Figure 7-2. They should be able to justify their choices. You may want to create a chart to help students in the class compare their choices with those of their classmates.

7. Student answers will vary as they list their individual human relations strengths and weaknesses. They should reflect the skills described in the text: self-understanding, understanding others, communication, team building, and developing job satisfaction. You may want the class to brainstorm ways of improving weaknesses in this vital area.

8. Students are to list the four kinds of influence (position, reward, expert, identity) and identify a person they have observed who illustrates each type, with an example of how each person uses his or her influence to achieve results in the organization.

9. Answers will vary. Students should justify their opinions as to whether individuals can have different levels of personal and business ethical behavior.

10. Answers will vary. Students should list their probable responses to unethical behavior by the four types of individuals mentioned. You may want to discuss whether differences in their responses are justified.

Develop Your Business Language Answers

11. d. formal influence
12. b. core values
13. f. implementing
14. n. staffing
15. g. influence

16. c. ethical business practices
17. j. management
18. e. human relations
19. i. leadership
20. a. controlling

21. m. planning
22. k. management style
23. l. organizing
24. h. informal influence

Make Academic Connections

25. **COMMUNICATION** Managers are responsible for establishing the importance of ethical behavior in a business. You are the CEO of a company that has a reputation of being a very ethical business. Prepare a two-minute speech that you will give to a group of newly hired employees that identifies the importance of that reputation and encourages each person to act ethically in all they do.

26. **PERSONAL DEVELOPMENT** The characteristics of effective leaders are shown in Figure 7-2. Create a three-column table. In the first column, list the characteristics from the figure. In the middle column, describe things you have done (hobbies, work, projects) that give evidence of each leadership characteristic. In the final column, list other things you can do in the next five years to further develop your capabilities as a leader.

27. **ECONOMICS** Some people believe that ethical behavior and a company's profitability do not go hand in hand. Use the Internet to locate research on the relationship between ethics and profits. Develop a one-page report on your findings. In the report, indicate whether you believe an ethical company can be profitable.

28. **MATH** The three levels of management spend different amounts of time on the five management functions. The records of one company show the average amount of time their managers spent on each function in a week. The results are shown in the table below. Calculate the total time spent per week by all levels of management for each of the five functions. Develop a graph that shows the percentage of the total hours each group devotes to each of the management functions during their workweek.

	PLANNING	ORGANIZING	STAFFING	IMPLEMENTING	CONTROLLING
Executives	22	6	2	4	18
Mid-Managers	10	12	7	14	7
Supervisors	5	8	3	20	6

Linking School and Community

There are many opportunities in your community to develop skills that will help you become an effective business leader. Select five of the leadership characteristics shown in Figure 7-2 that you would like to develop. For each characteristic selected, identify a community activity in which you can participate that will help you develop the characteristic. List the community group or organization that offers the activity and the requirements to participate in the activity.

Web Workout

Leadership and leadership development are important topics in business today. Many business executives maintain personal blogs to discuss their ideas, beliefs, and leadership experiences. Most of the leadership blogs encourage feedback and discussion of leadership from blog readers both inside and outside of the executive's company.

Think Critically

1. Locate two blogs written by business executives on the topic of leadership. Read several postings by the executive and responses from blog readers. Write a one-paragraph description of each blog, including the blogger's name and job title, company, the purpose of the blog, and the types of topics or discussions included.

2. Identify and write a brief description of one blog posting that discusses an aspect of leadership that you studied in this chapter. Identify and briefly describe another blog posting that provides information on leadership you did not study in the chapter.

3. How can reading blogs of business executives help develop your leadership skills?

Decision-Making Strategies

Valencia Price has just become a supervisor in the Roxbury Manufacturing Company, where she has worked for 11 years. She had often heard employees complain that their supervisors were not interested in employees' ideas and did not involve them in decision-making. As a result, Valencia felt it was important to avoid using power and reward influence and to try to adopt a strategic leadership style. From the first day of work as a supervisor, Valencia asked employees to discuss how the work could be improved. She knew that the other employees respected Manny, a long-time member of the work team. She would often ask Manny to lead the discussion when she wanted the team to make a decision so the employees would not think she was trying to influence them. After a month, Valencia started to hear that employees believed she could not make a decision on her own and wasted too much time in meetings. Several even suggested that maybe Manny should be the supervisor. They said that if Valencia had to ask Manny to run her meetings, she must not have any confidence in her own supervisory skills.

29. What principles of effective leadership was Valencia demonstrating as a supervisor?

30. Why were the employees not satisfied with the way Valencia was leading? What would you recommend she do?

Partnership with Business Project

Networking with leaders in the business community contributes to success. You may shadow business leaders and develop positive relationships within the business community. FBLA members can benefit greatly by forming positive relationships with business leaders.

This event recognizes FBLA chapters that develop and implement the most innovative, creative, and effective partnership plan for increasing sustained communication and interaction with the business community.

This class project will be performed by teams of two or three members. Each team must propose a Partnership with Business Project for the FBLA Chapter to consider.

The report you prepare will include Development (description of the goals, planning activities, and roles of business leaders and chapter members), Implementation (description of the activities implemented to learn concepts of business operations, level of involvement from business leaders, and roles of business leaders and chapter members in implementing the project), Results (description of concepts learned from the project and the impact of the project), Degree of Involvement (hours spent, personal contact, executives, and department heads contacted), and Evidence of Publicity (examples of publicity and recognition received from the partnership).

The format of the report should be clear and concise with logical arrangements of information. The written presentation should use a creative design with graphics.

PERFORMANCE INDICATORS EVALUATED

- Understand the importance of the business partnership.
- Demonstrate creative strategy for networking in the business community.
- Demonstrate a relationship that is important to the business and FBLA members.

You will be evaluated for

- Creativity and variety of partnership activities.
- Organization of your oral presentation.
- Outcome from the partnership between the business and FBLA.

For more detailed information about performance indicators, go to the FBLA web site.

Think Critically

1. What is the definition for professional networking?
2. Successful partnerships must provide a win-win situation for all participants. What does this mean?
3. List two types of activities that FBLA members can participate in with a business partner that are beneficial to both parties.

http://www.fbla-pbl.org/

Portfolio Activity
school.cengage.com/business/introtobiz

Access the web site shown here to find portfolio activities for this chapter. Use the activities to provide tangible evidence of your learning.

---

3. Answers will vary. Two possible activities could be (1) having students shadow and work at businesses and (2) an education partnership in which businesspeople participate in career fairs and speak to classes. Students will gain real-life insight into possible career fields and the business will be making contacts with bright students who will make excellent employees some day, as well as spreading good will and increasing publicity for the business.

Decision-Making Strategies Answers

29. Valencia was doing many things correctly. She was trying to work with Manny, who wielded informal influence. She was being sensitive to workers' concerns that she had heard expressed over the years. She chose a strategic management style because the employees were experienced. This style of management should have allowed her to improve group relationships.

30. Employees did not feel that Valencia was leading them. It appeared that she was transferring her responsibility to others. Valencia could adopt a mixed management style. She could make most of the day-to-day decisions and hold employee meetings only when major new decisions or changes needed to be implemented. She should continue to communicate and seek input from the informal leader, Manny; however, she could do this in less formal settings than meetings.

Winning Edge
Partnership with Business Project

The event encourages students to build positive relationships with business leaders.

Think Critically Answers

1. Professional networking means meeting and associating with other business leaders for mutual benefit.

2. All participants in the project must feel like they are benefiting from participation in the project.

CHAPTER OVERVIEW

In this chapter, students will learn about the role and importance of human resources and how to manage a diverse workforce and an effective organizational culture.

8-1 Human Resources Basics

This lesson describes the changing workforce in today's businesses and introduces the work of human resources personnel.

8-2 Managing Human Resources

This lesson focuses on how to identify and hire personnel, the types of compensation and benefits plans used in business, and the steps in employee performance management.

8-3 Organizational Culture and Workforce Diversity

After studying this lesson, students will recognize the benefits of diversity to a business, employees, customers, and society. The important factors leading to an effective organizational culture are presented.

CHAPTER 8

Human Resources, Culture, and Diversity

8-1 Human Resources Basics

8-2 Managing Human Resources

8-3 Organizational Culture and Workforce Diversity

172

Planning a Career in...

HUMAN RESOURCES

Today's businesses recognize the importance of their employees to the company's success. A highly skilled, motivated workforce provides a competitive edge. Companies usually spend more money on their personnel than on any other resource. With that large investment, they need professional human resources personnel to recruit, train, motivate, and compensate employees.

The goal of human resources is to have the right people in the right jobs at the right time. This is accomplished by hiring the best people, providing a work environment that encourages productivity and satisfaction, and offering programs that allow employees to develop skills to meet the job requirements of today and tomorrow.

Large human resources departments are made up of a number of specialists. They work closely with managers and employees. They ensure that employees are skilled, motivated, and rewarded for their work.

Employment Outlook

- There are many jobs in human resources, but also high interest in those jobs from college graduates and people with experience in industry.
- People with abilities in a specialized area of human resources are in greater demand than generalists.
- Job opportunities exist from entry-level clerks and assistants to the vice president of human resources.

Related Job Titles

- Director of Human Resources
- Benefits Specialist
- Employment Recruiter
- Employee Relations Representative
- Organizational Development Consultant
- Training Specialist
- EEO/Affirmative Action Representative
- Mediator
- Job Analyst

Needed Skills

- A college degree with broad preparation in business, social sciences, and behavioral sciences
- Specialized preparation in one or more specific areas of human resources management
- Ability to work with people at all levels of an organization
- Skill in problem solving, negotiations, and conflict resolution
- Ability to deal with detailed information, while maintaining confidentiality

What's it like to work as a... Corporate Trainer

Emiko is a lead trainer for the Orbis Company. She has had an interesting career path, starting as a high school science teacher, followed by five years as a laboratory specialist in industry. Last month, she applied to fill an open training position in the company. The new job allowed her to combine her passions for teaching, science, and helping her coworkers.

As a lead trainer, Emiko meets with managers to identify training needs. Those needs might be helping new employees learn their jobs, preparing experienced employees for new processes, or developing a teamwork course. Emiko works with instructional designers and media specialists to prepare training materials. She must stay up to date with the latest educational technology because training is often delivered using computers and the Web.

What about you? Why is Emiko's position so important to the success of the Orbis Company? Would you be interested in a career as a corporate trainer? Why or why not?

Additional Career Information

Additional information on careers can be found in the *Occupational Outlook Handbook,* an online publication (www.bls.gov/oco) of the federal government. Tell your class about this resource and how to use it. This description of job duties can be used to demonstrate the relevancy of skills learned in this course.

Planning a Career in...

HUMAN RESOURCES

Human resources is a very complex and important area of business, presenting many interesting career opportunities. Human resources personnel work with managers and employees in recruiting and hiring new employees, establishing pay systems and benefits programs, managing payroll and other records systems, and assisting with performance management and performance improvement.

What About You? Answers

Answers will vary. Emiko's position is important because quality training helps employees perform well, allowing the company to achieve its goals. She also represents the company to new employees; therefore, when she makes a good first impression and properly equips them to succeed in their jobs, the company will retain employees longer and avoid costly retraining. By using the latest educational technology, she helps the company train employees better and faster.

The level of interest in a career as a corporate trainer will vary. Some students might suggest that a career as a trainer would be interesting and would allow them to use many different skills. Other students might suggest that they are more interested in other careers or that they are not interested in teaching and training others.

Focus on Real Life

Remind students that many terms are used to describe the people who work in business—*labor, personnel, human resources.* All refer to a very important resource. The work of business is not accomplished without people. Employees determine how much work is done, the quality of that work, and its cost.

TEACH

Before beginning the discussion, ask students what they believe have been the most important changes in the workforce in the past 20 years and how those changes have affected employees and business. Have students compare their ideas with the information presented in the lesson.

TEACH

Obtain a copy of the *Occupational Outlook Handbook* and show it to students. Allow them time to page through the handbook to see the vast amount of information available on careers. Show them the web site for the handbook (www.bls.gov/oco) and tell them that the web site is a source of some of the most up-to-date information on the changing workforce.

Goals

Describe the nature of today's workforce.

Identify important goals and activities of human resources.

Key Terms

workforce

downsizing

outsourcing

Focus on Real Life

The contributions of the people who provide the labor in businesses are vital to the economic growth of the United States and the international economy. Labor includes all people involved in producing and marketing products, providing services, completing business operations, or managing business activities and people. Labor refers to anyone who works. This includes the chief executive officer of a huge corporation as well as a self-employed web designer.

Businesses use three types of economic resources to produce goods and services. These resources are natural resources, human resources, and capital resources. Many people think of human resources as the most important of these. Without people working, businesses could not operate. Goods and services could not be delivered to consumers. Labor is the workforce—a vital ingredient in the production of goods and services for economic health.

---

main idea

Describe the nature of today's workforce.

THE CHANGING WORKFORCE

The **workforce** is made up of all the people 16 years and older who are employed or who are looking for a job. More than 150 million people have full-time or part-time jobs in the United States workforce.

Most jobs today require at least a high school education. They often require some special training. Some jobs require only basic skills and a willingness to work hard, but those jobs are becoming scarce. Some jobs are high paying and some are low paying. Some involve working mainly with machines and technology. Others involve working mainly with people and information.

Types of Jobs

The business world consists of hundreds of thousands of companies. These companies provide a wide variety of jobs.

The jobs in the business world may be arranged in many ways. The Bureau of Labor Statistics (BLS) is part of the U.S. Department of Labor. It researches thousands of different jobs. The BLS publishes many useful materials about the workforce. The *Occupational Outlook Handbook* is one of these. It offers up-to-date information about the U.S. workforce.

There are two major types of industries analyzed in the *Occupational Outlook Handbook*. The *service-producing industries* include businesses that perform services that satisfy the needs of other businesses and consumers. Service companies include health care facilities, insurance companies, retail stores, and transportation businesses. *Goods-producing industries* include businesses that produce or manufacture products used by other businesses or purchased by final

174   **CHAPTER 8   HUMAN RESOURCES, CULTURE, AND DIVERSITY**

Teaching Strategies

Expand Beyond the Classroom Have students interview a family member or neighbor who has worked for more than 20 years. The student should ask about the changes the person has seen in the workforce in his or her lifetime, as well as the things that have not changed.

Industry Categories	
SERVICE-PRODUCING INDUSTRIES	**GOODS-PRODUCING INDUSTRIES**
• Information	• Agriculture, mining, and construction
• Finance activities	• Manufacturing
• Professional and business services	• Trade
• Education and health services	• Transportation and utilities
• Leisure and hospitality	
• Government	

Source: Occupational Outlook Handbook

FIGURE 8-1
Which category, service-producing or goods-producing, accounts for more jobs in your community?

consumers. These companies are involved in construction, manufacturing, mining, and agriculture. Figure 8-1 highlights the industry categories from the *Occupational Outlook Handbook*.

The U.S. economy has experienced a change. It has moved from an emphasis on goods-producing businesses to service-producing businesses. The BLS estimates that nearly all job growth over the next 10 years will occur in service businesses. Four out of five workers will be employed in those businesses.

Another way of looking at the workforce is to think about groups of occupations. Occupations are affected by industry trends and current developments in certain types of businesses. Occupations in groups are affected differently. Eleven occupational groups used by the BLS, along with future employment prospects for each group, are shown in Figure 8-2.

Occupations also are referred to in terms of two very broad types of workers: white-collar and blue-collar.

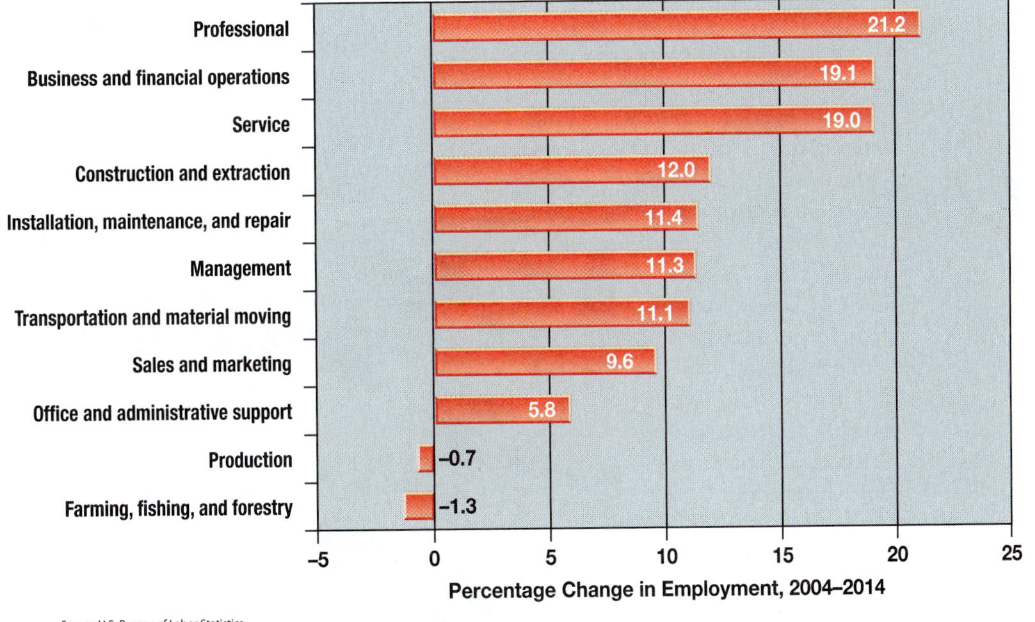

Employment Projections for Occupational Categories

Source: U.S. Bureau of Labor Statistics

FIGURE 8-2
What factors other than the rate of employment growth would you consider when choosing an industry in which to work?

Work as a Team

Each year, *Fortune* magazine identifies the "Best Companies to Work For" based on high rankings from each company's employees. As a team, make a list of things a company can do that you believe would help it make it to the "Best Companies…" list.

A *white-collar worker* is one whose work is more mental than physical and involves the handling and processing of information. Most white-collar workers are employed in offices, stores, and professional services businesses. They include professional, managerial, and clerical workers. A *blue-collar worker* is one whose job involves a great deal of manual work, including the operation of machinery and equipment or other production activities. Blue-collar workers are employed in factories, on construction sites, on farms, and in the delivery of many basic services.

Changing Job Requirements

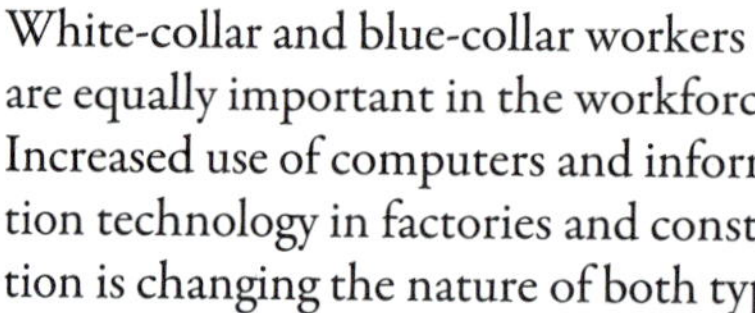

White-collar and blue-collar workers are equally important in the workforce. Increased use of computers and information technology in factories and construction is changing the nature of both types of work. It is resulting in a need for higher levels of education and training. Both types of workers are needed to satisfy economic needs and wants.

The jobs in the workforce are subject to a variety of factors that can cause the need for these jobs to change. Some of these influences may cause jobs to be eliminated. Others will cause the work to be modified. Changes may require

employees to develop new skills and get different training. Consumer preferences, economic conditions, new technology, and business competition are strong influences on the workforce.

Consumer Preferences Consumers regularly cast their "dollar votes" in the marketplace. Preferences by consumers have an important effect on available jobs. Jobs are affected by consumer demand for a product or service. Sometimes new products entering the market make those already available obsolete. Workers making the old product may find that their jobs will be eliminated. New jobs would be created by the demand for the new products.

Business Cycles Stages of the business cycle affect job opportunities. When businesses expand and consumers buy more goods and services, new jobs are created to meet the growing demand. More workers are employed and earn more money. In turn, they spend more on goods and services that they need and want. The growing demand continues.

High prices cause consumers to decrease their buying. When interest rates increase, both businesses and consumers find it difficult to borrow money. Demand for goods and services decreases. As a result, jobs may be eliminated or the

Name ways in which computers could change the way an industry operates.

number of workers reduced. Consumer spending and demand is decreased even more.

New Technologies *Technology* refers to the use of automated machinery, electronic equipment, and integrated computer systems to help increase the efficiency of producing goods and services. Technology is important in the workplace. It improves efficiency so that businesses may stay competitive in international markets. Computerized systems and robots have greatly reduced the need for production workers in many manufacturing industries. These include steel, autos, tires, and consumer electronics. Sophisticated computer and communications systems have also reduced the need for office employees such as typists, bookkeepers, and clerks. New technology continues to change the types of jobs in production and manufacturing. It has also changed how office workers and professionals perform their jobs.

Business Competition Companies must be competitive to stay in business. Costs are a major factor. The cost of running a business affects jobs and workers. When costs begin to increase, the business must look for ways to stay profitable. Installing new equipment and streamlining processes make workers more productive. Businesses may also decide to downsize. **Downsizing** is a planned reduction in the number of employees needed in a firm in order to reduce costs and make the business more efficient. **Outsourcing** removes work from one company and sends it to another company that can complete it at a lower cost. Today, many U.S. jobs are being outsourced to companies in other countries that pay much lower wage rates.

checkpoint »
What are several strong influences on changes in the workforce?

HUMAN RESOURCES OVERVIEW

The work of every company is completed by the people who work for the organization. Employees who have the knowledge and skills needed, who are motivated to work efficiently, and who complete their jobs with quality contribute to the success of the business. Companies that have difficulty finding qualified employees, have a poor work environment, and suffer from quality issues, waste, and employee errors will have difficulty remaining competitive or meeting customer needs.

Human resources are the people who work for a business. Human resources include management and employees, full-time and part-time workers. People hired to fill temporary positions as well as those who have worked for the company for many years are human resources. Managing human resources is one of

Think of the places you frequent regularly. What types of workers are visible? Are there "behind the scenes" employees?

© Getty Images/PhotoDisc

Identify important goals and activities of human resources.

ONGOING ASSESSMENT

checkpoint » **ANSWER**

Strong influences for change in the workforce include consumer preferences, economic conditions (business cycles), new technology, and business competition.

TEACH

Point out to students that many companies have a hard time finding qualified employees. Ask them whether they believe this problem relates more to a lack of knowledge and skills, a lack of motivation to perform quality work, poor human relations skills, or some other reason.

THINK CRITICALLY THROUGH VISUALS

Answers will vary depending on what types of businesses they patronize regularly. Have them list some of the visible employees, as well as the types of work that would occur "behind the scenes."

Different Learning Abilities

At-Risk Have students list two or three ways that technology is affecting a job they are interested in as a career. Have them think of ways they can develop the technology skills that will be needed for that work.

THINK
CRITICALLY
THROUGH
VISUALS

Answers will vary. Some of the many challenges human resources managers might encounter include a lack of qualified applicants for positions that need to be filled, difficulties in training and motivating employees, the need to stay current with the many federal and local laws pertaining to human relations, planning for safety in a dangerous industry, excessive employee turnover, and keeping the necessary records for payroll and benefits.

TEACH

Divide students into teams and assign each team one or two of the major goals of human resources. Ask the team to suggest ways they can work with other managers in a company to successfully accomplish that goal.

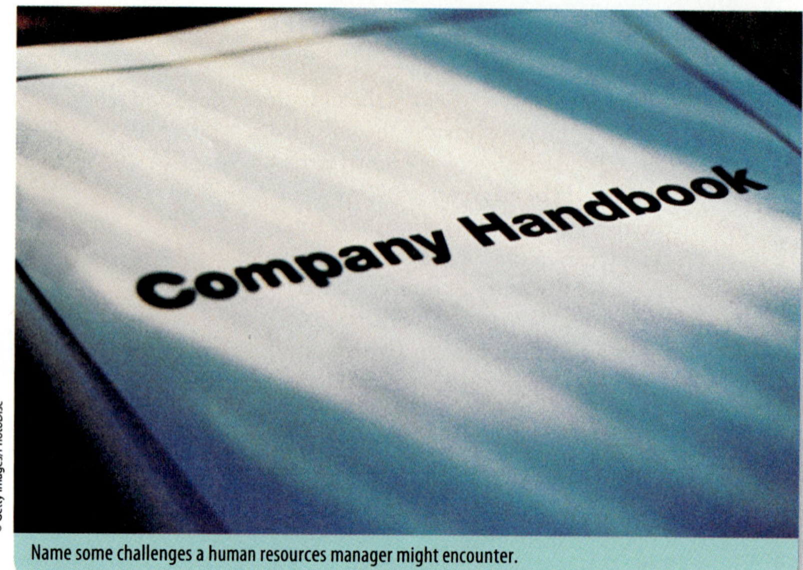

© Getty Images/PhotoDisc

Name some challenges a human resources manager might encounter.

the most important responsibilities of a business. Most medium- to large-sized businesses have a department devoted to human resources management and activities. The owner of a small business will be responsible for managing human resources or will hire others to complete the work.

Human Resources Goals

Human resources are different from almost every other resource needed by businesses. Each person is different. They bring varied knowledge, skills, experience, and motivation to their jobs. People are used in different ways in a company. Some will be required to do hard, physical labor. Others will operate sophisticated equipment. Some employees will work in groups where they must have effective interpersonal skills and demonstrate teamwork. Others will work independently, relying on their own abilities. Managers will direct the work of others and make long-term plans that affect the entire company. New employees must be willing to follow directions and will

have few decision-making responsibilities at first.

Human resources must be able to work with the vast differences and unique capabilities of each employee and develop a workforce that is productive and efficient. There are seven major human resources goals.

1. Identify the personnel needs of the company.

2. Maintain an adequate supply of people to fill those needs.

3. Match abilities and interests with specific jobs.

4. Provide training and development to prepare people for their jobs and to improve their capabilities as job requirements change.

5. Develop plans to compensate personnel for their work.

6. Protect the health and well-being of employees.

7. Maintain a satisfying work environment.

Human Resources Activities

Managing human resources involves four broad categories of activities. The categories are planning and staffing, performance management, compensation and benefits, and employee relations. Specific human resources activities for each of the categories are listed in Figure 8-3.

Planning and staffing activities are directed at identifying and filling all of the jobs in the company with qualified people. *Performance management* involves evaluating the work of

---

Applied Skills

Communication Have students use the information from the lesson to develop an advertisement for the manager of human resources in a business. The advertisement should include a description of the major duties plus the preparation and experience expected of applicants. The ad should be prepared and printed in the format of a classified advertisement in a newspaper.

Human Resources Activities			
PLANNING & STAFFING	**PERFORMANCE MANAGEMENT**	**COMPENSATION & BENEFITS**	**EMPLOYEE RELATIONS**
• Job analysis • Recruitment and selection • Job placement	• Performance assessment • Performance improvement • Managing promotions, transfers, and terminations	• Wage and salary planning • Benefits planning • Payroll, benefits, and personnel records management	• Health and safety planning • Labor relations • Employment law and policy enforcement • Organizational development

FIGURE 8-3

Which activities do you think are the most important? Explain your answer.

employees and improving performance through training and development. *Compensation and benefits* is responsible for planning and managing payroll, personnel records, and benefits programs. *Employee relations* is responsible for maintaining a safe, healthy, and productive work environment for all employees.

> *checkpoint* >>
> What are the major goals of human resources?

8-1 Assessment

Key Concepts

Determine the best answer.

1. The U.S. workforce is made up of about _?_ people.
   a. 80 million
   b. 100 million
   c. 150 million
   d. 190 million

2. The Bureau of Labor Statistics publication that provides detailed and up-to-date information about the U.S. workforce is the
   a. *Occupational Outlook Handbook*
   b. *IRS Publication 15*
   c. *Congressional Record*
   d. *Business Report*

3. A person whose work is more mental than physical and involves the handling and processing of information is a
   a. blue-collar worker
   b. human resource manager
   c. white-collar worker
   d. service employee

4. Which of the following would *not* be a part of a company's human resources?
   a. Managers
   b. Full-time employees
   c. Temporary employees
   d. All could be included in human resources.

Make Academic Connections

5. **Math** The population of the United States is approximately 301,700,000. If 150,000,000 people are not employed, what percentage of the total population is not currently working? What accounts for the difference in that percentage and the approximate 5 percent unemployment rate that is typically reported?

6. **Art** Create a collage on poster board that illustrates the many activities that are a part of human resources. Clip pictures from newspapers and magazines that represent the four broad categories of activities. Show your collage to other students and describe the activities you have illustrated.

RETEACH

Have students use Figure 8-3 to discuss the role of human resources and the activities performed by human resources personnel.

ENRICH

Have students use Internet career information to identify five jobs that did not exist 20 years ago.

FIGURE 8-3 *ANSWER*

Answers will vary, but reasons should be specific. The reasons can relate to business needs, the needs of employees, or both.

ONGOING ASSESSMENT

checkpoint >> **ANSWER**

The seven major goals of human resources are listed on page 178.

ASSESS

Key Concepts Answers

1. c. 150 million

2. a. *Occupational Outlook Handbook*

3. c. white-collar worker

4. d. All could be included in human resources.

Make Academic Connections

5. About 50 percent of the population is not working: $150{,}000{,}000 \div 301{,}700{,}000 = .497$ or 49.7%. The reported unemployment rate reflects only persons aged 16 and older who are actively seeking employment. Children, stay-at-home parents, and the retired, for example, are not included when computing the unemployment rate.

6. Designate a location for displaying collages and allow time for students to discuss their work.

CLOSE

Ask students to identify reasons why human resources is one of the fastest growing career areas in business today.

8-2 Managing Human Resources

Goals

Identify important planning and staffing activities.

Describe compensation and benefits plans.

Recognize the goals of performance management.

Key Terms

job analysis

compensation

salary and wages

benefits

incentive systems

promotion

transfer

termination

Focus on Real Life

Jaqueline Perez had come to the end of a busy week as she locked the door to her bookkeeping service. She knew her work wasn't finished. For the third time this year, she was going to have to replace one of her best employees who had resigned to take a position with a larger competitor. She owned a small company of 15 full-time and 12 part-time employees. The business had been more successful than she had hoped in its first three years, but the personnel problems were challenging.

Jaqueline had tried to support her employees with a good work environment. She even gave them time off from work to get advanced training. Because of it, the employees had become very skilled at using computer systems for maintaining business records. But it seemed that just as an employee got to the point where he or she was really doing a good job, the employee would be hired by a larger business paying higher wages or offering better benefits. Jaqueline wondered what she could do as a small-business owner to compete with the economic advantages offered by larger businesses.

---

main idea

Identify important planning and staffing activities.

HUMAN RESOURCES PLANNING AND STAFFING

Human resources management ensures that needed employees are available, productive, paid, and satisfied with their work. If human resources management does its job well, the company will have employees who do their jobs well. This will result in a successful, profitable business.

Planning and Job Analysis

Human resources management begins by analyzing where the business currently is in terms of its personnel and where it wants to be. The decision to hire people must be made carefully. Once an employee is hired, the person's salary must be paid whether the company is profitable or not. An employee should be hired when the work of that employee will add more to the company's profitability than it will cost.

Classifying Employees The company must decide whether the person to be hired will be permanent or temporary. A *permanent employee* is one to whom the company makes a long-term commitment. It is expected that the employee will work for the business as long as the business is profitable and the employee's performance is satisfactory. A *temporary employee* is one hired for a specific time or to complete a specific assignment.

Because permanent employees feel that they are a part of the business, they are often more productive than

---

Applied Skills

Mathematics A company currently has 2,550 employees. Eighty-five percent are permanent and 63 percent are full-time. Have students calculate the number of employees in all four employment categories and present the results in a chart or graph.

temporary employees. On the other hand, there is more control over the company's resources when temporary employees are hired. The employee is paid only until the temporary assignment ends. Temporary employees are usually hired during a busy time for the business or when a special task needs to be done.

Whether permanent or temporary, employees can be hired full-time or part-time. A *full-time employee* regularly works a schedule of 30 hours or more a week. A *part-time employee* has a shorter work schedule with either fewer hours each day or fewer days each week.

Determining Job Requirements Before starting the hiring process, human resources staff studies the work that must be done in the job. Specific information about each job is needed in order to hire people with the right skills. That information is often collected by completing a job analysis. A **job analysis** is a specific study of a job to identify in detail the job duties and skill requirements.

First, human resources staff reviews the current job in detail. They identify all important job duties, as well as the knowledge and skills required to successfully complete the job. Next, they add any new activities planned for that job to the analysis. The job analysis will help determine if the needs of the business can best be met with temporary, permanent, part-time, or full-time employees.

Recruiting and Hiring

Once the specific need and skill requirements are determined, prospective employees meeting the requirements must be located. If this search is not done carefully, an employer may spend a great deal of time and expense and an appropriate employee may still not be found. Several good sources of prospective employees exist and are identified in Figure 8-4. Businesses should use sources

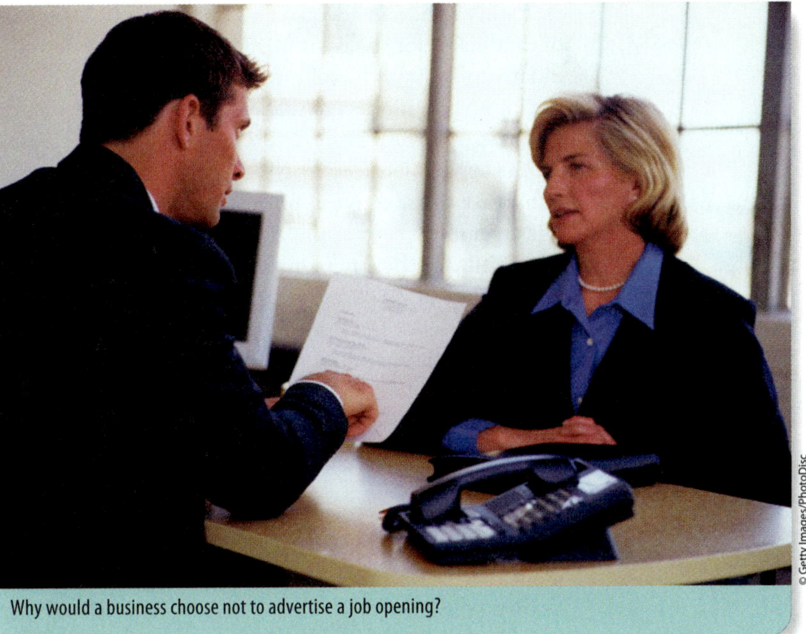

Why would a business choose not to advertise a job opening?

© Getty Images/PhotoDisc

Effective Sources for Locating Prospective Employees	
• Newspaper classified advertising	• Internet career services
• Public and private employment agencies	• Radio and television advertising
• High school and college placement offices	• Industry publications
• Job and career fairs	• Company web sites
• Referrals by employees	• Company employment office

FIGURE 8-4

Which sources would you most likely use to look for a job?

that will provide an adequate number of candidates for the position. The candidates must have the skills required for the job and an interest in working for the business.

The Application Process Most companies ask prospective applicants to fill out an employment application. The application gathers personal information, information on education, and work experience history. It may also ask for specific skills related to the job and names of people who can serve as references. For career-level jobs, the applicant may be asked to submit an application letter and a resume as well. Applications are used to remove people who are clearly not qualified for the job and to identify those who appear to be especially qualified.

Once applications have been reviewed, the top applicants are studied more carefully. Information is checked for accuracy. References are contacted. The employer selects a few applicants to interview. The applicant may be asked to complete special tests related to needed job knowledge and skills. During the interview, the applicant will be introduced to the work area, managers, and coworkers. The applicant will be given more detailed information about the company and the job. Finally, the applicant whose qualifications best match the job requirements will be offered the job.

New Employee Orientation The final step in the hiring process is to help the new employee get a good start in the company. As a part of the orientation, the new employee will meet with human

CORPORATE SOCIAL RESPONSIBILITY

What About Corporate Profits?

As energy prices rose rapidly in 2006, consumers paid more to heat their homes, the price of gasoline went up, and businesses passed on higher costs to customers. Most people were shocked when oil companies announced their 2006 annual profits. ExxonMobil Corporation reported $39.5 billion in net income, the largest profit ever by a U.S. corporation. That figure eclipsed the profit of a major competitor, ConocoPhillips. It reported 2006 profits of $15.6 billion, its largest ever.

At the same time, as consumers were struggling to pay the increasing energy prices, top executives of oil companies received salaries that most people could not comprehend. In 2006 the average yearly compensation of CEOs of the largest U.S. corporations was $6.5 million. The average for oil company CEOs was significantly higher at $11 million. The compensation for the CEO of Occidental Petroleum was well above the industry average—he received $460 million.

While people believe in the free enterprise system and recognize profit as the reward for taking business

risks, the size of the oil industry's profits caused a great deal of debate. Should the government impose an extra tax on companies with such high profits? Should the petroleum companies artificially reduce prices to help consumers and bring profits to a more reasonable level? The companies argued that their industry is very risky and prices can fall as rapidly as they rise. The 2006 profits made up for years when little or no profits were earned. They also note that they annually pay billions as taxes on their profits as well as other taxes and fees on their operations.

Think Critically

1. If a company operates legally, do you believe there should be a limit to the amount of profit it earns? Explain your answer. How would you feel if you were a company stockholder?
2. Do very profitable companies have any extra responsibilities to their customers and the communities in which they do business? Why or why not?

Applied Skills

Language Arts Have students write a paragraph about the importance of effective communication skills when completing the application process for a new job. Ask them to provide some specific examples of how good communication skills help the process and how poor communication skills hinder it.

resources specialists to complete all of the paperwork needed to receive pay and benefits. In turn, the company will have a complete employee record. There will usually be at least several days of training. The employee may be paired with an experienced coworker, or mentor. The mentor answers questions and helps the new employee solve problems and build confidence for the new job. The company may have a probationary period of several weeks to several months. At the end of that time, the new employee is evaluated to be sure job performance is meeting the company's expectations.

COMPENSATION AND BENEFITS

One of the reasons people work is to earn money. **Compensation** is the amount of money paid to an employee for work performed. Compensation is made up of two parts. **Salary and wages** are direct payment of money to an employee for work completed. Compensation in forms other than direct payment is known as **benefits**. Examples of benefits are insurance, vacations, retirement plans, and health and fitness programs.

Compensation Methods

A *time wage* pays the employee a specific amount of money for each hour worked. A *straight salary* pays a specific amount of money for each week or month worked. Neither of these types of compensation are based on the amount or quality of work done, but are determined by the amount of time spent on the job. For that reason, it is a simple system to manage. The business just has to keep records on the amount of time each employee works.

Work as a Team

Automobile dealerships have traditionally paid their salespeople with a straight commission. Recently some dealerships have started to pay each salesperson a salary and an incentive based on customer satisfaction surveys. As a team, discuss how this change might affect the performance of the salespeople and why the dealerships have chosen to make the change.

Incentive systems connect the amount of compensation to the quality or quantity of an employee's performance. Some businesses pay a *commission* in which an employee is paid a percentage of sales for which he or she is responsible. Salespeople are often compensated with commissions. Another pay-for-performance plan is known as a *piece rate*. An employee receives a specific amount for each unit of work produced. Piece rates are most often used in factories and data processing or telephone call centers.

Some companies use a *base plus incentive* compensation system. This system combines a wage or salary with an additional amount based on the

main idea

Describe compensation and benefits plans.

If you were a telemarketer, would you rather be paid commission on your sales or by the hour? Explain your answer.

TEACH

Have students list each of the types of compensation methods, write a definition of each, then develop an example of how the amount of money paid to an employee would be calculated using each method.

Work as a Team

Invite a representative of each team to summarize the team's findings. Ask students if the way salespeople are compensated may influence which dealership you visit when you are shopping for a car.

THINK CRITICALLY THROUGH VISUALS

Answers will vary. Some students will prefer to be paid hourly in order to have a reliable income. Others would prefer to be paid on commission so they have the opportunity to earn more than the hourly rate based on their ability to make sales.

Different Learning Abilities

Limited English Proficiency (LEP) Have students write each of the bold and italicized terms on a sheet of paper, then write the definition of each.

Have students work in pairs to read each of the terms and its definition, working on correct punctuation and understanding of each definition.

FYI

At any time, about 66 percent of the U.S. population age 16 and older is in the workforce. This includes individuals who are unemployed but looking for work. The remainder of the population age 16 and older that is not in the workforce is made up of students, parents who do not work outside the home, people who choose not to hold a job, individuals who are sick or disabled, and those who have retired.

employee's performance. One type of base plus incentive plan is profit sharing. With profit sharing, employees receive their regular compensation plus a share of the profits earned by a company. This system encourages commitment, teamwork, and effective customer service so that profits will be high.

Employee Benefits

Employee benefits can be an expensive addition to the cost of compensation. On average for all businesses, an additional 20 to 40 percent of an employee's wages is spent on benefits. If an employee earns $7.00 an hour, 30 percent added for benefits increases the hourly cost to $9.10. If the employee works 40 hours a week for 50 weeks, the additional cost is $4,200.

State and federal laws require some benefits. Most businesses must offer and pay the cost of these required benefits. Benefits include compensation for overtime hours worked, social security, Medicare, and contributions to funds for injured employees and for unemployed workers. Full-time employees may expect companies to offer insurance plans including health, life, dental, and disability insurance. Many companies, especially small businesses, cannot afford the cost of all of those types of insurance. The rapidly rising cost of health insurance has been particularly difficult for businesses to handle. As a result, many companies are reducing health insurance benefits. They may also require employees to pay a large part of the monthly insurance premiums.

Time off for vacations is another popular benefit for employees. Paid vacations are a costly benefit because employees are paid for time when they are not working. On the other hand, the time off may result in a more content and productive employee. Other benefits offered by businesses include retirement programs, employee savings plans, personal or sick days, and flexible work schedules.

The costs of benefits programs are very high and continue to increase. Each employee may prefer different benefits. As a result, human resources departments have developed cafeteria plans. A *cafeteria plan* allocates a certain amount of money to each employee that can be spent on benefits. The employee selects the preferred benefits. If the cost of the benefits does not use all of the allocated money, the employee can receive the difference in additional pay. If the costs are higher, the employee pays the difference.

© Getty Images/PhotoDisc

What kinds of benefits are important to you?

checkpoint >>
List three types of incentive systems for employee compensation.

Applied Skills

Building Study Skills Have students prepare a study guide that outlines the types of compensation systems and employee benefits that employers frequently offer.

PERFORMANCE MANAGEMENT

Managers work closely with their employees to make sure work is being finished as planned. Every employee is expected to meet quality standards as well as work efficiently. In addition, employees must demonstrate effective working relationships with coworkers, managers, and customers. As jobs change, new equipment and procedures will be introduced. Employees must upgrade their skills to meet the changing job requirements. Most companies offer training and development programs to help employees perform their work well.

Employee Evaluation

The manager evaluates the work of all employees on a regular basis. The human resources department is in charge of developing the evaluation procedures and forms. Managers will be trained to complete objective evaluations and hold evaluation conferences with employees. Human resources maintains the results of employee evaluations in the employee's personnel file.

The Evaluation Process Performance evaluations focus on the specific job duties of each employee. They also review the important work qualities expected of all employees. Those qualities include factors such as communication, interpersonal relationships, quality and quantity of work, and ethical behavior.

Managers are given evaluation forms to complete. Evaluation decisions are based on observations of the employee's performance and evaluation of the quality of the work produced. Some companies ask coworkers to provide feedback that is considered in the evaluation process. Using the evaluation form, the manager identifies each employee's strengths and areas that need improvement.

The Evaluation Conference After the manager completes the evaluation form, a conference is scheduled with the employee. The purpose of the conference is to review and discuss the results of the evaluation and to plan for any needed performance improvement. Often, both the manager and employee are concerned about the conference. They might not be comfortable with a specific discussion of performance. Human resources personnel should work with all employees to help them prepare for evaluation conferences. The conference should be meaningful and positive. The conference should result in reasonable agreement on the employee's performance, goals, and plans for the future. It should identify the support the employee can expect from the manager and the company in order to improve performance.

Promotions, Transfers, and Terminations

Employees expect that if they work for a company for a long time and perform well, they should be rewarded with increased pay

Is earning a good wage or salary enough for you to be satisfied with your work? What else do you expect?

TEACH

Discuss with students the problems that can occur if an employee evaluation process is not planned and handled well by a manager and an employee. Have students brainstorm things managers and employees can do to improve the effectiveness of the employee evaluation and evaluation conference.

THINK CRITICALLY THROUGH VISUALS

Answers will vary. Some students will say that earning money is reason enough to work, although they may also expect benefits, such as health insurance and paid vacation. For true satisfaction in their work, others will want affirmation of their contributions to the company's success and opportunities to improve their skills and advance in their careers.

Different Learning Styles

Kinesthetic Learners Organize students into teams of three. Have them take turns role-playing an effective employee evaluation conference with one person acting as the employee, one as the manager, and one as an observer who identifies the strengths and weaknesses of the conference.

and the chance of promotion. A **promotion** is the advancement of an employee to a position with greater responsibility. Companies want to keep good employees. They want to place good employees in positions where they can provide the most benefit to the company. When possible, companies should fill open positions with current employees. Those employees are familiar with the company and will view the promotion as a reward. They will be motivated to continue to work for the company and continue to work effectively.

In some cases, promotional opportunities do not exist, but employees want to change jobs. It is not unusual for some jobs in a company to be cut due to changes in competition while other jobs are created. In that case, employees may accept a job transfer. A **transfer** is the assignment of an employee to another job in the company with a similar level of responsibility. The job may provide a new challenge for the employee or may be a better match with the person's skills.

If performance does not meet the company's expectations or if jobs are being reduced, the company may have to terminate the employee. A **termination** ends the employment relationship between a company and an employee. The termination may be a *discharge* that ends employment due to inappropriate work behavior. Another type of termination is a *layoff*, which is a temporary or permanent reduction in the number of employees due to changing business conditions. The company should complete all terminations carefully. The terminations must meet legal requirements and be as helpful as possible to the employee who is asked to leave the business.

> *checkpoint* >>
> What is the purpose of an evaluation conference?

8-2 Assessment

Key Concepts

Determine the best answer.

1. An employee to whom a company makes a long-term commitment is considered to be
   - **a.** full-time
   - **b.** part-time
   - **c.** permanent
   - **d.** temporary

2. True or False. Companies should interview all prospective employees who apply for a job.

3. On average, the percentage of employees' wages spent on benefits is
   - **a.** less than 5%
   - **b.** 10%–20%
   - **c.** 20%–40%
   - **d.** more than 50%

4. The employment relationship between a company and an employee is ended with a (an)
   - **a.** termination
   - **b.** interview
   - **c.** evaluation
   - **d.** lawsuit

Make Academic Connections

5. *Math* Augusta is paid $3,100 a month and a commission of 2 percent on all sales. She also is given a yearly bonus of $4,500. If Augusta's sales for the year are $186,200, what is her total earnings for the year?

6. *Research* Use the Internet to locate four different sources of current job opportunities. Develop a table that compares the sites in terms of their effectiveness in providing information about the job, the company, and the procedure applicants should follow in applying for a job.

7. *Critical Thinking* You are a human resources specialist giving advice to a new supervisor on how to conduct a performance evaluation conference with an employee. List three recommendations you would make to the supervisor that would result in an effective conference.

RETEACH

Have students review the lesson and list all of the human resources activities discussed.

ENRICH

Ask a human resources professional to speak about the use of technology in human resources.

CLOSE

Ask students to complete this sentence: "Human resources management activities are important to an organization because…"

Organizational Culture and Workforce Diversity

Goals

Recognize factors that contribute to an effective organizational culture.

Describe the benefits of diversity to an organization, individuals, and society.

Key Terms

organizational culture

work environment

labor union

diversity

glass ceiling

Focus on Real Life

"Three years of related experience required."
"Must be very energetic and eager."
"Requires heavy lifting."

Each of these statements is from employment advertisements. Do the statements reflect important qualifications for a job? On the other hand, are the requirements designed to eliminate certain people as job applicants? Lack of related work experience excludes many high school students and recent graduates. A requirement of high energy or stamina might discourage older workers from applying. Women might avoid applying for a position when heavy lifting is a job requirement. Job recruitment should focus on the job. It should not focus on the type of person thought to be best qualified to fill the position. If a manager believes a female is most appropriate for the job, the requirements stated to fill the position will often reflect that belief. If physically disabled people are viewed as unsuitable for a job, those applicants will seldom be considered. Businesses should avoid any employment practice that discourages or eliminates applicants who may actually be effective employees.

Focus on Real Life

Show students an employment advertisement that is very general and one that is very specific. Ask them which would be most helpful in locating the most applicants. Which would be most helpful in locating the best qualified applicants?

TEACH

Write the term "organizational culture" and its definition on the board. Have students provide examples of each of the parts of the definition—atmosphere, behaviors, beliefs, and relationships. Discuss how those factors contribute to a positive or negative place to work.

DEVELOPING AN EFFECTIVE CULTURE

Businesses today are far different from those of the past century. Some of the changes that have occurred are obvious. Technology has reduced the need for low-skilled employees and demanded that current workers have much greater skills. The Internet has changed the way you communicate, share information, and shop. Globalization of business has resulted in greater competition. It has also resulted in more opportunities for every business to reach many new customers.

Other changes are just as important but not as clear. The workforce is more diverse, with growth among both younger and older workers. Jobs are changing, with a larger temporary and part-time workforce and a rise in entrepreneurship. Jobs are being shifted to other countries in an effort by businesses to cut costs. The number of manufacturing jobs is declining. Service jobs are growing at a rapid pace. Some of the service jobs are low skill. Others are professional-level jobs or require a great deal of technical knowledge.

Businesses have to respond to all of the changes and maintain a positive organizational culture. An **organizational culture** is the environment in which people work, made up of the atmosphere, behaviors, beliefs, and relationships. An organizational culture shows people how they will be treated and how they are expected to treat others. It identifies what is acceptable behavior and what is not. If a company has a positive organizational culture,

> **main idea**
>
> Recognize factors that contribute to an effective organizational culture.

Different Learning Styles

Visual Learner Have students locate pictures of different work settings in business—a factory, an office, a farm, a service business. Have them use the pictures to point out factors that make up the business' organizational culture.

FYI

employees enjoy going to work. They have positive working relations with coworkers and managers. They believe the company values them and their work. They are motivated to do a good job for the company.

Work Environment

The **work environment** is the physical conditions and the psychological atmosphere in which employees work. The physical conditions are the work area, offices, break rooms, storage areas, and all other spaces where employees spend time while at work. Tools and equipment, lighting, temperature, and air quality are also a part of the physical work environment. The physical conditions must be safe and healthy. That is certainly a legal requirement of businesses. It is also important in assuring employees that the company has their best interests at heart. If employees believe the physical environment is unsafe or unhealthy, they will likely look for another job.

In addition to the physical conditions, companies need to provide a positive psychological atmosphere. Employees do not want to work in a place where they feel they are mistreated or where their work and ideas are not valued. An atmosphere of mistrust or fear is likely to result in low morale and poor performance among employees.

Not all jobs can be physically comfortable. Some require people to work outside in very hot or cold conditions. Other jobs require a great deal of physical effort or can be quite hazardous. Even in those jobs, the business needs to find ways to provide as much physical comfort as possible. They should offer protective clothing and equipment, allow needed breaks, and ensure that every employee receives adequate safety training.

Offering a positive psychological environment means that managers are trained in effective communications and interpersonal skills. They are honest, fair, and ethical in their treatment of each employee. Employees get important information from their managers rather than from rumors through the grapevine. They believe their work is important and valued. They are recognized and rewarded for their contributions to the company.

Would you rather work inside or outside? Alone or in a group?

Different Learning Styles

Tactile Learner Have students walk around the classroom and point out physical conditions that contribute to making a positive work environment and those that contribute to making it a less positive work environment.

Work–Life Relationships

People seem to be working more days and longer days. Some people hold two jobs. There are many two-career families. Balancing work and personal life is a very important issue for most employees. A recent survey revealed that a majority of people would give up additional income to be able to spend more time with their families.

A positive organizational culture is one that respects the demands on employees from outside of the job. It offers ways for employees to meet those demands while also fulfilling the requirements of the job. Some of those ways include personal time, family leave, flextime, job sharing, and flexplace.

Many companies now offer personal time for employees to complete non-job activities that can only be done on work time. It is hard to schedule a dental or medical appointment, visit a child's school, or renew a driver's license while working. *Personal time* is a few hours each month that can be scheduled for non-job activities. Some companies even offer paid employee time to volunteer at schools or other community organizations.

Family leave policies allow employees to take a leave of absence for the birth or adoption of a child, to care for a sick family member, or for other personal emergencies. In 1993, the U.S. Congress passed the Family and Medical Leave Act. It requires companies employing 50 or more people to provide up to 12 weeks of unpaid leave for employees who face specific family or personal circumstances.

Flextime allows employees some choice in how their work days and work hours are arranged. Some employees may start and end their work day earlier or later than normal. They may be able to work a longer day and thereby work fewer days each week. *Job sharing* offers one job to two people. Each person works a part-time schedule. They share the work space and duties of the job. *Flexplace* means that some employees can complete part or all of their work away from the business site. Telecommuting is becoming increasingly popular. Employees who primarily use personal computers and other technology can work from home. They communicate with managers, coworkers, and customers using the Internet, telephone, and fax machine.

Some of the strategies for improving work–life relationships cost companies very little. Others do have a cost but often result in reduced absenteeism, lower employee turnover, and happier and more productive employees.

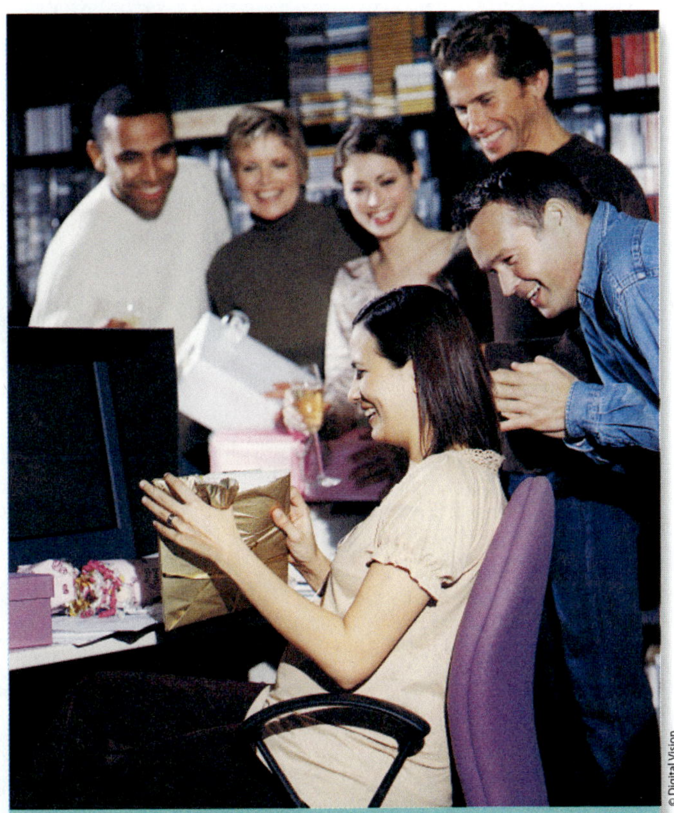

The Family and Medical Leave Act has limits on who may benefit—only 45 percent of Americans are eligible.* Are there other ways an employee might negotiate time with family?

*Economic Opportunity Institute

Different Learning Abilities

Visually Impaired Type the name and definition for each of the strategies for improving work–life relationships on a computer-generated slide so they can be projected on a screen in a size large enough for students to be able to read.

TEACH

Have students describe why work–life relationships are important for a part-time employee who is also a college student, for a single mother with two children, for a middle-aged worker with elderly parents who are quite ill, and for a retired person who is working part-time.

TEACH

As you discuss each of the ways employees are trying to meet employee work–life relationship needs, have students write each method and its definition in their notes.

 **PROJECT**

Provide the following instructions to students. (These instructions also appear on page xxiv of the textbook.)

How important do you believe family leave policies, flextime, or job sharing would be to you in choosing a career? Explain why work–life relationships are important when people set their life-span goals.

Life-Span Plan Answer

Answers will vary. Students might indicate that the importance of work–life relationships varies at different times in worker's lives.

THINK CRITICALLY THROUGH VISUALS

Employees can negotiate more time for their families through personal time, family leave, flextime, job sharing, and flexplace policies.

Students will identify five different employment laws that would apply to teens holding part-time jobs. They should briefly describe each law and explain how an employer or employee could comply with the law.

TEACH

Explain to students that businesses with poor employer–employee relations will have a difficult time being successful in the long run. People will work for the company only until they can find a better job and may not give their best effort. Even when many people are available to work for a company, the business should work to develop effective relationships with its employees.

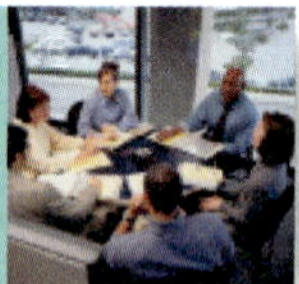

THINK CRITICALLY THROUGH VISUALS

Employee input gives a manager many advantages. Insights from the people actually performing the job can help managers make better decisions. Employees are more likely to support management decisions if they feel their ideas and suggestions are valued.

Employer–employee relations are governed by a number of federal laws administered by the Department of Labor. Those laws relate to wages and salaries, benefits, employment age, health and safety, and many other issues. Access the web site shown below and click on the link for Chapter 8. Identify five different employment laws that would apply specifically to you and your classmates if you held a part-time job. Prepare a brief description of each law and what an employee or employer must do to comply with the law.

school.cengage.com/business/introtobiz

Employer–Employee Relations

Both managers and employees want their business to succeed. Unprofitable businesses have to reduce the number of employees they hire. They must limit salary and benefit increases. If everyone can work together to make the business successful, all should benefit. Managers and employees do not always have the same immediate goals. Managers must make sure that a company makes a profit. They try to get more work done at a lower cost. Employees are most concerned about pay, working conditions, and job security.

Many years ago, a boss made all of the important decisions and told employees what to do. This characterized employer–employee relations. Employees had little input as to what they did or how they did it. Each person was assigned a specific job. They often had little interaction with other employees while they worked.

That approach often left employees thinking that their ideas were not welcome or appreciated. They believed they knew a great deal about their jobs and the business and could offer suggestions to improve the way work was done. Those differences led to disagreements and conflicts between many employers and their employees.

Much is often made of the differences between management and employees. Still, there may be more things that are alike than different between the two groups. Managers and employees have discovered that as they work together, they find ways to accomplish the goals of both the organization and the individuals who work for it. Managers who involve employees in decision-making find that better decisions are made. Employees are more likely to support those decisions. Employees discover that when they cooperate with management, managers have a better understanding of their needs and expectations. Both groups benefit through cooperation.

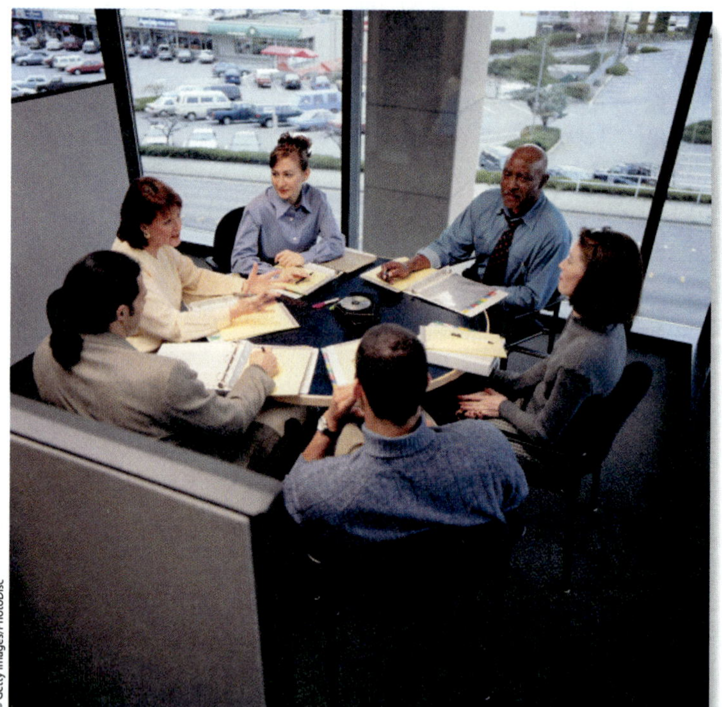

What are the advantages a manager might experience by gaining employee input?

Different Learning Abilities

Gifted Have students study several companies that have been identified as one of the "best places to work." Ask students to determine what the companies do to develop effective employer–employee relations and report on their findings to other class members.

Labor Unions

Early in the 20th century, many U.S. businesses did not treat their employees well. Low wages and poor working conditions caused employees to band together and form labor unions. A **labor union** is an organized group of employees who negotiate with employers about issues, such as wages and working conditions. Unions can be effective because they represent large numbers of employees. The popularity of labor unions peaked in the 1940s and 1950s when more than one-third of the U.S. labor force was unionized. The percentage of U.S. workers who belong to a union has been steadily declining since the 1960s and is now about 12 percent.

Occupations with strong union membership today include police and firefighters, government employees, communications workers, transportation workers, construction trades, manufacturing occupations, and utilities employees. Unions and management resolve issues through *collective bargaining*, which is formal negotiation between members of both groups. When agreement is reached, both groups sign a written labor contract. There are also federal and state laws that regulate the relationships of businesses and unions.

Relationships between many companies and their unions are very positive today. They work together on issues that affect the success of the business and the work life of employees such as job training to keep employee skills up to date, employee assistance if a business site closes, and how to improve product quality to make businesses more competitive.

checkpoint »
What are some ways that companies help employees meet personal demands outside the job?

How might a company recruiter ensure diversity in the workplace? What if only one type of person applies for positions?

© Getty Images/PhotoDisc

WORKFORCE DIVERSITY

Imagine a world where everyone looked, thought, and acted alike. The world is diverse, and the United States is the most diverse country in the world. That diversity continues to grow. Not all businesses reflect that diversity. Even in companies with a diverse workforce, that diversity is not always reflected in various job categories or in management positions.

Prospective employees and customers are attracted to work and shop in businesses where the employees are similar to themselves. When people with diverse backgrounds and characteristics are promoted into leadership and management positions, it will encourage others like them to work hard to achieve that same success.

main idea

Describe the benefits of diversity to an organization, individuals, and society.

TEACH

Discuss with students why many characteristics of employees beyond gender and race should be considered as businesses work to improve the diversity of their workforce. Ask them whether they believe focusing on many characteristics may reduce the importance of gender and race in that company.

Work as a Team

Ask students what a company can do in addition to developing a diversity statement to demonstrate their commitment to diversity.

Benefits of Diversity

"Workplace diversity" has many definitions. The basic definition of **diversity**, as it applies to businesses and organizations, is the comprehensive inclusion of people with differences in personal characteristics and attributes. The federal government has recognized important personal characteristics in equal employment legislation. Those laws are identified in Figure 8-5. Today, businesses working to build a diverse workforce use a much broader view of diversity. They try to build a broad workforce that reflects the communities in which they operate and the markets they want to serve. Diversity includes race, ethnicity, gender, age, and disability. It also includes socio-economic status, culture, religion, and even personal interests, abilities, and values.

When people in an organization are more alike than different, there is often reduced creativity and innovation. There will be limited understanding of people who are different including their attitudes, experiences, and needs. It will be difficult to recognize and plan for those differences when developing products and services for customers who are different from the people in the company. Companies that build a diverse workforce see several benefits. The benefits can be classified as organizational, individual, and societal.

Organizational Benefits *Prospective employees and managers are drawn from the broadest possible employment pool.* The greatest increase in the labor force in the future will be women, ethnic and racial minorities, and immigrants. If people from those groups are not considered, the company will have fewer and fewer employees from which to choose.

The company will have a broader base of knowledge and understanding when making decisions. People with very different backgrounds, experiences, and even ways of thinking and planning will be a part of the organization. They will bring new ideas on how to design processes, plan products, work and communicate with others, and provide leadership.

Prospective customers will have a more positive image of the company. Customers with diverse characteristics will see a company that values that diversity. They will have a greater level of respect and trust for the company and its products. They will see a company that has their interests at heart. They will see that their views and interests are represented within the company.

The company will be better at serving diverse markets. The company will understand similarities and differences in needs, decision-making processes, and communication strategies among diverse customer groups. Traditional stereotypes that upset consumers will no longer be used.

Federal Laws Regulating Discrimination

- The **Civil Rights Act of 1964** prohibits job discrimination based on race, color, religion, gender, and national origin.

- The **Age Discrimination in Employment Act of 1967** protects individuals who are 40 years of age or older.

- The **Americans with Disabilities Act,** which took effect in 1992, prohibits discrimination based on disabilities.

FIGURE 8-5

How have these laws increased employment opportunities for all Americans?

Work as a Team

Most companies and organizations have developed diversity statements to reflect their beliefs about the importance of diversity. As a team, use the Internet to identify and study examples of those statements from several companies. Select one that your team agrees is the best statement. Justify your choice.

 CHAPTER 8   HUMAN RESOURCES, CULTURE, AND DIVERSITY

Applied Skills

Communication Have students create an advertisement for a company that illustrates its commitment to diversity and the benefits to employees and customers. Consider allowing students to work in pairs or small groups to develop an ad for a magazine, newspaper, television, radio, or the Internet.

Global business strategies will improve. The United States is the most diverse country in the world and a country of immigrants. That offers American businesses a unique advantage to recognize and understand global needs and differences. They can do this much easier than companies from countries with limited diversity.

Individual Benefits *Each employee will have the opportunity to develop to their full ability.* In the past, women and other minority employees have faced a glass ceiling. A **glass ceiling** is an artificial limit placed on minority groups moving into positions of authority and decision-making. Businesses that value diversity remove those obstacles so everyone has an opportunity to advance based on their ability and performance.

Individuals will feel they are respected and supported despite their differences. Employees who are different from the typical employee do not have to hide those differences. They do not have to be uncomfortable because they are different. Individual differences will be expected and viewed as a valuable part of the organization. Employees can comfortably represent their uniqueness when participating in planning and decision-making.

Societal Benefits *Prejudice and discrimination will be reduced as a societal problem.* People involved in diverse organizations learn to recognize and value diversity. This is true for neighborhoods, schools, and businesses alike. They lose their stereotypes and recognize the strength that comes from the full participation of every person.

The country has a more talented, experienced, economically successful workforce. Diversity opens more job opportunities for everyone. It allows people to develop and use all of their abilities. It increases access to higher-paying jobs. Diversity in business leads to greater opportunities in society.

Developing a Diverse Organization

An organization's culture develops over many years. Employees and managers become comfortable with the way things have always been done. It may be hard to recognize all of the ways that an organization makes it difficult for people from diverse backgrounds to be successful in the organization. The whole organization will need to be committed to diversity in order for the necessary changes to occur. An example of a written commitment to diversity is shown in Figure 8-6.

The following steps have been used successfully in a number of businesses and other organizations to develop diversity.

FIGURE 8-6

Abbott Laboratories Diversity Statement

Abbott offers more than just a job—our diversity allows us to offer employees unlimited career opportunities in a variety of disciplines and across many health care specialties. We are proud to say that our efforts have been recognized by many distinguished publications and organizations.

Abbott provides equal opportunities for every employee—no matter which role they play or how long they've been with the company—and works hard to nurture an atmosphere that fosters creative thinking and helps employees develop to their full potential. We believe the simple reason why any organization—or individual—reaches its full potential is because diversity is valued, appreciated, and supported at all levels.

At Abbott, we offer extensive learning and development programs and resources, and a variety of educational opportunities to ensure that our employees are equipped with the latest information in their functional areas of expertise.

Copyright © 2006, 2007 Abbott Laboratories, Abbott Park, Illinois, U.S.A.

Would you include anything else to demonstrate the company's commitment to diversity? Explain your answer.

FIGURE 8-6 ANSWER

Answers will vary. Some possible additional ideas that could be included are the company's commitment to seeking and hiring a diverse group of employees, the belief that a diverse workforce positions the company for increased success in the global economy as well as the ability to reach broader markets, assurances that all company policies and procedures are designed to promote diversity, the availability of diversity education for employees at all levels, and the recognition and celebration of diversity as part of the organization's culture.

TEACH

Ask students how they could determine whether a company has a "glass ceiling."

Teaching Strategies

Expand Beyond the Classroom Have students visit with people who lead diversity training sessions in business in order to learn more about the methods and activities they use to build understanding of and appreciation for individual differences.

TEACH

As each step used by companies to develop diversity is discussed, have students identify how they believe that activity contributes to a successful organization.

ONGOING ASSESSMENT

checkpoint >> **ANSWER**

Organizations benefit from having a larger employment pool from which to select qualified applicants, the ability to project a positive image, and enhanced capability to serve diverse markets. Individuals benefit by having the opportunity to develop to their full potential and to feel respected and supported despite their differences. Society benefits by a reduction in the social unrest and upheaval caused by prejudice and discrimination. The entire society benefits as diversity opens more job opportunities for everyone.

ASSESS

Key Concepts Answers

1. True
2. b. flexplace
3. d. inclusion

Make Academic Connections

4. Actual reports, tables, and charts will vary. Encourage students to use the most current data they can find.

5. Bulletin boards, exhibits, and displays will vary. Consider making arrangements for the works to be displayed for several days.

6. Features will vary. You may want to have students use desktop publishing software to "publish" their reports.

---

1. **Develop a written commitment to diversity.** Prepare a mission statement that clearly communicates the company's values.

2. **Have the full support of top executives.** The top managers in the business must make diversity a priority in their written and oral communications and in their actions.

3. **Review evidence of diversity in the company.** Gather data on the diversity characteristics of all employees, managers, and companies. If any part of the organization does not reflect the diversity expectations, determine what is standing in the way and make changes.

4. **Update policies and procedures.** Make sure that recruiting, hiring, performance evaluation, and promotion practices encourage diversity.

5. **Provide continuing diversity education.** All managers and employees should participate in programs to increase their understanding of inclusion and diversity and to prepare them to work effectively in a diverse organization.

6. **Recognize and celebrate diversity.** Make diversity a part of the organization's culture. Have visible evidence of the variety of languages, music, art, celebrations, and customs of employees and customers.

checkpoint >>
Identify several organizational, individual, and societal benefits of diversity.

8-3 Assessment

Key Concepts

Determine the best answer.

1. True or False. There are greater numbers of both younger and older employees in the workforce today than in the past.

2. Some employees can complete part or all of their work away from the business site under
   a. flextime
   b. flexplace
   c. job sharing
   d. personal time

3. The term most closely related to diversity is
   a. affirmative action
   b. discrimination
   c. minority
   d. inclusion

Make Academic Connections

4. **Social Studies** Use the Internet to identify data that describes the changing characteristics of the U.S. population in terms of age, gender, race, religion, and immigration status. Develop a written report of your findings. Include at least five tables and charts to support your written report.

5. **Art** Working with other students in your class, create a bulletin board, exhibit, or display that illustrates the diversity in your school and community.

6. **Journalism** Select a business in your community and contact a company executive to schedule an interview. Prepare several questions on the steps the company has taken to increase diversity and the results of those steps. Record your interview. Use the information to prepare an 800- to 1,000-word feature for a newspaper.

RETEACH

Have students review the lesson goals. For each goal, have students prepare sentences that summarize the key information presented in the lesson.

ENRICH

Have students plan a diversity celebration that could be held in your school or community.

CLOSE

Ask students to point out any personal experiences that have demonstrated the benefits of diversity to them.

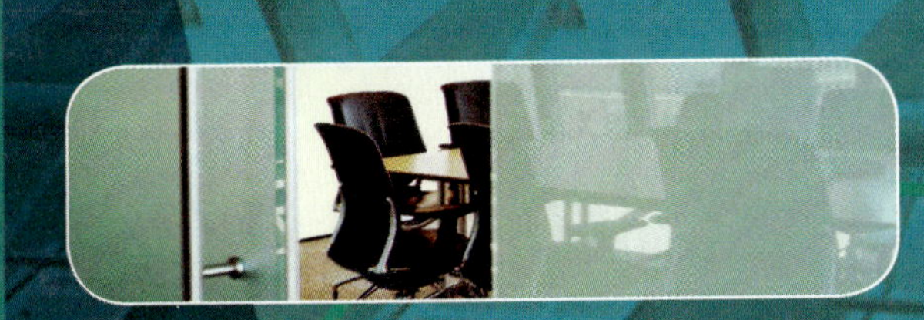

Coffee and a Conscience

In 1981, while on a skiing trip in Vermont, Robert Stiller stopped at a coffee shop for a cup of coffee. He liked the coffee so much that he decided to buy the business. Green Mountain Coffee Roasters is no longer a small-town coffee shop. It has expanded to become a major wholesaler of specialty coffees with a large direct-mail business and an e-commerce site. The company has been recognized by *Forbes* magazine as one of the best 200 small companies in America and by *Business Week* and *Fortune* as one of the fastest-growing small businesses.

Mr. Stiller was not only interested in developing a successful business. He had a belief that a company can be profitable and still have a social conscience. He wanted to operate a company that demonstrated a concern for the environment, for the people who grow and supply the coffee, and for the local and global community. Green Mountain Coffee is a partner and advocate in Businesses for Social Responsibility and the Fair Trade Partners.

Most coffee growers are small family farmers who are at the mercy of large coffee companies. Those companies had pushed the price paid for coffee beans to less than 70 cents a pound. The result was a drop in the income of small farmers to a level that didn't allow them to maintain their families' nutrition, health care, or education. Fair Trade Partners guarantee a minimum fair price when they purchase a farmer's coffee beans, as much as $1.40 per pound. In return, they ask the farmers to use farming practices that result in high-quality

products and that protect the environment.

Another program supported by Green Mountain is Coffee Kids, a nonprofit international organization. It is committed to improving the lives of children and families in the small mountain towns of coffee-growing regions around the world. The organization offers health care, nutrition training, educational scholarships, and money for local schools to improve the lives of children living in poverty. In 2001, Green Mountain employees personally donated more than $100,000 to Coffee Kids.

Through the Community Action For Employees (CAFÉ) program, Green Mountain encourages employees to perform volunteer work while on company time. Employees average 6.5 work days a year of community service.

Social responsibility is an ongoing focus and commitment of the company. The following are examples of Green Mountain's principles.

Ethics Do the right thing. Integrity is the foundation of all our decisions, actions, and relationships.

Sustainability Pathway to our future. We use resources wisely and make decisions that take into account the well-being of people, profit, and the planet.

World Benefit Creating positive change. We are a force for good in the world. We celebrate and support the power of businesses and individuals to bring about positive changes, locally and globally.

Think Critically

1. Why would Green Mountain be willing to pay farmers almost twice as much for their coffee beans than the large coffee companies pay?

2. How do you believe social programs, such as those supported by Green Mountain Coffee, affect customers' views of the company? Do you believe it affects the sales of their products? Why or why not?

Have students read about the personal experience of Robert Stiller and how he was able to accomplish his goals as an entrepreneur while holding to important personal values. Point out to students that businesspeople can maintain a strong social conscience and work to solve important world problems while operating a successful business.

Think Critically Answers

1. The practical reason for paying the farmers more is that Green Mountain can then influence the growers to use sustainable agricultural practices that result in high-quality products. Paying more than the market rate also allows the company to achieve its goal of creating positive change.

2. Answers will vary. Students might suggest that Green Mountain's support of social programs encourages customer goodwill and loyalty. Many people want to help solve the problems caused by poverty and to feel good about their consumer choices.

Communicate Business Concepts Answers

1. New technology has made manufacturing more efficient so that fewer workers are needed. Many goods-producing industries have moved their operations to countries with lower labor costs. The large, aging baby boomer generation needs an ever-increasing number of services. Over the next 10 years, people will need more proficiency in technology, more specialized job training, and top-notch human relations skills.

2. Consumers "vote" with their dollars on which industries should thrive and which should wither. The 1960's trend away from wearing hats caused many people who made or sold hats to lose their jobs. Another example of an industry that has lost jobs is newspaper publishing as consumers opted to learn the news from television and radio. On the other hand, jobs related to DVD and CD players, home computer systems, Internet service, cable television, video cameras, overnight package delivery service, wide-screen televisions, online shopping, airbags and global positioning systems in cars, and an endless list of new products and services exist today because of consumer demand.

3. Small businesses can compensate by offering more flexible work schedules, the opportunity to perform a wider variety of tasks, and a more creative and personable environment in which to work.

CHAPTER 8 Assessment

Business Notes

8-1 HUMAN RESOURCES BASICS

1. There are more than 150 million people who have full-time or part-time jobs in the United States workforce. Changes in the economy may require employees to develop new skills and get different training. Consumer preferences, economic conditions, new technology, and business competition are strong influences on the workforce.

2. Human resources are the people who work for a business. The major goals of human resources are to (1) identify the personnel needs, (2) maintain a supply of people to fill needs, (3) match abilities and interests with specific jobs, (4) provide training and development, (5) develop compensation plans, (6) protect the health and well-being of employees, and (7) maintain a satisfying work environment. The activities of human resources are planning and staffing, performance management, compensation and benefits, and employee relations.

8-2 MANAGING HUMAN RESOURCES

3. Human resources management ensures that needed employees are available and that they are productive, paid, and satisfied with their work. If human resources management does its job well, the company will have employees who do their jobs well, resulting in a successful, profitable business.

4. Compensation is the amount of money paid to an employee for work performed. Compensation is made up of two parts. Salary and wages are direct payment to an employee for work completed. Compensation in forms other than direct payment for work is known as benefits.

5. The manager regularly evaluates the work of all employees. Performance evaluations focus on the specific job duties of each employee as well as the important work qualities expected of all employees.

8-3 ORGANIZATIONAL CULTURE AND WORKFORCE DIVERSITY

6. An organizational culture is the environment in which people work, made up of the atmosphere, behaviors, beliefs, and relationships. An organizational culture shows people how they will be treated and how they are expected to treat others. A positive organizational culture is one that respects the demands on employees from outside of the job.

7. Prospective employees and customers are attracted to work and shop in businesses where people like them work. Companies that build a diverse workforce see several benefits. The benefits can be classified as organizational, individual, and societal.

Communicate Business Concepts

1. Why are service-producing industries growing more rapidly than goods-producing industries? What effect will this trend have on the skills people need for careers in the next 10 years?

2. Provide several examples of the effect of consumer "dollar votes" on jobs. What are some jobs that have increased and decreased in importance due to those "votes?"

3. Small businesses usually cannot offer the same levels of wages and benefits to employees as large businesses. In what other ways can small businesses compete to hire and retain highly qualified employees?

4. In addition to offering insurance benefits, what types of activities should businesses undertake to protect the health and safety of their employees?

5. What are the advantages and disadvantages for a company in hiring part-time and temporary employees rather than full-time and permanent employees?

4. The first step is compliance with all local, state, and federal health and safety regulations. The physical layout of the workplace should be ergonomically correct. A competently managed work environment will also reduce mental and emotional stress that could lead to illnesses or careless injury.

5. Part-time and temporary employees do not have to be maintained on the payroll if the amount of work decreases, giving management great flexibility. Also, they usually do not receive as many costly benefits as permanent workers. They may not understand or embrace the organization's values and they may not have the experience or skills of full-time employees.

6. Use a business directory to identify several nonprofit corporations that provide services to the public in your area. What public service is each providing? Why do you think each is a nonprofit rather than a for-profit corporation?

7. You are the human resources manager for a company and want to hire several accountants. List three good recruiting sources and justify your choices. If you wanted to hire several web designers, would your sources change? Why or why not?

8. Make a list of three benefits you would like to see a company offer its employees. How do you believe that list would change if you were married with a spouse and young children? If you plan to retire in 10 years?

9. Do you believe the physical conditions or psychological atmosphere of a business are more important to maintaining an effective work environment? Justify your choice.

Develop Your Business Language

Match the terms listed with the definitions.

10. Ends the employment relationship between a company and an employee.

11. Removes work from one company and sends it to another company that can complete it at a lower cost.

12. Amount of money paid to an employee for work performed.

13. Environment in which people work, made up of the atmosphere, behaviors, beliefs, and relationships.

14. Compensation in forms other than direct payment for work.

15. The assignment of an employee to another job in the company with a similar level of responsibility.

16. The comprehensive inclusion of people with differences in personal characteristics and attributes.

17. An organized group of employees who negotiate with employers about issues, such as wages and working conditions.

18. All the people 16 years and older who are employed or who are looking for a job.

19. Physical conditions and psychological atmosphere in which employees work.

20. The advancement of an employee to a position with greater responsibility.

21. Connect the amount of compensation to the quality or quantity of an employee's performance.

22. Direct payment to an employee for work completed.

23. A planned reduction in the number of employees needed in a firm in order to reduce costs and make the business more efficient.

24. A study of a job to identify in detail the specific job duties and skill requirements.

25. An artificial limit placed on minority groups moving into positions of authority and decision-making.

KEY TERMS

a. benefits
b. compensation
c. diversity
d. downsizing
e. glass ceiling
f. incentive systems
g. job analysis
h. labor union
i. organizational culture
j. outsourcing
k. promotion
l. salary and wages
m. termination
n. transfer
o. work environment
p. workforce

Develop Your Business Language Answers

10. m. termination
11. j. outsourcing
12. b. compensation
13. i. organizational culture
14. a. benefits
15. n. transfer

16. c. diversity
17. h. labor union
18. p. workforce
19. o. work environment
20. k. promotion
21. f. incentive systems

22. l. salary and wages
23. d. downsizing
24. g. job analysis
25. e. glass ceiling

Make Academic Connections

26. a. Last year's total training budget was $3,580 (6 × $130 = $780 plus 35 × $80 = $2,800).

b. Around 22 percent of the budget was spent on new employee training (780 ÷ 3,580 = 0.217 multiply by 100 for 21.7%).

c. It will cost $143 to train a new employee and $88 to train existing employees.

d. The new training budget for all employees will be $3,652 (35 × $88 = $3,080 plus 4 × $143 = $572).

27. Answers will vary. A good source of the demographic information requested in this exercise can be found at the Bureau of Labor Statistics web site.

28. Answers will vary.

29. Answers will vary. A word processing program with a table feature can make this task easier.

30. a. Monday, $46.70; Tuesday, $28; Wednesday, $36.40; Thursday, $21; Friday, nothing; Saturday, $67.

b. $182

c. $17.10

d. $199.10

Linking School and Community

Answers will vary depending on the individuals interviewed.

Make Academic Connections

26. **MATH** A small business budgets $80 per employee per year for training costs. The training cost for new employees is $130 for their first year. Last year the firm had 35 employees and added 6 new employees. It is considering increasing both parts of the training budget by 10 percent for the next year.

  a. What was the total training budget for last year?
  b. What percentage of the budget is spent on new employee training?
  c. With the proposed increase, how much will be spent for training each experienced employee and each new employee?
  d. What will be the total new training budget for all employees if four new employees will be hired?

27. **TECHNOLOGY** Use a spreadsheet and graphics program to make a chart or graph showing current data for the U.S. workforce using the following characteristics: (a) part-time versus full-time employees; (b) gender of employees; (c) racial classification of employees.

28. **COMMUNITY SERVICE** Companies participate in community activities to demonstrate that they value diversity. Using your community, develop a written description of a community service project that the employees of a business could complete to demonstrate that value.

29. **ADVERTISING** Use the Internet or a newspaper to locate classified advertising for employment opportunities. Select a job of interest to you and find listings from three different companies for that type of job. Develop a table that compares the three opportunities based on job duties, wages or salary and benefits, and work environment of the company.

30. **MATH** Nicole Miller works for a store that pays her an hourly wage of $7 plus a commission of 2 percent on all sales over $500 per day. Her hours worked and daily sales for the past week are shown in the table.

  a. How much did Nicole earn in base salary and commission for each of the days she worked?
  b. How much was the total of her base salary for the week?
  c. How much was the total of her commissions for the week?
  d. What were Nicole's total earnings for the week?

Monday	6 hrs	$735 total sales
Tuesday	4 hrs	$320 total sales
Wednesday	5 hrs	$570 total sales
Thursday	3 hrs	$450 total sales
Friday	0 hrs	$0 total sales
Saturday	8 hrs	$1,050 total sales

Linking School and Community

Identify several people from your community who work full time. Ask them their views on the importance of maintaining a balance between their work life and their personal life. Have them identify ways they believe the company they work for supports or does not support a balance in work–life relationships. Based on your discussions, do you believe most of the companies are or are not sensitive to work–life relationships?

Web Workout

Each year *Fortune* magazine publishes a list of the "100 Best Companies to Work For." This is not the only list that ranks employers. Several organizations, magazines, and websites publish lists of outstanding employers in specific industries or for particular types of workers. Because each set of rankings is based on different criteria, different companies appear on different lists.

Looking at these lists and the criteria used to rank employers can provide insight into these businesses for consumers, investors, and potential employees. Business owners, executives, and managers can use these lists to learn about the characteristics of companies that are considered the best.

Think Critically

1. Think about the criteria you might use to rank companies as the best places to work. Compare and discuss your ideas with your classmates.

2. Locate the web site of an organization or magazine that provides an annual ranking of the best places to work. Review the rankings, the criteria, and the companies included in the list. Write a short summary of your findings. Include the official name of the list and your source.

3. Choose a company from the list you found and visit the company's web site. Locate information about organizational culture, work environment, and work–life relationships. Describe our findings and offer your opinion about this company as a great place to work.

Web Workout

1. Characteristics will vary. Encourage discussion and try to elicit specifics related to organizational culture, work environment, and work–life relationships.

2. Summaries will vary depending on the list. Examples of lists include the best places to work in the federal government, the best companies to work for if you are over 50, the best companies for working mothers, and the best companies for entry-level jobs. Consider having students meet in small groups to discuss their findings and compare them to the characteristics they identified in the first item.

3. Descriptions and opinions will vary. Invite interested students to share their findings with the class.

Decision-Making Strategies

Arte Malik has operated a lawn care business for many years. The business offers landscaping services including seeding and sodding lawns, applying chemicals and fertilizer, and regular lawn mowing. Mr. Malik has 25 employees. Many of them have worked for him for 5 to 10 years. He usually hires two or three new employees each year. In the past, Arte was not concerned about the skills of new employees. He prefers to find people who are interested in the work and want to learn. Yet the machinery he uses is getting more complex, and employees must know a great deal about safe handling of chemicals, detecting plant diseases, and effective lawn care. The local community college has a two-year degree program in lawn care management. Arte is deciding whether to continue his present hiring procedure of allowing new employees to learn on the job, develop a training program to be offered to all employees, or hire only people who have completed the community college program.

31. What are the advantages and disadvantages of each of the choices Mr. Malik is considering?

32. If you were Mr. Malik's human resources manager, what choice would you recommend? Why?

Portfolio Activity

school.cengage.com/business/introtobiz

Access the web site shown here to find portfolio activities for this chapter. Use the activities to provide tangible evidence of your learning.

Think Critically
Answers

1. Mexico provides inexpensive labor that reduces production costs and provides employees for jobs that are often difficult to fill at the wages employers want to pay.

2. Answers will vary. It can be argued that if Americans are unemployed, any illegal workers might have taken away possible jobs. The question is whether the jobs would be filled by American workers if there were no illegal workers.

Decision-Making Strategies Answers

31. If Mr. Malik decides to hire only persons who have completed the community college program, he will be able to choose from more qualified applicants, but he would be decreasing the size of his employment pool and might miss the opportunity to hire some excellent, if untrained, employees. Developing a training program for all employees has the advantage of ensuring standard and up-to-date employee knowledge, but it might be considered a waste of time by experienced employees. It will also be a new expense.

32. A human resources manager might advise Mr. Malik to offer a higher starting wage to applicants who have completed the two-year degree in lawn care management (because they will need less on-the-job training), but to continue to accept applications from the general public. Frequent, brief training sessions for all employees might be less disruptive and would keep all employees current on the latest developments. Or Mr. Malik could develop a mentor program in which experienced employees are paired with new hires to facilitate training.

Winning Edge
Emerging Business Issues Event

The ability to debate using information and logical arguments is an important business skill. Business-people need to be aware of important economic and political issues and form opinions and beliefs after careful study.

Career Planning and Development

CHAPTER OVERVIEW

Students study the variety of career opportunities in business and learn how prepare a career plan and apply for a secure a job.

9-1 Career Opportunities

This lesson presents an overview of career planning activities.

9-2 Planning Your Career

While studying this lesson, students will consider various personal factors, career experience, and information sources about jobs.

9-3 Applying for Employment

This lesson introduces employment application forms, resumes, and cover letters. Applying for employment online is also addressed.

9-4 Securing a Job

The interview process, factors to assess when accepting employment, and successful career attitudes provide the focus of this lesson.

200

Teaching Resources

Activities and Study Guide, Ch. 9
Chapter and Unit Tests, Ch. 9
Spanish Resources, Ch. 9

ExamView ® *CD,* Ch. 9
Instructor's Resource CD
- PowerPoint Slides, Ch. 9
- Lesson Plans, Ch. 9

Xtra! Web Site

school.cengage.com/business/introtobiz
- Study Tools, 9-1, 9-2, 9-3, 9-4
- Quiz Prep, Ch. 9
- Net Bookmark, Ch. 9
- Crossword Puzzle, Ch. 9
- Portfolio Activity, Ch. 9

Planning a Career in…
EMPLOYMENT ASSISTANCE

Most jobs involve some aspect of planning, creating, or distributing goods and services. But some jobs involve helping people obtain employment and helping them advance in their careers. The field of employment assistance includes a variety of activities. Some workers are employed by schools and companies to help people explore career options. Others assist people with preparing a resume, writing a cover letter, or practicing interview skills.

Many states have employment bureaus to help workers who have lost their jobs or who require retraining if they are injured on the job. Employment assistance workers are available to help identify, encourage, and plan advanced training for persons who have jobs. The field of career counseling is especially important as employment opportunities change due to technology, global competition, and demographic trends.

Employment Outlook

- Overall employment is expected to grow faster than average for all occupations.
- Employment for counselors in schools will show average growth.
- Career specialists who provide career planning assistance will be in strong demand as economic conditions and technology result in people seeking new employment fields.

Related Job Titles

- Career Counselor
- Career Placement Advisor
- Career Planning Instructor
- Career Coach
- Resume Writer
- Interviewing Trainer
- Vocational Testing Center Manager

Needed Skills

- School counselors need a college degree along with state school counseling certification.
- Knowledge of employment trends and job search techniques are fundamental for most careers in this field.
- Communication and human relations skills are important for effective interaction with students and clients who are being served.

What's it like to work in…
Career Counseling

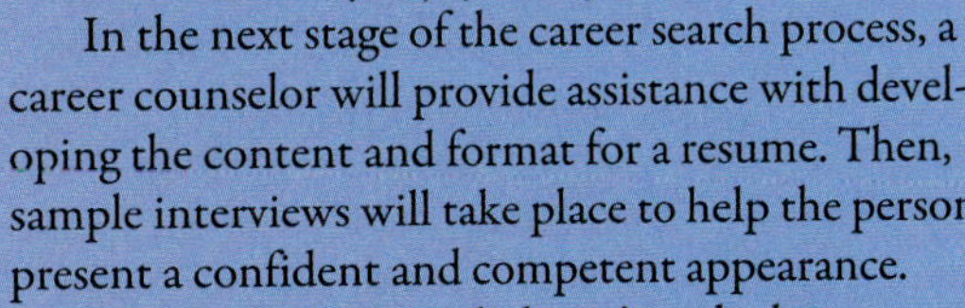

"You are very capable in mathematics and computer technology. But your interests seem to lie in working with people." These comments from a career counselor can help people better understand what they do well and what they enjoy doing.

In the next stage of the career search process, a career counselor will provide assistance with developing the content and format for a resume. Then, sample interviews will take place to help the person present a confident and competent appearance.

The counselor's work doesn't end when a person gets a job. A desire to advance in a career field can result in additional interaction with a counselor. Or, if a need exists to change careers, the counselor can direct you to needed resources for education and training.

What about you? Have you ever helped someone with finding a job or preparing for an interview? Is this something you enjoy?

Planning a Career in…
EMPLOYMENT ASSISTANCE

As various economic and technological factors change the types of jobs that are available and the application process, many people seek assistance. The employment assistance field involves helping others to obtain or change jobs. A strong knowledge of career planning activities is required. Use this career feature to give students a more specific profile of work in this field. Use the follow-up questions to encourage further student discussion.

What About You? Answers

Answers will require thinking beyond what is presented and formulating their own reactions. Students who have some experience with job interviews will be able to provide opinions. Helping someone prepare for an interview with role-playing can be enjoyable.

Additional Career Information

Additional information on careers can be found in the *Occupational Outlook Handbook,* an online publication (www.bls.gov/oco) of the federal government. Tell your class about this resource and how to use it. This description of job duties can be used to demonstrate the relevancy of skills learned in this course.

Goals

Describe the steps in the career planning process.

Identify the main sources of career information.

Discuss career fields with the most growth potential.

Key Terms

career

informational interview

mobility

Focus on Real Life

While reading the Sunday newspaper, Dan Capparus noticed a large amount of space devoted to employment ads. He was impressed by the number of help wanted ads placed by businesses in his community. The ads indicated that certain kinds of training were needed or that applicants needed experience in certain business operations. He observed that the ability to use certain computer programs was mentioned quite often.

Dan thought about his own situation. He wondered if he was taking the right courses to get the career that he wanted in the future. He then realized that he did not know for sure what kind of career he really wanted. For some reason or other, he had not given this important subject a lot of thought. He wondered what strategies he might use to improve his awareness of careers.

main idea

Describe the steps in the career planning process.

THE CAREER PLANNING PROCESS

An *occupation* is a task or series of tasks that is performed to provide a good or service. People are hired to fill occupations, and they are paid for the work they perform.

A **career** is a goal for work that is fulfilled through an occupation or series of occupations. You actually have a kind of career goal now: "to complete your schooling and get ready for your future."

Career planning is the process of studying careers, assessing yourself in terms of careers, and making decisions about a future career. As shown in Figure 9-1 on the next page, this process begins by carrying out a personal assessment. Your interests, values, talents, and abilities provide the basis for a career choice as you develop new interests and abilities.

Your search for the right career could continue for a long time. In the years ahead, some of your values and goals will change. You will develop new interests and abilities.

Do you want a career or an occupation? Explain your answer.

Your Study of Careers

Too often, a career choice is not made until full-time work begins. This is too late, especially if certain training and education are required.

The study of careers is a continuous process. New career opportunities occur all the time. You do not just decide to study careers for one day or one week. It is important to view learning about careers as a lifelong activity. It is something that continues even after you begin your career.

Your first decision will likely be a *tentative career decision*—a decision that is subject to change as new information is received. A tentative decision is much better than no decision at all. Your career decision will give you a direction that is needed.

Making initial career decisions while you are in school has many advantages. One is that, in school, you have a lot of information readily on hand. More importantly, early career planning will help you choose the right courses. An early career decision can also encourage you to become involved with organizations such as Future Business Leaders of America (FBLA), DECA, and Junior Achievement (JA). These organizations teach you about business and careers.

Career Training

Many careers require education and training beyond high school. These educational alternatives include:

- Two-year schools, usually called community colleges or junior colleges, offer training in many areas.

- Four-year colleges and universities, both public and private, provide education for many careers and professions.

- Private business schools and other institutions specialize in training students for specific occupations such as court reporter, computer technician, barber, or medical assistant.

The Career Planning Process	
Step 1	**Personal Assessment** • Determine interests and values • Identify talents and abilities
Step 2	**Employment Market Analysis** • Geographic influences • Business and economic trends
Step 3	**Application Process** • Application form • Resume and cover letter
Step 4	**Interview Process** • Prepare for interview • Follow-up activities
Step 5	**Employment Acceptance** • Salary and financial factors • Organizational environment
Step 6	**Career Development and Advancement** • Practice career success behaviors • Develop strong work relationships

Consider the cost for further schooling as an investment in your future that will help you earn higher wages and expand your potential. Many ways exist to help finance additional schooling. Most schools have financial aid programs including scholarships, student loans, and work-study opportunities.

Some financial aid programs are based on your academic record. Others are based on financial need. You should assess these methods for financing an education as you continue your career planning and decision-making.

How can you be sure that you are making the best career decision? There is no way to guarantee a perfect decision. Those who follow the right steps generally make good decisions.

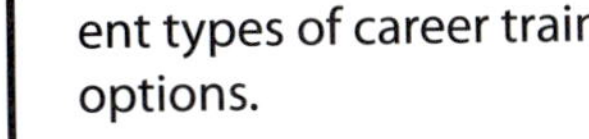

checkpoint »

List the steps in the career planning process.

TEACH

Emphasize the personal, social, and economic benefits of studying careers and effective career planning.

Use Figure 9-1 to discuss the various activities in the career planning process.

Provide an overview of the various benefits of different types of career training options.

FIGURE 9-1 *ANSWER*

Answers will vary. Resources that can be used in planning a career include research tools on the Internet or in the library, organizations such as FBLA or BPA, school guidance counselors, and talking with people who work in various careers.

 **PROJECT**

Provide the following instructions to students. (These instructions also appear on page xxiv of the textbook.) Describe a career planning process you might complete that would help you achieve your life-span goals.

Life-Span Plan Answers

Answers will vary. Students should describe a process that includes personal assessment, employment market analysis, application process, interview process, employment acceptance, and career development and advancement.

ONGOING ASSESSMENT

checkpoint » *ANSWER*

The steps in the career planning process are personal assessment, employment market analysis, application process, interview process, employment acceptance, and career development and advancement.

NETBookmark

The Riley Guide offers information and links on various career-planning topics. Access the web site shown below and click on the link for Chapter 9. Click on one of the Riley Guide links and obtain information from two different sources. Is the information provided similar or are conflicting findings evident?

school.cengage.com/business/introtobiz

main idea

Identify the main sources of career information.

CAREER INFORMATION SOURCES

Many information sources for career planning are easily available. Your school may have a career resource center with magazines, books, videos, and CDs on careers. Some information covers careers in general. Other sources provide specific coverage about occupations and careers in your area.

Print and Media Sources

The *Occupational Outlook Quarterly* or other print publications from the

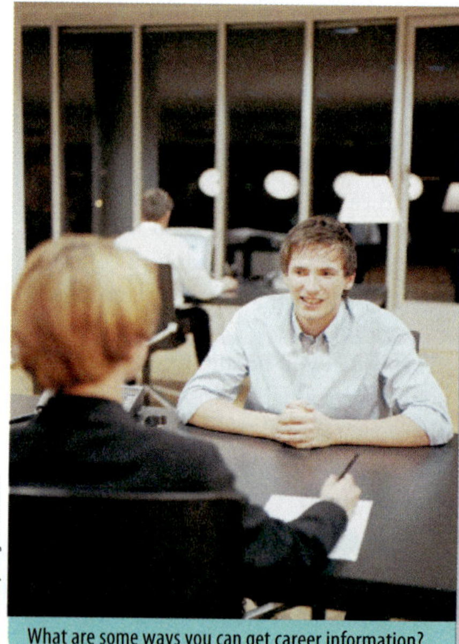

What are some ways you can get career information?

Bureau of Labor Statistics can be helpful. The *Occupational Outlook Handbook* gives in-depth information on hundreds of occupations including job duties, working conditions, education and training requirements, advancement possibilities, employment outlook, and earnings. These resources are also available online.

Career World magazine publishes information about a variety of careers. It often looks at careers of the future. *The Encyclopedia of Careers and Vocational Guidance* can give you basic information about many occupations.

Newspaper help wanted ads (both in print and online) can be useful in career planning. Reading the help wanted ads in newspapers gives you an idea of what jobs are in demand. The ads help you find out what training and skills are needed. The career and business sections of newspapers publish articles on a range of career planning topics.

Online Sources

Web sites are available to help you with career planning. A search may be performed to gather information about "resumes," "effective interviewing," and "creating a career portfolio."

Informational Interviews

A very useful method to get career information is with an informational interview. An **informational interview** is a planned discussion with a worker who is willing to help you find out about the work that a person does, the preparation needed for that career, and the person's feelings about the career. Informational interviews will help you gain insight into what actually happens in a specific career area.

You will find that most workers like to talk about their career experiences. Be sure to plan your questions for a career information interview. Some suggested questions might include:

- How did you get your current job?
- In what ways do you find your work most satisfying? What are your main frustrations?
- What tasks and activities are required in your work?
- What are the most important qualifications for working in this field?
- What advice would you give a young person who is thinking about this type of work?

Keep notes on what you learn in your informational interviews. The experiences of others can provide key career planning information.

If a specific career interests you, ask your teacher or guidance counselor about the possibility of becoming a *job shadow* at a company employing workers that reflect your career interest. Job shadowing allows you to spend time with a worker

Using Figure 9-2, select three of the career areas listed. For each career area: (1) create a list of additional jobs, and (2) describe various skills that would be necessary to work in this career area.

for a day or a week to learn about a certain occupation.

Business Contacts

The process of talking to other people about their jobs is called *networking*. The advantage of networking is that your contacts are not limited to the people you know personally. Every person you meet is a potential contact for career information. The contacts in your network can provide support when you start work as well as later in life.

> *checkpoint* >>
> What are the main sources of career information?

Career Areas with Greatest Growth Potential					
Sales and retailing	marketing representatives and sales managers in the areas of electronics, medical products, financial services	**Health care**	medical assistants, physical therapists, home health workers, lab technicians, health care administrators	**Social services**	child care workers, elder care coordinators, family counsellors, social service agency administrators
Business services	web consultants, language translators, employee benefits managers, data analysts	**Hospitality and food service**	resort and hotel administrators, customer service representatives, food service managers, meeting planners	**Financial services**	risk assessment managers, actuaries, e-commerce accountants, investment consultants
Management and human resources	supervisors, interviewers, employee benefits administrators	**Computer technology**	systems analysts, computer operators, web site developers, service technicians	**Education**	corporate trainers, special education teachers, educational administrators

FIGURE 9-2

Which of the career areas shown above interest you? Do you think you should limit your career exploration to these career areas?

This activity will allow students to share their knowledge with others in the class.

TEACH

Explain the value of the suggested informational interview questions.

Use Figure 9-2 to provide an overview of the career areas with the most potential. Remind students that jobs will be available in every career area, and they should be encouraged to pursue their interests and abilities.

Describe how business contacts can assist in the career planning process.

FIGURE 9-2 *ANSWER*

Answers will vary. Some students may be interested in a career that is not on the list—one without much growth potential. This could provide an interesting discussion on how to prepare for and succeed in a less common career. Point out that, while demand for a field may be low, a person's ability and perseverance can make a difference.

ONGOING ASSESSMENT

checkpoint >> **ANSWER**

Print, media, and online sources, informational interviews, and business contacts are the main sources of career information.

Different Learning Styles

Auditory Learner Have students work in pairs or small groups. Ask them to discuss the career areas and job titles in Figure 9-2. Ask students to (1) name other types of jobs in these fields and (2) suggest needed skills in these career areas.

TEACH

Explain how geographic factors can influence career opportunities.

Ask students to name recent social, economic and technological trends that could affect demand for various jobs.

ONGOING ASSESSMENT
checkpoint >> **ANSWER**

Future employment opportunities are influenced by geography and economic trends. Consumer demand, changing demographics, and new technology all affect employment trends.

ASSESS

Key Concepts Answers

1. c. determine your interests and abilities

2. a. obtain information about a career area

3. d. job shadowing

Make Academic Connections

4. Answers will vary. Students should identify several areas with strong demand for various careers and draw logical conclusions about the factors that affect job opportunities in these geographic regions.

5. Answers will vary depending on when the assignment is completed and the scientific developments identified.

CLOSE

Ask students to name the most important actions in the career planning process.

main idea

Discuss career fields with the most growth potential.

GROWTH CAREER AREAS

The life work you choose could be affected by the careers available in a field. Future employment opportunities are influenced by geography and business trends.

Geographic Influences

You may have to decide whether you want to work in the geographic area in which you now live or whether you are willing to move to where the job you really want is located. There may be reasons why you would prefer to live and work near your home. People who successfully pursue the careers of their choice often have mobility. **Mobility** is the willingness and ability of a person to move to where jobs are located.

The lack of mobility can lead to *locational unemployment*. This occurs when jobs are available in one place but go unfilled because those who are qualified to fill those jobs live elsewhere and are not willing to relocate.

Economic and Industry Trends

Career areas with the most potential are influenced by economic trends and current business activities. Consumer demand, changing demographic trends, and new technology are factors that often affect career opportunities. As shown in Figure 9-2 on the previous page, service industries are expected to have the greatest employment potential.

While these are fields with strong future demand, do not limit yourself. Every career area will need new employees. Think about your personal interests and abilities in addition to economic and business trends.

checkpoint >>
What factors affect the career areas that will be in demand in the future?

9-1 Assessment

Key Concepts

Determine the best answer.

1. The first step of the career planning process is to
a. prepare a resume and cover letter
b. interview for a job
c. determine your interests and abilities
d. obtain career training

2. The purpose of an informational interview is to
a. obtain information about a career area
b. apply for a job with a nonprofit organization
c. research salaries for starting employees
d. gain career training experience

3. Spending time with a worker on the job to learn about a career is called
a. networking
b. personal assessment
c. career training
d. job shadowing

Make Academic Connections

4. *Geography* Conduct research to identify areas of the country with strong demand for various careers. What factors have affected job opportunities in these geographic regions?

5. *Science* Identify recent scientific developments. Explain how these discoveries might affect (a) the type of career opportunities available in the future and (b) how people work in organizations.

RETEACH

Use Figure 9-1 to provide additional reinforcement of career planning activities.

ENRICH

Based on Figure 9-2, have students prepare a summary of their plans to work in one or more of these fields.

Doing Business in... Ukraine

Official name
Ukraine

Capital
Kyiv (Kiev)

Population
46.3 million

Currency
hryvnia

Major exports
metals, petroleum products, machinery, transport equipment, food products

Major export partners
Russia, Turkey, Italy

Major imports
energy, machinery, equipment, chemicals

Major import partners
Russia, Germany, Turkmenistan, China

Source: CIA World Factbook

As the country of Ukraine moved from using the Russian ruble to its current currency, the hryvnia, something rather unusual occurred. To prevent a shortage of money, the government issued coupons to use when buying some of the limited food and other products. While the coupons were not intended to become currency, their acceptance grew as the ruble became less attractive. The people of Ukraine desired to separate themselves from their past as a Russian state.

Today, the hryvnia is a fairly strong currency, reflecting an expanding economy and encouraging business investment from around the world. Ukraine's strategic location, between Europe and Asia, is also attractive. More than 300 U.S. companies have business operations there. Ukraine's economy benefits from fertile farmland, rich natural resources, a well-developed industrial base, and a highly trained labor force.

Ukraine has seen extremes in its history. The country was the major political and cultural center in Eastern Europe until conquered in 1240. More recently, Ukraine was part of the Soviet Union for 70 years. It became independent in 1991 and has expressed interest in being considered for membership in the European Union.

Visitors to the country often comment on the friendliness and generosity of the Ukrainian people. In business, however, be sure to use formal titles, such as Mr., Mrs., Miss, Ms., or Dr., until you are told to use a first name. When conducting business negotiations, don't accept the first "no." This initial "no" may be quick and automatic. Instead, be pleasant and ask again using a different phrasing. In addition, "final offers" may not be final. Be prepared to wait. Ukrainian businesspeople may walk out or shout. While responding in a similar dramatic way might be useful, patience will usually be more effective.

Social events are important in the business process. As you develop trust, acceptance of you will develop. Meetings will usually include highly sweetened coffee or tea along with chocolates or cookies. Some of the most popular dinner foods of Ukrainians include pork, chicken, seafood, potatoes, and many types of bread—white, brown, rolls, bagels, pita, and flat bread.

Think Critically

1. How does Ukraine's history affect current business and economic activities?
2. What aspects of Ukrainian culture might create difficulties for international companies?
3. Conduct library or Internet research to obtain additional information about business and economic activities in Ukraine.

Doing Business in...

Focus on **Real Life**

Explain to students that they have many school and personal experiences that can be the basis for planning a career.

TEACH

Provide an overview of interests, values, talents, and abilities.

Explain how interests can be identified and enhanced.

Have students name some interests that could be the basis of future employment.

THINK CRITICALLY THROUGH VISUALS

Answers will vary. When students allow their own interests and values to influence their choices, it will likely result in a rewarding career rather than choosing a career on the advice of someone else.

Goals

Describe factors of a personal assessment for career planning.

Discuss methods for obtaining career experience.

Identify information sources for available jobs.

Key Terms

values

talent

ability

Focus on **Real Life**

Brianna Bunton learned about career planning in a number of ways. Brianna prepared a career report on becoming a corporate lawyer as a requirement for her Introduction to Business class. She also interviewed the legal counsel for a local corporation. Her report gave her doubts about whether she really wanted to pursue a career in law and whether she could afford the additional schooling.

A course in marketing that Brianna finished in her junior year led her to believe that the marketing field was one that she would like to enter. She did some reading about careers in this area. With her various skills, she was able to get a part-time job as a marketing assistant the following summer. While on the job, she learned about more about the marketing process. Her job gave her a chance to talk to several sales and marketing workers about their careers. When school began again in the fall, she took more courses related to her interest in marketing.

---

main idea

Describe factors of a personal assessment for career planning.

PERSONAL ASSESSMENT

How can you make sure you select a job you will enjoy and that fits your life situation? Your career planning activities should start with a self-assessment of your interests, values, and abilities. These three areas will help you better understand the careers that will be the best for you. With a thorough self-assessment, you will be more likely to have a satisfying and successful career.

Interests

Many resources are available in print and online to determine the activities that give you satisfaction. Your *interests* provide a basis for your employment goals and possible career paths.

People with strong social tendencies may be best suited for work interacting with people. If you enjoy investigating situations, a career in some type of research should be considered. What are some topics or activities of interest to you?

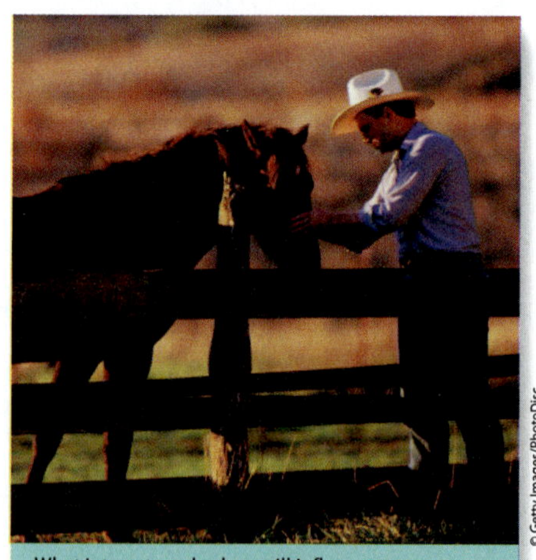

What interests and values will influence your choice of career?

Different Learning Abilities

At-Risk Have students name some topics and activities that are of interest to them. Help them name jobs related to these interest areas. Pair students and ask them to work together to learn more about these jobs and what education or training is required.

Values

Your **values** are things that are important to you. You can learn about your values with exercises or activities. These exercises show how you rank items such as prestige, money, power, achievement, independence, security, belonging, or serving others. Each of these may influence you, directly or indirectly, when you select your life's work.

You can begin to look at your values by answering some questions. Your answers will help you understand what you consider important. Examples of questions include:

- Is it important for me to earn a lot of money?

- Am I mainly interested in work that provides a service for others?

- Is it important for me to have an occupation that others think is important even if I do not really care for it?

- Do I want an occupation that is very challenging and may require additional schooling?

- Would I be willing to start in a job that pays a lower salary than another if that job was more challenging and offered better opportunities for future advancement?

- Do I consider investing money in education or occupational training as important as spending for other things?

Another question to better understand your values is: "What would you do if someone gave you a large sum of money to be used in any way you desire?" Would you start your own business? Would you hire a jet and travel around the world? Would you set up a foundation to support athletics for underprivileged children? Would

Prepare a list of common values of people in our society. For each item on your list, describe career situations that would be appropriate for people with this value.

you buy the trendiest wardrobe ever? Would you use the money to finance an expensive education? Your answers will reveal something about your personal values.

Talents and Abilities

Each of you has certain talents and abilities. A **talent** is a natural, inborn aptitude to do certain things. People often say someone has a "natural talent." **Ability** is the quality of being able to perform a mental or physical task. Your talents and abilities, along with your career goals and interests, are important in career planning.

How can your natural abilities help you get a job?

Mathematics Point out various calculations that will be of importance in most job situations. Use Appendixes A, B, C, and D to highlight some of the math competencies needed by students.

Explain the role of values when making career decisions and other choices in life.

Point out the importance of certain values for success in a career.

Ask students to describe some talents and abilities that are necessary for various types of careers.

This activity will help students see a relationship between values and their future employment.

 PROJECT

Provide the following instructions to students. (These instructions also appear on page xxiv of the textbook.) Complete a personal assessment of yourself. It should include listings of your interests, values, talents, and abilities. Explain how these lists may help you create your own life-span plan.

Life-Span Plan Answer
Answers will vary. Students should complete personal assessments that identify their interests, values, talents, and abilities and explain how these are related to their life-span plans.

Answers will vary, but could include discussion of the fact that talents are inborn aptitudes, while abilities can be developed and strengthened.

TEACH

Explain how various courses in high school and college can help people develop their abilities.

Point out the importance of various abilities (writing, researching, speaking, math, computer applications) for certain types of careers.

ONGOING ASSESSMENT

checkpoint >> **ANSWER**

One might have several areas of interest; talents, however, are inborn abilities that can assist in narrowing career interests.

TEACH

Explain some of the ways in which people can obtain work skills and organizational experiences before getting their first job.

A QUESTION OF ETHICS

This feature will help students better understand some of the difficulties a person might face in the career planning process.

Ask students to offer examples of discriminatory practices that job seekers might encounter.

Think Critically
Answers

1. Race, gender, age, and disabilities are areas in which discrimination can occur.

2. By staying focused on relevant career skills, training, and experience, both employers and potential employees can avoid unethical topics during the interview process.

You can learn about your abilities in a number of ways. Think about the courses you have taken and the grades you have received in school. What kinds of courses have you taken? In which ones have you done your best work? Which courses have been easiest for you? Which have been the most difficult? Which do you like the best? Answers to questions such as these will identify your talents and abilities.

Abilities can be developed, and that is important to keep in mind. If you are weak in a certain area, you may want to take courses that will improve that area. For instance, employers continually report that writing, reading, and computing skills are very important.

If you are not strong in preparing reports, take extra courses in English and Business Communication. If reading is a concern, get help in that area. If working with fractions and decimals is not easy for you, more courses in math,

main idea

Discuss methods for obtaining career experience.

including business math, would be desirable. Work to strengthen your weak areas *before* you go into full-time work. You can plan your courses and future activities to help you grow toward your chosen career.

> *checkpoint* >>
> What is the difference between an interest and a talent?

EMPLOYMENT EXPERIENCE

Most people have more career skills than they realize. Your involvement in a range of school and community activities provides the basis for employment experiences. You can obtain further career-oriented abilities in four main ways: work-study programs, part-time employment, volunteering, and school activities.

A QUESTION OF ETHICS

Discriminatory Hiring Practices

Tomas Novak applied for a position as a regional sales manager for a technology company. Tomas was born and educated in Prague, located in what is now the Czech Republic. He has lived and worked in the United States for eight years and recently became an American citizen. He has more than 10 years of computer sales experience.

After the interview, Tomas was told that other applicants were more qualified. He did not receive a job offer. While it would be difficult to prove, Tomas feels he was a victim of discrimination due to his slight Czech accent. He believes his ability and skills were comparable to others who were hired.

According to the Civil Rights Act and the Americans with Disabilities Act (ADA), it is illegal for employers to make hiring decisions based on personal characteristics such as age, marital status, ethnicity, race, and gender. You can help reduce illegal hiring practices. Be cautious when deciding what kinds of personal information you include in a resume or cover letter. Never include a picture of yourself on a resume.

Most potential employers do not want to see this personal information related to characteristics that might be a basis for hiring bias. Instead, only offer personal information that is related to the job and your career skills, such as hobbies,

community activities, memberships, or personal interests.

Think Critically

1. Describe other situations in which a person might be discriminated against when applying for a job.
2. What actions can be taken by companies and workers to eliminate discriminatory hiring practices?

Different Learning Abilities

Limited English Proficiency (LEP) Obtain translations of various key terms and concepts in this lesson to reinforce these ideas in both English and other dominant languages used by students. Discuss how some career planning words may not translate exactly.

Work-Study Programs

Cooperative education combines school with work-related experience. These programs provide an occasion to develop a variety of on-the-job skills. You will not only learn about technical aspects of the job, but will also learn to interact in work settings.

In a similar way, *internships* involve work experience in organizations while learning about a career field. Internships for careers in accounting, finance, marketing, and communications are available with many companies and nonprofit organizations.

Applying for an internship is similar to applying for a job. First, identify potential positions. Then prepare a resume and cover letter to communicate your background and interest in participating in an internship.

Part-Time Employment

Summer and part-time work can provide valuable experience. In addition, these work situations will allow you the chance to see if you enjoy a particular career field. Your part-time work experience also helps you make contacts. These people will be able to guide you and offer support throughout your working life.

Volunteer Activities

Involvement in community service can result in gaining career experiences and improving work habits. Volunteering in community organizations also helps you develop organizational skills while making future career contacts.

School Activities

Class assignments can provide work-related experiences. For example, research and communication skills are developed when you prepare reports and oral presentations. Working on team projects offers you a chance to interact with others, a skill vital in every career.

School clubs and organizations can result in a range of valuable skills. Goal setting, planning, supervising, and delegating responsibility are activities needed in many employment settings.

> *checkpoint* »
> What are methods for obtaining employment experience?

Name some volunteer and part-time activities that could help in a career search.

© Brand X Pictures

FYI

Career experts estimate that more than 70 percent of available jobs are not advertised to the public. Talk to people you know, attend career fairs, and contact companies directly to identify possible job opportunities.

main idea

Identify information sources for available jobs.

SOURCES OF AVAILABLE JOBS

Finding available positions is a common concern for job hunters. Several sources are often used to obtain leads. Your ability to find job openings is a key part of career planning activities.

The Media

The sources you use for information about career planning can help you get job leads, too. Newspaper want ads are a common starting point. Many newspapers post employment ads on their web sites. Some papers have partnered with career web sites that have searchable databases of currently advertised positions. Be aware that most available positions are not advertised to the general public. Therefore, other job search actions are very important.

© Getty Images/PhotoDisc

Name some ways you can find out about job openings.

Personal Contacts

You need to let as many people as possible know that you are looking for a job. Your school counselors and business teachers can be very helpful. If your school has a placement office, be sure to register with that office. Your relatives, friends, neighbors, and others will be good potential sources of job leads.

Business Contacts

You should visit businesses and ask about their openings. Some businesses post help wanted signs in their windows. Some retail businesses, including restaurants, accept applications continuously. They make it easy for prospective employees to pick up and turn in applications. Employment kiosks, where you can apply for a job online, are common in large stores. Getting a job means going out and looking around. During a visit, you will be able to observe the types of activities performed by employees. You may also be able to make contacts for future career information.

Use phone books, business directories, and web sites to find names of organizations that may have unadvertised jobs. Communicating with these companies can produce business contacts that can result in current or future employment opportunities.

Career Fairs

Career fairs are often held at schools or community centers. These events allow a chance to contact several prospective employers in a short time. You will be asked a few questions to determine if you qualify for a longer interview.

Get ready for job fairs by being prepared to quickly communicate your potential contributions to an organization. Knowing something about the company will help set you apart from other applicants.

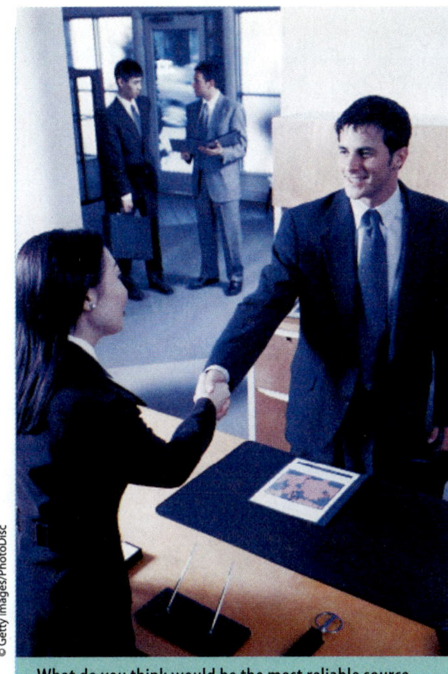
What do you think would be the most reliable source of job information?

Government Employment Offices

Local and state government employment offices are another source for information about available jobs. These tax-supported agencies help people find jobs and provide career information, and work with employers to find qualified workers.

Employment offices can provide up-to-date information about the job market in your area. They can help you look for part-time, summer, or full-time work.

No one source is necessarily better than others. You need to let as many people as possible know that you are looking for a job. Your relatives, friends, neighbors, and others are all potential sources of job leads.

checkpoint »
What are the main sources of information about available jobs?

9-2 Assessment

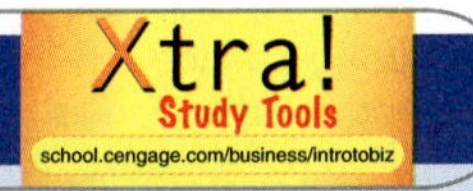

Key Concepts

Determine the best answer.

1. True or False. A person's values are also called natural talents.

2. True or False. Volunteering experience can result in obtaining career skills.

3. A desire to assist others in your job is an example of your
   a. talents
   b. interests
   c. abilities
   d. values

4. A(n) _?_ is an event that allows a person to contact several prospective employers in a short time.
   a. career fair
   b. informational interview
   c. network
   d. career resource center

Make Academic Connections

5. *Research* Use library research or an Internet search to locate a career assessment tool. After answering the questions, describe what you learned about yourself in relation to potential future careers.

6. *Communication* Look at the classified advertising section in your Sunday newspaper. Find three jobs that include an international factor. Prepare a paragraph summary explaining actions a person might take to prepare for these jobs.

TEACH

Explain the value of government employment agencies in the job search process.

Remind students that some for profit employment agencies may charge a fee.

THINK CRITICALLY THROUGH VISUALS

Answers will vary. Personal and business contacts are often considered to be the most reliable source of job information.

ONGOING ASSESSMENT

checkpoint » **ANSWER**

Business and personal contacts are the main sources of employment information. Others include newspapers and other publications, career fairs, employment agencies, and online sources.

ASSESS

Key Concepts Answers

1. False. Values are different from talents.

2. True

3. d. values

4. a. career fair

Make Academic Connections

5. Results will vary. Ask volunteers to share their findings with the class.

6. Paragraphs will vary depending on the classified advertisements used.

CLOSE

Ask students to compare values, interests, and abilities. Ask for student opinions regarding which of the three would most affect their career goals.

RETEACH

Explain various actions that a person might take to obtain employment experience.

ENRICH

Have students debate which source of job information would be most valuable to various groups: students, college graduates, a person looking to change careers.

Emphasize the importance of making effective presentations. Ask students to explain effective presentations from the perspective of the audience. When observing presentations, what are some actions that can make a talk memorable?

Think Critically
Answers

1. Plan and practice your presentation. When making your presentation, speak openly rather than reading from your notes, project your voice without repetition, stand up straight, and make eye contact.

2. Answers will vary because the need to present ideas effectively is useful in a variety of professional and casual arenas. The classroom, in sales, development meetings, professional trade conventions, and interviews are common areas in which presentations are used.

Effective Presentations

"Please prepare a presentation about the recent changes in our product line for the executive committee meeting."

This request and others point out your need to be able to make oral presentations. Your ability to communicate orally is a vital skill that can be enhanced by considering these actions.

Plan Your Presentation
- **Clearly define your purpose.** Organize the main sections. Conduct research to get needed information.
- **Plan a creative introduction.** Use a story, quote, statistic, or involvement activity to get the audience's attention and to communicate your main theme.
- **Develop a clear conclusion.** Summarize the main ideas and key findings.

Practice Your Presentation
- Prepare an outline of key ideas and main phrases. Do not memorize or read your entire presentation.
- Present your complete presentation several times. Record your presentation to determine areas for improvement.
- Consider using a handout with key ideas, graphs, tables, maps, or other visuals.

Make Your Presentation
- Talk to the audience, don't read to them. Don't read from your visuals—posters, slides, or other items.
- Use effective voice projection, expression, and enthusiasm. Avoid repetitious phrases such as "OK," "you know," and "like."
- Look and talk professionally—dress appropriately and stand up straight.

You are likely to make many presentations throughout your life. At first it may seem difficult. As you prepare, practice, and present more talks, your ability and comfort level will increase.

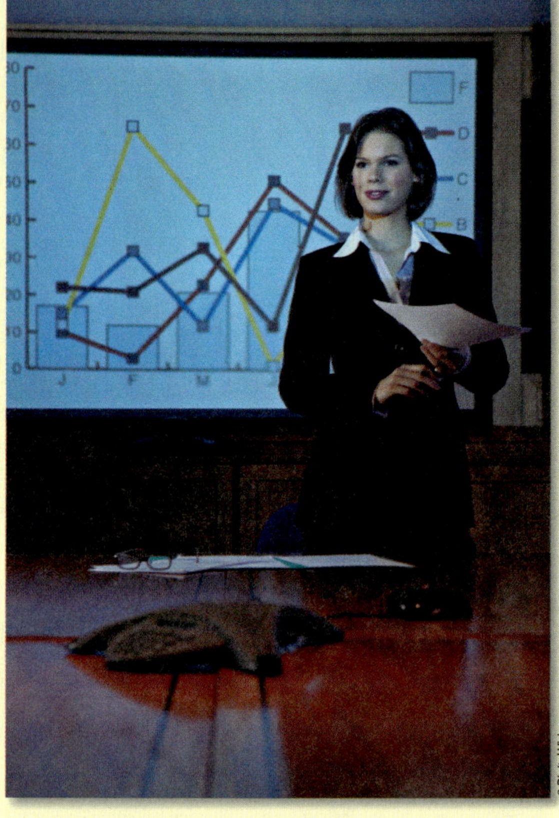

Think Critically
1. What are the main suggestions you should follow for making an effective presentation?
2. Describe some situations in which you may make presentations during your life.

Teaching Strategies

Expand Beyond the Classroom Have students talk to people about making presentations as part of their job or in other settings. Instruct students to ask these people how they prepare for a presentation. Ask students to report their findings to the class.

Applying for Employment

Goals

Prepare an application form and a resume.

Identify the parts of an application cover letter.

Discuss the online application process.

Key Terms

application form

resume

career portfolio

cover letter

Focus on Real Life

Francisca Negalo just graduated from high school. Her work experience includes a summer job and employment through a cooperative education program. Francisca is now ready for full-time employment. Her high school business education program included computer applications and two years of accounting. She is familiar with computer-based accounting systems, and she is proficient with the most recent version of Windows and Microsoft Office.

Francisca plans on continuing her accounting studies in an evening program at a local two-year college. She wants to earn an associate's degree in accounting. In time, she will transfer to a university and work toward a bachelor's degree in business administration. For now, she needs to get a job and earn some money.

APPLICATION ACTIVITIES

The application process may start in several ways. You might fill out an application form you have received from the employer. Some businesses use online application forms. You may also apply by submitting a resume and cover letter. As an alternative to mailing these documents, you might send them via e-mail or post them to a web site.

Personal Data Sheet

The application process starts by preparing a *personal data sheet*. A personal data sheet is a summary of your important job-related information. It should list your education and work experience, as well as your references. Preparing your personal data sheet will ensure you have all the necessary information to fill out the application form.

Application Form

An employer often has each applicant complete an application form. An **application form** asks for information related to employment. The form gives the employer standard information about each job applicant. The form will likely ask for your name, address, Social Security number, education, work experience, the job for which you are applying, and references.

main idea

Prepare an application form and a resume.

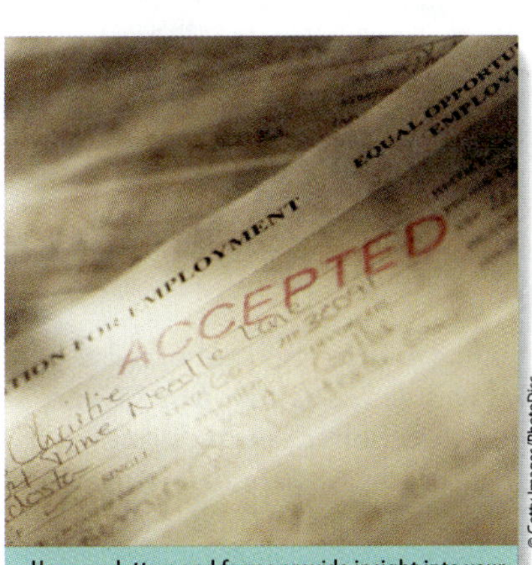

How can letters and forms provide insight into your personal attributes?

© Getty Images/PhotoDisc

Focus on Real Life

Ask students to identify steps taken in this scenario that may be of value to them in the future.

TEACH

Describe the purpose of a personal data sheet. Ask students to explain how it will be used when applying for a job.

Explain the role of the applications form in a job search. Point out that application forms are used in some settings and not in others.

THINK CRITICALLY THROUGH VISUALS

Answers will vary. The high-quality forms and letters students produce show they are neat, orderly, and can follow directions—all positive attributes for any job.

Different Learning Styles

Kinesthetic Learner Have students create an employment application form they might use if they owned a small business. Ask them to explain why certain information is requested on the form they create.

216

TEACH

Use Figure 9-3 to explain the various sections of an application form. Ask students to relate their experiences with completing an application form.

Provide an overview of the purpose and main sections of a resume.

FIGURE 9-3 *ANSWER*

Answers will vary. If the form is filled out carefully and all questions are answered fully, it reveals a person who is neat and pays attention to details.

Sample Application Form

The following is a reproduction of the completed application form shown in Figure 9-3.

LAKEVIEW TECHNICAL COLLEGE
APPLICATION FOR EMPLOYMENT

Name *Francisca Negalo*
(First)   (Middle)   (Last)

Social Security No. *399-48-6951*

Date *July 15, 20--*

U.S. Citizen *X* yes
____ no, if not, type of visa ____________

Do you have any physical condition that may prevent you from performing certain kinds of work *No*

Have you ever been convicted of a felony or misdemeanor or are there any felony charges against you pending disposition? *No*

If yes, give date(s) and nature of the act(s) and disposition ____________

Have you ever been compensated for an on-the-job accident? *No* If yes, explain ____________

Have you served in the U.S. armed forces? *No* What branch ____________ Type of discharge ____________ Rank ____________

Dates of service ____________ If you were deferred—why? ____________

In case of emergency, notify *Marianne Negalo* *520 Nancy Blvd. Sun Prairie, WI* *(608) 555-1710*
(Name) (Address) (Phone)

List all employment within the past ten years **EMPLOYMENT HISTORY**

NAME OF EMPLOYER and Immediate Supervisor	ADDRESS and Telephone Number	POSITION HELD		Dates Employed		Reason for Living
		Occupation and Duties	Monthly Rate	From	To	
Tempest Tea Pot Company Mrs. Phillis Lipton	707 Coffee Lane Middletown, WI 555-1010	General office work including some record keeping	$5/hr.	9/9--	6/20--	Temporary Coop.
City Assessor's Office Mr. Dan Verwith	16 Capitol Avenue Madison, WI 555-1122	Record Clerk Recorded data using computer	$6/hr.	6/20-	present	

EDUCATION

Level	Name	Address	Years Attended		Date Graduated	What did you specialize in? Degree(s) Received
			From	To		
Elementary	Hillside Elementary	16 N. 45th St.	19--	19--		
High School	Four Lakes	1234 Monona Drive	19--	19--	June 10	
Trade School						
Business College						
College						
Graduate						
Other						

PERSONAL REFERENCES
Other Than Immediate Relatives

Name	Address	Telephone Number	Occupation	Years Known
Mr. Tim Schilling	1234 Monona Drive, Madison	555-1099	Teacher	3
Rev. David Crane	937 Culpepper Ct. Madison	555-4661	Pastor	12
Mrs. Susan Collins	1602 Woodrale, Madison	555-0065	Secretary	5

Type of work you would consider *Accounting*   Full, or part time? *Full time*

Minimum salary you would consider *$14,000* Would you consider temporary work? *No* Date available for employment *Immediately*

The information contained here is true to the best of my knowledge and belief. I realize that any falsification in this application constitutes grounds for dismissal. In this connection, I authorize all previous employers to provide Lakeview Technical College with any information concerning my employment. I further authorize Lakeview Technical College to verify any other information I have provided in this application. I FURTHER UNDERSTAND THAT THIS APPLICATION BECOMES INACTIVE AFTER THREE MONTHS.

Signature *Francisca Negalo*   Date *June 15, 20--*

Filling out the application form should be viewed as your *first job task.* Follow directions carefully. Print answers neatly. Answer all questions completely. Carefully study the completed application form in Figure 9-3.

Resume

A **resume** is a tool that provides information about you to a potential employer. Two of the most popular types of resumes are *experience-based* and *qualifications-based.* In an experience-based resume, experiences are usually listed in order of work history. In a

Different Learning Abilities

Dyslexia Prepare short written explanations of the various elements of an application form. Have students carefully read each item and explain it in their own words.

FIGURE 9-4

How will the information in this resume help an employer who wants to hire the best person possible?

qualifications-based resume, your abilities and experiences related to the job for which you are applying are highlighted.

As shown in Figure 9-4, a resume usually includes the following sections:

- **Personal information** Name, address, phone, e-mail
- **Career objective** Personal employment goal
- **Education** Schools attended, dates, degrees, programs of study
- **Experience** Work and volunteer activities with dates and responsibilities
- **Career-related honors and other activities** Awards, school and community involvement

Be sure your resume is presented in a professional manner—clean, organized, with no errors. Limit your resume to one page. Use a format that highlights how your skills will contribute to the company's needs.

Applied Skills

Word Processing/Office Technology Have students use a resume template in a word processing software program. Ask students to comment on the benefits and drawbacks of using this kind of preformatted document.

TEACH

Use Figure 9-4 to explain the various sections of a resume.

Point out that a career objective might not be included on the resume. Instead, this information might be communicated in a cover letter.

Have students suggest various tips to follow when creating a resume.

Ask students for suggestions that might improve the resume presented in Figure 9-4.

FIGURE 9-4 ANSWER

Answers will vary. The information in a resume shows an employer whether the applicant's education, experience, activities, and interests would be a good fit for the job.

PROJECT

Provide the following instructions to students. (These instructions also appear on page xxiv of the textbook.) Complete a resume for yourself similar to the one in Figure 9-4 in your text. Identify steps you could take over the next year that would improve your resume and increase your chances of being hired. Explain how these short-term steps might help you achieve your life-span goals.

Life-Span Plan Answer

Resumes will vary and should include their personal data, employment history, education, and personal references. Steps for improving a resume should focus on things students can do to enhance their value to potential employers and how each relates to life-span goals.

Discuss some of the points to remember when preparing a resume.

Ask students to share their experiences in preparing a resume.

Use Figure 9-5 to point out the action verbs that can help students better communicate their experiences in a resume or cover letter.

Explain the use of a career portfolio for various types of job application settings.

FIGURE 9-5 *ANSWER*

Answers will vary. Additional verbs may include *wrote, completed, engineered, maintained, determined, conducted, recommended, executed, provided,* and *authorized*.

ONGOING ASSESSMENT

checkpoint >> **ANSWER**

The typical resume includes personal information, career objective, education, experience, career-related honors, and other activities.

TEACH

Explain the purpose of a *cover letter*.

Ask students to name some actions that might be taken before starting to write a cover letter.

Remember that resumes are usually skimmed quickly. Some companies even use scanners to check for keywords. Important phrasing might include: fluent in Japanese, proficient with Adobe Illustrator, Cisco network certification, research ability, team projects, leadership skills, overseas study, and international experience.

Use action words that demonstrate what you have achieved. See Figure 9-5 for examples of strong action words.

When preparing your resume, be completely honest about your qualifications. Remember that employers check resume information. Providing false information can cause you to lose a job. False information, found after you have been hired, can lead to your dismissal and long-term career problems.

Many career experts suggest not including a career objective on the resume. Often, a career objective is too vague or too general. Instead, this goal is better addressed in the cover letter when you connect your abilities to the organization's needs.

References are not usually included on the resume. Have this information on hand when requested by a prospective employer. Prepare a list of people who can give a report about your character, education, and work habits. These individuals may be teachers, previous employers, supervisors, or coworkers. Be sure to obtain permission from the people you plan to use as references.

main idea

Identify the parts of an application cover letter.

Career Portfolio

Many job applicants prepare a career portfolio. A **career portfolio** provides tangible evidence of your ability and skills. A career portfolio may include the following items:

Action Verbs for Resumes and Cover Letters		
Achieved	Directed	Organized
Accomplished	Edited	Planned
Administered	Facilitated	Produced
Coordinated	Initiated	Researched
Created	Implemented	Supervised
Designed	Managed	Trained
Developed	Monitored	Updated

FIGURE 9-5

What are some other action verbs that might be used on a resume or in a cover letter?

- Resume, cover letter, and answers to sample interview questions
- Sample reports, presentation materials, and research findings from school projects
- Web site designs, creative works from school activities or previous employment such as ads, packages, and promotions
- News articles of community activities or other experiences in which you have participated
- Letters of recommendation

A career portfolio can show your abilities in a tangible manner to prospective employers. In addition, these materials will communicate your initiative and uniqueness.

checkpoint >>
What are the main sections of a resume?

APPLICATION COVER LETTER

The application **cover letter** expresses your interest in a specific job. Think of this as a sales letter for the purpose of obtaining an interview. Like any good sales letter, a cover letter should draw attention and interest. It should build a desire to meet you. Your letter should urge the reader to invite you to come for an interview. Figure 9-6 on the next page shows a cover letter that is neat, courteous, and to the point. A carelessly written letter may cause the

Different Learning Abilities

At-Risk Ask students to name some of their work experiences or school activities. Have them explain how these experiences might be described in a cover letter when applying for a job.

employer to think that you will be a careless worker. A cover letter usually involves three main sections: introduction, development, and conclusion.

Introduction

Your cover letter should start by getting the reader's attention. Next, indicate the reason for writing. Refer to the job or type of employment in which you are interested. Give a brief summary of your experience and qualifications. If applicable, mention the name of the person who referred you to this organization.

Development

This section should highlight your background and experiences that specifically qualify you for the job. Refer the employer to your resume for more details. At this point, summarize information about your experiences and training. Connect your skills and background to specific organizational needs.

Conclusion

The final section is designed to request action—ask for the opportunity to discuss your qualifications in more detail. In other words, request an interview! Include your contact information, telephone numbers, times when you are available, and e-mail address. Make sure your e-mail address is professional. Close the letter with a summary of how you could benefit the organization. Create a personalized cover letter for each position for which you apply.

Targeted Letter

In recent years, some job applicants are using a *targeted application letter* instead of a resume and cover letter. This letter provides a quick summary of your ability to meet the needs of an organization. A target letter will usually include a list of major skills and competencies. Once again, your goal is to emphasize achievements and skills so you will be invited for an interview.

Sample Cover Letter

1602 Collegewood Drive
Madison, MI 53711-2821
June 25, 20--

Dr. David Haugen
Vice President of Finance
Lakeview Technical College
Madison, WI 53706-3692

Dear Dr. Haugen:

The advertisement in the *Daily Chronicle* for an accounting clerk describes a position in which I am interested. Please consider me as an applicant for that position.

The ad stated that you are looking for a bright and alert person who is conscientious and interested in long-term employment. My record at Four Lakes High School and part-time employment record will show that I have the qualities you desire. My career goal is to someday become a Certified Public Accountant. An accounting clerk's position in your office will allow me to get an important start on my career.

My business education program at Four Lakes High School included courses in Introduction to Business, Computer Applications, Office Procedures, and Accounting. I also completed four years of English and three years of math. For each of my last semesters, I was on the honor roll. In our work experience program, I worked ten hours a week during my senior year for the Tempest Tea Pot Company, where I learned a great deal about office work and human relations. My summer job in the city assessor's office is helping me to work accurately with figures.

Enclosed is a personal data sheet giving my qualifications in more detail. I would appreciate an opportunity to interview with you. I may be reached by telephone at (608) 555-0308 anytime during the day.

Sincerely yours,

Francisca Negalo

Francisca Negalo

Enclosure

FIGURE 9-6

What aspects of this letter would cause a reader to want to meet the applicant in person?

---

checkpoint »

What is the purpose of a cover letter?

Work as a Team

Plan an online portfolio. Design a web site that could serve as a career portfolio. Describe the format, elements, graphics, and links of this electronic portfolio. Talk about how an online portfolio could be used when applying for various types of careers.

TEACH

Explain how computers and technology are changing the job search process. Highlight some of the examples mentioned in the textbook.

Describe how an online resume might differ from a traditional one.

Ask students to suggest ways that career planning activities might be different in the future.

ONGOING ASSESSMENT

checkpoint >> **ANSWER**

Job seekers may learn job-seeking skills, post resumes, learn more about a company, and apply for jobs online. Employers may post positions, review resumes, and perform screening interviews online.

ASSESS

Key Concepts Answers

1. b. your references

2. a. request an interview.

Make Academic Connections

3. Answers will vary. In general, employers cannot discriminate on the basis of age, race, religion, marital status, national origin, religion, or disability.

4. Answers will vary. Invite students to share their findings with classmates.

CLOSE

Ask students to name mistakes that might be made when preparing an application form, resume, or cover letter.

ONLINE APPLICATION PROCESS

Many people are using the Internet for career planning activities. While researching potential employment is the most common use, job seekers also apply and interview online. Because an Internet resume is less personal, do not overlook other job search methods—phone calls, ads, job fairs, and personal contacts.

Online Applications

Many organizations allow you to apply online. In addition to the basic application, you may also be asked some preliminary questions to determine your suitability for the position available. When posting your resume online or sending it by e-mail, consider the following:

- Use a simple format. Avoid bold, underline, italics, and tabs.

- Do not use attached files that may be difficult to open.

Cyber resumes are posted on various web sites. They are scanned for keywords to identify candidates with the necessary job qualifications. The words and phrases that might make you an attractive job candidate vary depending on the company and the position. One company might search for words such as *leader, interpersonal,* and *team* and another might scan for *word processing, database,* and *spreadsheet.*

Cyber Interviewing

Many organizations hold screening interviews using video conferencing. Others require that you post preliminary interview responses online. These "e-interviews" may involve questions such as: "Would you rather have structure or flexibility in your work?" and "What approach do you use to solve difficult problems?"

Online interviewing may also be used to test a person's ability in job-related situations. For example, an applicant may be asked to respond to tasks such as those that a bank teller or retail clerk might encounter.

checkpoint >>
How is the Internet used in the job application process?

9-3 Assessment

Key Concepts

Determine the best answer.

1. The item *least* likely to be included on a resume is
   a. a school award
   b. your references
   c. schools attended
   d. your work experience

2. The main purpose of a cover letter is to
   a. request an interview
   b. obtain career information
   c. ask a person to be a reference
   d. apply for a government job

Make Academic Connections

3. *Law* Conduct library or online research to obtain information on laws that protect people during the hiring process. What actions are illegal when selecting among various people for a job?

4. *Technology* Locate an online application form. What types of questions are asked? Are you pre-pared to answer these questions? How?

RETEACH

Use Figures 9-3, 9-4, 9-5, and 9-6 to highlight major ideas about application forms, resumes, and cover letters.

ENRICH

Have students develop answers for interview questions that might be asked online.

Goals

Describe activities involved in the interview process.

Compare factors to consider when accepting a job offer.

Identify attitudes and actions for success on the job.

Key Terms

employment interview

mentor

exit interview

Focus on Real Life

Barda Yang received a phone call asking her to come in for an interview. She had recently applied for a part-time job to assist the administrator of a child care facility. Barda has always enjoyed working with children. Her volunteer work at the park district, helping to coach soccer, helped her get this interview.

Although this position doesn't involve working directly with children, she is excited about the opportunity to work in this environment. Barda has not had many interviews in her life, but has practiced answering sample questions with her aunt. This experience has given her more confidence as well as an improved ability to answer unexpected questions.

THE INTERVIEW PROCESS

"We want to meet with you in person." This is your goal after submitting an application or resume. An **employment interview** is a two-way conversation in which the interviewer learns about you and you learn about the job and the company.

Before You Interview

Prepare for an interview by obtaining more information about your prospective employer and the job for which you are applying. Prepare questions to ask in the interview. These might include

- What training opportunities are available to employees?

- What qualities do your most successful employees possess?

- What new opportunities are your company considering in the next few years?

Successful interviewing requires practice. Record yourself so you will answer questions in a smooth and complete manner. Prepare concise answers for specific questions you might be asked. Ask friends to help you practice your interview skills. Attend workshops on interviewing skills. Work to organize your ideas. Speak clearly and calmly. Be sure to communicate enthusiasm.

main idea

Describe activities involved in the interview process.

What kinds of information can you learn about a position in an interview?

Focus on Real Life

Use this feature to explain to students various activities involved with the interview process.

TEACH

Ask students to name some actions that might be taken when preparing for an interview.

THINK CRITICALLY THROUGH VISUALS

An interview can provide information on the responsibilities of the position, the pay and benefits, the opportunities for training and advancement, and the goals of the company.

Different Learning Abilities

Hearing Impaired Encourage students to seek out resources about successful interviewing of job applicants who are deaf or have a hearing impairment. Make sure to include all students in practice interviews and role-playing activities.

TEACH

Use the FYI feature to highlight what an interviewer can and cannot ask an applicant.

Ask students for some of their experiences when preparing for a job interview.

Discuss some of the activities that might take place during the actual interview.

FIGURE 9-7 *ANSWER*

Ask students to share their thoughts regarding possible answers for the various interview questions listed in the figure.

An interviewer cannot ask

1. *Where you were born*
2. *Your age*
3. *If you have any disabilities*
4. *Your marital status*
5. *Your religion*
6. *Your responsibility for children*

An interviewer can ask

1. *If you are a U.S. citizen*
2. *For proof that you are over 18*
3. *If you have the physical ability to perform the job*
4. *If there are any days or times when you can't work*

As part of your interview preparation you should plan to make a good first impression. It is important to arrive on time for your appointment and dress appropriately. Make sure you know how to get to the interview location and give yourself plenty of time to get there. You should go alone to the interview even if someone else is providing transportation. Wear the type of clothing that is appropriate for the company and the job for which you are applying.

During the Interview

The person who interviews you wants to find out such things as your appearance, manners, use of language, and general ability for the job. An interviewer may take a number of different approaches. Most interviewers will try to put you at ease when your interview begins. Interviews may include situations or questions to determine how you react under pressure. Answer clearly in a controlled manner. Use of *behavioral interviewing* is expanding to better evaluate an applicant's on-the-job potential. Questions typically begin with "describe" or "tell me about . . ." Some common interview questions are shown in Figure 9-7.

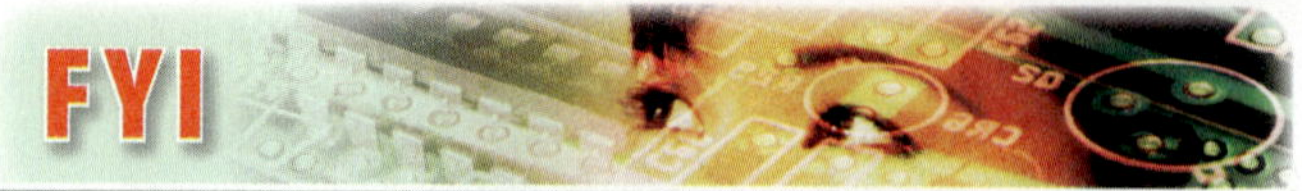

Some employers use pre-employment tests to screen applicants for skills and abilities needed on the job. Examples of pre-employment tests include keyboarding, word processing, calculating, and other skills. The interviewer may review your test results and discuss specific job requirements with you.

Avoid talking too much, but answer each question completely using good eye contact. Stay calm during the interview. Remember, you are being asked questions on a subject about which you are the world's expert—you! Finally, thank the interviewer for the opportunity to discuss the job and your qualifications.

Common Interview Questions

Education and Training Questions

- What qualifies you for this job?
- Why are you interested in this company?
- What activities have helped you to expand your interests and knowledge?

Work and Other Experience Questions

- In what situations have you done your best work?
- Describe the supervisors who motivated you most.
- Which of your past accomplishments are you most proud of?
- Describe people with whom you have found it difficult to work.

Personal Qualities Questions

- What are your major strengths?
- What are your major weaknesses? What have you done to overcome these?
- What do you plan to be doing 5 or 10 years from now?
- Which individuals have had the greatest influence on you?

FIGURE 9-7

Think of answers to each question and write them down.

Applied Skills

Communication Ask students to prepare sample answers for the interview questions in Figure 9-7. Invite students to participate in a role-playing activity using the questions from the figure and their prepared answers. Consider having students work in groups of three, taking turns as an interviewer, a job applicant, and an observer.

After the Interview

Within a day or two, send a *follow-up letter* to express your appreciation for the opportunity to interview. Even if you don't get the job, this thank-you letter will make a positive impression for future consideration.

Next, evaluate your interview performance. Try to remember questions that you were not expecting or not prepared to answer. Write notes about areas in which you need improvement. The more interviews you have, the better you will present yourself. More interviews will also increase the chance of being offered a job.

Be patient after the interview. It may take several weeks for the company to complete all of its interviews and make its selection.

checkpoint >>
What actions should be taken when preparing for an employment interview?

JOB OFFERS

"We'd like you to work for us." When you hear those words, remember to consider several factors before accepting or declining the position. The financial aspects of a job should be assessed along with some organizational factors.

Salary and Financial Factors

The type of work and your experience will affect your rate of pay. The position may include *employee benefits*. Insurance, vacation time, and retirement programs are examples of common employee benefits. Some companies offer free parking, on-site fitness centers, discount gym memberships, and other programs and services. Ask what benefits, services, and programs will be available to you and how much you will be expected to pay for them. Part-time and seasonal employees may or may not be offered benefits.

Organizational Environment

While the financial elements of a job are very important, also consider the working environment. Leadership style, dress code, the physical workspace, and the social atmosphere should be explored.

Advancement potential and training programs should be assessed. Some companies take pride in promoting from within and work hard to provide career and personal growth opportunities for workers.

checkpoint >>
What factors should a person consider when accepting a job?

main idea
Compare factors to consider when accepting a job offer.

What kind of work environment appeals to you?

Answers will vary. Ask students to describe work environments that they may find both positive and negative.

Applied Skills

Building Study Skills Suggest the following activities to build study skills: (1) Develop a list of items to obtain when researching an organization for which a student might work. (2) Create sample questions that might be asked in an interview. (3) Prepare a summary of factors to consider when evaluating a job offer.

TEACH

Ask students to name attitudes or behaviors they have observed or experienced that can contribute to success on the job.

Highlight examples of the "Job Success Strategies" listed.

THINK CRITICALLY THROUGH VISUALS

Answers will vary, but one of the most often cited reasons for leaving a job is an inability to get along with coworkers. A congenial work atmosphere is one of the most important aspects contributing to employee satisfaction. Hours, pay, benefits, and opportunity for advancement are also important.

main idea

Identify attitudes and actions for success on the job.

ON-THE-JOB BEHAVIOR

Attitude can make a big difference in your career success. A positive attitude helps you learn and cooperate with others. Always think, speak, dress, and act in ways that project a positive image. Then, you will likely find your job more satisfying and enjoyable.

Job Success Strategies

As you prepare for your first day of work, remember the following:

- **Ask questions.** If you do not understand directions, have them repeated and listen carefully. You probably will make mistakes when learning your job. Be sure to learn from each mistake and avoid repeating it.

- **Avoid complaining.** If you seem to have more work to do than you can handle, talk with your supervisor.

- **Honor the time for breaks.** Don't abuse rest periods and lunch breaks by extending the time limit.

- **Consider your appearance.** Dress neatly and be well groomed. Employers often observe that sloppy appearance reflect sloppy work habits.

- **Be on time.** Arriving late or leaving early is a poor practice.

- **Be friendly with everyone.** Respect your coworkers and learn to get along. Each person in an organization is important. Any coworker may be of help to you in the future.

- **Show you are dependable.** Do quality work that is completed on time. Sloppy work or work turned in late affects others. You are part of a team—take pride in that. Pay attention to details. Return phone calls and e-mails promptly to show that you care about your work.

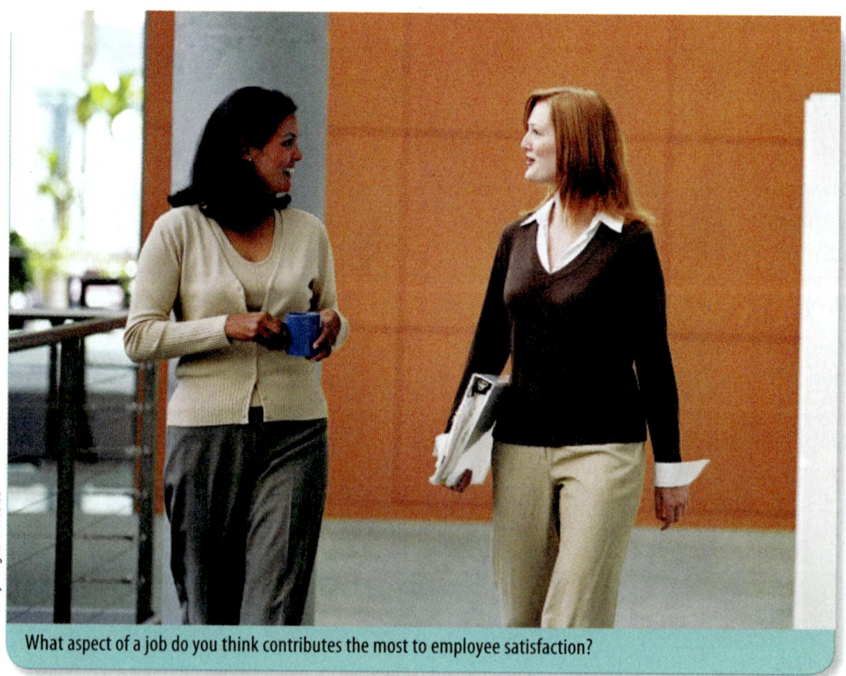

What aspect of a job do you think contributes the most to employee satisfaction?

Teaching Strategies

Expand Beyond the Classroom Ask students to interview several adults about job success strategies they have used or have witnessed other workers use. Invite students to share their findings. Make a list of the strategies mentioned and ask students to compare it to the strategies listed in the textbook.

- **Follow the rules.** If a rule seems unfair or unreasonable, discuss it with others and find out why it was created.

Many successful people get assistance from a person with more experience. A **mentor** is an experienced employee who serves as counselor to a person with less experience. Mentors frequently offer specific advice related to work assignments as well as general career guidance. For example, your mentor might help you develop skills needed in your current position and provide insight about future opportunities.

Leaving a Job

When the time comes to leave a job, it is important to depart on good terms. The following tips can help you leave a job in an appropriate manner.

- Give at least a two-week notice. Write a short, polite letter of resignation; include the date of the last day you will be working.

- Try to finish all of your current projects. If they are not completed, leave a note explaining to the next person where to begin.

Is it possible that your new job may bring you back in contact with a former employer?

- If there is an **exit interview**, in which your employer asks questions about your work, be constructive and cooperative.

- Let coworkers know that you appreciated the opportunity to work with them.

Leaving on a positive note is good for you and for those you are leaving.

checkpoint >>
How does a mentor assist less experienced employees?

9-4 Assessment

Key Concepts

Determine the best answer.

1. A commonly suggested action to take after an interview is to
   a. contact the organization about the salary
   b. evaluate your performance in the interview
   c. revise your resume
   d. estimate the cost of career training for the job

2. The _?_ interview occurs when leaving a job.
   a. informational
   b. exit
   c. employment
   d. coaching

Make Academic Connections

3. **Communication** Work with another person to improve your interview skills. Ask each other some of the questions in Figure 9-7. Describe strengths and needed improvements to each other.

4. **Culture** Describe questions and actions that might occur in the interview process in different countries. How could body language be interpreted differently in various cultures?

TEACH

Explain the role of a *mentor*. Describe actions that might be taken to identify a potential mentor.

Discuss appropriate actions to take when leaving a job. Ask students to describe their experiences when leaving a job.

THINK CRITICALLY THROUGH VISUALS

A new job might bring a person in contact with a former employer, so it makes sense to leave a job with a positive attitude.

ONGOING ASSESSMENT

checkpoint >> **ANSWER**

A mentor can provide insight into how to find opportunities for promotion. He or she will have an understanding of the current demands within your company or chosen field.

ASSESS

Key Concepts Answers

1. b. evaluate your performance in the interview

2. b. exit

Make Academic Connections

3. Ask volunteers to share what they learned. Encourage them to describe strengths and areas that need improvement.

4. Answers will vary. For example, job applicants in other countries should be prepared for differences in the etiquette of greeting one another, in the duration of the interview process, and in the types of questions permitted.

RETEACH

Highlight the main actions to take before, after, and during an interview.

ENRICH

Have students describe a work environment that they might enjoy in the future.

CLOSE

Ask students to name the most important actions that might be taken that could result in obtaining a job offer.

CHAPTER 9 Assessment

Business Notes

9-1 CAREER OPPORTUNITIES

1. The career planning process involves a self-assessment, an analysis of the employment market, application activities, the interview process, a comparison of job offers, and career development activities.

2. Important sources of career information include print and media sources, online sources, informational interviews, and business contacts.

3. Career fields with the most growth potential include computer technology, health care, business services, social services, sales and retailing, education, hospitality and food service, financial services, management, and human resources. Service industries are expected to have the greatest employment potential in the future.

9-2 PLANNING YOUR CAREER

4. Your interests, values, talents, and abilities should be assessed when making a career decision.

5. Employment experience may be obtained through work-study programs, part-time employment, volunteer activities, and school activities.

6. Information sources about available jobs include the media, personal contacts, business contacts, career fairs, and employment agencies.

9-3 APPLYING FOR EMPLOYMENT

7. The application process may start with completing an application form or with the use of a resume and cover letter.

8. There are three main parts to an application letter. The introduction gets the reader's attention. The development highlights your background and the skills that qualify you for the job. The conclusion asks for an interview.

9. Online application activities include the application process, e-resumes, and cyber interviewing.

9-4 SECURING A JOB

10. The interview process involves preparing for the interview, participating in the interview, and follow-up activities.

11. Factors to consider when accepting a job offer are salary, benefits, leadership style, dress code, social atmosphere, and advancement potential.

12. A positive attitude is the foundation of success on the job. Other success strategies include asking questions, avoiding complaints, giving attention to your appearance, following the rules, and being on time, dependable, and friendly.

Communicate Business Concepts

1. Who are some people you know that you might consider for an informational interview?

2. Give examples of how consumer demand, changing demographic trends, and new technology might affect career opportunities.

3. Make a list of your talents and abilities. Specify whether you believe each one is strong or weak. Indicate how you might use your strengths in career planning. Also indicate what actions you might take to improve your weak areas.

4. What actions might a person take when preparing to attend a career fair?

5. Your personal data sheet should list several references. Application forms also ask references to be listed. Make a list of three or more references you could use right now. Then note the type of information each reference could give that would be of help to a potential employer.

6. Prepare a list of items that you might include in a career portfolio when applying for a job.

7. If you were in charge of hiring people, what information would you want to obtain from applicants? How would you go about getting this information? What are some specific questions you would ask if you were to interview the applicants?

8. Job applicants may encounter role-playing situations in an interview. What types of situations may be used to assess the skills and abilities of prospective employees?

9. Information has been received about three job openings in your community. Each is quite different. Assume that you are qualified for only one position. Make up whatever qualifications you think you would like to present to a prospective employer. Then write a letter of application for the position.

   a. Reliable person is needed to handle a variety of responsibilities in a small business office. Must be able to work without supervision and communicate effectively with people who call for information. Word processing and other office skills are desirable. Salary is better than average in this community.

   b. Salespeople are needed for the auto parts and cosmetics departments of a large retail store. Applicants should have some familiarity and/or experience with selling. Hours are flexible, although some evening and weekend work will be required. Benefits are especially attractive; incentive bonus policy can provide a good income for the right person.

   c. Ours is a leading bank in this region. We are in need of capable people who want to begin a career in banking. Our training program starts at the bottom, but provides a great opportunity to learn about the banking industry. Salary is competitive.

10. What kinds of questions would you ask in an exit interview if you were the supervisor interviewing a sales clerk who is leaving?

Develop Your Business Language

Match the terms listed with the definitions.

11. A planned discussion with a worker to find out about the work that person does, the preparation necessary for the career, and the person's feelings about the career.

12. The willingness and ability of a person to move to where jobs are located.

13. The things that are important to you in life.

14. A natural, inborn aptitude to do certain things.

15. A goal in life that is fulfilled through a job or a series of occupations.

16. The quality of being able to perform mental or physical tasks.

17. A sales letter about an applicant written for the purpose of getting an interview.

18. A summary of job-related information about yourself.

19. An experienced employee who serves as counselor to a person with less experience.

20. A document used by employers that asks for information related to employment.

21. A two-way conversation in which the interviewer learns about you and you learn about the job and the company.

22. An interview in which an employer asks questions about how an employee liked his/her work and inquires about job improvements that might be made.

23. Tangible evidence of your ability and skills provided when applying for a job.

KEY TERMS

a. ability
b. application form
c. career
d. career portfolio
e. cover letter
f. employment interview
g. exit interview
h. informational interview
i. mentor
j. mobility
k. resume
l. talent
m. values

6. A portfolio should contain a resume, cover letter, answers to sample interview questions, sample reports, presentation materials, research interests, creative works from school activities or previous employment, evidence of community activities, and letters of recommendation.

7. Answers will vary, but should include typical resume information; recruitment activities, such as advertising; and appropriate questions, such as those found in Figure 9-7.

8. Employers might utilize a variety of interview techniques including role-playing, behavioral interviewing, and skills assessments. Situations might include on-the-job activities or interactions with customers.

9. Answers will vary. Encourage students to connect their training and experiences to the specific needs of the position.

10. Answers will vary, but should express continued respect for the exiting employee. They could include questions about how the company might improve—specifically, what changes should be made to the job he or she is leaving?

Develop Your Business Language Answers

11. h. informational interview
12. j. mobility
13. m. values
14. l. talent
15. c. career
16. a. ability
17. e. cover letter
18. k. resume
19. i. mentor
20. b. application form
21. f. employment interview
22. g. exit interview
23. d. career portfolio

Make Academic Connections

24. Paragraphs will vary. Students should summarize the topic and explain the value of the information in career planning activities.

25. Answers will vary and should include information about the application process and hiring activities in a different culture.

26. a. $3,500 + ($9,500 \div 2) + $5,300 = $13,550

b. $9,500 + $1,200 + $11,600 = $22,300

c. $13,550 \div $22,300 = 0.605 or 61%

d. $22,300 − $13,550 = $8,750

27. Presentations will vary and should include examples of strong and weak interview behaviors. Consider allowing students to work in pairs.

28. Answers will vary and should include information about the procedure, cost, and other information.

29. a. Total: 7 + 6 + 9 + 5 + 8 = 35; Average: 35 ÷ 5 = 7

b. Total: 50 + 40 + 40 + 35 + 35 + 35 + 35 + 45 + 45 = 360 minutes or 6 hours; Average: 360 ÷ 9 = 40 minutes.

30. Answers will vary. Answers could include the demand for various jobs in different areas, the cost of living, and the number of qualified applicants.

31. Explanations will vary depending on the world event selected.

Make Academic Connections

24. **ECONOMICS** The web site for the Bureau of Labor Statistics presents a wide variety of data on employment and wages. Select a topic area and present a two-paragraph summary. Explain how this information could be useful in your career planning activities.

25. **CULTURE** Talk to someone who has worked in another country. Obtain information about the application process and hiring activities in a different culture.

26. **MATH** Nancy Sisterrse attends a college where the tuition and fees amount to $9,500 per year. The books and supplies she buys total $1,200 per year. In addition, she has general living expenses of $11,600 per year. She has three sources of income: financial aid of $3,500 per year, a scholarship that pays one-half of her tuition, and a work-study job from which she earns $5,300 per year.

a. How much income does Nancy receive each year from her three sources of income?

b. How much does it cost Nancy to go to this college each year?

c. What percentage of her annual college costs is covered by her three sources of income? (Round off your answer.)

d. If her uncle David said that he would lend her the money she needs beyond her three sources of income, how much money would Nancy have to borrow each year?

27. **COMMUNICATION** Prepare an in-class presentation or video with examples of strong and weak interview behaviors.

28. **TECHNOLOGY** Visit a web site that allows people to post their resumes. Prepare a summary of the procedure, cost (if any), and other information from the web site.

29. **MATH** Emilie Antoine is a personnel interviewer. On Monday, she interviewed seven job applicants; on Tuesday, six applicants; on Wednesday, nine applicants; on Thursday, five applicants; and on Friday, eight applicants.

a. How many job applicants did Emilie interview that week? What was the average number per day?

b. On Wednesday, the first interview took 50 minutes; the next two each took 40 minutes; the next four took 35 minutes each; and the last two took 45 minutes each. How many total hours did Emilie spend in these interviews? What was the average length of the interviews?

30. **GEOGRAPHY** Obtain information about the salaries of workers in different geographic regions of the United States. What factors affect the differences that exist?

31. **HISTORY** Research a significant world event. Explain how this event affected the location and types of careers available around the world.

Linking School and Community

Talk to two or three people in your community to obtain information about their job search and interviewing experiences. Use the following questions in your discussion with these people:

- What are some ways that you have learned about available jobs?
- What actions did you take to improve your chances of being selected for a job?
- How did you prepare for job interviews?

Prepare a one-page summary of your findings. Which of these ideas did you find most interesting and potentially useful in the future?

Web Workout

The Internet can be a very useful source of career planning information. Select a career topic area (such as preparing a resume, identifying job opportunities, or effective interviewing) and compare the advice given on two different career web sites.

Think Critically

1. Prepare a summary of the main ideas from each web site.
2. What are the similarities and differences between the advice presented on the two web sites?
3. How might the information obtained be of value to you in the future?

Linking School and Community

Summaries will vary and should reflect responses to the three questions. Reactions to the information gathered during interviews also will vary.

Web Workout

1. Summaries will vary.
2. Similarities and differences will vary.
3. Answers will vary.

Decision-Making Strategies

Jeff Barbson is looking to his future and wondering what kind of career he should prepare for. His father is the city's civil engineer. His mother is a buyer for a major department store. Both of his parents are successful and enjoy their careers. Both of them have talked with Jeff about their work. He has visited his father's office and has worked as a sales clerk in his mother's store. Jeff's favorite subjects are computers, economics, and art. His least favorites are history, English, business law, and math. He earns his best grades in computers and art. Jeff's father wants him to be an engineer because there is a need for engineers in their state. His mother wants him to go into retailing. Jeff would like to go to medical school and become a heart specialist.

32. Based on his school record, which of the three career areas do you think he should choose?

33. What advice would you give Jeff regarding career planning?

Job Interview Event

You are applying for a position at the Winning Edge Corporation, a large fictional financial corporation headquartered in Washington, DC. Company benefits include paid holidays and vacations, sick leave, a retirement plan, and health insurance. Salary will be based upon experience and education. The event consists of three parts:

- Letter of application and resume
- Job application form
- Interviews

You are required to prepare a one-page letter of application. Your resume should not exceed two pages in length. The resume, letter of application, and job application should be put together in a file folder with the student's name on the tab of the folder. You will be required to complete a job application form with the use of your resume and a one-page reference sheet. No other reference materials may be used. Your initial interview with a member from the business community will last 10 minutes. Finalists from the first round of interviews will have a 15-minute second interview. Total scores will be calculated for the letter of application, resume, job application, and interview to determine which students will be hired.

PERFORMANCE INDICATORS EVALUATED

- Understand the importance of a professional portfolio that includes a resume and letter of application.

- Demonstrate strong interviewing skills necessary to earn a job.
- Prepare a business resume and letter of application that generate results.

You will be evaluated for

- Organization of your professional portfolio
- Performance during the interview
- Quality of participation in the interview

For more detailed information about performance indicators, go to the FBLA web site.

Think Critically

1. Why is the letter of application important?
2. Why should you research a company before going on the interview?
3. Give two good examples of questions a candidate can ask the interviewer.
4. List the major sections of the resume.

http://www.fbla-pbl.org/

Portfolio Activity

school.cengage.com/business/introtobiz

Access the web site shown here to find portfolio activities for this chapter. Use the activities to provide tangible evidence of your learning.

Decision-Making Strategies Answers

32. Answers will vary. For example, students might suggest that Jeff should think about a career related to his interests and abilities.

33. If he is serious about medicine, Jeff should consider what steps he needs to take to improve his math skills; he should shadow a heart specialist or do an informational interview to learn more about what is involved. If he wants to use his abilities in computers and art, he might consider a career in graphic arts where he could illustrate medical publications, thus incorporating all of his interests.

Winning Edge
Job Interview Event

Think Critically Answers

1. The letter of application introduces the applicant to the prospective employer.

2. The more you know about the company, the more intelligent you will be at the interview. You will be able to communicate more intelligently and ask better questions.

3. Answers will vary, but could include: What is the possibility for promotion of hard-working employees? What types of training do you offer employees?

4. Parts of a resume include personal/contact information (name, address), objective, education, work experience, skills, extracurricular or community service activities, and references.

This project involves organizing and planning international business activities. This experience can help students work as a team and develop better group decision-making skills.

Explain to students that this team project can provide (1) improved understanding of others, (2) increased creativity from diverse points of view, and (3) expanded awareness of global business activities.

Remind students that effective teams

- clearly define roles and behavior guidelines,

- adapt to differences to allow a focus on tasks of the project,

- value diverse points of view, and

- plan for unexpected situations

For the outcome, select one or more items in the "Present" section of the project.

Global Business Project

Organize International Business Activities

Goals

- Select an organization type that would be most appropriate for an international business setting.

- Outline a business plan for a global entrepreneurial enterprise.

- Identify leadership traits and managerial skills needed when doing business in other countries.

- Research needed training and skills for working in various international settings.

- Prepare a resume, cover letter, and answers to interview questions for an international business employment opportunity.

Activities

Use your textbook, library materials, web sites, interviews with people, and other resources to complete the following:

1. Companies commonly organize as a sole proprietorship, a partnership, or a corporation. Based on the business idea that you developed in the previous unit (or another international business idea), analyze the positive and negative aspects of these three types of business structures.

2. A business plan is vital when starting a new enterprise. Based on your international business idea, obtain information on these business plan components:

   - overview of the business idea

   - main competitors

   - description of customers

   - discussion of the organization's major operations

   - preliminary marketing activities

   - summary of start-up costs

3. Some leadership skills may be appropriate for several cultural settings. Other career competencies are unique to various regions and industries. Using the country from your portfolio (or select a country), describe two leadership traits unique to the geographic area or business you have chosen.

4. A person's ability to understand and work with people in different cultures is a necessary for international business success. List skills and training that would be of value to a person working for a multinational company.

5. In preparation for a global business career, prepare a list of your current skills and training you hope to obtain in the future. Identify abilities and experiences needed to work in an international business setting.

6. Create a list of questions and preliminary answers that might be the basis of an interview with a multinational company.

© Getty Images/PhotoDisc

Present

1. Prepare a portfolio (folder, file, or notebook) to store the information and materials you created in the activities above.

2. Describe in writing or with a visual display the benefits and drawbacks of the three types of business structures when doing business in a foreign country.

3. Create a resume for yourself as it might look in the future. Also, write a cover letter that expresses your interest and ability to work for an international company.

4. Prepare a video (or in-class presentation) showing strong interviewing skills and common job interview weaknesses when applying for a position with an international business organization.

UNIT 3 BUSINESS OPERATIONS AND TECHNOLOGY	OVERVIEW	SPECIAL FEATURES	LESSON ASSESSMENT	
Chapter 10 Marketing, pp. 234–263	Chapter 10 presents information on how marketing is planned and executed to satisfy customer needs at a profit.	Corporate Social Responsibility: Marketing Ethics, p. 247; Focus on Real Life, pp. 236, 243, 250, 255; FYI, pp. 242, 257; Life-Span Plan, p. 240; Net Bookmark, p. 245; Planning a Career in Marketing, p. 235; A Question of Ethics: The Price of Success, p. 258; Sharpen Your Life Skills: Resolve Conflict, p. 249; Winning Edge FBLA: Business Plan, p. 263; Work as a Team, pp. 237, 248, 251, 256	Checkpoints, pp. 238, 240, 242, 245, 246, 248, 252, 254, 256, 259 Key Concepts, Make Academic Connections, pp. 242, 248, 254, 259	
Chapter 11 Business and Technology, pp. 264–289	In Chapter 11, students will obtain a basic knowledge of the use of computer systems and technology in various business settings.	Business Improving Society: Co-op America, p. 285; Doing Business in Egypt, p. 273; Focus on Real Life, pp. 266, 274, 280; FYI, pp. 269, 277; Life-Span Plan, pp. 267, 278; Net Bookmark, p. 282; Planning a Career in Information Technology, p. 265; Winning Edge FBLA: Web Site Development, p. 289; Work as a Team, pp. 271, 276, 284	Checkpoints, pp. 268, 271, 272, 276, 277, 279, 281, 282, 284 Key Concepts, Make Academic Connections, pp. 272, 279, 284	
Chapter 12 Financial Management, pp. 290–315	Chapter 12 presents information on financial planning decisions and procedures used in business.	Corporate Social Responsibility: How Much Is Enough?, p. 310; E-Commerce in Action: Taxing Online Purchases, p. 294; Focus on Real Life, pp. 292, 298, 303, 308, 310; FYI, pp. 295, 304; Life-Span Plan, p. 302, 310; Net Bookmark, p. 310; Planning a Career in Accounting, p. 291; A Question of Ethics: Disclosing Employee Performance Information, p. 304; Winning Edge BPA: Human Resource Management, p. 315; Work as a Team, pp. 296, 299, 306, 311	Checkpoints, pp. 293, 296, 297, 299, 302, 305, 306, 309, 311 Key Concepts, Make Academic Connections, pp. 297, 302, 307, 311	
Chapter 13 Production and Business Operations, pp. 316–341	Chapter 13 describes how production occurs in businesses and how businesses organize and manage their operations.	Business Improving Society: Designs That Make a Difference, p. 337; Focus on Real Life, pp. 318, 323, 329; FYI, pp. 321, 332; Life-Span Plan, p. 324; Net Bookmark, p. 326; Planning a Career in Industrial Engineering, p. 317; Technology in Action: Philips HomeLab, p. 325; Winning Edge BPA: Small Business Management Team Event, p. 341; Work as a Team, pp. 320, 324, 335	Checkpoints, pp. 319, 322, 326, 328, 333, 336 Key Concepts, Make Academic Connections, pp. 322, 328, 336	
Chapter 14 Risk Management, pp. 342–365	Chapter 14 discusses the risks faced by businesses and how to deal with insurable and uninsurable risks.	Corporate Social Responsibility: Business Response to a Disaster, p. 357; Doing Business in Costa Rica, p. 361; Focus on Real Life, pp. 344, 350, 355; FYI, pp. 346, 356; Life-Span Plan, p. 351; Net Bookmark, p. 353; Planning a Career in Risk Analysis, p. 343; Sharpen Your Life Skills: Reducing Personal Risks with Lifestyle Choices, p. 349; Winning Edge BPA: Advanced Interview Skills Event, p. 365; Work as a Team, pp. 348, 351, 359	Checkpoints, pp. 345, 348, 352, 354, 358, 360 Key Concepts, Make Academic Connections, pp. 348, 354, 360	

<table>
<tr><th>CHAPTER ASSESSMENT</th><th>TEACHING RESOURCES</th><th>TEACHING STRATEGIES</th></tr>
<tr>
<td>Business Notes, Communicate Business Concepts, Develop Your Business Language, Decision-Making Strategies, Make Academic Connections, Linking School and Community, Web Workout, pp. 260–263</td>
<td>*Activities and Study Guide,* Ch. 10
Chapter and Unit Tests, Ch. 10
Spanish Resources, Ch. 10
Exam*View*® CD, Ch. 10
Instructor's Resource CD
Xtra! Web Site</td>
<td>**Applied Skills** Communication, p. 253, 258; Language Arts, p. 239; Mathematics, p. 251; Performing Arts, p. 247; Word Processing/Office Technology, p. 245; Writing Across the Curriculum, pp. 244, 256
Different Learning Abilities At-Risk, p. 246; Attention Deficit Disorder, p. 241; Gifted, p. 243; Hearing Impaired, p. 250; Limited English Proficiency, p. 240; Specific Learning Disability, p. 255; Visually Impaired, p. 238
Different Learning Styles Kinesthetic Learner, p. 237; Tactile Learner, p. 257; Visual Learner, pp. 236, 252
Teaching Strategies Collaborative Learning, p. 249</td>
</tr>
<tr>
<td>Business Notes, Communicate Business Concepts, Develop Your Business Language, Decision-Making Strategies, Make Academic Connections, Linking School and Community, Web Workout, pp. 286–289</td>
<td>*Activities and Study Guide,* Ch. 11
Chapter and Unit Tests, Ch. 11
Spanish Resources, Ch. 11
Exam*View*® CD, Ch. 11
Instructor's Resource CD
Xtra! Web Site</td>
<td>**Applied Skills** Geography, p. 273; Mathematics, p. 282; Science, p. 281; Technology, pp. 274, 278; Word Processing/Office Technology, p. 270; Writing Across the Curriculum, p. 276
Different Learning Abilities Dyslexia, p. 280; Gifted, p. 277; Limited English Proficiency, p. 268; Specific Learning Disability, p. 266; Visually Impaired, p. 271
Different Learning Styles Auditory Learner, p. 269; Kinesthetic Learner, p. 275; Print Learner, p. 283; Visual Learner, p. 267
Teaching Strategies Expand Beyond the Classroom, p. 281</td>
</tr>
<tr>
<td>Business Notes, Communicate Business Concepts, Develop Your Business Language, Decision-Making Strategies, Make Academic Connections, Linking School and Community, Web Workout, pp. 312–315</td>
<td>*Activities and Study Guide,* Ch. 12
Chapter and Unit Tests, Ch. 12
Spanish Resources, Ch. 12
Exam*View*® CD, Ch. 12
Instructor's Resource CD
Xtra! Web Site</td>
<td>**Applied Skills** Communication, pp. 296, 306; Language Arts, p. 310; Mathematics, pp. 300, 301; Technology, p. 293; Writing Across the Curriculum, p. 304
Different Learning Abilities At-Risk, p. 299; Dyslexia, p. 294; Limited English Proficiency, p. 305; Specific Learning Disability, p. 303
Different Learning Styles Auditory Learner, p. 298; Tactile Learner, pp. 295, 308
Teaching Strategies Collaborative Learning, p. 309; Expand Beyond the Classroom, p. 292</td>
</tr>
<tr>
<td>Business Notes, Communicate Business Concepts, Develop Your Business Language, Decision-Making Strategies, Make Academic Connections, Linking School and Community, Web Workout, pp. 338–341</td>
<td>*Activities and Study Guide,* Ch. 13
Chapter and Unit Tests, Ch. 13
Spanish Resources, Ch. 13
Exam*View*® CD, Ch. 13
Instructor's Resource CD
Xtra! Web Site</td>
<td>**Applied Skills** Building Study Skills, p. 318; Communication, pp. 321, 335; Technology, p. 332; Word Processing/Office Technology, p. 334; Writing Across the Curriculum, p. 324
Different Learning Abilities At-Risk, p. 319; Attention Deficit Disorder, p. 330; Limited English Proficiency, p. 331; Specific Learning Disability, p. 326; Visually Impaired, p. 327
Different Learning Styles Kinesthetic Learner, p. 323; Print Learner, p. 333; Visual Learner, pp. 320, 329
Teaching Strategies Collaborative Learning, p. 325</td>
</tr>
<tr>
<td>Business Notes, Communicate Business Concepts, Develop Your Business Language, Decision-Making Strategies, Make Academic Connections, Linking School and Community, Web Workout, pp. 362–365</td>
<td>*Activities and Study Guide,* Ch. 14
Chapter and Unit Tests, Ch. 14
Spanish Resources, Ch. 14
Exam*View*® CD, Ch. 14
Instructor's Resource CD
Xtra! Web Site</td>
<td>**Applied Skills** Building Study Skills, p. 352; Communication, p. 355; Language Arts, p. 347; Mathematics, p. 346; Technology, p. 356; Writing Across the Curriculum, p. 349
Different Learning Abilities At-Risk, p. 351; Attention Deficit Disorder, p. 344; Gifted, p. 359; Hearing Impaired, p. 358; Limited English Proficiency, p. 350; Visually Impaired, p. 353
Different Learning Styles Kinesthetic Learner, p. 357; Visual Learner, p. 345</td>
</tr>
</table>

Business Operations and Technology

In this unit, students learn about specialized operations areas of business and how technology affects those operations.

Chapter 10 · Marketing This chapter presents information on how goods and services are planned, promoted, distributed, and sold to customers.

Chapter 11 Business and Technology In this chapter, students will learn about computers and other technology applications in business.

Chapter 12 Financial Management This chapter focuses on financial planning and decision-making and the financial records used by businesses.

Chapter 13 Production and Business Operations Students will study the forms of production and how businesses complete production planning. They will also learn about tools and procedures for managing business operations.

Chapter 14 Risk Management In this chapter, students will learn about the types of risks that businesses encounter, how insurance helps protect against losses, and other ways businesses reduce and manage risks.

UNIT 3

Business Operations and Technology

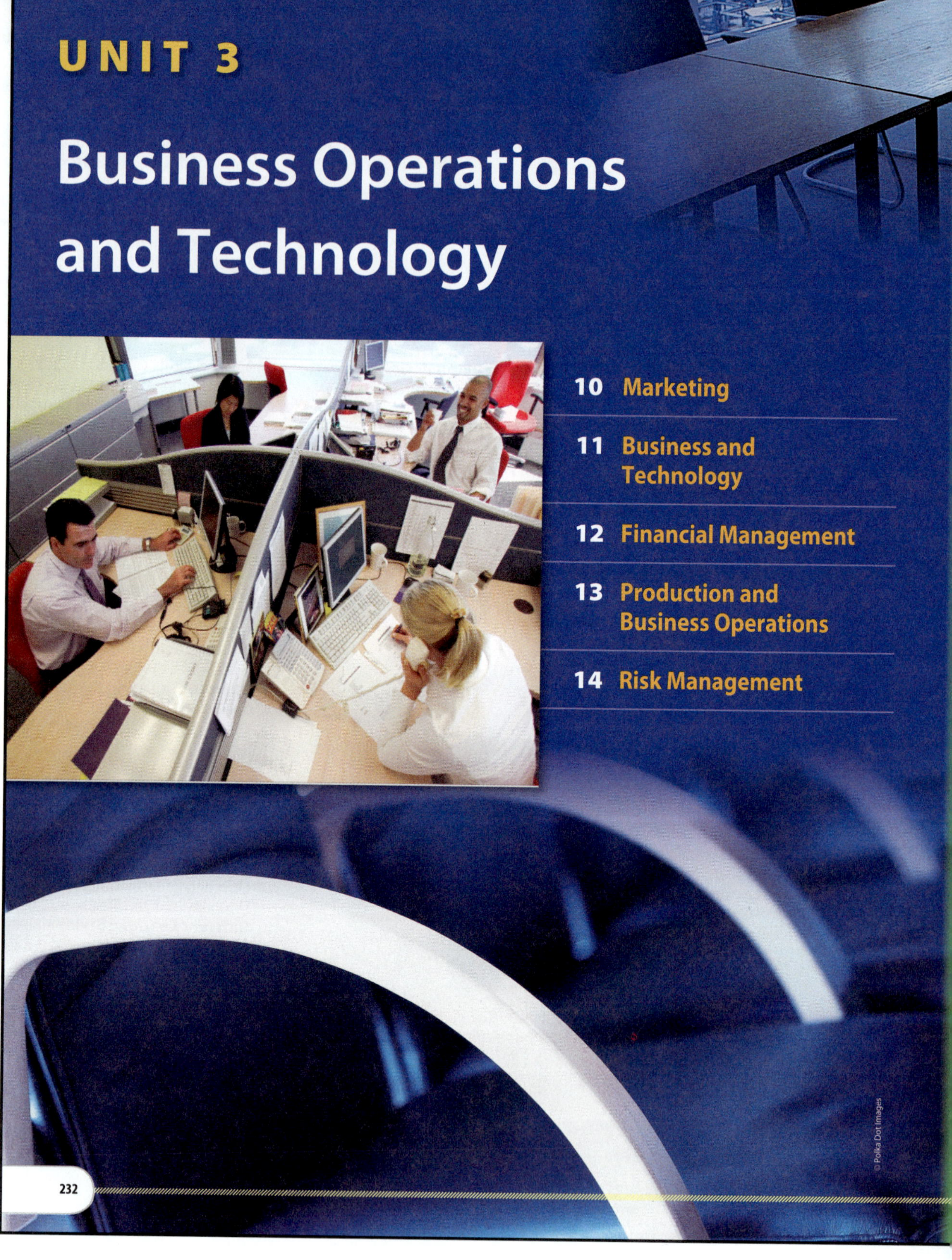

© Polka Dot Images

232

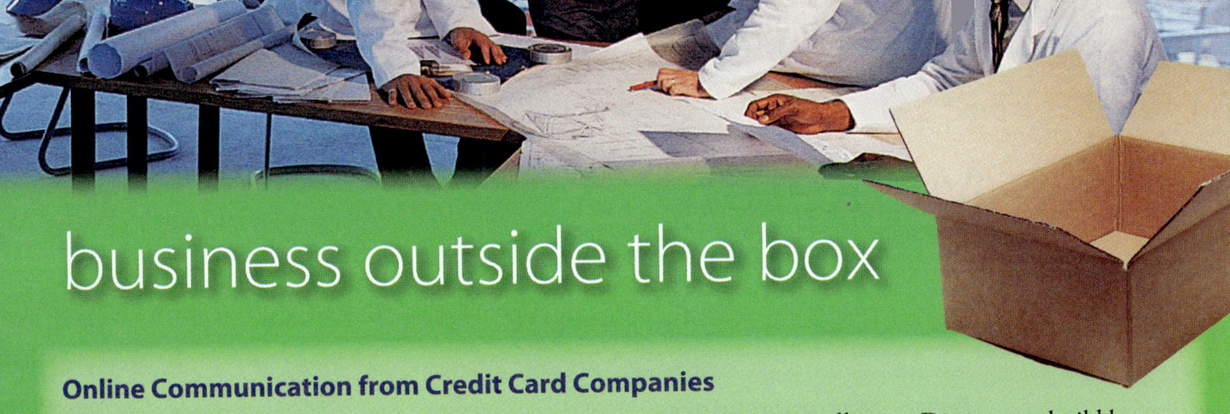

business outside the box

Online Communication from Credit Card Companies

No one is pleased to receive a late notice from a credit card company. In an effort to reduce the trauma, Discover Card allows customers to sign up for online reminders. These reminders include notices that a new statement is available, a warning that an account is near its credit limit, and a message that a payment is due soon.

This approach helps Discover keep in touch with customers. Online communications allow Discover Card to personalize its communication at a low cost. This strategy has resulted in more timely payments and is allowing Discover to build long-term relationships with many customers.

Think Critically

What are some other messages that a credit card company such as Discover might use to enhance relationships with customers?

It's Not a Bank, but…

PayPal handles more than 100 million accounts worldwide each year. While the online payment service is not a bank, it provides similar services.

The process starts with customers providing details of a credit card or bank account. PayPal, serving as a financial intermediary, verifies the transactions. Then payment amounts are transferred from the buyer to the seller.

Although PayPal mainly serves customers using eBay, other organizations also make use of this service. Some local governments are allowing citizens to make tax payments using PayPal. Various charities accept donations through the system.

PayPal has expanded internationally and is now serving customers in more than 100 markets around the world. The global challenges PayPal will face include different regulations in various countries and differing consumer preferences for making payments.

Think Critically

Why is a payment service such as PayPal particularly useful for eBay buyers and sellers?

Marketing

CHAPTER OVERVIEW

Marketing is an increasingly important activity in all businesses. This chapter presents information on how marketing is planned and executed to satisfy customer needs at a profit.

10-1 Marketing Basics

Students will be introduced to basic marketing concepts, the importance of a marketing strategy, and how consumers make buying decisions.

10-2 Develop Effective Products and Services

This lesson describes the importance of marketing research in developing new products and how products and services are different.

10-3 Price and Distribute Products

Students will study how to determine an effective selling price and the characteristics of channels of distribution.

10-4 Plan Promotion

Students will learn about the importance of communication in marketing and the common types of promotion used by businesses.

234

Teaching Resources

Activities and Study Guide, Ch. 10
Chapter and Unit Tests, Ch. 10
Spanish Resources, Ch. 10

Exam*View* ® CD, Ch. 10
Instructor's Resource CD
- PowerPoint Slides, Ch. 10
- Lesson Plans, Ch. 10

Xtra! Web Site

school.cengage.com/business/introtobiz
- Study Tools, 10-1, 10-2, 10-3, 10-4
- Quiz Prep, Ch. 10
- Net Bookmark, Ch. 10
- Crossword Puzzle, Ch. 10
- Portfolio Activity, Ch. 10

Planning a Career in…
MARKETING

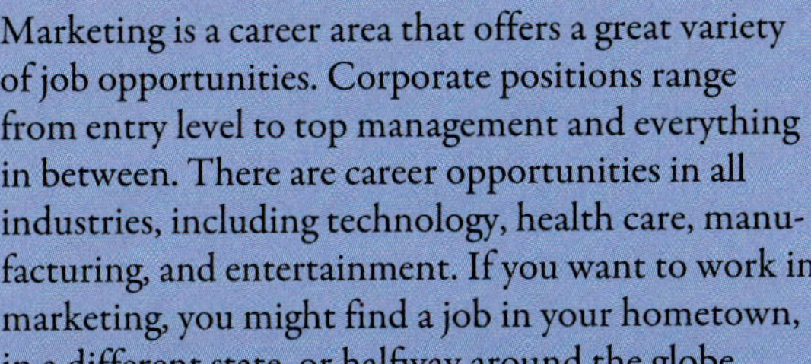

Marketing is a career area that offers a great variety of job opportunities. Corporate positions range from entry level to top management and everything in between. There are career opportunities in all industries, including technology, health care, manufacturing, and entertainment. If you want to work in marketing, you might find a job in your hometown, in a different state, or halfway around the globe.

The work of marketers is diverse and exciting. A marketing researcher conducts focus group interviews in a mall or for a political candidate. A marketing team designs a multi-million dollar advertising campaign for a new product. An international sales representative for a pharmaceutical company travels the world to introduce a life-saving drug. A distribution center manager develops a plan to reduce shipping costs. Not only are marketing careers available to people with a wide range of interests, talents, and education, they also include some of the highest-paying business careers.

Employment Outlook

- The employment outlook for marketing jobs is varied, with some high-growth areas and others facing increasing competition.
- Employment in advertising, marketing, promotions, public relations, and sales is expected to grow faster than the average due to intense domestic and global competition.
- Opportunities in marketing research will be very good but require a master's degree or PhD and strong math and statistics skills.

Related Job Titles

- Financial Securities Sales Agent
- Merchant Wholesaler
- Marketing Consultant
- Manager of Corporate Brands
- Trade Show and Special Events Coordinator
- Marketing Database Manager
- Media Relations Specialist

Needed Skills

- Creativity, analytical communication, and human relations skills
- A college degree in business or marketing is needed for some positions
- Some employers prefer people with broad work experience

What's it like to work in… Sales Management

Before Kerri Snodgrass boards a flight to Cairo, she returns a call to Ferris Joachum. As vice president of sales, Kerri knows Ferris is in final negotiations with a major customer for a $1.5-million order of environmental monitoring equipment.

Ferris says, "If we can get the order shipped within two weeks and spread the payments over two years, I think I can make the sale."

Kerri uses the airline's Internet connection to communicate with her company's production manager and with a loan officer of the international bank they use for customer financing. After several discussions, they get approval on the shipping date and are able to offer free financing for one year. As she gets off the plane, Kerri receives a text message from Ferris that the sale has been completed and the order has been placed.

As a sales manager, Kerri needs to understand all aspects of her business, gather information, and make quick but effective decisions to support her salespeople and satisfy the customers. Salespeople and sales managers are the face of the company to its customers.

What about you? What skills and personal qualities do you believe make Kerri Snodgrass a successful sales manager?

Planning a Career in…
MARKETING

Not all marketing careers are well known, but selling is one that most people recognize. Effective salespeople work to understand customers and sell them products and services they need. If they do that well and make a profit for the company, they will be well compensated for their work.

What About You? Answer

Answers will vary. Examples of skills and qualities include her understanding of the business and experience, her ability to make quick decisions, her trust in her employees, and her attention to customer service.

Additional Career Information

Additional information on careers can be found in the *Occupational Outlook Handbook,* an online publication (www.bls.gov/oco) of the federal government. Tell your class about this resource and how to use it. This description of job duties can be used to demonstrate the relevancy of skills learned in this course.

236

Focus on Real Life

Ask students to compare selling today with selling hundreds of years ago. How is it the same and how is it different? Ask the same question about advertising. Tell students that businesses continue to use things that work, but must adapt to changes in consumer needs and technology.

TEACH

Ask students to list as many words as they can think of that describe marketing. As a class, review the lists and help students determine which terms actually describe marketing or marketing activities. Explain that marketing is very important to businesses and involves a large number of activities.

TEACH

Divide the class into small groups and assign a local business to each group. Have them make a list of all activities the company needs to perform to sell its products and services to its customers. Have the groups compare the lists.

Goals

Define important marketing concepts.

Identify the steps in a marketing strategy.

Describe the consumer decision-making process.

Key Terms

marketing

marketing strategy

target market

marketing mix

marketing orientation

final consumers

business consumers

consumer decision-making process

buying motives

Focus on Real Life

Marketing is as old as business itself, yet it continues to be one of the most innovative areas of business. Salespeople have worked in businesses for centuries to persuade customers to buy. Today, many salespeople use video-conferencing equipment on their computers to demonstrate a product to customers and answer their questions.

United Parcel Service (UPS) started as a local parcel delivery service for retail stores in Seattle, Washington, more than a century ago. Today it delivers packages around the world. UPS uses the Internet to allow customers to schedule pickups, track packages, and verify package deliveries and signatures.

Advertising has moved from flyers and roadside billboards to targeted e-mail messages and huge electronic displays on the sides of buildings.

Companies continually change and improve the way they provide marketing services to attract customer attention and meet changing customer needs.

---

main idea

Define important marketing concepts.

UNDERSTAND MARKETING

Marketing may be the most visible set of business activities to consumers. Yet it may also be the most misunderstood business function. When asked to define marketing, people often use terms such as advertising or selling. While both of these are important, many other activities are a part of effective marketing.

The American Marketing Association's definition of marketing shows how complex it is: " **Marketing** is an organizational function and a set of processes for creating, communicating, and delivering value to customers and for managing customer relationships in ways that benefit the organization and its stakeholders." These words describe a complex but key part of every business. Marketing includes a range of activities and a number of businesses in the U.S. economy.

Marketing Activities

As a consumer you are exposed to marketing activities all of the time. You take part in many of these activities. You see or hear advertisements for products and services. You see the brand names on the packages of foods you eat and on the clothes that you and your friends wear. You read product descriptions on a company's web site. You interact with salespeople in your favorite retail store. These are all examples of marketing.

There are less obvious but equally important marketing activities. These include storing products in warehouses and distribution centers and moving the products to the places where they will be sold or used. Establishing and accepting

---

Different Learning Styles

Visual Learner Prepare the background for a bulletin board and label it "The Many Faces of Marketing." Have students use magazines, newspapers, advertisements, promotional materials, and the Internet to locate pictures of people completing a variety of marketing activities. Have them cut out the pictures and display them on the bulletin board.

credit and arranging means of online payment are marketing activities. Businesses use marketing when they gather data on consumer needs, use that information to improve products, and test new products before they are sold.

A great deal of marketing is not even aimed at final consumers. Businesses market products and services to other businesses. These businesses then use the products and services in their own business processes or sell them to final consumers. More time and money is spent in business-to-business marketing than in marketing products and services to final consumers.

Marketing Businesses

All businesses must complete some marketing activities even if that is not their focus. Many businesses are directly involved in marketing. Marketing businesses include advertising agencies and marketing research firms. Transportation companies such as trucking, railroad, and air freight move products from producers to consumers. Shipping and delivery companies provide express pickup and delivery of documents and packages. Financial services companies issue and manage credit cards. They can also provide loans to businesses for purchasing raw materials and finished goods. Wholesalers and retailers participate in the distribution, storage, and sale of products to connect manufacturers and their customers. Marketing activities, marketing businesses, and marketing careers are an important part of the U.S. economy.

Marketing Functions

Marketing activities can be organized into seven functions as shown in Figure 10-1. Each function occurs every time a product or service is developed and sold. Businesses provide many of the marketing functions. Consumers often take part in one or more

of the marketing functions when they make purchases.

Product and service management is designing, developing, maintaining, improving, and acquiring products and services that meet consumer needs. Producers and manufacturers develop new products. Other businesses are also involved in product/service management when they obtain products for resale. Services are created and provided by the employees of service businesses.

Distribution involves determining the best ways for customers to locate, obtain, and use the products and services of an organization. Careful shipping, handling, and storing of products are needed for effective distribution.

FIGURE 10-1

Why is each marketing function needed whenever a product or service is sold?

Selling is communicating directly with potential customers to determine and satisfy their needs. Selling can be face to face, such as when a customer visits a business or when a salesperson goes to the home or business of a potential customer. Selling is also performed using a telephone or other technology such as instant messaging or videoconferencing to communicate directly with a customer.

Marketing-information management is obtaining, managing, and using market information to improve business decision-making and the performance of marketing activities. Marketing-information management includes marketing research and the development of databases with information about products, customers, and competitors.

Financial analysis is budgeting for marketing activities, obtaining the necessary funds needed for operations, and providing financial assistance to customers so they can purchase the business' products and services. Customers must have the resources and methods to pay for their purchases. Businesses must receive timely payments so they can continue to operate.

Pricing is setting and communicating the value of products and services. Customers must be able to easily identify the price of items that interest them or they will move on to another choice. Consumers want to know that they are getting a fair value for the money they are spending. Prices must be set low enough that customers are willing to pay but high enough that the business makes a profit.

Promotion is communicating information about products and services to potential customers. Advertising and other promotional methods are used to encourage consumers to buy. Advertising may occur in a variety of ways—television, newspapers, magazines, radio, direct mail, and the Internet. Other methods include contests, product displays, sponsorships, and public relations activities.

MARKETING STRATEGY

Marketing is an important and costly part of business operations. Marketing activities often cost 50 percent or more of the selling price of a product or service. In order for a company to make a profit, marketing must be carefully planned. It must be done well, yet at a low cost. Consumers usually have many choices of products and services. If they are not satisfied with the offering of one company, they will look to a competitor to meet their needs. Careful marketing will aid a company in understanding

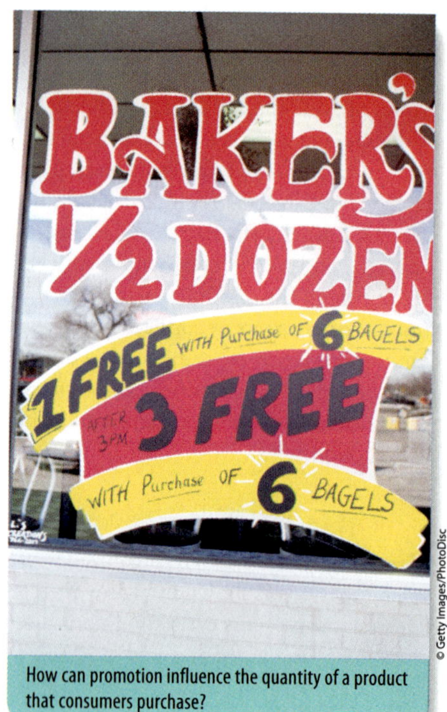

© Getty Images/PhotoDisc

How can promotion influence the quantity of a product that consumers purchase?

Different Learning Abilities

Visually Impaired Record the term and definition for each of the seven marketing functions on an audiotape. Have the student listen to the definitions as many times as needed to remember the meaning of each. Make the recording available to all interested students.

and meeting customer needs. Successful marketing results in satisfying exchanges between businesses and consumers. Businesses offer products and services that satisfy their customers' needs. Customers pay for those products and services, providing the businesses with revenues and profit.

Marketing Planning

Marketing planning is aimed at satisfying customer needs better than competitors do, resulting in sales and profits. A company's plan that identifies how it will use marketing to achieve its goals is called a **marketing strategy** .

Developing a marketing strategy is a two-step process. The first step is to identify a target market. A **target market** is a specific group of consumers who have similar wants and needs. Many companies try to promote their products to a wide audience whose wants and needs are quite varied. It is not easy for the company to meet all of those needs. The result is that many people will not want the company's products or will be dissatisfied with them. Focusing on a target market makes it easier to develop products and services that specific groups of customers want.

The second step in developing a marketing strategy is to create a marketing mix. A **marketing mix** is the blending of four marketing elements—product, distribution, price, and promotion. A successful marketing mix satisfies the wants and needs of the target market. It also provides a profit for the company.

Develop a Successful Marketing Strategy

Many businesspeople believe they know what consumers want. They produce a product and then begin to plan how they will market it to consumers. This approach to marketing typically results in an emphasis on advertising and promotion in order to attract the attention of

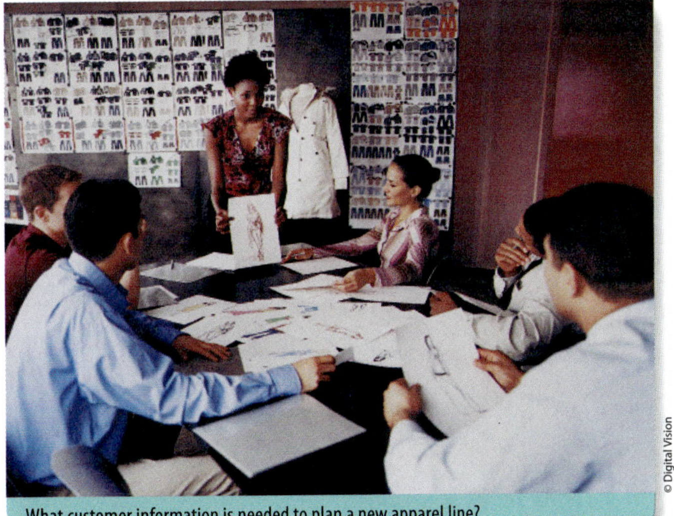

What customer information is needed to plan a new apparel line?

potential customers and convince them to buy the company's product. If the product does not appeal to consumers, the business will be forced to cut the price. Lower profits or even losses may be the result.

To increase the chances of developing a product or service that meets customer needs and can be sold at a profit, companies adopt a marketing orientation. A **marketing orientation** considers the needs of customers when developing a marketing mix. With a marketing orientation, businesspeople don't assume they know what customers want. They use research to study customers and their needs. The results of the research are used to plan a marketing mix designed to satisfy those needs.

A company that owns a fleet of cruise ships gathers information on people who might consider a cruise as a vacation choice. Families with young children, young singles, and retirement-age adults usually will want different kinds of vacation experiences. First-time cruisers will need different information than experienced cruisers. Menu items, entertainment, travel arrangements to and from the port, and payment options all must be planned to appeal to potential customers.

TEACH

As you introduce the terms "target market" and "marketing mix" to the class, have each student draw an image of each of the terms on a sheet of paper. Have each student show the illustration to other class members and explain how it fits the definition.

THINK CRITICALLY THROUGH VISUALS

Planning a new apparel line requires information about which customers might buy the apparel, how much they may be willing to pay, what qualities they look for in their clothing, and what styles are in fashion.

TEACH

Ask students why some businesses do not offer products and services that seem to satisfy customers. Have them suggest ways that these businesses could better understand customer needs in order to provide satisfying products and services. Explain that the process of considering customer needs when planning a marketing mix is known as a marketing orientation.

Answers will vary, but could include costs, destinations, duration, dates, amenities, and activities.

ONGOING ASSESSMENT

checkpoint >> **ANSWER**

The two steps are identifying a target market and developing a marketing mix.

TEACH

Write the following sentence on the board, "Effective marketing begins with customers." Ask students to discuss the meaning of the sentence.

Ask students to discuss the similarities and differences between final consumers and business consumers. Have them identify products and services that would appeal to both types of consumers and others that would appeal to one or the other type.

PROJECT

Provide the following instructions to students. (These instructions also appear on page xxiv of the textbook.) How easily are you able to communicate with other people? Explain how an ability to communicate with other people can affect the life-span goals you set and your ability to achieve them.

Life-Span Plan Answers

Answers will vary. Students should describe their communication abilities and explain how these abilities may affect their life-span goals.

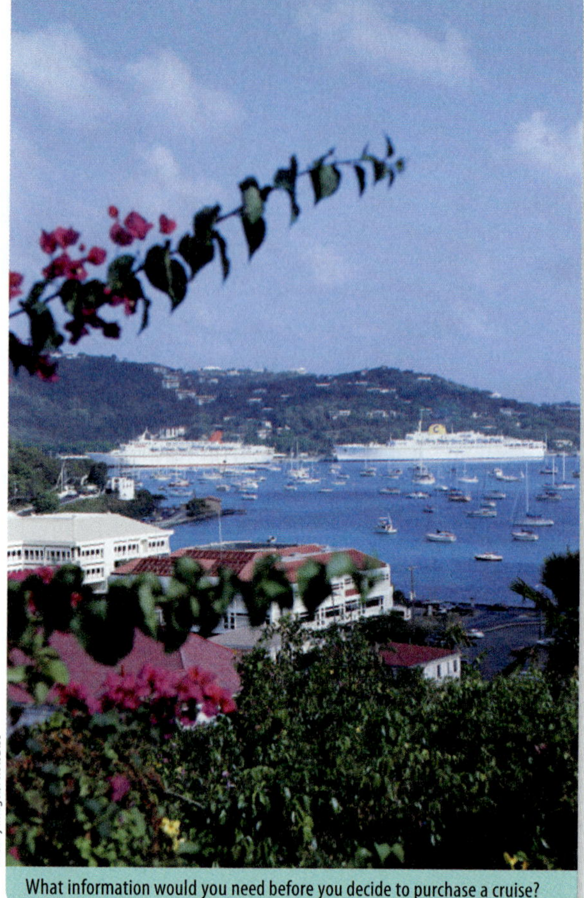

What information would you need before you decide to purchase a cruise?

main idea

Describe the consumer decision-making process.

The company will first study possible customers and the similarities and differences in vacation wants and needs. Then it will select the target market that presents the best opportunity for planning a successful cruise. Using the information gathered about the target market, the company then develops the marketing mix. The product will be an exciting and relaxing cruise experience. There will be enjoyable onboard activities and interesting onshore excursions at cities on the ship's schedule. Distribution will include providing all of the documents needed by travelers, arranging customer travel to and from the port city, handling baggage, and ensuring effective customer service throughout the process. Pricing decisions provide an affordable cruise with payment options to meet the budgets of the target customers. Promotion offers information to interest prospective customers in the cruise and persuade them to decide it is the best vacation choice.

The cruise company will make each of these marketing mix decisions to meet the specific needs and expectations of their target market. The decisions will be different in many ways than if the cruise was planned for a different group of consumers.

checkpoint >>
What are the two steps in developing a marketing strategy?

UNDERSTAND CUSTOMERS

Effective marketing begins with customers. Think of a recent product or service you purchased and why you made the choice you did. You likely had several products that would generally meet your needs. You considered those choices and selected the one that you believed would provide the most satisfaction for the money you had to pay.

Many new businesses fail because the owners have an idea for a product but fail to consider customers and their needs. If a product appeals to a group of customers with unsatisfied needs, it has a real chance to succeed. If customers do not see a need for a product or believe they have other choices that are better or less costly, the product will likely not succeed.

Businesses can develop products for two types of consumers. **Final consumers** are persons who buy products and services mostly for their own use. **Business consumers** are persons, companies, and organizations that buy products for the operation of a business, for incorporation into other products and services, or for resale to their customers.

Different Learning Abilities

Limited English Proficiency (LEP) Have students write each marketing term and its definition in their notebook. Then ask a student whose first language is English to work with the student to understand the correct pronunciation of each term and its definition.

Consumer Decision-Making

The specific sequence of steps consumers follow to make a purchase is known as the **consumer decision-making process**. Both the steps and the sequence of decisions are the same for all consumers. The length of time taken to complete the process and the information used to complete each step might be quite different from one consumer to the next. The five steps in the consumer decision-making process are shown in Figure 10-2.

Decision-making begins with a need. You may be hungry or thirsty, or you may want to plan an evening's entertainment with friends. Maybe you need a summer job or are trying to choose a college to attend. If the need is urgent, you will try to satisfy it right away. If it is less important you may put it off or even ignore it. If the need is one that is familiar to you and you have satisfied it before, you will often use that past experience to help make a decision. If it is a new need, you may have a hard time deciding how to make the best choice because you have no similar experience.

People use information to make decisions. You may talk to friends or a trusted adult. An advertisement, magazine article, or Internet site may catch your attention because it provides information related to an important need. You choose sources that you trust and that provide information you understand. Using this information, you will select a very few products that seem to meet your needs. Once the choices are narrowed, you will compare them to determine if one appears to be a better choice or a greater value than the others.

Based on the information you have obtained and the urgency and importance of the need, you will make a decision. The decision is usually to buy the product you have decided is best for you. The decision may be not to buy because you have not found a satisfying choice or you do not have the money you need at the time. You may then go back to a previous step and look at other choices or gather more information.

If you decide to purchase a product, you will complete the purchase and use the product you chose. Based on that

Steps in the Consumer Decision-Making Process

1. Recognize a need.
2. Gather information.
3. Select and evaluate alternatives.
4. Make a purchase decision.
5. Determine the effectiveness of the decision.

FIGURE 10-2

How might you use these steps to help you make your next consumer decision?

How do you decide which products to purchase when you visit a supermarket?

TEACH

Have each student think of their most recent purchase of a product they bought for the first time. Have them list in order every activity they completed to identify the product they would buy and make the purchase. Then have them compare their lists with the five steps in the consumer decision-making process. After reviewing the five steps, ask students whether it represents the way they usually make purchase decisions.

FIGURE 10-2 *ANSWER*

Answers will vary. Encourage discussion about using the process when making consumer decisions such as what clothes to buy, where to eat, or which concerts to attend.

THINK CRITICALLY THROUGH VISUALS

Answers will vary, but could include the price of the products, what is on the shopping list for that day, what looks attractive at the store, or nutritional content or ingredients.

Different Learning Abilities

Attention Deficit Disorder As each step of the consumer decision-making process is discussed, ask two students to present a short role-play of a consumer completing that step.

Since Fortune magazine began its list of Most Admired Companies in 1997, only three companies have appeared in the top 10 every year. They are Southwest Airlines, Berkshire Hathaway, and General Electric.

experience you will decide if you made a good choice. If you liked the product, you will probably make the same decision the next time you have the same need. You may also make the decision more quickly and easily. If the product was not what you expected, you will be unlikely to purchase that product again.

Buying Motives

Why do you shop in a certain store or choose one brand of a product over another? The reasons consumers decide what products and services to purchase are called **buying motives**. Understanding the motives of consumers helps businesses plan a marketing mix.

Some purchases are guided by emotions. *Emotional buying motives* are reasons to purchase based on feelings, beliefs, and attitudes. If you are concerned about protecting your family and possessions, you may decide to buy a home security system. Purchases of gifts and cards for holidays and occasions are triggered by feelings of love and affection.

Rational buying motives are guided by facts and logic. You may want the most cost-effective car, so you consider fuel use and repair costs of various models. When choosing a college to attend, you can compare the costs of tuition and the reputation of the college in the major you plan to study.

checkpoint >>
What are the steps in the consumer decision-making process?

10-1   Assessment

Key Concepts

Determine the best answer.

1. The best definition of marketing is
  a. promotion and selling
  b. producing and distributing products and services to customers
  c. finding customers and convincing them to buy your products
  d. none of the above is correct.

2. The two steps in a marketing strategy are
  a. developing a product and promoting it to consumers
  b. identifying a target market and developing a marketing mix
  c. conducting marketing research and planning production
  d. pricing a product and distributing it to customers

3. Which of the following is an example of a rational buying motive?
  a. love
  b. fear
  c. economy
  d. self-image

Make Academic Connections

4. *Marketing* List the seven marketing functions. Using a business directory or a telephone book, identify a business that specializes in providing each service for final consumers or other businesses. Briefly describe what the business does and the types of customers it serves.

5. *Technical Writing* Select one of your recent purchases. Using computer software, develop a chart or illustration that identifies the steps in the decision-making process and how you completed each step to make the purchase decision.

Develop Effective Products and Services

Goals

Justify the importance of marketing research.

Identify the components of a product.

Describe how services differ from products.

Key Terms

marketing research

product

services

intangible

inseparable

perishable

heterogeneous

Focus on Real Life

When you go to a store or use a catalog or the Internet to make a purchase, you will usually find several choices of the product you want. What makes the products offered by one company different from those offered by other companies? In some cases, it is little more than the brand name of the product. In other cases, there are differences in the design of the products, the features, and the options available.

Products can become so specialized that making choices that meet the needs of each customer becomes a very complex process. Companies need to develop tools to help consumers sort through their choices. Purchasing a shirt or pair of slacks on the Internet can involve creating a virtual "model" of your body size and shape and then comparing styles, colors, and fabrics by viewing them on the model. These types of online tools help customers develop a picture of their choices and make complicated decisions easier.

CREATE AND IMPROVE PRODUCTS

How do businesses develop new products? In many cases, products that are identified as new in a company's advertising are not new at all. Some type of change has been made in the product that may be a major improvement. The change may also be a minor one that provides little benefit to the customer. The business calls the product new to attract the attention of customers and encourage them to buy.

Totally new products that have never been seen before by customers are not often introduced. What new products can you recall having been introduced during your lifetime? The Internet, airbags in automobiles, scanning equipment used in retail stores, and artificial hearts did not have similar substitutes before they were introduced. They were the result of research by engineers and scientists seeking to find solutions to important problems. Most products you use today are minor or major improvements in existing products. A CD or MP3 player uses new technology to store and replay music. Handheld personal digital assistants are new versions of past computer models. Even cellular phones are improved versions of older wireless telephones. These and many other product improvements occur through the development of new technology or redesign of current products.

Scientists and other researchers often develop product improvements. Many ideas for product improvements result from the ideas of consumers and from their experience in using current products. Finding solutions to problems through carefully designed studies involving consumers is known as **marketing research**.

main idea

Justify the importance of marketing research.

Focus on Real Life

Suggest to students that the products offered by most companies have competitors that are quite similar. Consumers may have difficulty deciding which of the choices will be best for them. Businesses must find ways to help consumers make good choices.

TEACH

Have students make a list of products that have been introduced in the last two or three years. Have them discuss which of the products were truly unique, meaning there was no other product like it, and which were improvements on existing products. Are they familiar with any products that companies promoted as "new" when they really did not appear to be different from older products? Based on the discussion, ask students how they believe companies can come up with ideas for really new products.

Different Learning Abilities

Gifted Have students use the Internet to research technology and processes that are currently being studied by scientists and engineers that may result in new products several years in the future. Have them report on their findings and discuss with other class members whether they believe the new product ideas will be successful or not.

TEACH

Present students with the following marketing problem: A manufacturer of athletic shoes learns that its brand is ranked in the top three by people over 25 years old, but is not in the top five for people between the ages of 15 and 24. Have students use the five steps in marketing research to plan a way to improve the ranking with younger consumers.

FIGURE 10-3 *ANSWER*

Answers will vary. Point out that none of the other steps can be completed without first defining the marketing problem.

THINK CRITICALLY THROUGH VISUALS

Personal interviews are an effective way to gather consumer information because people are more likely to give complete and information answers to another person than they would when answering survey questions in an objective format.

TEACH

Explain that a company wants to test a new product to determine whether customers will buy it. Have students describe how each of the types of research studies can be used by the company to test the product.

Plan Marketing Research

Many types of research procedures can be used to solve marketing problems. Each type of research follows the scientific problem solving process outlined in Figure 10-3.

Steps in Marketing Research
1. Define the marketing problem.
2. Study the situation.
3. Develop a data collection procedure.
4. Gather and analyze information.
5. Propose a solution.

All marketing research studies involve gathering and analyzing information. A great deal of information about consumers and competitors is available to businesses without doing new studies.

Why are personal interviews an effective way to gather consumer information?

Analyzing existing information gathered for another purpose but used to solve a current problem is known as *secondary research*. Studies carried out to gather new information specifically directed at a current problem is *primary research*.

Types of Research Studies

The most common type of marketing research study involves consumer surveys. *Surveys* gather information from people using a carefully planned set of questions. The surveys are often sent to consumers through the mail or using the Internet. They can also be conducted over the telephone.

Another less structured way of gathering the ideas, experiences, and opinions of consumers is through *focus groups*. In this research method, a small number of consumers take part in a group discussion. A focus group leader acts to identify areas of agreement and disagreement and to develop new ideas. Focus group members might discuss their experiences with a product, react to new product ideas, or make suggestions for product improvements.

Observations of consumers provide useful information for marketing researchers. *Observations* collect information by recording the actions of consumers rather than asking them questions. A store may be interested in how customers study and choose products in a display case or the routes they take through a store when shopping. A product design team may observe any problems consumers have using a product to make design improvements.

A final method of marketing research is conducting experiments. An *experiment* presents two carefully controlled alternatives to subjects in order to determine which is preferred or has better results. A marketing experiment may compare two sizes of packages to see if one size results in more sales than the

Applied Skills

Writing Across the Curriculum Have students prepare a paragraph that shows the connection between the process used to obtain marketing research to the research process used in another class, such as a science class.

other. A study could determine the effect of offering a 50-cent coupon to grocery shoppers on their choice of cereal brands.

PRODUCT PLANNING

Each part of the marketing mix is important when you decide to buy a product. The product must be available through effective distribution and must have an affordable and fair price. You must be aware of the product through effective promotion and know how it will meet your needs better than other choices. However, one mix element is more critical than the other three. If the product itself is not what you want, the effectiveness of the other mix elements does not matter. A business must carefully plan each of its products to make sure it meets the needs of the target market better than similar products offered by competitors.

Parts of a Product

A **product** is everything a business offers to satisfy a customer's needs. A product is made up of several components. It starts with the *basic product,* which is the simplest form of a product. The basic product is not unique and is usually available from several companies. Additions and improvements to the basic product are known as *product features.* One model of cellular telephone offers a built-in digital camera, voice dialing, and a web browser as features. When customers are offered choices of features, the choices are known as *options.* When buying an automobile, customers can choose options such as color, engine size, and manual or automatic transmission.

A *brand name* provides a unique identification for a company's products.

Companies try to develop a memorable brand name with an appealing image.

Packaging is a part of many products. *Packaging* provides protection and security for the product before it is used. It also may make product storage and use easier. A new container for ground coffee is created with indentations that allow customers to pick it up easily with one hand. Some customers struggled with handling the original round container. The package is a convenient way to provide information to customers that help them make a purchase decision or explain how to use the product.

A way to build customer confidence in a company's products is by offering a *guarantee* or *warranty.* If the product breaks or does not meet customer expectations, the company will repair, replace, or provide a refund.

Product Planning Procedures

New product planning is a costly and time-consuming process. It is not unusual for a company to invest several million dollars and spend years to develop a new product. Many people are involved in creating the product idea, determining how it will be produced

main idea

Identify the components of a product.

NETBookmark

The U.S. Census Bureau provides very detailed data that helps businesses make marketing strategy decisions. Access the web site shown below and click on the link for Chapter 10. Click on the American FactFinder link and locate census information on your community. Study the data and locate (1) the number of people who are 15–19 years old and the number of people who are 20–24 years old and (2) the number of renter-occupied and owner-occupied homes in your community. How might that information be used by businesses?

school.cengage.com/business/introtobiz

ONGOING ASSESSMENT
checkpoint » ANSWER

The steps in marketing research are to define the marketing problem, study the situation, develop a data collection procedure, gather and analyze information, and propose a solution.

TEACH

Bring a product to show the class that illustrates the components of a product described in the lesson. As you discuss each of the components, have students identify them on the example product.

NETBookmark

Explain to students that the government and other organizations, such as professional associations, provide a great deal of useful information that businesses can use to make marketing decisions. The U.S. Census Bureau is an excellent resource to help people understand more about prospective customers in a market.

Applied Skills

Word Processing/Office Technology
Ask students to use statistics similar to the information gathered in the Net Bookmark feature to create a graph or chart that illustrates the characteristics of people in your community. For example, they might make a chart using all the age ranges presented in the Fact Finder for a particular community.

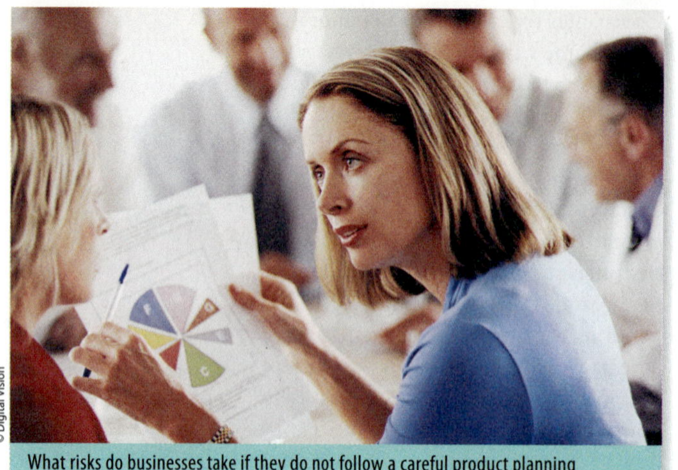

What risks do businesses take if they do not follow a careful product planning procedure?

and marketed, analyzing costs, and predicting sales. When that much money is at stake, companies need a procedure that results in products customers want and that can make a profit for the company for several years.

The steps in new product planning are:

- **Idea Development** Generating new product ideas is a creative process. Ideas come from the work of scientists, from the suggestions of salespeople and other employees, and from consumer surveys and focus groups. Most ideas are for improvements to existing products.

- **Idea Screening** Companies encourage the development of a large number of new product ideas. Then they evaluate the ideas to determine which have the best chance to be successful. Ideas are screened to determine if a demand exists for the new product. Do other companies offer similar products? Can the product be produced at a reasonable cost? Is the product legal and safe?

- **Strategy Development** If a product idea appears to be workable, the next step is to develop a full marketing strategy. The target market for the product is studied carefully. There must be a strong need for the new product. Alternative marketing mixes are developed and tested with potential customers. The costs of the alternatives are compared to determine which provide the greatest value.

- **Production and Financial Planning** Next, the company develops a production procedure and identifies the facilities, equipment, and people that will be needed to produce the product. The costs of production and marketing are determined and a financial plan is developed to be sure the product will make a profit.

- **Limited Production and Test Marketing** If a new product idea makes its way through the planning process, a company may produce a limited quantity of the product and test it in a small part of the market. This step allows the company to make sure the product can be produced and marketed as planned before a large investment is made for full production.

- **Full-Scale Production** If each of the preceding steps is completed successfully, the new product will move into full-scale production and marketing. The company will continue to gather information on production and sales to be sure financial projections are being met. Competitors will also be watched because they will likely introduce competitive products if the new product is successful. Few unsuccessful products should make it through. Products that are fully screened have a much greater chance of being successful than new products that do not go through a planning procedure.

checkpoint >>
What are the components of a product?

Different Learning Abilities

At-Risk Have students use the Internet or library resources to gather information on careers in product planning. For example, they might investigate opportunities related to product testing. Have them describe the jobs and what would be interesting about that career area.

SERVICES

Products are tangible items you can see and examine such as books, boats, and hamburgers. Marketing is used for both products and services, but services are more difficult to market. **Services** are activities that are consumed at the same time they are produced.

Services are **intangible**, meaning that they have no physical form. Because services are intangible, it is more difficult to examine a service and determine if it will meet your needs. Marketers must find ways to describe the service in understandable ways to prospective customers.

Effective service marketing is done in much the same way as product marketing. Using the two-step marketing strategy, service marketers first identify target markets for services. They then develop a marketing mix that appeals to the market. In addition to the service itself, the market mix includes distribution, pricing, and promotion of the service. The nature of services compared to the nature of products requires a change in the way they are marketed.

Services are **inseparable**, meaning that they are consumed at the same time they are produced. The person or technology producing the service must be available when and where the customer

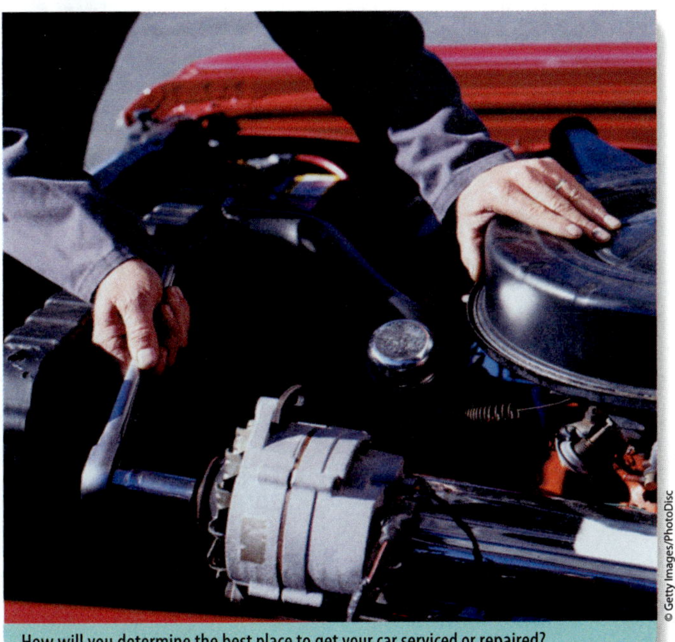

How will you determine the best place to get your car serviced or repaired?

© Getty Images/PhotoDisc

CORPORATE SOCIAL RESPONSIBILITY

Marketing Ethics

Some people may think that the term "marketing ethics" is an oxymoron, or a contradiction in terms. Many people have a low opinion of marketers. Individuals receive unsolicited sales calls, junk mail, and spam. They watch advertisements that don't tell the whole story on products. They encounter salespeople who only seem to be interested in their own commissions.

Marketers, however, play a very important role in society. They deliver a standard of living. Marketers identify new products. They find ways to get those products into customers' hands through convenient distribution and at low costs. If marketers did not work within a society, customer's choices would be very limited.

Ethical marketers abide by a set of standards outlined by the American Marketing Association. These standards require that marketers must do no harm and adhere to all applicable laws and regulations. Marketers must make products that work and advertising should not be intentionally deceptive or misleading. Marketers also must be honest, responsible, fair, have respect, be open, and be good corporate citizens.

Think Critically

1. Describe why individuals may have a low opinion of marketers.
2. Explain why marketers play an important role in society.
3. Describe ethical standards that marketers should follow.

Applied Skills

Performing Arts Have students work in groups to write, produce, direct, and perform a short skit related to ethical marketing. Suggest that they draw on their own experiences. Encourage students to develop interesting characters and realistic dialogue to deliver their message. Arrange for groups to perform their skits in front of the class.

TEACH

List the four characteristics of services that make them different from products. Have students identify several well-known services. For each service, have students describe each of the four characteristics as it applies to that service.

THINK CRITICALLY THROUGH VISUALS

Answers will vary, but could include recommendations from family or friends, the prices charged, or whether the location of the business and its hours of operation are convenient.

CORPORATE SOCIAL RESPONSIBILITY

Have students describe how they feel about their own experiences with marketers.

Think Critically Answers

1. Many people think marketers communicate unnecessarily, aren't truthful, and are only interested in making money.

2. Marketers deliver a standard of living by identifying new products and getting those products into customer's hands conveniently at low costs.

3. Ethical marketers must do no harm and adhere to all applicable laws and regulations. Marketers must make products that work and advertising should not be intentionally deceptive or misleading. Marketers must also be honest, responsible, fair, have respect, be open, and be good corporate citizens.

Ask students whether they believe that maintaining the quality of a product would be easier or more difficult than maintaining the quality of a service.

THINK CRITICALLY THROUGH VISUALS

The server in a restaurant can make the experience pleasant and ensure repeat customers by being attentive and providing good service.

ONGOING ASSESSMENT

checkpoint >> **ANSWER**

Products are tangible and may be nonperishable; it is generally easier to control the quality and marketability of these items. Services, however, are intangible, more difficult to market, and perishable.

ASSESS

Key Concepts Answers

1. True

2. False. The first step in marketing research is to define the marketing problem.

3. c. inseparable

Make Academic Connections

4. Letters regarding a product that failed will vary.

5. Results will vary.

CLOSE

Ask students to list ways that companies can increase customer satisfaction with their products and services.

Work as a Team

The employees of a company that provides a service to consumers are responsible for the quality of the service. If your team owned a pet-sitting business, what would you do to make sure the employees provided high quality service for each customer?

© Getty Images/PhotoDisc

How can a server affect your perception of a restaurant?

needs it. Marketers must determine where and when consumers want a service and must be able to provide it at that location and time.

Services are **perishable**, meaning that the availability of a service must match the demand for that service at a specific time. A service cannot be stored for later consumption like many products. If all seats at a concert are filled, no more people will be able to hear that performance. If a hairstylist does not have a client, the service goes unused.

Services are **heterogeneous**, meaning that there will be differences in the type and quality of service provided. Because people usually provide services at the time they are consumed, there is less control over quality than is possible with products. The skill, training, and motivation of the service provider affect service quality.

checkpoint >>

In what ways are services different from products?

10-2 Assessment

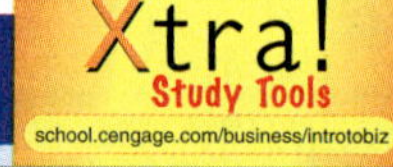

Key Concepts

Determine the best answer.

1. True or False. Most new products introduced by companies are not totally new, but are improvements on existing products.

2. True or False. The first step in marketing research is to develop a data collection procedure.

3. The availability of a service must match the demand for that service at a specific time because it is:
   a. heterogeneous
   b. perishable
   c. inseparable
   d. intangible

Make Academic Connections

4. *Critical Thinking* Use the Internet to locate an article describing a new product that failed. Review the information to determine the possible reasons for failure. Write a short memo to the company describing how using the new product planning process may have reduced the likelihood of failure for the product.

5. *Research* Identify a product that many of your classmates use regularly. Prepare a five-question survey to determine their feelings about the strengths and weaknesses of the product and possible ways the product could be improved. Give the survey to at least 10 students. Present the results in a short report including at least one table, graph, or chart.

RETEACH

Have one group of students list and summarize the steps in the marketing research process and another group list and summarize the steps in the product development process.

ENRICH

Have students use the Internet to locate information on the top-rated brand names in several product and service categories based on customer satisfaction.

Sharpen Your Life Skills

Resolve Conflict

Conflict can be defined as competing differences between two or more people. These differences are often caused by struggles over goals, motives, values, ideas, and resources. Believe it or not, conflict can be both good and bad, depending upon the results of the conflict. The costs of negative, unresolved conflict include decreased productivity, low employee morale, and heightened workplace tensions. These all have the potential to damage the success of a business. But conflict of the right nature can be beneficial to business. For example, friendly conflict can encourage competition, diverse thinking, creativity, and a wider variety of solutions to business problems. Prevention is the solution to many problems, including workplace conflict. Some tips for preventing negative conflict in the workplace include the following:

© Getty Images/PhotoDisc

- Be open to others' ideas. Listen before making up your mind.
- Avoid stereotyping your coworkers and superiors.
- Do not use language or expressions that may be offensive or demeaning to others.
- Disagree constructively. Offer alternative suggestions or solutions rather than simply rejecting others' ideas.
- Above all, treat your coworkers and superiors with the respect you want them to show you.

Unfortunately, conflict cannot always be avoided. All types of conflict can arise, from personality clashes to conflict over business ideas. The following strategies can be helpful in managing conflict with coworkers.

- **Intervention** Ask a coworker or supervisor to provide a setting for conflict resolution between you and those with whom you are in conflict. A supervisor also might speak on your behalf to the coworker with whom you are in conflict.
- **Confrontation** Approach the coworker with whom you are having trouble. Both of you must

recognize the problem and then work together toward a solution.

- **Compromise** If the conflict involves a disagreement over a particular business issue, you might work out a compromise solution. For example, you may agree to your coworker's idea in exchange for similar treatment during the next conflict.
- **Avoidance** The avoidance technique should be your last solution, but in some situations it may be best. If you simply cannot solve a personality conflict, deal with the individual when you need to, but otherwise steer clear.

Conflict between a worker and a superior is acceptable, and in some cases even beneficial, if it leads to increased mutual respect. Conflict with superiors must be handled with care and should not be seen as a challenge to the superior's authority. Conflict with superiors should be kept professional and private.

Think Critically
1. What is conflict?
2. What are the consequences of negative conflict?

Unresolved conflicts in business, even if they involve only very minor issues, can build into serious problems for the people involved and even for the company. Employees and managers need to recognize when conflicts are developing into problems and work to resolve them in positive ways. Having the ability to resolve conflicts is a skill valued by employers.

Think Critically Answers

1. Answers may vary. The article defines conflict as competing differences between two or more people.

2. Answers may vary. The article lists decreased productivity, low employee morale, heightened work place tensions, and, ultimately, loss of business success.

Teaching Strategies

Collaborative Learning Divide students into small work teams. Have each team identify a common conflict that could occur in business. The team should prepare a skit that shows how the conflict develops and how it can be resolved effectively. Each team should deliver its skit to the other teams.

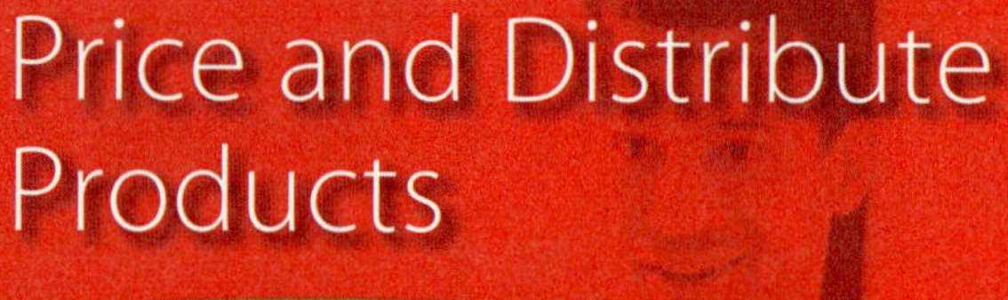

10-3 Price and Distribute Products

Goals

Discuss how the selling price of a product is calculated.

Differentiate between a direct and an indirect channel of distribution.

Key Terms

price

distribution

channel of distribution

channel members

Focus on Real Life

Many product failures result from distribution problems rather than a poor product. A product isn't available when and where customers want it, it is damaged in shipment, or the costs of shipping are higher than customers want to pay. Each of the situations is a distribution problem, but may result in lost sales.

Companies track the distribution of their products and set benchmarks that identify the expected level of performance. Distribution benchmarks can include how long a product stays in storage, how many times it is handled as it is being moved from the manufacturing plant to the customer, the percentage of items damaged during distribution, and many other measures of performance. Distribution personnel are judged on whether they meet the benchmarks or not.

main idea

Discuss how the selling price of a product is calculated.

VALUE AND PRICE

When you decide to purchase a product, how do you determine what to pay? Do you always pay the price that is marked on the product by the seller? Do you compare prices of several businesses to find the lowest price? Do you consider how much money you have available to spend in determining what price to pay? Are you concerned whether the seller is making a profit and whether that profit is low or high? Buyers usually want to pay the lowest price possible and sellers want to charge the highest price possible. Determining the best price for a product is a difficult marketing challenge.

Pricing Factors

Many factors go into a decision about a fair price. What you might consider an appropriate price may be different from the decision of other customers. It probably is very different from the price the seller believes is appropriate. There are both general and specific factors that influence the price paid for a product.

Supply and Demand A product that has a ready supply will have a lower price than a product with a very limited supply. If demand for a product is high, prices will increase. Products with low levels of demand will have comparatively low prices.

Uniqueness When a product has few close competitors because it is unique, the price will be higher than products that are very similar to others.

Age When products are first introduced to the market, prices will be quite high. As products age, the price gradually decreases.

Season Many products are used at a particular time of the year. Winter apparel, air conditioners, and holiday decorations have high levels of sales for a short time and then almost no sales for the rest of the year. Prices will be highest just before and at the beginning of the season. Prices will be lower during other times of the year.

Complexity Highly complex and technical products have higher prices than simple products. Products with many features and options will also command higher prices.

Convenience People pay for convenience. If a product is easily available and the seller provides a high level of customer service, prices will go up. Customers expect to pay low prices if they shop at a large warehouse store that is not as conveniently located and offers little service.

Price a Product

Price is the money a customer must pay for a product or service. The price of a product changes as it moves from producer to consumer. The manufacturer sets a price that is paid by other businesses that will sell the product to the final customer. The price is set by the business following a formula that identifies the components of the price. The formula is:

$$\frac{\text{Selling}}{\text{price}} = \frac{\text{Product}}{\text{costs}} + \frac{\text{Operating}}{\text{expenses}} + \text{Profit}$$

Selling price is the price paid by the customer for the product.

Product costs are the costs to the manufacturer of producing the product or the price paid by other businesses to buy the product.

Operating expenses are all expenses of operating the business that are associated with the product. They can include salaries, storage and display equipment, facilities, utilities, taxes, and many others.

Profit is the amount of money available to the business after all costs and expenses have been paid.

Gross margin is an important factor in product pricing. The *gross margin* is the difference between the selling price and the product costs. It represents the amount of money on hand to pay for operating expenses and provide a profit.

Markup A pricing concept related to gross margin is markup. A *markup* is the amount added to the cost of a product to set the selling price. The markup is equal to the expected gross margin. A markup is stated as a percentage of the product's cost or as a percentage of the product's selling price. If a product costs 15 dollars and has a 100 percent markup on cost, the selling price is $30.00.

$$(\$15 \times 1.00) + \$15 = \$30$$

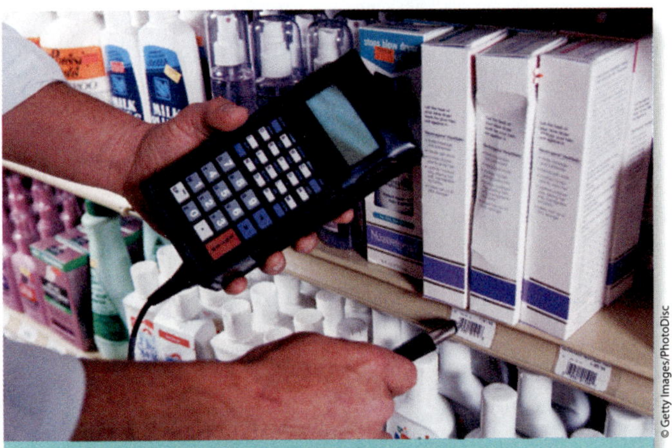

Why should businesses be very careful when raising or cutting prices?

TEACH

Write each of the components of price on a separate sheet of paper. Tape each one on the board as you describe its meaning. Once all of the components are taped on the board, have students identify the math functions that need to be added in order to calculate selling price. Then have students rearrange the items to develop formulas for calculating each of the other components.

Work as a Team

Have students discuss the advantages and disadvantages that a retail store has compared to an e-commerce business that doesn't have a local facility in which consumers can shop.

THINK CRITICALLY THROUGH VISUALS

Businesses must be careful when raising or cutting prices because the price affects consumer buying decisions and the perceived value of the product.

Applied Skills

Mathematics Give students several examples of the amounts of the components for a product price, but leave out the amount of a different component each time. Have students use the pricing formula for calculating the missing figure for each of the examples.

That $30 product would have a markup on selling price of 50 percent.

$$\$15 \div \$30 = 0.50 \text{ or } 50\%$$

Markdown Businesses are not always able to sell products at the original price they set. If customer demand is not as high as projected, if the selling season is ending, or if there is a flaw in the product, the business may have to take a markdown. A *markdown* is a reduction from the original selling price.

A markdown should be thought of as a pricing mistake because it reduces the amount of money the business has to cover operating expenses and profits. However, the original selling price can be set high because the product is new and there is higher demand. Small markdowns result in most of the remaining products being sold while still making a profit. The leftover products may need to be sold at large mark-downs that still provide some money to cover the product cost and expenses.

checkpoint >>

What is the formula for calculating the selling price of a product?

How have parcel delivery services influenced the success of many e-commerce businesses?

© Digital Vision

CHANNELS OF DISTRIBUTION

Do you own any products that were produced in China, India, or New Zealand? If so, the process of getting the product from that country to your city was probably both difficult and time consuming. In contrast, have you or your family shopped at an area farmers' market? Here, local producers sell fruits, vegetables, and other homegrown products. The products have to be transported only a short distance and may be harvested the same morning they are sold. Each situation describes a distribution process.

Distribution involves determining the best methods and procedures to use so customers can find, obtain, and use a product or service. As a marketing mix element, **distribution** is the locations and methods used to make a product or service available to the target market. The route a product follows and the businesses involved in moving a product from the producer to the final consumer are known as a **channel of distribution**.

Need for Distribution Channels

In the earliest economic exchanges, people often bartered to exchange goods and services. If two people each had something the other person wanted, they would agree on how much of each product would be exchanged and the trade would be made. For example, a bushel of apples might be traded for a yard of fabric. The distribution process was relatively simple. In complex economies, exchanges are much more difficult due to several differences that exist between producers and consumers.

- **Differences in Quantity** Businesses produce or sell large amounts of each product to many customers. Each consumer needs only a very small number of products at a given time.

- **Differences in Assortment** Businesses typically specialize in producing a specific type of product while consumers want to purchase a variety of products.

- **Differences in Location** In today's global economy, thousands of miles often separate producers and consumers. Businesses may need to distribute their products to customers in many countries.

- **Differences in Timing** Businesses gain efficiency by producing large amounts of a product at one time. Some agricultural products can only be produced at a specific time of the year. Consumers may want to buy products at different times than when they are produced.

Distribution channels develop to make adjustments in these differences. An effective channel of distribution takes the large quantities produced and breaks them into quantities customers want to buy. The channel gathers products from many producers to offer customers the array of products they need in convenient locations. They move products efficiently from where they are produced to where they can be sold. Distribution channels store products from the time they are produced until customers want to buy them.

Channels and Channel Members

The businesses that take part in a channel of distribution are known as **channel members**. All marketing functions and activities are performed by a channel member or by the consumer. Businesses join a channel of distribution when either the producer or consumer does not want to perform one or more marketing activities or when the business can perform the activities better or at a lower cost.

Channels are either direct or indirect. In a *direct channel of distribution,* products move from the producer straight to the consumer with no other organizations participating. An *indirect channel of distribution* includes one or more other businesses between the producer and consumer. These other businesses provide one or more of the marketing functions.

In indirect distribution channels for products that are sold to business customers, typical channel members are specialists in providing one of the marketing functions. The channel member may be a transportation company, a sales organization, or a financial institution. Some channel members may be responsible for almost all of the marketing functions. They obtain products from a number of small manufacturers and market them to many business customers.

Retailers are a well-known and important part of distribution channels for consumer products. *Retailers* are the final business organization in an indirect channel of distribution for consumer products. Retailers offer a

Name several ways a distribution center improves the exchange process between businesses and consumers.

THINK CRITICALLY THROUGH VISUALS

A distribution center can provide products in quantities consumers want, in convenient locations, and at the time the products are wanted.

Applied Skills

Communication Have students write a four-paragraph essay titled, "Why distribution is important to producers and consumers." Remind students that an essay reflects the perspective of the author.

A knowledgeable salesperson provides the information the consumer needs to make an informed purchase decision.

ONGOING ASSESSMENT

checkpoint >> **ANSWER**

In a direct channel of distribution, products move directly from the producer to the consumer. In an indirect channel, others may participate in the movement of products from the producer to the consumer, such as transportation services and retailers.

ASSESS

Key Concepts Answers

1. b. a large quantity of available products

2. c. assortment

Make Academic Connections

3. Spreadsheets will vary depending on the five products selected.

4. Answers will vary depending on the businesses selected.

CLOSE

Ask students to define and compare the advantages and disadvantages of a direct and indirect channel of distribution.

How can a knowledgeable salesperson increase customer confidence in their decision to purchase a product?

range of products at convenient locations for consumers. They help consumers to select the best products. They can provide financing and delivery services. They may even offer repairs and other customer services. Retailers assist manufacturers by storing, displaying, and advertising the products and often paying the manufacturer well before final consumers buy the products.

checkpoint >>
What is the difference between a direct and an indirect channel of distribution?

10-3 Assessment

Key Concepts

Determine the best answer.

1. Which of the following conditions will result in a lower rather than a higher price?
   a. a high customer demand
   b. a large quantity of available products
   c. a product that has very few similar competing products
   d. All would result in lower prices.

2. When businesses specialize in producing a specific type of product, a channel of distribution will be needed to adjust differences in
   a. timing
   b. location
   c. assortment
   d. quantity

Make Academic Connections

3. *Math* Visit a department store or the online catalog of an Internet business. Identify five products that have been marked down and for which the original price and sale price are listed. Prepare a spreadsheet on which you list the product, the original price, and the sale price. Calculate the amount of the markdown and the markdown percentage. Determine the amount you would pay if you purchased all five items at the original price and if you purchased them at the sale price. What is the total savings in dollars and as a percentage of the original prices?

4. *Research* List the seven marketing functions. Use a business directory or the Internet to locate a business that specializes in the first function on your list. Choose a business that is part of an indirect channel of distribution. Do this for each function on your list.

RETEACH

Ask students to review the lesson and develop two multiple-choice questions from the lesson information. Have students in turn ask one of their questions to the class and then identify the correct answer.

ENRICH

Have students use the Internet to learn how technology is being used to improve the quality and speed of distribution activities.

10-4 Plan Promotion

Goals

Justify the importance of communication in marketing.

Identify and describe the common types of promotion.

Key Terms

promotion

effective communication

personal selling

advertising

Focus on Real Life

The most powerful marketing tool influencing consumer behavior is promotion. It can attract your attention and remind you of important needs. It can tap your emotions and encourage you to buy. It is so powerful that it can even influence you to purchase a product you later decide was not the best choice.

Advertising is a promotional tool often used to influence emotions. The image created with a picture or other graphic, the language used to communicate information, even the colors of the headline, text, picture, or background can establish feelings of pleasure, happiness, fear, or sadness. An advertisement that leaves you with a positive feeling toward the product based on your emotions will be memorable and often will influence your feelings about the product or company.

COMMUNICATION AND PROMOTION

Promotional messages from businesses, organizations, government agencies, and political candidates bombard you on a regular basis. Each day newspapers, television and radio programs, and mailboxes are filled with advertisements. Sides of buses, tops of taxis, even posters in restaurant restrooms contain promotional messages asking you to buy something, support a cause, or change an opinion. Every time you visit the World Wide Web, you are exposed to a variety of virtual promotions. It is apparent that businesses and organizations believe in the power of promotion, but is it always effective? What determines whether promotion is used well or not?

Promotion is any form of communication used to inform, persuade, or remind. Businesses, organizations, groups, or individuals use promotion. It is used to influence knowledge, beliefs, and actions about products, services, or ideas. To plan effective promotion, marketers must first understand the communication process. They then must apply effective communication to interact with consumers in a way that results in information, understanding, and action.

The Communication Process

Most of you have played the game where one person starts a message by whispering in the ear of a second person. That person whispers to the next and so on until several people have heard the message. When the last person states what he or she heard, it is seldom the same as the initial message. The game makes the point that effective communication is not easy. **Effective communication** is the exchange of information so there is common understanding by all participants. Effective communication is illustrated in Figure 10-4 on the next page.

> **main idea**
>
> Justify the importance of communication in marketing.

Different Learning Abilities

Specific Learning Disability (SLD) Have students describe or find an example of a promotion they believe is effective and one they believe is not effective. Ask them to describe what makes the promotion effective or ineffective in their opinion.

Focus on Real Life

Ask students why promotion is considered the most powerful marketing tool. Have them discuss how promotion can be used effectively and ineffectively by businesses.

TEACH

Have students make a list of all of the different types of promotion they can think of. Remind them to consider non-business promotions as well as those provided by businesses.

TEACH

Ask students to describe differences between effective communication and effective promotion. Ask them if a promotion by a business has to result in the sale of a product or service in order to be considered successful.

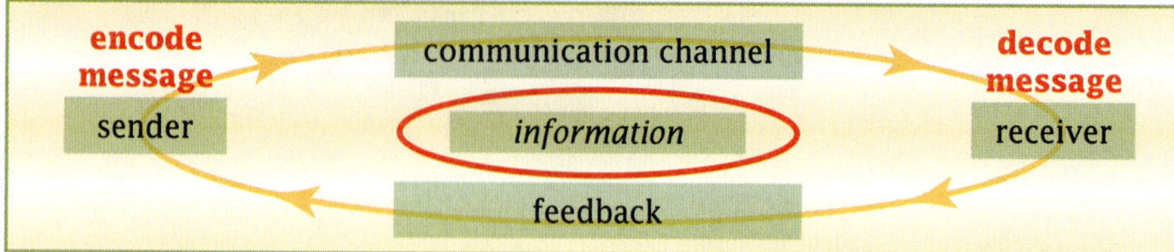

Communication begins with a person or organization (*the sender*) that has information to communicate to another person or organization (*the receiver*). The sender chooses the way (*communication channel*) the information will be transmitted to the receiver. Before sending the message, the sender decides the form in which the information will be sent—text, spoken words, pictures. Preparing the information to be communicated is called *encoding*. The receiver obtains the information from the channel and interprets it for understanding (*decoding*). To be sure that the communication achieved the desired result, the sender needs to have a response from the receiver (*feedback*). If the receiver understood the information and responds in a way the sender wanted, communication was effective. If the receiver does not respond or acts in an unexpected way, communication failed.

Communicating Through Promotion

Promotion is an important form of communication. A business needs to provide information to consumers in order to persuade them to make a purchase. As the sender, the business decides what information to provide. The consumer is the receiver. The information is encoded in the form of a promotional message such as an advertisement. The business chooses an information channel. Common promotional channels include advertising media, salespeople, and the Internet. If the customer sees or hears the message, it is decoded. The response of the consumer gives feedback to the business about the effectiveness of the promotion.

Choosing target markets and studying their needs and decision-making process can make promotion more effective. When the focus of a business is a target market, communication can be very specific to the needs of that group using media that are familiar to and trusted by those consumers. The business will understand where the customers are in the decision-making process. It will tailor promotional messages at that stage. Early messages get attention and give simple information about the product or service and the needs it satisfies. Later promotions can compare the product to competing brands. They may point out advantages that are important to the target market. When customers purchase the product, promotions can switch to providing reinforcement of their decision and offering after-sale services.

Work as a Team

Choose a newspaper, television, or magazine advertisement that is familiar to each person. Using that advertisement, identify each of the components of the communication channel. Discuss whether the advertiser seems to be demonstrating effective or ineffective communication.

Writing Across the Curriculum Have students write a paragraph that demonstrates how the communication process applies in another class they are currently taking. Invite students to share their ideas with the class.

TYPES OF PROMOTION

An inventor asks you for advice on how to promote a new type of cellular telephone that combines high-speed video and audio. What types of promotion would you recommend? Would it be a glitzy television campaign or direct mail to cellular service subscribers? Maybe you would suggest text messaging delivered to cell phones. What about salespeople ready to demonstrate the new product to customers who visit shopping mall kiosks? There are many choices for promotional communications. The types of promotion are divided into personalized promotion and mass promotion. *Personalized promotion* communicates directly with each customer using information tailored to that person. *Mass promotion* communicates with many people at the same time with a common message.

Personalized Promotion

Personalized promotion is the most effective form of marketing communication. It is also the most expensive. The most well known type of personalized promotion is personal selling. **Personal selling** is direct, individualized communication with prospective customers to assess their needs and assist them in satisfying those needs with appropriate products and services. Personal selling usually is done face-to-face with each customer. The customer visits the business to meet with a salesperson or the salesperson goes to the home or business of the customer. Personal selling also can be completed using telephone calls or live audio and video Internet connections. Because personal selling is often used for complex and expensive products and services, it may require several contacts between the salesperson and the customer to complete the sale.

A 2004 survey by the Promotion Marketing Association found that consumer products companies spent twice as many of their marketing dollars on promotions, such as contests, coupons, and product samples, than they did on advertising.

To prepare for a sale, salespeople gather information on the prospective customer they will visit. They study product information. They need to be able to make the best match of products to customer needs. When a customer is qualified, meaning they appear to have the need for and resources to buy a product, the salesperson schedules a meeting with the customer. During the meeting, the salesperson asks questions, provides information, and demonstrates the product for the customer. If the product meets the customer's needs, the salesperson helps the customer make a decision to purchase. The salesperson may also arrange payment

main idea

Identify and describe the common types of promotion.

© Digital Vision

What questions would help a salesperson determine the best computer system to recommend for a particular consumer?

TEACH

As a class, have students develop a list of the characteristics they believe are important to an effective sales person. Ask them if they believe most salespeople are concerned about making sure their customers are really satisfied with their purchases. Ask students to explain their answers.

THINK CRITICALLY THROUGH VISUALS

Answers will vary. Students should realize that a salesperson would want to determine who would be using the computer, how the computer will be used, and how much the consumer is willing to spend. Examples of questions include: Are you buying this computer for your home or office? What kinds of things do you plan to do with the computer? Are you replacing another computer? What's your budget for this purchase?

Different Learning Styles

Tactile Learner Give students a familiar consumer product such as a calculator, camera, cell phone, PDA, or MP3 player. Have them develop a short sales presentation that emphasizes three important product features and the benefits of each feature for the consumer. Invite volunteers to give their presentations to other students acting as consumers.

TEACH

Have students use library resources or the Internet to locate a recent listing of top-rated television commercials. Have students discuss the commercials on the list that they are familiar with and decide whether they agree that they deserve the top rating or not.

Have students prepare a table to compare the three types of mass promotion described: publicity, public relations, and sales promotion. Suggest the following table headings: Uses, Strengths, Weaknesses.

A QUESTION OF ETHICS

Ask students whether they believe companies can be so successful that they cause problems for themselves because other businesses find it difficult to compete. Explain that Microsoft finds itself in that position. The feature asks students to consider what actions are ethical and unethical in reducing the amount of competition a company faces.

Think Critically Answers

1. Answers will vary. Students may cite antitrust laws, or they may side with Microsoft on the grounds of free enterprise.

2. Competition generally benefits consumers in that it decreases prices while increasing quality and assortment.

3. Findings will vary depending on when the assignment is completed. Provide direction for how students are to report their findings.

or financing as well as product delivery and any services the customer requires. After the customer has used the product, the salesperson contacts the customer to answer additional questions and determine that the customer is satisfied.

Mass Promotion

Mass promotion is directed to many people at the same time. If the people are from the same target market, they will have like needs. Because the promotional message is aimed at many people, it cannot be as individualized and specific as personalized promotion. However, reaching many people with the same message through mass media is much less expensive. While a large company may spend hundreds of thousands of dollars on a television advertisement, it reaches more than a million people. Therefore the cost of the message for each customer is quite low.

Advertising is the most known and used type of mass promotion. **Advertising** is any paid form of communication through mass media directed at identified consumers to provide information and influence their actions. The most common advertising media are television, radio, newspapers, magazines, mass mailings, outdoor displays, and the Internet.

Consumers are exposed to hundreds of communications including promotional communications in the media each day. These messages are not developed for or delivered directly to individuals. For this reason, the advertisements must be designed to attract attention and focus the consumer on a small amount of specific information. Most advertisements do not result in an immediate sale. Rather, they attempt to influence prospects to take additional action such as visit a store, gather more information, or test the product.

A QUESTION OF ETHICS

The Price of Success

Should a successful company be penalized because it has developed a successful product? An important principle of private enterprise is that businesses and consumers benefit from competition. The belief is that competition increases the choices and quality of products and reduced prices for consumers. European courts recently stepped in to fine Microsoft for trying to reduce competition for several of its products.

Microsoft develops and sells the operating system used in most personal computers. Because computer manufacturers know that consumers expect to buy computers that have the Microsoft operating system installed, they must purchase the systems from Microsoft. Microsoft includes many features that are added to the operating system such as an Internet browser, e-mail and productivity programs, and a media player. All of the added programs are owned and sold by Microsoft. It is not easy for consumers to uninstall the programs once they buy a computer and difficult for Microsoft's competitors to get computer manufacturers and consumers to purchase and use their programs because Microsoft has already included them in the system.

Microsoft argues that its programs are popular among consumers, the features improve the operating system, and when pre-installed are easier to use and cheaper for consumers than if they had to buy all of the added programs separately. Its competitors argue that Microsoft is monopolizing the market by forcing computer manufacturers to include its products and reject the similar products of competitors.

Think Critically

1. Should courts step in to prevent Microsoft from requiring computer manufacturers to install the additional Microsoft software in order to buy its popular operating system?

2. Do you believe competition among businesses usually benefits consumers? Why or why not?

3. Use the Internet to gather the latest information on legal actions taken by governments and competitors against Microsoft designed to encourage greater competition.

Applied Skills

Communication Have students choose a popular consumer product and create a print advertisement for the product. Make sure they identify a target market that serves as a focus for the advertisement.

Other types of mass promotion are publicity, sales promotion, and public relations. *Publicity* is non-paid promotional communication presented by the media rather than by the business or organization that is being promoted. *Public relations* is an ongoing program of non-paid and paid communications. It is planned to favorably influence public opinion about an organization, marketing effort, idea, or issue. *Sales promotion* includes activities and materials designed to reinforce a company's brand and image. It is also a direct incentive to take an action likely to immediately increase sales of a product or service. Sales promotion includes contests and games as well as the many products companies give away to consumers or sell at a low cost that highlight a brand name or product.

Mass Personalization

Businesses can combine the advantages of personalized and mass promotion by using mass personalization promotion. Mass personalization begins with promotion through mass media such as newspapers, mass mailings, or the Internet. Prospective customers see the advertisement and become interested in the product or service. The company then provides an easy-to-use method for the consumer to gather more personalized information.

A customer who views an Internet advertisement or uses a search engine to gather information can be encouraged to complete an online survey. The questions provide the business with more specific information about the consumer, including their interests and needs. When the survey is submitted, the consumer is taken to a more specific web site tailored to their profile or they are sent specific information via e-mail. They can even contact an online customer service representative who can answer detailed questions. A simpler form of mass personalization on the Internet is a set of links that take customers with specific questions to other web pages. The links can help them choose a specific product and complete an online purchase.

> *checkpoint* »
> Describe the advantages and disadvantages of the major types of promotion.

ONGOING ASSESSMENT

checkpoint » **ANSWER**

Personalized promotion allows the provider to meet customers and identify customer needs. It is, however, the most expensive type of promotion. Mass promotion reaches a larger target market and is much less expensive. It does not, however, provide for individualized service, and sales (results) are often not immediate.

ASSESS

Key Concepts Answers

1. c. the advertisement
2. a. personal selling

Make Academic Connections

3. Illustrations will vary depending on the examples.

4. Answers will vary depending on the products or services identified. Provide students with suggestions for how to communicate their answers. For example, they might prepare a short report, a bulleted list, a display, or a short presentation.

CLOSE

Ask students: "What should a business do to make sure its promotion is effective?"

10-4 Assessment

Key Concepts

Determine the best answer.

1. Which of the following is *not* a part of effective communication?
   a. the sender
   b. the receiver
   c. the advertisement
   d. information

2. The most expensive but also most effective type of promotion is:
   a. personal selling
   b. advertising
   c. publicity
   d. public relations

Make Academic Connections

3. *Critical Thinking* Use Figure 10-4 to illustrate three different examples of business communications: a business-to-business communication, a business-to-final consumer communication, and a consumer-to-business communication.

4. *Research* Identify three different products or services you would consider buying. For each product, identify the information you need to help you make a purchase decision and what media or information source you would choose to gather the information. Describe how a business could use promotion to influence your decision.

RETEACH

Ask students to use Figure 10-4 to discuss how businesses can plan to use each of the promotional methods described in the chapter.

ENRICH

Ask students to describe ways that promotion can be used to increase the effectiveness of each of the other three marketing mix elements.

Communicate Business Concepts Answers

1. Answers will vary. Students are to identify businesses from their community as being marketing businesses or not marketing businesses.

2. Answers will vary. Students are to find local businesses whose work relates to each of the marketing functions.

3. A business consumer for this product could be an office supply chain, and a final consumer could be a salesperson who is frequently on the road. Both consumers would be interested in a good price. The business consumer would want to know how the printer could be sold with other products, while the final consumer would want to hear about its convenience and reliability.

Business Notes

10-1 MARKETING BASICS

1. Marketing is an organizational function and a set of processes for creating, communicating, and delivering value to customers and for managing customer relationships in ways that benefit the organization and its stakeholders. The seven marketing functions are product and service management, distribution, selling, marketing-information management, financial analysis, pricing, and promotion.

2. A marketing strategy is a two-step process used to plan and market products. The first step is to identify a target market and the second step is to develop a marketing mix.

3. The steps in the consumer decision-making process are: recognize a need, gather information, select and evaluate alternatives, make a purchase decision, and determine the effectiveness of the decision.

10-2 DEVELOP EFFECTIVE PRODUCTS AND SERVICES

4. The steps in a marketing research study are: define the marketing problem, study the situation, develop a data collection procedure, gather and analyze information, and propose a solution.

5. The components of a product are the basic product, product features, options, brand name, packaging, and a guarantee or warranty.

6. Products are tangible items that you can see and examine. Services are intangible activities that are consumed at the same time they are produced.

10-3 PRICE AND DISTRIBUTE PRODUCTS

7. Businesses use the following formula for setting the price of a product: Selling price = Product costs + Operating expenses + Profit.

8. A direct channel of distribution moves products from the producer directly to the consumer with no other organizations participating. An indirect channel of distribution includes one or more other businesses between the producer and consumer. These other businesses provide one or more of the marketing functions.

10-4 PLAN PROMOTION

9. When the focus of a business is a target market, communication can be very specific to the needs of that group using media that are familiar to and trusted by those consumers.

10. There are two major types of promotion. Personalized promotion communicates directly with each customer using information tailored to that person. Mass promotion communicates with many people at the same time with a common message.

Communicate Business Concepts

1. Some companies are not marketing businesses, but complete marketing activities as a part of their business operations. Other businesses are marketing businesses because their primary activities are to complete marketing activities. Identify three businesses from your community that are not marketing businesses and three that are marketing businesses. Justify your choices.

2. Use the Yellow Pages of the telephone directory for your town or city. For each of the seven marketing functions, locate a business whose primary work relates to that function. Identify the work of the business to show how it relates to the marketing function.

3. You are planning the marketing strategy for a new portable printer that weighs less than two pounds and can fit in a backpack or briefcase. Identify one target market for the printer that is a business consumer and one that is a final consumer. Describe how the marketing mix would be similar and different for each target market.

4. Often it is believed that people will purchase the lowest-priced product available, but experience shows people will pay more for a product if they believe the higher-priced product is better than the lowest-priced products. Think of several products you purchase for which you know you pay more than you would have to. List the features of the products that cause you to pay a higher price. After you have developed the list, classify the reasons according to the four elements of the marketing mix: product, distribution, price, promotion.

5. The price charged for a product is affected by a number of factors. For each of the following situations, identify whether you believe it will result in a higher or lower price. Write one or two sentences to justify each answer.

a. One customer purchases a very large quantity of a product.
b. A business provides a high level of customer service.
c. The product is very fragile and requires special handling.
d. The product moves through many businesses in the channel of distribution before it reaches customers.

6. Internet services have the same traits as those provided by bricks and mortar businesses. Locate an Internet service business. Review the company's web site and find information that describes how the service is intangible, inseparable, perishable, and heterogeneous.

Develop Your Business Language

Match the terms listed with the definitions.

7. Any paid form of communication through mass media directed at identified consumers to provide information and influence their actions.

8. The exchange of information so there is common understanding by all participants.

9. A specific group of consumers that have similar wants and needs.

10. Everything a business offers to satisfy a customer's needs.

11. The locations and methods used to make a product or service available to the target market.

12. The blending of the marketing elements.

13. Intangible activities that are consumed at the same time they are produced.

14. An organizational function and a set of processes for creating, communicating, and delivering value to customers and for managing customer relationships in ways that benefit the organization and its stakeholders.

15. The route a product follows and the businesses involved in moving a product from the producer to the final consumer.

16. Finding solutions to problems through carefully designed studies involving consumers.

17. A company's plan that identifies how it will use marketing to achieve its goals.

18. The reasons consumers decide what products and services to purchase.

19. Direct individualized communication with prospective customers to assess their needs and assist them in satisfying those needs with appropriate products and services.

20. Any form of communication used to inform, persuade, or remind.

21. The money a customer must pay for a product or service.

KEY TERMS

a. advertising
b. buying motives
c. channel of distribution
d. consumer decision-making process
e. distribution
f. effective communication
g. marketing
h. marketing mix
i. marketing research
j. marketing strategy
k. personal selling
l. price
m. promotion
n. services
o. target market

---

4. Answers will vary. Students are to come to some conclusions about why they (and people in general) are sometimes willing to pay more for a product than necessary.

5. a. Buying in quantity generally results in a lower price.

b. High levels of personalized customer service often result in a higher price.

c. A product that requires special handling often has a higher price.

d. A product that passes through many businesses generally has a higher price because each business must make its profit.

6. Answers will vary. Students are to find an Internet service business and analyze how its service is intangible, inseparable, perishable, and heterogeneous.

Develop Your Business Language Answers

7. a. advertising
8. f. effective communication
9. o. target market
10. d. consumer decision-making process
11. e. distribution

12. h. marketing mix
13. n. services
14. g. marketing
15. c. channel of distribution
16. j. marketing research

17. i. marketing strategy
18. b. buying motives
19. k. personal selling
20. m. promotion
21. l. price

Make Academic Connections

22. a. 3 manufacturers × 1,000 customers = 3,000 exchanges

b. 3 manufacturers × 10 retailers = 30 exchanges; 10 retailers × 100 customers = 1,000 exchanges; 30 + 1,000 = 1,030 exchanges

23. Findings will vary.

24. Advertisements will vary. Encourage interested students to work with classmates to produce their ads using live or recorded performances.

Linking School and Community

Students are to talk to several people of different ages about the consumer decision-making process, then compare how they made buying decisions and whether there were differences based on age.

Web Workout

1. Answers will vary. Students should find information from research studies directed at specific topics.

2. Students should find research related to branding, marketing communication, e-business, and product testing and evaluation.

3. Answers will vary. The names of some of the specialty panels are Affluent, Automotive Insights, Chronic Illness, IT Decision Makers, Pet Companion, Physicians, and Travelers. Companies are interested in these market segments because each represents a viable market segment for business.

Make Academic Connections

22. **MATH** The use of intermediaries reduces the number of exchanges needed to distribute products from producers. Consider a situation where three manufacturers produce products that are purchased by 1,000 customers. Use the following information to determine the number of exchanges needed for each customer to purchase one product from each manufacturer.

a. How many exchanges will be needed if each manufacturer sells one product to each of the 1,000 customers?

b. How many exchanges will be needed if each manufacturer sells its products to 10 retailers and each of the retailers sells all three products to 100 customers?

23. **RESEARCH** Use the Internet, business magazines, or newspapers to locate a report on a marketing research study. Review the research and prepare a two-page analysis. The report should include the purpose of the research, the characteristics of the people studied, the data collection method, important findings, and the sponsor of the research. Describe how a business could use the research to improve their marketing strategy.

24. **COMMUNICATION** Promotion is used for three purposes: to inform, to persuade, and to remind. Select a product or service with which you are familiar. Write three short radio advertisements for the product. Direct each advertisement at one of the three purposes of promotion.

25. **MATH** Calculate the missing amounts in the table below for each product.

PRODUCT	PRODUCT COST	MARKUP PERCENT	MARKUP AMOUNT	SELLING PRICE	TOTAL COST	NET PROFIT
A	$30	40	$12			$2
B		50	$50			$25
C	$60			$84	$72	

Linking School and Community

Interview three people from your community to learn more about the consumer decision-making process. One person should be approximately your age or younger, another at least 10 years older than you, and the third at least 20 years older than you. Ask each to identify a product they recently purchased. Then ask them questions about how they decided they needed to make the purchase, how they gathered information about choices, and how they made the decision, as well as their satisfaction following the decision. Ask them if they believe they made an effective decision or not and why. When you have completed all of the interviews, compare the procedures they followed with the steps of the consumer decision-making process.

Web Workout

The Internet is becoming a very strong tool for marketing research. Companies can place surveys online, run online focus groups, and deliver alternative web pages to see which ones are most effective. Harris Interactive has more than 6 million members from more than 125 different countries in its Harris Pole Online Panel. Visit the Harris Interactive web site. Evaluate the benefits that their research services offer customers.

Think Critically

1. Read an article that appears under the "Headlines" banner. Describe how the information that Harris has collected could help a business.

2. Browse through the Harris site and list all the marketing functions where Harris provides marketing research services.

3. List three of the specialty groups that Harris Pole Online uses to collect information for companies. Why would companies be interested in these market segments?

25.

Product	Product Cost	Markup Percent	Markup Amount	Selling Price	Total Cost	Net Profit
A				$42	$40	
B	$100			$150	$125	
C		40%	$24			$12

Decision-Making Strategies

DeeLites is a popular bakery in a small Iowa town. The bakery produces a variety of fresh pastries, cakes, pies, and other specialty desserts that have reduced calories. Loyal customers say that the low-calorie baked goods are better tasting than similar higher-calorie products they can purchase elsewhere. Customers have encouraged the owner of DeeLites to allow ordering over the Internet so their friends and relatives from other cities and states can purchase the products. The owner would like to increase sales, but is concerned whether the Internet is a good way to expand.

26. What would be the advantages of using the Internet to expand sales?

27. What changes in the marketing mix would have to be made to sell products using the Internet?

Business Plan

Business plans are the key to acquiring financing for a start-up business. The business plan gives entrepreneurs a tool for evaluating, organizing, and selling a new business concept.

After conducting the appropriate research, select a business to start in your community and write a business plan. Your business plan should include an Executive Summary (brief synopsis of the key points and strengths included in the plan), Company Description, Industry Analysis, Target Market, Competitive Analysis, Marketing Plan and Sales Strategy, Operations, Management, and Organization, Long-Term Development, and Financials. You may also include attachments such as certifications, licenses, and tax requirements. The business plan can be single- or double-spaced, but cannot be longer than 30 pages.

The oral presentation will include five minutes for setup and 10 minutes to present your business plan. Visual aids may be used during the presentation. Following each oral presentation, the judges or class may ask questions for five minutes.

PERFORMANCE INDICATORS EVALUATED

- Understand the complete business plan.
- Present the business plan with confidence and authority.
- Reinforce the business plan with appropriate research.
- Reinforce the presentation with appropriate visual aids.
- Produce a clear and concise written document that follows grammar, punctuation, spelling, and business style rules.

For more detailed information about performance indicators, go to the FBLA web site.

1. Why is the business plan so important for an entrepreneur?
2. Why does a financial institution want to know the long-term goals for a business?
3. List three good sources of information when writing a business plan.

http://www.fbla-pbl.org/

Access the web site shown here to find portfolio activities for this chapter. Use the activities to provide tangible evidence of your learning.

school.cengage.com/business/introtobiz

2. The financial institution wants to know that the entrepreneur has seriously considered the future. The financial institution wants to make sure that they will receive a return on their investment.

3. Answers will vary and could include SBA, Internet, businesses, franchise plans, college and university faculty.

Decision-Making Strategies Answers

26. Using the Internet would allow DeeLites to expand its market. It would also allow DeeLites to increase awareness of its products and communicate quickly with customers.

27. By carefully designing its web site, DeeLites could maintain its concept of a sweet shop, but it would become a virtual shop. Pricing may have to be adjusted to include shipping and any additional expenses involved. Promotions would have to include keyword use on the web site to attract hits, and DeeLites would want to advertise the web site to existing customers. Distribution would include new shipping methods. The goods probably would not change unless there were adjustments needed to ensure freshness and stability in shipping, and services would have to increase to include personnel to handle incoming orders. Services would also have to shift to include phone or e-mail communication.

Winning Edge
Business Plan

This is a long-term project in which students develop a full business plan and make an oral presentation of the key features of the plan.

Think Critically Answers

1. The business plan sells the entrepreneur's idea. The business plan must be well written to capture possible financing.

In this chapter, students will obtain a basic knowledge of the use of computer systems and technology in various business settings.

11-1   Computer Systems

In this lesson, an overview of computer systems, along with various software applications, is presented.

11-2   Business Applications of Technology

Management information systems and other uses of technology, including e-commerce, are discussed in this lesson.

11-3   Other Technology Issues

This lesson considers some of the workplace and personal applications of technology, along with various social concerns.

CHAPTER 11

Business and Technology

264

Teaching Resources

Activities and Study Guide, Ch. 11
Chapter and Unit Tests, Ch. 11
Spanish Resources, Ch. 11

ExamView® CD, Ch. 11
Instructor's Resource CD
- PowerPoint Slides, Ch. 11
- Lesson Plans, Ch. 11

Xtra! Web Site

school.cengage.com/business/introtobiz
- Study Tools, 11-1, 11-2, 11-3
- Quiz Prep, Ch. 11
- Net Bookmark, Ch. 11
- Crossword Puzzle, Ch. 11
- Portfolio Activity, Ch.11

Planning a Career in...
INFORMATION TECHNOLOGY

In your lifetime, thousands of new jobs have been created because of the increased use of computers. Computer and technology workers must meet the demands for information within their organizations. People with a variety of skills and educational backgrounds can find career opportunities working with computers and technology.

How can you gain the training you need to compete? Most high schools offer a number of computer classes. Instruction is also available at computer training centers. Some employers will pay for employees to take computer courses. Self-paced and online programs are also available.

Employment Outlook

- The Bureau of Labor Statistics expects faster than average growth in jobs related to computers and technology.

- More than 83 percent of the labor force work in service industries, and most computer-related jobs are in service organizations.

Related Job Titles

- Computer Technician
- Information Systems Manager
- Computer Programmer
- Software Engineer
- Software Sales Representative
- Data Entry Clerk
- Computer Support Specialist
- Information Systems Teacher
- Network Administrator
- Systems Analyst
- Computer Scientist
- Database Administrator
- Web Developer

Needed Skills

- Most computer-related jobs require more than a high school education. This training may be achieved through a specialized vocational program or a college degree program.

- Knowledge of computer systems, computer languages, application software, and other technology is required for specialized positions.

What's it like to work in ... Information Technology

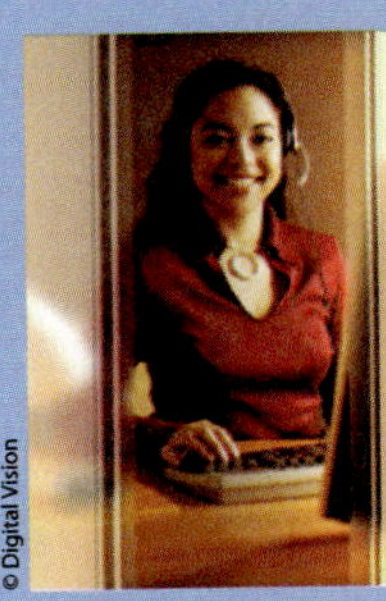

"Should we use a Flash intro? Will a banner heading be most appropriate? What functions are required to serve the needs of this new customer?" Kellye, a web developer, is in a morning brainstorming session with her team. They are planning to have some ideas ready in time for a meeting with the customer tomorrow.

Around the world, more than a billion people access the Internet for information, entertainment, and business activities. Web sites are the basic element of the Internet. Web developers analyze, plan, design, implement, and support the web sites of their organizations. Many businesses use outside vendors like Kellye's company to create and maintain their web sites.

Knowledge of multimedia software is a key requirement for web developers. Graphics, digital imagery, audio, and video are vital to the appeal and effectiveness of a web site. Web developers are often involved with creating web sites for online selling and other e-commerce activities.

What about you? In what ways do you use computers and technology each day that might be the basis for a future career?

Planning a Career in...

INFORMATION TECHNOLOGY

Computers and technology influence nearly every job in our society. This feature provides a focused look at employment positions directly related to information technology.

Ask students to describe some work duties for the job titles listed. Also discuss the types of skills and experiences needed for these positions. Be sure to emphasize both technology skills and other career competencies.

After reading the Career feature, ask students what they think about the position described. Do they know anyone who holds a similar job? At the conclusion of the discussion, direct students to answer the What About You question that follows the feature.

What About You? Answer

Answers will vary. Students may not realize that their daily use of computers and technology could be preparing them for future careers.

Additional Career Information

Additional information on careers can be found in the *Occupational Outlook Handbook,* an online publication (www.bls.gov/oco) of the federal government. Tell your class about this resource and how to use it. This description of job duties can be used to demonstrate the relevancy of skills learned in this course.

Focus on Real Life

This opening situation can help to show the influence of technology in various settings in our society.

TEACH

Ask students to elaborate on the statement, "Computers are everywhere." Ask them to provide examples of where they see computers. Also have them identify situations where they don't actually see the computer, but they know a computer is being used. For example, they might not see a computer, but they know that a standardized test is being scored by a computer.

THINK CRITICALLY THROUGH VISUALS

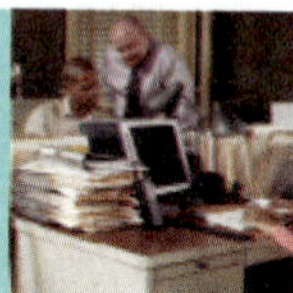

Computerized records management uses electronic folders and files instead of paper files. Computers access and search records much more quickly than manual methods. Computers can pull information from a vast number of records and quickly prepare reports. Computers also make it easier to share file information with people in other offices.

Goals

Identify the main elements of a computer system.

Describe input devices and processing activities.

Explain computer storage media and output types.

Key Terms

computer system

hardware

software

computer network

central processing unit (CPU)

program

computer language

operating system software

application software

Focus on Real Life

Ms. Jenkins announced to her class, "The French Club will meet today during sixth period. The topic for discussion will be computers and new technology."

Fran looked at Brenda and said, "That doesn't make sense! What do computers have to do with the French Club?"

"Recently our club decided to use a database program to keep track of our membership records," said Brenda. "In addition," she went on, "the club is using e-mail to talk to students in France. Then, we are planning a videoconference with other French clubs around the United States. We will also use our computer network to…"

"Wait a minute!" Fran exclaimed. "OK. OK. Computers do have a lot to do with the French Club."

"Well then, I guess you'll be coming to the meeting today after school," responded Brenda.

---

main idea

Identify the main elements of a computer system.

COMPUTERS IN SOCIETY

Computers are everywhere. These electronic devices process store receipts, test scores, and sports statistics. Computers in business are used to store, process, and report information. Computers are also used to design factories, control traffic patterns, and measure medical test results.

Nearly every business uses some type of computer. A company needs quick, efficient processing to control its operating costs, manage resources, and stay competitive. When you think about the billions of business transactions, checks, and school records that are processed each day, you realize the importance of computers.

Each day in banks, stores, offices, factories, homes, and nonprofit organizations, the use of computer systems is expanding. As managers plan and implement computerized activities, they must decide how best to use technology to serve the production and distribution needs of the organization.

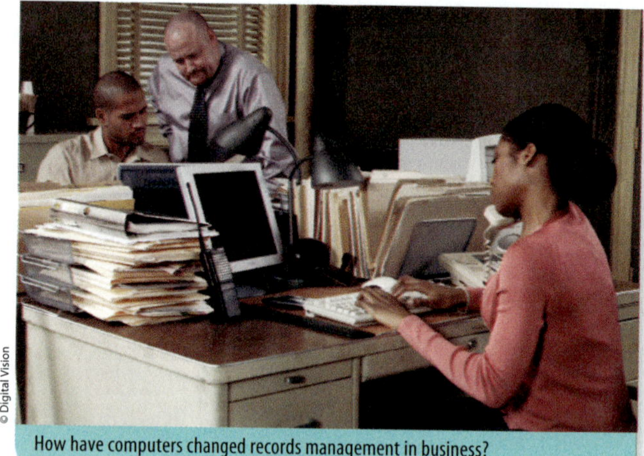
How have computers changed records management in business?

Different Learning Abilities

Specific Learning Disability (SLD) Motivate passive students and those lacking confidence by asking them to name some uses of computers they have observed. Encourage them to discuss some of the business applications of computers in our society.

Elements of a Computer System

Video games, personal digital assistants, and automated highway toll collection systems all have four basic components:

1. Input device
2. Processing unit
3. Memory and storage
4. Output device

As shown in Figure 11-1, these four basic components make up what is called a **computer system**. The physical elements of a computer system are called the **hardware**. Examples of computer hardware include keyboards, cameras, microphones, speakers, monitors (or screens), chips, and printers.

Hardware is constantly changing and expanding. For example, today most computers can handle sound, graphics, animation, and video. In the past, these features were only offered on large computers. Multimedia computer systems are now common in small businesses and homes.

In contrast to hardware, **software** refers to the instructions that run the computer system. Businesses commonly use several types of software. These include word processing, spreadsheet, database, presentation, and communications programs.

Computer Networks

Computers in businesses and schools are commonly linked together in a **computer network**. Organizations link computers together so users can share hardware, software, and data.

The Internet is the largest and best-known computer network in the world. The Internet is most often used for two activities: (1) the exchange of e-mail and (2) for accessing the World Wide Web.

The World Wide Web (WWW) is also called the Web. It allows computer users to access information on almost every topic. The Web uses text, images, hyperlinks, graphics, frames, animation, video, and audio. It is an extensive information source. This global computer network provides product information, travel assistance,

Why is it easier to manage information with computers than without computers?

Different Learning Styles

Visual Learner Encourage visual learners to discuss each of the main elements of a computer system. Ask them to use drawings or photos to create a display that represents the main elements of a computer system.

TEACH

Explain each element of a computer system. Ask students to name examples of items in each element of a computer system.

Contrast the difference between hardware and software. Have students describe the main purposes of hardware and software.

Provide a basic explanation of computer networks. Point out the various types of computer networks that students may have experienced in school, at home, and in stores.

PROJECT

Provide the following instructions to students. (These instructions also appear on page xxv of the textbook.) Do you believe that you are *computer literate* (able to understand and use computers efficiently)? Are you comfortable using computers? Describe how the computerization of our society and economy may affect your ability to achieve your life-span goals.

Life-Span Plan Answer

Answers will vary. Students should explain why computer skills are important for achieving life-span goals.

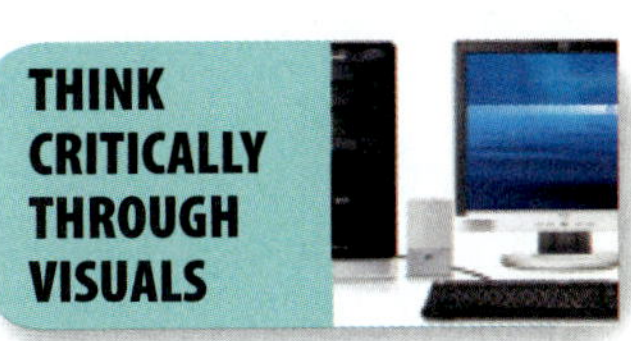

THINK CRITICALLY THROUGH VISUALS

It is easier to manage information with computers than without them because computers can access and store a vast amount of information very quickly.

268

TEACH

Explain the difference between the Internet and an intranet. Ask students to try to describe situations when each might be used.

Ask students to suggest possible uses of local computer networks in businesses and other organizations.

ONGOING ASSESSMENT

checkpoint >> **ANSWER**

The four main elements of a computer system are the input device(s), processing unit, memory and storage, and output device(s).

TEACH

Explain the various types of input devices.

Ask students to describe input devices they have used.

THINK CRITICALLY THROUGH VISUALS

Student answers will vary and will hopefully be quite creative. So many once unimaginable input devices have already been invented that this might be a difficult question.

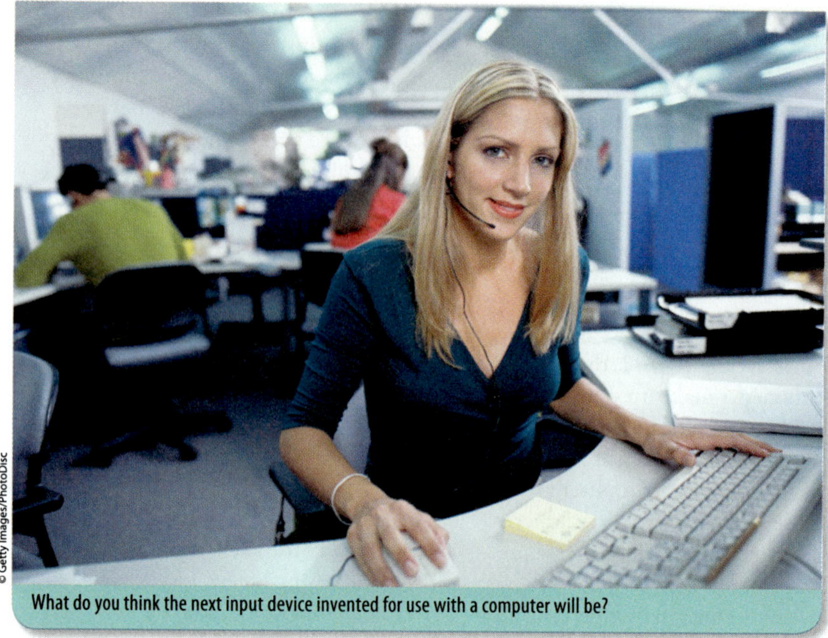

What do you think the next input device invented for use with a computer will be?

© Getty Images/PhotoDisc

main idea

Describe input devices and processing activities.

music, government publications, current news, weather, and sports. The World Wide Web is also an important source for handling business transactions.

A local computer network, sometimes called an *intranet,* is an organization's private computer network. It is based on the same communication standards as the Internet. An intranet is a smaller version of the Internet. Only members or employees can utilize an intranet. An intranet's web site looks and functions just like a typical web site, but it is private and only accessible to authorized users.

Like the Internet, an intranet is primarily used to share information. An intranet is an effective tool for saving time and money for companies. It can bring many benefits to an organization.

checkpoint >>

List the four main elements of a computer system.

INPUT AND PROCESSING

Computer systems start with the entering of data or other input items. Operation of the system continues with the processing of the data.

Input: Getting Started

The first major component of a computer system is known as input. While people are mostly concerned with the results of computer operations, there has to be a starting point. Data is entered into a computer system with an input device.

The keyboard is a common input device. Keyboards are generally used to enter text and numbers. Another common input device is the *mouse,* a hand-controlled device used to point to commands or images on the computer screen.

Other input devices are often used for specific activities. The following list includes some common examples.

Different Learning Abilities

Limited English Proficiency (LEP) Obtain translations of the four components of a computer system, as well as other key terms in the lesson, to reinforce these concepts in both English and other dominant languages used by students. Use visuals and have students name the items in both English and other languages.

- Touchpads built into laptop computers allow you to point and click just as you would with a mouse.
- Controllers and joysticks for video games allow you to direct the actions of game characters.
- Touch-sensitive screens allow you to use finger contact to enter data, give commands, and make selections.
- Light pens, which are handheld input devices that detect the presence of light, can be used to draw on a computer screen. They can also be pointed at the screen to enter data, make a selection, or give a command.
- Scanners translate words and images into computer-readable formats.
- Voice-activated systems allow words spoken into a microphone to be entered as data or to be translated into instructions or commands.
- Microphones and cameras allow input of audio and video.

Processing: Making Things Happen

How does data become meaningful information to be used by organizations and individuals? *Processing* is the second major component of a computer system. This activity occurs in the **central processing unit (CPU)**, which is the control center of the computer.

The CPU is the "brain" of a computer system. In a personal computer, the CPU consists of tiny wafers or chips. These chips carry instructions and data using electronic pulses.

The most common way to give instructions to a computer is with a program. A **program** is a series of detailed, step-by-step instructions that tell the computer what functions to complete.

FYI

Biometric input devices are used to recognize fingerprints, facial features, voices, and eye patterns. These personal characteristics are scanned and processed to allow access to buildings, offices and other secured areas. They are also used to authorize access to computers, files, and specific transactions, including purchases.

Most powerful computer programs are in formats that are difficult to understand. The format of a computer program is a computer language. **Computer language** is a system of letters, words, numbers, and symbols used to communicate with a computer.

The two main types of computer programs are operating system software and application software. **Operating system software** translates commands and allows application programs to interact with the computer's hardware. The most commonly used operating system is Windows®. **Application software** refers to programs that perform specific tasks such as word processing,

What types of computer application software have you found most useful in your daily life?

database management, or accounting. Commonly used application software includes word processing, desktop publishing, database, spreadsheet, and presentation software.

Word Processing An organization's reports, correspondence, and other information are created with word processing software. This type of program allows the user to enter, store, revise, and print text for letters, memos, reports, or standard business forms.

Desktop Publishing Word processing activities may be expanded to produce newsletters, brochures, and other publications. Desktop publishing usually includes graphics software to prepare charts, graphs, and other visual elements. Today, computer graphics are commonly used in television commercials, movies, training materials, and in other settings with a need for visuals.

Database Software "Create a list of employees who speak a language used in Asia." This type of request would involve the use of *database software*. A database is an organized collection of information with data items related to one another in some way.

In recent years, *database marketing* has become popular. Software is used to maintain, analyze, and combine customer information files. The information about customers is then used to increase sales by better serving customer needs. For example, a household with young children might receive advertising about educational software. Using a database increases the chance of reaching potential customers who are likely to buy the product.

Spreadsheet In the past, accountants used worksheet paper with many rows and columns. Such a worksheet is an

FIGURE 11-1

How can spreadsheet software improve accuracy?

	A	B	C	D	E	F	G	H	I	J	K
1							PROFIT & LOSS - ACTUAL VS. BUDGET				
2											
3							Jan - Dec '04		Budget		$ Over/(Under) Budget
4											
5		Income									
6					Product Sales		432,144		450,000		(17,856)
7					Service Sales		471,866		500,000		(28,134)
8				Total Income			904,010		950,000		(45,990)
9				Cost of Goods Sold							
10					Payroll-Direct Labor		186,433		200,000		(13,567)
11					Subcontractors		201,074		172,500		28,574
12					Other Cost of Goods Sold		34,975		42,500		(7,525)
13				Total Cost Of Goods Sold			422,482		415,000		7,482
14		Gross Profit					481,528		535,000		(53,472)
15				Overhead Expenses							
16					Advertising		742		500		242
17					Bad Debts		1,050		0		1,050
18					Depreciation		17,433		17,500		(67)
19					Employee Benefits		32,876		35,000		(2,124)
20					Insurance		32,777		33,500		(723)
21					Office Expense		2,192		2,000		192
22					Payroll-Administrative		153,044		175,000		(21,956)
23					Professional Fees		12,125		11,750		375
24					Rent		67,200		67,200		0
25					Taxes-Business		16,433		17,000		(567)
26					Taxes-Payroll		34,362		38,000		(3,638)
27					Travel Expenses		15,273		12,200		3,073
28					Utilities		8,924		9,475		(551)
29				Total Expenses			394,431		419,125		(24,694)

Applied Skills

Word Processing/Office Technology Have students describe experiences with various software application programs. Ask them to prepare a brief demonstration of the software or to show a sample of output from these various applications.

example of a manually prepared spreadsheet. *Spreadsheet software* is a program that formats data in columns and rows in order to do calculations.

The location where a column and row intersect is called a *cell*. A spreadsheet is created with specific information, words, numbers, or formulas entered into the cells. Spreadsheets are used to prepare payroll records, financial statements, budgets, and other financial documents. (See Figure 11-1.)

Spreadsheet software may also be used to do a *what-if* analysis of a situation. For example, a manager may want to see the effect of different prices on profit. The spreadsheet automatically recalculates for each price.

Presentation Software Creating slide shows for educational and business seminars has become very common. The use of *presentation software* allows a speaker to show text, data, photos, and other visuals. These images may be accompanied by sound effects, music, or other audio. The use of multimedia elements adds to the value and enjoyment of presentations.

> *checkpoint* »
> What are common input devices?

MEMORY AND OUTPUT

Various programs must be stored for use in the computer system. Memory is also used for data processing activities.

Memory and Storage: Saving for Later

The third major component of a computer system is the *memory*. When in use, a program is stored in the computer's memory. This memory within the computer is also called *internal* (or *primary*) *storage*. During

Your school experiences are continually changing because of technology. Create a list of ways in which you have used computers and other technology in school settings and when doing homework. Discuss ways in which technology might be used to enhance the school learning environment.

processing, both the program and any data entered with an input device are stored in memory.

As shown in Figure 11-2 memory capacity is measured using units such as *bit, nibble, byte,* and *kilobyte (K).* To give you an idea of a computer's internal storage capacity, it would take at least a 1K computer to store the information on an average page in this book.

Primary storage cannot hold all of the programs and all of the data needed by computer users. Therefore, *external (or auxiliary) storage* that is not part of memory is available for storing both programs and data.

A hard disk is housed inside the computer allowing storage of billions of characters. CDs, DVDs, magnetic tapes, and flash memory sticks are examples of commonly used auxiliary storage devices.

Output: Obtaining Results

The final component of a computer system is known as *output.* This element is of greatest interest to most people. Your score on a video game, the results of a

main idea

Explain computer storage media and output types.

Memory Capacity	
Bit:	smallest unit
Nibble:	4 bits; a ½ byte
Byte:	8 bits
Kilobyte:	1,024 bytes
Megabyte:	a million bytes
Gigabyte:	a billion bytes
Terabyte:	a thousand gigabytes

FIGURE 11-2

Why is it important to know the number of bytes of memory capacity in a computer?

TEACH

Ask students to describe situations, other than a talk or lecture, in which presentation software might be used.

ONGOING ASSESSMENT

checkpoint » **ANSWER**

Common input devices include keyboard, mouse, game controller, joystick, touch-sensitive screen, scanner, voice-activated system, microphone, and camera.

Work as a Team

Encourage students to think of new ways to use technology in schools.

TEACH

Explain the importance of the memory component of a computer system.
Ask students to name various output devices. Discuss the benefits of various output devices.

FIGURE 11-2 *ANSWER*

It is important to know the number of bytes of memory capacity in a computer to determine whether there is room on the system for files or programs you wish to add.

Different Learning Abilities

Visually Impaired Make arrangements for students to touch and hold samples of various output devices and media to allow students to better understand these elements of a computer system.

TEACH

Provide explanations of the major output items listed on this page.

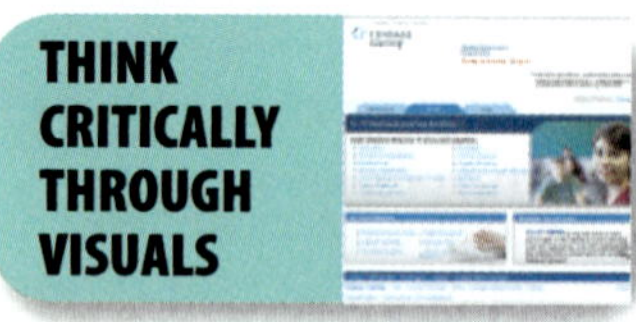

THINK CRITICALLY THROUGH VISUALS

A company web site can provide text, graphics, audio, and video output. Other examples are printed letters, forms, receipts, reports, mass mailings, and medical or school records.

ONGOING ASSESSMENT

checkpoint » **ANSWER**

Internal memory is inside the computer and holds a fixed amount of data. External memory is not stored within the computer and it is highly portable.

ASSESS

Key Concepts Answers

1. a. input
2. d. database
3. b. DVD

Make Academic Connections

4. If your class has the equipment and software, presentations can be created using software such as Microsoft PowerPoint.

5. After an initial investment, computer technology should help businesses run more efficiently with fewer people, so operating costs should decrease and profit should increase. Highly skilled computer workers might see an increase in their earnings. However, computer technology might decrease the need for unskilled labor.

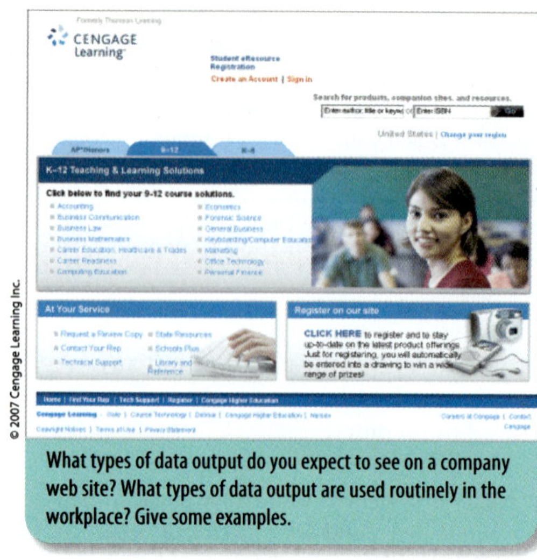

What types of data output do you expect to see on a company web site? What types of data output are used routinely in the workplace? Give some examples.

test, or the sales for a new product are important outcomes of data processing activities.

Output devices present data in a form that can be retrieved later or may be communicated immediately. There are four common types of output:

1. Text output, which includes processing results displayed on a computer screen (monitor) or in a printed report

2. Graphics output, which might include company logos, photos, drawings, scrolling messages, and animated graphics

3. Audio output, which involves music and broadcast clips as well as presentations for training seminars

4. Video output, which may be in the form of a training film, television commercial, or news report

Quite often, a single output source, such as a web site, includes more than one of these categories.

checkpoint »
How do internal and external memory differ?

11-1 Assessment

Xtra! Study Tools
school.cengage.com/business/introtobiz

Key Concepts

Determine the best answer.

1. An optical scanner is a device in the _?_ component of a computer system.
   a. input
   b. output
   c. memory
   d. processing

2. A list of potential customers for your new product would be created using _?_ software.
   a. desktop publishing
   b. word processing
   c. spreadsheet
   d. database

3. Which of the following is an example of auxiliary storage?
   a. CPU
   b. DVD
   c. monitor
   d. software

Make Academic Connections

4. **Technology** Prepare a visual presentation of a computer system and explain how each part works in the system.

5. **Economics** Describe how technology might affect the operating costs and profits of a company. What are possible effects of technology on the wages of workers?

RETEACH

Divide the class into four groups, each representing one component of the computer system. Have each group describe various activities associated with this element.

ENRICH

Have students develop a computer system for a local business or a company of their choice.

CLOSE

Ask students to compare computer systems that might be used in different business settings.

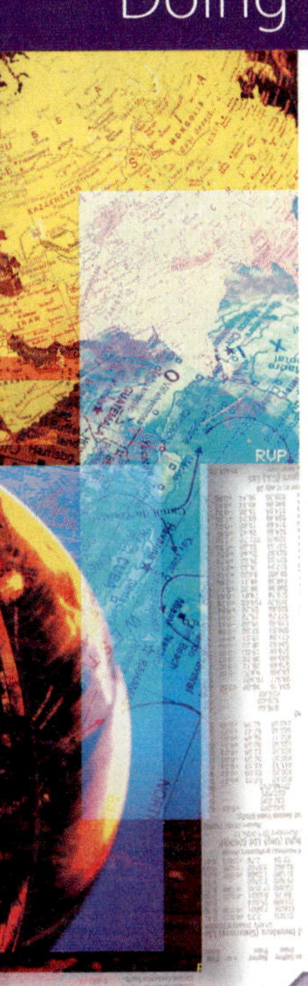

Official name
Arab Republic of Egypt

Capital
Cairo

Population
80.3 million

Currency
Egyptian pound

Major exports
crude oil and petroleum products, cotton, textiles, metal products, chemicals

Major exports partners
United States, Italy, Spain, Syria

Major imports
machinery and equipment, chemicals, wood products, fuels

Major import partners
United States, Italy, Germany, Spain, China

Source: CIA World Factbook

© Khaled El-Fiqi/Epa/Landov

Protected by deserts on both sides, Egypt has a tradition of architecture and culture. Today, the country is dependent on the fertile land along the Nile River. The Suez Canal provides a vital trade route between the Atlantic Ocean and the Indian Ocean.

As you enter a meeting in Egypt, several greetings may be used. The handshake is most common. Expect to see some traditional clothing, but foreign business-people should wear business suits. Clothing styles should always be modest and conservative. Even though it can be extremely hot, most of the body must remain covered. Even shirt collars are expected to be buttoned. You may be expected to take off your shoes, but only after following the lead of your host.

The workweek in Egypt runs from Saturday to Wednesday. Friday is the Muslim holy day, and most people also take off Thursday. In your negotiations, the pace will start slowly. Do not rush the situation. Because Egyptians must get to know you and like you before doing business, the decision process will take time. Also, be ready to compromise in your negotiations.

While the main language of Egypt is Arabic, many business discussions may be carried out in English or French. Business cards will be better received if one side is English and the other side is Arabic. Language mean-ing will not always be direct. A "yes" may in fact mean "possibly."

Be cautious of body language. The left hand is considered unclean in the Arab world. Always use your right hand unless both are needed, such as for lifting a heavy object. While Egyptians may gesture with their hands when speaking, pointing is considered very rude. The "thumbs up" sign is offensive.

Your conversations may include talk of soccer, basketball, and boxing. Avoid talking about political issues. In regard to food, many of the most popular Egyptian recipes are thousands of years old. Wheat and barley are the basis for many breads, pastries, and cakes. Peas, beans, lettuce, cucumbers, leeks, and other vegetables are often served with oil and vinegar dressing. Figs, dates, pomegranates, and grapes are important parts of the Egyptian diet, as are fish, poultry, lamb, and beef.

Think Critically

1. How does doing business in Egypt differ from business activities with which you are familiar?
2. What common mistakes might a person make when doing business in Egypt?
3. Conduct library or Internet research to find additional information about business and economic activities in Egypt.

Doing Business in…

While geographically located on the continent of Africa, Egypt is culturally linked to the Middle East. Remind students that most international business mistakes are the result of cultural differences.

Think Critically
Answers

1. Student answers will vary, but they will probably comment on the workweek running from Saturday through Thursday instead of from Monday through Friday, having a long getting-to-know-you phase before beginning negotiations instead of the western "let's get right down to business" approach, and the fact that "yes" can mean "possibly."

2. Because the left hand is considered unclean, a two-handed handshake, considered warm in the west, would be offensive. The cheerful thumbs up sign would be considered rude. Discussing hot political issues, which Americans do freely, would also be a mistake. Scheduling business meetings on Thursday or Friday or wearing short sleeves or shorts on a hot day would also send negative messages.

3. Students will find varied information about Egypt depending on what sources they locate during their library or Internet research. You may want to have each student share his or her most interesting findings.

Applied Skills

Geography Use maps in class or have students locate maps online to identify the location of Egypt and surrounding countries. Based on information derived from the map, have students suggest some types of business that might be common in this region.

TEACH

Ask students to explain why information is important for making decisions in business and other settings.

Explain the purpose of a management information system (MIS).

THINK CRITICALLY THROUGH VISUALS

Computer systems and software are essential parts of an MIS because they organize, process, and store an organization's vital information.

11-2 Business Applications of Technology

Goals

Describe the components of a management information system (MIS).

Identify computer applications in service industries.

Discuss e-commerce activities.

Key Terms

management information system (MIS)

computer-assisted instruction (CAI)

e-commerce

Focus on **Real Life**

Josh Aki arrived on the first day of his new part-time job at NBI Distributors. This retailing company sells an array of products by mail, telephone orders, and via the Internet.

During orientation, Josh met the sales manager and learned that some of the firm's products were doing well and others were just sitting in the warehouse. After he got settled at his desk, Josh's supervisor said, "Josh, please outline a report with the sales results of the new products we have introduced over the past six months. Alicia will help you get started."

After some initial pleasantries, Alicia showed Josh how to check the database for sales results. She suggested that he summarize the data on the spreadsheet program and prepare his report with word processing software.

"Thanks, will you be around if I need more help?" Josh asked.

Alicia smiled and said, "Sure, Josh. Welcome to the NBI team."

---

main idea

Describe the components of a management information system (MIS).

MANAGEMENT INFORMATION SYSTEMS

Managers need information to make business decisions. A **management information system (MIS)** is a coordinated system of processing and reporting information in an organization. Computer systems and software are essential parts of management information systems.

A company may need a departmental budget that provides information on expected income and expenses for the next three months. Using an accounting program, past company data and future projections can be processed to create this budget. Budgets help with day-to-day decisions and planning for the future.

Components of an MIS

As shown in Figure 11-3 on the next page, the four main components of an MIS are gathering data, analyzing data, storing data, and reporting results. These activities

© Digital Vision

Why are computer systems and software essential parts of an MIS?

Applied Skills

Technology Ask students to explain why information needs vary for different types of industries. Help start the discussion by asking students to think about the information needs of a particular business such as a local manufacturing company.

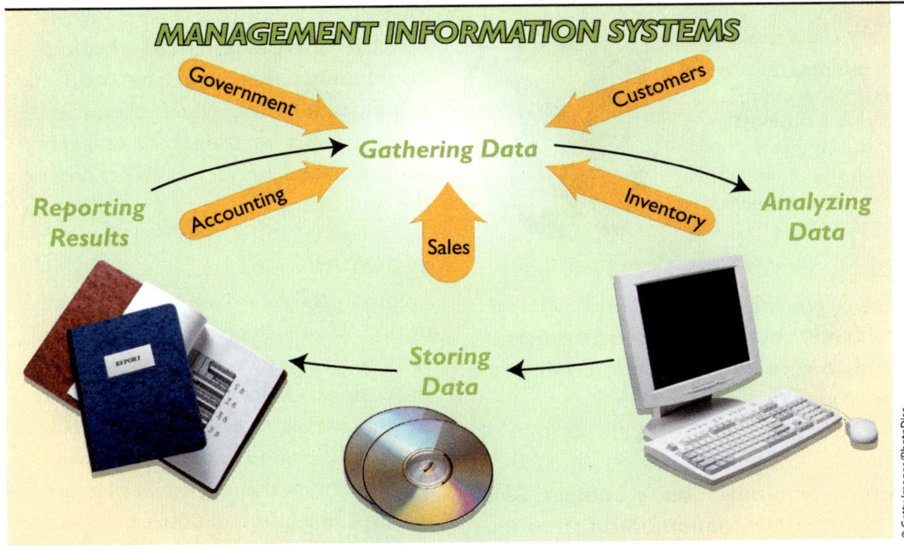

allow an organization to obtain needed information in four main categories—financial, production and inventory, marketing and sales, and human resources.

1. *Financial information,* including budgets, sales reports, and financial statements

2. *Production and inventory information,* including production summaries, lists of tools and supplies, and finished goods reports

3. *Marketing and sales information,* including data on customer needs, current economic conditions, and actions of competitors

4. *Human resources information,* including salaries, employee benefit data, and employee evaluations

Data Sources

The information for an MIS comes from several sources. *External* data sources are outside an organization. Financial institutions, government agencies, and customers are examples of external data sources.

In contrast, *internal* data sources provide input from within the organization. Internal data includes accounting records, inventory information, and company sales figures. While gathering raw data may be an easy task, changing these facts and figures into meaningful information is the major goal of an MIS.

The MIS in Action

What activities are involved in a management information system? How is needed information communicated to managers? The operation of the MIS involves the following steps:

1. Identify the information needs of the organization.

2. Obtain facts, figures, and other data.

3. Process, analyze, and organize data in a useful manner.

4. Distribute information reports to those who make decisions.

5. Update data files as needed.

Computer networks are often used in an MIS to distribute information to

TEACH

Use Figure 11-3 to provide an overview of elements of a management information system (MIS).

Explain the four types of information most commonly used by businesses.

Contrast the difference between external and internal data sources. Ask students to name examples of each.

Describe the five steps of a management information system (MIS).

FIGURE 11-3 *ANSWER*

Students should respond that information is often collected from multiple sources. Information must then be analyzed and stored so it can be accessed for developing reports. Provide examples of how information is used to make decisions in business, schools, government, and other organizations.

Different Learning Styles

Kinesthetic Learner Have students use Figure 11-3 and the steps involved in the operation of an MIS to create a poster, tabletop display, or slide presentation. Provide an opportunity for students to display their work.

managers, employees, and others. These networks connect computers, printers, and other equipment within a company or around the world.

Worldwide networks are set up through telephone lines, satellites, and other communication technology. Also important for communicating information is e-mail. E-mail gives users the ability to send data quickly through a computer system. After an employee prepares a letter or report, the document is sent electronically to another computer on the local or worldwide network.

checkpoint >>

What are the four components of a management information system?

main idea

Identify computer applications in service industries.

TECHNOLOGY IN SERVICE INDUSTRIES

More than 60 percent of workers in the United States are employed in service industries. The use of computers in these organizations is extensive.

Public Service

Government agencies use computers to keep records. For example, the federal government keeps social security records for all past and present workers in the United States and military records for people who have served in the armed forces.

Agencies are always expanding their use of computers. Medical information can be found within seconds to save lives. Police records can be sent to other locations minutes after a crime has occurred, helping to solve the crime. Schools and other agencies can transfer records easily when someone moves to another area of the country.

Education

Computers have become vital teaching devices. Computers make it possible to train and test workers in a range of professions. Office workers learn to use word processing software in their daily tasks. At the same time, they receive instruction on the proper use of grammar, spelling, punctuation, capitalization, and document formats. Airline pilots use computerized simulators to learn and improve skills needed for flying new types of aircraft.

Computer-assisted instruction (CAI) is the use of computers to help people learn or improve skills at their own pace. With CAI, students work at a speed that best serves their needs. The student does not have to go to a school building for instruction. The student

How have computers changed the classroom in recent years?

can learn at home on a computer network system connected to a central training location.

The demand for computer and *information technology* (IT) training in the workplace continues to grow. With the proper computer skills, you will be able to compete for some of the best-paying jobs in the business world.

Health Care

Computers are widely used in hospitals and other medical facilities. Uses range from keeping patient records to monitoring medications during surgery.

Medical professionals are also able to see to the healthcare needs of people in rural areas without leaving the city. The use of *telemedicine* with videoconference equipment allows diagnosis by a doctor in a different location, followed by treatment provided by a local healthcare professional. Technology of this type helps to expand the availability of health care in remote areas of less developed economies.

Financial Services

Paying bills online, checking your credit report, and selling stocks and bonds are just a few examples of computerized financial activities. Electronic banking and other financial services have made it possible for consumers to do business beyond usual banking hours. Each day, computers transfer billions of dollars. Payments to workers, businesses, and government flow through local and global computer networks.

Most people are familiar with credit cards and cash cards. You may not be aware of the existence of *smart cards*. These plastic cards with a silicon chip are used to store information. The chip within the card stores such data as your current account balance and credit history. It may even store medical information for emergencies.

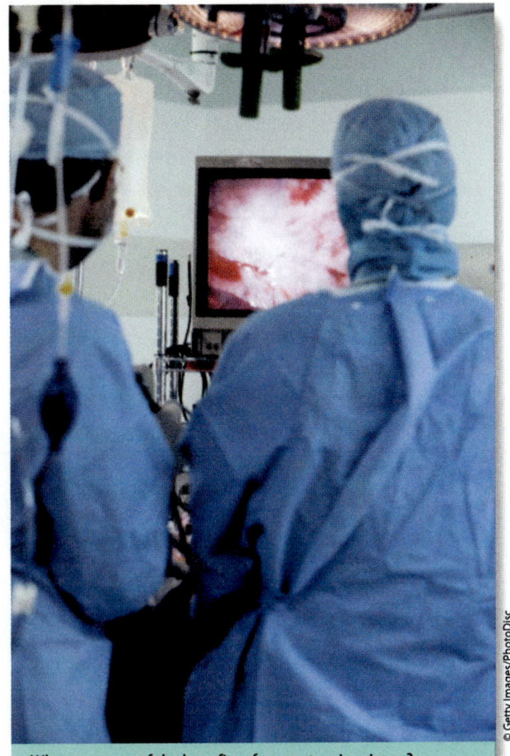

What are some of the benefits of computers in science?

The card could serve as a personal record keeper for travel and other expenses. In addition, a smart card can be used to prove you paid for merchandise you want to exchange, to gain admittance to your place of work, or to unlock and start your car without keys.

checkpoint >>

What service industries make extensive use of computers?

FYI

The use of mobile phones and other wireless technology is sometimes called "m-commerce" (m for mobile). Various handheld devices are expanding and enhancing e-commerce activities. Instant messaging, stock trading, banking, online buying, music, and sports video clips are most common. About one-third of the world's population will be using wireless technology in the near future.

TEACH

Explain the importance of information technology (IT) departments in every type of organization.

Ask students to share some experiences or observations of technology use in health care and medical fields.

Describe uses of computer systems for banking, insurance, and other financial services.

Use the FYI feature to point out the expanded use of wireless technology in various business settings.

THINK CRITICALLY THROUGH VISUALS

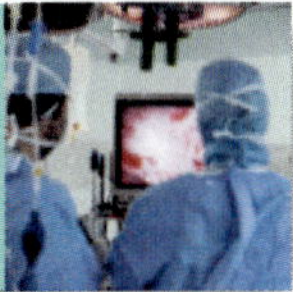

Computers allow scientists to work with large and complex calculations and vast amounts of data so they can quickly and accurately draw conclusions from experiments and extrapolate their findings to solve challenging problems.

ONGOING ASSESSMENT

checkpoint >> ANSWER

Service industries that make extensive use of computers include public service organizations such as government, military, and police agencies; educational institutions such as local school districts, community colleges, and universities; health care facilities, such as hospitals and doctors' offices; and financial services industries, such as banks and insurance companies.

PROJECT

Provide the following instructions to students. (These instructions also appear on page xxv of the textbook.) Explain how you believe the growth of e-commerce will affect the life-span goals you set or your ability to achieve them.

Life-Span Plan Answer

Answers will vary. Students should describe how the growth of e-commerce has changed the life-span goals they might set for themselves.

TEACH

Explain the basics of e-commerce. Point out that e-commerce involves more than buying and selling online. Point out the e-commerce activities listed on this page.

Describe examples of B2C and B2B transactions— the most common e-commerce patterns.

THINK CRITICALLY THROUGH VISUALS

Many students may assert that e-commerce provides more opportunities for today's entrepreneur because it allows for easy entry into markets at low costs. It also opens up the entire world as a possible market.

FIGURE 11-4 *ANSWER*

Answers will vary. Students should discuss how the Internet allows buyers and sellers to communicate, exchange information about products and prices, and facilitate purchases.

---

main idea

Discuss e-commerce activities.

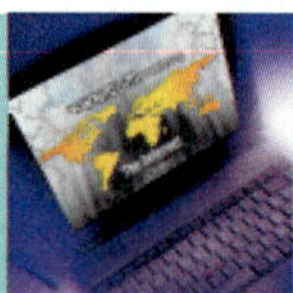

E-COMMERCE

You are walking through the mall. As you pass a clothing store, a message appears on your cell phone screen. "Now on special for spring, waterproof jackets, $34.95." This targeted promotion is just one example of the fast, powerful capabilities of e-commerce and wireless technology.

E-commerce (e for *electronic*) refers to conducting business transactions using the Internet or other technology. These online business activities come in a range of forms. Almost every function of a company has been adapted to e-commerce. The most common e-commerce activities include:

- Providing product information
- Promoting a company
- Selling online
- Conducting market research
- Making payments
- Obtaining parts and supplies
- Tracking shipments

Types of E-Commerce

E-commerce opens up opportunities to companies previously limited by geographic, financial, or political

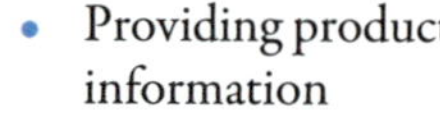

Do you think e-commerce provides more opportunities for the entrepreneur?

restrictions. These online economic activities involve four basic models with two selling and buying parties: businesses (B) and consumers (C). See Figure 11-4.

The first and most familiar model is Business-to-Consumer, or B2C. Expanded sales of products in different geographic markets will create B2C growth. Examples are online companies such as Amazon.com and Dell.

The second e-commerce model is Business-to-Business, or B2B. These online exchanges are the largest and fastest-growing segment of e-commerce. They account for more than 80 percent of Internet transactions. Examples are Ford and General Motors buying parts online from their suppliers.

Consumer-to-Business (C2B) is the third e-commerce model. In C2B, consumers originate online transactions through price offers to businesses. The online company Priceline was one of the first companies in this category. Priceline

FIGURE 11-4

How does the Internet help each of these e-commerce models operate efficiently?

E-Commerce Matrix

		Seller	
		Business	Consumer
Buyer	Business	B2B	B2C
	Consumer	C2B	C2C

Applied Skills

Technology Have students investigate the use of blogs (web logs) on various topics. What are the benefits and drawbacks of this communication activity?

allows shoppers to make bids for products and services such as airline tickets and hotels. The airline and hotel companies then decide whether to accept the offers. While small at this stage of online development, C2B could expand with new technologies and consumer initiatives.

Finally, Consumer-to-Consumer (C2C) is the fourth e-commerce model. In the long economic tradition of bartering and auctions, buying and selling among consumers is growing in cyberspace. The ease and speed of transactions among online parties is encouraging more C2C exchanges. An example is the online company eBay.

Global E-Commerce

Internet-based computer systems, along with software that translates information from one language to another, make it possible to do business around the world without leaving your computer. Instant transmission of data with the use of satellites makes even the farthest point on earth as close as a button on your computer. Increased global business can have an important impact on world trade and international relations.

Importing and exporting can take place using a computer system. The goods are shipped from the closest location to save time and money. For example, you may order an item from a company in Italy using your computer. When the Italian marketers receive your order on their computer, they check a database and find there are five such items in stock in Canada. They instruct the Canadian importers through the Internet to ship the items to you. You receive them the next day.

You pay the Italian company. Later, the Italian and Canadian companies settle their accounts through the computerized banking system.

Another way of bringing people together to do business is *videoconferencing*. This system allows people in different geographic locations to meet "face-to-face" by satellite. It is used for sales presentations, training sessions, and other types of meetings. A sales staff in Peru can make a presentation to potential customers in Spain, South Africa, Pakistan, and the United States without leaving their offices in Lima.

> *checkpoint* >>
> What do the notations B2C and B2B mean?

11-2 Assessment

Key Concepts

Determine the best answer.

1. An example of external data would be
   a. a company sales report
   b. a list of employee qualifications
   c. a government economic forecast
   d. payroll records

2. CAI refers to
   a. paying bills online
   b. electronic inventory control
   c. providing health care to remote areas
   d. individualized instruction

3. When a packaged food producer sells items to a restaurant, this is considered to be a _?_ e-commerce transaction.
   a. B2C   c. C2B
   b. B2B   d. C2C

Make Academic Connections

4. **Visual Art** Create a visual presentation of a management information system for a specific information flow for a company of your choice.

5. **Culture** Research other cultures to determine how people in these societies might react to various aspects of e-commerce.

Ask students to point out benefits and limitations of global e-commerce.

Have students list the types of businesses that would best be served by global e-commerce.

ONGOING ASSESSMENT

checkpoint >> **ANSWER**

The notation B2C refers to the Business-to-Consumer e-commerce model, while B2B means the Business-to-Business e-commerce model.

ASSESS

Key Concepts Answers

1. c. a government economic forecast

2. d. individualized instruction

3. b. B2B

Make Academic Connections

4. Presentations will vary depending on the companies whose management information systems they choose to illustrate.

5. Findings will vary. For example, potential buyers in Middle Eastern and African cultures who value face-to-face negotiation before closing a business deal might resist the impersonal nature of e-commerce.

CLOSE

Ask students to describe the uses of technology by various businesses in your community.

RETEACH

Ask students to discuss the purpose and elements of a management information system (MIS).

ENRICH

Have students design a product that might be sold online to consumers around the world. Invite interested students to plan a web site to accommodate e-commerce for this product.

11-3 Other Technology Issues

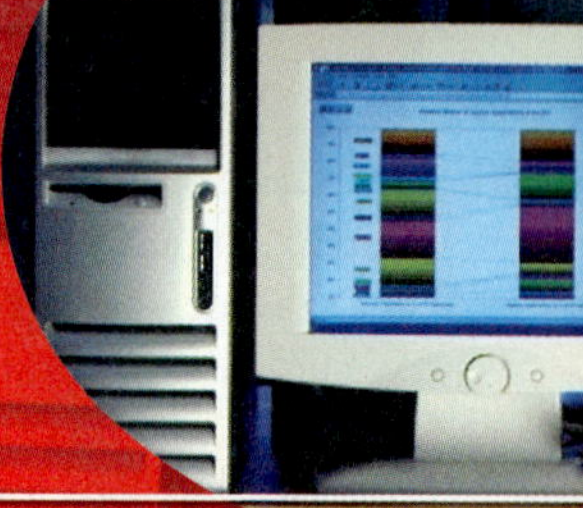

Goals

Explain workplace uses of technology.

Identify home and personal applications of technology.

Discuss social concerns related to technology.

Key Terms

robotics

artificial intelligence (AI)

expert system

computer-aided design (CAD)

telecommuting

piracy

computer virus

Focus on Real Life

Herb Cunningham has just lost his third job in seven years. Although he is a talented worker, demand for his skills as a bookkeeper is declining. Computerized accounting systems keep track of sales and expenses in most companies.

"I guess it's time to upgrade my skills," Herb commented to his son, Joe. "I'm going to enroll in a training class for accounting software while I'm looking for another job."

"That's a good idea, but it might not be enough, Dad," responded Joe. "You should learn how to use spreadsheets, work with tax software, and download information from the Internet."

"I'm not sure I'll be able to learn how to do all of those things," was Herb's reply.

"But, Dad, I'll be here to help you," said Joe, "and you can start by letting me show you how to use the computer to apply for jobs."

---

main idea

Explain workplace uses of technology.

WORKPLACE TECHNOLOGY

Computers are present in almost every business situation. They help improve efficiency and productivity. Computers can be found in oil fields, warehouses, retail stores, hospitals, offices, and factories.

Robotics

Most of you have seen robots and other computer systems in science fiction movies set in outer space and in the future. In real life, **robotics** involves mechanical devices programmed to do routine tasks, such as those in many factories. An example of work where robots are used is assembly line work that requires repetitive tasks.

Early robots did only simple tasks such as tightening a bolt on an automobile. Today, robots exist that can see, hear, smell, and feel. Robots are able to work 24 hours a day. These computerized workers can perform in dangerous situations such as in outer space, underwater, or underground. The use of robots is also growing to include automated checkout clerks, airline ticket agents, and hotel desk clerks.

Expert Systems

Have you ever wanted a quick answer to a question without having to find a book or person who knew the answer? **Artificial intelligence (AI)** is software that enables computers to reason, learn, and make decisions. It uses logical methods similar to the methods humans use. An example of artificial intelligence is computer programs that make decisions about complex topics. For example, software exists that asks people questions about their health in order to determine solutions for potential medical problems.

Different Learning Abilities

Dyslexia Prepare some short assignments requiring answers with a few words to help students understand robotics and expert systems. For example, ask students to make a list of specific uses of robotics. Encourage all students to participate.

This software allows people in areas without doctors to receive better medical care.

Computer programs that help people solve technical problems are called **expert systems.** They are now available for medical services, financial planning, and legal matters. Expert systems are based on the knowledge of human experts in many specialized areas. These systems provide intelligent answers as effectively as human experts in those subject matters. For example, employees of the Internal Revenue Service use an expert system to quickly answer questions from taxpayers.

Computer-Aided Design

Computers created many of the products you use each day. **Computer-aided design (CAD)** refers to the use of technology to create product styles and designs. CAD allows you to try different sizes, shapes, and materials for a new machine, automobile, or food package. This process can be used to experiment with many variations before spending time and money building a model or going into production.

Telecommuting

Each morning, more than 20 million Americans travel to their offices—in another room of their homes! These people do all or part of their work at home. **Telecommuting** involves the activities of a worker using a computer at home to do a job. Telecommuting saves travel time and costs. It results in less traffic along with reduced noise and air pollution.

Each year more and more people become telecommuters. This working arrangement is especially attractive to people who have a hard time leaving their home to go to work. These include workers who are disabled or parents who desire to be with their young children. A work-at-home arrangement is most common

© Digital Vision

What types of businesses might use computer-aided design?

among workers such as writers and editors, researchers, accounting clerks, sales representatives, computer programmers, and web site designers.

These workers can easily send their reports, documents, and ideas to their employers by computer. Telecommuting is made possible with computers and other technology. E-mail and faxes allow a person to communicate with the company's main office.

checkpoint »
How is computer-aided design (CAD) used by businesses?

TEACH

Ask students to name situations in which expert systems might be used.

Explain the uses of computer-aided design (CAD) in various settings.

Have students describe work situations that would be appropriate for *telecommuting.*

THINK CRITICALLY THROUGH VISUALS

Computer-aided design (CAD) is a wonderful tool for businesses such as architects, engineering firms, packaging designers, manufacturers, and any business that needs to create a three-dimensional object.

ONGOING ASSESSMENT

checkpoint » **ANSWER**

Businesses use CAD to experiment with many variations of different sizes, shapes, and materials before spending time and money on building prototypes or starting actual production.

Applied Skills

Science Have students research the use of computer-aided design (CAD) in various laboratory and production settings.

Teaching Strategies

Expand Beyond the Classroom
Invite a local business professional to speak to students about robotics, expert systems, computer-aided design, or telecommuting.

HOME AND PERSONAL TECHNOLOGY

Computers not only change the way you work, but technology also affects almost all aspects of life.

School and Homework

Internet studies reveal that computers are a key homework tool for students. For many students, more than one-third of homework time involves the computer. More than half of all students think the computer is their most important homework resource.

Students today find many uses for the computer. Online encyclopedias, presentation software, and other technology are increasing your skill to communicate and use ideas.

Home Robotics

Robots are no longer just in factories and businesses. Computerized systems now exist for repetitive chores such as vacuuming and mowing the lawn. Toys and other electronic devices for children can both entertain and educate. In the future, you can expect home robots to monitor household appliances, roll trash cans to the street, and assist the elderly with lifting heavy items.

Household Record Keeping

Computer systems are becoming information centers in people's homes. They

What are some types of software that can make household activities easier?

are used for sending and receiving e-mail, shopping online, keeping financial records, completing homework assignments, and downloading music and videos.

Programs can keep a list of names and addresses of people to whom you send greeting cards. You may store your favorite recipes by categories. A family's medical history can be kept on file. You can have an inventory of household items for insurance records in case of theft or damage. In addition, computer programs may be used for personal financial record keeping, budgeting, writing checks, and preparing your income tax return.

checkpoint >>
What types of technology tools are available to students?

NET Bookmark

Finding fast and accurate information on the Internet is the goal of most Web searches. With several search engines available, how do you select the one that is best for your needs? Access the web site shown below and click on the link for Chapter 11. Obtain suggestions to follow when conducting a Web search.

school.cengage.com/business/introtobiz

Applied Skills

Mathematics Have students survey friends and relatives to obtain data on the types of software most commonly used in homes. Have students work in small groups to combine their data and create a graph reporting the results of their surveys.

SOCIAL CONCERNS OF TECHNOLOGY

New technology will continue to expand the potential uses of computers in business. New software will eliminate some jobs while increasing job growth in others. It will also continue to change the way work is done.

Expanded computer use has resulted in concerns about health and safety, criminal activities, and privacy. While computers are beneficial to society, the wise person will not place complete faith in the reliability or safety of computer systems.

Employment Trends

Many people think computers are taking away their jobs. What is actually occurring is a shift in the job duties and skills needed to work in business and industry. When computers replace workers, companies need to retrain the workers with skills in programming, operating, or repairing computer systems.

Displaced workers are workers who are unemployed because of changing job conditions. They must adapt to the changing job market in order to have continued employment. What actions can companies and workers take to be ready for the new jobs of the future?

Computers and other technology are becoming more important in our lives each day. The ability to use this technology is vital to each person's economic survival. *Computer literacy* is the ability to use computers to process information or solve problems. You do not have to understand how to program a computer in order to use it. You do need to know how to enter, store, process, and retrieve information.

Health Concerns

Various products and substances can be dangerous. While little danger exists from using computers and other technology, some people have encountered discomfort resulting from on-the-job activities. For example, eyestrain and vision problems have been linked with prolonged work at computer screens. Muscle tension and nerve damage can occur from too many hours at a keyboard. These and other concerns have resulted in guidelines from labor organizations and government agencies for safe computer operation.

Computer Crime

Widespread use of computers has led to an increase in white-collar crime. *White-collar crime* is illegal acts carried out by office or professional workers while at work. Workers may steal money, information, or computer time through improper use of databases or illegal access to computer systems.

While the typical bank robbery results in a loss of $10,000, computer crimes involving bank records average hundreds of thousands of dollars. Theft of a physical item is obvious. Theft of computer time

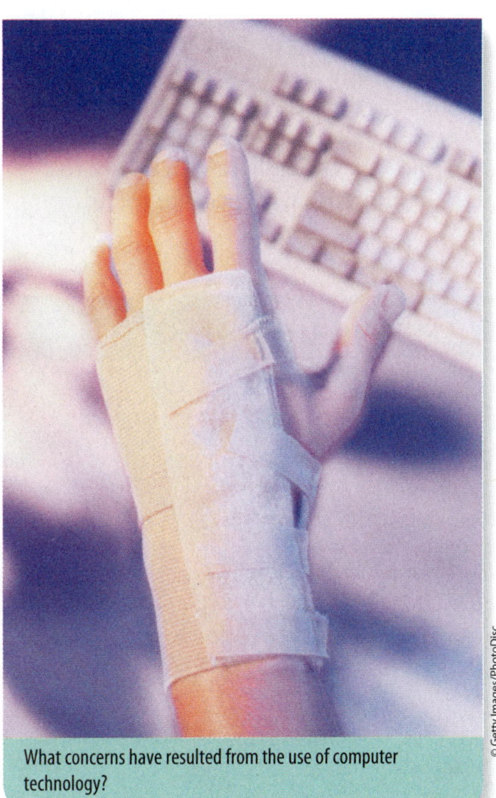

What concerns have resulted from the use of computer technology?

Discuss social concerns related to technology.

TEACH

Ask students to name some concerns that could result from technology.

Point out the need for continuing education related to technology.

Explain potential health concerns related to technology.

Ask students to explain the costs to society that result from criminal activity using computers.

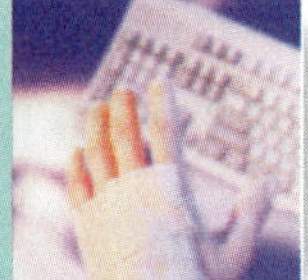

THINK CRITICALLY THROUGH VISUALS

The use of computer technology has brought benefits but also concerns. Repetitious motions in non-ergonomic computer work environments have led to carpal tunnel syndrome, possible eyestrain, and other health problems. Other areas of concern are the displacement of some workers by new computer technology and new opportunities for white-collar computer crime, identity theft, piracy of computer software and other copyrighted materials, identity theft and other privacy concerns, and the ravages of computer hackers and virus creators.

Different Learning Styles

Print Learner Use the headings on pages 283 and 284 to emphasize the main social concerns associated with computers and technology.

In addition, encourage students to use library and Internet resources to read more on these topics.

Work as a Team

The workplace is constantly changing because of technology. Some jobs are eliminated, while others are created. Describe various career skills and activities that will be needed to work with technology in the future.

or information from a database is usually harder to detect.

Piracy is stealing or illegally copying software packages or information. It can be a significant problem. In some countries, between one-third and one-half of the software used is obtained illegally. Companies that develop software may lose more than half of their profits to information pirates who violate the law. Copyright laws apply to software as well as books and music.

Destructive efforts are also a concern to computer users. A **computer virus** is program code hidden in a system that can later do damage to software or stored data. The virus may be programmed to become active on a certain date or when certain data is accessed. Some computer viruses are harmless, only showing up as a funny message. Others have been known to destroy critical government records.

Privacy Concerns

One of the greatest challenges facing computer users is the need to guarantee privacy. Some dishonest people have learned how to illegally access computer databases. While some laws exist to protect your privacy, many concerned people believe these regulations are not strong enough. Some businesses are becoming stricter about who can access and use company information. Tighter security systems are being developed. Some organizations change the password needed to access information several times a day to protect their databases.

In recent years, *identity theft* has become a major concern for consumers and companies. Thieves obtain information online about a person. They apply for a credit card in the person's name or access the bank account of that person. Each day, more than 1,000 people have their identities stolen in the United States. Con artists illegally obtain millions of dollars each year through identity theft.

> *checkpoint* >>
> How do companies suffer from software piracy?

11-3 Assessment

Key Concepts

Determine the best answer.

1. Telecommuting refers to
   a. the use of computers to design products
   b. working at home by computer
   c. difficulties from overusing computers
   d. illegal acts of office workers

2. Hidden software code that can damage computer operations is
   a. piracy
   b. a displaced worker
   c. a virus
   d. computer literacy

3. Illegal acts carried out by office or professional workers while at work are referred to as
   a. computer crime
   b. identity theft
   c. piracy
   d. white-collar crime

Make Academic Connections

4. *Communication* Prepare a memo that sets out the benefits of telecommuting for an organization. In your memo, present specific details of a job that would be appropriate for telecommuting.

5. *Music* Select three different types of music. Discuss how each might be appropriate or inappropriate for an office setting to reduce stress associated with working on computers.

RETEACH

Ask students to name the major uses of computers and technology in homes.

ENRICH

Have students explain the use of technology in developing economies to improve quality of life.

CLOSE

Ask students to describe actions that might be taken to address various concerns associated with technology.

Co-op America

"Every time you make a purchase, the money that leaves your hands goes to work."

In an effort to make sure these dollars work to better serve the interests of consumers, workers, and society, Co-op America was created based on the belief that your purchases can support businesses that create jobs, care about their communities, engage in fair trade, and protect the environment. The organization's mission is "to harness economic power—the strength of consumers, businesses and the marketplace—to create a socially just and environmentally sustainable society."

Co-op America was started in 1982 and provides practical tools to address today's social and environmental problems. While many environmental organizations fight political and legal battles, Co-op America educates people and business about making improvements through the economic system.

The main programs of Co-op America are:

- The Green Business Program, designed to start small socially and environmentally responsible businesses

- The Responsible Shopper Program, which informs people about how to vote with their dollars to make changes

- The Boycotts Program, which encourages corporations to become socially and environmentally responsible and provides information about boycotts and shareholder

resolutions against irresponsible companies

- The Living Green Program, providing information about practical measures people can take to make their personal, community, and work lives more meaningful and sustainable

Co-op America publishes a variety of materials. The organization's *National Green Pages* is a directory of America's leading socially and environmentally responsible businesses.

Co-op America has 65,000 individual members and 2,500 member businesses that work together to achieve the goals of the organization. In addition, Co-op America manages the Social Investment Forum, a trade organization for socially responsible investing professionals.

Each day, Co-op America encourages consumers to rethink their buying habits. Your purchases should be with companies that are trying to become more socially and environmentally responsible. Investors are encouraged to support socially responsible companies. Most importantly, Co-op America wants consumers, investors, and businesses to demand change—change that starts in their own homes and businesses.

Think Critically

1. How does Co-op America serve consumers and businesses in our society?

2. What aspect of Co-op America do you believe is most valuable for people in your state or community?

3. Go to the web site of Co-op America to obtain additional details about the activities of this organization.

Explain the benefits of cooperatives for consumers and society. Describe how co-ops might better serve the needs of consumers, small businesses, and society in general.

Think Critically Answers

1. Co-op America serves consumers and businesses in our society by helping them make informed decisions so that they can "vote" for environmentally and socially responsible companies through their purchases.

2. Answers will vary depending on the state in which you live.

3. Students visit the Co-op America web site to gain additional information about this innovative service. You may want to have them search the site for information about companies and activities in your state.

Communicate Business Concepts Answers

1. a. monitor—hardware

b. word processing program—software

c. chips—hardware

d. keyboard—hardware

e. operating system program—software

f. disk drive—hardware

g. mouse—hardware

h. printer—hardware

2. Examples include bank tellers, cashiers, order takers, and teachers.

3. a. spreadsheet software

b. database software

c. word processing software

d. graphics software or any program containing a chart feature

e. spreadsheet software

f. database software

g. word processing software (could merge data from database software).

4. External data would include government reports and information provided by customers and financial institutions. Internal data could include a company's own accounting records, inventory information, employee records, and sales figures.

5. Schools could benefit because each teacher could reach more students. Schools would not have to provide facilities. Students could benefit because they could continue their education while employed, save time and money by not commuting, and learn at their own pace.

6. Workers benefit because they save time and money by not having to commute. They also gain flexibility in their schedules. Employers benefit because they do not have to provide resources for employees who are not in the office. They also gain employee loyalty. Society benefits because more workers are able to adjust their schedules to care for family. Companies operate more efficiently, possibly leading to lower prices. Also, home-based workers do not commute, taking some pressure off of city rush hours and the environment.

7. E-commerce has expanded global business by providing a lower-cost way to enter the business world. E-commerce allows a business owner to serve customers anywhere that packages can be delivered, lessening the disadvantage of a remote location.

Business Notes

11-1 COMPUTER SYSTEMS

1. Computer systems consist of four main components: the input device, the processing unit, the memory and storage facilities, and an output device.

2. Commonly used input devices include the keyboard, mouse, video game controllers, touch-sensitive screens, scanners, and voice-activated mechanisms.

3. The main types of storage devices are the internal memory in a computer and external memory such as disks, CDs, DVDs, magnetic tape, and flash memory sticks. Data processing results are reported as text output, graphics output, audio output, or video output.

11-2 BUSINESS APPLICATIONS OF TECHNOLOGY

4. The four main components of a management information system (MIS) are gathering data, analyzing data, storing data, and reporting results. The goal of an MIS is to change raw data (facts and figures) into information that can be used by managers.

5. Service industries that make extensive use of computers and technology include public service organizations, educational institutions, healthcare facilities, and financial service organizations.

6. E-commerce involves the conducting of business transactions over the Internet or through other electronic technology.

11-3 OTHER TECHNOLOGY ISSUES

7. Robotics, expert systems, computer-aided design (CAD), and telecommuting are used in a variety of business situations to help improve efficiency and productivity.

8. Personal technology applications include schoolwork, home robotics, and household recordkeeping.

9. Expanded technology and computer use can result in concerns about job loss, health and safety, criminal activities, privacy, and identity theft.

Communicate Business Concepts

1. Identify each of the following items as either *hardware* or *software*.

  a. monitor (screen)
  b. word processing program
  c. chips
  d. keyboard
  e. operating system program
  f. disk drive
  g. mouse
  h. printer

2. What are possible business activities currently performed by people that might be performed in the future using a computer system?

3. Identify whether word processing software, database software, spreadsheet software, or graphics software would be used to perform the following computer applications.

  a. Preparing a report of new equipment purchased for each office of a company
  b. Preparing a list of employees that is sorted by ZIP code
  c. Creating a form letter to go to new customers of a mail-order business
  d. Creating a pie chart showing the portion of sales of each product
  e. Preparing a document listing the total sales for each geographic area of the country
  f. Listing the employees who have not missed a day of work in five years
  g. Sending a letter to each employee who has not missed a day of work in five years

4. List examples of (a) external data and (b) internal data used by most companies.

5. Who would benefit from schools that would allow students to take classes at home by computer?

6. Describe the benefits to workers, employers, and society when an organization allows some of its employees to do all or part of their work at home.

7. How has e-commerce expanded global business in countries that previously had limited economic activity?

8. How is it possible for the increased use of computers to create more jobs than are lost?

9. How might expert systems be used in the future to help people solve medical, legal, financial, and other technical problems?

10. What are potential benefits from the use of smart cards in handling everyday transactions?

11. What actions could be taken by organizations to prevent computer crime?

Develop Your Business Language

Match the terms listed with the definitions.

12. Several computers linked into a single system.

13. Computer programs that perform specific tasks such as word processing, database management, or accounting.

14. Instructions that run a computer system.

15. The control center of the computer.

16. The combination of an input device, a processing unit, memory and storage facilities, and an output device.

17. Conducting business transactions over the Internet or using other technology.

18. Software that translates a computer user's commands and allows application programs to interact with the computer's hardware.

19. A system of letters, words, numbers, and symbols used to communicate with a computer.

20. The components or equipment of a computer system.

21. A series of detailed step-by-step instructions that tell the computer what functions to complete and when to complete them.

22. The use of computers to help people learn or improve skills at their own pace.

23. A term used to describe the activities of a worker using a computer at home to perform a job.

24. Mechanical devices programmed to do routine tasks.

25. Technological assistance used to create product styles and designs.

26. Stealing or illegally copying software packages or information.

27. Programs that assist people in solving technical problems.

28. An organized system of processing and reporting information in an organization.

29. A program code hidden in a system that can later do damage to software or stored data.

30. Programs that enable computers to reason, learn, and make decisions using logical methods similar to the methods humans use.

KEY TERMS
a. application software
b. artificial intelligence (AI)
c. central processing unit (CPU)
d. computer language
e. computer network
f. computer system
g. computer virus
h. computer-aided design (CAD)
i. computer-assisted instruction (CAI)
j. e-commerce
k. expert systems
l. hardware
m. management information system (MIS)
n. operating system software
o. piracy
p. program
q. robotics
r. software
s. telecommuting

8. It creates new jobs in programming, computer systems analysis, and operating and repairing computers. Expert systems might help solve medical problems by logically deducing the best possible courses of treatment and could also help scientists draw conclusions from medical research. Expert systems could research volumes of case law to help lawyers prepare cases for their clients.

9. Expert systems could connect potential borrowers with the best lenders for their needs or help investors choose the most promising investments.

10. One benefit of using smart cards for everyday transactions is improved personal record keeping. The smart card could replace your car keys and open the door for you at work. It could alert you when your checking account is low and streamline the process of applying for a loan.

11. Organizations can have employees use pass words to log on to their computers, monitor employee e-mail, and encrypt sensitive data when it is sent over the Internet.

Develop Your Business Language Answers

12. e. computer network
13. a. application software
14. p. program
15. c. central processing unit
16. f. computer system

17. j. e-commerce
18. n. operating system software
19. d. computer language
20. l. hardware
21. r. software

22. i. computer-assisted instruction
23. s. telecommuting
24. q. robotics
25. h. computer-aided design
26. o. piracy

27. k. expert systems
28. m. management information system
29. g. computer virus
30. b. artificial intelligence

Make Academic Connections

31. **TECHNOLOGY** Research types of input, output, and memory devices that have recently been developed for use by businesses and individuals.

32. **COMMUNICATION** Talk to people who make online purchases. What types of products do they buy most frequently? What concerns do they have about buying online? Prepare a table with a summary of your findings.

33. **TECHNOLOGY** Prepare a list of daily activities and information items that might be included in the processing and storage capabilities of a smart card.

34. **SCIENCE** Investigate various uses of *telemedicine* and *telesurgery* in the United States and in other areas of the world.

35. **MATH** The Barkley Corporation usually sends about 3,800 pieces of mail per month at $0.42 each. If the firm switches to electronic mail service at a cost of $1,250 per month, how much money would it save or lose? What other factors should the company consider before making this change?

36. **GEOGRAPHY** Many nations around the world do not have reliable telephone service. As a result, cell phones and wireless communication has grown at a fast pace in these countries. Conduct research and prepare a map reporting the countries with a significant usage rate of wireless communication.

37. **TECHNOLOGY** Research recent computer viruses. What types of damage do various viruses do to computer systems?

38. **LAW** Conduct an Internet search to obtain information about avoiding identity theft. Make a list of 10 ways to protect your identity.

Linking School and Community

Talk with a few members of your community about the computers and technology they use on the job. Ask them to describe technology changes they have seen in their jobs during the last year and during the last three years. Also ask them to identify the computer skills they think are important for career success. Prepare a one-minute presentation that summarizes your findings.

Web Workout

The number and popularity of social networking sites on the Internet continue to grow. Social networking web sites allow multiple users to communicate through an individual's web site. There are a wide variety of social networking sites with many users. MySpace alone has over 180 million users worldwide. The enjoyment and convenience of a social networking site is tempered by concerns about illegal and unethical behavior. All users need to take precautions when using these sites.

Think Critically

1. Make a list of the activities that people participate in while using social networking sites.
2. Make a list of problems that might arise when using social networking sites.
3. Use the Internet or library resources to identify recommendations for safe social networking practices. Create a one-page flyer of tips for social network users.

Decision-Making Strategies

The Kendall Manufacturing Company assembles electronic devices used in offices and homes. They employ about 600 people in various office, factory, and warehouse positions. Currently, all factory and warehouse jobs are done manually.

Managers at Kendall are considering replacing 150 assembly line workers with a computerized system. The company can save $135,000 a year in operating costs by using this new technology.

39. What factors should the company consider before using the computerized assembly line system?

40. If the company uses this new system, what should the company do to help workers who are displaced by this technology?

Web Site Development

Business success depends on the ability to communicate ideas and concepts using the Internet and related technologies. This event challenges students to design a web site for a business.

Command Performance is a new company that specializes in electronic presentations and teleconferencing for corporate meetings. Command Performance takes care of the following business meeting details:

- Securing the teleconference format
- Preparing the agenda
- Negotiating meeting/hotel room prices
- Designing all electronic presentations and handouts necessary for the meeting

You have been hired to design a web site to advertise the services offered by Command Performance. The introduction to the web site should use Flash or Flash-type animation. The company overview should include a Mission Statement, Company Services, New Products, Company History, Staff, and one additional element. The web site must include customer service information. Current clients and a portfolio of presentations should be available on the web site (March of Dimes and FBLA-PBL, Inc. are two current clients). The site should include links, site map, FAQs, pricing and/or rates, and a Contact Us link.

PERFORMANCE INDICATORS EVALUATED

- Understand effective page layout and design.
- Produce a site with functional links that are consistent and support the theme.
- Include content that makes the site effective.
- Demonstrate proper use of grammar, spelling, and punctuation.
- Produce a site that is compatible with multiple browsers.
- Respect copyrights laws.

You will be evaluated for:

- Thoroughness of all important concepts on the web site
- Validity of links included on the web site
- Navigation ease of your web site

For more detailed information about performance indicators, go to the FBLA web site.

1. List two things that frustrate customers about web sites.
2. Why should a web site list current customers and projects?
3. What web site elements can close the sale with prospective customers?
4. Identify two benefits of using Command Performance that should be emphasized on the web site.

http://www.fbla-pbl.org/

Access the web site shown here to find portfolio activities for this chapter. Use the activities to provide tangible evidence of your learning.

Decision-Making Strategies Answers

39. The company may want to phase in the new system, one assembly line at a time. They will want to be sure they have employees who are trained to operate the new system.

40. Employees with technical aptitude could be retrained and transferred to new jobs. To maintain as much goodwill as possible, Kendall will want to give employees who cannot be switched to other jobs training and severance pay.

Winning Edge
Web Site Development

Think Critically Answers

1. Customers are frustrated by slow downloading time or too many clicks of the mouse being needed to reach information.

2. Listing current customers and projects validates the success of the company.

3. Answers will vary. Personal testimonies from satisfied customers, honest important information readily available to customers, and company history can all help close a sale.

4. Answers will vary. For example, benefits include saving time, saving money, professional expertise, and peace of mind.

CHAPTER 12

Financial Management

Teaching Resources

Activities and Study Guide, Ch. 12
Chapter and Unit Tests, Ch. 12
Spanish Resources, Ch. 12

ExamView® *CD,* Ch. 12
Instructor's Resource CD
- PowerPoint Slides, Ch. 12
- Lesson Plans, Ch. 12

Xtra! Web Site

school.cengage.com/business/introtobiz
- Study Tools, 12-1, 12-2, 12-3, 12-4
- Quiz Prep, Ch. 12
- Net Bookmark, Ch. 12
- Crossword Puzzle, Ch. 12
- Portfolio Activity, Ch. 12

Planning a Career in...
ACCOUNTING

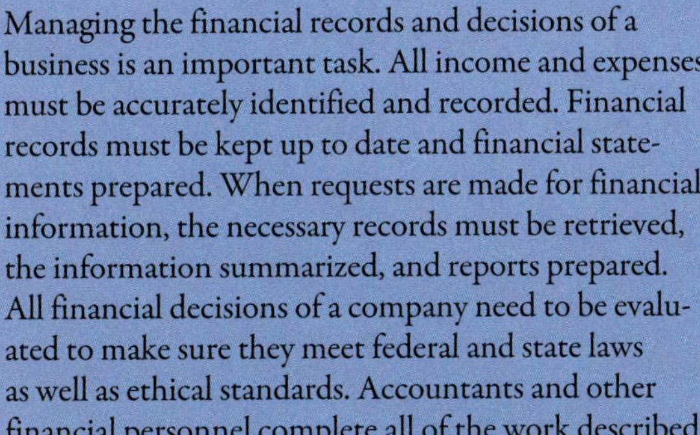

Managing the financial records and decisions of a business is an important task. All income and expenses must be accurately identified and recorded. Financial records must be kept up to date and financial statements prepared. When requests are made for financial information, the necessary records must be retrieved, the information summarized, and reports prepared. All financial decisions of a company need to be evaluated to make sure they meet federal and state laws as well as ethical standards. Accountants and other financial personnel complete all of the work described.

Public accountants perform accounting, auditing, tax, and consulting activities for their clients. Management accountants record and analyze the financial information of the companies for which they work. They advise executives and other managers to help them make good business decisions. A unique and growing area is forensic accounting. Forensic accountants investigate crimes such as securities fraud, embezzlement, and money laundering. They often appear as expert witnesses in criminal and civil cases.

Employment Outlook

- There are more than one million accountants working in the United States. Nearly 10 percent are self-employed.

- Employment opportunities are expected to grow rapidly in both private and public accounting.

- Accountants with advanced computer skills and a specialized knowledge of business operations and legal issues will be in especially high demand.

Related Job Titles

- Accountant
- Auditor
- Budget Analyst
- Financial Analyst
- Management Analyst

Needed Skills

- Bachelor's degree in accounting, with a master's of accounting or MBA preferred

- Ability to efficiently analyze and interpret facts and figures

- Ability to deal with detailed information

- Accountants can earn a certification of Certified Public Accountant (CPA) by passing a series of tests, completing advanced coursework, and documenting successful accounting experience.

What's it like to work as an... Accountant

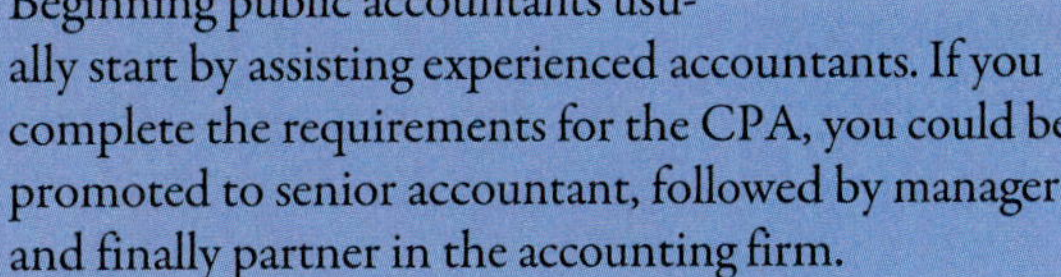

When you graduate with an accounting degree, you will often start as a junior accountant or accounting technician. Demonstrating your accounting skills on the job provides you with opportunities to advance. Beginning public accountants usually start by assisting experienced accountants. If you complete the requirements for the CPA, you could be promoted to senior accountant, followed by manager and finally partner in the accounting firm.

If you are entrepreneurial, you might decide to open your own public accounting firm. Another choice is an executive position in management accounting or internal auditing in a corporation. Management accountants often start as cost accountants or junior auditors. With experience, you can become an accounting or auditing manager, a controller, a chief financial officer, or even the president.

What about you? Why are both math and computer skills important to people who want to work in accounting? If you decided on a career in accounting, would you be more interested in public or management accounting? Why?

Planning a Career in...
ACCOUNTING

One of the most popular and challenging career areas in business is accounting. It combines mathematics skills with business understanding to prepare and maintain the financial records of a business and help business managers make effective financial decisions. Technology is having an important impact on accounting practice, so accountants need to develop skills in using a variety of business computer software.

What About You? Answers

Math and computer skills are essential for accountants because they must be able to work with figures and use accounting software to prepare reports. Answers regarding careers in accounting will vary. Some students will be attracted to the challenge and independence of a public accounting firm or even starting their own public accounting business, while others will appreciate the relative security and opportunity for career advancement that one might find working for a corporation.

Additional Career Information

Additional information on careers can be found in the *Occupational Outlook Handbook,* an online publication (www.bls.gov/oco) of the federal government. Tell your class about this resource  and how to use it. This description of job duties can be used to demonstrate the relevancy of skills learned in this course.

12-1 Financial Planning

Goals

Recognize important financial questions that must be answered in a business.

List the steps in budget preparation.

Describe three types of business budgets.

Key Terms

revenue

expenses

budget

start-up budget

operating budget

cash budget

Focus on Real Life

Ernest enjoyed everything about being a manager except for one thing. Each day he received a number of financial reports. Some described the financial condition of the entire business and some were specific to his department. He saw the payroll expenses for his employees, the changing costs of materials and supplies, as well as all other expenses of his department. The reports showed whether he was over or under budget for every expenditure.

Ernest wasn't always sure what he should do with the information. He usually asked questions of other managers or one of the company's accountants. He was told that the financial decisions he made would probably be among the most important to the success of his department and his career. Ernest decided to attend classes to reduce his anxiety and improve his financial management skills.

---

main idea

Recognize important financial questions that must be answered in a business.

FINANCIAL PLANNING

Picture yourself as a business owner. One of the constant problems you face is the need to have adequate financial resources to operate the business. From the first day you begin planning the business and each day it operates, financing questions must be addressed. Financial questions never go away. Even the most successful businesses are continually active in financial planning.

Beginning a Business

The moment a decision is made to start a business, financial planning begins. How much money will be needed to start the business? Where will that financing come from? How will adequate funds be obtained to operate the business for the months or years until the business becomes profitable? What will be the best sources of sales and other income? What will be the major expenses? When must they be paid?

Many new businesses fail due to poor financial planning. Experts in business finance should be consulted to help the new business with its financial planning. The business owner needs to know the importance of financial planning and must develop financial management skills.

Ongoing Operations

Finances are a key part of the operations of all businesses. Every business activity costs money. Without careful planning and management, those costs can grow to a level where the business income cannot cover the expenses. All income that a business receives over a period of time is called **revenue**. Businesses also have expenses. **Expenses** are the costs of operating a business. Every business is guided by the basic financial equation

Revenue − Expenses = Profit or Loss

If revenue is greater than expenses, the business will make a *profit*. If expenses exceed revenue, the business will suffer a *loss*.

The difference between revenue and expenses determines whether a business makes a profit or loss. If a company's annual revenue is $2 million and expenses were $1.5 million, did the business make a profit or suffer a loss?

All managers are responsible for the costs of the part of the business they manage. Each employee should also be concerned about those costs. The profitability of the business is directly linked to the number of employees and the wages the business can pay. Managers and employees should find ways to reduce waste and control expenses. They can also make suggestions about ways to increase sales and income through better products and services and higher customer satisfaction.

Ongoing operations require that employees be paid, supplies and materials ordered, and buildings maintained. Equipment must be repaired and technology updated. Each decision related to ongoing operations requires careful attention to costs.

Business Expansion

Successful businesses expand to be able to serve more customers, reach unserved markets, and sell new products. Yet expansion costs money. The hope is that the income generated by the expansion will be far greater than the cost. A more profitable business is the result.

Business expansion calls for research to develop new products and locate new markets. New factories and equipment may be needed to produce the products. Additional employees must be hired and trained. Marketing activities will be planned and implemented to distribute and promote the products. Most expansion plans occur over a long period and can cost thousands or even millions of dollars. Each time business expansion is anticipated, careful financial planning must be completed. The planning must anticipate the costs associated with the expansion, the source of the funds to pay for the expansion, and the expected income that will result from the new plans. If the planning is not correct and the expansion results in heavy losses rather than profits, the previously successful business may fail.

The difference between revenue and expenses determines whether a business makes a profit or a loss. If a company's annual revenue is $2 million and expenses were $1.5 million, did the business make a profit or suffer a loss?

checkpoint >>
What is the basic financial equation for businesses?

The business has a profit of $500,000. Have students insert numbers into each side of the basic financial equation to demonstrate how the business will experience a profit or loss.

TEACH

List the following areas of a business and ask students how managers and employees working in each of those areas can help to control costs: production, transportation, sales, accounting, information management, and customer service.

ONGOING ASSESSMENT

checkpoint >> **ANSWER**

The basic financial equation for businesses is revenue minus expenses equals profit or loss.

Applied Skills

Technology Have students use a spreadsheet program to build a model that demonstrates the basic financial equation. The model should include cells for revenue, expenses, and profit/loss with a formula in the profit/loss cell.

TEACH

List the two main purposes of a business budget on the board. Have students discuss why each of the purposes is important to a business and what happens if they are not able to accomplish one or both of the purposes.

E-Commerce in Action

For many years, government officials have been trying to encourage the development of e-commerce with hopes it would expand the economy. Reducing taxes paid by consumers was viewed as a way to encourage online purchasing. Now, those officials and traditional businesses are concerned about the results of those decisions due to lost tax revenues and the possibility of a pricing advantage for businesses.

Think Critically Answers

1. Answers will vary. Some will probably maintain that taxing online purchases would be too complicated to be cost effective. They may also point out that, because of shipping charges, adding online taxes to Internet sales will pose an unfair burden on the ability of e-commerce companies to be competitive. Others will maintain that taxing Internet orders is necessary so that traditional retailers can compete successfully and also so that states will receive much needed tax money.

2. Answers will vary depending on the state.

List the steps in budget preparation.

DEVELOPING BUSINESS BUDGETS

A **budget** provides detailed plans for the financial needs of individuals, families, and businesses. A *business budget* has two main purposes:

1. Anticipate sources and amounts of income.

2. Predict the types and amounts of expenses for a specific business activity or the entire business.

The business must be able to identify and predict the amount of each source of income and each type of expense. In addition, the business will need to determine when each expense must be paid and when income will be received. For the business to succeed, enough revenue must be available to pay all expenses.

Sources of Budget Information

To develop an effective budget, information to predict income and expenses is needed. If a business has operated for several years, identifying sources of income and types of expenses will not be difficult. The main source of that information is the financial records of the business. Budgeting is much harder for a new business. No financial records exist to serve as a guide. Other sources of information must be used.

Taxing Online Purchases

Forty-five states and the District of Columbia collect sales taxes. However, sales taxes are often not collected when purchases are made online. From their beginning, many Internet businesses argued that they were not required to collect sales taxes except in the states where their businesses were located. The U.S. Supreme Court agreed when it ruled that states are prohibited from collecting sales tax from businesses that have no physical presence in their state unless Congress specifically passes a law to allow it. Congress has not yet enacted such a law.

Traditional businesses argue they are at a competitive disadvantage because they are required to collect the sales taxes and online businesses are not. Internet businesses respond that their customers have the additional cost of product shipping, so there is no real price advantage. State governments contend that they are losing billions of dollars of tax revenue each year because they cannot impose sales taxes on e-commerce.

Rather than waiting for Congress to pass a law, the National Governors Association and the National Conference of State Legislators developed the State Sales and Use Tax Agreement (SSUTA) to create uniformity and to simplify the more than 8,000 different state and local sales tax laws. SSUTA suggests that states ask retailers to voluntarily collect and submit sales taxes based on customer addresses. The agreement also outlines procedures that could be used if the U.S. Congress passes the necessary legislation to allow states to collect sales tax on Internet sales. Currently, 15 states have changed their laws to conform to the agreement and other states are planning changes.

Software development companies have taken notice of the current situation and have created programs that make it easy for businesses to calculate, collect, and process sales taxes. These software programs are currently being used by businesses that are voluntarily collecting sales taxes for Internet purchases. Depending on what Congress does, the demand for these programs could increase if online businesses are required to collect the sales taxes for multiple states and localities.

Think Critically
1. Do you believe sales taxes should apply to online sales? Why or why not?
2. Use library or Internet resources to determine if your state has laws and procedures related to e-commerce sales tax.

Different Learning Abilities

Dyslexia Have students review the lesson and prepare a short outline that lists financial planning decisions for a business for each of the following situation: beginning a business, ongoing operation, and business expansion.

The Small Business Administration (SBA) provides many planning tools for new businesses. Among those tools are guides to developing a budget and financial information to help the new business owner predict income and expenses. Another source of information is private businesses that collect and publish financial information on similar businesses and industries. Examples of those companies are Dun and Bradstreet, Value Line, and Standard and Poor's. Some information is also available from business magazines and newspapers including *Fortune, Forbes, Entrepreneur, Black Enterprise,* and *The Wall Street Journal.*

Professional associations, such as the National Federation of Independent Business and the National Retail Merchants Association, offer resources to help with financial planning. A new franchise will typically receive assistance with financial planning from the franchisor. This help might include a complete beginning budget. A bank or other financial institution where a new business has established accounts is another source of financial planning. Franchisors and financial institutions want to see businesses succeed, so they typically require careful financial planning.

Budget Preparation

The most important step in financial planning is developing a budget. You can compare the use of a budget to the use of a road map when you are traveling to an unfamiliar location. Without the map, you will have little idea where you are going while you travel. If you take a wrong turn, you will have difficulty knowing your mistake. It will be hard to get back to the correct road without the map. In the same way, a budget identifies where a business is going. It allows the owner to determine if the business is making progress toward its financial destination. By regularly comparing the business'

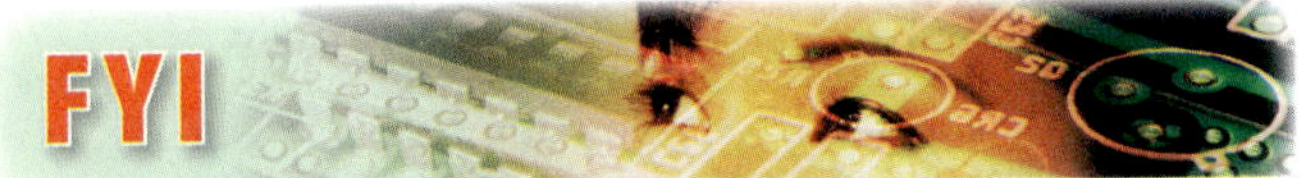

U.S. businesses spend more than $1 trillion dollars each year on investments in buildings, equipment, and technology. The industry with the greatest level of spending is manufacturing. Most of their purchases in recent years were for equipment and technology rather than buildings.

financial performance to the budget, the owner can determine if the budget goals are being met. If not, the owner can make corrections before serious financial problems occur.

A business budget has the same basic goals as a personal or family budget developed to manage the household finances. The goals are to determine the sources and amounts of income, to identify the types of expenses and predict their costs, to determine how income will be distributed to cover those expenses, and to reward investors if there is a profit.

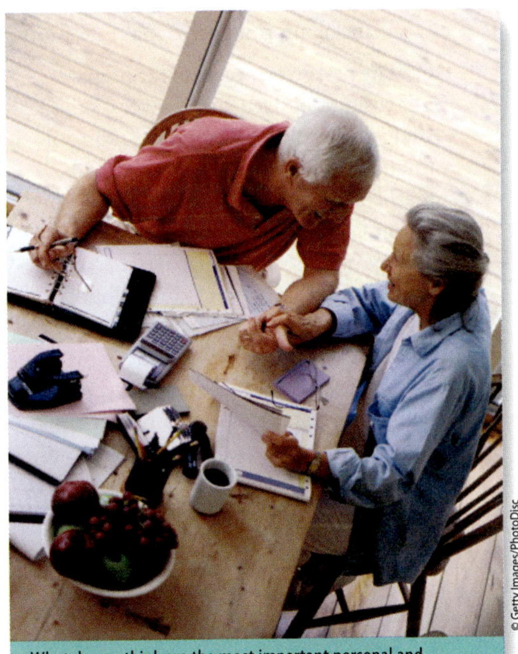

What do you think are the most important personal and family budget categories for most people? How might they differ from a business budget?

TEACH

Tell students that the personal characteristics of many entrepreneurs make them unwilling to ask for help and advice. That often leads to problems with financial planning and decision-making. All businesspeople should be willing to gather information and ask for help and advice, especially in the important area of business financing.

THINK CRITICALLY THROUGH VISUALS

Answers will vary as to which budget categories are most important. Budget categories for both businesses and individuals would include sources of income, utilities, taxes, insurance, and investments. Businesses would have categories for employee-related expenses and capital investments such as computers, equipment, and buildings, while individuals would have housing, transportation, education, and child care expenses.

Different Learning Styles

Tactile Learners Have students visit a library or bookstore with an extensive business collection and locate books and magazines that provide useful financial information for new business owners. Ask students to make a list of the resources they located.

Before the teams begin their work, ask them to discuss and agree on the major categories of income and expenses they should include in their budgets.

TEACH

Review the skills that are needed by people responsible for preparing a budget. Have students identify ways these skills could be developed.

ONGOING ASSESSMENT

checkpoint >> ANSWER

The four steps are (1) preparing a list of each type of income and expense that will be a part of the budget, gathering accurate information from business records and other information sources for each type of income and expense, creating the budget by calculating each type of income, expense, and the amount of net income or loss, and (4) explaining the budget to people who need financial information.

TEACH

Have students list the three types of budgets. As each is discussed, have students write the definition of each and note the differences among the budgets.

THINK CRITICALLY THROUGH VISUALS

Budget items that need to be considered include sales tax, title and license fees, insurance, maintenance and repairs, fuel, parking fees, and tolls.

Work as a Team

Individually prepare a personal budget for the next three months by anticipating the types and amounts of income and expenses you will have. Compare your budget with those of other team members and discuss ways to make your budgeting process more accurate.

main idea

Describe three types of business budgets.

The budgeting process involves four fundamental steps.

1. Prepare a list of each type of income and expense that will be a part of the budget.

2. Gather accurate information from business records and other information sources for each type of income and expense.

3. Create the budget by calculating each type of income, expense, and the amount of net income or loss.

4. Explain the budget to people who need financial information to make decisions.

The person responsible for preparing business budgets needs several skills. Budgeting requires an understanding of financial information, computer skills, mathematical abilities, and effective communications skills. New small business owners often seek the help of an accountant or banker when preparing a budget for the first time. Small- and medium-sized businesses may hire an accounting firm to maintain financial records and to help with budget development. Larger businesses employ accountants and other financial planning experts to maintain the business' financial records. They also help with budgeting and using budget information.

checkpoint >>
What are the four steps in preparing a business budget?

    CHAPTER 12   **FINANCIAL MANAGEMENT**

TYPES OF BUDGETS

A large business will have many specialized budgets. Each manager will be responsible for one or more budgets in his or her area of operations. For every business, three particular budgets are essential. They are the start-up budget, the operating budget, and the cash budget. The **start-up budget** plans income and expenses from the beginning of a new business or a major business expansion until it becomes profitable. Most start-ups require expenditures of thousands or even hundreds of thousands of dollars in order to open. Buildings and equipment must be purchased or leased. Inventory, supplies, and materials are needed. New employees will be hired or existing employees retrained. Expenses for utilities, licenses, advertising, and transportation will be incurred before the company can sell its new products and services. Sources of financing for these expenditures must be identified from either inside the company or from outside financial sources. The amount of start-up expenses must be predicted correctly so that ample start-up financing is available until the new activities produce adequate income.

What additional budget items would need to be considered when buying a car?

Communication Have students use a computer software program to prepare a slide presentation that compares the three types of business budgets. Organize students into small groups and have them share their presentations within their group.

The **operating budget** describes the financial plan for ongoing operations of the business for a specific period. The operating budget is usually planned for three months, six months, or a year. An operating budget is prepared for the entire business. Each department and division of a large business will also develop and follow its own operating budget.

When planning an operating budget, income and expenses from prior budgets are reviewed. Planners look for possible changes that could increase or decrease income and expenses. Then the budget for the next period is prepared. It is used to manage the operations of the company for the period covered by the budget.

A **cash budget** is an estimate of the actual money received and paid out for a specific period. A cash budget anticipates that cash will come into a business and that cash will be paid out during each week or month of operation. If a new business is losing money, it still must have adequate cash on hand to pay current expenses. Even profitable businesses may have times when adequate cash is not available due to high expenses or a delay in receiving payments from customers.

A cash budget will determine if a business has adequate financial resources on hand to pay bills as they become due or if they will need to borrow money. It will also show when there is so much cash on hand that some of it can be invested. Investing cash on hand provides another source of business income.

> *checkpoint* >>
> Identify and describe the three types of budgets needed by all businesses.

12-1 Assessment

Key Concepts

Determine the best answer.

1. True or False. Financial planning is needed by small businesses only until they begin to make a profit.

2. The basic financial equation is
   a. revenue − profit = loss
   b. expenses + revenue = profit or loss
   c. profit − loss = revenue and expenses
   d. revenue − expenses = profit or loss

3. True or False. A cash budget is an estimate of the actual money received and paid out for a specific period.

Make Academic Connections

4. *Math* Use the basic financial equation to determine the profit or loss for each of the following:
   a. revenue $85,695; expenses $72,624
   b. revenue $1,824,300; expenses $2,183,680
   c. revenue $729,655; expenses $499,220

5. *Technology* Use the Internet to locate a sample business budget. Enter the entire budget into a spreadsheet program. Develop a new budget by adjusting each of the income and expense items in the budget with a 3 percent increase. Then develop another budget by adjusting the original income and expense items with a 1.5 percent decrease.

6. *Economics* Locate a newspaper or magazine article that describes an anticipated change in the economy that might result in higher or lower income or expenses for businesses. Write two paragraphs discussing how financial planners should use the information when developing an operating budget.

TEACH

Ask students why a business has a problem when it does not have enough cash on hand, even if it is making a profit. Remind them that they may be late with payments, making their suppliers unhappy, or they will have to borrow money, thus adding to the business expenses.

ONGOING ASSESSMENT

checkpoint >> **ANSWER**

All businesses need the start-up budget, which plans income and expenses from the beginning of a new business or a major business expansion until it becomes profitable; the operating budget, which describes the plan for ongoing operations for a specific period; and the cash budget, which is an estimate of the actual money received and paid out for a specific period.

ASSESS

Key Concepts Answers

1. False. Even the most successful businesses are continually active in financial planning.

2. d. revenue − expenses = profit or loss

3. True

Make Academic Connections

4. a. Profit: $85,695 − $72,624 = $13,071

   b. Loss: $1,824,300 − $2,183,680 = −$359,380

   c. Profit: $729,655 − $499,220 = $230,435

5. Answers will vary depending on the business budget used.

6. Answers will vary depending on the articles selected.

RETEACH

Ask students how budgets help people plan for items in the basic financial equation.

CLOSE

Ask each student to identify a way that a budget can help businesspeople make better decisions.

ENRICH

Have students search the Internet to locate computer software programs that can help businesspeople with financial planning and budgeting.

TEACH

Tell students that many people are not in the habit of keeping financial records for their personal lives. Therefore, it is difficult to get in the habit of recordkeeping when starting a new business. If you develop and use records for your personal finances, you will have experience that will be helpful in your business career.

Write the names of each of the types of records in random order. Then, as you read the definition of each type of record from the lesson, have students match the definition with the correct record name.

Goals

Identify several types of financial records needed by businesses.

Describe the differences between an income statement and a balance sheet.

Key Terms

financial records

assets

liabilities

owner's equity

balance sheet

income statement

Focus on **Real Life**

Paulette received a call from her banker. She had a payment due on the loan she had taken out to buy the building for her printing business. The banker informed her that there was currently not enough cash in her accounts to make the loan payment. While Paulette was not currently behind in her payments, the bank was increasingly concerned about her ability to meet the payment schedule. Paulette had been late in making payments four of the past 10 months. Paulette knew she had enough printing orders to cover the cost of the loan payment, but her customers did not always pay on time either. She was reluctant to ask customers to pay cash for large orders. She felt it might encourage them to take their business to a competitor. On the other hand, she didn't know how she would come up with the money to pay the bank loan. Paulette called her accountant to set up a meeting to review the financial status of her business. Hopefully, they would be able to develop a solution that would satisfy the bank.

---

main idea

Identify several types of financial records needed by businesses.

FINANCIAL RECORDS

Budgets reflect the financial plans of businesses. To determine if those plans have resulted in success, financial records are needed. **Financial records** are used to record and analyze the financial performance of a business. Several types of records are maintained. They provide detailed information about the financial activities of the company. Local, state, and federal governments require some records. Other records provide information needed by owners and managers to aid their decision-making.

Types of Records

The following records are commonly maintained to document the performance of a business.

- *Asset records* name the buildings and equipment owned by the business, their original and current value, and the amount owed if money was borrowed to purchase the assets.

- *Depreciation records* identify the amount assets have decreased in value due to their age and use.

- *Inventory records* identify the type and number of products on hand for sale. Adequate records are crucial to correctly determine the number of products sold, damaged, or lost and the current value of that inventory.

- *Records of accounts* identify all purchases and sales made using credit. An *accounts payable record* identifies the companies from which credit purchases were made and the amount purchased, paid, and owed. An *accounts receivable record* identifies customers that made purchases using credit and the status of each account.

Different Learning Styles

Auditory Learner Provide students with the opportunity to read each of the types of records and their definitions aloud to help them distinguish among the types. Consider allowing students to work in pairs or small groups.

- *Cash records* list all cash received and spent by the business.
- *Payroll records* contain information on all employees of the company, their compensation, and benefits.
- *Tax records* show all taxes collected, owed, and paid. As a part of payroll, employers must withhold a percentage of employees' salaries and wages for income taxes, Social Security and Medicare taxes, and, in some cases, unemployment compensation insurance. In addition to the taxes withheld from employees, businesses must pay the employer's share of Social Security and Medicare taxes, and other taxes that are calculated as a percentage of payroll. Depending on the type of business and the location, a company may have to collect and pay state and local sales taxes. Businesses may have to pay several types of taxes on their income and value of their assets. Adequate records must be maintained to accurately calculate any taxes owed and to file the necessary tax forms.

Maintaining Financial Records

Business records have to be accurate and should be kept up to date. In the past, the preparation and maintenance of financial records was an expensive and time-consuming process. It was often done manually using paper documents that had to be carefully completed, saved, and protected. Then those documents were sent to the people responsible for preparing the company's financial records.

Technology is changing the way financial information is collected. Much of the information is now collected using point-of-production and point-of-sale technology such as scanners, touch screens, and personal digital assistants (PDAs). Data files are transferred from the places information is collected to the computers

of the people who prepare the financial records. Technology is also changing the way financial records are prepared and maintained. Businesses use computerized financial systems that have templates for each financial record. The software completes the necessary mathematical calculations. It updates records and compares those records with budgets. The software can even complete what-if comparisons to help managers determine the impact of changes in budgets and financial performance.

checkpoint »

How has the process of maintaining financial records been affected by technology?

What are the differences between keeping records manually and on a computer?

FINANCIAL STATEMENTS

The three most important elements of a company's financial strength are its assets, liabilities, and owner's equity. In simple terms, **assets** are what a company owns, **liabilities** are what a company owes, and **owner's equity** is the value of the owner's investment in the business.

Reports that sum up the financial performance of a business are *financial statements*. A company reports its assets, liabilities, and owner's equity on the *balance sheet*.

Three other key financial elements for a business are the amounts of *sales*, *expenses*, and *profits*. Sales, expenses, and profits (or losses) for a specific period are reported in the company's *income statement*.

The Balance Sheet

The assets, liabilities, and owner's equity for a specific date are listed on the **balance sheet**. The balance sheet is usually prepared every six months or once a year. Figure 12-1 shows a balance sheet.

The left side of the balance sheet lists all assets. *Assets* are anything of value owned by the business. There are two common divisions of assets. *Current assets* include cash and those items that can be readily converted to cash such as inventory and accounts receivable. *Long-term assets* (also known as *fixed assets*) are the assets with a lifespan of more than a year. Common fixed assets are land, buildings, equipment, and expensive technology.

The right side of the balance sheet is divided into two categories. *Liabilities* are amounts owed by the business to others. As with assets, there are two types of liabilities. *Current liabilities* are those that will be paid within a year. *Long-term liabilities* are debts that will continue for longer than a year. Current liabilities include payments owed to banks and other financial institutions for short-term loans. Also included are

FIGURE 12-1

What can you tell about the success of this business based on this balance sheet?

The ProfitCo Company
Balance Sheet
July 31, 20xx

Assets			Liabilities		
Current Assets			**Current Liabilities**		
Cash	$22,225		Accounts payable	$18,250	
Accounts receivable	42,200		Payroll taxes payable	1,900	
Inventory	98,200		Wages payable	23,525	
Prepaid expenses	5,340		Short-term bank loan payable	5,700	
Total Current Assets		$167,965	**Total Current Liabilities**		$49,375
Long-Term Assets			**Long-Term Liabilities**		
Vehicles	68,500		Long-term notes payable	85,200	
Furniture and fixtures	21,450		Mortgage payable	120,600	
Equipment	33,000		**Total Long-Term Liabilities**		$205,800
Buildings	320,000				
Land	82,500		**Total Liabilities**		$255,175
Total Long-Term Assets		$525,450			
			Owner's Equity		$438,240
Total Assets		$693,415	**Total Liabilities and Owner's Equity**		$693,415

Applied Skills

Mathematics Have students use Figure 12-1 and decrease each of the assets by 5 percent and increase each of the liabilities by 3 percent. Using the new amounts, have students calculate the totals for each of the categories of assets, liabilities, and owner's equity.

payments due to suppliers for inventory purchases, supplies, and inexpensive equipment. Long-term liabilities are debts owed for land, buildings, and expensive equipment.

Finally, *owner's equity* is the value of the business after liabilities are subtracted from assets. It shows how much the business is worth on the date the balance sheet is prepared. Another way of looking at owner's equity is that it shows the value of the investments owners have made in the business.

The Income Statement

To report the revenue, expenses, and net income or loss from operations for a specific period, a business prepares an **income statement**. An income statement usually covers six months or a year, but may also encompass a shorter period such as a month. Figure 12-2 shows a sample income statement.

Revenue is all income received by the business during the period. Sources of income include the sale of products and services, plus interest earned from investments. *Expenses* are all of the costs of operating the business during the period. Expenses include things such as rent, supplies, inventory, payroll, and utilities. The business has *net income*

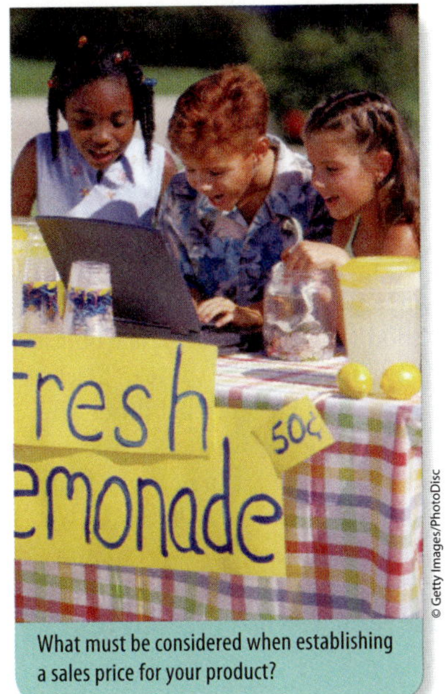

© Getty Images/PhotoDisc

What must be considered when establishing a sales price for your product?

Anticipated expenses and projected revenue must be considered when establishing a sales price for a product so that the seller can recoup all operating expenses and make a profit on the sales.

TEACH

Have students compare Figures 12-1 and 12-2. Ask them to point out the differences. What can they learn about the business from an income statement that they cannot learn from a balance sheet?

FIGURE 12-2 ANSWER

Students should be able to study this income statement and determine that the business financially successful because revenue is greater than expenses, resulting in a profit for the identified time period.

The Netinc Company
Income Statement
For the 6-month Period Ending December 31, 20xx

Revenue			
Sales	$1,289,650		
Sales returns and allowances	−20,200		
Net sales		$1,269,450	
Cost of goods sold		−325,650	
Interest earned		80,263	
Total Revenue			$1,024,063
Expenses			
Selling expense		$32,050	
Marketing expense		282,954	
Administrative expense		52,445	
Rent expense		38,220	
Utilities expense		22,900	
Payroll expense		184,908	
Total Expenses			$613,477
Income taxes			−68,250
Net Income			$342,336

FIGURE 12-2

What can you tell about the success of this business based on this income statement?

Applied Skills

Mathematics Ask students to use the income statement in Figure 12-2 to demonstrate what happens if sales decrease by 5 percent, while all expenses increase by 10 percent. Invite interested students to set up a spreadsheet with the data shown in Figure 12-2 and demonstrate the impact of changing the figures for sales and expenses.

PROJECT

Provide the following instructions to students. (These instructions also appear on page xxv of the textbook.) Describe ways in which the financial planning functions of a business are similar to the financial planning that must be done by people to achieve their life-span goals. Evaluate the status of your own financial planning. How will you know if you have the financial resources to achieve your life-span goals?

Life-Span Plan Answer

Answers will vary. Students should describe similarities between financial planning and life-span planning.

ONGOING ASSESSMENT

checkpoint >> **ANSWER**

A balance sheet reports assets, liabilities, and owner's equity as of a specific date. An income statement reports sales, expenses, and net profit or loss for a specified time period.

ASSESS

Key Concepts Answers

1. b. asset records

2. True

3. c. one year

4. b. balance sheet

Make Academic Connections

5. Tables will vary.

6. Personal balance sheets and income statements will vary.

CLOSE

Have students complete the following sentences: "The purpose of a balance sheet is. …" "The purpose of an income statement is. …"

when revenue is greater than expenses. A *net loss* occurs when expenses are greater than income.

Business managers review financial statements carefully to determine how their businesses are performing. Because the statements summarize financial performance for a specific time, the owner can compare the performance of the current period with the performance of last month or last year. If the value of assets is increasing in relation to liabilities, the business is in a better financial position. It may be able to invest in new products, buildings, and equipment. A rapid rise in liabilities or decline in owner's equity should cause concern. The business must carefully evaluate what is causing the

change. If net income is increasing, the owner will want to maintain and improve that performance. On the other hand, if expenses are increasing but revenue is not, the owner will want to determine the reasons for the problem and make changes.

In addition to comparing financial performance from one time period to another, the owner will want to make comparisons with similar businesses. A business that is less profitable than similar businesses, or with lower sales or higher expenses, may have difficulty competing.

checkpoint >>
What is the difference between a balance sheet and an income statement?

12-2 Assessment

Key Concepts

Determine the best answer.

1. The value of the buildings and equipment owned by a business can be determined in the
  a. inventory records   **c.** records of accounts
  b. asset records   **d.** tax records

2. True or False. The two most common and important financial records for businesses are the income statement and the balance sheet.

3. Current liabilities are amounts owed that will be paid in less than
  a. one month   **c.** one year
  b. six months   **d.** five years

4. The current value of investments made by the owners of a business can be found in the
  a. income statement   **c.** tax records
  b. balance sheet   **d.** record of accounts

Make Academic Connections

5. *Government* A business is required to collect taxes and make payments to local, state, and federal governments for its employees. Use the Internet to gather information on payroll taxes (local, state, and federal) that must be collected by a business in your community. Prepare a table that identifies each type of payroll tax, how the amount of tax to be collected is determined, and when and to whom the payments must be made.

6. *Accounting* Using the examples in Figures 12-1 and 12-2, any records, and your best memory, create a personal balance sheet and income statement. The balance sheet should reflect your personal financial status as of the current date. The income statement should represent your income and expenditures for the past three months.

302   CHAPTER 12   FINANCIAL MANAGEMENT

RETEACH

Display Figures 12-1 and 12-2. Have students offer definitions of each of the major headings on the two financial statements and describe how each statement helps in understanding the financial condition of the business.

ENRICH

Have students enter the financial statements shown in Figures 12-1 and 12-2 into a spreadsheet program and insert the formulas to make the necessary calculations. Then have them demonstrate how the spreadsheet can be used to update each financial statement after six months.

12-3 Payroll Management

Goals

Describe the components of a business' payroll system.

Identify information included in payroll records and paychecks.

Key Terms

payroll

payroll record

direct deposit

Focus on Real Life

Zena picked up her paycheck from the human resources office on her way to the parking lot. She had finished a hard week of work and was looking forward to a meal and a movie with friends. She would stop by her bank on the way to the restaurant to deposit her paycheck in her savings account and get some cash for the weekend.

Zena almost hated to look at her paycheck each time she received it. In addition to the check, the company provided detailed information on her earnings and deductions. The information was so detailed that it became confusing. The report showed she had earned an extra day of vacation, but the sick day she had to take last week also was listed. The cost of all of her benefits, including health and dental insurance, reduced her take-home pay by $62 each pay period. In addition, taxes and other required government deductions totaled $143. Halfway through the year, Zena's deductions and withholding already had topped $3,500. She knew the benefits were important to her, but she didn't know if she really wanted to look at their cost each time she was paid.

PAYROLL SYSTEMS

One of the most important financial duties of a business is maintaining a payroll. A **payroll** is the financial record of employee compensation, deductions, and net pay. A payroll system maintains information on each employee to be able to calculate the company's payroll and to make the necessary payments to each employee.

Most businesses pay every employee on a weekly, bi-weekly, or monthly basis. A majority of employees in most businesses receive an hourly wage, but the wage rate may be different for each employee. Some employees work part time while others work a full 40 hours or more a week. The rest of the employees, especially managers and others in professional positions, receive a weekly or monthly salary. Again, the amount of salary for each person may be different. Some may earn additional payments in the form of commissions, bonuses, and profit sharing.

> **main idea**
>
> Describe the components of a business' payroll system.

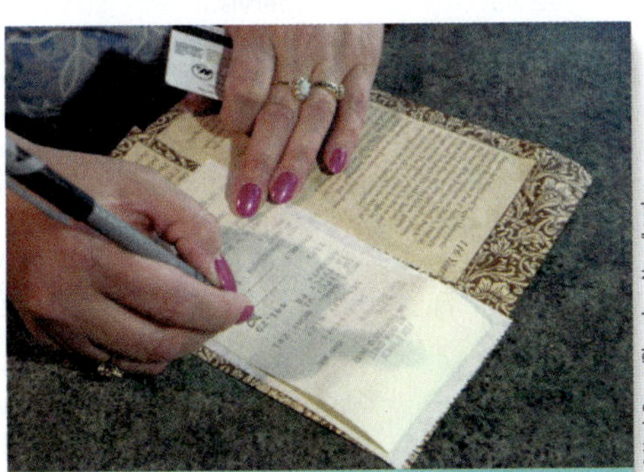

Can you think of the various types of income people earn in addition to wages and salaries? For instance, waiters receive a large portion of their income from tips.

© Noah Berger/Bloomberg News/Landov

Focus on Real Life

Ask students what they believe companies should do to make the information on paychecks, including deductions and benefits, more understandable.

TEACH

Before beginning a discussion of payroll, show students Figure 12-3. Have them study the figure carefully and identify all of the information that is included in the payroll record. Ask them why each of the types of information in the record is needed by the business and the employee.

THINK CRITICALLY THROUGH VISUALS

Other sources of income students may suggest in addition to the typical standard paycheck are royalties for creative works, dividend income from investments in stocks and bonds, payment for freelance work, fares and tips for taxi drivers, bonuses for outstanding performance or end-of-year holidays, profit sharing and pension payments, sales commissions, and signing bonuses when sought-after new employees are hired.

Different Learning Abilities

Specific Learning Disability (SLD) Give students several math problems that involve an hourly wage rate and the number of hours an employee works each week. Have students calculate the amount that would be earned in one week for each example. Provide a calculator for students if needed.

A QUESTION OF ETHICS

Explain to students that confidentiality is important in business. Employees and managers need to be very careful not to disclose personal and confidential information about other employees, customers, and the business. Confidentiality is both a legal issue and a matter of ethical behavior.

Think Critically Answers

1. Answers will vary. Some will probably feel the probationary employee deserved more feedback about the co-workers' opinions and an opportunity to tell her side of the story. Others will feel that it is the employer's right to hire or fire employees as he or she thinks best. You may want to ask students who have jobs to share their experiences with and feelings about work evaluations.

2. The supervisor could have asked the employees who complained about the new hire to provide specific examples of their concerns to report to the new employee so that she could have an opportunity to make improvements during the probationary period. Specific examples of negative behavior should have been documented. The decision to hire or fire should not have been made based on general, vague feelings. As for the new employee, she should have asked for candid feedback from her supervisor throughout the probationary period. Perhaps if she had made noticeable efforts to fit in with the other employees, the supervisor would have made a more favorable decision.

FYI

In addition to income taxes, people who are employed by companies and people who are self-employed all pay taxes for Medicare and Social Security. Employers pay half of the required payment for each employee. The other half is deducted from the employee's paycheck. Proprietors must pay self-employment taxes, which cover their contributions to Medicare and Social Security. Because they are self-employed they pay the full amount.

As a part of the compensation system, most businesses provide employees a range of benefits. Benefits may include insurance options, paid or unpaid vacation, sick leave and personal leave, retirement plans, and education assistance. A business must keep records of employee benefits used. Many benefits are a part of payments made to employees as a part of the payroll.

The final part of payroll is tax records and payments. Businesses are responsible for making required federal and state payments for each employee. These taxes consist of income taxes, Social Security, Medicare, and unemployment taxes and are commonly referred to as *payroll taxes*.

Income Taxes The Federal government, most states, and some local governments require employers to withhold income tax from their employees' pay. The taxes are based on the amount of wages and income and the number of employee dependents.

Social Security and Medicare These payments are often referred to as FICA (Federal Insurance Contributions Act). The government requires employers to withhold and deposit these contributions from employees' paychecks along with matching contributions by the employer.

Unemployment Taxes Employers pay Federal Unemployment Tax (FUTA) to the unemployment insurance system. The amount owed is based on the

A QUESTION OF ETHICS

Disclosing Employee Performance Information

Following a three-month probationary period, a new employee was fired. The supervisor had heard from several employees that the new worker was hard to get along with and was not carrying her full share of the work. While two work evaluations completed by the supervisor rated her performance as above average, her performance was not outstanding so the decision was made to terminate her employment. When the employee was notified of the decision, she was shocked and asked why she was being fired. Not wanting to create problems for the current employees who had complained or to disclose that the evaluations had not shown serious problems, the supervisor declined to provide reasons. Should the employee have a right to know why she was fired?

There are federal and state laws that regulate an employee's right to information. An employee generally can examine information in his or her personnel file that relates to work performance. That includes any written notes and formal performance evaluations. An employer should be careful about making judgments that are heavily influenced by the opinions of others without direct evidence. Also, providing regular feedback on evaluations and discussing any issues or concerns before they become major problems are important management responsibilities.

Think Critically

1. Do you believe the supervisor was right in not disclosing the information gathered from the new employee's coworkers? Why or why not? Do you feel the same way about the results of the work evaluations?

2. What recommendations would you make to the supervisor to prevent the type of situation from occurring again? As a new employee, what would you do to make sure you have adequate feedback on how you are doing?

Applied Skills

Writing Across the Curriculum Have students write a paragraph that shows the connection of ethics in working with confidential information to another class they are currently taking.

business' total employee wages. Many states also have their own unemployment taxes.

Employers must withhold taxes from employee wages and salaries as well as make their own required contributions. Businesses must prepare and maintain tax records. They also have to send required payments to the government on time.

Most payroll systems are part of a larger personnel records system. That system is a central location for all information the company maintains on all employees from the time they are hired until well after they no longer work for the business. Personnel records include personal information, employment history, performance evaluations, compensation records, and other information needed by the company. Most information in personnel files is confidential. Because of this, the businesses must carefully and securely maintain the records.

How do payroll records relate to vacations?

© Getty Images/PhotoDisc

PREPARING A PAYROLL

Maintaining payroll records and preparing paychecks is an ongoing and time-consuming task for businesses. In the past, each employee completed and submitted a time card. Payroll clerks entered the information into each employee's payroll record. When paychecks were to be issued at the end of each pay period, employee compensation and deductions had to be calculated, withholding and benefits records completed, and paychecks prepared. Today, computerized payroll record systems make the process more efficient and accurate. The software needed to manage a basic payroll system can be purchased at a relatively low cost. The system can collect employee work records each day. At the time paychecks need to be prepared, all information on benefits and deductions is entered and each employee's pay is calculated. All payroll records are updated and individual paychecks are prepared electronically.

Payroll Records

The form used to track each employee's pay history is a **payroll record**. Each payroll record holds the employee's name, Social Security number, address, and other needed personal information. It also includes individual tax information and a record of benefits such as vacation and sick days available and used. The employee's current and year-to-date earnings, deductions, gross pay, and net pay are maintained in the

main idea

Identify information included in payroll records and paychecks.

Most businesses use their payroll system to keep track of each employee's vacation time.

ONGOING ASSESSMENT

checkpoint >> **ANSWER**

The purpose of the payroll system is to maintain information on each employee to be able to calculate the company's payroll and make the necessary payments to each employee, taking the proper legal state and federal deductions from each paycheck.

TEACH

Invite a human resources specialist who is responsible for preparing a company payroll to speak to the class. Ask the person to describe the procedures that are completed, the technology used, and the amount of time it takes to process the entire company payroll each time.

Different Learning Abilities

Limited English Proficiency (LEP) Have the student review the lesson and write any terms related to payroll and payroll records that he or she has difficulty pronouncing or understanding on a sheet of paper. Review each of the words with the student to help with comprehension.

Work as a Team

Review the information in the Focus on Real Life at the beginning of the lesson. Discuss with your team what you could say to Zena to help her feel better about the deductions shown on her paycheck that reduced the amount of her take-home pay.

payroll record. A similar payroll record is kept for each part-time and full-time employee. An example of an automated payroll record is shown in Figure 12-3.

Preparing Paychecks

After all employees' payroll records have been completed and pay amounts have been calculated, a paycheck is prepared for each person. Employees will want to know how the amount of pay they receive is determined and the type and amount of deductions made. Most businesses print an *earnings report* that is included with the employee's paycheck. The earnings report usually includes information for the current pay period as well as the cumulative amounts for the year. An example employee paycheck and earnings report is shown in Figure 12-4 on the next page.

Businesses may offer a direct deposit service for employees. With **direct deposit**, the employer transfers net pay electronically into the employee's bank account. The employee does not receive a printed paycheck but is given a receipt of the funds transfer and an earnings report. The receipt may be posted on a benefits web site where the employee can print it out, if desired.

> *checkpoint* >>
> What is the difference between a payroll record and an earnings report?

FIGURE 12-3

Why is a payroll record needed for each employee?

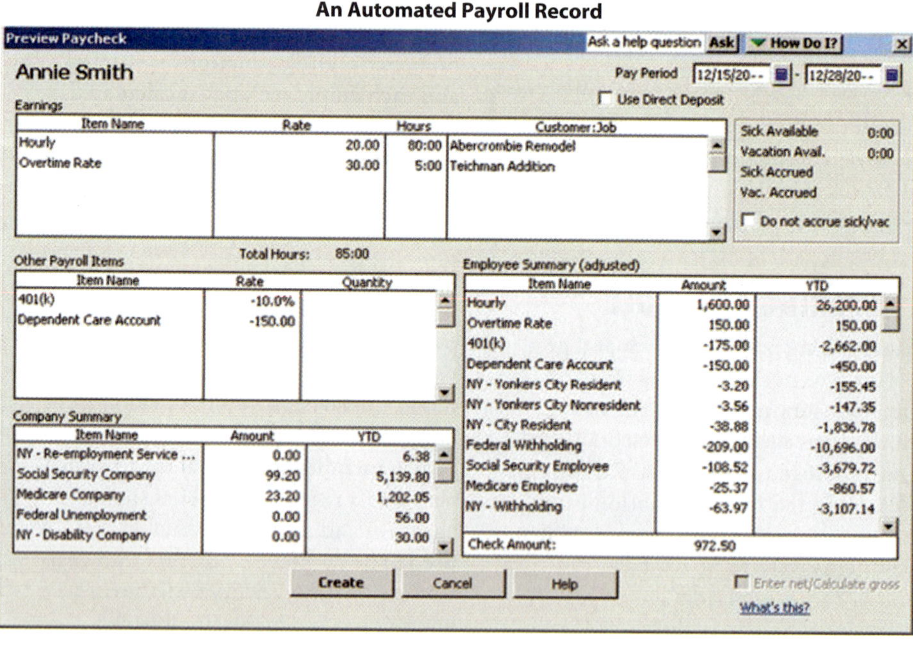

An Automated Payroll Record

Earnings

Item Name	Rate	Hours	Customer:Job
Hourly	20.00	80:00	Abercrombie Remodel
Overtime Rate	30.00	5:00	Teichman Addition

Sick Available 0:00
Vacation Avail. 0:00
Sick Accrued
Vac. Accrued
Do not accrue sick/vac

Total Hours: 85:00

Other Payroll Items

Item Name	Rate	Quantity
401(k)	-10.0%	
Dependent Care Account	-150.00	

Company Summary

Item Name	Amount	YTD
NY - Re-employment Service ...	0.00	6.38
Social Security Company	99.20	5,139.80
Medicare Company	23.20	1,202.05
Federal Unemployment	0.00	56.00
NY - Disability Company	0.00	30.00

Employee Summary (adjusted)

Item Name	Amount	YTD
Hourly	1,600.00	26,200.00
Overtime Rate	150.00	150.00
401(k)	-175.00	-2,662.00
Dependent Care Account	-150.00	-450.00
NY - Yonkers City Resident	-3.20	-155.45
NY - Yonkers City Nonresident	-3.56	-147.35
NY - City Resident	-38.88	-1,836.78
Federal Withholding	-209.00	-10,696.00
Social Security Employee	-108.52	-3,679.72
Medicare Employee	-25.37	-860.57
NY - Withholding	-63.97	-3,107.14
Check Amount:	972.50	

Applied Skills

Communication Have students create a communication designed to encourage employees to use direct deposit for their paychecks. Offer suggestions for the medium that students might consider for communicating their message. For example, they might prepare an insert for pay envelopes, a poster, a bulletin board, or a feature article for the employee web site or newsletter.

Marquese Co.
Anchora, IN

Pay Begin Date 11/14/20--
Pay End Date 11/20/20--

Employee Jan Exraee
2346 Transport Dr.
Tollboard, IN

Employee ID 83-221

Check No. 18925

Description	Current	Year-to-Date	Taxes	Current	Year-to-Date	Deductions	Current	Year-to-Date
Regular Wage	$480.00	$22,560.00	Fed	$91.20	$4.012.85	FICA	$31.99	$1,430.96
Overtime	$36.00	520.00	State	24.00	1.006.45	OASDI	7.48	334.66
						Net Pay		$361.33

Marquese Co.
Anchora, IN

No. 18925

Date November 20, 20--

Pay to the
Order of _____ Jan Exraee _____ $ 361.33

Amount Three Hundred Sixty One and 33/100 _____ dollars

BankCo, USA
Evincey, IN

Paula Morris
Paula Morris, Marquese Co.

12-3 Assessment

Key Concepts

Determine the best answer.

1. The financial records of employee compensation, deductions, and net pay are known as
   a. compensation
   b. payroll
   c. earnings report
   d. paycheck

2. True or False. Businesses are responsible for making required federal and state payments for each employee.

3. The electronic transfer of net pay into an employee's bank account is known as
   a. tax withholding
   b. FICA
   c. direct deposit
   d. an automated payroll system

4. True or False. Payroll records need to be maintained for all full-time employees, but not for part-time employees.

Make Academic Connections

5. *Math* Calculate the amount of employee withholding for Social Security (6.2%) and Medicare (1.45%) for each of the following employee's wages.
   Marjorie Elder: $865.00
   Antoine Fresher: $726.40
   Amelda Francois: $1,480.90

6. *Art* Create a poster or flowchart that illustrates the steps in the payroll process from the point that employees complete their work until their paychecks are issued.

FIGURE 12-4 *ANSWER*

The employee's net pay is determined by subtracting all deductions from the gross pay. In this figure, the deductions include federal and state withholding taxes, FICA, and OASDI.

ASSESS

Key Concepts Answers

1. b. payroll
2. True
3. c. direct deposit
4. False. Payroll records need to be maintained for all employees.

Make Academic Connections

5. Marjorie Elder: $53.63, Social Security; $12.54, Medicare.
   Antoine Fresher: $45.04, Social Security; $10.53, Medicare.
   Amelda Francois: $91.82, Social Security; $21.47, Medicare.

6. Posters and flowcharts should clearly illustrate the steps. Consider allowing students to work in pairs.

CLOSE

Ask students to identify one important fact about payroll that they have learned as a result of the lesson.

RETEACH

Have students review the lesson and write one true/false question related to each of the lesson objectives. Organize the students into two teams. Have the teams alternate asking the other team a question. At the end, determine which team answered the most questions correctly.

ENRICH

Some businesses issue paychecks to employees weekly, some bi-weekly, and some monthly. Have students discuss reasons why a business might choose a longer time period than weekly to calculate and issue paychecks.

308

THINK CRITICALLY THROUGH VISUALS

The advantage of making decisions with a team is that, by having more than one person look at the same financial data, different insights and creative solutions to problems are possible. The cons include the risk of power struggles over the final decision and the possibility that the team will not reach consensus.

12-4 Financial Decision-Making

Goals

Recognize important financial information managers use to make decisions.

Identify the steps in making financial decisions in business.

Key Terms

financial performance ratios

discrepancies

Focus on Real Life

There are an increasing number of computer applications and online tools that can make managing financial information easier. One such tool is the electronic budget. Available online or in software programs, budgeting tools can help manage finances and assist with financial decision-making. Electronic budgets are easy to use. They save time and offer managers more useful information than a budget done on paper. Electronic budgets provide detailed reports of various financial data. They can even do the math for you! One key benefit of electronic budgets is that you can look at what-if projections. For instance, you could determine how your business's expenses would be affected if you decided to increase your advertising budget. You could compare the results of hiring a temporary employee versus a full-time employee. Electronic financial tools help make a difficult management task easier and more accurate.

---

main idea

Recognize important financial information managers use to make decisions.

USING FINANCIAL INFORMATION

Financial statements are important management tools for business owners and managers. Financial statements present summaries of the financial activities of a business. Managers who understand the information in financial statements will be able to make decisions that result in the wise use of the company's money.

Important Financial Information

As previously discussed, the three most important elements of a company's financial strength are its assets, liabilities, and owner's equity. Three other key financial elements for a business are the amount of sales, expenses, and profits. A company reports its assets, liabilities, and owner's equity on the balance sheet. Sales, expenses, and profits for a specific period are reported on the company's income statement.

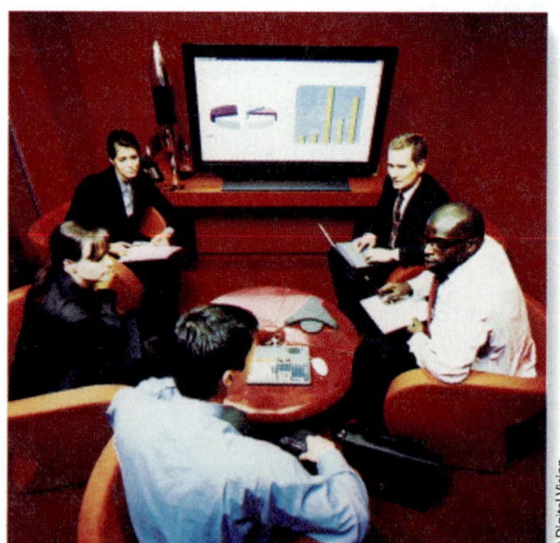
What are the pros and cons of having a team of people help make decisions?

Different Learning Styles

Tactile Learners Print copies of Figures 12-1 and 12-2. Have students review the copies to remind themselves how the important financial information is organized and presented in the two main financial statements.

Understanding Financial Performance Ratios

Managers use the financial elements found on the financial statements to calculate financial performance ratios. Financial performance ratios are comparisons of a company's financial elements that indicate how well the business is performing. Some important financial performance ratios are the current ratio, debt to equity ratio, return on equity ratio, and net income ratio. Figure 12-5 shows the formulas used to calculate each ratio.

Current Ratio Current assets compared to the current liabilities is the *current ratio.* Current assets are those that the business could convert to cash within one year. Current liabilities are all payments that the business must make within one year. The current ratio tells you if the business can pay its debts when they become due. The current ratio should be at least 1:1 for a healthy business. A 1:1 ratio means that there are at least as many current assets as current liabilities.

Debt to Equity Ratio The company's liabilities divided by the owner's equity is the *debt to equity ratio.* The debt to equity ratio tells you how much the business is relying on money borrowed from others that will have to be paid back rather than money provided by the owners. Most banks want to see a debt to equity ratio no higher than 2:1. Too much debt puts a business at risk because it may have trouble meeting its obligations to its lenders.

Return on Equity Ratio The net profit of the business compared to the amount of owner's equity is the *return on equity ratio.* The return on equity ratio shows the rate of return the owners are getting on the money they invested in the company. It should be compared to the return they could receive if they used their money in other ways such as savings, investing in other companies, or purchasing stocks and bonds.

Financial Performance Ratio	Formula
Current Ratio	Current Assets / Current Liabilities
Debt to Equity Ratio	Total Liabilities / Owner's Equity
Return on Equity Ratio	Net Profit / Owner's Equity
Net Income Ratio	Total Sales / Net Income

Net Income Ratio The total sales compared to the net income for a period such as six months or a year is the *net income ratio.* The net income ratio shows how much profit is being made by each dollar of sales for the period being analyzed. You should compare the net income ratio to past periods and to competing companies. The ratio will show if additional sales are as effective in adding to the company's profit as those in the past.

checkpoint »
Identify four important financial performance ratios used by managers to determine how well the business is performing.

What does it mean if your company's net income ratio increases from one year to the next?

© Getty Images/PhotoDisc

TEACH

Financial performance ratios are an advanced topic and may be difficult for some students to immediately understand. As some students demonstrate their understanding of the ratios, use peer learning to pair that student with another student who has not yet grasped the concept to help with the explanation and understanding.

FIGURE 12-5 ANSWER

A debt ratio higher than 2:1 indicates that a business might have too much debt. This puts a business at risk because it may have trouble meeting its obligations to its lenders.

ONGOING ASSESSMENT

checkpoint » **ANSWER**

Four important financial performance ratios used by managers to determine how well a business is performing are (1) current ratio, (2) debt to equity ratio, (3) return on equity ratio, and (4) net income ratio.

THINK CRITICALLY THROUGH VISUALS

If your company's net income ratio increases from one year to the next, it shows that additional sales have been more effective in adding to the company's profit than those in the past.

Teaching Strategies

Collaborative Learning Organize students into learning teams and have each team answer the following question: How can a business experience increases in both sales and assets and still have financial problems? Use the financial performance ratios to answer the question.

TEACH

Explain that financial conditions can change rapidly, and managers can be more prepared to deal with problems or take advantage of opportunities if they have the most current financial information.

Think Critically
Answers

1. Answers will vary. Discuss earnings of top professional athletes.

2. Answers will vary. Discuss how the success of corporate executives should be determined.

3. Government involvement reflects the growing public concern about executive compensation.

PROJECT

Provide the following instructions to students. (These instructions also appear on page xxv of the textbook.) Explain why making good financial decisions is no less important to individuals than it is to businesses. How do you make your financial decisions? Will this process help you achieve your life-span goals?

NET**Bookmark**

Decision-making is an important skill for managers. It is a skill that is needed by and useful for everyone. Access the web site shown below and click on the link for Chapter 12. Study several of the decision-making techniques introduced on the web site. Select one of the tools and try it out on an important decision you are facing. Now use one other tool and compare the results.

school.cengage.com/business/introtobiz

MAKING FINANCIAL DECISIONS

Managers are responsible for the financial health of their company and for the specific areas of the company under their control. If adequate finances are not available, the work that is required will not be done as well or as quickly as needed. On the other hand, if more money than is needed is used for certain operations, there many not be enough for other parts of the company.

The first step in financial decision-making is preparing a budget. The budget identifies the amount of money needed for all parts of the business to complete planned activities. It also projects what types and amounts of income will be earned from the sale of the company's products, services, and other investments.

Once a budget is developed and approved, managers use the budget as a guide to operate the business. They regularly check to see if income and expenses are meeting budgeted amounts. Income should be as high as or higher than planned. Expenses should not exceed the budgeted amount. Managers get regular financial reports and examine them carefully, looking for discrepancies. **Discrepancies** are differences between actual and budgeted performance.

CORPORATE SOCIAL RESPONSIBILITY

How Much Is Enough?

In 2006, the average compensation of the top executives of the largest 500 U.S. companies was almost $15 million. That was nearly a 10 percent increase from the previous year. Executive compensation is climbing much faster than employee pay. In 1968, the average corporate CEO made 20 times more than the average worker. Today the ratio is 400 to 1. As companies reduce the number of employees and make cutbacks to wage and benefit packages, many people are questioning the appropriateness of big paydays for company executives. They are asking, "How much is enough?"

Corporate boards of directors set executive compensation levels. Some critics, including shareholders, accuse board members of having close relationships with executives that result in higher pay levels than needed. Board members respond that managing a large corporation is extremely difficult and requires huge personal sacrifices, and the compensation levels reflect those demands. They point out that total compensation for executives is a tiny percentage of overall company revenues and that successful management increases profits and shareholder value.

In response to concern about excessive executive compensation, regulations have been enacted that require more disclosure. Also, legislation has been proposed. For example, the Shareholder Vote on Executive Compensation Act would require public companies to submit executive pay plans to a nonbinding shareholder vote to give shareholders a "say on pay" in their companies.

Think Critically

1. If multinational companies have annual revenues of tens or even hundreds of billions of dollars, is it appropriate for the top CEO to make $10 million or more in a year? Why or why not?
2. Do you believe there should be a relationship between compensation of a company's CEO and employees' wages? Justify your answer.
3. Why do you believe the government is getting involved in how executive salaries are determined? Do you agree or disagree with that action?

Life-Span Plan Answer

Answers will vary. Students should recognize the value of preparing a budget, using the budget, and making adjustments.

Applied skills

Language Arts Have students complete the sentence: I believe the most important financial information needed by managers is _____ because _____.

Discrepancies let managers identify problems before they become serious enough to harm the business. They might also see areas where financial performance is better than what was budgeted.

The final step is to make needed adjustments. If income and expenses are similar to the budget, the manager will not need to take action. If there are financial problems, managers will take corrective action to try to bring performance back in line with the budget. That might include finding ways to improve revenue as well as seeking ways to cut expenses. In some cases, performance cannot be improved or factors outside the managers' control are responsible for the poor performance. The managers may have to adjust the budget. This should be done as a last resort because the budget was carefully planned.

Use the information from Figures 12-1 and 12-2 to calculate each of the four financial performance ratios described in this lesson. Use decimals to express your answers. Discuss what the results mean for the businesses.

At the end of the period covered by the budget, the business will prepare new financial statements. It will use the results to determine the financial success of the operations. The company will also use the results to improve the budgeting process in the future.

checkpoint >>
List the three steps in financial decision-making.

12-4 Assessment

Key Concepts

Determine the best answer.

1. Which of the following is *not* one of the three most important elements of a company's financial strength?
   a. assets
   b. owner's equity
   c. payroll
   d. liabilities

2. True or False. Sales and profits for a specific period are reported in a company's income statement.

3. True or False. Employees rather than managers are responsible for the financial health of a company.

4. Differences between actual and expected performance are
   a. ratios
   b. budgets
   c. profit or loss
   d. discrepancies

Make Academic Connections

5. **Communication** You are responsible for helping a new manager understand financial statements. Prepare and present a short presentation explaining the importance of the balance sheet and income statement. Use a computer and presentation software to develop several slides for your presentation.

6. **Critical Thinking** In comparing current operating costs with the budget, you see that payroll expenses are much higher than budgeted, but income has not increased. How would you attempt to identify the problem? What might be some reasons for the discrepancy?

Work as a Team

The performance ratios are:
Current ratio: 3.4
Debt to equity ratio: .0.58
Return on equity: cannot be calculated from the information provided
Net income ratio: 3.77

ONGOING ASSESSMENT

checkpoint >> **ANSWER**

The three steps are (1) preparing a budget, (2) using the budget as a guide to the operations of the business, and (3) making needed adjustments to bring performance in line with the budget.

ASSESS

Key Concepts Answers

1. c. payroll

2. True

3. False. Managers are responsible for the financial health of a company.

4. d. discrepancies

Make Academic Connections

5. Share several students' presentations with the class to reinforce the concept.

6. Answers will vary. For example, the manager would need to carefully study the balance sheet and income statement in an attempt to discover the reason for the discrepancy. Perhaps a new product was introduced that had high start up costs, unanticipated overtime was needed to handle rush orders, or sales did not hit their projected targets.

CLOSE

Ask students to compare the management of their personal finances to the management of a company's finances.

RETEACH

List the three steps in financial decision-making on the board. Have students discuss how managers should complete each step and how the step contributes to the financial health of the business.

ENRICH

Ask students to identify how they believe employees can help to improve the financial performance of an organization. Ask for examples in the areas of revenues, expenses, and profits. Discuss why employees should be concerned about the financial performance of the company they work for.

Communicate Business Concepts Answers

1. Some expenses for the start-up phase could be patent fees for a new product, equipment purchases, computer hard ware and software, office furnishings, or registering the new business with state and local authorities. Expenses for the ongoing operations phase might include hiring consultants, attending conferences to keep current with industry trends, or replacing computer equipment. Expansion phase expenses could be similar to start-up expenses, or they could include opening branch locations, registering to do business in another state, or moving production to another country.

2. A budget is a future projection based on financial history and current trends. A financial record is an accounting of the actual financial performance of the company.

A budget charts the future, and financial records keep the company on track to meet performance goals.

3. A business needs an accurate cash budget so that it will know how much money was received and paid out for a specified period and whether it has enough money on hand to pay bills. It will also show when a business may have excess cash on hand. A business needs access to cash so that it can pay current expenses and remain solvent. Even profitable businesses need access to cash for unexpected expenses or when they experience a delay in receiving payments.

Business Notes

12-1 FINANCIAL PLANNING

1. The financial questions that must be answered in a business include: How much money is needed to start the business? From where will the financing come? How will funds be obtained to run the business for the months or years until it becomes profitable? What will be the best sources of sales and other income? What will be the expenses? When must they be paid?

2. The four main steps in budget preparation are: prepare a list of the income and expenses that will be a part of the budget; gather accurate information for each income and expense; create the budget by calculating each type of income, expense, and amount of net income or loss; and show and explain the budget to people who need financial information to make decisions.

3. There are three types of business budgets. The start-up budget plans income and expenses from the beginning of a new business or a major expansion until it becomes profitable. The operating budget describes the financial plan for ongoing operations of the business for a specific period. A cash budget is an estimate of the actual money received and paid out for a specific period.

12-2 FINANCIAL RECORDS AND FINANCIAL STATEMENTS

4. Financial records are used to record and analyze the financial performance of a business. The types of records maintained include asset, depreciation, inventory, account, cash, payroll, and tax records.

5. The two most common and important financial statements for businesses are the income statement and balance sheet. The business' assets, liabilities, and owner's equity for a specific date are listed on the balance sheet. An income statement reports the revenue, expenses, and net income or loss from operations for a specific period.

12-3 PAYROLL MANAGEMENT

6. A payroll is the financial records of employee compensation, deductions, and net pay. A payroll system maintains information on each employee to be able to calculate the company's payroll and to make the necessary payments to each employee.

7. A payroll record is a form used to document each employee's pay history. It includes such information as name, Social Security number, address, and tax and benefit records. After all payroll records have been completed and pay amounts have been calculated, a paycheck is prepared for each person. A paycheck usually includes the current and cumulative pay amounts and the type and amount of deductions.

12-4 FINANCIAL DECISION-MAKING

8. The three most important elements of a company's financial strength are assets, liabilities, and owner's equity. Two other key elements for a business are the amount of sales and profits. Managers use those financial elements to calculate financial performance ratios to make decisions that result in the wise use of the company's money.

9. The first step in financial decision-making is preparing a budget. Second, managers use the budget as a guide to the operations of the business. The final step is to make needed adjustments.

Communicate Business Concepts

1. Identify several unique business expenses for the three times in a business' life: start-up, ongoing operations, and expansion.

2. What is the difference between a budget and a financial record? Why are both needed in a business?

3. Why is it important to maintain an accurate cash budget for a business? What happens to a business if it does not have access to cash even though it has other assets worth a lot of money?

4. What information is contained in a balance sheet that is not in an income statement?

5. Confidentiality of the personal information of employees is very important in businesses and other organizations. If you were the payroll manager of a large company and had several employees who had access to personnel and payroll records, what would you do to protect the confidentiality of the information that they could access as a part of their work?

6. The use of direct deposit for employee paychecks saves businesses and banks a large amount of time and money. Many employees are still reluctant to use it. What are some reasons people may not want to use this system? What could you say to a friend to convince them to use direct deposit?

7. Why are the assets, liabilities, and owner's equity more important to the financial strength of a business than the amount of profit they earned in a particular period?

8. If you were a stockholder in a business, which of the four financial performance ratios would be most important to you? Why? If you were a banker considering loaning money to a business, which ratios would be most important to you? Why?

9. Do you believe the financial performance of a business is a more important measure of a manager's effectiveness than other factors, such as customer satisfaction or employee satisfaction or turnover? Justify your answer.

Develop Your Business Language

Match the terms listed with the definitions.

10. Reports the revenue, expenses, and net income or loss from business operations for a specific period.

11. Provide detailed plans for the financial needs of individuals, families, and businesses.

12. The employer electronically transfers net pay into the employee's bank account.

13. Plans income and expenses from the beginning of a new business or a major business expansion until it becomes profitable.

14. Used to record and analyze the financial performance of a business.

15. All income that a business receives over a period of time.

16. Lists the business' assets, liabilities, and owner's equity for a specific date.

17. Differences between actual and budgeted performance.

18. Describes the financial plan for ongoing operations of the business for a specific period.

19. What a company owns.

20. The costs of operating a business.

21. An estimate of the actual money received and paid out for a specific period.

22. A form used to document each employee's pay history.

23. Comparisons of a company's financial elements that indicate how well the business is performing.

24. The financial records of employee compensation, deductions, and net pay.

25. The value of the owners' investment in the business.

26. What a company owes.

KEY TERMS

a. assets
b. balance sheet
c. budget
d. cash budget
e. direct deposit
f. discrepancies
g. expenses
h. financial performance ratios
i. financial records
j. income statement
k. liabilities
l. operating budget
m. payroll
n. payroll record
o. owner's equity
p. revenue
q. start-up budget

Develop Your Business Language Answers

10. j. income statement
11. c. budget
12. e. direct deposit
13. q. start-up budget
14. i. financial records
15. p. revenue
16. b. balance sheet
17. f. discrepancies
18. l. operating budget
19. a. assets
20. g. expenses
21. d. cash budget
22. n. payroll record
23. h. financial performance ratios
24. m. payroll
25. o. owner's equity
26. k. liabilities

4. A balance sheet contains information about assets, liabilities, and owner's equity. The balance sheet sums up the financial picture of the company, while the income statement focuses on profitability.

5. Answers will vary. Payroll managers could have employees sign confidentiality agreements. Payroll employees should have passwords on their computers, and hard-copy paper files and folders should be kept in locked cabinets.

6. People may be reluctant to use direct deposit because they like receiving a paycheck, want the freedom to deposit it in varying banks, fear it will be more difficult to resolve problems with inaccuracies and do not like or trust change. Arguments for using direct deposit include security and the money would enter bank accounts more quickly.

7. Profits are determined for a specific shorter period of time. The balance sheet shows the financial health of a company in terms of its major resources and liabilities.

8. A stockholder would be most interested in a company's return on equity ratio as it would show whether this investment is as profitable as other available investment options. A banker would be most interested in the debt to equity ratio to be sure the business does not already have too much debt.

9. Answers will vary, but most students will probably agree that financial performance is the most important measure of a manager's effectiveness.

Make Academic Connections

27. MATH Lee Chan has owned a video business for three years. The first year, Mr. Chan barely earned a profit. The next year's profit was more substantial. As shown in the table, he has just received the financial results from the third year and wants to compare them to those of the second year of operations.

a. How much money in sales did Mr. Chan earn each year?
b. What was his total cost of doing business each year?
c. What profit or loss did Mr. Chan earn this year? What is the difference with the profit or loss from last year?

	LAST YEAR	THIS YEAR
Rent	$28,000	$28,000
Sales	78,250	80,725
Inventory	15,000	13,750
Payroll	17,850	18,210
Utilities	10,010	7,075
Supplies	1,020	2,020

28. TECHNOLOGY Use the Internet to identify two software programs that can be used by a small business to manage payroll. Evaluate the two programs and prepare a table that compares the features of the two programs. Prepare a written recommendation to a business owner on the software you believe would be the best choice with reasons for your decision.

29. ECONOMICS The budgets of a business are affected by events and changes outside the business, including the actions of competitors, and the strength and weakness of the local, national, and global economies. Review recent newspapers and business magazines. Find several articles that report on the economy and competition that could have a positive or negative effect on businesses in your community. Prepare a note card for each article on which you summarize the key points of the article and describe how the information could affect the financial decisions made by business managers.

Linking School and Community

Meet with someone in your community who is familiar with payroll, such as a small business owner, a certified public accountant, or a payroll service provider. Ask to see a sample of an earnings report (pay stub) from a paycheck. Identify the total amount of wages or salary earned during the pay period. Then identify the amount of each deduction listed. Calculate the percentage of the total wage or salary represented by each deduction. Then calculate the percentage represented by the total of all deductions. Finally, determine the percentage of the total wage or salary represented by the net pay.

Web Workout

Visit the web site of the United States Internal Revenue Service. Locate information about the following tax forms related to business payroll: W-2, W-4, 940, 941, and 944.

Think Critically

1. Prepare a brief description of the purpose of each form. Include answers to the following questions:

Who is responsible for completing the form? When must it be completed? Where is it sent or distributed?

2. Other than sending checks, how do businesses make payroll tax payments to the federal government?

Decision-Making Strategies

Dominique sat at his office computer reviewing the financial statements for his three-year-old business. He had yet to make a profit. He was able to pay himself a small salary but still had to hold a part-time job to maintain his family's lifestyle. He had added a part-time employee and needed another, but didn't have the money to pay another person right now. Dominique studied the business' balance sheets and income statements side by side. The balance sheets showed that the value of assets was increasing. Liabilities had increased as well due to the need to continue to borrow money to purchase inventory as his sales increased. He had been able to make regular payments on his building and equipment loans, so long-term liabilities were decreasing. There had been no change in the value of the owner's equity, so his investment was not paying off. When he shifted his attention to the income statement, he could see that sales were up sharply, but so were the costs of his inventory and operating expenses. He did notice that he had more cash on hand to pay bills as they came due and that the losses were getting smaller and smaller.

30. What financial information that Dominique reviewed do you believe is positive? What information is negative?

31. Based on the financial information provided, do you believe Dominique's business is successful or not? Justify your answer.

Human Resource Management

The hospitality industry requires employees to strive to satisfy the needs of customers. You are the Human Resources Director for a new 500-room luxury hotel that will be celebrating its first anniversary in three months. You have the responsibility to design a professional development meeting that not only recognizes employees for good performance, but also teaches more about customer service and teamwork. The meeting must cover company goals, strategies, and incentives and involve employees in team activities that strengthen employee relationships. Team games, activities or challenges, and prizes/rewards for accomplishment should be incorporated. You must create the agenda for team participation and corporate understanding. You have 30 minutes to outline your strategy and seven minutes to present the plan to the hotel general manager or students in the class. Up to three minutes will be allowed for judges' questions.

PERFORMANCE INDICATORS EVALUATED

- Demonstrate understanding of human relations skills.
- Describe why professional development is the responsibility of the business and its employees.
- Demonstrate successful evaluation techniques.
- Discuss compensation, benefits, and incentive programs.
- Demonstrate effective and informative communication and presentation skills.

Your team will be evaluated for

- Knowledge of human resources management and management concepts
- Application of critical thinking skills to interpret personnel policies
- Demonstration of effective oral communication skills
- Communication of employee benefits and compensation

For more detailed information about performance indicators, go to the BPA web site.

Think Critically

1. Why must professional development meetings include games and prizes?
2. What is the main purpose for professional development activities?
3. What strategy can be used to provide associates with essential new information while strengthening the company team concept?
4. What prizes or gifts can the hotel provide at the professional development meeting?

http://www.bpanet.org/

Portfolio Activity

school.cengage.com/business/introtobiz

Access the web site shown here to find portfolio activities for this chapter. Use the activities to provide tangible evidence of your learning.

---

event provides the opportunity for a team of students to plan an employee meeting to accomplish several important objectives.

Think Critically
Answers

1. Prizes and games will help break down negative stereotypes associated with professional development meetings.

2. Successful professional development provides current education and information and brings company employees together as a team.

3. Group involvement can be used to teach new concepts. Employee involvement in presentations is another effective approach.

4. Meal certificates at the restaurant and hotel room certificates are prizes the hotel could provide.

Decision-Making
Strategies Answers

30. The positive information that Dominique found is that he is able to pay himself some salary, the value of the company's assets was increasing, he had been able to make regular payments on his loans so that long-term liabilities were decreasing, sales were up so that he had more cash on hand to pay bills as they came due, and the losses were getting smaller and smaller. Negative information is that he still has to work a part-time job, he doesn't have enough money to hire another employee that he needs, his liabilities have increased, there has been no change in the value of the owner's equity, and the costs of his inventory and operating expenses have increased.

31. Dominique's business is successful in the sense that it is improving and moving in the right direction. However, the business is at the three-year mark where it should begin to show a profit. He might want to reevaluate the company's financial situation at the end of the third year to determine whether the business just needs a little more time or whether his investment and energies could be better spent elsewhere.

Winning Edge
Human Resource Management

Human resource managers have responsibilities for employee development and employee motivation and satisfaction. Meetings provide opportunities to recognize and reward employees and establish a positive organizational culture, as well as to offer training about new information and procedures. This

Production and Business Operations

13-1 Types of Production

13-2 Production Planning

13-3 Planning and Managing Business Operations

CHAPTER OVERVIEW

Chapter 13 describes how production occurs in businesses and how businesses organize and manage their operations.

13-1 Types of Production

This lesson addresses the role of producers and production in the economy and the various methods used to manufacture products.

13-2 Production Planning

Major production activities and how manufacturing procedures are organized are the focus of this lesson.

13-3 Planning and Managing Business Operations

This lesson helps students understand the importance of effective business operations and tools used to manage those operations.

Teaching Resources

Activities and Study Guide, Ch. 13
Chapter and Unit Tests, Ch. 13
Spanish Resources, Ch. 13

Exam*View*® CD, Ch. 13
Instructor's Resource CD
- PowerPoint Slides, Ch. 13
- Lesson Plans, Ch. 13

Xtra! Web Site

school.cengage.com/business/introtobiz
- Study Tools, 13-1, 13-2, 13-3
- Quiz Prep, Ch. 13
- Net Bookmark, Ch. 13
- Crossword Puzzle, Ch. 13.
- Portfolio Activity, Ch. 13

Planning a Career in...
INDUSTRIAL ENGINEERING

Industrial engineers work to improve the ways that businesses use the factors of production to develop products and services needed by businesses and consumers. They are involved in designing new products and improving the quality and usability of existing products. They help to improve the operations of businesses by introducing new technology, reorganizing work, and promoting the health and safety of workers.

Industrial engineers are highly educated scientists. They conduct research and apply mathematical and statistical models to problems. They work with managers and other experts in businesses to solve problems, reduce costs, and improve operations.

Although most industrial engineers work in manufacturing industries, they also work as consultants in health care, government, and higher education.

Employment Outlook

- While the number of manufacturing companies and jobs is declining, the demand for industrial engineers is stable.
- Because businesses need to make higher-quality products efficiently and safely, the services of industrial engineers should remain in demand.
- The concern for worker and consumer safety, environmental protection, and energy conservation should increase the need for industrial engineers with those specialties.

Related Job Titles

- Project Engineer
- Operations Analyst
- Quality Engineer
- Ergonomist
- Standards Engineer
- Systems Analyst
- Business Process Manager

Needed Skills

- Mechanical aptitude
- Math and quantitative abilities
- Scientific abilities
- Computer skills
- Organization skills
- Excellent communication skills
- Creative problem solving

What's it like to work in ... Industrial Engineering

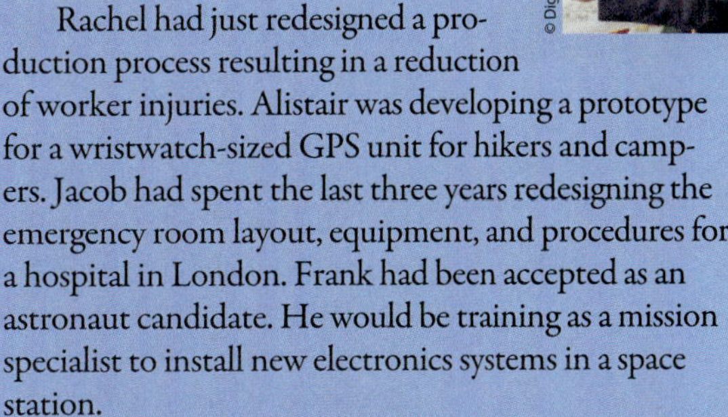

Four industrial engineers were gathered at the national conference of the Institute for Industrial Engineering. They had all graduated 10 years ago and were discussing their recent projects.

Rachel had just redesigned a production process resulting in a reduction of worker injuries. Alistair was developing a prototype for a wristwatch-sized GPS unit for hikers and campers. Jacob had spent the last three years redesigning the emergency room layout, equipment, and procedures for a hospital in London. Frank had been accepted as an astronaut candidate. He would be training as a mission specialist to install new electronics systems in a space station.

They realized, as they talked about their work, that they were in an exciting professional area. They were making important contributions to their organizations and to society. They agreed to meet again in a few years and see where their careers had taken them.

What about you? Why do you think industrial engineers are able to work in such varied types of businesses?

INDUSTRIAL ENGINEERING

Engineering is one of the most important career areas in manufacturing and production. In addition to helping design new products, engineers plan the production processes plus the equipment and tools needed. They also test products and check procedures to improve the quality of products and efficiency of production.

What About You? Answer

Student answers will vary. Industrial engineers are able to work in varied fields because almost every business enterprise needs to design new products that meet important needs of individuals and society. They also develop efficient manufacturing and production methods, as well as to improve the performance of existing operations and manufacturing processes.

317

Additional Career Information

Additional information on careers can be found in the *Occupational Outlook Handbook,* an online publication (www.bls.gov/oco) of the federal government. Tell your class about this resource and how to use it. This description of job duties can be used to demonstrate the relevancy of skills learned in this course.

">

Focus on Real Life

The production of most products we use today is very complex. It often involves several companies that may be located in different parts of the world. They must work together to plan and produce all of the parts and pieces of a complicated product and bring them all together for assembly. Ask students to consider a familiar product. Have them try to determine all of the components that need to be produced and assembled to form the final product they purchase and consume.

TEACH

Write this statement on the board: "The economy begins with production." Have each student write a paragraph that describes what the statement means to them based on the understanding of economics they developed in previous chapters.

List the three categories of products on the board: natural resources, agricultural products, and processed goods. Have students work as a group to name products produced in your state that fit within each of the categories.

13-1 Types of Production

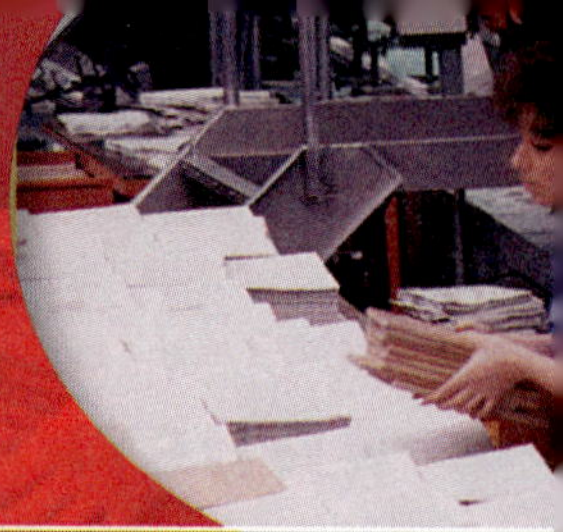

Goals

Describe the role of producers in the economy and the forms of production.

Differentiate among the various types of manufacturing.

Key Terms

- extraction and cultivation
- processing
- manufacturing
- mass production
- custom manufacturing
- materials processing

Focus on Real Life

When you buy a pair of jeans, you probably do not think about the activities and businesses involved in making them. An interesting sequence of events occurs. First, farmers plant and harvest the cotton and sell it to a textile company. The textile company makes it into cloth and dyes it different colors. Other companies make thread, rivets, zippers, and leather. The jeans are designed. The cloth and other materials are used to make the jeans in various styles, colors, and sizes. They are labeled, inspected, and boxed before they are ready to be shipped to retailers and sold.

Different businesses, large or small, complete all of these processes. They are often located in different parts of the world. These businesses are different in many ways, but are alike in that they all are a part of the production process. They help put a product or service that you want on the market. Producers are an important, but often less visible, part of the economy that supplies the goods and services you want.

main idea

Describe the role of producers in the economy and the forms of production.

PRODUCTION AS AN ECONOMIC ACTIVITY

The economy begins with production. Consumers need products and services to satisfy their needs and wants. Businesses also need products and services. They incorporate products and services into the products they produce and use them in operations. They also resell them to their customers.

Role of Producers

The role of producers can be described by the categories of products produced and the types of businesses that make products. The three categories of products used by businesses and consumers are natural resources, agricultural products, and processed goods. *Natural resources* are raw materials supplied by nature. *Agricultural products* are crops and animals raised by farmers. *Processed goods* are products that have been changed in form to increase their value and usefulness.

There are four types of businesses that are responsible for production: producers, extractors, farmers, and manufacturers. *Producers* develop products to sell to other businesses or consumers. *Extractors* obtain natural resources, such as water, oil, coal, and timber, from the earth for processing and use. *Farmers* tend land and other natural resources to grow crops and livestock that are later sold and processed. *Manufacturers* obtain materials from other producers and convert them into products for sale to consumers and other businesses.

Forms of Production

The forms of production are extraction and cultivation, processing,

Applied Skills

Building Study Skills Before students begin their study of the chapter, have them go through the chapter and develop an outline in their notebooks by copying the major headings and subheadings. Then, as they study the chapter, have them complete the outline by organizing key information under the appropriate heading. They can then use the completed outline for reviewing the chapter.

and manufacturing. In **extraction and cultivation**, products are obtained from nature or grown using natural resources. Extraction and cultivation ensure that there is an available supply of natural resources and the crops, livestock, fish, and other agricultural products needed. This is the most basic form of production.

Processing involves changing and improving the form of another product. Few products are used exactly as they are found in nature or grown on farms. Most are processed in some way before they are used. Water must be filtered and treated before it can be consumed or used in the production of other products. Timber is cut and formed into lumber or processed into paper or other materials. Oil is pumped from deep in the earth. The oil is then sent to refineries to be converted into gasoline, heating oil, and petroleum-based products. They are then used in the production of other products such as plastics, cosmetics, medicines, and food. The crops and livestock raised by farmers are sent to processing plants. They are inspected, packed, and shipped to supermarkets or are processed and combined with other products. This gives you the variety of foods you prepare at home or order in a restaurant.

Manufacturing combines raw materials and processed goods into finished products. Either other businesses or final consumers use those finished products. Manufacturing can be as simple as a cabinetmaker using tools and materials to build an entertainment center. It also can be as complex as designing a microchip for a computer or building a high-speed rail system.

Describe a process that farmers and other producers must use to turn a crop into a saleable good.

Each of these forms of production is needed to make all of the goods and services demanded by businesses and consumers. Each requires specialized tools and equipment, in addition to well-trained and often highly skilled personnel. The requirements to locate and pump oil from miles below the ocean floor, to design and build the equipment needed to create artificial diamonds, or the ability to plan and build a small aircraft that can be piloted from the Earth's atmosphere to the beginnings of space are hard to comprehend. But they are no more important to your quality of life than the expertise of the production team on an assembly line installing airbags into automobiles or the capability of the person inspecting the prescription drugs as they are processed and packed for distribution to hospitals and pharmacies.

checkpoint »

What are the three forms of production?

TEACH

Organize the class into three teams—extraction and cultivation, processing, and manufacturing. Have each team plan and draw a mural that illustrates their form of production so that the finished mural provides an accurate view of production.

THINK CRITICALLY THROUGH VISUALS

Answers will vary depending on students' knowledge of agriculture. Students should recognize that few crops go directly from the farm to the consumer. For example, after a farmer harvests soybeans, the beans are dried to the proper moisture content in bins and then carried by large trucks to a grain depot, where the soybeans are inspected and shipped via train or river barge to processing plants. From there, the soybeans are sold to companies with factories that use them in a wide variety of food products.

ONGOING ASSESSMENT

checkpoint » **ANSWER**

The three forms of production are (1) extraction and cultivation, (2) processing, and (3) manufacturing.

Different Learning Abilities

At-Risk Have students list the three forms of production. Then have them use the *Occupational Outlook Handbook* to locate one job or career area that interests them for each of the forms of production. Ask them to write a short statement that explains why each job interests them.

Work as a Team

In your team, create a table with three columns. Label each column with one of the types of manufacturing procedures. Agree on five products that would be manufactured using each procedure and list them in the column under the correct heading.

main idea

Differentiate among the various types of manufacturing.

MANUFACTURING

Manufacturers get products or raw materials from other businesses. They combine and change them into a form that their customers can use. One manufacturer might use steel, plastic, and other materials to make many parts into products such as skis or snowmobiles for winter sports. Another may purchase meat, vegetables, and fruit from farms to create frozen entrees you can heat in your microwave. A third takes timber from a forest and processes it into lumber and plywood. A construction company then purchases those building materials to build the houses for a new neighborhood.

A Manufacturing Process

Usually, several manufacturers are a part of the total activity needed to produce goods that are purchased by consumers or other businesses. Think about the jeans described in Focus on Real Life. The whole process calls for several steps performed by a number of businesses. For example, a textile mill in North Carolina buys cotton grown on an Alabama farm. It spins the cotton into yarn and makes the yarn into fabric. A plant in New England then dyes and prints the cloth. A clothing manufacturer in New York buys the cloth and makes it into jeans.

Increasingly, businesses around the world complete those activities. The raw materials and processed goods move long distances as they are produced, processed, and prepared for sale. Working together, producers each add their unique processes that change the form of raw materials into products that fulfill consumers' needs.

Types of Manufacturing Procedures

Manufacturing businesses can set up production in several ways to make their products. The number of products needed and the characteristics of the products will determine the type of manufacturing procedures.

Mass Production An assembly process that makes a large number of identical products using a continuous, efficient procedure is **mass production**. Mass production is sometimes called repetitive production. Automobile assemblies or beverage bottling plants often use this

What makes an assembly line a more efficient way of manufacturing?

---

type of production. Mass production allows a business to assemble products in a very large quantity and at a low cost.

With mass production, employees usually have precise tasks. They use specialized tools and equipment as they work on product assembly. That allows training costs to be lower and quality to be higher. It can also result in monotonous work and reduced motivation. Companies have been testing ways to add variety and raise the quality of work in factories that use mass production. Computers and mechanized equipment now assist with or perform many of the procedures on an assembly line.

Custom Manufacturing

Building a specific and unique product to meet the needs of one customer is done with **custom manufacturing**. Manufacturers make products ranging from dentures to a concert hall to meet particular design standards. When each customer has quite different needs or someone is building the product for a specific use, it may require custom manufacturing.

A business using custom manufacturing works closely with the customer to plan and design the product. It may call for unique materials or a special assembly process. With products such as buildings, bridges, or landscaping, the construction takes place at a new site each time. In other situations, such as the design of a unique tool for the space program or a special running shoe for a professional athlete, the design and assembly of the unique product will occur at the manufacturer's site. Sometimes, a small team of designers, toolmakers, and assemblers take part in highly specialized custom manufacturing. This team works closely with the customer and each

What kinds of everyday products are often custom made?

other to create a particularly unique product such as a musical instrument or race car.

Materials Processing Changing the form of raw materials so they can be consumed or used to make other products is **materials processing**. Oil companies refine crude oil to form gasoline and other petroleum products. Mills process grain into flour, cereal, and feed for animals. Digital editors convert a variety of audio and image files into films, CDs, and other multimedia presentations.

There are two types of materials processing. With *continuous processing,* the raw materials constantly move through

FYI

In 2005, 350,000 U.S. manufacturers produced and sold $4.7 trillion dollars of products. Ten years earlier, there were 10,000 more manufacturers, but they produced nearly a trillion dollars less. Reorganization, new technology, and production efficiency result in more products from fewer businesses.

Ask students to make a list of products that are produced using custom manufacturing. Have them identify the characteristics of the products and the needs of consumers that require customization. Discuss why customization results in higher costs and the reasons consumers are willing to pay those higher costs.

THINK CRITICALLY THROUGH VISUALS

Student answers will vary. Dentures and crowns, tailored business suits, duct work installed in older homes when upgrading the heating and air conditioning system, draperies, special occasion cakes, landscaping, decks, wedding rings and other jewelry, musical instruments, floral arrangements, and even computers are a few of the things that can be custom made.

Applied Skills

Communication Have students use computer software to prepare a visual presentation that compares the three major types of manufacturing procedures.

TEACH

Ask students why continuous processing is more efficient than intermittent processing. Why do businesses use intermittent processing if it is slower and more expensive?

THINK CRITICALLY THROUGH VISUALS

Materials used include flour, water, milk, eggs, oil, salt, and yeast. Commercial bakeries may add preservatives.

ONGOING ASSESSMENT

checkpoint >> **ANSWER**

Custom manufacturing is building a unique product to meet the needs of one customer. Materials processing is changing the form of raw materials so they can be used to make other products. Custom manufacturing involves a smaller amount of materials; materials processing involves larger quantities.

ASSESS

Key Concepts Answers

1. d. All of the answers are correct.

2. False. Extraction and cultivation is the most basic form of production.

3. d. custom manufacturing

4. c. textbooks

Make Academic Connections

5. Reports will vary.

6. Results will vary depending on the item selected. Product labels provide much of the information on the materials used.

---

specially designed equipment. This changes them into a specific product useable for consumption or for further manufacturing. Raw milk is sprayed into huge drying machines to produce powdered milk. Mills dry corn and then grind it for use in the production of feed for cattle or flakes for cereal.

Intermittent processing uses short production runs to produce a precise amount of a variation of a product. The machinery or materials are reconfigured each time to provide the required variation. A printer uses intermediate processing to complete a special order of stationary or to print and assemble a uniquely designed brochure. A baker resets the equipment to blend and bake wheat bread after making a batch of pumpernickel loaves.

What raw materials are used when making bread?

checkpoint >>
What is the difference between custom manufacturing and materials processing?

13-1 Assessment

Key Concepts

Determine the best answer.

1. Which of the following is *not* one of the categories of products used by consumers and businesses?
   a. natural resources
   b. agricultural production
   c. processed goods
   d. All of the answers are correct.

2. True or False. The most basic form of production is manufacturing.

3. Building a specific and unique product to meet the needs of one customer is known as
   a. materials processing
   b. mass production
   c. extraction
   d. custom manufacturing

4. Intermittent processing would most likely be used in the production of
   a. automobiles
   b. customized houses
   c. textbooks
   d. televisions

Make Academic Connections

5. *History* Gather information and prepare a two-page written report on the early use of mass production and automation in manufacturing.

6. *Geography* Select an article of clothing or a popular food item. Conduct research to determine the major raw materials and natural resources that are used in the production of the product. Identify the country or countries that are the major sources of the production or supply of those materials.

RETEACH

Organize students into teams to review the lesson and create a study tool.

ENRICH

Have students write a short story communicating their ideas about the future of manufacturing.

CLOSE

Remind students that production and manufacturing are still at the heart of business. Without them, most consumer needs would go unsatisfied.

13-2 Production Planning

Goals

Identify the activities involved in production planning.

Describe how manufacturing is organized.

Key Terms

applied research

pure research

production process

Continuous Process Improvement (CPI)

benchmarks

Focus on Real Life

Today, American businesses see W. Edwards Deming as a hero. That was not always the case. In the 1950s and 1960s, people thought that U.S. manufacturers were the best in the world. Dr. Deming had devoted his life to studying quality issues and applying quality improvement procedures. In 1946, he formed the American Society for Quality Control. He tried to talk with American businesspeople about his ideas, but they were not interested.

At the same time, Japanese managers were trying to rebuild their industries. They asked Dr. Deming for assistance. His work helped Japanese businesses become international leaders in product development and product quality. Deming is a folk hero in Japanese society. Because of the Japanese success, U.S. businesses began to study Dr. Deming's ideas and implement his quality-improvement processes. Today, businesspeople worldwide are aware of W. Edwards Deming's 14 points for management.

PRODUCTION ACTIVITIES

Production and manufacturing processes are very complex. They involve a number of activities and resources that businesses must carefully plan and coordinate. Before a company can manufacture a product, it must have the facilities and equipment needed to carry out the production activities. The company must obtain the materials needed for production. It must hire enough people with the required skills. It must check finished products for quality and store them until sold. The business must then distribute them to customers when and where they are needed.

Product Development

Before any production planning can occur, the company decides what products it will produce. A business cannot rely on selling the same products year after year. As customer needs and competition changes, new products will have to be developed. Product planning involves two steps—new product research and product design.

Product Research Companies devote a large amount of their resources to discovering new product ideas. For example, U.S. businesses spent more than $208 billion for research in 2005. Many scientists and engineers devote all of their work time to research and development activities. Their goals are to develop new products that will meet the needs of customers and improve the current products offered by the company and its competitors.

Companies carry out two types of research to discover new product ideas. **Applied research** studies existing

Focus on Real Life

Tell students that, based on Dr. Deming's work, almost all businesses and organizations today are concerned about quality improvement. Service businesses, government agencies, and even schools now have quality teams and are all studying important processes using Dr. Deming's principles.

Deming was also a composer and organist. He used his interest in music to provide an example of quality improvement. "Don't blame the singers (workers) if the song is written poorly (the system is the problem); instead, rewrite the music (fix the system)."

TEACH

Have students brainstorm activities that must be completed in order to produce a product and move it to customers. As each activity is named, write it on the board. When students have named as many activities as possible, have them review the list and try to put the activities in order from the first thing that needs to be done to the last.

Different Learning Styles

Kinesthetic Learner As you introduce and discuss the major production activities, have students use flowcharting symbols to prepare a visual depiction of the sequence of activities in the production process.

Work as a Team

Make a list of several new products that some members of your team like and some do not. Discuss the differences among the products and determine what makes some products appealing and others unappealing.

products to develop design improvements or new product uses. Engineers working for an automobile manufacturer will study the current designs to improve the efficiency of engines or increase passenger safety. **Pure research** is research done without a specific product in mind with the goal of discovering new solutions to problems. For example, scientists working for drug manufacturers study diseases and immune systems of the body. Their goal is to uncover treatments and cures.

Product Design When scientists develop a new product idea, businesses must turn that idea into a product that they can make and sell profitably. Design engineers create models and test them to come up with the best possible design. They select materials that make the product useable and durable.

After engineers build and test a model, the business determines all of the materials and parts needed for the final product. Financial experts determine the cost of making the product. They will get information from customers and competitors to decide the price at which they can sell the new product. By comparing cost and pricing information, the business can determine whether they will be able to make and sell the product profitably.

Production Planning

If a company develops and tests a new product idea and concludes that it can sell the product at a profit, the company then develops plans to produce the product. Production planning includes three activities. First, the company develops a

production process. Next, it obtains production resources. Finally, the company selects and prepares production personnel.

Production Process The activities, equipment, and resources needed to manufacture a product are part of the **production process**. If the business will make the product using mass production, it must organize the assembly line. Customized manufacturing requires that the company identify the changes in materials and assembly procedures that will be required for customizing each product.

Production Resources Next, the business orders or builds the machines, tools, and other equipment required for each of the production processes. Often, new products will call for customized equipment. The business must locate and organize adequate space to perform the needed production activities. This allows employees to complete work efficiently and safely. In some cases, a business will have to buy or construct a new building. In other situations, it can remodel current facilities from the production of older products that are being discontinued.

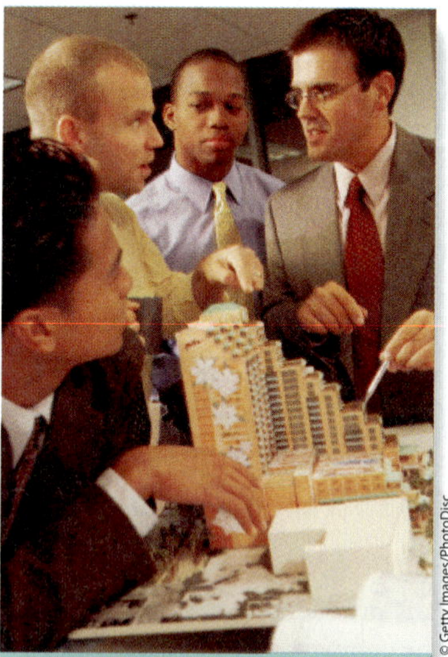
What are the benefits of making a model of your product first?

 CHAPTER 13 PRODUCTION AND BUSINESS OPERATIONS

Another planning step is to determine the sources of the raw materials, parts, and supplies needed to make the product. Often the manufacturing company will not have the needed resources. It will have to identify suppliers and negotiate agreements to make sure an adequate and timely supply is available at an appropriate price. The company may decide it can produce some of the parts and materials needed.

Personnel Finally, the company focuses on personnel planning. It estimates the number of employees needed to complete all production activities. It determines the skills required of each employee. The company will check to see if there are enough employees in the company and if they have the needed abilities. If not, it must hire and train new employees. Another option is to find a separate company with the capability and employees needed to complete some or all of the production activities rather than using its own employees and facilities.

Inventory Management

Inventory is a detailed account of a company's materials, supplies, and finished products. *Inventory management* maintains the supply of all resources needed for production and the products produced. Inventory management is a vital manufacturing activity. Most products are assembled using many different parts and supplies. Each of the items needed to make a product must be available at the time and place needed for assembly. If an item is not on hand,

Can your home sense that you are too hot or cold and automatically adjust the temperature? As you fix a meal in the kitchen, can you use voice commands to choose menu items, measure ingredients, and control appliances? That is the vision guiding research in the Royal Philips electronics company. Their scientists created a laboratory called HomeLab in Eindhoven, The Netherlands. HomeLab is an actual two-story house occupied by people who live there 24 hours a day. They are observed as they interact with prototypes of products the company is designing.

Philips calls the technology it is studying ambient intelligence. They believe that, in the home of the future, technology and people will be united in a way that the technology responds to the movements, sounds, gestures, and physical characteristics of the home's residents. They anticipate that their research will allow them to develop products ranging from lighting and appliances to entertainment units and even clothing that can interpret and respond to individual expectations and actions.

While the HomeLab is a very expensive research investment, the company believes it provides an ideal setting to conceive, test, and improve new products in an environment that reflects the way consumers live. They also believe it will speed the new product development process because the products are tested at the same time they are being developed. According to Philips' Chief Technology Officer, "Our innovation is centered around what consumers want. By observing them using our technology in their natural habitat—the home—we can better adapt that technology into real-world products."

Think Critically

1. What problems might the researchers encounter when observing people who know they are being observed? How might they overcome these problems?
2. Other than those listed, what types of products do you believe could benefit from study in this type of research laboratory?

Teaching Strategies

Collaborative Learning Have students form learning teams. Have each team create a product idea they would like to have tested in the Philips HomeLab. Ask students to describe why the HomeLab would present a good research environment for the product and what information they would need from the research to determine whether the product could be successful.

TEACH

Explain to students that maintaining an inventory of the raw materials, parts, supplies, and equipment needed in manufacturing is very important. Ask students to identify three different problems that could occur in managing an inventory for manufacturing. Examples could be late delivery, inventory being stolen or damaged, and poor record keeping. Have them discuss how each problem would affect the manufacturing process and what the company should do to make sure the problem does not occur.

Technology in Action

Many consumer products manufacturers are creating "living laboratories" where consumers can test new products the company is developing. Philips HomeLab is an example. While it is expensive, the company believes the type of research they can do in the home provides important benefits in new product development.

Think Critically Answers

1. People who know they are being observed may behave differently, perhaps reacting more favorably to products in a subconscious effort to "please" the company. This can be over come by making the observations as noninvasively as possible and by conducting the observations over a long period of time so that the research participants will let down their guard and interact naturally with the products.

2. Answers will vary. Any type of consumer product could be tested in a research facility such as HomeLab.

NETBookmark

A number of data collection and reporting tools are used to study quality issues and make quality improvements in business. Access the web site shown below and click on the link for Chapter 13. The web site provides examples of seven quality tools. Click on each example for a description and example of how the tool is used.

school.cengage.com/business/introtobiz

main idea

Describe how manufacturing is organized.

the assembly process must be stopped. Conversely, if a supply of any of the items is larger than the business can use in a short time, inventory and storage costs will be too high.

Inventory managers keep records of the supply and cost of all resources used in production. They work to ensure that suppliers deliver orders on time and in the correct quantities and price. The business maintains adequate storage space to make sure it can easily locate parts and materials and move them to production lines as needed. The space is planned to make sure that materials are safe and secure and can be moved quickly, safely, and easily.

After the business completes product assembly and inspection, it moves the products into storage or distributes them to customers. The business must keep an accurate finished product inventory in order to make sure it can fill customer orders. If there are not enough products available, it will miss sales. Too many products in inventory raise costs. In addition, products run the risk of becoming outdated.

> *checkpoint* >>
> Describe the three activities that are a part of production planning.

MANUFACTURING PROCEDURES

One of the biggest changes in manufacturing businesses is the production procedures used. Pictures of old factories show long assembly lines with employees located at workstations along the line. Employees are surrounded by tools and a supply of any parts they need to complete their part of the product assembly. Products moved slowly along the line and frequently stopped because additional time was needed to complete a procedure, correct a problem, or repair equipment.

Today, assembly is quite different. Employees often work in teams, completing many procedures together. Each employee is trained to be able to perform several assembly procedures. Supplies and parts move along conveyor belts or on robot-driven carts to arrive just as they are needed. Many products are customized to meet specific customer requirements as they are assembled. Managers, team leaders, and employees look at the screens of computers that monitor the assembly process and provide production information. Other employees quickly step in when needed to repair equipment or help to solve problems. Products move rapidly through the assembly process. Employees check products for quality at several points. When assembly is completed, the products are packaged, labeled, and moved to a loading area for immediate shipment to customers.

Organizing the Work Area

The type of product and production process will determine how the work area is organized. Mass production requires a large building. There must be space for the assembly line, equipment, tools, employee workstations, and storage for parts needed for assembly and

Different Learning Abilities

Specific Learning Disability (SLD) When assigning the Net Bookmark activity, ask another student to work with each SLD student to locate the Internet site, review the examples of quality tools, and discuss the examples of how the tools are used.

finished products. If the company completes customized production of small products, such as eyeglasses, there will often be a larger workspace for each employee. They will have easy access to the variety of parts and materials needed for each product assembly. Often, as production of each customized product is planned, one employee will be assigned to collect the materials needed for an order. With the order in hand, the employee will wheel a cart through the room that stores the parts and quickly select those needed. Then the employee will move the cart to the work area of the other employees who will complete the product assembly.

Building or assembling a product at the customer's location provides different challenges. Some examples are home construction, landscaping, and telephone system installation. In these activities, employees, equipment, and supplies must be moved to the customer's location. Transportation, storage, and security become major issues. Managers at the construction site must be able to communicate with inventory managers and with people responsible for transporting the supplies and materials needed. Often companies have an overall project manager who works in the company's office and visits the work site from time to time. Other managers are located at the various work sites. They supervise the construction and are in regular communication with the project manager.

Improving Manufacturing

Manufacturers face challenges today as they cope with rising costs, greater competition in the global marketplace, and growing customer demands. The challenges include the need for faster production, increased quality, and reduced costs. Companies are responding with improved manufacturing procedures, better employee training, and more attention to quality.

Manufacturing is made up of a series of processes. One process follows another until production is complete. In the past, if there was a problem within a process, managers and employees would try to identify the problem and attempt to correct it. This was a slow process. It affected all of the processes that followed. Improvements were not made until problems were discovered.

Manufacturers have now adopted Continuous Process Improvement, detailed in Figure 13-1, as a way to make sure manufacturing processes are completed as effectively and efficiently as possible. **Continuous Process Improvement (CPI)** increases the quality of work by reducing errors, inefficiencies, and waste. Rather than waiting for a problem to occur, processes are continuously reviewed with the goal of finding ways to improve them and reduce defects and production errors.

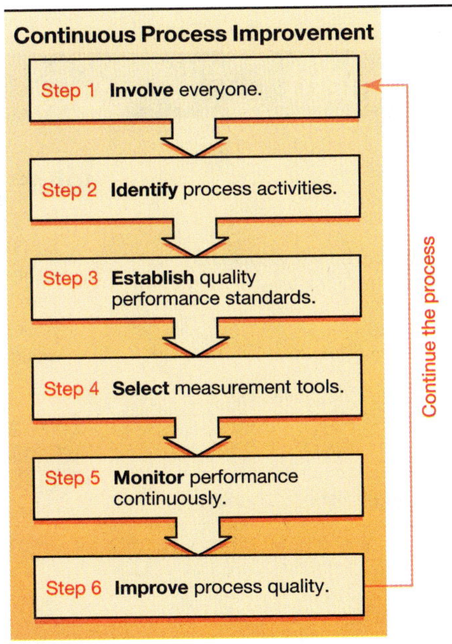

Continuous Process Improvement

Step 1 **Involve** everyone.

Step 2 **Identify** process activities.

Step 3 **Establish** quality performance standards.

Step 4 **Select** measurement tools.

Step 5 **Monitor** performance continuously.

Step 6 **Improve** process quality.

Continue the process

FIGURE 13-1

How would Continuous Process Improvement affect the prices that consumers pay for products?

TEACH

Ask students why it would benefit an organization to involve everyone in CPI activities rather than just the managers.

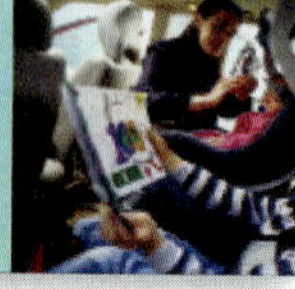

Answers will vary. Consumer products of all kinds have been recalled by the manufacturer or by the government.

ONGOING ASSESSMENT

checkpoint >> **ANSWER**

Manufacturers have implemented CPI because it can help meet the need for faster production, increased quality, and reduced costs. CPI increases the quality of work by reducing errors, inefficiencies, and waste.

ASSESS

Key Concepts Answers

1. False. As customer needs and competition change, new products have to be developed.

2. True

3. c. production resources and finished products

4. b. benchmarks

Make Academic Connections

5. Answers will vary.

6. a. January: 0.92%; February: 0.90%; March: 0.72%

b. Average production: 3,821. Average number of defects: 32.3. Average defect rate: 0.85%.

c. Graphs and charts should accurately illustrate the data.

CPI is designed to help an organization achieve its goals by improving the quality of work. CPI should involve everyone linked to work processes. That includes employees, managers, other businesses involved in the process, and even customers. It begins by listing all of the activities involved in the process. Standards for quality performance are developed. Often the standards are based on **benchmarks,** or the best practices among all competitors. Measurement tools are chosen and measurements are taken to determine if activities are meeting the standards that have been set. Based on those results, the people involved look for ways to improve each procedure to meet and exceed the standards. They also consider ways to improve the overall process by changes in activities, equipment, and resources.

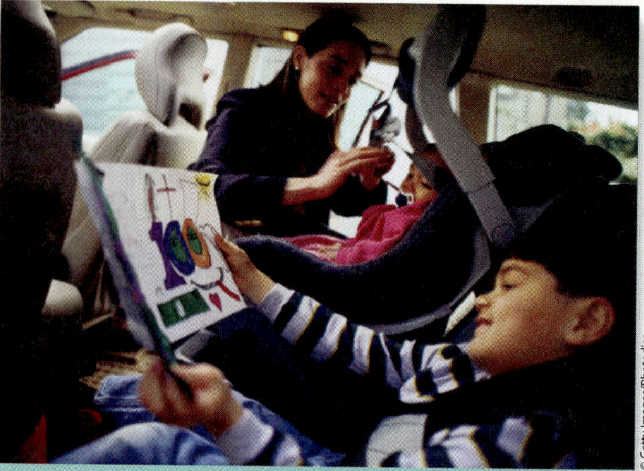
Some children's car seats have been recalled because they did not meet safety standards. Can you think of any other products that have recently been recalled?

checkpoint >>
Why have manufacturers implemented Continuous Process Improvement (CPI)?

13-2 Assessment

Key Concepts

Determine the best answer.

1. True or False. Once a company has developed successful products, it should be able to continue to sell them year after year.

2. True or False. Pure research is done without a specific product in mind.

3. Inventory managers keep records of
a. personnel
b. customers
c. production resources and finished products
d. All of the answers are correct.

4. The best practices among all competitors are
a. standards
b. benchmarks
c. CPI
d. quality measures

Make Academic Connections

5. *Art* Choose a small household product that you or your family use regularly. Evaluate the product and determine a design improvement for the product. Sketch a new design that illustrates the improvement. Show your sketch to other students and explain the product design.

6. *Math* A company keeps track of the number of defective products as part of its CPI program. For three months, the number of products and defects were

January: 3,358 products, 31 defects
February: 4,210 products, 38 defects
March: 3,895 products, 28 defects

a. Calculate the percent of defects for each month.
b. Calculate the average production and defect rates for all three months.
c. Create a graph or chart that illustrates and compares the three months of data.

RETEACH

Have students read each of the lesson checkpoints and prepare written answers for each.

ENRICH

Have students use the Internet to gather information on a company or organization that has adopted CPI. Have students report on the company, the CPI tools and procedures used, and the benefits reported by the company.

CLOSE

Remind students that manufacturers are constantly looking for ways to reduce costs and improve quality to remain competitive.

13-3 Planning and Managing Business Operations

Focus on Real Life

Have students discuss their experiences with the products from several manufacturers that are not compatible with each other such as video games, computer software, or cellular telephones. Ask them to consider why manufacturers may believe they benefit from that situation even though it is frustrating to consumers.

TEACH

Have students identify the day-to-day operating problems that many businesses face that are listed in the lesson. Ask them to identify ways that managers and employees can attempt to prevent each of the problems.

Goals

Discuss the importance of effective business operations.

Describe tools used to manage business operations.

Key Terms

logistics

just-in-time

operational plan

schedule

standard

Focus on Real Life

You put a CD in your computer and receive an error message. You purchase a memory card to use in your digital camera, but when you try to install it, the camera won't format the card. A digital cassette isn't compatible with the new digital video recorder you purchased. What's going on? Why can't manufacturers get together and agree on standard designs, sizes, and formats for their products?

Product incompatibility has been frustrating consumers and businesses for years. The International Organization for Standardization (ISO) was formed to address the need for standardization. ISO is a network of the national standards institutes from 157 countries. They develop consensus agreements among suppliers, users, government regulators, and consumers. They agree on specifications and criteria to be applied to the manufacture of products and the provision of services. As more agreements are reached and standards are issued by the ISO, there will be more cooperation and consistency among businesses and less frustration for consumers.

THE IMPORTANCE OF BUSINESS OPERATIONS

The day-to-day operations of a business often determine its success or failure. The company may have products that meet customer needs. They may have competitive prices. Still, several things can go wrong in daily operations that result in problems. Work procedures may not be efficient. Security issues may result in product thefts or damage to buildings and equipment. Lack of maintenance can lead to costly repairs or safety hazards for employees and customers. A poor work environment can result in dissatisfied employees who are less productive than they could otherwise be.

Businesspeople need to plan business operations as carefully as they work to satisfy their customers or plan for new products.

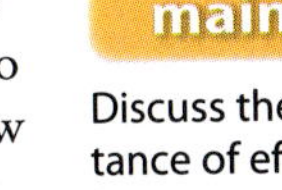

Discuss the importance of effective business operations.

What are some jobs where safety is a concern?

Students should have no trouble thinking of jobs in which safety is a concern: sanitation worker, electrician, welder, press operator, farmer, and employee in a nuclear power plant are just a few examples. Point out that any job can be unsafe if sensible safety precautions are not taken.

Different Learning Styles

Visual Learner Ask students to look around the school, businesses, and their home to locate examples of safety warnings, labels, posters, and the like. Have them make a list of the types of safety issues that are identified by the warnings.

TEACH

Ask students to start an outline in their notes using the common types of business operations as the major headings. Then, have students add a description of each to their notes during discussion, plus descriptions of the important activities that need to be completed for each type.

THINK CRITICALLY THROUGH VISUALS

Students should list improvements businesses could make to their facilities in order to attract more customers. Some examples are additional parking, more seating, better lighting, fresh paint, indoor plants, landscaping, new flooring, and updated signage.

Types of Business Operations

Some business operations are specific to the type of business. The production activities of a manufacturer are different from the merchandise display and promotion activities of a retailer. They are different from the patient care activities of a hospital. Even among those very different types of businesses, there are some common types of business operations. They are facilities management, logistics, scheduling, and safety and security.

Facilities Management Buildings are one of the largest investments of a business. Buildings house the work and workers. They provide space for all of the business operations as well as storage of materials, supplies, and products. Facilities management protects the company's investment of thousands or even millions of dollars.

Facilities management begins with making economic decisions about the buildings needed. Some companies buy existing facilities. Others build new buildings to house their operations. It may be more cost-effective to rent some or all of the facilities needed. Facilities managers continually study the long-term plans of the company. They must determine if the current buildings are adequate, if more space is needed, or if some facilities are no longer needed or are out-of-date. It may be necessary to buy additional buildings or expand existing facilities. The expansion may require that expensive land be purchased. Some companies purchase land many years in advance at a cheaper price in anticipation of expansion.

Building maintenance and repair is another vital task of facilities management. A regular cleaning schedule is followed. From time to time, walls must be painted, carpets cleaned or replaced, and equipment updated. Exterior maintenance, including landscaping, is another ongoing task. A business must maintain a professional appearance for visitors and employees. It must also make repairs to facilities and equipment immediately so the problems don't affect operations. Failure to maintain and repair buildings and equipment on a regular basis will result in higher costs in the future.

Another key area of facilities management is energy and environmental management. Energy costs are a rapidly growing expense. Companies need a ready supply of electricity, gasoline, heating oil, and water. Yet they also need to keep utilities costs under control. Facilities managers study ways to conserve energy resources. They also monitor the quality of air, building temperature, and other environmental factors to maintain a healthy and productive workforce. Many businesses are actively involved in implementing green management practices. *Green management* is concerned with protecting the

Give an example of an improvement a business could make to its facility in order to attract more customers.

Different Learning Abilities

Attention Deficit Disorder Have students look around the classroom and identify two things that require maintenance and two things that require repair.

environment through conservation of natural resources, wise energy use, and reduction of emissions, waste, and pollution.

Logistics Large quantities of products and materials move in, around, and out of a business on a daily basis. **Logistics** is managing the acquisition, movement, and storage of supplies, materials, and finished products in a business. Logistics has become a very important part of business operations. A newer term for logistics is *supply chain management*. A supply chain is all of the businesses involved from the time raw materials are obtained until finished products are sold.

The major activities that make up logistics are locating sources of supplies, purchasing, transportation, and sales. In addition to the physical movement of resources, logistics is responsible for effective communications and information among all participants in the supply chain. One important logistics process is just-in-time. Using **just-in-time**, goods arrive when needed (just in time) for production, use, or sale rather than sitting in storage. Just-in-time logistics requires careful planning and coordination among supply chain members. It also requires an effective information system.

Scheduling Even in small businesses, many activities occur at the same time. Scheduling involves determining the activities that need to be completed, the people who will complete the work, and the resources needed for the task. Consider a factory that produces a number of products to fill hundreds of customer orders. The factory must maintain the right inventory of products to fill each order. If customers have to wait too long, they may cancel their order. If too much time is spent producing one type of product, supplies of others may run low. If raw materials needed to produce a particular product arrive late, production of that product must be halted. Retail and service businesses find the same types of scheduling problems as they make sure they can match their resources with customer demand.

An important part of logistics planning is employee scheduling. Companies have a workforce made up of full-time, part-time, and temporary employees. The company assigns each employee to a work area. Each employee has a specific set of skills to meet job requirements. The company depends on having the right number of people available at any time to complete the scheduled work. The human resources department is responsible for making sure enough employees are available with the skills needed. They balance the workforce by determining the number of full-time, part-time, or temporary employees needed. They may need to hire more employees at certain times or reduce the number of employees at other times. A key human resource activity is training. Training ensures employees have the skills needed for their job assignments.

What are some complications in scheduling transportation of goods?

TEACH

Locate an illustration of a chain or draw a simple diagram of a chain on the board. Tell students that *supply chain* is a relatively new term to describe all of the businesses that must work together to supply a customer's needs. Ask them why the image of a chain is appropriate to describe the relationships among the businesses. Ideas include the strength of each link, many links are required, the order of the links, and how the links are connected.

THINK CRITICALLY THROUGH VISUALS

Complications in scheduling transportation of goods could include finding the proper amount of space on carriers (air, truck, train, or ship) and negotiating contracts, packaging products for shipment, having products ready on time, loading and unloading equipment and personnel, and arranging insurance on goods in transit.

TEACH

Ask students to consider the advantages and disadvantages to a business and its supplier of using a just-in-time system to deliver products from the supplier to the business rather than carrying large inventories of the products.

Different Learning Abilities

Limited English Proficiency (LEP) Have students use a language translation dictionary to determine the word in their primary language that has a similar meaning to *logistics*. Ask them to look up the full definition of *logistics* in a dictionary and then write the meaning of the term in their own words.

The National Retail Security Survey reports that retailers lose more than $30 billion of their inventories each year. The sources and proportion of those losses are

- Employee theft: 46.0%
- Shoplifting: 30.6%
- Administrative errors: 17.6%
- Vendor fraud: 5.8%

Safety is another main business concern. The business wants to prevent accidents and injuries to employees and customers. Businesses work to maintain safe work areas and work procedures. They provide safety training and enforce rules and regulations designed to reduce accidents. Many businesses place safety posters around the workplace. They recognize work units that have a record of no accidents or injuries for a period of time.

Information Management

Effective business operations require the coordination of many activities, resources, and people throughout the business. It usually involves the activities of other businesses. For a growing number of businesses, operations in many locations and even in several countries need to be coordinated. *Information management* uses technology to access and exchange information to complete the work of an organization.

Managers, supervisors, and team leaders are responsible for the weekly and daily work schedules. They determine the work that is required. They also prepare the work schedule. If a heavier than usual workload is expected, employees may be scheduled to work more hours. The schedule must anticipate employee vacations and the possibility that employees will be absent or leave the company. Most managers have a specific wage and salary budget they are expected to meet. They must schedule carefully so as not to exceed the budget but still get the work finished.

Safety and Security Companies are responsible for protecting people and property. Many events and circumstances can result in injury to people or damage to property. Companies devote a great deal of effort to providing security and safety.

Security procedures and personnel protect both people and property. Damage and injury can occur because of crime, unintentional actions, or natural causes, such as tornados, hurricanes, and earthquakes. Security personnel study the resources and activities of a business to identify potential security problems. They then prepare security plans and procedures to prevent problems whenever possible. The plans also minimize the amount of loss if a security problem occurs.

What can retailers do to recover losses suffered from shoplifting?

© Getty Images/PhotoDisc

TEACH

Remind students that, based on the recent terrorist threats in the United States and worldwide, companies are focusing even more attention on safety and security. Companies need to protect employees, facilities, equipment, customers, and products. Companies are spending large amounts of money and time and hiring additional personnel to increase security and safety.

THINK CRITICALLY THROUGH VISUALS

Retailers can recover losses suffered from shoplifting by charging customers higher prices. Alternatively, they could lower or freeze employees' wages and try to reduce other operating expenses. Retailers invest in electronic security tags, video cameras, and undercover security personnel in an attempt to reduce the amount of shoplifting.

Applied Skills

Technology Have students gather information on innovative products that are being developed to help solve safety and security concerns of businesses, government, and other organizations. Ask students to provide a picture or illustration of the technology and a description of its potential use.

Can you think of other ways that technology has made communication easier?

Information management has four goals.

1. To collect, organize, and securely maintain all needed information.

2. To provide instantaneous access to information required to perform work and make decisions.

3. To prevent access to information by those unauthorized to use it.

4. To use technology to improve communication and information sharing.

There are many types of information used in businesses. They include text, data, graphics, pictures, and video. Businesses exchange information in a number of ways. Oral communications include telephone, voice mail, face-to-face meetings, and now voice-over-Internet. Written communications take the form of letters, memos, reports, brochures, product manuals, e-mail, text and instant messages, and many others.

Information managers are responsible for designing, purchasing, installing, and maintaining the many types of technology used in the business. They must develop procedures for collecting, storing, and using information. They make sure the information is accessible yet secure. They provide training to all employees on the use of technology as well as on effective communications skills.

The Internet has become a vital resource for information management. The Internet provides a method for worldwide and continuous access to a company's information by employees, customers, business partners, and even competitors. Virtual communication using the Internet replaces face-to-face meetings. It saves time and reduces travel budgets. Yet the Internet also presents a number of security challenges for information managers. Those challenges include viruses, attacks by hackers on the business web site and computers, and equipment and software failures. Advances in technology and an understanding of how the Internet can be used encourage businesses to rely on it more often for effective communications and information sharing.

> **checkpoint »**
> Identify four important types of business operations.

Have students read the four goals of information management. Ask them to consider how the development of the Internet has made it easier to accomplish each goal. Then have them identify problems the Internet has created for businesses related to each of the goals.

THINK CRITICALLY THROUGH VISUALS

Technology has made communication easier by making it faster and more convenient. Instant messaging allows employees to communicate in real time. Documents can be sent instantly by fax or attached to e-mail messages. Voice mail can take messages for a person who is talking on the phone. Voice-over-Internet is another exciting new form of oral communication. Web cameras and videoconferencing technologies allow both face-to-face and oral communication to occur even at great distances.

ONGOING ASSESSMENT

checkpoint **» ANSWER**

Four important types of business operations are (1) facilities management, (2) logistics, (3) scheduling, and (4) safety and security.

Different Learning Styles

Print Learner Ask students to reread the definition and four goals of information management. To reinforce the lesson, suggest that students locate and read an article about information management and write a one-paragraph summary.

Risk Management

CHAPTER OVERVIEW

Chapter 14 discusses the risks faced by businesses and identifies ways to deal with insurable and uninsurable risks.

14-1   Overview of Risk Management

After studying this lesson, students will be able to identify important business risks and learn how businesses deal with these risks.

14-2   Insurable Risks

In this lesson, students will study important insurance concepts and the primary types of business insurance.

14-3   Uninsurable Risks

This lesson describes risks businesses face that cannot be insured and strategies businesses can employ to reduce risks in national and international activities.

Teaching Resources

Activities and Study Guide, Ch. 14
Chapter and Unit Tests, Ch. 14
Spanish Resources, Ch. 14

ExamView® *CD,* Ch. 14
Instructor's Resource CD
- PowerPoint Slides, Ch. 14
- Lesson Plans, Ch. 14

Xtra! Web Site

school.cengage.com/business/introtobiz
- Study Tools, 14-1, 14-2, 14-3
- Quiz Prep, Ch. 14
- Net Bookmark, Ch. 14
- Crossword Puzzle, Ch. 14
- Portfolio Activity, Ch. 14

Planning a Career in…

RISK ANALYSIS

Consumers and businesses buy insurance for protection against risks. When people who have insurance are injured, need health care, or suffer property damage, insurance companies pay for some or all of the costs. Insurance companies rely on actuaries to determine the premiums needed to cover the costs. An actuary determines the amount of risk insurance companies face and sets the rates charged. They evaluate investments to maximize the company's return.

Although actuaries work in all parts of the economy, many work in financial services businesses. Corporations and state and federal governments also employ actuaries. Many work for consulting firms. In order to demonstrate knowledge and skill to employers, colleagues, and clients, actuaries need to pass professional exams. Since 1988, the *Jobs Rated Almanac* has rated the job of actuary as one of the five best jobs in the United States.

Employment Outlook

- Actuarial positions are expected to grow more than 20 percent, which is much faster than average for all careers through 2014.
- Actuaries complete research for the insurance industry to develop, price, and evaluate products such as life, auto, health, or homeowners insurance.
- The fastest employment growth is expected in industries including finance, investments, software development, data processing services, health services, management, and consulting.
- Consulting jobs in the healthcare and retirement planning field are expected to grow faster than the average.

Related Job Titles

- Actuarial Assistant
- Actuarial Analyst
- Chief Actuarial Consultant
- Chief Actuary
- Chief Risk Officer
- Enrolled Actuary

Needed Skills

- A degree in mathematics, actuarial science, statistics, or computer science
- Courses in business, economics, and finance to understand business operations and costs
- Courses in English, speech, and business writing to develop communication skills

What's it like to work as an … Actuary

After Janine graduated from college, she obtained her first job working for a large insurance company as an actuarial assistant. During the first year, she worked on three projects. The projects involved evaluating the company's expenses to process claims, reducing time to review and update rates for group medical insurance, and developing an online insurance rate calculator for customers.

The company encouraged its actuaries to prepare for and pass the series of professional exams. New employees met twice a month with experienced actuaries for study sessions. Janine completed the first of seven exams while in college. Since she started working, she has passed three more exams and is preparing for the next one.

While her work is hectic, she enjoys the variety of the projects. "No day is like any other day," Janine stated. "You have to like pressure and tight deadlines." Eventually, she hopes to move into a management position and then maybe into consulting, with the goal of owning her own business.

What about you? What do you think are the benefits to Janine of passing the professional exams? How does her employer benefit?

Planning a Career in…

RISK ANALYSIS

Most people are aware of the career of insurance salesperson, but many are not aware of the variety of other insurance careers. One of the most important insurance career areas is in risk analysis. Insurance companies rely on expert risk analysts, known as actuaries, to determine the potential costs of damages the company will have to pay to the individuals and organizations it insures. If the analysis is not accurate, the insurance company can lose a great deal of money.

What About You? Answers

The benefit to Janine for passing the professional exams is that she will gain credibility and will have more career options, whether to advance into management with her present employer or to realize her dream of starting her own consulting business. The company benefits because having a competent and highly trained actuarial staff means it will make the best and most profitable decisions possible when underwriting risks.

Additional Career Information

Additional information on careers can be found in the *Occupational Outlook Handbook,* an online publication (www.bls.gov/oco) of the federal government. Tell your class about this resource and how to use it. This description of job duties can be used to demonstrate the relevancy of skills learned in this course

Overview of Risk Management

Goals

Identify the types of risks facing businesses.

Describe ways that businesses can deal with risks.

Key Terms

risk

economic risk

personal risk

property risk

liability risk

pure risk

controllable risk

insurance

Focus on **Real Life**

As Jamie walked away from the cell phone kiosk, he was facing two important decisions. He had found a cell phone with all of the features he wanted. It was a bit more expensive than he anticipated, but he had enough money. The monthly plan was affordable with the services he wanted. The salesperson told Jamie he could save $100 on the price of the phone if he would sign a two-year contract with the wireless service provider. Yet if he cancelled the service during that time, he would have to pay the company $200. The service provider was a new company and Jamie wasn't sure he would like their service enough to commit to two years.

In addition, the salesperson offered Jamie a protection plan that would provide a replacement if Jamie's phone were lost or stolen for a cost of $4.95 a month. Jamie had never lost his phone but knew of several friends who had. He knew he could not afford to replace the phone.

As Jamie walked away, he was thinking about the contract and the protection plan. He would have to think about the costs versus the risks before making a final decision.

main idea

Identify the types of risks facing businesses.

IDENTIFYING RISKS

Every day you face risks. **Risk** is the possibility of incurring a loss. You face many types of risks and possible losses. Some are very important to you and can have long-term effects. The risk of a serious illness or an accident that results in an injury would have a major impact on your life. A hurricane, tornado, or fire can leave homes, businesses, and even entire communities damaged or ruined.

Other risks are inconvenient but have little lasting effect. If you are caught in traffic, you risk being late for an appointment. When you buy a new product, you risk that it might go on sale in two weeks. Even if you are very careful, you cannot avoid all risks and losses. Still, individuals and businesses need to be aware of risks and try to reduce possible losses, especially for those risks that may result in physical or financial harm.

Can you think of reasons for buying a warranty on a product you just purchased?

© Getty Images/PhotoDisc

Different Learning Abilities

Attention Deficit Disorder Have students write the term *risk* and its definition. Then have them identify three risks they currently face and three that may be faced in the future. Have students work in pairs or small groups to discuss the risks they have identified.

344

Types of Risks

There are many ways of viewing risks. Being able to identify the type of risk helps to determine how to plan for the risk. Planning for a risk may reduce the chance that it will occur or reduce its impact if it does occur.

Economic and Non-Economic Risks

A risk that can result in financial loss is an **economic risk**. There are three categories of economic risks. A **personal risk** can result in personal losses such as health and personal well-being. A **property risk** can lead to loss of personal or business property including money, vehicles, and buildings. A **liability risk** relates to harm or injury to other people or their property because of your actions.

Non-economic risks may result in inconvenience or embarrassment but do not have a financial impact. A traffic accident is an economic risk. It can result in expenses such as medical care, automobile repairs, and higher insurance rates. Deciding with your friends to perform at the school talent show is a non-economic risk. You may be uncomfortable or embarrassed if the show does not go well, but you won't suffer financially.

Pure and Speculative Risks

A risk that presents the chance of loss but no opportunity for gain is a **pure risk**. Severe weather is an example of a pure risk. The storm may pass with no harm to a business. A heavy snowstorm that causes the business to close for a day or two will reduce sales. Wind and rain damage to a building will add to expenses because of the cost of repairs.

Speculative risks offer the chance either to gain or to lose. Suppose you invest your money in a new business. If it is successful, you will make a nice profit. On the other hand, if it fails you can lose all of the money you invested.

Controllable and Uncontrollable Risks

A risk that you can reduce or eliminate by actions you take is a **controllable risk**. To prevent loss from theft, businesses install security systems, hire guards, and train employees to be alert for possible problems. *Uncontrollable risks* cannot be reduced by your actions. A sudden hailstorm or early freeze can affect a farmer's crops and little can be done to reduce the losses suffered.

Insurable and Uninsurable Risks

People look for ways to protect themselves from the negative effects of risks. A common form of protection is insurance. **Insurance** exchanges the uncertainty of a possible large financial loss for a certain smaller payment. If a large number of people face a given risk and the cost of possible losses can be predicted, it is an *insurable risk*. If a risk is not common or if it is impossible to predict the amount of loss that could be suffered, it is an *uninsurable risk*.

What unexpected economic and non-economic issues may result from a traffic accident?

checkpoint »
What is risk?

TEACH

Have students prepare an outline of the terms related to the types of risks discussed in the lesson. Have them record each of the major types of risks and the categories for each of the types. Ask students to list the examples from the lesson under each category and then identify one additional example of each.

THINK CRITICALLY THROUGH VISUALS

Unexpected economic issues that may result from a traffic accident include: the cost of repairing the vehicles and other damage; the cost of medical care for anyone who was injured; time away from work to get estimates and have repairs made; the cost of replacement transportation while the vehicle is in the shop; fines and court costs; and higher insurance rates. Non-economic issues could include pain and mobility problems if an injury occurred, and possibly frustration and anger.

ONGOING ASSESSMENT

checkpoint » **ANSWER**
Risk is the possibility of incurring a loss.

Different Learning Styles

Visual Learner Have students create a poster that visually identifies each of the types and categories of risks described in the lesson. Instruct students to locate a picture or illustration that represents each risk and add it to the poster.

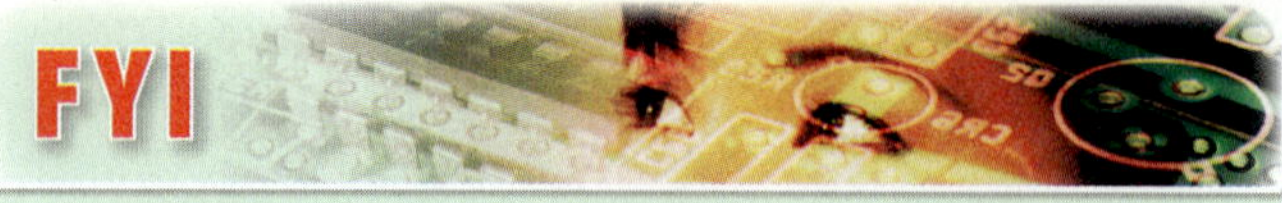

The Insurance Services Office (ISO) defines catastrophes as events causing at least $25 million in insured property losses to a significant number of insurers and policyholders. A record 24 catastrophes, including four major hurricanes, hit the United States in 2005, resulting in total losses of $61.9 billion.

main idea

Describe ways that businesses can deal with risks.

DEALING WITH RISKS

Suppose you and nine of your friends each have a new set of golf clubs. Each set is worth about $600. You all decide to form an organization called the Golf Club Owners Insurance Association (GCOIA) as shown in Figure 14-1. The purpose of the GCOIA is to reduce the risk of a large financial loss should one member's clubs get stolen. To provide protection, each member agrees to share the cost of replacing any stolen clubs. Therefore, if your golf clubs were stolen, each member (including yourself) would contribute $60 to buy new clubs for you. If you are not a member of the GCOIA and your clubs are stolen, you would have to pay the total cost ($600) of new clubs. As a member, replacing your stolen clubs would only cost you $60. When a member loses golf clubs, each member suffers only a relatively small economic loss. In that way, the members help one another by sharing the risk of economic loss.

Everyone faces risks. Many of these risks will result in financial damage or possible disaster if the loss is severe. Individuals and businesses must determine how they will deal with the risks and possible losses they face. Figure 14-2 shows that there are four possible ways to deal with risks.

Avoid the Risk

With thought and planning, you might be able to avoid some risks. If you don't believe you have enough experience or skill to start your own business, you can decide not to become an entrepreneur. If a snowstorm is in the forecast, you can choose not to drive your car to avoid a possible accident. If market research suggests there may not be enough demand for a new product to cover the costs, a business can choose not to make that product.

In order to avoid risks, decision-makers need to be aware of risks that can threaten a decision. They must determine the costs and possible rewards of their decisions. They must estimate the size of losses if anticipated problems occur. If the likelihood of risk or the amount of loss is too great, they may make the decision to avoid the action. This ensures that there will be no loss.

FIGURE 14-1

Would you want to pay for someone else's clubs if you took care of your own clubs to make sure they were not stolen?

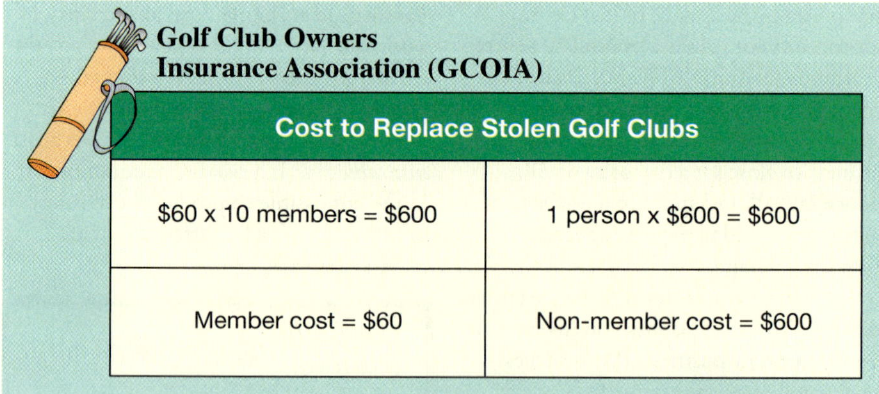

Sharing the Risk of a Financial Loss

Cost to Replace Stolen Golf Clubs	
$60 x 10 members = $600	1 person x $600 = $600
Member cost = $60	Non-member cost = $600

Applied Skills

Mathematics An insurance company insures eight businesses for fire loss in one city. Each business has insured property valued at an average of $340,000. The insurance company estimates that there will be fire losses of 12 percent of the insured value in any year, but they budget 110 percent of the estimated losses each year in case losses are higher than average. How much should the insurance company budget to cover the fire losses of the eight businesses each year?
Answer: $8 \times \$340{,}000 \times 0.12 \times 1.1 = \$359{,}040$

Transfer the Risk

Sometimes an activity must occur even though there is a risk that can have serious financial consequences. If a business is not in a position to assume the risk, it may choose to transfer it. When a business transfers a risk, someone else assumes the risk. A company may not be able to afford losses that it could suffer if the company offers customer credit and several credit customers do not pay their bills. In that situation, the company may transfer the risk of poor credit to a bank or credit card company. These businesses already have a credit operation. They are able to manage credit customers more effectively. They are also in a position to handle larger credit losses. The bank or credit card company will be willing to accept the risk of credit sales with the likelihood that they can make a profit on the interest paid by the credit customers.

A company can transfer the risk of product damage by using other channel members to store and distribute products. A manufacturer can transfer the risk of a costly or unsuccessful research process by forming a joint venture with an experienced research firm. The cost of the research will be shared with the other company that already employs experienced researchers. If the research is successful, the manufacturer will produce and sell the product. It will then share the profits with the research partner.

Insure the Risk

If a business faces the same type of risk also faced by others and the size of losses can be reasonably predicted, it is possible to purchase insurance. In the case of the Golf Club Owners Insurance Association described earlier, each club owner insured the risk of stolen clubs by paying a small amount to the Association. In the same way, businesses that face the risk of fire damage to their buildings, equipment, and inventories can pool those risks with other businesses by purchasing fire insurance.

It is possible that a few businesses will have losses from fires during a specific period. Based on the history of fires in businesses, it is possible to reasonably estimate the total amount of fire damage among a number of businesses for that amount of time. Each business will pay a small amount for insurance that will cover the losses of the businesses that suffer a loss from fire.

Assume the Risk

Some companies decide that they are willing to assume certain risks. That means that if they suffer a loss, they will deal with the result. Typically, if a business decides to assume a risk, it means that the result of damage will not have serious negative consequences on the business. The company believes available funds can cover any financial loss.

A very large business may choose to set aside a small amount of money each month rather than purchasing insurance. They believe that if a financial loss occurs because of a risk, there will be enough money saved to cover the amount of the loss.

Four Possible Ways to Deal with Risk	
Method	**Activity**
Avoid	Choose not to completed the risky activity
Transfer	Find another business to complete the activity
Insure	Purchase insurance to pay for any losses
Assume	Completed the activity with full responsibility

FIGURE 14-2

What method would you use to avoid the risk of your cell phone being stolen?

TEACH

Ask students why one company would want to assume risks faced by another company. In almost all cases, it is because they can manage the risk better and believe they can make a profit or obtain another benefit for their business.

FIGURE 14-2 ANSWER

Students could choose the avoid method by simply not owning a cell phone. They might be able to choose the insure method by paying a monthly fee to insure the phone against loss or theft. Or they may assume the risk, use the cell phone as carefully as possible, and hope it is not lost or stolen. They might even be able to transfer the risk by renting or borrowing a phone.

TEACH

Divide the class into four groups. Assign each group one of the methods of dealing with risks. As a group, think of possible risks faced by individuals and businesses. For each of the identified risks, have each group try to identify an example of how to deal with the risk using their assigned method.

Applied Skills

Language Arts Have students write a paragraph explaining why it is important for businesses to identify the risks they face and how they plan to deal with those risks. Invite several students to read their paragraphs aloud.

Work as a Team

After teams have completed their work, invite a school administrator who is familiar with the types of insurance carried by the school or school district to meet with the class and discuss how the school identifies its insurance needs.

ONGOING ASSESSMENT

checkpoint >> **ANSWER**

Business can deal with risk by (1) avoiding the risk, (2) transferring the risk, (3) insuring the risk, or (4) assuming the risk.

ASSESS

Key Concepts Answers

1. False. The loss may not occur. Speculative risks even offer the chance to gain.

2. d. All are economic risks.

3. c. transferring

4. True

Make Academic Connections

5. Tables will vary depending on when the assignment is completed.

6. Student answers will vary depending on the 10 risks they choose for their lists.

CLOSE

Have students describe reasons why understanding risks and how to deal with the risks they face are very important to businesses.

Work as a Team

Work with your team to recognize several risks that could affect your school, students, staff, and visitors. Identify one or more risks that fit each of the following types: economic, non-economic, controllable, and uncontrollable. Discuss how the identified risks could be reduced.

In other situations, it may not be possible to avoid, transfer, or insure a risk. If that is the case, the business will need to assume the risk. Once a business produces or purchases a product for resale, it must be able to sell the products at a reasonable price in order to cover its costs. If the sales goals are not met, the business suffers a loss. It assumes the risk of being able to sell its inventory at a profit.

Some risks are so unlikely that the company decides to do nothing. It assumes a problem will not occur. The company may be forced to take emergency actions if it is wrong. A company hires enough employees to operate the business. It knows a few extra employees are needed because at any time a certain number will be on vacation, on sick leave, or out for other reasons. If the company is suddenly hit with a major flu epidemic, there may not be enough employees available to run the business for a few days. Managers will have to decide whether to hire temporary employees, reduce some operations, or even close the business until employees recover.

checkpoint >>
Identify four ways that a business can deal with risks.

14-1   Assessment

Key Concepts

Determine the best answer.

1. True or False. Every risk you face results in a loss.

2. Which of the following is *not* a type of economic risk?
  a. personal risk
  b. property risk
  c. liability risk
  d. All are economic risks.

3. Using another business to complete a risky activity is known as _?_the risk.
  a. assuming
  b. avoiding
  c. transferring
  d. insuring

4. True or False. To be insurable, the same type of risk must be shared by a large number of businesses or individuals.

Make Academic Connections

5. *Environment* Storms, earthquakes, and other natural disasters are often very costly to individuals, businesses, and communities. Millions of dollars in damages are suffered. It takes months and even years to recover. Use the Internet to identify the most costly natural disasters that have occurred in recent years. Identify the type of disaster, the country or region affected, and the estimated financial costs of each. Prepare a table to report your findings.

6. *Critical Thinking* Think carefully about the types of risks you and other family members face as a part of your daily lives. Make a list of 10 such risks. Classify each risk as controllable or uncontrollable and justify each of your classification decisions. For each of the controllable risks, describe actions you and your family members can take to reduce the risk or the possible damage that could occur.

RETEACH

Have students write each of the key terms in their notebooks, then locate the definition of the term and record it beside the term. Have students write a sentence that demonstrates their understanding of each term.

ENRICH

Have students use the Internet to find examples of unusual items that have been insured.

Sharpen Your Life Skills

Sharpen Your Life Skills

Reducing Personal Risks with Lifestyle Choices

The decisions people make about lifestyles are by far the most important factors influencing their health. The U.S. Centers for Disease Control and Prevention report that several key factors influence a person's well-being.

- Quality of medical care, 10%
- Heredity, 18%
- Living and working environment, 19%
- Lifestyle choices, 53%

People want to live long, healthy, and happy lives. Even so, the day-to-day choices you make can result in poor physical and emotional health, accidents, and relationship problems. Your lifestyle reflects your activities, values, beliefs, and behaviors. Day-to-day choices also have an impact on your long-term health and happiness. Making risky choices or failing to be concerned about your physical and emotional health can have negative consequences. These consequences may be hard to overcome or even life-threatening.

Areas where people can make positive lifestyle choices include nutrition, physical activity, medical care, emotional health, interpersonal relationships, and personal development. Making positive lifestyle choices is key to reducing personal risks.

Nutrition Eat a balanced diet that includes a variety of foods. Select foods that promote energy and health. Don't overeat or eat too little. Avoid excessive snacking or foods and beverages filled with "empty" calories.

Physical Activity Maintain an active schedule involving enjoyable physical activities. Take part in activities that exercise your heart, strengthen muscles, and build flexibility. Develop skills in physical activities you can enjoy all of your life.

Medical Care Schedule regular visits with your family doctor, dentist, and eye-care specialist. Actively participate in your medical care by providing accurate and complete information, asking questions, and following the advice of your health care providers.

Emotional Health Stay active mentally and emotionally. Develop friendships, but also take time for yourself. Take on creative activities. Don't bottle up your emotions. Don't be afraid to discuss your feelings or seek help from counselors and mentors.

© Getty Images/PhotoDisc

Interpersonal Relationships Spend time with family and friends. Avoid using negative communications that others can easily misinterpret. Be open to people with different backgrounds and experiences. Resolve conflicts before they affect long-term relationships.

Personal Development Set personal, academic, and career goals. Make plans to achieve them. Think about the short- and long-term consequences of your decisions and actions. Avoid risky behaviors including the use of tobacco, alcohol, and drugs. Drive safely, wear your seat belt, and avoid distractions. Think before participating in activities that can lead to accidents or injuries to you or others.

Think Critically

1. How can decisions made today affect your lifestyle in the future?
2. What additional recommendations can you make for a healthy and happy lifestyle?

Often we don't think about risks until it is too late. Then we suffer the consequences of that risk. By anticipating risks and thinking about their consequences, we might decide to do things differently so that negative results are greatly reduced or even eliminated. This type of planning can be especially important for the many personal risks we face and the way our lifestyle choices can either increase or decrease the results.

Think Critically Answers

1. Many lifestyle choices will appear to have little impact on students' health and well-being today but will have enormous effects on their health in the future.

2. Student answers will vary. This should make for a lively discussion. They should be able to supply specific reasons for their suggestions.

Applied Skills

Writing Across the Curriculum Have students write a paragraph that shows a connection of the information in the Sharpen Your Life Skills feature to one or more classes they have taken in the past or in which they are currently enrolled.

Explain that technology now offers many ways for businesses to increase security or monitor other risks. Many of those technologies help businesses control access to buildings, equipment, and data by carefully screening the people who are trying to gain access. Technologies developed and tested by researchers and government agencies usually quickly spread to other businesses and organizations if they prove successful.

TEACH

Remind students that a common way of reducing the amount of possible financial loss from a risk is to purchase insurance. Insurance is available to individuals and to businesses. The same basic principles and features apply to both types of insurance. Consumers and businesspeople need to understand the basics of insurance to make wise decisions about the type, amount, source, and cost of insurance.

14-2 Insurable Risks

Goals

Recognize important insurance concepts.

Describe several types of business insurance.

Key Terms

insurers

insured

policyholder

insurance policy

premium

claim

Focus on Real Life

Businesses must protect against damage to buildings, equipment, and inventory. They must also guarantee the safety of employees. Access control security systems can help guard against some of these risks. One of the most effective security systems today utilizes hand geometry scanners. These scanners record more than 90 measurements of the length, width, thickness, and surface area of the human hand. Doors and gates protecting secure sites open only when the system recognizes the hand measurements of someone authorized to enter the premises.

In addition to controlling access, these systems can be used to track arrival and departure times and to identify people in a building or other secured area. The popularity of hand geometry scanners is proven, as nuclear power plants, hospitals, day care centers, and even schools are benefiting from their use.

main idea

Recognize important insurance concepts.

PURCHASING INSURANCE

Most individuals and businesses cannot pay for large economic losses. Instead, they share the risk with other individuals or businesses. They buy insurance to provide the financial protection they need in the event they suffer a financial loss. When people buy insurance, they have peace of mind knowing that even if they have an accident, injury, or other loss, they will be able to concentrate on recovery. They will not have to worry about how to pay for the costs of the loss.

Insurance Basics

Insurance companies provide planned protection against economic losses. The company, called an **insurer,** agrees to take on certain economic risks and to pay for losses if they occur. The person or business for which the insurer assumes the risk is the **insured.** To show that it has taken on the risk, the company issues a written contract, or insurance policy. The person or company buying the policy is the **policyholder.** An **insurance policy** states the conditions to which the insurance company and the policyholder have agreed. The amount the policyholder must pay for insurance coverage is a **premium.** The policyholder makes payments monthly, quarterly, every six months, or once a year. A **claim** is a policyholder's request for payment for a loss that the insurance policy covers.

Insurance Companies

In addition to offering financial protection for policyholders, insurance companies are also investment companies. The premiums collected from the policyholders make up the funds from which the insurance company pays for claims. The company invests these premiums. The additional amount earned from these investments allows the company to make a profit and to cover the costs of claims.

Different Learning Abilities

Limited English Proficiency (LEP) Have students study each of the insurance terms and their definitions. Then have students pronounce each term to you and describe their understanding of the meaning of each term. Clarify any misunderstandings.

You can get insurance protection in several ways. Individuals can buy insurance directly from an insurance company. Employers may provide insurance as an employee benefit. Professional organizations and other groups may offer insurance coverage to members. Businesses often offer insurance for customers to provide protection for related risks. When using credit, customers may want credit insurance. Shippers may offer transportation insurance. Security companies may provide theft insurance.

Most people purchase insurance from an insurance agent. An *insurance agent* represents the insurance company and sells insurance policies to individuals and businesses. A key part of an insurance agent's job is to help each client choose the proper kind and amount of protection from possible economic losses. Based on the client's choices the agent submits information to the insurance company that will prepare the policy.

There are two basic types of insurance agents. One works for a large insurance company and sells only policies written by that company. The other is an independent agent who may sell many kinds of policies from a number of different companies. You can also purchase insurance directly from an insurance company or through an agent using the Internet.

Most people are concerned about the type and cost of insurance when choosing an insurance company. Any time you purchase insurance, the offerings of several companies should be compared for features and prices. Another key factor is the service provided by the company if a loss occurs. When a loss is suffered, policyholders want to be able to rely on the insurance company to act quickly in providing help. It should be easy to contact the

Have team members locate the web sites of several insurance agents in your community. Identify the insurance company or companies that the agent represents and the types of insurance sold by each for consumers and for businesses. Compare the results of the searches.

company. Their response should be prompt. The process used to file a claim needs to be easy and understandable. Full reimbursement for losses covered by the policy should be processed as quickly as possible.

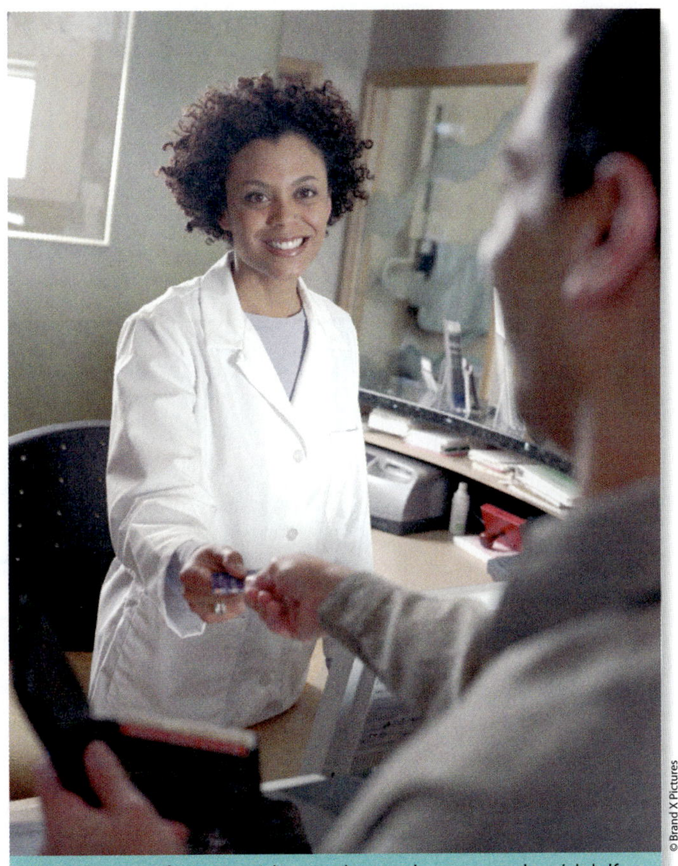

What other types of insurance might an employer purchase on an employee's behalf besides health insurance?

© Brand X Pictures

Different Learning Abilities

At-Risk Encourage students to talk with family members to identify whether they have insurance or are insured by others and the types of insurance coverage held.

TEACH

Ask students which of the following terms best describes an insurance agent in their view: salesperson, risk analyst, paperwork processor, customer service representative, or problem-solver. Tell them that each term applies to the job.

Work as a Team

Ask students to use the information they gathered to classify the insurance agents as independent agents or employees of an insurance company. Does the classification seem to be different based on the types of insurance sold?

THINK CRITICALLY THROUGH VISUALS

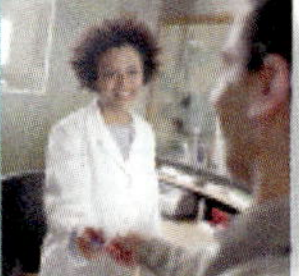

An employer might purchase unemployment, life, or disability insurance for an employee.

 **PROJECT**

Provide the following instructions to students. (These instructions also appear on page xxv of the textbook.) Describe several examples of losses you might suffer that would prevent you from achieving your life-span goals. Explain why buying adequate insurance and taking other measures to reduce risks is an important part of every person's life-span plan.

Life-Span Plan Answers

Answers will vary. Students should describe significant losses such as sickness, accidents, and death, that could prevent them from achieving their life-span goals.

ONGOING ASSESSMENT

checkpoint >> **ANSWER**

When selecting an insurance company, one should collect information about the type and cost of insurance and the quality of service provided by the company if a loss occurs.

TEACH

Before beginning the discussion, tell students that businesses normally carry insurance to protect against risks to their major assets. Ask students to identify what they believe the major assets of most businesses are that would need to be insured. After the students have responded, have them compare their responses to the categories listed in Figure 14-3.

FIGURE 14-3 *ANSWER*

Answers will vary. Most examples will be financial losses resulting from increased expenses or reduced revenues in each of the categories. Costs related to personnel include in reduced productivity, medical expenses, and liabilities from lawsuits. Property expenses could increase due to the need to rebuild or repair damages to equipment and buildings. Losses in the operations category may be from lower sales due to the inability to operate the business.

Point out that businesses risk catastrophic losses if their personnel, property, and operations are not properly insured. Businesses that experience a major loss will not be able to meet customers' expectations and could cease to be a viable commercial enterprise.

main idea

Describe several types of business insurance.

Insured Losses

Both consumers and businesses can buy insurance to cover almost any kind of economic loss. Violinists can insure their fingers. Professional athletes can insure against injuries. Writers may insure their manuscripts. Businesses can insure against the loss of rent from property damaged by fire, injury to consumers resulting from the use of the company's product, or theft by employees.

The kinds of insurance protection that will be important to most consumers are vehicle, property, health, and life insurance. Businesses also insure their vehicles and property. They may provide health and life insurance for some or all employees. They also need liability insurance. *Liability insurance* protects against losses from injury to people or property resulting from the products, services, or actions of a business.

checkpoint >>

What information should be considered when selecting an insurance company?

FIGURE 14-3

What types of losses might a business face if each of these categories is not properly insured?

BUSINESS INSURANCE

A company uses its financial resources to invest in land, buildings, operating equipment, inventory, and people. If the business suffers a serious loss of any of these resources, the business may have trouble replacing the resources and continuing to operate. Businesses buy many types of insurance to obtain financial protection for their assets. Figure 14-3 illustrates the three major business insurance categories of personnel, property, and business operations.

Insuring Personnel

The health and well-being of managers and employees are important to a business. If workers are sick or injured, they will not be able to work. The costs of medical care are high. Costs will need to be paid by either the employee or the company. If an accident occurs on the job, the business will often be responsible for the cost of medical care and lost wages while the employee recovers. Businesses purchase or offer to employees several types of insurance to provide protection for the costs of those risks.

Applied Skills

Building Study Skills As students study and discuss each of the major categories of business insurance, have them prepare a written summary that describes each category.

Health Insurance Many businesses offer *health insurance,* which provides protection against the high costs of individual health care. Health insurance covers routine costs of medical care. It may also cover costs of hospitalization or other needed medical treatments. Businesses often offer group health insurance. With *group insurance,* a large number of employees and their family members are covered under one policy. The policy covers many people, and premiums are paid for all members of the group. Therefore, the cost of insurance is lower than if each person bought a separate policy. Some companies pay for the entire cost of employee health insurance. Most pay a percentage of the cost and employees pay the remainder of the premium.

Disability Insurance Another type of insurance that businesses may offer is disability insurance. *Disability insurance* provides payments to employees who are not able to work for an extended period due to serious illness or injury. The amount of payment is usually a percentage of the employee's income. It is based on the number of years worked and the seriousness of the disability. A special type of disability insurance is known as workers' compensation. *Workers' compensation* is a system of insurance set up by state law that pays employees who are injured on the job. Each business makes payments to the insurance fund based on the number of employees.

Life Insurance Many businesses also offer *life insurance,* which pays the amount of the insurance policy upon the death of the insured. The payment is made to people named in the policy known as beneficiaries. Beneficiaries are usually family members of the insured. Partnerships often purchase a life insurance policy on each partner with the company named as beneficiary. This provides money that will be used

to maintain the business operations that the deceased partner performed. Corporations often insure the lives of key executives because of their importance to the company's success. Businesses may offer a small amount of life insurance for each employee or allow employees to purchase low-cost life insurance as a benefit.

Insuring Property

Businesses buy various types of insurance policies to protect their property. They obtain protection for buildings, equipment, and building contents, including inventory, through commercial property insurance.

Commercial property insurance covers property losses resulting from fire, storms, accidents, theft, and vandalism. Special policies can also provide coverage for flood damage and earthquakes.

Vehicle insurance covers the automobiles, trucks, and other business vehicles. Damages to the vehicles and occupants resulting from accidents are covered. Vehicle insurance pays the costs of damage to the property of others. It also pays medical costs for those injured if people driving the company's vehicles cause an accident.

An increasing amount of consumer information is available to help you compare companies before purchasing insurance. The Better Business Bureau and J.D. Power and Associates have joined to provide ratings of home and auto insurance companies. Access the web site shown below and click on the link for Chapter 14. Review the ratings of Homeowners Insurance Providers and Auto Insurance Providers. Locate information on how J.D. Powers determines its ratings. How do the ratings help consumers make better decisions about which company to choose for their insurance needs?

school.cengage.com/business/introtobiz

Different Learning Abilities

Visually Impaired Provide students with an audio recording of the lesson information. After students listen to the lesson, discuss the information to clarify any misunderstandings. Make the audio recording available to all interested students.

TEACH

Ask students why the cost of health insurance for a large group of employees is usually lower than the cost if each employee tried to purchase the same coverage individually. Remind them that the administrative costs to the insurance company would be less because the company pays one premium for everyone and does much of the paperwork. The risks are also spread across a large number of people, so the chances of a loss for any one group member is less.

Student answers will vary. The J.D. Powers ratings could help consumers make better decisions when choosing an insurance company by allowing them to compare information about several companies at once.

TEACH

Explain to students that, even if a business insures many types of property with one insurance company, the insurer will need to determine the risk of loss on each type of property and usually will write a specific policy for each type. Some policies cover a number of related risks to a property type. For example, a commercial package policy allows businesses to combine a number of types of property insurance coverage such as fire, windstorms, snow and ice, vandalism, and liability in one policy.

Insuring Business Operations

Employees' actions or business operations may result in accidents, injuries, property damage, or other losses. The business can purchase various types of insurance to protect against those losses. *Business interruption insurance* provides compensation for ongoing business expenses that occur if a business has a temporary shutdown due to a fire, flood, or other major problem.

Liability insurance provides coverage for claims by others based on damages suffered because of business operations, employees, or products. A customer may be injured while visiting the business. The use of a product may result in physical injury, illness, or even death. An employee may be dishonest or take action that injures another person. The business may be held financially liable for any of those situations.

Can you think of several types of insurance that a business owner might make a claim against in order to recoup damages from a fire?

checkpoint >>

What are the three major areas that can be covered by business insurance?

14-2 Assessment

Key Concepts

Determine the best answer.

1. The reason businesses and individuals purchase insurance is to
  a. make a profit
  b. provide financial protection
  c. reduce taxes
  d. increase sales

2. True or False. Another term for an insurance company is the policyholder.

3. True or False. An insurance agent can work for only one company or may represent several insurance companies.

4. Insurance that provides coverage for claims by others based on damages suffered as a result of business operations, employees, or products is
  a. health insurance
  b. property insurance
  c. vehicle insurance
  d. liability insurance

Make Academic Connections

5. *Debate* The high cost of liability insurance is a controversial topic. Form two teams to study and debate the following issue: "The maximum amount of damages that a company should have to pay to one individual for any liability claim should be $1 million."

6. *Math* A new employee had an individual health insurance policy that costs $180 per month plus $125 per month for his spouse and two children. The company offers a group policy that costs $165 a month for an individual or $286.50 for the entire family. The company contributes 10 percent of the cost of the individual policy toward either choice.
  a. How much does the group policy reduce the cost of health insurance for the entire family without the company's contribution?
  b. What will be the amount the employee will pay for family health insurance for an entire year? What is the annual savings compared to the previous policy?

RETEACH

Assign teams of students one of the categories of business insurance in Figure 14-3. Have the group review the lesson information and develop a presentation to be delivered to the other teams.

ENRICH

Invite an insurance agent to speak about the impact of technology on his or her work.

CLOSE

Discuss ways that businesses can reduce the cost of insurance while still protecting against risks.

14-3   Uninsurable Risks

Goals

Describe why some business risks are uninsurable.

List the strategies a company can use to reduce the risks of doing business internationally.

Key Terms

property rights

counterfeiting

Focus on Real Life

Microsoft has a greater share of the software market in China than it does in the United States. Surprisingly, it is not happy with this statistic. Most Microsoft software being used in China has been pirated. Chinese companies have stolen it and then sold it to Chinese consumers often at a very low cost.

The problem is not exclusive to Microsoft. It is estimated that 92 percent of business software and 96 percent of entertainment software used in China has been pirated. When software is pirated, the companies that developed the software receive no money for their products. As a result, honest consumers around the world pay higher prices.

Microsoft is responding by adding sophisticated anti-piracy security features to its software and filing lawsuits against software pirates. Microsoft is also working to establish business operations in China, including a large research center, production facilities, and sales. The company hopes its presence in the country will reduce the amount of illegal activity.

IDENTIFYING AND REDUCING RISKS

Businesses cannot insure many of the risks they face. Some are too expensive to insure. If the chance that a risk will occur cannot be reasonably predicted or the possible financial loss to the business cannot be calculated, it is not likely that an insurance company will provide coverage. The costs of some risks are so high that a business cannot afford the cost of insurance protection. In that case, the business must determine other ways to deal with those uninsurable risks.

Types of Uninsurable Risks

Several circumstances can lead to business risks that can be very costly to a company. These circumstances are economic conditions, consumer demand, competitors' actions, technology changes, local factors, and business operations.

main idea

Describe why some business risks are uninsurable.

What are the economic results of pirating music and entertainment software?

TEACH

For each of the categories of uninsurable risks, have students describe why the risks are uninsurable and what companies can do to try to reduce or manage the risk.

THINK CRITICALLY THROUGH VISUALS

Bricks-and-mortar stores can compete with Internet retailers by offering better customer service longer hours, discounts, liberal and convenient return policies, interesting product displays, knowledgeable and helpful sales people, and a fun atmosphere that makes people want to come into the store. They can also offer online shopping services through a web site in addition to their local stores.

FYI

Insurance companies offer educational services by preparing brochures and videos, conducting training sessions in business, and providing public service announcements on safety, health, and accident prevention. They conduct these activities to help reduce risks and lower the cost of insurance.

Economic Conditions When the economy is strong, consumers and business customers are more willing to spend money. Sales will be strong and profits high. A downturn in the economy can quickly reduce sales and profits. If the company does not cut production and expenses, it can experience real problems. Managers need to study the economy carefully. They must be prepared to respond to improvements or declines in economic conditions.

Consumer Demand Companies produce products that they think will meet consumer demand. They study customer needs and preferences. If they can predict a change in demand, they may be able to take advantage of the need with new products. If consumer tastes change, the company may end up with products in inventory that they are unable to sell at a profit.

Competitors' Actions Businesses function in a competitive environment. The actions of competitors can affect the success of a business. If a competitor starts a major advertising campaign or decides to reduce prices, a business will have to decide whether it needs to respond or not. The wrong decision can result in lost sales and profits or additional unneeded expenses. A new competitor may enter the market or a current competitor may introduce a new product. If a company is not prepared for these types of competitive actions, its share of the market can quickly decline.

Technology Changes What happened to traditional businesses when other companies started to use the Internet? If a company is not prepared to accept debit cards as a form of payment, will customers take their business elsewhere? When consumers can download music and movies from web sites, will brick and mortar music and video stores be affected? Anytime technology changes, there is a possible effect on a business. The cost of putting new technology in place is usually high, but if the business doesn't adopt the technology, it may lose sales.

Local Factors The highway that runs in front of a fast-food business closes for a month for repair. The utility company serving the city has a 5 percent rate increase for the cost of electricity. The county zoning board rejects a business' request to expand its production

What can bricks-and-mortar stores do to retain traditional customers who have turned to the Internet for shopping?

Applied Skills

Technology Have students visit the web sites of e-commerce businesses and identify ways that the business is attempting to reduce risks the company and its customers face when they engage in online shopping. Ask students to discuss their findings.

facilities. The laws, regulations, taxes, and infrastructure of a local community can have an influence on the operations of a business. Some businesses decide to move from one community to another to get conditions that are more favorable. Businesses work with government officials and community organizations to keep a positive environment for business.

Business Operations The day-to-day operations of a business can have a major impact on its success or failure. A poorly run business will have higher costs, low morale, increased turnover, and a poor customer image. A lack of employee training and poor management can lead to production errors, safety problems that result in accidents and injuries, poorly maintained equipment and facilities, and labor relations problems. If managers and employees are not committed to the success of the company, they will miss opportunities to improve operations, increase customer satisfaction, and control expenses.

Businesses Respond to a Disaster

In 2005, federal, state, and local governments struggled to respond to the devastation caused by Hurricane Katrina in New Orleans and along the gulf coast of the United States. Faced with a growing crisis, businesses sprang into action with the same efficiency and effectiveness they use in their day-to-day operations to respond to emergencies in communities affected by the storm and its aftermath. Thousands of businesses, large and small, demonstrated their commitment to aiding people in need with donations of money, equipment, materials, and employee time.

Before Katrina made landfall, Wal-Mart had 45 trucks loaded with supplies in its Brookhaven, Mississippi, distribution center and ready for delivery. With 34,000 of its own employees affected by the storm, Wal-Mart immediately promised and delivered $20 million in cash donations, 1,500 truckloads of free merchandise, and food for 100,000 meals.

Two home improvement giants, Home Depot and Lowe's, experienced Katrina's wrath as they saw some of their own stores heavily damaged or destroyed from high winds and flooding. All along the storm's path managers and dedicated employees opened less-damaged stores within hours to provide generators and emergency supplies for their neighbors. In addition, Home Depot pledged more than

$11 million and worked with volunteer organizations to rebuild more than 100 playgrounds and athletic fields that had been damaged or destroyed. Lowe's teamed with designer Marianne Cusato to develop plans and materials for small, permanent homes called Katrina Cottages as affordable alternatives to FEMA trailers for displaced residents and emergency workers.

Marriott Corporation committed to help its 2,800 employees who worked at 15 New Orleans hotels as they faced the loss of their jobs and in some cases their homes. Many employees were bused to Houston where they were housed and fed in the ballroom of the Houston Airport Marriott while the company helped them find temporary housing and jobs.

These are just a few examples of the efforts made by businesses following Hurricane Katrina. They illustrate ways businesses respond to disasters and how their efforts can help communities and individuals recover.

Think Critically

1. Why are businesses willing to commit resources to help deal with emergencies that affect other areas as well as their own communities?
2. How might the expertise of businesses be used by government agencies to improve responses to future disasters and emergencies?

Different Learning Styles

Kinesthetic Learner Have students locate an online questionnaire or application for purchasing automobile or life insurance. Ask them to review the questions asked and other information needed to complete the questionnaire or application. Remind students not to enter personal information while working on this assignment.

TEACH

Have students collect examples from local newspapers of activities by government agencies and departments that are having negative affects on businesses. Have students discuss why businesses are affected, why the government is taking the action described, and what businesses are doing to try to reduce the impact on them.

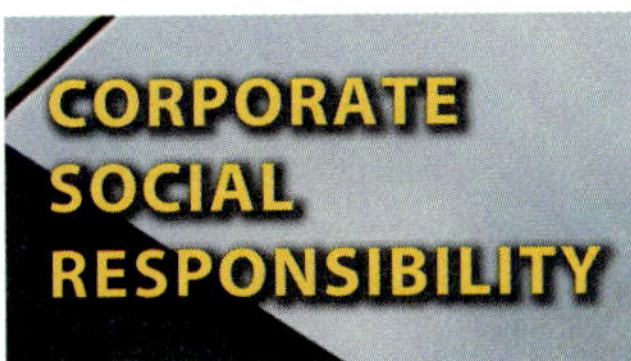

When communities, states, and countries are hit by huge natural disasters there are usually losses in property, jobs, and even lives. While insurance provides some protection, many of the losses are either too large or are not covered by insurance. Individuals, community organizations, and businesses are usually quick to jump in to offer a variety of types of help to those affected.

Think Critically Answers

1. Businesses have a financial incentive to help deal with emergencies. Recovery will mean customers can once again spend money. In addition, when a disaster strikes, businesses in the community want to help their employees and neighbors because they are all part of the same community.

2. Governments may ask businesses to share expertise and help with training to be better prepared for disasters. They also can coordinate their efforts with businesses during the recovery to speed up their response and increase the available resources.

358

TEACH

Have students study the section "Managing Risks" and develop an outline of the main ways businesses and their employees can identify, manage, and reduce risks.

THINK CRITICALLY THROUGH VISUALS

Stores deter theft by employing security personnel, prosecuting shoplifters, installing security cameras and alarms, and using electronic security tags on merchandise. They maintain tight inventory control to deter employee theft.

ONGOING ASSESSMENT

checkpoint >> **ANSWER**

Businesses can make employees aware of uninsurable risks, gather information, and spot problems quickly. Managers should monitor changes in the economy, competitors' actions, and technology. Businesses should review customer information, including complaints and requests, and identify products whose sales are increasing or decreasing. Businesses should monitor operating costs, inspect facilities and equipment, and take care when hiring employees. Businesses should implement security measures to prevent theft and vandalism and to protect employees and customers. Company records should be protected with backup copies of important information stored in safe locations. Businesses should be aware of any proposed changes in laws and regulations that could affect operations.

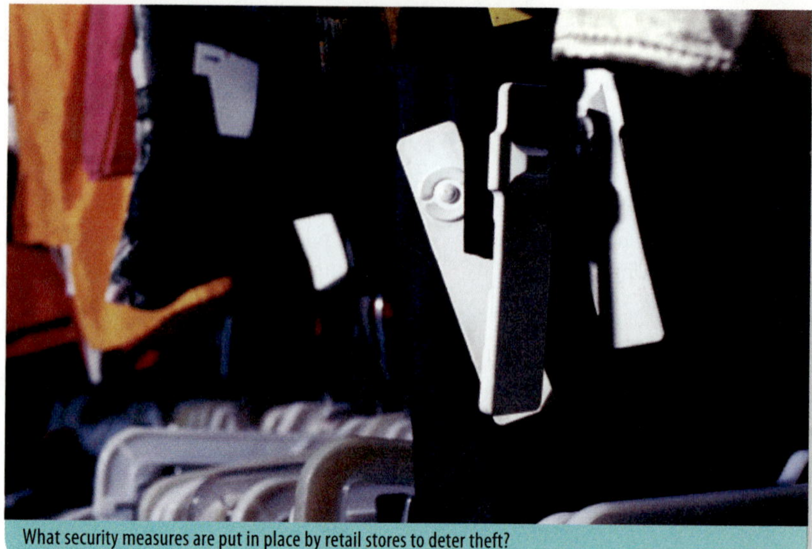

What security measures are put in place by retail stores to deter theft?

Managing Risks

Each of the situations just described poses a risk to businesses. Alone, any of the risks can cause serious financial problems. If several occur at the same time, it is not likely the business will survive. Uninsurable risks present important challenges to managers and employees.

Everyone in a business needs to be aware that there are many uninsurable risks. The business must inform them of the types of risks that are particularly important to their part of the operations. All employees must be watchful for changes that can lead to problems.

Businesses need to implement measures to gather information and spot possible problems. They should continually study all of the risk areas. Managers need to be aware of changes in the economy, competitors' actions, and technology. The business should collect and review customer information, including complaints and requests. It should carefully watch sales to identify which product sales are increasing and which are decreasing. It should monitor all operating costs to make sure they do not get out of control.

Businesses should inspect facilities and equipment to make sure they are running properly and safely. Careful employee hiring and ongoing training will also add to effective and safe operations. Businesses should put security measures in place to prevent theft and vandalism and to protect employees and customers. Important information and company records should be protected from all forms of possible damage. Backup copies should be prepared and stored in safe locations.

Businesses should be active in their local communities. They should work to develop and maintain a positive image. They should build relationships with local, state, and national government officials. Businesses must be aware of any proposed changes in laws and regulations that could affect operations. Careful study and planning followed by positive actions will have the greatest effect on reducing business risks.

checkpoint >>
What are several things businesses can do to manage risks?

Different Learning Abilities

Hearing Impaired Prepare computer-generated slides or printed handouts containing key points and discussion details and provide them to the students in advance of the discussion.

Give the students ample opportunities to ask questions or seek clarification for the information provided.

RISKS IN INTERNATIONAL BUSINESS

As an international business manager, would you be willing to ship automobiles to a company in another country before receiving the payment? Would you agree to take another country's currency for payment instead of U.S. dollars? These are examples of risks faced by every organization involved in international business.

Strategies for Reducing Risk

To reduce international business risk, management experts advise the use of four strategies. First, carry out business in many countries. This approach reduces the risk faced when doing business in only one country or a single region. If turmoil occurs in one nation, causing lost sales and profits, the global company is covered with profits from other markets.

Next, offer a range of products. When an organization broadens its product line, reduced sales of one item will not mean complete failure for the company. Successful global organizations continually create new products, seek new uses for existing products, and look for new markets for their products.

Third, involving local business partners may reduce risk. Joint ventures with local companies help to reduce political and social risks. An agreement between a global company and a local business can help both organizations. In addition, the citizens and government of the host nation will not feel as threatened by outsiders if a company they are familiar with is involved.

Finally, employ local management in order to lower global business risk. Executives and other managers who are native to a country or region better understand cultural norms and political

Work with your team members to describe a possible joint venture between companies in two different countries. Explain why the businesses might want to work together. What are possible benefits for each organization? How might the venture reduce risks facing each company?

actions. This knowledge can help the international company adapt its product and business activities to the needs of the market being served.

International Property Rights

In some South American countries, local companies not connected to the National Basketball Association make shirts celebrating the championship of an NBA team. In China, street vendors illegally duplicate and sell copies of popular movies, music videos, and books. These are both examples of violations of property rights.

Property rights are the exclusive rights to possess and use property and its profits. This excludes everyone else from interfering with the use of the item. *Intellectual property* refers to technical knowledge or creative work. It includes software, clothing designs, music, books, and movies. For many companies, their intellectual properties are valuable assets that generate sales and profits. A *patent* is the exclusive right of an inventor to make, sell, and use a product or process. An inventor may obtain a patent on a computer component, a new package design, or a prescription drug. These inventions can give a company a competitive advantage. Patents are designed to encourage innovation and progress.

A *trademark* is a distinctive name, symbol, word, picture, or combination of these that a company uses to identify products or services. Common trademarks known around the world include

main idea

List the strategies a company can use to reduce the risks of doing business internationally.

TEACH

Tell students that companies that participate in international business face different risks as well as more of the same types of risks they face in their home countries. If business people are not aware of these new risks and do not prepare for them, the international business activities have a greater chance of failing.

Work as a Team

Ask students if they believe forming a joint venture with a company in another country reduces or increases the number of risks faced by each company alone. Have them provide reasons for their decision.

TEACH

Have students refer to the intellectual property rights problem faced by Microsoft presented in the Focus on Real Life feature at the beginning of the lesson. Why is Microsoft encountering problems in China? International property rights are a particularly challenging issue in international business. Countries do not all have the same laws dealing with property rights, and it is more difficult to enforce property rights laws in some countries. Also, it is difficult to monitor intellectual property all over the world in order to recognize when property rights are being violated.

Different Learning Abilities

Gifted Have students use library or Internet resources to locate information on a court case where a U.S. company tried to enforce its intellectual property rights in another country. Have them provide an oral summary of the case to the other class members.

the McDonald's golden arches and Kellogg's Tony the Tiger. A *copyright* protects the original works of authors, composers, playwrights, artists, and publishers. In the United States, a new copyright gives originators sole rights to publish and exhibit their creative works for their lifetime plus 70 years.

Most other countries have similar laws. There may be differences in the definitions and type of protection. Some countries do little to enforce property rights laws, especially when the products of a foreign company are involved. **Counterfeiting** refers to illegal uses of intellectual property, patents, trademarks, and copyrights. For example, a company may make slight changes in a well-known product and sell it in other countries. They are using the product illegally so they don't have to pay for the development costs of their own products or pay the original company for the product. By using the actual product name or trademark illegally, they are trying to profit from the reputation of the famous company. When property rights laws are not enforced, companies can lose profits. This discourages them from participating in international trade.

checkpoint >>

Why do U.S. companies have difficulty enforcing intellectual property rights in some international markets?

14-3 Assessment

Key Concepts

Determine the best answer.

1. True or False. Every risk a business faces can be insured.

2. The growing use of the Internet as a business tool is an example of what type of business risk?
   a. economic conditions
   b. technology change
   c. consumer demand
   d. business operations

3. True or False. To reduce the risks of international business, a company should conduct business in many countries.

4. The exclusive right of an inventor to make, sell, and use a product or process is a
   a. trademark
   b. copyright
   c. patent
   d. None of the above is correct.

Make Academic Connections

5. *Economics* Use the business section of newspapers and business magazines to gather information on predictions for changes in the economy for the next 6 to 12 months. Based on this information, prepare a two-page written report for small business owners in your community identifying how the changes might affect their businesses in a positive or negative way.

6. *International Relations* Use the Internet to gather information on the fraudulent use of the intellectual property of U.S. businesses in other countries. Develop a table that identifies the U.S. company, the product that has been misused, the country or countries in which the fraud has occurred, and any action taken by the company to protect its property rights. Present the information in your table to other class members. Discuss the effect of the fraud on businesses and consumers.

Doing Business in…Costa Rica

Official name
Republic of Costa Rica

Capital
San Jose

Population
4.1 million

Currency
colon

Major exports
bananas, pineapples, coffee, melons, ornamental plants, sugar, textiles

Major export partners
United States, Hong Kong, Netherlands, Guatemala

Major imports
raw materials, consumer goods, capital equipment, petroleum

Major import partners
United States, Japan, Venezuela, Mexico

Source: CIA World Factbook

With more than 130 protected parks, refuges, and reserves, the natural beauty of Costa Rica is the foundation of this country's pride and its main tourist attraction. When you are having a casual conversation with local business associates, the country's tourist sites and natural beauty are acceptable topics.

Business negotiations and decision-making usually involve people at various levels of an organization, not just the top officials. In business settings, wear dark, conservative suits. Your business cards should have a Spanish translation on the back. Be sure to present the cards so they can be read by the people receiving them in their own language. While business gifts may not be expected, small presents are appropriate when you are invited to someone's home. The most common gifts are flowers, candy, fruit, or a plant.

Expect to dine between 7 and 8:30 p.m. Always be on time for a business meal and other meetings. These visits are usually prearranged. In rural areas of the country, life is less formal. Quite often, people visit unannounced. When you arrive at the door, don't knock. Instead, shout "Upe!" This greeting in Costa Rica means "let me in" or "anybody home?"

The stable political and economic environment of Costa Rica makes it an attractive location for investors. Full ownership of real estate and businesses by foreigners is allowed. This freedom is different from many countries where local ownership must exceed 50 percent. The high educational standards of Costa Rica also make it appealing to international companies. High-tech businesses are adding to the economic base of the country. As technology exports increase, traditional products, such as coffee and bananas, will become a smaller portion of the country's total trade.

Black beans and rice are foundation elements of the Costa Rican diet. Breakfast may consist of gallo pinto (a combination of rice and beans). At lunch, rice and beans might be mixed with salad, eggs, or meat. Then, for your evening meal, you may have rice with chicken and, of course, beans.

Think Critically

1. How does doing business in Costa Rica differ from other countries?
2. What elements of Costa Rican society help to enhance the country's economic development?
3. Conduct library or Internet research to find additional information about business and economic activities in Costa Rica.

Doing Business in…

Every country provides unique business opportunities for international trade, including markets for exporting the products and services of the country. Costa Rica is a small country in terms of both geography and population. However, due to its close proximity, agricultural production, and positive view of foreign investment, it has become an important trading partner for the United States.

Think Critically Answers

1. Business negotiations involve people at various levels of an organization. The ability to speak Spanish would be a definite plus. The country welcomes business investment by allowing full ownership of real estate and businesses by foreigners, while many other countries require at least 50 percent local ownership. The high educational standards mean there is a well-educated workforce.

2. The country's investment in education, gracious social customs that promote solid relationships, and stable political and economic environment enhance Costa Rica's economic development.

3. Student answers will vary depending on what additional information they locate about business and economic activities in Costa Rica.

">

CHAPTER 14 Assessment

Business Notes

14-1 OVERVIEW OF RISK MANAGEMENT

1. There are many types of risks and possible losses. The main types of risks are economic and non-economic, pure and speculative, controllable and uncontrollable, and insurable and uninsurable. Individuals and businesses need to be aware of risks and attempt to reduce possible losses, especially for those that may result in physical or financial harm.

2. Individuals and businesses must determine how they will deal with the risks and possible losses they face. There are four possible ways to deal with risks: avoid the risk, transfer the risk, insure the risk, or assume the risk.

14-2 INSURABLE RISKS

3. Most individuals and businesses cannot pay for large economic losses, so they share the risk with other individuals or businesses. They purchase insurance to provide the needed financial protection in the event they suffer a financial loss.

4. Businesses purchase a variety of types of insurance to obtain financial protection for their assets. The types of insurance can be categorized within three major areas: personnel, property, and business operations.

14-3 UNINSURABLE RISKS

5. If the chance that a risk will occur cannot be reasonably predicted or the possible financial loss to the business calculated, it will be unlikely that an insurance company will provide coverage. The costs of some risks are so high that a business cannot afford the cost of insurance protection.

6. To reduce international business risks, companies should conduct business in many countries, offer a variety of products, involve local business partners, and employ local management.

Communicate Business Concepts

1. Identify one personal, property, and liability risk faced by a family. Identify one of each that is faced by a business. Now identify a non-economic risk for an individual and for a business.

2. What are several controllable risks you and your friends might face? What are some uncontrollable risks you and your friends might face? What makes the risks you identified controllable or uncontrollable?

3. People and businesses can deal with risks in four ways. Identify the four ways and describe the advantages and disadvantages of each.

4. Under what circumstances should you consider buying insurance? Are there circumstances where you are facing an insurable risk and you would choose not to buy insurance? Why would you make that decision?

5. List several questions you would want answered about an insurance company before you decided to purchase insurance from the company.

6. Visit the web site of a company that sells automobile insurance. What are the procedures you should follow if you are involved in an automobile accident and that company insures you? Are the procedures different depending on who is at fault?

7. Visit the web site of a large employer in your community or region. Locate information about the insurance benefits that the company offers its employees. Determine the types of insurance offered, who is eligible for the insurance benefits, and whether the company pays some or all of the costs for the insurance premiums.

8. Identify a type of business you would consider owning or managing. What are some specific risks the business could face that would be uninsurable because the chance of the risk or the amount of loss cannot be easily predicted? Are there some risks facing the business that could be very expensive to insure?

9. What information sources are available that could be used by businesspeople to keep track of changes in economic conditions that could affect their companies? What are some current economic conditions that could have a positive or negative effect on U.S. businesses?

10. Suggest several ways that a retail business can improve security to prevent theft of merchandise by customers and employees. Are there ways operations can be changed or improved to reduce the chances of theft?

11. You own a small business that produces computer games. You are considering selling the games in several foreign countries. What risks might you face as you begin international trade that you didn't face in the United States? Which of the risks are controllable and which are uncontrollable? Identify several steps you could take to reduce these risks.

Develop Your Business Language

Match the terms listed with the definitions.

12. Agrees to take on certain economic risks and to pay for losses if they occur.

13. Those that can be reduced or eliminated by actions you take.

14. Illegal uses of intellectual property, patents, trademarks, and copyrights.

15. The amount the policyholder must pay for insurance coverage.

16. The person or business for which the risk is assumed.

17. Those that can result in financial loss.

18. The possibility of incurring a loss.

19. A policyholder's request for payment for a loss that is covered by the insurance policy.

20. The person or company purchasing the policy.

21. Presents the chance of loss but no opportunity for gain.

22. The exclusive rights to possess and use property and its profits.

23. States the conditions to which the insurance company and the policyholder have agreed.

24. Exchanges the uncertainty of a possible large financial loss for a certain smaller payment.

25. Can result in losses, such as health and personal well-being.

26. Can lead to a loss of personal or business items such as money, vehicles, and buildings.

27. Related to harm or injury to other people or their property because of your actions.

KEY TERMS
a. claim
b. controllable risk
c. counterfeiting
d. economic risk
e. insurance
f. insurance policy
g. insured
h. insurer
i. liability risks
j. personal risks
k. policyholder
l. premium
m. property rights
n. property risks
o. pure risk
p. risk

Make Academic Connections

28. **ECONOMICS** Speculative risks offer the chance to gain or to lose. People invest their money hoping to get a good return on the investment. Still, most investments have some risk, which means the money can be lost. Common investments are savings accounts, stocks, and real estate. Identify two additional investments. Prepare a table that compares each of the investments in terms of their risk and possible gain or loss.

29. **WRITING** You have been asked by a business owner to give advice on how to deal with a risk the business is facing. During the winter after an ice storm, the parking lot and sidewalks are often very slippery. There is a risk that employees and visitors may slip on the ice and be injured. Prepare a memo to the business owner describing some ways the business might deal with the risk. Recommend the actions that should be taken and reasons for your recommendations.

8. Answers will vary, depending on the types of businesses students choose. They should demonstrate that they understand that companies cannot insure themselves against all risks.

9. Sources of information that businesspeople could use are newspapers and financial magazines, such as the Wall Street Journal and Fortune; online news groups; services that provide stock market information; trade publications specific to a particular industry; conferences and seminars; trade shows and conventions; government reports; and organizations' annual reports.

10. Answers will vary. Students should suggest various ways retailers can curb theft, such as hiring security personnel, including undercover security officers; using electronic tags on merchandise; using computer software to maintain tight control of inventory; and installing video surveillance cameras.

11. Risks would include currency exchange fluctuations, financing difficulties, the prospect of having the games pirated and the host country not enforcing property rights laws, the product not being appropriate for the market (perhaps the games would offend the local culture or not enough homes would have computers), and political and economic turmoil. Students are to list whether the risks they identify are controllable or uncontrollable and several steps they could take to reduce the risks.

Develop Your Business Language Answers

12. h. insurer
13. b. controllable risk
14. c. counterfeiting
15. l. premium
16. g. insured
17. d. economic risk
18. p. risk
19. a. claim
20. k. policyholder
21. o. pure risk
22. m. property rights
23. f. insurance policy
24. e. insurance
25. j. personal risks
26. n. property risks
27. i. liability risks

30. **TECHNOLOGY** Use your local telephone or business directory or the Internet. Identify five insurance agents that sell business insurance in your area. Use a computer to create a database of information about the agents. Include the agent's name, agency name, address, telephone number, e-mail address, insurance company represented, and types of business insurance sold.

31. **MEDICINE AND LAW** The medical profession has been faced by rapidly increasing costs for malpractice insurance. There is a debate about the reasons for these increases which include increasing medical costs, poor practices by some health professionals, expensive judgments ordered by juries against doctors in court cases, and high fees charged by lawyers. Conduct research on medical malpractice and prepare a two-page report on your findings. Include recommendations on how to reduce the cost of malpractice insurance.

32. **GRAPHICS** Businesses try to reduce the number of accidents and injuries in their buildings by continually reminding employees of the importance of safety. Prepare a poster that could be displayed in a local business that has an attention-getting message about safety and accident prevention.

33. **CONSUMER RESEARCH** Visit a store in your community that sells clothing for men, women, and children. Study the items that have been reduced in price. Identify factors that explain why the merchandise is not selling and needs to be placed on sale. Note any differences in these factors for women's, men's, and children's apparel. Based on your research, develop several recommendations that can be used by the company in the future to select products that will respond to consumer needs and preferences.

34. **INTERNATIONAL BUSINESS** Several unique types of insurance are available for companies that participate in international commerce. Use the Internet to identify five types of insurance company buying or selling products in another country. Prepare a table that identifies each type of insurance, its purpose, and a company or organization that offers the insurance for sale.

Linking School and Community

Read, watch, and listen to news reports and identify the types of risks that are affecting your community. Make a list of the risks you identify and determine if they are mainly controllable or uncontrollable, insurable or uninsurable. Determine what plans are being made by community leaders, including government, business, social service organizations, and others, to deal with the risks and reduce their potential impact on the community.

Web Workout

Insurance companies benefit when their policyholders work to reduce the risks that are covered by insurance policies. Many nonprofit organizations and government agencies also try to help individuals and businesses reduce the risks they face. Use an Internet search engine to identify web sites that offer information on how to reduce a specific risk facing individuals or businesses.

Think Critically

1. Select the web site of (a) an insurance company, (b) a government agency, and (c) a non-profit organization that provides information on reducing risks.

2. Prepare a table that identifies the sponsor of the web site; the type of risk discussed; whether it is a risk facing individuals, businesses, or both; and whether it is an economic or non-economic risk.

3. For each web site selected, write one paragraph explaining why you think the business, agency, or organization is interested in reducing the particular risk or risks for businesses and individuals. What are their goals or how do they benefit if there are fewer losses?

Decision-Making Strategies

The Chrismann Company is a manufacturer of lawn equipment that it sells through garden centers in a 10-state region of the upper Midwest. To distribute its products, it maintains a fleet of 25 trucks. It also has 18 cars driven by its sales people. The company recently finished a review of its vehicle insurance costs. Records show that the average cost to insure each truck is $960 a year and $725 for each car. Insurance claims filed for the past eight years averaged $31,200 a year. When studied closely, data shows that claims in two of those years were less than $10,000 and for three years exceeded $45,000. The company's executives are considering canceling their vehicle insurance. They want to set up a fund using the money they currently pay to the insurance company. This fund would be used to pay costs of repairs and injuries resulting from any vehicle accidents.

35. If the average costs related to repairs and injuries continue for the next five years, how much will the company save using their new plan?

36. Develop reasons for and against the new plan. If you were an executive, would you be in favor of or opposed to the plan?

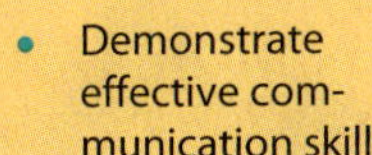

Advanced Interview Skills Event

Advancement in the workforce depends on skills, work ethic, and an organized career portfolio.

You have been employed by Secure Insurance for five years. You started soon after high school graduation and have continued working while attending college. File clerk was your first position with the company. Your strong work ethic and quick understanding of the industry earned you a promotion to the position of insurance adjuster. You will earn your college degree in Business Administration next month. Because you have thoroughly enjoyed working for Secure Insurance, you would like to apply for a management position. You take great pride in your work ethic and understanding of the insurance industry.

You must create a career portfolio to sell your qualifications. You also will participate in an interview to prove your qualifications. The application letter must be addressed to
Ms. Cassandra Smith
Human Resources Department Manager
Secure Insurance
2345 Old Cheney Road
Lincoln, NE 68502

PERFORMANCE INDICATORS EVALUATED

- Demonstrate knowledge of job search skills.
- Apply technical writing skills to produce an application letter and resume.
- Demonstrate effective communication skills.
- Demonstrate the ability to create and effectively use an employment portfolio.
- Complete a job application form.
- Discuss understanding of work ethics and work environment.
- Describe knowledge of job advancement.
- Demonstrate interpersonal skills.
- Create an attractive portfolio for use during a job interview.

For more detailed information about performance indicators, go to the BPA web site.

Think Critically

1. What is your definition of a strong work ethic?
2. Why is experience during college important for career advancement?
3. How will you dress for this interview? Describe an appropriate outfit, including colors, garments, and styles.

http://www.bpanet.org/

Access the web site shown here to find portfolio activities for this chapter. Use the activities to provide tangible evidence of your learning.

Decision-Making Strategies Answers

35. If average costs continue for the next five years, the company will save $29,250 over the five-year period (present cost to insure the trucks and cars for five years is $185,250; under the new plan they would spend $156,000 to pay for repairs and injuries).

36. Answers will vary. One reason to adopt the new plan is for the cost savings. When claims are low, the savings will be even greater. The major reason not to self-insure is that, in the event of a catastrophic loss (such as multiple accidents involving bodily injuries), the costs could be much higher than the premiums.

Winning Edge
Advanced Interview Skills Event

Many companies encourage their employees to continue their education and offer opportunities for advancement to experienced and effective employees. To prepare for advancement, employees should maintain a portfolio that offers evidence of their work and abilities. They also need to be well prepared to complete an application and interview when advancement opportunities appear.

Think Critically Answers

1. Answers will vary. A strong work ethic means total focus on doing the job correctly and honestly, plus respecting the company, employees, and customers.

2. College internships or work experiences are essential for the fast track to employment. Companies prefer students who have actual work experience as well as academic degrees.

3. Answers will vary. Students should recognize that a business suit is appropriate for an interview for most management positions. The suit should be navy, black, or gray. Men should wear a white or light blue shirt and a conservative tie. Women should wear a modest blouse. Some students might suggest less formal clothing might be acceptable depending on the culture of the company.

Global Business Project

Students conduct research on various aspects of international business operations and plan global marketing activities, identify technology uses, list items necessary to create and market an international product, describe common production methods used in various locations, and catalog risks a company might face when doing business internationally.

Students prepare portfolios to store the information from the Activities exercises. They create visual summaries of their international marketing activities and develop package designs or advertisements to communicate their global business ideas. They describe the information they will need to implement their business ideas and make flowcharts to represent the movement of information within their business organizations. They create presentations listing startup costs, projected revenue, and expenses and prepare in-class presentations or videos to communicate production methods and business risks from around the world.

Implement International Business Operations

Goals

- Identify international marketing activities.
- Explore technology uses of business in varied global settings.
- Name income sources, operating expenses, and financing sources for international business operations.
- Research production methods used in countries with varied levels of economic development.
- Analyze risks faced by companies involved in international business.

Activities

Use your textbook, library materials, web sites, interviews with people, and other resources to complete the following:

1. Plan global marketing activities. Marketing has four main elements: (1) the product, (2) pricing methods, (3) promotional activities, and (4) distribution channels. Develop a plan to market a product or service outside the United States. Briefly describe each component of marketing for this product or service in a specific country or region of the world.

2. Identify technology uses. Research information needs of companies involved in international business. Describe types of computer systems, networks, and software used by multinational companies in various countries.

3. For your business idea, list items (with estimated amounts) that would be necessary to create and market this international product. Research start-up costs and financing sources (such as loans, money from investors, or personal assets). Identify sources of income and operating expenses.

4. Production methods around the world vary based on tradition, technology, economic conditions, and local labor skills. Describe common production methods used in various regions of the world.

366

5. Create a list of economic, social-cultural, and political-legal risks a company might encounter when doing business around the world.

Present

Prepare a portfolio (folder, file, or notebook) to store the information and materials you created in the activities above.

1. Create a visual summary (poster, computer presentation, or web site) of your international marketing activities. Also, develop a package design or advertisement to communicate the main parts of your global business idea.

2. Based on your global business idea, describe information needs for these categories: (1) financial information, (2) production, (3) sales and marketing, and (4) human resources. Create a flowchart to communicate the movement of information within your planned business organization. Show sources of data, such as customers, sales records, and employee time cards, as the input section. The output section might include information items such as financial statements, inventory records, and payroll reports.

3. Create a presentation (with visuals) listing start-up costs, projected monthly revenue, and monthly expenses for your business idea. Spreadsheet software may be used to prepare a summary of the financial data.

4. Prepare an in-class presentation (or video) to communicate production methods and business risks from around the world.

UNIT 4 PERSONAL FINANCIAL MANAGEMENT OVERVIEW	OVERVIEW	SPECIAL FEATURES	LESSON ASSESSMENT	
Chapter 15 Consumers in the Global Economy, pp. 370–395	Chapter 15 focuses on wise buying activities and protecting consumer rights.	Business Improving Society: Consumers Union, p. 386; Focus on Real Life, pp. 372, 380, 387; FYI, pp. 383, 388; Life-Span Plan, p. 377; Net Bookmark, p. 373; Planning a Career in Customer Service, p. 371; A Question of Ethics: Frauds by Consumers, p. 382; Technology in Action: Electronic Package Tags, p. 375; Winning Edge BPA: Global Marketing Team Event, p. 395; Work as a Team, pp. 378, 382, 390	Checkpoints, pp. 374, 378, 379, 381, 384, 385, 388, 389, 391 Key Concepts, Make Academic Connections, pp. 379, 385, 391	
Chapter 16 Money Management and Financial Planning, pp. 396–419	Chapter 16 provides students with the information needed to better understand money management activities, budgeting strategies, and future financial decisions.	Doing Business in Nigeria, p. 402; Focus on Real Life, pp. 398, 403, 409; FYI, pp. 399, 405; Life-Span Plan, pp. 404, 410; Net Bookmark, p. 412; Planning a Career in Financial Planning, p. 397; Sharpen Your Life Skills: Effective Interviewing, p. 415; Winning Edge BPA: Graphic Design Promotion, p. 419; Work as a Team, pp. 400, 408, 410	Checkpoints, pp. 399, 400, 401, 403, 406, 408, 411, 413, 414 Key Concepts, Make Academic Connections, pp. 401, 408, 414	
Chapter 17 Banking and Financial Services, pp. 420–447	Chapter 17 introduces and explains various financial institutions and bank services commonly used by consumers.	Business Improving Society: Microfinance, p. 434; Focus on Real Life, pp. 422, 428, 435; FYI, pp. 433, 443; Life-Span Plan, p. 424; Net Bookmark, p. 432; Planning a Career in Banking and Financial Services, p. 421; Technology in Action: Biometric Banking, p. 429; Winning Edge BPA: Presentation Management Individual Event, p. 447; Work as a Team, pp. 423, 429, 438	Checkpoints, pp. 424, 426, 427, 430, 431, 433, 437, 439, 442, 443 Key Concepts, Make Academic Connections, pp. 427, 433, 443	
Chapter 18 Consumer Credit, pp. 448–477	Chapter 18 presents coverage of types of consumer credit accounts along with information on the wise use of credit.	Corporate Social Responsibility: Marketing Credit Cards to Students, 453; Focus on Real Life, pp. 450, 457, 462, 469; FYI, pp. 451, 465; Life-Span Plan, pp. 450, 460; Net Bookmark, p. 460; Planning a Career in Consumer Credit, p. 449; A Question of Ethics: Pawnshops, Payday Loans, and Credit Repair, p. 471; Technology in Action: Databases, Personal Privacy, and Identity Theft, p. 455; Winning Edge FBLA: Impromptu Speaking Event, p. 477; Work as a Team, pp. 453, 461, 466, 472	Checkpoints, pp. 454, 455, 456, 460, 461, 464, 466, 468, 470, 472, 473 Key Concepts, Make Academic Connections, pp. 456, 461, 468, 473	
Chapter 19 Savings and Investment Strategies, pp. 478–507	Chapter 19 presents information for identifying and analyzing investment alternatives, which is the main subject of this chapter.	Doing Business in Thailand, p. 500; E-Commerce in Action: Buying a House Online, p. 498; Focus on Real Life, pp. 480, 486, 491, 495, 501; FYI, pp. 483, 502; Life-Span Plan, pp. 481, 489, 498; Net Bookmark, p. 487; Planning a Career in Investments, p. 479; Winning Edge BPA: Presentation Management—Team Event, p. 507; Work as a Team, pp. 482, 489, 494, 499, 503	Checkpoints, pp. 481, 483, 485, 487, 488, 490, 492, 493, 494, 497, 498, 499, 502, 503 Key Concepts, Make Academic Connections, pp. 485, 490, 494, 499, 503	
Chapter 20 Insurance, pp. 508–539	Chapter 20 describes the types of insurance that consumers should consider based on their personal circumstances and resources.	Focus on Real Life, pp. 510, 516, 523, 529; FYI, pp. 512, 519; Life-Span Plan, pp. 517, 524; Net Bookmark, p. 527; Planning a Career in Insurance, p. 509; Sharpen Your Life Skills: Enhancing Presentations with Visuals, p. 522; Technology in Action: Telemedicine, p. 532; Winning Edge FBLA: Entrepreneurship Case Study, p. 539; Work as a Team, pp. 515, 521, 528, 533	Checkpoints, pp. 511, 513, 515, 517, 519, 521, 524, 527, 528, 531, 534, 535 Key Concepts, Make Academic Connections, pp. 515, 521, 528, 535	

CHAPTER ASSESSMENT	TEACHING RESOURCES	TEACHING STRATEGIES
Business Notes, Communicate Business Concepts, Develop Your Business Language, Decision-Making Strategies, Make Academic Connections, Linking School and Community, Web Workout, pp. 392–395	*Activities and Study Guide,* Ch. 15 *Chapter and Unit Tests,* Ch. 15 *Spanish Resources,* Ch. 15 **Exam***View*® CD, Ch. 15 *Instructor's Resource CD* *Xtra! Web Site*	**Applied Skills** Building Study Skills, p. 383; Communication, p. 375; Mathematics, p. 376; Science, p. 386; Technology, p. 387; Word Processing/Office Technology, p. 389; Writing Across the Curriculum, p. 380 **Different Learning Abilities** At-Risk, p. 388; Dyslexia, p. 384; Hearing Impaired, p. 381; Limited English Proficiency, p. 378; Specific Learning Disability, p. 377; Visually Impaired, p. 372 **Different Learning Styles** Auditory Learner, p. 373; Tactile Learner, p. 382 **Teaching Strategies** Expand Beyond the Classroom, pp. 374, 390
Business Notes, Communicate Business Concepts, Develop Your Business Language, Decision-Making Strategies, Make Academic Connections, Linking School and Community, Web Workout, pp. 416–419	*Activities and Study Guide,* Ch. 16 *Chapter and Unit Tests,* Ch. 16 *Spanish Resources,* Ch. 16 **Exam***View*® CD, Ch. 16 *Instructor's Resource CD* *Xtra! Web Site*	**Applied Skills** Building Study Skills, p. 410; Communication, p. 412; Geography, p. 402; Mathematics, pp. 399, 406; Writing Across the Curriculum, p. 398 **Different Learning Abilities** Attention Deficit Disorder, p. 404; Gifted, p. 407; Limited English Proficiency, p. 409; Visually Impaired, p. 405 **Different Learning Styles** Auditory Learner, p. 413; Kinesthetic Learner, p. 411; Print Learner, p. 400; Tactile Learner, p. 403
Business Notes, Communicate Business Concepts, Develop Your Business Language, Decision-Making Strategies, Make Academic Connections, Linking School and Community, Web Workout, pp. 444–447	*Activities and Study Guide,* Ch. 17 *Chapter and Unit Tests,* Ch. 17 *Spanish Resources,* Ch. 17 **Exam***View*® CD, Ch. 17 *Instructor's Resource CD* *Xtra! Web Site*	**Applied Skills** Building Study Skills, p. 430; Communication, p. 425; Culture, p. 434; Geography, p. 423; Office Technology, p. 441; Technology, p. 429 **Different Learning Abilities** At Risk, p. 435; Gifted, p. 432; Limited English Proficiency, p. 426; Specific Learning Disability, p. 422; Visually Impaired, p. 440 **Different Learning Styles** Auditory Learner, p. 428; Kinesthetic Learner, pp. 431, 436, 442; Print Learner, pp. 424; Tactile Learner, p. 437; Visual Learner, p. 438 **Teaching Strategies** Expand Beyond the Classroom, p. 439
Business Notes, Communicate Business Concepts, Develop Your Business Language, Decision-Making Strategies, Make Academic Connections, Linking School and Community, Web Workout, pp. 474–477	*Activities and Study Guide,* Ch. 18 *Chapter and Unit Tests,* Ch. 18 *Spanish Resources,* Ch. 18 **Exam***View*® CD, Ch. 18 *Instructor's Resource CD* *Xtra! Web Site*	**Applied Skills** Building Study Skills, p. 471; Communication, pp. 464, 472; Mathematics, p. 458; Office Technology, p. 465; Technology, p. 459; Writing Across the Curriculum, p. 454 **Different Learning Abilities** At Risk, p. 450; Dyslexia, p. 467; Gifted, p. 455; Hearing Impaired, p. 463; Limited English Proficiency, p. 452; Specific Learning Disability, p. 469; Visually Impaired, p. 457 **Different Learning Styles** Auditory Learner, p. 453; Kinesthetic Learner, p. 462; Print Learner, p. 470; Tactile Learner, p. 451; Visual Learner, p. 460 **Teaching Strategies** Expand Beyond the Classroom, p. 466
Business Notes, Communicate Business Concepts, Develop Your Business Language, Decision-Making Strategies, Make Academic Connections, Linking School and Community, Web Workout, pp. 504–507	*Activities and Study Guide,* Ch. 19 *Chapter and Unit Tests,* Ch. 19 *Spanish Resources,* Ch. 19 **Exam***View*® CD, Ch. 19 *Instructor's Resource CD* *Xtra! Web Site*	**Applied Skills** Communication, p. 484; Geography, p. 488; Law, p. 495; Mathematics, p. 481; Office Technology, p. 493; Science, p. 502; Technology, p. 487; Writing Across the Curriculum, p. 501 **Different Learning Abilities** At-Risk, p. 480; Dyslexia, p. 491; Gifted, p. 486; Hearing Impaired, p. 496; Limited English Proficiency, p. 483; Visually Impaired, p. 498 **Different Learning Styles** Auditory Learner, p. 492; Kinesthetic Learner, p. 500; Visual Learner, p. 482 **Teaching Strategies** Expand Beyond the Classroom, pp. 489, 497
Business Notes, Communicate Business Concepts, Develop Your Business Language, Decision-Making Strategies, Make Academic Connections, Linking School and Community, Web Workout, pp. 536–539	*Activities and Study Guide,* Ch. 20 *Chapter and Unit Tests,* Ch. 20 *Spanish Resources,* Ch. 20 **Exam***View*® CD, Ch. 20 *Instructor's Resource CD* *Xtra! Web Site*	**Applied Skills** Building Study Skills, p. 513; Communication, p. 517; Mathematics, pp. 520, 530; Technology, pp. 519, 532; Word Processing/Office Technology, p. 512; Writing Across the Curriculum, p. 522 **Different Learning Abilities** At Risk, p. 524; Attention Deficit Disorder, p. 525; Gifted, p. 514; Limited English Proficiency, p. 518; Specific Learning Disability, p. 510; Visually Impaired, p. 526 **Different Learning Styles** Kinesthetic Learner, p. 529; Print Learner, pp. 523, 534; Tactile Learner, p. 527; Visual Learner, pp. 516, 531 **Teaching Strategies** Expand Beyond the Classroom, pp. 511, 533

Personal Financial Management

In this unit, students will learn about personal business skills including consumer buying, money management, banking, consumer credit, saving and investing, and insurance.

Chapter 15 Consumers in the Global Economy This chapter covers the basics of buying along with consumer rights and responsibilities.

Chapter 16 Money Management and Financial Planning The basics of budgeting and personal financial planning are addressed in this chapter.

Chapter 17 Banking and Financial Services Savings, payment, and other banking services are covered in this chapter.

Chapter 18 Consumer Credit The types of credit along with the wise use of credit are the main focus of this chapter.

Chapter 19 Savings and Investment Strategies Savings plans, stocks, bonds, mutual funds, real estate, and other investment alternatives are the basis for this chapter.

Chapter 20 Insurance Motor vehicle, home, life, and health insurance coverages are the major topics of this chapter.

UNIT 4

Personal Financial Management

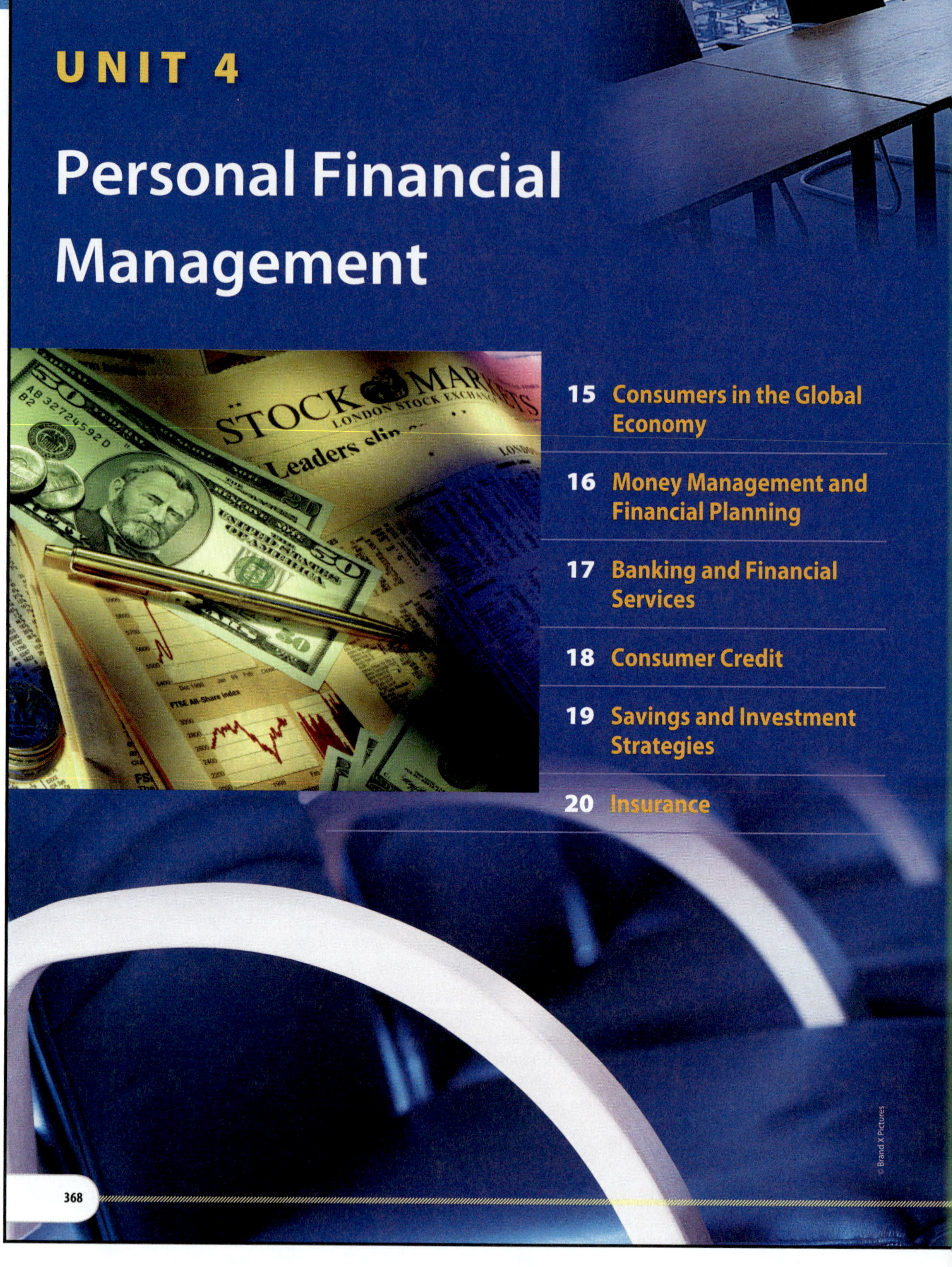

© Brand X Pictures

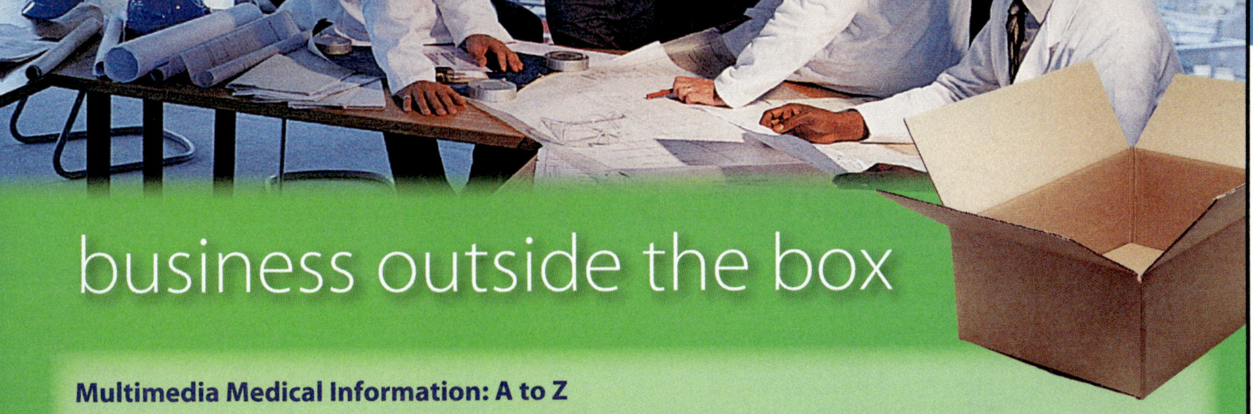

business outside the box

Multimedia Medical Information: A to Z

Health care organizations, including hospitals and medical centers, are spending millions to develop user-friendly, content-rich web sites for a wide range of audiences. Rather than developing all of their own content, they are buying some content from sources such as A.D.A.M. (Animated Dissection of Anatomy for Medicine). This Atlanta-based company provides interactive medical information for health care organizations, medical professionals, consumers, the media, and students.

A major product of A.D.A.M. is its extensive multimedia medical encyclopedia database covering thousands of diseases and conditions. Other products include graphics, 3-D image models, virtual tours of the human body, and broadcast-quality animation. Physician-reviewed text ensures the highest quality of medical information.

Efforts by A.D.A.M. for global expansion have been successful. Within a few months of starting to look at international opportunities, the company sold its interactive medical software in Singapore, Switzerland, and Malaysia. They also have representatives in Spain, Chile, Japan, Korea, Mexico, Norway, and Sweden.

Think Critically

Create a plan to provide professionals and consumers with other types of vital information they might need in their daily activities.

A Sweet Idea

Joe Semprevivo worked in the ice cream shop owned by his parents, but was not able to eat the product he served to others—he had had juvenile diabetes since he was nine years old. Joe was motivated to change that. By age 12, he developed the first sugar-free ice cream. Within three years of creating the ice cream, Joe placed his product in about 75 stores. He visited with supermarket managers and convinced them to carry the product. He explained that his product would serve the needs of diabetics and other health-conscious consumers.

Joe also wanted to have a snack he could take with him to school. At age 15, he and his parents developed a cookie appropriate for those with his same medical condition. Today, Joseph's Sugar-Free Cookies come in eight flavors. His product line has expanded to include sugar-free cakes, brownies, syrup, sweeteners, and peanut butter and fat-free cookies.

Think Critically

What are some special needs that might be met with new products?

CHAPTER 15

Consumers in the Global Economy

© PhotoDisc / Getty Images

370

Teaching Resources

Activities and Study Guide, Ch. 15
Chapter and Unit Tests, Ch. 15
Spanish Resources, Ch. 15

ExamView® *CD,* Ch. 15
Instructor's Resource CD
- PowerPoint Slides, Ch. 15
- Lesson Plans, Ch. 15

Xtra! Web Site

school.cengage.com/business/introtobiz
- Study Tools, 15-1, 15-2, 15-3,
- Quiz Prep, Ch. 15
- Net Bookmark, Ch. 15
- Crossword Puzzle, Ch. 15
- Portfolio Activity, Ch.15

Planning a Career in...
CUSTOMER SERVICE

Each day, millions of customers seek service, all kinds of service. For example, they might want to purchase a computer, return a defective toaster, exchange a gift, schedule a delivery, complain about poor service, request information, apply for a loan, or pay a parking ticket. Employment opportunities in customer service include careers in business, in government, or with a nonprofit organization. Customer service employees work directly with customers in places such as banks, hospitals, and retail stores. They also work in offices and call centers. The specific focus of customer service positions vary widely. For example, there are customer service professionals who help people check into hotels, buy products, make insurance claims, and register for social services. They even offer suggestions for how to cook a turkey.

Employment Outlook

- Employment in customer service is expected to increase faster than the average through 2014.
- Bilingual job seekers have increased opportunities for jobs.
- There are many new openings expected as well as the need to replace experienced customer service representatives who transfer to other occupations.

Related Job Titles

- Customer Service Representative
- Bank Teller
- Catalog Sales Agent
- Computer Support Specialist
- Customer Assistance Coordinator
- Customer Service Specialist
- Financial Service Representative
- Internet Customer Service Representative
- Hotel Desk Clerk
- Receptionist
- Retail Sales Clerk

Needed Skills

- Educational requirements vary. Most customer service positions require only a high school diploma. Some employers require an associate or bachelor's degree.
- Basic computer skills are required and advanced skills are necessary for some positions.
- Good oral and written communication skills along with interpersonal and problem-solving skills are needed.
- Most customer service positions require a basic understanding of business activities, marketing, and consumer behavior.

What's it like to work in... Customer Service

Before he even takes off his coat, Brian starts his day by checking e-mail messages. Today, several messages request information about identity theft. Yesterday, it was complaints about online auctions. Tomorrow, it could be comments about a proposed consumer protection law.

As an Internet customer service specialist with the state consumer protection office, Brian must be ready for a variety of activities. Research, responding to requests, and report preparation are just a few of his daily responsibilities.

When talking to people about his job, Brian always mentions the satisfaction he gets from helping others. He also mentions how much he likes having variety in his day. He never knows what he will find in his mailbox.

What about you? Would working in the field of customer service be of interest to you?

Planning a Career in...
CUSTOMER SERVICE

The complexity of the U.S. economy and business activities can result in many consumer concerns. A wide range of job opportunities are available to inform and assist consumers when planning and making buying decisions.

What About You? Answer

Some students would find the job's high level of human contact stimulating and the ability to do something to help people rewarding. Others might see this job as merely dealing with other people's problems Encourage students to share their experiences with customer service professionals. Refer them to the related job titles that appear on this page to get the conversation started. Ask which aspects of the jobs they think they would enjoy and which they would dislike.

Additional Career Information

Additional information on careers can be found in the *Occupational Outlook Handbook,* an online publication (www.bls.gov/oco) of the federal government. Tell your class about this resource and how to use it. This description of job duties can be used to demonstrate the relevancy of skills learned in this course.

15-1 Consumer Buying Decisions

Goals

Identify major sources of consumer information.

Explain wise buying actions.

Describe the main types of shopping locations.

Key Terms

unit price

brand

impulse buying

Focus on Real Life

"I am going on a wilderness retreat with a community service group and I have to buy a sleeping bag," Kristen said to Joshua.

"I don't know much about sleeping bags, but I want to get the best one for my trip. I stopped by the sporting goods store and they had many varieties and prices. I was confused. Can you help?"

"I don't know much either, but I expect your choice depends on where you will use the bag," said Joshua. "Did you gather information before you began looking? There are consumer groups that test products. If you want, I can help you look online, or we can go to the library to find magazine articles."

"That sounds like a good idea," Kristen replied. "A salesperson at the store might be able to help, but researching in advance should help me ask the right questions."

main idea

Identify major sources of consumer information.

CONSUMER INFORMATION SOURCES

Consumers have the power to decide to buy or not to buy. Businesses must serve the needs of consumers. Without satisfied consumers, businesses would not make sales, earn profits, or remain in business. Several information sources are available to help consumers with their buying decisions.

Product Testing Organizations

Product testing organizations test products and services for the benefit of consumers and business. Manufacturers pay these organizations to perform safety tests on products. Underwriters Laboratories tests electrical components of products from all over the world for fire and electrical safety. The UL symbol indicates that the product has been tested and judged safe for normal use.

The Association of Home Appliance Manufacturers (AHAM) develops and maintains performance standards for appliances such as refrigerators, air conditioners, and freezers. The AHAM seal indicates that a product has met performance standards. The Carpet and Rug Institute and the Motorist Assurance Program issue other seals of quality.

Consumers Union reports scientific, technical, and educational information about products and services. This nonprofit organization performs independent tests on consumer goods. It publishes articles in a monthly magazine called *Consumer Reports*.

Media Sources

Each day, you have access to a range of media sources offering consumer information.

Print Publishers Many magazines and newspapers provide various types of consumer assistance. General interest magazines such as *Consumers Digest, Good*

Housekeeping, and *Parents* provide articles and product information. For money management, financial planning, and investment advice, you could read *Money* or *Kiplinger's Personal Finance Magazine.*

Specialty magazines and newspapers also provide information about specific types of products or services. These publications cover topics such as motor vehicles, computers, boats, electronic equipment, travel, and education. Readers can obtain a better understanding of the technical aspects of these products and services.

Broadcast Organizations Radio and television are valuable sources of consumer information. Most stations carry programs to inform you about product safety, care and use of products, and shopping tips.

The Internet Online information has become a very valuable resource for consumers. Most consumer information sources can be accessed through the Internet. The use of a search engine allows you to obtain specific answers for your consumer questions.

Government Agencies

Federal, state, and local governments also inform consumers. The federal government has the Consumer Information Center, which serves as headquarters for consumer information. This agency puts out a quarterly catalog of publications. It also maintains an extensive web site to assist consumers.

The United States Department of Agriculture (USDA) offers publications and online information about food buying, meal planning, and nutrition. The USDA also inspects and grades meat and other foods. It makes that information available to consumers.

Other federal government agencies that provide consumer information include the Federal Trade Commission (FTC), Food and Drug Administration

(FDA), Consumer Product Safety Commission (CPSC), National Highway Traffic Safety Administration, Department of Housing and Urban Development, and Environmental Protection Agency.

Every state has consumer protection agencies. These agencies have web sites

Name some ways in which you are protected on a daily basis by the activities of a government agency.

NETBookmark

Students explore the federal government's consumer information resources. Ask whether students were surprised at the amount of information available on their chosen consumer topic. Was it more or less information than they expected?

TEACH

Ask students to name various magazines and newspapers that could be of value to consumers.

Point out the value of various radio and television programs when planning a consumer purchase.

Explain the value to consumers of the government agencies listed.

THINK CRITICALLY THROUGH VISUALS

Student answers will vary. For example, government agencies protect consumers by setting and enforcing safety standards for products, assuring the safety of the foods and drugs, providing police and fire protection in local communities, safeguarding our economy by watching the activities of those who invest in securities, protecting U.S. interests at home and abroad, enforcing workplace health and safety laws, and enacting and enforcing environmental laws.

Different Learning Styles

Auditory Learner Encourage auditory learners to repeat the names of the main consumer information sources discussed on pages 372–374.

In addition, have students read out loud some examples of materials from various consumer information sources.

TEACH

Explain the value of various business sources for consumer information.

Ask students to describe experiences of obtaining consumer information from friends or relatives.

THINK CRITICALLY THROUGH VISUALS

A product label is a more reliable source of information than advertising because it contains factual, specific information. Advertising, on the other hand, may simply appeal to emotions and will attempt to encourage you to buy the product.

ONGOING ASSESSMENT

checkpoint >> **ANSWER**

The main sources of consumer information are product testing organizations, media sources, government agencies, business sources, and personal contacts.

to provide information and handle consumer questions. State departments of banking and insurance are available to assist with those areas. Large cities and counties also have consumer assistance offices.

Business Sources

As a public service and in an effort to sell goods and services, businesses make consumer information available.

Advertising Advertising is widely available. It is a popular source of consumer information. The main purpose of an advertisement is to encourage you to buy. Because of this, you should carefully evaluate this information source.

Advertising can be helpful. Useful advertisements tell you what the product is, how it is made, and what it will do. Advertisements give facts that you can use to compare the product with other competing products. Beware of advertising claims that really tell you nothing about the product. If an advertisement states that a product is better, ask, "Better than what?"

Would you find more reliable information in an advertisement or on a product label? How do you know?

Product Labels A label, attached to or printed on a product, provides useful information. A label will report the nature or content of a product. The label will also likely tell you what the product is made of, its size, how to care for it, and when and where it was made. Clothing labels must tell you what the product is made of and must give instructions for washing or cleaning.

Customer Service Departments Many businesses have special departments focused on customer service. Some firms provide customers with booklets on a range of consumer topics. For example, banks and insurance companies publish booklets to help consumers manage their money. Some large retail firms provide printed materials to help consumers with their buying problems.

Better Business Bureau The Better Business Bureau (BBB) can provide helpful information. If you plan to buy a used car from a particular dealer, you could call the BBB to find out what experiences others have had with that dealer. If consumers have reported problems with the firm, you could find out about these complaints. BBBs give facts only. They do not recommend products or firms.

Personal Contacts

An often-used information source is "word of mouth." This includes information received from other people. You often trust information provided by others who have bought and used a product. When planning a purchase, you may talk to someone who already owns the product or has used the service. This word-of-mouth consumer information can be a valuable resource when making consumer decisions.

checkpoint >>
What are the main sources of consumer information?

Teaching Strategies

Expand Beyond the Classroom Have students obtain examples of various product labels (food, clothing, appliances, other items). Ask them to report on the most useful information presented on these labels.

WISE BUYING STRATEGIES

Whenever you plan to buy something, think about several key decisions. These include the following. Do you really need the item now or can you wait? Which stores should you consider? What quality do you want? What price are you willing to pay? Should you pay cash or use credit? If you make the purchase, what other important item may you have to do without?

Use Decision-Making Steps

As a consumer, you should follow the decision-making steps when making a purchase.

1. *Identify your needs or wants.* Be able to state clearly why you intend to buy something.

2. *Know the choices available.* These choices include price, quality, location, variety, reputation, and other factors.

3. *Determine your desired satisfaction.* You should develop answers to questions such as, "How much am I willing to pay?" "What quality level do I want?" and "How long am I willing to wait for the item?"

4. *Evaluate alternatives.* At this stage, you will shop for the products and services that could satisfy your needs. You will compare them in terms of the criteria you have identified.

5. *Make the decision.* Decide whether to buy or not. Determine what product or service is most satisfying. Decide from which business you will make the purchase.

Good buying skills will make you a better consumer. You can get greater value for your money each time you make a purchase.

Explain wise buying actions.

Electronic Package Tags

You are walking along and suddenly you receive a text message on your cell phone. You are informed that a certain item is on sale at a store as you walk by that exact store. This message could be both convenient and frightening.

Radio frequency identification devices (RFIDs) in clothing labels and other products will allow keeping track of things and people. Currently, RFIDs are being used in highway toll lanes, and for pet identification, library book circulation and retrieval, and baggage tracking by airlines. They are also used in warehouses to monitor the location of inventory. Companies are able to identify the exact location of their products. Using RFID technology reduces theft and misplaced inventory.

Two components make up an RFID system. First, the data-loaded tag (called the transponder) is attached to the item to be tracked. Second, a reader (the transreceiver) captures the tag's data using radio waves. These data are then sent to a computer for processing.

In the future, RFIDs could be used in homes to turn on appliances and monitor heating and security. Tagging of individual consumer products and clothing is also expected. A purchase you make could be tracked from the store to your home and everywhere else it is used.

Think Critically

1. What are possible uses of RFIDs that could benefit consumers?
2. What concerns might be associated with RFIDs?

TEACH

Ask students to name some actions that might be considered as wise buying actions.

Describe consumer actions related to each decision-making step.

Have students give examples for each of the decision-making steps listed.

Technology in Action

The use of radio frequency identification devices continues to expand. Point out the benefits of these devices along with potential concerns.

Think Critically Answers

1. Students should be able to think of many uses for RFIDs. For example, they could be used to locate children or Alzheimer's patients who wander away from their homes, to simplify taking attendance in schools or punching time cards in the workplace, or to alert consumers to product recalls or upgrades.

2. Perhaps the most serious concern students will raise is the invasion of privacy. They may object to the idea that their movements could be tracked by RFIDs. Also, if the technology is not working properly, it may be difficult to revert to manual methods of attendance or record keeping while the problem is being fixed. Also, companies could use RFIDs to inundate individuals with unwanted and excessive advertising messages.

Applied Skills

Communication Have students prepare a poster or other visual presentation identifying the decision-making steps a consumer should use when making a purchase. Instruct students to include a specific example showing how to use the decision-making steps. Consider allowing students to work in pairs and make arrangements to display students' work.

Comparison Shopping

Smart consumers are comparison shoppers. They compare price, quality, services, and brands.

Compare Prices A **unit price** is a price per unit of measure. Most stores help consumers compare among various brands and sizes of the same product. Shelf labels show both the total price and the price of one standard measure, or unit, of the product.

If you need to calculate a unit price, divide the price of the item by the number of units per measure. For instance, in the supermarket, you see that a 16-ounce bag of Golden Frozen Corn costs $1.26. An 8-ounce box of Yellow Perfection Corn sells for $0.69 per box. Which is the better buy for the dollar?

If you compare the total prices only, it is not easy to decide. Because stores usually post the cost per ounce, the unit price, you could quickly compare the two package sizes. In this case, the 16-ounce bag would show a unit price of 7.9 cents an ounce ($1.26 ÷ 16). The 8-ounce box would be 8.6 cents per ounce ($0.69 ÷ 8). Unit pricing would quickly tell you that the 16-ounce bag is a better buy per ounce for the dollar.

Prices of products can vary greatly. The cost of the same item often differs from store to store and in different geographic regions. For example, an identical camera may be available with prices ranging from $25 to more than $40. These price differences emphasize the need for comparison shopping.

Compare Quality High-quality products and services often cost more. Buying lower-quality items can sometimes turn out to be more expensive than buying higher-quality items. For example,

Name an instance when you spent time comparing prices, quality, and service on an item before making a purchase. How did you determine which item was the best choice?

© PhotoDisc/Getty Images

if you buy a lower-quality pair of shoes, they may wear out in a short time. You will have to replace the lower-quality shoes sooner. You may end up buying two pairs of low-quality shoes in a short span of time.

Compare Services Most businesses try to provide good service, but types of services can differ. Some businesses sell for cash only. Others offer credit. Some businesses provide free delivery. Other services offered may include layaways, repairs, and special orders. Service is important, but be careful not to pay for more service than you need.

Compare Sales The word "sale" is perhaps the most overused, and least trusted, word in marketing. You have probably seen sale signs a thousand times. When an item is really on sale, it is offered at a price lower than its normal selling price. Some "sales" may not really be sales at all.

Promotional sales are used to promote the selling of regular merchandise with short-term price reductions. This type of sale may be used when a new store opens or when new products are introduced. Retailers may use promotional sales in hopes that customers will buy the sale items as well as other products not on sale.

A *clearance sale* is used to clear merchandise that stores no longer wish to carry. This may be end-of-season items, odd sizes and models, or discontinued merchandise. Clearance sales usually offer some bargains. Be sure that you need a sale item before you buy it.

Compare Brands A **brand** is a name given to a product or service to distinguish it from other similar and competitive items. The company that makes the product or service usually creates a *brand name.* Brand names are designed to help build customer loyalty.

National brands are advertised all over the country. They are sold in almost every community. Among these goods are items such as food, clothing, shoes, tools, and cosmetics. Manufacturers of such goods often place brand names on the items they make. Well-known brand names include Kellogg's, Jell-O, Colgate, The Gap, and L'Oreal. Recognizing national brand names allows you to expect uniform quality. Buying brand-name goods is especially helpful when it is hard to inspect for quality, such as packaged products.

Some stores have their own brand names, called *store brands* or *private label brands.* For example, Craftsman has long been one of the brand names on tools sold by Sears. Store brands are usually sold at a lower cost than national brands. Buying store brands may save you money and offer good quality at the same time.

Stores may also carry unbranded items at reduced prices, called *generic products.* Generic products are less expensive because they do not require advertising and fancy packaging. These lower costs result in lower prices. Differences in quality between generic and branded products may be small, making these items a good value.

Wise Buying: A Summary

Skillful consumers are efficient in their shopping activities. They save time, energy, and money by planning.

Take Your Time "I just don't have the time" is something many people say. Spending time planning purchases usually results in savings. Taking your time will allow you to look for the best values. As a good shopper, you should refuse to be hurried. Then, you can avoid buying things that you really do not want or need.

Compare different brands of similar items. Name similarities and differences. Is one better than the other? Why?

Different Learning Abilities

Specific Learning Disability (SLD) Encourage students to locate and bring to class examples of various types of brands that are available to consumers. Ask them to explain possible differences of quality and price among the brands.

Life-Span Plan Answer

Answers will vary. Students should explain that funds wasted through bad buying decisions are funds that cannot be used to help them achieve their life-span goals.

TEACH

Provide an overview of the types of brands (national, store brands, generic). Ask students about their experiences and preferences for various brands.

Highlight the key points in the wise buying summary.

THINK CRITICALLY THROUGH VISUALS

Those who say the store brand items are just as good may argue that if the ingredients are the same the products are the same. Others will contend that the name brand products have gone through extensive consumer testing and are made with better formulas and processes. These students may have also found brand name items to be of more consistent quality. Other students will be willing to give store brand products a chance, having found that they are often just as good.

PROJECT

Provide the following instructions to students. (These instructions also appear on page xxv of the textbook.) Explain why an ability to make wise buying decisions is important for achieving your life-span goals. Do you believe buying skills contribute to your ability to reach your life-span goals? What could you do to improve your buying skills?

Work as a Team

This activity will help students develop a better awareness of shopping locations.

TEACH

Point out situations in which consumers might consider the timing of purchases.

Ask students for some of the factors that influence Impulse buying.

ONGOING ASSESSMENT

checkpoint >> **ANSWER**

Decision-making steps that should be taken when making a purchase are (1) identifying your needs or wants, (2) knowing the choices available, (3) determining your desired satisfaction, (4) evaluating alternatives, and (5) making the decision.

TEACH

Describe product lines and services of traditional retailers.

Ask students to describe their experiences in contemporary retailers.

Work as a Team

Today, consumers have more ways to buy than ever before. Using the three main categories of buying locations (traditional retailers, contemporary retailers, and non-store shopping), create a list of businesses in your community. Then, discuss the advantages and disadvantages of using each of the three categories.

main idea

Describe the main types of shopping locations.

Time Your Purchases For some items, prices are lowest at predictable times. Certain seasons and conditions favor goods and services being sold at reduced prices. Some examples include:

- Fresh fruits and vegetables are usually lower in price during the peak of their growing season.

- Winter clothing is often on sale in January.

- Firewood often costs less in the summer.

Consumer information sources can help you add to this list.

Avoid Being Impulsive The opposite of spending time and effort is buying too quickly and is called **impulse buying**. Impulse buying should be avoided. It often happens when an item is nicely displayed where customers are likely to see it, such as near the checkout counter.

Some impulse buying is harmless when the cost is small and the item is worth the price. Be aware that buying more expensive items on impulse can be costly. One of the best ways to avoid impulse buying is to use a shopping list. You can save money with a list whether it is for groceries, hardware, or clothing.

checkpoint >>
What decision-making steps should be taken when making a purchase?

SHOPPING LOCATIONS

When deciding where to buy, you have many choices. The types of stores and other buying locations expand every day because of competition and technology.

Traditional Retailers

Many of the stores in which you shop have developed over the past 100 years. *Department stores* have an extensive product line and emphasize service. They may have personal shoppers, make deliveries, and wrap gifts.

Discount stores emphasize lower prices on their products. Most discount stores base their success on a high volume of sales and low prices. If service is not important to you, this may be where you should shop.

Specialty stores have a special line of products for sale. They carry a wide variety of products in a narrow line such as sporting goods, jewelry, or women's shoes. Some specialty stores may also be discount stores.

In food retailing, a *supermarket* is the large, full-service store that carries many brands. *Convenience stores* are small stores that emphasize the sale of food items, an accessible location, and long operating hours. These stores usually stock popular items at higher prices.

Contemporary Retailers

Today, *specialty superstores* offer low prices and a wide variety of a limited product line. These include retailers such as OfficeMax, Home Depot, and Best Buy.

Discount stores have expanded to include a wide array of food products. These *superstores* may also include other retail services such as a bakery, restaurant, pharmacy, video rentals, and banking.

The *warehouse club* is a no-frills outlet focusing on the sale of large quantities at

---

Different Learning Abilities

Limited English Proficiency (LEP) Obtain translations of wise buying activities to reinforce these concepts in both English and other dominant languages used by students. Also use ads, labels, packages, and other visuals in their native language as examples.

reasonable prices. Products are displayed in simple settings resembling a warehouse. These stores target small business owners who are looking to buy various supplies and equipment.

Factory outlets have been popular. These stores have a reputation for selling high-quality merchandise at low prices. Products are direct from the factory and sometimes have minor flaws.

Non-Store Shopping

Shopping at home started with door-to-door sales. Then, *mail order* catalogs became very popular. People sent in their orders by mail and later called by telephone. Now, you can buy using your television, computer, or fax machine.

Non-store shopping also includes *vending machines*. Each year, more and different products are available through these automated devices. In Japan, a person can buy everything from eggs and toys

What are some advantages to shopping in a store rather than using a catalog or shopping online?

© Getty Images/PhotoDisc

to flowers and toilet paper from a vending machine.

checkpoint »
What are the main categories of shopping locations?

15-1 Assessment

Xtra!
Study Tools
school.cengage.com/business/introtobiz

Key Concepts

Determine the best answer.

1. The most reliable consumer information source will usually be
   a. advertising
   b. comments from salespeople
   c. comments from other consumers
   d. reports from consumer testing organizations

2. The first step in the buying decision-making process is to
   a. identify product alternatives
   b. evaluate the services at different stores
   c. decide whether to use cash or credit
   d. identify your needs

3. Which of the following is an example of a non-store shopping location?
   a. club warehouse
   b. vending machine
   c. factory outlet
   d. hypermarket

Make Academic Connections

4. **Math** A 12-ounce package of cereal is priced at $3.20. A larger container of the cereal costs $5.20 for 1½ pounds. What is the unit price for each item?

5. **Communication** Select several advertisements. Develop a list of questions to ask when evaluating advertising. Use these guidelines to evaluate the ads you selected. Prepare a one-page summary of your findings.

Focus on Real Life

Ask students to comment on this scenario and to provide their own experiences in various shopping situations.

TEACH

Ask students to name common concerns of consumers. Explain how actions in the consumer movement have helped address these concerns.

FIGURE 15-1 ANSWER

Examples will vary. Students might mention nutrition labels as an example of their right to be informed. You may want to discuss times when they have been denied these rights, perhaps by stores that refuse to let students enter without an adult or limit the number of students they allow in the store at one time. If time allows, you may want to ask whether there are limits on these rights and, if so, what those limits are.

15-2 Consumer Rights and Responsibilities

Goals

Explain the consumer movement.

Explain seven consumer rights.

Describe consumer responsibilities.

Key Terms

consumer movement

fraud

guarantee

express warranty

implied warranty

Focus on Real Life

Juan met Michelle after school. "Hi, Michelle. Have you decided which computer to buy?"

"I don't know," replied Michelle. "I looked at the computers at Bayside Computer Store and they have the lowest price. But I got the impression they didn't take me seriously because of my age."

Young people often comment that businesses do not respect them as customers or treat them as well as adults. Successful businesses recognize that teens are a powerful consumer group with purchasing power. They not only choose where they want to spend their money, but often influence the buying decisions of family and friends.

Businesses that ignore or disrespect younger customers jeopardize sales. They may also lose long-term customers who don't feel comfortable when shopping in these stores. You can be sure that businesses that are aware of consumer rights and buying power will welcome teen customers.

---

main idea

Explain the consumer movement.

THE CONSUMER MOVEMENT

In the past, some businesses were viewed as often trying to take advantage of consumers. False claims were sometimes made about products. Prices were often too high. Some products were unsafe. To fight against unfair business practices, consumers united to demand fair treatment from businesses, giving rise to what is known as the **consumer movement**.

Because of this movement, public and private agencies, policies, laws, and regulations were developed to protect consumer interests. In 1962, President John F. Kennedy presented his Consumer Bill of Rights and declared that every consumer has the first four rights shown in Figure 15-1. In 1969, President Richard M. Nixon added the fifth right to the list. In 1975, President Gerald R. Ford added the sixth. In 1994, President William J. Clinton added the seventh.

Consumer Bill of Rights
1. The right to be informed.
2. The right to safety.
3. The right to choose.
4. The right to be heard.
5. The right to a remedy.
6. The right to consumer education.
7. The right to service.

FIGURE 15-1

Give examples of how your rights as a consumer are respected.

Applied Skills

Writing Across the Curriculum Write a paragraph that demonstrates the connection between various concerns faced by consumers in the past and the development of the Consumer Bill of Rights. Suggest that interested students create a timeline to put things in historical perspective.

YOUR CONSUMER RIGHTS

As a consumer, you have the right to expect honesty and fair treatment from businesses. Few businesses are intentionally dishonest. Being a skilled consumer means that you know the Consumer Bill of Rights and how to exercise these rights.

The Right to Be Informed

Most products and services are described in advertisements, on labels, or by a salesperson. You have a right to know what the product or service is and what it will do for you.

Fraud occurs when consumers are given false information in an effort to make a sale. If a salesperson knowingly sells you a car on which the odometer has been turned back 30,000 miles, fraud has occurred.

Not all product information you receive can be expected to be perfectly accurate. Suppose you were looking for a used car for transportation to and from school. If a salesperson told you she thought the car would get about 20 miles to the gallon but it only got 18, you were not deceived. The salesperson may not have been accurate in estimating gas mileage, but no guarantee was made.

When a salesperson exaggerates the good qualities of a product and says, "It's the best" or "It's a great buy," there is no fraud. On the other hand, if the salesperson tells you a car has new brakes and it does not, this is fraud.

The Right to Safety

Consumers have a right to be safe from harm associated with using products or services. Several agencies work to assure the safety of consumers. The Consumer Product Safety Commission has the authority to set safety standards, ban hazardous products, and recall dangerous products from the market.

The Food and Drug Administration (FDA) makes certain that food, drug, and cosmetic products are not harmful to consumers. This federal agency enforces laws and regulations that prevent the distribution of unsafe or misbranded foods, drugs, and cosmetics.

The FDA also works to ensure that product labels do not mislead consumers. The United States Department of Agriculture (USDA) helps ensure consumer safety by setting quality standards for farm products. The USDA also controls the processing, inspection, and labeling of meat products.

The Right to Choose

The right of consumers to choose from a variety of goods and services has become well established. In fact, one of the main activities of the Federal Trade Commission (FTC) is to prevent one firm from using unfair practices to force competing firms out of business. When a business has no competitors and controls the market for a product or service, it is said to have a *monopoly*. Competing firms encourage customers to buy from them by

main idea

Explain seven consumer rights.

Why is it important for consumers to have choices?

Work as a Team

Your consumer rights are commonly taken for granted. As a team, create a table with three columns and seven rows. List the seven consumer rights in the left column. In the center column, describe situations in which each consumer right is involved. In the right column, describe actions that people can take to more effectively use each consumer right.

offering a choice of products and services at a range of prices. By driving away this competition, monopolies limit the right to choose.

The Right to Be Heard

Most businesses have a customer service department to hear the concerns or complaints of customers. Some smaller businesses have a specific person assigned to that duty. Businesses are usually happy to take care of problems you have with their products or services.

Several federal government agencies, such as the FTC, also assure your right to be heard. As a consumer, you can complain directly to the FTC if you believe that your consumer rights have been violated. The FTC regulates advertising and encourages informative and truthful advertising.

State government agencies, such as the Office of the Attorney General or the Department of Consumer Affairs, have responsibility for protecting the rights of consumers. They can prosecute businesses for breaking state consumer protection laws. These offices also inspect advertising practices. They handle consumer problems related to automobile repairs, credit, and door-to-door sales practices.

Privately funded groups also help to make certain you are heard. Various national and local groups inform and protect consumers in a variety of

A QUESTION OF ETHICS

Frauds by Consumers

Most people are familiar with bait-and-switch tactics, work-at-home schemes, and "lose weight fast" scams. These frauds against consumers result in lost money for consumers and are usually illegal. Various actions by consumers can also cause higher prices. People who would not think of shoplifting may be dishonest in other ways. Deceptive actions by consumers include the following.

- Eating items in a store without paying for them
- Buying a book, reading it, and returning it for a full refund
- Sitting on the floor in a bookstore and reading an entire magazine without buying it

- Making photocopies of sheet music and passing them out to all the members of your chorus
- Buying clothing, wearing the item, and then returning it
- Asking for a cup for water and using it to take a soft drink from a self-serve dispenser
- Switching price tags from lower-priced items and putting them on the more expensive items

While most of these actions are illegal, all affect the operating costs of businesses. Each of these "frauds by consumers" results in higher prices. Many of these practices have become more difficult with

technology. While new electronic devices have improved store security, this equipment has also added to business costs and higher prices.

Think Critically
1. What other actions by consumers can result in higher prices for the things you buy?
2. Describe how businesses and individual consumers might help reduce these actions that result in higher prices for everyone.

purchasing areas. Some groups specialize in auto safety or consumer credit. Others will assist with any consumer problem.

The Better Business Bureau is concerned with problems arising from false advertising or misrepresented products and services. Dues paid by member businesses support BBBs. They work to maintain ethical practices and combat consumer fraud. If you believe your consumer rights have been violated, you can get help from one of 120 Better Business Bureaus around the country. After reporting your concern, the bureau will try to persuade the business to fix the problem. Most businesses willingly carry out the BBB request.

The Right to a Remedy

The Fair Packaging and Labeling Act, National Traffic and Motor Vehicle Safety Act, Truth in Labeling Act, and Fair Debt Collection Practices Act all protect consumers. These and other laws are designed to provide assurances that consumers can seek a legal remedy when a problem occurs.

Consumers also have protection provided through a guarantee. With some purchases, a consumer can expect a guarantee or a warranty. A **guarantee** is a promise by the manufacturer or dealer, usually in writing, that a product is of a certain quality. A guarantee may apply to the entire item or only to some parts of it. It may promise that defective parts will be replaced only if a problem occurs during a specified period. No guarantee covers damages caused by misuse.

When making a purchase, a skillful consumer asks about a guarantee. A guarantee is frequently in the form of statements like these: "The working parts of this watch are guaranteed for one year." "This sweater will not shrink more than 3 percent." These kinds of guarantees

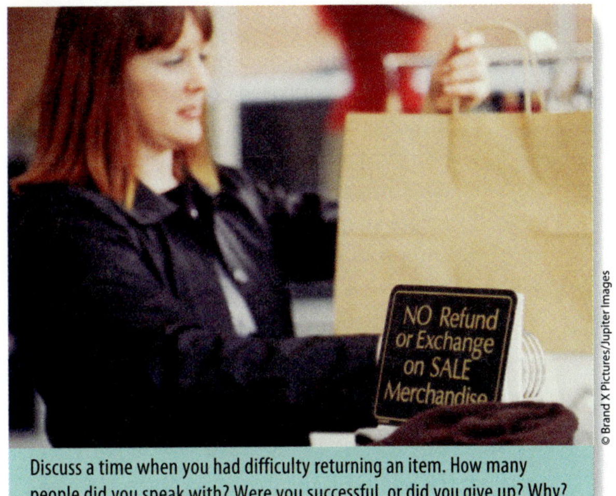

© Brand X Pictures/Jupiter Images

Discuss a time when you had difficulty returning an item. How many people did you speak with? Were you successful, or did you give up? Why?

are sometimes called express warranties. An **express warranty** is made orally or in writing and promises a specific quality of performance.

You should review the guarantee before buying an item. You can also require the business to put in writing any other guarantees that have been offered orally. Written guarantees are useful if you need to return a faulty product. Read the guarantee carefully to find out exactly what is covered and for what period.

Some guarantees are not written. They are called implied warranties. An **implied warranty** is imposed by law and is understood to apply even though it has not been stated. In general, the law requires certain standards to be met. For example, it is implied that health care products purchased over the counter at a pharmacy will not harm you when used according to the directions.

FYI

Teenage consumers spend more than $200 billion each year. The main categories of their spending are food and snacks, clothing, entertainment, school items, and automobile expenses.

TEACH

Explain the various types of guarantees and warranties. Contrast the difference between an express warranty and an implied warranty.

Use the FYI feature to point out the buying influence of young consumers. Ask students to name actions that young consumers might take to make wiser use of their consumer rights.

THINK CRITICALLY THROUGH VISUALS

Student answers will vary. Invite a few volunteers to share details of their experiences when attempting to return unsatisfactory items they had purchased.

Applied Skills

Building Study Skills Have students create review questions for this lesson. Ask each student to contribute one question for each of the main ideas related to consumer rights and responsibilities. Use the questions as the basis for an in-class competition.

TEACH

Ask students to name some of the topics and activities that might be used in a consumer education class.

ONGOING ASSESSMENT

checkpoint >> **ANSWER**

An express warranty is made orally or in writing and promises a specific quality of performance. An implied warranty is imposed by law and is understood to apply even though it has not been stated.

THINK CRITICALLY THROUGH VISUALS

The company that sells you a cell phone should provide you with convenience, courtesy, and responsiveness to any problems you might have with the phone.

TEACH

Provide an overview of the main consumer responsibilities. Ask students to explain why these actions are important to society.

Describe consumer responsibilities.

The Right to Consumer Education

Although individual buying decisions are important, educated consumers need to understand how their choices affect the economy. Consumer education should take into account how buying actions create an interaction between consumers and producers. Educated consumers are aware that their decisions not only affect their personal situation, but also have economic and social implications.

The Right to Service

This latest right suggests consumers can expect convenience, courtesy, and responsiveness to consumer problems and needs. The right to service encourages businesses to take steps necessary to ensure that products and services meet the quality and performance levels claimed for those products and services.

checkpoint >>

How does an express warranty differ from an implied warranty?

What kind of service should you expect from the company that sells you a cell phone?

YOUR CONSUMER RESPONSIBILITIES

Just as some businesses have not met their responsibilities to consumers, some consumers try to take advantage of businesses. Even consumers who are not unethical or dishonest may have expectations that businesses cannot meet. Consumers also have responsibilities in business relationships.

Be Honest

Most people are honest, but those who are not cause others to pay higher prices. Shoplifting losses are estimated to be in the billions of dollars each year. Businesses make up losses from shoplifting by charging higher prices.

As a responsible consumer, you must be as honest with a business as you want it to be with you. You should be as quick to tell the cashier that you received too much change at the checkout counter as you are to say that you received too little.

Be Reasonable

As a buyer, you are usually responsible for what you buy if the business has been honest. If you are dissatisfied and wish to complain, you should complain in a reasonable way.

You should first be sure that you have a cause for complaint. Be sure that you have followed the directions for using the product. After you have confirmed the details of your complaint, calmly explain the problem to an employee of the business from which you bought the item. In most cases, the business will be glad to correct the problem because it does not want to lose you as a customer.

Be Active

As a responsible consumer, you should report unethical business practices to prevent other consumers from becoming victims. By reporting the matter to

---

a consumer agency, you might be able to get the shop to keep its word both to you and to future customers.

Be Informed

The most important responsibility you have as a consumer is to be informed. Just having the right to be informed will not make you an informed consumer. You must find and use the information available to you.

You should also keep informed about your rights as a consumer. Learn about the laws and agencies that protect your rights and how to report a violation of your rights. Being an informed consumer is hard work, but the extra effort spent in making your dollars go as far as possible will be worth it.

Be Involved

In the United States, involvement is an important consumer activity. As a citizen, you have a responsibility to participate in government, which starts by being an informed voter.

As a consumer, you also have responsibilities. When the opportunity arises, make your concerns known to government officials or consumer agencies. Only when you become involved as a consumer can agencies do their jobs and legislative bodies pass appropriate laws.

You have an obligation to society to be a wise and efficient consumer. The world has only a limited supply of natural resources such as petroleum, metals, clean air, and clean water. Sometimes, uninformed consumers unnecessarily waste these resources and contribute to damaging the environment.

checkpoint »
What actions can be taken to be an involved consumer?

15-2 Assessment

Xtra! Study Tools
school.cengage.com/business/introtobiz

Key Concepts

Determine the best answer.

1. True or False. The U.S. Consumer Product Safety Commission is responsible for regulating the safety of food.

2. True or False. An implied warranty is usually printed in the owner's manual of a product.

3. A person who compares product information on labels is using the consumer right to
   a. service
   b. be informed
   c. be heard
   d. a remedy

4. If a person returns an item as new for a refund after using it, this violates the consumer responsibility to be
   a. honest
   b. involved
   c. informed
   d. active

Make Academic Connections

5. *Research* Go to the web site of the FTC's Bureau of Consumer Protection. What services does this government agency provide? How do you and other consumers benefit from the actions of the FTC?

6. *Law* The Truth in Labeling Act requires that certain information be presented on food labels. Using a label from a food product in your home, identify some of these required items. How would you make food labels more informative for consumers?

ONGOING ASSESSMENT

checkpoint » **ANSWER**
To be an involved consumer, you should be honest, reasonable, active, informed, and involved.

ASSESS

Key Concepts Answers

1. False. The Consumer Product Safety Commission regulates the safety of products. (The Food and Drug Administration regulates the safety of food.)

2. False. An implied warranty is understood to apply even though it is not written.

3. b. be informed

4. a. honest

Make Academic Connections

5. Answers will vary.

6. Answers will vary. Suggestions for making food labels more informative might include inclusion of information about country of origin, genetically modified ingredients, and use of antibiotics and pesticides.

CLOSE

Have students explain or dramatize actions that represent irresponsible consumer behavior.

RETEACH

Form 12 small groups. Ask each group to prepare a summary for one of the rights or responsibilities addressed in this lesson.

ENRICH

Ask students to create a list of government agencies that might be contacted for various consumer concerns.

BUSINESS IMPROVING SOCIETY

Consumers Union provides information that is considered by many to be some of the most objective available to consumers. The organization accepts no advertising for its magazine to avoid business influence on its testing and reporting activities.

Think Critically Answers

1. Consumers Union assists consumers by providing information on products and services, sorting out low-quality and unsafe products from those that offer solid value. It publishes a monthly magazine, *Consumer Reports,* and a number of web sites where consumers can read the results of extensive testing of all kinds of consumer products and services. Consumers Union also advocates for improved consumer protection laws. The advocacy arm of Consumers Union conducts research, offers educational programs on consumer topics, publishes reports, organizes conferences, and testifies at government hearings.

2. Answers will vary depending on what issues are currently being investigated by Consumers Union.

Consumers Union

Imagine 24 different washing machines all operating in the same room. Envision 32 digital cameras being used by a small group of people. These are scenes you might encounter in one of the 50 testing laboratories of Consumers Union in Yonkers, New York.

Consumers Union was created in 1936 to provide information on products and services to help buyers get the most for their money. Today, Consumers Union continues to sort out low-quality and unsafe products from those items that will give you the best value. Each month, the results of these consumer tests are reported in *Consumer Reports* magazine and on the Consumer Reports web site.

Consumers Union also conducts extensive testing on motor vehicles. Each year, the organization buys the vehicles the same way you would buy a car. That is, Consumers Union has shoppers bargain with dealers for the best price. After an inspection of the vehicle's features, road testing occurs on a 195-mile course. Engineers record various performance data. Finally, crash tests are conducted to assess safety and the possibility of a rollover. All of these findings are then published to help consumers make wiser car-buying choices.

In recent years, as consumers spend more of their income on services, Consumers Union has expanded its activities. Every month in the magazine, consumers are provided with information about banking services, health care, insurance, lawyers, and other personal and financial services.

Consumers Union is involved with protecting consumers in other ways. Offices in Washington, DC, California, and Texas promote improved consumer protection laws. The Washington office works to build support for laws related to telecommunications, product safety, food safety, financial services, health care policy, energy, international trade, and other consumer issues.

The advocacy arm of Consumers Union conducts research and offers educational programs on consumer topics. This group also publishes reports, organizes conferences, and testifies at government hearings.

Think Critically
1. How do the activities of Consumers Union assist consumers?
2. Conduct research to create a list of current consumer issues that are of concern to Consumers Union.

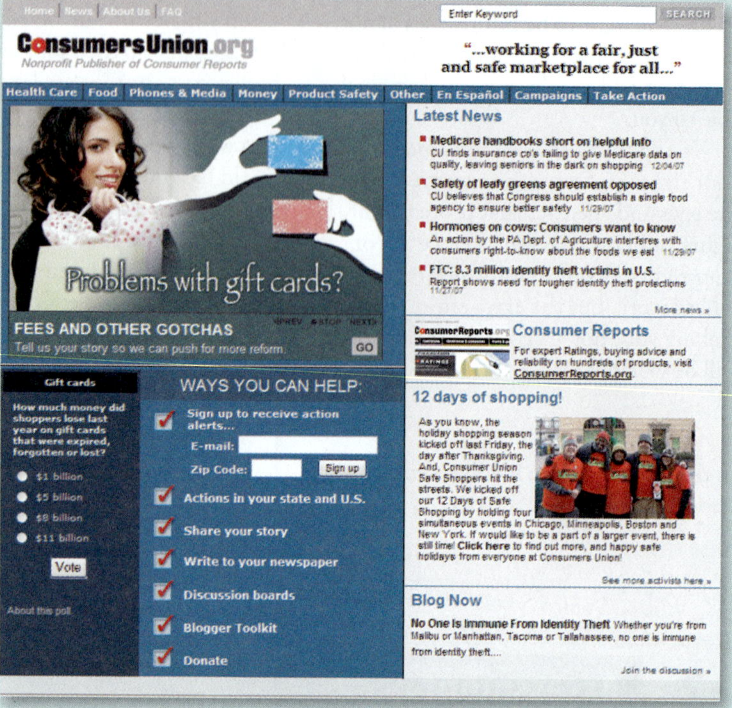

© 2007 by Consumers Union of U.S., Inc. Yonkers, NY 10703-1057, a nonprofit organization. Reprinted with permission from www.ConsumersUnion.org for educational purposes only. No commercial use or reproduction permitted. www.ConsumerReports.org, and www.ConsumersUnion.org.

Applied Skills

Science A variety of scientific methods are used when testing consumer products. Have students describe how various products might be analyzed based on the ingredients of these items.

Focus on **Real Life**

Use this feature to point out common problems faced by consumers.

TEACH

Ask students to name various problems commonly encountered by consumers. Describe examples of consumer problems related to the categories listed on this page.

15-3 Consumer Protection Actions

Goals

List common consumer concerns.

Describe the steps of the consumer complaint process.

Explain legal actions available to assist consumers.

Key Terms

mediation

arbitration

class action suit

small claims court

Focus on **Real Life**

Monica Robinson bought an expensive leather purse. Unfortunately, after she used the purse for a few weeks, the zipper broke. She took the purse back to the store from which it was purchased. Monica very politely and calmly described to the salesperson how the zipper broke. She also had her receipt from the purchase to show that the purse was only six weeks old. The salesperson looked at the purse and the receipt and offered Monica a replacement, a store credit, or a refund. Monica chose a replacement.

This consumer problem had a pleasant ending. Most of them do. You should not get upset or angry in order to get satisfactory results from a business. In fact, most businesses are eager to solve problems that consumers have. They want happy, satisfied customers who will return.

Solving consumer problems is usually a matter of practicing good two-way communication. Let the business know what you want. The job of the business is to tell you what you can expect to get. If both consumer and business are honest and fair, the problem can be solved.

COMMON CONSUMER PROBLEMS

Consumers hope that their purchases will always result in a satisfactory transaction. Still, problems sometimes arise. The item may have been damaged in transit. The wrong size sweater may have been shipped. These types of consumer problems are usually resolved quite easily.

Sometimes, problems that are more serious might occur. Your credit card payment may not be properly recorded to your account. A product you purchased might stop working after just a few days of use.

Sources of Complaints

Various consumer agencies report that the main sources of consumer complaints involve the following types of business.

- Motor vehicle purchases, repairs
- Debt harassment
- Identity theft and credit card fraud
- Guaranteed and advance-fee loans
- Credit repair scams
- Telemarketing, catalog, and magazine sales
- Internet auctions, online purchases
- Prizes, sweepstakes, and phony lottery promotions
- Work-at-home and start-your-own-business opportunities
- Travel and vacation promotions
- Health and diet gimmicks

main idea

List common consumer concerns.

Applied Skills

Technology Have students locate a blog (web log) with information about various consumer problems or complaints. What information is presented that might be useful?

FYI

"Phishing" is a high-tech scam that uses spam or pop-up messages to deceive you into revealing your credit card number, bank account information, Social Security number, passwords, or other sensitive information. The Federal Trade Commission warns consumers never to disclose personal data online to a questionable source.

Deceptive Business Activities

Consumer fraud can be discovered in media ads, in the mail, or even on a city street corner. Various scams, cons, and swindles have been around for a long time. When a deal seems like it's too good to be true, it probably is! Each year, federal government agencies report consumers losing billions of dollars on phony investments and other deceptive offers.

The Internet has become the number one source of fraudulent offers. Consumers may not know the identity or location of all online merchants. This makes it difficult to track down the con artist after you have already lost your money.

The most common online scams involve sales of Internet services and general merchandise. Online auctions, non-delivery of products, credit/debit card scams, and work-at-home offers are also common sources of fraud.

Internet scams can also take the form of prizes, sweepstakes, and credit card offers. Consumers have lost as much as $10,000 through Internet fraud. Be cautious when making your online purchases.

Protection for Shoppers

With the increasing popularity of e-commerce comes the concern for consumer rights. Federal laws that protect Internet and TV shoppers are the same as those that govern purchases made by telephone. The seller must send you the item within 30 days or within another period specifically stated by the company. If there is a delay, the seller must notify you. You then have the right to cancel your order.

If an unreceived or returned item is billed to your credit card, you have 60 days to dispute it. The credit card company then has 30 days to respond. Within 90 days of your letter, the credit card company must investigate the matter and explain why the bill is correct or incorrect.

You do not have to pay the part of your credit card bill under dispute until the matter is resolved. To avoid finance charges, you must pay the rest of your bill on time.

checkpoint >>
What are sources of common consumer complaints?

Describe some Internet scams or other suspicious schemes. How do you know that they are probably not legitimate offers?

Different Learning Abilities

At-Risk Connect various topics (consumer complaints, deceptive business practices) to student experiences. Point out the importance of understanding these potential problem areas.

THE COMPLAINT PROCESS

While no one wants consumer problems, they do occur. When they happen, a person should be prepared. Consumer protection experts suggest four steps when trying to resolve a purchasing problem.

Step 1 Contact the Place of Purchase

Most consumer complaints are settled by returning to the place of purchase. Calmly explain the situation. Provide evidence of your purchase and the problem. A receipt or other dated documents will help you convince the store to take action in your favor.

Step 2 Contact the Company Headquarters

If communicating with the place of purchase does not bring satisfaction, you should move up in the organization. Contact the customer service department or other office within the company. The address, phone, and e-mail of most organizations can be obtained on the package or through a search.

When contacting the company, once again provide facts about the situation. Tell what happened in a brief letter or e-mail. Include copies of any documents that back up your story. Be specific about what action you would like them to take.

Step 3 Involve a Consumer Agency

If communication with the business fails to satisfy your demands, consider using the services of a consumer agency or public interest organization. Contacting a local, state, or federal government agency can encourage the business to take action.

Some agencies and organizations specialize in specific consumer topics such as consumer credit, health care, motor vehicles, or telecommunications. Other groups, such as state consumer protection offices, will help you with almost any consumer concern.

Step 4 Take Legal Action

When the first three steps do not work, more extreme actions may be required. Several legal actions are available to consumers. These include the use of a third party for dispute resolution, class action suits, small claims court, and hiring a lawyer.

> *checkpoint* >>
> List the steps of the consumer complaint process.

Describe the steps of the consumer complaint process.

© Digital Vision

Why might someone decide not to pursue a lawsuit against a company even when the company has been fraudulent?

TEACH

Ask students to describe the actions they would take to solve a consumer problem.

Provide an overview of the complaint process.

Point out methods that students could use to obtain company contact info, such as package information, toll-free telephone numbers, Web search, or company web site.

ONGOING ASSESSMENT

checkpoint >> **ANSWER**

Steps of the consumer complaint process are (1) contact the place of purchase, (2) contact the company headquarters, (3) involve a consumer agency, and (4) take legal action.

THINK CRITICALLY THROUGH VISUALS

Not every consumer problem is worth pursuing to the fourth step of taking legal action against the fraudulent company. If the amount of money involved is small, the consumer might not consider it worth the time and expense of entering the legal system to attain satisfaction.

Applied Skills

Word Processing/Office Technology Have students use word processing software to create a complaint letter to a company based on an actual or potential consumer problem. Be sure students clearly describe the situation and explain the action they would like the company to take.

Work as a Team

Each day, many consumers encounter consumer difficulties. Based on your experiences and observations, prepare an individual list of consumer problems of which you are aware. Then, compare your list with others on your team. How did most people become aware of various consumer problems? What actions were taken to resolve some of these concerns?

main idea

Explain legal actions available to assist consumers.

LEGAL ACTIONS FOR CONSUMERS

If contacting the business or a consumer agency does not resolve the problem, various legal actions may be considered.

Third-Party Settlements

A third party may be used to settle consumer differences. **Mediation** involves the use of a third party who tries to resolve the complaint between the consumer and the business. A mediator suggests a compromise between the two parties. This process helps the parties work out their own mutually agreeable solution to the dispute.

If the parties agree to it in advance, another third-party action may be used. **Arbitration** results in a decision that is legally binding. After hearing both sides and considering evidence, the arbitrator makes a decision. Both the consumer and business must abide by the arbitrator's verdict.

Class Action Suits

What would you do if you are overcharged a couple of dollars? Maybe nothing, but what if this same injustice occurred to thousands of consumers?

A **class action suit** is legal action by one party on behalf of a group of people who all have the same grievance. In this type of lawsuit, one person or a small group represents the interests of many others (the *class*). The settlement may result in a refund to all consumers involved. If they cannot all be identified, the funds are sometimes given to public education programs or schools.

Name some benefits of joining a class action suit rather than trying to win a case alone.

© Getty Images/PhotoDisc

Small Claims Court

In every state, a court system exists to resolve cases involving small amounts. These courts are called small claims court. In these courts, disputes are resolved quickly and inexpensively.

The rules are simple and informal, and the dispute involves less than a set amount. The limits for cases heard in small claims court vary by state. The amount ranges from less than $1,000 in some states to $10,000 in others.

Most often, lawyers are not involved. Individuals present the facts of the situation and provide written and other evidence. Witnesses may also be used.

Using a Lawyer

If all else fails, a final step might be to hire a lawyer. When a situation involves larger amounts of money or severe injuries from a product, the use of an attorney may be appropriate. Information about potential lawyers may be obtained from advertisements or referrals from other people.

Name some types of cases that would be appropriate for small claims court.

Before using the services of a lawyer, you should ask various questions. Is the lawyer experienced in this type of case? Will you be charged a flat fee or an hourly rate? When will you be required to make payment for services?

checkpoint »
How does mediation differ from arbitration?

15-3 Assessment

Key Concepts

Determine the best answer.

1. Most consumer complaints are resolved by
   a. taking legal action
   b. using arbitration
   c. hiring a lawyer with consumer protection experience
   d. returning to the place of purchase
2. A company refused to refund $10 to more than 4,000 customers. This situation might result in the use of
   a. mediation
   b. arbitration
   c. a class action suit
   d. small claims court

Make Academic Connections

3. **Visual Communication** Create a poster or other visual that communicates the four steps in the consumer complaint process. Use a specific consumer problem as the basis for your visual presentation.

4. **Research** Use library materials or an Internet search to determine the small claims court limit amount in your state. Also, obtain information about filing a case in small claims court.

Explain situations in which small claims court and using a lawyer would be appropriate.

THINK CRITICALLY THROUGH VISUALS

Answers will vary. Types of cases that might be heard in small claims court could include landlord/tenant disputes, automobile accident issues, property damage, collection of personal debts, and consumer complaints.

ONGOING ASSESSMENT

checkpoint » **ANSWER**
Mediation involves the use of a third party who tries to resolve the complaint, while arbitration results in a decision that is legally binding on both parties in a dispute.

ASSESS

Key Concepts Answers

1. d. returning to the place of purchase

2. c. a class action suit

Make Academic Connections

3. Students create a visual to illustrate the four steps in the consumer complaint process for a specific consumer problem.

4. Students use the library or the Internet to learn the small claims court monetary limit and filing procedures in your state.

RETEACH

Provide examples of comparison shopping activities.

ENRICH

Have students describe situations that might be appropriate for mediation or arbitration.

CLOSE

Emphasize steps that might be taken to resolve consumer problems.

Communicate Business Concepts Answers

1. Well-informed consumers have realistic expectations and understand their own responsibilities in the purchasing transaction. This action also creates a more pleasant transaction environment. Well-informed consumers will likely become return customers when they have a satisfying experience.

2. Answers will vary. Students will probably admit that they sometimes skip one or more steps when comparison shopping to save time or to purchase an item they desperately want.

3. Answers will vary. Students should list factors such as the reliability, independence, and the current accuracy of the consumer information source.

4. Answers will vary but could include a product testing organization's rating, recommendation of friends and family who have purchased cellular phones, and a salesperson's advice.

5. Mrs. Franklin could contact the Better Business Bureau to see if the company is a member or has any complaints against it. She could ask for a written estimate and if the chimney sweeps refuse or start to pressure her to make an immediate decision she might suspect that they are not a reputable company. She could check their credentials with an industry trade group to learn if they are a member in good standing or a member at all. She should proceed very cautiously because it is unusual for reputable service companies to solicit door-to-door offering to perform immediate work.

Business Notes

15-1 CONSUMER BUYING DECISIONS

1. The main sources of consumer information are product-testing organizations; media sources such as print publishers, broadcast organizations, and the Internet; government agencies; business sources such as product labels, customer service departments, and Better Business Bureaus; and personal contacts.

2. Comparison shoppers will evaluate price, quality, service, sales, and brands when making a purchase. Wise consumers take their time when making purchases, buy when prices are lowest, and avoid impulse buying with shopping lists.

3. The main shopping locations used by consumers can be viewed in three categories. Traditional retailers include department stores, discount stores, specialty stores, supermarkets, and convenience stores. Contemporary retailers include specialty superstores, warehouse clubs, and factory outlets. Non-store shopping options include door-to-door, mail order, phone, computer, and vending machines.

15-2 CONSUMER RIGHTS AND RESPONSIBILITIES

4. The consumer movement emerged to fight unfair business practices. Because of this movement, public and private agencies, policies, laws, and regulations were developed to protect consumer interests.

5. The Consumer Bill of Rights declares that every consumer has the right to be informed, to safety, to choose, to be heard, to a remedy, to consumer education, and to service. Being a skilled consumer means that you know the Consumer Bill of Rights and how to exercise these rights.

6. Consumers also have responsibilities in business relationships. The five basic responsibilities of consumers are to be honest, to be reasonable, to report unethical practices, to be informed, and to be involved.

15-3 CONSUMER PROTECTION ACTIONS

7. The main consumer complaints are related to automobiles, deceptive investments, identity theft and consumer credit, telemarketing and catalog sales, work-at-home schemes, contests, vacation promotions, phony diets, and buying online.

8. Four steps are suggested when encountering a consumer problem: (1) contact the place of purchase, (2) contact the company headquarters, (3) involve a consumer agency, and (4) take legal action.

9. A variety of legal actions is available to help consumers. Mediation and arbitration involve the use of a third party to resolve a consumer complaint. Class action suits allow a small group of consumers to act on behalf of many. Small claims court allows a person to take legal action without the use of a lawyer.

Communicate Business Concepts

1. Why do you think most businesspeople like to have well-informed customers?

2. Do you go through all of the steps of comparison shopping on every purchase you make? Explain.

3. List factors you might consider when evaluating the usefulness of a consumer information source.

4. If you were planning to buy a cellular phone, what information sources might be most valuable?

5. One autumn day, a woman and a man came to Carrie Franklin's door. They said they were chimney sweeps and would like to clean her chimney before she began using her fireplace. The man said it would be inexpensive and make her home safer, reducing the chances of a chimney fire. Mrs. Franklin looked out her window and saw the name "Chim Chim Chimney Sweeps" on their truck. How can she find out if the firm is reliable?

6. An impulse purchase could be a harmless activity if the cost is very low and the item is not an important, long-term acquisition.

7. Answers will vary. Factors that influence a student's decision of where to shop could include convenient and attractive location, product line, prices, reputation for quality merchandise and service, and safety.

8. Answers will vary, but it is likely that students will have used many of the consumer rights, perhaps without being aware of it.

9. Consumer fraud still exists because disreputable companies see an opportunity for financial gain by

6. When would you consider an impulse purchase a harmless activity?

7. What are some factors you might consider when deciding where to shop?

8. Which of the consumer rights have you recently used?

9. Why, with all of the laws and organizations to protect consumers, do you continue to hear of examples of consumer fraud?

10. Which of the following situations would be considered fraud? Why?

   a. A salesperson says the sound system you are looking at is the best on the market. After you buy it, you find it rated in a consumer magazine as second best.
   b. An advertisement for a bookcase cabinet claims it is made of solid walnut. Upon close inspection after buying the bookcase, you see that it is only walnut veneer glued over less expensive plywood.
   c. The person who sells an electric corn popper says it is completely washable. Before using it, you put it into a sink filled with water to wash it. The first time you try to make popcorn, there is a flash and the popper's electrical unit catches fire. When you return the popper to the store, the salesperson tells you that she did not mean the popper could be put under water. She says you should have known that electrical appliances should not be put in water. She refuses to give you either a refund or an exchange.

11. Describe situations in which a person might use (a) a class action suit and (b) small claims court.

12. When might you use a lawyer to resolve a consumer dispute? What are some of the pros and cons of using a lawyer versus other dispute resolution methods?

Develop Your Business Language

Match the terms listed with the definitions.

13. Use of a third party who attempts to resolve the complaint between a consumer and business.

14. Buying too rapidly without much thought.

15. A name given to a product or service to distinguish it from other similar products or services.

16. A legal system for resolving cases involving small monetary amounts.

17. The price per unit of measure of a product.

18. When false information is given to a customer in an effort to make a sale.

19. A lawsuit brought by one party on behalf of a group with the same grievance.

20. Guarantees made orally or in writing that promise a specific quality of performance.

21. Third-party settlement resulting in a decision that is legally binding.

22. A promise by the manufacturer or dealer, usually in writing, that a product is of a certain quality.

23. Guarantees imposed by law that are not stated orally or in writing and that require certain standards to be met.

24. Banding together of consumers to demand fair treatment from businesses.

KEY TERMS

a. arbitration
b. brand
c. class action suit
d. consumer movement
e. express warranty
f. fraud
g. guarantee
h. implied warranty
i. impulse buying
j. mediation
k. small claims court
l. unit price

Develop Your Business Language Answers

13. j. mediation
14. i. impulse buying
15. b. brand
16. k. small claims court
17. l. unit price
18. f. fraud
19. c. class action suit
20. e. express warranty
21. a. arbitration
22. g. guarantee
23. h. implied warranty
24. d. consumer movement

cheating customers. Many consumers are uneducated about their rights and possible methods of recourse if a purchase results in a problem, and some companies hope to take advantage of this ignorance.

10. a. This would not be considered fraud because the salesperson may have genuinely believed the sound system to be the best on the market and could claim he or she was unaware of the magazine's rating.

b. This would be fraud because a specific written description of the item was substantially inaccurate.

c. This would not be considered fraud. However, the store may nurture customer loyalty by giving the consumer a new corn popper to restore good will and avoid possible fraud accusations.

11. Answers will vary. Class action suits are useful when the amount of the fraud is small for each individual member of the class but large when the class is considered as a whole. Small claims court is useful in resolving complaints involving relatively small amounts of money or damage.

12. A lawyer could be used to resolve a consumer dispute that involves a large purchase or when significant harm was done because of the purchase. The advantage of using a lawyer is that he or she has the legal expertise to thoroughly understand the consumer's legal rights and how best to present the case in court. Sometimes simply receiving a letter from a lawyer will cause a company that has broken the law to make restitution to the consumer. The disadvantage of using a lawyer is the cost and time spent if the matter proceeds to court.

Make Academic Connections

25. **LAW** Prepare a summary of various federal consumer agencies and laws designed to protect consumers related to product safety, motor vehicles, food, medical products, and consumer credit.

26. **VISUAL COMMUNICATIONS** Select a magazine advertisement. Create a poster describing various elements of the ad. Highlight the sections of the ad that would be useful or deceptive to consumers.

27. **RESEARCH** Collect examples of advertisements with the word "sale" included. Group the ads into categories based on the type of sale being displayed. What types of sales are most common?

28. **ART** Design a label for a food product with your own brand, product name, graphics, nutritional information, and other features.

29. **MATH** Berri purchased a new cell phone that stopped working one month after the warranty expired. When she returned to the store, she was offered the choice of purchasing a new phone for 5 percent off the list price of $98 or a reconditioned phone that carried the same warranty as a new phone for $75.

  a. What would be the price of the new phone with the discount?

  b. What percent of the price of a new telephone is the price of the reconditioned phone?

  c. How much money would Berri save by purchasing the reconditioned phone?

30. **TECHNOLOGY** Conduct an online search of Internet frauds. What types are most common? How can a person avoid these deceptive online business practices?

31. **MATH** The Jones family ordered a new car from Germany. The express warranty said the average driver would get 48.3 kilometers for every 3.85 liters of gasoline used.

  a. How many miles per gallon is this?

  b. If they traveled 90 miles and used 10.5 liters of gas, did the car perform better or worse than the warranty claimed?

32. **HISTORY** Conduct research on the way that people shopped in the 1800s to mid-1900s. Comment on some of the cultural, geographic, economic, and social factors that contributed to these customs.

Linking School and Community

Talk to people in your community about the types of consumer problems they have encountered. What was the nature of the situation? What actions did they take to resolve the problem? What suggestions do they have for other consumers? Prepare a short written or oral summary of your findings.

Web Workout

Many web sites provide online reviews from customers. Reading reviews by satisfied and dissatisfied customers can be helpful when a consumer is researching or planning to purchase a product or service. Past customers can post their positive and negative comments and even, in some cases, photographs. Some web sites allow customers to rate products or services using a scale such as one to five stars.

Think Critically

1. Identify two different web sites that use customer reviews or ratings to help others with their purchase. Write a brief description of the sites and how their systems work.
2. Explain how the number of opinions offered might influence consumer purchasing decisions. Also address the issue of fraud or manipulation of review and rating systems.

Web Workout

1. Descriptions will vary depending on the sites selected. Students might select booksellers, music sites, and hotel booking sites.

2. Answers will vary. Students might suggest that finding very few comments might mean the product has not sold well or it could mean that customers have not participated in the review or ranking system. They should recognize the opportunity for a business or its competitors to manipulate the system.

Decision-Making Strategies

Pierre needs a new digital camera to take on his trip to Mexico as an exchange student. He is not a photography expert, but he has taken some pictures for the school newspaper. He intends to use the camera to take indoor and outdoor pictures of people as well as scenery.

Pierre has about $150 to spend on the camera. He wants the camera to be sturdy, easy to use, and to take good-quality pictures.

33. What sources of information could Pierre use to find out what cameras are in his price range?

34. What two sources of information do you believe are best? Why?

Global Marketing Team Event

Marcella is interested in providing nutritious meals that are easy to prepare. She has created a line of meals called Marcy's Gourmet. These meals do not require freezing. Each meal takes into consideration a well-balanced diet. Selections include meat and vegetarian choices. Each meal takes five minutes to prepare in a microwave or 20 minutes in an electric oven. Prices for Marcy's Gourmet meals range from $3.00 to $5.00.

Your team of two will develop an international marketing plan for this new product. The marketing plan must not exceed 10 single-spaced pages. Team members will present before a panel of judges (class members) and a timekeeper. The length of the presentation will be no more than 10 minutes. The completed plan should include, but is not limited to: Title Page and Table of Contents, Synopsis or mini-plan, Company Goals, Description of Customers and Their Needs, Description of Pricing Strategy, Competition, and Price Selection Methods.

PERFORMANCE INDICATORS EVALUATED

- Develop an international marketing plan.
- Identify a customer base, including consumer and organizational markets.
- Illustrate fundamentals of consumer behavior in different cultures.

You will be evaluated for your

- Knowledge of demographics in the international market
- Understanding of the marketing mix
- Understanding of economic, social, legal, and technological trends
- Use of appropriate research and accompanying documentation
- Description of timeline for business success

For more detailed information about performance indicators, go to the BPA web site.

Think Critically

1. Can the product be a success in America, internationally, or both?
2. What groups of individuals will this product appeal to (consider gender, age, education, and income)?
3. What is the most appropriate method of distribution for this product?
4. What demographic and cultural issues must be considered when marketing this product?
5. Will the name "Marcy's Gourmet" have any effect in the international marketplace?

http://www.bpanet.org/

Access the web site shown here to find portfolio activities for this chapter. Use the activities to provide tangible evidence of your learning.

school.cengage.com/business/introtobiz

Decision-Making Strategies Answers

33. Pierre could include independent reports from product testing organizations, in-store displays of various cameras, talking to knowledgeable friends and family, and the Internet.

34. Answers will vary. Students may consider product testing organizations and experiences of family and friends to be reliable sources.

Winning Edge
Global Marketing Team Event

Think Critically Answers

1. Answers will vary.

2. This product will appeal to busy families wanting healthy meals and single people with tight schedules.

3. Answers will vary. Major supermarkets, retail outlets, and convenience stores are all possible methods of distribution for this product.

4. Answers will vary. Students should demonstrate their understanding of the demographics and cultures of the countries in which they plan to market the new product.

5. Answers will vary. Marcy's may not mean anything on the international market. Gourmet could mean expensive or high quality.

CHAPTER 16

Money Management and Financial Planning

16-1 Personal Financial Statements

16-2 Budgeting Techniques

16-3 Your Financial Future

Planning a Career in...
FINANCIAL PLANNING

People have many questions about their finances: *How much should I save for retirement? What is the best type of life insurance for my family situation? How can I get out of debt?*

These and many other questions are answered by people who work in personal financial planning. Employment in this field has a wide range of opportunities. If you choose a career in financial planning your work may involve providing financial planning services through a large financial services corporation, a small consulting firm, or a neighborhood bank. As an alternative, you might work for a social service agency or consumer advocacy organization that helps people deal with financial difficulties and develop a plan for avoiding future problems.

Employment Outlook

- Faster than average growth in employment is expected as the personal financial choices faced by people become more complex.
- Employment of financial analysts in large firms will grow as fast as the average growth for most occupations.
- Jobs for community-based and nonprofit budget counselors will expand as various economic conditions and personal situations result in needed services.

Related Job Titles

- Credit Counselor
- Certified Financial Planner
- Financial Data Analyst
- Personal Financial Advisor
- Family Money Management Counselor
- Tax Preparer
- Chartered Financial Analyst
- Chartered Financial Consultant
- Insurance Agent
- Stock Broker
- Private Banking Specialist

Needed Skills

- College degrees with emphasis in accounting, finance, economics, or other business fields are required for some positions.
- Communication and interpersonal skills are needed for dealing with clients.
- Mathematical, computer, analytical, and problem-solving skills are essential for success.
- Certification, designations, and other credentials demonstrate competencies.

What's it like to work in ...
Financial Planning

At 8 a.m., Carl leaves for work, in the next room. Carl runs a personal financial planning business out of his home. This morning he is reviewing the files of several clients before advising them about various personal financial decisions. Then it's time to get on the road. At 10 a.m., Carl is scheduled to meet with a person who just retired but does not have enough income to cover current living expenses. At noon, he meets with several small business owners who want to create a retirement fund for their employees.

The afternoon is open so Carl can relax or take care of personal errands. In the evening, things get busy. Right after dinner, Carl meets with a family who wants to create a savings and investment program to set aside funds for their children's college education. His day ends with a phone call from a client who has a question about recent tax law changes.

What about you? What personal financial situations might result in a need for hiring someone trained as a financial planner or budget counselor?

Planning a Career in...

FINANCIAL PLANNING

Financial planning and money management activities affect every person in our society. Consumer demand for expert advice provides many employment opportunities.

What About You? Answer

Answers will vary. Personal financial situations that might result in a need for hiring someone like Carl could include starting a business, beginning a career after college and needing to pay student loans, getting married, buying a house, planning for retirement, expecting a child, or saving for college for a child.

Additional Career Information

Additional information on careers can be found in the *Occupational Outlook Handbook*, an online publication (www.bls.gov/oco) of the federal government. Tell your class about this resource and how to use it. This description of job duties can be used to demonstrate the relevancy of skills learned in this course.

Goals

Explain the basics of money management.

Create a personal balance sheet.

Develop a personal cash flow statement.

Key Terms

money management

personal assets

net worth

cash flow statement

Focus on Real Life

"My financial situation is just fine—or it is a disaster! It all depends on what day of the week it is."

"Tell me; what's the problem, Yung-su?" asks his neighbor.

"Mr. Liang, I can't seem to get a grip on my finances. I work 10 hours a week and make about $10 per hour. That seems like a lot of money for a part-time job while going to school. But I always seem to run out of money before I get paid."

"I suppose that also means you are not saving any money, but rather spending everything you make. My advice is to get some lessons in money management. I'd be glad to help."

The one thing most people have in common is a desire to use money wisely so that needs, wants, and goals will be satisfied. While no individual, family, or organization is likely to have every desire met, several money management techniques can help you wisely use your financial resources.

main idea

Explain the basics of money management.

MONEY MANAGEMENT BASICS

Right now $1,000, or maybe $100, seems like a lot of money to you. Once you graduate from high school, and perhaps college, and have a full-time job, your thinking about what is a large amount of money will change. You probably will earn much more than one million dollars in your lifetime. As a college graduate, you will likely make even more.

While this may seem like a lot of money, remember that you will be responsible for many living expenses. You will have to pay for food, housing, clothing, and transportation as well as other goods and services you need and want. Upon beginning a career and living on your own, you will face the same problem you face now—having a limited amount of money to pay for all the goods and services you want and need.

Do you keep track of how you spend your money? What method do you use?

© Getty Images/PhotoDisc

Money management refers to the day-to-day financial activities associated with using limited income to satisfy your unlimited needs and wants. Money management involves getting the most for your money through careful planning, saving, and spending. It involves making and using a plan for spending.

Some people have the wrong idea about money management. They think it means never spending, doing without things, and not having any fun. If you learn to manage your money well, you will be able to buy what you really want. Planning ahead and deciding what is important will help you have money for things you enjoy. If you set goals, make wise decisions, buy wisely, and live within your income, you will be a successful money manager.

The process of good money management should start with knowing your current financial status. When watching a baseball or soccer game, most people want to know the score. In the money management game, score is kept with the use of two financial statements: the balance sheet and the cash flow statement.

FYI

According to the Bureau of the Census, the main assets of U.S. households are motor vehicles, homes, savings accounts, U.S. savings bonds, certificates of deposit, mutual funds, stocks, corporate bonds, and retirement accounts.

PERSONAL BALANCE SHEET

"How much money do you have?" might be the first question many people would ask when measuring your financial situation.

The answer to that question would not give the entire picture because most people have other items of value besides money. A *balance sheet* is a record of assets and liabilities at a point in time. It reports what a person or family owns as well as owes. The main parts of a balance sheet are displayed in Figure 16-1.

Assets

Items of value are **personal assets**. Assets include such things as money in bank accounts, investments, furniture, clothing, automobiles, jewelry, and rare coins. The current value of all assets of an individual or family is the first thing stated on a balance sheet.

main idea

Create a personal balance sheet.

Personal Balance Sheet

Assets		Liabilities	
Checking account	$450	Home mortgage	$45,000
Savings account	2,300	Credit card balance	230
Home	97,000	Education loan	1,800
Automobile	4,600	*Total liabilities*	$47,030
Household items and furniture	6,200		
Personal computer	1,600		
Jewelry	1,100	**Owner's Equity (Net Worth)**	
Total assets	$113,250	Total assets – Total liabilities	$66,220

FIGURE 16-1

What accounts for the bulk of this family's assets, liabilities, and equity?

TEACH

Describe various actions that might be considered wise money management.

ONGOING ASSESSMENT

checkpoint » **ANSWER**

Wise money managers get the most from their limited incomes through careful planning, saving, and spending. They set goals, make wise decisions, buy wisely, and live within their incomes.

TEACH

Provide an overview of the elements of a personal balance sheet—assets, liabilities, and equity.

Ask students to name various assets that might be listed on a personal balance sheet.

Use the FYI feature to point out the assets commonly reported on a personal balance sheet.

FIGURE 16-1 ANSWER

The largest of this family's assets is its house. Its greatest liability is its home mortgage. The percentage of the home already paid for constitutes most of the family's equity.

Applied Skills

Mathematics Have students create a list of personal assets and liabilities. Ask them to total each and determine the net worth. Ask students to explain how their personal balance sheet might change in the future.

Liabilities

Amounts owed to others are *liabilities*. These debts may include credit card balances, car loans, a home mortgage, or personal loans. A listing of your liabilities is the second item on a balance sheet.

Net Worth

The difference between a person's assets and liabilities is your **net worth**. This difference represents the amount of money that could be claimed if all assets were sold for cash and all debts were paid off. For example, if a family has $189,000 in assets (including the value of a home) and has $87,000 in debts (mainly their home mortgage), the family has a net worth of $102,000. Net worth is also referred to as *owner's equity*.

A balance sheet is a helpful way to measure financial strength. Businesses commonly prepare a balance sheet either once a month or quarterly to determine the financial condition of the business. In the same way, a balance sheet can help in measuring financial progress.

> *checkpoint* >>
> What are three main categories of a personal balance sheet?

PERSONAL CASH FLOW STATEMENT

A balance sheet reports assets, liabilities, and net worth on a given date. Almost every day, business transactions occur that change these balance sheet items. For example, when you make a loan payment, your liabilities decrease. If you save part of your earnings, your assets and net worth increase by the amount of the savings.

To examine changes in a person's net worth, another financial statement can be helpful. A **cash flow statement** reports net wages and other income along with spending for a period, such as for a month. Figure 16-2 on the next page includes typical items found in a cash flow statement.

Cash Inflows

The first part of a cash flow statement reports cash inflows, or your income. *Cash inflows* is the money you have available to spend as a result of working or from other income, such as interest earned on your savings.

When preparing a cash flow statement, first report your *net pay* or *take-home pay*, which is the amount of a paycheck after taxes and other payroll deductions. These deductions may include retirement contributions, charges for health benefits, and other things, as well as local, state, and federal taxes. Your take-home pay is the amount you actually have available to spend. Be sure to include any other income, such as interest.

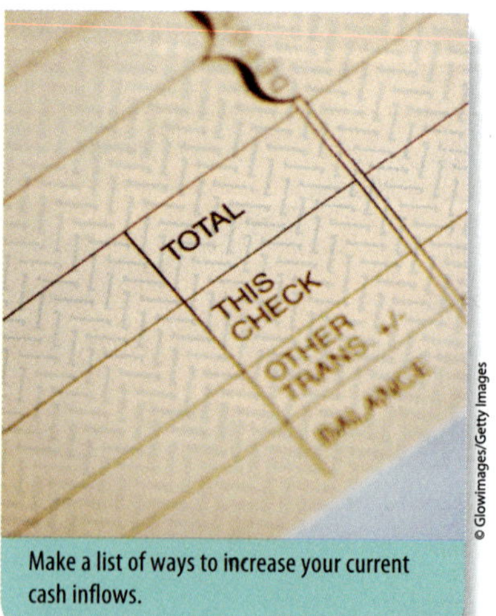
Make a list of ways to increase your current cash inflows.

Cash Outflows

The second part of a cash flow statement reports your cash outflows, or your expenditures. Amounts spent for food, clothing, transportation, and other living costs are *cash outflows*. Keeping track of how much is spent for various living expenses will help you plan and control your spending. Your personal cash flow statement can be used to develop a budget, which can help you avoid cash flow problems.

Compare Inflows and Outflows

The final step in preparing the cash flow statement is to subtract the cash outflows (total spending) from the cash inflows (total income). If you spent less than you had in income, the difference represents an increase in your net worth. Most likely, this amount will be kept in savings for future needs or wants. If you spent more than you had in income, you either had to use some of your savings or had to use credit to pay these additional expenses.

Personal Cash Flow Statement	
Cash Inflows (Income)	
Net income (take-home pay)	$1,300
Other income (interest)	10
Total Income	$1,310
Cash Outflows (Expenditures)	
Rent	$300
Food	400
Clothing	50
Utilities	60
Telephone	30
Transportation	120
Personal care	30
Recreation/entertainment	75
Total Spending	$1065
Net Cash Flow	**$245**

FIGURE 16-2

What percentage of total income did this person spend on basic needs?

> *checkpoint* >>
> What do cash outflows represent?

16-1 Assessment

Key Concepts

Determine the best answer.

1. Savings accounts and a home are examples of
   a. liabilities
   b. assets
   c. net worth
   d. cash outflow

2. A payment for rent represents
   a. a cash inflow
   b. a cash outflow
   c. a liability
   d. an asset

Make Academic Connections

3. **Math** Calculate the missing amount.
   a. Assets $7,000
      Liabilities $1,800
      Net worth   __?__
   b. Assets $26,000
      Liabilities   __?__
      Net worth $19,000
   c. Assets   __?__
      Liabilities $5,600
      Net worth $67,800

4. **Research** What types of liabilities are commonly listed on the personal balance sheets of households in the United States?

TEACH

Describe common cash outflows for an individual or household.

Ask students to describe what actions a person might take after comparing cash inflows and outflows.

FIGURE 16-2 *ANSWER*

The person depicted in this cash flow statement spent about 76% of his or her total income on basic needs ($990 ÷ $1,310 = 0.7557; 0.76 × 100 = 76%).

ONGOING ASSESSMENT

checkpoint >> **ANSWER**

Cash outflows represent amounts spent for food, clothing, transportation, and other living expenses.

ASSESS

Key Concepts Answers

1. b. assets
2. b. a cash outflow

Make Academic Connections

3. a. $5,200
   ($7,000 − $1,800 = $5,200)

   b. $7,000
   ($26,000 − $19,000 = $7,000)

   c. $73,400
   ($67,800 − $5,600 = $73,400)

4. Answers will vary. Students might mention credit card balances, automobile loans, home mortgages, student loans, and personal loans.

CLOSE

Ask students to explain the importance of a cash flow statement when planning money management activities.

RETEACH

Explain the difference between a personal balance sheet and personal cash flow statement.

ENRICH

Have students list various items that might appear on a personal balance sheet and a personal cash flow statement.

Doing Business in…

Learning about U.S. trading partners can help students better understand the interdependence of the global economy. Encourage students to learn more about doing business in other African countries.

Think Critically
Answers

1. Nigeria has more than 250 languages and ethnic groups, which could complicate business communication. Important business is conducted in face-to-face meetings where traditional dress might be worn in addition to traditional business attire. Formal titles, respect for older persons, and lengthy greetings are very important in business dealings. The conversation at the beginning of business negotiations may be more personal than in other cultures. Use of the left hand is offensive and should be avoided in situations such as handshakes or passing food dishes. The underground economy may impact business transactions.

2. Benefits of informal economic activities include employment and the availability of needed goods and services. Concerns related to informal economic activities include the government's inability to collect taxes, regulate businesses, and protect consumers and workers.

3. Answers will vary depending on the information students locate.

Doing Business in…Nigeria

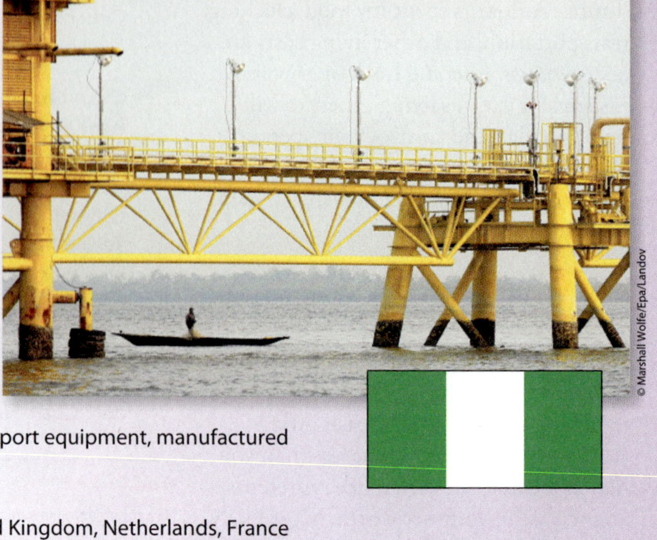

Official name
Federal Republic of Nigeria

Capital
Abuja

Population
135 million

Currency
naira

Major exports
petroleum, petroleum products, cocoa, rubber

Major export partners
United States, Spain, Brazil

Major imports
machinery, chemicals, transport equipment, manufactured goods, food, live animals

Major import partners
China, United States, United Kingdom, Netherlands, France

Source: CIA World Factbook

Imagine trying to do business in a country with more than 250 languages and ethnic groups. In Nigeria, the most populous country in Africa, you are likely to encounter a variety of business situations.

When in Nigeria, you will conduct important business in face-to-face meetings. In these settings, you may see Nigerian businessmen wearing a suit and tie. Or, they might wear traditional clothing such as a buda, a loose-fitting shirt that extends to the knees.

As you greet business associates in Nigeria, remember that formal titles are very important. Be ready to address someone as "Chief," "Prince," or "Alhaji." Respect for older persons is vital. It is offensive in Nigerian society to pass an elderly person without a greeting. Handshakes are the most appropriate greeting.

At the first meeting with a business contact, be patient and expect many ongoing greetings. At first the conversation might seem overly personal, because Nigerians like to know the people with whom they are doing business.

If you are having lunch with a business acquaintance, make sure you always use your right hand (or both hands) to pass and accept dishes. The left hand is taboo and is rarely used for interpersonal transactions. Left-handers are especially advised to practice the use of their right hand. Foods that you will likely encounter include yams, cassava (a starchy root), and rice. Meats you are offered might include beef, chicken, turkey, goat, goose, and fish.

Nigeria is one of the world's largest oil producers. Due to political turmoil and unstable financial conditions, the country has continually faced economic difficulties. The informal economy (also called the underground economy) accounts for more than half of the business activities in Nigeria. Large numbers of workers make their living in unregulated settings. The items they produce and sell create income not reported to the government.

Think Critically
1. How does doing business in Nigeria differ from doing business in other countries?
2. What are the benefits and concerns related to informal economic activities?
3. Conduct library or Internet research to obtain additional information about business and economic activities in Nigeria.

Applied Skills

Geography Have students use the Internet or library resources to locate a map of Nigeria and its neighboring countries. Ask students to make a list of the countries that border Nigeria. Lists should include Benin, Cameroon, Chad, and Niger.

Budgeting Techniques

Goals

Identify purposes of a budget.

Describe steps for preparing a budget.

Describe characteristics of successful budgeting.

Key Terms

fixed expenses

variable expenses

allowance

budget variance

Focus on **Real Life**

Brandon Zeng has been practicing his Chinese through written communication with relatives in Hong Kong and conversations with his parents. He also has taken several business courses in high school. Brandon hopes to have a career in international business working in the Pacific Rim countries.

"I can't wait to go to Asia next summer, but the trip is going to cost me a fortune! The air transportation, housing, food, and other living expenses will cost $4,000. My parents have agreed to pay half. Fortunately for me, I developed a plan to save money for this trip. By the end of the year I will have the $4,000 I need. It's going to be a great experience. Hey Josh, why don't you go with me?"

"Are you kidding? I'm not as disciplined as you! I would never be able to save enough money. You are a pro at managing money. Maybe you can give me a few tips."

BUDGET ACTIVITIES

A *budget* allows you to meet your personal goals with a system of saving and wise spending. By developing a plan for saving and spending income, you will be able to make wise and rewarding personal economic decisions. The main purposes of a budget are to help you do the following:

- Live within your income.
- Achieve your financial goals.
- Buy wisely.
- Avoid credit problems.
- Plan for financial emergencies.
- Develop good money management skills.

Having a written budget is a key part of successful money management. Your budget may be a simple record of how much you make, how much you plan to spend, and how much you want to save. On the other hand, your budget may be a more detailed record with specific amounts to be spent in categories such as food, clothing, and transportation. A good budget should take very little of your time, but it should provide needed information on your spending and savings plans.

main idea

Identify purposes of a budget.

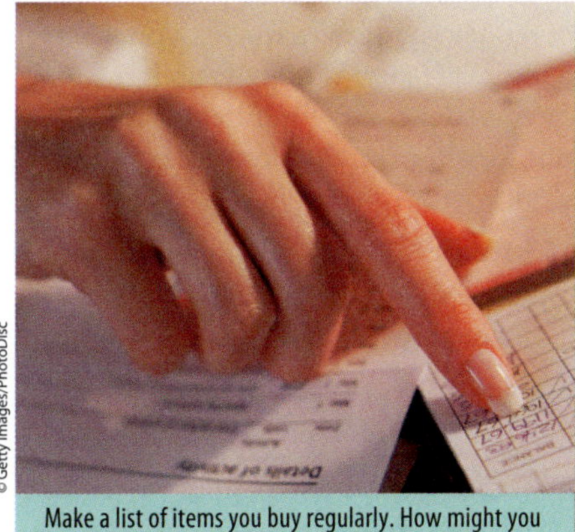

Make a list of items you buy regularly. How might you start spending less on these items?

checkpoint >>
What are the main purposes of a budget?

Focus on **Real Life**

Use this situation to encourage students to think about better planning for spending and saving their money.

TEACH

Ask students to describe situations that might occur as a result of poor budgeting activities.

Highlight and explain the purposes of a budget that are listed on this page.

THINK CRITICALLY THROUGH VISUALS

Answers will vary. Most students should be able to discover ways to spend less on the items they buy through planned spending, careful comparison shopping, postponing purchases, or eliminating unnecessary purchases.

ONGOING ASSESSMENT

checkpoint >> **ANSWER**

The main purposes of a budget are to help people live within their incomes, achieve financial goals, buy wisely, avoid credit problems, plan for financial emergencies, and develop good money management skills.

Different Learning Styles

Tactile Learner Use sample items or objects to represent the purposes of a budget. Ask students to identify these purposes based on the tangible items they are given.

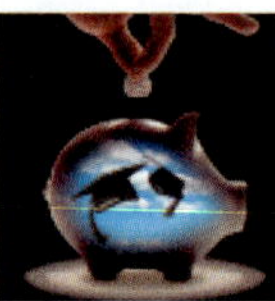

TEACH

Provide an overview of the four steps of the budgeting process.

Ask students to name financial goals for themselves today and five years from now.

Have students give examples of fixed and variable expenses.

Answers will vary depending on the personal short- and long-term goals of students. Actions to achieve goals can include savings, budgeting, buying insurance, and reducing credit use.

PROJECT

Provide the following-instructions to students. (These instructions also appear on page xxv of the textbook.) Explain why it is important for people to create and use a budget process when they are young even if they have only small amounts of income and only have a few expenditures. Do you have a budget process that you use? How can a budget process help you achieve your life-span goals?

Life-Span Plan Answer

Answers will vary. Students should point out that people who learn to create and use a budget when they are young are often better able to manage their funds when they are adults.

Describe steps for preparing a budget.

THE BUDGET PROCESS

The process of creating and using a budget involves four main steps.

1. Set financial goals.
2. Plan budget categories.
3. Maintain financial records.
4. Evaluate your budget.

Any individual, family, or organization can use these steps to aid them in using available financial resources.

Set Financial Goals

Setting financial goals is the first step for any financial action. Goals identify results you want to achieve. When you can see where you would like to be financially, you can develop a budget accordingly.

Writing down short-term and long-term goals will help you decide how to spend and save your money. If your goals include going to college, your budget will require more for savings. If you are currently working at a job that requires you to spend a large amount for transportation, you will likely budget more for this item.

Plan Budget Categories

Most financial advisers recommend that an amount be set aside for savings as the first part of a budget. If savings are not considered first, other expenses may use all available income.

After savings, two types of living expenses must be considered: fixed and variable expenses. **Fixed expenses** are costs that occur on a regular basis and are for the same amount each time. Examples of fixed expenses are rent, mortgage payments, and insurance premiums.

Variable expenses involve living costs that differ each time and may not be as easy to estimate. These types

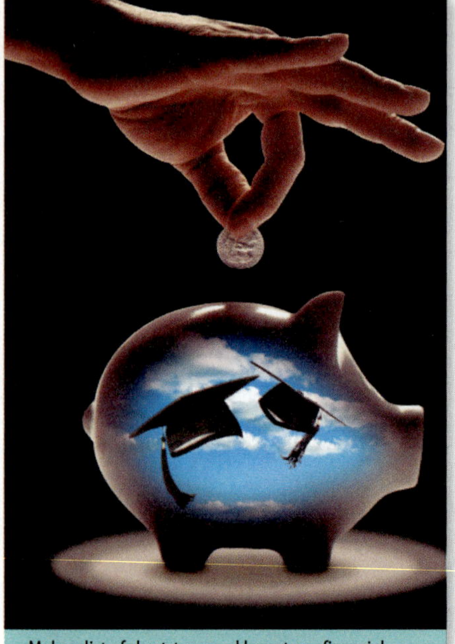

Make a list of short-term and long-term financial goals. What steps do you need to take to reach these goals?

of expenses include food, clothing, and utilities (such as telephone and electricity). Some variable expenses, such as medical and dental costs, occur less often and may be large when they do occur. Such expenses must be provided for in the budget.

The amount budgeted for savings and other expenditures is referred to as an allowance. An **allowance** is the amount of money you plan to use for a certain budget category. While the budget categories can vary for different situations, eight main divisions are commonly used.

1. **Savings**   Savings accounts, government bonds, stocks, and other investments
2. **Food**   Food eaten at home and meals eaten away from home
3. **Clothing**   Clothing, shoes, dry cleaning, and repairs

Different Learning Abilities

Attention Deficit Disorder Provide clear directions to students, asking them to write down two financial goals they have for the future. Ask them to explain actions that might be taken to achieve those goals.

4. **Household** Rent, mortgage, property taxes, insurance, utilities, furnishings, household supplies, painting, and repairs

5. **Transportation** Auto payments, insurance, operating costs, maintenance, repairs, and public transportation

6. **Health and Personal Care** Medical and dental expenses, medications, eyeglasses, health insurance, and personal care costs

7. **Recreation and Education** Books and other reading materials, theater tickets, concerts, vacations, school expenses, hobbies, and club dues

8. **Gifts and Contributions** Charitable contributions and personal gifts

At this point, ask yourself, "How much should I set aside for each category?" Planned spending for various budget categories will depend on income, family size, ages of children, cost of living in your area, and work-related expenses.

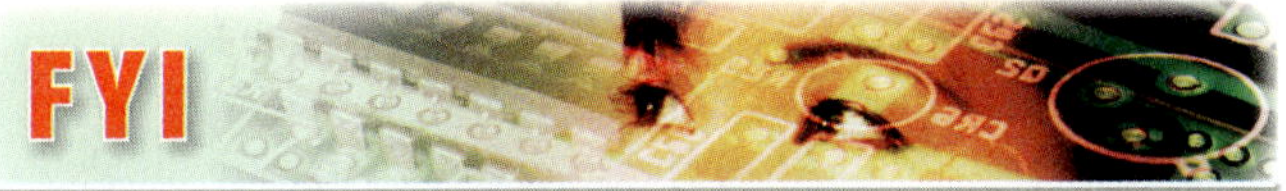

A once-popular system for family budgeting required envelopes marked with labels of different expenses such as "Food," "Housing," and "Automobile." Each envelope contained the budgeted amount of money, and expenses were paid from the money in the envelopes. This system allows a person to see where the money is going. Unfortunately, a danger exists with keeping large amounts of cash at home.

It will also depend on personal values, needs, and goals. A cash flow statement, similar to the one shown in Figure 16-2, can help you develop budget categories. This financial statement reports the categories in which your money has been spent. It provides a basis for your budget.

Other help for developing a budget can come from government reports on family spending or from articles in magazines, such as *Kiplinger's Personal Finance* and *Money*. An example of a family budget for one month is shown in Figure 16-3.

Family Budget for One Month				
Chung Household Monthly Budget January, 20--				
Estimated Income		**Estimated Expense**		
Manuel's net income	$4,225	Savings	$2,225	
Lydia's net income	4,350	Food	1,100	
		Clothing	475	
		Household	1,825	
		Transportation	1,275	
		Health & personal care	450	
		Recreation & education	800	
		Gifts & contributions	425	
Total income	$8,575	Total Expenses	$8,575	

FIGURE 16-3

What percentage of income have the Chungs budgeted for savings? How do people decide how much to save?

TEACH

Ask students to suggest methods that might be used for personal financial recordkeeping.

Explain how a budget variance is calculated. Describe actions that might be taken when a budget variance occurs.

ONGOING ASSESSMENT

checkpoint » **ANSWER**

Eight commonly used budget categories are (1) savings, (2) food, (3) clothing, (4) household, (5) transportation, (6) health and personal care, (7) recreation and education, and (8) gifts and contributions.

TEACH

Point out the main characteristics of an effective budget listed on this page.

Ask students to describe budgeting activities they have experienced or observed.

THINK CRITICALLY THROUGH VISUALS

Answers will vary depending on their current situation. Reduced spending for certain items, reduced use of credit, and increased income sources are common answers.

Maintain Financial Records

After planning a budget, individuals and families should record their income and expenses to find out if the plan is working. An example is shown in Figure 16-4. The first line shows the monthly income available to the family ($8,575 after taxes and other paycheck deductions) and the budget allowances for each category.

During the month, entries for expenditures were recorded. Because the family pays most bills by check, a checkbook is an easy reference for the information needed to prepare the income and expense summary.

Evaluate Your Budget

All columns were totaled at the end of the month. Actual spending is compared with the budgeted amounts. Any difference between these amounts is a **budget variance**.

If actual spending is greater than planned spending, such as for the "Household" category, it is referred to as a *deficit*. When actual spending is less than the budgeted amount, as with the "Food" category, a *surplus* occurs.

A category-by-category comparison allows you to find areas where changes in the budget may be appropriate. A variance in the actual amount spent and the budgeted amount does not always mean a change in your spending plan is necessary.

Your budgeted amount may still be appropriate with a slight deficit or surplus occurring every few months in some categories. If you expect necessary higher or lower spending in a certain category, a change in your budget is probably needed.

checkpoint »
What are eight commonly used budget categories?

SUCCESSFUL BUDGETING

Effective budgeting will be an ongoing learning process for you.

Characteristics of an Effective Budget

The following are common characteristics of a successful budget.

- *Must be realistic.* It should reflect current income and planned spending.

- *Should be flexible.* When unexpected expenses arise, your spending plan should be able to adapt for these living costs.

- *Should be evaluated regularly.* Every few months, evaluate the budget to determine whether it still is appropriate.

- *Must be well planned and clearly communicated.* All family members should discuss financial goals, wants and needs, and plans for spending.

- *Should have a simple format.* If it is too detailed and difficult to understand, family members may not be willing to use the spending plan.

What kinds of adjustments would you have to make to live within a budget?

© Getty Images/PhotoDisc

Applied Skills

Mathematics Have students create situations in which a budget *deficit* or a *surplus* is present. Have students calculate the amount of the deficit or surplus. Invite interested students to set up a budget worksheet using spreadsheet software.

FIGURE 16-4

In which categories did the Chung's expenditures exceed the amount they had budgeted? In which were they less than the amount budgeted?

Chung Household

Income and Expense Record

Date		Explanation	Totals: Receipts	Totals: Payments	Distribution of Savings and Expenditures: Savings	Food	Clothing	Household	Transport.	Health/Per.	Rec./Edu.	Gifts & Con.
		Budget	$8,575.00		$2,225.00	$1,100.00	$475.00	$1,825.00	$1,275.00	$450.00	$800.00	$425.00
January	1	**Balance**	1,300.00									
		Manuel's net income	2,112.50									
		Lydia's net income	2,175.00									
	2			$2,225.00	2,225.00							
	7			1,075.00		210.00	140.00	100.00	100.00	150.00	225.00	150.00
	14			950.00		230.00	90.00	200.00	145.00	125.00	90.00	70.00
	15	Manuel's net income	2,112.50									
		Lydia's net income	2,175.00									
	17	Mortgage payment		1,200.00				1,200.00				
	21	Car payment		850.00					850.00			
	22			925.00		200.00	150.00	190.00	75.00		160.00	150.00
	29			1,055.00		300.00	95.00	220.00	50.00	200.00	90.00	100.00
	31	**Totals**	$9,875.00	$8,280.00	$2,225.00	$940.00	$475.00	$1,910.00	$1,220.00	475.00	$565.00	$470.00
February	1	**Balance***	$1,595.00									

*Balance = January's total receipts - total payments = $9,875.00 – $8,280.00

TEACH

Use Figure 16-4 to highlight the various activities in the budgeting process.

Ask students to evaluate the Chung's budgeting process. What are the benefits and drawbacks of the system they use?

FIGURE 16-4 *ANSWER*

The Chung's expenditures exceeded the amounts they had budgeted in the household, health and personal care, and gifts and contributions categories. Their expenditures were less than budgeted in the food, transportation, and recreation and education categories. Expenses were equal to the budgeted amounts in the remaining categories.

Different Learning Abilities

Gifted Have students conduct online research regarding money management activities and budgeting procedures. The findings may be reported in a written format or oral presentation to the class.

Encourage students to think of situations that could affect budgeting activities. Ask representatives from the various teams to report to the class.

TEACH

Explain each of the budgeting formats discussed on the page. Ask students to point out the benefits and drawbacks of each one.

ONGOING ASSESSMENT

checkpoint >> **ANSWER**

Five characteristics of an effective budget are that it is (1) realistic, (2) flexible, (3) evaluated regularly, (4) well planned and clearly communicated, and (5) in a simple format.

ASSESS

Key Concepts Answers

1. False. Retirement planning is usually considered a long-term goal.

2. b. achieve financial goals

3. a. estimating variable expenses

Make Academic Connections

4. a. The total amount spent for food was $331.

b. Mary and Fred had a budget surplus of $9.

5. Posters and presentations will vary.

CLOSE

Highlight the purposes and process of creating and implementing a budget.

Work as a Team

For a budget to be successful, it must be followed. Work as a team to identify some situations in which a person or household may not be able to stay within their budget. Then explain actions that might be taken to resolve the situation.

Types of Budgeting Formats

Most money management software programs have a budgeting feature. They allow you to develop a budget, keep track of your accounts, and pay your bills. They may also aid in financial planning. Such software often can be linked to income tax software programs so that annual tax forms can be completed more quickly.

While handwritten or computerized budgets are most common and usually the most appropriate, some people believe a checkbook is an effective budgeting system. Be aware that a checking account does not serve the purpose of planning for spending. Your checks are a record of purchases and paid bills. You still need a plan for using income.

Others say they keep their budgets in their heads rather than on paper. This simple system may work for an individual with limited income and few financial commitments. A family with a larger income and more living expenses would find it ineffective. A person with a mental budget also risks forgetting how much is to be spent or has been spent on certain items.

checkpoint >>
What are five characteristics of an effective budget?

16-2 Assessment

Xtra!
Study Tools
school.cengage.com/business/introtobiz

Key Concepts

Determine the best answer.

1. True or False. Retirement planning is usually considered a short-term goal.

2. A major purpose of a budget is to
  a. assist with comparison shopping
  b. achieve financial goals
  c. reduce a person's enjoyment of life
  d. gather data for using credit cards

3. The most uncertain aspect of the budgeting process involves
  a. estimating variable expenses
  b. determining net worth
  c. estimating fixed expenses
  d. setting financial goals

Make Academic Connections

4. *Math* Mary and Fred James budgeted $340 a month for groceries. During the month, they spent $87, $93, $38, $61, and $52 at the supermarket.
  a. What was the total amount spent for food?
  b. Did Mary and Fred have a budget deficit or surplus? What was the amount?

5. *Visual Art* Talk to several people about various short-term and long-term goals they have had in their lives. Prepare a poster or computerized presentation summarizing various types of goals, both financial and personal.

RETEACH

Ask students to name examples of fixed and variable expenses.

ENRICH

Have students create a budget for their current income or for an assumed amount in the future.

16-3 Your Financial Future

Goals

Describe the financial planning process.

Explain actions for implementing a financial plan.

Identify actions for reviewing a financial plan.

Key Terms

financial plan

individual retirement account (IRA)

estate planning

Focus on Real Life

"Hey Gloria, are you going to the Business Speakers Series monthly luncheon on Friday?"

"I really hadn't given it much thought, Maria. Are you?"

"Yes! The speaker is from the local college and is supposed to be very dynamic and informative. The topic is financial planning, and if I am going to go to college, I need some help in planning right now! Why don't you meet me there?"

"Great idea, Maria. I always thought of financial planning as something for people out of college. But it certainly makes sense to start now! I guess if I start planning early, I can get a head start on my future!"

TEACH

Explain that financial planning, while similar to budgeting, is more comprehensive and involves a long-term perspective.

Ask students to name financial planning activities. Also, ask them to list items that might be included in a financial plan.

DEVELOPING A FINANCIAL PLAN

To successfully reach financial goals, you must have a plan. Successful coaches have a game plan. Travel agents refer to vacation plans. Builders must have house plans. Successful consumers and businesspeople must have a financial plan. A **financial plan** is a report that summarizes your current financial condition, acknowledges your financial needs, and sets a direction for your future financial activities.

Financial planning includes evaluating one's financial position, setting financial goals, and guiding activities and resources toward reaching those goals. Everyone should have a carefully developed financial plan.

Your financial plan should include all that you know about good money management. This plan should be developed carefully. It should be evaluated and updated frequently. A well-developed financial plan can make your financial life more satisfying.

Talk with an older person who started saving when he or she was your age. What can you learn from this person's financial successes or mistakes?

© Getty Images/PhotoDisc

main idea

Describe the financial planning process.

THINK CRITICALLY THROUGH VISUALS

Answers will vary. Students might report that saving regularly helped someone achieve financial goals. They also might report that not having a plan has resulted in disappointment.

Different Learning Abilities

Limited English Proficiency (LEP) Obtain translations for various key terms in this chapter to reinforce these concepts in both English and other dominant languages used by students.

TEACH

Explain the advantages of financial planning listed on this page. Highlight the steps in the financial planning process.

Ask students to name items that might be included in a financial inventory.

Name some of the financial documents that students will encounter now and in the future.

Point out differences in financial activities in various stages of a person's life cycle.

Work as a Team

This activity can help students become more aware of the various financial documents and records they will use throughout their lives.

 **PROJECT**

Provide the following instructions to students. (These instructions also appear on page xxv of the textbook.) Describe the role of financial planning in the creation of a person's life-span plan. Do you have a financial plan? Explain why people who fail to create and follow a financial plan often fail to achieve their life-span goals.

Life-Span Plan Answer

Answers will vary. Students should point out that most life-span goals require a significant allocation of funds that can only be accumulated through careful financial planning over time.

Work as a Team

Having an organized system of financial records is important for financial planning success. As a team, (1) develop a list of financial records in addition to those in Figure 16-5, (2) discuss where you might keep various documents in addition to a home file, (3) decide how long various documents should be kept.

Financial planning offers several specific advantages.

- Your financial uncertainties will be reduced.

- You will gain more control of your financial activities.

- Your family and household members will know more about your financial situation in case they need to assume control of your finances.

- Earning, spending, protecting, and saving your resources will be more systematic.

Financial Planning Process

Financial planning experts recommend the following steps.

1. *Analyze your current financial condition.* You should create a balance sheet and cash flow statement.

2. *Develop financial goals that are responsive to your vision.* What short-term and long-term objectives do you have? How much money will you need, and when?

3. *Create your financial plan.* This activity will require that you plan various actions for your saving and spending goals. This step may require help from a financial planner or other financial specialists.

4. *Implement the plan.* This may involve buying or selling property or investments, moving bank accounts, acquiring insurance, or any number of financial activities.

5. *Revise your financial plan.* As time goes on, you will frequently evaluate and revise your financial plan.

Financial Inventory

Think of a financial inventory as a financial checkup. When you get a medical checkup, the physician assesses your health. A financial inventory is a careful assessment of your finances.

A financial inventory will usually include the creation of a personal balance sheet and cash flow statement. This process will provide information about your current financial position in terms of income, savings, investments, property, living expenses, insurance, and money owed.

Personal Financial Filing System

To keep your financial inventory and other records in order, you should create a personal financial filing system. Well-organized files are key to financial planning. These files should contain all of the documents and records related to such things as contracts, bills, receipts, bank balances, and legal papers. The files will become an invaluable resource to you as you progress with your financial planning. The contents may be organized in categories as shown in Figure 16-5 on the next page.

Financial Life Cycle

Most people's lives follow a predictable pattern called a *life cycle.* Each stage of life is distinguished by unique characteristics, requirements, and expectations. For example, during the teen years, people are exploring career options, developing plans for independence, and evaluating future financial needs. In your twenties, you will likely train for a career, set up a household, and perhaps marry and have children.

Applied Skills

Building Study Skills Ask students to prepare three multiple choice questions from the lesson to help other students review the material. Encourage students to meet in small groups to discuss the lesson and quiz each other.

A Filing System for Personal Financial Records

Personal records
- Birth certificate
- Social Security card
- Current resume

Money management records
- Current budget
- Personal balance sheet
- Cash flow statement

Housing records
- Lease
- Mortgage papers
- Property tax records

Tax records
- Pay stubs, W-2 forms
- Receipts for tax deductions
- Income tax forms

Consumer purchase records
- Warranties
- Receipts for major purchases
- Motor vehicle registration

Financial services and credit records
- Bank statements
- Certificates of deposit
- Credit contracts
- Monthly credit card statements

Insurance records
- Insurance policies
- Medical information
- Claim reports

Investment, retirement, and estate records
- Investment account statements
- Pension plan information
- Will, trust information

Name some ways computers have made financial record keeping more efficient.

Later in life, you may decide to obtain additional career training or make plans for paying for children's education. Then retirement plans, investing, and estate planning will likely become a priority.

Each life stage has financial matters that need attention. That attention can be provided through the development of a good financial plan. Remember, a good plan is one that is flexible and useful throughout several life stages.

Using a Financial Planner

Creating a financial plan is not a simple task. Doing your own financial planning requires time, information, and patience. Financial planners are professionals who can help you. A financial planner should have studied and passed examinations on various topics, including investments, insurance, taxes, real estate, and estate planning.

Questions you might ask when choosing a financial planner include the following:

- What experience and training do you have?

- Are you willing to supply references from past clients?

- How are your fees determined?

checkpoint >>
List five recommended steps for financial planning.

FIGURE 16-5 *ANSWER*

Computers have made financial record keeping more efficient by calculating personal income and expenses quickly and accurately. Computers can prepare detailed reports of all income and expense categories and simplify record keeping for budgeting and tax purposes.

TEACH

Relate the categories of documents in Figure 16-5 to various financial planning activities in different stages of a person's life.

Describe actions that might be taken when deciding whether to use the services of a financial planner.

ONGOING ASSESSMENT

checkpoint >> **ANSWER**

Five recommended steps for financial planning are (1) analyze your current financial condition, (2) develop financial goals that are responsive to your vision, (3) create your financial plan, (4) implement the plan, and (5) revise your financial plan.

Different Learning Styles

Kinesthetic Learner Have students draw samples for two or three of the documents listed in Figure 16-5. Ask students to explain the information included in the document they created.

NETBookmark

An extensive amount of financial planning information is available on the Internet. Access the web site shown below and click on the link for Chapter 16. Select a financial planning topic. Why is this area of financial planning of interest to you? What information did you learn about this topic? What additional answers do you need about this topic?

school.cengage.com/business/introtobiz

main idea

Explain actions for implementing a financial plan.

IMPLEMENT A FINANCIAL PLAN

Implementing your plan may involve a wide variety of actions. You may need to move your savings to an account in which you will earn a higher interest rate. You may buy a bond. Maybe you will begin to work more hours at your part-time job to earn more money.

The list of financial planning actions can seem almost endless. For your plan to lead to achieving your financial goals, several common areas should be considered.

Insure Current Income

Protecting your income so that it contributes to your goals is a key financial planning action. Insurance is available that will provide an income to those who fear the two most common causes of loss of income: disability and unemployment.

Disability Income Insurance To replace income that is lost when you cannot work because of an illness or injury, you can purchase *disability income insurance.* Many different disability income policies are available. Most disability income insurance will pay 60 to 70 percent of your salary while you are disabled. Before the benefits begin, there is usually a waiting period from one week to 90 days after you are disabled. Many employers provide this type of insurance.

Unemployment Insurance

Unemployment is another hazard to a financial plan. To reduce the financial hardship of unemployment, most states have an *unemployment insurance* program, operated in cooperation with the federal government. This coverage provides cash payments for a limited time to people who are out of work for a reason other than illness. A local unemployment office will provide guidance to help find a new job. If no suitable job is found, you may qualify for payments to replace part of your lost wages.

Plan for Future Income

The success of any financial plan also calls for a stream of future income. Once people retire, their salaries stop, but they continue to need money to cover living expenses. Workers can ensure that they will have enough income during their retirement years through Social Security, pensions, individual retirement accounts, and annuities.

Social Security A key form of income protection comes through the federal government's Social Security system called *retirement, survivors,* and *disability insurance.* This part of Social Security provides pensions to retired workers and their families, death benefits to dependents of workers who die, and benefits to disabled workers and their families.

Social Security benefits are funded by payroll taxes from both workers and employers. The taxes are deducted from employees' paychecks. Employers match the amounts paid by their employees. Self-employed people, such as farmers and small business owners, pay the entire tax themselves.

When a worker retires, becomes disabled, or dies, monthly payments are made from the trust fund. The amount of benefits received depends on how long a worker was employed and how much a worker earned while employed.

Applied Skills

Communication Have students prepare a short written report about one of the topics presented on pages 412–413. Encourage students to use Internet and library resources to obtain additional information on their topic. Invite interested students to share one or two things they discovered about their topics.

Pensions A *pension* is a series of regular payments made to a retired worker under an organized plan. Some employers offer plans that provide monthly payments to retired workers. Unions often establish similar plans. To qualify under most pension plans, you must work for the same organization for a minimum number of years.

Retirement Accounts People can also develop their own retirement income plans. The most popular of these plans is the **individual retirement account (IRA)**. An IRA is a tax-sheltered retirement plan in which people can annually invest earnings up to a certain amount. Contributions to traditional IRAs are tax-deductible. The investment gains are tax-deferred and the funds are taxed when they are withdrawn after age 59½. Contributions to a Roth IRA are not tax-deductible. However, all funds, including any investment gains, are tax-free when withdrawn after age 59½.

Other types of retirement accounts for self-employed workers and people who run their own businesses include the 401(k), Keogh, SIMPLE, and SEP plans. Each of these involves tax-deferred retirement income. *Tax-deferred* means the investment earnings will be taxed later, after retirement. The type of retirement plan for which you qualify will depend on your employment situation and income level.

Annuities An amount of money an insurance company pays to a person who has previously deposited money with the company is called an *annuity*. This financial agreement is an investment plan for retirement income. You pay the insurance company a certain amount of money either in a lump sum or in a series of payments. In return, the company agrees to pay you a regular income beginning at a certain age and continuing for life or for a specified number of years.

What are common sources of income during retirement?

REVIEW YOUR FINANCIAL PLAN

A financial plan must be flexible. View your financial plan as a changeable document. Your plan should be evaluated and adjusted on a regular basis to produce the outcomes you desire.

Revise Financial Goals

Once you have an understanding of changes in your financial or personal situation, you should consider changes in your financial goals. These goals may be short-term or long-term. They are usually stated in dollar amounts. An example of a short-term goal is "saving $1,000 in one year." This goal is simple, straightforward, and fairly short-term.

How much money per month will you need to live comfortably when you retire? Where will this money come from?

© Getty Images/PhotoDisc

main idea

Identify actions for reviewing a financial plan.

TEACH

Explain the process and benefits of pensions and retirements accounts.

Ask students why many people do not have adequate income when they reach retirement age.

ONGOING ASSESSMENT

checkpoint >> **ANSWER**

Common sources of income during retirement are Social Security, pensions, individual retirement accounts, Roth IRAs, 401 (k) plans, Keogh plans, and annuities.

TEACH

Point out the importance of reviewing a financial plan on a periodic basis.

Ask students to describe situations that might create a need for a person to revise financial goals.

THINK CRITICALLY THROUGH VISUALS

Answers will vary and will depend on the income they plan to achieve and the lifestyle they hope to maintain in retirement. Students may not have thought about possible sources for this money—sources that depend in large part on their choices of employment and consistency in saving.

Different Learning Styles

Auditory Learner Have students work in pairs to review this lesson. Encourage them to take turns reading the headings aloud and explaining the content.

By contrast, long-term financial goals are often more complex and involve a longer period. These might include "owning a home by age 30."

Often, short-term goals may need to be given up in order to achieve long-term ones. For example, you may have to forgo buying a bicycle in order to save for an automobile.

Review Financial Activities

Changes in your goals will require changes in spending and saving habits. Although retirement may be years away, preparing for it is a vital part of financial planning. Chances are very good that you will spend many happy and healthy years in retirement. Those years will be happier and healthier if you have an adequate supply of money.

Estate planning. involves the accumulation and management of property during one's lifetime and the distribution of one's property at death. During your life you build your estate through savings, investments, and insurance. You also plan how you wish your estate to be transferred when you die.

Remember to Save and Share

Money management and financial planning are ongoing activities. Every decision you make will affect both current spending and long-term financial security. The only way to have money in the future is to spend less than you receive. The overuse of credit and other poor spending habits are the basis for long-term financial disaster. Your budget and spending activities should also involve sharing some resources. This may involve religious donations or contributions to local and global organizations that provide food, housing, and other necessities to people in need.

> *checkpoint* >>
> What activities are involved when reviewing a financial plan?

16-3 Assessment

Key Concepts

Determine the best answer.

1. A common source of retirement income is
    a. disability income insurance
    b. a mortgage
    c. pensions
    d. unemployment insurance
2. A long-term financial goal usually involves
    a. less than two years
    b. buying with a credit card
    c. using the services of a financial planner
    d. saving over many years

Make Academic Connections

3. *Research* Use library or online research to determine common financial planning activities for different stages of life. Prepare a poster to summarize your findings for people in their 20s, 30s, 40s, 50s, 60s, and older.

4. *Oral Communication* Conduct an interview with another student. Ask that person about her or his financial goals. Suggest actions to help the person achieve those goals.

Sharpen Your Life Skills

Effective Interviewing

As a job applicant, you will be interviewed. You will be asked questions to determine your experiences and knowledge. In contrast, your ability to interview others can be of value in several ways. Someday you may interview potential employees for a company. Or, you may interview people for information for class assignments or in work situations.

When conducting an interview to make a business decision or to obtain information, follow these guidelines.

1. Create four or five open-ended questions related to the topic to get the person talking.
2. Develop questions that cannot be answered with one or two words.
3. The best interview questions start with "why," "what," "when," "where," "how," and "describe."
4. Listen for major themes or key ideas. Give the respondent time to answer. Don't interrupt.
5. Use follow-up questions to obtain additional information.
6. Do not ask leading questions—ones that suggest an answer for which you are looking.

Probing and Clarifying

Two valuable interviewing techniques are probing and clarifying. Probing is a technique to obtain additional information from a respondent. Probing starts with careful questioning by the interviewer. Probing can be achieved with repeating a question. Probing phrases include:

- Anything else?
- Please tell me more.
- What do you mean by that?
- Why do you feel that way?

Clarifying is a process to get an explanation about an answer that has already been given. You want to know

specifically what is meant by an answer. One clarifying technique is to ask, "What do you mean by…" and then repeat the respondent's exact words. Another way to clarify is to ask the respondent to provide additional information about some response that has already been given.

Think Critically

1. What are situations in which your ability to interview others would be useful?
2. What actions could you take to improve your interview skills?
3. Conduct an interview to obtain information about a career, company, or country. Write an essay about your experience.

Point out the importance of developing effective interviewing skills. Explain that interviewing skills can be used to gain information in a wide variety of situations.

Think Critically
Answers

1. Situations in which an ability to interview others would be useful include hiring employees; reporting stories for a newsletter, magazine, or journal; and gathering information for class assignments or work challenges.

2. To improve interviewing skills, practice interviewing people of varying ages and backgrounds. When interviewing people you know fairly well, try to discover facts about that person that you didn't know.

3. Essays will vary depending on the person interviewed and the topic selected.

1. **a.** Money owed to the dentist is a liability.

   b. An automobile is an asset.

   c. Clothing is an asset.

   d. Savings account is an asset.

   e. Credit card balance is a liability.

   f. Amount due for a personal loan is a liability.

   g. 100 shares of stock are assets.

2. Answers will vary. If you learn to manage your money well, you will be able to buy what you really want. Planning ahead and deciding what is important will help you have money for things you enjoy.

3. Answers will vary. Short-term goals are goals for the near future, such as paying back a $200 debt in six months. Long-term goals look farther into the future, for example, paying off a mortgage in 15 instead of 30 years.

4. Answers will vary, but could include things such as increasing income by finding a better paying job, getting a roommate, or foregoing non-essential expenses.

5. Chris is not following good money management because he does not have a plan for how much he spends or saves.

6. **a.** Answers will vary. Fixed expenses could include rent, insurance, utilities, car payments, or savings.

   b. Answers will vary. Variable expenses could include food, clothing, car repairs and recreation.

CHAPTER 16 Assessment

Business Notes

16-1 PERSONAL FINANCIAL STATEMENTS

1. You can manage your money wisely by planning carefully, using information to help you better understand and take action on your money matters, comparing products and prices, and making wise decisions.

2. A balance sheet is a record of assets and liabilities at a point in time. Assets are items of value. Liabilities are amounts owed to others. Net worth is the difference between assets and liabilities.

3. A cash flow statement is a record of cash inflows (income) and cash outflows (payments for living expenses) for a given period, such as a month.

16-2 BUDGETING TECHNIQUES

4. The main purposes of a budget are to help you live within your income, achieve your financial goals, buy wisely, avoid credit problems, plan for financial emergencies, and develop good money management skills. Having a written budget is an important phase of successful money management.

5. The process of creating and using a budget involves setting financial goals, planning budget categories, maintaining financial records, and evaluating your budget.

6. A successful budget will be realistic, flexible, evaluated regularly, well planned, clearly communicated to those involved, and in a simple format.

16-3 YOUR FINANCIAL FUTURE

7. The five main steps in the financial planning process are to analyze your current financial condition, develop financial goals, create a financial plan, implement the plan, and evaluate and revise the plan over time.

8. Two key areas to consider when implementing a financial plan are protecting current income and providing for future income. Current income can be protected by disability income insurance and unemployment insurance. Sources of future income during retirement include Social Security, pensions, individual retirement accounts, and annuities.

9. When reviewing your financial plan, view it as a fluid, changeable document that will accommodate opportunity. You should revise financial goals as your financial or personal situation changes. Changes in your goals will require changes in spending and saving habits. Most importantly, remember to save. The only way to have money in the future is to spend less than you receive.

Communicate Business Concepts

1. Identify each of the following items as an asset or a liability:

   a. Money owed to the dentist
   b. An automobile
   c. Clothing
   d. Savings account
   e. Credit card balance
   f. Amount due for a personal loan
   g. 100 shares of stock

2. "Money management means never spending, doing without things, and not having any fun." Do you agree with this statement? Explain your answer.

3. Describe the difference between short-term and long-term goals. Give two examples of each type.

4. What two actions could you take if your expenditures were consistently greater than your income?

5. Every week, Chris Thorson puts any amount he has not spent during the week into a savings account. If he needs more money than he has during a week, he withdraws it from his savings. Is Chris following a good money management plan? Explain.

---

c. Answers will vary. Families with younger children might have child care expenses and more doctor visits. Families with no children would have lower expenses in many categories, such as food and clothing.

7. Insuring one's income is a key financial planning action. Disability income insurance and unemployment insurance will pay for living expenses in the event that the insured cannot work or loses his or her job.

8. Assuming one has an income, doing nothing about financial planning is in effect doing something, possibly spending unwisely and neglecting to save for the future.

6. Consider a family of four people: mother, a super-market manager; father, a department store sales-person; and two children, ages 14 and 11.

   a. List four fixed expenses that this family would likely have each month.
   b. What are some variable expenses that they are likely to have?
   c. How are the family's expenses different from those of other families with younger children or no children?

7. Why would you want to insure your income?

8. One financial planner has said, "Doing nothing about financial planning is equivalent to making a decision about financial planning." What do you think she meant by this?

9. How does a budget differ from a financial plan?

10. Give examples of activities that might be involved in implementing a financial plan.

11. Some people claim that living by a budget is too structured and restrictive. That is, they do not like to live such a planned and strict economic life. What would you say to those individuals who have that point of view in order to convince them that budgets can be helpful to everyone?

12. Tell in your own words how people's financial goals change throughout their life cycle.

13. List some items that might be a want for one person but a need for someone else.

Develop Your Business Language

Match the terms listed with the definitions.

14. The difference between a person's or family's assets and liabilities.

15. A report that summarizes your current financial condition, acknowledges your financial needs, and sets a direction for your future financial activities.

16. Living costs involving differing amounts each time.

17. Accumulation and management of property during one's lifetime and the distribution of one's property at death.

18. Costs that occur regularly and are for the same amount each time.

19. A difference between actual spending and planned spending.

20. The financial statement that reports net wages and other income along with spending for a given period.

21. A tax-sheltered retirement plan in which people can annually invest earnings up to a certain amount. The earnings contributed and interest earned are tax-free until the funds are withdrawn.

22. Items of value.

23. The day-to-day financial activities associated with using limited income to satisfy your unlimited needs and wants.

24. The amount of money you plan to use for a certain budget category.

KEY TERMS
a. allowance
b. budget variance
c. cash flow statement
d. estate planning
e. financial plan
f. fixed expense
g. individual retirement account (IRA)
h. money management
i. net worth
j. personal assets
k. variable expense

Develop Your Business Language Answers

14. i. net worth
15. e. financial plan
16. k variable expense
17. d. estate planning
18. f. fixed expense
19. b. budget variance
20. c. cash flow statement
21. g. individual retirement account (IRA)
22. j. personal assets
23. h. money management
24. a. allowance

9. A budget is a plan for saving and spending income that will help a person or family live within its income and achieve financial goals. A financial plan summarizes one's current financial condition, acknowledges financial needs, and sets a direction for future financial activities. A budget helps manage day-to-day decisions, while a financial plan guides an individual into the future.

10. Examples include meeting with a financial planner, insuring current income, planning for future income, moving money into accounts that will better meet financial goals, and making employment and education decisions.

11. Students might tell financially careless individuals that reckless spending and sporadic saving will actually make them less financially secure and less able to purchase the things they want.

12. Students should be able to describe how financial goals might change throughout a person's lifetime, from saving for college, a car, and a rental deposit to purchasing a home, getting married, and having children, to saving for travel and retirement.

13. Answers will vary. An example of something that is a want for one person and a need for another would be a professional athlete's jersey that is a need for the athlete, but a want for a fan. A high-powered computer is a necessity for a graphic design business, but a luxury item for a teenager who wants to play video games. Fine tailored suits might be a necessity for a salesperson, but a want for a factory worker.

Make Academic Connections

25. **ECONOMICS** Use newspaper ads and Web research to determine the current value of various assets such as homes, motor vehicles, jewelry, antiques, and rare coins.

26. **CULTURE** Conduct research using personal interviews and other sources to determine the main assets (possessions) of typical households in other countries.

27. **MATH** The Gage family's assets total $268,400. Their total liabilities are $166,300. What is the amount of their owner's equity? What actions could they take to increase their net worth?

28. **TECHNOLOGY** Conduct an Internet search for budget guidelines suggested for various categories of spending such as food, housing, transportation, clothing, health care, and others.

29. **RESEARCH** Locate in-store or online information about available money management software. Prepare a brief written summary comparing the prices and features of different programs.

30. **VISUAL ART** Create a flowchart to communicate the five steps of the financial planning process.

31. **RESEARCH** Conduct research to determine various professionals who might help you with your financial planning in the future. Prepare a summary table reporting the name, title, training and background, area of specialization, and cost of services for various financial planners.

32. **LAW** Obtain information about recent changes in Social Security taxes and benefits. Prepare a two- to three-paragraph summary.

33. **HISTORY** Locate a copy of a budget or financial report for your school, church, city government, or a public company from at least five years ago, as well as a copy of the current budget for the same entity. Compare the two budgets. Prepare a brief summary comparing assets, liabilities, and net income. Discuss what factors may have caused these differences.

34. **ECONOMICS** Interview fellow students, your parents, or other adults who are employed. Gather information about the deductions that are taken from their paychecks. Prepare a table listing the various deductions. Indicate which deductions are required and which are optional.

35. **PERSONAL FINANCE** Assume you have been given a three-year-old car as a gift. Research the monthly costs associated with owning a car. Include items such as insurance, license, local annual use taxes, cost of gasoline based on 10,000 miles per year, and regular maintenance costs. Use a spreadsheet to present your findings.

36. **CULTURE** Select one city each in North America, South America, Europe, and Australia. Conduct Web research to determine the per-person cost of an afternoon out with your friends in each city. Use the current exchange rate to convert the costs to U.S. dollars. Include items such as transportation (subway, taxi, or gas per gallon cost), lunch, a movie, and a new music CD. Present your findings in a table.

Linking School and Community

Talk with people in your community about their money management activities. What are their main budgeting concerns? How do they cope with these? What actions do they take to save money for the future? What types of investments do they recommend?

Web Workout

You can find many sources of information about money management and personal financial planning on the Internet. The web sites vary widely in the types and quality of information provided. Choose a topic from this chapter and find two web sites offering information or advice related to the topic.

Think Critically

1. Write a short summary of the main ideas from each web site.
2. How does the information presented address differences related age and household situations?
3. What additional information could be added to the site related to your topic?

Decision-Making Strategies

Joan Leitzel just graduated from college and got her first job as a speech therapist. Joan wants to make sure she manages her income wisely so that she can be independent and eventually buy a house on her own. She lives with her parents now, so her only expenses are payments on a college loan and an auto loan.

37. What advice would you give Joan if she wants to buy a house in the future?

38. When she eventually goes to the bank for a loan, how should Joan organize her financial information?

Graphic Design Promotion

The banking industry has become highly competitive. Banks are constantly creating promotional brochures to attract the attention of new customers.

You have been hired by First Bank of America to design a promotional brochure describing the bank's services. The bank offers free checking accounts for high school students and retired customers. Other customers who maintain a minimum balance of $500 at all times also receive free checking services.

Your bank provides money management and other financial services to customers. First Bank of America is open six days a week. The Monday–Friday hours are 9 a.m.–7 p.m. and Saturday hours are 9 a.m.–1 p.m. The bank has convenient locations throughout the community that feature drive-up windows and ATMs.

Your final product may be black and white or color and printed on white or colored paper. All graphics must be computer generated. You may not use any items, such as photographs or logos, that are protected by copyrights or trademarks. Judges will have 10 minutes to ask participants about their brochures.

PERFORMANCE INDICATORS EVALUATED

- Use principles of design, layout, and typography in graphic design.
- Generate a promotional flyer for marketing purposes.
- Demonstrate knowledge of graphic design and rules for layout.
- Demonstrate effective use of color, lines, text, graphics, shapes, etc.
- Use appropriate artwork and design techniques to effectively illustrate a theme.
- Apply technical skills to manipulate graphics, artwork, and images.

For more detailed information about performance indicators, go to the BPA web site.

Think Critically

1. What do customers want from their banks?
2. Why have banking hours changed so dramatically?
3. Where is the best place to distribute promotional brochures for a bank?

http://www.bpanet.org/

Access the web site shown here to find portfolio activities for this chapter. Use the activities to provide tangible evidence of your learning.

school.cengage.com/business/introtobiz

Decision-Making Strategies Answers

37. Answers will vary. Students might suggest that Joan should begin a consistent savings plan to accumulate a down payment on a house. She should invest her savings wisely so that her future down payment fund grows steadily. She should pay her car loan and college loan on time in order to establish a good credit rating.

38. When Joan finally goes to the bank seeking a mortgage loan, she might want to prepare a personal balance sheet and cash flow statement to demonstrate her financial health. She will also need to be able to provide the potential lender with any financial records needed to process the loan application, such as payroll stubs or copies of past tax returns.

Winning Edge
BPA Graphic Design Promotion

This activity will provide students with an opportunity to experience the process of planning and preparing business visuals.

Think Critically Answers

1. Customers want respectful service, security, honesty, accuracy, and royal convenience from their banks.

2. Banking hours have changed to meet the changing needs of a busy workforce. Hours have become more flexible due to increased competition in the industry.

3. Answers will vary and could include at the bank, major shopping malls, and busy locations throughout the community. The brochures could also be mailed to community residents.

CHAPTER 17

Banking and Financial Services

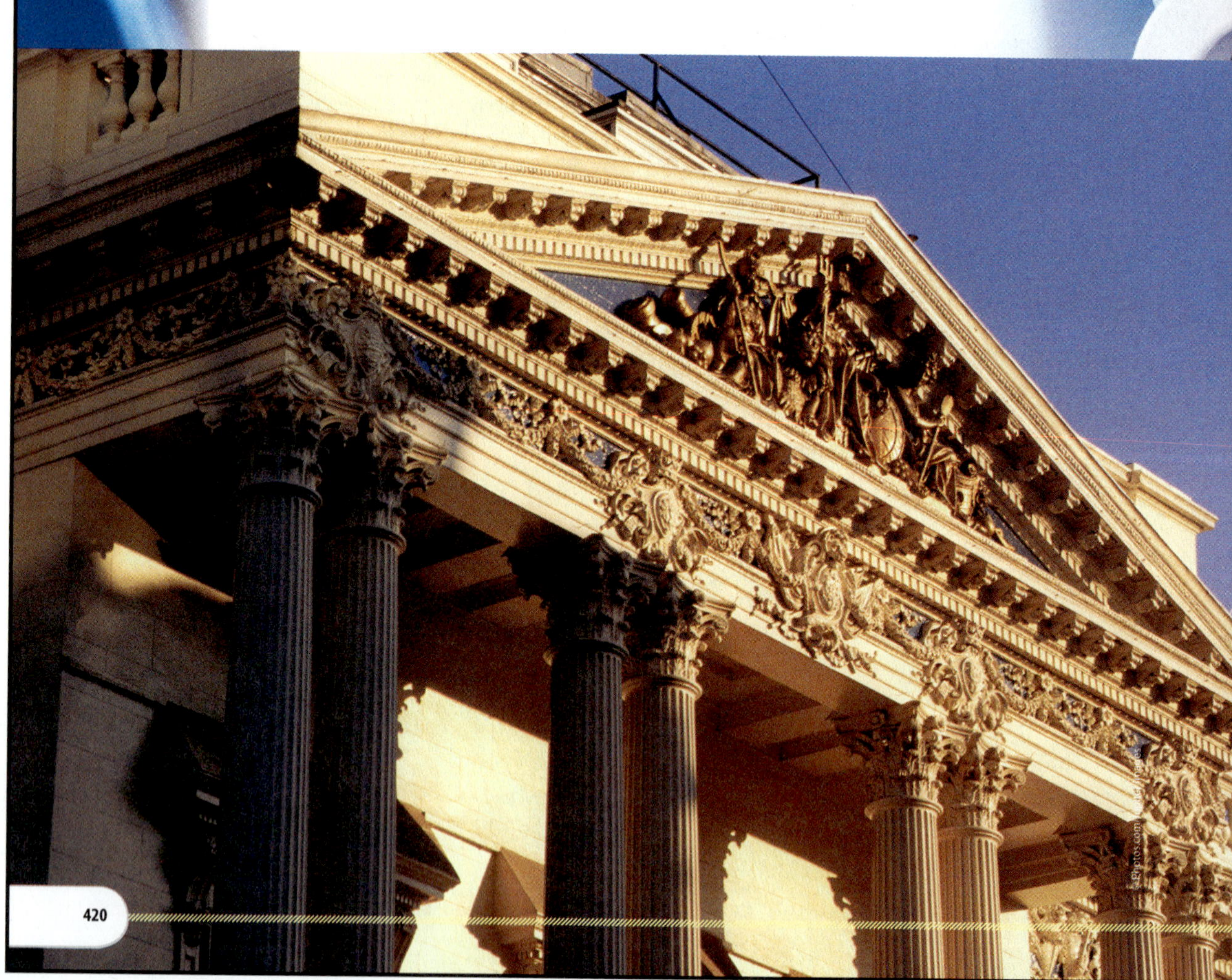

Planning a Career in...
BANKING AND FINANCIAL SERVICES

The banking and financial services industry offers many career opportunities. Numerous financial workers are employed in commercial banks. Others work in specialized banks, savings and loan associations, credit unions, and finance companies. Work activities in the financial services industry range from serving customers and researching economic trends to planning marketing activities for financial institutions.

Employment Outlook

- Career opportunities in banking and financial services are expected to see continued growth.
- Slower growth is expected for certain banking jobs due to industry consolidation and technology.
- Employment of bank branch managers will grow as banks open branches in areas with strong population growth.
- Electronic banking activities will influence the need for employees with technology skills.

Related Job Titles

- Branch Manager
- Teller
- Head Teller
- Loan Officer
- Customer Service Representative
- Financial Services Sales Agent
- Financial Manager
- Information Processing Manager
- Economist

Needed Skills

- Entry-level jobs may require only a high school education, with college business courses needed for advancement.
- Bank officers, professional personnel, and executive positions require a college degree.
- Continuing education in cash management, financial analysis, and international banking should be considered.
- Interaction with customers requires strong communication skills and the ability to speak a second language is an asset.
- Accuracy, professional appearance, and computer competencies are vital for success.

What's it like to work in... Financial Services

Each morning, Ken Li goes online to see how various economic factors are affecting interest rates. He knows that when money is more expensive, borrowing by businesses and consumers declines. But if interest rates are lower, the use of credit will likely increase. This additional borrowing can result in higher earnings for banks.

Changing interest rates are just one area of research for Ken, who works for a bank with offices in 23 states. Today, he must also investigate current trends for employment, consumer spending, and retail sales. These economic indicators provide managers with information to better plan strategies for their banking organizations.

What about you? What knowledge of banking and financial services do you have that might be of value when selecting a career?

Additional Career Information

Additional information on careers can be found in the *Occupational Outlook Handbook,* an online publication (www.bls.gov/oco) of the federal government. Tell your class about this resource and how to use it. This description of job duties can be used to demonstrate the relevancy of skills learned in this course.

Planning a Career in...
BANKING AND FINANCIAL SERVICES

Competition and technology are affecting the banking industry. Many large banks have taken over smaller competitors. In addition, computers and other automation systems are affecting needed skills and employment opportunities in this industry.

What About You? Answer

Answers will vary depending on their experiences with managing their own finances. Point out that understanding banking and financial services is useful in many career areas.

17-1 Banks and Other Financial Institutions

Goals

Explain the purpose of the Federal Reserve System.

List the types of financial institutions.

Discuss factors for selecting a financial institution.

Key Terms

Federal Reserve System (Fed)

commercial bank

credit union

Federal Deposit Insurance Corporation (FDIC)

Focus on Real Life

"I finally got a job for the summer," Gerri told Mike. "I can save money and go on that trip."

"Where are you going to save your money?" asked Mike.

"At home, of course," responded Gerri.

"Are you kidding?" Mike went on to say. "That's dangerous! Your money can get lost, or you might spend it before summer comes."

"Well, what should I do with my money?" asked Gerri.

"Deposit it in a bank," answered Mike.

"Will it be safer?" asked Gerri.

"For sure," said Mike. "Banks and other financial institutions provide safety and growth for your money. Plus they help their customers in many ways with other financial matters."

"You're kidding! I guess it's time I learn about banking," Gerri responded.

---

main idea

Explain the purpose of the Federal Reserve System.

THE BANKING SYSTEM

Have you ever thought of a bank as a business? Many people do not think of banks in this way. Yet, a bank is a business just like a store or factory. As a business, a bank sells services such as checking and payment accounts, savings accounts, loans, and investments.

Banks are regulated more strictly than most other businesses. If a business fails, some people lose money. If a bank fails, thousands of people are affected.

The Federal Reserve System

Most banks attempt to attract the deposits of customers. However, as an individual, you cannot open an account in a Federal Reserve Bank because it is a *bank for banks*.

What is the purpose of the Federal Reserve?

The federal government set up the **Federal Reserve System (Fed)** to supervise and regulate member banks and to help banks serve the public efficiently. All national banks are required to join the Federal Reserve System, and state banks may join. Banks that join the system are known as *member banks*. The United States is divided into 12 Federal Reserve districts, with a central Federal Reserve Bank in each district, as shown in Figure 17-1.

Federal Reserve Activities

A Federal Reserve Bank serves member banks and the economy in several ways. One service provided by the Fed is the holding of *reserves*. Banks cannot lend all of the money they receive from customers. They are required to keep a part of the money deposited by customers on deposit with the Federal Reserve System. The Fed holds these deposits in case the banks need additional funds to meet the daily customer demand.

As a result, a bank will lend only a certain percentage of deposited funds. It keeps the

Banks are considered one of the most important types of businesses in any economy. Prepare a list of ways in which the banking system affects (1) businesses, (2) consumers, and (3) workers.

rest in reserve. This regulation is designed to help the banking system and the economy operate efficiently and to protect deposit.

For example, suppose a customer deposits $1,000 and the bank is required to hold 15 percent of all deposits in reserve. This means the bank can lend $850, which is 85 percent of the new deposit.

$$85\% \times \$1,000 = \$850$$

Another service of the Federal Reserve System is clearing checks for member banks. *Clearing* refers to the paying of checks among different banks in different locations. The Fed processes millions of checks each day to make sure that the correct amounts are added to and subtracted from the appropriate accounts.

Work as a Team

This activity can help students better understand the role of banking and financial services in an economy.

TEACH

Explain how *reserves* create additional funds in the economy.

Describe the importance of the *clearing* process for checks and other payments.

FIGURE 17-1 *ANSWER*

Answers will vary depending on where your school is located.

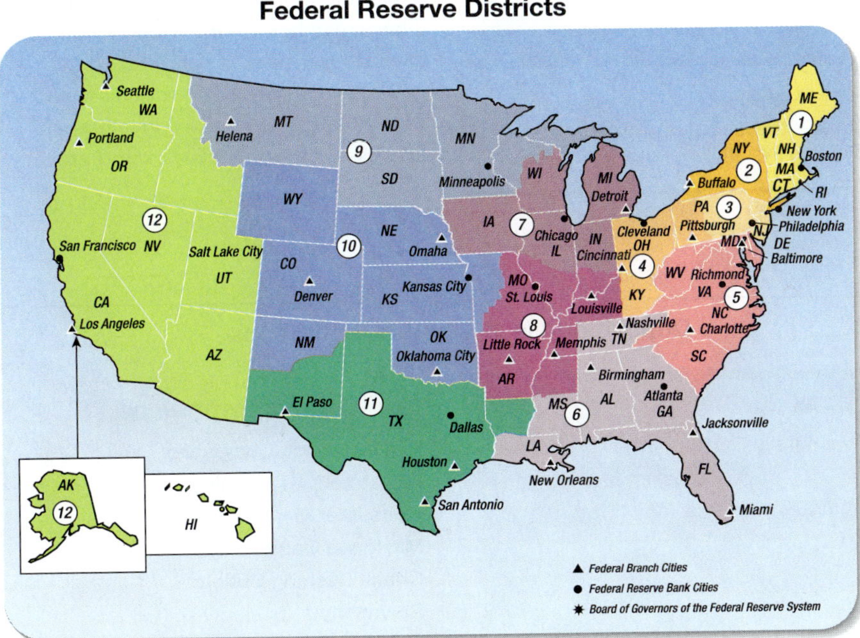

Federal Reserve Districts

FIGURE 17-1

Which Federal Reserve Regional Bank serves banks in your community?

Applied Skills

Geography Explain that the Federal Reserve district identification appears to the left of Washington's image on the face of the one-dollar Federal Reserve note. Use several one-dollar bills from different Federal Reserve Banks to demonstrate that money from several districts is likely to be in circulation in your area.

TEACH

Highlight the banking activities that can promote economic growth.

ONGOING ASSESSMENT

checkpoint >> **ANSWER**

The Federal Reserve System was created by the federal government to supervise and regulate member banks and to help banks serve the public efficiently by holding reserves and clearing checks.

TEACH

Use Figure 17-2 to provide an overview of the main categories and types of financial institutions.

Describe the major services provided by a commercial bank.

FIGURE 17-2   *ANSWER*

Answers will vary depending on which institutions students have done business with in the past.

PROJECT

Provide the following instructions to students. (These instructions also appear on page xxv of the textbook.) Do you believe that people need a safe and reliable banking system to achieve their life-span goals? Describe how you expect to use banks and other financial institutions to reach the goals you set in your life-span plan.

Life-Span Plan Answer

Answers will vary. Students should point out that people need a reliable banking system as a place to store their savings with safety and obtain credit when necessary.

List the types of financial institutions.

Banking and the Economy

The actions of the banking system affect you in many ways. Several million people work in banks, savings and loan associations, credit unions, and other financial institutions. The following activities are just some of the ways that individuals, businesses, and governments use banking services.

- Borrow money to build roads
- Borrow money to buy seeds for crops
- Deposit cash from business operations
- Finance a college education
- Invest for retirement
- Obtain a mortgage
- Process credit card transactions
- Save for a vacation

The savings you and others deposit make banking services possible. Deposits do not remain idle in bank vaults. They are put to work. When you and others deposit money in a bank, you are helping to create jobs and economic growth that benefit your community and your society.

checkpoint >>
What is the main purpose of the Federal Reserve System?

FIGURE 17-2

Which of these types of institutions have you done business with?

TYPES OF FINANCIAL INSTITUTIONS

When someone says, "I'm going to the bank," the person might actually mean a credit union or a cash machine. There are many types of financial institutions that provide a wide range of products and services. Figure 17-2 shows how financial institutions are classified.

Deposit Institutions

Deposit institutions, also called *depository intermediaries*, accept deposits from people and businesses and use them to finance their business.

Commercial Banks The most common way for a bank to be organized is as a **commercial bank**. Commercial banks are often called *full-service banks* because they offer a wide range of financial services. Commercial banks offer checking accounts, provide savings accounts, make loans to individuals and to businesses, and offer other services. In large banks, different departments may handle these services. There may be a savings department, a trust department, a real estate department, and an investment department. Many banks have full-service branch offices in shopping centers and grocery stores.

Deposit and Non-Deposit Institutions

Deposit Institutions	Non-Deposit Institutions
Commercial Banks	Life Insurance Companies
Savings and Loan Associations	Investment Companies
Mutual Savings Banks	Consumer Finance Companies
Credit Unions	Mortgage Companies
	Check Cashing Outlets
	Pawnshops

Different Learning Styles

Print Learner After reading the information about banking and the economy, ask students to use their own words to explain how banking services contribute to the economy of a country. Encourage discussion and ask for other examples of the ways that individuals, businesses, and governments use banking services.

Savings and Loan Associations

Traditionally, a savings and loan association (S&L) specialized in savings accounts and making loans for home mortgages. Deregulation in the 1980s allowed these institutions to expand the array of services they could offer. They have become more like banks. Today, many S&Ls use the words *savings bank* in their names.

Mutual Savings Banks A *mutual savings bank* is a savings bank that is owned by, and operated for the benefit of, its depositors. The profits are distributed in proportion to the amount of business each participant does with the company. While a mutual savings bank provides a variety of services, it is organized mainly for savings and home loans. Mutual savings banks are located mainly in the northeastern United States.

Credit Unions A user-owned, not-for-profit, cooperative financial institution is called a **credit union**. People in the same company, government agency, labor union, or profession often form credit unions. Serving members only, credit unions accept savings deposits and make loans for a variety of purposes. When people deposit money in a credit union, they become members because deposits are considered partial ownership in the credit union. Today, credit unions also offer a wide range of financial services. The National Credit Union Administration (NCUA), a federal agency, regulates these financial institutions.

Non-Deposit Financial Institutions

The other major category of financial institutions is *non-deposit institutions* or *non-depository intermediaries*. They do not take or hold deposits. They earn their money selling specific services or policies.

Life Insurance Companies People commonly buy life insurance to provide financial security for their dependents. Besides protection, many life insurance companies also offer financial services such as investments. Through careful investing in new and existing companies, life insurance companies help to expand business in the economy.

Investment Companies People can choose investment opportunities for long-term growth of their money through investment companies. Many investors own shares of one of the more than 60,000 mutual funds worldwide. Investment companies make these mutual funds available.

Consumer Finance Companies A business that specializes in making loans for long-lasting or durable goods, such as cars and refrigerators, and for financial emergencies is a consumer finance company. Because consumer finance companies make loans, they are a part of the financial services industry. Unlike banks and other financial institutions, consumer finance companies do not accept savings deposits.

What is unique about a credit union?

TEACH

Describe the services provided by savings and loan associations, mutual savings banks, and credit unions. Ask students to describe their experiences with various financial institutions.

Explain how non-deposit financial institutions differ from deposit institutions.

Contrast the services offered by life insurance companies, investment companies, and consumer finance companies.

THINK CRITICALLY THROUGH VISUALS

Unlike banks, credit unions are user-owned, not-for-profit, cooperative financial institutions that serve members only.

Applied Skills

Communication Have students create a poster or computer presentation to communicate the various types of financial institutions used by consumers. Consider allowing students to work in pairs.

TEACH

Caution students about using check-cashing outlets and pawnshops. Also warn students about the high costs of payday loan companies and rent-to-own businesses.

ONGOING ASSESSMENT

checkpoint >> **ANSWER**

Examples of non-deposit financial institutions include life insurance companies, investment companies, consumer finance companies, mortgage companies, check-cashing outlets, and pawnshops.

THINK CRITICALLY THROUGH VISUALS

Banks are safe places for valuables because their well-guarded vaults provide more security than a home. Most bank deposits are insured up to $100,000 by the Federal Deposit Insurance Corporation (FDIC).

TEACH

Provide an overview of the factors to consider when selecting a financial institution.

Explain the major services offered by various financial institutions.

Point out the main function of the Federal Deposit Insurance Corporation.

main idea

Discuss factors for selecting a financial institution.

Mortgage Companies Buying a home is an important activity in society. Mortgage companies, along with other financial institutions, provide loans for buying a home or other real estate.

Check-Cashing Outlets People who do not have bank accounts may use check-cashing outlets (CCOs) to cash paychecks and to obtain other financial services. CCOs offer a wide range of services such as electronic tax filing, money orders, private postal boxes, utility bill payment, and the sale of bus and subway tokens. Some services provided at a CCO are more expensive than at other businesses.

Pawnshops Pawnshops make loans based on the value of some tangible object, such as jewelry or other valuable items. Pawnshops commonly charge higher fees than other financial institutions and should usually be avoided.

checkpoint >>

What are some examples of non-deposit financial institutions?

Why is a bank a safe place for your valuables? Are there any risks?

© Getty Images/PhotoDisc

SELECTING A FINANCIAL INSTITUTION

To obtain the best value for your financial services dollar, comparison shop. You should think about the services offered, safety, convenience, fees and charges, and restrictions.

Services Offered

As financial institutions offer additional financial services, your choices may become confusing. There are four basic types of banking services you will use.

1. Savings accounts
2. Checking and payment accounts
3. Loans and other credit plans
4. Other services, such as safe-deposit boxes and investment advice

As you work through the marketplace maze, it is important for you to determine which banking services meet your needs. Do not be attracted by fancy financial product names or flashy services that you might never need or use.

Safety

The federal agency that helps to regulate banks and other financial institutions is the **Federal Deposit Insurance Corporation (FDIC)**. It protects depositors' money in case of the failure of a bank or financial institution that it regulates. The FDIC insures all accounts in the same name at each bank up

---

Different Learning Abilities

Limited English Proficiency (LEP) Obtain translations for the list of financial services presented on this page. Use these translations to reinforce these concepts in both English and other dominant languages used by students. Some banks provide brochures about services in several languages, and many banks offer a Spanish-language version of their web site.

to an amount of $100,000. Although the FDIC is a government agency, banks provide money for its operation. Almost 99 percent of all banks are FDIC members.

The National Credit Union Administration (NCUA) regulates credit unions. NCUA insures a depositor's funds, up to $100,000, through its National Credit Union Share Insurance Fund. Some state-chartered credit unions use a private insurance program. Recently, the FDIC and the NCUA increased deposit coverage for certain types of retirement accounts from $100,000 to $250,000.

Although most banks and financial institutions have federal deposit insurance, do not assume that this is the case at every financial institution. Make sure the institution where you keep your savings is insured.

Convenience

Do you want 24-hour banking services? Do you want branch offices near your home or work? These are some of the factors you will need to think about as you decide about convenience. There is usually a trade-off. While more convenience may mean higher costs, in recent years online banking has resulted in lower costs for many consumers.

Fees and Charges

Financial services have costs. Compare your needs with the price you pay. Remember, seemingly low fees for using an ATM or having a checking account can add up to hundreds of dollars in a short time.

Restrictions

Costs are not always measured in dollars. If you must keep $500 on deposit to get "free" checking you may be losing the chance to earn interest on those funds at another institution.

If you must keep money on deposit for two years to earn a higher rate, you are restricted from using those funds for some unplanned purpose. Always balance your needs with the conditions imposed upon you. When you are not satisfied, shop around!

checkpoint >>
What factors should be considered when selecting a financial institution?

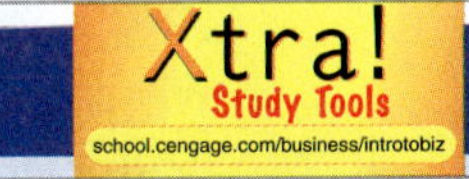

17-1 Assessment

Key Concepts

Determine the best answer.

1. The financial institution most likely to charge the highest rate for a loan would be a
   a. bank
   b. pawnshop
   c. credit union
   d. mortgage company

2. If deposit insurance is most important to you when selecting a financial institution, you are most concerned with
   a. safety
   b. convenience
   c. services
   d. fees

Make Academic Connections

3. **Research** Conduct library and online research about the Federal Reserve System. When and why did it start? What are the main responsibilities of the Fed?

4. **Technology** Visit the web site of the Federal Deposit Insurance Corporation to obtain current information on deposit insurance. What other information on the FDIC web site would be of value to consumers?

TEACH

Describe the insurance coverage available for savings accounts through the FDIC and the NCUA.

Ask students to name actions that might be taken to reduce the fees paid for various financial services.

ONGOING ASSESSMENT

checkpoint >> **ANSWER**

Factors to consider when shopping for a financial institution include the services offered, safety, convenience, fees and charges, and restrictions.

ASSESS

Key Concepts Answers

1. b. pawnshop
2. a. safety

Make Academic Connections

3. The Federal Reserve System was created in 1913 to provide a safer, more flexible, and more stable monetary and financial system. The main responsibilities of the Fed are to conduct monetary policy, supervise and regulate the banking industry, and provide financial service to depository institutions.

4. Findings will vary. The FDIC web site includes information, alerts, and advice for consumers. The site has information about specific topics such as identity theft and privacy.

RETEACH

Review the main functions of the Federal Reserve System.

CLOSE

Ask students to name the main types of financial institutions.

ENRICH

Have students describe situations when a person might use various non-deposit financial institutions.

Financial Services and Electronic Banking

TEACH

Ask students to name various financial services that they or family members use.

Provide an overview of the purpose of savings and payment services.

THINK CRITICALLY THROUGH VISUALS

To reduce or eliminate bank fees, shop for banks with the lowest fees, use only ATMs affiliated with your bank that charge no fees or, if this is not possible, use ATMs only in emergencies.

Goals

Identify the financial services used by consumers.

Explain types of checking accounts.

Describe electronic banking activities.

Key Terms

safe-deposit box

service charge

debit card

Focus on Real Life

"Sixteen dollars for cash machine fees!" exclaimed Hans George as he opened his bank statement. "I guess the cost of those cash withdrawals adds up fast!"

Hans George has a routine of using his cash card at an automatic teller machine several times a week. He really likes the convenience of obtaining cash.

Hans also finds that when getting cash is easy, he easily overspends. While automatic teller machines are convenient and easy to use, you must also consider fees and the potential for impulse buying. In recent years, cash machine fees have risen from nothing to $1 or $2 per withdrawal.

How much can cash machine transaction fees cost? If you have two $1 transaction fees a week, you will pay $104 in fees over a year.

---

main idea

Identify the financial services used by consumers.

TYPES OF FINANCIAL SERVICES

A financial institution can provide services for various personal and business activities. The services you use depend on your needs.

Savings Services

Safe storage of funds for future use is a common need. One of the main services that financial institutions offer is accepting money from customers for safekeeping. A range of savings plans is available for this purpose.

Payment Services

The ability to transfer money to others is necessary for daily business activities. Types of payment services include checking accounts, debit cards, online payments and automatic withdrawals.

What can you do to reduce or eliminate bank fees?

Different Learning Styles

Auditory Learner Encourage students to review the types of financial services discussed on pages 428–430 by listening to a partner read aloud. Suggest that students listen without taking notes.

Lending Services

Most people, businesses, and governments borrow money at some time. A business may want to borrow money to build a new warehouse or buy products to resell. Individuals may borrow to buy a car or pay college tuition. Banks make loans because most of their income is from the interest they charge borrowers.

Banks offer many types of lending services. These include auto loans, business loans, and mortgages. Credit cards allow a person to buy items without having the cash. When paying with a bank credit card, you are borrowing money from the bank.

Another way that banks lend money is by sending several checks with a customer's credit card statement. This allows the customer to use one of the checks to obtain cash or to pay a bill. If the customer uses the checks, the bank charges the amount of each check to the customer's credit card account. In effect, the amount of the check is a loan.

Electronic Banking

Electronic funds transfer (EFT) refers to the use of computers and other technology for banking activities. Electronic banking services include the use of automated teller

The future of banking includes expanded services available through online sources. As a team, create a written description of ways in which banks will offer savings, loans, and other financial services online.

Technology in Action

Biometric Banking

"Place your finger on scanner to authorize payment." This is an example of biometry at work in the real world. Biometry is the analysis of biological observations, and its use in identification is not new. For centuries, scars, complexion, eye color, and height have been used to identify people. Today, technology known as biometrics allows banking and other security activities based on physical features.

Fingerprint Verification Bank of America created a program to use a person's fingerprint to give individuals access to their online banking services. Law enforcement agencies have long used fingerprint identification techniques. For banking, a chip is used to store a customer's fingerprint. A payment or funds transfer is authorized when the customer places a finger on a small scanner.

Iris Scanning The pattern of every iris is unique. Scanning the characteristics of your eyeball may someday be used as a bank account password or to allow access to your computer. Today's technology includes cameras that can scan an iris from a distance of two or three feet.

Voice Recognition Customers at the American Savings Bank in Hawaii no longer have to enter a number to access their account. Using a voice-activated response system, customers are able to obtain an account balance or make a money transfer.

Hand Geometry Instead of tapping out a password on a keypad or swiping a card, hand geometry is used to measure physical characteristics of the hand or fingers. Using a three-dimensional view, this technology allows workers to access a secure area and may be used in the future to permit banking transactions.

Face Recognition The Mr. Payroll face recognition system uses machines to compare two images of the face to authorize check cashing.

Think Critically

1. What concerns might be associated with biometric banking activities?
2. Conduct an Internet search to obtain additional information on new technology currently being used in banking transactions. Choose one technology and write a short report.

Encourage students to think of ways to use existing and future technology for delivering additional types of online banking services.

TEACH

Have students name reasons that individuals, businesses, and governments use lending services.

Provide an overview of the main electronic banking services.

Technology in Action

This feature discusses several technological innovations using body parts for banking and other security systems.

Think Critically
Answers

1. Answers will vary. Privacy, personal information, and potential computer crime issues may be mentioned.

2. Reports will vary.

Applied Skills

Technology Have students create a flowchart to explain various components and movement of funds for several electronic banking services. Ask a group of volunteers to share their findings with the class.

machines (ATM), point-of-sale transactions, direct deposit, and automatic bill payment. Online computer banking allows a customer to access many financial services.

Storage of Valuables

Banks offer **safe-deposit boxes** for storage of valuables. Because these safe-deposit boxes are in well-guarded vaults, they are very safe places to keep jewelry, rare coins, investment certificates, birth records, a list of insurance policies, and other valuable documents.

Only you or someone to whom you have given the right to open the box may open it. Not even a bank has the right to open your safe-deposit box unless it is ordered to do so by a court. You rent safe-deposit boxes by the year. They come in a variety of sizes.

Investment Advice

Many financial institutions help customers by offering financial advice and investment services. Banks can assist customers with decisions about buying a home, offer tips on money management, and help customers exchange U.S. funds for foreign currency.

Most banks offer advice on investments. This involves savings that are put to work to earn more money. Types of investments include government bonds, stocks, and mutual funds.

Management of Trusts

Many banks manage investments on behalf of customers. When they do this, the money or other property that is turned over for the bank to manage is said to be held in *trust*. This service can be offered through a trust company or through trust departments in banks.

Trusts are used by people of all ages. They are especially useful for very young people and for some elderly people. A young person who inherits money may not have the skill and experience to manage it wisely. Elderly people who are ill may ask the trust department of a bank to manage

their money. The bank makes investments and keeps the customers informed about what is happening to their money.

> *checkpoint* >>
> What are the main financial services used by consumers?

TYPES OF CHECKING ACCOUNTS

While checking accounts vary from one bank to another, three types are most common.

Regular Checking Accounts

If you write a lot of checks each month, consider a regular checking account. A **service charge** is a fee a bank charges for handling a checking account. With most banks, there is no service charge for a regular checking account as long as you maintain a certain minimum balance. This amount varies and is often $300 or higher.

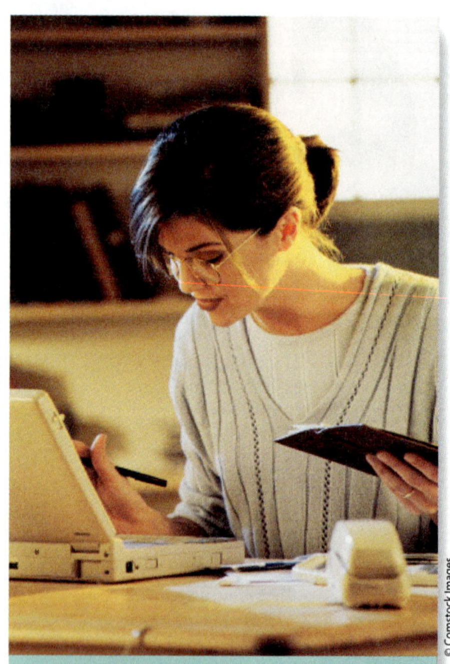

How does online banking make managing your checking account and paying bills more convenient?

main idea

Explain types of checking accounts.

A checking account at a credit union may be called a *share draft* account because the members are called *shareholders*.

Interest-Earning Checking Accounts

Many financial institutions offer checking accounts that earn interest. These accounts may require a higher monthly balance than regular checking accounts. If the account falls below the required amount, the bank usually pays no interest and may add a service charge.

The rates of interest that banks pay their customers also vary. Usually, a bank will offer a higher rate of interest when a higher balance is kept in the account. Very often, interest rates on checking accounts are quite low. When you are depositing larger amounts of money, consider other savings alternatives.

Special Checking Accounts

If you only write a few checks each month, consider a *special checking account*. Also called *activity* accounts, banks charge customers about 10 to 20 cents for each check written. A monthly service charge may also be added.

Comparing Checking Accounts

When selecting a checking account, evaluate the following items.

- Minimum balance
- Interest rate earned, if any
- Monthly service charge
- Fees for other services, such as printing checks and stop payment orders
- Other restrictions

When choosing a checking account, be careful. A bank may attract you with a low minimum balance, but fees can result in a higher total cost.

> *checkpoint* >>
> What are three main types of checking accounts?

ELECTRONIC BANKING

Each day, the use of electronic banking services expands. You can do your banking from an ATM, from a home computer, or from a wireless Internet connection on your cell phone.

E-Banking Services

Over the years, banks have expanded their hours of operation to meet the demands of their customers. Traditional "banker's

main idea

Describe electronic banking activities.

Examples of Electronic Banking Activities				
	ATM ACTIVITIES	PREAUTHORIZED ACTIVITIES	ONLINE ACTIVITIES	POINT-OF-SALE ACTIVITIES
Check account balances	✓		✓	
Withdraw cash	✓			
Make deposits	✓			
Transfer funds	✓		✓	
View account history			✓	
Pay bills			✓	
Apply for loans			✓	
Manage investments			✓	
Accept direct deposits		✓		
Pay bills automatically		✓		
Make debit card purchases				✓

FIGURE 17-3

Has electronic banking made it easier for you to manage your finances? Explain your answer.

TEACH

Explain the features of interest-earning and special checking accounts.

Provide an overview of the main factors to consider when comparing checking accounts.

ONGOING ASSESSMENT

checkpoint >> ANSWER

Three main types of checking accounts are (1) regular checking accounts, (2) interest-earning checking accounts, and (3) special checking accounts.

TEACH

Use Figure 17-3 to provide an overview of electronic banking services.

FIGURE 17-3 ANSWER

Answers will vary. Students might mention the convenience of getting cash from an ATM or checking account balances online. Some students might report that they like having paychecks and tax refunds deposited directly to their accounts.

Different Learning Styles

Kinesthetic Learner Have students work in pairs to demonstrate electronic banking services described on pages 431 and 432. Encourage them to create scenarios to explain how and why a person would use e-banking services.

TEACH

Explain the various components of electronic banking: ATMs, point-of-sale payments, direct deposit, and automatic bill payments.

Ask students whether people are writing fewer checks than a few years ago. Point out that debit card transactions and online payments are being used instead of checks in many situations.

NET Bookmark

Many types of banking services are available from many types of financial institutions. Access the web site shown below and click on the link for Chapter 17. Access the "Checking and ATM" section. What information is available to help consumers select a checking account when using electronic banking services?

school.cengage.com/business/introtobiz

hours" of 9 a.m. to 3 p.m. are a thing of the past. Banks have evening and weekend hours, ATM machines dispense cash 24 hours a day, and e-banking services are available any time of the day or night. Figure 17-3, on page 431, illustrates some common electronic banking services.

Automatic Teller Machines Commonly called a *cash machine*, an automatic teller machine (ATM) allows many banking services. The most common use of an ATM is withdrawing cash from a bank account or getting a cash advance from a credit card. Bank customers also can use ATMs to check account balances, make deposits, or transfer funds from one account to another.

A **debit card**, or *cash card*, is used for ATM transactions. A debit card is different from a *credit card*. With a debit card issued by your bank, you are using money that is in your account. With a credit card, you are borrowing from the bank to pay later.

A lost or stolen debit card can be expensive. If you notify the financial institution within two days of the lost card, your liability for unauthorized use is $50. After that, you can be liable for up to $500 of unauthorized use for up to 60 days.

ATM services have expanded to provide other types of transactions. You can use these machines to buy bus passes, postage stamps, and gift certificates.

Be aware that many banks charge fees for ATM usage. To minimize ATM fees, compare rates at several financial institutions. Use your bank's ATMs to avoid surcharges. Withdraw larger amounts to avoid fees on several small transactions.

Payments at the Point-of-Sale In a *point-of-sale transaction*, a merchant accepts a debit card to pay for purchases. Most gas stations, stores, and restaurants accept this type of payment. Vending machines that accept debit cards are also becoming more common.

Direct Deposit A major portion of society uses *direct deposit* of paychecks and government payments. Funds are deposited electronically and available automatically for your use.

Automatic Bill Payments Each month, many people pay their rent, mortgage, loans, utilities, and other bills without doing anything. *Automatic bill payment* requires a bank customer to authorize preset amounts of monthly expenses. The bank deducts the payments from your account and transfers them to the appropriate companies. With automatic bill payments, be sure to check each month that the correct amounts have been deducted.

Electronic Payment Options

The use of cash, checks, and credit cards is declining. These payment methods are being replaced by newer electronic alternatives.

Debit Card Transactions Most stores, restaurants, and other businesses accept debit cards issued by Visa and MasterCard. You may also know these cards as *check cards*. When the debit card transaction is processed, the amount of the purchase is deducted from your checking account.

Online Payments Various Web companies and banks now provide online bill payment services between buyers and

Different Learning Abilities

Gifted Encourage students to obtain additional information about technology and government regulations for electronic banking. Invite interested students to prepare a display or presentation based on their research.

sellers. When using these services, be sure to think about the monthly charge as well as online security and customer service availability.

Also on the Web are "cybercash" or "e-cash" services designed to serve as financial intermediates. These organizations create their own *e-money* that serves as a medium of exchange for online transactions.

Stored-Value Cards The gift card your aunt sent you for your birthday is a stored-value card. Prepaid cards for phone service, transit fares, highway tolls, and school lunches are common. Some stored-value cards are disposable. Others can be reloaded with additional funds. Some employers use prepaid cards instead of paper paychecks to help employees avoid check-cashing fees. Employees can use the cards to make purchases and to withdraw cash at ATM machines.

Smart Cards These "electronic wallets" are similar to ATM cards. Their imbedded microchip stores prepaid amounts as well as account balances, transaction records, insurance information, and medical history.

Mobile payment systems through cell phones and other wireless devices are expanding. This usually occurs through an existing bank account. Most banking activities accessed by computers soon also will be able to occur via cell phone. In the future, transactions may bypass banks and appear as charges on your phone bill.

Banking in the Future

The way you use banks and money will continue to change. Electronic financial services will be combined with wireless technology. You will be able to do almost any transaction away from the financial institution.

An access card or a handheld device will provide a large number of services. The technology will create a personalized system for obtaining, transferring, and using funds. Expanded information related to financial activities, health care, education, careers, travel, and recreation will also be a key element.

checkpoint >>
What are common electronic banking services?

17-2 Assessment

Xtra!
Study Tools
school.cengage.com/business/introtobiz

Key Concepts

Determine the best answer.

1. True or False. Using a debit card is similar to writing a check.

2. True or False. Automatic payments are made through automatic teller machines.

3. True or False. If you write only a few checks each month you should consider a regular checking account.

Make Academic Connections

4. **Visual Communication** Conduct a survey of 20 students to determine the types of financial services they use. Create a table or graph to report your findings.

5. **Technology** Locate examples of online payment services and "cybercash" companies. What services are provided? What concerns might be associated with these services?

TEACH

Discuss the features benefits associated with online payments, stored-value cards, and smart cards.

Use the FYI feature to explain new payment options.

ONGOING ASSESSMENT

checkpoint >> **ANSWER**

Common electronic banking services include automatic teller machines (ATMs), point-of-sale payments, direct deposit, and automatic bill payments. E-banking also includes electronic payment options such as debit card transactions, online payments, stored-value cards, and smart cards.

ASSESS

Key Concepts Answers

1. True

2. False. A bank deducts an automatic payment from a customer's account and transfers the money to the appropriate company to pay the customer's bill.

3. False. If you write many checks each month you should consider a regular checking account.

Make Academic Connections

4. Tables and graphs will vary.

5. Answers will vary. Services mentioned may include sending money, paying for goods and services, and collecting payments from buyers. Concerns may include identity theft, fraud, and phishing.

RETEACH

List the major services provided by financial institutions.

ENRICH

Have students describe situations that illustrate how consumers use various banking services.

CLOSE

Explain actions that might be taken to reduce the fees and charges for various financial services.

While many attempts have been made to improve economic development in poor countries, few have been successful. The use of microlending has been of value in various settings.

Think Critically Answers

1. Microfinance programs allow very low-income people who have no access to formal financial institutions to generate enough income to provide for life's necessities and family needs. By providing affordable loans, microfinance programs improve the economy of rural areas. Some microfinance programs have expanded to provide other financial services, such as savings accounts and insurance coverage, thus helping borrowers build assets and protect against risks.

2. If a microfinance program is too successful, it could supplant traditional banking companies. Unscrupulous operators of microfinance programs could cheat poverty-stricken clients more easily than affluent clients.

3. Students will search the Internet for more examples of microfinance programs around the world.

Microfinance

How could a loan of $50 result in a life-changing experience? In countries such as Bangladesh, Nepal, the Philippines, and Zimbabwe, microfinance has helped improve the economy and society.

Microfinance, also called microlending and microcredit, involves programs of small loans to people for self-employment projects. The resulting business activities generate enough income to provide for life necessities and family needs. Most microcredit efforts involve nonprofit organizations, which helps avoid political influences.

Most microfinance clients have little income and no access to formal financial institutions. They are usually self-employed, household-based entrepreneurs. In rural areas, clients are small farmers or food-processing workers. In urban areas, microfinance clients include shopkeepers, service providers, artisans, and street vendors.

In southeastern Bangladesh, one of the poorest regions in the world, BRAC (formerly the Bangladesh Rural Advancement Committee) helps women obtain loans. Loans help them farm fish, keep cows for milk production, grow vegetables, raise poultry, buy rickshaws, and sew clothing. The women pay 15 percent simple interest on loans, which is much less than they would have to pay to loan sharks. The banking is done in the village through an agent of the microfinance institution. Loans are not secured through collateral. Repayment is made in 52 weekly installments in a year's time, and simple interest is used rather than compound interest.

BRAC also works to improve the health of women and children. More than 30,000 volunteers have been trained by BRAC to recognize and treat 10 common illnesses such as anemia, diarrhea, ringworm, and scabies.

The success of microfinance is not limited to Bangladesh. Organizations around the world provide affordable financing to improve the economy of rural areas. Using a model similar to the one used by BRAC, an organization offers a small inexpensive loan to help an entrepreneur start or grow a small business. Income generated by the business is then used to cover living expenses, operate the business, and repay the loan.

Over time, some microfinance programs have expanded to include other financial services. In addition to loans, savings accounts and insurance coverage may be provided. These services help borrowers build assets and protect against risks.

Think Critically

1. What are the main benefits of microfinance programs?
2. What are some possible concerns of microfinance?
3. Conduct an Internet search to find other examples of microfinance around the world.

Applied Skills

Culture Have students talk to people who have lived in or visited other countries. How do people's attitudes and behaviors differ regarding the use of banking services?

Goals

Describe three main types of endorsements.

Describe proper check-writing procedures.

Explain the bank reconciliation process.

Identify other payment methods.

Key Terms

endorsement

check register

stop payment order

bank statement

bank reconciliation

outstanding checks

Focus on Real Life

Alicia Garcia made her first deposit in her new checking account. Her friend Joni asked her, "If I write you a check, could you give me the cash? You can deposit my check in your account later."

"How do I know your check is good?" Alicia asked.

"What! We've been friends for more than 10 years," Joni responded. "Don't you trust me?"

"Of course I trust you," said Alicia. "Just remember that if a check isn't good, it can result in some expensive service fees."

The next day, Laura came up to Alicia and said, "I can't wait to send away for this sweater, but the ad says 'no personal checks.' How can I pay for it?"

"Let me tell you about money orders," responded Alicia.

OPENING A CHECKING ACCOUNT

The following are some of the benefits that checking accounts provide for consumers.

- Convenience and ease of making payments

- Safety to make payments with less risk than using cash

- Proof of payment

- A record of finances for managing your money

The First Deposit

Opening a checking account starts with signing a *signature card*. This document is used to verify your signature. The bank compares the signature on checks to the one on the signature card. A sample signature card is shown in Figure 17-4.

Sometimes two or more people have an account together called a *joint account*. Each person who will write checks on the account must sign the signature card. Any signer of the card in a joint account can write checks on

> **main idea**
>
> Describe three main types of endorsements.

Signature Card

Second National Bank
PERSONAL CHECKING ACCOUNT

○ JOINT AND SEVERAL (Payable to the order of either or the survivor)
● INDIVIDUAL (If payable on death to named survivors, fill in section below)
___ Indicate number of signatures required

SIGNATURE: *Alicia Garcia*

SIGNATURE:

PRINT OR TYPE NAME(S)
Alicia Garcia   or
ADDRESS: 19684 Absaroka Dr., Houston, TX 77083-5549   CITY AND STATE   ZIP CODE
HOME PHONE: 555-6403
HOW LONG? MO. YRS.: 2 years
DRIVERS LICENSE NO./STATE: 720J64—TX

PAYABLE ON DEATH OF DEPOSITOR TO SUCH OF THE FOLLOWING NAMED AS SURVIVE DEPOSITOR:

(PRINT OR TYPE NAME — DESIGNATION BY OTHER MEANS IS NOT SUFFICIENT.)
Office: ___   Date: April 10, 20--

OFFICER APPROVAL

SOCIAL SECURITY NUMBER: 201-24-1590

ACCOUNT NUMBER: 1648-7214

FIGURE 17-4

Do you understand how a signature card protects you and the bank?

Focus on Real Life

This situation can be used to discuss some of the activities involved with checking accounts.

TEACH

Explain the main benefits of checking accounts. Use Figure 17-4 to point out the actions required to open a checking account.

FIGURE 17-4   *ANSWER*

A signature card protects account holders and the bank by giving the bank a way to verify that checks are signed by the account holders and not by imposters.

Different Learning Abilities

At-Risk Explain the importance of understanding checking account and other financial services. Ask students to name situations in which these services would be needed.

the account as if he or she were the only owner.

When you deposit money in a checking account, you fill out a *deposit slip*. This form lists all items you are depositing—currency, coins, or checks. The deposit slip shows your name, account number, the date, the items deposited, and the total amount of the deposit.

Types of Endorsements

Before you can deposit a check, it must be endorsed. This involves writing your name on the back of the left end of the check. An **endorsement** is written evidence that you received payment or that you transferred your right of receiving payment to someone else.

When you endorse a check, your responsibilities are almost as great as if you had written the check yourself. As an endorser, you are actually making this promise: "If this check is not paid by the bank, I will pay it."

Your endorsement must be made in the 1½-inch space on the left side of the check. If you write outside this limit, the bank may return the check. Different endorsements have different purposes. Figure 17-5 shows some examples.

Blank Endorsement An endorsement that consists of only the endorser's name is a *blank endorsement*. To endorse a check, sign your name in ink exactly as it is written on the face of the check. If the name on the check is different from your official signature, you will need to endorse the check twice. First, use the name as given on the check. Then, write your name as it appears on the account.

A blank endorsement makes a check payable to anyone who has the check. While you can use this endorsement to transfer any check, sometimes another type of endorsement is better.

FIGURE 17-5

Describe the benefits of each type of endorsement.

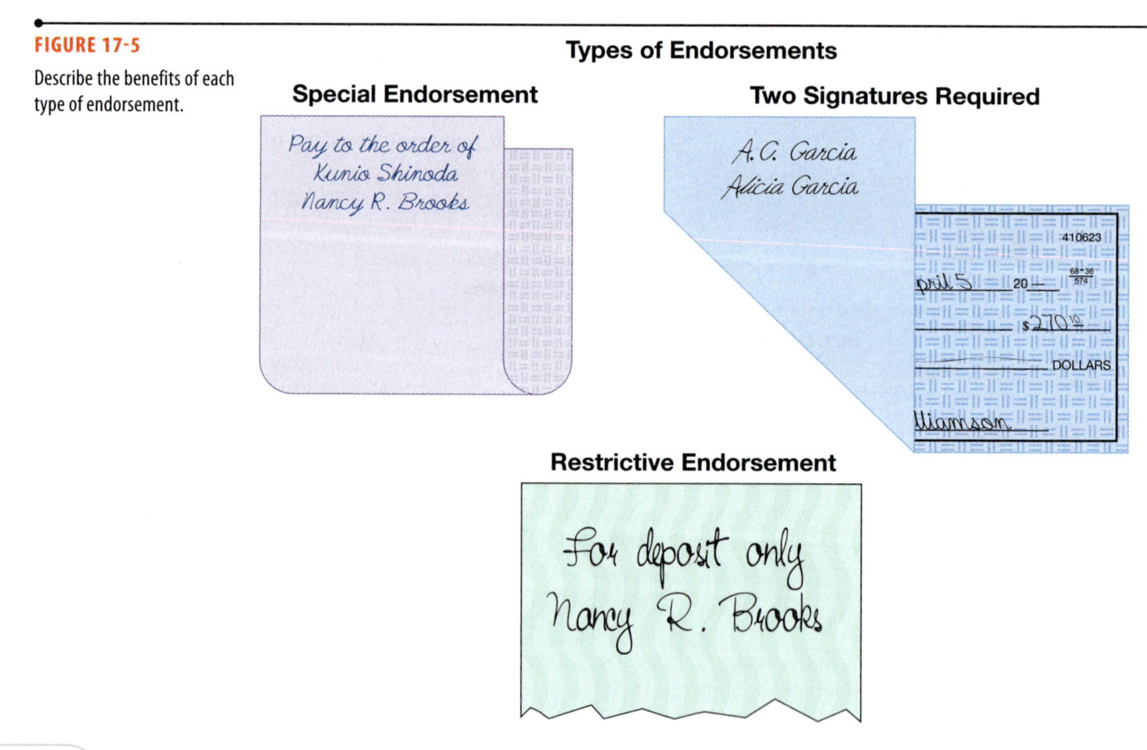

Full Endorsement The use of a *full endorsement*, also called a *special endorsement*, allows you to transfer a check to another person. You write the words "Pay to the order of…" followed by the name of the person or business to which the check is being transferred. This is followed by your signature. This phrasing results in only the specified person being able to sign and cash the check.

Restrictive Endorsement A *restrictive endorsement* limits the use of the check to the purpose given in the endorsement. For example, you may have several checks that you want to mail to the bank. You could write "For deposit only" above your signature, followed by your account number. This endorsement restricts use of the check so it can only be deposited to your account.

> *checkpoint* »
> What are the three types of endorsements?

USING A CHECKING ACCOUNT

Checking accounts are an easy way to access funds. Still, to use a checking account correctly, you must understand certain information and follow some simple procedures.

Check-Writing Procedures

Some checks are light blue or green in color. Others have a picture of a forest, a sports team logo, or an inspirational quote. No matter what they look like, all checks contain essentially the same information.

Elements of a Check Figure 17-6 shows some terms that are used to identify the parts of a check. Three parties are shown on each check.

- The *drawer* is the owner of the account who signs the check.
- The *payee* is the person to whom the check is written.

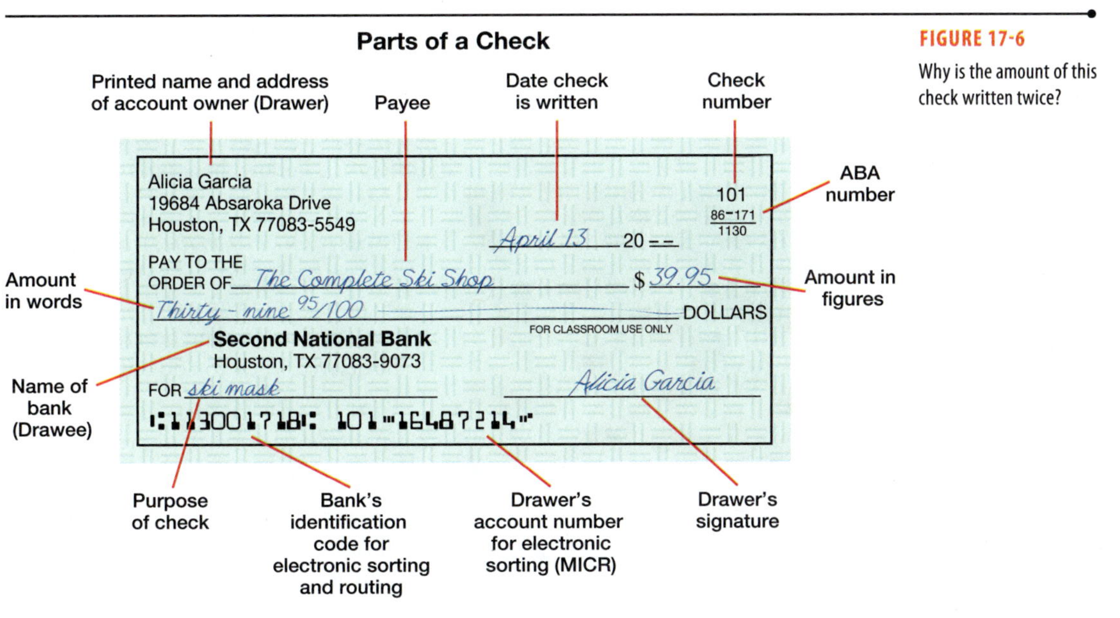

Parts of a Check

FIGURE 17-6

Why is the amount of this check written twice?

Different Learning Styles

Tactile Learner Use samples of checks to allow students to practice correctly writing checks for various payment situations. Have students also practice endorsing the backs of the sample checks.

TEACH

Explain the importance of a check register. Also describe how a check stub and duplicate check copy serve a similar purpose.

Highlight the steps for writing a check. Ask students to name various errors that might be made when writing a check.

THINK CRITICALLY THROUGH VISUALS

Checks must be filled out properly because they are legal documents. Carefully filling out a check also ensures that the bank can process it correctly.

Work as a Team

Many people carelessly write checks, making it easy for others to alter the checks. Review the steps for proper check writing and discuss the importance of each item. Write a list of common errors of check writing and what problems might occur.

- The *drawee* is the bank or other financial institution that pays the check.

The Check Register Your checkbook will have a place for recording account activities. One of three formats may be used for this purpose. The *check stub* is a form attached to the check by a perforated line. A **check register** is a separate book, usually the same size as the checkbook. Note that both forms provide blanks to fill in the same type of information about the check. A *duplicate copy* of the check may also be automatically created when you write the check.

Always fill out the stub or register first. If you write the check first, you may forget to record the information before you transfer the check.

Writing a Check Fill out the check completely and carefully using the following seven steps.

Why is it important to fill out a check properly?

1. Write checks in order by number so you know which checks have been paid.

2. Write the date in the proper space.

3. Write the payee's name on the line following *Pay to the Order of.*

4. Write the amount of the check in figures after the printed dollar sign. Write the amount close to the dollar sign to prevent someone from altering your check. Write the cents figures close to the dollar figures so that additional numbers cannot be inserted.

5. Write the dollar amount in words on the line below the payee's name. Write the cents in figures as a fraction of a dollar. Begin writing at the far left end of the line. Draw a line from the fraction to the printed word *Dollars* to fill all unused space.

6. Write the purpose of the payment on the line at the bottom of the check.

7. Sign your checks with the same signature you wrote on your signature card.

Proper Check Writing Poor check writing can cause problems and financial difficulties. Follow these tips to avoid trouble.

1. *Write checks only on the forms provided by your bank.* Checks can be written on just about anything—even a paper bag—but sorting and processing can be delayed when you do not use the proper form.

2. *Write checks in ink.* This prevents someone from altering the amount.

3. *Only write checks if money is available.* Writing a check for more than is in your account can result in an *overdrawn account.* The bank may not pay the check and you will most likely be charged a fee.

Different Learning Styles

Visual Learner Encourage visual learners to close their eyes and mentally picture the process of writing a check. Then have them write a check using a blank sheet of paper.

4. *Use the current date.* A *postdated* check is one that is dated later than the date on which it is written. This business practice is unwise and can result in additional service charges.

5. *Avoid making checks payable to "Cash" or to "Bearer."* Such a check can be cashed by anyone. Instead, make the check out to yourself or to the bank as payee.

6. *Always fill in the amount.* If you leave it blank, you may be held responsible for amounts filled in by others.

7. *Void checks on which you make errors.* Do not try to erase or retrace your writing. Write "Void" across the check. Make note of the voided check in the check register.

8. *Record every payment from your checking account, whether the payment is by check or EFT.* Some people carry a few blank checks. When one of these checks is used, make a note of it and record it in the register. Also, promptly record all transactions made at an ATM.

Stopping Payment

In certain situations, you may not want your bank to pay a check that you have written. To do so, you will fill out a **stop payment order**, a written notice that tells the bank not to pay a certain check. Because banks charge a high fee for stopping payment on a check, use this process only for good reason. You may learn, for example, that a check you have written to pay a bill was lost in the mail. A check you have written may have been stolen. Before you write a new check, you should stop payment on the one that was lost or stolen.

checkpoint »
What is the purpose of a check register?

THE RECONCILIATION PROCESS

As a depositor, you will need to review the record of your account that the bank keeps. At regular intervals, usually monthly, the bank will send you a report on the status of your account known as a **bank statement**.

Bank Statement Information

While bank statement formats vary, most present the following information.

- The balance at the beginning of the month.
- The deposits made during the month.

How can a computer program help with reconciling your checkbook?

Explain the bank reconciliation process.

TEACH

Describe the steps for proper check writing.

Explain the purpose of a stop payment order.

ONGOING ASSESSMENT

checkpoint » **ANSWER**

The purpose of a check register is to record all account activities so that the account holder will always know the account balance. The check register is also used for reconciling a checkbook with a bank's monthly statement.

TEACH

Explain the purpose of a bank statement.

THINK CRITICALLY THROUGH VISUALS 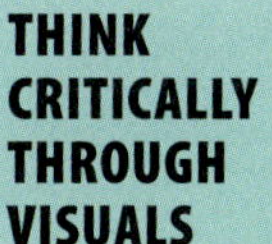 

A computer checking program can help with reconciling a checkbook by providing accurate, detailed records of all account activity.

TEACH

Use Figure 17-7 to highlight the various items reported on a bank statement. Ask students to share observations from their own bank statements.

Explain how a person might use a bank statement to serve as a proof of payment.

FIGURE 17-7 *ANSWER*

Twelve checks were paid by the bank and posted to Alicia's account.

- The checks paid by the bank during the month.
- Any automated teller transactions made during the month.
- Any electronic fund transfers (EFT) or special payments the bank has made.
- Service charges for the month, including charges for services such as stopping payment on a check.
- Any interest earned on the account.
- The balance at the end of the month.

Examples of some of these items appear on the bank statement shown in Figure 17-7.

Determine Checks Paid

When your bank statement arrives, compare the checks you wrote to those that have been paid by your bank. Banks might not return actual *canceled checks* that have been paid. Instead, banks can use a *substitute check*, which is a digital reproduction of the original paper check. In some cases banks do not return checks or provide substitute checks unless the customer requests them.

There are times when you need to show proof of a payment. In most cases, information on the statement will be sufficient to prove payment. If the check showing the endorsement is needed, a substitute check is considered a legal equivalent of the original check.

FIGURE 17-7

How many checks were paid by the bank and posted to Alicia's account?

Monthly Account Statement

Second National Bank

Checking Account Statement

ACCT. 1648-7214
DATE 5/1/- -
PAGE 1

Alicia Garcia
19684 Absaroka Drive
Houston, TX 77083-5549

Please examine at once. If no errors are reported within 10 days, account will be considered correct.

BALANCE FORWARD	NO. OF WITH- DRAWALS	TOTAL AMOUNT	NO. OF DEP.	TOTAL DEPOSIT AMOUNT	SERVICE CHARGE	BALANCE THIS STATEMENT
0 00	14	433 89	4	826 95	3 00	390 06

CHECKS AND OTHER DEBITS		DEPOSITS AND OTHER CREDITS	DATE	BALANCE
		331.85	4/10	331.85
101	39.95		4/13	291.90
102	50.00		4/15	241.90
		50.00	4/16	291.90
103	32.97		4/22	258.93
104	.87		4/22	258.06
	50.00 ATW		4/23	208.06
106*	16.30		4/24	191.76
107	25.78		4/24	165.98
		175.00	4/24	340.98
109*	65.33		4/26	275.65
110	33.46		4/27	242.19
111	24.33		4/27	217.86
112	5.80		4/27	212.06
113	12.85		4/27	199.21
		270.10 AD	4/29	469.31
114	4.25		4/30	465.06
	72.00 AP TexPower		4/30	393.06
	3.00 SC		4/30	390.06

KEY TO SYMBOLS

AD-	AUTOMATIC DEPOSIT	PC-	PAID OVERDRAFT CHARGE
AP-	AUTOMATIC PAYMENT	PR-	PAYROLL DEPOSIT
ATD-	AUTOMATIC TELLER DEPOSIT	RC-	RETURN CHECK CHARGE
ATW-	AUTOMATIC TELLER WITHDRAWAL	RT-	RETURN ITEM
CC-	CERTIFIED CHECK	SC-	SERVICE CHARGE
EC-	ERROR CORRECTED	ST-	SAVINGS TRANSFER
OD-	OVERDRAFT	TC-	TRANSFER CHARGE

*Where this asterisk is shown, a preceding check is still outstanding or has been included on a previous statement.

Different Learning Abilities

Visually Impaired Create an enlarged version of a bank statement to allow students to see the details. Consider contacting a local bank to get information about services they offer for customers with visual impairments.

Find Differences

You keep your own record of your checking account, usually in a check register. The bank statement is the bank's record of your account.

The document created to show how the two balances were brought into agreement is called the **bank reconciliation**. Bringing the balances into agreement is known as *reconciling the bank balance*. The bank often prints forms for reconciling on the backs of bank statements. Figure 17-8 shows an example of a bank reconciliation.

The balances shown on your records and the bank statement may be different. Following are some of the most common reasons for the difference.

- Some of the checks you wrote may not have *cleared* (been paid). These checks, which have not been deducted from the bank statement balance, are called **outstanding checks**.

- You may have forgotten to record a transaction in your register, such as an ATM deposit or automatic bill payment.

- A service charge may appear on the bank statement.

- You may have mailed a deposit to the bank that has not yet been received.

- Interest earned may have been added.

- You may have recorded the amount of a check incorrectly in the check register. You may have added or subtracted incorrectly.

Reconciliation Form

YOU CAN EASILY
BALANCE YOUR CHECKBOOK
BY FOLLOWING THIS PROCEDURE

FILL IN BELOW AMOUNTS FROM YOUR CHECKBOOK AND BANK STATEMENT

BALANCE SHOWN ON BANK STATEMENT	$ 390.06	
ADD DEPOSITS NOT ON STATEMENT	$	
TOTAL	$ 390.06	

SUBTRACT CHECKS ISSUED BUT NOT ON STATEMENT

108	$ 10.00
115	21.00
116	17.50

| TOTAL | $ 48.50 |
| BALANCE | $ 341.56 |

BALANCE SHOWN ON YOUR CHECKBOOK $ 416.56

ADD ANY DEPOSITS NOT ALREADY ENTERED IN CHECKBOOK $

TOTAL $ 416.56

SUBTRACT SERVICE CHARGES AND OTHER BANK CHARGES NOT IN CHECKBOOK

$ 3.00
Tex Power 72.00

| TOTAL | $ 75.00 |
| BALANCE | $ 341.56 |

THESE TOTALS REPRESENT THE CORRECT AMOUNT OF MONEY YOU HAVE IN THE BANK AND SHOULD AGREE. DIFFERENCES, IF ANY, SHOULD BE REPORTED TO THE BANK WITHIN TEN DAYS AFTER THE RECEIPT OF YOUR STATEMENT.

FIGURE 17-8

What does the $341.56 balance represent? Is it always less than the balance shown on the statement? Explain your answer.

TEACH

Ask students to describe reasons why a person's checkbook balance might differ from the bank statement. Explain the items listed on this page that could cause a difference between the checkbook balance and the bank statement.

FIGURE 17-8 *ANSWER*

The $341.56 balance represents the actual amount of cash available at this point in time, after taking into account all checks that have been written, bank fees and charges, and any errors. The balance shown at the bottom of the bank reconciliation form can be more or less than the balance shown on the statement. It would be more if there were a deposit in transit.

Applied Skills

Office Technology Explain how spreadsheet software might be used to prepare a bank reconciliation. Invite interested students to set up a spreadsheet using the numbers in Figure 17-8.

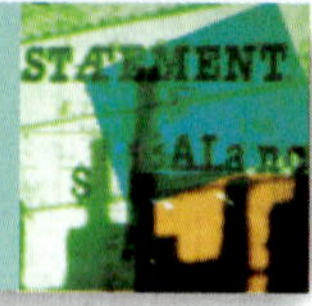

Bank statements typically include the balance at the beginning and end of the month, the deposits made and checks paid by the bank during the month, ATM transactions, EFT transfers, service charges, and any interest earned.

TEACH

Explain the calculation for completing the bank reconciliation process. Describe the actions to take if the adjusted checkbook balance and the adjusted bank balance do not agree.

ONGOING ASSESSMENT

checkpoint >> **ANSWER**

Common causes of differences between the bank statement balance and a person's check register occur because of checks that have not cleared, transactions that may not have been recorded in the check register, service charges, deposits mailed to the bank that may not have arrived by the time the statement was issued, interest earned, or transactions whose amounts were not recorded correctly.

TEACH

Describe situations in which a person might use a certified check, a cashier's check, or traveler's checks.

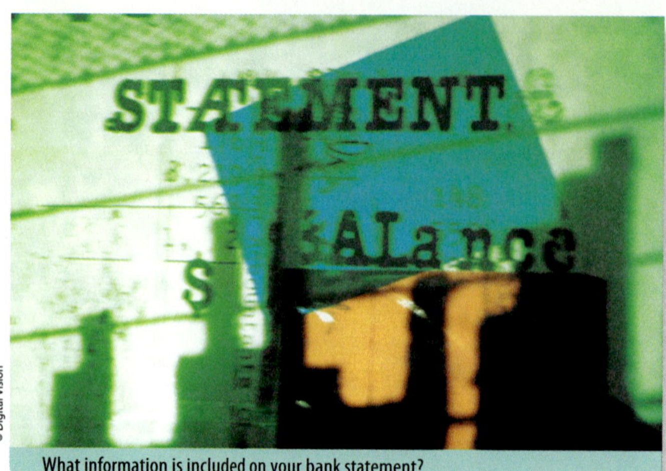

What information is included on your bank statement?

main idea

Identify other payment methods.

Calculate Adjusted Balance

To determine the true balance in your account, take the following steps.

1. Subtract the total of the outstanding checks from the bank statement balance.

2. Add any *deposits in transit* to the balance statement balance.

3. Subtract service charges, fees, and automatic payments from your checkbook balance.

4. Add any interest earned to your check register balance.

At this point, if the balances do not agree, either you or your bank has made an error. You should check each of the steps again. Then, carefully go over the calculations in your check register. If you do not find an error in your calculations, contact your bank.

After you have reconciled your bank statement, correct any errors that you made on your register. The new balance now agrees with the bank statement. With your account updated, you can write checks on the new balance.

OTHER TYPES OF PAYMENTS

Often, you might need to make a payment in a situation when a personal check is not acceptable. Several payment alternatives are available.

Certified Checks

A *certified check* is a personal check for which a bank has guaranteed payment. The certification is stamped on the face of the check and is signed or initialed by a bank officer.

Cashier's Checks

A bank usually keeps funds in an account of its own on which it writes its own checks. A *cashier's check* is a check that a bank draws on its own funds. A cashier's check costs the amount of the check plus a service fee. These banker's checks are more acceptable than the personal checks of an individual whom the payee may not know.

Traveler's Checks

Carrying a large sum of money when you travel is risky. In addition paying traveling expenses with personal checks may be difficult. *Traveler's checks* are special forms designed for making payments when away from home. You can buy them at banks, credit unions, and travel bureaus. Traveler's checks are sold in several denominations such as $10, $20, $50, and $100. In addition to the value of the checks, a fee of 1 percent may be charged. This means that $100 worth of traveler's checks will cost $101.

Traveler's checks require your signature in two places. First, you sign each one when

---

Different Learning Styles

Kinesthetic Learner Invite students to create a short presentation about one of the payment methods mentioned on page 442 and 443. Encourage students to include examples of situations where the payment method might be used. Consider allowing students to work in pairs.

they are bought. Then, when you cash a check or pay for a purchase with it, you sign it again in the presence of the person accepting it. Businesses throughout the world commonly accept traveler's checks.

Money Orders

A person who does not have a checking account and wants to send a payment through the mail may purchase a money order. A *money order* is a form of payment that orders the issuing agency to pay the amount printed on the form to another party.

Several types of organizations commonly sell money orders.

- A *bank money order* is sold by a bank stating that money is to be paid to a specific person or business.

- A *postal money order* purchased from the U.S. Post Office can be sent safely through the mail. It can be cashed only after the payee signs it.

- An *express money order* is issued by various organizations including traveler's check companies, travel agencies, and many supermarkets, pharmacies, and convenience stores.

- A *telegraphic money order* involves buying a message to direct a telegraph office to pay a sum of money to a certain person or business.

If a money order is lost or stolen, the receipt copy that you receive may be used in making a claim.

FYI

The Check Clearing for the 21st Century Act (known as Check 21) shortens the processing time of checks using electronic systems. The actual paper check will no longer be processed.

> *checkpoint* >>
> How does a certified check differ from a cashier's check?

17-3 Assessment

Xtra! Study Tools
school.cengage.com/business/introtobiz

Key Concepts

Determine the best answer.

1. The first document that must be completed when opening a checking account is the
   a. deposit slip
   b. reconciliation statement
   c. check register
   d. signature card

2. A personal check with guaranteed payment is a
   a. cashier's check
   b. money order
   c. certified check
   d. traveler's check

Make Academic Connections

3. **Math** Service charges for Tom Harding's regular checking account at Second National Bank are based on the bank's rate schedule:

Minimum Balance	Charge
0–$199	$6
$200–$399	$4
$400 and over	no charge

During a recent six-month period, Tom's balances were: April, $148.00; May, $201.97; June, $101.61; July, $418.53; August, $248.29; and September, $154.36.
   a. How much was Tom's service charge for each month?
   b. What was the total service charge for the six-month period?

TEACH

Explain the various sources of money orders.

Use the FYI feature to explain the effect of Check 21 on check processing activities.

ONGOING ASSESSMENT

checkpoint >> **ANSWER**

A certified check is a personal check for which a bank has guaranteed payment. A cashier's check is a check that a bank draws on its own funds.

ASSESS

Key Concepts Answers

1. d. signature card
2. c. certified check

Make Academic Connections

3. a. Tom's service charges were April, $6; May, $4; June, $6; July, no charge; August, $4; and September, $6.

   b. Tom's total service charge for the six-month period was $26.

CLOSE

Highlight the main points to remember when writing checks.

RETEACH

Explain the process of reconciling a bank statement.

ENRICH

Have students design a format for a bank statement that might be more informative to consumers.

Communicate Business Concepts Answers

1. Answers will vary. Arguments for more government controls on banks could focus on making the banking system safer, free from corruption, and less likely to take advantage of poor or uneducated consumers. Arguments against increased government regulation are that banks are freer to offer innovative new services and can pay higher interest rates without additional restrictions.

2. A major factor is the location and availability in your community. Other factors would be comparing fees, services, and interest rates offered by both credit unions and banks.

3. a. A person planning to open a fitness center—checking account, small business loan

b. A musical group—checking account, savings account, small business loan, safe deposit boxes to store important records while the group is on the road

c. A wealthy senior citizen—checking account, savings account, safe deposit box, investment advice, trust.

d. A buyer of a van—automobile loan, checking and savings accounts

e. A high school recycling club—a checking account

4. Jake will need to ask himself whether he plans to make many withdrawals or payments to others using the money in the account. If so, he needs a checking account. If the $1,000 is his savings and he does not foresee many withdrawals, he will want a savings account that pays interest.

5. Answers will vary. One suggestion for Cher is to

Business Notes

17-1 BANKS AND OTHER FINANCIAL INSTITUTIONS

1. The Federal Reserve System serves member banks by accepting their deposits, lending them money, clearing checks, and providing other services.

2. The main deposit-type institutions are commercial banks, savings and loan associations, mutual savings banks, and credit unions. Non-deposit financial institutions include life insurance companies, investment companies, consumer finance companies, mortgage companies, check-cashing outlets, and pawnshops.

3. To obtain the best value for your financial services dollar, investigate and compare services offered, safety, convenience, fees and charges, and restrictions.

17-2 FINANCIAL SERVICES AND ELECTRONIC BANKING

4. The most common services offered by financial institutions are accepting deposits, transferring funds, lending money, electronic banking, storing valuables, providing financial advice, and managing trusts.

5. The main types of checking accounts are regular checking accounts, interest-earning checking accounts, and special checking accounts.

6. Electronic banking services include the use of automated teller machines (ATM), point-of-sale transactions, direct deposit, automatic bill payment, online payments, stored value cards and smart cards.

17-3 CHECKS AND PAYMENT METHODS

7. The purpose of an endorsement is to allow the recipient of the check to cash, deposit, or transfer it to someone else. A blank endorsement consists of only the endorser's name. A full endorsement, also called the special endorsement, allows you to transfer a check to another person. A restrictive endorsement limits the use of the check to the purpose given in the endorsement.

8. Reconciling a checking account involves finding the differences between the balance on the bank statement and the balance in your checkbook.

9. Other types of payment methods include certified checks, cashier's checks, traveler's checks, and money orders.

Communicate Business Concepts

1. Some people believe that banks need more regulations and control by the government. Others would like fewer regulations for banks. What are some arguments for each point of view?

2. What factors might affect whether you use a commercial bank or a credit union for your banking activities?

3. List the type of banking service that you think each person would be most likely to use. Explain your answer.

a. A person planning to open a fitness center
b. A musical group
c. A wealthy senior citizen
d. A buyer of a van
e. A high school recycling club

4. Jake Olsen has decided to put $1,000 in the bank. List several questions Jake might want to ask before choosing whether to put the money in a checking or a savings account.

5. Cher Alonso often makes deposits and withdrawals at the ATM that she passes on her way to work. She frequently forgets to record these banking activities in her check register and never seems to know how much money she has in the bank. In addition, she

always use the ATM's option to print a receipt for each transaction. She could place the receipt in her check register and remove it only when she has recorded the transaction. An even better plan would be to record the transaction in her check register before leaving home and visiting the ATM.

6. Answers will vary, but could include important papers such as birth, marriage, and death certificates; social security cards; important financial documents, such as insurance policies and stock certificates; valuable jewelry; and rare coins.

7. Answers will vary. Debit cards do make it easier to forget to properly record transactions in the check register, increasing the possibility of an overdraft.

has overdrawn her account twice and has had to pay a fee each time. Can you suggest a plan for Cher to follow that would allow her to use the automatic teller services and still be sure of having an accurate record?

6. Name items that a person might keep in a safe-deposit box.

7. While using a debit card increases the speed and efficiency of business transactions, what effect can this have on a person's money management skills?

8. Isaac Ahlred has received his bank statement for the month of May. The bank statement shows a balance of $401.19, but his check register shows a balance of only $364.52.

   a. What is the most likely reason that the bank balance is larger than Isaac's?

Develop Your Business Language

Match the terms listed with the definitions.

12. A bank that offers a full range of financial services.

13. A nationwide banking plan set up by the federal government to supervise and regulate member banks.

14. A written notice telling the bank not to pay a certain check.

15. A separate form on which the depositor keeps a record of deposits and checks.

16. A device used for cash machine transactions.

17. A secured area in a bank vault for storing valuables.

18. Written evidence that you received payment or that you transferred your right of receiving payment to someone else.

19. A report sent by the bank to a depositor showing the status of his or her account.

20. A federal agency that protects deposited money in case of the failure of a bank or financial institution that it regulates.

21. A fee a bank charges for handling a checking account.

b. What steps should Isaac take to bring his balances into agreement?

9. While on a trip, the Mendoza family decided to buy furniture, which cost $500. The dealer would not accept a personal check or credit cards. What method could be used to pay for the furniture?

10. "You should shop for the best place to open a checking account as carefully as you shop for the best buy in any product or service." Give two reasons to support this statement.

11. Matt Huffman believes that it is a waste of time to record information on check stubs. "The bank sends me a statement each month. That's all I need," he says. How could you convince Matt that he should keep records?

22. Checks that have not been deducted from the bank statement balance.

23. A not-for-profit financial institution formed by people who have like occupations or live in the same community.

24. A statement showing how the checkbook balance and the bank statement were brought into agreement.

KEY TERMS

a. bank reconciliation
b. bank statement
c. commercial bank
d. check register
e. credit union
f. debit card
g. endorsement
h. Federal Deposit Insurance Corporation (FDIC)
i. Federal Reserve System
j. outstanding checks
k. safe-deposit box
l. service charge
m. stop payment order

8. a. The most likely reason the bank's balance is larger than Isaac's is that his account has some outstanding checks.

b. Isaac should deduct the amount of all outstanding checks in his check register from the bank's balance. Also, he should determine whether there are any fees he needs to deduct or add any interest that was earned.

9. If the Mendoza family's ATM agreement allowed a large withdrawal, they could electronically withdraw that much cash to pay for the furniture. They could use a debit card, if accepted by the dealer, or obtain a cashier's check at a local bank that would accept their check or credit card. Traveler's checks or a money order may also be possible.

10. One reason for carefully shopping for the best checking account is because even small monthly fees will add up. Conversely, even slightly higher interest rates on interest-bearing checking accounts will add to savings over the months and years. Good service and convenient hours also will have a large impact on the account holder's daily life.

11. Explain to Matt that data entry errors can occur at even the best banks. Checks can also be lost or their amounts altered. If he does not balance his checkbook, he will never be aware of such problems. Balancing his checkbook will allow him to spot trends in his spending that will help him better manage his finances.

Develop Your Business Language Answers

12. c. commercial bank

13. i. Federal Reserve System

14. m. stop payment order

15. d. check register

16. f. debit card

17. k. safe-deposit box

18. g. endorsement

19. b. bank statement

20. h. Federal Deposit Insurance Corporation (FDIC)

21. l. service charge

22. j. outstanding checks

23. e. credit union

24. a. bank reconciliation

Make Academic
Connections

25. Answers will vary
depending on the bills students examine. The seal is
located to the left of George
Washington's portrait.

26. Answers will vary as
students research financial
services and payment methods common in other parts
of the world.

27. Posters will vary.

28. Answers will vary
depending on the credit
unions in your area.

29. Answers will vary
depending on the state in
which your students live.

30. Answers will vary
depending on the economic
measures students select.

31. Findings will vary.

32. Role-play situations will
vary.

33. First, Tom needs to subtract the outstanding checks
($7.16 + $15.10 + $9.95)
from the bank balance:
$378.65 − $32.21 = $346.44.
Then, he needs to subtract
the $3 service charge from
his checkbook balance
($349.44 − $3.00 = $346.44)
to equal the bank's balance.

Make Academic Connections

25. **GEOGRAPHY** Locate a map of the United States. Use this map to show the districts of the Federal Reserve System. Look at several U.S. one dollar bills. Which Federal Reserve Banks are noted on the seal of this currency?

26. **CULTURE** Research financial services and payment methods commonly used in various countries around the world.

27. **COMMUNICATION** Collect advertisements and promotional information from several financial institutions. Analyze these materials to deter-mine information that is useful for consumers. Create a poster to highlight and report your findings.

28. **HISTORY** Investigate the availability of credit unions in your community. Who may join? What services are offered?

29. **LAW** Check cashing outlets and pawnshops fre-quently charge fees and rates much higher than other financial institutions. Research laws that regulate these financial institutions. Prepare a one-page summary of your findings.

30. **ECONOMICS** Select various economic measure-ments of the economy, such as interest rates and consumer prices. Describe how changes in these economic factors might affect the use of financial services.

31. **RESEARCH** Several states require that banks offer basic checking accounts for low-income consum-ers. In Illinois, Massachusetts, Minnesota, New Jersey, New York, Rhode Island, and Vermont, checking services with minimal fees must be made available for consumers who make a limited number of transactions. These are called life-line accounts. Research the availability of this service in your area.

32. **COMMUNICATION** Work with a partner to present role-playing situations to describe when you might use a certified check, a cashier's check, traveler's checks, and a money order.

33. **MATH** In October, Tom Jarez received his bank statement that showed a balance of $378.65. The service charge was $3. In examining his state-ment, he found that the following checks were outstanding: No. 31, $7.16; No. 34, $15.10; and No. 35, $9.95. His checkbook balance at the end of the month was $349.44. Reconcile his bank statement.

Linking School and Community

Talk to people in your community about the financial institutions and financial services they use. Which of these have you learned about in this chapter? Are there other financial services that you need to learn about? Create a two-paragraph summary of your findings.

Web Workout

Most major banks offer many services to meet the needs of various groups in the economy. Banks often organize their services based on three types of cus-tomers: consumers, small businesses, and corpora-tions and institutions. Consumer services include checking, saving, and loans. Small business services include lines of credit, SBA loans, retirement plans, and cash management. Banks serve commercial banking customers, including corporations and insti-tutions, by servicing new loans, assisting with fund transfers, documenting legal requirements, and sug-gesting risk management strategies. Some banks also offer a variety of global financial services, which may include foreign currency exchange services, payment services for importers and exporters, and sending money electronically to international locations.

Think Critically

1. Locate the web site of a large bank that offers financial services for several types of customers. Prepare a brief written summary of the features of the bank's web site.
2. Make a list of the loan services offered to each type of customer.
3. Identify a service that is only offered to com-mercial customers. Write a brief statement explaining the service.

Linking School and Community
Summary paragraphs will vary.

Web Workout

1. Summaries will vary.

2. Answers will vary depending on the categories used by the bank. For example, a bank might offer auto, home, and school loans for personal bank-ing customers. The bank might offer lines of credit and SBA loans to small business customers. For commercial and institutional customers, the bank might offer equipment leasing, commercial real estate financing, and asset-based lending.

3. Answers will vary. Students might report cur-rency exchange services or letters of credit.

Decision-Making Strategies

Fran and Bill Hamilton recently moved to a new community. They are having trouble deciding whether to use a financial institution near their workplaces or near their home. The Hamiltons have the opportunity to do business with a credit union, a national bank with many branches, a local bank with strong personal service, or a savings and loan association.

34. What factors should the Hamiltons consider when selecting a financial institution?

35. How could Fran and Bill obtain information about the financial institution that would best serve their needs?

Presentation Management Individual Event

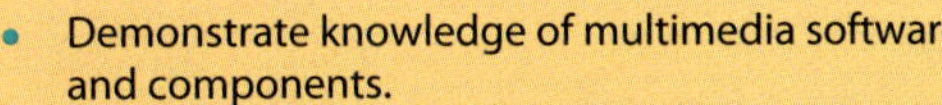

This event will assess your use of current desktop technologies and software to prepare and deliver an effective multimedia presentation.

You will design a multimedia presentation. You have 15 minutes for preparation and setup. The presentation will last a minimum of 7 minutes and a maximum of 10 minutes. Up to 5 minutes will be allowed for questions from the judges. The contestant must make effective use of current multimedia technology in the presentation. In preparation of the presentation, contestants should use space, color, and text as design factors. No VCR or laserdisc may be used in the presentation. Charts and other graphics should be used in the presentation. The student is responsible for securing a release form from any individual whose name, photograph, and other information is included in the presentation.

Topic: Banks are encouraging customers to do business using the Internet. They stress the convenience of paying bills online. Many individuals are suspicious of handling their banking business online. Computer fraud and theft of identity are issues that some customers feel override the convenience of banking online.

You must prepare an electronic presentation that encourages customers to bank online. Factors to emphasize include convenience, security, and timeliness. Your presentation should show how the positive aspects outweigh the negative concerns of banking online.

PERFORMANCE INDICATORS EVALUATED

- Demonstrate knowledge of multimedia software and components.
- Demonstrate effective oral communication.
- Apply technical skills to create a multimedia presentation that enhances the oral presentation.

You will be evaluated for your

- Knowledge of the topic
- Organized presentation of the topic
- Confidence, quality of voice, and eye contact
- Relationship of the topic to business strategy

For more detailed information about performance indicators, go to the BPA web site.

Think Critically

1. List three advantages for banking online.
2. List three disadvantages for banking online.
3. What can the bank do to make customers more comfortable with banking online?

http://www.bpanet.org/

Access the web site shown here to find portfolio activities for this chapter. Use the activities to provide tangible evidence of your learning.

Decision-Making Strategies Answers

34. The Hamiltons will want to consider the services offered, the convenience of each institution's locations and hours, any fees and charges, the quality of service, and any restrictions on accounts.

35. Fran and Bill could ask questions over the phone. They could visit the establishments to evaluate the facilities and talk with employees who could explain the various accounts and services. The Hamiltons could visit each institution's web page, read brochures, and talk to neighbors about area financial organizations.

Winning Edge
Presentation Management Individual Event

This activity provides students an opportunity to make a presentation in a simulated business setting. Encourage students to research the situation, prepare a professional presentation, and practice their presentations.

Think Critically Answers

1. Answers may vary. Three advantages of banking online are the ability to stay at home to conduct business, to get up-todate information on bank accounts, and to pay bills online immediately.

2. Answers may vary. Three disadvantages of banking online are computer fraud, not having computer access at home, and insufficient directions/training.

3. To make customers more comfortable with banking online, banks can offer training sessions and prepare informational brochures teaching customers about electronic banking.

This chapter presents coverage of types of consumer credit accounts along with information on the wise use of credit.

18-1 Credit Fundamentals

This lesson explains the types of consumer credit along with the advantages and disadvantages of using credit.

18-2 Cost of Credit

Calculating interest and finance charges is the main focus of this lesson.

18-3 Credit Application and Documents

Credit applications, loan contracts, monthly statements, and other credit documents are covered in this lesson.

18-4 Protection of Credit Rights

Various regulations protecting credit users and problems of using credit are the basis of this lesson.

CHAPTER 18

Consumer Credit

© Getty Images/PhotoDisc

448

Teaching Resources

Activities and Study Guide, Ch. 18
Chapter and Unit Tests, Ch. 18
Spanish Resources, Ch. 18

ExamView® *CD,* Ch. 18
Instructor's Resource CD
- PowerPoint Slides, Ch. 18
- Lesson Plans, Ch. 18

Xtra! Web Site

school.cengage.com/business/introtobiz
- Study Tools, 18-1, 18-2, 18-3, 18-4
- Quiz Prep, Ch. 18
- Net Bookmark, Ch. 18
- Crossword Puzzle, Ch. 18
- Portfolio Activity, Ch. 18

Planning a Career in...
CONSUMER CREDIT

Credit is important in most economies. Many individuals and businesses use credit for various purchases. Consumer credit involves loans for housing, motor vehicles, and college expenses. Business loans are vital for companies to start operations, purchase inventory, and buy equipment. As a result, many workers employed by banks and credit card companies are involved in approving, processing, servicing, and collecting credit transactions. Workers in consumer credit also find jobs in credit counseling, helping people regain control of their finances and plan for their financial future.

Employment Outlook

- Most occupations in the credit industry will have average growth.
- Slower growth is expected for loan officers because technology is making loan processing simpler and faster.
- Demand for bill collectors and loan counselors is expected to increase because people do not always make wise credit and buying choices.

Related Job Titles

- Bill and Account Collector
- Credit Authorizer
- Credit Clerk
- Loan Officer
- Interviewer
- Credit Analyst
- Loan Counselor
- Information and Record Clerk
- Customer Service Representative
- Credit Counselor
- Credit Administrator
- Credit and Collections Manager
- Commercial Credit Analyst

Needed Skills

- Four-year college degree with an emphasis in finance and economics
- On-the-job training and industry courses for loan officers and other credit workers
- Computer skills, especially in spreadsheet and database application programs
- Excellent communication skills for interaction with customers

What's it like to work in ... Consumer Credit

"We're not sure where our money goes each month. We just know we owe more than $8,000 in credit card bills," was the response of Joan and Hank Salvatore.

Joan and Hank have a monthly income of $3,750, but their expenses are more than $4,400. That's why they came to the community credit counseling service. Joan and Hank were assigned to Bev Gonzalez. Bev worked for a consumer loan company for more than 15 years. Today, instead of granting credit to people, she helps them with credit problems.

Bev recommends that the Salvatores set up a budget to help them plan purchases and reduce spending. For example, Joan and Hank can eat at home more often and make occasional restaurant meals a treat. The extra money the Salvatores will have as a result of following a budget can be used to pay off their debt. In addition to offering a strategy for getting out of debt, Bev will help Joan and Hank learn how to manage their money in the future. No more arguing about money and no more calls about late bill payments.

What about you? What work activities in the consumer credit field appeal to you? What will you have to do to achieve success in this career field?

© Getty Images/PhotoDisc

Planning a Career in...
CONSUMER CREDIT

The many borrowing opportunities available to consumers create a variety of career opportunities.

What About You? Answers

Answers will vary. To achieve success in the consumer credit career field, a student will need an understanding of finance and economics, proficiency with spreadsheet and database application programs, and good interpersonal skills.

Additional Career Information

Additional information on careers can be found in the *Occupational Outlook Handbook*, an online publication (www.bls.gov/oco) of the federal government. Tell your class about this resource and how to use it. This description of job duties can be used to demonstrate the relevancy of skills learned in this course.

Focus on **Real Life**

This feature provides an opportunity to point out that credit is used by individuals, businesses, and governments.

TEACH

Ask students to name the best thing about using credit. Then ask them about the major concern. Provide an overview of the use of credit by explaining the terms *debtor* and *creditor*.

Explain the difference between trade credit and consumer credit.

Use the FYI feature on the next page to explain credit terms commonly used when companies sell on account. Explain that when speaking, "2/10, n/30" is read as "two ten, net thirty."

Explain the *installments* of loan credit.

PROJECT

Provide the following instructions to students. (These instructions also appear on page xxv of the textbook.) What life-span goals might you set that would require you to use credit? Describe steps you can take in the next few years to create a credit history that will help you borrow funds in the future.

Life-Span Plan Answer

Answers will vary. Students should identify major expenditures, such as buying a house or paying for higher education, that few people could afford without credit.

Goals

Identify the types of consumer credit.

Describe the benefits of using credit.

Explain some disadvantages of using credit.

Key Terms

credit

finance charge

down payment

installment loan

promissory note

collateral

cosigner

credit rating

Focus on **Real Life**

In most economies, consumers, businesses, and governments use credit. For example, a person buys gas with an oil company credit card. A student applies for and receives a government loan to help with college expenses. A business receives a $2 million loan to build a new store. Another company borrows $150,000 to finance the purchase of additional inventory. The state of Louisiana may borrow $35 million through a bond issue to build new college buildings. A county board might borrow $250,000 to make emergency road repairs.

What do these people, businesses, and governmental institutions have in common? They all have wants, but lack the money to satisfy those wants. If they borrow money to satisfy their wants, they will be using credit.

---

main idea

Identify the types of consumer credit.

USING CREDIT

Credit is the privilege of using someone else's money for a period of time. That privilege is based on the belief that the person receiving credit will honor a promise to repay the amount owed at a future date. Two parties are involved in a credit transaction. Anyone who buys on credit or receives a loan is a *debtor*. The one who sells on credit or makes a loan is the *creditor*.

Although the credit system uses forms and legal documents, it also depends on trust between the debtor and creditor. This trust means that the creditor believes that the debtor will honor the promise to pay. Without that trust, the credit system could not operate.

Types of Credit

Businesses use trade credit. *Trade credit* occurs when a company receives goods from a supplier and pays for them later.

Businesses may secure long-term loans for land, equipment, and buildings. They may also borrow money for shorter periods, usually for 30 to 90 days, to meet short-term needs for cash.

Local, state, and federal governments often use credit to provide goods and services that benefit the public. Governments may use credit to buy items such as cars, aircraft, and police uniforms. They may also borrow funds to build highways, parks, and airports.

Most consumers use credit. You may use credit to buy expensive products that will last a long time. You may also use credit for convenience in making smaller purchases.

If you borrow money to use for some special purpose, you are using *loan credit*. Loans are available from several kinds of financial institutions. Loan credit usually involves a written contract. The borrower agrees to repay the loan in specified amounts, called *installments*, over a period of time.

If you charge a purchase at the time you buy the good or service, you are using *sales credit*. Most businesses offer

---

Different Learning Abilities

At-Risk Describe careers and personal finance activities related to consumer credit. Emphasize the importance of knowing and understanding the various topics in this lesson.

sales credit. Sales credit involves the use of charge accounts and credit cards by consumers.

Charge Accounts

A charge account represents a contract between the firm offering the account and the customer. Three types of charge accounts are generally available: regular, budget, and revolving.

Regular Accounts A regular charge account requires the buyer to make full payment within a stated period—usually 25 to 30 days. The seller may set a limit on the total amount that may be charged during that time. People use regular accounts for everyday needs and small purchases. Service providers, such as doctors, dentists, lawyers, and plumbers, commonly offer this type of credit.

Budget Accounts Some stores and utility companies offer *budget* charge accounts. This credit agreement requires that a customer make payments of a fixed amount over several months. One budget plan that businesses offer is the 90-day, three-payment plan. Under this plan, you pay for your purchase over a 90-day period, usually in three equal monthly payments.

With a utility company budget plan, the company makes an estimate for gas or electricity charges during a certain period, such as a year. You then agree to pay a certain amount each month to cover those charges. This plan avoids large payments during some times of the year. You pay the same amount each month.

Revolving Accounts The most popular form of sales credit is the *revolving* account. You may charge purchases at any time, but only part of the debt must be paid each month. Features of revolving credit include the following.

- A maximum amount may be owed at one time, called a *credit limit*.

Trade credit terms are often stated "2/10, n/30." This means that the business can take a 2 percent discount if the bill is paid within 10 days from the billing date. The full or net amount must be paid within 30 days.

- A payment is required once a month, but the total amount owed need not be paid at one time.

- A finance charge is added if the total amount owed is not paid. A **finance charge** is the total dollar cost of credit, including interest and all other charges. You must pay this additional amount for the convenience of using credit.

What are some reasons that a business would borrow funds?

TEACH

Contrast the difference between regular charge accounts and budget accounts. Explain the features of a revolving charge account.

THINK CRITICALLY THROUGH VISUALS

Businesses might borrow funds to pay for goods they will resell at a profit or for new equipment, building projects, and facility upgrades that will make them more profitable in the long run. Businesses also sometimes borrow money for short periods to meet short-term cash needs.

Different Learning Styles

Tactile Learner Use various objects to represent the use of credit among individuals, businesses, and governments. Ask students to describe the use of credit based on the object they are holding.

Revolving charge accounts are convenient, but they can make overspending easy. The finance charges on unpaid balances can be quite high, sometimes 1½ percent per month (18 percent per year) or higher. There is rarely a finance charge if balances are paid in full within a specified period, such as within 25 days.

Credit Cards

Charging purchases with credit cards is common. Most credit cards issued today are multipurpose cards. Consumers can use them at thousands of stores, restaurants, and other businesses, as well as to pay for goods and services online.

Bank Cards Bank credit cards have become very popular all over the world. MasterCard and VISA are two of the best known. Sometimes an annual fee must be paid for the privilege of using these cards.

While banks and various merchants may issue credit cards, most credit card processing is done through *Independent Sales Organizations (ISOs)*. When you use your bank credit card, electronic terminals typically send the transaction data to an ISO which then authorizes payment. At the end of the day, credit sales information is submitted electronically and the banks then pay the business for the sales amount minus a service fee.

This fee covers the bank's expenses of processing the sales receipts and collecting amounts owed from customers. The bank is doing the work that the business' own credit departments would have to do otherwise.

Business owners like bank credit cards because the bank takes on the liability and expense of granting credit. Customers like bank charge cards because they are accepted by many businesses all over the world.

Charge Cards American Express and Diners Club, once called travel and entertainment cards, are widely used charge cards. Subscribers pay a yearly membership fee that is usually higher than the fee for bank cards. Cardholders are not given a spending limit. They are usually expected to pay the full balance each month. Business travelers like to use charge cards because the detailed records they receive are useful for business and tax record keeping. They offer proof of travel expenses.

Affinity Cards Some organizations allow their names to be affiliated with a credit card. These affinity cards are *co-branded* with an issuing bank. They allow an organization, such as a charity, sports team, or oil company to receive a small percentage of credit sales.

Retail Store Cards Many retail stores offer their own credit cards to customers. These cards show the name of the store

What are the different types of credit cards that a person can apply for?

that issues them. Customers can only use these cards at the issuing stores.

Installment Credit

For some expensive purchases, consumers often use a different type of credit. *Installment sales credit* is a contract issued by the seller that requires periodic payments at specified times. The seller adds finance charges to the cost of the items purchased. The credit agreement shows the total amount to be paid. Consumers often purchase furniture and household appliances with installment sales credit.

Using installment sales credit differs from using credit cards. The following are some features of installment credit.

- Signing a sales contract that shows the terms of the purchase.

- Receiving the purchased item at the time of the sale. Be aware that the seller has the right to *repossess*, or take back, an item if payments are not made on time.

- Making a **down payment**, which is a payment of part of the purchase price. It is usually made at the time of the purchase.

- Paying a finance charge on the amount owed.

- Making regular payments at stated times, usually weekly or monthly. For example, if a total of $120 is to be repaid in 12 monthly installments, $10 is paid each month.

CORPORATE SOCIAL RESPONSIBILITY

Marketing Credit Cards to College Students

Credit card companies are looking for customers. In 2005, more than six billion credit card offers were mailed to prospective customers. Some of those offers were sent to college-aged young adults because research shows that individuals develop their first brand loyalties between the ages of 18 and 25. The marketing efforts of credit card companies in the college market are successful. More than 83 percent of college students hold credit cards and more than 70 percent keep their first credit card.

Card companies make it easy for college students to get a credit card. In fact, it is not uncommon for a college student to receive 50 offers per semester. In addition to marketing their cards through the mail, credit card companies have a presence on campus. They have booths, displays, tents, and tables during orientation and other campus events. They sponsor activities and often offer free gifts with pre-approved credit applications. Credit card companies make it easy for students to get a credit card. It is up to students and their families to decide when to get a card and which card is right for them.

Some students arrive on college campuses with a credit card in their wallet. Even if the student's name is on the card, the card actually might belong to the student's parents. Getting a credit card in your own name has advantages. It allows you to establish credit in your own name and demonstrate financial responsibility and independence.

NellieMae, a student loan company, offers a variety of services for college students and their families. One of these services is credit education, including information about obtaining and using credit cards. NellieMae recommends that students shop for the best interest rate, look for a card with no annual fee, and request a low credit limit.

Think Critically

1. Why are credit card companies interested in college-aged customers? Do you think credit card companies are acting in a socially responsible way by making it so easy for college students to obtain credit?
2. Use Internet and library resources to learn about strategies for selecting a credit card and using it wisely. Create a poster or brochure targeted at college-aged customers that incorporates tips for using credit cards wisely.

Different Learning Styles

Auditory Learner Encourage auditory learners to work with a partner to learn about the types of credit cards presented on pages 452 and 453.

Suggest that students use rhymes or rhythms to help them remember material.

Describe the features of installment credit.

Explain the purpose of a down payment.

Ask students to name reasons why a person might apply for a loan.

Contrast the difference between an installment loan and a single-payment loan.

CORPORATE SOCIAL RESPONSIBILITY

The credit card industry tries to maximize its revenue by bringing in new customers. Other companies in the finance industry are trying to be socially responsible by helping young people gain control over their credit.

Think Critically
Answers

1. Credit card companies market to college-aged consumers because they know that 70 percent of young people will remain loyal to their first card. They hope to lock in long-term customers. Student's opinions about social responsibility will vary.

2. Posters and brochures will vary.

TEACH

Ask students to name items that could serve as *collateral* for a loan.

ONGOING ASSESSMENT

checkpoint >> **ANSWER**

The major types of consumer credit are loan credit and sales credit.

TEACH

Highlight the main benefits of using credit.

Ask students to name actions that could affect a person's credit rating.

Work as a Team

This feature will require students to think about various positive and negative aspects of a business offering credit.

In some cases, the seller charges a penalty if a payment is received after the due date. In others, all remaining payments may become due at once if only one payment is missed.

Consumer Loans

A loan is an alternative to charge account buying or installment sales credit. The terms of the loans and the requirements for securing the loans differ.

An **installment loan** is one in which you agree to make monthly payments in specific amounts over a period of time. The payments are installments. The total amount you repay includes the amount you borrowed plus the finance charge on your loan.

Another kind of loan is a *single-payment loan*. With this type of credit, you do not pay anything until the end of the loan period, possibly 60 or 90 days. At that time, you repay the full amount you borrowed plus the finance charge.

A lender needs some assurance that each loan will be repaid. If you are a good credit risk, you may be able to sign a promissory note. A **promissory note** is a written promise to repay based on a debtor's excellent credit history. The amount borrowed, usually with some interest, is due on a certain date. Promissory notes should include the following components:

main idea

Describe the benefits of using credit.

- **Principal** The amount that is promised to be paid

- **Time** The days or months from the date of the note until it should be paid

- **Date of maturity** The date on which the note is due

Work as a Team

Most businesses sell on credit. Create a list of situations in which a company may not offer credit to customers. What would be benefits and drawbacks of this action?

- **Payee** The one to whom the note is payable

- **Interest rate** The rate paid for the use of the money

- **Maker** The one who promises to make payment

In some cases, the lender may ask you to offer some property you own, such as a car, a house, or jewelry, as *security*. Property that is used as security is called **collateral**. You give the lender the right to sell this property to get back the amount of the loan if you do not repay it. This type of loan is a *secured loan*.

What if you do not have an established credit history or any property to offer as security? You may be able to get a relative or friend who has property or a good credit history to sign your note. They become the legal **cosigner**. The cosigner of a note is responsible for payment of the note if you do not pay as promised.

> *checkpoint* >>
> What are the major types of consumer credit?

BENEFITS OF CREDIT

Both businesses and consumers can benefit from credit use. The main advantages of credit for consumers include the following.

- **Convenience** Credit can make it easy for you to buy. You can shop without carrying much cash.

- **Immediate Possession** Credit allows you to have the item now. A family can buy a dishwasher on credit and begin using it at once.

- **Savings** Sometimes credit allows you to buy an item on sale at a good price. Some stores, especially department and furniture stores, send notices of special sales to credit customers.

Applied Skills

Writing Across the Curriculum Have students prepare a paragraph that connects the benefits of consumer credit to other business topics or to another class they are taking.

- **Credit Rating** A person's reputation for paying bills on time is known as a **credit rating**. If you buy on credit and pay your bills on time, you gain a reputation for being dependable. In that way, you establish a favorable credit rating. A credit rating is valuable when you might need to borrow money or when you want to make a major purchase.

- **Useful for Emergencies** Access to credit can help in unexpected situations. Sometimes you may not have enough cash and have an urgent need for something. For example, your car might need repairs.

What are the main advantages of consumer credit?

CREDIT CONCERNS

Buying on credit is convenient and can be beneficial. There are also some disadvantages if you are not careful.

- **Overbuying** A common spending hazard of credit involves buying something that is more expensive than you can afford. Attractive store displays and advertisements invite you to make purchases.

- **Careless Buying** If you become impatient or distracted in your shopping, you may not shop carefully. You may fail to make comparisons, causing you to buy at the wrong time or the wrong place. Credit can tempt you not to wait for a better price on an item you want now.

- **Higher Prices** Stores that only accept cash may sell items at lower prices than stores that offer credit. Extending

Explain some disadvantages of using credit.

Technology in Action

Databases, Personal Privacy, and Identity Theft

Information about you is readily available to many people. Businesses and governments all over the world use computer databases and electronic networks to store and exchange this information about you.

How is this information obtained? Most databases are created from information given voluntarily. For instance, you offer information when you apply for credit, obtain telephone service, apply for a driver's license, obtain insurance, and answer survey questions.

Privacy is a basic right to have information about you kept confidential. Like most consumers, you are probably concerned about your privacy. While there is some reason to be concerned about databases and personal privacy, protections exist. Decisions about granting credit or obtaining insurance are most often based on accurate, up-to-date information. The information gathered is used for legitimate business reasons.

Various state and federal privacy laws continue to be under review. Government officials must decide what information is private and when consumers should be asked to give permission before credit or medical reports are released to others. In recent years, stronger privacy protection laws have been enacted.

Identity theft is the fastest-growing financial crime. That's the bad news. The good news is that the technology that is used to steal a person's identity can also be used to protect it. Each year, credit card companies, retail stores, and online businesses improve their security systems. These efforts help to ensure that your personal information and financial data will not be viewed or used by unauthorized individuals or companies.

Think Critically

1. What dangers are involved with having private information easily accessible to others?
2. Conduct a web search to determine actions you can take to protect your privacy.

The main advantages of consumer credit are convenience (shopping without carrying cash), immediate possession of items bought on credit, savings (when stores offer special prices to credit customers), the chance to build a favorable credit rating, and for emergencies.

TEACH

Explain the main concerns associated with using credit.

Technology in Action

Privacy concerns and identity theft are major concerns. Use this feature to expand student awareness of these issues.

Think Critically Answers

1. Private information that is easily accessible to others could be misused. For example, a criminal could steal a person's identity or stalk an individual whose personal information is easy to get.

2. Answers will vary. Their research should help students create lists of practical measures they can take to protect their privacy. Ask what actions they plan to take and whether any of the measures seem too extreme or impractical for the privacy benefit gained.

Different Learning Abilities

Gifted Have students conduct research about identity theft. Encourage students to explore the methods used to commit the crime, how stolen identities are used, and the impact on individual victims, businesses, and society. Their findings may be reported in a paper or in an oral presentation to the class.

TEACH

Have students comment on the questions to ask before using credit. Which of these questions are most important?

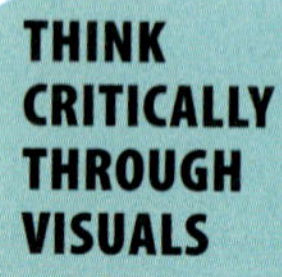

THINK CRITICALLY THROUGH VISUALS

Stores offer discounts to attract customers who may buy on credit. While the store may not earn much on the sale, selling on credit can result in earnings from interest.

ONGOING ASSESSMENT

checkpoint >> **ANSWER**

Potential drawbacks of buying on credit include overbuying, careless buying, paying higher prices, and overuse of credit.

ASSESS

Key Concepts Answers

1. b. installment credit
2. c. a loan
3. b. convenience

Make Academic Connections

4. Findings will vary.

5. Tables will vary. The benefits of credit include convenience, immediate possession, savings, credit rating, and usefulness in emergencies. Credit concerns include overbuying, careless buying, higher prices, and overuse of credit.

---

credit is expensive for stores. When customers do not pay as agreed, there are collection costs. Sometimes businesses must write off consumer debts as uncollectible. These increased costs often result in higher prices.

- **Overuse of Credit** Buying now and paying later may sound like a good idea. If too many payments need to be made later, the total amount due can become a problem. Consumers must keep records of the total amount owed so that they do not have monthly payments that exceed their ability to pay.

Questions to Ask

Before making a final decision about whether to buy on credit, think about these important questions.

- How will you benefit from this use of credit?
- Is this the best buy you can make or should you shop around?

Why do you think stores offer discounts to consumers?

- What will be the total cost of your purchase, including the finance charges?
- What would you save if you paid cash?
- Will the payments be too high for your income?

Answering these questions will help you make wise credit decisions.

checkpoint >>
What are potential drawbacks of buying on credit?

18-1 Assessment

Xtra!
Study Tools
school.cengage.com/business/introtobiz

Key Concepts

Determine the best answer.

1. Large purchases (such as appliances and automobiles) are commonly bought using
   a. a bank credit card
   b. installment credit
   c. a charge account
   d. trade credit

2. Signing a promissory note occurs when using
   a. a credit card
   b. a charge account
   c. a loan
   d. trade credit

3. Which of the following is an advantage of using credit?
   a. overbuying
   b. convenience
   c. higher prices
   d. lower credit rating

Make Academic Connections

4. **Marketing** Collect advertisements from newspapers, magazines, and web sites for companies that offer credit. What types of credit are offered? Is the company selling credit as its primary product or using credit to promote the sale of other goods and services?

5. **Economics** Create a table showing the benefits of credit and credit concerns. For each benefit and each concern, describe the effect consumer credit has on individuals and businesses.

RETEACH

Have students name the benefits and concerns of consumer credit.

ENRICH

Describe uses of credit by your local government.

CLOSE

Ask students to name the major types of consumer credit.

Cost of Credit

Goals

Calculate interest in consumer credit situations.

Explain finance charges when using credit.

Key Terms

interest

annual percentage rate

Focus on **Real Life**

Using credit to purchase goods and services may allow you to be more efficient or more productive. Valid reasons exist for using credit. A medical emergency may cause financial need. You may be offered a new job and need a car to get to work.

There are many choices about when and where to borrow. Wise credit shopping involves careful analysis of the cost of credit. If you are thinking of borrowing money or obtaining a credit card, consider two factors. First, figure out how much it will cost you. Second, determine whether you can afford it.

After deciding to use credit, you should shop around for the best terms. Consumer credit enables you to have and enjoy goods and services now and to pay for them with future income. Always remember that credit is not free.

Focus on **Real Life**

Point out that the financial cost of credit should be a major factor when planning and selecting among borrowing alternatives.

TEACH

Explain the three elements that are used to calculate interest. Show sample calculations for interest.

THINK CRITICALLY THROUGH VISUALS

The longer it takes to pay back borrowed money, the more interest the borrower will pay. Time increases the amount of interest owed.

FINDING INTEREST

Borrowing money has a cost. **Interest**, *I*, is the cost of using someone else's money. The amount of interest paid on a loan or charge account should be clearly understood. To determine this amount, you need to know the following.

1. **Principal, *P*** Amount of the loan.

2. **Interest Rate, *R*** Percent of interest charged or earned. Remember that a percent can also be expressed as a decimal or a fraction. The symbol for percent is %.

3. **Time, *T*** Length of time for which interest will be charged, usually expressed in years or parts of a year.

Simple Interest

On single-payment loans, interest is usually *simple interest*. The formula for computing simple interest is shown below.

$$\text{Interest} = \text{Principal} \times \text{Rate} \times \text{Time}$$
$$I = P \times R \times T$$

A simple interest rate of 12 percent per year means you are paying 12 cents for each dollar you borrow for a year. At this rate, if you borrow \$1, you pay 12 cents in interest. If you borrow \$2, you pay 24 cents. If you borrow \$10, you pay \$1.20, and so on.

main idea

Calculate interest in consumer credit situations.

© Getty Images/PhotoDisc

How does time affect the amount of interest that you pay?

Different Learning Abilities

Visually Impaired Prepare enlarged materials with the main components and formula to explain interest calculations. Consider asking all students to participate in preparing tapes or audio files that can be used for review.

Suppose you borrow $100 ($P$) at 12 percent ($R$) for one year ($T$). To calculate the amount of interest, first change 12 percent to a decimal, 0.12. Using the formula, the interest is $12.

$$I = P \times R \times T$$
$$I = \$100 \times 0.12 \times 1 = \$12$$

If you borrow $100 at 12 percent for two years, you pay twice as much interest, or $24.

$$I = \$100 \times 0.12 \times 2 = \$24$$

If you borrow the money for three years, you pay $36, and so on.

Time in Months Your loan may be for one month instead of one year. How is simple interest calculated for less than a year? The amount of interest is based on the portion of the year. There are 12 months in a year, so one month is one-twelfth of a year, regardless of the number of days in the particular month.

If you borrow $100 at 12 percent for one month, the interest is

$$I = P \times R \times T$$
$$I = \$100 \times 0.12 \times \frac{1}{12} = \$1$$

Time in Days A loan may be for a certain number of days such as 30, 60, or 90 days. To make the computation easy, a year is often considered as 360 days. The interest on a loan of $100 at 12 percent for 60 days is $2.

$$I = P \times R \times T$$
$$I = \$100 \times 0.12 \times \frac{60}{360} = \$2$$

Maturity Dates

The date on which a loan must be repaid is the *maturity date*. When the time of the loan is stated in months, the date of maturity is the same day of the month as the date on which the loan was made. A one-month loan made on January 15 will be due February 15. A two-month loan will be due March 15, and so on.

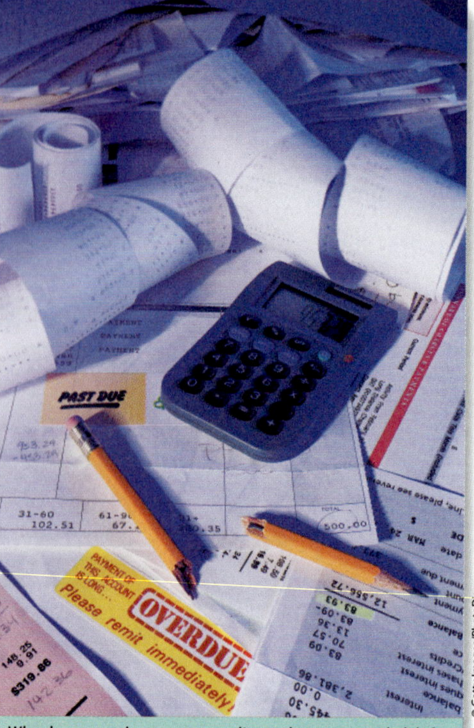

What happens when you use credit to take on too much debt?

© Getty Images/PhotoDisc

When the time is in days, you must count the exact number of days to find the date of maturity. First, determine the number of days remaining in the month when the loan was made. For example, if the loan was made on January 10, there would be 21 days counted in January, because there are 31 days in January. Then add the days in the following months until the total equals the required number of days.

Suppose you want to find the date of maturity of a 90-day loan made on March 4. First find the number of days remaining in March. Then add the days in the following months until you reach 90 days.

March	27 days (31 – 4)
April	30 days
May	31 days
June	2 days
Total	90 days

Therefore, the due date is June 2.

Installment Interest

When you borrow money, you usually make several partial payments instead of one large single payment. A loan that you repay in partial payments is an installment loan (or consumer loan). Each payment is an *installment*.

Banks, credit unions, and consumer finance companies all offer installment loans. With an installment loan, the bank gives the borrower a schedule of payments. It shows how much the borrower must pay each month.

With some loans, the lender adds the amount of the interest to the amount you borrow. You sign a *promissory note* for the total amount. You then repay the note in equal monthly installments.

Suppose you borrow $100, sign a note for $110, and agree to repay the loan in 12 monthly installments of $9.17 each. If you had borrowed $100 for one year and paid $110 at maturity, the interest rate would be 10 percent.

$$\$10 \div \$100 = 0.10$$

However, you paid off just part of the loan each month. You had the use of the entire $100 for one month and a smaller amount each succeeding month as you repaid the loan. In this case, the true interest rate amounts to 18.5 percent.

Amortization Schedules

On some installment loans, interest is calculated on the amount that is unpaid at the end of each month. The payment table of principal and interest over time is called an *amortization schedule*.

Suppose that a person obtained a loan for $1,000 and agreed to repay $100 per month. The lender applies the payment to principal and interest. The borrower makes payments each month on a level payment schedule. Figure 18-1, on page 460, shows this amortization schedule.

What large purchases often require an individual to apply for an installment loan?

© Digital Vision

Answers will vary depending on the two topics selected.

TEACH

Use Figure 18-1 to explain how a constant payment is often used to pay off a loan plus the interest.

ONGOING ASSESSMENT

checkpoint >> **ANSWER**

To calculate interest, one must know the principal (amount of the loan), the interest rate, and the length of time for which interest will be charged.

FIGURE 18-1 ANSWER

A level loan payment schedule is most often used for very large loans paid back over a number of years.

 **PROJECT**

Describe why the excessive use of credit can prevent people from achieving their life-span goals. How would you decide when or when not to borrow funds?

Life-Span Plan Answer

Answers will vary. Students should point out that an excessive use of credit might prevent them from saving funds they need to achieve their life-span goals.

TEACH

Explain the importance of knowing and using the annual percentage rate.

Point out other fees and costs that may be associated with a loan.

Consumers need to stay informed about using credit wisely. Access the web site shown below and click on the link for Chapter 18. Select two topic areas. Prepare a summary of the main ideas presented for each area. Explain how this information might be valuable to consumers who use credit.

school.cengage.com/business/introtobiz

main idea

Explain finance charges when using credit.

Amortization schedules show that when loans are first taken, a larger percentage of the payments go to interest. At the end of the schedule, more goes to principle. For example, the first payment includes more than $9 in interest and the ninth payment includes only $1.57 in interest. Only $90.90 from the first loan payment is applied to the principal. The ninth payment includes more than $98 in principal.

checkpoint >>

What three things are necessary to calculate interest?

FIGURE 18-1

Which kind of loan schedule would be best for very large loans paid back over a number of years?

Amortization Schedule
$1,000 loan, 12% interest rate, monthly payments are $100

Payment	Interest	Applied to Principal	Loan Balance
			$1,000.00
$100.00	$10.00	$90.00	910.00
100.00	9.10	90.90	819.10
100.00	8.19	91.81	727.29
100.00	7.28	92.72	634.57
100.00	6.35	93.65	540.92
100.00	5.41	94.59	446.33
100.00	4.46	95.54	350.79
100.00	3.51	96.49	254.30
100.00	2.54	97.46	156.84
100.00	1.57	98.43	58.41
58.99	0.58	58.41	-------

FINANCE CHARGES

Before you borrow money or charge a purchase, you should know the exact cost of using credit. Three things to consider are the annual percentage rate, the total dollar charges, and the alternative sources of credit.

Annual Percentage Rate

The **annual percentage rate** (APR) is a disclosure required by law. It states the percentage cost of credit on a yearly basis. All credit agreements, whether for sales credit or loan credit, require disclosure of the APR.

In addition to interest, the APR includes other charges that may be made. *Service fees* involve the time and money it takes a creditor to investigate your credit history, process your loan or charge account application, and keep records of your payments and balances.

The costs of collecting from those who do not pay their accounts may also be passed on to other borrowers. *Uncollectible accounts* are frequently referred to as *bad debts* or *doubtful accounts*.

Different Learning Styles

Visual Learner Use Figure 18-1 to highlight the payment amounts, interest, amount applied to principal, and loan balance for the situation presented. Ask students to point out and explain trends they see when they look at the amortization schedule.

Lenders may also add an amount to cover the cost of credit insurance. This coverage repays the balance of the amount owed if the borrower dies or becomes disabled.

Total Dollar Charges

To make you aware of the total cost of credit, federal law requires that the lender must tell you the finance charge. The *finance charge* is the total dollar cost of credit, including interest and all other charges. Either your contract or your charge account statement must state this finance charge.

Compare Credit Costs

If you have to borrow money or buy on credit, be sure to compare the total cost of credit among alternative sources. Check with several lenders and compare the APRs.

If you make a purchase with a credit card, know which card has the lowest APR. If an installment sales contract is required, think about whether an installment loan from a financial institution may be cheaper for you.

Various factors affect interest rates. Create two lists: (1) What economic factors can affect interest rates? (2) What personal factors can affect the rate a lender charges a borrower?

When getting a loan, shop around just as carefully as you would for any major purchase. Borrowing money is costly, so make sure that you get the best loan. Some of the things you should check include the annual percentage rate, the amount of the monthly payments, and the finance charge.

Always remember that when you use credit, you are spending future income. If you decide to use credit, the benefits of making the purchase now should outweigh the costs of using credit. Effectively used, credit can help you have more and enjoy more. Misused, credit can result in too much debt, loss of reputation, and even bankruptcy.

checkpoint >>
What does APR represent?

18-2 Assessment

Key Concepts

Determine the best answer.

1. True or False. The principal of a loan is the total amount of interest that will be paid.

2. True or False. Interest rates are stated on the basis of one year even if a loan is for several years.

3. The most valuable number to consider when comparing credit among various borrowing sources is the
   a. total finance charge
   b. maturity date
   c. annual percentage rate
   d. principal

Make Academic Connections

4. *Math* Calculate the amount of interest for each of the following loans.
   a. $6,000 borrowed for 1 year at 7% APR
   b. $2,000 borrowed for 4 months at 8% APR
   c. $1,100 borrowed for 2½ years at 6% APR

5. *Economics* Several types of interest rates exist in every economy. Use library materials or an Internet search to determine common reported interest rates. Which of these rates are related to consumer credit?

This activity can help students understand that both economic and personal factors can affect the interest rate for a loan or other credit.

TEACH

Point out that the "finance charge" is the total *dollar* value of using credit as opposed to the rate communicated with the APR.

Emphasize the importance of comparing the cost of credit at various lenders.

ONGOING ASSESSMENT

checkpoint >> *ANSWER*

APR represents the annual percentage rate, which is the percentage cost of credit on a yearly basis. This disclosure is required by law.

ASSESS

Key Concepts Answers

1. False. The principal of a loan is the total amount borrowed.

2. True

3. c. annual percentage rate

Make Academic Connections

4. a. The interest is $420 ($6,000 × 0.07% × 1).

   b. The interest is $53.33 ($2,000 × 0.08% × 1/3).

   c. The interest is $165 ($1,100 × 0.06% × 2.5).

5. Answers will vary depending on when the assignment is completed.

RETEACH

Explain APR and total finance charges.

CLOSE

Ask students to name the three factors needed to calculate interest.

ENRICH

Have students list factors that can affect interest rates for a loan.

18-3 Credit Application and Documents

Goals

Explain the credit application process.

Describe the activities of a credit bureau.

Discuss commonly used credit documents.

Key Terms

credit application

credit bureau

statement of account

Focus on Real Life

"I don't get it. How do you get credit if you never had it? It seems like you have to have a good credit history before you even have credit."

When Amy Compton mentioned her concerns during her business class, a few students said they were already working on establishing good credit. Some students said they had credit union and bank accounts in their own names. Others reported that they had part-time jobs.

Everyone agreed that the first step toward getting credit was opening a bank account and demonstrating your ability to repay a debt.

---

main idea

Explain the credit application process.

CREDIT APPLICATION PROCESS

To obtain a loan or credit card, you must prove that you are a good credit risk. Not everyone who wants credit will receive it. Lenders need certain information in order to make a decision about granting credit. They want to be assured of two things: your ability to repay a debt and your willingness to do so.

The Three Cs of Credit

In deciding whether to grant you credit, businesses consider three main factors, known as the three Cs—character, capacity, and capital.

Character refers to your honesty and willingness to pay a debt when it is due. If you have a history of paying bills on time, creditors believe that you are a good credit risk.

Capacity refers to a person's ability to pay a debt when it is due. The lender or seller must decide if you have enough income to pay your bills. If your income is too small or unsteady, granting you credit may not be wise. In contrast, your income may be high, but if you have other debts, you may not be able to handle more payments.

Capital is the value of the borrower's possessions. Capital includes the money and property you own. Your capital may include a car that is paid for and a house on which a large amount has been paid. A checking account and savings also add to your capital. The amount of capital gives the lender some assurance that you will be able to meet your credit obligations.

Credit Applications

When you apply for credit or a loan, the lender will ask you to fill out an application. A **credit application** is a form on which you provide information needed by a lender to make a decision about granting credit. Figure 18-2 shows an example of a credit card application. In addition to printed applications, some companies take credit card applications online.

One of the most important parts of a credit application is your *credit references*—businesses or individuals who are able and willing to provide information about your creditworthiness. Your signature on the application gives a lender permission to contact your credit references to inquire about your credit record.

Different Learning Styles

Kinesthetic Learner Have students create a credit application. Ask students to explain why certain items are requested on the form they develop.

CREDIT CARD APPLICATION

Important: Fill in all information requested below.

Second National BankCorp

1. Information About Yourself *(Name of person in whose name card will be issued)*

☐ Mr. ☐ Mrs. ☐ Miss ☐ Ms.   First Name   Middle   Last Name
(Courtesy titles are optional)

Home Address   Apt.   City   State   ZIP Code   How Long? Years ___ Mos. ___

Previous Address (if less than 2 years at present address)   Apt.   City   State   ZIP Code

Home Telephone ( )   Business Telephone ( )   Social Security Number   Date of Birth / /   No. of Dependents (Exclude Yourself)

Are You a U.S. Citizen? ☐ Yes ☐ No   If No, Explain Immigration Status   Are You a Permanent Resident? ☐ Yes ☐ No   Do You: ☐ Own ☐ Rent ☐ Other   Monthly Rent or Mortgage $

2. Employment Information *(Your total yearly income from all sources)*

Employer   Address   City   State   ZIP Code

How Long? Years ___ Mos. ___   Occupation   Yearly Gross Salary $ Other Income*   Source

Former Employer (if less than 1 year with present employer)   How Long? Years ___ Mos. ___   *Note: Alimony, child support or separate maintenance income need not be disclosed if you do not wish to have it considered as a basis for paying this obligation.

Nearest Relative Not Living with You   Address   City   State   Relation   Telephone

3. Other Credit

Major Credit Cards (Visa, MasterCard, etc....)   Account Number

Other Credit Cards (Dept. Stores, etc....)   Account Number

Other Credit   Account Number

4. Banking Information

☐ Checking   Name of Bank   City   Account Number

☐ Savings   Name of Bank (if different from above)   City   Account Number

☐ Other (Check here if you have any of the following:)   IRA   CD   Money Market Account   Stocks/Bonds   Investments   Cash Management Account

5. Joint Account Information *(Complete for joint account or if you are relying on the income of another person to qualify for an account)*

First Name   Middle   Last Name   Relation

Home Address   Apt.   City   State   ZIP Code

Home Telephone ( )   Business Telephone ( )   Social Security Number   Date of Birth / /

Employer   Address   City   State   ZIP Code

How Long? Years ___ Mos. ___   Occupation   Yearly Gross Salary $ Other Income*   Source

Former Employer   How Long? Years ___ Mos. ___   *Note: Alimony, child support or separate maintenance income need not be disclosed if you do not wish to have it considered as a basis for paying this obligation.

6. Additional Cards *(Complete this section if you want cards issued to additional buyers on your account.)*

1. Spouse   First Name   Middle   Last Name

2. Other   First Name   Middle   Last Name

7. Signatures

I authorize the Second National BankCorp to check my credit record and to verify my credit, employment and income references.
I have read the important information on the reverse side.

X ________________   X ________________
Applicant's Signature   Joint Applicant's Signature

I understand that Second National BankCorp may amend the account terms and charges specified in the Cardmember Agreement in the future.

FIGURE 18-2

Why is it important to fill in all the blanks and to do so accurately?

TEACH

Ask students to explain why certain information is requested on the credit application. Describe how information on the credit application is used by providers of credit.

FIGURE 18-2 ANSWER

It is important to accurately fill in all the blanks on a credit card application so that the lender can make the best possible decision about whether to extend credit. If you do not sign the application, the potential creditor cannot contact your credit references. You are building a credit history, and your credit cannot be reported accurately to credit bureaus if you do not supply the lender with correct information. Finally, supplying false information on a credit application is illegal.

Different Learning Abilities

Hearing Impaired Prepare a visual aid that includes a written description of the various sections of a credit application. Encourage students to ask questions about the form.

A landlord wants to rent to tenants with good credit histories because they are more likely to pay their rent on time and in full. Anyone who is considering loaning you money—car dealers, credit card companies, and so forth—and even employers may request a copy of your credit report.

TEACH

Explain the process used to verify various items reported on a credit application.

Ask students to suggest some actions that might be taken to establish credit by a person who has never had credit. Highlight commonly suggested actions that might be taken to establish credit.

ONGOING ASSESSMENT

checkpoint >> **ANSWER**

The three Cs of credit are (1) character, (2) capacity, and (3) capital.

Why is good credit important to a landlord? Who else might request a copy of your credit report?

Your signature also indicates that you understand the type of credit and that the information you have provided is true. You need to fill out the credit application completely, accurately, and honestly. You should only sign it when you understand it and have provided the requested information.

Documenting Credit Data

Information provided on credit applications must be verified to assure its accuracy. Present and former employers can verify employment dates and salary figures. Banks and other financial institutions can report whether the applicants have the accounts they listed. Landlords can indicate how long tenants have been renting and if they pay their rent on time. Other creditors can report how an applicant makes payments on accounts.

You may list a personal reference because you do not have sufficient business credit references. The person you list can indicate how he or she feels you conduct your personal business activities. In each case, the reference helps the credit manager to get a better picture of you as a credit risk. The credit manager can then make an accurate appraisal of your creditworthiness.

Actions to Establish Credit

Building a good record of creditworthiness can be important. You can begin while you are still in school. Trust and reliability are important in matters of credit. You can help to establish yourself by having a good record of grades and attendance. Both employers and lenders know that school behavior patterns tend to carry on later in life.

In addition, start a checking and savings account. If you keep a balance in each account, a lender can see that you can handle money. Making regular deposits to your savings account also suggests that you will be a good credit risk.

Some people establish credit records by charging small purchases. You may buy a sweater on credit and make the payments according to the agreement. This action is an important step toward proving you are a good credit risk. You may want to pay off your account within 30 days and avoid an interest charge. Either way, you will be building a good credit record.

Having a good part-time or full-time employment record also helps to start a favorable credit record. Changing jobs often does not look good. Being on a job for two or more years is a positive part of a good credit record.

Other information that lenders will want to know relates to your finances. You will need to report how much you earn, what kinds of savings and investments you have, and whether you have any other sources of income. A lender may also want to know about your reliability. In other words, they will want to know your occupation, how long you have been with your present employer, how long you have lived at the same address, and whether you own or rent your home.

checkpoint >>
What are the three Cs of credit?

Applied Skills

Communication Have students create a public service announcement for radio, television, or webcast with suggested actions to take when establishing credit. Encourage students to use scripts and storyboards for planning.

CREDIT BUREAU

In addition to checking with your credit references, a lender will usually check with a credit bureau. A **credit bureau,** or credit reporting agency, is a company that gathers information on credit users. It sells this information to businesses offering credit. Banks, finance companies, and retail stores are among the customers of credit bureaus.

Credit bureaus keep debt records of consumers. They can record only information that is officially reported to them. The information shows if payments are up to date or overdue and if any action has been taken to collect overdue bills. Other credit bureau information may be added to create a month-by-month credit history for the consumer accounts.

Credit bureaus cooperate with each other. They provide information to other credit bureaus. If you are new to an area, the local credit bureau can obtain information from the bureau in your previous community.

Credit Report

A credit bureau uses your record to grade you as a credit risk. Your *credit report* shows the debts you owe, how often you use credit, and whether you pay your debts on time. Figure 18-3 shows a credit report that a credit bureau may issue to a

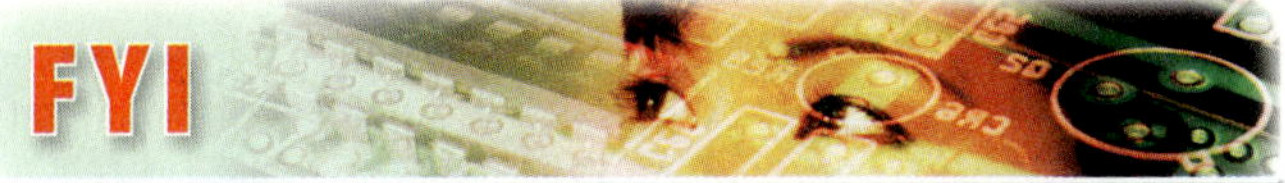

The three major companies that store data on consumers and provide information to lenders are Experian, Equifax, and Trans Union. Equifax maintains more than 190 million credit files on U.S. consumers.

Describe the activities of a credit bureau.

Credit Report

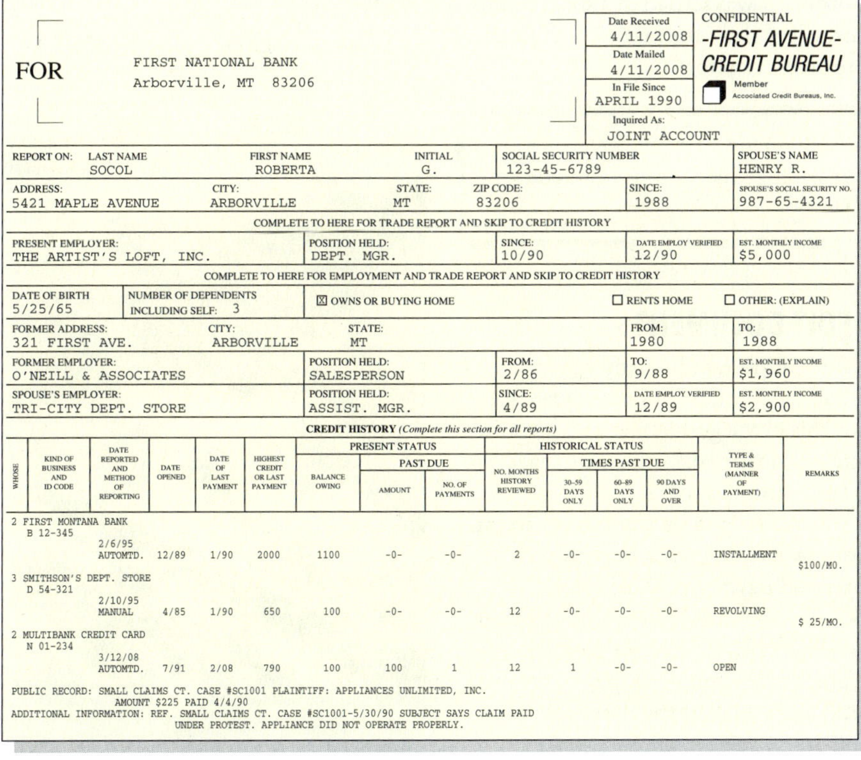

WHOSE	KIND OF BUSINESS AND ID CODE	DATE REPORTED AND METHOD OF REPORTING	DATE OPENED	DATE OF LAST PAYMENT	HIGHEST CREDIT OR LAST PAYMENT	BALANCE OWING	PAST DUE AMOUNT	PAST DUE NO. OF PAYMENTS	NO. MONTHS HISTORY REVIEWED	TIMES PAST DUE 30–59 DAYS ONLY	TIMES PAST DUE 60–89 DAYS ONLY	TIMES PAST DUE 90 DAYS AND OVER	TYPE & TERMS (MANNER OF PAYMENT)	REMARKS
2	FIRST MONTANA BANK B 12-345	2/6/95 AUTOMTD.	12/89	1/90	2000	1100	-0-	-0-	2	-0-	-0-	-0-	INSTALLMENT	$100/MO.
3	SMITHSON'S DEPT. STORE D 54-321	2/10/95 MANUAL	4/85	1/90	650	100	-0-	-0-	12	-0-	-0-	-0-	REVOLVING	$ 25/MO.
2	MULTIBANK CREDIT CARD N 01-234	3/12/08 AUTOMTD.	7/91	2/08	790	100	100	1	12	1	-0-	-0-	OPEN	

PUBLIC RECORD: SMALL CLAIMS CT. CASE #SC1001 PLAINTIFF: APPLIANCES UNLIMITED, INC.
AMOUNT $225 PAID 4/4/90
ADDITIONAL INFORMATION: REF. SMALL CLAIMS CT. CASE #SC1001-5/30/90 SUBJECT SAYS CLAIM PAID
UNDER PROTEST. APPLIANCE DID NOT OPERATE PROPERLY.

FIGURE 18-3

What kind of information would be on your credit report?

TEACH

Describe the functions of a credit bureau.

Use the FYI feature to inform students of the major credit reporting organizations.

Use Figure 18-3 to point out the information commonly contained in a credit report. Use an online search engine to show students examples of credit reports.

FIGURE 18-3 ANSWER

Answers will vary depending on their employment and credit histories. Some students may have no credit reports at this time in their lives.

Applied Skills

Office Technology Ask students to describe how a credit bureau might use database software to process various information items on a credit report.

lender. Credit bureaus do not make value judgments about any individual. The bureau simply gathers facts as reported to them.

Your credit record is confidential. That is, only you or those who have a legitimate reason for examining it can obtain it.

The top half contains background information about the individual. The bottom half lists information about the individual's accounts and payment history. Note that at the bottom there is a reference to a public record. It shows a dispute between the consumer and a creditor that was settled in a small claims court. All of this information is of interest to credit grantors.

> *checkpoint* >>
> What is the main purpose of a credit bureau?

CREDIT DOCUMENTS

Credit is important in many ways. Millions of consumers and businesses enjoy this privilege. No matter what kind of credit is involved, both parties have legal responsibilities.

You can help maintain a good credit record by keeping track of your purchases and payments. When you buy on credit, you should keep a copy of the sales slip, credit card receipt, or other documents. As you make payments by check, keep track of the date and check number.

Credit Contracts

"KWYS" are four letters to keep in mind when signing any legal form. These letters stand for "know what you're signing." This principle applies to all credit contracts. An installment contract is one of the most important forms you may sign. Before signing one, consider the following questions.

- How much are the finance charges? Are they clearly shown on the contract?
- Does the contract include the cost of services you may need, such as repairs to a television or a washing machine?
- Does the contract have an add-on feature so that you can later buy other items?
- If you pay the contract in full before the ending date, will the finance charge be reduced?
- Is the contract completely filled in before you sign? Be sure to draw a line through any blank space before signing.
- Will you be given a copy of the contract?

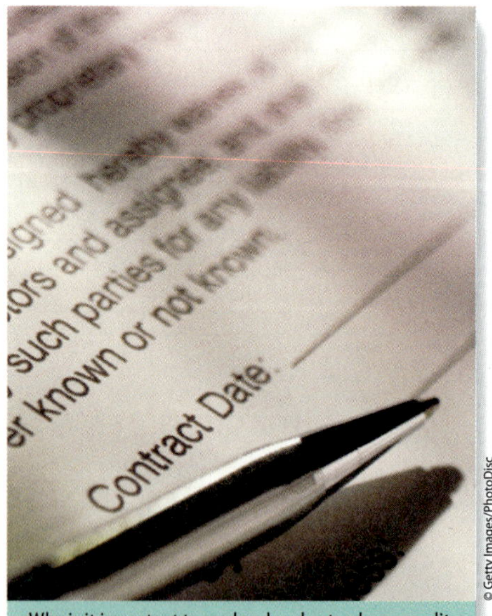

Why is it important to read and understand your credit documents before signing them?

- Under wht conditions can the seller repossess the merchandise if you do not pay on time?

Statement of Account

As a credit card or charge account customer, you will receive a monthly summary of your account. The **statement of account**, or simply the *statement,* is a record of the transactions completed during the billing period. Most statements report the following information.

- The balance that was due when the last statement was mailed

- The amounts charged during the month

- The amounts credited to your account for payments or for returned items

- The current balance, which is the old balance + finance charges + purchases – payments

- The minimum amount of your next payment and when it is due

Figure 18-4 shows a sample of a monthly statement of a charge account.

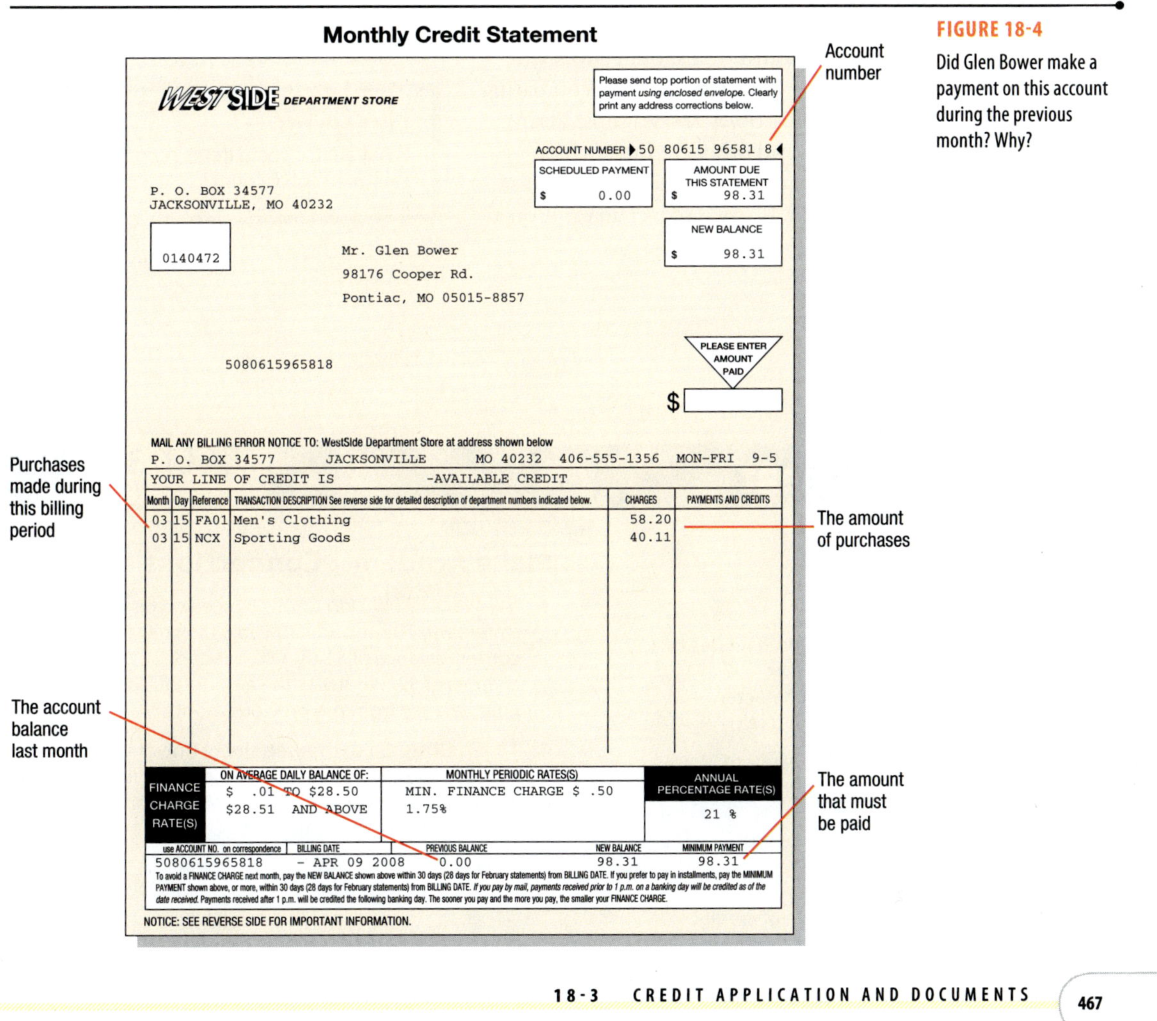

Monthly Credit Statement

Different Learning Abilities

Dyslexia Prepare a series of short assignments requesting students to locate various information items on the credit statement presented in Figure 18-4.

Accuracy of Records

Keeping accurate records will help you avoid credit record problems. Accurate record keeping is a good personal business practice.

Many errors are simply honest mistakes. Businesses are as eager to correct them as you are. Your creditworthiness may be at stake. Bad publicity may also hurt the reputation of the business if errors are not corrected.

Avoiding Fraud

The Federal Trade Commission reports that credit card fraud is a major problem. To avoid loss due to fraud, you should check your credit card account statements very carefully for errors.

Each month, you should check the accuracy of your statement by comparing it with your copies of sales slips. Verify payments and other credits, such as amounts subtracted when merchandise is returned. If you discover an error on a statement, you should notify the business at once. To help prevent Internet fraud, online credit card transactions require account numbers, expiration dates, and printed security numbers. The data transfer is also encrypted.

> *checkpoint* >>
> What are the main items reported on a statement of account?

What safety precautions are in place on the Internet to prevent credit card fraud?

© Photographer's Choice/Getty Images

18-3 Assessment

Xtra! Study Tools
school.cengage.com/business/introbiz

Key Concepts

Determine the best answer.

1. A reputation for paying bills on time relates to a person's
   a. capacity
   b. collateral
   c. character
   d. capital

2. The main activity of a credit bureau is to
   a. calculate the cost of credit for lenders and borrowers
   b. determine when a person is overusing credit
   c. contact a government agency when lenders overcharge for credit
   d. report information on the use of credit by consumers

Make Academic Connections

3. *Business Math* Don Ghonski received his credit card statement. This report showed $45 in new purchases, a current balance of $178, a payment of $70, and finance charges of $2. What was the amount of Don's beginning balance from the previous month?

4. *Technology* Go to the web site of one of the major credit reporting agencies. What services does the agency provide for businesses? What information is available to assist consumers?

18-4 Protection of Credit Right

Goals

Identify credit application regulations.

Explain credit use regulations.

Discuss credit problems and available assistance.

Key Terms

credit counselor

bankruptcy

Focus on Real Life

Ben Khan mistakenly leaves a credit card lying on a counter at a store. After asking at the store and waiting a few weeks, he realizes the card will not be returned. On his next statement, more than $200 worth of merchandise was charged.

Julie Roma checks her charge account statement and finds several errors on it. One charge is for a purchase she did not make, and this is the third month in a row that this charge has shown up on the statement.

Your friends, Monique and Gary Buckman, had their loan application turned down. The loan officer explained that their credit bureau report was not good. Monique and Gary were shocked. They always pay their bills on time, with only a few minor exceptions. They need this loan for home improvements.

These credit problems can happen to anyone. If consumers know about credit laws and regulations, they can take actions to avoid and correct problems.

CREDIT APPLICATION REGULATIONS

Most businesses are honest in their business dealings. Unfortunately, some are not. Because of this, it became necessary for federal and state governments to pass laws to protect credit consumers.

Truth-in-Lending Act

The *Truth-in-Lending Act of 1968* was the first of a series of credit protection laws. Truth-in-Lending requires that you be told the cost of credit before signing an agreement. The law requires that the lender clearly state the annual percentage rate (APR) and total finance charge.

The Truth-in-Lending Act also protects consumers against unauthorized use of credit cards. The law limits your liability to $50 for unauthorized credit card purchases made prior to notifying the card issuer. You are not liable for any fraudulent charges made after you have notified the credit card company. You can notify the company by telephone, but you should also put your notification in writing.

> **main idea**
>
> Identify credit application regulations.

© Brand X Pictures

What are some reasons that a loan application would be turned down?

TEACH

Have students describe factors that might result in a person being discriminated against when applying for credit.

ONGOING ASSESSMENT

checkpoint >> **ANSWER**

The Truth-in-Lending Act assists consumers by requiring that they be fully informed of all of the costs of credit before signing an agreement. Borrowers must be informed of the annual percentage rate and total finance charge. The Law also limits consumers' liability for unauthorized use of credit cards to $50 for unauthorized purchases made prior to notifying the card issuer, and card holders are not liable for any purchases made after notifying the credit card company.

TEACH

Explain the features of the Fair Credit Billing Act.

THINK CRITICALLY THROUGH VISUALS

The Equal Credit Opportunity Act is important because it prohibits creditors from denying a person credit because of age, race, sex, or marital status. A creditor must investigate an applicant's creditworthiness and, upon request, give any person who is denied credit a written statement of the reasons for the denial.

Equal Credit Opportunity Act

The *Equal Credit Opportunity Act* prohibits creditors from denying a person credit because of age, race, sex, or marital status. Young people who may have just entered the labor market cannot be denied credit based only on age. Older, possibly retired, people also have special protection under this act.

Married women who previously found it difficult to establish credit in their own names now have a legal right to do so. Under this law, a woman has a right to her own credit if she proves to be creditworthy.

Unless your state still requires a person to be at least 21 to enter into a contract, a creditor cannot deny you credit based on your age alone. A creditor must look into your creditworthiness. Upon request, a creditor must give any person who is denied credit a written statement of the reasons for denial.

main idea

Explain credit use regulations.

CREDIT USE REGULATIONS

Several laws have been created to protect your rights when using credit.

Fair Credit Billing Act

The *Fair Credit Billing Act* requires prompt correction of billing mistakes. To get a correction of an error, you must notify the creditor in writing within 60 days after your statement was mailed. A good rule is to report errors as soon as you discover them. After you report an error, remember the following points.

- While waiting for an answer, you are not required to pay any amount in question.
- The creditor must acknowledge your complaint within 30 days unless your statement is corrected before that time.

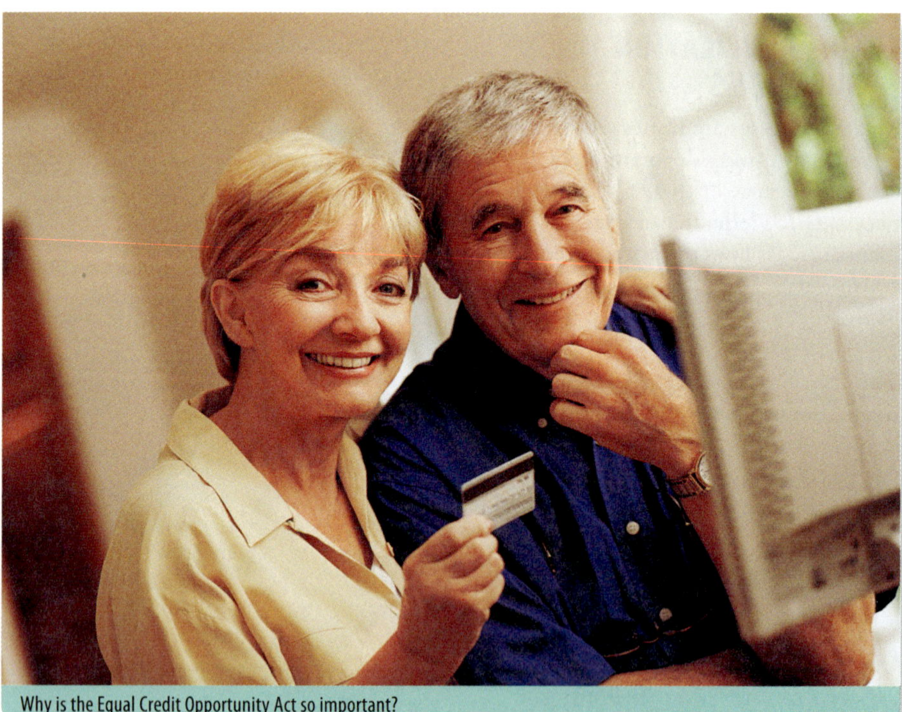

Why is the Equal Credit Opportunity Act so important?

© Digital Vision

Different Learning Styles

Print Learner Suggest that students focus their attention on the list of provisions of the Fair Credit Billing Act on this page. Ask them to develop a scenario that illustrates all four points.

- You do not pay finance charges on any amount in error.

- If no error is found, the creditor must bill you again. The bill may include finance charges that have accumulated plus any minimum payments that were missed while the statement was being questioned.

The Fair Credit Billing Act also provides that you may withhold payment of any balance due on defective merchandise or services purchased with a credit card. Your first step should be to contact the business and try to resolve the problem. You can correct many situations if your complaint is made in a courteous but firm manner. The law protects you if you have made this "good faith" effort to work with the business.

Fair Credit Reporting Act

The *Fair Credit Reporting Act* is the law that gives consumers the right to know what information credit bureaus are giving to potential creditors, employers, and insurers. This law provides that if credit is denied based on information in a credit report, the applicant must be given the name, address, and phone number of the credit bureau that provided the information. In addition, credit records for both a husband and wife are kept if both are responsible for the debt. This allows a credit history to be developed for each spouse.

Prior to the passage of this law, many consumers were unaware that potential lenders had access to reports on their bill-paying habits. This act makes those reports available to the consumer. It provides ways in which consumers can access and correct information.

The Fair Credit Reporting Act also requires that credit bureaus must delete any information dealing with a personal bankruptcy that is more than 10 years old. The credit bureau must also delete any other adverse information if it is more than seven years old.

A QUESTION OF ETHICS

Pawnshops, Payday Loans, and Credit Repair

Consumer credit is an area where unfair and deceitful business credit practices thrive. Pawnshops lend money based on the value of property, such as jewelry. These small loans are usually repaid in a month or two, but typically at a high interest rate. Some states allow pawnshops to charge 3 percent a month—that's 36 percent a year.

People in need of a small amount of money for a short time may use a *payday loan*. Nearly 10,000 of these companies now operate in the United States. The interest rate for this cash advance can be more than 600 percent. With a payday loan, a consumer may write a personal check for $230 to borrow $200 for 14 days. The lender agrees to hold the check until the next payday. This $30 finance charge for the 14 days translates into an APR of nearly 400 percent. Often, a customer continues to borrow without paying anything back. Within a few weeks, the finance charge can exceed the amount borrowed.

"Credit Repair—Are you in trouble with past due payments? Is your credit record being ruined? We can fix all problems quickly—come in today." Every day, credit repair companies offer to help consumers with poor credit histories. They promise to improve your credit rating, for a fee. Too often, after paying hundreds of dollars, consumers get nothing. Companies disappear with your money. To protect consumers, the Credit Repair Organizations Act requires that credit repair companies cannot collect their fee until completing the promised services.

Think Critically

1. Why are people attracted to these credit situations?
2. Conduct research to obtain additional information about pawnshops, payday loans, and credit repair companies. Report your findings in a short report.

TEACH

Describe the purpose of the Consumer Credit Reporting Reform Act.

Ask students to describe situations in which a debt collector uses inappropriate behavior or tactics.

Explain the provisions of the Fair Debt Collections Act.

Highlight the suggested actions to take when a person is facing credit problems.

THINK CRITICALLY THROUGH VISUALS

A reputable credit counselor can help individuals assess their credit problems and suggest actions to take to reduce spending and eliminate credit difficulties.

ONGOING ASSESSMENT

checkpoint >> **ANSWER**

The purpose of the Fair Credit Reporting Act is to give consumers the right to know what information credit bureaus are giving to potential creditors, employers, and insurers. The Act requires credit bureaus to keep records for both a husband and wife if both are responsible for the debt so that each spouse can develop a credit history. It also requires credit bureaus to delete information dealing with a personal bankruptcy that is more than 10 years old and any other adverse information that is more than 7 years old.

main idea

Discuss credit problems and available assistance.

Consumer Credit Reporting Reform Act

An unfavorable credit report can force you to pay a higher interest rate on a loan or you might be denied a loan. *The Consumer Credit Reporting Reform Act* places the burden of proof for accurate credit information on the credit reporting agency rather than on you. Under this law, the creditor must certify that disputed data is accurate. If a creditor or the credit bureau verifies incorrect data, you can sue for damages. The federal government and state attorneys general can also sue creditors for civil damages.

What can a credit counselor do for people with credit problems?

Fair Debt Collection Practices Act

A *debt collection agency* attempts to obtain money that is past due. The agency may contact people who are overdue with credit payments.

To prevent threats and other inappropriate actions, the *Fair Debt Collection Practices Act* requires that debt collectors treat you fairly. It bans various debt collection actions. This law does not take away the debts that are owed.

A debt collector may contact you in person, by mail, telephone, telegram, or fax. A debt collector may not contact you at inconvenient times or places, such as before 8 a.m. or after 9 p.m. They also may not contact you at work if your employer prohibits such contact.

checkpoint >>

What is the purpose of the Fair Credit Reporting Act?

CREDIT PROBLEMS AND ASSISTANCE

A person who cannot pay his or her bills when they are due might take these four steps.

1. Contact creditors and explain the situation.

2. Make a realistic proposal for when and what you can pay. Don't just say, "I can't pay."

3. Keep any promises you make.

4. Make a written copy of your agreement to avoid problems later.

You may be able to work out a *debt repayment plan.* A creditor and a debtor develop this agreement to reduce payments to a more manageable level and still pay off the debt. This is good for both the creditor and the debtor.

One thing to avoid is being misled by advertisements that tell you, "Erase bad credit! 100% guaranteed." Claims such as these are fraudulent. No one can unconditionally correct a bad credit record—it does not work that way. If you need help with a credit problem, contact a reputable credit counseling organization.

Credit Counseling

Different kinds of help are available to people with credit problems. A **credit counselor** discusses and suggests actions to take to reduce spending and eliminate credit difficulties.

Various nonprofit counseling services are available around the country. The National Foundation of Consumer Credit can direct you to a local credit assistance program. This nonprofit organization has hundreds of member agencies that operate local offices around the country. Many of the member agencies are known as Consumer Credit Counseling Service (CCCS). Consumers are warned to be cautious of for-profit credit counseling services.

Bankruptcy

Consumers may take one additional step when facing credit problems. They should use this final option only for extreme situations. **Bankruptcy** is the legal process of reducing or eliminating an amount owed. This process is costly and requires legal assistance. Consumers can usually avoid bankruptcy by using credit wisely and practicing sensible money management.

checkpoint >>
What actions can a person take when facing credit problems?

18-4 Assessment

Key Concepts

Determine the best answer.

1. A person may be denied credit on the basis of his or her
   a. gender
   b. age
   c. income
   d. type of job

2. The federal law that provides protection when an error occurs on a monthly statement is the
   a. Truth-in-Lending Law
   b. Fair Credit Reporting Act
   c. Fair Credit Billing Act
   d. Equal Credit Opportunity Act

3. The legal process of reducing or eliminating an amount owed is
   a. credit
   b. credit reporting
   c. bankruptcy
   d. financing

Make Academic Connections

4. *Statistics* Obtain current data about the number of people who have declared personal bankruptcy in recent years. Prepare a chart to show the trend of these data. Give an explanation as to why the trend occurred. What are the costs of bankruptcy to a society?

5. *Communication* Create a role-playing situation in which you are denied credit. Have one person explain how he or she encountered credit problems. Have the other person suggest actions to eliminate the credit problems.

TEACH

Warn students about companies that claim to easily solve your credit problems. Describe credit counseling services that are available to consumers.

Explain situations when bankruptcy may be appropriate. Emphasize the drawbacks of bankruptcy for both consumers and society.

ONGOING ASSESSMENT

checkpoint >> **ANSWER**

When facing credit problems, a person can contact creditors and explain the situation, make a realistic proposal for when and what he or she can pay, keep any promises made, and make a written copy of agreements to avoid later misunderstandings. A person with credit problems may be able to work out a debt repayment plan. He or she could also contact a credit counselor for advice. Bankruptcy is a final option for extreme debt situations.

ASSESS

Key Concepts Answers

1. c. income
2. c. Fair Credit Billing Act
3. c. bankruptcy

Make Academic Connections

4. Charts will vary depending on when the assignment is completed. Answers should indicate that students understand that the societal costs of bankruptcy include financial loss to businesses and the individual's loss of creditworthiness.

5. Students engage in role-play to explore credit problems and solutions.

RETEACH

Highlight the main provisions of the credit protection laws discussed in this lesson.

ENRICH

Have students prepare a list of questions that a credit counselor might ask a client.

CLOSE

Ask students to describe the major causes of credit problems.

Communicate Business Concepts Answers

1. a. Students will probably say Debbie's plan is safer.

b. Answers will vary. Students might suggest that Edward not make more purchases with credit cards than he can pay for. They might suggest that Debbie use credit cards wisely to take advantage of special sales on products she needs and to avoid carrying large amounts of cash while shopping.

2. Extending credit could help Gerry's business because customers will be more likely to make large purchases. Her business could be hurt if customers do not pay their debts. She could offer credit card options to her customers; even though she will have to pay the credit card company a small percentage of her sales, she will not risk a loss if a customer does not pay.

3. Answers will vary. Here are some possible responses:

a. Most students will agree that this can be a convenience as long as the credit user does not accumulate too much debt.

b. Most students will agree that this is a wise approach, but may not always be possible.

c. Although this is true, sometimes there are valid reasons for postponing paying for a purchase when the borrower has a plan for paying off the debt.

d. Some students may agree; however, they may not realize that even a small finance charge may represent a very high interest rate.

Business Notes

18-1 CREDIT FUNDAMENTALS

1. Credit is the privilege of using someone else's money with the obligation to repay it at a future time. The major types of consumer credit are charge accounts, credit cards, installment credit, and consumer loans.

2. Credit used wisely makes some buying more convenient, gives the purchaser immediate possession rather than waiting until later, allows buyers to take advantage of special sales, and establishes a person's credit rating.

3. Credit is misused if it results in overbuying, careless buying, paying higher prices in stores that grant credit, or incurring excessive debt.

18-2 COST OF CREDIT

4. The amount of interest expense is calculated by multiplying the interest rate times the principal times the number of days or months.

5. The annual percentage rate (APR) states the percentage cost of credit on a yearly basis. Costs of credit in addition to interest include service fees, the cost of collecting bad debts, and credit insurance. The finance charge is the total dollar cost of credit including interest and all other charges.

6. The cost of credit varies among lenders. You can save money by shopping around to compare the APR, amount of monthly payments, and total finance charge.

18-3 CREDIT APPLICATION AND DOCUMENTS

7. A credit application is a document on which you provide information needed by a lender. A business considers a person's character (honesty and willingness to pay debts), capacity (the ability to pay debts), and capital (the value of the person's possessions) in reviewing an applicant for credit.

8. A credit bureau gathers information on credit users. A credit record documents your credit history. You can maintain a good credit history by paying your bills on time.

9. Two commonly used credit documents are the installment contract and the statement of account. Before signing an installment contract, consider the finance charges and other features of the loan. Credit statements should be checked carefully and errors reported as soon as they are discovered.

18-4 PROTECTION OF CREDIT RIGHTS

10. The Truth-in-Lending Law and the Equal Credit Opportunity Act provide information and protection when applying for credit.

11. The Fair Credit Billing Act, the Fair Credit Reporting Act, the Consumer Credit Reporting Act, and the Fair Debt Collections Act protect consumers when using credit.

12. Assistance with credit problems is available from counselors, debt consolidation, and, as a last option, bankruptcy.

Communicate Business Concepts

1. Edward Adiska buys everything he possibly can on credit. If he does not have enough money to cover his monthly payments when they are due, he borrows money to pay them. His sister, Debbie, likes to buy things only after she has saved enough money to pay cash for them.
a. Whose plan do you think is better? Why?
b. What suggestions about the use of credit might you make to Edward and Debbie?

2. Gerry Shadle owns and operates a flower shop. She is considering expanding her shop to include home decorating items. At present, Gerry sells for cash only. How might extending credit help or hurt her business?

3. Read the following statements and explain why you agree or disagree.
a. "A credit card is nice to have. If I'm out of cash, I can still buy what I want."

b. "I don't believe in using credit for most purchases. I pay cash for everyday items and use credit only for expensive items, such as a new refrigerator."

c. "If I can't pay cash, I can't afford it. I won't buy anything unless I can pay cash."

d. "I often don't pay the full amount of my charge account when it is due; the finance charges are quite reasonable."

4. Les Heddle needed to borrow $15,000 to do some remodeling in his store and has three options:

OPTION 1: The Thrifty Loan Company offered him an APR of 16 percent for a three-year loan. Monthly payments, including finance charges, would be $555.

OPTION 2: The Greenback Bank offered him a five-year loan at 15 percent APR with a total monthly payment of $375.

OPTION 3: The Silk Purse Finance Lending Shop did not quote an APR figure but said, "We have a 'no frills' loan policy, and you can have a four-year loan with monthly payments at the amazingly low figure of $496 per month."

Construct a loan comparison chart showing the lender, APR, loan length, monthly payment, total payment, and cost of credit. Then decide which loan would be the best for Les Heddle. Give reasons for your decision.

5. Suzanne Winters does not believe in buying anything on credit. She says too many people get into trouble with credit and many errors are made in credit transactions. Explain to Suzanne ways in which laws protect consumers who engage in credit transactions and tell her about some of the help that is available for consumers who have credit problems.

Develop Your Business Language

Match the terms listed with the definitions.

6. Your reputation for paying your bills on time.

7. Someone who becomes responsible for payment of a note if you do not pay as promised.

8. The privilege of using someone else's money for a period of time.

9. A loan in which you agree to make monthly payments in specific amounts over a period of time.

10. The legal process of reducing or eliminating an amount owed.

11. A person who suggests actions to reduce spending and eliminate credit difficulties.

12. A payment of part of the purchase price that is made as part of a credit agreement.

13. A written promise to repay based on the debtor's excellent credit rating.

14. Property that is offered as security for some loan agreements.

15. The total dollar cost of credit, including interest and all other charges.

16. The percentage cost of credit on a yearly basis.

17. A company that gathers information on credit users and sells that information in the form of credit reports to credit grantors.

18. A record of the transactions that you have completed with a business during a billing period.

19. A form in which you provide information needed by a lender to make a decision about granting credit.

20. The cost of using someone else's money.

KEY TERMS

a. annual percentage rate (APR)
b. bankruptcy
c. collateral
d. cosigner
e. credit
f. credit application
g. credit bureau
h. credit counselor
i. credit rating
j. down payment
k. finance charge
l. installment loan
m. interest
n. promissory note
o. statement of account

4. The loan comparison chart appears at the bottom of this page.

This exercise should convince students that it is worth the time it takes to shop for credit. The Thrifty loan has the lowest cost, but the Greenback loan could be paid back with the lowest monthly payments.

5. Suzanne should be told about consumer credit protection laws, consumer credit counseling services, and debt-repayment plans.

Develop Your Business Language Answers

6. i. credit rating

7. d. cosigner

8. e. credit

9. l. installment loan

10. b. bankruptcy

11. h. credit counselor

12. j. down payment

13. n. promissory note

14. c. collateral

15. k. finance charge

16. a. annual percentage rate (APR)

17. g. credit bureau

18. o. statement of account

19. f. credit application

20. m. interest

Lender	APR	Loan Length	Monthly Payment	Total Payment	Cost of Credit
Thrifty	16%	3 yrs.	$555	$19,980	$4,980
Greenback	15%	5 yrs.	$375	$22,500	$7,500
Silk Purse	?	4 yrs.	$496	$23,808	$8,808

Make Academic Connections

21. **HISTORY** Research the use of credit throughout history. When was credit first used in various civilizations? How has credit been used to influence the development of retailing and other business activities in the United States?

22. **CULTURE** People in different countries have different attitudes toward credit. Based on web searches, library research, and talking with people who know about other countries, prepare a summary of how credit is used around the world.

23. **RESEARCH** Collect credit applications, advertisements, and online offers. Create a table to compare the different APRs reported in the various credit information sources.

24. **COMMUNICATION** Prepare a one-minute oral summary of the activities of a credit bureau. Explain how credit bureaus serve both consumers and businesses.

25. **MATH** Find the date of maturity for each of these loans:

DATE OF LOAN	TIME OF LOAN
March 15	4 months
May 26	3 months
July 31	5 months
April 30	30 days
October 5	45 days

26. **RESEARCH** Some credit contracts include the "Rule of 78." This condition results in a "prepayment penalty" if a loan is paid off early. Conduct a web search to obtain a basic understanding of the Rule of 78.

27. **TECHNOLOGY** Conduct a web search to locate a sample of a credit contract. What features of the contract provide consumers with clear information about the cost of credit and other terms of the loan agreement?

28. **LAW** Several federal agencies, including the Federal Trade Commission and the Federal Reserve Board, administer consumer credit protection laws. Conduct research on the laws discussed in the chapter. Prepare a table with a summary of which agency to contact when your rights are violated.

29. **MATH** Before borrowing $200, Laura Demetry visited a small loan company and the loan department of a bank. At the loan company, she found that she could borrow the $200 if she signed a note agreeing to repay the balance in six equal monthly installments of $36.50. At the bank, she could borrow the money by signing a promissory note for $215 and repaying the balance in six equal monthly payments.

 a. What would be the cost of the loan at the small loan company?

 b. What would be the cost of the loan at the bank?

Linking School and Community

Obtain information on the responsibilities involved with cosigning a loan. Talk to people in your community. What do they know about being a cosigner? What precautions should be taken when cosigning? Talk with a credit counselor to obtain information about problems associated with cosigning a loan.

Web Workout

Individuals should give considerable evaluation to choosing a credit card and not react to free offers, temporary low interest rates, or pre-approved cards. Individuals should choose a credit card offer that meets their needs. Use the Internet to identify a wide variety of card types. Evaluate different card offerings using at least three different credit card sources such as a bank, a credit card company, or other businesses that offer reward cards (airlines, hotels, etc.).

Think Critically

1. Develop a table to evaluate at least three different cards. Choose from this list a card you would like to use and justify your choice.

2. Identify cards that are directed toward students. Compare interest rates for cards directed toward students versus cards for individuals with good credit ratings. Explain why there are differences.

Decision-Making Strategies

Samantha Mae has been out of school for three years and has held four different jobs with different employers. She has been on her present job for two months. Her monthly take-home pay is $1,362. She shares an apartment with two friends to keep expenses down, but she is always in debt. Each month, she is short of the money she needs to pay all of her charge accounts. Her checking account is frequently overdrawn. Samantha has decided it would be better to live by herself. She blames her roommates for her credit spending sprees. She has come to you for a loan of $2,000. Her new apartment will cost $400 a month, and she wants to pay off some of her bills that are past due. She assures you that she will pay you at least $50 each month.

30. What are some criteria you would use to determine whether a personal loan for Samantha would be a good idea? What additional information might you want?

31. Would you loan the money to Samantha? Why or why not?

Impromptu Speaking Event

Leaders have the special skill to express their thoughts without prior preparation. Poise, self-confidence, and organization of facts are three valuable skills that are beneficial for articulate leaders.

Participants will draw a current event and will be given 10 minutes to organize their speech. One 4" by 6" index card will be given to the participant and may be used during the preparation and performance of the impromptu speech. Information may be written on both sides of the note card. Your speech should be four minutes in length, and no reference materials may be brought to or used during the preparation or presentation. No microphone will be used for your speech. Participants will receive a five-point deduction for any time under 3:31 or over 4:29 minutes. Some impromptu topics:

- Importance of Credit
- Minding Your Cs of Credit
- Credit Protection and Rights
- Avoiding the Disasters of Credit

PERFORMANCE INDICATORS EVALUATED

- Understand the three Cs of credit.
- Differentiate the pros and cons of credit.
- Define the role of credit in the market economy.
- Explain credit concepts in a clear, concise manner.

For more detailed information about performance indicators, go to the FBLA web site.

Think Critically

1. List two advantages and two disadvantages of credit.
2. What are the three Cs of credit? How can individuals protect their credit?
3. Do you believe that consumers are addicted to credit in a negative way? Explain your answer.

http://www.fbla-pbl.org/

Access the web site shown here to find portfolio activities for this chapter. Use the activities to provide tangible evidence of your learning.

school.cengage.com/business/introtobiz

Information for identifying and analyzing investment alternatives is presented in this chapter.

19-1 Saving and Investment Planning

Types of investments and factors to consider when selecting an investment are the main topics in this lesson.

19-2 Stock Investments

Type of stock, investing in stock, and stock values are the focus of this lesson.

19-3 Bonds and Mutual Funds

This lesson provides explanations of government bonds, corporate bonds, and mutual funds.

19-4 Real Estate Investment

Various housing options, along with discussion of home buying activities, are covered in this lesson.

19-5 Other Investments

This lesson explains investing in commodities and collectibles.

CHAPTER 19

Savings and Investment Strategies

© Stockbyte/Getty Images

478

Teaching Resources

Activities and Study Guide, Ch. 19
Chapter and Unit Tests, Ch. 19
Spanish Resources, Ch. 19

Exam_View_® CD, Ch. 19
Instructor's Resource CD
- PowerPoint Slides, Ch. 19
- Lesson Plans, Ch. 19

Xtra! Web Site

school.cengage.com/business/introtobiz
- Study Tools, 19-1, 19-2, 19-3, 19-4, 19-5
- Quiz Prep, Ch. 19
- Net Bookmark, Ch. 19
- Crossword Puzzle, Ch. 19
- Portfolio Activity, Ch. 19

Planning a Career in...
INVESTMENTS

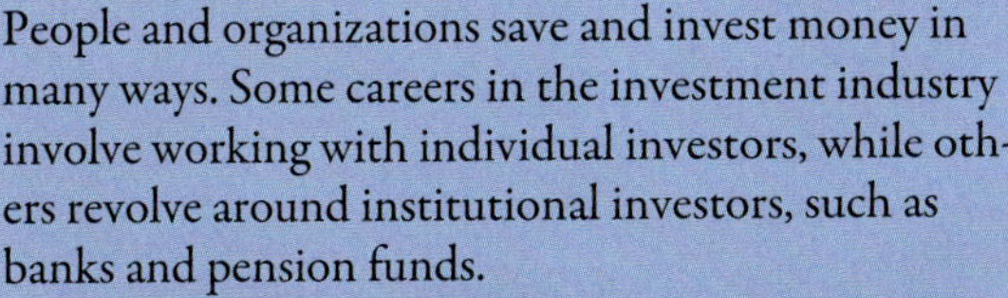

People and organizations save and invest money in many ways. Some careers in the investment industry involve working with individual investors, while others revolve around institutional investors, such as banks and pension funds.

Career opportunities exist for workers who want to work directly with clients and those who prefer to work behind the scenes. Positions are located in diverse settings such as retail outlets, call centers, and corporate headquarters. Although some positions are located in major financial centers, there are career opportunities around the country and around the world.

New and different investment products continue to be created. These investment alternatives result in employment opportunities for those interested in helping others plan their financial futures.

Employment Outlook

- As more people seek investment opportunities, the demand for securities sales workers will increase.
- Clerical and research workers with computer skills and finance knowledge will have average growth.
- Nationally, demand for real estate sales workers will grow more slowly than average, with some regions, especially in the south and west, having greater job opportunities than others.

Related Job Titles

- Brokerage Account Executive
- Brokerage Clerk
- Economist
- Financial Analyst
- Fund Manager
- Investment Banker
- Real Estate Appraiser
- Real Estate Agent
- Securities Research Analyst
- Securities and Commodities Sales Agent
- Stockbroker

Needed Skills

- Understanding economic conditions and global business trends is fundamental.
- Knowledge of investment terms and the legal aspects of investing is necessary.
- Workers involved in selling securities and commodities must pass licensing exams and they need strong sales skills and communication ability.
- Real estate agents and brokers must pass a state test for their licenses and need to be knowledgeable about the housing market in their community.

What's it like to work as an...
Investment Broker

"Do you think I should sell my health care stocks? Or will they continue to be a good investment for my future? How will changing interest rates affect my investment holdings? What will be the charges to sell my stocks?"

These questions are commonly asked of Roberto Jiminez, an investment broker. He has found that an understanding of economic conditions and business trends is the foundation of success in this field.

Each day, financial markets around the world process millions of actions to buy and sell investments. Stocks, bonds, mutual funds, real estate, currencies, commodities, gold, and silver are bought and sold by investors. The people who research, sell, and record these transactions are employed by a variety of investment companies and related businesses.

What about you? How could economic conditions affect the demand for investment jobs? What training and knowledge would be important for success in investment careers?

Planning a Career in...

INVESTMENTS

Global business activities, technology, and other factors have created increased interest in personal investing. Many career opportunities have been created by this trend.

What About You?
Answer

When the economy is strong, many people will be looking for ways to invest their money and the demand for investment jobs will increase. Training and knowledge that would be important for success in investment careers would include a thorough understanding of economics and how business systems work. Fluency with investment terms and a grasp of the legal aspects of investing will also be essential.

Additional Career Information

Additional information on careers can be found in the *Occupational Outlook Handbook*, an online publication (www.bls.gov/oco) of the federal government. Tell your class about this resource and how to use it. This description of job duties can be used to demonstrate the relevancy of skills learned in this course.

19-1 Saving and Investment Planning

Goals

Explain the basics of saving and investing.

Identify types of savings and investments.

Discuss factors to consider when evaluating savings and investment alternatives.

Key Terms

saving

investing

yield

liquidity

Focus on Real Life

"I'd sure like to buy that MP3 player," said Mel. "It has all the features I want. But it costs about $150. I can't afford it."

"Try saving your money," Hank said in an encouraging voice. "Maybe if you cut back on some of your other spending, you could save enough money to buy it."

"That would take forever," sighed Mel.

"It's easier than you think," responded Hank. "If you put aside just a dollar a day, within six months you'd have more than $150. If you save even more each day, you could buy the player fairly soon."

"You're kidding!" exclaimed Mel.

"Really," said Hank. "Most people don't realize that saving small amounts of money on a regular basis can result in large amounts in the future, and that doesn't even include the interest you can earn."

---

main idea

Explain the basics of saving and investing.

SAVING AND INVESTMENT BASICS

Creating a personal saving and investing strategy is vital for every financial plan. Putting money aside in a systematic way is the basis for achieving financial goals.

When savings are invested and used, the economy benefits. Individuals, businesses, and governments borrow money from financial institutions. People commonly borrow the savings of others to pay for homes, motor vehicles, and college. When this money is spent, demand for goods and services increases. This results in more jobs and creates more spending by workers.

Businesses borrow funds to operate or expand their operations. Building a new factory, replacing old equipment, or selling a new product are common reasons for business borrowing. These actions create jobs and expand economic activity.

Governments may borrow for highways, schools, or other public services. An economy would be significantly weakened without savings and investments.

Savings and Investment Activities

Saving is the storage of money for future use. How much you save, where you put your savings, and what you save for are important decisions. People save different amounts of money for different reasons and in different ways.

Some people save for years and then use those funds for a down payment to buy a home. Saving is also important to have money available for emergencies. Financial planning experts encourage people to deposit 10 percent of their income into a savings account or other investment each month.

Different Learning Abilities

At-Risk Emphasize to students the importance of saving and investment knowledge for various aspects of their lives. Ask students to explain how investing might benefit them in the future. Ask students to focus their attention on the next year and the next five years

After building up some savings, most people want to earn more. **Investing** means using your savings to earn more money. While a savings plan is a simple type of investing, many other investment choices are available.

Determine Investment Goals

Every saver and investor has one of two major financial goals: income and growth. People who want income for current living expenses desire *current income*. People select various types of savings plans and investments to provide current income.

In contrast, *long-term growth* is the other main investment goal. This goal is for those who desire financial security in the future. Investors who desire long-term growth choose investments that they hope will increase in value over time.

The Growth of Savings

In addition to putting money aside as savings, you should have those savings working for you. *Interest* is money you receive for letting others use your money.

If you save $50 a month, in a year, the savings will amount to $600. Suppose you deposit this money in a savings program that earns 6 percent simple interest, paid quarterly. You will earn $9 every three months. You will earn $36 each year. The interest is not added to your account, but rather is paid directly to you. At the end of 10 years, you will still have $600 in the account but will have earned $360 in interest.

Compound Interest Earning interest on previously earned interest results in faster growth of savings. *Compound interest* is computed on the amount saved plus the interest previously earned. For example, simple annual interest of 10 percent on $1,000 is $100.

If the interest is compounded, then the interest computed at the end of the next year is based on $1,100 ($1,000 + $100 first-year interest). The 10 percent interest earned in the second year is $110.

Interest the third year is based on $1,210 ($1,100 + $110 second-year interest) and is $121. When interest is compounded, the amount of interest paid increases each time it is calculated. Without compounding, the interest paid would be only $100 each year.

Interest can be compounded daily, monthly, quarterly, semiannually, or annually. The more frequent the compounding, the greater the growth in your savings. Figure 19-1 shows how quickly monthly savings of different amounts increase when interest is compounded quarterly at 6 percent.

> *checkpoint* ››
>
> How does saving influence economic activity?

Compound Interest (Quarterly)

Monthly Savings	End of First Year	End of Second Year	End of Third Year	End of Fourth Year	End of Fifth Year	End of Tenth Year
$ 5.00	$ 61.98	$ 127.76	$ 197.76	$ 271.68	$ 350.32	$ 822.16
10.00	123.95	255.52	395.15	543.35	700.47	1,644.32
25.00	309.89	638.79	987.87	1,358.38	1,751.62	4,110.79
30.00	371.86	766.55	1,185.45	1,630.05	2,101.94	4,932.95
35.00	433.84	894.30	1,383.02	1,901.73	2,452.26	5,755.11
50.00	619.77	1,277.58	1,975.74	2,716.75	3,503.24	8,221.59

FIGURE 19-1
What would be the effect if the interest was compounded monthly or weekly?

Applied Skills

Mathematics Explain the difference between simple and compound interest for a person's savings and investments. Use visuals to show the faster growth of money with compounding. Invite interested students to construct tables similar to Figure 19-1 for interest compounded weekly and monthly.

TEACH

Emphasize the importance of investing for economic growth.

Explain the two main goals of investing: current income and long-term growth. Have students describe situations for each of these two types of goals.

Use Figure 19-1 to illustrate the growth of savings.

FIGURE 19-1 *ANSWER*

This savings account would grow more quickly if the interest were compounded more frequently.

PROJECT

Provide the following instructions to students. (These instructions also appear on page xxv of the textbook.) Explain why people who have created life-span plans are often more successful in saving than those who have not. How might your life-span plan help you save?

Life-Span Plan Answers

Answers will vary. Students should point out that most people are better able to work and save when they have a clear idea of what they want to achieve.

ONGOING ASSESSMENT

checkpoint ›› *ANSWER*

Saving benefits the economy by making more money available for borrowing by individuals, businesses, and governments. When this money is spent, demand for goods and services increases, resulting in more jobs and more spending by workers.

TEACH

Provide an overview of the main categories of savings plans. Ask students to describe situations in which different savings plans would be appropriate.

Have students create a list of various types of investments.

THINK CRITICALLY THROUGH VISUALS

In addition to the classic piggy bank shown here, many banking institutions allow young people to open savings accounts. Some families buy a small amount of inexpensive stock for their children and then teach the children how to follow the stock's progress in the financial pages or over the Internet.

main idea

Identify types of savings and investments.

SAVING AND INVESTMENT CHOICES

Many choices are available for your saving and investing dollars. The choices range from very safe savings accounts to rather risky investments.

Savings Plans

Banks, credit unions, and other financial institutions offer a choice of savings plans. Regular savings accounts, certificates of deposit, and money market accounts all provide a safe location for storage of your money.

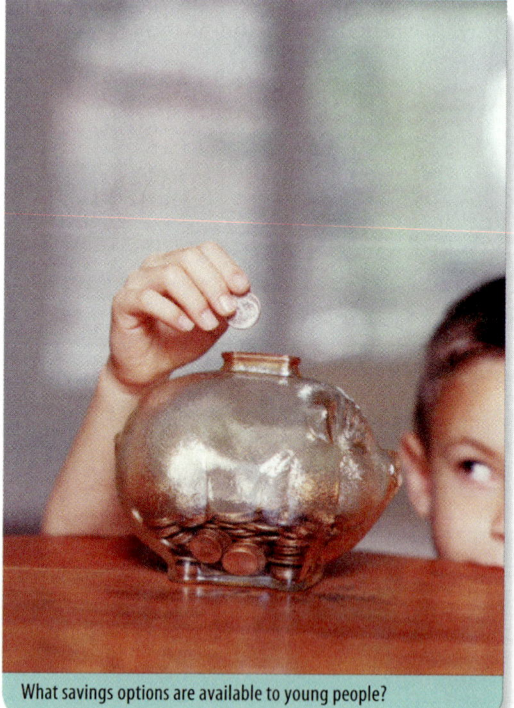
What savings options are available to young people?

© Getty Images/PhotoDisc

Savings Account A savings plan with a low or zero minimum balance is a regular savings account. Usually, you may deposit and withdraw money as needed. These accounts pay interest while keeping money safe.

Certificate of Deposit A *certificate of deposit* allows you to earn a higher interest rate than a regular savings account. This savings instrument usually requires a minimum deposit of $100 to $1,000 or more. You must leave the money on deposit for a specified period, from a few days to several years. Penalties, in addition to loss of interest, may be assessed if the money is withdrawn early.

Money Market Account A *money market account* pays a variable interest rate based on various government and corporate securities. Interest paid on money market accounts reflects the current rates of interest being paid in the money markets.

In general, money market accounts do not require long-term deposits. They may have a large minimum balance requirement. The earnings on money market accounts are higher than regular savings but slightly less than long-term certificates of deposit.

Securities

Investments in securities include stocks, bonds, and mutual funds. Corporations and governments sell these securities to raise money.

Stock Investments When you buy a share of stock, you become part owner of a company. A stock purchase, made directly or indirectly through mutual funds, is a very common way of investing. If a stock increases in value and is then sold for more than its original cost, a *capital gain* results. When an investment is sold for less than its original cost, a *capital loss* is the result.

Bond Investments Lending money for use by businesses and governments is

---

another common investment. *Bonds* represent debt. When you purchase a bond, you are lending funds to a company or government agency to use for their business activities.

Mutual Funds Instead of buying individual stocks and bonds, people can buy shares in a mutual fund managed by an investment company. Money from many investors is used to invest in a variety of securities. Mutual funds allow investors to spread out their risk among many investments.

Alternative Investments

Other investment choices include real estate, commodities, and collectibles. These choices often carry greater risk than savings or securities choices. As with all investments, you should carefully review your situation and options before investing in these areas.

Real Estate People invest in real estate for numerous reasons. Many people purchase their own home for the sense of security and stability. Some purchase property for rental income. Others buy vacant property in hopes that its value will increase. Housing, farmland, apartment buildings, and shopping malls are some examples of real estate investments.

Commodities Grain, livestock, precious metals, currency, and financial instruments are all commodities. Investors purchase commodity contracts in anticipation of higher market prices for the commodity in the near future. Commodity investing is considered very risky.

Collectibles Old coins, works of art, antique furniture, and other rare items are often bought with the hopes that their value will increase.

FYI

To determine how many years it will take your savings to double, use the "Rule of 72." To use this rule, divide 72 by the interest rate on your investment. The result is the number of years it will take you to double you money. For example, if your investment is earning 6 percent interest, you divide 72 by 6. At an interest rate of 6 percent, your money will double every 12 years.

EVALUATING SAVINGS AND INVESTMENTS

As you decide which investments are best for you, four main factors should be considered: safety, return, liquidity, and taxes.

Safety and Risk

Today, savings accounts at most financial institutions are insured up to $100,000 by the federal government. This insurance is a promise that your money will be available when you need it. *Safety* is assurance that the money you have invested will be returned to you.

Suppose you lend $100 to someone who promises to pay it back with 10 percent interest at the end of one year. If the loan is paid back, you will receive $110 ($100 + $10 interest). If the borrower has no money at the end of the year, you may get nothing back. You may lose both the $100 you loaned and the $10 interest you should have earned.

Not all investors require the same degree of safety. Someone may have enough money to make 20 different investments. If one of them loses value, the investor still has the other 19. Another person may only have a small amount of money and can make only one investment. One loss would be serious. Most people want to make investments that are relatively safe.

main idea

Discuss factors to consider when evaluating savings and investment alternatives.

TEACH

Explain the main categories of securities and other investment alternatives.

ONGOING ASSESSMENT

checkpoint >> **ANSWER**

The nine main categories of saving and investment alternatives are (1) savings accounts, (2) certificates of deposit, (3) money market accounts, (4) stock investments, (5) bond investments, (6) mutual funds, (7) real estate, (8) commodities, and (9) collectibles.

TEACH

Provide an overview of the factors that can be used to evaluate investments.

Use the FYI feature to explain the Rule of 72, which is a shortcut for estimating saving and investment growth.

Different Learning Abilities

Limited English Proficiency (LEP) Obtain translations for the names of savings plans and investments to reinforce these concepts in both English and other dominant languages used by students. Also consider using visuals to communicate these ideas.

The price of investing in high-yielding securities is that, as the opportunity for return goes up, so does the risk.

TEACH

Explain the meaning of *yield*.

Point out the value of the Truth in Savings Act (TISA).

Use Figure 19-3 to communicate risk levels for various types of investments.

A person might invest in a high-risk investment if he or she perceives an opportunity for a high return on the investment.

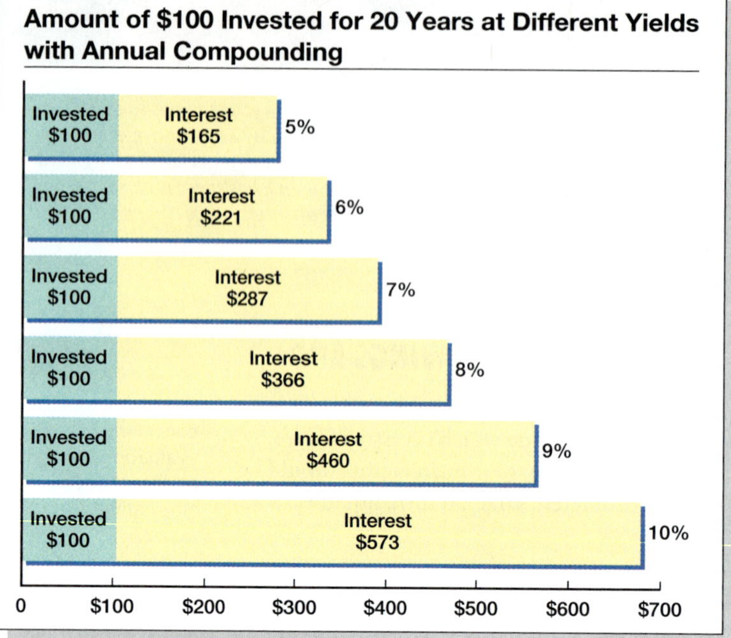

FIGURE 19-2

What is the price of investing in higher-yielding securities?

Potential Return

A good savings plan or investment should earn a reasonable return. The **yield** is the percentage of money earned on your savings or investment over a year. Other common names for yield are the *rate of return* or the *annual yield*. Figure 19-2 shows the value of an investment of $100 after 20 years at several different yields.

Usually, higher yields and greater risk of loss go together. Investments you make with the federal government are the safest. When you invest money with individuals or businesses, it usually earns higher interest than that paid by the government because there is less safety. For example, the government may pay 3 percent interest on an investment. At the same time, one business may pay 5 percent while a business with even greater risk may have to pay 10 percent.

Investors will not accept higher risks unless the yields are greater. However, a low rate of return on an investment does not guarantee safety. Similarly, high rates of interest do not mean that a loss will surely occur. Higher yields mean that investors believe the situation involves a higher risk. Figure 19-3 shows the risk level for various investments.

The Truth in Savings Act (TISA) requires that financial institutions give consumers information to compare savings accounts. The law defines

FIGURE 19-3

Why would a person make a high-risk investment?

Applied Skills

Communication Have students create a visual presentation to communicate the major factors to consider when evaluating savings and investing alternatives. Encourage them to use photos and other graphics to enhance their presentation.

the *annual percentage yield* (APY) as the percentage rate equal to the total amount of interest that a $100 deposit would earn based on a 365-day period. APY helps eliminate confusion caused by different interest calculation methods. Some financial institutions used 360- or 366-day years to calculate interest.

Liquidity

Sometimes cash is needed quickly to pay unexpected bills. Investments that can be turned into money quickly are called *liquid*. **Liquidity** is the ease with which an investment can be changed into cash without losing its value.

Suppose you have $5,000 on deposit in a bank. If you need money right away, you usually can go to your bank and withdraw it. On the other hand, suppose you own a piece of land that you bought for $5,000. The land may be a safe investment. However, if you need money immediately, you may find it difficult to sell the land right away. You might even have to sell it for less than $5,000 if you cannot wait for a buyer who is willing to pay your price.

If you have several investments, not all of them need high liquidity. The amount of liquid investments you need will depend upon your expected need for cash.

Taxes

Earnings from most savings and investments are taxed. Taxes reduce your rate of return. For example, if you earn $100 in interest but 20 percent is taken in taxes, you have only earned $80, $100 − ($100 × 0.20). Some investments have *tax-exempt* earnings, meaning you don't have to pay taxes on that income. These investments are attractive because the tax-free yield may actually be higher than a comparable taxable investment.

> *checkpoint* >>
> What are four factors to consider when selecting an investment?

19-1   Assessment

Key Concepts

Determine the best answer.

1. Which of the following is investing for current income?
   a. retired person who needs to pay living expenses
   b. business manager planning for retirement
   c. student putting away money for college
   d. family that wants to buy a vacation home

2. The most liquid investment listed here is
   a. rare coins
   b. real estate
   c. a savings account
   d. a house

3. A person who desires high income from an investment would be most concerned with
   a. safety   c. liquidity
   b. return   d. risk

Make Academic Connections

4. **Math** To determine the annual yield (rate of return) on an investment, divide the income from the investment for the year by the original amount invested. Look at the example. Then, calculate the annual yield for the other investments.

INVESTMENT	ANNUAL INCOME	AMOUNT INVESTED	ANNUAL YIELD
Example	$80	$800	10%
Savings account	$4	$200	
Bond	$85	$1,000	
Real estate	$6,400	$40,000	

5. **Economics** Prepare a list of benefits of saving and investing for (a) consumers, (b) business, and (c) government.

TEACH

Ask students to name some of the reasons a person might buy stock in a company.

Explain the differences between preferred and common stock.

Explain the process presented that might be used to determine the dividends for stockholders.

19-2 Stock Investments

Goals

Compare the two major types of stock.

Describe the activities involved with buying or selling stock.

Identify factors that affect the value of a stock.

Key Terms

preferred stock

common stock

stockbroker

stock exchange

market value

Focus on Real Life

Josie's older brother buys stock with part of his wages. He is planning for his retirement years. One day, Josie asked her brother about the benefits of investing in stock.

"You have the opportunity for big growth of your money over the years," he responded, "if you pick the right stocks."

"That's for me," Josie said. "I'm putting all my savings I have earned from babysitting in stock!"

"Wait a minute," warned her brother, "it's not that easy! You have to determine which companies have stocks with the most growth potential. Then you have to contact a broker or open an online account. Next you should…"

"That's enough," was Josie's response. "I'm really not interested in something that complicated."

"Don't give up," encouraged her brother. "While investing in stock may not be best for you right now, it is a topic that you should start learning about."

---

main idea

Compare the two major types of stock.

TYPES OF STOCK

When you buy shares in a corporation, you become a *stockholder*. If a business is profitable, it may pay out part of the profits in cash to the stockholders. These payments are *dividends*. The opportunity to earn a high rate of return attracts people to invest in stocks. Keep in mind that the risk of losing money on a stock investment also exists.

Before it can pay any dividends to stockholders, a corporation must pay bondholders the rate of interest promised to them. Sometimes there is not enough money left to pay dividends. If the corporation decides to put the money it earns toward business expansion, stockholders receive no dividends. If a corporation goes out of business, a stockholder may get little or nothing back from the investment.

Preferred Stock

The two main classes of stock issued by corporations are preferred stock and common stock. **Preferred stock** has priority over common stock in the payment of dividends. The dividends paid to preferred stockholders are usually limited to a set rate. Investing in preferred stock is less risky than common stock, but preferred stockholders generally have no voting rights.

Common Stock

The second main class of stock is common stock. **Common stock** represents general ownership in a corporation and a right to share in its profits. Common stock has no stated dividend rate. As part owners of the corporation, common stockholders are invited to the annual meeting of the corporation. They are entitled to one vote per share of common stock owned.

Different Learning Abilities

Gifted Have students conduct research to obtain additional information about preferred and common stock. The findings may be reported in a written format or in a presentation to the class.

Common stockholders receive dividends only after preferred stockholders are paid their dividends. Yet, if the profits of a company are large, the common stockholders may receive higher dividends than preferred stockholders. Suppose that a company has issued $100,000 worth of common stock and $100,000 worth of preferred stock with a dividend rate of 6 percent. The company earns a profit of $20,000 and pays all the profit out as dividends. Preferred stockholders would be paid $6,000 in dividends, $100,000 × 0.06. The remaining $14,000 ($20,000 − $6,000) would be available to pay dividends to the common stockholders. The common stockholders would earn a return of 14 percent.

checkpoint »
How does preferred stock differ from common stock?

STOCK TRANSACTIONS

Each day, people buy and sell hundreds of millions of shares of stock. Buying a stock that is right for you is an important decision.

Using a Stockbroker

A licensed specialist in the buying and selling of stocks and bonds is a **stockbroker**. Through brokers, stockholders state the price at which they are willing to sell their shares. Interested buyers tell brokers what they would be willing to pay for those shares. The brokers then work out a price that is acceptable to both buyers and sellers. For their services, brokers charge a fee called a *commission*.

Two types of brokers are common. A *full-service broker* provides information about securities you may want to buy. Full-service brokers work for brokerage houses with large research staffs.

In contrast, a *discount broker* just places orders and offers limited research and other services. They charge lower commissions than full-service brokers. Investors who do their own research can save money by using a discount broker.

Online Investing

Numerous brokers operate online services. These services allow investors to access account information as well as buy and sell securities. By investing online, you are essentially your own financial planner.

These transactions are usually less expensive and more convenient than using a financial planner or broker. There are also disadvantages to investing online. Inexperience in making investment trading decisions can result in a large financial loss. Many online investors buy or sell stocks too quickly because making trades is only a click away.

Stock Exchanges

Brokers work through a **stock exchange**, which is a business organization that accommodates the buying and selling of securities. The best-known stock exchange is the New York Stock Exchange in New York City. The American Stock Exchange is also in New York City. Regional stock exchanges operate in Boston, Chicago, Philadelphia, and San Francisco. More than 170 stock exchanges are in operation around the world.

main idea

Describe the activities involved with buying or selling stock.

ONGOING ASSESSMENT
checkpoint »» ANSWER

Preferred stock has priority over common stock in the payment of dividends. Investing in preferred stock is less risky than common stock, but preferred stockholders generally have no voting rights within the corporation. Common stock, on the other hand, represents general ownership in a corporation and a right to share in its profits. Common stockholders are entitled to one vote per share of common stock owned. Although preferred stockholders are paid first, their dividends usually are limited to a set rate. If the profits of a company are large, the common stockholders may receive higher dividends than preferred stockholders.

TEACH

Describe the services provided by a stockbroker. Explain the differences between a full-service broker and a discount broker.

Point out some of the benefits and limitations of online investing.

Ask students to describe the purpose of a stock exchange.

NETBookmark

Answers will vary depending on the types of investments students select for this exercise.

Applied Skills

Technology Have students locate information on the services provided by online brokers. Ask them to determine the benefits and costs of the services provided.

Usually, stocks of smaller companies are not traded on a stock exchange. The *over-the-counter* (OTC) market is a network where securities transactions occur using telephones and computers rather than on an exchange. The OTC market in the United States is the NASDAQ, which stands for the National Association of Security Dealers Automated Quotations. Today, the NASDAQ includes many large companies.

Changing Stock Values

The **market value** of a stock is the price at which a share of stock can be bought and sold in the stock market. The market value indicates the current value of a share of stock.

The prices at which stocks are being bought and sold are available through stock market listings in newspapers and from online sources. Figure 19-4 shows a stock market listing.

The market value can change rapidly. If the business is doing well, the market value is likely to go up. If the business has a poor record, the market value usually goes down. The market value also may be affected by current economic conditions as well as national and global politics.

Another measurement of investment values is a *stock index*. These indicators of stock values are commonly reported on television, radio, and in newspapers. The Dow Jones Industrial Average (DJIA) includes 30 of the largest U.S. companies. Another commonly reported stock index is the Standard & Poor's (S&P) 500, which is based on stock values of 500 major companies.

checkpoint >>
What is the purpose of a stock exchange?

STOCK SELECTION

Buying stocks follows a process similar to the one shown in Figure 19-5. By viewing various economic and

FIGURE 19-4
How is a stock's yield different from a bond's yield?

Stock Market Quotations

1	2	3	4	5	6	7	8	9	10	11	12
52-Week					Yld.		Vol.				Net
Hi	Lo	Stock	Sym.	Div.	%	PE	100s	Hi	Lo	Close	Chg.
74.93	56.72	Deere	DE	1.12	1.6	15	21823	70.14	67.38	68.01	−0.42
95.64	64.84	FedExCp	FDX	0.28	0.3	27	14555	94.54	91.78	93.74	+1.22
45	35	Kellogg	K	1.01	2.3	21	6791	44.82	43.67	44.74	−0.24
20.50	15.94	Mattel	MAT	0.40	2.1	16	21682	19.23	17.77	18.80	−0.15
42.95	31.25	Reebok	RBK	0.30	0.8	14	4501	40.47	37.82	39.22	+0.12

1 – Highest price paid for stock during past 52 weeks
2 – Lowest price paid for stock during the past 52 weeks
3 – Abbreviated company name
4 – Symbol used to report company
5 – Current dividend per share (in dollars)
6 – Dividend yield based on current selling price
7 – Price-earning ratio
8 – Number of shares traded, expressed in hundreds, on the trading day
9 – Highest price for a share on the trading day
10 – Lowest price for a share on the trading day
11 – Closing price for the day
12 – Change in closing price compared to previous trading day

social trends in the United States and around the world, you will determine what types of companies would benefit from those trends. For example, as people live longer, they require increased health care. Companies involved in health care products may be a wise investment.

Stock Information Sources

When choosing stocks, you should learn about the company. Several sources are available to assist you. These include *Moody's Handbook of Common Stocks, Value Line,* and *Standard and Poor's Encyclopedia of Stocks*. Publications like these provide data about net worth, debt, sales revenue, profits, dividend history, and the future prospects of companies. Many web sites are also available to provide valuable information on companies.

The U.S. Securities and Exchange Commission (SEC) oversees the financial markets. It requires all companies that issue publicly traded securities to electronically file detailed reports. You can access these reports at the SEC web site.

Discuss various business and economic trends. Prepare a list of stocks that your team believes would be good investments. Explain what factors influenced the selection of these companies.

Economic Factors

Many economic conditions affect stock prices. Awareness of these factors will help you make better choices about stock investments. You should consider the following economic factors.

- **Inflation** Higher prices can result in lower spending by consumers, reducing company profits.

- **Interest rates** As the cost of money changes, company profits can increase or decline.

- **Consumer spending** Profits of companies that sell products and services to households are directly affected by buying habits.

Four-Step Process for Deciding Stock Purchases

1. Observe and analyze economic and social trends.

2. Determine industries that will be affected.

3. Identify companies in those industries.

4. Decide whether to buy, sell, or hold the stock of those companies.

FIGURE 19-5

Name a company or industry that has profited from a trend in recent months?

- **Employment** As people obtain or lose jobs, the amount of money they have for spending will affect company profits.

Company Factors

If you are considering investing in a company, ask the following questions.

- Has the company been profitable over a period of years?

- Have the company's managers made good business decisions?

- Does the company have growth potential in coming years?

- Does the company have an unusually large amount of debt?

- How does the company compare with others in its industry?

Other information about a company should also be considered. The *yield* of a stock is important if your goal is to earn a good return from your investment.

Suppose a company is paying a quarterly dividend of $0.60 a share. The total dividend for the year would be $2.40. If the stock were selling for $40 a share, the current yield (return) would be calculated as

$$\frac{\text{Dividend per share}}{\text{Market price per share}} = \text{Dividend Yield}$$

$$\frac{\$2.40}{\$40} = 0.06 \text{ or } 6\%$$

The price of a stock should also be considered. Many investors look at the stock's *price-earnings (P/E) ratio*, which is the relationship between a stock's selling price and its earnings per share. The P/E ratio gives you an indication of whether the stock is priced high or low in relation to its earnings per share.

> *checkpoint* ››
>
> How do various economic factors affect stock prices?

19-2 **Assessment**

Xtra!
Study Tools
school.cengage.com/business/introtobiz

Key Concepts

Determine the best answer.

1. Which of these statements best describes preferred stock?
   a. vote at the annual meeting of the company
   b. first priority for receiving dividends
   c. low priority for receiving dividends
   d. no stated dividend rate

2. Higher spending for recreation in the economy would most benefit the stock prices for companies in the __?__ industry.
   a. electronics
   b. health care
   c. office equipment
   d. automobile

Make Academic Connections

3. **Math** Based on Figure 19-4, answer the following:
   a. What number of shares was traded for Deere on this day?
   b. What is the highest price of a share of Kellogg's during the past year?
   c. What was the closing price of Mattel on the previous trading day?

4. **Communication** Conduct a survey of people about what they believe are the most important factors to consider when selecting a stock. Prepare a summary data table and written analysis of your findings.

19-3 Bonds and Mutual Funds

GOVERNMENT BONDS

To raise money for current operations or future expansion, most governments and corporations sell bonds. A *bond* is a certificate representing a promise to pay a definite amount of money at a stated interest rate on a specified due date. The due date is also called the *maturity date*. Bonds are similar to promissory notes issued by individual borrowers. When you buy a bond, you are lending money to the organization selling the bond. You become a *creditor* of the organization. Governments issue bonds to raise money for funding public services. The federal, state, and local governments issue a variety of bonds.

Municipal Bonds

A city may want to build a new park or new school. A state may need funds to build or repair highways and bridges. Bonds issued by local and state governments are called **municipal bonds**, or *munis*.

main idea

List types of government bonds.

Why do state and local governments issue bonds?

Different Learning Abilities

Dyslexia Prepare some short fill-in assignments asking about various types of bonds. Clearly present the material and encourage students to provide the correct answer.

Focus on Real Life

This feature will introduce students to some of the issues associated with investing in bonds and mutual funds.

TEACH

Ask students to explain why governments often borrow money.

Explain the features of a municipal bond.

THINK CRITICALLY THROUGH VISUALS

State and local governments can raise money for public service projects by issuing municipal bonds.

492

Municipal bonds have an advantage over bonds issued by companies. Usually, interest earned on municipal bonds is exempt from federal and most state income taxes. In order to avoid taxes, people buy municipal bonds even though the interest rates usually are not as high as the rates offered on corporate bonds. In general, municipal bonds are considered safer investments than corporate bonds.

U.S. Savings Bonds

For people with small amounts of money to invest, U.S. government savings bonds are one of the safest investments. Series EE savings bonds come in denominations ranging from $50 to $10,000. They pay interest through a process called *discounting*.

A Series EE bond is bought at half its face value. A $50 bond costs $25. At the end of its full term, it pays at least $50. The difference between the purchase price and the redemption value is the interest earned. The length of time the bond is held determines the interest earned. The time it takes for a savings bond to mature will vary depending on the current interest rate being paid.

Until 2004, the U.S. government also sold Series HH bonds. These were called *current-income* bonds, with interest paid every six months. The interest was automatically deposited to the bondholder's bank account.

Interest payments for Series HH bonds were different from EE bonds. With EE bonds, interest is only paid when the bond is cashed. With HH bonds, bondholders received interest payments twice a year. Many investors favor this semiannual income, especially retired people.

One other type of savings bond is the *I bond*. These investments pay an interest rate that is lower than the rate of other savings bonds, but it is a variable rate that increases with inflation.

Other Federal Securities

The federal government also borrows using Treasury bills and notes. The difference between these debt securities is the length of time to maturity. Treasury bills, or *T-bills*, involve short-term borrowing with maturities from 91 days to one year. Treasury notes, or *T-notes*, have maturities from 1 to 10 years.

The U.S. government also issues treasury bonds, called *T-bonds*. These involve long-term borrowing, with a maturity of 30 years.

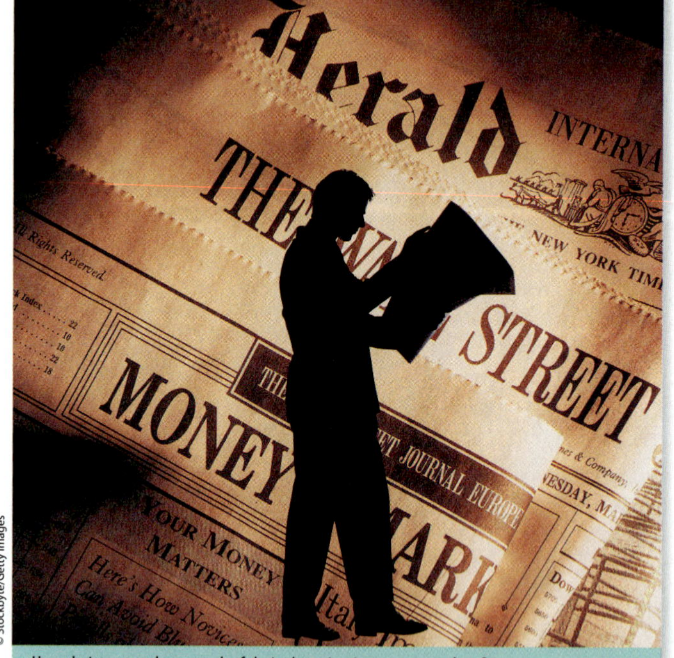

© Stockbyte/Getty Images

How do investors keep track of their changing investment values?

Different Learning Styles

Auditory Learner Encourage auditory learners to repeat the names of the types of bonds discussed on pages 491–492. Ask them to explain each type of bond.

CORPORATE BONDS

Investing in bonds for a company is quite different from investing in stock. When you invest in stock, you become an owner. When you buy a bond, you are lending money to the company. Bonds issued by corporations are **corporate bonds**.

Bond Components

Each bond has a *face value*, also called the *maturity value*. This is the amount being borrowed by the corporation issuing the bond. Most corporate bonds are issued for $1,000.

Interest is paid to the investor periodically (usually twice a year) based on the face value and the stated interest rate. On the bond's maturity date, the face value is repaid to the investor.

Bond Values

Bonds are bought and sold in the bond market. The market value of a bond varies based on changing interest rates and the credit rating of the borrowing organization.

Bond values are reported similarly to the way stocks are reported. Corporate bond prices are stated in 100s, but the bonds are sold in $1,000 denominations (10 times the listed amount). For example, a bond reported at 100 is selling at its face value—$1,000. A bond selling at 105 has a market value of $1,050.

The price investors are willing to pay for a bond depends upon the *stated interest rate*. If the bond's stated rate is lower than interest rates on similar bonds, investors will want to buy the bond for less than its face value. If the bond's stated interest rate is higher than interest rates on similar bonds, the seller of the bond will want to receive more than its face value.

MUTUAL FUNDS

Many people who are interested in investing do not have the time or expertise needed to make wise investment decisions. A **mutual fund** is an investment fund set up and managed by a company that receives money from many investors. The mutual fund is managed by a professional who uses the investors' money to buy and sell a wide variety of stocks or bonds. A portion of the income generated by the investments is paid to the investors.

Types of Mutual Funds

More than 60,000 different mutual funds are available to investors around the world. These funds have many different objectives. For instance, some emphasize investing in growth stocks, some emphasize stocks that pay high dividends, and some emphasize international stocks. The following list includes some of the main types of mutual funds.

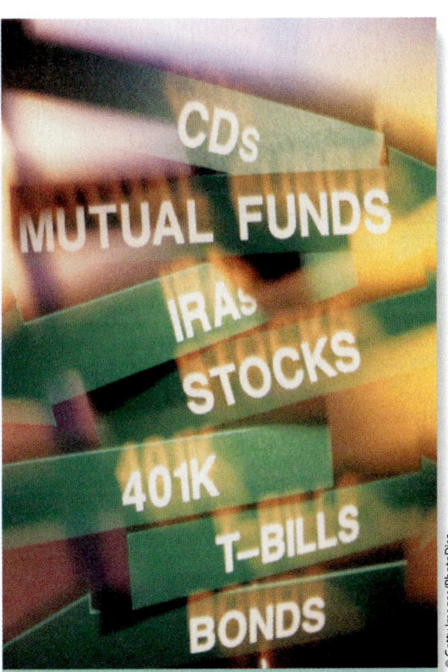

© Getty Images/PhotoDisc

Make a list of long-term investment options. What are the pros and cons for each type?

Describe features of corporate bonds.

Describe various types of mutual funds.

TEACH

Describe the purpose of corporate bonds. Explain how bond values change as a result of changing interest rates.

ONGOING ASSESSMENT

checkpoint >> ANSWER

The value of a bond is affected by changing interest rates. If the bond's stated rate is lower than interest rates on similar bonds, investors will want to buy the bond for less than its face value. If the bond's stated interest rate is higher than interest rates on similar bonds, the seller of the bond will want to receive more than its face value.

TEACH

Ask students to explain the purpose of a mutual fund. Describe the purpose of different types of mutual funds.

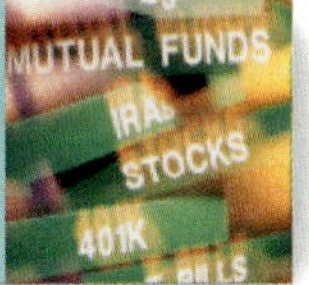

THINK CRITICALLY THROUGH VISUALS

Long-term investment options are certificates of deposit, mutual funds, individual retirement accounts, stocks, 401(k) and other retirement plans, T-bills and T-notes, T-bonds, and corporate bonds. These all have the advantage of being vehicles to grow savings over time. The disadvantage of all these instruments is lack of liquidity.

Word Processing/Office Technology Have students use presentation software to communicate different types of mutual funds. Encourage students to use photos and other graphics in their presentation.

493

Work as a Team

Review the list of types of mutual funds. Describe situations in which each type might be appropriate for a particular individual or family. Explain how this type of mutual fund could meet various investment goals.

- Aggressive-growth stock funds seek quick growth, but also have higher risk.

- Income funds specialize in stocks that pay regular dividends.

- International funds invest in stock of companies from around the world.

- Sector funds buy stocks of companies in the same industry such as health care, energy, or telecommunications.

- Bond funds specialize in corporate bonds.

- Balanced funds invest in both stock and bonds.

When selecting a mutual fund in which to invest, match your personal investment goals to the type of mutual fund.

Mutual Fund Values

Mutual fund investors own shares of the mutual fund. The value of each share is based on the total value of all investments made by the mutual fund company. For example, if the investments were worth $400,000 and 80,000 shares existed, each share would be worth $5, $400,000 \div 80,000 = \$5$. This amount is called the *net asset value (NAV)* of a mutual fund.

A part of the dividends and interest received from the fund's investments is used to pay operating expenses of the fund. The major portion of earnings is distributed to the mutual fund shareholders or reinvested in the fund.

checkpoint >>

What are the main types of mutual funds?

19-3 Assessment

Xtra! Study Tools
school.cengage.com/business/introtobiz

Key Concepts

Determine the best answer.

1. Municipal bonds are issued by
   a. corporations
   b. the federal government
   c. international companies
   d. state and local governments

2. The price of a mutual fund share is most affected by
   a. current tax rates
   b. the value of investments
   c. current foreign rates
   d. the value of housing

3. True or False. A bondholder is part owner of a company.

4. True or False. Interest rates in an economy affect the value of a bond.

Make Academic Connections

5. *Technology* Go to the web site for U.S. savings bonds to obtain information about how to buy savings bonds online. What features are available online to calculate the current value of savings bonds?

6. *Research* With thousands of mutual funds available to investors, how could a person evaluate them? Locate library and online information that could provide assistance when deciding in which mutual funds to invest.

19-4 Real Estate Investments

Goals

Describe home buying activities.

Explain the benefits of home ownership.

Discuss the costs of home ownership.

Key Terms

real estate

mortgage

equity

assessed value

Focus on Real Life

Driving home from their honeymoon, Joshua Moskowitz turned to his bride Carrie. "You know, we have some money that we received as wedding gifts," said Joshua. "We should buy some stocks for our long-term financial future. I have heard of a lot of people who made fortunes with stocks."

"What do you know about stocks? Are you sure we won't lose our money?" asked Carrie.

"Well, it's true, I don't know much about stocks," responded Joshua. "But I do know baseball cards! Let's invest our money in baseball cards."

"That's kind of risky, isn't it?" was Carrie's next question.

"OK…OK. Then let's buy gold bars. Gold can be a solid investment," replied Joshua. "You can't go wrong with gold."

"Hold on. We both want what's best for our future, but don't you think that first we'd better find a place to live?" responded Carrie.

SELECTING HOUSING

Real estate—land and anything that is attached to it—is one investment that many people eventually acquire. Getting started with real estate usually means finding a place in which to live.

Renting Your Residence

Most people start by renting an apartment. As renters, you are freed from much of the work and expense of property maintenance. Renting also makes it easier for you to move when needed. As a tenant, you must take care of the rented property, but you are not able to call the apartment your own.

Many people want to own a house and yard that they can maintain and fix up just the way they want. To realize this goal, they must save money for a down payment on a house.

What are the pros and cons of renting compared to buying your residence?

main idea

Describe home buying activities.

Focus on Real Life

This situation can encourage students to start thinking about various future financial decisions, including their housing.

TEACH

Have students describe real estate decisions they might make in the future.

Ask students to name some benefits and potential drawbacks of renting a place of residence.

THINK CRITICALLY THROUGH VISUALS

Renters are liberated from the work and expense of property maintenance and are freer to move whenever they desire. Renters also do not have to come up with a large down payment, as when purchasing a house, and rent payments are typically lower than mortgage payments. However, rent payments do not purchase anything tangible, but simply allow the renter to live in the property for a specified amount of time. Many people prefer to buy a house as an investment. Part of the money spent on a home mortgage payment goes to pay for the house, which is usually increasing in value. Homeowners often prefer to do their own home maintenance, gardening, and decorating so that things can be done according to their personal specifications.

Applied Skills

Law Provide students with a copy of an apartment lease or rental agreement. Have them describe the information that is presented in this legal document. Encourage discussion about the obligations spelled out in the document.

What are the advantages and disadvantages of owning a mobile home?

Owning a Mobile Home

Some people find houses too expensive. They might consider a mobile home in a good location that they can afford. A mobile home can be a first step toward becoming a real estate owner.

An advantage of owning a mobile home is having a place to call your own. As time passes, a family may need more space and look to purchase a house.

Buying a Home

Unless you have thousands of dollars available, you will need to borrow to buy a house. A **mortgage** is a legal document giving the lender a claim against the property if the principal, interest, or both are not paid as agreed.

Mortgages are usually long-term loans—for 15, 20, or 30 years—that require monthly payments. These payments are usually higher than rent. A mortgage payment includes a portion of the principal and interest charges. In addition, it often includes money to be used to pay property taxes and insurance. Money used for a down payment reduces the amount of loan needed with the mortgage.

Interest rates on mortgages may be set for the term of the loan. This type of mortgage is called a *fixed-rate mortgage*. Market interest rates generally increase or decrease during the life of a mortgage depending on economic conditions. Therefore, lenders also offer an *adjustable-rate mortgage (ARM)*. The interest rate of an ARM is raised or lowered from time to time depending upon the current interest rate being charged by lenders. Monthly payments for ARMs often are lower, especially in the early years of the mortgage, compared with fixed-rate mortgages.

Services of Real Estate Agents

Buying a house is not a simple matter. Most homebuyers use a real estate agent. This person is trained and licensed to help with the buying and selling of real estate. Someone who wants to buy a house contacts a real estate agent. The agent helps the person decide what they want in a house. The agent will also arrange for the prospective buyer to view homes offered for sale.

Different Learning Abilities

Hearing Impaired Communicate the main types of housing choices available to a person using a variety of visuals. Consider using photographs, illustrations, and floor plans. Make copies of the visuals available to all interested students.

Sellers of real estate may also use the services of a real estate agent. Someone who wants to sell a house contacts an agent. The real estate professional helps to set the selling price and promotes that the house is for sale.

Other Real Estate Professionals

Legal matters are also a part of the real estate purchase process. A lawyer, working with the real estate agent, will help you with the transaction. A lawyer assures that your property has no claims against it, such as back taxes. Having a lawyer represent you in the transaction can help to avoid legal problems.

When buying a house, an appraiser's report on the home's value is also important. An *appraiser* is someone trained to estimate the value of property and who can give an official report on the value. Factors such as the quality of construction, the location, and the price of similar houses are considered when doing the appraisal.

Buying a Condominium

In some areas, *condominiums*, or *condos*, are popular. This is an individually owned housing unit in an apartment-like complex. The maintenance and yard work are normally taken care of with a service fee paid by condo owners.

> *checkpoint* >>
> What are four available housing alternatives?

BENEFITS OF HOME OWNERSHIP

The advantages of home ownership include tax benefits, increased equity, and pride of ownership.

Tax Benefits

Although you may pay both mortgage loan interest and property taxes on real estate you own, these costs can be to your

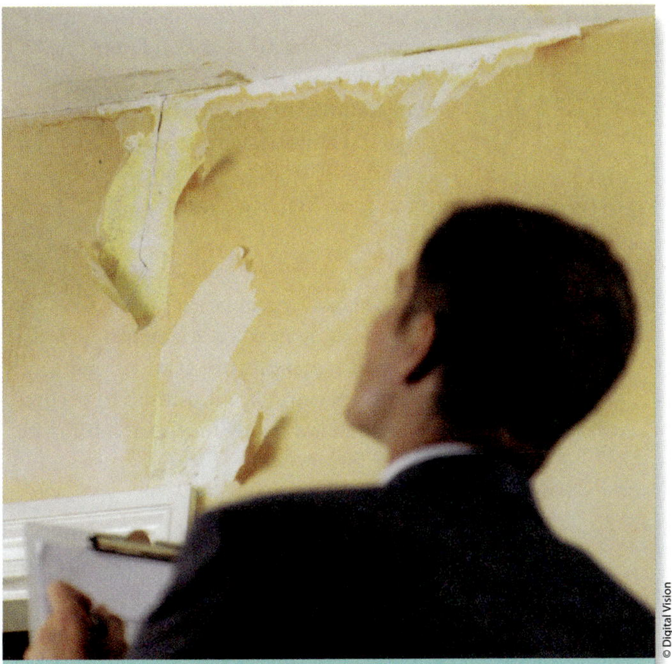

What real estate professionals will you need when purchasing real estate?

benefit. Reduced income taxes result when the interest paid on a mortgage is included as a deductible expense. Real estate property taxes are usually also deductible when computing your federal income taxes.

Increased Equity

From an investment standpoint, the potential increase in home value is an important aspect of ownership. **Equity** is the difference between the price at which you could currently sell your house and the amount owed on the mortgage. Equity builds up over the years. It increases rapidly in the last few years of a mortgage.

Because of *appreciation*, a general increase in the value of property that occurs over time, homes increase in value. During the 10 years that one family had lived in their home, its market value had increased to $244,000 and their debt decreased to $165,000. Therefore, their equity was $79,000.

Many factors affect the value of a home. Most important is location.

main idea

Explain the benefits of home ownership.

TEACH

Ask students to explain the benefits of using a lawyer and an appraiser when buying a home.

Explain the benefits of owning a condominium.

ONGOING ASSESSMENT

checkpoint >> **ANSWER**

Four housing alternatives are (1) renting, (2) owning a mobile home, (3) buying a traditional home, and (4) buying a condominium.

THINK CRITICALLY THROUGH VISUALS

In addition to a real estate agent, you may need the services of a real estate appraiser, a home inspector, a lawyer, an insurance agent, and a loan officer when purchasing a house.

TEACH

Ask students to name some benefits of home ownership. Explain how mortgage interest and property taxes reduce a person's income taxes.

Describe the benefits of equity to a homeowner. Explain how equity in a home is calculated.

Teaching Strategies

Expand Beyond the Classroom Arrange for a class speaker who is a real estate agent, lawyer, insurance agent, or home inspector. Ask that person to explain information needed when buying or owning a home.

497

498

TEACH

Provide an overview of home ownership costs.

Explain how the assessed value is used to calculate property taxes.

ONGOING ASSESSMENT

checkpoint >> **ANSWER**

The main benefits are tax benefits, increased equity, and pride of ownership.

E-Commerce in Action

As in all types of business transactions, computerized activities are being used when buying a home.

Think Critically Answers

1. Benefits are the reduced paperwork and processing time and the ability to easily compare mortgage rates. Concerns are that a consumer might not be as aware of important details or negotiate as skillfully as a real estate professional.

2. Reports will vary.

PROJECT

Provide the following instructions to students. (These instructions also appear on page xxv of the textbook.) Will home ownership be one of your life-span goals? Explain how buying a home is different from other types of investments you may make.

---

main idea

Discuss the costs of home ownership.

In addition, the quality of schools, maintenance of the property, and home features increase home values. Features that can add to the value of a home include an updated kitchen, remodeled bathrooms, a master bedroom suite, a finished basement, and a large garage.

Pride of Ownership

Another advantage of owning real estate is pride of ownership. Many people feel a sense of accomplishment when they buy a home. Having a home to use and decorate as desired is a strong motivation for many home buyers.

> *checkpoint* >>
> What are the main benefits of home ownership?

COSTS OF HOME OWNERSHIP

While there are important benefits to owning your own property, various costs also exist. Home ownership has costs such as property taxes, interest payments, property insurance, and maintenance.

Property Taxes

Property taxes vary greatly from state to state and community to community. Generally, real estate taxes range from 2 to 4 percent of the market value of the property. Taxes are based on the **assessed value**, which is the amount that your local government determines your property to be worth for tax purposes. Assessed values normally are lower than the market value, often the assessed value is only about half.

Although still rare, e-commerce home buying is expanding. When you buy a house online, the process starts by viewing homes online. You then go to see several homes in person.

The financing also involves online activities. First, you determine the mortgage amount for which you are eligible. Next, compare mortgage rates among lenders. Finally, you complete the application and are approved within a few hours.

After negotiating the final price by e-mail, the next step is the *closing*. The lender prepares the closing documents and sends them electronically to the closing agent.

The deed is scanned and delivered by computer image. All completed documents are forwarded to the appropriate parties, with the buyer receiving electronic versions of all files.

The Electronic Signature in Global and National Commerce Act enables this process to take place. This law allows an *electronic signature*, such as an electronic sound, symbol, or process, to be attached to a contract or other online record.

The time needed for this entire process will be greatly reduced. The paper-based recording of documents usually takes 45 days. Online, the process can be completed in about three hours.

Think Critically
1. What benefits and concerns are associated with buying a home online?
2. Conduct an online search to obtain additional information about online home buying. Prepare a report about your findings.

Life-Span Plan Answer

Answers will vary. Students should point out that a home is different because it provides a current benefit instead of only the hope of a future return.

Different Learning Abilities

Visually Impaired Prepare or obtain enlarged materials to communicate the benefits and costs of home ownership. Ask students to explain the various items with additional information or an example.

A home with a market value of $180,000 may be assessed at $90,000. If the tax rate is $60 per $1,000 of assessed value, the annual taxes are $5,400.

$$90,000 \div \$1,000 \times \$60 = \$5,400$$

The tax rate is 6 percent of the assessed value, but only 3 percent of the market value.

Interest Payments

Interest payments add to the cost of the house. A 30-year mortgage for $100,000 at 8 percent interest would result in more than $164,000 in interest payments over the life of the loan.

Property Insurance

Property insurance is an essential home ownership cost. The value of the house, the construction material, the location in respect to other buildings, and the availability of fire protection are some factors that affect the cost of homeowners insurance. Typical annual home insurance costs are less than 1 percent of the market value of the house. Property insurance provides protection from fire, theft, accident, or other losses of your home or property.

Maintenance

The cost of *upkeep*—maintaining your property in good condition—is important in home ownership. Annual upkeep costs average about 2 percent of the property's value. Postponing repairs or not taking good care of the house and yard through regular maintenance can be very costly in the long run.

> *checkpoint* »
> What are common costs of home ownership?

19-4 Assessment

Xtra! Study Tools
school.cengage.com/business/introtobiz

Key Concepts

Determine the best answer.

1. The person who reports on the value of a home is a(n)
   a. lawyer
   b. real estate agent
   c. appraiser
   d. mortgage broker

2. A common financial benefit of home ownership is
   a. low property insurance costs
   b. tax deduction for your down payment
   c. increased property value
   d. low maintenance costs

Make Academic Connections

3. **Finance** Find the asking price for three different homes that are currently for sale in your community. Use an online mortgage calculator to calculate the monthly payments for each home for a 30-year fixed rate mortgage with a 10 percent down payment and with a 20 percent down payment. Report your findings in a table.

4. **Math** A home worth $123,000 and a mortgage of $72,400 would have equity of $_?_. A home with an assessed value of $178,000 with a tax rate of $52 per $1,000 would have a property tax bill of $_?_.

Asia provides a very diverse region with regard to culture, religion, foods, and other factors. Encourage students to talk to people who have lived in or visited this region of the world to obtain a better understanding of the people and business environment.

Think Critically Answers

1. When doing business in Thailand, one should expect to spend up to two hours at a business lunch, from 1 to 3 p.m. Use the time to develop relationships with business associates. Sports are a good topic of conversation in Thailand. English is the second most common language after Thai, so language should be less of a problem here than in some other countries. When negotiating, remember that Thais will never say "no."

2. When negotiating with business associates in Thailand, one should maintain a sense of humor and a pleasant attitude. Greet others with a *wai* to communicate respect. Never touch another person's head as the head is considered sacred. Avoid pointing one's feet toward others as feet are thought to be the least sacred body part; remove shoes before entering a home. Don't speak loudly or show anger in public, which are considered offensive. Avoid confrontation.

3. Answers will vary depending on what students uncover in their research on business and economic activities in Thailand.

Doing Business in…Thailand

Official name
Kingdom of Thailand

Capital
Bangkok

Population
65.1 million

Currency
baht

Major exports
footwear, fishery products, rice, rubber, jewelry, automobiles, computers

Major export partners
United States, Japan, China, Singapore, Hong Kong, Malaysia

Major imports
capital goods, raw materials, consumer goods, fuels

Major import partners
Japan, China, United States, Malaysia, United Arab Emirates, Singapore.

Source: CIA World Factbook

Known as Siam until 1939, Thailand is the only nation in Southeast Asia that was never colonized. The country's name means "land of the free." Thailand is also known as the "Land of Smiles." A sense of humor, laughter, and a pleasant attitude are highly regarded.

While Thailand guarantees freedom of religion with many religions represented, 95 percent of the population is Buddhist. Traditionally, all young men are expected to become monks for at least three months to study Buddhist principles.

Monks in Thailand are highly respected. The first rows of the theater are reserved for them and for high-ranking officials. People are also expected to give up their seats on a bus or train to a monk who is standing.

Greet others in Thailand with a wai (pronounced *why*), in which you place the palms of your hands together at chest level, fingers extended, and bow slightly; women curtsy. A wai communicates respect.

The head is considered very sacred in Thailand. Never touch another person's head or pass an object over it. In contrast, the bottoms of the feet are least sacred. Avoid pointing your feet toward others. Stamping your feet is considered very improper. Removing your shoes is customary when entering a Buddhist temple or private home.

A business lunch may last two hours, from 1 to 3 p.m. The time is used to develop relationships with business associates. You may discuss sports such as soccer, table tennis, badminton, volleyball, and basketball, which are popular in Thailand.

Dinner may extend from 7 to 10 p.m. with an eight- or nine-course meal. Rice is served with nearly every meal. In addition, you will likely have spicy dishes consisting of meat, vegetables, fish, eggs, and fruits.

English is the second most common language after Thai. Remember that speaking loudly or showing anger in public is offensive. During negotiations, Thais will never say "no." Avoiding confrontation is a high priority.

Think Critically
1. What actions might be necessary when doing business in Thailand?
2. How might a person negotiate with business associates in Thailand?
3. Conduct library or Internet research to find additional information about business and economic activities in Thailand.

Different Learning Styles

Kinesthetic Learner Have students draw a flowchart, map, or other visual that communicates the trade relations of Thailand with other countries in its region or around the world. Ask students to explain what factors might affect the creation and success of a trade route.

Goals

Discuss types of commodity investments.

Explain the use of collectibles as an investment.

Key Terms

commodities

futures contract

collectibles

Focus on Real Life

"Take a look at this one! It must be more than 100 years old," said Colin. "Now that's a great investment."

"But how do we know these coins are genuine and whether they will increase in value?" asked Paul.

"Well, we could check on the Internet or get another opinion," responded Colin.

"But that's a lot of money to invest in something with that much risk," cautioned Paul. "I'm not sure that's how I want to invest my college savings."

"Come on," urged Colin. "You have to take a risk to make big bucks."

"But I could also lose 'big bucks'!" noted Paul.

"OK, that's enough 'buts.' I guess you need to consider other types of investments that match your risk level and investment goals," Colin said.

COMMODITIES AND FUTURES

Another type of investment considered by experienced investors is commodities. **Commodities** include grain, livestock, and precious metals. Generally, commodity investing is considered to be speculative. A *speculative investment* is one with an unusually high risk.

Commodity investors buy and sell futures contracts. An agreement to buy or sell an amount of a commodity at a specified price in the future is a **futures contract**. Futures contracts also involve the buying and selling of currencies and financial instruments.

Commodity Exchanges

Commodities are bought and sold on exchanges similar to stock exchanges. Buyers and sellers are represented by traders on the exchanges.

One of the best known exchanges is the Chicago Board of Trade (CBOT).

Established in 1848 to provide a market for agricultural products, CBOT helps to avoid the huge price variances for these products.

Other commodity exchanges around the world include the Chicago Mercantile Exchange, the Kansas City Board of Trade, Brazilian Futures Exchange, and the Russian Commodity and Raw Materials Exchange.

Agricultural Commodities

Agricultural products, such as corn, soybeans, and wheat, are some of the items traded on commodity exchanges. Agricultural producers sell their crops in advance of a harvest at what they believe is a good price. Farmers will then know in advance how much they will receive for a crop.

The futures contract buyers hope the price of the crop will go up when harvested so that they can earn a profit.

main idea

Discuss types of commodity investments.

Applied Skills

Writing Across the Curriculum Prepare a paragraph that shows the connection of agricultural commodities to various business topics or to another class such as math, history, science, or foreign language.

Focus on Real Life

This feature can help students to become aware of other types of investments.

TEACH

Ask students to name products they use each day that include various agricultural products.

Point out that investing in commodity futures is very risky. Explain the purpose of a commodity exchange.

501

Describe how food companies use agricultural futures contracts to protect themselves from extreme price changes.

Explain the value of investing in precious metals. Explain that the spot market refers to the current value of an item, in contrast to the value in a futures contract.

Point out how foreign currencies and other financial items are used as investments.

Use the FYI feature to clarify confusion between the euro and the Eurodollar.

ONGOING ASSESSMENT

checkpoint >> **ANSWER**

Types of commodities commonly used with futures contracts are agricultural commodities, such as grain and livestock, and precious metals.

THINK CRITICALLY THROUGH VISUALS

Answers will vary. They should have no trouble thinking of collectibles that have increased in value such as stamps, coins, sports cards, dolls, antiques, and fine art paintings.

Conditions that affect agricultural commodity prices include weather, international trade agreements, and worldwide demand and supply.

Gold, Silver, and Precious Metals

Precious metals have worldwide importance. Investors have traded gold and silver on commodity markets for centuries. Gold has the longest history as a monetary commodity, going back to gold coins that were circulated as early as 500 B.C. Gold is highly prized for both ornamental and industrial reasons. More recently, other metals, such as copper and platinum, have also become valuable commodities.

Prices of these metals are affected by economic conditions as well as supply and demand. For example, in 1879, gold sold for $18.79 per ounce. Since 1979, the price of an ounce of gold has ranged from more than $800 to less than $300.

Precious metals are quoted as *spot prices* per one troy ounce. This is the current price quoted for precious metals in the world markets. You can find the spot price for gold in London and New York in newspapers and online.

Money invested in precious metals does not earn interest. If you hold gold, silver, or platinum, you might profit by selling them later at a price higher than what you paid. Gold and other precious metals have another advantage—many view them as protection against currency becoming worthless. Gold could be used for buying goods and services when paper money might not be accepted.

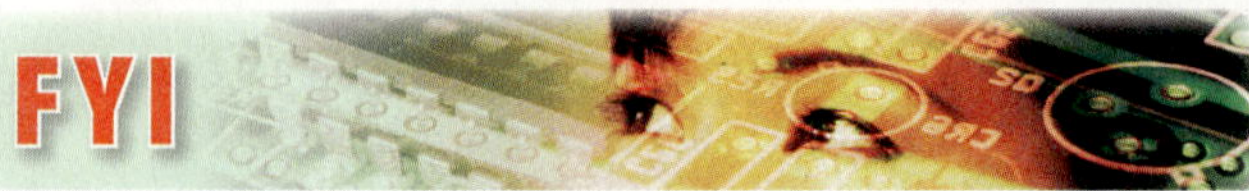

People often confuse the euro and a Eurodollar. The euro is the official currency of the European Union. A Eurodollar is a U.S. dollar deposited in a bank outside the United States. It was originally called the Eurodollar because most of those deposits occurred in Europe. Today, the U.S. dollar is used in all regions of the world.

Currency and Financial Instruments

Currencies, such as the U.S. dollar, euro, and Japanese yen, and financial instruments, such as Treasury bills and notes, are traded on the futures markets. The price of currency and financial instruments is affected by a country's economic outlook and current interest rates. Again, investors buy currency or financial instruments expecting the prices to increase in the future so that they can sell them to others at a profit.

checkpoint >>
What types of commodities are commonly used with futures contracts?

Can you think of some collectibles that may be worth more now than when they were acquired? Provide some examples.

© Getty Images/PhotoDisc

Applied Skills

Science Have students research the use of gold, silver, and other precious metals in various products. Ask students to explain what features of these metals create long-term value.

COLLECTIBLES

Another form of investment that is popular with many people is collectibles. **Collectibles** are items of personal interest to collectors that can increase in value in the future.

An advantage of collectibles is the personal pleasure of buying, collecting, storing, arranging, and displaying what is collected. Often, collectors even form organizations. For example, stamp clubs around the country bring together stamp collectors who buy, sell, trade, display, and discuss their stamps. Baseball card trading takes place at scheduled events in huge arenas as well as over kitchen tables. Antique dealers and collectors gather for major events at which they buy and sell their items.

Types of Collectibles

A wide variety of collectible items may serve as investments. Commonly obtained items are stamps, coins, sport trading cards, and antiques. In addition, unusual items purchased as an investment include autographs and letters of famous people, Chinese ceramics, movie posters, glassware, rare books, and toys.

Collectible Values

The possibility of the average buyer of collectibles making a large profit is not great. Only rare stamps, coins, art, and antiques—which may cost hundreds or thousands of dollars—tend to be items on which the investor can make a considerable profit. The wise investor in collectibles studies the market, knows the product well, and analyzes the potential risk.

main idea

Explain the use of collectibles as an investment.

checkpoint »
What are common types of collectibles?

19-5 Assessment

Key Concepts

Determine the best answer.

1. The spot price for gold or silver refers to the
   a. interest for borrowing to buy the precious metal.
   b. current market price of the precious metal.
   c. future market price of the precious metal.
   d. global price for the precious metal set by the World Bank.

2. The value of collectibles is most influenced by
   a. the current tax rate on investments.
   b. government regulations of the market.
   c. the futures market for commodities.
   d. interested buyers and potential sellers.

Make Academic Connections

3. **Research** Go to the web site of the Chicago Board of Trade, the Chicago Mercantile Exchange, or another commodity exchange. Prepare a summary of the commodities and financial instruments traded on this exchange.

4. **Art** Identify paintings and other works of art that would be considered valuable investments.

RETEACH

Emphasize the risks associated with commodity futures and collectibles.

ENRICH

Have students describe how economic conditions might affect the value of commodities and collectibles.

Business Notes

19-1 SAVING AND INVESTMENT PLANNING

1. Savings plans help buy needed goods and services as well as prepare for future expenses and emergencies. Savings help the economy by making funds available to individuals, businesses, and governments for borrowing. The main investment goals are current income and long-term growth.

2. The major categories of savings and investments are savings accounts, certificates of deposit, money market accounts, stocks, bonds, mutual funds, real estate, commodities, and collectibles.

3. When evaluating savings and investments, consider safety, yield, liquidity, and taxes.

19-2 STOCK INVESTMENTS

4. Stock is equity and represents ownership. Preferred stock has priority over common stock in the payment of dividends. Preferred stockholders receive dividends paid at a set rate. Common stock represents general ownership in a corporation and a right to share in its profits. Common stockholders vote to elect the officers of the corporation.

5. Stockbrokers work through stock exchanges to buy and sell shares of stock for investors.

6. When selecting stock investments, consider a company's profitability, debt, growth potential, yield, and price-earnings ratio (P/E). Also consider economic factors such as inflation, interest rates, consumer spending, and employment.

19-3 BONDS AND MUTUAL FUNDS

7. A bond represents a debt owed by an organization. Government and companies sell bonds to raise funds to finance current operations or future expansion. Local and state governments sell municipal bonds. The federal government sells savings bonds, Treasury bills, and Treasury notes.

8. Companies issue corporate bonds to raise funds. Investors are paid interest for lending money to the company.

9. Mutual funds allow people to combine their funds to buy a variety of securities, which reduces risk and increases potential returns. Types of mutual funds include aggressive-growth stock finds, income funds, international funds, sector funds, bond funds, and balanced funds.

19-4 REAL ESTATE INVESTMENTS

10. A person can get started in real estate by renting a place to live or buying a mobile home. When buying a home, you may need to obtain a mortgage and use the services of a real estate agent and lawyer.

11. The advantages of home ownership are tax benefits, increased equity, and pride of ownership.

12. The major costs associated with owning a house include property taxes, interest payments, property insurance, and maintenance.

19-5 OTHER INVESTMENTS

13. Commodities commonly used as investments include corn, soybeans, wheat, gold, silver, copper, platinum, foreign currencies, and Treasury debt instruments.

14. Collectibles can combine a hobby with an investment that may increase in value.

Communicate Business Concepts

1. What actions could employers and government take to encourage saving in society?

2. How does inflation increase the risk of an investment?

3. Ella Chapman, a wealthy businessperson, invests $5,000 in a newly organized company. Frank Brokaw earns an average moderate salary and has $5,000 in a savings account. Because Ella has a reputation for being a good investor, Frank decides to also invest in that company. Does the fact that the investment may be a good one for Ella mean that it is also a good investment for Frank? Explain your answer.

4. What are some reasons people buy stocks even though they are not as safe as other types of investments?

5. Why do municipal bonds usually pay a lower rate of interest than corporate bonds?

6. Susan Haugen bought $5,000 of gold mining stocks a few years ago. Last week, she received a letter saying that the company went out of business. It could not operate profitably, so it closed down. How much of her investment might Susan lose?

7. People who buy and sell land and houses commonly say that the three most important factors to consider when buying real estate are "location, location, and location!" Why do you think this is their belief?

8. Blair Vazquez owns a house that has a value of $180,000. For the past three years, the upkeep has averaged less than $800 a year. Can Blair assume that his expenses will be only $800 in future years?

Develop Your Business Language

Match the terms listed with the definitions.

9. The amount that your local government determines your property to be worth for tax purposes.

10. Licensed specialist in the buying and selling of stocks and bonds.

11. Land and anything that is attached to it.

12. Represents general ownership in a corporation and a right to share in its profits.

13. Investments set up and managed by companies that receive money from many investors.

14. A legal document giving the lender a claim against real estate property.

15. Items of personal interest to collectors that can increase in value in the future.

16. Using your savings to earn more money.

17. The percentage of money earned on your savings or investment over a year, also called the rate of return.

18. Bonds issued by local and state governments.

19. Storage of money for future use.

20. The difference between the price at which you could currently sell your house and the amount owed on the mortgage.

21. Business organizations that accommodate the buying and selling of securities.

22. Bonds issued by corporations.

23. Agreements to buy or sell an amount of a commodity at a specified price in the future.

24. The price at which a share of stock can be bought and sold in the stock market.

25. Grain, livestock, and precious metals.

26. Stock that has first priority in the payment of dividends.

27. The ease with which an investment can be changed into cash without losing its value.

KEY TERMS

a. assessed value
b. collectibles
c. commodities
d. common stock
e. corporate bond
f. equity
g. futures contract
h. investing
i. liquidity
j. market value
k. mortgage
l. municipal bond
m. mutual fund
n. preferred stock
o. real estate
p. saving
q. stock exchange
r. stockbroker
s. yield

4. People buy stocks because, even though they do not have a guaranteed rate of return, they have the possibility of earning a much higher return than safer investment choices.

5. Municipal bonds are considered safer investments than corporate bonds, and interest on municipal bonds is tax exempt from federal and most state income taxes.

6. Susan could lose all of her $5,000 investment.

7. People will buy a less than-perfect home in a desirable area, but they will not buy a home in an undesirable area with poor schools, poor public services, or lack of convenient access to jobs and shopping.

8. No, Blair may have to pay much more than $800 in some future year if his home needs a major repair, such as replacing the roof or the heating and air conditioning system, which could cost thousands of dollars.

Develop Your Business Language Answers

9. a. assessed value
10. r. stockbroker
11. o. real estate
12. d. common stock
13. m. mutual fund

14. k. mortgage
15. b. collectibles
16. h. investing
17. s. yield
18. l. municipal bond

19. p. saving
20. f. equity
21. q. stock exchange
22. e. corporate bond
23. g. futures contract

24. j. market value
25. c. commodities
26. n. preferred stock
27. i. liquidity

Make Academic Connections

28. **LAW** The Truth in Savings Act was created to provide consumers with clear, accurate information on the earnings of savings accounts. Conduct an online search to obtain additional information about this law.

29. **MATH** Small amounts add up to large sums in a short time. How much will each person below save in one year (365 days) if he or she saves the following amounts without interest being added?

  a. Charles Jason: 20 cents a day
  b. Carla Spivak: 95 cents a week
  c. Alice Farney: $10 every two weeks
  d. Nolan Robinson: $20 a month

30. **TECHNOLOGY** Buying investments online can be convenient and reduce commission costs. Locate a web site that allows you to buy and sell stock and other investments online. What services are provided by this e-broker? What costs are involved?

31. **MATH** The price-earnings (P/E) ratio is calculated by dividing the price per share by the earnings per share. If a company has 100,000 shares of stock and earns a net profit of $150,000, (a) what is the earnings per share? (b) If the company's stock is selling for $30 per share, what is the P/E?

32. **GEOGRAPHY** Research the location of stock exchanges around the world. Identify one in Europe, one in Asia, one in Africa, and one in Latin America. Prepare a map showing the locations of these stock exchanges.

33. **ECONOMICS** Select a company and research its stock price for one day a week for the past eight weeks. Prepare a table showing the changing market value of the stock. Describe situations that may have affected the market value of this stock.

34. **COMMUNICATIONS** Talk to a person who is a member of an investment club. What is the purpose of an investment club? How do these groups help investors earn money while learning about stocks and bonds?

35. **ECONOMICS** Locate current bond prices in the newspaper or online. Select a bond for a company. Identify the following: (a) company name, (b) stated rate of the bond, (c) bond maturity date, (d) current yield, and (e) current market value of the bond. What economic and company trends are likely affecting the current market value of the bond?

36. **RESEARCH** Junk bonds are investments with high risk but also potential for a high return. Conduct library or online research to obtain information about these risky bonds.

37. **BUSINESS** Commodity trading is governed by the Commodity Futures Trading Commission (CFTC) and the National Futures Association (NFA). Conduct library and online research to obtain additional information on these agencies.

Linking School and Community

Talk to people in your community about their investments. What types of investments do they own? (Do not ask the value of the investments.) How did they decide to obtain these investments? What types of investments do they recommend for people of various ages? Prepare a one-paragraph summary of your findings.

Web Workout

Investment advice is available from many sources. An investment blog can help you research investments and plan for the future. These web logs provide comments and other information based on experiences of various investors.

It is important to evaluate any information posted on a blog. You should be concerned about the accuracy of postings. It is also important to view posting in light of your own your specific situation.

Think Critically
1. Locate a blog that discusses investments. Describe several typical postings.
2. What actions might be taken to make sure the information presented on this blog is valid?
3. Write a comment you might post on this blog.

Decision-Making Strategies

Jennie Wolfe has inherited $18,000. She graduated from high school three years ago, has an accounting job, is renting a small apartment, and saves regularly.

Jennie understands the need to evaluate stock and bond investments based on safety, liquidity, and rate of return. In addition, she realizes that the investments she selects must be guided by her personal financial needs and goals. Jennie also believes that she will not need any large amounts of cash for the next several years.

38. Jennie wants to invest in stocks that will be very safe, highly liquid, and earn a high return. Is there anything wrong with this investment goal?

39. What advice would you give Jennie to help her study the companies from which she is considering buying bonds and stocks?

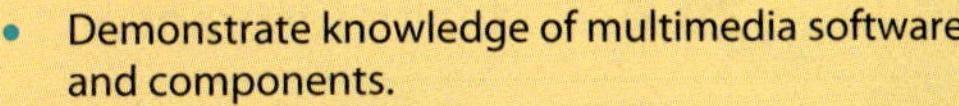

Presentation Management—Team Event

This event will assess your use of current desktop technologies and software to prepare and deliver an effective multimedia presentation.

You will design a computer-generated multimedia presentation. You have 15 minutes for preparation and setup. The presentation will last a minimum of seven minutes and a maximum of 10 minutes. Up to five minutes will be allowed for questions from the judges. The contestants must make effective use of current multimedia technology in the presentation. In preparation for the presentation, contestants should use space, color, and text as design factors. No VCR or laserdisc may be used in the presentation. Charts and other graphics should be used in the presentation. The student is responsible for securing a release form from any individual whose name, photograph, and other information is included in the presentation.

Topic: You are an investment advisor who helps individuals decide where to invest money based upon the amount available to invest risk factor, and rate of return. Your presentation must cover stocks, bonds, real estate, futures, commodities, and collectibles. You must discuss the safety, liquidity, and possible rate of return for each investment.

PERFORMANCE INDICATORS EVALUATED

- Demonstrate knowledge of multimedia software and components.
- Demonstrate effective oral communication skills.
- Apply technical skills to create a multimedia presentation that enhances the oral presentation.

You will be evaluated for your

- Knowledge of the topic
- Organized presentation of the topic
- Confidence, quality of voice, and eye contact
- Relationship of the topic to business strategy

For more detailed information about performance indicators, go to the BPA web site.

Think Critically
1. What does liquidity of an investment mean?
2. Which investments involve greater risk?
3. What is the advantage of investing in real estate?
4. Why are futures markets and collectibles classified as riskier investments?

http://www.bpa net.org/

Access the web site shown here to find portfolio activities for this chapter. Use the activities to provide tangible evidence of your learning.

school.cengage.com/business/introtobiz

Decision-Making Strategies Answers

38. Jennie might want to invest at least a portion of her money in investments that are slightly less safe but could provide a much higher rate of return. Because she does not plan to spend the money in the next few years, she does not need a highly liquid investment. She will likely realize a higher return by giving up some safety and liquidity.

39. Jennie should first determine her current and future financial goals. She might want to use the services of a full-service stock broker. She will also want to learn about the companies through publications such as *Moody's Handbook of Common Stocks, Value Line,* and *Standard and Poor's Encyclopedia of Stocks* that provide data about companies' net worth, debt, sales revenue, profits, dividend history, and future prospects. Many web sites also provide valuable information on companies.

Winning Edge
Presentation Management—Team Event

This activity offers students an opportunity to use technology to develop a visual presentation. Encourage students to carefully integrate visuals that effectively enhance the content of their presentation.

Think Critically
Answers

1. Liquidity means how readily the investment can be exchanged for cash.

2. Futures and collectibles involve greater risk. Any investment that is not insured involves greater risk.

3. Real estate usually goes up in value.

4. Futures markets and collectibles depend on possible demand or desire for the items. They are both risky investments.

Insurance

CHAPTER OVERVIEW

Chapter 20 describes the types of insurance that consumers should consider based on their personal circumstances and resources.

20-1 Vehicle Insurance

Students will learn the types of risks they face as automobile owners and the insurance coverage related to each risk.

20-2 Property Insurance

This lesson discusses the various types of coverage available through property insurance and the factors that affect the cost of that insurance.

20-3 Life Insurance

Students will study life insurance principles and learn the process used to buy insurance.

20-4 Health Insurance

The lesson offers information on health, disability, and long-term care insurance as well as the providers of health insurance.

<table>
<tr><td>20-1</td><td>Vehicle Insurance</td></tr>
<tr><td>20-2</td><td>Property Insurance</td></tr>
<tr><td>20-3</td><td>Life Insurance</td></tr>
<tr><td>20-4</td><td>Health Insurance</td></tr>
</table>

508

Teaching Resources

Activities and Study Guide, Ch. 20
Chapter and Unit Tests, Ch. 20
Spanish Resources, Ch. 20

ExamView® *CD*, Ch. 20
Instructor's Resource CD
- PowerPoint Slides, Ch. 20
- Lesson Plans, Ch. 20

Xtra! Web Site

school.cengage.com/business/introtobiz
- Study Tools, 20-1, 20-2, 20-3, 20-4
- Quiz Prep, Ch. 20
- Net Bookmark, Ch. 20
- Crossword Puzzle, Ch. 20
- Portfolio Activity, Ch. 20

Planning a Career in...
INSURANCE

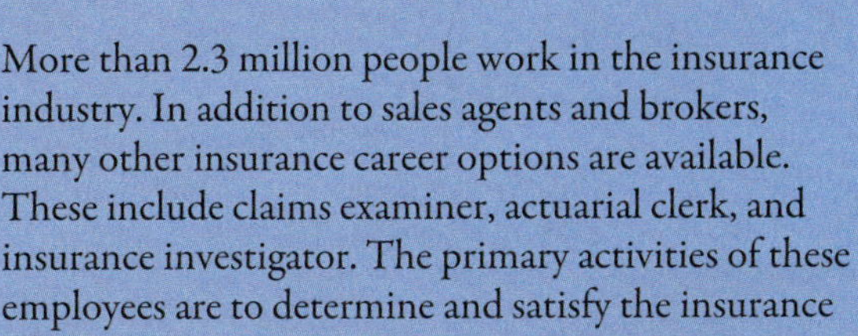

More than 2.3 million people work in the insurance industry. In addition to sales agents and brokers, many other insurance career options are available. These include claims examiner, actuarial clerk, and insurance investigator. The primary activities of these employees are to determine and satisfy the insurance needs of consumers and business organizations.

Employment Outlook

- There will be slower than average employment growth for insurance agents.
- Employment for support workers in the insurance industry will require strong technology competencies.
- As insurance agents offer additional financial planning services and investment products, expanded opportunities will be available.

Related Job Titles

- Insurance Sales Agent
- Actuary
- Insurance Broker
- Insurance Underwriter
- Claims Examiner
- Claims Clerk
- Auto Damage Insurance Appraiser
- Insurance Policy Processing Clerk
- Customer Service Representative
- Insurance Fraud Investigator

Needed Skills

- Sales, management, and professional positions usually require a college degree. Graduation from high school or a two-year postsecondary business program is adequate for most office and administrative support jobs.
- Software skills and general ability with technology are important as most insurance activities are computerized.
- Sales ability and strong communication skills are vital for those involved in selling and customer service.
- Specialized insurance training may be obtained through courses offered by the Insurance Institute of America and other insurance organizations.

What's it like to work in... Insurance

"Now that we have your life, car, and home insured, how about considering a portfolio of mutual funds for your retirement plan?" asked Valerie Esposito.

"Wait a minute, I thought you were an insurance agent, not an investment broker," responded Jane Conley.

© Digital Vision/Getty Images

"Well, we now do a lot more than just sell insurance," responded Valerie. "My company offers all types of insurance for businesses and individuals. In addition, we can help you with various financial services and investment products. We also make car loans and mortgages, and we issue credit cards."

"That's nice to know," commented Jane. "I'll be able to get assistance from you about my insurance needs, but I will also be able to borrow and invest through your company. How convenient!"

What about you? What aspects of the insurance business might interest you for a future career?

Planning a Career in...
INSURANCE

The insurance industry is very large and is growing with a variety of career opportunities. Many types of insurance coverages are available to consumers, and each type needs to be carefully planned, sold, and managed. From beginning jobs to highly technical careers, students can find interesting opportunities that match their interests and abilities.

What About You? Answer

Answers will vary depending on their career interests. Encourage students to match their specific interests and educational plans with possible insurance careers.

Additional Career Information

Additional information on careers can be found in the *Occupational Outlook Handbook*, an online publication (www.bls.gov/oco) of the federal government. Tell your class about this resource and how to use it. This description of job duties can be used to demonstrate the relevancy of skills learned in this course.

Vehicle Insurance

Focus on Real Life

Ask students to identify expenses associated with owning or driving a car or truck. Ask them which of the expenses are the highest. If insurance is near the top, discuss why the cost is so high for teenagers.

TEACH

Plan and print the map for a 100-mile trip from your city following a variety of types of roads. Show the map to students and ask them to identify the possible risks and hazards they might face if they had to drive a car over the route.

THINK CRITICALLY THROUGH VISUALS

Automobile insurance can protect a policyholder from the economic risk of expensive car repairs and perhaps medical intervention in the event of an accident.

Goals

Discuss motor vehicle risks.

Explain auto insurance coverage.

Identify factors that affect auto insurance costs.

Key Terms

bodily injury liability

medical payments

uninsured motorist

property damage liability

collision coverage

deductible

comprehensive coverage

Focus on Real Life

"Chris! What a great-looking car! How did you ever afford it?"

"It's not easy, Roberto, to afford a car and still be in school. Not only do I have to make car payments, but I also have to pay for insurance. It's been quite a shock! I did save enough money from a part-time job last summer to buy the car, but I didn't plan on how much insurance would cost. I'm looking for a job right now so I can afford to keep the car."

Purchasing car insurance can be expensive, but not everyone has to pay high premiums. Drivers who insurance companies view as low risks pay significantly less than those in the high-risk category.

---

main idea

Discuss motor vehicle risks.

MOTOR VEHICLE RISKS

Owning a vehicle puts you in a position of high economic risk. You might have an accident and injure yourself or other people. You might damage your vehicle or others' property. Your vehicle might be vandalized or stolen. Someone could sue you because of an accident.

Treating injured people and repairing damaged property resulting from an automobile accident can take all of the assets of a person who does not have insurance. The amount of money paid to injured people and to owners of damaged property has increased dramatically in recent years. Vehicle insurance provides protection from the financial risks involved with owning and driving a car.

Sometimes you cannot avoid an accident. No one may be directly blamed for it. However, in most cases someone is at fault. The person who is legally at fault is liable for damages and financial losses that result from the accident. Although you may think you are faultless, you can be sued. If you are insured, your insurance company will provide legal defense for the suit. If the court decides that you are legally liable for injuries or damage to property, your insurance company will pay up to the limits stated in your insurance policy.

Individual states regulate laws related to vehicle insurance. Most of these laws benefit responsible drivers. Owners of vehicles should know about financial responsibility laws and compulsory insurance laws.

In what ways can automobile insurance protect you?

Different Learning Abilities

Specific Learning Disability (SLD) Have students list one risk they could face in each of the situations: (1) as the driver of a car, (2) as the passenger in a car, (3) as a pedestrian crossing a street, and (4) as a vehicle owner who loans a vehicle to another driver.

Financial Responsibility

All states have some type of *financial responsibility law*. These laws protect the public from financial loss caused by drivers. If you cause an accident and cannot pay for damages or injuries through insurance, the legal system may take other action. Your savings or property may be taken. Your driver's license will also likely be suspended or taken away. Financial responsibility laws make you legally responsible for any injuries you cause to people. You are also responsible for damage to the property of others.

Compulsory Insurance

Most states require drivers to carry certain types of automobile insurance before they can get a license for their car. In these states, it is compulsory that an automobile owner have insurance for personal injury and property damage. Compulsory insurance laws may not allow a driver to register a car or get a driver's license without proof of the required insurance coverage.

checkpoint >>
What are financial responsibility laws?

AUTOMOBILE INSURANCE COVERAGE

Insurance companies offer several types of auto insurance protection. The two main categories are personal injury coverage and property damage coverage. Figure 20-1 summarizes the types of automobile insurance coverage.

Personal Injury Coverage

Personal injury coverage includes bodily injury liability, medical payments, and uninsured motorist protection. These three types of coverage are the main source of money paid in claims by automobile insurance companies.

Bodily Injury Liability Protection Insurance that protects a driver from claims resulting from injuries or deaths for which the insured is at fault is **bodily injury liability** coverage. This type of insurance covers people in other cars, passengers riding with the insured, and pedestrians. The insured and, in most cases, the insured's immediate family are not covered.

Explain auto insurance coverage.

ONGOING ASSESSMENT

checkpoint >> **ANSWER**

Financial responsibility laws exist in some form in every state. These laws protect the public from the financial loss caused by uninsured drivers by making drivers legally responsible for any injuries or property damage they cause.

TEACH

Obtain a brochure from an automobile insurance agent or the Internet that lists and describes the types of automobile insurance coverage offered by the company. Have students compare those listed with the types described in the lesson.

FIGURE 20-1   ANSWER

Answers will vary. Some students might suggest liability coverages are the most important because not having liability coverages can result in the highest potential financial loss.

Summary Chart of Automobile Insurance Coverage

Types of Coverage	Coverage On	
Personal Injury Coverage	**Policyholder**	**Others**
Bodily injury liability	No	Yes
Medical payments	Yes	Yes
Uninsured motorist protection	Yes	Yes
Property Damage Coverage	**Policyholder's Automobile**	**Property of Others**
Property damage liability	No	Yes
Collision insurance	Yes	No
Comprehensive physical damage	Yes	No

FIGURE 20-1
Which types of auto insurance coverage do you think might be the most important? Why?

Teaching Strategies

Expand Beyond the Classroom Have students use library resources or the Internet to determine what the state's financial responsibility and compulsory insurance requirements are for automobile ownership and how they are enforced.

TEACH

Tell students that there are many types of auto insurance coverage, but that those coverage in total can be quite expensive. Have students rank the types of coverage in terms of which they believe are most important if they didn't have enough money to buy all coverage. What could happen financially to them if they didn't carry some of the coverage?

Dollar amounts of bodily injury coverage are generally expressed as two numbers, such as 100/300. The first number refers to the limit in thousands of dollars that the insurance company will pay for injuries to any one person in an accident. For example, with 100/300 bodily injury liability coverage, the insurance company would pay up to $100,000 for injuries to one person.

The second number, 300, is the maximum amount that the company would pay for injuries to multiple people because of the accident. If more than three people were injured, each person may not receive the full $100,000. The insurance company is only liable for $300,000 in this case. You may obtain larger amounts of bodily injury protection for a slight increase in your premium.

Medical Payments Protection

Policyholders and family members are covered if they are injured while riding in their car or another car through **medical payments** coverage. This protection may also cover them if they are walking and are hit by a car. In addition, the policy protects guests in the insured car.

Medical payments insurance covers the costs of medical, dental, ambulance, hospital, nursing, and funeral services. Payment, up to the limit stated in the policy, is made no matter who is at fault. Car owners usually purchase medical payments insurance along with bodily injury liability coverage.

Uninsured Motorist Protection

In some cases, injuries are caused by hit-and-run drivers or by drivers without insurance or money to pay claims. To protect against these drivers, insurance companies offer **uninsured motorist** coverage.

This coverage is available only to those people who carry bodily injury liability insurance. Uninsured motorist protection covers the policyholder and family members. It also covers guests in the policyholder's car. Uninsured motorist protection covers the insured person only if the uninsured motorist is at fault. This is different from medical payments coverage, which pays regardless of who is at fault.

Insurance companies also offer *underinsured motorist* coverage. This insures you for losses caused by another driver whose coverage is insufficient.

Property Damage Coverage

Three types of automobile insurance protect you from economic loss as a result of property damage. The three types of coverage are property damage liability, collision, and comprehensive damage.

Property Damage Liability

Insurance that protects a driver against claims if the insured's car damages someone else's property and the insured is at fault is **property damage liability** coverage. The damaged property is often another car, but it may also be property such as telephone poles, fire hydrants, or buildings. Property damage liability insurance does not cover damage to the insured's car.

Collision Insurance
Insurance that protects a car owner against financial loss resulting from a collision or rollover is **collision coverage**. This insurance does not cover injuries to people or damage to the property of others.

Collision coverage is usually written with a **deductible** clause. You must pay this amount before the insurance

---

Applied Skills

Word Processing/Office Technology Have students use a word processing program to recreate Figure 20-1 as a table. Ask them to add an additional column on the right side of the table and add a brief description of each type of cover age in that column.

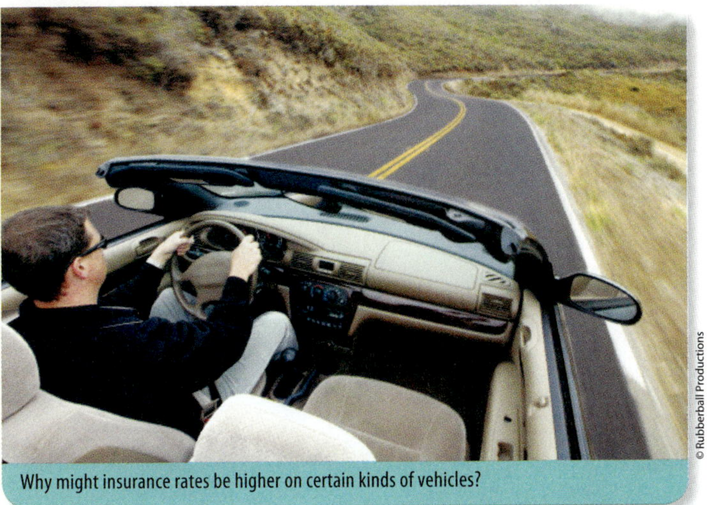

Why might insurance rates be higher on certain kinds of vehicles?

company pays a claim. For example, suppose your car suffers $2,500 damage in an accident and your deductible amount is $500. You would pay $500 and the insurance company would pay $2,000, $2,500 damages − $500 deductible = $2,000 claim. Deductible amounts are often $200, $500, or more. Deductibles reduce the premium cost.

Collision coverage does not provide for payment of damages greater than the car's value. Suppose the insured's car incurs $6,500 in damages in a collision with another vehicle. If the car has a value of only $6,100, the collision coverage would pay only $6,100, not $6,500.

Collision coverage may not be worthwhile on a car that is of little value. In some situations, the cost of repairing the car may be more than the car is worth.

Comprehensive Coverage Your car can be damaged or destroyed in other ways. Common perils include theft or damage from fire, tornado, flood, vandalism, or falling objects. Comprehensive coverage protects the insured against almost all damage losses except those caused from a collision or rollover.

If the insured's car is stolen or destroyed, the amount paid by insurance is not necessarily equal to the amount paid for the car. Rather, it is equal to the car's estimated value at the time of the loss. Suppose the insured's car cost $15,000. It is stolen soon after it is purchased. The insurance company will probably pay almost as much as the car cost—perhaps $14,500. If the car is stolen two years after it is purchased, the insurance company may pay only $10,500. The car has grown older and has a decreased value.

No-Fault Insurance Laws

In an effort to reduce insurance costs and speed up claim settlements, *no-fault insurance* has been adopted by some states. Under this program, people injured in an automobile accident collect for their financial losses from their own insurance companies no matter who is at fault. These losses include their medical bills, loss of wages, and other related expenses.

> *checkpoint* >>
> What are the two main categories of automobile insurance coverage?

Insurance rates might be higher on vehicles that are more expensive to repair, that are more likely to be driven at high speeds, or that perform more poorly in crash safety tests.

TEACH

Have students debate the advantages and disadvantages of carrying a very high deductible amount, such as $1,000, to get a substantial savings in the auto insurance premium.

ONGOING ASSESSMENT

checkpoint >> **ANSWER**

The two main categories of automobile insurance coverage are (1) personal injury coverage and (2) property damage coverage.

Applied Skills

Building Study Skills Have students discuss automobile insurance coverage. Ask them to develop a study outline that lists each coverage and provides an outline of what protection it offers.

TEACH

As each of the factors used to determine insurance rates is identified, ask students to suggest why the factor can lead to higher or lower rates.

THINK CRITICALLY THROUGH VISUALS

Actions drivers can take to increase their driving safety include obeying all traffic laws, observing posted speed limits, wearing safety belts, and lessening in-car distractions, such as cell phones and rowdy passengers.

main idea

Identify factors that affect auto insurance costs.

AUTOMOBILE INSURANCE COSTS

Automobile insurance is expensive. You should spend this money wisely and carefully. It is important to understand how to get the most protection for your insurance dollar.

Insurance Rates

Insurance companies use several factors to determine automobile insurance costs. Examples of these factors include:

What are some actions you can take to increase your driving safety?

- Your age and other characteristics such as accident record, marital status, academic standing, and credit rating

- Purpose for which you use your car

- Number of miles you drive each year

- Value and type of your car

- Community in which you live

- Amount of coverage and deductibles

Because some drivers are more likely to have accidents than others, they pay higher premiums. To determine premium rates, drivers are classified according to age, marital status, driving record, and scholastic achievement.

The lowest rates are reserved for the best risks—those least likely to have an accident. When a driver in the family is under age 25, the cost of insurance is usually higher than if all drivers are over age 25.

The purpose for which a car is driven and the number of miles it is driven in a year also affect insurance rates. Cars used for business purposes are generally driven more miles in a year than are cars driven for pleasure. This increases the chances of an accident.

The value of your car has an important effect on the cost of insurance. Premiums for collision coverage and comprehensive physical damage coverage are higher for a car worth $18,000 than for a car worth only $11,000. The insurance company runs the risk of paying out much more to the insured if the $18,000 car is destroyed or stolen. The type of car also affects the rate. Drivers of a luxury car or a sports car will pay higher rates.

Rates for automobile insurance vary from state to state. They vary from city to city within a state. The population in a particular area and the number of accidents that occur in the area also affect insurance rates. Insurance companies gather statistics on the amount of claims paid for in an area. They base their rates on this information.

The cost of your automobile insurance will vary according to the coverage you have and the deductibles you choose. The more coverage you carry, the higher the cost.

Reducing Auto Insurance Costs

By planning your automobile insurance purchase carefully, you can save money. For example, insurance companies often decrease the extra amount charged for young drivers if they complete a driver education course. Companies in most states also offer young people a good student discount.

Different Learning Abilities

Gifted Have students use the Internet site of an insurance company that allows rate comparisons. Ask them to make a list of several types of coverage they would need to insure an automobile. They should then compare the cost of the same coverage for several different automobile models and several different ages of the same model.

Selecting a Company

Automobile insurance premiums also vary from company to company. Be sure to compare rates. Companies may offer lower rates if the family insures more than one car or if the insured buys other types of insurance from the same company. Also, paying premiums on a monthly basis is usually more expensive than paying a premium for six months or one year.

Assigned-Risk Plans

Usually as a result of a poor driving record, some drivers are unable to buy automobile insurance in the normal fashion. Because of this, every state has an *assigned-risk plan*. Every automobile insurance company in the state is assigned a certain number of high-risk drivers, based on the amount of insurance each company sells. Each company has to insure a fair proportion of high-risk drivers. Drivers in high-risk categories pay much higher premiums.

Insurance for Other Vehicles

Insurance on motorcycles, recreational vehicles, and snowmobiles is similar to automobile insurance. Bodily injury liability, property damage liability, collision, and comprehensive physical damage insurance are the most important types of coverage. The engine size and value of the vehicle are the key factors in determining the cost. Generally, the larger and more expensive the vehicle, the higher the insurance cost.

checkpoint >>

What factors affect the cost of automobile insurance?

20-1 Assessment

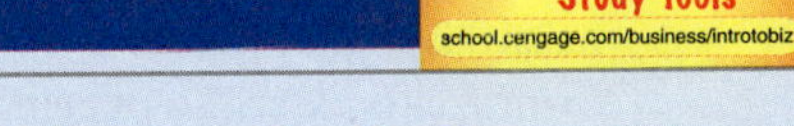

Key Concepts

Determine the best answer.

1. Health care costs for a person you hit while driving would be covered by
   a. collision
   b. medical payments
   c. bodily injury liability
   d. uninsured motorist

2. While driving, you damage a fence. The repair costs would be covered by
   a. collision
   b. property damage liability
   c. comprehensive
   d. no-fault insurance

Make Academic Connections

3. *Math* Joan Nordland is a college student who took a driver education course in high school. She has a B + average in her college work. She qualifies for a driver education discount of 20 percent and a good student discount of 15 percent off the premium for her automobile insurance. If the standard premium for her policy is $850 per year, how much will Joan save?

4. *Communication* Research automobile accident rates for various age groups. Create a graph to communicate the data.

Property Insurance

Goals

Describe property insurance coverage.

Explain property insurance policies.

Identify factors that affect property insurance costs.

Key Terms

personal liability coverage

homeowners policy

depreciation

Focus on Real Life

"I love our new apartment! We have spent a lot of money getting it ready to move into when school starts, but now I'm broke! Are you sure we really need renters insurance?"

"Trust me, Susan, with three college girls sharing an apartment, we need insurance. If our belongings were stolen or destroyed in a fire, we would be out a lot of money. I couldn't afford to replace all my personal items if they were stolen or destroyed. And with three of us sharing the insurance expense, it really won't cost us that much money."

"I guess you're right, Ashley. I know I couldn't replace all my personal belongings either. Go ahead and call your mom's insurance agent and find out what we need to do to get the process started."

main idea

Describe property insurance coverage.

PROPERTY INSURANCE COVERAGE

Insurance that protects you from the financial loss you would incur if some of your property were lost or destroyed due to fire, theft, vandalism, flood, or other hazard is *property insurance*. Property owners also are at risk of being sued by other people who are injured on their property. Because the risks of loss in such situations are high, everyone should carry property insurance.

Home and property insurance protect you against three kinds of economic loss.

1. Damage to your home or property

2. Expenses you must pay to live somewhere else if your home is damaged and must be repaired or rebuilt

3. Liability losses related to your property

Damage to Home or Property

You should insure your home and other expensive property for damage from fire, vandalism, unavoidable accidents, and natural disasters such as lightning, wind, and hail. If your property is damaged and you are insured, the insurance company will pay all or a portion of the cost of repair or replacement.

What kinds of weather might cause property damage in your area?

© Getty Images/PhotoDisc

Additional Living Expenses

If a fire or other disaster strikes your home, one of the first shocks you will experience is that you do not have a place to live. You may have to move into a hotel, motel, or furnished apartment while your home is being repaired.

Property insurance often includes coverage for *additional living expenses*. This insurance feature helps to pay for the living costs you would incur if something happened to your home.

Liability Protection

The third kind of loss, liability loss, is protected by personal liability insurance. **Personal liability coverage** covers claims from injuries to people or damage to property caused by you, your family, or even your pets. Suppose a neighbor slips on your icy sidewalk and it is proven you are at fault. Personal liability coverage will pay for any medical and legal costs up to a stated limit. What if a child damages a car in an adjacent driveway with a tricycle? Claims will be paid through the policy of the child's family. Specifically, the provisions that cover liability for physical damage to the property of others will be used to determine the claim amount.

These kinds of events may seem remote and rather petty. Yet court awards to those who suffer the damage or injury often are neither remote nor petty. In fact, these awards (and therefore premiums) are increasing so quickly that the insurance industry often refers to it as the insurance liability crisis. Awards to injured people for millions of dollars are not uncommon. Everyone should have some form of liability protection from economic loss.

PROPERTY INSURANCE POLICIES

When purchasing property insurance, you must first decide what you should insure. You must also decide the perils from which you should insure your property. *Perils* are the causes of loss such as fire, wind, or theft.

Property permanently attached to land, such as a house or garage, is *real property*. Property not attached to the land, such as furniture or clothing, is known as *personal property*. You may insure real and personal property with a homeowners policy.

Homeowners Policies

The most common form of home and property insurance policy sold today is a **homeowners policy**. This coverage provides a very convenient package-type insurance policy designed to insure homes and property. Homeowners policies come in several forms.

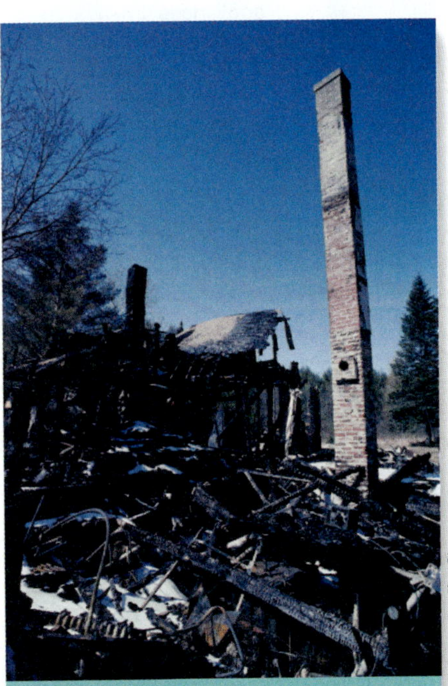

What different kinds of perils should a home be insured against?

Explain property insurance policies.

ONGOING ASSESSMENT
checkpoint >> **ANSWER**

The three main types of property insurance coverage are coverage for (1) damage to home or property, (2) additional living expenses, and (3) liability protection.

TEACH

Ask students why renters need to purchase insurance coverage for personal property, but not real property. Use their answers to make sure they understand the differences between the two types of property insurance.

THINK CRITICALLY THROUGH VISUALS

Homes should be insured against perils such as wind, fire, or theft. Floods and earthquakes are perils not usually included in typical policies, but homeowners can purchase special policies to cover these threats.

PROJECT

Provide the following instructions to students. (These instructions also appear on page xxv of the textbook.) Why is the purchase of property and liability insurance important to all life-span plans? What amounts and types of insurance should you plan to buy in the next few years?

Life-Span Plan Answers

Answers will vary. Students should point out that losses of a person's personal property or harm they cause others can prevent them from achieving their life-span goals unless they are appropriately insured.

Applied Skills

Communication Have students create a magazine advertisement that encourages first-time renters to consider purchasing personal property insurance.

Types of Perils

Basic	1. Fire or lightning 2. Volcanic eruption 3. Windstorm or hail 4. Explosion 5. Vehicles 6. Riot or civil commotion 7. Aircraft 8. Smoke 9. Vandalism or malicious mischief 10. Theft 11. Breakage of glass constituting a part of building
Broad	12. Falling objects 13. Weight of ice, snow, sleet 14. Collapse of buildings 15. Sudden and accidental tearing apart, cracking, burning, or bulging of a steam or hot water heating system or of appliances for heating water, an air conditioning system, or automatic fire-protective sprinkler system 16. Accidental discharge, leakage, or overflow of water or steam from within a plumbing, heating, or air-conditioning system or domestic appliance 17. Freezing of plumbing, heating, and air-conditioning systems, automatic fire-protective sprinkler system, and domestic appliances 18. Sudden and accidental injury from artificially generated currents to electrical appliances, devices, fixtures, and wiring (does not include loss to a tube, transistor, or similar electronic components)
Special	All perils EXCEPT earthquake, flood, war, nuclear accidents, and certain others (Check policy for details.)

The *basic form* of a homeowners policy insures property against the first 11 perils listed in Figure 20-2. The *broad form* covers 18 different risks. The *special form* is even more comprehensive. It covers all perils shown in Figure 20-2 and many more. The special form is sometimes referred to as an *all-risk policy*. It costs from 10 to 15 percent more than the basic policy. Such a policy insures against all perils except those excluded by the policy.

Personal liability coverage is included with all forms of the homeowners policy. With a homeowners policy, you are as protected as you would be if you bought several separate policies.

Renters Policies

Many people rent homes, condominiums, or apartments. Their dwellings are filled with personal property. Renters have many of the same property and liability insurance needs as homeowners. A *renters policy* is a property and liability policy suitable for renters.

This policy covers household goods and personal belongings. This coverage provides protection against the same kinds of perils covered by homeowners policies. A renters policy may include personal liability coverage, but it doesn't protect the actual dwelling. The dwelling should be covered under the owner's policy.

Special Coverage

You can purchase policies for damage caused by flood in a flood-prone area. You can also obtain insurance to protect against economic losses caused by earthquakes. Neither of these two perils is typically covered in other policies.

Making a Claim

If you have to make a claim for a property loss, you will want to be well prepared. You should keep a list, called an *inventory*, of personal property that you have insured. The list should include the following information.

1. The brand name and description of each item

2. The purchase price

3. The date and place of the purchase

In addition to an up-to-date personal property inventory, insurance agents suggest keeping receipts for purchases. Taking photographs or making videos of your furniture and other property can also help to support claims.

Inventory records along with photographs or videos should be stored in a location that cannot be damaged by fire, water, or smoke. If the records are lost or damaged, it will be hard to provide the insurance company with the information it needs to make a payment for your claim. A safe deposit box in a bank or other safe location away from your home is a good storage area for property records.

The age of a personal property item is quite important. Most property becomes old, gradually wears out, and decreases in value. This decrease in value is **depreciation**. It may affect the amount an insurance company will pay if the property is destroyed.

For example, a sofa costing $700 that is expected to last 10 years would depreciate $70 each year ($700 cost ÷ 10 years = $70 depreciation per year). Its value after six years would be $280 (depreciation per year $70 × 6 years = total depreciation

FYI

$420; original cost $700 − total depreciation $420 = $280).

In recent years, homeowners have begun to purchase *replacement insurance*. With this method, the insurance company actually replaces an item that has been destroyed. No depreciation is deducted. Instead, the item is actually replaced no matter what the current cost may be. A replacement cost policy would pay whatever it cost to replace your property.

checkpoint >>

How does a renters policy differ from homeowners insurance?

What is the value of homes in your neighborhood? How does this affect insurance rates in your area?

© Getty Images/PhotoDisc

ONGOING ASSESSMENT

checkpoint >> **ANSWER**

A renters policy may include personal liability coverage, but unlike homeowners insurance, it doesn't protect the actual dwelling, which should be covered under the owner's policy.

THINK CRITICALLY THROUGH VISUALS

Answers will vary depending on the value of homes in your community. Generally, the more expensive the home is, the more costly the insurance protection. However, high crime can cause higher rates even in a neighborhood of less expensive homes.

Applied Skills

Technology Have students conduct an Internet search to locate a web site that features forms that can be used to create a personal property inventory. Forms are often available on the web sites of insurance or moving companies. Have students begin the process of completing a personal inventory for themselves or their family by adding information for several items they own.

Have students discuss the difference between insuring property for its current value and its replacement cost. Ask them which type of insurance would cost more and why.

THINK CRITICALLY THROUGH VISUALS

A detailed household inventory can help a homeowner remember every covered item in the event of a claim. Such an inventory should include the date each item was acquired, the purchase price, and receipts or appraisals of items.

main idea

Identify factors that affect property insurance costs.

PROPERTY INSURANCE COSTS

As with any insurance purchase, a wise consumer should seek the proper protection at the lowest cost. This process involves making sure that you insure the property for the correct amount. You should also carefully consider the factors affecting property insurance costs. The value of a home and furnishings represents the largest investment that many people make. The purchase of a carefully selected insurance plan to protect these items makes good sense.

Coverage Selection

Suppose a family had a house built in 2004 for $180,000. They insured it for that amount. If today's cost of building a similar house is $220,000, the current replacement value of the house is $220,000. Yet if the house is destroyed by fire, the insurance company may pay the family only $180,000.

Some insurance companies provide for automatic increases in property coverage as the price level increases. Others will pay the current replacement value if the property is insured for at least 80 percent of that replacement value.

Building costs and property values increase almost every year. Property owners should review the value of their homes and insurance coverage on a regular basis. They should determine the cost of replacing their property. They must make sure that their insurance policies provide enough protection.

Special care should be taken to correctly estimate the value of personal property. Because personal property includes many items, some may be overlooked. Most homeowners policies provide personal property coverage at 50 to 70 percent of policy value. For example, if your home is insured for $100,000, your personal property is insured for 60 percent of this, or $60,000. The value of personal property that you obtain over the years is often high. In many cases, a homeowner's personal property is worth a great deal more than the coverage provided. Additional coverage is available for a slightly higher premium.

Why is a detailed household inventory helpful if you need to submit an insurance claim?

Applied Skills

Mathematics Provide the following scenario and questions to students. A home was valued at $165,000 when it was purchased. If the value of the home has increased by 8 percent, what is the current value of the home? ($165,000 × 1.08 = $178,200) If the home must be insured for at least 80 percent of the replacement value, what is the amount of insurance coverage required at the time of purchase ($165,000 × 0.8 = $132,000) and today ($178,200 × 0.8 = $142,560)

Insurance Premiums

Premiums paid for homeowners insurance have increased over the years. Several factors determine the price that you pay for insurance on a home and furnishings. The most important factor is the estimated danger of loss based on the insurance company's past experiences. In addition to the loss experiences, an insurance company considers the following factors in determining homeowners' insurance premiums.

- Value of the property insured
- Construction of the building: whether it is made of brick, wood, or concrete, and the construction of the roof
- Number of claims on the property
- Type of policy (basic, broad, or special)
- Distance to the nearest fire department and water supply
- Amount of deductible (the higher the deductible, the lower the premium)
- Credit rating of the insured

When items are stolen or damaged, insurance companies require that you prove the value of the item. Prepare a list of possessions that are commonly found in a home. Describe actions that might be taken to prove the value of these items.

You should consider these items before purchasing or building a home. You should also keep them in mind when you are shopping for insurance on a home you already own. In addition, homeowners insurance discounts are often available for policyholders who are nonsmokers, for installing smoke detectors and burglar alarms, and for buying multiple policies, such as life and auto insurance, from the same company.

checkpoint >>
What factors affect the cost of home insurance?

20-2 Assessment

Xtra! Study Tools
school.cengage.com/business/introtobiz

Key Concepts

Determine the best answer.

1. True or False. Most property insurance policies will pay for living somewhere else while a damaged home is being repaired.

2. True or False. A garage is an example of personal property.

3. The most coverage is provided by the _?_ form of homeowners insurance.
   a. basic
   b. special
   c. broad
   d. renters

4. Renters would *not* be covered for
   a. living expenses
   b. personal liability
   c. personal property
   d. real property

Make Academic Connections

5. *Visual Art* Use photos, drawings, and other visual images to create a display that communicates the various perils covered by property insurance.

6. *Research* Contact a local insurance agent to obtain information on the costs of renters insurance in your community.

Work as a Team

Have the teams list recommendations they would make to property owners to ensure they have adequate information for filing a claim with an insurance company.

ONGOING ASSESSMENT

checkpoint >> **ANSWER**

Factors include the estimated danger of loss based on the insurance company's past experiences, the value of property insured, construction of the building, number of claims on the property, type of policy, distance to the nearest fire department and water supply, amount of deductible, and credit rating of the insured. Sometimes discounts are available for policyholders who are nonsmokers, who have installed smoke detectors and burglar alarms, and who buy multiple policies from the same company.

ASSESS

Key Concepts Answers

1. True
2. False. A garage is real property because it is attached to land.
3. c. broad
4. d. real property

Make Academic Connections

5. Displays will vary. The various perils covered by property insurance should be represented.
6. Findings will vary.

CLOSE

Ask students to describe three reasons why property owners should purchase insurance.

RETEACH

Divide students into learning teams of three or four students. Have each team review the lesson and create a study outline of the important information about property insurance.

ENRICH

Have students compare the similarities and differences between automobile insurance and property insurance.

521

Sharpen Your Life Skills

Have students identify five different ways that visual information can be presented and compare the advantages and disadvantages of each in terms of ease of use and effectiveness of communication.

Think Critically Answers

1. Visuals can enhance the effectiveness of a presentation by communicating data more effectively than mere written information. The audience will grasp the information more clearly and quickly and will recall it longer when visuals are used.

2. Visual presentations will vary. They should reflect the guidelines outlined in this feature.

Enhancing Presentations with Visuals

An audience benefits from the visual presentation of data, ideas, and concepts through improved clarity and stronger recall. A graph can illustrate the importance of sales figures. A map can help participants get their bearings. An interesting graphic can capture people's attention.

Commonly used visuals include slides, transparencies, posters, videos, models, photographs, flip charts, computer images, chalkboards, dry erase boards, maps, and demonstrations. To create effective visuals, be sure to use the following guidelines.

- Keep the design simple. Include only one major idea per visual.
- Limit how many visuals you use.
- Be concise and accurate. Proofread text and check calculations.
- Choose the visual that is most appropriate for the information or data you are presenting.
- Make sure that data are represented accurately.
- Make visuals large enough to be seen by the entire audience.
- Position yourself so the audience can clearly see the visuals.

Charts and graphs can enhance a presentation by creating a visual representation of data. They are particularly helpful in demonstrating relationships and trends. Commonly used charts and graphs include pie charts, organization charts, bar graphs, flow charts, line graphs, and pictographs.

Presentation software such as PowerPoint® can enhance an oral report. Templates and designs should be selected carefully to create audience appeal and limit distraction. When creating a presentation using software, consider these guidelines.

- Limit the text quantity to six lines per slide and approximately six words per line.
- Choose text and background colors that contrast for easy reading.
- Use a consistent font style with a size that can be read.
- Add images, such as photos, maps, graphs, and illustrations, to emphasize key ideas.
- Avoid distracting transitions, animation, and sound effects.

When presenting, do not read from the screen or your notes. Talk to your audience with enthusiasm, expression, and voice projection.

Think Critically
1. How can visuals enhance the effectiveness of a presentation?
2. Create a visual that could be used with a presentation for a class or other situation.

Applied Skills

Writing Across the Curriculum Have students write a paragraph that illustrates how they could use the information contained in the "Sharpen Your Life Skills" feature to create an effective presentation for another class.

Goals

Discuss the principles of life insurance.

Explain the types of life insurance.

Describe the process of buying life insurance.

Key Terms

beneficiary

term life insurance

permanent life insurance

Focus on Real Life

"I was shocked when I heard that one of my fraternity brothers died. He was only 30 and he had young children—just like me. Now, I can't stop worrying about my own family. What would they do if something happened to me?"

"Rafael, I know this is upsetting, but I'm sure you have life insurance. Maybe you need to check to make sure you have enough coverage." replied Steve.

"You probably won't believe this, Steve, but I don't have any life insurance. I have other kinds of insurance, but I thought I was too young to worry about life insurance."

"Everyone needs life insurance to protect their family against economic loss. Julie and I just met with our insurance agent to make sure we had the right kind of coverage. She talked to us about some policies that combine insurance and investments. Do you want her name and phone number?"

This seems like a good time for Rafael to consider purchasing life insurance. He will need to decide what kind of life insurance to buy, how much to buy, and where to buy it.

LIFE INSURANCE PRINCIPLES

Life insurance protects survivors against financial loss associated with death. Specifically, it is designed to replace a loss of income for family members who are financially dependent upon another person. Life insurance can also be considered a means of saving or investing, but its primary purpose is always protection against financial loss.

The Life Insurance Policy

A life insurance policy is a contract between the insurance company and the person buying the insurance, called the *insured*. The following are the major elements of a life insurance policy.

- Name of the insured
- Amount of coverage, also called the face value or death benefit of the policy
- Cost of the insurance, called the premium amount
- Name of the beneficiary

Beneficiary Selection

When you buy life insurance, you must name a beneficiary. A **beneficiary** is the person named in the policy to receive the insurance benefits. The beneficiary is most often a spouse, children, or other dependents. You may insure not only your own life, but also the life of any person in whom you have an insurable interest. To have an *insurable interest* in the life of another person, you must receive some kind of financial benefit from that person's continued life.

> **main idea**
>
> Discuss the principles of life insurance.

Focus on Real Life

Ask students what they believe is the appropriate age for someone to consider purchasing life insurance. Are there factors more important than a person's age that could determine whether life insurance is needed or not?

TEACH

Ask students: Why should life insurance be viewed as a way to provide financial protection for survivors first rather than as a method of investment? Tell them there are many other options for investing that provide a greater return, but insurance offers immediate financial protection for survivors no matter how many premiums have been paid.

Different Learning Styles

Print Learner Have students prepare written definitions for each of the following insurance terms: face value, premium amount, and beneficiary.

You have, for example, an insurable interest in the lives of your parents. You do not have an insurable interest in a stranger's life. A partner in a business has an insurable interest in the lives of other partners.

> *checkpoint* >>
> What is an insurable interest?

main idea

Explain the types of life insurance.

TYPES OF LIFE INSURANCE

Insurance companies offer a variety of life insurance plans that meet different needs. The two basic types of life insurance policies are term life and permanent, or cash value, life.

Term Life Insurance

Insurance that provides financial protection from losses resulting from a death during a definite period, or term, is **term life insurance**. This coverage is the least expensive form of life insurance. Term insurance is also the *only* form of life insurance that is purely life insurance. All other forms of insurance also have savings or investment features.

Term policies may run for a period of 1 to 20 years or more. If the insured dies during the period for which the insurance was purchased, the amount of the policy is paid to the beneficiary. If the insured does not die during the period for which the policy was purchased, the insurance company is not required to pay anything. Protection ends when the term expires.

By paying a slightly higher premium, a person can buy *renewable* term insurance. This type of policy allows the policyholder to continue term insurance for one or more terms without taking another physical examination.

Term insurance policies may be level term or decreasing term. With *level* term insurance, the amount of protection and the premiums remain the same while the insurance is in effect. With *decreasing* term insurance, the amount of protection gradually becomes smaller, but premiums remain the same during the term. This is often appropriate because the need for insurance normally declines as children become independent and other savings and investments grow.

Permanent Life Insurance

The common characteristics of **permanent life insurance** are that it has cash value and an investment feature. Part of the premium you pay for permanent life insurance is used for insurance that provides protection. This feature is just like term insurance. The insurance company invests the remaining part of the premium that is not needed to pay for the coverage. It adds to the cash value of the insurance policy.

Describe some of the various types of dependents who might be protected by life insurance.

Different Learning Abilities

At-Risk Have students ask a parent or adult friend if they have life insurance coverage and how they made the decision to buy or not to buy the insurance.

Cash value refers to the amount of money that the insurance company will pay if the policyholder decides the insurance is no longer needed. The cash value is much less than the death benefit that would be paid to beneficiaries. As long as permanent policies are kept in force, they accumulate cash value in addition to providing life insurance.

The longer you keep your permanent life insurance policy, the higher its cash value will be. If you give up or surrender your policy, you receive the amount of the cash value. If you need money but do not want to cancel your policy, you can borrow an amount up to the cash value from the insurance company. If you should die before the loan is repaid, the insurance company will withhold the unpaid amount from the face value of the policy when it pays your survivors. *Face value* is the amount of insurance coverage that was originally purchased and that will be paid upon the death of the insured.

The cash value of permanent life insurance can be seen as a savings plan. Usually, the return on your money in the cash value portion of permanent life insurance is not large. Nevertheless, permanent insurance plans have a built-in savings feature that encourages people to save for the future. Permanent life insurance comes in the form of whole life, variable life, and universal life policies. Each type builds up cash value.

Whole Life Insurance Permanent insurance that extends over the lifetime, or whole life, of the insured is *whole life insurance*. One type of whole life insurance is an *ordinary life policy*. Premiums for ordinary life insurance remain the same each year as long as the policyholder lives.

Some whole life insurance policies are meant to be paid in full in a certain number of years. *Limited-payment policies* may be designated by the number of years the policyholder agrees to pay on them, such as 20-payment life policies. They are like ordinary life policies except that premiums are paid for a limited number of years or until a person reaches a certain age. Limited-payment policies free the insured from paying premiums during retirement when income may be lower.

Variable Life Insurance An insurance plan that resembles an investment portfolio is *variable life insurance*. This plan lets the policyholder choose among a broad range of investments. These investments include stocks, bonds, and mutual funds. The death benefits and cash values of variable life policies vary according to the yield on the investments that the policyholder selects.

The insurance company first designates an amount of the variable life premiums to cover the cost of insurance. It places the remaining amount

Why do people's insurance needs change at different times in their lives?

People tend to need more life insurance when they are younger because they are more likely to have dependent children and large debts, such as mortgages. Older individuals may need less life insurance because they do not have dependents, they own their homes, and their investments and savings have grown.

TEACH

Tell students that borrowing against the cash value of an insurance policy should be done only after a great deal of thought. If the money is borrowed and not repaid, the beneficiaries will not receive the full value of the insurance policy. If money is borrowed, plans should be made to repay the loan as quickly as possible.

Different Learning Abilities

Attention Deficit Disorder Have students describe the main difference between an ordinary life policy and a limited payment policy in terms of the payment of premiums.

in an investment account. Both the death benefit and the cash value rise and fall with the success of the investment account.

A variable life policy might guarantee a minimum death benefit. There is no guaranteed cash value. The minimum death benefit, in relation to premiums paid, is well below other types of life insurance. On the positive side, a strong rate of return on the investment account can increase the cash value and the death benefit.

Universal Life Insurance *Universal life insurance* provides both insurance protection and a substantial savings plan. The premium that you pay for universal life insurance is split in three ways. One portion of it pays for insurance protection. The insurance company takes a second portion for its expenses. The third portion goes into interest-earning investments for the policyholder.

The most important feature of universal life insurance is that the investment portion of the policy earns a variable rate of return. This rate is usually higher than is paid on other types of cash value life insurance. This yield on the investment portion tends to rise or fall based on changing economic conditions. Figure 20-3 compares the features of the different types of life insurance.

FIGURE 20-3

Which kind of insurance is least expensive for a given amount of death benefit?

Types of Life Insurance Policies

| POLICY FEATURES | TERM LIFE INSURANCE | PERMANENT LIFE INSURANCE | | | |
| | | Whole Life Insurance | | | |
		Ordinary Life Insurance	Limited Life Insurance	Variable Life Insurance	Universal Life Insurance
Premium	Begins low but increases gradually	High, but usually stays constant	Higher than ordinary life insurance but constant	Fixed and regular	Varies at the discretion of the policyholder
Payment Period	Specified number of years—normally 5, 10, or 15 years	Life of the insured	Specified number of years—normally 20 to 30 years	Specified period	Specified period
Cash Value	None	Some cash value	More cash value than ordinary life but less than variable life	Varies with the rise or fall in the value of the investment account	Varies with the interest rate paid on the cash value
Death Benefit	Fixed	Fixed	Fixed	Death benefit always exceeds cash value	Can vary at the discretion of the policyholder
Purposes	Protection for a specified period of time	Protection for life, some cash value for policyholder	Protection for life, some cash value for policyholder	Life insurance plus an opportunity to select different cash value investment options	Life insurance with a fairly high rate of return on cash value

Group Life Insurance

Some individuals are fortunate to have an employer or some other group offer the opportunity to buy group life insurance. An insurance policy that covers a group of people is called *group life insurance*. The group acts as a single unit in buying the insurance.

The cost of group life insurance is less than the cost of a similar individual policy. This savings results from the insurance company covering many people in one policy.

Most group life insurance plans offer term rather than permanent insurance. The insurance company works with an employer or other organization, such as a union, to develop the insurance plan. Then, each employee or member of the organization may purchase individual life insurance coverage.

> *checkpoint* »
> What is the difference between term and permanent life insurance?

BUYING LIFE INSURANCE

Many people need the protection offered by life insurance. Without insurance, few people have the financial resources needed to pay for a funeral and other related expenses when someone close to them dies. For a life insurance program to be effective, it must fit your needs and those of your family.

Coverage Amount

Anyone with dependents should consider life insurance. A *dependent* is a person who must rely on another for financial support. In the future, you will need to ask the question, "What would happen to the people who are financially dependent on me if I die tomorrow?" If they could

Insurance can be confusing, but many valuable online information sources are available. Access the web site shown below and click on the link for Chapter 20. Select a link for one type of insurance. Explain how this information might be used in your life now or in the future.

school.cengage.com/business/introtobiz

not live financially in the way in which they lived before your death, you most likely need life insurance.

The following questions will help to determine the need for life insurance.

- How much money is required for your dependents' financial stability if your income is lost?

> **main idea**
>
> Describe the process of buying life insurance.

Why do people working in dangerous occupations cost more to insure?

528

Explain that the phrase *insurance poor* describes people who buy much more insurance than they really need or can afford.

ONGOING ASSESSMENT

checkpoint >> **ANSWER**

Factors include the number of dependents who rely on the person, the amount of savings the person has to leave to those dependents, and the amount of the person's debts.

TEACH

Ask students to discuss why the premium paid for a whole life policy stays the same, while the cost for a term policy gets higher as the purchaser ages.

ASSESS

Key Concepts Answers

1. c. Term
2. c. receives money when the insured dies

Make Academic Connections

3. Findings will vary. Encourage students to discuss their findings and compare the answers they found for common questions.

4. The cash value of the investment portion will be $18,784.50 at the end of the year ($17,643 × 0.0647 = $1,141.50; add that amount to the original cash value: $17,643 + $1,141.50 = $18,784.50).

CLOSE

Ask students to list reasons why a person would or would not decide to purchase life insurance.

Work as a Team

Knowing how much life insurance to have can be a difficult decision. As a team, prepare a list of factors that a person might consider when determining the amount of life insurance to obtain.

- How much income will you need when you retire and what will be the sources of your income?

- What can you afford to pay for your life insurance needs?

Answers to these questions will help you purchase the best life insurance program for you.

Life Insurance Application

To buy individual life insurance coverage, you need to complete a life insurance application. You apply for this coverage through an insurance agent representing an insurance company.

You may be required to take a physical exam to assess your health. If you have no serious health problems, you then pay a premium and receive your life insurance policy.

If you are in poor health or work in a dangerous job, you may be considered a poor risk. Even so, you likely will be able to get insurance. You will probably pay higher premiums than people who are in good health and are employed in less hazardous jobs.

Premium Payments

In addition to the health and occupation of the insured, the type of policy affects the cost of life insurance. The age of the person being insured also affects premiums. In purchasing a whole life policy, for example, the premiums for ordinary life insurance are higher than those for term insurance, but the annual premium stays the same throughout the insured's life. The premiums on limited-payment life insurance are higher than those for ordinary life insurance, but they are payable for only a limited number of years.

> *checkpoint* >>
> What factors affect the need for life insurance?

20-3   Assessment

Key Concepts

Determine the best answer.

1. _?_ life insurance is considered temporary coverage.
  a. Whole
  b. Universal
  c. Term
  d. Variable

2. The beneficiary of a life insurance policy
  a. is the cost of insurance
  b. makes the premium payments
  c. receives money when the insured dies
  d. is the period for which the policy is in effect

Make Academic Connections

3. *Technology* Use the Internet to find an insurance company web site that includes frequently asked questions about life insurance. Find three questions that interest you. Copy the questions and their answers along with the name of the company and the URL.

4. *Math* The rate of return on the investment portion of a life insurance policy is 6.47 percent for a given year. If the investment portion (cash value) was $17,643 at the beginning of the year, what will it be worth at the end of the year? Round to the nearest cent.

RETEACH

Have students review the information in Figure 20-3 and clarify any questions they have about the different types of life insurance policies.

ENRICH

Have students prepare a description of the type and amount of life insurance they believe they should have at age 20, 35, and 65. Have them justify their decisions.

20-4 Health Insurance

Goals

Describe health insurance coverage.

Discuss health insurance providers.

Explain disability and long-term care insurance.

Key Terms

hospital insurance

surgical insurance

regular medical insurance

major medical insurance

coinsurance

comprehensive medical policy

disability income insurance

Focus on Real Life

"Carlotta! Welcome back to work! We really missed you. How is your back?"

"My back is doing great. Thanks for asking. I can't believe I hurt it and had to have surgery. I am almost feeling normal again, and the insurance company paid nearly all of my bills. You don't realize how important health insurance is until you need it. If I didn't have such great coverage, I would be out more than $40,000."

Almost no one has enough money to pay the medical bills associated with a serious illness. Health insurance provides protection against the economic risks associated with paying for medical care. Health insurance is similar to the other forms of insurance. You pay premiums for a policy that guarantees protection. When you are ill and need money to pay medical bills, the insurance company will pay the bills up to specified amounts.

HEALTH INSURANCE COVERAGE

Several types of health-related insurance are available to provide different kinds of coverage. One type of health insurance is *medical insurance*. It can be classified as (1) hospital insurance, (2) surgical insurance, (3) regular medical insurance, (4) major medical insurance, and (5) a comprehensive medical policy. Insurance companies also offer combination policies.

Hospital Insurance

An illness or injury may require you to be hospitalized. In this situation, **hospital insurance** usually pays most or all of the charges. These include expenses for your room, food, and medical items such as use of an operating room, anesthesia, X-rays, laboratory tests, and medications. Because of the high cost of hospitalization, people purchase hospital insurance more than any other kind of health insurance.

You can buy hospital insurance from insurance companies or from nonprofit corporations, such as Blue Cross. If expenses are more than the amount covered by the hospital insurance plan, the patient must pay the difference.

Surgical Insurance

Surgery is a major reason for hospitalization. It can be very expensive. **Surgical insurance** covers all or part of the surgeon's fees for an operation. The typical surgical policy lists the types of operations that it covers and the amount allowed for each. Some policies allow larger amounts for operations than others. This, of course, requires that a higher premium be paid. Surgical insurance is often bought in combination with hospital insurance.

> **main idea**
>
> Describe health insurance coverage.

Focus on Real Life

Tell students that insurance companies and companies that provide health insurance for employers are working to reduce the costs of health insurance. Ask students to describe things people can do to reduce the costs of their medical care.

TEACH

Ask volunteers to share things that have happened to them that have required a trip to a physician or hospital. Get the discussion going by asking if anyone has broken a bone or had a tonsillectomy. As the types of insurance coverage are introduced, match the student experiences to the correct type of health insurance coverage.

Different Learning Styles

Kinesthetic Learner Have students use a variety of resources to locate advertisements for health insurance companies. Have them match the types of insurance offered by each company with the coverage descriptions from the lesson.

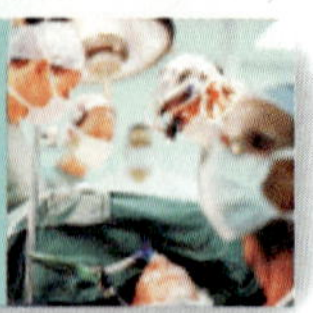

Hospital insurance is expensive because the cost of medical procedures keeps rising as new treatments are discovered. The escalating cost of malpractice insurance also plays a role. With today's high-tech medical care, hospital stays can easily cost tens of thousands or even hundreds of thousands of dollars.

TEACH

Explain to students that coinsurance is sometimes called a "copayment" or "copay." Some insurance policies require policyholders to pay a small copay of $10–$25 dollars for each visit to a doctor and each prescription. Have students discuss why the use of that small copay might reduce the costs of health care by causing the policyholders to think carefully about whether a trip to a doctor is needed or not.

Again, you can buy surgical insurance from insurance companies or from non-profit organizations. Surgical plans cover mainly medical and surgical treatment rather than hospital care. These plans list the maximum amounts that they will pay for different types of surgery. They also cover the doctor's charges for care in the hospital. Some plans pay the doctor's charges for office or home care. The coverage generally does not provide for preexisting conditions or for illnesses or injuries that are covered by other insurance.

Regular Medical Insurance

Sometimes normal care provided by a physician can be quite expensive. **Regular medical insurance** covers fees for nonsurgical care given in the doctor's office, the patient's home, or a hospital. The policy states the amount payable for each visit or call. It also lists the maximum number of visits covered. Some plans provide payments for diagnostic and laboratory expenses.

Regular medical insurance is usually combined in one policy with hospital and surgical insurance. The protection provided by regular medical, hospital, and surgical insurance is often referred to as *basic health coverage*.

Major Medical Insurance

Long illnesses and serious injuries can be very expensive. Bills of $50,000 to $100,000 and higher are not unusual. **Major medical insurance** provides protection against the high costs of serious illnesses or injuries. This coverage complements the other forms of medical insurance.

Major medical insurance helps pay for most kinds of extended and specialized health care prescribed by a doctor. It covers the cost of treatment in and out of the hospital, special nursing care, X-rays, psychiatric care, medicine, and many other health care needs. Maximum benefits may

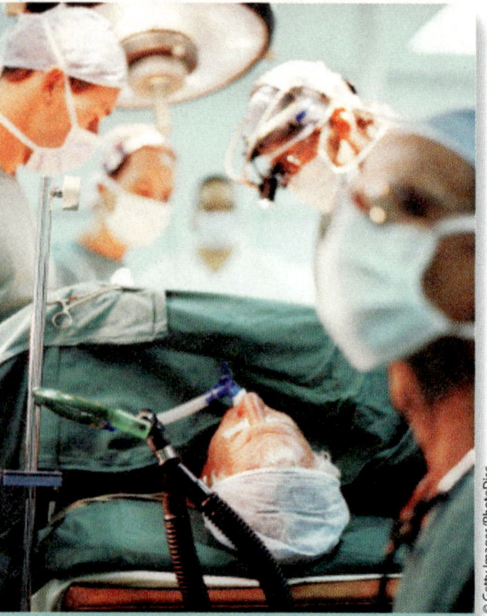

© Getty Images/PhotoDisc

be limited, but usually extend to a high amount, such as $500,000 or $1,000,000.

All major medical policies have a *deductible* clause. The clause is similar to the one found in automobile collision insurance. With this clause, the policyholder agrees to pay the first part of the expense resulting from sickness or injury. The deductible may be $500 or more.

Major medical policies usually contain a *coinsurance* clause. **Coinsurance** is the sharing of expenses by the policyholder and the insurance company. The policyholder typically pays a deductible and then shares the remaining cost with the insurance company.

For example, the insurance company may pay 80 percent of the cost for medical treatment after the deductible is paid. The policyholder will then pay the remaining 20 percent. The policyholder's share is limited to a specific dollar amount stated in the policy. Once the deductible and the coinsurance amounts are met, the insurance company reimburses 100 percent of the cost up to the policy's coverage limits.

Mathematics Provide the following scenario and question to students. A consumer has an insurance policy with a $500 deductible and coinsurance of 20 percent of the costs above the deductible. If the total bill is $5,300, how much must the consumer pay? (The consumer pays $1,460. Subtract the deductible from the total bill, $5,300 − $500 = $4,800. Multiply the difference by 20 percent, $4,800 × 0.2 = $960. The consumer pays $960 plus the $500 deductible.)

The deductible clause discourages the filing of minor claims. The coinsurance clause encourages the policyholder to keep medical expenses as reasonable as possible. Thus, both clauses help to lower premiums because they help to reduce payments of insurance claims.

Comprehensive Medical Policy

Insurance providers have developed a **comprehensive medical policy** that combines the features of hospital, surgical, regular, and major medical insurance. This coverage retains the features of each separate coverage, such as amounts-payable limits. The policy has only one deductible. A combination of coverages will likely be less expensive than the total of the separate coverage.

Dental Insurance

As dental expenses have increased over the years, insurance companies now offer coverage to help pay for normal dental care. Dental insurance usually includes examinations, X-rays, cleaning, and fillings. It may cover part or all of complicated dental work such as crowns or bridges. This policy also covers dental injuries resulting from accidents.

Most dental plans contain deductible and coinsurance provisions to reduce the cost of premiums. Dental insurance is offered mainly through group plans. It continues to grow in popularity.

Vision Care Insurance

In anticipation of eye care expenses, many individual consumers and groups purchase vision care insurance. These policies cover eye examinations, prescription lenses, frames, and contact lenses. Some vision care plans now cover the cost of laser eye surgery, which can eliminate the need for glasses.

New medical developments may result in additional vision care coverage. Some plans now cover the cost of laser eye surgery that eliminates the need for glasses.

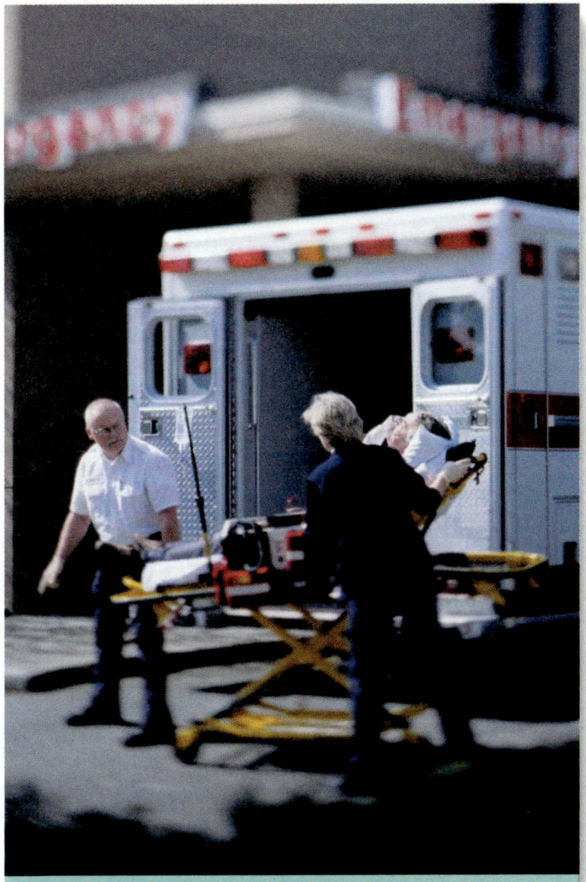

Why do most people need some kind of health insurance?

> *checkpoint* >>
> What four types of health insurance would be included in a comprehensive medical policy?

HEALTH INSURANCE PROVIDERS

main idea

Discuss health insurance providers.

Health insurance is available from several sources. These options include group health insurance, individual health insurance, health maintenance organizations, preferred provider organizations, and government programs.

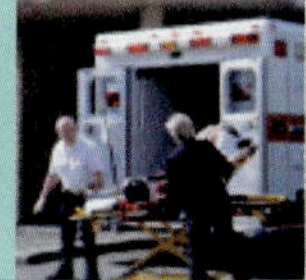

Most people need some kind of health insurance because they do not have enough assets to pay for the soaring costs of today's high-tech medical care. Even a relatively routine hospital stay could cause financial ruin for many people.

TEACH

Ask students if they believe that purchasing medical, dental, and vision care insurance results in people taking better care of themselves or not. Some will suggest that, because they are spending money for the insurance, they will try to take better care of themselves. Others will suggest that those who don't have insurance will be more careful because they know they don't have insurance protection.

ONGOING ASSESSMENT

checkpoint >> **ANSWER**

A comprehensive medical policy would include the following four types of health insurance: (1) hospital, (2) surgical, (3) regular, and (4) major medical insurance.

Different Learning Styles

Visual Learner Have students visit the employment section of the web sites of three different companies that describe the health care benefits provided to employees of the company. Ask them to develop a chart or table that compares the health care policies of the companies.

Group Health Insurance

The most popular way to buy health insurance is through a group. As with group life insurance, employers, unions and other organizations offer group health insurance policies.

Companies that sponsor group policies often pay part or all of the insurance premiums for their employees. They provide this as an employment benefit. Employees can usually buy coverage for family members as well.

The cost of group health insurance is lower per insured than the cost of a comparable individual policy. The costs are lower because insurance companies can manage group plans more economically.

Individual Health Insurance

Some people are not eligible for group health insurance. They may be self-employed and have no employer to help buy health insurance. One alternative is to buy individual health insurance. These policies are available to individuals and are adapted to individual needs. Individual health insurance policies are usually rather expensive. They may require a physical exam and have a waiting period before the policy takes effect.

Technology in Action

Telemedicine: One Way Technology is Shaping Medicine

A physician in a rural hospital learns new surgery techniques by viewing live images of a procedure being performed by a surgeon halfway around the world. A nurse in an emergency room prepares for the arrival of a heart attack patient while receiving real-time data from diagnostic equipment being used by paramedics in the field. While sitting at a home computer, a teenager with cancer participates in a support group with young people from 10 different states.

These are just a few examples of how telemedicine works. "Telemedicine" is an umbrella term that refers to a wide range of activities involving medicine, communication technology, and distance. The American Telemedicine Association classifies telemedicine services in five categories:

Specialist referral services most often involve a specialist helping another physician to diagnose a patient's condition. For example, a radiologist, a physician who specializes in the interpretation of diagnostic images, can read a chest X-ray from a remote location across town or in a different country.

Patient consultations involve direct interaction between a patient and a health care provider. A typical scenario involves a patient in a rural clinic staffed by an allied health professional communicating with a physician in another location such as a private medical office or a hospital.

Remote patient monitoring relies on the use of monitoring devices to collect data from a patient and transmit it to another location for interpretation. Home health agencies use this technology to monitor chronic conditions such as diabetes and congestive heart failure.

Medical education focuses on providing continuing education and special training to health professionals. Telemedicine is a convenient and cost-effective way to participate in classes, seminars, workshops, and demonstrations.

Consumer medical and health information includes online medical and health resources for the general public as well as specialized service for specific patients or groups. Some examples include online chats with midwives, web-based food diaries for nutritional counseling, blogs focused on issues family caregivers face, and e-mail follow-up after an office visit.

The use of telemedicine is growing and changing with the introduction of new technologies and innovations. Although there are concerns about cost-effectiveness, insurance coverage, and privacy, it is likely that some telemedicine services will become routine.

Think Critically

1. How might the availability of telemedicine services impact the cost of health care?
2. Use library or Internet resources to find three examples of telemedicine being used in different settings. Write a short summary of your findings.

Applied Skills

Technology Ask students to investigate the use of telemedicine in your community. Ask students to focus their attention on business activities related to telemedicine. For example, they might learn more about a company that manufactures equipment that facilitates telemedicine, a medical practice or hospital that markets telemedicine services, or an insurance company that covers telemedicine services.

Managed Care Plans

Various alternative health insurance plans have grown in popularity. Known as *managed health care* or *managed care*, these programs cover more than two-thirds of Americans who have insurance through their employer. These plans often provide lower-cost, comprehensive health care through networks of medical professionals.

Managed care plans usually have higher monthly premiums. Yet the overall cost of health care may be lower for the consumer because of low or no deductibles, low copayments, and little or no paperwork. A potential drawback is that patients have less control and limited choices of whom they see for health care. Managed care plans have various names, such as HMOs (health maintenance organizations) and PPOs (preferred provider organizations).

The growth of managed care has resulted from large companies trying to control the rising cost of providing health care coverage for employees. Today, many managed care plans are run by insurance companies.

Health Maintenance Organization (HMO)

One managed care choice is a health maintenance organization. A *health maintenance organization (HMO)* commonly consists of a staffed medical clinic to serve members. You join an HMO for a fixed monthly fee. As a member, you are entitled to a wide range of prepaid health care services, including hospitalization. HMOs emphasize preventive health care. Early detection and treatment of illnesses help reduce hospital visits and keep costs down. Generally, HMOs do not cover treatment or care that is not authorized by a physician or procedures that are above the average cost for the area.

Preferred Provider Organization (PPO)

A popular alternative is the *preferred provider organization (PPO)*. This system involves several health care providers, such as a group of physicians, a clinic, or a hospital. These medical professionals contract with an insurance company to provide services to members. These providers agree to charge set fees for services.

Members are encouraged, but not required, to use the PPO services through financial incentives. Members are able to get medical treatment through the PPO at a significant discount. They may seek medical treatment elsewhere. However, expenses for treatment outside the PPO may be only partially reimbursed.

State Government Assistance

An important health insurance program by state governments is *workers' compensation*. This insurance plan provides medical and survivor benefits for people injured, disabled, or killed on the job. Accidents can occur on almost any job. Employees may suffer injuries or develop some illness because of working conditions. Workers' compensation laws provide medical benefits to employees who are injured on the job or become ill as a direct result of their working conditions. Under these laws, most employers are required to provide and pay for this insurance for their employees.

State governments also administer a form of medical aid to some low-income individuals and families known as *Medicaid*. The federal government shares with states the cost of providing health benefits to eligible individuals

Everyone is affected by rising health care costs. As a team, prepare a list of actions that might be taken by (a) individuals, (b) businesses, and (c) government to (1) improve the health of people in society and (2) reduce costs for medical services.

Work as a Team

Ask students to discuss the effects on individuals and businesses of rapidly rising health care and health insurance costs.

TEACH

Write "HMO" and "PPO" on the board. Have students list the similarities and differences between the two types of managed care. Have them decide which of the two they would personally prefer and why.

Teaching Strategies

Expand Beyond the Classroom Have a team of students act as an investigative news group and prepare a story on ways companies are attempting to improve the health of their employees. The group should prepare a video "news story" and play the video for the other class members.

and families. The services covered by Medicaid include hospital care, doctor services, X-rays, lab tests, nursing home care, and home health care services. States may also offer a health insurance program for people who have trouble obtaining coverage. Past health conditions can result in a person being turned down by most health insurance providers.

Federal Government Assistance

The nation's Social Security laws provide a national program of health insurance known as *Medicare*. This insurance is designed to help people aged 65 and older and some disabled people pay for health care. Medicare has two basic parts: hospital insurance and medical insurance.

The hospital insurance plan includes coverage for hospital care, service in an approved nursing home, and home health care up to a certain number of visits. No premium payments are required for the hospital insurance. Almost everyone 65 years old and older may qualify.

The medical insurance portion of Medicare is often called supplementary or voluntary medical insurance. The services covered under this plan include doctor services, medical services, supplies, and home health services. The medical insurance requires a monthly premium. The federal government pays an equal amount to help cover the cost of the medical insurance.

Cost Containment

The cost of health insurance is very high. In fact, health care costs consistently increase two to three times faster than the overall cost of living. The cost of health insurance is determined by four main factors: extent of the coverage, number of claims filed by policyholders, age of the policyholder, and number of dependents. You have little control over your age

What can you do to reduce your health insurance costs?

and the number of people dependent on you. You can make sure you buy only the kind and amount of insurance you need. You can also take good care of yourself and not use your medical benefits unnecessarily.

Insurance companies encourage policyholders to play an active role in *cost containment*, or keeping costs down. The most common methods are coinsurance and deductibles.

Some policyholders have coverage under both their employer's and their spouse's insurance. Insurance providers coordinate benefits to prevent two or more insurers from making payments on the same charges. The health insurance industry encourages second opinions to ensure the necessity of procedures.

Another cost-containment strategy is the use of outpatient services such as surgery. In the past, people undergoing some forms of surgery might have been admitted to the hospital for one or two days. Now, the person comes to the hospital or an outpatient center in the morning. After the surgery, the patient returns home the same day.

checkpoint >>
Who are the main providers of health insurance?

Different Learning Styles

Print Learner Have students look through recent newspapers and magazines to find articles on efforts undertaken by consumer groups, government, businesses, and the health care industry to contain health care costs. Have them clip or copy the articles and organize them for others to read.

DISABILITY AND LONG-TERM CARE INSURANCE

The need for health insurance goes beyond various medical expenses. Disability income and long-term care insurance programs protect people in other types of situations.

Disability Income Insurance

For most people, income from employment is their single most important economic resource. Protecting your income is very important. One form of health insurance provides periodic payments if the policyholder becomes disabled. **Disability income insurance** protects you against the loss of income caused by a long illness or an accident. The insured receives weekly or monthly payments until they are able to return to work.

Disability income policies often include a waiting period. This requires the policyholder to wait a specified time after the disability occurs before payment begins. Monthly payments under disability insurance plans are usually much smaller than the income people earn from their jobs. The amount may be 40–60 percent of the normal income, but many disability payments are not subject to income taxes.

Long-Term Care Insurance

With people living longer, *long-term care insurance* is the fastest-growing type of protection. This coverage provides *long-term care*, which is daily assistance needed because of a long-term illness or disability. This assistance may involve a stay in a nursing home. It may cover help that is provided at home for daily activities such as dressing, bathing, and doing household chores.

What effect does our longer lifespan have on the health insurance industry?

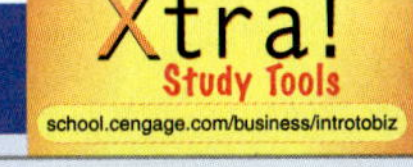

Explain disability and long-term care insurance.

---

checkpoint >>
What is the purpose of disability income insurance?

20-4   Assessment

Key Concepts

Determine the best answer.

1. Health insurance coverage for a long illness is __?__ insurance.
   a. hospital
   b. surgical
   c. regular medical
   d. major medical

2. If you are injured on the job, you are likely to be covered by
   a. Medicare
   b. Medicaid
   c. workers' compensation
   d. an HMO

Make Academic Connections

3. *Government* Investigate health insurance resources provided by your state government. Write a short report about your findings.

4. *Visual Communication* Create a poster or video that addresses one of the concepts presented in this lesson.

TEACH

Ask students to compare benefits provided by health insurance, disability income insurance, and long-term care insurance. Why should a person consider purchasing all three types of insurance?

THINK CRITICALLY THROUGH VISUALS

Our longer lifespan means people are using medical insurance longer. Also, older persons usually require more medical intervention to remain healthy than younger persons.

ONGOING ASSESSMENT

checkpoint >> **ANSWER**

The purpose of disability income insurance is to provide periodic payments if the policyholder becomes disabled and loses his or her income.

ASSESS

Key Concepts Answers

1. d. major medical
2. c. workers' compensation

Make Academic Connections

3. Findings will vary.
4. Posters will vary.

CLOSE

Ask students: Why is the cost of health care and health insurance such an important issue in the United States today? What can businesses and consumers do to reduce those costs?

RETEACH

Divide the class into study teams and assign each team one type of insurance discussed in the chapter. Have the team review the information and develop a written study outline of the important information. Have each team distribute their outline and discuss it with the other teams.

ENRICH

Ask each student to prepare a personal health insurance plan identifying the type of insurance coverage needed and the reason for each type of insurance. If the student chooses not to have a type of insurance discussed in the lesson in his or her plan, ask the student to provide a reason for that decision.

Communicate Business Concepts Answers

1. a. Personal injury coverage (bodily injury liability)

b. Personal injury coverage covers the family member (bodily injury liability) and property damage coverage covers the parked car (property damage liability)

c. Property damage coverage (property damage liability)

d. Property damage coverage (comprehensive coverage)

2. The coverage was enough for all but $5,000 of the total $105,000 in bodily injury costs. The 50/100 coverage means the insurance company will pay up to $50,000 per bodily injury and up to $100,000 in total bodily injury costs when more than one person is injured in an accident.

3. Collision coverage does not pay for damages greater than the car's current value. The 10-year-old car probably has a low current value so that, even if the insurance company paid the policyholder the entire amount, it might not be enough to make a needed car repair. If the 10-year-old car is very valuable, however, its owner may still want to pay for collision coverage.

Business Notes

20-1 VEHICLE INSURANCE

1. Motor vehicle risks include having an accident, having your vehicle stolen, injuring yourself or another person, or damaging another's property.

2. Personal injury insurance covers bodily injury liability, medical payments, and uninsured motorist protection. Property damage liability protects you against claims if you damage another person's property.

3. Automobile insurance rates are affected by age, accidents, marital status, academics, credit rating, car use, number of miles driven a year, value of car, and where you live.

20-2 PROPERTY INSURANCE

4. Home and property insurance protect against three economic losses: (1) damage to home or property, (2) expenses to live somewhere else if your home is badly damaged, and (3) liability losses.

5. A homeowners insurance policy provides coverage for various perils. Renters insurance is available for those who rent.

6. Wise consumers select the most appropriate protection at the lowest cost.

20-3 LIFE INSURANCE

7. Life insurance protects survivors against the financial loss associated with dying. It replaces a loss of income for a family who is financially dependent upon another person.

8. Term life insurance provides financial protection from losses of life during a definite period. Permanent insurance has both cash value and an investment feature.

9. To buy individual life insurance coverage, a person applies to an insurance agent. A physical exam may be required to assess the person's health. Life insurance premiums depend on the type of policy and the age and health of the person being insured.

20-4 HEALTH INSURANCE

10. Five common types of medical insurance are hospital insurance, surgical insurance, regular medical insurance, major medical insurance, and a comprehensive policy. Dental and vision care insurance provide specific coverage for these medical needs.

11. Health insurance providers include group health insurance, individual health insurance, health maintenance organizations, preferred provider organizations, and government programs.

12. Disability income insurance protects against income loss due to illness or accident. The insured receives payments until able to return to work. Long-term care insurance provides daily assistance needed because of a long-term illness or disability.

Communicate Business Concepts

1. Which type of automobile insurance would cover the following situations?

  a. A pedestrian is injured by a driver.
  b. A family member is injured when you run into a parked car.
  c. You, in an attempt to avoid hitting a dog in the street, run into a parked car.
  d. Winds cause a tree branch to break your windshield and dent the hood.

2. A driver was at fault when three passengers were badly hurt. The court awarded two of the people $30,000 each and $45,000 to the third person. The driver had bodily injury liability coverage of 50/100. Was this enough coverage for financial loss? Why or why not?

3. Why is collision coverage on a 10-year-old car less important than on a three-year-old car? Why may a person still want to have collision coverage on a 10-year-old car?

4. What type of property insurance would cover these situations?

   a. Damage to furniture because of a fire
   b. The cost of staying at a hotel after your home was damaged by fire
   c. Injury to a repairperson on your property

5. Recently, homes in an Iowa valley were destroyed when heavy rains caused the Mississippi River to rise above flood level. Do you think those Iowa residents who had homeowners policies suffered any financial losses? Why or why not?

6. What type of life insurance policy would your recommend for these people?

   a. Carlos Medina, age 27, wants a policy with premiums as low as possible for the next 10 years.
   b. Julie Hovel, age 45, wants a policy with no premium payments after she retires.

7. Why is a physical examination not usually required when buying group life insurance coverage?

Develop Your Business Language

Match the terms listed with the definitions.

8. Health insurance that covers all or part of surgeon's fees.

9. The person named in the life insurance policy to receive the benefits.

10. Covers claims for injuries or damage to property caused by you or your family.

11. The amount the insured pays before the insurance company pays a claim.

12. Coverage that provides protection against the high costs of serious illnesses or injuries.

13. Coverage for claims resulting from injuries or deaths for which the insured is at fault.

14. Health coverage for your room, food, and other hospital expenses.

15. The decrease in value of property.

16. Insurance coverage for medical expenses of a policyholder and family members if they are injured while riding in a car.

17. Coverage for injuries caused by hit-and-run drivers or by drivers without insurance.

18. Protection against the loss of income caused by a long illness or an accident.

19. Life insurance coverage with a cash value and an investment feature.

20. Coverage that protects a driver against claims if the insured's car damages someone else's property.

21. Health insurance for non-surgical care in a doctor's office, patient's home, or hospital.

22. A package-type insurance policy designed to insure homes and property.

23. Auto coverage for a loss resulting from a collision with another car or object.

24. A health policy combining hospital, surgical, regular, and major medical insurance.

25. Auto coverage for almost all damage losses except those caused from a collision.

26. Life insurance that provides financial protection during a set period.

27. The sharing of expenses by the policyholder and the insurance company.

KEY TERMS
a. beneficiary
b. bodily injury liability
c. coinsurance
d. collision coverage
e. comprehensive coverage
f. comprehensive medical policy
g. deductible
h. depreciation
i. disability income insurance
j. homeowners policy
k. hospital insurance
l. major medical insurance
m. medical payments
n. permanent life insurance
o. personal liability coverage
p. property damage liability
q. regular medical insurance
r. surgical insurance
s. term life insurance
t. uninsured motorist

4. a. damage to home or property insurance coverage

b. additional living expenses coverage

c. personal liability coverage

5. Typical homeowners policies do not include flood insurance, so the homeowners in the Iowa valley probably did suffer a significant financial loss unless they had purchased special flood insurance policies.

6. a. Carlos should investigate term insurance options because term insurance has the lowest premiums and can be purchased in terms of 10 years.

b. Julie Hovel should purchase a limited-payment whole life insurance policy.

7. Most group life insurance is term insurance, which does not usually require a physical examination. Also, the rates for group life insurance are based on the life expectancies of a large group of people instead of an individual person's health status.

Develop Your Business Language Answers

8. r. surgical insurance

9. a. beneficiary

10. o. personal liability coverage

11. g. deductible

12. l. major medical insurance

13. b. bodily injury liability

14. k. hospital insurance

15. h. depreciation

16. m. medical payments

17. t. uninsured motorist

18. i. disability income insurance

19. n. permanent life insurance

20. p. property damage liability

21. q. regular medical insurance

22. j. homeowners policy

23. d. collision coverage

24. f. comprehensive medical policy

25. e. comprehensive coverage

26. s. term life insurance

27. c. coinsurance

Make Academic Connections

Make Academic Connections

28. LAW Obtain information on the financial responsibility and automobile insurance requirements in your state.

29. RESEARCH Contact a local insurance agent to obtain information on the costs of automobile insurance for young drivers.

30. MATH Orien was involved in an automobile accident. The total damage to both vehicles was $3,228. The state in which Orien lives assigns a percentage of fault to each driver involved in an accident. Each driver must pay the percentage of damages based on the percentage of fault assigned. If Orien was assigned 35 percent of the fault in the accident, how much of the damages will he be required to pay? How much must the other driver pay?

31. LAW Describe in writing or present in class various liability situations that would be covered by a person's homeowners or renters insurance policy.

32. ACCOUNTING The value of personal property declines due to time and use. Using newspaper advertisements and other information sources, compare the value of various new and used items. What observations can you make about depreciation?

33. MATH If Ellen Williams owned a home worth $98,000 and wanted to be certain it was insured for at least 80 percent of its value, for how much should it be insured?

34. COMMUNICATION Working with other students, write a script and present a short skit that communicates the need for life insurance in various family situations. Consider using simple props and costumes to help communicate your message.

35. RESEARCH Conduct library or online research about actions that might be taken to reduce the costs of health care.

36. VISUAL ARTS Create a poster to educate and remind classmates about financial and social responsibilities that come with owning or driving a car or truck. Consider including concepts related to insurance, safety, and the environment.

37. MATH Fran Markowitz had her annual medical examination. According to her insurance plan, she paid a portion of the costs of the services. The total costs and her share of each were as shown in the table.

SERVICE	TOTAL COST	PATIENT SHARE
Doctor visit	$80	$15 deductible
Lab work	$220	20% copay
Prescriptions	$120	$20 copay
Vision exam	$65	$10 deductible
New lenses	$180	5%

a. What was the total cost of the medical examination?
b. How much of the total cost did Fran pay?
c. What percent of the total cost did the insurance company pay?

Linking School and Community

Ask several people in your community about the types of insurance coverage they have. What coverage has been obtained through group policies? What coverage is through individual policies? What suggestions do they have for you when buying various types of insurance?

Web Workout

The Internet can be a valuable source of information about insurance. Select an insurance topic that you would like to learn more about. Find two web sites that offer tips or advice related to the topic you have selected.

Think Critically

1. Prepare a summary of the information about your topic for each web site. Be sure to clearly identify your topic and provide the URL for each web site.
2. What are the similarities and differences of the advice presented on the two web sites?
3. How might the information obtained be of value to you in the future?

Make Academic Connections

28. Findings about financial responsibility and automobile insurance requirements will vary by state.

29. Findings about costs of automobile insurance for young drivers will vary. Consider inviting a local insurance agent to speak to the class.

30. Orien will be required to pay $1,129.80 ($3,228 × 0.35). The other driver will pay $2,098.20 ($3,228 − $1,129.80).

31. Answers will vary as students explain various liability situations covered by homeowners or renters insurance policies.

32. Students make observations about depreciation. They may notice that costs of certain items depreciate quickly (such as automobiles), while that of houses appreciate (increase in value).

33. Ellen should be insured for $78,400 ($98,000 3 0.80).

34. Scripts and skits will vary.

35. Findings will vary.

36. Posters will vary.

37. a. The total cost of the medical examination was $665.

b. Fran paid $98 of the total cost ($15 + $44 + $20 + $10 + $9).

c. The insurance company paid $567, or 85 percent, of the total cost ($567 ÷ $665 = 0.85).

Linking School and Community

Answers will vary. Encourage students to share the suggestions they heard about buying various types of insurance.

Web Workout

1. Summaries will vary. The topic and the URL for each web site should be included.

2. Similarities and differences will vary.

3. Answers will vary. Students should recognize that insurance needs change over time and that the information they found might be helpful in the future.

Decision-Making Strategies

Jane is a rather careless driver. She is a 17-year-old with a late-model compact car that looks sporty and is equipped for speed. Jane loves to drive fast and has compiled a rather poor traffic record. In only one year, she has had two "fender bender" accidents and received two speeding tickets. Those who care about Jane have suggested that her reckless driving habits are putting her and others at risk.

38. What potential property and liability risks are associated with Jane's driving habits?

39. How is Jane's driving affecting her auto insurance premiums?

40. What suggestions do you have for Jane about her driving?

Entrepreneurship Case Study

This event is composed of two parts: a written objective test and a decision-making problem (case study). Teams consisting of three participants will present and defend their solution to a business challenge.

Once you receive your business topic, you have 30 minutes to prepare your presentation and argument. Each participant will be given two 4" by 6" index cards that may be used during the preparation and presentation to the judges/students. No reference materials or visual aids may be brought to or used during the preparation or performance.

Your team has 10 minutes to present the case. One member should introduce the team and describe or summarize the case study. All team members must participate in the presentation. Note cards may be used to explain decisions and rationales to the judges. After the presentation, five minutes are allowed for questions and answers.

Your case study involves the rising cost of insurance. Health insurance is an important fringe benefit that you provide your employees. The cost of health insurance is rising at a rapid rate, and now your company is faced with determining strategies to continue paying for employee health insurance. You must determine how you will pay for the increasing costs. What will you do to keep employees healthy? How will you shop around for insurance? What other expenses are you willing to cut in order to continue funding health insurance?

PERFORMANCE INDICATORS EVALUATED

- Understand the importance of health insurance for employees.
- Prepare a concise plan for funding the rising costs of health insurance.
- Explain the sacrifices that must be made to fund health insurance.
- Explain the importance of shopping around for health insurance.

For more detailed information about performance indicators, go to the FBLA web site.

Think Critically

1. Why is health insurance such an important fringe benefit?
2. What can a company do to encourage employees to follow healthy lifestyles?
3. What fringe benefits are you willing to cut in order to save health insurance?

http://www.fbla-pbl.org/

Access the web site shown here to find portfolio activities for this chapter. Use the activities to provide tangible evidence of your learning.

school.cengage.com/business/introtobiz

2. To encourage healthy lifestyles, companies can provide memberships to health clubs, incentives for healthy lifestyles, and lower insurance rates for healthy employees.

3. Answers will vary (e.g., company vehicle, vision or dental insurance, less paid vacation).

Global Business Project

Students conduct research on buying habits in other cultures, banking systems and payment activities in another country, attitudes toward credit around the world, and the expected economic conditions and business opportunities for a selected country. They next choose a company involved in international business, obtain its recent financial statements, and then write a summary of its financial situation and international operations. Finally, students describe the liability and property insurance a global company might need to manage its risks.

Students prepare portfolios to store the information from the Activities exercises. They create visuals showing buying behaviors in other countries and describe how a product or service might need to change based on another country's culture and traditions. Students develop a flowchart or graph to show the banking system and payment activities in another country and explain how individuals and businesses use the various payment methods. They prepare written reports (with visuals) to describe to investors another country's investment potential, economic strengths, and areas of concern. Finally, students create in-class presentations explaining a possible joint venture in another country.

Manage International Business Operations

Goals

- Identify consumer buying habits in various cultures.
- Research common financial institutions in other countries.
- Explore cultural attitudes toward the use of credit.
- Analyze the investment environment of a foreign country.
- Create a global risk management plan and recommend insurance coverage.

Activities

Use your textbook, library materials, web sites, interviews with people, and other resources to complete the following:

1. Buying habits in other cultures can be different. Using the country in your portfolio (or select a country), research customs, traditions, and beliefs that affect buying behaviors or eating habits in that nation. Describe various goods and services that might need to be adapted when being sold in this country.

2. Banks and other financial institutions provide funds and transfer money for business transactions. Research the banking system and payment activities in the country from your portfolio (or another country). To what extent is electronic banking used in that country?

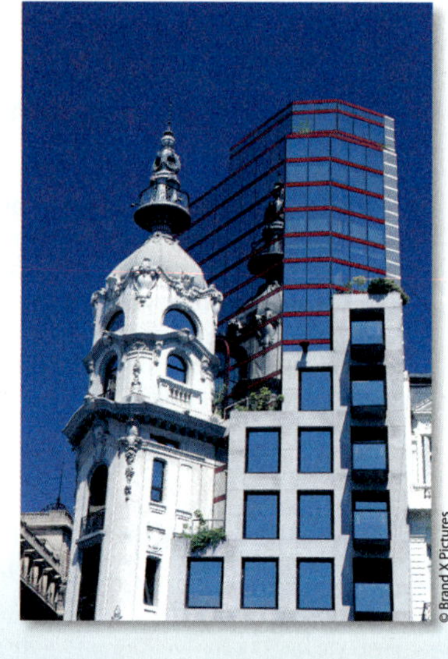

3. Attitudes toward credit vary around the world. Obtain information about the cultural feelings toward the use of credit in another country. How might this information affect a company's international business activities?

4. Individuals and companies want to invest in countries with strong economic and business potential. Using the country you have studied

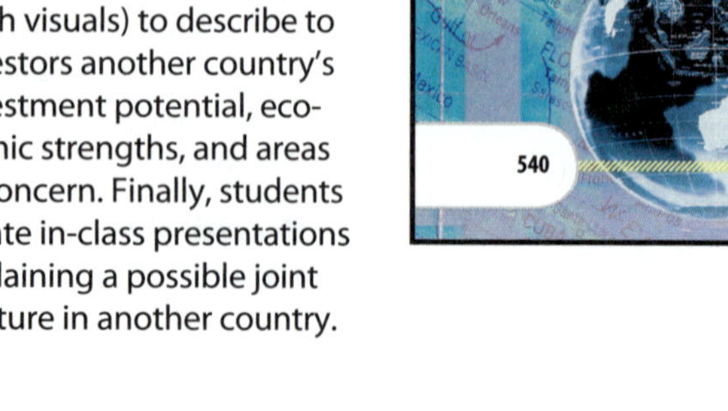

(or another one), research expected economic conditions and business opportunities for this nation. What recommendations would you make to investors about this country?

5. Select a company involved in international business. Obtain recent financial statements for the company. Prepare a summary of its recent financial situation and the international operations of the company.

6. The use of insurance is a common part of a risk management plan. Describe the liability and property insurance a global company might need.

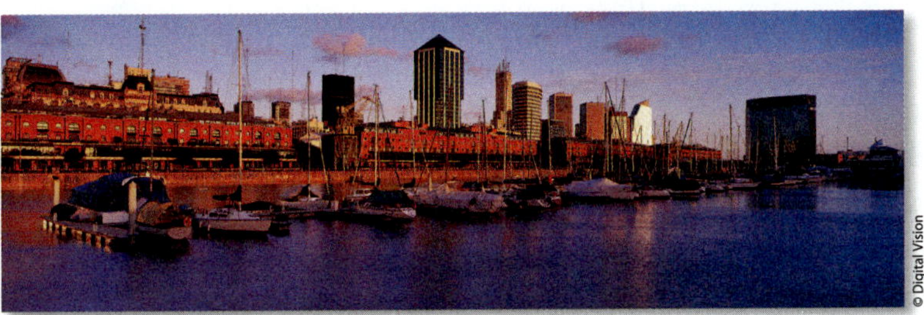
© Digital Vision

Present

Prepare a portfolio (folder, file, or notebook) to store the information and materials you created in the activities above.

1. Create a poster, slide presentation, web site, or video showing different buying behaviors in other countries. Describe how a product or service might need to be changed based on the culture and traditions in another country.

2. Develop a flowchart or graph that shows the banking system and payment activities in another country. Explain how various payment methods (the country's currency, checks, credit cards, and electronic banking) are used by individuals and businesses.

3. Prepare a written report (with visuals) describing the investment potential of another country. Describe economic and business strengths of the country. Point out areas of concern about which investors should be aware. Use visuals (photos, tables, maps) to communicate the strengths and weaknesses of the country's investment environment.

4. A common method for reducing global business risk is working with a partner in another country. Create an in-class presentation (or video) explaining a joint venture that might be established when doing business in another country.

Using a Calculator and Computer Keypad

KINDS OF CALCULATORS

Many different models of calculators, both desktop and hand held, are available. All calculators have their own features and particular placement of operation keys. Therefore, it is necessary to refer to the operator's manual for specific instructions and locations of the operating keys for the calculator being used.

HAND-HELD CALCULATORS

There are many different kinds of hand-held or pocket calculators. They come in all shapes and sizes with a variety of keys and functions. All calculators have number keys (0 to 9), operation keys ($+$, $-$, $\times$, $\div$), and clear keys (C or CE). Most calculators have a percent key (%). Some hand-held calculators come with a memory for storing numbers and calculation results. These are shown as M+, M−, and MR. Others, such as scientific calculators, have many more keys including x^2, $1/x$, and $\sqrt{}$.

It is important to read the operator's manual to learn how your particular calculator works. Be sure to keep the manual in a safe place so you can refer to it for help in solving various mathematical problems.

DESKTOP CALCULATORS

Several operating switches on a desktop calculator must be engaged before it will produce the desired results.

The *decimal selector* sets the appropriate decimal places for numbers that will be entered. For example, if the decimal selector is set at 2, both the numbers entered and the answer will be displayed with two decimal places. If the decimal selector is set at F, the calculator automatically sets the needed decimal places. The F setting allows the answer to be unrounded and carried out to the maximum number of decimal places possible.

The *decimal rounding selector* rounds the answers. The down arrow position will drop any digits beyond the last digit desired. The up arrow position will drop any digits beyond the last digit desired and round the last digit up. In the 5/4 position, the calculator rounds the last desired digit up only when the following digit is 5 or greater. If the following digit is less than 5, the last desired digit remains unchanged.

The *GT* or *grand total switch* in the on position accumulates totals.

Ten-Key Touch System

Striking the numbers 0 to 9 on a desktop calculator or numeric keypad on a computer without looking at the keyboard is called the *touch system*. Using the touch system develops both speed and accuracy.

The 4, 5, and 6 keys are called the *home row*. If the right hand is used for the key-board, the index finger is placed on the 4 key, the middle finger on the 5 key, and the ring finger on the 6 key. If the left hand is used, the ring finger is placed on the 4 key, the middle finger on the 5 key, and the index finger on the 6 key.

Place the fingers on the home row keys. Curve the fingers and keep the wrist straight. These keys may feel slightly concave or the 5 key may have a raised dot or bar. The differences in the home row allow the operator to recognize the home row by touch rather than by sight.

Maintain the position of the fingers on the home row. The finger used to strike the 4 key will also strike the 7 key and the 1 key. Stretch the finger up to reach the 7 and stretch the finger down to reach the 1 key. Visualize the position of these keys.

Again, place the fingers on the home row. Stretch the finger that strikes the 5 key up to reach the 8 key and down to reach the 2 key. Likewise, stretch the finger that strikes the 6 key up to strike the 9 key and down to strike the 3 key. This same finger will stretch down again to hit the decimal point.

If the right hand is used, the thumb will be used to strike the 0 and 00 keys and the little finger to strike the addition key. If the left hand is used, the little finger will be used to strike the 0 and 00 keys and the thumb to strike the addition key.

Performing Mathematical Operations on Desktop Calculators

Mathematical operations can be performed on any calculator both quickly and efficiently. The basic operations of addition, subtraction, multiplication, and division are used frequently on a calculator. Here is how these operations are completed on a typical desktop calculator.

Addition Each number to be added is called an *addend*. The answer to an addition problem is called the *sum*.

Addition is performed by entering an addend and striking the addition key (+). All numbers are entered on a calculator in the exact order they are given. To enter the number 4,375.68, strike the 4, 3, 7, 5, decimal, 6, and 8 keys in that order, and then strike the addition key. Commas are not entered. Continue in this manner until all addends have been entered. To obtain the sum, strike the total key on the calculator.

Subtraction The top number or first number of a subtraction problem is called the *minuend*. The number to be subtracted from the minuend is called the *subtrahend*. The answer to a subtraction problem is called the *difference*.

Subtraction is performed by first entering the minuend and striking the addition key (+). The subtrahend is then entered, followed by the minus key (−), followed by the total key.

Multiplication The numbers being multiplied together are called *factors*. The answer to a multiplication problem is called the *product*.

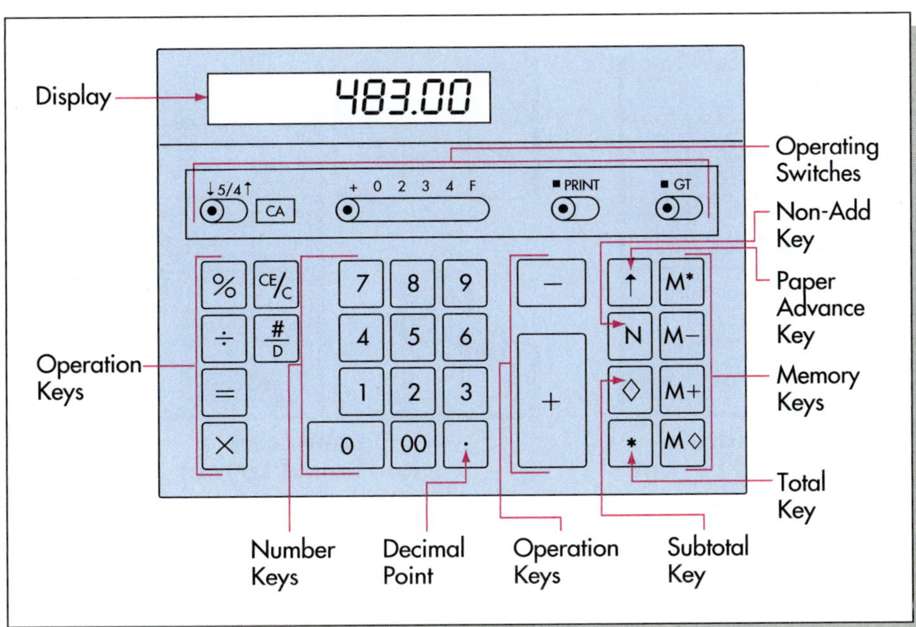

Multiplication is performed by entering one factor, striking the multiplication key (×), entering the other factor, and then striking the equals key (=). The calculator will automatically multiply and give the product.

Division The number to be divided is called the *dividend*. The number the dividend will be divided by is called the *divisor*. The answer to a division problem is called the *quotient*.

Division is performed by entering the dividend and striking the division key (÷). The divisor is then entered, following by the equals key (=). The calculator will automatically divide and give the quotient.

Correcting Errors If an error is made while using a calculator, several methods of correction may be used. If an incorrect number has been entered and the addition key or equals key has not yet been struck, strike the clear entry (CE) key one time. This key will clear only the last number that was entered. However, if the clear entry key is depressed more than one time, the entire problem will be cleared on some calculators. If an incorrect number has been entered and the addition key has been struck, strike the minus key one time only. This will automatically subtract the last number added, thus removing it from the total.

when the keys on the keypad are pressed. When Num Lock is not on, the arrow, Home, Page Up, Page Down, End, Insert, and Delete keys can be used. Enhanced keyboards allow you to keep the Num Lock key activated at all times.

The asterisk (*) on the computer is used for multiplication. The slash key (/) is used for division.

Performing Mathematical Operations On Computers

Calculations with a computer keypad are performed in much the same way as on a desktop calculator. However, after the + key is depressed, the display usually shows the accumulated total. Therefore, the total key is not found on the computer keypad. Some computer programs will not calculate the total until the Enter key is pressed.

Subtraction is performed differently on many computer keypads. The minuend is entered, followed by the minus (−) key. Then the subtrahend is entered. Pressing either the + key, the = key, or the Enter key will display the difference.

Multiplication and division are performed the same way as on a desktop calculator. Keep in mind that computers used the * for multiplication and / for division.

COMPUTER KEYPADS

The computer has a keypad on the right side of the keyboard called the *numeric keypad*. Even though there are several styles of computer keyboards, there are two basic layouts for the numeric keypad, as shown in the illustration on this page.

Most computers have a small light that indicates when the *Num Lock* key (above the 7 key) is on. When the Num Lock key is turned on, numbers are entered

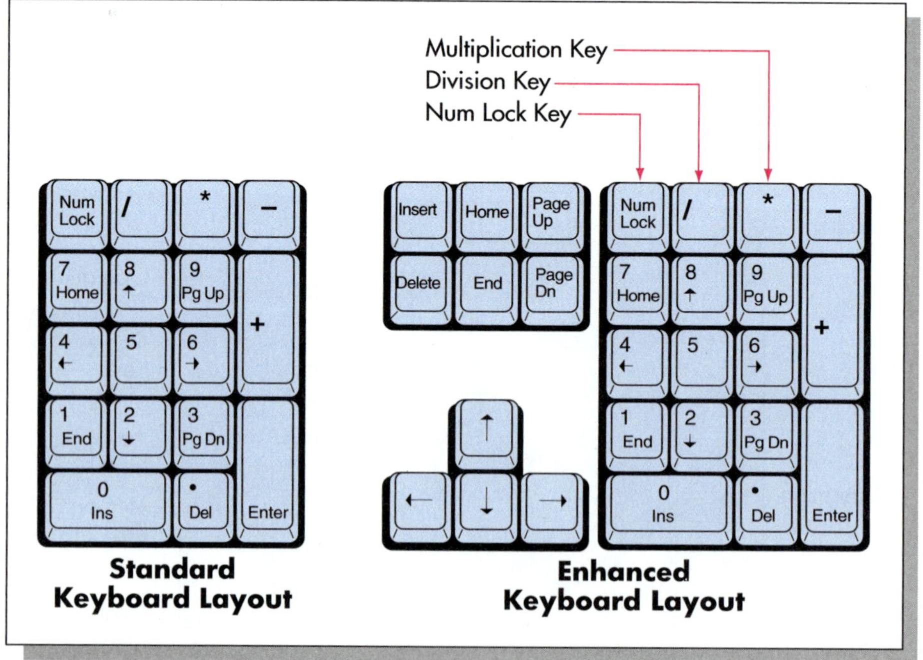

Standard Keyboard Layout

Enhanced Keyboard Layout

APPENDIX B

Math Review

This arithmetic review will help you solve many of the end-of-chapter problems in this text as well as common arithmetic problems you may encounter in business.

ESTIMATING SUMS AND DIFFERENCES

In some situations, an **estimate** may be useful. Sometimes an exact answer is not needed, so you can estimate. Other times, estimation can be used to check mathematical calculations, especially when using a calculator.

Most people estimate by **rounding** numbers. Rounded numbers are easier to work with. Rounded numbers usually contain one or two non-zero digits followed by all zeros.

Examples

The U.S. Bureau of the Census estimated the 1997 population of Texas at 19,385,699.

- Round 19,385,699 to the nearest ten million.

  19,385,699 $\longrightarrow$ 20,000,000

  9 is greater than or equal to 5, so round up to 20,000,000.

- Round 19,385,699 to the nearest million.

  19,385,699 $\longrightarrow$ 19,000,000

  3 is less than 5, round down to 19,000,000.

One new car has a list price of $15,209.50.

- Round $15,209.50 to the nearest thousand dollars.

  $15,209.50 $\longrightarrow$ $15,000

  2 is less than 5, round down to $15,000.

- Round $15,209.50 to the nearest dollar.

  $15,209.50 $\longrightarrow$ $15,210

  5 is greater than or equal to 5, round up to $15,210.

Examples

- Estimate the answer to 24,432 + 15,000.

	Option 1:	Option 2:
24,432	Round to the	Round to the
+ 15,000	nearest ten	nearest
	thousand.	thousand.
	20,000	24,000
	+20,000	+15,000
	40,000	39,000

- Estimate the answer to $32.23 − $17.54.

	Option 1:	Option 2:
$32.23	Round to the	Round to the
−17.54	nearest ten	nearest
	dollars.	dollar.
	$30.00	$32.00
	−20.00	−18.00
	$10.00	$14.00

- Estimate how much change you should get if you give the clerk $20 to pay for a bill of $6.98.

  $20.00 $\longrightarrow$ $20.00

  −6.98 $\qquad$ −7.00

  $\longrightarrow$ $13.00

MULTIPLYING NUMBERS ENDING IN ZEROS

When you multiply numbers that have *final zeros*, you can use this shortcut:

> Multiply the numbers by using only the digits that are not zeros. Then write as many final zeros in the product as there are zeros in the numbers being multiplied.

Examples

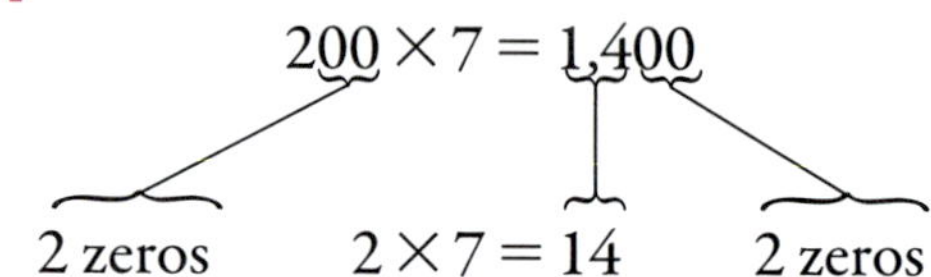

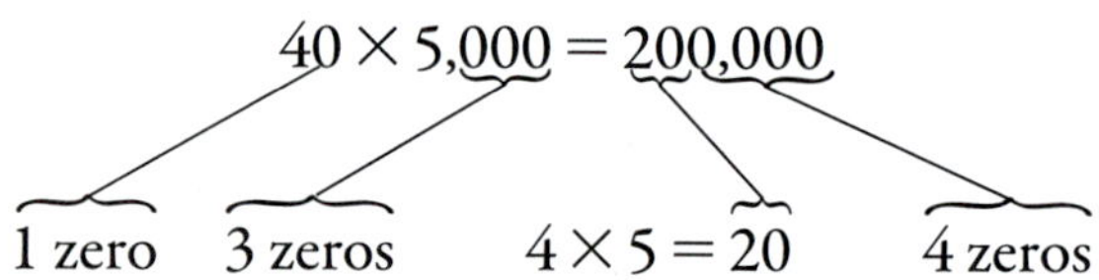

When multiplying larger numbers, use an imaginary line to separate zeros from the rest of the digits.

$36 \times 2,500$

```
    36 |
  × 25 |00 ◄
   180 |        ──► 2 zeros
    72 |
  ─────
   900 |00 ◄         90,000  Answer
```

$3,600 \times 25,000$

```
    36 |00    ◄──── 2 zeros
  × 25 |000   ◄──── 3 zeros
   180 |            2 + 3 = 5 zeros
    72 |
  ─────
   900 |00000  ◄─ 5 zeros
       90,000,000  Answer
```

ESTIMATING PRODUCTS

There are various ways to estimate the answer to a multiplication problem.

- Option 1: Round both numbers **up**. Estimate will be greater than the actual product.

- Option 2: Round both numbers **down**. Estimate will be less than the actual product.

- Option 3: Round each number to the nearest unit with one non-zero digit. The estimate will be close to the actual product.

Examples

Estimate $82,543 \times 653$.

Option 1: $90,000 \times 700 = 63,000,000$
Option 2: $80,000 \times 600 = 48,000,000$
Option 3: $80,000 \times 700 = 56,000,000$

DIVIDING WHOLE NUMBERS

Division is the opposite of multiplication. Division is shown in several ways. To show that 18 divided by 3 is 6, you may use any of these forms:

$$18 \div 3 = 6 \qquad \frac{18}{3} = 6 \qquad 3\overline{)18}\,{}^{6}$$

In each case, 18 is the dividend, 3 is the divisor, and 6 is the quotient.

$$\text{dividend} \div \text{divisor} = \text{quotient}$$

$$\frac{\text{dividend}}{\text{divisor}} = \text{quotient} \qquad \text{divisor}\overline{)\text{dividend}}^{\,\text{quotient}}$$

DIVIDING NUMBERS ENDING IN ZEROS

When you divide multiples of 10, there are several shortcuts you can use. Try either of the shortcuts discussed below:

- Write the numbers as a fraction. Cross out the same number of zeros in both the numerator and denominator of the fraction.

- Move the decimal point in the dividend to the **left** the same number of places as there are zeros in the divisor.

Examples

- $1,000,000,000 \div 10,000 = \dfrac{1,000,000,000}{10,000}$

$$= 100,000$$

- $1,000,000,000 \div 10,000$

$$= 100000.0000. \div 1.0000. = 100,000$$

ESTIMATING QUOTIENTS

One way to estimate the answer to a division problem is to start by rounding the divisor to a number with one non-zero number followed by all zeros. Then round the dividend to a multiple of that rounded divisor.

Examples

- Estimate $609 \div 19$.

  Round 19 to 20 and 609 to 600.

  $600 \div 20 = 30$

- Estimate $19,876,548 \div 650$.

  650 rounds up to 700.

  Multiples of 7 are 7, 14, 21, 28, 35, and so on. Use the closest multiple, 21.

  $$21,000,000 \div 700 = \frac{21000000}{700}$$

  $$= \frac{210000}{7} = 30,000$$

ADDING AND SUBTRACTING DECIMALS

When adding and subtracting decimals, align the decimal points. Then add or subtract as for whole numbers. Place the decimal point in the answer directly below where it is located in the computation. A number like 532 can also be written as 532. or 532.0. When writing decimals less than one, a zero is placed before the decimal point to show that there are no ones.

Examples

- Find the sum of 33.67, 72.84, 0.75, and 43.34.

  $$\begin{array}{r} 33.67 \\ 72.84 \\ 0.75 \\ + \ 43.34 \\ \hline 150.60 \end{array}$$

- Find the sum of 320.5471, 1.4, and 82.352.

  $$\begin{array}{r} 320.5471 \\ 1.4 \\ + \ 82.32 \\ \hline 404.2991 \end{array}$$

- Find the difference between 952.1 and 34.2517.

  $$\begin{array}{r} 952.1 \\ - \ 34.2517 \end{array}$$

  Add 0s to the **right** after the decimal point.

  $$\begin{array}{r} 952.\mathbf{1000} \\ - \ 34.2517 \\ \hline 917.8483 \end{array}$$

MULTIPLYING DECIMALS

When multiplying decimals, align the numbers at the right. Multiply as if you are multiplying whole numbers. To locate the decimal point in the answer, count all digits to the right of the decimal point in each number being multiplied and place the decimal point so there are that many digits after the decimal point in the answer.

Remember: Estimation can be used to check that your answer is reasonable and that you have correctly located the decimal point in the answer.

Examples

- Multiply 7.46 by 3.2.

  $$\begin{array}{r} 7.46 \quad \longleftarrow 2 \text{ decimal places} \\ \times \ 3.2 \quad \longleftarrow 1 \text{ decimal place} \\ \hline 1492 \qquad 2 + 1 = 3 \\ 2238 \quad \\ \hline 23.872 \quad \longleftarrow 3 \text{ decimal places} \end{array}$$

- Multiply 0.193 by 0.2.

  $$\begin{array}{r} 0.193 \quad \longleftarrow 3 \text{ decimal places} \\ \times \ 0.2 \quad \longleftarrow +1 \text{ decimal place} \\ \hline 0.0386 \quad \longleftarrow 4 \text{ decimal places} \end{array}$$

  If needed to get enough decimal places, add a zero before the numeric answer but after the decimal point.

  Remember that the zero before the decimal point shows that there are no ones in the product. The answer is less than one.

  Estimate to check your answer.

  $0.2 \times 0.2 = 0.04$

  0.04 is close to 0.0386, so the answer is reasonable.

MULTIPLYING BY POWERS OF 10

Numbers like 100,000,000, 10,000, 100, 0.1, 0.01, and 0.00001 are powers of 10. To multiply by these, simply move the decimal point in the number being multiplied.

When multiplying by a power of 10 greater than one, move the decimal point to the right. The answer is larger than the number you started with.

When multiplying by a power of 10 less than one, move the decimal point to the left. The answer is smaller than the number you started with.

Examples

- Multiply 25,397 by ten thousand.

  $25,397 \times 10,000 = 253,970,000$

  Think: 25397.0000.

- Multiply 0.078 by one hundred.

  $0.078 \times 100 = 7.8$

  Think: $= 0.07.8$

- Multiply 192,536 by one ten-thousandth.

  $192,536 \times 0.0001 = 19.2536$

  Think: 19.2536.

- Multiply 0.293 by one hundredth.

  $0.293 \times 0.01 = 0.00293$

  Think: 0.00.293

SHORTCUTS WHEN MULTIPLYING WITH MONEY

Businesses price items at amounts such as 49¢, $5.98, or $99.95. A price of $99.95 seems less to the buyer than an even $100. When finding the cost of several of such items, you can use a mathematical shortcut.

Examples

- Find the cost of 27 items at 98¢ each.

  normal multiplication

  $$\begin{array}{r} \$0.98 \\ \times\ 27 \\ \hline 686 \\ 196 \\ \hline \$26.46 \end{array}$$

  Shortcut: Think: 98¢ = $1−2¢

  $(27 \times \$1) - (27 \times 2\text{¢}) = \$27 - 54\text{¢}$

  $54\text{¢} = \$0.54$

  $$\begin{array}{r} \$27.00 \\ -0.54 \\ \hline \$26.46 \end{array}$$

- Find the cost of 32 items at $6.95 each.

  Shortcut: Think $6.95 = \$7 - \$0.05$

  $(32 \times \$7) - (32 \times \$0.05)$

  $= \$224 - \$1.60 = \$222.40$

- Find the cost of 101 items at $9.99 each.

  Shortcut: Think $9.99 = \$10 - \$0.01$

  $(101 \times \$10) - (101 \times \$0.01)$

  $= \$1,010 - \$1.01 = \$1,008.99$

  Alternate Shortcut:

  Think: $101 = 100 + 1$

  $(100 \times \$9.99) + (1 \times \$9.99) =$
  $\$999 + \$9.99 = \$1,008.99$

MULTIPLYING A WHOLE NUMBER BY A FRACTION

To multiply a whole number by a fraction, multiply the whole number by the numerator (top number) and then divide that answer by the denominator (bottom number).

Examples

- $180 \times \dfrac{2}{3} = \dfrac{180 \times 2}{3} = \dfrac{360}{3} = 120$

- $500 \times \dfrac{3}{4} = \dfrac{500 \times 3}{4} = \dfrac{1500}{4} = 375$

- $768 \times \dfrac{1}{8} = \dfrac{768 \times 1}{8} = \dfrac{768}{8} = 96$

- $90 \times \dfrac{4}{5} = \dfrac{90 \times 4}{5} = \dfrac{360}{5} = 72$

Simplifying Fractions

When working with fractions, you can simplify the fractions by dividing the numerator and the denominator by a common factor (a number that will divide into both numbers evenly). Division by such common factors is called **canceling** or **cancellation**.

Examples

- Simplify $\frac{10}{12}$.   **Think:** 2 is a factor of both 10 and 12.

$$10 \div 2 = 5$$
$$\frac{10}{12} = \frac{5}{6}$$
$$12 \div 2 = 6$$

- Simplify $\frac{75}{100}$.   **Think:** Use 25 as a common factor.

$$75 \div 25 = 3$$
$$\frac{75}{100} = \frac{3}{4}$$
$$100 \div 25 = 4$$

- Simplify $\frac{280}{60}$.   **Think:** Use 20 as a common factor.

$$280 \div 20 = 14$$
$$\frac{280}{60} = \frac{14}{3}$$
$$60 \div 20 = 3$$

Using Fractional Parts of $1.00 in Multiplying Mentally

While goods and services may be priced at any figure, prices are frequently expressed in fractional parts of $1, $10, or $100. For instance, 2 items for $1 is the same as $\frac{1}{2}$ of 100¢, or 50¢ per item, and 3 items for $10 is the same as $\frac{1}{3}$ of $10, or $3.33\frac{1}{3}$ per item.

You can also use fractional parts of $1.00 to find the cost of multiple items mentally.

24 items selling for $1.00 would cost $24.00

24 items at 50¢ each = $\frac{1}{2}$ of $24 or $12.00

24 items at 25¢ each = $\frac{1}{4}$ of $24 or $6.00

24 items at $33\frac{1}{3}$¢ each = $\frac{1}{3}$ of $24 or $8

Many similar calculations can be made mentally. While there are many fractional parts of $1.00, a chart of those most commonly used follows.

Fraction	Part of $1.00
$\frac{1}{8}$	$0.12\frac{1}{2}$
$\frac{1}{6}$	$0.16\frac{2}{3}$
$\frac{1}{5}$	$0.20
$\frac{1}{4}$	$0.25
$\frac{1}{3}$	$0.33\frac{1}{3}$
$\frac{3}{8}$	$0.37\frac{1}{2}$
$\frac{2}{5}$	$0.40
$\frac{1}{2}$	$0.50
$\frac{3}{5}$	$0.60
$\frac{5}{8}$	$0.62\frac{1}{2}$
$\frac{2}{3}$	$0.66\frac{2}{3}$
$\frac{3}{4}$	$0.75
$\frac{4}{5}$	$0.80
$\frac{5}{6}$	$0.83\frac{1}{3}$
$\frac{7}{8}$	$0.87\frac{1}{2}$

Examples

- Find the cost of 16 items at $12\frac{1}{2}$¢ each.

  Think: $12\frac{1}{2}$¢ $= \frac{1}{8}$ of $1

  $$16 \times \frac{1}{8} = 2$$

  16 items at $12\frac{1}{2}$¢ each will cost $2.

- Find the cost of 33 items at 25¢ each.

  Think: 25¢ $= \frac{1}{4}$ of $1

  $$33 \times \frac{1}{4} = \frac{33}{4}, \text{ or } 8\frac{1}{4}$$

  33 items at 25¢ each will cost $8\frac{1}{4}$, or $8.25.

- Find the cost of 48 items at 75¢ each.

  Think: $75¢ = \frac{3}{4}$ of $1

  $$48 \times \frac{3}{4} = \frac{\overset{12}{\cancel{48}} \times 3}{\cancel{4}_1} = \frac{12 \times 3}{1} = \frac{36}{1} = 36$$

  48 items at 75¢ each is $36.

- Find the cost of 34 items at $62\frac{1}{2}$¢ each.

  Think: $62\frac{1}{2}¢ = \frac{5}{8}$ of $1

  $$34 \times \frac{5}{8} = \frac{\overset{17}{\cancel{34}} \times 5}{\cancel{8}_4} = \frac{17 \times 5}{4} = \frac{85}{4} = 21\frac{1}{4}$$

  34 items at $62\frac{1}{2}$¢ each is $21\frac{1}{4}$, or $21.25.

Fractional Parts of Other Amounts

You can use the table on this page to find fractional parts of multiples of 10.

Examples

- Find $\frac{5}{6}$ of $1,000.

  $$\frac{5}{6} \text{ of } \$1,000 = 1000 \times \frac{5}{6} \text{ of } \$1$$
  $$= 100 \times \$0.83\frac{1}{3}$$
  $$= \$83\frac{1}{3}$$

  So, $\frac{5}{6}$ of $1,000 is $.83.33.

  $\left(\frac{1}{3} \text{ dollar} = \$0.33\frac{1}{3}, \text{ which is } \$0.33 \text{ when rounded to the nearest cent.}\right)$

- Find $\frac{3}{4}$ of $100.

  $$\frac{3}{4} \text{ of } \$100 = 100 \times \frac{3}{4} \text{ of } \$1$$
  $$= 100 \times \$0.75$$
  $$= \$75$$

  So, $\frac{3}{4}$ of $100 is $75.

- Find $\frac{7}{8}$ of $10.

  $$\frac{7}{8} \text{ of } \$10 = 10 \times \frac{7}{8} \text{ of, } \$1$$
  $$= 10 \times \$0.875$$
  $$= \$8.75$$

  So, $\frac{7}{8}$ of $10 is $8.75.

Dividing Decimals

Division involving decimals is completed like division of whole numbers, except for dealing with the decimal point.

When you divide a decimal by a whole number, you divide as for whole numbers and place the decimal point directly above the location of the decimal point in the dividend.

Examples

- Divide 12.944 by 8.

  $$8\overline{)12.944} = 1.618$$

  To check division, multiply your quotient by the divisor. The result should be the dividend.

  $$\begin{array}{r} 1.618 \\ \times \quad 8 \\ \hline 12.944 \end{array} \checkmark$$

- Divide 37 by 4.

  $$4\overline{)37.00} = 9.25$$

  Add zeros as needed.

  Check:
  $$\begin{array}{r} 9.25 \\ \times \quad 4 \\ \hline 37.00 \end{array} \checkmark$$

To divide by a decimal, move the decimal point to the right the same number of places in both the divisor and the dividend so you are dividing by a whole number.

Examples

- Divide 12.944 by 0.8.

  Think: 0.8 has one decimal place, move the decimal points in the divisor and the dividend right one place.

  $$
  \begin{array}{r}
  1\,6.18 \\
  0.8.\overline{)12.9.44} \\
  \underline{8} \\
  4\,9 \\
  \underline{4\,8} \\
  1\,4 \\
  \underline{8} \\
  6\,4 \\
  \underline{6\,4} \\
  0
  \end{array}
  $$

- Divide 37 by 0.004.

  $$
  \begin{array}{r}
  9.250. \\
  0.004.\overline{)37.000.} \\
  \underline{36} \\
  1\,0 \\
  \underline{8} \\
  2\,0 \\
  \underline{2\,0} \\
  0
  \end{array}
  $$

  Add zeros as needed.

  Remember: Estimation can be used to check that your answer is reasonable and that you have correctly located the decimal point in the answer.

Determining Percentages and Interest in Business

Finding percentages and calculating interest are frequent functions in business. Every career in business demands some knowledge of percentages and interest. The well-prepared business person is comfortable with percentages and interest.

MEANING OF PERCENT

Percent is derived from two Latin words, "per centum," meaning "by the hundred." You can express a percent as a common fraction or a decimal fraction. When the percent involves a fraction, like $7\frac{1}{4}\%$, change the mixed number to a decimal and move the decimal point two places to the left.

$$7\frac{1}{4}\% = 7.25\% = 0.725$$

Examples

- Write 19% as a fraction and a decimal.

  Percent means *per one hundred*, so write it as a fraction with a denominator of 100.

  $$19\% = \frac{19}{100} = 0.19$$

- Write 0.98 as a fraction and a percent.

  $$0.98 = \frac{98}{100} = 98\%$$

- Write $\frac{3}{100}$ as a decimal and a percent.

  $$\frac{3}{100} = 0.03 = 3\%$$

- Write $8\frac{1}{2}\%$ as a decimal and a fraction.

  $$8\frac{1}{2}\% = 8.5\% = 0.085 = \frac{85}{1000}$$

  Notice that 0.085 is 85 *thousandths*, so the fraction has a denominator of 1000.

FINDING A PERCENT OF A NUMBER

To find the percent of a number, change the percent to a fraction or decimal and multiply. Using a calculator simplifies the process.

Examples

- Find 18% of 117,334.

  With fractions:

  $$117,334 \times \frac{18}{100} = \frac{117334 \times 18}{100}$$
  $$= \frac{2112012}{100} = 21,120.12$$

- Find 18% of 117,334.

  With decimals:

$$
\begin{array}{r}
117,334 \\
\times\ \ \ \ 0.18 \\
\hline
938672 \\
117334\ \ \ \\
\hline
21,120.12
\end{array}
$$

- Find 10% of 359.

  $$359 \times 0.10 = 35.9$$

CALCULATING SIMPLE INTEREST

Interest is money paid for the privilege of using someone else's money. Interest is always expressed as a percent. The *principal* is the amount of money borrowed. Simple interest (I) is calculated by multiplying the principal (P) times the annual interest rate (R) times the length of time in years (T). The formula is written as:

$$I = P \times R \times T$$

Examples

- Find the amount of simple interest due on $400 borrowed for 2 years at 8%.

  $I = \$400 \times 0.08 \times 2 = \$64$

- Find the amount of simple interest due on $600 borrowed for 1 month at 18%.

  Think: 1 month is $\frac{1}{12}$ of a year.

  $I = \$600 \times 0.18 \times \frac{1}{12} = \$9$

- Find the amount of simple interest due on $3,000 borrowed for 6 months at $9\frac{3}{4}$%.

  $I = \$3,000 \times 0.0975 \times \frac{6}{12} = \$146.25$

COMPOUND INTEREST

With the advances in the use of computer, compound interest is more common than simple interest. For example, a credit card may say that it charges 1.5% interest per month. It then seems that you are paying $12 \times 1.5\%$, or 18% interest per year. However, in reality you are charged more than 18% interest per year because you are paying interest on interest.

Example

Suppose that you owe $100 on your credit card and do not make any payments for one year. Assuming there are no late fees, your balance at the end of each month would look as shown in the following table. When the interest is calculated, all amounts are rounded up to the next cent.

Month	Beginning Balance	Interest (1.5% per month)	Ending Balance
Jan.	$100.00	$1.50	$101.50
Feb.	$101.50	$1.53	$103.03
Mar.	$103.03	$1.55	$104.58
Apr.	$104.58	$1.57	$106.15
May	$106.15	$1.60	$107.75
June	$107.75	$1.62	$109.37
July	$109.37	$1.65	$111.02
Aug.	$111.02	$1.67	$112.69
Sept.	$112.69	$1.70	$114.39
Oct.	$114.39	$1.72	$116.11
Nov.	$116.11	$1.75	$117.86
Dec.	$117.86	$1.77	$119.63

So in 12 months you have paid $19.63 in interest on $100, or 19.63%, not 18% interest.

FINDING WHAT PERCENT A NUMBER IS OF ANOTHER

To find what percent a number is of another, divide the one number (the part) by the other number (the whole). Then show the result as a percent.

Example

- 50 is what percent of 200?

  Divide 50 by 200.

$$
\begin{array}{r}
0.25 \\
200\overline{)50.00} \\
\underline{40\ 0} \\
10\ 00 \\
10\ 00
\end{array}
$$

  $0.25 = 25\%$

  50 is 25% of 200.

Using Measurements in Business

The metric system of measurement is used in business by most nations in the world. Because of our great amount of trade with other countries, the United States has taken some steps toward conversion to the metric system. Some U.S. businesses and industries have already made the change, and you should become familiar with the metric system.

There are some things about the metric system that may already be familiar to you. For example, if you have been to a track meet or swimming meet or have seen one on television, you know that distances can be measured in meters, not just in feet, yards, or miles. Food is often labeled to show amounts in grams as well as pounds or ounces. Meters, kilometers, and grams are examples of metric units of measurement.

BASIC METRIC UNITS

The basic metric units are the meter (length), the liter (capacity), and the gram (mass or weight). All measurements can be expressed in terms of these three basic units. However, prefixes are used with the basic units to avoid dealing with very large and very small numbers. The most common prefixes used in the metric system are:

Kilo- ⟶ one thousand times
Centi- ⟶ one one-hundredth of
Milli- ⟶ one one-thousandth of

Look at the charts below. The same prefixes are used for length, capacity, and mass or weight.

Length
1 kilometer = 1000 meters
1 meter = 100 centimeters
1 meter = 1000 millimeters
1 centimeter = 10 millimeters
1 centimeter = 0.01 meter
1 millimeter = 0.001 meter

Capacity
1 kiloliter = 1000 liters
1 liter = 100 centiliters
1 liter = 1000 milliliters
1 centiliter = 10 milliliters
1 centiliter = 0.01 liter
1 milliliter = 0.001 liter

Mass (Weight)
1 kilogram = 1000 grams
1 gram = 100 centigrams
1 gram = 1000 milligrams
1 centigram = 10 milligrams
1 centigram = 0.01 gram
1 milligram = 0.001 gram

The abbreviations, or symbols, for metric measurements are also uniform, changing only to show whether you are measuring length, capacity, or mass.

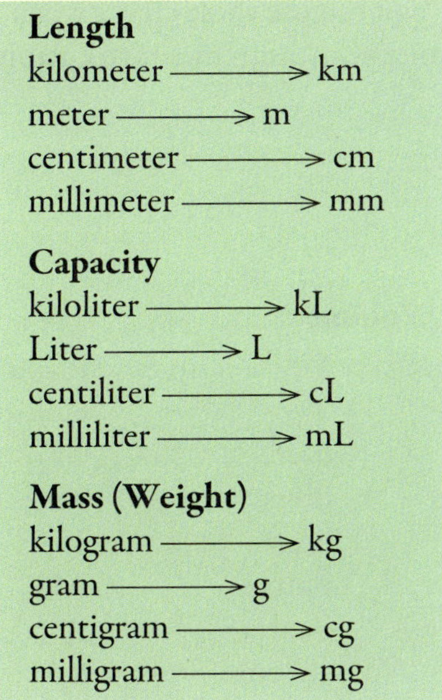

Length
kilometer ——————⟶ km
meter ——————⟶ m
centimeter ——————⟶ cm
millimeter ——————⟶ mm

Capacity
kiloliter ——————⟶ kL
Liter ——————⟶ L
centiliter ——————⟶ cL
milliliter ——————⟶ mL

Mass (Weight)
kilogram ——————⟶ kg
gram ——————⟶ g
centigram ——————⟶ cg
milligram ——————⟶ mg

CONVERTING UNITS WITHIN THE METRIC SYSTEM

Using the tables above, you can see that one kilometer is 1000 times as long as a meter and that one millimeter is one-thousandth of a meter. Since the relationships between the prefixes are multiples of 10, you can change from one unit to another by multiplying by a power of ten, which can be done by moving the decimal point.

Examples

- Change 0.36 meters to centimeters.

  Think: 1 meter = 100 centimeters

  To get from 1 to 100, move the decimal point to the right 2 spaces.   0.36.

  So 0.36 meters = 36 centimeters

- Change 5000 grams to kilograms.

  Think: 1000 grams = 1 kilogram

  To get from 1000 to 1, move the decimal point to the left 3 spaces.   5.000.

  So 5000 grams = 5 kilograms

- Change 4.5 liters to milliliters.

  Think: 1 liter = 1000 milliliters

  To get from 1 to 1000, move the decimal point to the right 3 spaces.

4.500.   Notice how zeros are added so the decimal can be moved the needed number of spaces to the right.

So 4.5 liters = 4500 milliliters

- Change 0.86 millimeters to centimeters.

  Think: 10 millimeters = 1 centimeter

  To get from 10 to 1, move the decimal point to the left 1 space.

0.0.86   Notice that a zero is added so the decimal can be moved the needed number of spaces to the left.

So 0.86 millimeters = 0.086 centimeters

CUSTOMARY MEASUREMENT

In the United States feet, pounds, and gallons are still common units of measure.

Below is a list of common customary measurements and their equivalents.

Length
1 foot = 12 inches
1 yard = 3 feet
1760 yards = 1 mile
5280 feet = 1 mile

Capacity
1 pint = 2 cups
1 quart = 2 pints
1 gallon = 4 quarts

Weight
1 pound = 16 ounces
1 ton = 2,000 pounds

MEASURING TEMPERATURE

Thermometers that measure temperature are marked in degrees Celsius (°C) or in degrees Fahrenheit (°F). The Celsius scale is a metric scale. The Fahrenheit scale is nonmetric

METRIC	EVENT	NONMETRIC
100°C	Water boils	212°F
37°C	Normal body temperature	98.6°F
0°C	Water freezes	32°F

CONVERTING BETWEEN SYSTEMS

Once in a while it may be necessary to convert from the metric system to the customary system or vice versa. You can use these charts when you need to change metric measurements to customary or vice versa.

Length/Distance

When you know:	You can find:	If you multiply by:
inches	millimeters	25.40
inches	centimeters	2.54
feet	meters	0.305
yards	meters	0.91
miles	kilometers	1.61
millimeters	inches	0.04
centimeters	inches	0.39
meters	inches	39.37
meters	feet	3.28
meters	yards	1.09
kilometers	miles	0.62

Weight/Mass

When you know:	You can find:	If you multiply by:
ounces	grams	28.35
pounds	kilograms	0.45
grams	ounces	0.035
kilograms	pounds	2.20

Capacity/Volume

When you know:	You can find:	If you multiply by:
pints	liters	0.47
quarts	liters	0.95
gallons	liters	3.78
liters	pints	2.11
liters	quarts	1.06
liters	gallons	0.26

Temperature

When you know:	You can find:	If you:
°F (degrees Fahrenheit)	°C (degrees Celsius)	subtract 32, multiply by 5, then divide by 9.
°C (degrees Celsius)	°F (degrees Fahrenheit)	multiply by 9, divide by 5, then add 32.

Examples

- You are in a 440-yard race. How many meters long is the race?

  To change from yards to meters, multiply by 0.91.

  $440 \times 0.91 = 400.4$

  The race is 400.4 meters long.

- A store shelf has a weight limit of 250 kilograms. What is that limit in pounds?

  To change kilograms to pounds, multiply by 2.20.

  $250 \times 2.20 = 550$

  The weight limit is 550 pounds.

- It is 10°C outside. What is the temperature in degrees Fahrenheit?

  To change from °C to °F, multiply by 9, divide by 5, then add 32.

  $10 \times 9 = 90; 90 \div 5 = 18; 18 + 32 = 50$

  The temperature is 50°F.

- It is 95°F outside. What is the temperature in degrees Celsius?

  To change from °F to °C, subtract 32, multiply by 5, then divide by 9.

  $95 - 32 = 63; 63 \times 5 = 315; 315 \div 9 = 35$

  The temperature is 35°C.

Taxes in Your Life

Each day, without thinking about it, you pay taxes. You pay taxes when you get a paycheck or make a purchase. Wise tax planning starts with knowing the types of taxes you pay and learning how to file a federal income tax return.

TYPES OF TAXES

A *tax* is a charge imposed by a government to finance various public services. Federal, state, and local governments levy taxes.

Most people pay taxes in four major categories: purchases, property, wealth, and earning. Common taxes on purchases are sales tax and excise tax. Real estate property tax and personal property taxes are examples of taxes on property. Taxes on wealth include estate tax, inheritance tax, and gift tax. Social Security tax and income tax are examples of taxes on earning. Examples of common taxes appear in the table below.

Not everyone pays every kind of tax. The types of taxes you pay and how much you pay is related to where you live, how much money you earn, and how you spend and save your money.

WHEN AND WHERE YOU PAY TAXES

Some taxes are paid as part of everyday living. Other taxes are due on specific dates. And some taxes, such as estate taxes, are triggered by an event.

Sales tax is collected at the time of purchase. If you buy a jacket for $80 you might pay more

Common Taxes		
CATEGORIES	**EXAMPLES**	**DESCRIPTION**
Taxes on purchases	Sales tax	A sales tax is a state or local tax on goods and services that is collected by the seller. Food and prescription drugs are often exempt.
	Excise tax	An excise tax is imposed on specific goods and services. For example, all states impose an excise tax on gasoline.
Taxes on property	Real estate property tax	This tax is based on the value of land and buildings. Most property tax revenue is used to pay for schools and local government services.
	Personal property tax	This tax is based on the value of personal property such as boats, cars, and trucks.
Taxes on wealth	Estate tax	This tax is based on the value of a person's property at death.
	Inheritance tax	This tax is based on the value of items received from a deceased person.
	Gift tax	This tax applies to gifts of any kind of property, including money, when the value of the gift exceeds a certain dollar amount. Generally the donor is responsible for the gift tax.
Taxes on earnings	Social Security tax	This tax is based on earnings and is used to finance retirement and disability benefits.
	Income tax	This tax is based on earnings and other sources of income and is a source of revenue for governments.

than $80. If your state has a 5 percent sales tax and you are shopping in a county with a 1 percent sales tax, you will pay the seller $84.80 for your coat. The seller will pay $4 to the state and $0.80 to the county.

In addition to paying sales tax at the cash register, you also pay taxes at the pump. The state price of gasoline includes various taxes. The tax may be hidden, but you still pay it.

Real estate taxes are usually due once or twice a year. Some property owners choose to pay the

No State Sales Tax
FIVE STATES DO NOT HAVE A STATE SALES TAX

- Alaska
- Delaware
- Montana
- New Hampshire
- Oregon

bill when it is due. Others choose to add money to their mortgage payments and ask the financial institution that holds the mortgage to set the money aside until it is time to pay the property tax. The financial institution then pays the bill when it is due.

Income Tax Payments

People make payments for federal, state, and local income taxes in two ways: withholding and estimated payments. Withholding is a "pay-as-you-go system" in which an employer deducts income tax from the earnings of workers each pay period. In January, workers receive a W-2 from each employer. A W-2 is a summary of a worker's earnings for the previous year and includes the amounts deducted for taxes.

Some people are required to make estimated payments for income taxes. Examples of income that may require estimated payments include significant income from savings and investments, income from royalties and pensions, and income from self-employment or working as an independent contractor. Estimated payments are made directly to the government and are due quarterly. Estimated payments for federal income tax are due on April 15, June 15, September 15, and January 15 of the next year.

No State Income Tax
SEVEN STATES DO NOT HAVE A STATE INCOME TAX

- Alaska
- Florida
- Nevada
- South Dakota
- Texas
- Washington
- Wyoming

PREPARING THE FEDERAL INCOME TAX RETURN

The Internal Revenue Service (IRS) is part of the U.S. Treasury. The IRS is the agency responsible for collecting federal income tax. In order to make sure that people pay the taxes they owe, the IRS requires taxpayers to file, or submit, a federal income tax return each year. With few exceptions, the filing deadline is April 15 of the next year.

The main purpose of preparing a federal income tax return is to determine the amount of tax a taxpayer is required to pay for a particular year. Because most people make tax payments throughout the year, the form is also used to determine if you have paid all that you owe, you need to pay more, or you are entitled to a refund or credit. The seven basic steps in the preparation of a federal income tax return are described below.

Federal Income Tax Return Preparation
Step 1 Determine gross income
Step 2 Calculate adjusted gross income
Step 3 Subtract deductions
Step 4 Determine exemptions
Step 5 Compute taxable income
Step 6 Calculate tax owed
Step 7 Make tax payments or ask for a refund or credit

Step 1: Determine Gross Income

The two main types of income for most people are earned income and investment income. Earned income results from wages, salary, commission, fees, tips, and bonuses. Investment income is the result of earnings from dividends, interest, and rent.

Federal income tax must also be paid on other types of income such as alimony, awards, lottery winnings, and prizes. For example, cash and prizes won on television game shows are subject to both federal and states taxes.

Tax-exempt income is income not subject to tax. Interest earned on most state and city bonds, for example, is exempt from federal income tax. In contrast, tax-deferred income will be taxed at a later date.

Step 2: Calculate Adjusted Gross Income

Certain items, called adjustments to income, are subtracted from gross income to obtain adjusted gross income (AGI). These reductions include deposits in retirement accounts and alimony payments.

Step 3: Subtract Deductions

A tax deduction is an amount that reduces taxable income. All taxpayers are eligible for a standard deduction, an amount on which no taxes are paid. As an alternative, a taxpayer may choose to itemize deductions. The rules regarding what can be included in itemized deductions are very specific and change to reflect tax policies and laws.

Example of items that might be included in itemized deductions include the following:

- Some medical and dental expenses
- Taxes paid for state and local income tax and property taxes
- Interest paid on a home mortgage or home equity loan
- Contributions to charitable organizations
- Casualty and theft losses
- Moving expenses when a new job is more than 50 miles away
- Certain job-related expenses such as union dues, required continuing education, work clothes, and tax preparation fees

The decision to use the standard deduction or to itemize your deductions depends on your income and your expenses for the year. In some cases it is worthwhile to calculate your tax liability both ways and choose the one that is more advantageous.

Step 4: Determine Exemptions

An exemption is a tax deduction for the taxpayer, a spouse, and each dependent. For each exemption, taxable income is reduced by a set amount. Therefore, the more dependents a taxpayer can claim, the greater the reduction in taxable income.

In most cases dependents are minor children, but specific criteria must be met. For a person to qualify as a dependent, all three of the following conditions are necessary:

1. The person must not earn more than a certain amount unless he or she is under age 19 or is a full-time student under age 24.
2. The taxpayer must provide more than half of the dependent's support.
3. The dependent must live with the taxpayer or be a relative.

Step 5: Compute Taxable Income

Taxable income is the amount on which taxes are calculated. This amount results from subtracting adjustments to income, deductions, and exemptions from gross income.

Step 6: Taxes Owed

Tax rates are the percentages used to compute the amount owed for taxes. In recent years, the federal income tax rates have ranged from 10 to 35 percent, depending on the level of taxable income.

A person's taxes can be reduced by a tax credit, an amount subtracted directly from taxes owed. Tax credits may be obtained for child- and dependent-care expenses. Low-income workers may qualify for the earned-income credit (EIC).

Remember that a tax credit differs from a deduction in that a tax credit lowers taxes by the full dollar amount. In contrast, a deduction reduces the amount on which the taxes are calculated.

Step 7: Make Tax Payments or Ask for a Refund or Credit

The final step of tax return is to compare the amount paid with the amount owed for taxes. You may owe an additional amount, or you may receive a refund or credit if you paid more than you owe for taxes. Many people like receiving a refund. However, it is important to remember, your money was being held by the government and you were not able to use it or earn interest on it.

COMPLETING THE FEDERAL INCOME TAX RETURN

The process of completing the federal income tax return requires taxpayers to determine their filing status and which tax form is appropriate for their situation. It is important to provide complete and accurate information and avoid common filing errors. The completed tax return must be filed with the IRS by mailing it to an IRS processing center or submitting it electronically.

Filing Status

All U.S. citizens and residents are required to file a federal income tax return if their income exceeds a certain amount. Marital status and the number of dependents determine a taxpayer's filing status. The five options for filing status are explained in the table on this page.

Tax Forms

Taxpayers use one of three forms to file their federal income tax return. Form 1040 is the basic form and Form 1040A and Form 1040EZ are shorter, less complicated versions.

Form 1040EZ Form 1040EZ allows a person with a simple tax situation to easily file a federal income tax return. Taxpayers who fall into one of the following groups can use this form:

- People who are single or married filing a joint return, under age 65, and claim no dependents
- People who have income only of wages, salaries, and tips and not more than $400 of taxable interest

Tax Filing Status	
1. Single	Single refers to individuals who are unmarried, divorced, or legally separated with no dependents.
2. Married Filing Jointly	Married filing jointly refers to a married couple filing a joint return.
3. Married Filing Separately	Married filing separately is an option available to a married couple when each spouse takes responsibility for his or her own tax return.
4. Head of Household	Head of household refers to an unmarried individual or a surviving spouse who maintains a household (paying for more than half of the costs) for a child or a dependent relative.
5. Qualifying Widow(er) with Dependent Child	Qualifying widow or widower refers to an individual whose spouse died within the past two years and who has a qualifying dependent child.

- People who have taxable income less than $50,000
- People who do not itemize deductions or claim any adjustments to income or any tax credits

Form 1040A A little more complicated than the EZ, Form 1040A may be used by people who have less than $50,000 in taxable income from wages, salaries, tips, unemployment compensation, interest, or dividends and use the standard deduction. This form will also allow deductions for individual retirement account (IRA) contributions and a tax credit for child and dependent care expenses.

Form 1040 The most detailed of the three forms, Form 1040 has sections for all types of income. A person must use this form if income is over $50,000 or if claimed as a dependent by a parent and had interest or dividends over a certain amount. Form 1040 is also used when itemizing deductions.

The decision regarding which tax form to use depends on your income level, the amount of your deductions, and other complexities of your tax situation.

Avoiding Common Filing Errors

Filing errors can cost time and money. An error might delay a refund or result in paying more tax than you really owe. Errors can also result in penalty and interest charges for not filing on time or underpayment of taxes.

When preparing a federal tax return, mistakes can be avoided by considering the following:

- Create a filing system for tax documents, receipts, and tax forms.

- Follow instructions carefully.

- Use the proper tax form, tax table, and correct filing status.

- Check, and recheck, calculations carefully.

- Include all required documents, such as a copy of your W-2 form.

- Sign the tax return.

- Make your check payable to the U.S. Treasury.

- Put your Social Security number and the tax year on your check.

- File online or mail your return before the deadline.

- Use the proper amount of postage.

- Keep a copy of the tax return.

Filing Taxes Online

The use of tax preparation software can save 10 or more hours of time. These programs allow taxpayers to use a computer to prepare federal and state tax forms by answering a series of questions or entering information on forms. The tax forms can be printed for filing by mail or the user may choose to file online. Filing online means that the tax return is submitted electronically.

The Internal Revenue Service now makes online filing easier and less expensive than it was a few years ago. The Free File Alliance provides online tax preparation and e-filing free to millions of taxpayers. This program is a partnership between the IRS and the tax software industry. Additional information is available on the IRS website.

TAX PREPARATION ASSISTANCE

Some taxpayers prepare their own federal income tax returns. Returns can be completed using paper and pencil or tax preparation software. Other taxpayers choose to have a tax professional prepare their returns. For some people this is a matter of convenience and others choose a professional because they are not comfortable completing their return on their own.

Many resources are available to help taxpayers with the preparation of their federal tax return and tax planning. Brief descriptions of the most commonly used resources are shown below.

IRS Services Tax information and assistance is available directly from the Internal Revenue Service. Examples of some of the resources are described below.

- Forms and publications including free booklets and pamphlets are available at local IRS offices and at the IRS web site. Forms and publications can also be requested by telephone or fax.

- Recorded tax tips can be heard by calling a toll-free number. These recorded messages are available 24-hours a day.

- Answers to specific questions can be obtained by calling a toll-free hotline. Taxpayers can ask questions about preparing or filing tax returns and tax-related rules and regulations. The hotline can also be used to get information about your refund, payments, or account.

- Walk-in service is available at the 400 local IRS offices around the country.

Tax Publications Commercial tax guides are available to assist taxpayers. These guides are usually well organized and cover a wide range of topics. Some are intended for specific groups such as small businesses. The publications are updated annually.

Online Sources The many web sites that focus on tax information may be located using an online search.

Tax Preparation Software Many taxpayers use tax preparation software on home computers to prepare tax returns. These software products allow users to print returns for filing or to file electronically. Data entry is quick and easy. There are options for updating information from last year's return and accessing earnings and interest data from employers and financial institutions. Tax preparation software also offer features that help taxpayers organize records, avoid common mistakes, and take advantage of appropriate deductions and credits. Tax planning features offer strategies for making financial decisions.

Some tax software products offer online versions of their products at their own web site. These Web-based tax programs are also available at the web sites of some large financial institutions. This allows users to work on their taxes from any computer linked to the Internet.

Tax Preparation Services Many taxpayers pay for professional tax preparation service. Some might pay as little as $35 and others pay thousands of dollars for these services. The fee varies based on the complexity of the tax return and the level of training of the tax preparer. Professional tax preparation and advice services can be grouped into several categories:

- Tax services include local, one-person organizations as well as national companies with hundreds of offices.

- Enrolled agents are government-approved tax preparers who meet training requirements.

- Certified public accountants (CPA) often have specific tax training to assist with tax planning and preparation of tax returns.

- Attorneys do not usually prepare tax returns, but their services are often used for assistance with tax planning and other tax-related legal matters.

Some tax preparation services and other businesses offer refund anticipation loans. In most cases the interest rate on this type of loan is very high. In some cases the annual interest rate is more than 100 percent of the amount being borrowed. You should be cautious of any loan or special financing that is dependent on a tax refund.

EFFECTIVE TAX STRATEGIES

Tax laws and tax forms change frequently. Reading newspapers, magazines, and books, using online resources, attending workshops, and consulting with financial professionals are all ways of being well informed about taxes and understanding your personal tax situation. Being knowledgeable can help you develop strategies and make decisions that limit the amount of taxes you are required to pay. It is also important to understand that your personal and financial situation will change over time and you will need to be aware of how these changes relate to taxes.

Three common ways to limit the amount of income tax you owe are home ownership, tax-exempt investments, and tax-deferred investments. The tax benefit of each of these strategies depends on the individual taxpayer's financial situation.

Home Ownership Home ownership may reduce taxable income if the taxpayer itemizes deductions. Amounts paid for real estate taxes and mortgage interest are itemized deductions that reduce taxable income. Interest on a home-equity loan of up to $100,000 is also an itemized deduction.

Tax-Exempt Investments Interest income from municipal bonds, issued by state and local governments, and other tax-exempt investments is not subject to federal income tax.

Tax-Deferred Investments Income from tax-deferred investments has the advantage of lowering current taxes. A common tax strategy for working people is the use of tax-deferred retirement plans to reduce their current taxes. These investment programs include:

- Traditional IRA
- Roth IRA
- SEP retirement plan
- SIMPLE retirement plan
- Keogh plan
- 401(k) plan

Investors need to understand the eligibility requirements and the tax advantages of investment programs before making any investment.

GLOSSARY

A

Ability the quality of being able to perform a mental or physical task.

Absolute advantage when a country can produce a good or service at a lower cost than other countries.

Accountability taking responsibility for the results achieved.

Accounts payable record a financial document that identifies the companies from which credit purchases were made and the amount purchased, paid, and owed.

Accounts receivable record a financial document that identifies customers that made purchases using credit and the status of each account.

Adjustable-rate mortgage (ARM) a mortgage in which the interest rate is raised or lowered from time to time depending on the current interest rate being charged by lenders.

Advertising any paid form of communication through mass media directed at identified consumers to provide information and influence their actions.

Agricultural products crops and animals raised by farmers.

AI. See **Artificial intelligence**

Allowance the amount of money you plan to use for a certain budget category.

All-risk policy. See **Special form**

Annual percentage rate (APR) the percentage cost of credit on a yearly basis.

Annual percentage yield (APY) the percentage rate equal to the total amount of interest that a $100 deposit would earn based on a 365-day period.

Annuity an amount of money an insurance company pays (usually monthly) to a person who has previously deposited money with the company.

Antitrust laws laws that prevent monopolies and promote competition and fairness.

Application form a form asking for information related to employment. It gives the employer standard information about each job applicant.

Application software programs that perform specific tasks such as word processing, database management, or accounting.

Applied research marketing research that studies existing products to develop design improvements or new product uses.

Appraiser someone trained to estimate the value of property and who can give an official report on the value.

Appreciation a general increase in the value of property that occurs over time.

APR. See **Annual percentage rate**

APY. See **Annual percentage yield**

Arbitration a third-party action resulting in a decision that is legally binding.

ARM. See **Adjustable-rate mortgage**

Articles of incorporation a written legal document that defines ownership and operating procedures and conditions for the business.

Artificial intelligence (AI) software that enables computers to reason, learn, and make decisions. It uses logical methods similar to the methods of human use.

Assessed value the amount that your local government determines your property to be worth for tax purposes.

Asset record a financial document used to name the buildings and equipment owned by the business, their original and current value, and the amount owed if money was borrowed to purchase the assets.

Assets what a company owns; anything of value owned by a business.

Assigned risk plan a plan in which every automobile insurance company in the state is assigned a certain number of high-risk drivers, based on the amount of insurance each company sells.

Audio output processing results involving music and broadcast clips as well as presentations for training seminars.

Authority the right to make decisions about how responsibilities should be accomplished.

Automatic bill payment requires a bank customer to authorize preset amounts of monthly expenses. The bank deducts the payment from your account and transfers them to the appropriate companies.

Balance of payments the difference between the amount of money that comes into a country and the amount that goes out of a country.

Balance of trade the difference between a country's total exports and total imports.

Balance sheet a report that lists a company's assets, liabilities, and owner's equity.

Bank money order a form sold by a bank stating that money is to be paid to a specific person or business.

Bank reconciliation the document created to show how your own record of your checking account and the bank's record of your account were brought into agreement.

Bank statement a report on the status of a bank account.

Bankruptcy the legal process of reducing or eliminating an amount owed.

Base plus incentive a compensation system which combines a wage or salary with an additional amount based on the employee's performance.

Basic economic problem the mismatch of unlimited wants and needs and limited economic resources.

Basic form a form of a homeowners policy that insures property against the basic perils.

Basic health coverage protection provided by regular medical, hospital, and surgical insurance.

Basic product the simplest form of a product. It is not unique and is usually available from several companies.

Behavioral interviewing an interview that evaluates an applicant's on-the-job potential. Questions typically begin with "describe" or "tell me about …".

Benchmark the best practices among all competitors.

Beneficiary the person named in the policy to receive the insurance benefits.

Benefits compensation in forms other than direct payment.

Blank endorsement an endorsement that consists of only the endorser's name.

Blue-collar workers workers who are employed in factories, on construction sites, and on farms.

Board of directors the people who make the major policy and financial decisions for the business.

Bodily injury liability insurance that protects a driver from claims resulting from injuries or deaths for which the insured is at fault.

Bond a certificate representing a promise to pay a definite amount of money at a stated interest rate on a specified due date.

Brand a name given to a product or service to distinguish it from other similar and competitive items.

Brand name a unique identification for a company's products.

Broad form a form of a homeowners policy that insures property against 18 different risks.

Budget detailed plans for the financial needs of individuals, families, and businesses.

Budget charge account a credit agreement that requires a customer to make payments of a fixed amount over several months.

Budget deficit occurs when a government spends more than it takes in.

Budget surplus occurs when a government spends less than it takes in.

Budget variance any difference between actual spending and budgeted amounts.

Business consumers persons, companies, and organizations that buy products for the operation of a business, for incorporation into other products and services, or for resale to their customers.

Business cycle the movement of the economy from one condition to another and back again. It has four cycles including prosperity, recession, depression, and recovery.

Business ethics rules about how businesses and their employees ought to behave.

Business interruption insurance compensation for ongoing business expenses that occur if a business has a temporary shutdown due to a fire, flood, or other major problem.

Business plan a written description of the business idea and how it will be carried out, including all major business activities.

Buying motives the reasons consumers decide what products and services to purchase.

Cafeteria plan employee benefit program that allocates a certain amount of money to each employee that can be spent on benefits.

CAI. See **Computer-assisted instruction**

Capacity refers to a person's ability to pay a debt when it is due.

Capital the value of the borrower's possessions, including money and the property owned.

Capital gain the result of a stock increase in value and then being sold for more than its original cost.

Capital loss the result of an investment that is sold for less than its original cost.

Capital projects spending by businesses for items such as land, buildings, equipment, and new products.

Capital resources the products and money used to produce goods and services.

Capitalism the private ownership of resources by individuals, rather than by the government.

Career a goal for work that is fulfilled through an occupation or series of occupations.

Career planning the process of studying careers, assessing yourself in terms of careers, and making decisions about a future career.

Career portfolio tangible evidence of your ability and skills.

Cash budget an estimate of the actual money received and paid out for a specific period of time.

Cash flow statement a report of net wages and other income along with spending for a period, such as for a month.

Cash inflow the money you have available to spend as a result of working or from other income, such as interest earned on your savings.

Cash machine an automated teller machine (ATM) that allows many bank services.

Cash outflow amounts spent for food, clothing, transportation, and other living costs.

Cash record a financial document that lists all cash received and spent by the business.

Cash value the amount of money that the insurance company will pay if the policyholder decides the insurance is no longer needed.

Cashier's check a check that a bank draws on its own funds. It costs the amount of the check plus a service fee.

Central processing unit (CPU) the control center of the computer.

Certificate of deposit a savings instrument that requires a minimum deposit for a specified period of time.

Certificate of deposit rate the rate for six-month time deposits at savings institutions.

Certified check a personal check for which a bank has guaranteed payment.

Channel members the businesses that take part in a channel of distribution.

Channel of distribution the route a product follows and the businesses involved in moving a product from the producer to the final consumer.

Character refers to a person's honesty and willingness to pay a debt when it is due.

Check cards. See **Debit cards**

Check register a separate book, usually the same size as the checkbook, for recording account activities.

Check stub a form attached to the check by a perforated line.

Claim a policyholder's request for payment for a loss that the insurance policy covers.

Class action suit a legal action by one party on behalf of a group of people who all have the same grievance.

Clearance sale sales used to clear merchandise that stores no longer wish to carry.

Clearing refers to the paying of checks among different banks in different cities.

Co-branded accounts company credit cards that are affiliated with bank card companies.

Code of ethics a set of rules for guiding the action of employees or members of an organization.

Coinsurance the sharing of expenses by the policyholder and the insurance company.

Collaboration software (groupware) software that provides real-time communications capabilities by voice, text, and video. It also allows team members working at their own computers from anywhere in the world to view the same documents on their computer screens and work on them as a team.

Collateral property that is used as security, giving the lender the right to sell this property to get back the amount of the loan if it is not repaid.

Collectibles items of personal interest to collectors that can increase in value in the future.

Collective bargaining formal negotiation between members of unions and management to resolve issues.

Collision coverage insurance that protects a car owner against financial loss resulting from a collision or rollover.

Command economy an economy in which resources are owned and controlled by the government.

Commercial bank the most common way for a bank to be organized. They offer checking accounts, provide savings accounts, make loans to individual and to businesses, and offer other services.

Commercial property insurance coverage of property losses resulting from fire, storms, accidents, theft, and vandalism.

Commission the amount of money an employee is paid based on a percentage of sales for which he or she is responsible; the fee stockbrokers charge for their services.

Commodities grain, livestock, and precious metals.

Common market (economic community) a market in which members do away with duties and other trade barriers.

Common stock stock that represents general ownership in a corporation and a right to share in its profits.

Communication channel the way the information being communicated from a sender is being transmitted to the receiver.

Comparative advantage a situation in which a country specializes in the production of a good or service at which it is relatively more efficient.

Compensation the amount of money paid to an employee for work performed, including salary and wages.

Compensation and benefits planning and managing payroll, personnel records, and benefits programs.

Competition the rivalry among businesses to sell their goods and services.

Competitors businesses offering very similar products to the same customers.

Compound interest interest computed on the amount saved plus the interest previously earned.

Comprehensive coverage insurance that protects the insured against almost all damage losses except those caused from a collision or rollover.

Comprehensive medical policy a policy that combines the features of hospital, surgical, regular, and major medical insurance.

Computer language a system of letters, words, numbers, and symbols used to communicate with a computer.

Computer literacy the ability to use computers to process information or solve problems.

Computer network a group of computers such as those in businesses and schools that are linked together so users can share hardware, software, and data.

Computer system all functional components of a computer, including an input device, processing unit, memory and storage, and an output device.

Computer virus a program code hidden in a system that can later do damage to software or stored data.

Computer-aided design the use of technology to create product styles and designs.

Computer-assisted instruction (CAI) the use of computers to help people learn or improve skills at their own pace.

Conditions of work clauses related to employee well-being while on the job that are often included in labor contracts and company policy manuals.

Condominium (condo) an individually owned housing unit in an apartment-like complex.

Conflict of interest occurs when an action by a company or individual results in an unfair benefit.

Conservation saving scarce natural resources.

Consumer a person who buys and uses goods and services.

Consumer Credit Reporting Reform Act a law that places the burden of proof for accurate credit information on the credit reporting agency rather than on the debtor.

Consumer decision-making process the specific sequence of steps consumers follow to make a purchase.

Consumer movement consumers united to demand fair treatment from businesses and to fight against unfair business practices.

Contingent worker one who has no explicit or implicit contract for long-term employment.

Continuous Process Improvement (CPI) a way to make sure manufacturing processes are completed as effectively as possible. It increases the quality of work by reducing errors, inefficiencies, and waste. Rather than waiting for a problem to occur, processes are continuously reviewed with the goal of finding ways to improve them.

Continuous processing changing the form of raw materials into a specific product useable for consumption or for further manufacturing by constantly moving the materials through specially designed equipment.

Contract an agreement to exchange goods or services for something of value, usually money.

Controllable risk a risk that you can reduce or eliminate by actions you take.

Controlling determines to what extent the business is accomplishing the goals it set out to reach in the planning stage.

Convenience stores small stores that emphasize the sale of food items, an accessible location, and long operating hours.

Cooperative a business formed to market products produced by members or to purchase products needed by the members. It is owned by members, serves their needs, and is managed in their interest.

Copyright protection of the creative work of authors, composers, and artists. Protection lasts for the life of the person receiving the copyright and extends for 70 years after the person's death.

Core values the important principles that guide decisions and actions in the company.

Corporate bond rate the cost of borrowing for large U.S. corporations.

Corporate bonds bonds issued by corporations.

Corporate bylaws operating procedures for the corporation.

Corporation a separate legal entity formed by documents filed with a state. It is owned by one or more shareholders and managed by a board of directors.

Cosigner the party responsible for payment of a note if the borrower does not pay as promised.

Cost containment keeping costs down.

Counterfeiting illegal uses of intellectual property, patents, trademarks, and copyrights.

Cover letter a letter expressing your interest in a specific job.

Credit the privilege of using someone else's money for a period of time.

Credit application a form on which you provide information needed by a lender to make a decision about granting credit.

Credit bureau a company that gathers information on credit users and sells that information to businesses offering credit.

Credit counselor a person who suggests actions to reduce spending and eliminate credit difficulties.

Credit limit a maximum amount that may be owed at one time.

Credit rating a person's reputation for paying bills on time.

Credit references businesses or individuals who are able and willing to provide information about your creditworthiness.

Credit report a document that shows the debts a person owes, how often credit is used, and whether he or she pays debts on time.

Credit union a user-owned, not-for-profit, cooperative financial institution.

Creditor one who sells on credit or makes a loan; the purchaser of a corporate or government bond.

Culture the accepted behaviors, customs, and values of a society.

Current assets cash and those items that can be readily converted to cash such as inventory and accounts receivable.

Current income income for current living expenses.

Current liabilities amounts owed by the business that will be paid within a year.

Current ratio current assets compared to the current liabilities.

Custom manufacturing building a specific and unique product to meet the needs of one customer.

D

Database marketing using information about customers to increase sales.

Database software software that allows you to maintain, analyze, and combine a collection of information.

Debit card (cash card) a bank-issued card used for ATM transactions.

Debt collection agency a company that attempts to obtain money that is past due.

Debt repayment plan an agreement between a creditor and a debtor to reduce payments to a more manageable level and still pay off the debt.

Debt to equity ratio the company's liabilities divided by the owners' equity.

Debtor anyone who buys on credit or receives a loan.

Decoding interpretating information for understanding.

Decreasing term insurance the amount of protection gradually becomes smaller, but premiums remain the same while the insurance is in effect.

Deductible the amount the insured must pay before the insurance company pays a claim.

Deficit when actual spending is greater than planned spending.

Deflation a decrease in the general level of prices.

Demand the quantity of a good or service that consumers are willing and able to buy.

Demand curve the graphic view of the demand for a product or service. The demand curve for a product, for example, illustrates the relationship between the price of the product and the quantity demanded by consumers.

Department stores stores that have an extensive product line and emphasize service.

Dependent a person who must rely on another for financial support.

Depository institution financial institution that accepts deposits from individuals and businesses and uses the money to finance its business.

Depreciation the decrease in value of a property as it becomes old and gradually wears out.

Depreciation record a financial document used to identify the amount assets have decreased in value due to their age and use.

Depression the phase of the business cycle that is marked by a prolonged period of high unemployment, weak consumer sales, and business failures.

Direct channel of distribution a channel in which products move from the producer straight to the consumer with no other organizations participating.

Direct deposit funds are deposited electronically and available automatically for your use.

Disability income insurance insurance that replaces income that is lost when you cannot work because of an illness or injury.

Discharge a type of termination that ends employment due to inappropriate work behavior.

Discount broker a stockbroker who places orders and offers limited research and other services.

Discount rate the rate financial institutions are charged to borrow funds from the Federal Reserve banks.

Discount stores stores that emphasize lower prices on their products.

Discounting the process in which savings bonds pay interest.

Discrepancies differences between actual and budgeted performance.

Displaced workers workers who are unemployed because of changing job conditions.

Distribution the locations and methods used to make a product or service available to the target market; determining the best ways for customers to locate, obtain, and use the products and services of an organization.

Diversity the comprehensive inclusion of people with differences in personal characteristics and attributes.

Dividends payments of profits in cash to stockholders.

Domestic business the making, buying, and selling of goods and services within a country.

Down payment a payment of part of the purchase price that is made as part of a credit agreement.

Downsizing a planned reduction in the number of employees needed in a firm in order to reduce costs and make the business more efficient.

Drawee the bank or other financial institution that pays the check.

Drawer the owner of the account who signs the check.

E

Earnings report a report, usually included with the employee's paycheck, that includes information for the current pay period as well as the cumulative amounts for the year.

E-commerce conducting business transactions using the Internet or other technology.

Economic decision-making the process of choosing which wants, among several options, will be satisfied.

Economic resources the means through which goods and services are produced.

Economic risk a risk that can result in financial loss, including personal risk, property risk, and liability risk.

Economic system a nation's plan for answering the three economic questions.

Effective communication the exchange of information so there is common understanding by all participants.

EFT. See **Electronic funds transfer**

Electronic funds transfer (EFT) refers to the use of computers and other technology for banking activities, including the use of automated teller machines (ATM), point-of-sale transactions, direct deposit, and automatic bill payment.

Embargo an action imposed by the government to stop the export or import of a product completely.

E-money a medium of exchange for online transactions.

Emotional buying motives reasons consumers decide what products and services to purchase based on feelings, beliefs, and attitudes.

Employee benefits compensation in forms other than direct payment such as vacation time, insurance coverage, and retirement programs.

Employee relations responsible for maintaining a safe, healthy, and productive work environment for all employees.

Employment interview a two-way conversation in which the interviewer learns about you and you learn about the job and the company.

Encoding preparing the information to be communicated.

Endorsement written evidence that a person received payment or transferred the right to receive payment to someone else.

Entrepreneur someone who takes a risk in starting a business to earn a profit.

Entrepreneurship the process of starting, organizing, managing, and assuming the responsibility for a business.

Equal Credit Opportunity Act a law that prohibits creditors from denying a person credit because of age, race, gender, or marital status.

Equity stock ownership; the difference between the price at which you could currently sell your house and the amount owed on the mortgage.

Estate planning a plan that involves the accumulation and management of property during one's lifetime and the distribution of one's property at death.

Ethical business practices practices that ensure the highest standards of conduct are observed in a company's relationships with everyone who is a part of the business or affected by the business' activities.

Ethics principles of morality or rules of conduct.

Exchange rate the value of a currency in one country compared with the value in another.

Executives top-level managers with responsibilities for the direction and success of the entire business.

Exit interview an interview in which your employer asks questions about your work upon your leaving the company.

Expenses costs of operating a business.

Experienced-based resume a resume in which experiences are usually listed in order of work history.

Experiment a method of marketing research which presents two carefully controlled alternatives to subjects in order to determine which is preferred or has better results.

Expert influence influence that arises when group members recognize that the leader has special expertise in the area.

Expert systems computer programs that help people solve technical problems.

Exports goods and services sold to other countries.

Express money order a form issued by various organizations including traveler's check companies, travel agencies, and many supermarkets, pharmacies, and convenience stores.

Express warranty a warranty that is made orally or in writing and promises a specific quality of performance.

External communications communications that occur between those inside the organization and outsiders such as customers, suppliers, and other businesses.

External data sources input provided to the management information system from outside an organization, such as financial institutions, government agencies, and customers.

Extraction and cultivation a form of production in which products are obtained from nature or grown using natural resources.

Extractor a business that takes resources from nature for direct consumption or for use in developing other products.

F

Face value the amount of insurance coverage that was originally purchased and that will be paid upon the death of the insured.

Factors of production economic resources, including natural resources, human resources, and capital resources.

Fair Credit Billing Act a law that requires prompt correction of billing mistakes.

Fair Credit Reporting Act a law that gives consumers the right to know what information credit bureaus are giving to potential creditors, employers, and insurers.

Fair Debt Collection Practices Act a law requiring that debt collectors treat you fairly. It bans various debt collection actions.

Family leave a policy that allows employees to take a leave of absence for the birth or adoption of a child, to care for a sick family member, or for other personal emergencies.

Farmers people who cultivate land and use other natural resources to grow crops and raise livestock for consumption.

Federal Deposit Insurance Corporation (FDIC) the federal agency that helps to regulate banks and other financial institutions.

Federal Reserve System (Fed) a system set up by the federal government to supervise and regulate member banks and to help banks serve the public efficiently. All national banks are required to join the Federal Reserve System, and state banks may join.

Feedback a response to the sender from the receiver.

Final consumers persons who buy products and services mostly for their own use.

Finance charge the total dollar cost of credit including interest and all other charges.

Financial analysis budgeting for marketing activities, obtaining the necessary funds needed for operations, and providing financial assistance to customers so they can purchase the business' products and services.

Financial performance ratios comparisons of a company's financial elements that indicate how well the business is performing.

Financial plan a report that summarizes your current financial condition, acknowledges your financial needs, and sets a direction for your future financial activities.

Financial records financial documents that are used to record and analyze the financial performance of a business.

Financial responsibility law a law that protects the public from financial loss caused by drivers.

Financial statements reports that sum up the financial performance of a business.

Fixed expenses costs that occur on a regular basis and are for the same amount each time.

Fixed-rate mortgage interest rates on mortgages that are set for the term of the loan.

Flexspace allows some employees to complete part or all of their work away from the business site.

Flextime allows employees some choice in how their work days and work hours are arranged.

Focus groups a marketing research study that gathers the ideas, experiences, and opinions from a small number of consumers who take part in a group discussion.

Foreign debt the amount a country owes to other countries.

Foreign exchange market banks that buy and sell different currencies.

Foreign trade. See **International business**

Formal communications communication methods that have been established and approved by the organization.

Formal influence a leadership role that is part of the organization's structure.

Franchise a written contract granting permission to operate a business to sell products and services in a set way.

Franchisee the company purchasing the rights to run the business.

Franchiser the company that owns the product or service and grants the rights to another business.

Fraud deception of consumers by providing false information in an effort to make a sale.

Freedom of choice the freedom to make decisions independently while accepting the consequences of those decisions.

Free-trade agreement an agreement between member countries to remove duties and trade barriers on products traded among them.

Free-trade zone a selected area where products can be imported duty-free and then stored, assembled, and/or used in manufacturing.

Full endorsement (special endorsement) an endorsement that allows you to transfer a check to another person.

Full-service broker a broker who provides information about securities you may want to buy. They work for brokerage houses with large research staffs.

Full-time employee one who regularly works a schedule of 30 hours or more a week.

Futures contract agreement to buy or sell an amount of a commodity at a specified price in the future; contract involving the buying and selling of currencies and financial instruments.

G

GDP per capita the output per person, calculated by dividing gross domestic product (GDP) by the total production.

GDP. See **Gross domestic product**

Generic products unbranded items at reduced prices because they do not require advertising and fancy packaging.

Glass ceiling an artificial limit placed on minority groups moving into positions of authority and decision-making.

Global strategy a strategy that uses the same product and marketing strategy worldwide.

Goal a precise statement of results the business expects to achieve.

Goods things you can see and touch; they are products you can purchase to meet your wants and needs.

Goods-producing industries businesses that produce or manufacture products used by other businesses or purchased by final consumers.

Graphics output includes processing results such as company logos, photos, drawings, scrolling messages, and animated graphics.

Green management facilities management using the practice of protecting the environment through conservation of natural resources, wise energy use, and reduction of emissions, waste, and pollution.

Gross domestic product (GDP) the total dollar value of all final goods and services produced in a country during one year.

Gross margin the difference between the selling price and the product costs.

Group insurance health insurance coverage offered to a large number of employees and their family members.

Group life insurance an insurance policy that covers a group of people. The group acts as single unit in buying the insurance.

Guarantee a promise by the manufacturer or dealer, usually in writing, that a product is of a certain quality.

H

Hardware the physical elements of a computer system.

Health insurance protection against the high costs of individual health care. It covers routine costs of medical care and may also cover costs of hospitalization or other needed medical treatments.

Health maintenance organization (HMO) a managed care plan whose members are entitled to a wide range of prepaid health care services, including hospitalization.

Heterogeneous characterized by the differences in the type and quality of service provided.

HMO. See **Health maintenance organization**

Homeowners policy a package-type insurance policy designed to insure homes and property.

Horizontal communications communications that move across the organization at the same level—employee to employee or manager to manager.

Hospital insurance insurance that usually pays most or all hospital charges if an illness or injury requires the insured to be hospitalized.

Host country the country in which the multinational company (MNC) places business activities.

Human relations the way people get along with each other.

Human resources people producing goods and services; people who work for a business.

I

I bond a bond that pays an interest rate that is lower than the rate of other savings bonds, but it is a variable rate that increases with inflation.

Identity influence influence that stems from the personal trust and respect members have for the leader.

Identity theft stealing information about a person from online sources to obtain money.

Implementing a manager's effort to direct and lead people to accomplish the planned work of the organization.

Implied warranty a guarantee imposed by law and is understood to apply even though it has not been written or stated.

Imports goods and services bought from other countries.

Improvement a designed change that increases the usefulness of a product, service, or process.

Impulse buying the opposite of spending time and effort is buying too quickly.

Incentive systems compensation systems connected to the quality or quantity of an employee's performance.

Income statement a report of revenue, expenses, and net income or loss from operations for a specific period.

Income tax taxes levied on the income of individuals.

Indirect channel of distribution a channel in which products move from the producer to the consumer through one or more other businesses.

Individual retirement account (IRA) a tax-sheltered retirement plan in which people can annually invest earnings up to a certain amount.

Inflation an increase in the general level of prices.

Influence power enabling a person to affect the actions of others.

Informal communications common but unofficial ways that information moves in an organization.

Informal influence a leadership role that is not part of a formal structure.

Information management using technology to access and exchange information to complete the work of an organization.

Informational interview a planned discussion with a worker who is willing to help you find out about the work that a person does, the preparation needed for that career, and the person's feelings about the career.

Infrastructure a factor that supports international trade in industrialized countries, including a nation's transportation, communication, and utility systems.

Innovation an invention or creation that is brand new.

Inseparable something that is consumed at the same time it is produced.

Installment loan a loan in which you agree to make monthly payments in specific amounts over a period of time.

Installment sales credit a type of credit contract issued by the seller that requires periodic payments at specified times. The seller adds finance charges to the cost of the items purchased.

Installments a specified amount a borrower agrees to repay for a loan.

Insurable interest a financial benefit from an insured person's continued life.

Insurable risk when a large number of people face a given risk and the cost of the possible losses can be predicted.

Insurance a form of risk protection that exchanges the uncertainty of a possible large financial loss for a certain smaller payment.

Insurance agent an agent who represents the insurance company and sells insurance policies to individuals and businesses.

Insurance policy a policy stating the conditions to which the insurance company and the policy-holder have agreed.

Insured the person or business for which the insurer assumes the risk.

Insurer a company that agrees to take on certain economic risks and to pay for losses if they occur.

Intangible something that has no physical form.

Intellectual property technical knowledge or creative work. It includes software, clothing designs, music, books, and movies.

Interest the money you receive for letting others use your money; the money you pay for using someone else's money.

Interest rates the cost of using someone else's money.

Interests activities that give you satisfaction and that can provide a basis for your employment goals and possible career paths.

Intermediaries businesses involved in selling the goods and services of producers to consumers and other businesses.

Intermittent processing using short production runs to produce a precise amount of a variation of a product.

Internal communications communications that occur between managers, employees, and work groups.

Internal data sources input provided to the management information system from within the organization, such as accounting records, inventory information, and company sales figures.

International business business activities needed for creating, shipping, and selling goods and services across national borders.

Internships the involvement of work experience in organizations while learning about a career field.

Interstate commerce business dealings involving companies in more than one state.

Intranet a local computer network based on the same communication standards as the Internet. It looks like and functions just like a typical web site, but it is private and only accessible to authorized users.

Intrastate commerce business dealings involving companies that do business in only one state.

Inventory a detailed account of a company's materials, supplies, and finished products.

Inventory management maintains the supply of all resources needed for production and the products produced.

Inventory records a financial document used to identify the type and number of products on hand for sale.

Investing using your savings to earn more money.

IRA. See **Individual retirement account**

J

Job analysis a specific study of a job to identify in detail the job duties and skill requirements.

Job shadow spending time with a worker for a day or a week to learn about that person's occupation.

Job sharing an arrangement in which one job is offered to two people. Each person works a part-time schedule. They share the work space and duties of the job.

Joint account when two or more people have an account together.

Joint venture a unique business organized by two or more other businesses to operate for a limited time and for a specific project. It is a type of partnership.

Just-in-time a logistics process in which goods arrive when needed for production, use, or sale rather than sitting in storage.

L

Labor union an organized group of employees who negotiate with employers about issues, such as wages and working conditions.

Layoff a type of termination which is a temporary or permanent reduction in the number of employees due to changing business conditions.

Leadership the ability to motivate individuals and groups to accomplish important goals.

Level term insurance the amount of protection and the premiums remain the same while the insurance is in effect.

Liabilities what a company owes.

Liability insurance protection against losses from injury to people or property resulting from the products, services, or actions of a business.

Liability risk a risk that relates to harm or injury to other people or their property because of your actions.

Licensing selling the right to use some intangible property (production process, trademark, or brand name) for a fee or royalty.

Life cycle when each stage of life is distinguished by unique characteristics, requirements, and expectations.

Life insurance insurance that pays the amount of the insurance policy upon the death of the insured. The payment is made to people named in the policy known as beneficiaries.

Light pens handheld input devices that detect the presence of light.

Limited liability company provides liability protection for owners. It has a simpler set of organizing and operating requirements than a corporation. No articles of incorporation or bylaws are needed. A simple document much like a partnership agreement must be developed.

Limited liability partnership a partnership that identifies some investors who cannot lose more than the amount of their investment, but they are not allowed to participate in the day-to-day management of the business.

Limited-payment policies a whole life insurance policy that is designated by the number of years the policyholder agrees to pay on it, such as a 20-payment life policy.

Liquidity the ease with which an investment can be changed into cash without losing its value.

Loan credit borrowed money for special use. It usually involves a written contract.

Locational unemployment occurs when jobs are available in one place but go unfilled because those who are qualified to fill those jobs live elsewhere and are not willing to relocate.

Logistics managing the acquisition, movement, and storage of supplies, materials, and finished products in a business.

Long-term assets (fixed assets) the assets with a lifespan of more than a year, such as land, buildings, equipment, and expensive technology.

Long-term care insurance insurance that provides long-term care including daily assistance needed because of a long-term illness or disability.

Long-term financing the money needed for the main resources of a business (such as land, buildings, and equipment) that will last for many years.

Long-term liabilities business debts that will continue for longer than a year.

M

Mail order catalogs catalogs whereby customers can shop and send in their orders by mail and by telephone.

Major medical insurance protection against the high costs of serious illness or injuries. It complements other forms of medical insurance.

Management the process of accomplishing the goals of an organization through the effective use of people and other resources.

Management information system (MIS) a coordinated system of processing and reporting information in an organization.

Management style the way a manager treats and involves employees.

Manufacturers businesses who get supplies from other producers and convert them into products. They sell their products to consumers and other businesses.

Manufacturing combining raw materials and processed goods into finished products.

Markdown a reduction from the original selling price.

Market economy an economy in which the resources are owned and controlled by the people of the country.

Market price the point where supply and demand are equal.

Market value the price at which a share of stock can be bought and sold in the stock market.

Marketing an organizational function and a set of processes for creating, communicating, and delivering value to customers and for managing customer relationships in ways that benefit the organization and its stakeholders.

Marketing mix the blending of four marketing elements—products, distribution, price, and promotion.

Marketing orientation an approach that considers the needs of customers when developing a marketing mix.

Marketing research finding solutions to problems through carefully designed studies involving customers.

Marketing strategy a company's plan that identifies how it will use marketing to achieve its goals.

Marketing-information management obtaining, managing, and using market information to improve business decision-making and the performance of marketing activities.

Marketplace anywhere that goods and services are exchanged.

Markup the amount added to the cost of a product to set the selling price.

Mass production an assembly process that makes a large number of identical products using a continuous efficient procedure.

Mass promotion communication to many people at the same time with a common message.

Materials processing changing the form of raw materials so they can be consumed or used to make other products.

Maturity date the date on which a loan must be repaid.

Maturity value (face value) the amount being borrowed by the corporation issuing the bond.

Mediation involves the use of a third party who tries to resolve the complaint between the consumer and the business.

Medicaid a form of medical aid to low-income individuals and families administered by state governments. The federal government shares the cost of providing health benefits to eligible individuals and families.

Medical payments insurance that covers policy-holders and family members if they are injured while riding in their car or another car.

Medicare a national health insurance program for people aged 65 and older and some disabled people.

Memory a component of a computer system that stores a computer program.

Mentor an experienced employee or "career coach" who serves as counselor to a person with less experience.

Microphones and cameras input devices that allow input of audio and video.

Mid-managers specialists with responsibilities for specific parts of a company's operations.

MIS. See **Management information system**

Mission statement a short, specific written statement of the reason a business exists and what it wants to achieve.

Mixed economy an economy that combines elements of the command and market economies.

Mixed management the combine use of tactical and strategic management styles.

MNC. See **Multinational company**

Mobility the willingness and ability of a person to move to where jobs are located.

Money management the day-to-day financial activities associated with using limited income to satisfy your unlimited needs and wants.

Money market account an account that pays a variable interest rate based on various government and corporate securities.

Money order a form of payment that orders the issuing agency to pay the amount printed on the form to another party.

Monopoly when a business has control of the market for a product or service.

Mortgage a legal document giving the lender a claim against the property if the principal, interest, or both are not paid as agreed.

Mortgage rate the amount individuals pay to borrow for the purchase of a home.

Multinational company (MNC) an organization that does business in several countries. It usually consists of a home country and divisions or separate companies in one or more host countries.

Multinational strategy a strategy that treats each country market differently. Firms develop products and marketing strategies that adapt to the customs, tastes, and buying habits of a distinct national market.

Municipal bonds bonds issued by local and state governments.

Mutual fund an investment fund set up and managed by companies that receive money from many investors.

Mutual savings bank a savings bank that is owned by, and operated for the benefit of, its depositors.

N

National brands brands that are advertised all over the country.

National debt the total amount owed by the federal government.

Natural resources raw materials supplied by nature.

Needs things that are required in order to live.

Negative or unfavorable balance of payments the result of a country sending more money out than it brings in.

Net income occurs when revenue is greater than expenses.

Net income ratio the total sales compared to the net income for a period such as six months or a year.

Net loss occurs when expenses are greater than income.

Net pay the amount of a paycheck after taxes and other payroll deductions; take-home pay.

Net worth the difference between a person's assets and liabilities.

Networking the process of talking to other people about their jobs.

No-fault insurance insurance allowing people who are injured in an automobile accident to collect for their financial losses from their own insurance companies no matter who is at fault. Those losses include their medical bills, loss of wages, and other related expenses.

Non-depository intermediaries a category of financial institutions that does not take or help deposits. They earn their money selling specific services or policies.

Nonprofit corporation a group of people who join to do some activity that benefits the public.

Non-renewable resource a natural resource that cannot be replaced when used up.

O

Observations a marketing research study that collects information by recording the actions of consumers rather than asking them questions.

Occupation a task or series of tasks that is performed to provide a good or service. People are hired to fill occupations, and they are paid for the work they perform.

Operating budget describes the financial plan for ongoing operations of the business for a specific period of time.

Operating expenses all of the expenses of operating the business that are associated with the product.

Operating system software a computer program that translates commands and allows application programs to interact with the computer's hardware.

Operational plan identifies how work will be done, who will do it, and what resources will be needed.

Opportunity cost the value of the next-best alternative that you did not choose.

Options choices of product features.

Oral communications communications that are spoken.

Ordinary life policy a type of whole life insurance in which premiums remain the same each year as long as the policyholder lives.

Organization chart a diagram that shows the structure of an organization, classifications of work and jobs, and the relationships among those classifications.

Organizational culture the environment in which people work, made up of the atmosphere, behaviors, beliefs, and relationships.

Organizing the function of a manager involving identifying and arranging the work and resources needed to achieve the goals that have been set.

Output a component of a computer system that presents data in a form that can be retrieved later or may be communicated immediately.

Outsourcing removing work from one company and sending it to another company that can complete it at a lower cost.

Outstanding checks checks that have not been deducted from the bank statement balance.

Over-the-counter (OTC) market a network where securities transactions occur using telephones and computers rather than on an exchange.

Owner's equity the value of the business after liabilities are subtracted from assets; the value of the owner's investment in the business.

P

Packaging protection and security for the product before it is used.

Partnership a business owned and controlled by two or more people who have entered into a written agreement.

Partnership agreement a written agreement among all owners detailing the rules and procedures that guide ownership and operations.

Part-time employee one who works a schedule with either fewer hours each day or fewer than 30 hours each week.

Patent the exclusive right of an inventor to make, sell, and use a product or process.

Payee the person to whom the check is written.

Payroll the financial record of employee compensation, deductions, and net pay.

Payroll record a financial document that contains information on all employees of the company, their compensation, and benefits.

Payroll taxes required federal and state payments for each employee, consisting of income taxes, Social Security, Medicare, and unemployment taxes.

Pension a series of regular payments made to a retired worker under an organized plan.

Performance management evaluating the work of employees and improving performance through training and development.

Perils the causes of loss, such as fire, wind, or theft.

Perishable the availability of a service to match the demand for that service at a specific time.

Permanent employee one to whom the company makes a long-term commitment. It is expected that the employee will work for the business as long as the business is profitable and the employee's performance is satisfactory.

Permanent life insurance life insurance that has cash value and an investment feature.

Personal assets items of value.

Personal data sheet a summary of your important job-related information.

Personal income salaries and wages as well as investment income and government payments to individuals.

Personal liability coverage insurance that covers claims for injuries to people or damage to property caused by you or your family.

Personal property property not attached to the land, such as furniture or clothing.

Personal risk a risk that can result in personal losses such as health and personal well-being.

Personal selling direct, individualized communication with prospective customers to assess their needs and assist them in satisfying those needs with appropriate products and services.

Personal time a few hours each month that can be scheduled for non-job activities.

Personalized promotion communication directly with each customer using information tailored to that person.

Piece rate a pay-for-performance plan in which an employee receives a specific amount for each unit of work produced.

Piracy stealing or illegally copying software packages or information.

Planning the function of a manager involving analyzing information, setting goals, and making decisions about what needs to be done.

Planning and staffing activities directed at identifying and filling all of the jobs in the company with qualified people.

Point-of-sale transaction a transaction in which a merchant accepts debit cards to pay for purchases.

Policies guidelines used in making consistent decisions.

Policyholder the person or company buying the policy.

Pollution occurs when the environment is tainted with the by-products of human actions.

Position influence the ability to get others to accomplish tasks because of the position the leader holds.

Positive or favorable balance of payments occurs when a nation receives more money in a year than it pays out.

Postal money order a form purchased from the U.S. Post Office that can be sent safely through the mail.

Postdated check a check that is dated later than the date on which it is written.

Preferred provider organization (PPO) a managed care plan that involves several health care providers, such as a group of physicians, a clinic, or a hospital.

Preferred stock stock that has priority over common stock in the payment of dividends.

Premium the amount a policyholder must pay for insurance coverage.

Presentation software a program that allows a speaker to show text, data, photos, and other visuals. The images may be accompanied by sound effects, music, or other audio.

Price money customer must pay for a product or service.

Price index a number that compares prices in one year with some earlier base year.

Price-earnings (P/E) ratio the relationship between a stock's selling price and its earnings per share.

Pricing setting and communicating the value of products and services.

Primary research studies carried out to gather new information specifically directed at a current problem.

Prime rate the rate banks make available to their best business customers, such as large corporations.

Procedure a list of steps to be followed for performing a particular work activity; a description of the way work is to be done.

Processed goods products that have been changed in form to increase their value and usefulness.

Processing changing and improving the form of another product.

Producers individuals and organizations that determine what products and services will be available for sale.

Product everything a business offers to satisfy a customer's needs.

 GLOSSARY

Product and service management designing, developing, maintaining, improving, and acquiring products and services that meet consumer needs.

Product costs costs to the manufacturer of producing the product or the price paid by other businesses to buy the product.

Product features additions and improvements to the basic product.

Production process the activities, equipment, and resources needed to manufacture a product.

Productivity the production output in relation to a unit of input, such as a worker.

Profit the amount of money available to the business after all costs and expenses have been paid.

Program a series of detailed, step-by-step instructions that tell the computer what functions to complete.

Promissory note a written promise to repay based on a debtor's excellent credit history.

Promotion any form of communication used to inform, persuade, or remind; communicating information about products and services to potential customers; the advancement of an employee to a position with greater responsibility.

Promotional sales sales used to promote the selling of regular merchandise with short-term price reductions.

Property damage liability insurance that protects a driver against claims if the insured's car damages someone else's property and the insured is a fault.

Property insurance insurance that protects you from the financial loss you would incur if some of your property were lost or destroyed due to fire, theft, vandalism, flood, or other hazard.

Property rights the exclusive rights to possess and use property and its profits.

Property risk a risk that can lead to loss of personal or business property including money, vehicles, and buildings.

Property tax a major source of revenue for local governments based on the value of land and buildings.

Proprietorship a business owned and run by just one person.

Prosperity the peak of the business cycle, it is a period in which most people who want to work are working, businesses produce goods and services in record numbers, wages are good, and the rate of gross domestic product (GDP) growth increases.

Public relations an ongoing program of non-paid and paid communications intended to favorably influence public opinion about an organization, marketing effort, idea, or issue.

Public utility an organization that supplies a service or product vital to all people including companies that provide local telephone service, water, and electricity.

Publicity non-paid promotional communication presented by the media rather than by the business or organization that is being promoted.

Pure research research done without a specific product in mind with the goal of discovering new solutions to problems.

Pure risk a risk that presents the chance of loss but no opportunity for gain.

Q

Qualifications-based resume a resume in which your abilities and experiences related to the job for which you are applying are highlighted.

Quota a government set limit on the quantity of a product that may be imported or exported within a given period.

R

Rational buying motives reasons consumers decide what products and services to purchase based on facts and logic.

Real estate land and anything that is attached to it.

Real property property permanently attached to land, such as a house or garage.

Receiver a person or organization that is being communicated to by another person or organization.

Recession the phase of the business cycle in which demand begins to decrease, businesses lower production, unemployment begins to rise, and gross domestic product (GDP) growth slows for two or more quarters of the calendar year.

Records of account a financial document used to identify all purchases and sales made using credit.

Recovery the welcome phase in the business cycle in which unemployment begins to decrease, demand for goods and services increases, and gross domestic product (GDP) begins to rise again.

References a list of people who can give a report about your character, education, and work habits. These individuals may be teachers, previous employers, supervisors, or coworkers.

Regular medical insurance insurance that covers fees for nonsurgical care given in the doctor's office, the patient's home, or a hospital. The policy states the amount payable for each visit or call. It also lists the maximum number of visits covered.

Renewable term insurance an insurance policy that allows the policyholder to continue term insurance for one or more terms without taking another physical examination.

Renters policy a property and liability insurance policy suitable for renters. It covers household goods and personal belongings and protect against the same kinds of perils covered by homeowners policies.

Replacement insurance insurance in which the insurance company actually replaces an item that have been destroyed. No depreciation is deducted.

Responsibility the obligation to complete specific work.

Restrictive endorsement an endorsement that limits the use of the check to the purpose given in the endorsement.

Resume a tool that provides information about you to a potential employer.

Retail sales the sales of durable and nondurable goods bought by consumers.

Retailers the final business organization in an indirect channel of distribution for consumer products.

Return on equity ratio the net profit of the business compared to the amount of owners' equity.

Revenue all income that a business receives over a period of time; government income.

Revolving account allows account holder to charge purchases at any time, but only part of the debt must be paid each month.

Reward influence influence that results from a leader's ability to give or withhold rewards.

Risk the possibility of incurring a loss.

Robotics mechanical devices programmed to do routine tasks, such as those in many factories.

S

Safe-deposit box a container for storage of valuables offered by banks.

Salary and wages direct payment of money to an employee for work completed.

Sales credit involves the use of charge accounts and credit cards by consumers purchasing goods and services.

Sales promotion activities and materials designed to reinforce a company's brand and image. It is also a direct incentive to take an action likely to immediately increase sales of a product or service.

Sales tax a state or local tax on goods and services that is collected by the seller.

Saving the storage of money for future use.

SBA. See **Small Business Administration**

Scanners input devices that translate words and photos into computer-readable formats.

Scarcity not having enough resources to satisfy every need.

Schedule a time plan for completing activities. It matches people with resources to make sure activities are finished on time.

S-corporation a corporate form of business that offers the limited liability of a corporation.

Secondary research analyzing existing information gathered for another purpose but used to solve a current problem.

Secured loan a loan in which you must put up property or collateral as security for repayment.

Selling communicating directly with potential customers to determine and satisfy their needs.

Selling price the price paid by the customer for the product.

Sender a person or organization that has information to communicate to another person or organization.

Service business a business that carries out activities that are consumed by its customers.

Service charge the fee a bank charges for handling a checking account.

Service fee a charge involving the time and money it takes a creditor to investigate your credit history, process your loan or charge account application, and keep records of your payments and balances.

Service-producing industries businesses that perform services that satisfy the needs of other businesses and consumers.

Services activities that are consumed at the same time they are produced.

Share draft a checking account at a credit union.

Shareholders members of credit unions.

Short-term financing the money needed to pay for the current operating activities of a business.

Signature card a document used to verify your signature.

Simple interest the interest on single-payment loans.

Single-payment loan a loan in which you do not pay anything until the end of the loan period, possibly 60 or 90 days. At that time, you pay the full amount you borrowed plus the finance charge.

Small business an independent business with fewer than 500 employees.

Small Business Administration (SBA) a government agency that helps small business owners develop business plans and obtain financing and other support for their companies.

Small claims court a court system in every state that exists to resolve cases involving small amounts.

Smart cards plastic cards with silicon chips that are used to store information. The chip within the card stores such data as a cardholder's current account balance, credit history, or medical information.

Social responsibility the duty of a business to contribute to the well-being of a community.

Software the instructions that run the computer system.

Span of control the number of employees who are assigned to a particular work task and manager.

Special checking account checking accounts for people who only write a few checks each month. Banks charge customers about 10 to 20 cents for each check written.

Special form a form of a homeowners policy that insures property against all perils except earthquakes, flood, war, nuclear accidents, and certain others.

Specialty stores stores that have a special line of products for sale.

Specialty superstores stores that offer low prices and a wide variety of a limited product line.

Speculative risk the chance either to gain or to lose.

Spreadsheet software a program that formats data in columns and rows in order to do calculations.

Staffing the function of a manager including all of the activities involved in obtaining, preparing, and compensating the employees of a business.

Standard a specific measurement against which an activity or result is judged

Start-up budget plans income and expenses from the beginning of a new business or a major business expansion until it becomes profitable.

Start-up financing the amount of money needed to open the business.

Statement of account a record of the transactions completed during the billing period.

Stock ownership in a corporation.

Stock exchange a business organization that accommodates the buying and selling of securities.

Stock index a measurement of investment values.

Stockbroker a licensed specialist in the buying and selling of stocks and bonds.

Stop payment order a written notice that tells the bank not to pay a certain check.

Store brands (private label brands) brands owned by stores. For example, Craftsman is one of the brand names on tools sold by Sears.

Straight salary a specific amount of money paid to an employee for each week or month worked.

Strategic management a style in which managers are less directive and involve employees in decision-making.

Substitute check a digital reproduction of the original paper check.

Supermarket in food retailing, it is the large, full-service store that carries name brands.

Superstores discount stores that have expanded to include a wide variety of food products. They may also include other retail services such as a bakery, restaurant, pharmacy, video rentals, and banking.

Supervisors the first level of management in a business, responsible for the work of a group of employees and some non-management duties.

Supply the quantity of a good or service that businesses are willing and able to provide.

Supply chain management software software that allows cooperating companies to share ordering, production, and shipping information.

Supply chain management. See **Logistics**

Supply curve the graphic view of the supply for a product or service. The supply curve for a product, for example, illustrates the relationship between the price of the product and the quantity businesses will supply.

Surgical insurance insurance that covers all or part of the surgeon's fees for an operation.

Surplus when actual spending is less than the budgeted amount.

Surveys a marketing research study that gathers information from people using a carefully planned set of questions.

T

Tactical management a style in which the manager is directive and controlling.

Take-home pay the amount of a paycheck after taxes and other payroll deductions.

Talent a natural, inborn aptitude to do certain things.

Target market a specific group of customers that have similar wants and needs.

Targeted application letter a letter that provides a quick summary of your ability to meet the needs of an organization. It usually includes a list of major skills and competencies.

Tariff a tax that a government places on certain imported products.

Tax record a financial document that shows all taxes collected, owed, and paid.

Tax-deferred earnings the investment earnings on a retirement plan that will be taxed later, after retirement.

Tax-exempt earnings earnings on which the recipient is not required to pay taxes.

T-bill rate the yield on short-term (13-week) U.S. government debt obligations.

T-bills. See **Treasury bills**

T-bonds. See **Treasury bonds**

Technology the use of automated machines, electronic equipment, and integrated computer systems to help increase the efficiency of producing goods and services.

Telecommuting allows employees who primarily use personal computers and other technology to work from home. They communicate with managers, coworkers, and customers using the Internet, telephone, and fax machines.

Temporary employee one hired for a specific time or to complete a specific assignment.

Tentative career decision a decision that is subject to change as new information is received.

Term life insurance insurance that provides financial protection from losses resulting from a death during a definite period or term.

Termination the end of an employment relationship between a company and an employee.

Text output includes processing results displayed on a computer screen (monitor) or in a printed report.

Time wage a specific amount of money paid to an employee for each hour worked.

TISA. See **Truth-in-Savings Act**

T-notes. See **Treasury notes**

Trade barriers restrictions to free trade.

Trade deficit a situation in which a country imports (buys) more than it exports (sells).

Trade surplus a situation in which a country exports (sells) more than it imports (buys).

Trademark a distinctive name, symbol, word, picture, or combination of these that a company uses to identify products or services.

Tradeoff what you make when you give something up to have something else.

Traditional economy an economy in which goods and services are produced the way they have always been produced. It is used in countries that are less developed and are not yet participating in the global economy.

Transfer the assignment of an employee to another job in the company with a similar level of responsibility.

Traveler's checks special forms designed for making payments when away from home.

Treasury bills (T-bills) bills that involve short-term borrowing with maturities from 91 days to one year.

Treasury bond rate the yield on long-term (20-year) U.S. government debt obligations.

Treasury bonds (T-bonds) bonds that involve long-term borrowing, with maturities ranging from 10 to 30 years.

Treasury notes (T-notes) note that involve borrowing with maturities from 1 to 10 years.

Truth-in-Lending Act of 1968 the first in a series of credit protection laws, it requires that borrower's be told the cost of credit before signing an agreement. It requires that the lender must clearly state the annual percentage rate (APR) and total finance charge. It also protects consumers against unauthorized use of credit cards.

Truth-in-Savings Act (TISA) a law requiring that financial institutions give consumers information to compare savings accounts.

U

Uncontrollable risk a risk that cannot be reduced by your actions.

Unemployment insurance insurance to reduce financial hardship of unemployment.

Unemployment rate the portion of people in the labor force who are not working.

Uninsurable risk when a risk is not common or if it is impossible to predict the amount of loss that could be suffered.

Uninsured motorist protection against hit-and-run drivers or drivers without insurance money to pay claims.

Unit price a price per unit of measure.

Unity of command a clear reporting relationship for all staff of a business.

Universal life insurance insurance that provides both insurance protection and a substantial savings plan.

Upkeep maintaining your property in good condition.

V

Values things that are important to you.

Variable expenses living costs that differ each time and may not be as easy to estimate.

Variable life insurance an insurance plan that resembles an investment portfolio. It lets the policyholder choose among a broad range of investments.

Vehicle insurance coverage of automobiles, trucks, and other business vehicles.

Vending machines non-store shopping where customers can shop for items by putting money into machines.

Venture capital money provided by large investors to finance new products and new businesses that have a good chance to be very profitable.

Vertical communications communications that move up or down in an organization between management and employees.

Video output processing results that may be in the form of a training film, television commercial, or news report.

Videoconferencing allows people in different geographic locations to meet "face-to-face" by satellite.

Voice-activated systems input devices that allow words spoken into a microphone to be entered as data or to be translated into instructions or commands.

W

Wants things that add comfort and pleasure to your life.

Warehouse club a no-frills outlet focusing on the sale of large quantities at reasonable prices.

White-collar crime illegal acts carried out by office or professional workers while at work.

White-collar worker one whose work is more mental than physical and involves the handling and processing of information.

Whole life insurance permanent insurance that extends over the lifetime, or whole life, of the insured.

Work environment the physical conditions and the psychological atmosphere in which employees work.

Workers' compensation an insurance plan that provides medical and survivor benefits for people injured, disabled, or killed on the job.

Workforce all of the people 16 years or older who are employed or who are looking for a job.

World trade. See **International business**

Written communications communication that include notes, letters, reports, and e-mail messages.

Y

Yield the percentage of money earned on savings or investment over a year.

Bank reconciliation, 441
Bankruptcy, 473
Bank statement, 439–440
Barriers. *See* International trade barriers
Base plus incentive, 183–184
Basic economic problem, 12–13
Basic form, homeowners' policy, 518
Basic health coverage, 530
Basic product, 245
BBB. *See* Better Business Bureau (BBB)
B2B. *See* Business-to-Business (B2B)
B2C. *See* Business-to-Consumer (B2C)
Behavioral interview, 222
Benchmark, 328
Beneficiary, 353, 523
Benefits, 304
    compensation and, 178–179
    defined, 183
    employee, 184, 188, 223
Better Business Bureau (BBB), 374, 383
Biometric banking, 429
Biometric input device, 269
Bit, 271
Blank endorsement, 436
Bloch, Henry, 130
Bloch, Richard, 130
BLS. *See* U.S. Bureau of Labor Statistics (BLS)
Blue-collar worker, 175–176
Board of directors, 111
Bodily injury liability, 511–512
Bond, 46, 91, 483
    components of, 493
    corporate, 493
    defined, 45
    government, 491–492
    values of, 493
Bond fund, 494
Bond investment, 482–483
Bond market, 45
Borrowing, 45–46, 91
Boycotts Program, 285
BRAC. *See* Bangladesh Rural Advancement
  Committee (BRAC)
Brand, 377
Brand name, 245, 377
Brazilian Futures Exchange, 501
Bribery, 57
Broad form, 518
Budget charge account, 451
Budget deficit, 46
Budgeting techniques, 403–408
Budget(s), 403
    characteristics of effective, 406
    defined, 294
    developing, 294–296
    electronic, 308
    formats, 408
    preparation for, 295–296
    process, 404–406
    sources of information for, 294–295
    types of, 296–297
Budget surplus, 46
Budget variance, 406
Burger King, 67
Business
    designing effective, 115–116
    ethics in, 79–80
    expansion of, 293
    ongoing operations of, 292–293
    organizational structure for, 115–118
    principles of effective, 116–117
    start, 292
Business activity, measuring, 44–47
    borrowing, 45–46
    future economic challenges, 46–47
    investment activities, 44–45
Business budget, 294–297
Business competition, 177
Business consumer, 240
Business contacts, 205
    as source of available jobs, 212
Business cycle, 38–40
    affecting job opportunities, 176–177
    defined, 38
    depression, 39–40
    prosperity, 38
    recession, 39
    recovery, 40
Business debt, 46
Businesses, U.S.
    activities, 104–106
    impact on community, 104
    roles of, 104
    services, 107
    size of, 103
    types of, 106–107
Businesses for Social Responsibility, 195
Business Improving Society features
    Architecture for Humanity, 337
    Consumers Union, 386
    Co-op America, 285
    delivering electricity, 119
    Heifer International, 27
    The Hunger Site, 69
    microfinance, 434
    social responsibility, 195
Business insurance, 352–354
Business interruption insurance, 354
Business operations. *See* Operations
Business Outside the Box features
    Discover Card, 233
    drinks for developing countries, 3
    Gene Wade and Platform Learning, 99
    Karen Neuburger, 99
    multimedia medical information, 369
    organic food, 3